MW01055621

Theatre Histories

This updated fourth edition of *Theatre Histories* offers a critical overview of global theatre, drama, and performance, spanning a broad wealth of world cultures and periods, integrating them chronologically or thematically, and showing how they have often interacted.

Bringing together a group of scholars from a diverse range of backgrounds and approaches to the history of global theatre, this introduction to theatre history places theatre into its larger historical contexts and attends to communication's role in shaping theatre. Its case studies provide deeper knowledge of selected topics in theatre and drama, and its "Thinking Through Theatre Histories" boxes discuss important concepts and approaches used in the book.

Features of the fully updated fourth edition include:

- Deeper coverage of East Asian and Latin American theatre.
- Richer treatment of popular culture.
- More illustrations, photographs, and information about online resources.
- New case studies, several written by authoritative scholars on the topic.
- Pronunciation guidance, both in the text and as audio files online.
- Timelines.
- An introduction on historiography.
- A website with additional case studies, a glossary, recordings of the pronunciation of important non-English terms, and instructor resources.
- A case studies library listing, including both those in print and online, for greater instructor choice and flexibility.

This is an essential textbook for undergraduate courses in theatre history, world theatre and introduction to theatre, and anyone looking for a full and diverse account of the emergence, development, and continuing relevance of theatre to cultures and societies across the world.

Tobin Nellhaus is an Independent Scholar. He writes mainly on the relationship between theatre and communication practices, and on critical realism in theatre theory and historiography.

Daphne P. Lei is a Professor of Drama and the Associate Dean for Graduate Affairs at the Claire Trevor School of the Arts, University of California, Irvine, USA. She is the 2022 recipient of the Distinguished Scholar Award, the lifetime achievement award from the American Society for Theatre Research.

Tamara Underiner is an Associate Professor in the School of Music, Dance and Theatre at Arizona State University, USA, and the Director of the PhD program in Theatre and Performance of the Americas.

Patricia Ybarra is the MacMillan Family Professor of the Humanities in the Department of Theatre and Performance Studies at Brown University, USA. She is a former president of the Association for Theatre in Higher Education.

Theatre Histories

An Introduction

Fourth Edition

General Editor: Tobin Nellhaus

Tobin Nellhaus, Daphne P. Lei,
Tamara Underiner and Patricia Ybarra

Routledge
Taylor & Francis Group

LONDON AND NEW YORK

Designed cover image: © Photographer: Fletcher Oakes. (l-r) Lisa Hori-Garcia, Velina Brown, Keiko Shimosato Carreiro in *Ripple Effect*, 2014. Courtesy of San Francisco Mime Troupe.

Fourth edition published 2024
by Routledge
4 Park Square, Milton Park, Abingdon, Oxon, OX14 4RN

and by Routledge
605 Third Avenue, New York, NY 10158

Routledge is an imprint of the Taylor & Francis Group, an informa business

© 2024 Tobin Nellhaus, Daphne P. Lei, Tamara Underiner and Patricia Ybarra

The right of Daphne P. Lei, Tobin Nellhaus, Tamara Underiner and Patricia Ybarra to be identified as authors of this work has been asserted in accordance with sections 77 and 78 of the Copyright, Designs and Patents Act 1988.

First edition published by Routledge 2006
Third edition published by Routledge 2016

British Library Cataloguing-in-Publication Data
A catalogue record for this book is available from the British Library

ISBN: 9781032027920 (hbk)
ISBN: 9781032027906 (pbk)
ISBN: 9781003185185 (ebk)

DOI: 10.4324/9781003185185

Typeset in Bembo
by codeMantra

Access the Instructor and Student Resources: www.theatrehistories.com

Contents

CONTENTS

CONTENTS

CONTENTS

CONTENTS

Figures

About the authors

Daphne P. Lei is a Professor of Drama and the Associate Dean for Graduate Affairs at the Claire Trevor School of the Arts, University of California, Irvine. Internationally known for her scholarship on Chinese opera, Asian American theatre, intercultural, transnational, and transpacific performance, she is the author of *Operatic China: Staging Chinese Identity across the Pacific* (Palgrave Macmillan, 2006), *Alternative Chinese Opera in the Age of Globalization: Performing Zero* (Palgrave Macmillan, 2011), *Uncrossing the Borders: Performing Chinese in Gendered (Trans)Nationalism* (University of Michigan Press, 2019), and coeditor (with Charlotte McIvor) of *The Methuen Drama Handbook of Interculturalism and Performance* (Bloomsbury, 2020). She is a former president of American Society for Theatre Research, and in 2022, she received the Distinguished Scholar Award from ASTR for outstanding achievement in scholarship in the field of Theatre Studies.

Tobin Nellhaus is an Independent Scholar and former Librarian for Performing Arts, Media and Philosophy at Yale University. He is the author of *Theater, Communication, Critical Realism* (Palgrave Macmillan, 2010) and co-editor (with Susan Haedicke) of *Performing Democracy: International Perspectives on Urban Community-Based Performance* (University of Michigan Press, 2001); and he was the General Editor of *Theatre Histories*, 3rd edition. His articles have appeared in *Theatre Journal*, *Journal of Dramatic Theory and Criticism*, *Journal of Critical Realism*, *Journal for the Theory of Social Behaviour*; the collections *Performance and Cognition* (Routledge, 2006), *Staging Philosophy: Intersections of Theater, Performance, and Philosophy* (University of Michigan Press, 2006), *Theatre, Performance and Change* (Palgrave Macmillan, 2018); and elsewhere.

Tamara Underiner is an Associate Professor in the School of Music, Dance and Theatre in the Herberger Institute for Design and the Arts at Arizona State University, where she directs the PhD program in Theatre and Performance of the Americas. She is the author of

Contemporary Theatre in Mayan Mexico: Death-Defying Acts (University of Texas Press, 2004), and has published on indigenous and Latina/o theatre and critical pedagogy in *Theatre Journal*, *Signs*, *Baylor Journal of Theatre and Performance*, *TDR*, and critical anthologies from academic presses in the U.S., Mexico, and Canada. She is active in the American Society for Theatre Research, the Association for Theatre in Higher Education, and the Hemispheric Institute for Performance and Politics.

Patricia Ybarra is the MacMillan Professor of the Humanities in the Department of Theatre Arts and Performance Studies at Brown University. She is the author of *Performing Conquest: Five Centuries of Theatre, History and Identity in Tlaxcala, Mexico* (Michigan, 2009), co-editor with Lara Nielsen of *Neoliberalism and Global Theatres: Performance Permutations* (Palgrave Macmillan, 2012; paperback 2015), and *Latinx Theatre in Times of Neoliberalism* (Northwestern University Press, 2018). She has also published articles in *Theatre Journal, Aztlán, Modern Drama, Theatre Topics*, and *the Journal of Dramatic Theory and Criticism*. She is a former President of the Association for Theatre in Higher Education. She is a first-generation college student of working-class parents.

Preface to the fourth edition

Theatre Histories continues to evolve. Carol Fisher Sorgenfrei and Bruce McConachie, who were with the book through its first three editions, rotated off; Daphne P. Lei and Patricia Ybarra joined the team, making this edition the first by a group entirely different from its original. We have greatly enriched the book's global coverage, especially of East Asia and Latin America, and improved the book's overview of popular performance forms such as musical theatre. We also reorganized Chapters 9 through 11, bringing related topics such as Naturalism and realism together. This change resulted in substantial differences in chapter length, but we hope it will make classroom discussions more focused, fluid, and comprehensive. In addition, there are more photos, and we replaced some of the older ones.

We have moved some of the third edition's case studies to the website, where they join other case studies, and added new ones to the book. Moreover, in previous editions, all case studies were written by the book's own authors; in this edition, we commissioned several from specialists, heightening the book's authoritativeness. Because of the growing number of case studies, we have included a list of the entire library, making it easier for instructors to select ones that suit their own priorities.

We dedicate this edition to the late Phillip B. Zarrilli, who passed away in 2020. He was one of the first to have the inspiration to write a new textbook on global theatre that became *Theatre Histories*. He will be greatly missed.

Acknowledgments

The authors want to express their gratitude to Claire Margerison and Steph Hines of Routledge, our picture researcher Emma Brown, and the rest of Routledge's textbook production staff. A book of this nature demands an extraordinary amount of work and consultation from many people, whose contributions are seldom known but remain essential.

We are also grateful for the work by the authors of the previous editions: Bruce McConachie, Carol Fisher Sorgenfrei, Gary Williams, and the late Phillip B. Zarrilli. Without their massive work on those earlier editions, this one would not have been possible.

A theatre history of this scope is feasible because of the specialized research of numerous dedicated scholars. We are indebted to them and quoted many. Their works are cited in this text and in the extended bibliographies on our website.

Many of our colleagues have been especially supportive. We wish to thank the many people we consulted for this edition, including Natalya Baldyga, Micky Bolaños, Charlotte Canning, Matthieu Chapman, Fiifi Coleman, Alicia del Campo, Jennifer Fisher, Lucía Guerra-Cunningham, Kellen Hoxworth, Amy B. Huang, Ketu Katrak, Margaret Knapp, Karen Jean Martinson, Jeff McMahon, Jayson Morrison, Jessica Nakamura, Alisa Solomon, Philip Thompson, Sarah Townsend, and Stacy Wolf. We have listened to and benefited from the external reviewers of our work, including our critics; they have helped us serve our readers better. We look forward to future conversations with our readers.

We are grateful to our students, who have helped to shape our thinking about theatre and performance history. Daphne P. Lei would especially like to thank Minwoo Park and Talin Abadian, as well as the PhD students who are devoted to teaching the theatre history series. Tamara Underiner expresses her gratitude to her doctoral students in the Theatre and Performance of the Americas program at Arizona State University who never failed to challenge her perspectives. Patricia Ybarra is grateful to her theatre history students at Brown University, who have changed the way she sees the world, and helped make her work more global.

We have also had the strong, enduring support of families and partners. Their considerable sacrifices made it possible for the work to get done, and we express our heartfelt thanks to all of them, including Eliana Danowski-Underiner, Gerry Magallan, Milo Schaberg, Rafe Schaberg, Milind Shah, and Naveen Shah.

Routledge would like to thank all those archives and individuals who have given permission to reproduce images in this textbook. In a few rare cases, we were unable, despite the utmost efforts, to locate owners of materials. For this, we apologize and will make any corrections in the next reprint if contacted.

General introduction

Tobin Nellhaus

The goals of *Theatre Histories*

Theatre has unusually strong connections with the other arts, technology, society, and individuals' situations, desires, and conflicts – it is a window into the entire human world. *Theatre Histories* aims to introduce the history of theatre, drama, and performance globally and in context. Because history isn't a simple thing, this book also discusses some of the complications in interpreting evidence and events.

Even our most basic terms can be understood in different ways. "Drama" is generally used to describe written plays with fictional characters and actions, even if based on historical people and events, that are performed live. Occasionally, it's used more broadly to refer to what is performed onstage, no matter how the fiction was devised; the drama might not be a script at all, just ideas and character types in the performers' minds. In contrast, for some people, "drama" carries the narrower sense of plays as literary works, to be read apart from performance. For the authors of this book, however, the connection to performance is essential.

"Theatre" usually refers to live performances of drama (or something drama-like) by skilled artists for live audiences. Such performances engage the spectators' imagination, emotion, intellect, and cultural perspectives, at varying levels. Theatre may or may not take place in buildings built specifically for performance. Sometimes, the audience members are also performers. In theatre, everyone involved is aware that the performance presents a fiction. Occasionally, people do use "theatre" to describe performances which present fictional situations (such as an argument at a café) before an unsuspecting public as though they were nonfictional, or even situations in which spectators observe other people as though they are fictional characters; but for the purposes of this book, these cases apply the term "theatre" metaphorically.

In *Theatre Histories*, "performance" generally refers to embodied presentation on stage (or with surrogates for the body, such as puppets). The term also has a special meaning today in the field of performance studies, where it includes *all* the ways in which humans represent themselves in embodied ways. Scholars apply that sense of "performance" not

DOI: 10.4324/9781003185185-1

only to the staging of plays but also to religious rituals, state ceremonies, carnivals, political demonstrations, athletic contests, customs at a family dinner table, the ways people portray themselves in social media, and many other activities. In that sense, theatre is but one of many kinds of performance.

Occasionally, *Theatre Histories* employs this broader sense of "performance." We think it is enlightening to make connections between theatre and other types of performance. For that reason, even though *Theatre Histories* is not a performance studies textbook, we consider a wide range of performances – from Hopi ritual clowns to Hip Hop theatre, from *jingju* ("Beijing opera") to productions of plays by Samuel Beckett, and from ancient Roman gladiators to plays in Japan using both human and robot actors.

We wrote *Theatre Histories* with the belief that today it's vital to know about theatre glob-ally. For example, it is not unusual for playwrights, directors, and designers to be inspired by the theatre of other cultures (possibly ancient ones), and sometimes actors are expected to know or quickly absorb acting methods from another tradition. In addition, cultural activ-ities and creations constantly cross into other cultures and influence each other, such as the importation of K-Pop music and Bollywood movies into Western countries, or the perfor-mance of Arthur Miller's *Death of a Salesman* in China; there are also deliberate fusions of cul-tural styles, such as a French theatre's staging of an ancient Greek tragedy using performance styles drawn from India. For those reasons, we strive to provide an understanding of theatrical performance around the world, throughout its known existence. We also believe that isolat-ing the study of Western from non-Western theatre respects neither our readers nor those traditions. Thus, most chapters in *Theatre Histories* include theatre from various parts of the world, with exceptions where thematic, historical pace, or other reasons made it unfeasible.

Theatrical performances occur within society. For that reason, *Theatre Histories* often discusses political, cultural, economic, and other social issues, and how they affected the-atre, drama, and performance. The relationships among these various social dynamics, and between them and theatre, are extremely complex. However, *Theatre Histories* will pay one element special attention: a society's communication practices (its uses of speech, handwrit-ing, printing, and electronics). We discuss this focus in more detail below.

More than simply determining facts, historians have to make decisions about what infor-mation is most important and develop an understanding of how events are related. In other words, the process of writing about history – **historiography** – always involves interpreta-tions of the past. One of the goals of *Theatre Histories* is to provide not just information about theatre, and not just our interpretations of that information, but also an understanding of how interpretations come into being – how history is written – in order to enable readers to evaluate historical writing. The remainder of this introduction surveys some of the core issues in historiography, the approach adopted by the authors, and its influence on our dis-cussions and the organization of the book.

The structure of *Theatre Histories*

Theatre Histories has three primary types of material: the main text, case studies, and boxes titled "Thinking Through Theatre Histories." There are also a few boxes concerning par-ticular points or important concepts. In addition, we also have a range of resources on the *Theatre Histories* website.

The main text describes the principal developments in theatre history, which broadly speaking we've organized chronologically. Because historical periods have no clear-cut boundaries, every chapter overlaps others (as the Table of Contents quickly shows). Chapters often begin with historical contexts and the forces driving the events that shape theatrical performance. Each chapter also has a theme. Chapter 4, for instance, observes that the flourishing cities of Europe and Asia from the thirteenth through seventeenth centuries were increasingly able to support theatre as a vocation. Theatre was no longer tethered to festivals, aristocratic courtyards, and similar venues, and increasingly relied on a paying public. Professional theatre troupes developed in China, Europe, and Japan, initially relying on touring, but in Europe and Japan, they eventually resided in buildings specially built for theatre. Sometimes, the chapter shows how performance can develop in two opposite directions at the same time: for example, Chapter 14 looks at how the late twentieth century saw the rise of both globalized theatre culture and performance based on local culture and history. Geographically, theatre often develops independently from continent to continent; within a continent, however, there's frequently plenty of traffic between countries – instructions on how to demonstrate religious devotion, touring theatre companies that display "how it's done," theories of the "best" type of theatre, and the like – so that discussing developments in a few countries can indicate the general pattern. However, seeing the similarities and dissimilarities between widely separated theatre traditions during a single time frame can help readers think about performance comparatively.

We have grouped the chapters into four parts. As we explain later in this introduction, the parts are characterized by developments in communication practices.

- Part I first addresses performance in oral cultures, such as rituals, and then turns attention to theatre when writing could only be produced by hand, and the cultures in many respects remained oriented around orality. Several societies developed major theatre traditions during this period, among them Europe, India, Japan, and China; and everywhere, there were forms of celebratory and commemorative performance.

- Part II surveys theatre during the first 250 years or so of the era when the printing press shaped culture in Europe, and contemporaneous developments in Asia. First, we consider the rise of professional theatre companies, which occurred in many parts of the world, mainly as the result of growing prosperity and urbanization. Our examination of the print revolution in Europe highlights the cultural changes and conflicts that arose out of it, and then the formation of highly centralized monarchies, which often utilized print as a way to shore up their power. These developments strongly influenced concepts of character and plot, and theatre professionals started seeking artistic realism in one sense or another.

- Part III concerns theatre in the next two centuries of print culture, from eighteenth through the early twentieth century, distinguished by the development of newspapers, magazines, and journals – the periodical press. This new use of print fostered new roles for theatre in European society, through which theatre contributed to and was influenced by the political structures that were emerging from capitalism, particularly nationalism. The trend toward globalization began, and the resulting intercultural contact had both innovative and oppressive effects. Realism became increasingly well-defined and established in Western theatre, and also spread to Japan, India, and eventually else-where, partially displacing the traditional performance genres that included music, sing-ing, and dancing. Toward the end of this era, entirely new media based mainly on electricity started to shatter print culture's modes of thought, promoting a new phe-nomenon: non-realistic, avant-garde theatre.

- Part IV picks up the thread as electric and then electronic communication – radio, sound recordings, film, TV, the internet, mobile phones, and more – played an increas-ingly prominent cultural role. On the one hand, various forms of realism dominated in mainstream theatre (except for musicals); on the other hand, non-realistic avant-garde genres were constantly being invented. Avant-gardes challenged nearly every aspect of theatre, such as the importance of the dramatic text versus performance, what counted as a performance space and how it could be used, what performance consisted of, and who could be a performer. In addition, within both the mainstream and the avant-garde, some forms of theatre sought to challenge the political ideologies, institutions and forces of their society. Often electronic communication provided models or tools for these developments.

Each of the four parts opens with a short introduction that briefly summarizes what that part will cover and raises philosophical issues stemming from the broad development of theatre in history.

Each chapter has one or two case studies, which look in depth at a particular type of performance, play, dramatist, practice, or some other aspect of theatre. These include topics such as the tradition of men playing women in Japanese *kabuki*, plays-within-plays during Shakespeare's time, mid-twentieth-century American musicals, and the work of the late Ghanaian playwright Ama Ata Aidoo.

The short "Thinking Through Theatre Histories" sections present subjects such as the-ories and methodologies in historiography (for instance, the ideas of literary critic Mikhail Bakhtin) and topical questions (such as theatre's origins). These sections aim to help the reader grasp the problems theatre historians face and the choices they make when studying historical events. Of course, these segments provide just an inkling of the enormous variety of historiographical theories, questions, and strategies, but we hope they help the reader gain awareness of the issues involved.

Historiography: Thinking about history

In the next two sections of this introduction, we explore aspects of historiography, and the connection between theatre and the history of communication. We discuss these issues for three reasons: it will clarify why *Theatre Histories* explains activities and events in certain ways; it informs the reader about how histories are written; and it guides students to issues they should consider when writing essays. At the end of the introduction, we discuss some of this book's features, such as pronunciation guidance, and explain our conventions for names, movements, and other matters.

Many people think history should be a neutral account of facts, and should not express opinions or impose values. In reality, that has never been possible and it can be misleading.

Consider this example attributed to the philosopher Isaiah Berlin about what happened in Germany under Nazi rule:

(a) The country was depopulated.
(b) Millions of people died.
(c) Millions of people were killed.
(d) Millions of people were massacred.

All four statements are true. The first is the most neutral – but only the last, which expresses the strongest value judgment, provides a precise and explanatory interpretation of history. It is the truest of the four, while in contrast, by obfuscating events the first statement is almost a lie. People who advocate neutral language may intend well by trying not to impose their views on others, but they can also open the door wide for arguments that are incorrect, misinforming, and/or malignant. Neutralization can even be a political tactic to downplay historical offences, such as by calling enslaved people "workers."

If historiography involves interpreting the past, then we need to consider what it means to "interpret." One view is that any claim that "X is true" is really "just an interpretation" – a complete matter of opinion. A similar idea is extreme cultural relativism, in which truth is *simply* what a culture decides it is, or activities can *only* be evaluated on a culture's own terms. According to this perspective, there is no way to choose between them – all opinions are equally valid, and whatever is "true for me" is inherently unassailable. The example above hints at how opinions can obscure facts. And nobody has stopped gravity or the climate crisis by not believing in it. Extreme relativism isn't even logically coherent, since the idea that every truth claim is merely an opinion is itself a truth claim.

But there are less extreme versions of relativism, and the notion that every claim is "just an opinion" does sound a useful cautionary note for historians. Determining exactly what, how, and why things happened is often extraordinarily difficult. Frequently, evidence is fragmentary and ambiguous, and it is hard to perceive one's own mistaken assumptions about what the evidence means. Although history may be imagined as a simple path of dry facts, people experience history as a realm of fierce argument. We know what happened in history, until we realize we don't or we discover that someone else knows it differently. Even at the personal level, when talking with someone about a shared event, we all encounter moments when we say: "I don't remember it that way!" There clearly are facts, but even if we agree on them, we can fit them together in different ways, bringing out different perspectives, illuminating different connections, or formulating different explanations. For instance, the standard U.S. view of the American Revolutionary War is that the British government was increasingly imposing itself on local governance and demanded oppressive taxes to pay for the French and Indian War (1754–1763, also called the Seven Years' War) in which many colonists had lost their lives; but to the British Parliament, the American colonials were ingrates refusing to pay their fair share for a war that had secured the colonies' very existence. Interpretation is intrinsic to historiography, and our understanding of history is necessarily always open to revision.

Social context and cultural relativity

What happens inside the theatre is deeply connected to what happens outside, not just as a matter of the topics playwrights present on stage, but also how plays are performed, who performs them, who attends them, and how social developments are manifested in stylistic shifts. For instance, approaches to acting can be rooted in physiological theories; the sorts of characters one sees in a play can be connected to the way people use the printing press; whether plays are written rather than improvised may be the result of the society's political and economic configuration. The theatre's doors are always open to the world, and the world always enters – the world is already part of theatre itself.

Let's take the question of characters in a play. What qualities should they have? Today, one might expect a "psychology" or "psychological truth" with motivations, fears, and so on; figures like Nora in Ibsen's *A Doll House* may spring to mind. But if we look at the long history and wide geographical expanse of drama, we discover that such characters are limited to the modern era, after realistic drama, a late child of print culture, conquered the world – and that conquest is shallower than one might expect. When understood in their original context, characters like Iago in Shakespeare's *Othello* turn out not to have psychologies in today's sense, although modern actors will frequently strive to build one for them. Psychologistic characters don't appear in the theatre traditions beyond the modern West either. Even within Western culture, if one doesn't grasp the medieval concept of self, the allegorical figure Good Deeds in the medieval play *Everyman* may seem almost like a placard. But it's very difficult to see the world through others' eyes, which can result in misunderstanding and even disparagement – a problem that has arisen quite often.

Characters must be created in a way that makes sense to their originating culture – they are culturally relative. The point is important because historians can unwittingly project their own perceptions, assumptions, and beliefs (which may seem like common sense in their own culture) onto earlier and foreign societies, leading to severe misinterpretations and distortions. The issue arises in many other areas. For instance, scholars may believe that religion involves the same type of concepts in other cultures as it does in their own, not realizing that there can be significant differences. There is a long history of historians projecting their ideas and values in a way that implies or even states outright that their own society is superior to others. We will discuss examples of this practice at several points.

For certain purposes, however, historians apply their perspective intentionally, particularly when they pursue questions such as "Who benefits?" and "Who is harmed?" Many scholars ask who benefits and who is harmed within various structures of gender, race, politics, and economics. Critiques of patriarchy, racism, gender conformism, imperialism, and authoritarianism are intense in most developed countries worldwide, and in many developing countries as well; in most continents, there is also a significant anti-capitalist tradition absent in the U.S. (although there, interest in socialism renewed in recent years). In the opposite direction, there has also been a resurgence of advocacy for systems of hierarchy and oppression. Each perspective leads to different ways of writing history, as does an approach that seeks to balance pros and cons somehow rather than say that one side outweighs the other. Such questions of benefit and harm arise in theatre history: for instance, in the past, many cultures allowed only men to perform in plays, which historians deemed insignificant until some argued that the practice was misogynistic, and others that it was homoerotic. (Its treatment as insignificant is itself often considered misogynistic.) Further interpretations emerged in response. Such debates force scholars to reexamine evidence and their own attitudes, and they have deepened our insight into theatre's complexity, even if they entail sharp criticism of earlier eras.

As we see, there is tension between the desire to avoid projecting our own society's views onto others and the desire to criticize earlier wrongs. There may be no completely satisfactory solution to that tension. In *Theatre Histories*, we present some examples of historical critique; we also strive to consider what performances meant to their original audience, although we can seldom be certain that we've succeeded – the people of third-century India, for instance, aren't around to tell us whether we got things right, and their judgments would be colored by their own perspectives on what is correct.

Evidence-theory connections

Evidence, then, is often subject to interpretation due to the historian's assumptions, values, and informational contexts. A historian's social position, possibly the need to justify one side's actions, and sometimes even wishful thinking can also slip into historiography.

One topic where historians' projections have strongly influenced their interpretations is the question of theatre's origins, especially in ancient Greece. In the early 1900s, Gilbert Murray and other classical anthropologists contended that Greek tragedy evolved from religious rituals. The hypothesis was surrounded by just enough apparent evidence to be taken as proved. By the late 1920s, however, classicists showed that the logic behind Murray's theory was flawed, much of the evidence it presented was misconstrued, and contrary evidence had not been considered. The problems with Murray's thesis are so acute that the classical scholar Gerald Else asserted that Murray had not accumulated evidence which he then realized could be explained by the "ritual origins" theory, but instead was driven by "the determination at all costs to find the origin of tragedy in religion, and therefore in ritual" (1965: 4) – in other words, that Murray selected and interpreted his evidence in order to fit the theory he already had in mind.

Although ancient Greek theatre may have had some sort of relationship to ritual, it was not the evolutionary one that Murray proposed. But the "religious ritual origins" theory captured many people's imagination and still appears in one form or another to this day, including among some classicists. (Some writers dub refuted yet tenacious theories "zombie ideas.") One reason it persists is that some theatre practitioners and scholars feel that the theory offers an inspiration for vitality in performance and a way to comprehend that vitality. Inspiration is always "true" in the sense that a lived experience cannot be falsified (if you feel excited, no one can demonstrate that you're actually bored), and some people find the inspiration more valid if they believe that "religious ritual origins" is correct. In other words, if an inspiration is true, then its source must be as well. For these practitioners and scholars, theatre's factual origin is not the most important truth: its value as a belief or subjective experience is. (Notice, however, that rejecting religious ritual as the *origin* of theatre does not exclude other possible relationships between them.)

In this example, we see that there can be different perspectives on "what actually happened," but these different perspectives are not equally valid, nor are they impervious to criticism. We can also see that for some people, there are different "kinds" of truth (a position that itself can be interpreted in various ways), and that not everyone thinks all kinds have the same level of importance. We will return to the question of theatre's origins in Chapter 1.

In another situation that arises, a historian may make an argument based on both strong argument and solid evidence and then the evidence changes. In one case of facts changing, the first known theatre building – the Theatre of Dionysus, in Athens, Greece – was long thought to seat 15,000–17,000 people but due to recent archaeological evidence, classical scholars now believe the theatre's initial capacity was closer to 3,700–6,000 spectators, and the larger figure refers to a later expansion (Roselli 2011: 64–5). As a result of this change in the evidence, an excellent theory about the role of theatre in ancient Athens based on the previous estimate might need to be revised or even rejected. Likewise, people may discover that some evidence about theatre is more recent than was thought, or valid for only one city; that other evidence must be considered; that a facet of theatre (say, the significance of the actors' gender) was left out of the picture entirely; that the source isn't reliable; or the evidence was misinterpreted in some other way.

Although historians usually strive to avoid forcing evidence into a predetermined theory, or at least to be aware that there may be contrary evidence, historical evidence is always sought, chosen, and interpreted. Evidence doesn't "speak for itself"; the historian makes it speak to us. Because historians must select and interpret, they can misunderstand or mis-represent historical events, but by the same token, historical revelations may arise through innovative interpretation as much as by new evidence.

Intelligibility, plausibility, and narrative

Historians do more than select and interpret evidence: they also organize the evidence in order to create an intelligible (and, they hope, persuasive) narrative. Chronological order is generally part of making history plausible, especially when the causes of change are central, although in practice much historical writing must shuttle back and forth in time in order to pick up threads of a complex story. Historians also make events understandable by casting them in a particular light or giving their narrative a particular tone. For example, a historian might highlight historical ironies, such as the way President George W. Bush (in office 2001–2009) once criticized "nation building," in which the U.S. rebuilds a country's economic and political structure when its government fails but later, after launching a misguided war in Iraq, Bush was forced to attempt exactly that. Historians can also romanticize events, as did those who described John F. Kennedy's term as President as "Camelot," alluding to a Broadway musical about the gallant King Arthur and the Knights of the Round Table. Sim-ilarly, one historian may view a certain chain of events as improvement, while another may perceive it as a decline. These are just a few of the ways historians may make narrative sense of history.

Of course, although historians strive to present a plausible narrative, "plausible" is not a synonym for "true." To take just one of the many complexities, discussions about historical causes can run into logical problems that are often hard to detect. Imagine that during a press conference, the head of the country's banking system commented on the stock market, and later that day the stock market indexes fell. It's easy to infer that the comment worried stockbrokers and led to the sell-off. But even though that interpretation is plausi-ble, it could be wrong: the traders might have actually been reacting to bad news coming from abroad. One would need additional evidence to show what really caused the market decline. (This error, in which one thinks that one event must have caused another event because it preceded the second, is called a *post hoc* argument, short for the Latin *post hoc, ergo propter hoc* – "after this, therefore because of this.") Another logical error is captured by the saying, "correlation does not mean causation": the fact that two things occur together is not proof that one causes the other. For instance, there is a correlation between taking baths and having lower rates of cardiovascular disease – but the one does not in fact cause the other. However, they could both be related to something else, such as relaxation time. To avoid such mistakes, historians have to think carefully about what evidence is required to support their analysis – and sometimes no further evidence is available, or at least known to the historian. Plausibility may be the best we can get. This is yet another reason why history is often subject to debate.

Causes of historical change

Narrative is intrinsic to any discussion of how and why societies change. True, to some observers societies don't fundamentally change at all: "the more things change, the more they stay the same." A less cynical and more truly historiographical view is that social changes operate in regular cycles such as rise and fall. A related idea is that social change consists of swings of a pendulum (say, between permissiveness and conformism). In contrast, sometimes history is depicted as progress toward some goal, at times perhaps delayed but ultimately inexorable – the "march of reason," for instance.

A problem facing all of these views is that they don't provide any reason why there would be stasis, cycles, pendulum swings, or progress, or why they should apply to the particular matter of interest: these things just happen on their own, guided by an invisible hand or abstract universal principle. One answer to this question is that there is no "why" – that instead, history is a matter of happenstance, contingency, and accident, without any particular direction or pattern: at most, change comes from personal interactions. And certainly at the micro level, little more than chance may explain why one person became a historical figure rather than another. But this view misses the "big picture" of historical developments. For instance, it is striking that during roughly 1550–1650, there were substantial changes in theatrical practices throughout Europe, not always in synchrony but in the same basic direction. Performance spaces increasingly moved indoors and used more scenery; characters became more psychologically driven. What drove this "change in taste"? Why had large numbers of people come to prefer it? How and why had the concept of "realistic" changed? Surely more than coincidence, personal influence, or the tides of fashion, was involved.

Those questions raise others. An admission that we don't know the cause of something is not the same as claiming there is no cause. If large forces lay behind cultural changes, one may ask what those forces were, or which of many forces was the most important. Various answers have been proposed, most of them boiling down to three kinds. One category points to material activities – for example, the production and exchange of goods and services (economics), relationships between and among the sexes and genders, technological developments, the methods of communication, and so forth. Another type focuses on institutions, such as political systems, religious organizations, or family structures. The third kind assigns primacy to ideas – theology, philosophy, science, or worldview. One can of course also see the three factors as interacting, although in the end, usually one is assigned the greatest weight. Historians' views of the main type of force that drives society, as well as the specific force they consider, lead to very different historical narratives.

Theories of society

A key element of historians' interpretations and narratives is their general concept of how individuals and society are related. Their concept may be difficult to detect, since it is seldom explicit (even to the historian) and sometimes several different concepts seem to be invoked. As we will see, a particular concept of society directly shaped *Theatre Histories*. Understanding these different theories helps explain some of this book's organization and themes.

Sociologist Margaret S. Archer (1995) identifies four broad concepts of the relationship between individuals and society. In brief, one is that society boils down to individuals. According to this view, known as "methodological individualism," talk about social groups, institutions, power relationships, and society as a whole is problematic or wrong because such things cannot be perceived: all that can be perceived are individuals' behaviors. History is essentially about "great men (and a few great women)."

The second theory of society focuses on the rules and systems that govern social activities, continue a society's existence, and keep it functioning as smoothly as possible. The rules and systems are embodied in systems such as a society's larger political and economic structures, and people just follow their roles within them. Maintaining social structures happens by default, in the same way that speaking English keeps the English language alive. Like "cogs in the machine," individuals and their activities are determined by their position within the social systems that they're part of.

A third position says that individuals and society shouldn't be viewed as different things. Rules and resources depend on the existence of people and their ideas about what they are doing, and equally, what individuals do is always within the context of a society. At every moment, individuals are constructing society, and society is constructing individuals. The two are inextricable, like the sides of a coin. Society exists only through individuals' acts of repeating the rules, in the present. However, individuals can introduce small changes, which can accumulate.

The final view agrees that individuals and society interact, but they aren't two sides of the same thing – they are different things, with different features. For instance, economic systems can have laws regarding property, but they don't have bodies, which people have. People can't wake up one day with new ideas about social roles and resources, and instantly transform the society they live in: they can change society, but only within the pre-existing circumstances that can enable or limit their actions; some of their legacy remains, influencing future generations (for better or worse). Thus, one historical era may begin long before the previous one closed, and incremental adjustments can suddenly spark radical upheavals. Under this theory, history is messy.

Although the authors of *Theatre Histories* have somewhat varying positions, on the whole we take the last view. Theatre history's messiness is reflected in every chapter, because cultures don't change at the same rate or in the same manner, and their genres of theatrical performance vary widely. Theatre history's untidiness is particularly conspicuous through our **periodization**. Chapters always overlap chronologically. Many different factors came into play in our decisions about where to draw the dividing lines (which are necessarily a bit arbitrary), and we often had to wrestle with questions about where to place certain topics. In fact among historians generally, periodization is often disputed. Was there a Renaissance in Europe, and if so, when, where, and for whom? It depends on what countries and social groups one has in mind, what activities one thinks distinguish that period, and whether one thinks "Renaissance" is even a valid description. Similarly, how does one periodize when developments in East Asia and Western Europe follow different paths? Sometimes, themes tell us more than chronology. For instance, in Chapter 3, we discuss commemorative drama in Judaism, Christianity, and Islam, even though these arose centuries apart.

The construction of history

The need to focus on particular aspects of historical events, the collection and interpretation of evidence, the development of a narrative, and the historian's perspective and concept of society can be summarized by the sentence "History is constructed." We piece it together and build an argument. However, even though any understanding of history is a construct and a range of interpretations may be supported by evidence and logic, interpreting the past is not a free-for-all: it possesses objective as well as subjective facets. Not all interpretations are valid, historians can make mistakes, and some theories are flat-out wrong, no matter how insistently they might be espoused. We may never know with *absolute* certainty that certain claims are correct. But absolute certainty isn't required in order for us to be confident that an account is true: truth is more like "certainty beyond a reasonable doubt."

Theatre and the history of communication

The interpretation of history adopted in *Theatre Histories* appears in the way we perceive an interplay between individuals and society; it is also manifested through how we handle social structures. Society has numerous structures, including the economic system, political power relations, sex/gender relationships, race and ethnicity, religion, education, transportation, agriculture, health care, international relations, and so on. Changes in one structure often affect the others, and several may be involved in a single historical change. The relative importance or weight one should give to a particular structure depends partly on what one is discussing, and the perspective one brings to it. To take one example, the history of American popular music might pay special attention to the role of race. Theatre, we believe, has been most deeply affected by communication practices, by which we mean the way a society develops and uses one or more means of communication, such as speech, handwriting, printing, and electric/electronic media.

Why communication? The principal reason is the primacy of practice, a theory which holds that many of our ideas and thought processes arise through ordinary practical activities rather than abstract reasoning. This has been demonstrated in cognitive science, linguistics, psychology, and other fields. It means that how we communicate – our use of speech, handwritten notes, text messages, etc. – affects our thoughts about the world, ourselves, our creation and access to knowledge, and many other aspects of culture. But how we communicate is more than the technological means of communication themselves, because as we will see, it involves the *overall* ways in which people in a particular society use the means of communication (even if particular expressions might not fit the general pattern). Since communication practices produce ways of understanding the world, they help define a culture holistically. The point is important for the study of theatre, because in its most commonplace, paradigmatic form, theatre involves the *oral* performance of a *written* script, thus combining the two most fundamental modes of communication. That blend forges a strong bond between theatrical performance and communication practices.

A key question, however, is how changes in communication affect culture. There are three basic views. One is that communication technologies affect everything that pertains to communication and culture, and their impact is the same everywhere – technologies are the only factor one needs to consider. This view is called technological determinism, and it is probably the most widespread. It often underlies claims that a technology will definitely have some specific effect or role in society (for instance, it was once thought that virtual reality would be "the next big thing"). A contrasting argument is that technologies have no particular effects or tendencies: instead, only social activities such as education have any role. *Theatre Histories* takes the third view that both technological and social aspects are at play. Technologies present various possibilities, but they aren't infinitely malleable, so they have some effects of their own. They are better suited for some purposes than for others, and they may serve or promote certain uses more than others (possibly inadvertently). Which specific possibilities become reality depends on things that people do in society at large. YouTube, for example, initially defined itself as an online dating site (unsuccessfully), but within weeks its creators discovered that people were uploading all sorts of videos, so it switched to a more open approach; mere months later, corporations were posting ads. Some people use YouTube as a sort of online radio with videos displaying a static image, but that's a weak usage of its capabilities. However, technologically YouTube cannot supplant person-to-person video calls.

Even though one can't separate communication technology from its social usage, its historical development is still important. One can periodize the history of communication in various ways. The most obvious approach is to distinguish between **oral cultures**, **manuscript cultures**, **print cultures**, and **electric and electronic cultures**. But there are other possibilities. From one perspective, there are really only two major eras: first, oral cultures, which have no form of writing whatsoever; then, the era of literate cultures, which has numerous sub-periods. However, as often happens, drawing a simple dividing line turns out to be not quite so simple. On the one hand, there have been cultures which had writing but gave it a minor role culturally, so in a technical sense they may have been literate, but for most practical purposes the cultures remained oral; on the other hand, oral communication is hugely important in even the most technologically sophisticated society with nearly universal literacy. Another approach to periodizing communication history might hold that there is a significant shift between the electronic culture of the television, radio, and telephone versus the socially networked culture of the computer, the internet, and especially mobile devices; in other words, one could break down the history of communication into shorter periods.

For *Theatre Histories*, we are using four periods, which are represented in the four parts of the book. Our focus, however, is on the connection between changes in a society's overall communication practices (not the technology), and the shifts and commonalities in performance and in the culture at large. For that reason, the book's parts don't exactly match the technological changes. First, after considering performance in oral culture, we examine theatre in various types of early literate and then manuscript cultures, when all writing had to be done by hand, but in all of the cultures discussed in Part I, to a greater or lesser extent, the spoken word still played a major cultural role. The next period hinges on the introduction of the printing press in Europe, which radically transformed the way books were produced and distributed, and made writing culturally dominant throughout the continent. Our third period arises from a change in how people used an existing technology: publishing on a re-current basis became logistically and financially viable, leading to the creation of newspapers, magazines, and journals of various sorts. Finally, we address the rise of electric and electronic modes of communication, which have continuously transformed. However, the effects of changing communication technology can take decades or even centuries to fully reshape a culture – *if* they do – and there's reason to think that electronic communication is not yet dominant, although that seems to be the direction world culture is taking.

But it's vital to remember that the dominance of any mode of communication is al-ways relative to other modes of communication, and specific to particular societies. What emerges in the industrialized parts of the world doesn't necessarily apply elsewhere. The reality is that in 2022 almost 10 percent of the world's population had no access to electric-ity, let alone computers; roughly 34 percent had never used the internet and hundreds of millions more could only do so intermittently. Even in technologically advanced countries, millions of people don't have home internet. Although mobile technologies are making rapid inroads, the digital divide between the truly connected and the unconnected will be extremely difficult to overcome and might never be eliminated. Speech, handwriting, and printing will continue to be used in one form or another. Their techniques and functions may change, but they will not vanish. This book's own readers to date have largely preferred the print edition, because it served them better or was more accessible than the electronic version.

What happened to YouTube is a good demonstration of the only indisputable law of history: the law of unintended consequences. People may believe that the intentions of great leaders and innovators are foremost in the "march of history," but at most that's only partly the case, and often not true at all. When the printing press was invented in Europe, nobody could have anticipated that it would facilitate a cultural renaissance, a scientific revolution, and the most savage religious schism the continent ever endured. Those effects and more had fundamental connections to the simple experience of using printed books. In the future too, history will have complex overlaps, multiple timelines, interweavings, lurches, and surprises. Theatre will trace a similarly unpredictable path as people absorb, respond to, act upon, and think within changing communication practices.

We will describe in more detail the specific ways in which communication has shaped theatre and drama within each of *Theatre Histories*'s four parts. Here, however, we need to observe that theatre not only has powerful ties to communication, it is also strongly affected by other social structures, such as economics, political structures, and the sex/gender system. The different factors influencing the stage interconnect in various ways and further complicate the history of theatre. To reflect that fact, within the larger context of communication that established this book's parts, the individual chapters pay great at-tention to other social structures. Because so much of theatre history has occurred during the dominance of a relatively stable print culture and the effects of electric and electronic technologies are still greatly in flux, communication naturally takes a less pronounced role in the book's second half.

We close this introduction by returning to our starting point. We began by discussing the meaning of some major terms in this book: theatre, drama, and performance. There has been and continues to be enormous diversity in the theatrical performance practices of the world, both geographically and chronologically. Diverse forces have shaped theatre's development throughout its history. And there is a diversity of theories, facets, emphases, and goals in theatre historiography. In writing this book, our aim has been to introduce all of these dimensions of writing about theatre in history. That is the meaning of the plural in the title, *Theatre Histories*.

FREE

INSTRUCTOR
& STUDENT
RESOURCES

FEATURES AND CONVENTIONS OF *THEATRE HISTORIES*

Theatre Histories has timelines at the beginning of each of the four parts. Glossary terms in the text are in boldface. However, the glossary itself now appears on the website to make room for the book's increase in photographs. Other features include online resources (both for the book and from elsewhere on the internet), pronunciation guidance, and suggestions for further reading.

Pronunciation guidance

We have provided pronunciation guidance for selected non-English terms both in the *Theatre Histories* companion website (www.theatrehistories.com) with recordings of native speakers, and through transcriptions in the book itself (also listed at the end of the book). For simplicity, the transcriptions use English spellings of speech sounds, while trying to avoid ambiguity. For instance, to distinguish between the *g* in "get" from the one in "gem," we use [gh] and [j], respectively. However, most languages include sounds not used in English, and/or don't use sounds that English does. For example, English doesn't have the *ü* sound in the German term *Einfühlung*, which we transcribe as [ahyn-FEW-lung]. In a few cases we use a similar English word (such as the guidance for *nanxi*, which is [nahn she], using the English "she"). In Japanese, syllables use length rather stress, so we transcribe *kabuki* as [kah-boo-kee], even though most English speakers stress the second syllable. Chinese uses tones, which we are unable to transcribe at all. For these reasons, the pronunciation guidance in the book is very rough, and it should be used in conjunction with the audio recordings on the website. We have not provided guidance for many other non-English words, but often one can find recordings of them online through translation sites and multilingual dictionaries.

Additional resources

At the end of the book, we list the books and articles that we cited in the text, and also selected online and other media resources, including websites and recordings of performances by famous twentieth- and twenty-first-century artists. (The online resources we list were active as of 2023.)

The website offers additional texts drawn from previous editions of this book, including short essays on various topics, and case studies which instructors may want students to read in addition to or instead of the ones in the current edition. In addition, we list books and articles that we used in writing *Theatre Histories* but didn't specifically cite in the text, or that a reader wanting more information would find useful. As noted above, the website also provides the book's glossary.

There is one caution about online resources. The internet can be an astonishingly rich source of valuable information, thoughtful analysis, and videos of brilliant performance. However, anyone can put up a website with information and opinions not based on expertise, present outdated or faulty scholarship, quote sources out of context, or even intentionally misrepresent facts. It is best to use websites in conjunction with current scholarly books and articles, which have been vetted by experts and often represent new research and ideas not reflected in websites.

Names and diacritics

Japanese and Chinese names place the family name first (e.g., Suzuki Tadashi), which we follow unless the person has adopted Western usage. The names for regions of the world, such as the West and the Global South, necessarily vary throughout the book, depending on the context.

We have followed common scholarly usage in diacritical markings and Romanized spellings of terms from the many languages used in this text. However, in some cases, there are two accepted approaches. For example, scholars of Japanese theatre use both *noh* and *nō*; we have adopted the latter because it is the spelling used for subject headings in library catalogs and (less consistently) journal databases, although in scholarly research one should always search both.

Capitalization

Scholarly practices for capitalization vary. To the extent possible, we capitalize the names of movements, reasonably identifiable groups, and geographical regions. Some examples are Romanticism, the Romantics, Realism (as an artistic movement), Symbolism, Asian, and Western. We leave in lower case the terms for ideas, theories, and styles, when they are not necessarily connected to a particular movement or group of people: for instance, realism (as a set of ideas and stylistic goals), symbolism (the use of symbols in general), positivism, and positivists. Occasionally, this convention leads to seemingly odd combinations, such as when we discuss "realism and Naturalism," but the reason should be clear from the text.

★

Performance in oral and manuscript cultures

DOI: 10.4324/9781003185185-2

PART I TIMELINE

DATE	THEATRE AND PERFORMANCE	CULTURE AND COMMUNICATION	POLITICS AND ECONOMICS
200,000–190,000 BCE			Beginnings of modern humans
100,000–60,000 BCE		Beginnings of language	
c.5500–c.4000 BCE			Ancient civilization in Sumer (southern Iraq)
c.3800 BCE			Ancient civilization in Crete
c.3200–1800 BCE			Earliest South American civilization (Peru)
c.3150–2686 BCE			First dynasty, Egypt
c.3000 BCE–[?]	Performance, festivals, Mesoamerica		
c.2700 BCE		Sumerian epic Gilgamesh Egyptian hieroglyphs	
c.2070–c.1600 BCE			Xia dynasty, China
c.2055 BCE–[?]	Ritual of Osiris at Abydos, Egypt		
c.2000–c.1000 BCE			Earliest Mayan civilization
c.1600–c.1046 BCE		Chinese writing	Shang dynasty, China
c.1180 BCE			Trojan War
c.1050 BCE		Phoenician script	
c.1000 BCE	Hopi katsina rituals, North America Celtic rituals, bardic festivals, Europe		
c.850 BCE		Greek alphabet	
c.800 BCE	Homer and bardic performance, Greece	Written Sanskrit	
776 BCE		Olympic games, Greece	
753 BCE			Founding of Rome
c.600 BCE		Writing in Mesoamerica	
c.563–483 BCE		Siddhartha Gautama (Buddha), India	
551–479 BCE		Confucius, China	

PART I TIMELINE

DATE	THEATRE AND PERFORMANCE	CULTURE AND COMMUNICATION	POLITICS AND ECONOMICS
534 BCE	Early form of Greek tragedy performed by Thespis		
c.525–c.456 BCE	Aeschylus, playwright		
509–27 BCE			Roman Republic
499–479 BCE			Greco-Persian wars
c.497–c.405 BCE	Sophocles, playwright		
c.480–406 BCE	Euripides, playwright		
460–429 BCE			Periclean age, Athens
c.448–c.387 BCE	Aristophanes, playwright		
431–404 BCE			Peloponnesian War
c.400	*Mahabharata* and *Ramayana*, Sanskrit epics, India		
c.380 BCE		Plato, *The Republic*	
356–323 BCE			Alexander the Great, Europe and Asia
c.342–c.291 BCE	Menander, playwright		
c.330 BCE	Aristotle, *The Poetics*		
323 BCE–31 CE			Hellenistic period, Europe
c.254–184 BCE	Plautus, playwright		
221 BCE			First Emperor, Qin dynasty
206 BCE–220 CE			Han dynasty, China
204 BCE–65 CE	Roman drama		
c.200 BCE–c.200 CE	Bharata Muni writes the *Natyasastra*, India		
196 BCE		Rosetta stone	
c.190–c.159 BCE	Terence, playwright		
27 BCE–476 CE			Roman Empire
27 BCE–14 CE			Caesar Augustus, first emperor of Roman Empire
c.4 BCE–29 CE		Jesus of Nazareth, Middle East/ Europe	

PART I TIMELINE

DATE	THEATRE AND PERFORMANCE	CULTURE AND COMMUNICATION	POLITICS AND ECONOMICS
c.4 BCE–65 CE	Seneca, playwright		
50–150 CE		Buddhism enters China	
250–710 CE			Yamato period, Japan
250–900 CE			Mayan classical period, Yucatán peninsula
476 CE			Western Roman Empire falls; Eastern (Byzantine) Empire continues
533 CE	Last known theatre performance within the former Roman Empire		
570–632 CE		Muhammad, Middle East	
618–907 CE			Tang dynasty, China
790–1066 CE			Viking exploration
800–1100 CE			Trans-Sahara trade routes
c.900 CE	*Kutiyattam* temple theatre, India		
900–1550 CE			Mayan post Classic Period, Yucatán peninsula
c.925 CE	Catholic liturgical tropes		
c.1040 CE		Movable type, China	
1066 CE			Normans (Northern French) conquer England
1095–1099 CE		First Christian crusade against Muslims	
c.1100 CE	Development of carnival, Europe		
1254–1324 CE		Marco Polo, Italian merchant traveler	
1266–1337 CE		Giotto, artist	
1279–1368 CE	Yuan *zaju*		Yuan dynasty, China
c.1300–c.1400 CE	*Ramlila*, India		
c.1300–c.1600 CE		Renaissance era begins in Italy; spreads throughout Europe in the sixteenth century	
1313–c.1600 CE	Passion plays, continental Europe		

PART I TIMELINE

DATE	THEATRE AND PERFORMANCE	CULTURE AND COMMUNICATION	POLITICS AND ECONOMICS
1343–1400 CE		Geoffrey Chaucer, English writer	
c.1350–1569 CE	Cycle plays, England		
1363–1443 CE	Zeami, actor-playwright		
1368–1644 CE			Ming dynasty, China
1368–1644 CE	*Zaju* and *kunqu*, China		
c.1374 CE	*Nō*, Japan		
1428–1521 CE			Aztec Empire, Central America
c.1440 CE	*Rabinal Achi*, Mesoamerica	Movable type (printing press), Europe	
1452–1519 CE		Leonardo da Vinci, artist	
1453 CE			Ottomans capture Constantinople
1456 CE		First printed Bible	
1468–1834 CE			Spanish Inquisition
1475–1564 CE		Michelangelo, artist	
1492 CE			Spanish encounter with the Americas
1492–1898 CE			Spanish colonization of Western Hemisphere
c.1500 CE	Professional theatre companies begin to appear in various European countries		
c.1500–1600 CE	*Kathakali* dance drama, India		

Introduction: Speech, writing, and performance

Tobin Nellhaus

Photo PI1
The Rosetta stone displays a decree of 196 BCE in three scripts: ancient Egyptian hieroglyphs, Demotic script, and ancient Greek.
Source: World History Archive/Alamy Stock Photo.

The focus of Part I is the transition from purely **oral culture** to **literate culture**. Its three chapters cover roughly 2,000 years of theatre history, from the fifth century BCE to the sixteenth century CE, in order to discuss performance in the context of oral culture and several early literate cultures. In this introduction to Part I, we first provide an overview of the path its chapters take through the earliest forms of theatre. Then, after scanning these births of theatre, we turn to a strange development. When Western theatre was born, it wasn't an only child: **antitheatricality** – opposition to theatre – was its sibling.

Because of the importance of oral culture, we begin Chapter 1 by considering storytelling and ritual, two primary types of performance for perhaps 100 millennia before writing even existed. Numerous cultures developed writing, but its importance and functions varied across the world and changed over time; as a result, its relationship with oral culture varied, and its cultural impact followed suit. In most of the world, writing's usage and significance were quite limited, as it was in the chapter's next two topics. Writing first appeared sometime around 3,500 BCE in a region of the Middle East. A few centuries later, hieroglyphic writing developed in Egypt. It was learned by portions of the society's upper echelons; the culture as a whole remained predominantly oral. As early as the nineteenth century BCE, a mass religious ceremony in Egypt may have had small theatre-like elements. Next, we leap forward chronologically to discuss performance in Central America and southern Mexico, where conditions of literacy were similar to those of ancient Egypt. Sometime during the fifteenth century CE, the Mayan people created a performance which commemorated a historical event and appears to have been more like theatre as we know it. We then return to the ancient world to examine the rise of theatre in Athens, where due to several unusual circumstances, literacy gained a far larger cultural role than ever before. Like Mayan performance, its topics drew from myths and known history, but it addressed these topics primarily as a way to focus on contemporary issues of civic life rather than commemorate the ancestors or the gods. In addition, Greek drama was strongly oriented around texts. When classical Greek plays became available in the West again 2,000 years later, they were highly influential, and they are performed even today.

Chapter 2 continues our study of early theatres. Rome in the second and first centuries BCE sought to imitate the culture of Greece, but its tragedies turned from civic commentary to sensationalism, and the comedies shifted from social satires toward domestic issues. Eventually, interest swung toward violent spectacles such as gladiatorial combat, presented to a mass audience in huge arenas. During India's classical era (roughly the first through the eleventh centuries CE), theatre was intended to be both popular entertainment and a source of good counsel, and the early plays often drew on two major epics for their narratives. Theatre practitioners in classical India paid exceptional attention to qualities of performance rather than the dramatic text. Around the fourth century CE, theatre began evolving in China, where transformation text, a storytelling form from India used to popularize Buddhism but also as secular entertainment, played an important role in the development of Chinese performance; by the eighth century, an academy of performing arts called the Pear Garden was established. In the fourteenth century, a Japanese troupe offering variety performances came under aristocratic influence and developed a genre of serious drama, which spread across the country. In the course of this development, early Japanese theatre absorbed religious and philosophical ideas. As in India, theatre artists were keenly aware of performance.

The developments in these diverse parts of the world show the complex interactions between oral culture and literate culture, and between elite and popular performance, which played out differently depending on the particular social circumstances.

In Chapter 3, our attention turns primarily to performance in a new type of literate culture, dominated by religions founded on holy scriptures. Judaism was based on the Torah; Christianity used the Bible, comprising the Torah as the "Old Testament" and many later texts called the New Testament; and Islam's holy book was the Qur'an, a work which assumes knowledge of the Jewish and Christian biblical literatures but is a separate set of texts. Unlike spiritual documents in other major religions and epic narratives such as India's *Mahabharata* and *Ramayana*, these books are considered holy in themselves – unalterable, doctrinal, and even thought to be dictated or revealed directly by God. As a result, these texts occupied extraordinary positions within their cultures and played a crucial role in the cultures' histories. That situation added to the complexity of the relationship between oral culture and literate culture in these societies.

Although the three religions all had a set of holy writings, both literacy and performance developed differently in each. Judaism and early Islam considered literacy part of religious practice, although in some contexts as a support to their oral traditions rather than an independent mode of communication. Jews were an oppressed, often ghettoized minority within Europe who had limited opportunities to develop performance practices, but even so, evidence indicates that some Jews acted, and a play was based on a biblical text. Islam reversed its stand on education during the eleventh century and to varying extents it condemned all representations of people, in theatre and elsewhere. However, Islamic thought about representation was complex and diverse, and important types of performance were permitted, such as shadow puppetry. Unlike Judaism and Islam, medieval Christianity had no imperative toward widespread literacy. As in Islam, however, the Church long prohibited theatrical performance. But in the fourteenth century, the Church began to find theatre useful, and allowed other types of performance as well. As a result, theatre developed extensively in Christian Europe. Many of the performances within all three religions commemorated events within each religion's sacred literature, honored major events in the religion's history, or enacted the religion's ideas and values. Within Europe, there were also important types of wholly secular performance such as farce, and several occasions for boisterous public celebration, feasting, and release, sometimes involving masks and/or role-play.

Part I covers nearly 2,000 years of theatre history. The period raises an interesting philosophical question. Through much of Islam's history, for over a millennium in Christianity, and occasionally in Judaism, theatre was prohibited. Why would a type of performance closely related to the rise of literacy be banned in cultures that depended on writing? There is little sign of anything similar in India or East Asia. The hostility toward theatre was occasionally venomous. For example, a few decades after the medieval Church began encouraging religious drama in England, an unknown author wrote an almost hysterical diatribe against it. It is as though theatre's adversaries found something fundamentally unnerving and disruptive about acting itself. Theatre, it seems, was too deeply tied to the body and a notion of personal falsity, and so actors were associated with licentious sex and considered similar to or the same as prostitutes. Such disapproval, which surrounded Western and Middle Eastern theatre for much of its existence, seems unfamiliar today.

But antitheatricality in Europe is quite old. Despite its frequent association with religion, antitheatricality isn't strictly a matter of faiths and holy books, for it arose soon after the creation of Western theatre itself, in a polytheistic culture without scriptures. In ancient Athens, the philosopher Plato (c.428–c.347 BCE), writing at a time when Greek drama was at its height, strongly condemned theatre, along with painting, sculpture, poetry, indeed anything that smelled of what he called *mimesis* (imitation). In fact, he decried writing as inferior to speech. Yet paradoxically, despite his distrust of writing, Plato wrote books, and stranger still, he wrote his books as dialogues – as near to drama as one can get without actual performance. Most ironically of all, according to classical scholar Eric Havelock (1963), Plato's antagonism toward theatre arose from the way literacy shaped his concept of rationality. These are only some of the peculiarities in Plato's antitheatrical arguments. Nonetheless, they strongly influenced Western attitudes toward theatre ever since.

Plato's prosecution of theatre was based on the belief that true reality is to be found in abstractions, not in the embodied material world. From this assumption, Plato staged two fundamental attacks on the stage. On the one hand, philosophically, Plato construed theatre's fictions as lies, or at best, feeble imitations of the truth. Thus, theatre trades in illusions and falsehoods, and the actor in particular violates personal identity by pretending to be someone else. On the other hand, moralistically, if truth resides in abstractions, then the mind as the seat of reason sharply contrasts with the body as the realm of unreason, passion, pleasures, and desires. Theatre, then, wrongly encourages audiences to enjoy unruly emotions and improper ideas instead of conducting rational thought.

Plato's antitheatrical ideas passed down through centuries of European thought. To a greater or lesser extent, theatre was seen as an affront to God and nature. The philosophical and moralistic strands in Christianity did not always have the same importance – in fact, the moralistic stance was usually expressed more vigorously – but they were always intertwined.

But why did Plato's antitheatrical prejudice arise in the first place, and why did later cultures accept it? Most likely, several factors lay behind the sometimes panicky assaults on theatre in the Western world. According to Havelock, one reason for Plato's animosity is that when writing developed in ancient Greece, it created a break with oral culture and reshaped the reasoning process. Plato was creating an analytical, "objective" mode of thought based on literacy, and opposed to the more "subjective," participatory oral culture, and mimesis was intrinsic to orality's participatory nature (Havelock 1963: 36–49). It appears that not only is there a connection between theatre and writing, there is also a connection between antitheatricality and writing.

Yet as we noted, in Plato's opinion, speech is superior to writing and more closely aligned with truth and nature. At first glance, Plato seems to be contradicting himself, opposing oral culture on the one hand but supporting it on the other. However, his opposition was to oral culture's embodied, performative element. In contrast, for Plato, writing was intrinsically objectionable because the written word is secondary, an imitation (mimesis) of speech sounds – living speech bore truth.

The embodiment necessary to communication in oral cultures seems to have long been distasteful or outright abhorrent to thinkers who believed that writing allowed the mind to become disembodied, creating a sharp body/mind division. This aversion continues in the later idea that although drama is good (not repugnant, as Plato had it), it's best read as literature, unconnected with performance. The earliest instance of that view is also from ancient Greece, where theatre remained popular, and as a result, it wasn't long before a more positive view of drama appeared in philosophy: Plato's former student Aristotle (384–322 BCE) argued that mimesis and the pleasure we take in it are vital to human learning, and based on this perspective, he wrote the first dramatic theory in history. But notably, Aristotle preferred the dramatic text over its performance, reiterating a form of antitheatricality.

Today, when actors are among the greatest celebrities and can even become presidents, antitheatricality may seem utterly foreign and archaic. Closer examination shows otherwise. We saw in the General Introduction that "theatre" is sometimes applied metaphorically, as is "drama." Some of those uses are decidedly derogatory. For example, a person who behaves over-emotionally might be called a "drama queen." Public events or statements meant mainly to impress people are occasionally described as "theatre," such as in "The candidate's demand for a recount was just political theatre" or even "*kabuki* theatre," insinuating that a Japanese genre is especially shady. The modern meanings of "hypocrite" and "histrionic" have antitheatrical roots as well.

Even in the history of Western theatre, key figures such as the seventeenth-century English dramatist Ben Jonson and the early twentieth-century French performer and writer Antonin Artaud have been sharply conflicted about theatricality. Strangely enough, antitheatricality can appear within theatricality itself.

As we see, the history of theatre in the West is shadowed by an antitheatricality founded on the history of writing. In contrast, generally speaking, non-Western societies seem to have taken much more straightforward pleasure in performance. Although people in classical India, China, and Japan sometimes scorned actors and classed them with prostitutes just as in the West, they seem to have done so out of a fear of social disorder or class mixing, and sometimes misogyny, but not a deep-seated suspicion of theatre as such. Why they didn't develop an antitheatrical prejudice is an open question. The absence of Plato's influence was undoubtedly one factor, but probably there were other reasons – perhaps a more fluid relationship between oral and literate cultures. We do not yet know. But as we begin surveying theatre's histories, we should be aware that it has always been dense with complexities rooted in fundamental communication practices.

★

CHAPTER 1

From oral to literate performance

Tobin Nellhaus

Contributors: Phillip B. Zarrilli,
Tamara Underiner, and Daphne P. Lei

Nobody knows for certain how theatre began. Probably nobody ever will. But we do know some things about the earliest theatre, the types of performance that preceded it, and sometimes the circumstances in which it arose. There is a striking difference between theatre and the types of performance that existed before theatre arose. Dance, music, storytelling, and ritual (along with most other arts, such as painting) are evidently as old as humanity itself. Perhaps the same is true of the comic scenes sometimes enacted during rituals, or costumed "monsters" who scare misbehaving children in order to discipline them. But theatre is different from those short scenes, partly in the ideas and moods it can create, and particularly in the amount of organization and resources needed to sustain it – and it seems to have begun after the invention of writing. Writing first appeared around 3600–3400 BCE in Mesopotamia, a region within the Middle East. Because writing produces permanent records (using stone, clay, papyrus, and other materials), it is used as the line between prehistory and history. Compared to all the other arts, theatre is very new.

The theme of this chapter is how performance was affected by the change from **oral culture** to cultures that also had writing, which varied because writing's role differed from culture to culture. In oral cultures, the importance of speech is also usually accompanied by a significant role for bodily movement and gesture – types of performance – and the major forms of performance in those cultures are ritual, storytelling, dance, and music. As we will see, features of ritual and storytelling are influenced by the nature of live speech. Even after societies developed writing, for a few millennia and sometimes longer it was so embedded within oral culture that it had few, if any, wide-scale cultural effects.

Even though oral culture began with the dawn of humankind, oral modes of performance are by no means solely part of the past: they are dynamic and adaptable practices that continue to shape peoples' personal and social identities, and numerous aspects of human thought and culture. Likewise, the rise of **literate culture** did not create a form of performance that was utterly separate from oral culture. The relationship between spoken and

DOI: 10.4324/9781003185185-3

written communication is complex and varies depending on its social context – oral culture is always present in literate culture and influence can go in both directions.

In this chapter, we will focus on how the introduction of writing affected performance in several different contexts. First, we will discuss ritual and storytelling in oral cultures. Then, we will turn to a huge ceremony in ancient Egypt, and another in Aztec society (located in Central Mexico) – cultures which used writing but restricted it to a small elite. We will also discuss a play-like performance in Mayan society (which resided in Central America and southern Mexico). Finally, we will look at theatre in ancient Greece, the earliest society where literacy had extended beyond the elite. Even though we may not be able to identify theatre's origins, these social and cultural differences can help explain some of early theatre's characteristics.

THINKING THROUGH THEATRE HISTORIES: THE PROBLEM OF BEGINNINGS

Nothing in society ever sprang from thin air, so historians often want to learn how and why an activity began or what led to it. Starting in the 1870s, many people have asked that question about theatre, and particularly about Greek tragedy, for which we have more evidence than any other kind of ancient performance. However, this doesn't prove the Greeks were the first to have theatre, only that it was the first to leave much evidence – enough to tantalize, but not enough to satisfy. The question of beginnings has three sides: identifying theatre's predecessor; explaining the process of change; and describing the relationship between theatre and its predecessor.

What *was* theatre's predecessor? There have been many hypotheses. Probably the most popular has been religious ritual. One reason for this theory is that Greek tragedy seems to have had some sort of connection to the cult of the god Dionysus in the city of Athens. One version of this idea is that theatre originated in choral songs and dances in honor of Dionysus. By the 1960s, classical scholars showed that the original forms of these theories faced major problems in their evidence and reasoning; however, revised versions developed, and debate rages on. There is far less information for other parts of the world; the common view is that theatre similarly arose from ritual, but the argument sometimes seems to be applying the theory about Greek theatre. Another frequent answer has been hero worship, in which people honored dead heroes and kings by imitating events in their lives. This view seems more straightforward, but it doesn't have a firm grounding in our historical and archeological knowledge about ancient Greece, and may be stronger in other regions. Various other theories have also been offered, some examining activities other than ritualistic ones, including the effects of writing. Although some ideas are better known than others, there is no true consensus.

The second side of any question about predecessors is the process of change and its possible implications. For example, if we accept the "religious ritual" theory of theatre's inception, we should clarify how the one developed into the other. Did the development occur in a smooth progression of a more or less evolutionary nature, along a continuum from highly ritualistic to un-ritualistic? If so, then given the universality of ancient ritual, one must wonder why theatre arose in so few cultures. Alternatively, perhaps theatre involved innovative steps that sought to accomplish something that rituals couldn't; rituals could still provide "raw materials," somewhat like the way many of the first movies were like stage plays. Religious ritual wouldn't be theatre's origin, merely something older. Theatre could be fundamentally different from ritual – a revolutionary cultural form. (Some scholars dismiss the process of change altogether, in effect saying "First there was religious ritual/choral songs/hero worship, then there was theatre, therefore there *must* be a connection even though we don't know how the former became the latter" – a version of the *post hoc* argument discussed in the General Introduction.)

Finally, one must consider the relationship between theatre and its predecessor. For example, what does it mean to say that X is the "origin" of theatre? Is that the same as saying it's the "earliest type" of theatre? One claim is that theatre's origin remains the essence of theatre itself (e.g., "theatre is fundamentally a religious ritual"). A converse view is that the origin was just the starting point: theatre was the goal or the final form of the previous activity ("religious ritual is fundamentally theatre"). A related position is that the origin of theatre is whatever caused it to develop. The validity of this idea depends on what the origin is thought to be: for example, if religious ritual is the origin of theatre, clearly it didn't drive theatre to become a more vigorous form of religion, so it's unlikely it caused theatre to develop; a type of performance that strove for (say) social self-reflection would be more likely to generate what we now recognize as theatre. As suggested above, theatre's predecessors could be the "raw material" – the familiar activities – that people reworked when they created theatre. This view focuses more on innovations than on origins. There are still further possibilities. Different ideas about the beginnings of theatre aren't mutually exclusive: much depends on what one is examining, and even on how one defines theatre. For instance, one can reject the ritual theory of theatre's origin, yet believe that today ritual and theatre still exist on a continuum, so that each has qualities of the other. Likewise, one can hold that certain features are essential to all theatre, including the very earliest, but something else caused theatre to arise.

The fact is, we have don't have enough evidence to be certain of any theory about theatre's beginnings. Even the evidence we do have is subject to interpretation. For example, we know that plays were performed at the Theatre of Dionysus. That obviously shows that the plays were in honor of that god. Or does it? Names don't necessarily prove consecration – for instance, from 2000 to 2024, one of the theatre buildings in New York City was named the American Airlines Theatre, but the plays performed there were not devotions to American Airlines. So, could there be any nonreligious reasons for incorporating theatre within a Dionysian festival, such as the advantages for attracting a large audience?

Theatre Histories does not commit to any origin theory and instead focuses on the connections between the development of theatre and changes in communication, in part because theatre is a form of communication. One important factor seems to be the interaction between orality and literacy that is embedded in the oral and embodied performance of a written text. As we will see, the mental strategies involved in maintaining an oral culture are different from those relying on texts, and ancient theatre reveals traces of both methods of thinking. Thus, understanding oral culture and the varieties of early literate cultures does help us understand several characteristics of ancient theatre. As we will see throughout this book, subsequent changes in communication practices similarly appear to have influenced theatrical performance.

Performance in oral cultures

For anyone silently reading this book (and for its authors too), it is difficult or impossible to completely grasp what oral culture is like because our own manner of thinking is already shaped by literacy. Sometimes people unfamiliar with oral culture assume it's simply a relative of literate culture, or else consider it a primitive form of thought devoid of abstraction and logical reasoning. However, studies conducted in Africa by cultural anthropologists, analyses of epic poetry from places ranging from ancient Greece to modern Serbia, and various other types of research have demonstrated that neither view is correct. Oral cultures can be sophisticated, but their methods of conceptualizing the world and people's relationships to it are very different from those common in highly literate societies. The research helps us to imagine what life and performance were like in cultures without writing and reading, and to see that some forms or features of oral culture exist in every culture today.

Many of oral culture's characteristics arise from practical aspects of speech. In everyday interactions, a living person must be present to speak, and another present to listen. Words have tones and rhythms, they can create rhymes or assonance, and they can be spoken softly or loudly. Speech uses not only the mouth, throat, and chest, but also facial expressions and usually gestures and other movements, potentially involving the whole body. One learns from others primarily by listening to them, so the sense of hearing has special importance. And crucially, speech only exists in the moment: after that, there is only memory. Consequently, in oral cultures, knowledge, historical legend, religious beliefs, mythology, and all other aspects of culture must be passed on by elders and by "cultural specialists" such as shamans and storytellers.

Memory aids in oral cultures

If knowledge in oral cultures can only be stored in memory and transmitted primarily through speech, how is that done? Although people in wholly oral cultures relied on their memories more than people in literate cultures and excellent memory was often prized, it was unusual to need verbatim recollection. Sometimes verbatim memorization did occur; for an example, see the discussion of the Indian Vedas in the "Primary Orality" essay on the *Theatre Histories* website. But in most situations, the goal was to express ideas in a way that made them easily remembered and easily learned, not to preserve the exact words.

Various techniques can aid memory, and many if not all of the same ones were used in cultures across the globe. The examples most familiar to Western readers are the ancient Greek epic poems *The Odyssey* and *The Iliad*, which were composed orally and probably written down in eighth century BCE. Open any page and you will discover examples of many of the strategies that oral cultures use to preserve and transmit ideas:

- *Verbal patterns, such as rhyme, rhythm, and formulas.* Ancient Greek oral poetry did not use rhyme, but it did use rhythm (called meter) which gives language an extra structure to aid memory and attract the audience's attention. Putting words to music makes cultural knowledge even easier to recall. Set phrases, called formulas, help too. In *The Odyssey* and *The Iliad*, for example, one finds recurrent formulas such as "said to her in answer," "the gray-eyed goddess Athena," and "rosy fingered dawn," which one can easily remember and fit into the rhythm.

- *Stereotypical characters, scenes, and stories.* Characters in oral cultures tend to be character-types – the wise, the evil, the innocent, the soldier – described with epithets such as "thoughtful Telemachos" and "resourceful Odysseus." Character-types don't have personalities in the modern sense: they are not "deep" or psychologically complex. Their nature is outward and publicly defined – which they must be, in order to communicate something memorable that can be passed down through the generations. Similarly, there are scene-types: standard events such as holding a feast or receiving a guest, which can be adapted as needed.

- *Strong, strange, and symbolic imagery.* Character-types condense traits down to a few strong qualities that are readily remembered. Even more memorable are strange and unnatural images, such as the many-armed Hindu goddess Kali, and Greek mythology's multi-headed monster Scylla. Scylla probably represented the dangers of the Strait of Messina between Italy and Sicily. Providing still greater symbolic and memorable aspects, Kali's arms and what each hand holds all have religious meanings. Symbolic elements make it possible for an image to pack a vast amount of knowledge, which one can recall by decoding the image's parts. (Of course, not all strong imagery was used symbolically.)

- *Narrative development through episodes.* Typically, long oral narratives consist of many episodes strung together. One event follows another without a necessary causal or logical connection, just an (actual or implied) "and then." As a result, one can often skip an episode in *The Odyssey* without radically harming the overall story of Odysseus, or recount just one or two episodes at a sitting to suit the occasion, audience, and time available. More literary plotlines, in contrast, have a closely knit causal sequence where skipping a scene could render the story incoherent. Sometimes oral narratives follow a standard pattern. One of the most common structures involves three elements, such as the major characters (as in "The Three Little Pigs"), personal interactions (lovers meet, separate, and rejoin), or objects (porridge that's too hot, too cold, and just right).

- *Codified gestures, actions, and bodily movements.* Customary physical actions can mark an event as memorable, identify relationships among people, and enact a culture's understanding of relationships among people or between people and deities; often, they accomplish all these things at once. Customary actions run the gamut: bowing upon meeting; shaking hands to seal an agreement; using beads (such as a rosary) to repeat prayers a set number of times; performing large rituals that involve chants, dances, and/or contests; and more. Inviting a stranger to a feast and giving them pride of place is a scene-type in *The Odyssey* that teaches the audience the culture's values. Our embodied interactions with the world also give us ways of understanding it. For instance, because human bodies are symmetrical, many cultures view left and right as opposites. Other world-based contrasts include night and day, male and female, hot and cold, and summer and winter. Thus in oral culture, ideas and expressions often involve pairing one thing against another (yet beings who combined or alternated between polarities such as male and female could be viewed as endowed with special powers or uniquely holy). Similarly, the idea of maintaining balance or equilibrium in society, nature, and/or the universe is central to many oral cultures, and a key part of their religious rituals, as we will see in our discussions of the Hopi and the Maya.

The techniques described above are only some of the features of oral communication, but they show that in order to preserve ideas, the structure of thought in oral culture must be very different from its structure in literate culture. But the difference does not lie simply in how one phrases language or constructs a story. Oral techniques orient an understanding of the world itself. Characters, for example, are flat or externally oriented not just because that's the easiest way to transmit them through history: people are actually understood as being psychologically flat or outward. In Europe, people only started to have psychological "depth" at the close of the Middle Ages and particularly during the Renaissance. We will recount that history in Chapter 5. (To read more about how oral cultures interpret the world, see the essay "Ritual" on the *Theatre Histories* website). Yet despite these crucial differences, verse, three-step narratives, codified behaviors, and other features of oral culture continue to play a role in human culture to the present. This is one example of the way that cultural elements connected to one mode of communication may endure when a new mode of communication arises.

Oral cultures vary in all sorts of ways, because many different social structures play a role in cultural development: economic systems, gender relations, political structures, religions, and more. But all oral cultures develop two major types of performance: storytelling and ritual. They are part of the background of oral culture that fed into the development of theatre.

Storytelling and ritual in oral cultures

The stories most cultures tell are generally brief, but some can be quite lengthy. Several ancient cultures produced extended epics, such as *Gilgamesh* (Sumeria, eighteenth century BCE), *Mahabharata* (India, eighth or ninth centuries BCE), *Popol Vuh* (Central America/southern Mexico, partly pre-third century BCE), *Beowulf* (England, seventh century CE), and *The Epic of King Gesar* (Tibet, twelfth century CE). In an oral culture, everyone would be familiar with many of the events that occurred in an epic and probably could link several together, but in some societies, a few people learned numerous stories and made storytelling their vocation, often delivering their stories with musical accompaniment or in song. Storytellers could become highly skilled not only in recounting tales, but also in selecting episodes, improvising stories, and even commenting on current events. However, evidence indicates that other societies did not develop the specialized role of storytellers; possibly their economy could not support even itinerant bards, or the shorter tales in their cultural repertory were sufficient for their needs.

An example of storytellers today is a group in western Africa (mainly in what is now Mali) known as griots (Figure 1.1). Griots could be male or female. The earliest reference to them was in 1352 CE, but they undoubtedly existed much earlier. "Storytellers" hardly begins to cover their numerous roles: they also served (and to some extent continue to serve) as historians, genealogists, advisors, spokespersons, diplomats, mediators, interpreters, musicians, composers, teachers, and other social functions. While any adult can perform most of a griot's general activities, professional griots are more skilled, knowledgeable, and engaging. They also tell lengthier stories. The longest recorded has almost 8,000 lines of verse; for comparison, *Beowulf* has roughly 3,200 lines, and *The Odyssey* has about 12,000 lines. The griots' epics have features shared by epics around the world – the requirements of this genre are very consistent, following the techniques described above (Hale 1998: 18–58, 135, 137).

Notably, storytellers usually present characters' dialogues not by enacting the characters, the way an actor plays roles, but via quoted speech. For instance, in a conversation we find introductory phrases like "in answer to him spoke Achilleus of the swift feet," or following a speech we encounter "So he spoke." The storyteller quotes what the characters said, rather than directly speaking as them. Sometimes the quoted speech is lengthy, such as when Odysseus recounts his voyage. Within his story, Odysseus himself quotes others' speech in the same manner. Though they may change their voice to distinguish characters, only occasionally do storytellers directly speak as a character. This is a significant distinction between storytelling and theatre: in theatre, actors speak as the character. However, theatre shares storytelling's focus on narrative.

Along with storytelling, a crucial form of oral culture is **ritual**. Ritual is a form of performance that draws participants' minds to ideas and feelings that have special social (often religious) importance. Rituals are essential for preserving a culture's memory of its identity, character, and beliefs. Both oral and literate cultures have rituals. Rituals can honor spiritual beings such as gods, spirits, or ancestors; conduct a rite or ceremony to mark an important life change such as puberty, marriage, or death; affirm or create a relationship toward someone (e.g., to a king or a guest) or

Figure 1.1

Mali: This Zoumana hunter is also a fetisher and griot.

Source: © Hemis/Alamy.

a social commitment (an oath, an agreement); spiritually purify a space, object, or person; demonstrate power; confer political office; and serve many other purposes.

Many rituals today are extremely old. One example is *nuo* [nu-oh], an ancient group of rituals, exorcisms of evil spirits, and thanksgiving to gods in China. Its exact origin is unknown – archeological findings trace *nuo* rites as far as 7,000 years ago, several millennia before China's earliest form of writing. Theories about the etymology of the ideogram "*nuo*" suggest that *nuo* was connected to ancient shamanism, animism, totem worship, or exorcism long before the establishment of today's best-known Chinese belief systems, such as ancestral worship, Confucianism, Taoism, and Buddhism.

The earliest written record appears in the *Analects*, indicating Confucius (551–479 BCE) witnessed a *nuo* rite. The first description of the performance aspects of *nuo* appears in *The Rites of Zhou*, compiled 300–100 BCE: a person wearing a black jacket, a red skirt, and a bearskin mask with four golden eyes holds a lance and a shield, leading 100 enslaved people in a seasonal *nuo* rite in order to repel pestilence and illness. Although there are diverse forms of *nuo* rituals and performances today, the initial form is believed to be an outdoor ritualistic masked dance with music, as seasonal rituals or for specific occasions. *Nuo* rituals were widely spread throughout history and can be found today from the Yellow River region, to coastal areas, to southern border provinces.

By the time it was recorded in *The Rites of Zhou*, *nuo* was already secularized and incorporated by the elite as part of the regularly performed court ritual. The latter then developed into a ritualistic masked dance, which, through cross-cultural transmission, was transformed into a forerunner of *nō* in Japan (see Chapter 2). As *nuo* developed, there was cross-fertilization between the Han (the ethnic majority) and the minority cultures. Different belief systems – cosmology, philosophy, local beliefs, and major religions such as Taoism and Buddhism – were integrated. Local stories and dramatic characters were also absorbed into the genre. The court ritualistic dance is an example of the adaptation of folk culture by the Han elite to form a type of political spectacle, which eventually was abolished in the seventeenth century. However, the folk forms of *nuo* continue to exist in countryside and remote areas occupied by ethnic minorities such as Tujia and Miao today, with religious ceremonies, ritualistic music, and masked dance with simple dramatization and improvisation. The folk forms, which were suppressed in modern China because of the Communist anti-superstition policy, are now revered and protected as part of the global trend of preserving the "oral and intangible heritage of humanity." Nowadays, there are also newly written "scripts" for *nuo* "opera."

An example of modern-day *nuo* rituals is from Tujia, a non-Han ethnic group from the mountainous area in central China. Its full-scale *nuo* rituals consist of a series of activities: building a sacred *nuo* shrine, inviting the gods to come to the shrine, exorcising evil spirits, offering thanks to the gods, and seeing the gods back to heaven. A typical ritualistic performance is "catching evil spirits," which involves two *nuo* masters wearing magical skirts made of eight pieces of fabric in different colors. They hold and move the skirts up and down while dancing with steps following a specific diagram, symbolically trapping all the evil spirits in the magic web they weave with their performance (Li 2015: 91, 97).

There are varying interpretations of ritual's primary social function, such as building cohesion within a society, releasing a culture's emotional tensions, hiding or justifying oppressive social relationships by giving them supernatural explanations and meanings, or creating opportunities to negotiate and sometimes transform social relationships. Whichever function(s) ritual serves, most societies require someone specialized in leading them. In oral cultures of both the past and present, at one end of the spectrum are **shamans**, who mediate between humans and the spirit world, heal people, and know most of the culture's mythology and history – but often live like everyone else in the village. (Occasionally most of the villagers can perform some shamanic duties, so the degree of specialization can be slight.) At the other end of the spectrum, a distinct priestly class develops, with high entrance requirements demanding years of preparation.

Rituals, especially religious ones, interest many people who study theatre because they require bodily performance. Tribal rituals frequently involve awe, emotional release, community bonding, and other feelings. In contrast to storytelling, such rituals may involve the impersonation or embodiment of deities, which is similar to the enactment of character in theatre; however, unlike both storytelling and theatre, religious rituals usually present or refer to very brief narratives, such as a single incident from a lengthy story already known to the participants. Rituals typically involve a special set of symbolic objects, words, or sounds (such as drumming), which create an element of spectacle. Often there are well-established rules of procedure or behavior, but sometimes the rules are loose, and ritual events can even provide a license for playfulness and misbehavior. The case study on the Hopi *Powamû* ceremony presents an example of a religious ritual that includes such playfulness. (The website has an additional example, the Yoruba *Egúngún* ritual.)

CASE STUDY: Hopi katsinas and clowns

Tobin Nellhaus

Contributor: Phillip B. Zarrilli

Of the hundreds of tribes native to North America, the Hopi have been the most able to maintain their ancient culture against Western impositions. They, the Zuni, and several other tribes form the Pueblo peoples, who live in the North American Southwest and share many cultural practices, yet have separate languages. The Hopi's homeland is on three mesas in what is now northeastern Arizona (Figure 1.2), which they occupied about 2,000 years ago, but the tribe itself is far older. Some Hopi were hunter-gatherers, but most were farmers, cultivating a variety of crops, including corn, kidney and tepary beans, cotton, pumpkins, and squash.

Farming required permanent settlement on the land rather than nomadically pursuing prey. Hopi villages, distinguished by their multistoried buildings made of limestone or adobe bricks, became thriving urban centers. The village of Oraibi dates from around 1125 CE, and may be the oldest continuously inhabited locale in what is now the United States. By the sixteenth century, the Hopi had at least 70 villages in the region, each of them independently governed by its own council. The Spanish, who began their invasion of the Americas at the beginning of that century, encountered the Hopi people in 1540. Over the decades, the Spanish imposed their rule throughout the region. Missionaries arrived in 1629 and converted many Hopi, increasingly by force. In 1680, the Pueblos rebelled and drove the Spanish out, but the Spanish re-conquered the area in 1691.

However, for over a century, the Hopi largely resisted religious conversion and lived in relative peace. Most of the Hopi along with the other Pueblo tribes adopted enough of Spanish culture to pacify the rulers. In 1850, the United States acquired the land that became the southwestern states, putting the Hopi under its jurisdiction. For some decades, their isolation and the scarce resources on their land spared them from the coerced removals and genocide by the United States that native tribes suffered elsewhere, but they were not left unscathed and eventually the pressures of their situation deeply fractured the community. Nevertheless, their religion never died out.

Traditional Hopi religion and beliefs are organized around an annual ritual calendar intended to maintain equilibrium with their environment. At the center of their religion are the ritual dances of the katsinas. These rituals helped the Hopi preserve

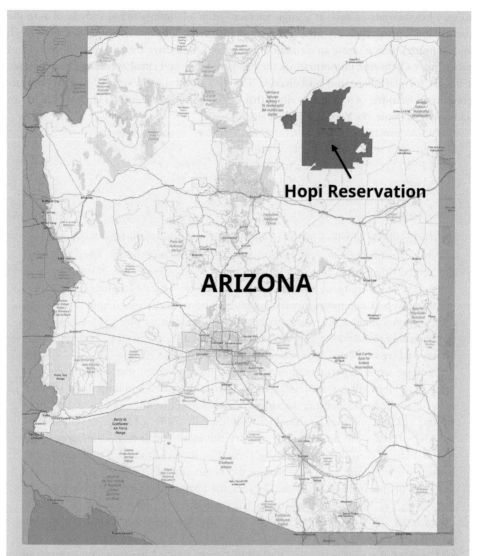

Figure 1.2
Map of the Hopi Reservation.
Source: © Tobin Nellhaus.

their culture and knowledge through the centuries. (Rituals performed both to secure environmental or cosmological balance and to sustain social values are a common part of oral cultures.) The descriptions of these dances by Spanish missionaries show that the katsina dances centuries ago were similar to those performed today. For a period of approximately seven months each year, Hopi interact with the katsinas – unseen spirits of all things good and kind, including the dead. (*Katsina* comes from *katsi*, life or spirit, and *na*, father. Usually *katsina* is anglicized as *kachina*, but most Hopi today prefer the correct phonetic form; however, we will not change spellings in quotations.) These seven months begin with the winter solstice (21 December), when *Soyala* ceremony is held. The first major katsina ceremony is *Powamû* (Bean Dance) in February. The final ritual with the katsinas is in July, when the Going Home Ceremony (*Nimán*) takes place. Many other ceremonies are held during the months when the katsinas visit. From August through November, non-katsina rites occupy the ritual calendar, with either the Snake-Antelope or the Flute Dance (*Chüchübti*) in August, women's society rituals in September and October (*Maraû* and *Oáqöl*), and tribal initiation (*Wüwüchim*) in November. The exact date and the structure of many ceremonies are flexible. Hopi religious ceremonies are conducted in the village's plaza and in underground chambers – *kivas* – reached by ladders. The kivas are both sacred spaces for ceremonies and communal lodges.

Katsinas have the power to "bring rain, exercise control over the weather, help in many of the activities of the villages, punish offenders of ceremonial or social laws, and in general act as a link between gods and mortals" (Dockstader 1985: 9). They are not gods themselves, but instead emissaries for the Hopi to the gods. As beneficent supernatural beings, the katsinas are thought to have always been with the Hopi, having come with the original Hopi ancestors when they emerged from underground at the beginning of time. They wandered together until the Hopi settled where they are located today in Arizona, with the katsinas residing in the mountains southwest. Each village may have katsinas of its own; new katsinas can be introduced, while others disappear.

Hopi interact with these beings, which can be male or female, via male masked dancers – also known as katsinas – who wear a costume and often a "helmet-mask" covering the entire head. It is a great honor and responsibility to become a katsina. "If [a dancer] understands the essence of the kachina, when he dons the mask he loses his identity and actually becomes what he is representing" (Sekaquaptewa 2001: 46). Sometimes the mask represents an animal or a bird; others may be known by a distinguishing feature, such as a long beard. At the time of the ceremonies, a katsina dancer must follow specific prescriptions for behavior and deportment, remaining pure and celibate in order to serve as a suitable messenger. The performers embody and impersonate these beings through a series of dances from their initial emergence at winter solstice until they return home in July. But they may also have nonreligious purposes, such as dancing (sometimes individually) for spectators' enjoyment. They bring gifts to children, but when a young child misbehaves, the parents may warn it that the katsinas could take away all the gifts.

The nine-day *Powamû* (Bean Dance) celebrates fertility and the Hopi's connection to the katsinas. It is the major ritual of the katsina cult. The ceremony is also thought to be medicine for rheumatism. Sixteen days before *Powamú*, beans are planted inside warm, humid kivas, and forced to grow. During *Powamú*, there are eight days of secret rituals. On the ninth day, the public ceremonies occur. As many as 50 or 60 masked katsinas perform the Bean Dance in the plaza, which lasts all night. The young bean plants in the kivas are cut and taken to a shrine. Finally, the katsinas distribute the beans to the households.

Every four years, selected children between the ages of six and ten are brought to the kivas to be initiated into the *Powamû* society. In those years, the ritual is longer and more complex. The children are taught the sacred history of the katsinas. They also discover that the katsinas they know from ceremonies are people in costume. After their initial shock and dismay, the children learn that the people performing as katsinas bear the katsina spirit, for all of reality has a spiritual aspect and is not always what it appears to be. Once they are initiated, the boys can perform the katsinas and the girls can be katsina maidens – but they are fiercely warned to keep their new knowledge secret.

The seven-month katsina cycle concludes in July with the *Nimán* (Going Home) ceremony, which lasts 16 days. Each village chooses a katsina to honor. Although the ceremony is similar to the earlier ones, it is more solemn and more gifts are distributed. At the end of the entire ceremony, a tribal representative makes a farewell speech, which ends with a prayer for rain. Then, the dancers remove their masks and return home. In the morning, the kivas are sealed and no more masked dances may be performed during the fall and winter, except for one paying homage to the katsina who represents death.

During Hopi katsina dances and at other times of the year, clowns appear. They are an excellent example of the way ritual can incorporate playfulness. Like the katsinas, they are always performed by males. As Barton Wright (2004) explains, there are several types of clowns, each with its own sort of costume and body-paint. Some wear masks, some don't, and some can do either. Many are considered sacred. The best-known type is the *koyemsi*, commonly known as "mudheads" since their heads are covered with sack-like masks, who occupy a special role (Figure 1.3).

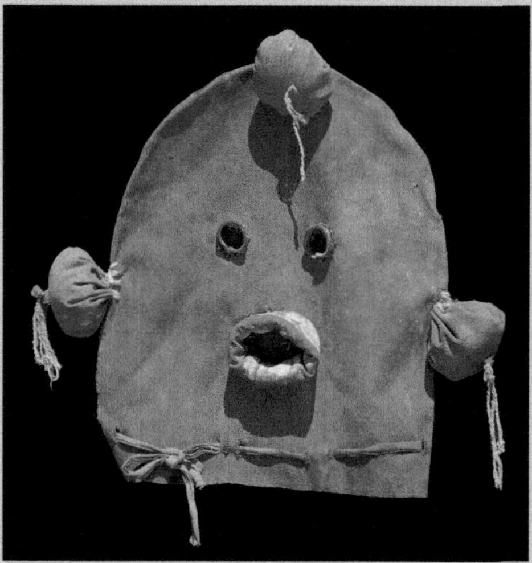

Figure 1.3
Hopi *koyemsi* (mudhead) katsina mask.

Source: © 2023 by the Second Face Museum of Cultural Masks. Reproduced with permission.

The clowns often enter the village plaza from the rooftops and descend in the most absurd and clumsy ways, such by the ladders headfirst or by trying to use an umbrella as a parachute. They literally stumble into the katsinas, try to "own" them, and pray to them for wrong things like pretty girls or cars. They dash around the village making crude jokes, tripping over themselves, and eating like gluttons, wasting much of the food. They search for someone standing right in front of them, walk backward, or stand on their heads in a puddle. They mime falling dead and are only revived by the performance of explicit sexual acts (although when performed while outsiders are present, these are often curtailed). They draw a house on the ground and get stuck inside. Some perform skits that are

> burlesques of the ordinary. A trifling occurrence is treated as a momentous event or the reverse, an exaggerated display of common emotion, is portrayed…. Essentially, the clowns isolate the core of a current event and reduce it to the ridiculous… often with a vulgar or even obscene version.
>
> (Wright 2004: 7)

Sometimes they impersonate obnoxious tourists pushing, taking photos, and shouting in crude English. Frequently, they satirize members of the tribe (for example, by performing mock college graduation ceremonies), and even burlesque the katsina dance itself. The katsinas, however, ignore them. But when the clowns' behavior becomes too outrageous, the Warrior katsinas arrive to threaten them; the clowns promise to behave but then forget. The Owl katsina throws little pebbles at them, representing pangs of conscience, and when the clowns do not improve their behavior, he imposes stronger and stronger punishments to discipline them. Finally, the exasperated katsinas whip them, strip them, throw them into a pile, and drench them with water.

The *koyemsi* mostly act like simpletons, unlike the other clowns, but they can also serve serious purposes, such as punishing wrong-doers, disciplining children, or curing the ill. They may also provide singing and drumming for the katsina dancers. The *koyemsi* are intermediaries between the katsinas and the humans, but they jumble katsinas' instructions, such as by telling men to do women's work and vice versa. Sometimes they lecture the spectators. They are never whipped, but instead given prayer-sticks. There are actually many different types of *koyemsi*, and some don't perform in a clownish manner at all – including the *Powamû koyemsi*, who is a katsina himself.

Some of the katsinas can be humorous too, at least to adults. For example, parents may arrange for the ogre katsinas (who play an important role in the *Powamû* ritual) to visit their home to discipline a misbehaving child. The ogres may demand the child recreate their bad behavior or threaten to snatch the child away or even eat it, and the parents bribe them with food, perhaps also persuading them that it's a bad time to make off with the child because it's about to be married (with an elderly grandparent playing the betrothed).

The clowns demonstrate, ridicule, and chastise the many ways people should *not* behave. In this way, they maintain the values of the village. But just as the more serious rituals do, the clowns also preserve essential aspects of Hopi culture and beliefs – the most basic function of rituals in oral cultures. As Emory Sekaquaptewa puts it, "the heart of the Hopi concept of clowning is that we are all clowns" (2016: 205).

Key references

Dockstader, F.J. (1985) *The Katsina and the White Man*, Albuquerque: University of New Mexico Press.

Sekaquaptewa, E. (2001) "Hopi Indian Ceremonies," in A. Gabriel Meléndez, M. Jane Young, Patricia Moore, and Pynes Patrick (eds.) *The Multicultural Southwest: A Reader*, Tucson: University of Arizona Press, 43–9.

Sekaquaptewa, E. (2016) "One More Smile for a Hopi Clown," in Susan Lobo, Steve Talbot, and Traci L. Morris (eds.) *Native American Voices: A Reader*, Upper Saddle River, NJ: Prentice Hall, 205–7.

Wright, B. (2004) *Clowns of the Hopi: Tradition Keepers and Delight Makers*, Walnut, CA: Kiva Pub.

Video

A Hopi Eagle katsina dance at Hotevilla, Arizona, in 2020: https://www.youtube.com/watch?v=VrLZt4SJ9Qo

Performance in oral cultures with writing

Writing has a complex history and has taken a variety of forms. The basic systems are logo-grams, syllabaries, and alphabets. Logograms use a simple image or (frequently) an abstract symbol to represent a whole word, the way that ☼ means "sun" and the emoticon ;-) means "wink." Syllabaries utilize one character for each syllable, phonetically – somewhat like using a letter name for a syllable, such as "R U OK?" for "Are you okay?" In syllabaries, the symbol is often derived from a logogram, like "I ♥ NY," which stands for "I love New York." Finally, alphabets give each individual speech sound its own letter, like *b* and *u*. (Writing systems can combine these basic approaches in various ways.) We will discuss a few of these below, and we offer a more detailed discussion of the history of language and the invention of writing in the essay "Human Speech and Early Writing" on the website.

In societies where writing developed, it stimulated economic and cultural growth. The extent, character, and rapidity of social transformation differed according to the context. In some societies, it appears that writing provided the means to create new forms of performance and new ways to encounter myths, epics, or narratives. This section examines performance in three ancient societies which used writing but kept it restricted to a small group of people (generally rulers, scribes, and priests), often for limited purposes. Important as those individuals often were, their literacy had little significant impact on people outside the courts and temples. Our first example of performance in such a culture is a massive ceremony conducted in Abydos, Egypt. The second and third are from societies in Mesoamerica (a region covering Central America and southern Mexico): the Aztecs' sacrificial ceremonies, and the Maya's dance-drama *Rabinal Achi*. Following these, we'll discuss performance in classical Greece, a society where writing was relatively widespread and used for numerous purposes.

The sequence of our discussion (Egypt, the Aztec and Mayan empires, Greece) does not signal progress or evolution. For example, there is no evidence that ancient Greek theatre had once been like the Abydos ceremony: it had a different path of invention. Instead, we are looking at forms of performance in connection with the relationship between orality and literacy in these societies. Both Egypt and Mesoamerica used forms of writing that were difficult to learn, and literacy extended only to a small elite. In Athens, however, because Greece used a more easily learned alphabetic script, literacy spread far more widely than was possible anywhere else at the time (although still far from universal). The differences between these societies' uses of writing had consequences for their types of performance.

Public life in these ancient societies was organized around elaborate annual religious or seasonal festivals featuring commemorative celebrations, rituals, and other performances. Some of these performances were highly choreographed and were believed necessary for maintaining social, civic, and cosmic cohesion. The idea that performances could have such power is related to the nature of religion in these early societies, which was less a matter of personal faith than the duties and actions which the gods or spirits required in order to receive their due and keep the universe in balance. To the religions of oral cultures, voice and gesture – especially in ritual – are themselves powerful, a view that could extend to other types of performance.

Many early forms of performance activities were part of commemorative religious ceremonies that celebrated or re-enacted a fundamental mythological, cosmic, or historical event, or a source of power. Commemorative ceremonies sometimes provided quasi-dramatic means of encountering a religious power or a past event in the present, reminding a community of "its identity as represented by and told in a master narrative … making sense of [its] past as a kind of collective autobiography" (Connerton 1989: 70). **Commemorative dramas** may be enacted to honor appropriate deities; to placate or celebrate cosmic or natural forces; to enhance communication with the divine; or to commemorate mythic, quasi-historical, or historical moments in the society's history.

Some early types of formalized performance not only have a ritual purpose, but also are highly sophisticated works of art, combining enactment, music or song, and dance or movement. They employ non-realistic modes of representation in acting, staging, and costuming (including masking and make-up) in order to depict larger-than-life figures, such as epic heroes, gods, and ghosts. They may blur the boundaries between spectating and participating. We will see additional examples of commemorative performance in Chapter 3, most of them in cultures more affected by literacy; here, we will consider two that arose in the context of highly restricted literacy.

Commemorative ritual performance in Abydos, Egypt

The religious background

By 3000 BCE, Egyptian civilization had evolved a highly complex set of religious practices and beliefs. For well over 3,000 years, Egyptian religious and cultural life exhibited a tolerant polytheistic openness to the worship of a spectacular array of many deities – gods and goddesses both old and new, local and foreign. Their myths and legends were often contradictory. Three distinct but interconnected accounts of creation existed, each focusing on a different group of deities and each considered equally valid.

As typical of ancient cultures, dualities were fundamental to the Egyptian worldview. Chaos was balanced by order. Life was associated with day and death with night. Their regular alternation demonstrated how the gods controlled the cosmos. The god Ra was both the lord of time and the sun-god who ruled the day. His counterpart was Osiris, ruler of death and the underworld. Death and life were not two different states, but two aspects of one state; therefore, life balanced death. The afterlife – an idealized version of Egyptian daily life – was an underworld (or in some versions, the sky) where the dead lived as eternally blessed spirits, transfigured both by their difficult journey to the afterworld and by their final judgment by the great god, Osiris. The daily rebirth of the sun mirrored the constant rebirth of the dead in the afterlife. In the afterworld, Ra and Osiris became one. According to the *Egyptian Book of the Dead* (a text used for funerals), "Osiris is yesterday and Ra is tomorrow."

Arguably the most important Egyptian myth is that of Osiris and his sister and consort, Isis. Before human-time, when Osiris and Isis ruled the world, prosperity and peace reigned. But Osiris's brother, Set, became jealous. He killed Osiris by sealing him in a coffin and drowning him in the Nile at a location near Abydos, thereby bringing conflict to the world. When Isis recovered Osiris's body, Set took the body from her, dismembered it, and scattered it over the far expanses of Egypt. Isis and her sister Nephthys (protectors and restorers of the dead), taking bird form, scoured the kingdom to reassemble Osiris's body. After Isis located every piece, with the help of other deities and fanning him with her wings she revived him. From their union was born their son, Horus, raised to avenge his father's death. Osiris left to become ruler of the afterworld.

This legend was central to Egyptian belief in the rebirth of the dead into an afterlife. In the Egyptian view, Set represented chaos and Horus the divine nature of kingship, always to be reborn. Osiris, the god who died and was restored to life, was associated with the annual flooding of the Nile, agriculture, and fertility.

The commemorative ritual of Osiris at Abydos

Cosmic equilibrium could be maintained only through the cooperation of the gods and goddesses. Chaos was kept at bay by the earthly representative of the gods – the pharaoh. As the intermediary between divine and mortal worlds, the pharaoh (male or female) possessed the inherent dualities of the cosmos. Only the pharaoh was empowered to intercede on behalf of humankind, and was therefore considered the main priest of every Egyptian temple. The pharaoh was at first regarded as a servant of the gods, but later was considered divinely conceived and equal to the gods. While alive, the pharaoh was considered an incarnation of Horus, son of Osiris, but upon death, the pharaoh was then identified with Osiris.

The elaborate ritual life of Egyptian temples was based on making offerings that nourished the gods: food, libations, song, dance, incense, and annual festivals. Before conducting daily worship or public ceremonies, priests and priestesses purified themselves by bathing, chewing mineral salts, and removing body hair. Song and dance were especially central to worship of Hathor, the goddess of music, motherhood, and beauty. One hymn describes how even the king danced and sang before the goddess while wielding a sacred, golden rattle:

> He comes to dance,
> comes to sing,
> Hathor, see his dancing,
> see his skipping!
> … O Golden One,
> how fine is the song
> like the song of Horus himself,
> which Ra's son sings as the finest singer.
> He is Horus, a musician!
> (Fletcher 2002: 83)

Figure 1.4
Ancient Egyptian carved and painted image of a golden barque boat. The craft was symbolic of the journey to the life after death. Temple of Medinet Habu, Luxor, Egypt.
Source: BasPhoto/Shutterstock.

The Egyptian calendar featured numerous seasonal, royal, religious, and other festivals, during which statues of gods and goddesses were housed in sacred barques (boat-shaped shrines) (Figure 1.4). These barques usually were hidden from sight and were the subject of secret rituals inside temples. When they were taken in procession by land and water to visit other temples or burial tombs, the barques were carried out of the temple on the shoulders of priests and accompanied by dancers and musicians (Figure 1.5), making that deity's power present for the people.

The deity most honored with great public ceremonies was Osiris, especially at the main center of his worship in Abydos during the period of the Middle Kingdom (roughly 2055–1640 BCE). Middle Kingdom rulers lavished patronage on the cult. Osiris's statue was re-housed in a new "everlasting great barque," constructed of "gold, silver, lapis lazuli, bronze, and cedar." Annually, the barque containing Osiris processed from the temple to the desert site of his tomb and back again. At the center of this liturgy, lasting days if not weeks, was a commemorative re-enactment of major moments of Osiris's story.

The way in which Egyptians understood their place within the world and cosmos was informed by two suppositions: the assumption that society was organized around "high centers," headed by divinely ordained monarchs, and the assumption that cosmology and

Figure 1.5
Fragment from a relief from a tomb at Sakkara (c.1250 BCE, 19th–20th dynasty) showing women and young girls playing tambourines and clapsticks and dancing at a festival procession (right), led by a baton-carrying official and other male officials, their arms raised in rejoicing.

Source: © Gianni Dagli Orti/Shutterstock.

history were indistinguishable. Both assumptions are evident in the commemorative ritual for Osiris at Abydos (Figure 1.6).

Sometimes a festival was described on a stele (a flat, inscribed stone). One stele, dating from the rule of Senusret III (1870–31 BCE), has attracted special attention. On it, a treasury official named Ikhernofret tells of his activities as overseer of the ceremonies:

> I arranged the expedition of Wepwawet when he went to the aid of his father. I beat back those who attacked the Barque of Neshmet. I overthrew the foes of Osiris. I arranged the Great Procession and escorted the god [Osiris] on his journey. I launched the god's ship … I decked the ship with gorgeous trappings so that it might sail to the region of Peker [near Abydos]. I conducted the god to his grave in Peker. I championed [avenged] Wenn-nefru [Osiris as the re-risen god] on the day of the Great Combat and overthrew all his adversaries beside the waters of Nedit. I caused him to sail in his ship. It was laden with his beauty. I caused the hearts of the Easterners to swell with joy, and I brought the gladness to the Westerners at the sight of the Barque of Neshmet.
>
> (Gaster 1950: 41–2)

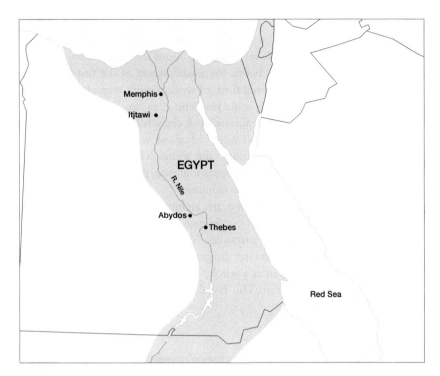

Figure 1.6
Map of Egypt c.1850 BCE.

The stele suggests that there was a spectacular procession that would have lasted for several days. It included an enormous mock battle representing the warring factions of Horus/Osiris and Set, the latter probably blocking the god's progress to his tomb, with thousands of participants on each side. The Greek historian Herodotus, writing about a similar event 14 centuries later, recorded that the massed armies at engaged in "a hard fight with staves.... They break one another's heads, and I am of the opinion that many even die of the wounds they receive; the Egyptians however told me that no one died."

This set of events has been called the "Abydos Passion Play," which sounds as though it was theatrical and akin to the medieval European Passion plays (discussed in Chapter 3). However, the title is now considered misleading partly because there is no evidence that it or any other Egyptian festival involved people playing characters – and some evidence against it. For example, Egyptian masks seldom had a mouth hole (Leprohon 2007: 270). Thus, if there were speeches, they were probably religious recitations or prayers by priests rather than in-character monologues or dialogues. Like the rituals and ceremonies of many ancient civilizations, the Abydos ceremony seems to have involved role-playing mythical narratives (as we saw with the Hopi katsina performances), but today scholars are more wary of phrases that imply that rituals had a more theatrical character than the evidence warrants. Great caution is needed when applying modern terminology to ancient forms of performance, especially when evidence is scarce, in order to avoid misinterpretation, anachronism, and perhaps ethnocentrism – such as by depicting the Abydos ritual as similar to the Christian Passion plays.

The role of hieroglyphic texts

No text has been located for the rites of Osiris at Abydos, but we note that like several other Egyptian festivals, there is writing on a stele recording the events after it had occurred, memorializing it. Starting around 3400 BCE, before the establishment of the first dynasty of the pharaohs, the Egyptians developed a mixed form of writing using hieroglyphs ("sacred carvings"), a system of logograms possessing some phonetic elements. Egyptians first used hieroglyphs for accounting and then as a bureaucratic tool; eventually colorful hieroglyphic inscriptions decorated tombs and temples and were elaborated with special symbols and images of animals, birds, and humans to "activate" the scenes. There were thousands of hieroglyphs, and with less than 1 percent of the populace literate, priests, scribes, and upper echelon administrators were a learned, specialist community.

The reign of Senusret III "was a time when art, architecture, and religion reached new heights, but, above all, it was an age of confidence in writing" (Shah 2000: 183). Many literary forms flourished, including narratives, "dream books," and texts devoted to astrology, law, history, mathematics, medicine, geography, and sacred liturgy. But as important as writing was for the elite, taken as a whole, Ancient Egypt had an oral culture with writing, rather than a literate culture. This is reflected in the form and content of the Abydos ceremony.

Mesoamerican performance

The early indigenous cultures of Mesoamerica – a region stretching from Central America up to southern Mexico (Figure 1.7) – provide not only another instance of performance in conditions of restricted literacy, but also powerful examples of the complexity of interpreting evidence noted in the General Introduction. The Mexica (Aztecs) and Maya ruled in parts of Mesoamerica until the late fifteenth and sixteenth centuries CE, when the Spanish invaded the Americas and conquered the indigenous peoples. The Maya reached their widest scope of power and influence, administrative sophistication, and cultural complexity during the Classic Period, 250–900 CE, and writing almost certainly contributed to their political control and economic growth.

Various writing systems were invented in Mesoamerica. The Mayan system, which most likely arose around 500 BCE, has only been partly translated, and we know little about its usage and the extent of reading and writing skills in Mesoamerica. The symbols changed over time and some were used only locally, but it seems that during any one place and time, scribes probably needed to know around 250 pictographic and syllabic signs. As in most ancient societies, only the scribes could write with much facility, although occasionally non-elites may have acquired some writing ability as well. Writing was read aloud, and most of Mayan culture and knowledge was transmitted orally. The scribes often sought to demonstrate their virtuosity; yet the pictographic aspect of Mayan writing may have made it interpretable (if unpronounceable) to a much larger population – highly advantageous in a multilingual region like Mesoamerica. In this manner, Mayan writing may have unified a large region within a single political and administrative control.

Performance was integral to Mesoamerican societies. Evidence from pyramid walls and the few extant sacred books point to a vigorous Mesoamerican performance culture

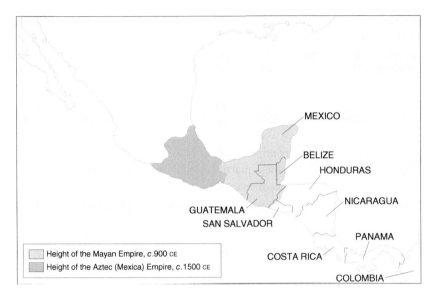

Figure 1.7
Map of the Mayan and Aztec Empires in Mesoamerica.

before the Maya had writing (Tedlock 1985: 151–2). Rigorous training in music and dance was normal for boys and girls from ages 12 to 15 and took place in "houses of song." Rulers performed "a 'princely dance' on special occasions," and priests "embodied god-figures" (Tedlock 1985: 358). Performances could involve thousands of highly skilled performers who "used elaborate and highly colorful costumes, masks, body make-up and, at times, puppets and stilts. The sets were lavishly adorned with arches, flowers, animals, and all sorts of natural and artfully designed elements" (Taylor 2004: 357). Performances were usually outdoors in public courtyards and temples, although some were in private patios.

The religious imperative for performance in Mesoamerica

Mesoamerican public celebrations always combined religion with spectacle. Ceremonies in the festivals were set against the great architectural spaces of Mesoamerican cities, which included massive pyramids. These temples were regarded as the "navel of the world" and "the human-made equivalent of nature's mountains … forming a living link that conjoined the heavens above, the earth, and the underworlds below" (Tedlock 1985: 364). Public ceremonies were synchronized with the movement of heavenly bodies, making cosmic time palpable and elaborate calendar-keeping essential. The performances were not entertainment, but offerings to the gods meant to fulfill a key purpose: to keep the lines of communication open between humans, their ancestors, and the gods they worshipped.

In many cultures the world over, an essential component of such communication has involved sacrifice, usually of animals. Among the Aztecs and occasionally among the Maya, these ceremonies could include human sacrifice. Recently scholars have begun to wrest an understanding of the meanings and purposes of human sacrifice away from the perspective of the Spanish military and missionaries, and attempt to grasp what it might have meant to the peoples themselves. According to performance studies scholar Diana Taylor, human sacrifice

> reflected the belief that there was no firm division between life and death.… The sacrificial victims would be joining the gods, at times taking messages from those on earth, while the victims' energy and force would be transferred to others on earth through the donning of the skin. Notions of continuity and constantly recycling life forces, rather than cruelty or revenge, sustained these practices. The Mayas, for example, referred to certain forms of sacrifice as *ahil* (acts of creation).
>
> (Taylor 2004: 361–2)

Religious rites create a synergy between the divine and human realms. If the gods sacrificed themselves for humans as the world was formed, then the gods require similar sacrifices in return. Sacrificial rites performed by divinely ordained priests or kings maintained the social and cosmological orders mandated by the gods at the time of creation. Human sacrifice was therefore considered a necessity.

Taylor's reference to "the donning of the skin" suggests how some Mesoamerican peoples understood concepts such as "embodiment" and "representation" in ways that are both similar to and different from European understandings. When the Aztecs wanted to honor their creator-deity Quetzalcóatl (the feathered-serpent god who gave his own blood to usher in the current incarnation of the human race, and the inventor of books and the calendar), they purchased a slave, who for 40 days was fêted, feasted, and worshipped *as* the god. At the end of the 40 days, the slave/god would be sacrificed in a public ceremony, in which his heart would be cut out and his body rolled down the temple steps. The body would then be skinned and the flesh donned by various onlookers, who *became* Quetzalcóatl while in the skin of the slave/Quetzalcóatl. According to Adam Versényi, the ritual accomplished several things at once: it re-enacted the god's original sacrifice on behalf of humanity; it performed a real sacrifice of human blood in honor of the same god; and it allowed the spectator/participants to be at once themselves, their fellow (sacrificed) man, and their god. As Versényi describes it, this rite and many others represented "a conflation of the entire matrix of actor/character/audience" (Versényi 1989: 219).

At the same time, as Taylor points out, "The massive performance festivals … made visible the very real economic and military power of a state that could afford to sacrifice hundreds – even thousands – of victims … . These spectacular synchronized acts were fundamental to maintaining power" (Taylor 2004: 364). Taylor's comments suggest that by describing sacrifices as "acts of creation," Mesoamerican rulers rationalized their use of violence, undoubtedly believing the rationalization themselves. Here, we see how evidence can have multiple meanings and reveal multiple social purposes.

THINKING THROUGH THEATRE HISTORIES: THE MULTIPLE MEANINGS OF EVIDENCE

Mesoamerican performance provides rich examples of the ways a single piece of evidence is frequently embedded with multiple meanings and can serve as evidence about a variety of social practices and concerns. There is nothing unusual about the presence of multiple meanings, known as *polysemy*: in fact, there are several ways in which evidence and activities can be polysemous.

The example we have just seen, in which the concept of *ahil* (acts of creation) simultaneously played a role in the Maya's religion and cosmology, but probably also helped Mayan rulers justify their use of violence and horror, illustrates one sort of polysemy. The function of ideas both as part of a society's understanding of itself and its world, and also as an expression of power and self-justification, is scarcely limited to the Maya – in fact, it is prevalent in most societies. It is common, for instance, in the expansion of national power through **colonization**. The Spanish conquerors of South and Central America used the claim of Christianity's superiority over indigenous religions in just such a manner: they truly believed in Christianity and its preeminence, but they also saw it as a rationale for killing Mayan people, suppressing Mayan religious practices while imposing their own, and censoring Mayan culture, all of which secured the conquerors' power. The term **ideology** points to such connections between ideas and power. (Later chapters will discuss colonization and its ideologies in more detail.)

Another type of polysemy involves ambiguity. One of the chief problems in understanding Mayan performance is the fact that much of our evidence comes from descriptions by the invading Spaniards, both military and missionary, who were unfamiliar with the cultures of the people they conquered and described what they saw in terms of their own concepts and values. In addition, they generally weren't interested in learning about the indigenous people's culture – in fact, the conquerors destroyed as much of Mayan culture as possible. Consequently, the Spaniards' descriptions may be distorted and biased; they may tell us more about the Spanish than they do about the Maya. At the same time, the descriptions cannot be written off. Some (possibly even all) parts may be substantially accurate, and they are almost all we have to guide us. As a result of these complexities, the documentary evidence about Mayan performance has uncertain meaning and value.

Activities can have multiple meanings in other ways. One of them is familiar to anyone who pays attention to politics. Proposed legislation (say, to cut taxes or to expand access to education) aims to address policy concerns – it strives to move the government and sometimes the entire society in a particular direction. Yet simultaneously, it often seeks partisan goals by advancing one political party's standing with the electorate or placing its opposition in an awkward position. Sometimes it's an open question which of these goals is foremost. As a result, one cannot take the legislation at face value: there may be other agendas behind it. A variant of this type of polysemy can be seen in consumer culture. A car is a means of transportation – but one's choice of car (say, a Porsche versus

> a Volkswagen) can be partly to obtain a status or sex symbol. In short, an artifact or document may be polysemous because it can serve multiple practical and social functions.
>
> Finally, every cultural object is the product of numerous processes. A book's text, for instance, can tell us many things about a culture's ideas and beliefs. In addition, however, its physical characteristics hint at the society's manufacturing capabilities, and its design may suggest what the society considers attractive (or whether it sees its attractiveness as necessary). Thus, a piece of evidence can tell a historian a variety of things or be used for a range of historical investigations.

Sung dance-drama: *Rabinal Achi*

While sacrificial rites performed by priests or kings maintained the social and cosmological orders mandated by the gods, more secular forms of performance – grounded in oral culture – were also common in Mesoamerica, entertaining the people and maintaining their collective memory. Farces ridiculed those who were ethnically different. In a performance from central Mexico entitled "Song of the Little Women," several concubines debate the pros and cons of living a life devoted to satisfying male prerogatives. Sung dance-drama, which incorporated music, song, and dance, celebrated collective and individual histories and glories. One important Mayan work of this type, the *Rabinal Achi* [drah-vee-NAHL ah-CHEE], commemorated certain political and military events in the history of the town of Rabinal. The history of its performance is also an example of the suppression of indigenous systems of belief and cultural performances that came with Spain's conquest of the New World.

Rabinal Achi is a K'iche' (also spelled Quiché) language dance-drama still performed today in the highlands of Guatemala. It is known both as *Rabinal Achi*, meaning "The Man of Rabinal," and as *Xajoj Tun*, "Dance of the Trumpets" – a reference to the fact that during parts of the performance characters dance to the playing of trumpets. It is one of few extant dramas with Mayan rather than Spanish dialogue. It relates the story of conflict between the noble warriors and leaders of two Mayan city-states, K'iche' and Rabinal, that reached a climax in the early fifteenth century, before the arrival of the Spanish.

The primary historical incident around which the performance score for *Rabinal Achi* evolved is the story of a famous king, Quicab – a member of the lineage of the house of Cawek of the Forest People. In the fourteenth and fifteenth centuries, Quicab ruled a confederation of the Rabinal, Cakchiquel, and Tzutuhil nations in what is now Guatemala. While Quicab was away on a military campaign expanding his kingdom, there was a revolt at home. One of those involved was his fifth son, who may have been the historical figure on whom the character Cawek in the dance-drama is based.

In the narrative, the main characters are Lord Five Thunder, ruler of the mountaintop fortress of Rabinal; the Man of Rabinal (serving at his behest), who upholds the traditional order; and the renegade who disrupts that order, Cawek, the son of the Lord of K'iche'. All three wear distinctive helmet-masks and carry axes and shields, symbols of royal power (Figure 1.8). Cawek's father was a noble who fought alongside the neighboring city-state of

Rabinal. Rabinal's boundaries are guarded by Eagle and Jaguar, priests in the service of Lord Five Thunder, whose names are taken from the source of their spiritual power to protect. At Lord Five Thunder's court resides his wife and his unmarried daughter, "Mother of Quetzal Feathers." Cawek becomes a renegade warrior when he betrays the people of Rabinal, causing much suffering. As the dance-drama opens, Cawek has already betrayed his father's former allies and been captured by Man of Rabinal. The performance presents the confrontation between Man of Rabinal and Cawek in the context of Cawek's trial. Cawek remains defiant toward his captors throughout, but at the end accepts his death by beheading. Before dying, he is allowed to view aspects of the world he will leave. He is shown the lovely daughter of Lord Five Thunder and dances depicting the beauty of nature.

Almost everything we know about *Rabinal Achi* derives from evidence dating after the Spanish conquest of the Mayan empire during the sixteenth century. Some of the evidence comes from accounts of performances seen through the Spanish colonizers' eyes. Most Spanish missionaries were wholly uninterested in the Maya's own views, but they recognized that the participation of the people in annual cycles of ceremonial performances (at which dance-dramas like *Rabinal Achi* were performed) had great meaning for the Maya, and they attempted to suppress and/or alter the performances by a variety of means. They insisted that Christian hymns be substituted for Mayan songs, and as early as 1593 and as late as 1770, they issued bans against indigenous ceremonies and dramatic performances, "warning that representations of human sacrifices would lead to real ones" (Tedlock 2003: 5). The bans, however, were never wholly successful. The Spaniards also introduced Christian biblical theatre from medieval Europe, possibly affecting indigenous performance.

The Maya never used their own system of writing to record what performers spoke in their performances. It was only under the influence of Christian missionaries that the Maya wrote down "texts" like *Rabinal Achi* in their own language, using the Roman alphabet. The missionaries had created handwritten scripts for the European Bible and saint plays that they introduced, translating some speeches into local Mayan languages. These alphabetic texts contained details and content never included in the older Mayan hieroglyphic texts. Anthropologist Dennis Tedlock attributes these differences not to alphabetic writing per se, but to the fact that indigenous authors were responding to the missionary suppression of their performances and the destruction of hieroglyphic texts. In order to save *Rabinal Achi* from complete censorship, the Mayan scribes separated the words of their version from its music, and removed "all but the main outlines of the original religious content from public view" (Tedlock 2003: 2). The Mayan scribes "sought to conserve the audible words of endangered performances for which those books provided prompts" (158). Their "texts" of

Figure 1.8

Rabinal Achi, or the Man of Rabinal, a conjectural image similar to that of an eighth-century lord found in the Mayan Temple of the Inscriptions at Palenque (not depicted). He wears a feathered headdress, mask, short cape and kilt, and he carries an upraised axe and a small round shield.

Source: Drawing by Jamie Borowicz. © Dennis Tedlock.

the sixteenth century were, then, written as records of oral performances and, according to Tedlock, are more like "a set of program notes than a libretto" (158). They are not single-author works but collectively created, memorable records of performance, which partici-pants would have elaborated upon in the moment of performance.

The available evidence does not provide a fully accurate picture of pre-Conquest Mayan performance, and we may never be able to apprehend the full scope, nature, and content of their dance-drama. Nevertheless, the performances of *Rabinal Achi* in Guatemala today hint at what Mayan drama might have been like before the Spanish conquest. Today and probably historically, the aesthetic conventions of *Rabinal Achi* are presentational – not rep-resentational or realistic. The audience is located on four sides of the playing space. "When the actors dance, they move around the perimeter of a square, and when they promenade they move in a circle. These pathways locate them all in one world" (Tedlock 2003: 14). The distinctive rhythms of the Mayan calendar are suggested in the counterclockwise movements within a square, together with their temporal marking of the 260 days of the divinatory calendar during which Cawek says farewell to his homeland by moving "on all four edges/ in all four corners." The overtly religious aspects of the performance today are the primary responsibility of the "Road Guide" – the native ritual specialist or priest-shaman whose prayers and offerings circumscribe and punctuate the performance. The characters deliver lengthy speeches as solos, similar to the renderings of ancient Mayan court songs. The main characters narrate more events from the past than they re-enact in the dramatic present. There is no fast-paced, realistic dialogue, and performers never attempt a conversational tone. When the Man of Rabinal captures Cawek with the rope he wears around his waist, he does not realistically lasso him, but rather, the two remain still and a stage assistant appears and ties the end of the rope carried by the Man of Rabinal around his prisoner.

Rabinal Achi never adopted the convention used in Spanish missionary plays, in which enemies are depicted in costumes indicating two different worlds – one "evil" and the other "good." Instead, the antagonists dress alike, and their arguments are shaped by a shared, rather than opposite set of values. One of the opponents may be misguided or wrong but he is not, as in the later dramas of the Christianizing missionaries, "evil" or living in "falsehood."

At the end of the storyline, Cawek is executed, which is depicted in modern perfor-mances as a beheading. To show this, the captive kneels and other characters dance around him. In a simple and unhurried manner, those with axes simply bring them toward but not to the prisoner's neck. Immediately following his "beheading," the performer stands, and joins the other dancers in a final collective dance. Shoulder to shoulder, they dance westward until they reach the foot of the steps leading to the door of the cemetery chapel. There, the actors all kneel, and the Road Guide leads them in a prayer to their ancestors (Tedlock 2003: 19).

While contemporary performances of *Rabinal Achi* seem to bear strong traces of pre-conquest practices, there is also evidence that it has changed over time. For example, an-thropologist Ruud van Akkeren (1999) has suggested that originally Cawek was likely put to death by arrows rather than by beheading. When and why it changed in performance is unclear.

Rabinal Achi seems to have different representational goals than the "drama" of human sacrifice described above. It commemorates a historic military conquest that resulted in a consolidation of power. In the Mayan empire, such conquests featured ceremonial executions, which served as a proof of their power. According to Tedlock, today's Mayan performers are speaking to and for their ancestors as much as to and for anyone else, including all those who ever acted in the *Rabinal Achi*. Performing in this dance-drama, then, is not so much a matter of impersonating historical individuals – as if their lives could be relived in realistic detail – as it is a matter of impersonating their ghosts (Tedlock 2003:14–5).

As a representation of Mayan royalty and culture, *Rabinal Achi* does reflect some pre-conquest local history. But its impulse is less toward full historical accuracy and more toward commemoration of the town of Rabinal's triumphal origins and ongoing cultural survival, as symbolized in its ability to withstand an internal threat to its cohesion. Instead of portraying an actual battle between ancient enemies, the enactment presents a montage of fragments of royal stories from across six different generations, gathered into the singular confrontation between the Man of Rabinal and the traitor Cawek. Generic character names allow the story and its examination of the power negotiations between rulers and city-states to remain open to interpretation.

Episodes from the history of royal lineages were the subject of many other pre-Spanish Mesoamerican performances. In them, the performers represented the main characters through costuming and dancing, while dialogue was sung or chanted by separate **choruses** (group performers) to musical accompaniment.

Rabinal Achi shares certain features with commemorative dramas elsewhere, of which we will present several more examples in Chapter 3. Like most commemorative performances, *Rabinal Achi* tells a story that has been carefully preserved both orally and in written form; it celebrates a moment in the past that is of great contemporary importance for the audience in the present who witnesses it; and it is meant to be staged on a regular basis as an aid against the loss of that heritage in social memory. In addition, however, commemorative performances in Mesoamerica were understood not as representations but as doing something fundamental in the world. Whether Mesoamerican commemorative performances constitute theatre is, according to Taylor, a matter of dispute among Latin American specialists (Taylor 2004: 366), but clearly it shares many of theatre's features.

Although *Rabinal Achi* was heavily censored in the early days of the Spanish conquest by missionaries suspicious of its "pagan" content, it survived and is meant to be staged every year on 25 January (the feast day of the town of Rabinal's Catholic patron saint, Paul). Its importance beyond the Mayan world is evidenced in the fact that in 2005, UNESCO – the United Nations' agency for education and culture – officially proclaimed it a "masterpiece of the oral and intangible heritage of humanity."

Performance in a literate culture: Theatre in the city-state of Athens

In Egypt, political and religious authority was vested in a single person, the pharaoh, and festivals honored gods like Osiris. In Mesoamerica, scattered kingdoms shared a culture and religion, and produced commemorative performances such as *Rabinal Achi* which were something close to theatre, although addressing the gods and understood as an actual intervention in the universe. A very different way of navigating the relationships between divine and civic authority, and the relationships among the citizens themselves, developed during the fifth century BCE in Athens, Greece, where distinctive forms of literary drama and theatre flourished. The forms of drama that developed in Athens represent conflicts over cultural issues that would have invited social, political, and aesthetic debates.

We have far more information about theatre in classical Athens than any other early theatre: documents, the remains of buildings, pottery, engravings, and over 40 plays. One reason we have so much information is the spread of literacy itself – documents provide much of our evidence. Yet there are many frustrating gaps in our knowledge. For instance, we know who did something important in theatre's development and the year in which they did it, but only vaguely what they did. We do know, however, that Greek theatre emerged during an era of major changes in political structures, economic systems, and communication methods.

Alphabetic writing and Athenian democracy

In the eighth and ninth centuries BCE, epic bards like Homer recited or sang versions of lengthy stories of the gods and epic heroes of bygone eras, such as *The Iliad* and *The Odyssey*. Their performances gave life to the deeds of a heroic aristocracy, populating a murky, distant, quasi-mythic, quasi-historical past. By the end of the fifth century BCE, however, the most important storytelling no longer appeared in solo oral epics or lyric poetry: instead, it was composed in tragedies or comedies in which multiple actors performed characters and spoke dialogue, and the chorus, with choreographed dancing and singing, played a slowly diminishing role. How and why did this transformation occur? The creation of an early form of democracy and probably the nature of Greek alphabetic writing played a part.

The alphabet started developing when, around 1200 BCE, the Phoenicians (who made their livelihoods trading along the Mediterranean coast) began to use a letter to indicate the initial consonant for a syllable, somewhat like a syllabary, but let the appropriate vowel be inferred by context. This approach radically reduced the number of characters needed to represent speech to just a couple dozen, few enough to be learned by anyone, not just priests and scribes – a great advantage for a trading people like the Phoenicians. However, because vowels had to be inferred, Phoenician script sometimes created ambiguity, which was resolved by inserting an extra consonant symbol to indicate the correct vowel.

Where the Phoenicians sailed, they brought their script with them. Probably around 850 BCE, the Greeks adopted Phoenician script. However, Greek words frequently have initial vowels, consonant clusters, and/or combined vowels (such as the *a*, *mn*, and *ia* in *amnesia*). Those weren't easily represented by the Phoenician script, even with its *ad hoc* approach to indicating vowels, so the Greeks introduced letters specifically for vowel sounds. That created the first full alphabet, which breaks speech into individual vowels and consonants. Although the script wasn't perfect, writing became more or less unambiguously pronounceable.

However, many features of modern writing took centuries to develop, including spaces between words, upper and lower cases, punctuation, and when drama was first written, clear indications when the speaker in a play changed. Just as in other early cultures with writing, reading aloud – even in private – was both a cultural norm and a practical necessity.

The social contexts of the alphabet's development gave it advantages beyond representing speech sounds. The social and political structures of ancient Greece were radically unlike those of its major neighbors (see Figure 1.9). In Egypt, a single, vast empire was ruled centrally by pharaohs for over 3,000 years. The lands to the east belonged to Greece's adversary

Figure 1.9

Map of the Mediterranean during the fifth century BCE.

in many wars: the Persian Empire, which eventually ruled Egypt itself. In contrast, Greece consisted of autonomous city-states, including Athens, Sparta, Thebes, and Corinth, that vied with one another for ascendancy and occasionally joined forces to face a common external threat, such as when they fought the Persians in 479 BCE. The small-scale political structure and independence of the ancient Greek city-state (*polis* [POH-lis]) probably worked against restricting literacy to an educated bureaucracy.

Central to Athens's creation of theatre was its route to democracy and its implications. Throughout the seventh and sixth centuries BCE, autocrats (*tyrannos*) took control in many cities. Hoping to prevent that, Athens reduced aristocratic power by establishing a written constitution, and fostered commerce and artisan manufacture. However, despite Athens' efforts, beginning in the 560s the autocrat Peisistratos seized control. He strove to tilt power from the aristocracy to the state by helping the lower classes, supporting popular religion and festivals, and promoting mercantile activity. The autocracy was finally deposed in a coup in 510 BCE. After further tumult, in order to distribute power and prevent autocracy from ever rising again, Athens abolished the hereditary tribes and replaced them with ten civic tribes based on place of residence. The *polis* also established legislative bodies and law courts with members chosen by lottery. These changes made Athens the first democracy. Citizenship in the new democracy excluded women, as well as the enslaved and resident immigrants – scarcely democratic in today's sense. Nevertheless, compared to all the other societies in the region, it was a democracy. At the new government's founding, Athens had perhaps 20,000 citizens.

Two aspects of Athenian society contributed to the rise of literacy and the culture behind theatre. Merchants and shopkeepers, although disparaged, were exceptionally important to

Athens's economy, and they found the simplicity of the alphabet enormously useful. Even more important was the democratic structure. All citizens were required to fulfill civic obligations as soldiers or sailors, athletes, financiers, participants, or spectators at annual religious festivals – and crucially, as legislators, debaters, judges, or jury members, which encouraged literacy.

Athenians grew increasingly interested in skillful public debate and oratory. At the same time, the legal and legislative need to consider issues from varying perspectives fostered diversity of ideas, which extended to all areas of thought – such as the view that the world is not governed by the whim of the gods but instead by natural, intelligible forces (although atheism itself was rare). Newly developing forms of education emphasized persuasive argument and eloquence, and some teachers, known as Sophists, expounded on their innovative and sometimes unconventional views. Instructors wrote manuals on persuasive oratory, called rhetoric – speeches were always given extemporaneously, not from a prepared text, but by studying rhetorical techniques a citizen could become a masterful speaker. Writing became so essential to the city's life that in the fifth century BCE, boys were required to attend school, where they learned writing, music, and math. "Everyday life was so overrun with books … that cheap editions of philosophy could be picked up from the bookstalls for a drachma" (Wise 1998: 21). Although in most of Greece probably no more than a few percent of the population was literate, in Athens it spread to possibly over 10 percent and found many new applications – enough that the first literate culture was born.

These circumstances tell us much about the meaning of performance there. The creation of democracy spurred not just literacy, but also theatre. As we will see, Greek drama drew from the same fountain of debate over civic matters as did the democracy. And as part of their civic duties, the wealthiest citizens were expected to undertake major responsibilities such as maintaining a warship, equipping a religious procession – or financing a chorus, which meant underwriting the production of a set of plays at the annual theatre festival honoring the god Dionysus.

The religious background

We mentioned that Athens's autocrat had promoted popular religion in Athens. As in Egypt and Mesoamerica, ancient Greek religion was polytheistic. Within the Greek pantheon, a complex host of gods and goddesses with their own spheres of influence vied for power, prestige, and influence. Greek gods behaved and misbehaved much like people, and they were often in conflict. However, each needed to be appropriately honored, propitiated, and worshipped to access their potential beneficence or prevent their wrath.

Most Greek cities had patron gods; in Athens's case it was Athena, goddess of wisdom, justice, military and heroic achievement, art and artisanal skills. But another god figures prominently in the history of Athens and its theatre: Dionysus, the god of wine. He was said to have dwelled in Athens for a time, and the cult of Dionysus was highly popular there. Dionysus "is associated with darkness, with nocturnal drinking bouts, and the loss of mental clarity in moments of collective emotion, with the loss of boundaries around the self experienced in a crowd." Dionysus plays music on "the haunting double oboe which can whip up wild dances" (Wiles 2000: 7–8). He was strongly associated as well with freedom and intoxicated abandon. Athens's democratic government officially sponsored the cult of Dionysus and established festivals in tribute. These festivals became occasions for theatrical performance.

Drama in the context of the Dionysian festivals in Athens

The theatrical performance of **tragedy** and **comedy** in ancient Athens needs to be understood in the context of the civic/religious ceremonies and festivals of which theatre was a part. Fifth-century Greek theatre was woven into the fabric of civic/religious discourse. Greek festivals typically included processions, sacrifices, celebrations, feasting, and the performance of choral laments – group singing and dancing. Some also included competitions, particularly athletic contests; later, especially in Athens, there were also competitions in what we now call the arts (in classical Greece, the arts weren't separate from religion and other aspects of the culture as they often are in Western cultures today).

Starting under the autocracy, every four years the Panathenaia festival honored Athena, which included processions, athletic contests, and a fully armored martial dance. Later, the Panathenaia added solo recitations of works by Homer and musical contests. But there were also four annual Dionysian festivals in Athens and the surrounding area. The largest was the City (or Great) Dionysia, which was second only to the Panathenaia in importance.

The City Dionysia was crucial in the history of Greek drama. It was long thought that the autocrat established it to curry favor with the populace, that competitions in tragedy were instituted in 534 BCE, and that the first winner was Thespis, who is also the first known actor (today "thespians" is a nickname for actors). Now, however, most classical scholars believe that the City Dionysia and the cult's state sponsorship were established later, probably 503–501 BCE – *after* the Athenian democracy was formed. According to this analysis, the City Dionysia was part of a program to celebrate and strengthen the new democracy by taking advantage of Dionysus's association with liberation. Thespis's performance in 534 BCE probably occurred at a rural Dionysia (Connor 1989).

The City Dionysia hosted the major drama competitions (eventually all the Dionysian festivals included plays). The festival lasted six days, and began with a raucous procession starting just outside the *polis*, reenacting Dionysus's arrival in Athens. According to the most likely order of events, on the next day, dithyrambs [DIH-thih-rams] – choral songs and dances in honor of Dionysus – were danced and sung by choruses of 50 boys and another of 50 men.

Most of the third day was devoted to comedy: five different playwrights competed with comedies that offered keen satirical commentary on current affairs, such as war, education, politics, the legal system, or even tragic poetry.

The next three days climaxed the festival. They began with important civic-religious ceremonies. Three playwrights then presented their sets of four plays (three tragedies and a final satyr play, described below), probably one set by each playwright per day. The judges announced the winners of the tragedy and comedy competitions and awarded prizes. At the festival's close, officials held an open public assembly to receive any criticism of the proceedings, including complaints about the plays selected or the judging.

The City Dionysia had not only religious significance, but tremendous economic, military, and political meaning as well. At its height in the fifth century, Athens was the leader of an alliance of cities, which turned into an empire. The member cities paid their tributes during the City Dionysia, and the Athenians showed off their military prowess. For example, the second-year cadets demonstrated their arms maneuvers, precision marching, and overall physical preparedness. Some of these young "citizen soldiers in training" then performed in the plays. The famous Pronomos Vase (Figure 1.10) shows them as members of the chorus in a satyr play.

Figure 1.10
This Greek vase for mixing wine, dating from the late fifth or early fourth century BCE, is famous for its theatrical figures, perhaps a company who performed a trilogy and satyr play. Called the "Pronomos Vase" after Pronomos, the aulos player seated at lower center, it shows (top center) the god of theatre, Dionysus, Ariadne (his wife), a muse, and to the sides, mature actors holding their masks – one costumed as a king, one as Herakles (with club), and the third as Silenus (leader of satyrs). Below left is a playwright (with scroll) and a choral trainer (with lyre). The young beardless men (*ephebes*) are costumed as satyrs with erect phalluses.

Source: Wiki/Furtwangler and Reinhold https://commons.wikimedia.org/wiki/File:Griechische_Vasenmalerei,_Taflen –_A._Furtwangler,_K_Reichhold.jpg.

Just as the City Dionysia was created as part of forming a democracy, so too was there an intense degree of civic participation as performers. Some 2,500–3,000 citizens took part in the processions, ceremonies, rites, or dramatic competitions constituting the festival. In 430 BCE, 40,000–60,000 men were citizens of Athens (adding women, the enslaved, and resident foreigners, the entire population was around 300,000). Thus, roughly one out of every 20 citizens directly participated in the City Dionysia.

Space and performance in the Theatre of Dionysus
The civic, political, and religious importance of the City Dionysia is emphasized by where the plays were performed. Originally, the performances were given in the city *agora* – a plaza which served as the center for social, business, political, and other parts of city life (located at the foot of the Acropolis, a high, rocky hill on which stands the Parthenon). Later, the Theatre of Dionysus Eleuthereus – a large outdoor amphitheatre – was built at the base of the Acropolis near the temple of Dionysus (Figure 1.11).

During the fifth century, the *theatron* [THAY-ah-tron; "seeing place"] was roughly divided into three sections (Figure 1.12). The *theatron* itself provided seating for 3,700–6,000 people. Prominent figures sat in a special section at the front. In the rest of the *theatron*,

Figure 1.11
Aerial photo of the Acropolis showing the Theatre of Dionysus (lower left) and the Parthenon (top).
Source: Greens and Blues/Shutterstock.

spectators paid to sit on wood benches behind them. And outside the official seating area, at least a thousand more people – including poor citizens, resident foreigners, and probably some enslaved people and women – found free seating on the hillside, in trees, and elsewhere. Many foreign visitors attended as well, increasing the festival's prestige.

If one assumes somewhat conservatively that between the *theatron* and the hillside seating, 6,000 people attended each performance, then at least a tenth of Athens's citizens and about 2 percent of its residents attended the City Dionysia each day – not counting the performers. The audience's size is another measure of the strong civic engagement in the festival.

The audiences responded vigorously to the quality of performance. Good shows received enthusiastic applause and accolades – but spectators in ancient Athens had no patience for poor performance or playwriting, and sometimes reacted with hissing, clucking, stomping, and prolonged noise-making. Occasionally actors and dramatists were driven off stage. Putting plays in a competition required audiences to judge the performances' artistic quality as well as their content. Unlike ritual performance, theatre most needed to please not the gods, but ordinary people.

As theatre's popularity climbed, inadequate space caused so many problems and even fistfights that in the fourth century BCE, the hillside was reshaped and benches were provided to enable 14,000–17,000 people to attend (Figures 1.13 and 1.14). However, all seats now required payment. Fewer poor citizens could attend, until a fund was established to assist them – another demonstration of the City Dionysia's civic importance.

All performers in Greek theatre were male, including those playing female characters. The very earliest form of tragedy, probably created by Thespis, consisted of a single actor before a chorus. It wasn't until decades later that the playwright Aeschylus added a second

Figure 1.12

Model of the early classical theatre of Dionysus at Athens.

Photograph after Hans R. Goette, in E. Pöhlmann, *Studien zur Buhnendichtung und zum Theaterbau der Antike: Studien zur Klassischen Philologie* 93, ed. M. V. Albrecht, 1995.

Source: © Rudolf Faist Productions/Deutsches Theatermuseum, München.

actor, and possibly the third as well, each of whom would play several roles. Three actors became the maximum permitted.

Masks were an essential part of classical Greek theatre (see Figure 1.10). None of the original masks from the classical era still exists, but vases, later masks, and other evidence suggest that tragic masks had formalized, expressionless faces. Comic masks, however, could present caricatures, grotesques, or even animal or bird heads. The mask in Figure 1.15, although later, is probably representative. Comic costuming was probably based on everyday wear, occasionally altered for amusing effect, and included a phallus. We have little information on tragic costumes, except that they included a tunic and sometimes a long or short cloak.

Music was a constant part of all performances. Played on a double pipe called an *aulos* that sounded somewhat like an oboe, music was essential for dancing the choral odes and probably accompanied individual speeches. Other instruments, such as the harp shown on the Pronomos Vase, were occasionally played as well. Musical styles may have had specific emotional associations for ancient Greek audiences, deeply shaping their responses to performances. The chorus not only sang, but also danced, giving what we call the stage its name: *orchestra*, "the place for dance."

The case study "Classical Greek Theatre: Space in *Oedipus the King*" on the *Theatre Histories* website offers more details on staging in fifth-century Athens.

Figure 1.13
Model of the Theatre of Dionysus after its expansion in the fourth century BCE.
Photograph: Hans R. Goette.

The plays and playwrights
Only 44 plays survive from the classical era, written by Aeschylus (c.543–456 BCE), Sophocles (497–406 BCE), Euripides (480–406 BCE), and Aristophanes (c.448–380 BCE). They constitute a tiny fraction of the 2,100 or more plays performed between the establishment of Athenian democracy and Aristophanes's death; we have titles for about a quarter of them, but most are now unknown. A vast number of plays were destroyed during a disastrous fire at the Great Library of Alexandria, Egypt, probably around 274 CE. The extant plays exist only as copies dating from the Middle Ages.

We noted above that during the City Dionysia, on each of the three days designated for tragedy, a playwright presented three dramas (initially, complete trilogies; later, separate tragedies) followed by a satyr play; on the day for comedy, five playwrights competed with one play each. Each tragedy was an original interpretation of a Greek narrative or historical event. The playwrights staged their own dramas, including the choreography, and thus had

Figure 1.14
The Hellenistic theatre at Epidaurus (340–330 BCE), showing the *theatron*, *orchestra*, and *parodoi* (see double gates right and left at the ends of the *theatron*). At the top of the circular *orchestra*, archeologists have laid out remaining fragments of the rectangular *skene*. The extant Greek stone theatres were built in the fourth century and after, although they likely derived some features from fifth-century theatres.
Source: © Gary Jay Williams.

no need to write out separate stage directions or other directions for the performers. The actors probably learned their lines from the author reading the text aloud.

Greek tragedies weren't "plays that end with a terrible event." Although they have a tragic situation at their heart, some close on an affirmative note. Many address the history and character of Athens itself. Aeschylus's *Oresteia* – the only complete trilogy to survive – drew on one of the stories about the aftermath of the Trojan War, and culminated with a new (though chronologically impossible) mythology of how Athens replaced cycles of vengeance with a superior, democratic judicial system. In Sophocles's *Oedipus at Colonus* (probably the conclusion of another trilogy), Athens takes Oedipus under its protection as an act of mercy, and his death sanctifies a cave near the city. Euripides's *The Bacchae* shows Dionysus's terrifying power as he exacts vengeance on the king of Thebes for having disregarded him, but the play is filled with ironies and paradoxes, such as proclaiming that Dionysus should be given his due but displaying him as repugnant, and presenting us with elderly men who have joined the Dionysian rites but whose reasons and enthusiasm are questionable. What, one might ask, is Euripides telling Athenians about their many Dionysian festivals?

The Bacchae is unusual in one respect: it's about Dionysus. According to classical scholar Scott Scullion (2002), we have titles for about 500 Greek tragedies, but less than 4 percent concerned the wine god, and the extant plays seldom refer to him. Nearly all Greek tragedies, including the earliest ones, are about secular figures. When Dionysian ecstasy arises in the action or language, which occurs only occasionally, it is usually treated ironically, as premature or misguided joy. There was a saying, well-known centuries later and possibly originating in our playwrights' time, that the plays had "nothing to do with Dionysus" – but it could have been either a complaint, a wry joke, or a clarification for the festival's numerous foreign visitors. This is an example of why some scholars think the connection between theatre and the cult of Dionysus has been overstated. In any case, Dionysus's absence wasn't a problem to most spectators or to the supervising authorities; otherwise, more plays would have made him their subject.

Figure 1.15

Ancient Greek theatre mask found in Athens, second century BCE. This mask was created after the death of the major Greek playwrights.

Source: Lefteris Papaulakis/Shutterstock.

There are considerable differences between the vision, structure, and poetic style of the plays of Aeschylus, written in the first half of the fifth century, and those of Euripides, written in the second half. Aeschylus was clearly very religious, but not doctrinal, and he staunchly supported Athens's democratic institutions. His work is also clearly indebted to the Homeric epic tradition. Euripides was influenced by the development of Sophism, the philosophical movement that brought disciplined processes of critical thinking to Athens. Controversially, his tragedies critiqued traditional values and religion, no longer showing reverence for the heroes and gods of the myths. Yet his plays were highly popular, especially after his death.

The **satyr plays** were send-ups of events in Homeric epics or tragedies, sometimes from the same narrative as the tragedies performed earlier in the day. These farcical, ribald pieces were named after the satyrs – the half-horse, half-human wine-drinking companions of Dionysus who constituted the chorus of these plays. Their costumes (Figure 1.10) included a horse's tail, an erect phallus, and a head-mask with pointed/equine ears, snub-nose, and wild hair and beard. Only one complete satyr play survives: Euripides's *Cyclops*. The satyr plays were characterized by broad physical sight-gags and scatological humor.

Fifth-century Greek comedy was just as concerned with public affairs as tragedy was. The only extant comedies are by Aristophanes, but his plays seem to have been typical of the genre: highly satirical and sometimes bawdy, obscene, fantastical, or absurd. The targets of its lampoons included politicians, militarists, "oracle mongers," and similar figures. Aristophanes caricatured the philosopher Socrates in *The Clouds*, and in *The Frogs* he made fun not only of Euripides, but also of Dionysus himself.

Beyond Athens, an independent comic tradition also developed in Syracuse during the fifth century, but since none of those comedies have survived, it is impossible to characterize them with any accuracy. However, the city was a second major center of performance; for instance, Aeschylus premiered some of his plays there.

Even though only men could be citizens of Athens, the plays include many strong women characters. In the surviving tragedies, they range from Clytemnestra in Aeschylus's *The Oresteia* to the protagonists of Sophocles's *Antigone* and Euripides's *Medea*. The women in Aristophanes's comedy *Lysistrata* protest against war by refusing to sleep with their husbands. These memorable female characters are, as Helene Foley has observed, quite surprising in a patriarchal society in which women were largely restricted to the domestic sphere (Foley 1981), although some scholars suspect an underlying misogyny because the characters were authored by men and played by male actors (Case 1985).

Performances of Greek drama were not simple acts of affirmation of the values of an ideally homogeneous community. Rather, the dramatists frequently addressed issues of concern to the *polis*, often reworking myths and epic narratives to do so. Aeschylus's *The Persians* (472 BCE), his prize-winning tragedy on the recent Battle of Salamis, could have been written either to praise the victorious Athenians or to express sympathy with the defeated Persians (Harrison 2000: 16–8). One year, a playwright was heavily fined for dealing with the painful subject of the Persians' destruction of Miletus, a city Athens had pledged to defend but did not. Its fall precipitated the Persian invasion of 492 BCE. Generals and the sons of fathers who died in battle engaged in ceremonies at the same City Dionysia where playwrights examined the conflict between the interests of state and those of the individual, the brutality of war and the suffering it brings, and other reasons for the citizens of Athens to reflect upon their city's decision-making. In this sense, the theatre's roots in Athenian civic powers and responsibilities were ultimately more fundamental than whatever linkage it had to Dionysus. One might well call Greek drama political theatre – theatre of and for the *polis*.

Greek theatre after the fifth century BCE

Fifth- and fourth-century Athens was a cauldron of new ideas in mathematics, astronomy, and philosophy. History, once the preserve of tales and epics, began to be written. The Sophists were refining methods of argument. Some thinkers (Euripides among them) cast doubt on traditional religious beliefs or even upon religion itself, particularly the idea that gods played a direct role in people's destinies. In opposition, the philosopher Plato (428–348 BCE) wrote vigorous criticisms of the Sophists and promoted older aristocratic values (including, paradoxically, scorn for writing). In *The Republic* (c.380 BCE), he imagined an ideal city where philosopher-kings ruled – and playwrights were expelled, launching a long history of antitheatrical prejudice in Europe.

At either the City Dionysia in 449 BCE or the Lenaia (another Dionysian festival) in 442 BCE, a competition among tragic actors was introduced, marking public recognition of the actor's art. An actor could win despite appearing in a losing tetralogy. Actors were celebrated or critiqued based on their day-long performances. By the fourth century BCE when, instead of new plays, previously authored plays were re-staged and/or toured other cities, the emphasis shifted further toward celebrating actors rather than playwriting. Reportedly, the famous late fourth-century Greek actor Polus performed in the title role of Sophocles's *Electra*, and in the scene when Electra takes the ashes of her brother Orestes from his tomb, Polus used the urn with the ashes of his own recently deceased son in his performance. According to the story, he "filled the whole place, not with the appearance and imitation of sorrow, but with genuine grief and unfeigned lamentation" (Gellius 1927: II:35–7).

Following Euripides's death in 406 BCE, Greek tragedy tended to use somewhat melodramatic plot devices. Only one play from this period survives. The satyr play seems to have declined, but comedy thrived. In the fourth and third centuries BCE, the satiric, smutty, and issue-oriented comedies of Aristophanes's time – **Old Comedy** – gradually gave way to comedies about private life, such as family, domestic slaves, prostitutes, and love. This more light-hearted genre was called **New Comedy**; we will look at it more closely in Chapter 2.

Between the appearance of early tragedy and New Comedy, Greek culture changed considerably. The rise of literacy shaped the development of both tragedy and comedy. We can identify some key changes:

- The chorus retained many characteristics of oral culture, but slowly lost its dramatic function, and relied on fewer formulaic phrases.
- In contrast, individual characters rose in prominence, and their speech became more colloquial and prose-like, although versification remained.
- Instead of the episodic, modular narratives of epics, plots adopted a linear and causally oriented structure focusing on a single event.
- In oral culture, imagery (especially strange imagery, such as monsters) often assisted memory, as the multi-headed Scylla in *The Odyssey* probably did; in literate culture such images often served the plot, such as the monstrous bull that rises from the sea to kill Hippolytus in Euripides's *Hippolytus*.

However, for decades, clear elements of oral culture continued in tragedy, most notably in the choruses whose performances included dance and song.

The first theory of theatre

Nearly a century after the pinnacle of Athenian theatre, Aristotle gave lectures that have come down to us as the *Poetics* (c.330 BCE), which even today is extraordinarily influential (in fact, all his work has powerfully affected philosophy, science, and other fields). The extant text is missing a section on comedy and has other corruptions, and there is speculation that it is Aristotle's lecture notes rather than a publication. Nonetheless, it is a vital document. He focused on the formal attributes and proper aesthetic effects of tragedy, discussing the kinds of plots, characters, and language appropriate to achieve the effects of a genre he considered a "natural" form, viewing Sophocles's *Oedipus the King* as the best example.

Probably Aristotle's most enduring idea is that **mimesis** – imitation or representation of action and characters – is the core of drama. Aristotle believed that there were six constituent elements of tragedy: plot, characters, verbal expression, thought (the characters' analyses or debates), song, and visual elements such as masks and costumes – in descending order of importance. Plots should consist of a necessary or plausible chain of events. The best plots, he claimed, involve a turning point (*peripety*), such as a reversal of circumstances or a dramatic irony and/or the recognition of some hidden fact, and the bad fortune that befalls the protagonist should not be caused by wickedness but by a serious mistake (*hamartia*).

One of tragedy's chief elements, Aristotle believed, was *catharsis* [kah-THAHR-sis], a term that has generated controversy due to its multiple meanings. Aristotle is frequently understood as saying that the audience is "purged" of fear, pity, or other emotions. But he might have meant that the events that caused the emotions were "clarified," or that the dramatic action "cleaned up" the wrongdoing that caused the tragedy. His phrasing is too ambiguous for us to know for sure. In fact, there are enormous difficulties in interpreting (let alone translating) the *Poetics*; countless misunderstandings and innumerable debates have followed.

The *Poetics* is the first known work of literary analysis, and the product of a literate culture. Aristotle's focus is on plays as a genre of literature, with only a little attention to theatrical performance, and still less on the plays' civic and religious contexts. Nevertheless, the *Poetics* provides clues about the performance context and early history of Greek tragedy.

The *Poetics* was unknown in Europe until the late 1500s, but after that, Aristotle's ideas were often considered authoritative, and are still drawn upon. As we will see in Chapter 5, Renaissance scholars portrayed the *Poetics* as rigidly prescriptive rather than a description of what Aristotle believed made for effective drama, and it became a model for European dramatic writing and analysis. Objections to Aristotle's theories have also been frequent, beginning in the early 1700s, but increasingly from the end of that century onward. Most of the criticism has been leveled against his views about plot structure and his indifference toward performance, but all his ideas, including the role of *mimesis*, have come under fire at some point. Even so, because of its historical role the *Poetics* is usually the starting point for studying dramatic theory.

Conquests, refugees, and resuscitation

Classical Greece is often glorified as the cradle of Western civilization. The facts, however, are more complicated, because Athens's massive cultural influence was not wholly of its own making.

Between 431 and 404 BCE, the Greek city-states of Athens and Sparta and their allies fought a series of devastating battles called the Peloponnesian War. The war occurred because Sparta (an oligarchy focused on military prowess) feared that Athens was growing too strong and imperialistic. Athens's defeat was hastened by poor military strategy and a disastrous plague. The city was never again the dominant power in ancient Greece.

In 338 BCE, King Philip II of Macedon (then part of northern Greece) subdued several of the Greek city-states, including Athens, placing them under his rule. His son Alexander the Great (356–323 BCE) – once Aristotle's pupil – widened his power over Greece, and then began a military campaign in which he conquered much of the Mediterranean region, Persia, and parts of India.

To make non-Greek lands more like Greece, Alexander began introducing Athenian culture, including theatre, throughout the area, a process called Hellenization. Actors became powerful, sometimes wealthy public figures, and some served as political negotiators or as ambassadors. At the end of the fourth century, instead of the old Athenian tradition of wealthy citizens supporting theatre as a civic duty, a state official oversaw the choruses and their budgets. Tragedy fossilized, but New Comedy grew highly popular. The plays by Aeschylus, Sophocles and Euripides survived because they were used in schoolbooks. The fate of the *Poetics* was more complicated, and it disappeared from Europe for centuries.

After Alexander's death, his empire was divided and eventually weakened. During the Hellenistic era (317–27 BCE), Rome arose as the major Mediterranean power. In 148–146 BCE, Rome formally annexed Greece. Roman authors sought to emulate the glory that was Macedonia, particularly its culture – that is, Athenian culture.

Eventually Romans lost interest in Greek literature, and after the crumbling Roman Empire's fall in 476 CE, little of ancient Greek culture was known in Europe until the twelfth century, when Aristotle commanded attention (in Latin translations), but lacking the *Poetics*. The situation was different in the Arabic world, encompassing the Mediterranean, the Middle East, and Persia (today, Iran). Even though few people knew Greek, the ancient texts were preserved across the centuries through storage and copying (Figure 1.16). Arabic scholars such as Avicenna (980–1037) and Averroes (1126–1198) studied Aristotle

Figure 1.16
Title page of *The Organon [Logic Books], Rhetoric and Poetics of Aristotle, and the Isagoge of Porphyry* (1027), commentary by Ḥasan ibn Sawar.
Source: Bibliothèque nationale de France.

intensively, including the *Poetics*, but they often used translations. However, because the Arabic world had nothing like Greek drama (as we will see in Chapter 3), the *Poetics* wasn't understood.

Ancient Greek literature might have remained an "Eastern" subject, but diplomatic gifts, the book trade, and the sacking of Constantinople (now Istanbul) in 1204 trickled classical Greek texts into Europe. After Constantinople's second sacking in 1453, Arabic scholars fleeing to Italy brought numerous manuscripts, possibly including the *Poetics*, along with much scholarship. The *Poetics* was published in a Latin translation in 1498; we will pick up its story in Chapter 5.

Ancient Athens had a long legacy, but one riddled with lengthy gaps and many losses, reinterpretations, and misunderstandings. And its legacy arose when the city was no longer powerful. Thanks largely to the preservation and scholarly work of the Arabic world, the culture of ancient Greece became part of the West's Renaissance construction of a classical heritage. Classical Greek culture was spread by others, as conquerors' imposition of their culture or the spoils of war, and the treasured belongings of refugees.

Summary

Among the numerous factors influencing the development of theatre, the way people communicate is especially significant. For most of humankind's existence, the spoken word was dominant. The primary forms of performance in oral culture were ritual and the solitary storyteller before an audience. When writing was invented, its significance and impact varied from society to society. In most cases, literacy was restricted to a minuscule elite and a limited effect on the wider culture. Writing's uses also changed over time – from little more than bookkeeping and administration, to religious texts for priests, to popular treatises on philosophy and oratory. Performance likewise transformed when writing became more central. Notable contrasts include oral culture's use of verse, formulas, and modular story structures, versus the Athenian literate culture's adoption of causality or probability for plot structuring, and prose-like texts.

But perhaps the most fundamental difference between ritual and theatre was that performance was no longer viewed as an offering to propitiate the gods or an act that preserved the balance of the universe: drama – even if it had deeply religious values, honored the gods, or portrayed their influence in human life – primarily served as commentary on human society. Plays approved or criticized human actions and sometimes challenged people's thought, even about the gods themselves. Although we have little information on how theatre arose outside of Greece, as we will see in Chapter 2, India, China, and Japan similarly made theatre a vehicle for human enjoyment and enlightenment. Many characteristics of oral culture continue within theatre to this day, but new cultural genres emerged and orality's role in performance and in society itself irrevocably altered.

★

Pleasure, power, and transmission: Scripted and non-scripted theatres

Daphne P. Lei

Contributors: Phillip B. Zarrilli and
Carol Fisher Sorgenfrei

Despite the invention of writing systems in Mesopotamia and the development of dramatic texts and theories in Greece, throughout history, oral traditions continued to be an essential element of performing arts, both due to the fact that literacy was limited and that orality and embodiment are necessary for transmitting performing arts. In this chapter, we discuss other early written theatres such as Sanskrit theatre and Roman comedy, along with some representative non-scripted performance genres. These non-scripted performances reflected local tastes, politics, and culture, and some became the predecessors of major traditional theatres, such as classical Chinese theatre. While the elite controlled the mainstream narratives – morals, values, and even aesthetics in written texts, the taste of the audience (public or selected groups) was also essential. We use Japan as an example to trace the development of performance from a pre-literate society with unscripted performances to the refined performance genre for the elite within the span about a millennium. Moreover, this chapter traces some of the significant cultural transmissions and artistic adaptation from one region to another.

We will look at the Roman Republic (509 BCE–27 BCE) and Roman Empire (27 BCE–476 CE), India (primarily c.200 BCE–c.200 CE), and East Asia – China and Korea (first millennium CE), and Japan (primarily mid-1300s to mid-1400s CE). We begin by showing how some forms of Greek performance were adapted by Roman playwrights and how Roman comedy and spectacular entertainments catered to the desires of the masses. We then turn to theatre in ancient India, looking at how significant cultural epics and the power of local political and religious leaders created several disparate genres. These culturally distinct genres influenced each other, arriving at significant new forms. The Hindu culture of ancient India gave birth to Buddhism, which spread rapidly throughout Asia, by sea to South and Southeast Asia, and by land along the Silk Road and other routes to East Asia. (The Silk Road is an ancient trade route, starting from northern China, through the Middle East, to Europe, connecting ancient civilizations such as the Chinese, Indian, Persian, and Roman). Along with

DOI: 10.4324/9781003185185-4

Buddhist stories and beliefs, artifacts, performance styles, and musical instruments traveled and took roots in different parts of Asia. Chinese philosophies, such as Taoism and Confucianism, along with their writing system and literature, were also influential in developing theatre in the neighboring countries. We will focus on non-scripted performances in China and both scripted and non-scripted theatre in Japan.

Ancient Roman performance: From the Republic to the Empire

To understand Roman performance, we must consider its debt to Greek civilization, even as the brilliance of Greek theatre declined. Rome, however, was a very different society. The Roman Republic was divided into three classes: the *patricians* (wealthy aristocrats), the *plebeians* (ordinary, lower-class citizens), and the enslaved population; the first two classes were citizens. The classes were strictly segregated, and intermarriage was forbidden; women did not enjoy the same legal rights as men. The most powerful branch of the Republic was the Senate. Senators were almost always patricians who were skilled in the arts of rhetoric. Although plebeians gained political power in the late Republic, the patricians retained control until the time of the Empire.

Every Roman institution operated as a sacred patriarchy, and each family was a state in miniature. The male head of each family (*pater familias*) legally held absolute power over members of his household. For example, in 340 BCE, Manlius Torquatus had his son executed for disobeying orders during the Great Latin War, even though his son's unauthorized attack resulted in military victory. Two types of behavior shaped and constrained Roman males during the Republican period: *pietas* and *gravitas*. *Pietas* is usually translated as "respect for elders," but also implies respect for authority, loyalty of wife to the husband, and devotion to the gods. *Gravitas* (a word related to "gravity") is usually translated as "dignity," and it implies seriousness.

Literacy in ancient Rome was perhaps 10 percent. Rhetorical skill was highly valued and greatly studied. In describing the funeral of Julius Caesar, the Roman historian Plutarch gives an account of a speech which used rhetorical skill to subtly shift the audience's point of view. For an imagined version of this event, see Mark Antony's famous eulogy beginning "Friends, Romans, countrymen, lend me your ears" in Shakespeare's *Julius Caesar* (III.2). All Roman playwrights exhibit such skill with language and actors were valued partly because of their skill in oral presentation.

Early Roman performance: Festivals, games, and mimes

The Romans adapted many aspects of Greek culture. The Olympian gods were transformed into Roman gods, with Zeus becoming Jupiter, Aphrodite becoming Venus. Mime (not to be confused with wordless pantomime) was a verbal and physical form of theatre from Syracuse, a town in Sicily, but could trace its origin to Athens in as early as the fourth century BCE. Unlike plays, which used only masked male actors (cross-dressed if depicting female characters), both males and female actors performed mime without masks. Some scholars suggest that because the face of the unmasked mime actor (Greek: *mimos*; Latin: *mimus*) was so expressive, mime fostered the development of a relatively more realistic acting style. Mimes used monologue, dialogue, dance, song, and skills such as acrobatics to elaborate on often sexually explicit scenes, political satire, everyday life, or farcical portrayals of incidents derived from mythology. Focusing on actors' expressive physical abilities, mime is sometimes compared to the variety shows, striptease, and slapstick of vaudeville.

Public holidays in ancient Rome were of two kinds. Those called *feriae* were primarily religious and serious, while others were called **ludi** ([LOO-dee]; sing. *ludus*) – "games," a term meaning both the holiday and the actual games, sports, and performances that were included along with religious observances.

Many *ludi* were held throughout the year. Some honored various deities, while others were held for secular reasons (such as dignitaries' funerals or birthdays) or to celebrate military victories. The largest public *ludi*, the *Ludi Romani* ("Roman Games"), was held early in September to honor the god Jupiter. Although originally celebrated on a single day, after 220 BCE it expanded, until by 51 CE the *Ludi Romani* took place over a period of 14 days, supported primarily by public funds.

The *Ludi Romani* far surpassed the Greek Panathenaea in diversity of events. Chariot and horse racing, boxing, singing, and parades were joined by bloody spectacles that resulted in the deaths of the participants. These included gladiatorial combats, staged animal hunts, and even mock sea battles (*naumachia* [naw-MAH-khee-ah]). Dramatic performances (*ludi scaenici*, meaning "stage games") were first included in 240 BCE. These first Roman plays were written by Livius Andronicus (c.284–c.204 BCE), a former Greek slave. Only fragments of his works survive, but we know that all of his plays were adaptations or translations of Greek plays, written in Latin (the language of ancient Rome).

Popular comedy in the Roman republic

In Greece, in the decades following Athens's defeat in the Peloponnesian War, the broad socio-political satire of Old Comedy was replaced by the New Comedy. Old Comedy had lampooned generals and politicians (exemplified by the plays of Aristophanes), but New Comedy focused on domestic issues, such as those written by Menander (c.342–c.291 BCE). Of the more than 100 plays written by Menander, only two complete or nearly complete New Comedies survive – *The Bad-Tempered Man* (also translated as *The Grouch*) and *The Woman of Samos* – and fragments of others (Figure 2.1). Their plots focus on love affairs and family relationships, with somewhat generic characters defined by gender, age, or class. Rather than the pointed political messages of Old Comedy, Menander's plays reflected everyday events.

Greek New Comedy was reinvented in Rome as *fabula palliata* – "plays in Greek dress" and Greek locations. Two notable Roman playwrights adapted Greek New Comedies from the previous 200 years for their Roman audiences: Titus Maccius Plautus, known as Plautus (c.254–184 BCE) and Publius Terentius Afer, known as Terence (c.190–c.159 BCE).

Plautus transformed Greek New Comedy with his first production, *Stichus*, in 205 BCE. Plautus wrote about 130 plays. Of these, 21 are extant. His adaptations are characterized by a taste for fast-paced, pun-filled, bawdy, and almost slangy Latin. Parts of his plays are in a meter designed to be sung to music, which might be considered as an early form of musical comedy. Plautus's plays also use certain indigenous Italian conventions, especially Atellan farce (*fabulae atellanae*) from southern Italy. Atellan farces were improvised from simple core narratives, with easily recognizable stock characters weaving together jokes and comical stage business. For example, the audience would expect an old man to oppose his son's amorous adventures and a slave to cleverly thwart his old master. Both early Atellan farces and Plautus's dramas were performed on temporarily constructed wooden stages set up for each *ludus*. This simple playing space was not bound by a realistic depiction of locale or space; it could represent a harbor front or a street. A scene building backed a simple playing space,

Figure 2.1
An image probably of the popular Menander, with three masks of Greek New Comedy: the mask of a young man (in his hand), and masks of a young woman and an older man or a comic slave. Marble relief sculpture of the first or second century BCE, after a third-century BCE work.

Source: Princeton University Art Museum. Museum purchase, Caroline G. Mather Fund y1951-1.

which can depict any locale. There are three openings in the scene building to allow many different plots. None of these wooden structures has survived.

Because dramatic performances took place in the context of public games, playwrights had to capture the attention of a popular audience. In Plautus's *Poenulus*, an actor steps on the stage and directly addresses the raucous audience. In comical language, he orders them to be silent, to sit still, to stop eating, and to wake up. He forbids prostitutes from sitting on the stage, old men from clomping around, and everyone from blocking the audience's view of the actor. And because he wants to have a paying audience, he says:

> Keep slaves from occupying the seats, that there be room for free men, or let them pay money for their freedom. If they can't do that, let them go home and avoid a double misfortune – being raked with rods here, and with whips at home if their masters return and find they haven't done their work.

> (Duckworth 1942: I, 727–8)

This prologue reveals how the Roman state/religious festival context was in essence a "marketplace" where the increasingly wide variety of popular entertainments had to vie for the short attention span of its mass public.

Plautus's comedies, known primarily for the fast traffic of their comic plots and low antic business, turn the traditional Roman values of patriarchal order and *gravitas* on their heads. Those with the least power in the Roman hierarchy – slaves, wives, and sons – are often those who win out (albeit the stakes are not large). In Plautus's plays, the clever slave often outsmarts his master. This is an example of "comic inversion" (discussed in the case study below) or the carnivalesque (discussed in Chapter 3) (see Figure 2.2).

The later comedies by Terence were more constrained, with more elegant and witty language and complex characters compared with those of Plautus. Because Terence had been a

Figure 2.2

This Roman marble relief shows a performance of masked characters typical of Roman comedy, including the two older men at left and the young man at right with a scheming servant at his side. Between them, a musician plays the double-reed *aulos*, suggestive of the use of music and song in some of the comedies. Behind the actors is a door in the façade backing the stage and a small curtain (*siparia*), perhaps concealing a painted panel not relevant to this particular scene. From the Farnese Collection on display in the National Archaeological Museum in Naples, Campania, Italy.

Source: Azoor Photo/Alamy Stock Photo.

slave brought to Rome from northern Africa and educated by a wealthy family, some scholars suggest that he may have been Black or Arab. From his first production in 166 BCE, Terence followed the model of the Greek New Comedy, with four of his six extant plays based on Menander's. He often combines plots and characters from several Greek sources into one play. His plays became key texts in Latin education during Europe's medieval period and greatly influenced the development of drama and performance during the early Renaissance. However, Terence at times had trouble holding the attention of his Roman audience. At the first performance of *Hecya*, written for the *Ludi Megalenses* in 165 BCE, the audience left to go and see the rope dancers. At a second staging, they left to see the gladiators fight.

CASE STUDY: Plautus's plays: What's so funny?

Gary Jay Williams, with Carol Fisher Sorgenfrei and Daphne P. Lei

Many critics and theorists have tended to value "serious" drama and literature over comedy; however, since it is comedy that audiences more often prefer, it might have a more direct social function than tragedy.

There are various types of comedy, not all of which can be considered here. Satire, for example, often has a serious or even political purpose, since it uses exaggeration to point out the flaws, foibles, and even the corruption of powerful people or institutions. Parody takes on familiar artworks or their genres and twists the originals to make fun of them. Farce focuses on wildly improbable characters and situations, fast-paced action and dialogue, and often involves mistaken identity and sexual situations. Slapstick relies more on physical humor such as clumsiness, a fall or a whack on the head. Some forms of comedy are only comic to specific audiences but are deeply offensive to others; comedy that uses jokes about sexual, physical, or racial stereotypes also raises ethical issues. Many comedy traditions also focus on remonstrance or social commentary and serve the similar functions as today's news-based comedy talk shows.

Aristotle's *Poetics*, which focuses on Greek tragedy, only briefly mentions comedy (some believe there was a lecture devoted to comedy but appeared to be lost); nevertheless, his view on comedy has influenced Western criticism in later generations. Distinguishing between tragedy and comedy, he reasoned that comedy will be populated by "characters of a lower type," while tragedy's chief characters will be from great and "illustrious" families (nobility or ruling families) (Else 1957: 376; Aristotle 1984: 2319, 2325). Aristotle suggests that comic characters, not unlike their tragic counterparts, are obsessed by some all-consuming idea that leads to their downfall, but in comedy, this defect is neither painful nor destructive, as its plots usually involve food, money, sex, or social status. For the Greeks and Romans, all comedies had a happy ending.

Some of the common comic elements – incongruity, reversal, repetition, misunderstanding, and mistaken identity – sometimes also appear in tragedies, but in comedy, potentially tragic events are reversed into happy results, leading to laughter and emotional release for the audience. Sigmund Freud (1856–1939) wrote about how laughter and comedy can have beneficial psychological effects. Northrop Frye (1937–1991) observed that many comedies end with some festive ritual, such as a dinner or wedding, signaling the formation of a stable, new society. Brandon J. Manning discussed comedy's function in addressing and subverting cultural and racial realities in marginalized groups, using examples from Black satire in American popular culture in the twenty-first century (Manning 2022).

Following Aristotle's mode of formal analysis, later Western theorists made distinctions between high and low comedies. High comedy, also called comedy of manners, generally concerns (and appeals to) aristocrats or the economically privileged, and it features clever ideas and witty language. In low comedy, such as farces and the plays of Plautus, the humor derives from fast-developing events and physical action, with the body being a major player. The erect phallus is a standing joke in the oldest of Western comic forms – built into the costumes of the characters in the Greek satyr plays.

In 1900, French philosopher Henri Bergson (1859–1941) summarized various theories of comedy. His main idea was that comedy results from incongruity – especially when our expectations differ from reality. The comic character is usually comic in proportion to his ignorance of his own faults, and continually repeats his mistakes in a mechanical way. For example, the central character of Plautus's *The Braggart Soldier* (*Miles Gloriosus*, 205 BCE) is totally infatuated with himself, bragging about his victories, strength (he says he killed an elephant with his fist), and sexual prowess. His slave, who struggles to carry his master's oversized shield, needs to feed his ridiculous appetite for flattery. The vain soldier demonstrates his ignorance of Roman religion by preposterously claiming that he was born only one day after Jupiter and that he is the grandson of Venus. When a servant girl greets him with "Hail, you gorgeous creature!/ Oh, man of every hour, beyond all other men / Beloved of two gods –" he interrupts her to ask, "Which two?" (1963: 90).

Another character who behaves mechanically (which, according to Bergson, is always comic) and who is unaware of his faults appears in Plautus's *The Pot of Gold*. Here, the miserly old Euclio is obsessed with money. He so fears that someone will steal the pot of gold he has hidden that he suspects everyone, including the rooster he finds scratching near it, which he instantly kills. The clever slave of his daughter's suitor manages to steal the gold, resulting in Euclio giving the suitor permission to marry his daughter so he can get it back. The play's serious issues – the cruel patriarchal control and excessive greed – can be twisted from a potential tragedy and end in a festive wedding.

According to Bergson, we laugh when "the history of a person or of a group … sometimes appears like a game worked by strings, or gearings, or springs" (Bergson 1956: 116). Plautus's *The Menaechmi* fits this description. It features another typical aspect of comedy – mistaken identity – by focusing on identical twin brothers (an easy practice since all actors wore masks). The plot of *The Menaechmi* is a calculus of complications set off by the presence of the twins, who long have lost to each other since childhood. In grief over the loss of Menaechmus, one of the twins when the boys were seven years old, his family renamed the remaining boy Menaechmus. Menaechmus II, who is from Syracuse, has been searching the world for his brother and arrives in Epidamnum where his brother, Menaechmus I, lives. The mistress of Menaechmus I, Erotium, mistakenly invites Menaechmus II into her house, supposing him to be her lover. So, too, the angry wife and all the servants of Menaechmus I mistake Menaechmus II for Menaechmus I. Each twin concludes that the world around him has gone mad. Everyone else believes the twins to be mad, including the doctor who is called in by Erotium's father. In exasperation at one point, Menaechmus II feigns madness to be rid of them all.

Plautus multiplies the confusions by repeatedly having one twin exit by one door just as the other enters by another. All the characters revolve in and out of the doors of the houses of Erotium and Menaechmus I like figures on a mechanical clock gone haywire. The audience is always in on the joke because Plautus is careful to have the entering twin identify himself clearly. At the play's climax, the twins finally meet at center stage, mirroring one another, and to the relief of everyone, they sort out the confusion.

Plautus's dialogue is also full of comic devices. Near the end of *The Rope*, Daemones and the slave Trachalio, who serves the suitor of Daemones's daughter, have a rapid-fire exchange of lines in which the response "All right" is repeated 17 times. After Trachalio exits, Plautus caps the sequence:

DAEMONES: All right, all right, nothing but "all right." He'll find all right's all wrong one of these days, I hope. [*Enter Gripus, another slave*]

GRIPUS: Will it be all right [*Daemones jumps*] if I have a word with you, sir?

(Plautus 1964: 145–6)

A moment later, Trachalio has a series of exchanges with his young master, Plesidippus, who is in love with Daemones's daughter:

PLESIDIPPUS: Do you think we shall be betrothed today?

TRACHALIO: I do.

PLESIDIPPUS: Do you think I should congratulate the old man on finding her?

TRACHALIO: I do.

PLESIDIPPUS: And the mother?

TRACHALIO: I do.

PLESIDIPPUS: And what do you think?

TRACHALIO: I do.

PLESIDIPPUS: You do what?

TRACHALIO: I think.

PLESIDIPPUS: You do think what?

TRACHALIO: I do think what you think.

PLESIDIPPUS: Don't you think you could think for yourself?
TRACHALIO: I do.

(Plautus 1964: 147–8)

In both cases, the robotic responses of the slave, Trachalio, produce a comic momentum that threatens to unravel language itself. Comedy results when humans act like wind-up mechanical dolls rather than living beings. Bergson called this type of momentum "the snowball effect," which occurs when some tiny thing (in the plot or even in dialogue) gets totally out of control and becomes a gigantic problem. (Compare Abbott and Costello's famous skit "Who's on First?" in which the two men are using simple words and names to mean very different things, producing comic frustration over a simple baseball game.) Plautus also employs parody and irreverence. He uses theatre to mock its own conventions. In Plautus's *Amphitryo*, the prologue is delivered by the god Mercury in disguise as a lowly servant:

> But I still haven't told you
> About this favor I came to ask of you –
> Not to mention explaining the plot of this tragedy.
> I must get on . . .
> What's that? Are you disappointed
> To find it's a *tragedy*? Well, I can easily change it.
> I'm a god after all. I can easily make it a comedy. . . .

(Plautus 1964: 230)

Plautus himself might have been a comic actor himself. His middle name, Maccius, may be derived from Maccus, the name of a clown figure in the ancient Atellan farces who was greedy and gluttonous, the type of character that Plautus might have played (see Figure 2.3).

Plautus's plays have had staying power. One century after his death, the critic M. Terentius Varro put together a collection of 20 of his 21 extant plays. Since Plautus borrowed many stock characters and plots from Menander, he is responsible for the survival of many classical prototypes. Among the many descendants of Plautus's *The Braggart Soldier* (*Miles Gloriosus*) are the Capitano and Scaramouche of the *commedia dell'arte* (see Chapter 4) and Shakespeare's Falstaff in *Henry IV, Part 1* (1598). Plautus's *The Menaechmi* is the source of Shakespeare's *Comedy of Errors* (1598), to which Shakespeare added a second set of identical twin slaves from Plautus's *Amphitryon*. *The Comedy of Errors* was the source for Richard Rodgers and Lorenz Hart's musical comedy *The Boys from Syracuse* (1938), with a script adapted by George Abbot, as well as a new adaptation, *La Comedia of Errors,* for the Oregon Shakespeare Festival, set at the US-Mexico border (2019). *Amphitryon* was widely adapted – 38 versions down to Jean Giraudoux's *Amphitryon 38* (1929), and Plautus's *The Pot of Gold* was the source of Molière's *The Miser* (1668). The 1962 American musical comedy *A Funny Thing Happened on the Way to the Forum* (by Burt Shevelove, Larry Gelbart, and Steven

Sondheim) was inspired by several of Plautus's plays. *Iran Man* (2005), Amy Richlin's translation and adaptation of Plautus's *The Persian*, is set in Los Angeles with dialogue in contemporary American slang and rap, interspersed with Spanish. (An unbridged version of this case study on Plautus is on the website.)

Key references

Aristotle (1984) *Poetics*, trans. I. Bywater in J. Barnes (ed.) *The Complete Works of Aristotle*, rev. edn, vol. 2, Princeton, NJ: Princeton University Press.

Bergson, H. (1956) "Laughter," in Wylie Sypher (ed.) *Comedy*, Garden City, NY: Doubleday Anchor Books.

Else, G. (1957) *Aristotle's Poetics: The Argument*, Cambridge, MA: Harvard University Press.

Frye, N. (1957) *Anatomy of Criticism*, Princeton, NJ: Princeton University Press.

Janko, R. (1984) *Aristotle on Comedy, Toward a Reconstruction of Poetics II*, Berkeley: University of California Press.

Manning, B.J. (2022) *Played Out: The Race Man in Twenty-First-Century Satire*, New Brunswick, NJ: Rutgers University.

Plato (1942) *Symposium*, in Plato, *Five Great Dialogues*, trans. B. Jowett, Roslyn, NY: Walter J. Black.

Plautus, T.M. (1958) *The Pot of Gold*, trans. Peter Arnott, New York: Appleton-Century-Crofts.

Plautus, T.M. (1963) *The Braggart Soldier*, trans. E. Segal, New York: Samuel French.

Plautus, T.M. (1964) *Amphityro*, in *The Rope and Other Plays*, trans. E.F. Watling, Baltimore, MD: Penguin Books.

Plautus, T.M. (1974) *The Twin Menaechmi*, trans. E.C. Wiest and R.W. Hyde, in O.G. Brockett and L. Brockett (eds.) *Plays for the Theatre*, 2nd edn, New York: Holt, Rinehart and Winston.

Slater, N.W. (1985) *Plautus in Performance*, Princeton, NJ: Princeton University Press.

Figure 2.3
Statue of a masked slave character from Roman comedy, leaning casually on a pillar. Archaeological Museum, Istanbul.

Source: © Gary Jay Williams.

Videos

Abbott and Costello comedy routine, "Who's on First?" in two versions, https://www.youtube.com/watch?v=2ve20PVNZ18; https://www.youtube.com/watch?v=sYOUFGfK4bU

Seneca's tragedies and Horace's Ars Poetica (The art of poetry)

Very few Roman tragedies have survived. What little we know of serious or tragic plays comes primarily from Seneca and Horace.

Lucius Annaeus Seneca (c.4 BCE–65 CE) was born in Spain and educated in Rome. He became a well-known politician, philosopher, and teacher who authored nine tragedies loosely based on Greek originals, including *Medea*, *Phaedra*, *Oedipus*, *Agamemnon*, and *Thyestes*. Unlike popular comedies, Roman tragedies were not performed in the marketplace. In fact, it is not clear if Seneca's tragedies were actually staged; they may have been merely recited at small or elite gatherings, or simply read as literature. Seneca's tragedies reflect the philosophy of Stoicism, which taught self-sufficiency and the avoidance of high emotion. Nevertheless, his plays are characterized by sensational violence and horror, far more than the Greek originals. This apparent contradiction may suggest a desire to condemn excessive emotion by demonstrating its horrific consequences, or it might support the theory that Seneca's plays were not actually staged – it is easier to describe violence and horror in detail than to act out the scenes (the Greeks avoided actual violent actions on stage). Alternatively, the gruesome violence in Seneca's plays may suggest that both high-minded patricians and plebeians enjoyed the gory spectacles, regardless of its occurrence in Senecan tragedies or in bloody *ludi*.

Like Terence, Seneca had a great impact on the Renaissance. His philosophical essays influenced the French humanist and essayist Michel de Montaigne (1533–1592), the "father of modern skepticism" who influenced many later writers, including French philosopher René Descartes (1596–1650), American essayist Ralph Waldo Emerson (1803–1882), and American science fiction writer Isaac Asimov (1920–1992). Seneca's plays were the only Roman tragedies to survive the Middle Ages and greatly influenced writers of the Renaissance and later, such as Shakespeare (see Chapter 5).

Quintus Horatius Flaccus, generally known as Horace (65–8 BCE), was an important poet whose *Ars Poetica* (*Art of Poetry*, published 18 BCE, also known as *Letters to Piso*) makes several demands on playwrights that have come to represent what we call "neoclassicism" in Western drama. While generally agreeing with Aristotle in most matters, his work is prescriptive while Aristotle's is descriptive: Aristotle looked at existing plays and tried to figure out what worked; Horace told playwrights what they should do, part of what the later generations knew as "the rules." (For sixteenth-/seventeenth-century neoclassical misunderstandings of Aristotle and Horace, and the controversies regarding "the rules," see Chapter 5.) Horace said that drama should not mix styles or genres (for example, no comic relief in a tragedy) and characters must be both consistent and recognizable (for example, playwrights should not deviate from the traditional image of well-known characters, such as Medea or Oedipus). Dramas should begin *in medias res* ("in the middle of things"), that is, not at the beginning of the story but closer to the climax, and tragedy should maintain a five-act structure. He disapproved of Plautus's bawdy language and plots, maintaining that drama must adhere to socially acceptable propriety, language, and what he termed "decorum."

Another important aspect of *Ars Poetica* is the idea of *dulce et utile*: combining "sweetness" (enjoyment) and "usefulness" (instructiveness). He said that instruction should be brief so our mind can retain it better. This idea is influential in the fields of both theatre and education: the most effective way to get a message across is through something that is entertaining. Prior to the mid-twentieth century, Latin was important for Western education, especially for the elites; therefore, Senecan tragedy and Horace's *Ars Poetica* (although often misinterpreted) were widely studied and had a profound impact on subsequent playwriting and dramatic theories, as well as theatre history in the West.

Imperial spectacles: Performance during the Empire

During the late Republic, dramatic performances had been sponsored by wealthy men who sought to enhance their reputations, but by the end of the first century BCE, both comedy and tragedy had ceased to be viable dramatic forms. Popular entertainment focused on spectacular re-stagings of extant dramas and on other events such as bloody contests.

The powerful patriarchy operating throughout the Roman Republic eventually gave way to a centralized authoritarian state with the establishment of the Roman Empire in 27 BCE, when Caesar Octavian (63 BCE–14 CE) received the honorific title of Augustus. The service due to one's family was now to be extended to the state, when noble/landed families surrendered their power to an emperor, later called the father of the country (*pater patriae*).

Rome's first permanent theatre was not built until 55 BCE by Pompey the Great (106–48 BCE) (Figure 2.4). This grand building seated 20,000 spectators and featured a stage 300 feet in width, backed by an architecturally elaborate three-story façade (*scaenae frons*),

Figure 2.4

Reconstruction of the Theatre of Pompey (55 BCE), Rome, in a nineteenth-century engraving after a drawing by Georg Rehlender. Connected to the rear of this theatre was an enormous public plaza with open colonnaded structures, which the Greeks had called a *stoa*. This can be seen in online interactive reconstructions.

Source: Interfoto/Alamy Stock Photo.

decorated with statues. It was a highly visible platform where Pompey (and subsequent rulers) could preside over the gathered populace, displaying his authority and the grandeur of Rome. Although a large temple was incorporated into the outer wall of the auditorium (*cavea*) for Venus Victrix, it seems that the *ludi* had lost almost all connection to religion.

Mime continued to be popular, as well as a relatively new art called **pantomime**. In pantomime, a chorus and/or musicians accompanied a solo, masked, non-speaking actor who played all the roles in a lavishly staged myth or the re-staging of a drama. In the second century CE, Lucian wrote of the pantomime actor:

> You will find that his is no easy profession, nor lightly to be undertaken; requiring as it does the highest standard of culture in all its branches, and involving a knowledge not of music only, but of rhythm and meter, and above all of your beloved philosophy, both natural and moral. . . . The pantomime is above all things an actor; . . . [S]uccess, as the pantomime knows, depends . . . upon verisimilitude . . . : prince or tyrannicide, pauper or farmer, each must be shown with the peculiarities that belong to him.
>
> (Nagler 1952: 28–9)

Like actors, pantomime and mime artists were often controversial figures denied citizenship, although they might be treated like stars by the public. When Julius Caesar served as the dictator of Rome (48–45 BCE), the noted producer and actor of mime, Laberius, was called out of retirement by Caesar himself to celebrate Caesar's victories. When Laberius appeared as a beaten slave in one mime performance, he dared to say on stage, "Henceforth, O citizens, we have lost our liberty!" And when Laberius said, "He must fear many, whom many fear," it is reported that the entire audience of 20,000 turned to see the reaction of Caesar, who showed tolerance for Laberius's performance. Not all performers were so lucky. Emperor Nero, who loved to perform, became so jealous of the skill of a pantomime dancer called Paris that he ordered the young dancer's execution.

Increasingly popular and bloody spectacles took place in "circuses," which in this context means a large, oblong, or rectangular stadium-like building with open-air seating used for entertainment. Rome's Circus Maximus was originally built during the second century BCE. Julius Caesar expanded it to 1,800-feet long and 350-feet wide, with wooden seating over arched stone vaults for around 150,000 spectators. Although destroyed by fire, when reconstructed in 200 CE, it had a seating capacity of 250,000. Spectacles included chariot racing, animal fights (*venationes*), and gladiatorial contests (*munera*). There was also staging of sea battles (*naumachiae*), which were based upon episodes from Greek history and performed by slaves, prisoners of war, or criminals condemned to death in a flooded circus. These "performers" were schooled in specialist forms of combat – some heavily armed wearing helmets, others lightly armed with sword and shield, and still others with net, dagger, and trident – usually with all fighting to the death. One of the sea battles staged in 46 BCE and commissioned by Julius Caesar re-enacted the battle between Tyre and Egypt on an artificial lake in Rome. In 52 CE, Claudius staged a fight between Rhodes and Sicily using 19,000 prisoners.

Those who survived the sea battles and gladiatorial contests might be saved from death because they had demonstrated great courage. It is estimated that about 50 percent of all human participants in these events were spared. Those who lived often became "stars." Some gladiators were in fact volunteers who craved the spotlight and, if victorious, were rewarded for their bravery and military skill. Female gladiators, often as highly trained in arms as the males, sometimes participated in the games. However, they were not always taken seriously and might be pitted against dwarves. The games were free – all citizens had a right to attend.

Animal fights included animals in combat with armed men, animals fighting animals, and condemned men and women exposed to animals that had been starved. During the reign of Augustus Caesar, 3,500 animals were killed in the course of 26 different festivals. To celebrate the completion of the Colosseum in 80 CE, 9,000 animals were killed in such games.

Roman society at this time was deeply divided between wealthy aristocrats and the rest of society, many of whom were very poor. Although legislation and official and semi-official educational propaganda attempted to constrain behavior and encourage a return to ancient virtues during the mid-Republic, the bawdy plays of Plautus and bloody spectacles at the amphitheatres remained popular. Spectacular entertainments such as those noted above may have helped to keep the poorer members of society occupied and help them "let off steam." "Bread and circuses," a term attributed to the poet Juvenal (late first to early century CE), is used to describe both the public taste and the political strategy of the ruling class.

Debating the ludi: Did violent spectacles serve a purpose?

Historian Paul Plass's analysis of the Roman games can help us understand how and why such massive public bloodshed with its "hideous damage done to men or animals" had both social and symbolic meanings. He makes several key points:

(1) The games and their bloody entertainments permitted daily "routines to be routinely broken" at festival time.
(2) The "intensity and scale" of violence made the games seem extraordinary.
(3) The public nature of the games allowed extreme violence to become the norm.
(4) Since they were mass public events, probably no individual felt responsibility for the lethal spectacles. Rather, a "mass identity" gave the participating citizens a sense of "power and gratification at survival."
(5) The spectators' mass attendance in public event "*was* the show in a political and social sense" (Plass 1995: 43).
(6) The extravagant games demonstrated an excess of "conspicuous consumption" that was fed by "copious supplies of [human and animal] blood." They indicated the unrestrained power of the emperor and the state (Plass 1995: 50).

(For a view of how another culture used such displays, see the discussion of Mayan human sacrifice in Chapter 1.)

Bloodshed always accompanies territorial expansion; for Romans, the genocide of Carthage in 146 BCE and the capture of 50,000 Carthaginians, who were sold to slavery, were part of the violent Roman history. It is worth noting that the people subject to the cruelty of *ludi* were usually the marginalized class (convicted criminals or enslaved people) and foreigners (war prisoners), although the survivors were able to ascend the social ladder and be admired by the crowd. Since slaves both wrote and performed in plays, scholar Odai Johnson thinks that Roman comedies "can be read as documents of repressed terror" to certain extent (Johnson 2010: 15). We can also read the bloody spectacles as a political strategy to use xenophobia and oppression to energize and unite the "normal" citizens to create a sense of social order and the empire. The thrill of watching the oppressed or disadvantaged

Other fight for their lives can be compared to today's popular (often very bloody) fights/spectacles such as the mega competitions of mixed martial arts (MMA) – the fighters are often ethnic minorities and/or from a lower economic status and the competitions are controlled by first-world capitalist corporations and consumed by the global spectatorship.

However, the games and the theatre had long been opposed by the growing Christian community, partially because Christians condemned to death had sometimes been thrown to wild animals. By the end of the second century, the Christian writer Tertullian (c.160–c.240) had urged Christians to avoid theatre and the spectacles at the amphitheatres. He believed that the *ludi* were dedicated to pagan deities, were filled with unchaste and inhumane activities, and did not offer viewers a chance to practice Christian virtues; attending them would pollute the viewer.

In 312, Emperor Constantine converted to Christianity and in 313 the practice of Christianity ceased to be a crime in the Empire. A decade later, it became the official religion of the Roman Empire. In 398, the Church decreed excommunication for anyone going to the theatre rather than church on holy days. Actors were forbidden the sacraments unless they renounced their profession, a decree that remained in force into the eighteenth century. Nevertheless, Roman *ludi* continued, with festivals in the fourth century lasting as long as 100 days. With the economic and political decay of the Empire and its division into independent parts ruled by Rome and Constantinople, a weakened Rome fell to the Visigoths in 476. Excessive blood spectacles gradually declined and the last record of a Roman theatre performance is dated 549 CE.

Many religions continued to have conflicted attitudes toward theatre: theatre competes with religions for attention and spreads "immoral" ideas; however, it is also a useful medium to preach religious beliefs, such as used in Hinduism, Buddhism, and Christianity.

Drama and theatre in ancient India

Alexander the Great had previously extended Hellenic influence to the northwest of the Indian subcontinent, and mutual influences can be discerned in Greek and Indian sculpture and painting during the Hellenic period. The huge Roman Empire did not reach as far as India; however, the Roman Empire traded extensively with India and China, importing luxuries such as spices and silk. Sanskrit (a language of ancient India) is linguistically related to Greek, Latin, and most European languages. While connections between ancient Greek and Indian performance are possible, except for some stories that traveled between cultures, there is no evidence of influence in either direction in the early period.

When we speak of **Sanskrit drama**, we are referring to a specific style of performance that originally used the Sanskrit language. The Sanskrit word for "story," *katha*, also means something "which is true" – that is, a story involving consequences that reverberate throughout cosmic history. It can also be translated as "telling or narration" (Lutgendorf 1991: 115). The performance of Sanskrit storytelling – and later, of Sanskrit drama – was always concerned with teaching moral lessons.

The *Mahabharata* and *Ramayana* are grand epics sacred to Hinduism (the major but not the sole religion of India). Both are important examples of *katha*. They began as narrated tales, and both have various written versions. The most respected Sanskrit version of the *Ramayana* dates between 200 BCE and 200 CE. When regional languages developed, this version was replaced with easily accessible vernacular versions. The same is true of the *Mahabharata*, which dates back to at least the mid-first millennium BCE. Many other compendiums of stories exist, forming a storehouse of sources for drama. These two Indian epics are some-times seen as the counterparts of the *Iliad* and *Odyssey* or compared with the *Bible*. Although they all tell complicated stories of both humans and deities in different cultural contexts, the scales are very different: *Mahabharata* alone is eight times as long as the two Greek epics combined and 15 times long as the Bible.

All traditional forms of Indian theatre use complex dances, music, and specific eye move-ments and hand gestures (*mudra*) to tell stories. The costume and makeup are non-realistic, elaborate, and colorful. Traditional Indian theatre is often referred to as Indian "dance" in the West in modern times because of the Western conception of spoken drama as the de facto theatre form.

The Natyasastra

The *Natyasastra* [NAH-tyah-SHAS-tr] – an encyclopedic work on all aspects of drama (*natya*) – dates from between 200 BCE and 200 CE. The author or authors are unknown but it is sometimes attributed to Bharata Muni. According to the *Natyasastra*, there were origi-nally only four Vedas (books of hymns sacred to Hinduism), but the god Brahma created the *Natyasastra* as the fifth Veda, gave it to the human sage Bharata and assigned Bharata's 100 sons the task of putting it into practice. Drama, therefore, is created by gods as a pastime for humans, to give them visual and auditory pleasure.

The *Natyasastra* maintains that drama was to represent people from all walks of life and be accessible to all. Its aim was to teach by offering "good counsel" and "guidance to people" (Ghosh, intro. to Bharata 1967: 2–3, 14–5) using interesting stories of life in all its diversity,

from war to sexual sensuality. The audience would "taste" (*rasa* [RAH-s(eh)]) the states of being/doing (*bhava* [PHAH-vuh]) conveyed by the characters.

The *Natyasastra* is composed of 36 chapters. It traces the origins of drama and explains how to construct an appropriate theatre building. It explains how to worship the gods prior to performance, discusses types of plays, playwriting, costuming and makeup, character types and behavior, movement, gesture, and internal methods for acting the moods and states of being of characters. While Aristotle's *Poetics* centers on dramatic texts, *Natyasastra* puts em-phasis on performance.

Early Sanskrit dramas

The scripts of Sanskrit plays reflect the social hierarchy of the period. Thus, only high-status male characters speak Sanskrit, while all women, children, men of inferior status, and a stock comic character (the *vidusaka*) speak in various dialects evolved from Sanskrit. The most common types of plays are heroic dramas, such as *Sakuntala* (sometimes written *Shakuntala*) by Kalidasa (c. late fourth century–early fifth century CE), a seven-act play based on well-known epic sources; plays such as *The Little Clay Cart* by Sudraka (active sometime between the third and sixth century CE); along with one-act farces (for example, *The Hermit/Harlot*) and other minor forms. All Sanskrit dramas begin with an invocation, followed by a prologue, and conclude with a ben-edictory prayer. Since the early nineteenth century, translations and adaptations of Sanskrit plays (for theatre, ballet, and opera) have been performed in Europe and North America.

The original story of *Sakuntala* appears in the *Mahabharata*. A king who is out hunting meets Sakuntala by chance and falls in love. They marry, and he gives her a distinctive ring. He leaves for the palace, promising to return for her. However, a curse has been laid upon them and he forgets all about her. She decides to go to the palace herself, but during the journey, the ring slips off her finger and falls into a river. Because of the curse, the king does not recognize her without the ring. Many years later, a fish with the ring inside its belly is caught. When the king sees the ring, the evil spell is broken, and the lovers are reunited.

In *The Little Clay Cart*, a poor but generous man, although a happily married father falls in love with a courtesan. At one point, she piles rich jewels on his son's humble toy cart made of clay. Through a series of complications and misunderstandings, her lover is accused of her murder. Just as he is about to be executed, it is revealed that she is not dead. The actual murderer of the real dead woman is arrested, the poor man and his lover are reunited, and the man's first wife and son happily welcome her into the family.

The one-act farce *The Hermit/Harlot* contains much witty dialogue and slapstick comedy. It was written by King Mahendravarman in the seventh century (Figures 2.5 and 2.6). A learned and austere yogi (the hermit) attempts to teach his comically wayward

Figures 2.5 and 2.6
The *Bhagavan* or Hermit (Figure 2.5), and his wayward student, Shandilya (Figure 2.6), played, respectively, by Raman Cakyar and Kalamandalam Shivan, in a *kutiyattam* production of *The Hermit/Harlot* in Thiruvananthapuram, Kerala, in 1977. From a reconstructed staging based on traditional acting and staging manuals, under the supervision of Ram Cakyar of the Kerala Kalamdalam. Shandilya's costume is the traditional one worn in *kutiyattam* by the stock comic character, the *vidusaka*, who plays Shandilya here.
Source: © Phillip B. Zarrilli.

disciple correct yogic practice, but the disciple can never learn correctly. In order to make his points, the yogi substitutes his own soul for that of a recently deceased prostitute (the harlot) with whom his disciple has fallen in love. Unbeknownst to the yogi, the harlot's soul had been mistakenly taken by the bumbling servant of the God of Death. The plot turns on farcical mistaken identities, ending with the souls being returned to their proper bodies.

More than 500 Sanskrit dramas exist today, composed in alternating simple prose and ornate verse, and chanted and/or sung to musical accompaniment, though some small prose sections may be spoken. The verse passages allow reflection, commentary, and a deepening of the state of mind of the main character(s) rather than forwarding the narrative.

Highly professional companies were composed of families that included male and female performers specializing in specific role types, led by a male manager/actor (*sutradhara*). According to *Natyasastra*, actors followed a rigorous training regime that included a special diet, full body massages, yoga, and extensive training in "dance postures, physical exercise . . . [and] rhythm" (Kale 1974: 57–8). Their regimen included training in body movement, voice, emotional expression, costumes, makeup, and the language of hand gestures. Actors learned physical vocabularies for representing both the ordinary things in nature, such as a deer or a flower, and abstract concepts. Actors moved from one part of the stage to another to indicate a shift in locale. This convention also allowed the action to shift back and forth between two groups of actors on stage. Scenery was minimal, but makeup and costume were specific and probably very elaborate.

Performances took place either in specially constructed theatres near temples as part of religious festivals (see Figure 2.7), or in small, intimate halls at court for other special occasions. The oldest outdoor spaces devoted solely to theatre were built between 300 and 50 BCE. They somewhat resemble Greek theatre architecture, but their locations (in central and eastern India) are well beyond the areas invaded by Alexander the Great in 325 BCE. Moreover, according to the *Natyasastra*, theatres for Sanskrit drama were square, rectangular, or triangular. Because none has survived, we don't know how many viewers these theatres held, but we do know that audiences came from all castes.

A person's caste indicated their hereditary place in society, including profession and level of ritual purity. Some contemporary scholars believe that prior to British colonization, it was relatively easy to move between the castes and the British solidified the system for their own political ends (Dirks 2001). We do know that ancient Sanskrit theatre was attended by people of all castes, including experts in various fields (such as archers, grammarians, actors, courtiers, kings, musicians, and courtesans) who were seated at the front of the stage. They gave criticism and awarded prizes based on their area of expertise.

Kutiyattam: *A new way to stage Sanskrit drama*

After the tenth century CE, the Sanskrit language became increasingly restricted to members of the priestly castes. New forms of regional performance using local languages appeared. One of these, *kutiyattam* ("combined acting") [KOO-tee-ah-TAHM], emerged in Kerala (in south India). The *kutiyattam* version of the Sanskrit play *The Hermit/Harlot* (discussed above) is one of the oldest plays in the *kutiyattam* repertory. For more information on staging and performing this play, see "*The Hermit/Harlot* as an Example of Sanskrit Drama" on our website.

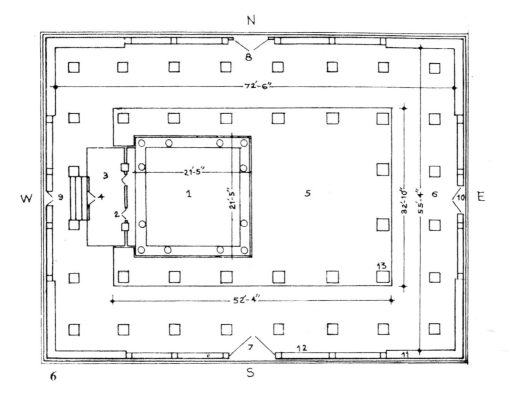

Figure 2.7

Floor plan of a playhouse for Sanskrit theatre in India, as described by Bharata in the *Natyasastra*, to be constructed on a consecrated piece of land on an east–west axis, and divided into equal halves for dressing room and acting areas. The audience is to be seated on the floor or a raked bank of seats in the east half.

Source: Line drawing. After Sketch No. 3, p. 47 in Tarla Mehta, *Sanskrit Play Production in Ancient India* (1995) New Delhi: Motilal Banarsidass.

It is said that King Kulasekhara Varman became the patron of *kutiyattam*. He was actively involved in the performances and introduced several controversial innovations to the staging of Sanskrit dramas:

(1) the use of the local language, Malayalam, by the main comic character (the *vidusaka*) to explain key passages;
(2) the introduction of each character with a brief narration of their past;
(3) permission for the performance to deviate from the script in order to elaborate the meaning and/or a character's state of mind/being; and
(4) the development of manuals for staging and acting in this emergent style.

Although it was written in the local dialect, *kutiyattam* was originally exclusively performed within a small number of high-caste temples in Kerala; the performance was a "visual sacrifice" to the deities of these temples (see Figure 2.8). Other changes included performing only sections of the full play. These sections have become dramas in and of themselves, with

Figure 2.8
A temple theatre, known as a *kuttampalam*, built for *kutiyattam* in the Lord
Vadakkunnathan (Siva) temple in Trissur, central Kerala. The temple compound containing
this one is set apart from the outside world by high walls and massive gates. The main
shrine housing Vadakkunnathan is to the right.
Source: © Phillip B. Zarrilli.

lengthy preliminaries and elaborations of the story featuring one of the main characters on
each night. Performing a single scene in the *kutiyattam* style can take from 5 to 41 nights.
During the final one to three nights, all the actors come on stage to perform the act or scene.
The term "combined acting" (*kutiyattam*) derives from this group appearance.

Not everyone approved of these innovations. Sometime in the fifteenth century, a highly
educated local connoisseur/scholar in his "Goad on the Actors" attacked the "unfounded
foul practices" of a specialized community of male and female actors. He wrote:

> Our only point is this – the sacred drama [*natya*], by the force of ill-fate, now stands
> defiled. The ambrosial moon and the sacred drama – both are sweet and great. A black
> spot mars the beauty of the former; unrestrained movements that of the latter. "What
> should we do then [to correct these defilements]?" The performance should strictly
> adhere to the precepts of Bharata [author of the *Natyasastra*]. Keep out the interruption
> of the story. Remove things unconnected. Stop your elaboration. . . . Reject the regional
> tongue. Discard the reluctance to present the characters.
>
> . . . Always keep the self of the assumed character. This is the essence of acting. One
> follows the principles of drama if things are presented in this way.
>
> (Paulose 1993: 158–9)

Despite such attacks, *kutiyattam* survived, and continues to be performed today.

Rasa-bhava *aesthetic theory and the actor/audience relationship*

The *Natyasastra* states, "nothing has meaning in drama except through *rasa*" (Bharata 1967: 105). *Rasa* means "taste." The analogy to tasting or savoring a meal explains how a theatrical performance is experienced by the audience. "The 'taste' of the various ingredient of a meal is both their common-ground and organizes them as its end" (Gerow 1981: 230). The "various ingredients" include each character's state of being/doing (*bhava*), which is specific to the ever-shifting context of the performance and the specific actor. As each *bhava* is embodied and elaborated in performance, the accompanying *rasas* are "tasted" by the audience.

The *Natyasastra* identified eight permanent states of being/doing, each with its accompanying *rasa* (see diagram). These basic states are enhanced by many other transitory and involuntary states.

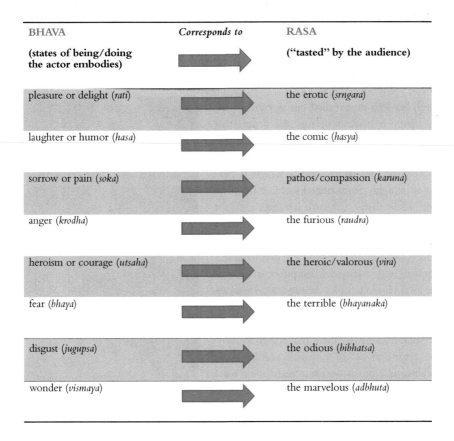

BHAVA	Corresponds to	RASA
(states of being/doing the actor embodies)	→	**("tasted" by the audience)**
pleasure or delight (*rati*)	→	the erotic (*srngara*)
laughter or humor (*hasa*)	→	the comic (*hasya*)
sorrow or pain (*soka*)	→	pathos/compassion (*karuna*)
anger (*krodha*)	→	the furious (*raudra*)
heroism or courage (*utsaha*)	→	the heroic/valorous (*vira*)
fear (*bhaya*)	→	the terrible (*bhayanaka*)
disgust (*jugupsa*)	→	the odious (*bibhatsa*)
wonder (*vismaya*)	→	the marvelous (*adbhuta*)

Rasa theory operates simultaneously on two levels:

(1) the audience's experience of the various states or moods arising from the actor's embodiment of the character; and

(2) the process of aesthetic perception of the whole. Playwrights and composers structure their work around those modes most useful for elaboration, and the actors bring these modes to life.

Although the emotions we experience in everyday situations form the basis, they differ from the ultimate aesthetic experience of *rasa*. To understand this dimension of *rasa* theory, we must go beyond Bharata's *Natyasastra*, which focuses pragmatically on the means for evoking *rasa*.

The most influential later theorist is the Kashmiri philosopher Abhinavagupta (tenth to eleventh century). For him, the ideal spectator is one whose heart/mind is "attuned" to appreciate the performance. He wrote that *rasa* is "[b]orn in the heart of the poet, it flowers as it were in the actor and bears fruit in the spectator." Moreover,

> [I]f the artist or poet has the inner force of the creative intuition, the spectator is the man of cultivated emotion, in whom lies dormant the different states of being, and when he sees them manifested, revealed on the stage through movement, sound and decor, he is lifted to that ultimate state of bliss, known as *ananda*.
>
> (Vatsyayan 1968: 155)

(An unbridged case study of *kutiyattam* and rasa-bhava theory is available on the website.)

The birth of kathakali

Although Sanskrit drama died out in most of India, its legacy is evident in regional genres that appeared between the fifteenth and seventeenth centuries. One of these is Kerala's **kathakali** [kah-TAHK-ah-lee] dance-drama, which is performed in a highly Sanskritized form of the local language, Malayalam – the same language used for *kutiyattam*. *Kathakali* developed from several earlier genres in the mid-1700s under the patronage of local rulers and wealthy landholders; performances were held in temporarily defined public spaces just outside local Hindu temples during annual festivals, making them accessible to a broad-based, popular audience. Over the years, *kathakali* was further refined until it became the form that is seen today.

The actor-dancers of *kathakali*, accompanied by vocalists and percussionists, create their roles using choreography, a complete gesture language to visually "speak" their character's lines, and expressive use of the face and eyes to communicate the characters' internal states (*bhava*). Performances begin at dusk and last all night. Costuming and makeup begin the process of transforming the actors into idealized, archetypal character types, each of which is individualized by the dramatic context and the actors' choices. An example of green (*pacca*) makeup, used for divine characters or epic heroes, appears in Figure 2.9.

Figure 2.9

The Progeny of Krishna, Scene 2. With the body of his eighth son lying before him, the Brahmin (M. P. Sankaran Namboodiri) pours out his tale of woe at court. Arjuna in green (*pacca*) makeup observes in the background.

Source: © Phillip B. Zarrilli.

While not an ancient genre, *kathakali* demonstrates many characteristics typical of Sanskrit performance. Since the 1960s, *kathakali* has participated in many international cultural exchanges. Controversial experiments have included a play about Adolf Hitler at the end of the Second World War and leftist *kathakali* dramas such as *People's Victory* (1987). French dancer Annette Leday and Australian playwright David McRuvie adapted *King Lear* into *kathakali*. This *kathakali King Lear* was performed throughout Europe and at international theatre festivals such as Edinburgh, Scotland, in 1989 and at Shakespeare's Globe (London) in 1999; it eventually went to India in 2018.

For further information on *kathakali*, see the case study "*Kathakali* Dance-Drama: Divine 'Play' and Human Suffering on Stage" on our website.

Early Chinese performances: From non-scripted to scripted performances

Nuo (see Chapter 1) is the earliest quasi-theatrical ritualistic rite and performance known in China. The inscriptions on the fragments of bones or turtle shells discovered in the nineteenth century uncovered a comprehensive ancient Chinese writing system (oracle bone script), which contains thousands of characters that bear resemblance to today's writing system. Before the rise of scripted dramatic performances with singing and movement (what the West would call "Chinese opera") around the twelfth century, there were many types of non-scripted theatrical performances. The term *you*, a general term for actor and performer, is documented as early as 800 BCE. Early *you* seems to have been a professional position sponsored by the court or elites; many records show that *you*, who often took on the task of remonstrance through comic storytelling, satire, impersonation, and sometimes with music and dance, seemed to enjoy the privilege of "free speech" and were able to intervene or alter a bad situation or even reverse an unwise political policy of the ruling class. While their witty speeches and acts are recorded, early *you* performances appear to have been impromptu.

Various states existed without a strong central government prior to the Qin (Chin) dynasty (221–206 BC) and the First Emperor (259–210 BCE) united all states to establish the first ethnic Han based Chinese empire. "China" thus became the name known to the West. Throughout history, the agricultural Han-based China strengthened itself from the cultures and materials from the neighboring non-Han nations, through trade, territorial expansion, and peace-alliance marriage, a "custom of marrying a Chinese woman from the royal family to the chieftain of another ethnic group" for the sake of peace (Lei 2019: 40). In terms of performing arts, India and Central Asia had significant influence over China.

Historical records show that dance, music, circus, fighting, magic, and puppetry were all common entertainments and some of them had strong dramatic quality. "Hundred games," a general term that covers miscellaneous art forms, appeared in the Han dynasty (202 BCE–220 CE). The Tang dynasty (618–907), often considered one of the highest points of Chinese civilization, was an empire with military strength, wealth, and vibrant arts, culture, and literature as well as a cosmopolitan view. Diverse imported arts, cultures, and religion – usually through the Silk Road – were celebrated and performing arts boomed. "Big Mask" (*damian*) is a form of dramatic masked dance which started in the sixth century. A representative piece "Lord Lanling" portrays the combat of Lord Lanling (541–573), who was a brave warrior but unfortunately had delicate facial features. In order to frighten the enemy, he wore fierce-looking wooden masks and often had great victories. The tradition gradually went out of fashion after the Tang dynasty and eventually disappeared in China; however, it went eastward to Japan and became part of the Japanese court dance tradition, *bugaku*, which is still alive today.

One of the ancient performance genres, "horn-butting play" evolved from the concept of animal fighting, to one-on-one types of human fighting such as wrestling, to dramatic skits, such as "Mr. Huang of the Eastern Sea," which dramatizes the fighting between Mr. Huang and an impersonated tiger (recorded by Ge Hong, 283–343 CE). Some believe that **canjun** (TSAN-jun) play (adjutant play), a comic genre popular in the Tang dynasty, evolved from this type of two-person "butting" concept along with the earlier *you* performance. *Canjun* is a comic sketch usually involving two male actors, who use witty language in a question-response form. The content is often about contemporary events and social commentaries. The two actors have distinctive role types and one actor always hits the other, adding a little slapstick humor. Music and female actors might be involved as well. Some believe that *canjun* is the predecessor of crosstalk (**xiangsheng**), a traditional form of two-person stand-up comedy that is still alive today (see Chapter 13).

The Tang dynasty also boasted the first royal academy of performing arts in China. Emperor Xuanzong (685–762), commonly known as Emperor Minghuang, founded the Pear Garden (**liyuan**) to systematically train male and female actors, dancers, and singers to entertain elite audiences at court. Even today, "Pear Garden" is a term to refer to the profession of traditional theatre and music and "children of the Pear Garden" to actors and actresses. Many traditional troupes today regard Emperor Minghuang as the founding father of theatre or worship him as a theatre god.

Tang dynasty is also famous for its poetry, with eminent poets such as Li Bai (701–762), Du Fu (712–770), and Bai Juyi (772–846), whose poetry is still memorized and recited by Chinese today. Tang poetry was also very influential in Korea and Japan; for instance, Bai Juyi's most famous poem "The Song of Eternal Sorrow" became the source of a famous *nō* play, *Yō Kihi* (*Imperial Consort Yang*, fifteenth century) by Konparu Zenchiku (1405–1468?).

Confucianism and the imperial examination

Confucius (551–479 BCE) is one of the most influential Chinese philosophers. He is also called "the supreme teacher" and *The Analects* (*Lunyu*), a compilation of his sayings and teachings – very often as dialogues with his students – became one of the most important classics still taught at school today. The sayings of Confucius and Mencius (372–289 BCE), a later thinker who held similar philosophy, were studied and debated by generations of scholars and "Confucianism" was gradually established. Confucianism is not a religion, but a practical philosophy and ethical system concerning human relations, such as among family members or between ruler and subjects. The central notion is *ren,* which has different definitions based on the contexts but generally aligns with the idea of humanity, humanness, or benevolence. Other important thoughts include filial piety, righteousness, royalty, propriety, and virtue. Confucian morals are common themes for drama or literature. Since Confucianism is based on human relations, sometimes it could be used as an oppressive doctrine regulating human behaviors in the name of virtue by the leaders in the domestic realm, in society, and even in government. Confucianism was not only a dominant belief system in premodern China; it was also prevalent in premodern Korea and Japan and influential in some Southeast Asian countries. It still plays a role in today's societies and politics.

The Imperial Examination, a nation-wide examination system to select scholars to serve at local or central governments, started in the late sixth century CE and lasted till 1905, with only brief interruptions. This difficult written exam requires comprehensive understanding

THINKING THROUGH THEATRE HISTORIES: SYMBOLIC CAPITAL

Pierre Bourdieu (1930–2002) coined the term "symbolic capital." Symbolic value is non-material resource such as knowledge, prestige, and honor that can be recognized within a social context and enhance a person's political and cultural status. For instance, a war hero might use his symbolic capital to run for political office. A talented poet or an artist whose work aligns with the ideology of the patron might win patronage and even a political career. In other words, symbolic capital can be legitimized and lead to actual financial capital within a specific social context. Throughout history, we can see how literature, art, and drama are used as symbolic capital by writers and artists.

Chinese literati were expected to work as government officials in premodern times. Literary knowledge and writing, therefore, were the symbolic capital that could lead to the financial capital in a direct way. It is not surprising that one of the most popular dramatic plots is about a poor but talented scholar who becomes a high-ranking official through the exam and wins the heart of a beauty. Sometimes, a poet's repudiation of the exam system (material value) and living as a hermit become a performative act of integrity, which, in turn, becomes another form of symbolic capital.

and memorization of Chinese classics, history, politics, and literature and excellent essay writing skills and calligraphy. Studying literature, therefore, could be a path to fame and fortune for *any* man, although the process was long and difficult and usually only elite families could afford schooling their children. The Imperial Examination ensured the longevity of Confucianism and created Confucian scholars for many generations. In the Yuan dynasty, the interruption of the practice negatively affected scholars' livelihood but shifted their energy to playwriting (see Chapter 4).

Transformation text

This chapter introduces a few performance genres that flourished in the Tang dynasty – masked dance, music and dance training, and speech-based comedy – all well-established but very distinctive genres, as well as literature with high symbolic value. For centuries, scholars did not understand what inspired the integration of the early different genres into the classical theatre form that we know today, whose earliest appearance could only be traced back to around the twelfth century. What was the catalyst? Were there any transitional forms? The answer was hidden in the caves in Dunhuang, a major trading city along the Silk Road in western China. The caves, which were sealed around the tenth century and reopened in the late nineteenth century, are full of handwritten scrolls of Buddhist texts, paintings and artifacts, sculptures and murals, and many scrolls of **transformation text** (*bianwen*). Transformation text is a storytelling form from India which was used to popularize Buddhism but also for secular entertainment. The original enigmatic Buddhist writing was "transformed" into an appealing storytelling and singing form with easier language, hence the name "transformation text." The text alternates between vernacular prose and rhymed verse and between narration and impersonation, with music, recitation, singing and visual aids. The literary pattern that mixes singing/speaking/recitation in prose and rhymed verse is similar to the classical theatre we know today. The artistic forms from India clearly inspired the creation of theatrical forms that integrate various artistic genres. Musical instruments and dance from Central Asia also played a significant role in shaping classical Chinese theatre. While the Dunhuang locals knew about the caves in the late nineteenth century, it was the visit of the British archeologist Aurel Stein and the French linguist and sinologist Paul Eugène Pelliot that got the attention of the scholars from China and the West. Unfortunately, a large quantity of the scrolls, along with other artifacts, were shipped to London, Paris, and St. Petersburg beginning in 1900s. The discovery of a lost Chinese tradition was lost again to Western expeditions, as the majority of the original scrolls are in Europe.

Buddhism was seen in China as early as in the late first century BCE but it became much more popular in the Tang dynasty. It is a major religion in China and Eastern and Southeastern Asian countries. Throughout history, the native Chinese religion Taoism (Daoism) and Buddhism co-existed and some rites and rituals are mixed in today's practice. Some Buddhist stories have been incorporated into part of the Chinese festivals, such as Mulian (see Chapter 3), some into dramatic repertoire (not as prevalent as Taoist stories), but the most influential element connecting Buddhism and drama is the transformation text.

Early Korean and Japanese performances

China has considerable cultural influence over Korea and Japan because of their geographical locations. In Korea, various forms of masked dance made up the early repertoire of Korean performing arts: some were native folk dance or shamanistic rituals; some were imported from China. One of the ancient forms of masked dance-drama, *talchum*, a UNESCO recognized oral and intangible heritage of humanity, is performed as a ritual and theatrical performance, taught at schools, and adapted into other modern performances such as K-pop (see Figure 2.10). Confucianism and Buddhism from China also had great impact on Korean culture. Prior to the development of Hangul, the Korean alphabet system, in the fifteenth century, Koreans used Chinese characters (*hanjia*) to write, even though Korean is a language very different from Chinese. Korean literati also had good knowledge of Chinese literature. After Japan invaded Korea in 370 CE, Korean scholars fluent in Chinese writing and literature were brought to Japan to educate the royalty. Like the Koreans, the Japanese also used Chinese characters (*kanji*) to write before they developed their own phonetic symbols (*kana*). Eventually, a complex system of writing developed, combining Chinese characters and two types of Japanese phonetic symbols.

Early Japanese performance and the development of *nō*

Japan's native religion was Shinto, in which it is assumed that everything – trees, birds, seas, animals, mountains, wind, and thunder – has its own soul or spirit, called *kami*. *Kami* are the natural energies and agents understood to animate matter and influence human behavior, and are sometimes identified as gods or goddesses. Chinese Buddhism became the official religion of Japan during the mid-sixth century, but it did not displace Shinto; rather, Buddhas and *kami* were and are often worshipped side by side, and Confucianism and Taoism incorporated into Japanese life. Modeling on the Tang system, the Taika Reform that started in 645 was to establish new systems for land, government, societal structure; Japan even established an exam system and a Confucian-based central administration.

Figure 2.10
Talchum, a traditional masked dance_drama performance in Andong City, South Korea.
Source: Joonsoo Kim/Alamy Stock Photo.

We see the combined influence of Shintoism, Buddhism, Taoism, and Confucianism in many aspects of Japanese theatre.

In Japan, many ancient theatrical and proto-theatrical genres are still performed. Every December in the city of Nara a festival that lasts for several days is devoted to presenting these early types of performance, as well as related martial arts such as horseback archery and sumo wrestling. The oldest performance genres are Shinto-inspired, shamanistic ceremonies and dances intended to harness *kami*. Various proto-theatrical court performances, including masked dance-dramas such as *bugaku* and *gigaku* that were originally introduced from China in the sixth century, are also performed at this festival and in special concerts. Masks dating from the Nara period (710–84) that depict warriors, gods, and semi-mythical beasts are preserved in temple collections.

Probably the greatest flowering of Japanese art and literature occurred during the Heian period (794–1185), after which the emperors, while still rulers in name, were gradually replaced by powerful warriors (samurai), and eventually by a single military leader called the shogun. Historical tales about the warring clans during the Heian period (such as *The Tale of the Heike*) were often chanted by blind musicians traveling the land. Such narrated stories joined literary

THINKING THROUGH THEATRE HISTORIES: ROOTS, ROUTES, ROADBLOCKS, DETOURS, AND U-TURNS

Culture travels; when one culture travels to another location by land, it affects both the local culture of the destination and the cultures along the way. James Clifford uses the concepts of "roots" and "routes" to help us understand diasporic cultures and communities and questions when the new culture can become "indigenous," that is, establish new roots (Clifford 2005: 524–58). In this chapter, we can see that Roman societies and theatre were significantly influenced by Greek cultures, even though the Greek gods had new names and plays were written in Latin. However, the local Roman taste for *ludi* also affected theatre.

Buddhism traveled the longest routes in Asia: via the Silk Road, Mahayana Buddhism went to China, co-existed with the native religion Taoism and other indigenous shamanistic beliefs, became "Chinese" Buddhism, which, in turn, had great impact on Korea and Japan, as we can see the prevalence of Buddhism in many *nō* plays. *Vajrayāna* Buddhism went to the Himalayan region, Tibet and Mongolia. Theravada Buddhism was developed in Sri Lanka and traveled to Southeast Asia and became the important religion in today's Thailand, Cambodia, and Myanmar (Burma). Hinduism, Buddhism, and Muslim also traveled and took roots in many regions, such as in Indonesia, where indigenous mythology mixed with newly rooted belief systems nurtured fascinating artistic forms.

While Buddhist stories did not become a significant part of Chinese theatre, the Buddhist storytelling form "transformation text" inspired and "transformed" Chinese theatre. Unfortunately, because of the rerouting and relocation of the Dunhuang treasure, the study of transformation text in the early twentieth century had to start with the diasporic texts in their new European homes.

Sanskrit theatre died but its elements can be found in *Kutiyattam* and *kathakali*. "Big mask" died in China but took roots in the Japanese court dance tradition. In the 1950s, the ancient dance-drama "Lord Lanling" was relearned and reintroduced by Chinese artists as a lost "Chinese" tradition, reversing the route of cultural transmission in the Tang dynasty when the Japanese deliberately imported Chinese culture (Lei 2015: 672). No culture is pure; however, there is always the desire to claim a pure national or cultural origin story and discount possible intercultural ("contaminated") influences. "Big Mask" in China might have a Uygur origin, and national symbol *sumo* wrestling in Japan might have a connection with the horn-butting play in China (the term *xiangpu*, which is used as the *kanji* for *sumo* existed in early Chinese texts). Cultural travels are rarely one-way and they are not always voluntary; culture travels back and forth, disappears and resurfaces, and always changes when being in contact with other cultures.

fiction written by court ladies (such as *The Tale of Genji* by Murasaki Shikibu), folk tales, religious stories, and even contemporary events, as key sources for playwrights in subsequent eras.

Zeami and nō

After 1185, brash samurai warriors rather than elegant aristocrats ruled Japan. In order to demonstrate their legitimate right to rule, they moved the government from Kamakura back to the old imperial capital of Kyoto, where the emperor still lived, and began to adopt the tastes and practices of the aristocrats they replaced. The once-powerful aristocrats feared dispossession. One of these, the court poet Nijō Yoshimoto, tried to retain power by transforming the military court into a bastion of cultural refinement. In 1374, he encouraged the 16-year-old shogun Ashikaga Yoshimitsu (1358–1408; ruled 1367–1395) – famous for his wild excesses and vulgar taste, such as *dengaku* [dehn-gah-koo] ("field music") – to attend a performance of popular *sarugaku* [sah-roo-gah-koo] ("monkey music") by the troupe headed by Kan'ami (1333–1384) and featured Kan'ami's talented, 11-year-old son Zeami (1363–1443).

By Zeami's time, masked *dengaku* was performed by both males and females. It had become associated with political turmoil and recurring bouts of mass hysteria called "*dengaku* madness." People of all classes would commit acts of larceny or lewdness, dance semi-naked in the streets for weeks on end, and dress in clothing forbidden to their class or gender. *Dengaku* actors were accused of being animal spirits disguised as humans. An eyewitness to a 1349 *dengaku* performance described golden curtains, exotic animal skins, and actors dressed in embroidered, silver brocade. The huge audience caused the wooden stands to collapse. The eyewitness described the chaos, confusion, violence, and commotion "as if Hell's unending battles and the tortures of its demons were being carried out before one's eyes" (O'Neill 1958: 75–7).

With its origin in native Shinto fertility dances, *dengaku* was also tied to supernatural female powers and unbridled female sexuality. In contrast, *sarugaku*'s origin was connected to calm Buddhist burial rites. Nijō and others hoped the samurai could be weaned from the irrational "female" madness and the agony of the dispossessed, and made to embrace the rational "masculine" values, so that they would become less of a threat to the aristocrats. *Sarugaku* (and eventually *nō*) would suggest victory of "rational" Buddhism and stoic male warriors over unruly, emotional female forces.

Asian names

Chinese, Korean, and Japanese names (as well as names in some other languages) are written with the family name first. Although publications in Western languages often use Western name order regardless of the original language, we will use the original name order unless the person has chosen to use Western order – usually because they were born and raised in a Western country.

As in the West, it is most common in scholarly writing to refer to Asian people by their family name. However, some famous Japanese artists and historical individuals are routinely referred to by their given name only or even by a well-accepted nickname. For example, the *kabuki* actor Bandō Tamasaburō V is generally called Tamasaburō, because there are many actors in the Bandō family but only one Tamasaburō in any generation.

When Ashikaga Yoshimitsu saw Zeami perform, he was so overwhelmed by the young actor's beauty and skill that he invited the entire troupe of rough and tumble, wandering, outcast performers to live in his court. Since sexual relations between males were not uncommon, Zeami became the shogun's lover.

Seeing Zeami as the shogun's favorite, Nijō took Zeami under his wing and tutored him in the aristocratic arts and culture, hoping to cultivate refined tastes in Zeami, who might influence the shogun. Nijō understood the complexity among the shogun, samurai (who felt culturally inferior to the aristocrats), aristocrats (who felt threatened by the samurai), and actors (who needed to please all sides), so his project ultimately benefited everyone.

Under Nijō's guidance, Zeami gradually altered the popular street entertainment *sarugaku* into the stately, poetic, all-male, Buddhist-oriented genre later known as *nō* (also spelled *noh*). After his father's death, Zeami continued to refine artistic practice and wrote many *nō* plays; he also wrote a series of sophisticated treatises on acting and playwriting in *Kadensho* (*The Transmission of Flowers*). These were meant for his descendants, and only came to public attention in the early twentieth century. Today, Zeami is acknowledged as one of the world's most important dramatic theorists.

The aesthetics of nō

Some of Zeami's most important aesthetic concepts are *monomane* [moh-noh-mah-neh], *yūgen* [yoo-ghehn], and *hana*. *Monomane* is the imitation of character. By imitating "the three roles" (male, female, or old person), the actor reveals the fictional character's invisible body. For Zeami, a mask allows the actor to become another character; his body becomes a vessel inhabited by another's "essence," which resides in the mask. According to Steven T. Brown, "Underneath the actor's costume and mask is the body of the actor transformed into the virtual body of the other" (2001: 26). *Yūgen* is a deep, quiet, mysterious beauty tinged with sadness. Zeami expands its meaning to refer to both text and performance, emphasizing the fleeting, melancholy nature of human existence. The greatest *yūgen* appears in plays about aged, dispossessed, or formerly beautiful women who are reduced to poverty, madness, or regret. *Hana* (flower) is the charm or beauty of actors: the *hana* of a youth actor is temporary; acquiring genuine *hana* as the actor matures is the lifelong cultivation. Like blossoms, the genuine *hana* will always appear fresh to the audience.

Performing and staging nō

Nō was originally performed in circular spaces similar to those used in *sumo* wrestling. As the *nō* stage evolved, it began to be modeled on the architecture of Shinto shrines (see Figure 2.11). In contrast, much of the philosophy in the plays is Buddhist.

The stage is a raised wooden platform covered by a roof held up by four pillars, even when indoors (see Figures 2.11 and 2.12; see also Figure 2.15). The main acting area is about 15 feet on each side. Beneath the floorboards, ceramic jars enhance the sound of the actors' stamping feet. The only décor is a painted pine tree on the back wall and a bamboo clump painted on the side. There are no special settings or lighting, and only minimal stage properties. A bridgeway (*hashigakari* [hah-shee-gah-kah-ree]) connects the stage with the curtained "mirror room" where the actors prepare; the *hashigakari* is seen as a passage from this world (the realm of the audience) to the world of spirits (embodied by the actor who crosses this bridge). The audience, usually about 400 people, sits on two sides of the stage. Steps lead from

Figure 2.11

A Japanese *nō* stage. It achieved the shape shown here by the sixteenth century. At first a separate structure, located in a courtyard, as seen here at the Buddhist temple of Nishi Honganji in Kyoto, it was housed within a larger building by the late nineteenth century. The stage proper remained covered by its own roof and linked to the green room by a raised passageway (*hashigakari*).

Source: Figure 1.9, p. 14 in *Dance in the Nō Theatre: Volume One. Dance Analysis* by Monica Bethe and Karen Brazell. Cornell University: China-Japan Program. Ithaca, 1982. The Cornell East Asia Papers series. Published with permission. © Monica Bethe and Karen Brazell.

the stage into the auditorium, a vestige of the Tokugawa era (also called the Edo era, 1603–1868) when actors would descend them to receive valuable gifts from the shogun and his entourage. The steps are not used today.

Since Zeami's time, almost all professional *nō* actors have been male, training from childhood with older relatives. The main character, called the *shite* [shih-teh] (literally "the doer"), and the secondary character, the *waki* [wah-kee] (meaning "the listener" or "sideman"), may have companions called *tsure* [tsoo-reh]. In reading *nō* plays, you will notice that some translators use the characters' names to indicate who is speaking, but others use only the traditional titles of *shite*, *waki*, or *tsure*. This is similar to the tradition of Chinese plays.

Three musicians (flute and two drums) and 8–15 chorus members enter in full view of the audience. The chorus kneels on the stage at the audience's right (opposite the *hashigakari*). Unlike the Greek chorus, they do not dance and have no specific identity. The musicians sit upstage, in front of the painted pine tree. They vocalize rhythmical sounds (*kakegoe*) as part of the musical score. Stage assistants (*kōken* [koh-kehn]) handle props, straighten costumes, or prompt actors. They are unobtrusive but clearly visible to the audience.

In most plays, after the chorus and musicians are in place, the *waki* enters on the *hashigakari* and establishes the situation; then the *shite* enters. The *shite* dances while retelling and reliving past woes; the *waki* is often a traveling Buddhist priest who is asked to pray for the release of the *shite*'s suffering soul. While the *shite* dances, the chorus chants his words.

When masks are used, they are usually worn only by the *shite* but sometimes also by the *shite*'s companion. Smaller than the adult male face, they allow the audience to see simultaneously the actor and the character. *Nō* masks, carved of light wood and carefully painted, are valued works of art handed down through the generations (see Figures 2.13 and 2.14). Costumes are elegant, costly, and conventional rather than realistic – even beggars are dressed in silks. The scripts are in an archaic language, using a "brocade style" that weaves together well-known stories, poetry, and Buddhist references.

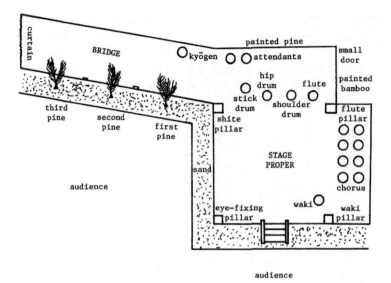

Figure 2.12

Nō stage plan, indicating locations of musicians, chorus, and attendants. The painted pine and bamboo on the upstage wall and the three pine trees arranged along the passageway reflect the outdoor origins of the theatre. Stage and passageway are separated from the audience by a strip of sand or gravel.

Source: Bethe and Brazell (as in Figure 2.11), p. 151. © Monica Bethe and Karen Brazell.

Zeami maintained that actors should gauge the style of performance to please the audience, changing it as needed. However, during the Tokugawa period, *nō* became a state ritual rather than entertainment, and no variations were permitted. Because *nō* was slowed down to satisfy ritual requirements, it is now performed about three times slower than it was during Zeami's day. In the past, a performance consisting of five *nō* plays with four short, comic plays (*kyōgen* [kyoh-ghen], literally "crazy words") in between them lasted all day. Today, most programs last two or three hours, and have one or two *nō* plays and one *kyōgen*.

Kyōgen actors belong to their own schools, and like *nō* actors, are traditionally male. In addition to performing entire comedies, *kyōgen* actors also perform minor roles during the interlude between two-part *nō* plays. *Kyōgen* plays emphasize comic inversions of social roles and stereotypical behavior. Unlike *nō*, *kyōgen* uses everyday speech, few masks, no chorus, and reserves song and dance for comic effect. Short, simple plots depict comic situations that are

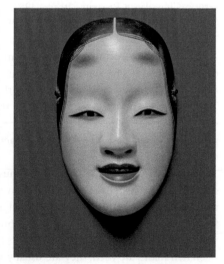

Figure 2.13

Each *shite* chooses the precise mask to wear from several possible ones. This *zo-onna* mask of a beautiful young woman is typical of what might be worn in the first part of *Dōjōji*.

Source: © kvap/iStock.

common to many cultures: powerless characters, such as women, thieves, servants, or sons-in-law, outwit masters, husbands, priests, or gods; the satires can sometimes be seen as social commentaries. They play practical jokes and are carried away by song, dance, and uncontrollable urges (for wine, food, prestige, mischief, or even cruelty). For example, in *Tied to a Pole* (*Bōshibari*), the master ties up his two servants to prevent them from drinking his wine. In a complex, physically comic sequence, they cleverly help each other get drunk anyway. Many of the Roman comedies discussed above feature a similar topsy-turvy world. As we will see in Chapter 3, such plots exist throughout the world, and are often called "carnivalesque."

Although the period of Ashikaga rule (1336–1573, also known as the Muromachi period) was created by samurai warriors, the *nō* plays they preferred seldom depicted military victory. Rather, in keeping with the tastes of the aristocrats they had displaced, the new rulers preferred plays dealing with tragic love affairs, unrequited passions, the agony of defeated warriors, the elegance of old age, or supernatural events. Most of the approximately 240 *nō* plays still performed were written during the Muromachi period.

Supernatural beings, ghosts, and traces of shamanic practices can be seen in many *nō* plays. An example is *Aoi no ue* (*Lady Aoi*), one of many *nō* plays derived from *The Tale of Genji*. It deals with the life-threatening attack on the pregnant Lady Aoi by another woman's jealous spirit that is so powerfully demonic as to require **exorcism**. The body of Aoi is represented by an empty kimono laid flat on the stage floor. Another famous *nō* play, *Dōjōji*, demonstrates similar concerns and is the focus of our case study.

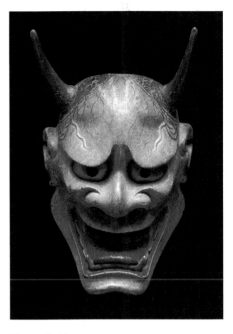

Figure 2.14

This *aka-hannya* ("red demon") mask is typical of what might be worn in the second half of *Dōjōji*.

Source: De Agostini/G. Sioen/Getty Images.

CASE STUDY: The *nō* play *Dōjōji*

Carol Fisher Sorgenfrei

Dōjōji is one of the most popular and theatrically flamboyant *nō* plays. The author is unknown; it was formerly attributed to Kanze Kojirō Nobumitsu (1435–1516). It has a prop used only in this play: a huge, silk-covered bell. Prior to the beginning of the play, stage assistants rig the bell to the roof of the stage. The action begins when the *waki*, the male Buddhist Abbot of Dōjōji (Dōjō Temple), calls the priests of the temple together. He announces that although there has been no bell in this temple for many years, today a new bell will be raised and dedicated. He leaves, forbidding the priests to admit women. The *shite* – an elegant woman – appears and convinces the foolish priests to let her enter in order to perform a celebratory dance at the dedication (Figure 2.15).

She dons a special hat normally worn only by male courtiers. Her dance gradually becomes chaotic and animalistic, entrancing the priests. The music, used only

Figure 2.15

In a performance of the *nō* play *Dōjōji* at the Kanze Theatre, Tokyo, 1962, the ghost of the maiden, dressed as a beautiful *shirabyōshi* dancer, approaches the bell at Dōjō Temple. Here, the actor moves from the *hashigakari* (bridgeway) toward the main stage, symbolizing her passage from the spirit world to this world.

Source: © Gary Jay Williams.

Figure 2.16

The ghost maiden dances around the bell which then descends over her and then is raised to reveal, as seen here, the differently costumed and masked actor (who has done a quick change inside the bell) as a horned, demon serpent which is the true form of the ghost maiden. The abbot and the priests, standing, are attempting an exorcism.

Source: © Gary Jay Williams.

in *Dōjōji*, is a secular version of the music of a Shinto demon-quelling ritual. Her feet move in triangular patterns, mimicking the fish-scale triangles on the actor's inner robe. Finally, the dancer knocks the hat from her head, stamps her feet, and looks at the bell as she stands directly beneath it. She swings her fan back and forth like the ringing hammer of a bell, as the chorus sings: "This loathsome bell, now I remember it!" (Brazell 1998: 199). She leaps up, and the giant bell falls crashing to the ground around her.

In the interlude, the priests discover that the bell is red hot. When the Abbot returns, he angrily explains why women were forbidden. Long ago, a girl's father told her that a priest who often visited would be her husband. One day, she asked the celibate priest when they would marry, and he fled in horror. She chased him by transforming herself into a serpent and swimming across a river. On the other shore, she followed him to the temple called Dōjōji, where he had hidden beneath an unraised bell. The serpent-woman entwined her body around the bell. The heat of her passion was so intense that the bell metal became fiery hot, burning alive the priest inside. The Abbot now explains that the dancer is this woman's furious ghost.

During this interlude, the *shite* remains inside the giant bell and changes mask and costume. When the bell rises for the second part of the play, we see a female snake-demon, the dancer's true form (see Figure 2.16). The Abbot and priests battle her, attempting an exorcism, but they cannot overpower her; they can only chase her off. As the play ends, the chorus chants:

> Again she springs to her feet,
> the breath she vomits at the bell
> has turned to raging flames.
> Her body burns in her own fire.
> She leaps into the river pool,
> Into the waters of the river Hidaka,
> And there she vanishes.
> The priests, their prayers granted,
> Return to the temple,
> Return to the temple.

(Brazell 1998: 206)

Zeami and the female origins of nō

Japanese performance is said to originate in the shocking dance of the goddess Uzume, a female Shinto deity. According to the myth, because the sun-goddess Amaterasu – the direct ancestor of the emperor and thus of the Japanese people – was angry with her trickster brother, she hid herself in a cave. Deprived of the sun's light and fertility, the world would have died. In desperation, Uzume leaped on to an overturned rain barrel, stamping her feet in dance and lifting her skirts to reveal her genitals. The other deities roared with laughter. The curious Amaterasu peeked out and light returned to the world. The laughter caused by Uzume's sexy dance had saved the world from eternal death. Zeami wrote that this myth proved *nō*'s divine origin and relationship to the royal household.

Amaterasu is identified with the life-giving sun, but her emotional, irrational response to the bad behavior of an unruly male dangerously disrupts the balance of nature. She cloaks her body in darkness. In contrast, Uzume intentionally displays her body in a kind of divine striptease and sexual spectacle that made the gods laugh. She is in control of her body and passions and of how she is viewed. These two female deities are reverse images that complement each other: light and dark, laughter and anger, life and death. Females have the power to give and to withdraw life.

However, patriarchal Buddhism challenged the female-oriented Shinto and powerful leaders allied themselves with these opposing religions, vying for political control. Many sects combined aspects of both religions. Eventually, Shinto rituals became associated with the female realm and with life-affirming acts (fertility, marriage, sex, and birth), while Buddhist rites were tied primarily to the male realm, death, and the afterlife. *Nō* theatre reflects this history. The texts are primarily Buddhist, emphasizing that actions in one lifetime determine how a soul is reincarnated in the next. They also emphasize salvation in the afterlife. In contrast, performance elements derive from aspects of Shinto (or Shinto-Buddhism). These female-oriented elements include demon-quelling dances, stamping feet, ritual purifications, possession by gods, the stage architecture, and most importantly, the presence of spirits and ghosts.

Nō also incorporated elements of earlier female dances. Shinto shrine maidens (*miko*) performed sacred *kagura* dances as well as ritual dances meant to pacify angry ghosts. Female prostitute-entertainers performed Buddhist funeral rituals for the imperial family and entertained aristocratic male clients on river boats. Their outcast status diminished as their religious importance grew. Zeami's family may have belonged to their clan (Kwon 1998).

Dances called *kusemai* and *shirabyōshi* were popular, secular entertainments mainly performed by women dressed in male clothing. Critics feared that their unconventional, disturbing musical rhythms and dance styles were contributing to "an age of turmoil" and were a sign of "a nation in ruins" (O'Neill 1958: 43–4). Like Uzume, these female ritualists and performers disrupted notions of social and religious stability.

Zeami praised and valued his female predecessors. He wrote that his father, Kan'ami, had trained with Otozuru, a female *kusemai* dancer. The *shite's* main dance is still termed *kusemai*, and many plays, including *Dōjōji*, feature characters who are female *shirabyōshi* or *kusemai* dancers.

When samurai warriors displaced the aristocrats, they needed to foster legal changes to centralize their military power and weaken the noble branch families. Among the new laws were those that shifted inheritance rights away from female aristocrats and toward first-born sons. Suddenly, a divorced or abandoned woman found herself dispossessed both financially and emotionally. Her fury at an unfaithful spouse would be intensified by the loss of property she would previously have retained. Many people believed that the angry spirits of such dispossessed females (along with those of the dispossessed male rivals of the ruling Ashikaga clan) were responsible for a century of natural disasters (earthquakes, plagues, typhoons, droughts, famines, fires, and floods) that devastated Kyoto.

Many nō plays, including *Dōjōji*, center on the agony, anger, or madness of dispossessed spirits (dead or alive), such as the loss and defeat of a warrior or uncontrollable madness of a woman. Buddhism is seen as a way to appease the often Shinto-identified female spirits and to bring peace and healing to the world.

Conclusion

In *Dōjōji*, the body of the male actor portraying a female dancer "enacts a complex double masquerade of both masculine and feminine" (Klein 1995: 118). The male nō actor's body stands in for the absent female body of the *shirabyōshi* dancer, which stands in for the absent male monk as well as the invisible demonic snake. By leaping into the bell, the *shirabyōshi* dancer imitates what happened to the male. However, instead of being burned to death, she is revealed in her true form. The climax of the play becomes a cosmic battle between demonic, female forces and holy, male forces, but it is not conclusive – the demon will continue to lurk in the river, able to resurface at any time. Female sexual power (or the potential power of the defeated and dispossessed aristocrats) can be contained but not destroyed.

The fear of women displayed in *Dōjōji* reflects the historical fact that "the position of women at the elite levels of Japanese society was taking a distinct downward turn" (Klein 1995: 117). The ambiguous ending suggests that chaos could erupt if the rulers failed to guard against all those (male as well as female) they had dispossessed.

Although originally only men wrote and performed *nō* and *kyogen*, beginning in the post-war era, women began to join the profession, bringing new life to the old traditions.

Key references

Brazell, K. (ed.) (1998) *Traditional Japanese Theater*, New York: Columbia University Press.

Brown, S.T. (2001) *Theatricalities of Power: The Cultural Politics of Nō*, Stanford, CA: Stanford University Press.

Klein, S.B. (1995) "Woman as Serpent: The Demonic Feminine in the Noh Play *Dōjōji*," in J.M. Law (ed.) *Religious Reflections on the Human Body*, Bloomington: Indiana University Press, 100–36.

Kwon, Y.H.K. (1998) "The Female Entertainment Tradition in Medieval Japan: The Case of *Asobi*," *Theatre Journal* 20: 205–16.

O'Neill, P.G. (1958) *Early Noh Drama*, London: Lund Humphries.

Sorgenfrei, C.F. (1998) "Zeami and the Aesthetics of Contemporary Japanese Performance," in B. Ortolani and S.L. Leiter (eds.) *Zeami and the Nō Theatre in the World*, New York: CASTA, 19–28.

Summary

In this chapter, we continued our discussion of the interactions between oral tradition, writing, and factors such as politics and social conditions in a few important performance traditions. We noted that not all cultures transform at the same speed or in the same way. We also discovered that not all cultures transmit in the same direction or influence each other at the same degree; we tried to trace the transmission of Buddhism as an example to show the intercultural complexity of artistic development. We referred to some of the most significant religions and belief systems in the world – Hinduism, Buddhism, Shintoism, Taoism, and Confucianism – and their impact on societies and performing arts. In theatre, the religious impact can be on plot, theme, dramaturgy, or performance form. The negotiation of various belief systems has interesting result in both form and content.

Although literacy was limited to elites in these societies, there were invaluable theoretical writings on theatre, such as *Natyasastra, Ars Poetica,* and *Kadensho*, which became the authority (or rules) imagined by scholars and artists of later generation to shape the development of some artistic traditions, despite the original performance traditions (such as Sanskrit theatre or Roman comedy) had long been lost. We also began to consider audience: is theatre inclusive or exclusive, that is, is theatre made for everyone or for a specific audience? The *Natyasastra* indicates that theatre is the gods' gift for all people, but most Sanskrit plays were written by elites and were often performed to exclusive audiences inside temples. In China, literary study seemed to be more widespread than in Europe during the first millennium CE because of the Imperial Examinations; however, scripted plays did not develop till around the twelfth century. Finally, we explained the fact that literacy came very late to Japan, and first only in the form of Chinese. *Nō* developed as an art that could please both the dispossessed aristocrats and the brash, relatively uncultured samurai. It also combined elements of the native belief system (Shinto) with imported ideologies (Buddhism, Taoism, Confucianism). In the next chapter, we will continue our discussion of how theatre works to please various types of audiences. As we will see, even in highly literate societies, orality does not vanish.

★

CHAPTER 3

Commemorative drama and Carnival

Tamara Underiner

Contributors: Daphne Lei, Tobin Nellhaus and Phillip B. Zarrilli

Virtually every society finds some way to keep its history alive by means of performance, dramatizing events recorded in its great epics, the stories of its predecessors, or more recent important events. Parades, pageants, and Founder's Days celebrations (replete with live re-enactments and tableaux) are still popular even among the most technologized of them. While these events may also be passed down orally and in written form, performance helps to ensure the continuity of social memory and plays an extremely important role in cultural preservation.

After writing becomes well established in a society, its relationship to oral culture can and often does change. In Chapter 2, we considered forms of performance that developed when writing had become socially prominent, even if still limited to scribes, priests, and the elite. In the period we cover here, however, writing was attaining an even more central role in society – usually for religious purposes – and all people were expected to know their content, whether or not they could read. These were now **manuscript cultures**, in which handwritten texts (generally on parchment or paper, often bound into a book rather than a scroll) were crucial for much of the society's functioning and culture. Nevertheless, there was considerable interaction between manuscript cultures' oral and literate realms, and performance was often the connective tissue between the two. This chapter focuses on two genres of performance – commemorative drama and Carnival – that have helped to connect people to their roots and impart cultural knowledge the world over.

Commemorative drama refers to a wide range of performance practices that share certain characteristics, all aimed at preserving and promoting some aspect of a society's heritage. While much commemorative drama is meant to promote deep reflection in a spirit of devotion or civic pride, another form of performance elicits a different kind of spirit: that of release from the constraints of civil and religious propriety, if only for a short time. Such performances can be broadly grouped under the category of the **"carnivalesque,"**

DOI: 10.4324/9781003185185-5

in which human nature is explored through the mingling of the sacred with the profane, often to hilarious and spectacular effect. (Recall our Chapter 1 discussion of Hopi katsina traditions in the U.S. southwest, which includes a variety of clowns whose antics are often earthy, crude, and sexual in nature – all in service of a larger socially normative aim and spiritual outlook.) Many of the commemorative performance traditions we discuss below incorporate and combine both devotional and carnivalesque aspects.

We begin with a discussion of **Carnival**, a public celebration with ancient roots. Here, we consider not only its history but also its spirit, asking what it is about "the carnivalesque" that seems to transcend time and place, and how its energies are constantly channeled anew into different forms. We then turn to a discussion of commemorative drama, which encompasses a variety of forms that can be formal and devotional, or can blend the serious with the carnivalesque. What they share is a commitment to preserving and performing the cultural and/or religious legacies of a society. Our discussion of commemorative drama centers on the dramas of Christianity, which gave birth to a plethora of performance forms in the West. But of course other religious and cultural traditions, before and after Christianity, also incorporate performance elements. Thus, we frame our discussion of Christian commemorative drama between two other traditions of such drama: the Jewish Purim play, which features both commemorative and carnivalesque aspects, and the Islamic *Ta'ziyeh,* a mourning ritual central to the Shi'ite faith. Our case studies consider how commemorative drama functions both to solidify and to challenge prevailing norms of belief and custom. One examines a dramatization of the historic conflict between Christianity and Islam, staged both as a straightforward commemoration and as a kind of allegory for more recent examples of cultural conflict. The other considers a commemorative drama based on a Hindu epic – the *Ramlila* of northern India.

Carnival and the carnivalesque

Carnival is a centuries-old tradition of lively, often rowdy public performance featuring deliberate misbehavior by masked characters in elaborate costumes. It may trace back to the Greek and Roman festivals of antiquity (e.g., the Dionysian celebrations in Greece, and the Bacchanalia and Saturnalia in Rome). In Europe and the Americas, it is associated with the Catholic season of Lent preceding Easter. But we can detect aspects of a carnivalesque spirit in other traditions, such as *kyōgen* (discussed in Chapter 2), and in the widespread celebrations associated with Chinese Lunar New Year, which include dragon dances (Figure 3.1) and the *Yuanxiao* Festival ([yu-AHN shao]) or Chinese Lantern Festival, celebrated on its fifteenth day. Celebrated throughout the Asian world, the Lantern Festival that closes the new year observation has roots extending back to the Han Dynasty (206 BCE to 220 CE) and was originally held in honor of the gods; today, it is a family-oriented festival that honors ancestors. Rooted in oral culture, the carnivalesque appears in all societies, including manuscript and print cultures (a matter taken up in more detail in the "Thinking through Theatre Histories" box).

Within Christianity, Easter marks the highest holy day, commemorating Jesus's resurrection from the dead. To properly prepare for this momentous day, early Christians were asked to observe an annual 40-day period of self-denial and deprivation, following an example from Jesus's own life. By the fourth century, in Old English this was called "Lent," from the word for the spring season. Before entering their season of self-denial, folks feasted heartily on meat and other good things, especially just before its official start on Ash Wednesday. The culmination of this pre-Lenten period – known as Shrovetide in English, *Mardi Gras*

Figure 3.1
Chinese dragon dancers perform in Beijing as part of the Chinese Lunar New Year celebrations of 2017.

Source: Kevin Frayer/Getty Images.

(Fat Tuesday) in French, as *Fastnacht* (Fasting Eve) in German and as Carnival in general – is still a time of highly theatrical celebration in Europe and throughout the Americas, and has itself been extended into its own season in some parts of the world. The word "Carnival" may derive from the Latin *carnem-levare* or *carne vale,* both of which refer to this "farewell to flesh or meat"; other explanations suggest a reference to the *carrus navales,* or floating cars, of ancient Roman festivals, that still feature in Carnival celebrations. The famous *Carnaval* of Rio de Janeiro, Brazil, is the largest in the world. In Brazil and the Caribbean, as in the Mardi Gras of New Orleans in the United States, Carnival has been transformed by the influence of African music, dancing, costuming, masking, and puppetry traditions that arrived in the Americas with the slave trade.

Carnival in Europe likely began in the urban centers and at court, in response to the increasingly stringent rules of Lent. It later spread to rural areas, and then spread again across the Atlantic with the arrival of the Catholic colonizers. In each of these regions, Carnival was flexible enough to incorporate the existing festival traditions of the local and, in the case of the Americas, enslaved populations. As a result, there were differences from place to place, and also within the various strata of society within a particular place. For example, among the European aristocracy and urban elite, Carnival included masked balls, comical theatrical performances, and public competitions. In the countryside events were organized by groups of friends, clubs, fraternities, and guilds, and often featured parades of peasants costumed as royalty. The well-known parades of today's Carnival celebrations have their roots in this period, which saw processions of costumed people on foot and on floats, performing masquerades in which they poked fun at certain segments of society.

Then as now, in both rural and urban settings, Carnival was a time when normal social strictures were suspended: aggressive and promiscuous acts were permitted, and reversals of social standing were enacted – with men and women crossdressing or masquerading as members of a different social or professional class. Carnivalesque humor reveled in life's fecundity, in sexuality and all the irrepressible life forces of the material body; its humor was full of images of copulating, defecating, dying, and birthing. Images of excessive eating and drinking were common (the clowns of early German farces, Hanswurst and Pickelhering, are named after folk foods). Images of the body, from nose to phallus, and lower bodily functions were writ large and grotesquely in Carnival folk humor; such representations, argued Mikhail Bakhtin, were not about the individual body/self but about the irrepressible and regenerative body of the people. (See Figure 3.2 and the "Thinking through Theatre Histories" box.)

Figure 3.2

This painting of *The Battle of Carnival and Lent* (1559) by Pieter Brueghel the Elder illustrates the worldly and "world-turned-upside-down" aspects of carnival, as revelers prepare to say their farewell to meat and other pleasures in the Lenten season of abstinence.

Source: Ryhor Bruyeu/Alamy Stock Photo.

These "rites of reversal" or "rites of misrule" were not confined to the Lenten season; the Church calendar also accommodated, if uneasily, other festivals in which social expectations were temporarily turned on their heads. For example, during Christmastime in many European countries, a "Feast of Fools" (sometimes called "Feast of Asses") was held in which the lower clergy mockingly impersonated their superiors (as well as women), played dice on the altar during the celebration of the Mass, and processed through town singing lewd songs. They may also have appointed a "Boy Bishop" from among the ranks of their choirboys, who performed a burlesque of the official Church service.

Church records show numerous attempts at banning these celebrations of misrule, and Carnival as well, both in Europe and in its American colonies – testaments to their enduring popularity. Scholars speculate that in the Americas, Carnival was an upper-class event until after independence from Spain and Portugal; this may explain why so many revelers in today's Brazilian *Carnaval*, for example, don the attire of eighteenth-century aristocracy.

Although the Church's concern about Carnival's excesses is well documented, many latter-day researchers suspect the Church needn't have worried. They argue that the chance to temporarily reverse the social order was in fact an important component for keeping it intact. Others want to see it for its imaginative and liberatory potential, as a rehearsal for a new world order rather than a safety valve that keeps the old one in its place, as discussed in the "Thinking through Theatre Histories" box.

THINKING THROUGH THEATRE HISTORIES: MIKHAIL BAKHTIN'S THEORY OF THE CARNIVALESQUE

One of the most important theorists of Carnival is the Russian literary critic Mikhail Bakhtin, who wrote between 1919 and the early 1970s, barely escaping the Soviet dictator Josef Stalin's infamous purges in the 1930s. His concept of Carnival folk humor was developed in his analysis of the evolution of the novel, but it is useful to theatre studies as well. Bakhtin sees Carnival as an elemental force, nurtured by a 1,000-year tradition of folk humor from satyr plays to medieval fools, liberating language and literature from the "official" ecclesiastical and feudal cultures and surging into the Renaissance. The culture of folk humor finds opportunities for expression in popular festivals all over the world.

Bakhtin based his theories on the Carnival traditions of Christian Europe. At the center of such celebrations was the false coronation and later deposing of a Carnival king (usually a slave or clown). His coronation is full of pomp and circumstance, his dethroning full of shame and disgrace. For Bakhtin, this embrace of contradictions is what characterizes a "carnivalesque" view of the world: one in which the sacred mingles with the profane, the new with the old, the high-born with the low-born, the wise with the foolish, and so forth. All of this is meant to reveal the hidden sides of human nature – and thereby to expose how social structures are relative, and social orders contingent rather than natural or God-given.

Bakhtin argued that the carnivalesque was central to medieval consciousness until the end of the sixteenth century, allowing Christians of the time to break free, for a time, from the many restraints upon their comportment that Church dogma demanded. As Carnival began to lose traction (at least in Europe) in the Enlightenment period, its dualistic impulses were channeled away from the public streets and into the realm of literature, formal theatre, and other forms of art and popular culture – extending to our own day, where it might be argued that some popular reality TV shows do the work of Carnival – conferring fame and glory on everyday people, if only for an episode, or season. Of course, the carnivalesque also wears its public face in the ongoing traditions of pre-Lenten Carnival and Mardi Gras parades, gay pride parades, public New Year's Eve celebrations, parades accompanying sports bowl games, and in Halloween parades and parties where disguise allows experimentation with alternate identities. Often, civic parades combine solemn patriotism with boisterous clowning and plenty of spectacle. Just as commemorative drama can include the carnivalesque, so can Carnival contain commemorative elements.

Commemorative performances

While commemorative drama may contain carnivalesque elements, it always shares certain elements that fulfill a more serious function: helping participants and observers learn and remember something important about their religious, civic or cultural heritage. Recall, for instance, *Rabinal Achi,* the Mayan drama introduced in Chapter 1. It is a performance of local history, but not in strictly chronological terms. Rather, it is more like a montage of many different historical events gathered into one central conflict from the distant past. Its yearly staging is meant to commemorate the origins and resilience of the town of Rabinal over the centuries, which is one reason why UNESCO (the United Nations' cultural agency) proclaimed it a masterpiece of the oral and intangible heritage of humanity. Both in its local meanings and in its more global UNESCO designation, *Rabinal Achi* highlights the notion of cultural heritage and continuity. As social anthropologist Paul Connerton argues in *How Societies Remember*, such performances have in common a key element: "they do not simply imply continuity with the past by virtue of their high degree of formality and fixity; rather, they have as one of their defining features the explicit claim to be commemorating such a continuity" (Connerton 1989: 48).

Rabinal Achi shares many features with commemorative drama in general:

- telling a story that has been carefully preserved both orally and in manuscript form;
- celebrating a moment in the past that is of great contemporary importance; and
- preserving that heritage in social memory through frequent staging, often through symbolic rather than realistic portrayal of people and events important to the community's sense of cultural continuity.

Commemorative performances often offer participants the chance to show how their present concerns relate to their past. In these kinds of performances, the carnivalesque can make a memorable appearance. An example is the centuries-old tradition of the Mexican *pastorela,* or Shepherd's Play. Annual *pastorelas* offer latter-day communities the opportunity

Figure 3.3
Latter-day performers of the Guatemalan *Rabinal Achi* wear masks suggesting the features of sixteenth-century Spaniards, even though the characters they portray are pre-Columbian Mayans. As such, these latter-day performances register both cultural continuity and change. Photo taken 23 January 2023.
Source: Esteban Biba/EPA–EFE/Shutterstock.

to inaugurate the Christmas season with a performance that both recalls the journey of the shepherds to the infant Jesus's birthplace, and comically treats and often satirizes local events of politics and popular culture of the previous year. In doing so these communities demonstrate that "continuity" can both accommodate and actually depend upon change. Seen this way, it is not surprising that the *Mayan* characters in contemporary productions of *Rabinal Achi* wear the masks of sixteenth-century *Spaniards* (see Figure 3.3). We consider another example of performance that foregrounds both continuity and change in our case study on the Moors and Christians.

Commemorative dramas are also a way of helping people remember to honor their ancestors. Although originally meant to honor the gods, the aforementioned *Yuanxiao* (Lantern Festival) soon became a performance of ancestral homage as well. But one of the most highly celebrated and theatricalized such traditions in today's Chinese-speaking world is **Zhongyuan** [zhong-yu-AHN], or "Ghost Festival," which combines Buddhist, Taoist, and Confucian beliefs with local exorcist customs. It takes place on the fifteenth of the seventh or "ghost" month of the lunar calendar every year. While the festivals vary region from region based on localized customs, all *Zhongyuan* share spectacular ritual performances and extravagant feasting as hallmarks.

Zhongyuan is often translated as the "Hungry Ghost" festival, and the hungry ghost has a rich oral, manuscript, and dramatic tradition in the Buddhist diaspora and in Taoism as well. Hungry ghosts are entities doomed to an eternal afterlife of insatiable appetite, due to their miserly or greedy habits in their earthly lives, and play a key role in the moral and ethical formation of followers. Dramas based on the "Mulian" character are exemplary of this tradition. "Mulian" is the Chinese translation of the Sanskrit name, Maudgalyayana, a disciple of Buddha. Mulian visited his mother in the underworld, only to find her wandering among hungry ghosts, due to all the bad things she did in her life. Saddened, he tried to bring her food, but it burst into flames as soon as she tried to eat it. Mulian was then instructed to prepare a sumptuous offering to monks, whose prayers eventually brought an end to his mother's suffering.

The Mulian sutra (text) was translated from Sanskrit into Chinese in the mid-third century CE and soon became very popular for its resonances with Chinese cultural beliefs in virtue and filial piety. Many spectacular religious rituals, which often involved dangerous acts with flames, evolved from the imagination of Mulian's encounter with ghosts. Eventually, by the early twelfth century the drama *Mulian Rescues His Mother* began to appear all over China. Mulian drama is full of astonishing and precarious stage action to depict the danger of the underworld. The food that Mulian provided for the monks became the excuse for generous feasting for everyone, especially the hungry, childless ghosts, who are customarily left out of ancestor worship. Like much commemorative drama in other cultures, *Zhongyuan* ghost festivals commemorate filial piety, celebrate good deeds and generosity, appease ghosts, and offer prayers for peace, while providing awe-inspiring theatricality and the occasion for magnificent feasting.

As these examples suggest, communal memory is often sustained through embodied performance in addition (or at times, contradiction) to what is preserved via the written word. We turn in the next sections to commemorative performance associated with the Abrahamic traditions of Judaism, Christianity, and Islam, which draw from sacred texts circulating in both written and oral forms.

Commemoration and the carnivalesque in the Jewish Purim *shpil*

One remarkable example of how commemorative drama can blend both the past and the present, and the serious with the carnivalesque, is the Jewish tradition of the **Purim *shpil(n)*** (play[s]). This annual festivity commemorates a great victory in a people's past with joy and laughter (and in some contexts, compels more serious contemplation) in the present day. Its source is the Book of Esther, from the Hebrew Bible, one of Judaism's central religious texts. Its story is of a Jewish victory over religious persecution, when the Jews were in exile in Persia in the fifth century BCE. The spirit of this victory – of a religious and ethnic minority over a hostile majority – is what is commemorated in Purim *shpiln*.

The Book of Esther is indeed rich in dramatic possibilities. It tells the tale of the beautiful young Esther who catches the eye of the Persian King Ahasuerus (in Greek, Xerxes), and foils his plans for the genocide of her people. The King's first wife, Vashti, was also beautiful – so beautiful he wanted to display her for all to see (in many accounts, naked) at a special banquet. When she refused, he decided to make an example of her disobedience and very publicly set out in search of a replacement. He chose the orphaned Esther, but to keep his favor she had to hide her Jewish identity. Later, unbeknownst to the King, her guardian Mordechai saved him from an assassination plot. But on an earlier occasion, Mordechai had refused to bow to the King's haughty prime minister, Haman, an act he never forgave. As a result, when Haman later learned that Mordechai himself was Jewish, he hatched a genocidal plot, with the King's approval, that on a certain day to come, everyone in the kingdom would have the right to murder and pillage any known Jews and their property. Eventually, two events transpired to mitigate the slaughter. First, the King discovered Mordechai had saved him from the earlier assassination plot. Second, to save her people, Esther revealed her true identity to her husband – and the threat to her life that Haman's antisemitic strategy represented. Outraged, the King ordered Haman to be hanged – on the very gallows Haman had intended for executing Mordechai. Since the decree against the Jews could not be rescinded, the King allowed the Jews to defend themselves. Granted this right, the Jews were able to kill thousands of their oppressors.

Readings of the Book of Esther commemorate the events of that day (usually corresponding to a date in March), with changing historical contexts sparking the need for re-evaluation and re-assessment of the text from generation to generation. As early as the 1400s, these readings were accompanied by what we might now call "audience participation," with congregants hissing and booing at every mention of Haman's name; performances of humorous monologues and skits loosely based on its events soon followed. Over time, the repertoire expanded to include carnivalesque elements parodying contemporary events in the local community, often relying on bawdy jokes and profanities. Troupes of Purim players would travel from home to home, collecting alms to support themselves and those less fortunate (Figure 3.4). Some towns supported only one troupe; larger towns, several. The actors, typically young unmarried men and boys, might perform year after year, often disguising

Figure 3.4

Orthodox Jews seen wearing costumes during Purim on the streets of Stamford Hill in north London.

Source: Dinendra Haria/SOPA Images/LightRocket via Getty Images.

themselves in order to "protect their freedom to be licentious" (Kirshenblatt-Gimblett 1980: 6). In the eighteenth century, biblical content returned to the Purim *shpil*, and in some parts of Eastern Europe the form expanded to full-length dramas with musical accompaniments and large casts (often featuring professional entertainers).

According to performance scholar Barbara Kirshenblatt-Gimblett, in the nineteenth and twentieth centuries, Purim *shpiln* took place in both private homes and public settings, and a single play could last up to five hours. In homes, where they were performed during the festive meals, they were often abbreviated so the troupes could reach as many homes as possible and collect more alms (Kirshenblatt-Gimblett 1980: 6).

In the nineteenth century, Queen Vashti became an early feminist icon for her refusal to subject herself to the patriarchal demands of her husband, and her role is slowly being reexamined in the Purim *shpil* in recent years. According to Melissa Kort, "Esther/Vashti Purim Flags" have begun to make an appearance in Purim plays to provide a counterpoint to the booing of Haman and cheering of Mordechai, Vashti banquets are being held during the Purim season, and women are being centered more in the Purim story.

For Jews around the world, the Purim *shpil* is still known for its entertainment value, allowing a commemoration of hope and humor in the face of adversity – not only the trials of the distant past, but all the tribulations faced by Jews between then and now. Today, video has become a new outlet for the mocking spoofery of Purim, and many "videoshpiln" have found their way to YouTube.

Commemorative performance in medieval Christian Europe

Because the early Christian Church opposed the popular entertainments of ancient Roman times, viewing them as sinful and the work of Satan, by the fifth century CE theatre had been banned outright; actors were excommunicated and denied Christian burial and sacraments. Drama as literature, however, was still permissible and could even be edifying. This is exemplified in the dramatic work of Hrotsvitha (c.935–73), a noble lay member of the all-female Abbey of Gandersheim, in Saxony (within what is now Germany). Her writings in Latin included six plays, based on the comedies of the Roman playwright Terence (discussed in Chapter 2). Her adaptations put them to use for the personal discipline of young Christian women, encouraging them to practice abstinence. The plays may well have been intended for reading, reflection, and semi-dramatic recitation, rather than performance.

Although a few small groups of traveling performers continued, theatre essentially ceased between the sixth and tenth centuries in Europe. When, where, and why it re-emerged at that point is a matter of debate. Some scholars see it as a re-emergence of older, pre-Christian rituals and performances co-opted by the Christian Church. Others argue that it emerged under the auspices of the Church as a part of the monastic worship service – but disagree about whether it developed organically out of the worship format, or was deliberately introduced in order to restore a faith in decline due to the Church's increasing power as a private landlord and broker of medieval social relations. And still others argue for a parallel emergence in the public realms of courtrooms of law and chambers of rhetoric, where the performance of forensic oratory took on highly theatrical forms (see Chapter 4). These "origin stories" suggest a complex interplay between textual authority and embodied performance.

Considering the function of writing in Christian Europe in the centuries before the invention of the printing press, Elizabeth L. Eisenstein notes an interesting dilemma, one that has particular relevance for the study of theatre and performance: if knowledge of the Church's most sacred mysteries was the domain of an exclusive society of literate scribes and priests, how then was it able to bring its doctrine to a population that was largely illiterate (Eisenstein 1979: 271)? In the "age of scribes" and well into the era of the printing press, oral culture and its embodied enactments remained lively and important, ultimately resulting in what theatre historian Ronald W. Vince has called a "bewildering array of performances of one kind or another that we find in medieval Europe" (Vince 1989: ix).

Turning first toward the religious context of such performance, we begin with the Christian ritual of the Mass, itself a performative commemoration, and continue with a discussion of the principal types of religious drama that emerged within Christendom: cycles or "mystery plays" plays based on the Bible; Passion plays devoted to the last days of Jesus's life, his death and resurrection; saint plays (sometimes called miracle plays) that commemorated the life and works of the Christian saints and martyrs; and morality plays that used allegorical devices to explore the human condition in terms of Christian values.

The Christian Mass as a performance of commemoration

At its essence, the Christian Mass is a commemoration of Jesus's last meal with his disciples before he was crucified by Roman authorities in Jerusalem. Much more has become interwoven with that simple ritual over time, so some context may be helpful. When Jesus of Nazareth (4? BCE–29? CE) began to carry out his public ministry in Galilee (Palestine), he was one of a number of Jewish prophets declaring the imminent arrival of a new kingdom of God, in territory then under Roman rule. His followers proclaimed him to be the Christ or the new messiah (Greek and Hebrew terms respectively for "anointed one" or savior). When he arrived in Jerusalem to celebrate the Jewish Passover at a feast (*seder*) with his followers, he extended his teaching and healing into an aggressive public protest by driving traders and moneychangers out of the main Jewish temple. He was arrested by the Roman authorities, put on trial, condemned to death, and crucified – a common mode of execution.

To the authorities of the period, whether Roman or Jewish, Jesus was a minor figure, the leader of a band of superstitious followers, and his crucifixion as an "enemy of mankind" was only one of many similar public spectacles of execution under Roman law. To his followers, the period immediately after Jesus's death was fraught with uncertainty. Was the new "Kingdom of God" imminent? Witnesses to his resurrection spread that good news, or "gospel," but few believed them at first. Thrown into turmoil by Jesus's death, his small group of disciples gathered to share a memorial meal that recreated their last supper with Jesus and that commemorated his crucifixion and resurrection. Similar memorial meals were established among converts as the new religion was brought to Greece. The meal also featured communal singing, perhaps a commentary by an elder in the community, and the blessing and distribution of bread and wine, as Jesus had at his last supper with his disciples. These activities are still part of the Christian Mass.

They became formalized into a liturgy, or order of Mass, conducted by a hierarchy of priests trained to conduct it, eventually in Latin. By the fourth century, after centuries of persecution, Christianity became the official religion of the Roman Empire. Over time, the liturgy began to expand past its initial focus on the sacrificial aspects of Jesus's life. By the tenth century, inventive clergy in monasteries – the main centers of learning and the arts – began elaborating on key moments of biblical history during the Mass. Many biblical passages were sung or set to music, and eventually, further small pieces of text were added to expand a melody through chant-and-response singing; these were called **tropes**. Over time, the tropes became increasingly dramatic, providing for the characterization not only of the emotional tone of the text being presented, but also of the personages being commemorated in the text.

Early troping practice in the tenth century set to music one biblical passage of key importance to Christians: Jesus's resurrection. It begins, "*Quem Quaeritis in sepulchro, o Christicolae?*" meaning "Whom do you seek in the tomb, followers of Christ?" The words are those of an angel greeting three such followers, all of them women, who had come to Jesus's tomb in order to properly anoint his body (Figure 3.5). The women (performed by men or boys) reply, "Jesus of Nazareth who was crucified, heavenly one." The angel's reply is of supreme importance for Christians, then and now: "He is not here. He is risen."

Figure 3.5

The Three Marys at the Tomb (1425–1435), an altarpiece by Jan and/or Hubert van Eyck, depicts the events commemorated in the *Quem quaeritis* tropes during the Easter service of the early Christian mass.

Source: incamerastock/Alamy Stock Photo.

This is the first confirmation of Jesus's resurrection from the dead, which for Christians carries with it the possibility of redemption for all humankind. Many versions of the sung text exist.

In the tenth century, the Bishop of Winchester wrote out detailed instructions for performing this scene in the all-male Benedictine monasteries. Tropes were soon used for other holy seasons, including the celebration of Jesus's birth. While moving and dramatic, tropes were not plays as such, but were designed for a heightened experience of personal/collective worship and devotion commemorating Christ. It was not long, however, before a few stories associated with Jesus's birth were being dramatized in Latin within churches.

Biblical dramas in Latin

Throughout the Middle Ages, literacy was confined to the learned language of Latin, and reading itself was dominated by one important text: the Christian Bible. The elite empowered to access its wisdom found much to appreciate and interpret on both religious and formal grounds. Medieval readers looked for connections between the Old (pre-Christian) and New Testaments in the stories and characters presented in both. They remarked on the similarities, for example, between the sacrifice of Isaac by his father Abraham (a patriarch of the Old Testament) and that of Jesus by his heavenly father in the New Testament, and came to see Isaac as an early "figure" for the later Christ. This figural turn of mind led readers to look for other kinds of patterns, such as symbolism, allegory, and analogy. These figurative devices would subsequently inform literature, art, political thought, theology, oral and written sermons based on that theology – and dramatic performances, in both Latin and later the vernacular.

Early biblical plays in Latin dramatized the visits to the manger to see the newborn Jesus, by both shepherds and Magi (the wise men or Three Kings who brought gifts to the Christ child); they were performed respectively on Christmas morning and January 6, the feast of the Epiphany. By the end of the eleventh century, the Procession of the Prophets was being performed, based on a popular sermon from the fifth or sixth century. After the initial spectacle of a musical procession, costumed priests playing Old Testament prophets stepped forward to deliver their prophecies of the coming of Christ. The monastery of Benediktbeuern in Germany combined this play with its Christmas plays from the New Testament (which told of the life and works of Jesus and his earliest followers).

One of the most sophisticated examples of biblical music-drama is *The Play of Daniel*, derived from the Old Testament story of Daniel in the lion's den. It was performed during the Christmas season in the Cathedral of St. Peter of Beauvais in northern France, in the twelfth and thirteenth centuries. Here, the Old Testament prophet Daniel prefigures the New Testament messiah. In this play, there are at least nine opportunities for processions through the cathedral, making use of harps, zithers, and drums to accompany chant singing. Daniel sings a musically compelling passage in which he deciphers the mysterious handwriting on the wall that predicts the fall of King Belshazzar. (A modern performance recording is available from Pro Musica.)

These early music-dramas were staged on elevated platforms set up near the altar in the open spaces of the cathedral normally used by the priest and choir (there were no fixed pews). Sometimes called **mansions** ("stations"), these bare platforms featured symbolic scenic devices rather than realistic settings. Actors moved freely from one *mansion* to another, using the common floor area, or ***platea*** [plah-TEH-ah] ("open space"). This was, in effect, a neutral, unlocalized playing area, with *mansions* bordering it. The *platea* could be whatever the text required at a given moment; the actor's lines identified the locale and atmosphere for the audience. The idea of the *platea* carried over into the later vernacular Bible plays staged outside the church (which we'll discuss later). The fluid, open stage that Shakespeare later wrote for was somewhat indebted to this staging tradition.

Christian drama in the vernacular

Over the centuries, regional dialects of Latin became the precursors to the modern languages of Italian, French, Spanish and Portuguese; English developed from Celtic origins into a new language combining Latin and Germanic roots. While Latin remained the official written language of Christendom, the "Word of God" came to the vast majority of lay people not via reading the Bible but through other activities, such as listening to sermons and reflecting on biblical scenes pictured in vivid detail on stained glass windows. During the Lenten season, the faithful could also participate in prayerful processions to the "stations of the cross" – depictions of episodes in the sequence of Jesus's suffering (called his Passion), such as Jesus carrying and being nailed to the Cross, his death, and the removal of his body for burial.

By the late twelfth century, innovative plays based on these and other biblical events began to be written in vernacular languages and performed outside churches. An important early example is *The Play of Adam* (c.1150) from northern France. It dramatizes the Old Testament story of the expulsion of the two first humans, Adam and Eve, from the Garden of Eden, and of the rivalry between their sons, Cain and Abel. The detailed stage directions make clear that it was performed adjacent to a church or cathedral, and they provide many details about scenic décor, costuming, and acting.

The fourteenth through sixteenth centuries saw a flowering of vernacular religious drama in towns throughout England and the European continent, whose themes were drawn from the Bible and from Christian doctrine. Such drama flourished for three reasons: (1) the institution of the new Feast of Corpus Christi; (2) the growth of towns and municipal governments as entities independent of feudal lords; and (3) the gradual development within towns of the medieval trade **guilds**. These were associations of tradesmen (such as bakers, tailors, and goldsmiths) who trained apprentices and eventually regulated wages and working conditions – and who sponsored the staging of certain plays. Alan E. Knight asserts that while on the surface the dramas of the period re-enact biblical history, behind that surface late medieval social structures, values, and political realities were being mirrored (Knight 1997: 1–2). Indeed, the staging of late medieval dramas was thoroughly urban, bourgeois, and informed by constant trade and transaction between continental Europe and England.

Christian feast days and biblical dramas

Key to the development of vernacular drama in the Middle Ages was the institution of the Feast of Corpus Christi – Latin for the "body of Christ." The sacrifice of Christ's body is commemorated in the climax of the Mass, when the Eucharist is celebrated: the priest raises bread and wine, and pronounces, as Jesus did during his last supper with his apostles, "This is my body" and "This is my blood." With these words, the bread and wine are believed to be transubstantiated into the actual body and blood of the risen Christ. Pope Urban IV instituted the Feast of Corpus Christi in 1264 in order to celebrate the redemptive power of this sacrament and the presence of Christ in the world; by 1350 it was widely observed, between late May and late June of every year. This festival invokes the theological doctrine of Incarnation, or God being made flesh in the person of Jesus Christ. The doctrine of Incarnation also extends to the Word of God, known through the Bible, embodied in Jesus and by extension the body of his followers, the Church. Thus the Feast of Corpus Christi is a celebration of a text turned into a performing (collective) body, a concept with figurative resonance in the domain of theatre, which also turns words (scripts) into flesh (actors acting).

In a common Corpus Christi ritual, priests process through the city displaying the "Host," a consecrated wafer encased in an elaborate vessel that signifies the presence of Christ in the world (Figure 3.6). From the beginning, the procession of the Host has often been accompanied by tableaux of biblical scenes representing Christian sacred history and testifying to the humanity of Christ. In Paris, in 1313, actors began to recite the story of the Passion as

Figure 3.6

A Corpus Christi celebration, showing a priest holding high the Host, or bread wafer symbolizing the miracle of transubstantiation, whereby the bread of the Host becomes one with the body of Christ. Note the witnesses to this miracle are lay people, demonstrating the message of this high holy day: Christ's redemptive sacrifice is available to all humankind.

Source: Bibliothèque nationale de France.

Figure 3.7

Detail from a painting by Denis van Alsloot of a city procession honoring the visit to Brussels in 1615 of Spain's Archduchess Isabella, then Governor of the Spanish Netherlands. This pageant wagon carries a scene of Christ's nativity with actors in tableau. Joseph and Mary hover over the Christ child at the corner of the stable; the scene includes admiring shepherds, animals, and apparently a blacksmith. This wagon was one of nine in the procession that represented subjects both religious and secular. The painting is an important source for our knowledge of medieval pageant wagons, although they are in use here to display tableaux rather than as stages for the performance of plays.

Source: Vicimages/Alamy Stock Photo.

part of a living tableau. Short speeches were introduced in Innsbruck, Austria, in 1391 with the appearance of Adam, Eve, and the 12 apostles of Jesus.

Meanwhile, in England and elsewhere on the continent, sets of plays based on key biblical episodes providing a whole history of salvation were being performed (see Figure 3.7). Among the Bible stories dramatized in these **cycle plays** were those of the creation of the world; the building of Noah's Ark; Abraham's sacrifice of his son; the Nativity, with the visits of the shepherds and the Magi; Herod's attempt to slay the new child-king by dispatching his army to kill all newborn children; Jesus's raising of his friend Lazarus from the dead; and Jesus's crucifixion and resurrection. While the latter plays occur as part of the overall cycle of plays, they should not be confused with the Passion plays staged during the Lenten season, which we discuss later on.

Not being attached to the liturgy as such, vernacular Bible dramas of all types combined instruction with dramatic freedom, often incorporating carnivalesque elements, inventing local characters, and providing comic relief. In some plays God talks like one's neighbor; in others, shepherds suffer from oppressive landlords; and in at least one other, Noah's wife seriously doubts her husband's big ark project. The plays are unlike Greek and Roman drama in that they are episodic, mix comedy and tragedy, and proceed according to God's plan of salvation rather than chronology. They abound in seeming anachronisms, introduced to make contemporary points.

Because of the later censorship of religious drama during the Protestant Reformation (see Chapter 5), the manuscripts of only four complete or nearly complete English cycles are extant: 48 individual plays in the York Cycle; 32 of the Towneley (sometimes called Wakefield) plays, 25 in the Chester Cycle, and 42 in the "N-Town" (unknown city) manuscript. We know an exceptional amount about the earliest of the four, the York Cycle; the evidence tells us much about its staging, the degree of civic involvement in performance, and the social and economic background to its production.

The first record of the York Cycle's performance is from 1376, but by then it was already a well-established part of York's civic and economic life. The extant scripts were written sometime between 1463 and 1477. The plays were performed on **pageant wagons**, which held the setting (such as Eden or the Nativity manger) and sometimes incorporated special effects. The wagons were pulled along a path starting at the outskirts and ending in the city center, stopping at "stations" to perform each play (or "pageant") before the audience gathered there. The number of stations isn't known for certain and probably changed now and then; estimates range from 8 to 16, but 12 seems the most likely. While a play was performed at a station, the subsequent wagon was queued up. Then when the performance was over, the first wagon was pulled to the following station and the next play was brought in. With 48 pageants (and possibly as many as 51), the York Cycle probably took around 20 hours to perform, though possibly not all plays were performed every year.

With a few exceptions these plays were sponsored and performed by one of the city's craft guilds; women did not perform. Often the guild had a connection to the biblical episode it performed: for example, the Shipwrights were responsible for "The Building of the Ark," the Fishers and Mariners performed "Noah and His Wife," and the Bakers dramatized "The Last Supper." Sometimes the connection lay deep in the play's production or symbolism: for instance, the reason the Armourers produced "The Expulsion from Eden" may have been that in medieval art, the archangel Michael typically wielded a sword when driving Adam and Eve out of Eden. In France, and later in England, these plays were also known as **mystery plays** mainly because of their spiritual character; however, another explanation may be that craft guilds often treated their methods and tools as trade secrets, referred to as "mysteries" that were carefully guarded.

Inventive means were used to stage religious plays, at York and elsewhere. Where pageant wagons were used, they provided stages for the tableaux in the processions and/or for performances at certain stations along the way ("processional staging"). Occasionally, some of the wagons might have been moved into (or next to) an open area such as a city square, a green, or even a large platform that would have provided a neutral playing space. (The overall arrangement, in which a platform or wagon with a set representing a relatively specific location is surrounded by a general playing area, is usually called *locus* [LAW-koos] and *platea* staging.) Some Corpus Christi cycles pageants were so elaborate that two wagons were needed; others evidently used no wagons at all. Usually the action was set on the wagon when there was one, but likely every once in a while an actor performed in the street in front of the wagon or strode in through the audience. Costuming and makeup conventions may seem familiar to those of today: devils and evil characters were often played with masks, helmets, or frightening makeup; God and angels may have had their faces painted gold. Music accompanied the performances.

Our only visual record of a medieval play in performance shows fixed, raised scaffolds – mansions – bordering the *platea*. A hand-painted illumination in a fifteenth-century French prayer book shows a scene from the lost saint play *The Martyrdom of St. Apollonia,* with actors in the *platea* and up on the scaffolds, possibly along with audience members (see Figure 3.8 and the discussion of saint plays below).

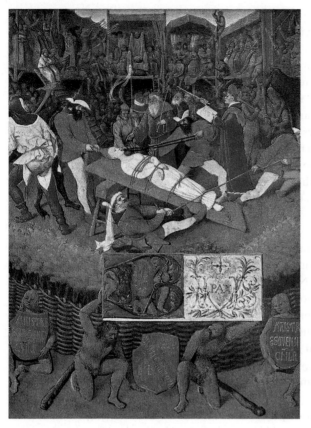

Figure 3.8

A scene from a lost medieval play, *The Martyrdom of St. Apollonia,* as represented in an illumination by Jean Fouquet in a French prayer book, the *Livre d'Heures pour maître Etienne Chevalier* (c.1452–1456). (According to legend, Apollonia was once tortured by the extraction of her teeth.) Among the scaffolds around the *platea* or playing area are those representing heaven (left) with its angels, and hell (right) with its devils and a hellmouth into which the damned were shepherded. The King's throne is at the rear, and the figure with book and baton may be the director, in ecclesiastical dress. The raised scaffolds seem to form a semi circle around the *platea,* but this and other details may be the painter's compositional strategies for representation in a book.

Source: Artefact/Alamy Stock Photo.

The production of cycle plays was far more than a side activity or entertainment for the trade guilds that sponsored them; the annual cycles were highlights of a festive season that attracted numerous visitors and provided a major economic boost for the community. Their staging was a major undertaking that required considerable financial resources and planning, organizational support and supervision by city officials. The York Cycle, for example, featured some 300 speaking parts. Due to the financial burden, sometimes two guilds had to combine their resources in order to produce one of the pageants. Why they chose to sponsor them at all is a matter of debate. Certainly piety played a role. But other pressures may have also been a factor. While the feast of Corpus Christi and the cycles of plays appealed to all sectors of society, recent studies suggest it may well have been the merchant/entrepreneurs who controlled, sponsored and even initiated these great "annual feat(s) of corporate ritual within their cit[ies]" (Dobson 1997: 105). Probably a combination of civic authority, economic motivation, civic pride, and religious devotion compelled the guilds to underwrite these major annual productions.

On the European continent, **Passion plays** were popular during the Lenten season. These plays treated the life of Jesus in his final days on earth (in contrast to the cycle plays, which covered the whole history of God's redemptive plan for humans, starting with Adam and Eve). Some were performed over several days on fixed stages in which all settings were visible at once (a convention known as **simultaneous staging**). The illustrations and stage directions of the text for the 1547 performance of the *Mystère de la Passion* in Valenciennes, France, indicate elaborate fixed stage arrangements that allowed complex scenic spectacles, including the descent of an angel,

Figure 3.9
Depiction of the setting for a passion play in Valenciennes, France, in 1547, as depicted by
the production's designer, Hubert Cailleau in 1577. Note the heavens on the one side of
the stage, and the hellmouth on the other.
Source: Bibliothèque nationale de France.

flying devils, and the ascension of Jesus into the clouds with angels (see Figure 3.9). The late
sixteenth-century Passion play at Lucerne, Switzerland, was performed in the city's Wein-
markt over two days. The Cornish play known as the *Ordinalia* used mansions in a circular
arrangement, perhaps within a circular earthen embankment, and its three parts played out
over as many days.

In the face of disasters or the horror of a plague like the "Black Death," some towns
organized Bible plays to give thanks for their deliverance. The Catholic community of
Oberammergau in the Bavarian Alps began to perform its Passion Play in 1634 in fulfillment
of a pledge to God that if the plague would cease, they would perform a play on Jesus's
sufferings every ten years. This the village has done until the present, with few exceptions
(e.g., during war and new plagues like COVID-19), changing the script in the 1960s to
remove antisemitic passages.

Saint plays, morality plays, and autos sacramentales

Three other types of dramas in this period helped to instruct and enlighten European
and newly colonized American Christians. One was the **saint** (or miracle) **play**, devoted
to the lives of the saints, especially their miraculous works. One such Spanish play, *El
Misterio de Elche*, dates from the late fifteenth century, and is still performed annually
over two days in the Basilica de Santa Maria in Elche (Spain), to celebrate the death and
miraculous Assumption (ascent) of Jesus's mother Mary into heaven. This event allows
both a glimpse into medieval European performance traditions and a sense of how they
have changed over time. Part I begins on August 14, the eve of her feast day, with *La*

Vespra, when Mary (still played today by a haloed boy in a curly wig), progresses through the church door accompanied by a wind band representing the apostles, and announces that she is about to die. Not long after, high above the congregants gathered below, the dome of the church – painted to represent the sky and heavens – opens as if by magic, allowing five angels (two boys, three men) to descend to Mary. The apparatus transporting the angels is known as *la magrana* (pomegranate), one of many inventive Spanish theatrical mechanisms of the time. On the following day, Part II, *La Festa,* commemorates her coronation after both her body and her soul arrive in heaven. The body of the silk-clad Virgin is transported heavenward in "the pomegranate," surrounded by four of the angels. As she rises toward the heavens the trap door opens once again, allowing the Holy Trinity (played by two boys and a man) to descend on a separate apparatus to the Virgin to fix the crown of heaven upon her head. Witnessing the performance in 2006, David Ward describes how

> [B]oth contraptions then rise and are steered carefully through the skycloth…. The audience holds its breath until the delicate double docking manoeuvre is complete. Then all heaven breaks loose: golden rain falls from paradise and again the organ plays, bells ring, fireworks bang and the audience claps and cheers.
>
> There are cries from all around the church of "Long live the mother of God!" and everyone shouts "Viva!"
>
> The apostles sing a Gloria of thanksgiving and we stagger out into the square, amazed.
>
> (Ward 2006: n.p.)

When congregant singers took over the performance from the priests and choirboys in the nineteenth century, they preserved the all-male performance tradition. As performed today, *El Misterio de Elche* is a montage of religious as well as secular performance elements which have accrued over the centuries. Its music ranges from medieval plainsong to Renaissance and Baroque musical styles. Melveena McKendrick observes how this major Church feast combines the procession of the penitents, fireworks, and other secular revelry to create a "potent mix of public fiesta and religious piety" (McKendrick 1989: 239) for the local congregants and numerous tourists who attend each year.

Morality plays developed widely during the fourteenth century, and came from a variety of sources, including folklore and didactic sermons given by the clergy to elaborate important lessons drawn from the day's scriptural readings. They were locally produced by groups of citizens, sometimes elaborately. Allegorical in nature, they usually focused on an "everyman" figure who faced a choice between good and bad behavior. Since God had given humankind free will to choose good or evil, the individual who chose badly would suffer the consequences – damnation and the fires of Hell. Often the entrance to this place was represented by a monstrous, fanged, mechanical "hellmouth" which would consume the fallen and the damned during the course of a play, and was meant to frighten the audience into choosing virtue (the place of "Paradise" at the opposite end of the playing space) over vice (see Figure 3.9). (Often a hellmouth was included in the Corpus Christi cycles as well.)

One of the earliest morality plays was authored by Hildegard of Bingen (1098–1179), a gifted Benedictine mystic, abbess, healer, and author. Like the dramas of Hrotsvitha, Hildegard's musical morality play *Ordo Virtutum* (or "Order of the Virtues," c.1155) was probably intended to be read or recited by nuns within her convent, not for a general public. It featured the battle for a human soul between the forces of evil (the Devil) and 16 personified virtues like Humility, Charity, Fear-of-God, Obedience, and so forth.

Perhaps the most famous morality plays in English are *The Castle of Perseverance* (c.1400–25, Figure 3.10) and *Everyman* (c.1495, likely based on an earlier Dutch version that was itself inspired by a Buddhist fable from a millennium earlier). In *The Castle of Perseverance,* the main character, Mankind, is seduced by the Bad Angel who tells him there will be time in old age to be virtuous. Mankind then encounters a wide range of allegorical characters who attempt to influence him. They include the Seven Deadly Sins (Wrath, Greed, Sloth, Pride, Lust, Envy and Gluttony); the figures of Conscience, Confession, and Penance; and the Virtues, including Meekness, Patience, Charity, and Chastity. At Mankind's trial before God, Mercy and Peace plead for him against Righteousness and Truth. God judges mercifully in the end. In *Everyman,* the title character is faced with his impending death. Fearful of going to eternity alone, he asks one worldly character after another to accompany him; in the end, only Good Deeds can do so, thereby providing justification for Everyman's entry into Heaven. A co-

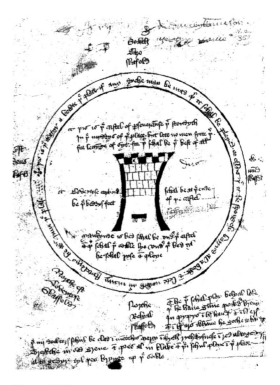

Figure 3.10

Plan of the mansions and playing area for the morality play, *The Castle of Perseverance*, c.1400–25, possibly for a performance in an ancient earthen round. Mankind's castle is at the center, the location of the five mansions is indicated outside the circle, and the direction within the double circles reads: "this is the water about the place [*platea*], if any ditch be made where it shall be played, or else let it be strongly barred all about."

Source: V.a.354. Folger Shakespeare Library.

medic 2017 adaptation by Branden Jacobs-Jenkins, *Everybody,* features a nine-character cast who must learn each other's parts; who plays which is chosen by lottery each night of the run, to symbolize the arbitrariness of fate. Love replaces Good Deeds in this version, which also interweaves a discussion between Everybody and everyone else about racism.

Within Spain, a new dramatic form, the ***auto sacramental*** [OW-toh sahk-rah-men-TAHL]*,* began to develop once Spain became a unified Christian nation in 1492. Prior to that year, Spanish territory had been divided among separate kingdoms, and large portions had been inhabited by Muslims and Jews. When Isabel I, queen of the Spanish kingdom of Castile, married her cousin Fernando II of Aragon in 1469, they set about unifying Spain under Catholic rule, aided both by military campaigns and by the Spanish Inquisition. In 1492, they defeated the Moors at Granada, and passed a law requiring all Jews to either convert to Christianity or be expelled from Spain.

As it had in other parts of Europe, theatre in Spain played its part in extending and solidifying Christian power. A unique form developed around the celebration of Corpus Christi there that combined elements of the cycle plays and the morality plays; these one-act plays became known as *autos sacramentales* (sacramental acts). Like the cycle plays, the *autos* dealt with important stories from biblical history to culminate in a celebration of the mystery of the Eucharist. But they also bore traces of earlier morality play devices, which had been popular in non-Islamic Spain from the thirteenth century.

Mounted on portable, wheeled stages called *carros,* the plays were presented several times in different locations throughout the principal cities of Spain. Sometimes, the city commissioned so many that performances took place over several days, for the benefit of the king, various governing councils, and the general public. The *carros* themselves were included in the Corpus Christi processions, where they were pulled along by bulls whose horns had been dipped in gold for the occasion.

Thousands of *autos sacramentales* were commissioned, to be staged and re-staged over the course of the centuries. As in England, they were under the control of trade guilds until the middle of the sixteenth century; after that, the city councils hired professional troupes to stage these plays, which were written by some of Spain's foremost dramatists, among them Gil Vicente, Juan del Encina, Lope de Vega, and Calderón de la Barca, who will be discussed further in Chapters 4 and 5. The most important of the *auto* authors was Calderón (1600–1681), who penned some 200, of which 76 survive. His work is remarkable not only for its quantity, but for its quality: Calderón is widely noted for his keen insights into human nature, which he viewed with great compassion, as well as his ability to blend serious religious philosophy and poetic language with inventive dramas embodying moral lessons. A fascinating example is *The Great Theatre of the World* (1635), in which God is viewed as a kind of cosmic stage director, putting the characters of King, Beauty, Rich Man, Peasant, Beggar and Child through their paces, noting that each has but one entrance and one exit from this particular "stage."

Interest in the *autos* began to wane after Calderón's death in 1681, but their influence was still felt halfway around the world. Perhaps the most famous *auto* is one that may never have been staged: the *Loa to the Divine Narcissus* by Sor Juana Inés de la Cruz, a Mexican nun who was also a celebrated philosopher, poet and dramatist in the seventeenth century (see the case study in Chapter 5). *Loas* are acts of praise that started as short monologues and dialogues serving as prologues to a principal work, then evolved into a form resembling a one-act play in their own right, artfully introducing a longer play with similar thematic material. Sor Juana's 1689 *loa* tells the story of the conversion to Christianity of the indigenous Mexicans by Spanish warriors and missionaries, and features such allegorical characters as Occident and America (a native prince and princess), Zeal (a Spanish soldier), and Religion (a Spanish lady), who argues that the "God of the Seeds" worshipped by the natives is an allegorical prefiguration of Christ himself.

Although the religious messages in the cycle plays and these other types of drama were strong, it is important to stress their entertainment value as well. The plots may have been familiar or didactic, but often farcical and topical humor crept in to keep the telling fresh. The characters may have been non-human abstractions, but the allegorical figures were fully fleshed and often disarmingly human in their characterization. The sets may have been limited by pageant wagon constraints, but clever costumers devised ways to hold audience interest, including leather bodystockings meant to suggest nakedness (for the plays about Adam and Eve), and others rigged so as to shed blood, as in the case of a play from the Chester cycle about the risen Christ. In France, because the reputation of the guilds depended in part on the quality of their productions, a "mixture of personal showmanship and the desire to dress the sacred characters as icons could lead to extravagances of silk, satin, and jeweled embroidery which we might find more appropriate to the Follies than to sacred drama" (Vince 1989: 69). For a population not yet literate in their own spoken language, all of these elements worked together to ensure an experience of Christian doctrine and values they hoped literally never to forget. However, the Church's approval of religiously oriented performance did not necessarily extend to theatre generally: suspicion continued, and particularly after the Reformation, the Church again condemned actors and denied them sacraments.

Dramas of Christian crusade and conquest

While the Christian Church in Europe was busy reaffirming its central tenets for believers through drama, it was also busy both at home and abroad trying to win new souls for the Christian God, with means both military and theatrical. When its power was eventually concentrated in Rome and in the figure of a pope, the Church constructed the idea of the "Holy Land," an area comprising the locations where its sacred history had unfolded (present-day Israel, Palestine, Lebanon, Syria, and Jordan). Soon, the Holy Land became a site of Christian pilgrimage. From the eleventh century, it also became a site of bitter, bloody struggles for power and ascendancy in a series of militarized engagements eventually described as the "Crusades," or holy wars. (The term, which means "marked with a cross" – the key symbol of Christianity – first appeared in Spain in the thirteenth century.) Until the late fifteenth century, Muslims were the principal targets of these campaigns.

When Christian kingdoms began to colonize the world, a variety of dramas of conquest resulted. In some, Western Christian modes of performance were imposed on indigenous populations, as happened in Mesoamerica. In their American colonies, the Spaniards introduced all manner of Christian biblical theatre from medieval Europe, in service of teaching and converting the natives. The first European play performed in the Americas was a morality play: *Juicio Final (Final Judgment)*, attributed to the Franciscan friar Andrés de Olmos, staged in Tlatelolco (c.1531–33, in what is now Mexico City). Written as a warning against local customs of concubinage, it threatened natives with eternal damnation if they did not marry within the Christian Church.

It is impossible to know exactly how the indigenous peoples of the Americas understood these religious dramas. Most scholars agree, however that drama played a strong role in the conversion project. Early Spanish conquerors were quick to adapt existent forms of indigenous theatricality to their own ends. Plays were performed in local languages,

Figure 3.11

A scissors dancer in a street in Chorrillos, Peru, c.2014. Some scholars trace this performance practice to a sixteenth-century "dancing sickness" performed as part of a resistance movement against Spanish occupation of Peru.

Source: Christian Vinces/Shutterstock.

and indigenous performers recruited to fill the roles. The Crusades themselves were a frequent topic of such drama, as noted in the case study below, about the Moors and the Christians.

Mexican theatre scholar Maria Sten once observed that "theatre was to the spiritual conquest of Mexico what the horses and gunpowder were to its military defeat" (Sten 1982: 14). But other scholars have noted that indigenous peoples living in the early period of the Spanish conquest did not uncritically accept new performance forms and content, nor abandon completely their own, as we saw with *Rabinal Achi,* and as our case study on the Christians and Moors suggests. In the Andes, for example, a Spanish "extirpator," charged with stamping out idolatry in the 1560s, was outraged to report that followers of an indigenous resistance movement known as *taki unquy* (or "dancing sickness") had hidden an image of one of their local deities on the very vessel that displayed the Host during a Cuzco Corpus Christi celebration. Scholars of this resistance movement, which had at its center a form of deity-possession of dancing bodies, have suggested that its impulse to reclaim local cultural identity has never disappeared – and may be visible in contemporary performance of the famous Andean *danza de las tijeras,* or scissors dance (see Figure 3.11).

CASE STUDY: Christians and Moors: Medieval performance in Spain and the New World

By Bruce McConachie, with Tamara Underiner

To celebrate their conquest in 1598 of what is now the American southwest, Spanish *conquistadores* threw themselves a week-long party, which included a variety of performances, including "A jolly drama, well composed,/Playing at Moors and Christians,/With much artillery, whose roar/Did cause notable fear and marveling,/To many bold barbarians …" (Harris 1994: 145). What was this "jolly drama" with "Moors and Christians" that involved noisy "artillery"? And why might a drama about Moors, the Spanish term for Muslims living in northern Africa, be performed to celebrate the conquest of land in North America?

At first glance, the answer might be a simple one: why not? As we have suggested in this chapter, Spain carried the Crusades to the Americas, where it sought to convert souls to Christ before the end-times came; the natives of the Americas, like the Muslims, can be seen as the "enemies" of Christianity who had to be defeated.

But upon closer examination, this explanation cannot account for the variety within and remarkable persistence of the tradition of the Moors and Christian dramas, both in Spain and in the New World, where the first record of such a performance dates back to 1538. At that performance, staged during a Corpus Christi procession in the town of Tlaxcala in central Mexico – by an all-native cast, in their native tongue of Nahuatl – the enemy "Sultan" was not an indigenous ruler but the Spanish conquistador Hernán Cortés himself, played by a native actor dressed as a Turk. At the end of the "play," he, along with all the other natives on stage and in the audience, were baptized in an act of compulsory conversion. What, exactly, was going on, and how do we understand such a performance?

This question too is not so simple. To begin to answer it we will cover the history of this genre of drama in both Spain and its colonies, and suggest an approach that will help to explain how this ancient dramatic form has survived half a millennium and more, on both sides of the Atlantic.

Historic background

By the time Spaniards in the New World crossed the Rio Grande to claim New Mexico, Christian kings, princes, and counts in Spain had been staging *moros y cristianos* spectacles for popular and aristocratic audiences for over 300 years. As in the Mexico and New Mexico productions of 1538 and 1598, performances of *moros y cristianos* in medieval Spain normally occurred in the midst of a festival. These choreographed battles typically pitted two groups of knights against each other – blackfaced Moors in exotic silk gowns and Christian crusaders in shining armor. Following exchanges of verbal abuse from both sides, the Moors usually won the initial battles, but the Christian knights always triumphed in the end, sometimes returning with facsimiles of Moorish heads on their lances. In other performances, the Moors would recognize the error of their ways, convert to Christianity, and bow down before a symbol of Catholic power.

Real battles between Christians and Moors began even before Spain had unified into a single country, and the Moors, at first, won most of them, establishing a culture and society in what is now present-day Portugal and most of Spain that was more advanced and tolerant than the rest of medieval Christian Europe (Figure 3.12). The warfare lasted until 1492, when the Moorish port city of Granada fell. In that momentous year, all Jews who refused to convert to Christianity were also expelled from the peninsula, and Columbus set sail under the flag of the new Spanish monarchs Fernando and Isabel.

This 700-year crusade left an indelible impression on Spanish history and culture. Hardened by constant warfare, a newly united Spain forged a culture of religious fanaticism and military valor that shaped the Catholic Inquisition at home, and conquest

Figure 3.12

Map showing extent of Christian and Moorish territories in 1490.

Source: © Bruce McConachie.

abroad. After 1492, the rulers of Spain expelled all infidels from the peninsula, tortured thousands of *morisco/as* (Christians of Moorish background) and *marrano/as* (Christians of Jewish background) whom they suspected of un-Christian belief, and extended their crusade of conversion or extinction to the natives of the New World. When the *conquistadores* of New Mexico performed the "jolly drama" of *moros y cristianos*, they were honoring a tradition of militant Christianity that had brought them victory for hundreds of years. There can be little doubt that the Spaniards rejoiced in the "fear and marveling" that the spectacle produced among the Native Americans who were watching the show.

The "low other" in medieval performance

Performances in medieval festivals and religious holidays often defined proper Christian behavior by denigrating and defeating its un-Christian opposite. Because hierarchical relations of authority and belief were so important in medieval Christian culture, stereotypes of "low others" proliferated in European performances from the twelfth through the sixteenth centuries.

Mummers plays, early Christianized versions of pagan rituals designed to en-sure the return of spring after the winter solstice, often featured a blackened Turk as the antagonist of a white Christian knight. Another winter solstice performance, the Sword Dance, symbolically sacrificed a hairy wild man or a "greenman" from the forest to incite the resurrection of the springtime sun (and the Christian Son of God). In the cycle plays, Jews, Romans, and infidels were often characterized as buffoons, villains, or other "low" types. Characters associated with vice in morality plays – the female temptress, Sloth, Gluttony, Pride, the rest of the Seven Deadly Sins, and Lucifer himself – were typically costumed and played in ways that aligned them with dirt, feces, and rampant sexuality (Figure 3.13). In medieval Spain, Moors and Jews became the primary symbols of the "low other" in festival performances. Medieval writers often characterized Moors as treacherous and cowardly in *moros y cristianos* plays, especially after 1492.

Figure 3.13
Stonework depicting a sexualized Lucifer tempting Christ. Carved on a capital of Autun Cathedral in France in the twelfth century by Gisilbertus.
Source: Azoor Photo/Alamy Stock Photo.

Moros y cristianos in New Mexico today:
conquest and re-conquest

The legacy of Spanish medieval theatre continues to shape popular and religious celebrations in Spanish-influenced regions of the world today. For example, every year during a June fiesta about two dozen men and women of Chimayó, New Mexico dress in medieval costumes, mount horses, wield swords and scimitars, and engage in a symbolic battle. To create the illusion of darker skin, the Latinos playing Moors also wear black veils. As during the days of Spanish imperialism, the ideology of militant Christianity continues to shape the ending of the play. Convinced by the outcome of

the battle that their own religion is false, the Moors convert to Christianity, and all performers join together in a hymn of praise to the Holy Cross.

Some Native Americans living in Mexico and the U.S. southwest also perform versions of *moros y cristianos*, partly to honor their conversion to Christianity under Spanish rule but also to gain a wry revenge against their historical persecutors. These performances typically involve Native Americans on hobbyhorses playing, as they did in Tlaxcala in 1538, both groups of antagonists, with historic Native Americans on one side and Spaniards and "white" Americans on the other (Figure 3.14). Instead of dramatizing conquest and conversion, however, the performance points up the foolishness of the "whites," who, in this revised version of *moros y cristianos*, flee a symbolic bull, portrayed by a Native American.

THINKING THROUGH THEATRE HISTORIES: READING FOR THE "HIDDEN TRANSCRIPTS"

Religious theatre scholar Max Harris has studied a wide variety of *moros y cristianos* dramas, both historical and contemporary, and offers a way to explain them in terms of both their resistance and their persistence. Harris compels us to consider two kinds of "transcripts" at work in performances in which power imbalances figure strongly, as they do in this case study: first, the "public," or official message of the performance, its stated intent; and second, the "hidden" transcripts that both powerful and powerless might employ to critique the public transcript, behind its back, either consciously or unconsciously.

Despite how the Spaniards in Europe and Mexico might have meant it, American variants on the *moros y cristianos* from the start have been staged with multiple hidden transcripts that allow its performers both to toe the official line of Christianity's triumph and to stage their own critique of that victory. Today, in situations in which Native Americans control and perform the dance, the drama of the Moors and Christians is no longer a "military theatre of humiliation" (Harris 2000: 27); instead, they have turned white soldiers, saints, and traders into the "low others" that Indians once had been.

Key references

Audio-visual resources

Short documentary from the Museum of International Folk Art and the Wisdom Archive, featuring archival footage from the 1976 *moros y cristianos* in Chimayo, New Mexico, as well as excerpts from scripted passages: https://www.youtube.com/watch?v=e_XUA3dFNjM

Books and articles

Glick, T.E. (1979) *Islamic and Christian Spain in the Early Middle Ages: Comparative Perspectives on Social and Cultural Formation*, Princeton, NJ: Princeton University Press.

Harris, M. (1994) "The Arrival of the Europeans: Folks Dramatizations of Conquest and Conversion in New Mexico," in C. Davidson and J. Stroupe (eds.) *Early and Traditional Drama: Africa, Asia and the New World*, Kalamazoo, MI: Medieval Institute Publications, 141–65.

——— (2000) *Aztecs, Moors and Christians*, Austin: University of Texas Press.

Holme, B. (1987) *Medieval Pageantry*, London: Thames and Hudson.

Scott, J.D. (1990) *Domination and the Arts of Resistance: Hidden Transcripts*, New Haven, CT: Yale University Press.

Shergold, N.D. (1967) *A History of the Spanish Stage from Medieval Times until the End of the Seventeenth Century*, Oxford: Clarendon Press.

Stallybrass, P., and A. White. (1996) *The Politics and Poetics of Transgression*, Ithaca, NY: Cornell University Press.

Stern, C. (1996) *The Medieval Theatre in Castile, Medieval and Renaissance Texts and Studies*, Vol. 156, Binghamton, NY: Center for Medieval and Renaissance Studies.

Wickham, G. (1987) *The Medieval Theatre*, 3rd edn, Cambridge: Cambridge University Press.

Islamic commemorative mourning dramas: The *Ta'ziyeh* of Iran and beyond

Just as the life of Jesus and biblical events played a central role in the development of commemorative liturgical and biblical dramas within Christianity, a major historical event in the history of Islam became the central inspiration for the development of the Islamic commemorative drama, **Ta'ziyeh** [TAH-zee-yeh] (also spelled *Ta'zieh*).

"Islam" is an Arabic word meaning submission to God, or Allah. In the Islamic tradition, Allah revealed his message to Muhammad in a series of visions from 612 CE. Muhammad said he merely transmitted the message of Allah, adding and removing nothing. For Muslims the Qur'an (often rendered as "Koran") is nothing less than the transmission in simple, clear Arabic language of a divine archetype that is kept in heaven for eternity, and is graven on the "guarded Tablet." It was that archetype that was directly revealed to Muhammad. Muhammad, a merchant living in the city of Mecca, probably did not read and would have transmitted what he received orally. The word "Qur'an" is from a verb originally meaning "vocal recitation"; it was only after 622 that some of Muhammad's disciples began to inscribe fragments of what they heard onto bits of leather. After the Prophet's death, the Qur'anic revelations were gathered into a set of texts, collected by the first Caliph, Abu Bakr.

For several centuries, written versions provided little more than a guide to memory for repeating aloud a text already memorized. The writing of the Qur'an grew in significance, becoming a sanctifying act and done in elaborate calligraphy, the most esteemed art in Islam (Figure 3.15). Islam generally prohibits pictorially representing the living or dead (people and animals) in order to maintain a clear distinction between the Creator and the created, but the Qur'an and other texts can be illuminated: texts are often decorated with geometric and plant-like patterns. Each of the Qur'an's 114 chapters can be marked by a decorative heading, and special marks to guide one's reading, indicating places for required ritual prostration.

Sultans, shahs, princes, and members of the aristocracy or wealthy merchants throughout the Islamic world have also valued secular Islamic books and manuscripts highly – and as we saw in Chapter 1, treasured, translated and preserved the work of non-Islamic scholars as well. From at least the ninth century onward, patronizing the production of fine manuscripts and maintaining a library were two key attributes of royalty in Persia (now known as Iran). Persian princes themselves were often artists or calligraphers. Other arts that flourished under the patronage of Islamic rulers included poetry, music, dance, storytelling (*naghali*), shadow theatre (*khayāl al-ẓill*), storytelling in front of an illustrated backdrop (*pardeh-khani and pardeh-dari*), and puppet theatre (*aragoz* in Egypt; shadow puppets called *karagöz* in Turkey and *karakouz* in Tunisia). Shadow and puppet theatre were exempt from the prohibitions against fully representational theatre; such plays were meant mainly for entertainment and based on written sketches on comedic, farcical, and satiric themes.

Despite prohibitions against representation, gifted *meddahs* (storytellers) in Turkey would use mimicry for comic effect, sometimes performing together as a kind of informal theatre in the countryside. Turkish sultans also patronized traveling troupes called **ortaoyunu** [OHR–toh-yu-nu], who from the thirteenth century performed comedic improvisational sketches based

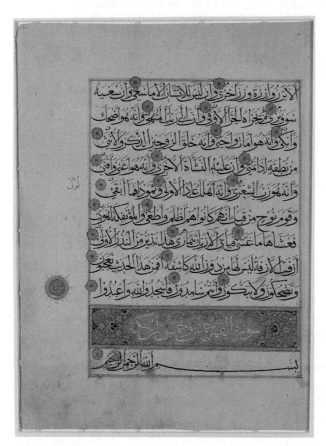

Figure 3.15
Qur'anic verses in Persian calligraphy from the sixteenth to seventeenth centuries. The round emblem at the left margin contains the word *sajdah* (prostration) in gold on a blue background, marking the place for prayer before reading the next chapter.

Source: Library of Congress, https://lccn.loc.gov/2019714487.

on standard plot scenarios and fixed character types that invite comparison to the Italian *commedia dell'arte* (see Chapter 4).

Commemorative mourning rituals and the development of Ta'ziyeh

Among Shi'ite Muslims, a form of commemorative performance known as *Ta'ziyeh* (Arabic for expressions of mourning, sympathy, or condolence) became central to their version of Islam. Its roots lie in the violent struggle over who would become successor, or *caliph,* to the Prophet Muhammad. When Muhammad died in 632, some of his followers believed that the Prophet passed special, divine knowledge to his son-in-law and cousin Ali (d. 661), as well as to his direct descendants, to serve as imams (prayer leaders and religious guides); these followers were called Shi'ites (members of the Shi'a sect). Others (members of the Sunni sect or Sunnis) held that the succession should fall to the best person, not necessarily to a direct relative of Muhammad. The two main branches of Islam – Shi'a and Sunni – reflect this historical and theological struggle over succession of the Prophet. Their fundamental disagreement was accentuated by both political and theological differences, which led to divergent legal and ritual practices. (Most Shi'ites live in present-day Iran, Iraq, Yemen, and Bahrain, with smaller communities in India, Pakistan, Bangladesh, and Afghanistan; while Sunnis, which constitute 85–90 percent of the world's Muslim population, live throughout the Middle East, North Africa, Central Asia, Indonesia, and the Americas.)

The *Ta'ziyeh* storyline begins in a rebellion sparked by the murder of the Prophet's son-in-law Ali's father and older brother, led by Hussein (Ali's son and Muhammad's grandson) in an ill-fated attempt to regain control. Hussein, his family and followers were surrounded by the opposing army on the plain of Karbala (in present-day Iraq). On the tenth day of Muharram in the Islamic year 61 (10 October 680), after ten battle-filled days without water in which all the males save one small boy were massacred, Hussein himself was killed and the women in his followers' encampment taken captive. The battle became a source for most Shi'ite rituals because all those martyred modeled the ideal behavior in the struggle to follow the right path toward Allah.

The first month of the Muslim lunar calendar, Muharram, soon became a period for Shi'ites to perform mourning rituals to commemorate the moment when Hussein, his family, and followers were martyred. Since at least the tenth century, ritual processions in Baghdad have featured mourners with black-painted faces and disheveled hair, singing songs of lamentation and beating their chests in mourning. (Acts of self-flagellation have remained a central part of participants' identification with the martyred Hussein to the present day.)

Shi'a practices were consolidated during the sixteenth century with the establishment of the Safavid dynasty on the Iranian Plateau. The popular orator Hussein Vaiz Kashefi composed *Rawzat al-shuhada (The Garden of Martyrs)* – a work which synthesized "various historical accounts, elegiac poems, theological tracts, and hagiographies into a chain of short narratives that together formed a much larger narrative" and which stressed "the courage, piety, and sacrifice of Hussein and his followers at Karbala." Reading it aloud at religious gatherings, orators improvised sermons based on the text whose intention "was to move the audience to tears through his recitation of the tragic deaths of the Battle of Karbala" (Aghaie 2005: 45–6).

Eventually, the events surrounding Hussein's martyrdom came to form the narrative core of an even more elaborate ritual performance called *Ta'ziyeh,* created during the Qajar period (1796–1925) (though some scholars suspect this storyline was melded onto an even more ancient mourning ritual for a legendary pre-Islamic prince). A cycle of ten *Ta'ziyeh* plays is performed during the first ten days of Muharram, one each day (for a translation of one play, see Pettys 2005). Each chronicles a single episode of the brutal events, or focuses on the heroic deaths of specific members of Hussein's family and followers. The only prescribed play is the death of Hussein – always performed on the tenth day. Observances often continue through the remainder of the month of Muharram and into the month of Safar, specifically to mourn the torment of Hussein's female relatives taken as captives to Damascus. Some communities produce less ornate *Ta'ziyeh* performances that are not necessarily about the events of Karbala throughout the year.

Non-representational reading and representation in Ta'ziyeh

Ta'ziyeh was originally performed at a crossroads or in other outdoor areas. Some staging elements may be remnants of pre-Islamic entertainments and rituals, including a mourning ritual for the legendary Iranian prince Siyâvash, a sinless hero unjustly killed, like Hussein. The blood shed by Prince Siyâvash, legend has it, caused a plant to spring up from the ground on the spot where he was slain, and over time he has become a powerful symbol linked to the spirit of vegetative growth. Some scholars see something of the regenerative spirit of Siyâvash at work in the impulse to perform *Ta'ziyeh* regularly, as a way to recall the pre-Islamic as well as Islamic past.

By the early nineteenth century, special gathering spaces (**takiyeh**) were built to house *Ta'ziyeh* performance. Under the Qajar kings of the nineteenth century, such stagings could be quite opulent and spectacular, to reflect the imperial ambitions of the sponsoring monarch. *Ta'ziyeh* is performed in the round, with a raised central platform surrounded by a huge circular, sand-covered space used for spectacular effects, such as equestrian events and foot battles. Additional raised stages erected around the edges of the circular space are used for subplots, enemy camps, or special scenes. These often extend into the audience area. Corridors stretch from the central stage through the audience so that messengers and processions of horses, camels, and vehicles can pass. Battle scenes can surround the entire audience. Audience and performers alike are immersed in a whirling, centrifugal experience of tumultuous action, songs, music, recitations, and battles (see Figures 3.16 and 3.17). Props and costumes are simple and sometimes symbolic. A basin of water represents the Euphrates River. Protagonists wear green or white and sing

Figure 3.16

A nineteenth-century performance of *Ta'ziyeh*. In the 1870s, the *Takiyeh Dowlat* shown here was erected in Tehran in the royal compound. Its walls, canvas ceiling, and circular stage were copied in *takiyeh* and *husseinyeh* (performance structures) all over the country.

Source: © Peter Chelkowski.

in lyrical Persian chants, while the antago-nists wear red and declaim in a fierce, un-couth manner. Women's roles are played by veiled men dressed in black. Some charac-ters, such as demons, are masked. *Ta'ziyeh* participant-performers are not "actors" who represent characters. They do not memorize lines. Rather, they are "readers" who sing or recite in a non-realistic manner from seg-ments of the script held in hand. Like many forms of commemorative ritual-drama, *Ta'ziyeh* has all the trappings of "theatre," as Westerners would understand the term, but in its most traditional form it is not theatre. Rather, it is a participatory, epic re-enactment of an historical event that makes the past present for Shi'ite participants and spectators.

To participate in *Ta'ziyeh* is to participate in a deeply religious event filled with intense grief, mourning, and lamentation. For his followers, Hussein's martyrdom at Karbala exemplified supreme self-sacrifice, human suffering, and a profound act of divine re-demption. The site of performance becomes the physical locus of martyrdom, and the pain participants inflict on themselves is the pain of Hussein.

Ta'ziyeh ties contemporary Shi'ites to their complex past, reminding them of their intimate connection with Hussein and the

Figure 3.17

In a *Ta'ziyeh* commemorative performance, Nabi-ollah Habibabadi (on horseback) is seen in the role of Shemr, the general who beheads Imam Hussein. In the background, Yazid, the Umayyid Sultan who ordered the killing. In Habibabad near Isfahan, Iran.

Shi'ite battle of resistance against a powerful, alien invader. *Ta'ziyeh* remains of central im-portance in Iran, but is also performed today in South Asia, other parts of the Arab world, and the Caribbean. Secular versions of the *Ta'ziyeh* were performed at theatre festivals in Avignon in 1991, Parma (Italy) in 2000, and in New York in 2002 at Lincoln Center.

CASE STUDY: Playful Gods: The *Ramlila* in North India

By Phillip B. Zarrilli, with Carol Fisher Sorgenfrei and Tamara Underiner

In this case study, we consider the Hindu commemorative devotional drama **Ramlila** [rahm-lee-lah] of North India. Unlike India's *kutiyattam*, considered in Chapter 2, which is patronized by relatively small, elite audiences interested in enhancing their aesthetic experience of performance, Hindu commemorative dramas are performed for mass, popular audiences. These dramas allow devotees immediate access to an encounter with one of many specific manifestations of the divine – an experience sometimes described as *bhakti rasa* (*bhakti* means devotion). This aesthetic experience of deep devotion is a creative interpretation of the *rasa* aesthetic considered in Chapter 2.

North India's *Ramlila* is an enormously popular, pluralistic form of open-air performance that re-enacts episodes from the life of Ram (also called Rama). Ram is considered to be one of the ten incarnations of the Hindu deity Vishnu (the preserver of the universe). *Lila* literally means an act of cosmic or divine "play"; that is, a moment when the divine interacts with the human world. In the case of *Ramlila* and its earlier quasi-dramatic precursors, the divine's vehicle for this interaction is Ram. The present form of the text used for the performance is called the *Ramcharitmanas* ("Sacred Lake of the Acts of Rama," c.1625), attributed to the poet Tulsidas (c.1532–1623) or one of his disciples. Its plot is based on the main elements of the much earlier Sanskrit epic *Ramayana* (fifth to fourth century BCE). *Ramlilas* occur every year, usually in September and October. All *Ramlilas* involve role playing and the re-enactment of specific events from Ram's life. Some are brief, while others are elaborated at length.

Origins of Ramlila

Since its first telling, the *Ramayana* has been a source for performance. Norvin Hein postulates that the earliest forerunners of today's immensely popular *Ramlila* were dramatizations of parts of the *Ramayana* under royal patronage. One early source, the *Harivamsa* (no later than 400 CE) relates how part of the *Ramayana* was sung by a background chorus while actor-dancers in the foreground enacted the story. Hein suggests that this early form of dance-drama eventually died out in North India under Muslim rule (1200–1500), but that elements of the early performance were still reflected in the popular Bhakti devotional drama that swept the region during the fifteenth and sixteenth centuries (Hein 1972: 124). The *Ramlila* makes a connection between performance and creation itself: the most revered version of the *Ramayana*, written by Valmiki sometime between 200 BCE and 200 CE, makes clear that the universe is a dramatic performance and that the god is the writer, director, star, and even the audience:

> The world is a show and you are the viewer.
> You make Brahma, Vishnu and Shiva dance.
> …
> Putting on a man's body for the sake of gods and saints,
> you talk and act like a natural king.
> Ram, when they see and hear your acts,
> the foolish are bewildered, the wise feel joy.
>
> (Qtd. in Hess 2006: 130)

A godly re-enactment

Ramlila is a highly participatory form of drama in which the devotee enters into "the fabric of mythic narrative" (Lutgendorf 1991: 251s). It draws millions of

Figure 3.18
Ravana, the ten-headed demon-king, is burned in effigy as part of *Ramlila*, as on-lookers try to capture the moment with their smartphones. Photo: Om Rathore.
Source: Om Rathore/iStock.

pilgrim-devotees from across India – especially the north and central regions – to the very site (Ayodhya) where it is assumed that Lord Ram was born and lived in the distant past. Re-enacting the trials and tribulations of Ram, some performances last three to five days and others for over a month. Audiences can exceed 100,000 – including not only Hindus, but (depending on the political climate) also minority Muslims and Christians. Performances culminate with the festival of Dussehra in which an effigy of the evil ten-headed demon-king, Ravana, is burned – a spectacular celebration of the victory of good over evil (see Figure 3.18). The performances are done by non-professional casts under the sponsorship of wealthy patrons.

In contrast to the highly decorative mode of composition of Sanskrit poetry still in use at the time he wrote, Tulsidas authored his version of the *Ramayana* in accessible language. In performance, Tulsidas's version of Ram's story is mapped onto the specific geographical locations understood to be dear to Lord Ram, so in effect, "the pageant came to express notions of cosmography and pilgrimage that aim at reclaiming and transforming the mundane world" (Lutgendorf 1991: 255). The entire performance becomes "a series of pilgrimages that re-enact the Lord's own movements and bring worshipers to the sites at which they reexperience his [holy] deeds" (Lutgendorf 1991: 250). Therefore, for the celebration of Ram and Sita's wedding anniversary, the ideal site is Mithila (Janakpur) in Nepal, the birthplace of Sita and the location of their wedding. Pilgrims who are able to travel there "identify themselves as members of Ram's

... wedding party, and they trade humorous insults with the people of the bride's hometown" (Lutgendorf 1991: 250). For worshippers in Ayodhya, the birthplace of Ram, there are also festivities. According to Hindi scholar Philip Lutgendorf,

> On the marriage day in Ayodhya ... wedding processions mounted by major temples wind through the city for hours. They consist of lampbearers, drummers and shehnai players, "English-style" marching bands (all requisites of a modern North Indian wedding), and of course the bridegrooms – Ram and his three brothers – astride horses or riding in ornate carriages. The grooms are usually *svarups* – young Brahman boys impersonating deities, but a few processions feature temple images borne on palanquins. After receiving the homage of devotees before whose homes and shops they briefly halt, the processions return to their sponsoring establishments, where a marriage ceremony is performed. The crowds of devotees attending these rites are not merely spectators; they are encouraged to take the roles of members of the wedding party.
>
> (Lutgendorf 1991: 251)

The Ramnagar Ramlila

Although hundreds of *Ramlilas* take place all over North India, the most famous (and the one that we will focus on) occurs in Ramnagar, which is across the river Ganga (Ganges) from the holy city of Varanasi (Benares). After a special set of offerings is given, Tulsidas's version of Ram's sacred story is chanted/sung in its entirety by a group of 12 men, known as Ramayanis, who are accompanied by a drum. A prescribed number of couplets are sung daily. Only on the tenth day of recitation do the Ramayanis arrive at couplet 175, when the *Ramlila* re-enactment of scenes *per se* begins. Their singing is then incorporated into the larger context of the *lila*, and continues until they reach the last book of the epic poem, when the *lila* ends. But the recitation of the full text is not complete, so the Ramayanis continue their quiet reading until each word of the text has been read, so that the final ritual passing of a flame is held in Ayodhya, closing the full performance of 30–32 days.

Since the text is chanted, the actors do not simply recite the text of the drama, but rather, like the dancers of old, they "bring to life and ... interpret the words of the recitation" (Hein 1972: 124). All actors are males, with the roles of Sita, Ram, and his brothers taken by prepubescent boys. They are worshiped as divine embodiments of those they impersonate. Other characters, such as Hanuman (the monkey king who helps Ram) and the ten-headed demon-king Ravana, wear masks, and all the performers are amateurs (see Figure 3.19). Some actors of a specific *Ramlila* claim that their roles are inherited within their families. The performance style is a combination of wordless tableaux and processional drama, in which actors move from place to place with occasional dialogue that most of the devotees will not hear. Some locations are specially constructed for a *lila* while others are actual landmarks in the town.

The Ramnagar *Ramlila* is considered by many participants to be the most powerful. Among the reasons for this distinction is the belief that in Ramnagar, Lord Ram, his

Figure 3.19
The figure of the monkey king Hanuman, who assists Ram and Sita in their trials
and tribulations during a *Ramlila* in Nepal.
Source: Filmlandscape/iStock.

three divine brothers, and his wife (the goddess Sita) are literally present in the bodies
of those who enact them, a perspective similar to that in the Aztec and Hopi ritual
performances we've discussed earlier. Here, five boy actors, spectacularly attired, are
carried around (either by grown men or in palanquins), because the gods' feet must
never touch the ground. At Ramnagar, the entire poem is presented, whereas some of
the other productions used shortened texts. Another reason for the dominance of the
Ramnagar version is the presence of thousands of *sadhus* (wandering, mendicant holy
men) who camp out in Ramnagar for the entire month.

Pilgrims as participants, not spectators
There are many ways that non-actor devotees can participate in the *Ramlila*. For example, when major characters begin to speak, thousands of participants shout a set cheer,
such as when Ram speaks, one hears a collective "*Bol! Raja Ramchandra ki jai!*" ("Say
it! Victory to King Ramchandra!"). Many people carry the entire text with them and
read it aloud along with the actors. At specific times in the performance, they sing out
holy praises of the names of god in repetitive melodies. They offer flowers, sweets, fruits,
or sacred basil leaves to the gods, touch the gods' feet whenever possible, and worship
in other ways. They travel – by bike, boat, bus, horse cart, rickshaw, car, motorcycle
or on foot – both to Ramnagar every day and following the performers as the story

unfolds. Each day's events may take 4–12 hours, and the most devoted participants follow along on foot, ideally barefoot. They act out the drama, playing the roles of crowds and wedding guests, or reciting poems of praise from the rooftops. People create special roles for themselves, such as making and donating flower garlands every year. While most people come on and off, there is a core group who attend every day, basically taking a holiday (which may be part of every day, several days in a row, or even an entire month, if they can afford it). They come dressed in special costumes, wear distinctive holy makeup (red and yellow on their foreheads), carry special staffs, and so on.

As religious studies scholar Linda Hess recounts:

> Again and again, the audience and citizens of Ramnagar act out what Tulsidas narrates. They drop their work and rush to gaze at the gods as they pass through town or village. They move with processions or climb on roofs to see. They illumine triumphant fireworks from their balconies as Ram's chariot returns slowly from exile. Some climb onto the chariot to make offerings. Others decorate their homes and shops just as the citizens of Ayodhya are said to have decorated theirs.
>
> (Hess 2006: 119)

Varieties of participant experience

A deep, personal piety and devotion is at the heart of the *Ramlila,* and motivates devotees to participate annually. In the past, the local Maharaja (the high king who sponsored and supported the performance) and Rama were considered "mirror images of each other, the twin heroes of the Ramnagar Ramlila" (Schechner and Hess 1977: 74). In modern, secular, democratic India, the identification of the Maharaja as upholder of the cosmos is a vestige of the past. Since Indian independence in 1947, kings no longer have any political power at all.

The staging of *Ramlila* for mass audiences is, however, not simply a devotional experience. Given the thousands of pilgrims who inundate locales where the *Ramlila* is staged, the area of its staging becomes an economically important marketplace for traders and vendors. Wherever festival performances are held, and whoever patronizes such performances, pilgrim/devotees must be fed and provided for. Local merchants are more than happy to accommodate the influx of pilgrims.

Many participants have posted videos on the internet, or have written about their experiences at the Ramnagar *Ramlila.* Hess, who has participated in several *Ramlilas,* notes that

> The Ramlila is what you make of it. If you come with devotion, you will see God. If you come with cynicism, you will see little boys in threadbare shorts. If you come looking for snacks, you will see refreshment stands. If you come for a spectacle, you will see fireworks. If you come with hostility or fear, that will also color what you see. "According to the feeling within, each one sees the Lord's form": such a statement admits the psychological nature of the Ramlila *darshan* ["vision" of the holy]. But it is not, as it might be in a different culture, "merely

psychological." It is gloriously, cosmically psychological. Every witness–participant creates the drama in her own mind, and in this drama is at once creator, actor and viewer. Thus the *Ramlila* teaches by experience that our realities are mind-made.

(Hess 2006: 135)

THINKING THROUGH THEATRE HISTORIES: RESURRECTIVE ASPECTS OF COMMEMORATIVE DRAMA

Hess's description of the experience of the *Ramlila* for participants is interesting to consider in light of other commemorative dramas like the Catholic Mass, *Rabinal Achi*, and the *Ta'ziyeh* – all of which understand themselves to be, in some important way, re-enactments rather than representations of the past.

For believers attending the Catholic Mass, the priest does not represent the historical Jesus as would an actor in a realistic drama; rather, he serves as the agent for bringing the living Christ back to material presence in the form of bread and wine, miraculously transubstantiated into the actual body and blood of Christ. In *Rabinal Achi*, the audience is understood to include the ghosts of the individuals portrayed in the action, as well as those of all the performers who ever played for them in the past; these ghosts are conjured forth by the staging of the drama. And in *Ta'ziyeh*, participant-performers do not understand themselves as actors representing characters; rather, they are literally making the past present, through the embodied experience of the pain of the slain Hussein.

For readers of this text who are accustomed to more secular or psychologically realistic kinds of performances, it may be difficult to understand the powerful effects of such performances on their participants. For them, there is no question that this is "only a play." For them, such performances – perhaps not quite literally but not merely symbolically either – have the power to raise the dead, and to bring the living face to face with their God.

Key references

Audio-visual resources

UNESCO provides an overview of the *Ramlila* story in performance, https://youtu.be/89dtCI4oNzU

Books and articles

Hein, N. (1972) *The Miracle Plays of Mathurā*, New Haven, CT: Yale University Press.

Hess, L. (2006) "An Open-Air Ramayana: Ramlila, the Audience Experience," in J. Stratton Hawley and V. Narayanan (eds.) *The Life of Hinduism,* Berkeley: University of California Press, 115–39.

Lutgendorf, P. (1991) *The Life of a Text: Performing the Ramcaritmanas of Tulsidas,* Berkeley: University of California Press.

Schechner, R. and L. Hess. (1977) "The Ramlila of Ramnagar," *The Drama Review* 21(3): 51–82.

Summary

Paul Connerton suggests that "if there is such a thing as social memory, we are likely to find it in commemorative ceremonies" (Connerton 1989: 71). As we have seen in this chapter, these ceremonies often take the form of dramatic performance – and these performances often combine elements of the serious and the comic, the devotional and the carnivalesque, the historic and the contemporary. They were particularly important in the medieval period, before literacy was widespread. We have focused primarily on religious observances that lend themselves to commemorative performances: the Jewish Purim *shpil*, the Islamic *Ta'ziyeh*, India's *Ramlila*, and the many forms of Christian ritual and drama designed to help followers of Christ learn that religion's most important traditions and moral lessons. We also touched on forms of ancestor worship in the Chinese diaspora. Of course, there are also many secular occasions for performances that honor a people's national or cultural heritage, some of which will form the basis of our discussion of theatre in Part II.

Throughout Part I, we have considered a number of performance traditions that depended for their continuance on oral and embodied "acts of transfer," even when a written text served as a basis, a referent, or a result. In so-called "traditional" or culturally homogeneous societies, the repetition of common values through regular, repeated performances serves a key purpose in fostering ongoing cultural cohesion. In the performances discussed in this Part of our textbook, the relationship between religion, power, and performance has been strong, with stagings occurring within sacred and shared civic spaces, under the watchful eye of authorities. Even so, enthusiastic devotees charged with maintaining and preserving cultural values in performance have always also appreciated its potential for transformation and critique.

In Westernized societies, for which life is not necessarily seen as a "structure of celebrated recurrence," the urge to commemorate may arise out of a sense of nostalgia for a lost past (Connerton 1989: 64). For such societies, commemorative performances not only provide compensation for this loss, but keep the past in its proper place, so that the unfolding future can continue to be embraced.

The invention of the printing press will capture some of the energies formerly reserved for preservation and dissemination by means of performance, and the social energies thus released are channeled into an increasingly professionalized class of theatre makers, as we shall see in Part II.

★

Theatre and performance in early print cultures

DOI: 10.4324/9781003185185-6

PART II TIMELINE

DATE	THEATRE AND PERFORMANCE	CULTURE AND COMMUNICATION	POLITICS AND ECONOMICS
1266–1337		Giotto, artist	
1279–1368			Yuan dynasty, China
1279–1654	*Zaju*, China		
c.1300–c.1400	*Ramlila*, India		
c.1300–c.1500		Renaissance era begins in Italy	
1313–c.1600	Passion plays, continental Europe		
1343–1400		Geoffrey Chaucer, writer	
c.1350–1569	Cycle plays, England		
1363–1443	Zeami, actor-playwright		
1368–	*Chuanqi*, China		Ming dynasty, China
c.1374	*Nō*, Japan		
1400–1500	*Rabinal Achi*, Mesoamerica		
1428–1521			Aztec Empire, Central America
c.1440		Movable type (printing press), Europe	
1452–1519		Leonardo da Vinci, artist	
1453			Ottomans capture Constantinople
1456		First printed Bible	
1468–1834			Spanish Inquisition
1475–1564		Michelangelo, artist	
1492			Spanish encounter with the Americas
1492–1898			Spanish colonization of Western Hemisphere
c.1500	Professional theatre companies begin to appear in various European countries		
c.1500–1600	*Kathakali* dance drama, India		
c.1500–c.1650	Classical humanist drama in universities, Europe		

PART II TIMELINE

DATE	THEATRE AND PERFORMANCE	CULTURE AND COMMUNICATION	POLITICS AND ECONOMICS
c.1500–c.1650		Renaissance era spreads throughout Europe	
1517–1648		Protestant Reformation	
1525–			Spanish expeditions to Asia; conquest of Philippines, 1565
1530s–1790s			Ottoman-Habsburg wars
1540–1623		William Byrd, composer	
1545–1648		Catholic Counter-Reformation	
c.1545–c.1800	*Commedia dell'arte*, Europe		
1548–1783	Hôtel de Bourgogne, Paris		
c.1550–	*Kunqu*, China		
c.1550–c.1765	Spanish Catholic drama		
c.1550–c.1750	Court spectacles and masques		
1550–1617	Tang Xianzu, playwright		
1558–1603			Reign of Queen Elizabeth I, England
c.1560–			Bourgeoisie become increasingly significant in Europe
1561		Julius Caesar Scaliger, *Poetics*	
1562–1635	Lope de Vega, playwright		
1564–1616	William Shakespeare, playwright		
1567	Red Lion, earliest English theatre building		
1567–1643		Claudio Monteverdi, composer (some operas)	
1570		Lodovico Castelvetro, *The Poetics of Aristotle*	
c.1572–c.1632	Alexandre Hardy, playwright		
1571			London Stock Exchange founded
1572–1637	Ben Jonson, playwright		
1576	The Theatre, England		
1577–1640		Peter Paul Rubens, artist	

PART II TIMELINE

DATE	THEATRE AND PERFORMANCE	CULTURE AND COMMUNICATION	POLITICS AND ECONOMICS
1585	Teatro Olimpico, first perspective stage scenery, Italy		
1588			English defeat the Spanish Armada
c.1590–c.1720s		Baroque era in Europe	
1598–1613; 1614–1642	The Globe Theatre, England		
c.1600	Okuni's performances begin *kabuki*, Japan		
1600–1681	Pedro Calderón de la Barca, playwright		
1602–1702		First newspapers – none are daily until 1702	
1603–1625			Reign of James I, England
1603–1868			Tokugawa (Edo) period, Japan
1606–1669		Rembrandt, artist	
1606–1684	Pierre Corneille, playwright		
1607			Jamestown, VA: First permanent English settlement in North America
1618–1648			Thirty Years' War, Europe
1618–1672	Madeleine Béjart, actor		
c.1620	Beginnings of neoclassicism		
1622–1673	Molière, playwright		
1625–1642			Reign of Charles I, England
1631–1700	John Dryden, playwright		
1632		Galileo Galilei, *Dialogue Concerning the Two Chief World Systems*	
1632–1687	Jean-Baptiste Lully, composer (many operas)		
1633–1668	Mlle. Du Parc, actor		
1635–1710	Thomas Betterton, actor		

PART II TIMELINE

DATE	THEATRE AND PERFORMANCE	CULTURE AND COMMUNICATION	POLITICS AND ECONOMICS
1637	*Le Cid* controversy establishes neoclassicism in France	René Descartes, *Discourse on the Method*	
1639–1699	Jean Racine, playwright		
1640–1689	Aphra Behn, playwright		
1640–1715	William Wycherley, playwright		
1642–1649	Suppression of theatre in England		English Civil War
1643–1715			Reign of Louis XIV, France
1644–1911			Qing dynasty, China
c.1650	Introduction of chariot-and-pole scenery system		
c.1650–c.1800		Enlightenment era in Europe	
1651		Thomas Hobbes, *Leviathan*	
1653–1729	Michel Baron, actor		
1653–1724	Chikamatsu Monzaemon, playwright		
1656–1743	Ferdinando Galli Bibiena, scenic designer		
1658–1713	Elizabeth Barry, actor		
1659–1695		Henry Purcell, composer	
1660			English Restoration; reign of Charles II (to 1685)
1660–1725		Alessandro Scarlatti, composer (some operas)	
1662	Re-opening of theatres in England; women begin to play female roles		
1662–c.1800	Neoclassicism in England, Germany, Russia		
1668–1733		François Couperin, composer	
1670–1729	William Congreve, playwright		
1694–1778		Voltaire	
c.1720		Beginnings of Enlightenment period in Europe	

Introduction: Performance, printing, and political centralization

Tobin Nellhaus

Photo PI2

A woodblock print of a Western European printing shop.

Source: Wiki, https://commons.wikimedia.org/wiki/File:Press1520.png

Part II covers the years from roughly 1250 to 1770. In the West, this era is sometimes called the "early modern" period, encompassing the **Renaissance**, the **Baroque**, and the **Enlightenment**. It was an age of massive economic, political, and cultural transformations. The system of agricultural production conducted by serfs laboring under a lord's power began to break apart, and the small-scale **capitalist** activities conducted by merchants living in the urban areas grew to economic and political dominance. The feudal political structure of the Middle Ages, which was structured around the lords' military duties and allegiances to kings and queens, was undermined as the royalty wrested power away from the nobility and placed legal, administrative, and sometimes religious functions into its own hands, establishing absolutist monarchies. To achieve both economic and political expansion, several of the absolutist regimes initiated explorations of the rest of the world, ultimately conquering huge parts of other continents and consolidating them within imperial power through colonies. Meanwhile, a major schism arose in Christianity, followed by proliferating religious sects. The invention of the printing press around 1440, a means of mass-producing writing by using movable type (pieces with a single letter or word that could be inserted into the equipment and then removed for reuse), facilitated or even provoked many of these upheavals, along with a variety of others.

In Asia too, the period was notable for political centralization and cultural flourishing. Economically and politically, the historical trajectories of Japan and China were long comparable to Europe's. Japan was in its own late medieval period in the mid-fifteenth century, similarly pairing a political structure founded on a hierarchy of warriors with an economic system based on peasant labor. Following over a century of social turbulence, the Tokugawa period (1603–1868) ushered in strengthened military political power and substantial governmental centralization, while merchants began to thrive. Japan's cultural activity centered on entertainment and leisure aimed at the merchant class (rather than the aristocracy), and some of its best-known cultural forms (including woodblock prints, the *geisha*, and *kabuki*) were born during this era. Japan had significant contact with Western merchants and missionaries, and it continued a practice of absorbing foreign elements into its culture rather than having them forced upon it. But troubled by the possibility of military incursions and ideological contamination, Japan's leaders decided to close off the country from most foreign contact.

Centralization coupled with expansionism began even earlier in China, during the Yuan dynasty (1271–1368). Unlike Europe and Japan, the massive state administration, staffed by highly cultured scholar-bureaucrats, possessed greater social esteem than the military. A new form of Chinese theatre matured during this period: *zaju* (variety play), which combined poetry, singing, dialogue, and dancing. Most of these popular plays were written by scholar-bureaucrats, many of whom had lost their status when the Mongols invaded China and abolished the Imperial Examination. State centralization continued further under the Ming dynasty (1368–1644), which is renowned as one of the finest periods of Chinese art, literature, and theatre. However, the government grew increasingly dependent on the prospering merchant class. A peasant rebellion brought the dynasty to its knees, and in 1644 it was replaced by the Qing dynasty (1644–1911), but China's economic and bureaucratic structures continued on roughly the same path as before.

China and Japan, like Europe, had printing with movable type. In fact movable type was first invented in China, around 1040 (the technique was developed further in Korea), and it was used extensively for bureaucratic functions; but for most other purposes, woodblocks were more practical – even money was printed using woodblocks. In Japan, there was some experimentation with printing with movable type during the early seventeenth century, but afterward woodblock printing again became standard. In neither case, however, did printing with movable type instigate the sort of upheavals it brought to Europe. There are two basic reasons. First, Chinese and Japanese scripts utilize a large number of characters since they are logographic rather than alphabetic (Japanese has two syllabic scripts as well). Thus printing with movable type required tens of thousands of type pieces, entailing a considerable financial investment. Printing with woodblocks was often more sensible because one needed to carve only the characters actually used. Second, all stages of printing in Asia were performed manually: paper was pressed on to the inked type or woodblock by hand, and sometimes rubbing was necessary to fully copy the page. In Europe, however, pages were printed by using a machine to press the inked metal onto the paper, which involved less time and labor. As media theorist Marshall McLuhan observed, printing probably gave Europe "the first uniformly repeatable commodity, the first assembly-line, and the first mass-production" (1962: 124). Printing in Europe may well be the earliest type of industrial capitalism.

Within theatre, the era covered by Part II is marked by three major transitions. One was the shift from performances connected with special events (such as festivals and commemorative occasions) or performed by touring companies, to professional theatre companies playing on a regular basis at permanent sites. Such companies arose in Europe, Japan, and China, often along with urbanization, which brought a large enough potential audience that permanent residence could make touring supplemental or unnecessary. By the end of the seventeenth century, theatre in many parts of the world had ceased being performed in the open air and moved indoors, partly to increase exclusivity, and partly because theatregoing became an ordinary leisure activity: during the daytime people worked, took care of their business, or tended to other duties, leaving the night free for entertainment. Chapter 4 provides an overview of these developments.

The two other major changes occurred only in Europe. As we saw in Chapter 3, in the Middle Ages, characters tended to be stereotypes, such as allegorical figures or simplified personages from religious history. Starting in the late sixteenth century, that approach to characterization began to be replaced by the creation of characters with a personal history and interior life – the bare bones of what would become psychological realism. (Some *kabuki* "domestic" and historical plays had similar qualities.) Likewise, the tradition of actors playing multiple roles was superseded by having each actor perform only one role. Scenery shifted away from generalized or stylized settings, and became more elaborate, taking strides toward the lifelike depiction of places. In France, a dispute on dramatic form arose, and when the royal administration intervened, the resulting decision set "the rules" for dramaturgy throughout the European continent and to some extent in England as well. As Chapter 5 explains, these changes were closely tied to the formation of **print culture**.

Finally, during the seventeenth century, in tandem with their centralization of power in other areas, the **absolutist** monarchs of France and England began to wield control over theatre, in ways that reverberated through the following century. They licensed two or three specific companies, giving them not just favor but even exclusive rights to perform in the capital. Theatre buildings were designed to give the ruler special treatment – not just a particularly favorable view of the stage, but also placed in easy view by the other spectators.

The fact that France's chief minister/cardinal, who managed the reins of power, interceded in a quarrel over dramatic structure demonstrates the extent to which absolutism shaped theatre. Although the Japanese and Chinese governments also licensed theatres and imposed restrictions, these were generally meant to prevent disruptions in society, rather than to control aesthetics and ideology. Thus even though monarchs in Europe, China, and Japan all centralized power, only in Europe did the theatre become both controlled by and an actual instrument of the state. Yet, at the same time that the French state set the "rules" for good theatre in Paris and beyond – they even influence playwriting today, whether or not playwrights are aware of them – within the palaces the king and his retinue blithely ignored those rules for their own flamboyant entertainments, including opera. Chapter 6 discusses these developments and more.

The notion that plays should follow certain strict rules for dramaturgy and staging may seem odd from a modern perspective, when originality is prized and "breaking the rules" is occasionally touted as essential to art itself. But even though the rules were purportedly derived from Aristotle (in actuality, distorting his ideas), his authority didn't automatically secure playwrights' obedience – in fact the rules were controversial until royal power stepped in. So something more was afoot when playwrights debated the rules.

The development of the rules was connected to the new approach to dramatic characters, actors' change to performing a single role, and the design of illusionistic scenery. At the heart of these trends was a new concept of realism – or rather, of reality – and how one obtains knowledge. This was the age of the "scientific revolution," in which the source of knowledge was deemed to be the direct, individual observation of nature. Such observations eventually disproved various classical theories of nature, many of which derived from Aristotle. However, when the rules were first articulated – in Lodovico Castelvetro's commentary on *The Poetics*, published in 1570 – Aristotle's authority was still almost wholly unquestioned. But how Aristotelian were the rules?

Aristotle aimed mainly to describe drama, employing some "best examples" sometimes leading to recommendations. It was Castelvetro and his followers who contorted those descriptions into requirements, often twisting Aristotle's words in the process. But there is more to the difference than that. Castelvetro's argument has three striking features. First, it declared that the purpose of literature is to delight "the crude multitude and the common people" (Castelvetro 1570: 109). Second, it insistently constricted the imagination; for example, it asserted that it's impossible to write tragedies about a fictional king, only a real one, for a tragedy about a fictional king would "sin against the manifest truth" (Castelvetro 1570: 112). Third, it justified the rules by claiming that the ignorant commoners would never accept the notion that (say) several days had passed when the performance lasted merely a couple of hours (Carlson 1993: 48–9). Clearly, the rules' justification had nothing to do with Aristotle, who hadn't said any of these things. Instead, the basic theory was that drama (or at least serious drama) must only encompass what an individual can perceive or read from concrete reality.

So, even though the rules claimed their authority from Aristotle, their underlying logic was founded on the same transformed concepts of knowledge and truth, hinging on the notion that reality must be observable and observed, that drove the scientific revolution – a revolution that included social conflict as well as ideas. The blatantly elitist emphasis on spectators' ignorance assumed that the upper classes possessed a superior type of knowledge, even though paradoxically the rules were rationalized by the lower classes' supposed lack of knowledge and imagination. In other words, the elite required its own imagination to be restricted to what it believed the lower classes could understand, as classical authority ostensibly required. Both the rules' elitism and their prescriptiveness reveal an upper-class determination to establish those ideas throughout the culture. The alterations in characterization, acting, and staging arose from the same basic concepts. As Chapter 5 will explain, those shifts emerged from the changes in communication practices brought by printing.

The early modern period was not the first time Europeans wrestled with the connection between theatre and truth. As discussed in the introduction to Part I, the connection lay at the heart of Plato's antitheatricality, because in his view theatre purveyed falsehoods and illusions. The issue would repeatedly arise again, such as in the nineteenth century with the movement known as Naturalism (to be discussed in Chapter 10). And Europe was not the only land where the question was ever considered important. For instance, as we pointed out in Chapter 2, the *rasa-bhava* aesthetic theory of early Sanskrit theatre relied on a particular understanding of reality, and *nō* had firm foundations in Buddhist philosophy. In fact, many theatre scholars today would agree that *all* theatre and drama – no matter where, when, or how performed – invoke concepts of reality, knowledge, and truth. Part II presents the history of theatre during an era when the use of printing in European society radically changed those ideas, but the issues are ever-present under the surface of performance.

★

CHAPTER 4

Secular and professional theatre, 1250–1650

Tamara Underiner

Contributors: Carol Fisher Sorgenfrei,
Daphne Lei and Tobin Nellhaus

From the fourteenth to seventeenth century, theatre outside of religious festivals, churches, temples, courts, and universities grew in popularity, eventually coming to serve as a livelihood for playwrights, performers, and theatre managers. In this chapter, we focus on the kind of theatre in Asia and Europe for which entertainment was at least as important as moral instruction, and for which troupes increasingly had to compete for audiences. To attract them, theatre artists deepened and extended their craft into new genres of drama and performance requiring new performance skills and new types of playhouses. Women's roles were showcased more (even if women themselves were still excluded from the stage in some countries). Enterprising managers developed new business models to sustain their companies. And as we'll see, everywhere that a secular and professional theatre developed, so too did suspicion about its power, so we'll also discuss the numerous forms of repression that accompanied these developments: legal or religious edicts against theatre in general and actors in particular, censorship of plays, and numerous anti-theatrical regulations.

Professional theatre developed in Europe during this period mainly in its populous, concentrated urban centers. Of course, the introduction of the printing press played a key role in European theatre developments: theatre scholar Julie Stone Peters observes that "after print, performance was never the same" (Peters 2000: 4). As more books became available and literacy increased, so did material available for adaptation into stage plays. The possibilities for dramatic exploration of secular topics began to multiply, in plays written mostly by men eager to draw on literary sources encountered during their time at university. In Europe, the forms these plays took eventually led to recognizable genres drawing on classic notions of tragedy and comedy, but also expanding into tragicomedy, pastorals or romances, and farce – as well as various combinations of each.

Print culture was also important in East Asia (China, Korea, and Japan), though with different impacts. Woodblock printing was well-established by the tenth century in China for the government-administered distribution of classics as well as the private printing of literary texts and Buddhist *sutras* (words of wisdom). Movable type printing was invented in China in the eleventh century; however, it did not revolutionize printing in China as it did in Europe, partially because the Chinese writing system requires thousands of ideographs, compared to the roughly two dozen letters of the Roman alphabet. In general, in China and Japan, playwrights were part of the literati circle or elite class, and plays were also read as literature. Over time, by the eighteenth century, famous actors eventually came to assume a more central role in Chinese and Japanese performances; this was also true in Europe, although playwrights' prestige and power also began to rise.

The period covered in this chapter overlaps with those of the chapters before and after it. This calls attention to an issue facing all historians: that of chronological periodization, a topic we explore in our "Thinking through Theatre Histories" box. The key differences among these three chapters are thematic rather than chronological. Chapter 3 focused on theatre and performance that was tied to some special occasion in the religious or civic calendar, or was used for the purpose of religious or moral instruction. Chapter 5 will focus on the development of print culture and its effects on the aesthetics and theories of theatre in the European Renaissance. In this chapter, we are more concerned with the "business" of the theatre, the various strategies undertaken to ensure its success – including the development of permanent playing spaces and an increased presence of female characters, actors, and audience members – and various countermeasures taken to restrict, regulate, and sometimes censor it. We also consider the opportunities the theatre provided for creating new social occasions and relations, and the plethora of new performance forms that emerged. We pay particular attention to Yuan *zaju* (variety plays) and later *kunqu* (*kun* opera) of China, the *commedia dell'arte* of Italy (a physical form of comedy which influenced theatre throughout Europe), and the *bunraku* (puppet plays) and *kabuki* (theatre) of Japan. Our case study considers the essential *kabuki* role of the *onnagata*, typically a male specialist in female roles.

THINKING THROUGH THEATRE HISTORIES: THE PROBLEM OF PERIODIZATION

How do theatre historians tell the story of theatre's long and varied past? One way is to break it up into various periods (hence the term "**periodization**"), tracing key moments of theatre's transformation and innovation as an art form over time. In most resulting historiographies, the focus tends toward important contributions made by or within different national traditions that characterize the period or age. Were we to adopt such an approach within this Part, we'd focus a great deal more than we do on France's neoclassical drama; on England's Elizabethan theatre; on Spain's Golden Age of drama; and on the various "renaissances" throughout the European continent. As you might infer, a strict chronology can lead to a kind of regional bias.

Other strategies then become useful. One is to show how theatre develops alongside other larger societal changes or movements, an approach this textbook takes, even as we acknowledge the key innovations described above. Specifically, we focus on how changes in theatre are related to changes in communication practices and also to a shift in cultural dominance from orality to literacy enabled by it. In this particular chapter, for example, we show how the technology of printing led to a wider circulation of texts available for both reading and staging, which, in turn, contributed to the growth of professionalization in the theatre.

But from a more global perspective, this approach does not resolve all problems of periodization. For example, China and Korea developed movable print long before Europe. In Japan, writing was introduced centuries after it appeared in other parts of the world, and was largely used by the elite and administrative classes, which influenced its literary theatre. So although changes in modes of communication did occur throughout the world in basically the same order, these changes often took place at different times in different cultures, in ways that don't make for easy generalization or global comparison.

Therefore, we adopt an additional strategy: that of a thematic organization, which helps us to draw comparisons, contrasts, and contextual insights from site to site within a given general time period, allowing for differential local timelines within. (The chapter titles of the Part give an idea of their principal organizing themes.) Thus, when we consider the histories of theatre throughout the world, we can acknowledge that theatre exists in various cultures in various ways, following its own timelines. We can recognize each culture's theatre tradition both for its deep roots and for the newer influences it may borrow from external sources. Respecting the timelines of various theatre traditions around the world within a thematic schema allows us to combine, as we do in this chapter, an examination of both European and different Asian theatres in ways other organizational schemes cannot.

Developments in Chinese drama, theatre, and performance

A unique confluence of circumstances, both cultural and political, led to the emergence of China's first golden age of drama in the thirteenth and fourteenth centuries. Recall from Chapter 2 that literacy had been important for the elite class starting with the Han dynasty (which ruled from 202 BCE to 220 CE with one brief interruption). Realms of literature, politics, and philosophy intersected; literary talent and skills (symbolic capital) could lead to actual financial capital. In addition to embracing such foreign inspirations as the transformation texts from India, the Song dynasty (Northern Song, 920–1127; Southern Song, 1127–1279) also cultivated its own fertile ground for theatre. For example, the maturity of a new poetic form, *ci*, brought Tang poetry much closer to singing (*qu*), and many urban entertainment centers became well-established. A thirteenth-century document records 280 titles of *zaju*, showing its popularity, although no scripts survived from the Song dynasty.

When the Mongols conquered China and founded the Yuan dynasty (1279–1368), it was the first time all of China was controlled by an ethnically non-Han government. These foreign military rulers distrusted the classically educated Confucian scholars and abolished the Imperial Examinations for a few decades, cutting off the familiar path from literature to politics. Many displaced and discontented literati invested their literary talent and energy in another venue – theatre. With the mature entertainment industry inherited from the Song, these Yuan playwrights ushered in the first golden age of Chinese theatre.

The dominant Yuan theatre, *zaju* ([zah-jyu], variety play) developed in the north, featuring song, dance, monologues and dialogues, and even farce and fighting. They typically consisted of four acts and a "wedge" (occasionally two "wedges"). Wedges are demi-acts that serve as a prologue or an interlude. Most plays only feature one singing role (the rest are speaking roles), so a play can be categorized as male or female, depending on the singing role. Generally, each act features music composed in a single musical mode with single-rhymed verse arias, though these modes and rhymes might change for each of the four acts. Spoken parts are largely in prose, except for the poetic recitation. Both men and women performed, and crossdressing was common. Distinctive role types were already developed: the major categories are male, female, *jing* (clownish or minor roles with distinctive features), and many sub-categories. Unlike modern American musicals which are collaborations between lyricists and composers, Chinese playwrights had comprehensive knowledge of music: they adapted existing tunes, worked with musicians and even wrote new music themselves. None of the tunes survived except for their titles. There are 170 extant Yuan *zaju* texts from a collection compiled in 1616; the 30 plays surviving from the Yuan period contain very few spoken parts so they only offer a partial picture. In other words, most Yuan *zaju* we have today probably had been "modernized" in the early seventeenth century. Performances took place in urban theatres or teahouses as commercial enterprises and sometimes as part of temple or court ritual occasions.

The Register of Ghosts (*Luguibu,* written around 1330) documents many Yuan *zaju* playwrights, including the renowned playwrights Guan Hanqing (c.1241–1320), Bai Pu (1226–c.1306), Ma Zhiyuan (1250–1321), Zheng Guanzu (c.1260–c.1320), and Ji Junxiang (fl. 1260–1290). Yuan playwrights often drew on literary and historical tales and popular legends. Two major clusters of stories and legends – *Water Margin* (originated in about twelfth century) and *Three Kingdoms* (originated in the third century) – were formalized into long novels during the Yuan dynasty. These familiar stories, which had similar function as the *Ramayana* and *Mahabharata* in India, provided rich source material and inspiration for performances from Yuan *zaju* to later genres, even beyond China, such as in Japanese animation. Yuan *zaju* contains both highly literate and highly entertaining elements, with diverse themes ranging from romantic adventures and supernatural rescues to moral stories.

Political allegory had long been a tradition in poetry, and Yuan literati found in theatre a new venue to express dissent. Guan Hanqing's *Injustice Done to Dou E* (*Dou E Yuan,* also known as *Snow in Midsummer*) perfectly describes the distaste for the new Mongol government. Dou E is a young widow who is framed for murder by a man she refused to marry. Since the court is corrupt, she is set to be executed. Before her death, she makes a chilling curse:

> If Dou E were indeed innocent, when the knife strikes and my head falls off, none of my warm blood would be spilled on the ground but fly onto the white cloth ... Heaven would send down three feet of snow to cover the corpse of Dou E . . . and Chuzhou [where the story takes place] would suffer three years of drought.
>
> Guan, V: 1511

Three years later, her ghost appears in the city under her curse to help her long-lost father, now a high-ranking official, to reopen her case and bring justice to the world.

This play reflects a complicated system in which gender, wealth, and power are intertwined. Dou E's father sold her when she was little, in exchange for the money for his journey to the capital for the Imperial Examination. The justice brought from his investigation (which will also end the curse) will further advance his political career. The multiple exchange and transformation of capital by trafficking and sacrificing a girl/woman addresses the power imbalance in the Yuan patriarchal society. It further may imply a connection between the corrupt government in the drama and the current Mongol regime, and Dou E's chastity can be compared to the resistance of the Han Chinese.

Another famous *zaju* known to the West is *Orphan of Zhao* by Ji Junxiang (thirteenth century), a story about the sacrifice of countless people to preserve an orphan – the only survivor of the Zhao clan – and the orphan's ultimate revenge. Since Zhao is the family name of the previous Song dynasty, the determination to save the orphan to restore a Han regime is a powerful political allegory. *Orphan of Zhao* is also the first known Chinese play introduced to the West, made famous by Voltaire as *Orphan of China* (*L'Ophelin de la Chine*, 1759, discussed in Chapter 6).

An important mural (dated 1324 (Figure 4.1)) preserved in Shanxi province of northern China revealed crucial visual and performance information about Yuan *zaju*. Above the image, a text (not included in the illustration) describes a performance of the actress with the stage name Zhongduxiu. The painting shows both male and female actors. Zhongduxiu (standing in the middle of the front row) wears a male official outfit; some actors clad in male outfits showed tiny feet (bound feet for Han women was a tradition that started in the Song dynasty). Some actors had exaggerated makeup and fake beards and some held props such as fans. The musicians, standing in the back, are in Mongolian outfit, which indicates that despite the general change of dress code in daily life under foreign regimes (in the Yuan and Qing dynasties), the stage remained a relatively timeless Han Chinese world. The costume, makeup, and props all bear a high resemblance to traditional Chinese theatre today.

Moreover, historically, the Han worldview situated themselves as the center state surrounded by non-Han ethnic groups viewed as inferior, "barbaric" others (the Chinese word for China, *zhongguo,* literally means "central state" or "middle kingdom"). Most Yuan *zaju* tells Han stories; however, minor "barbarian" characters (played by Han actors) often appear as racial caricatures speaking gibberish (invented Mongolian – think of the "low others" we discussed in the last chapter's case study). This tradition continued into later drama, even when Mongols were no longer the contemporary "barbarians," such as in the Qing dynasty under the Manchurian government. Going to theatre under a foreign regime was itself a political act.

The growth of kunqu

Although the Yuan *zaju* performance tradition eventually faded, its influence remained in many later genres. Today, **kunqu** [kwun chyu] (or *kun* opera) is the best genre for us to trace the earlier theatrical traditions. *Kunqu* originated from *chuanqi* [chwan chee] (marvel plays), which continued the tradition of *nanxi* [nahn shee] Southern Drama, which started around the twelfth century. Among all *chuanqi* forms, *kunqu* was the dominant from the late fourteenth to the sixteenth century. Focusing on beautiful singing, elegant poetry, and graceful dancing, *kunqu* was performed at public venues such as temples, teahouses, and brothels, and in private residences of wealthy aristocrats. Many believe that the ideal staging of *kunqu* is in

Figure 4.1
Portion of a Guangsheng Temple mural in Shanxi province (dated 1324) depicting a Yuan *zaju* performance. It shows the conventions of acting, costume, makeup, props, and musical instruments of the Yuan dynasty.

Source: CPA Media Pte Ltd/Alamy Stock Photo.

an elegant garden in a private residence for the selected audience. Many aristocratic families supported their own troupes of about 12 actors, even buying children and training them. These private troupes often maintained a higher level of sophistication and artistic skill than those performing in public venues.

As in *zaju*, *kunqu* featured male and female performers, crossdressing, and the tradition of recognizable role types: male, female, *jing* (painted face), clown, and many sub-categories. *Kunqu* actors also donned the timeless Han costume, with both real and symbolic props, with simple or no sets. The stage could be a square carpet, or a raised platform, with the audience on one side or surrounding the actors. *Chuanqi* plays are much longer and have complicated plots compared with *zaju*.

Probably the most famous *kunqu* play is *The Peony Pavilion* (*Mudanting*, 1598) by Tang Xianzu (1550–1617). In it, a young woman named Du Liniang dies of love for a young man she has only met in a dream. After her death, the dream lover – who is actually a real person – sees her self-portrait and immediately falls in love. With the intervention of gods and sorcery, he travels to the underworld and succeeds in having her resurrected. After some plot twists, the lovers triumph and harmony is restored. The long play has 55 scenes and no records indicate that it was ever done in its entirety. The most performed scene is "The Interrupted Dream," which dramatizes the romantic rendezvous of the young lovers in Du Liniang's dream.

Kunqu, like most traditional art forms, declined in modern times, but has enjoyed something of a renaissance since the late twentieth century. In 1999, a 22-hour version of *Peony*, which claimed to be "complete and traditional," was directed by Chen Shi-Zheng (1963–) and presented over three days at New York's Lincoln Center. The audacious attempt drew applause from the general public but criticism from *kunqu* connoisseurs as it was neither complete nor traditional. In 1998, Peter Sellars (1957–) directed the most experimental *Peony Pavilion* with parallel lovers (traditional and contemporary), multimedia, modern dance, and music by Tan Dun (1957–), sung in Western opera style), and the celebrated *kunqu* actress Hua Wenyi (1941–2022) performing the most famous scenes in modern dress. In 2001, *kunqu* became the first Chinese theatre genre to receive the status of UNESCO's "Masterpiece of Oral and Intangible Heritage of Humanity" and Hua Wenyi was honored at the White House.

The version with the most significant and long-lasting impact was *The Peony Pavilion: The Young Lovers' Edition* by Taiwanese writer Kenneth Hsien-yung Pai (Bai Xianyong, 1937–) in 2004. Pai, best known for his short stories and novels, is also a *kunqu* aficionado. His *Peony* brought together illustrious *kunqu* masters with younger actors, as well as transnational philanthropical support from China, Taiwan, and Hong Kong, and took place over three evenings (three hours each night). In the following twenty years, the extremely successful production toured around the world with over 500 performances, many of which took place in university campuses, successfully cultivating a young generation of *kunqu* lovers.

Secular performance and the emergence of professional theatre in Europe

During the European Renaissance, it was common to find people offering their singing, dancing, or storytelling talents in return for coin, performing on street corners and at village fairs, in princely banquet halls and in local taverns. But some scholars locate the precursors

Figure 4.2

"Mountebank distributing his wares on the stage." Some scholars speculate that men who hawked remedies on street corners and, later, stages, were the forerunners to modern professional actors. Artist unknown.

Source: Hulton Archive/Getty Images.

of the modern professional actor and actress in an unlikelier source: street mountebanks (also called charlatans) who sold remedies on street corners, often accompanied by a musician, and sometimes by a female accomplice who helped to demonstrate the effectiveness of the potions on offer (Figure 4.2). They enticed buyers through storytelling and feats of magic and physical prowess, making a living year-round as much from their performing talents as from the dubious health benefits of their products. (For a lively theatrical introduction to such a character in a play from this period, read Ben Jonson's *Volpone* [1606].)

But it was not possible to make a living through the more complex arts of formal theatre, involving casts acting out plots either scripted or improvised, until the middle of the sixteenth century. It was then that theatre companies began to form, often under royal or ducal **patronage**, and permanent theatre structures were built to showcase plays all year long, not just during religious occasions. The seeds for such theatre were likely planted in the prior century, when secular themes began to be introduced into religious and moral drama.

Religious plays such as the Corpus Christi cycles remained very popular well into the sixteenth century, especially in Catholic countries like Spain, Italy, and France. But theatre also began to be developed for occasions outside of the Church calendar as the **Protestant Reformation** took hold after 1517. This religious movement, discussed in more detail in Chapter 5, ushered in new varieties of Christianity that opposed the representations of divinity in any form; some opposed theatre altogether (notably the Puritans and the Quakers). In England, religious and political controversy was the order of the day; as a result, Elizabeth I (born 1533; reigned 1558–1603) issued decrees constraining plays with religious and political subjects, ultimately succeeding in suppressing the cycle plays during the 1560s and 1570s. (Nevertheless, Shakespeare seems to be remembering a performance of a religious play – the *Play of Herod* – in Hamlet's advice to the players.)

The morality plays, lacking representations of God and Jesus, could more readily be converted to post-Reformation purposes, and contributed to the development of secular plays, written by individual authors for professional theatres, well into the **Elizabethan era**. By the early sixteenth century, there were plays on frankly secular themes such as the importance of learning, nature, and so forth. For example, John Heywood's *The Play of the Weather* (published 1533) features a series of petitioners asking the Roman god Jupiter to provide the weather best suited to their needs. While such a plot may seem rather trivial, medieval studies scholar Pamela M. King (2012) argues that the play was actually a political satire about a tense moment in the reign of Henry VIII. Other morality plays were used to expose the alleged hypocrisies of the Catholic Church. But even in strongly Catholic countries, secular theatre developed in response to both increasing urbanization and new discoveries about the classical past, made possible by the rise of print culture.

In northern France and the Netherlands, "**chambers of rhetoric**" offer an example of a more clearly secular genre of performance we might call "pre-professional." These were societies devoted to the literary and dramatic arts, originally associated with the Church, which were pressed into service to help organize religious festivals, the entries of royal personages into the cities, and the performance of plays on festive occasions. Located in the urban centers, the chambers drew their members from the professional, merchant, and artisan classes, who were literate in French, Dutch, and/or Flemish. They originally met to exchange work; soon they began to hold literary competitions among themselves and, eventually, among different chambers, which then expanded to dramatic contests for public performance. There were prizes across a number of categories, including best play, best farcical entertainment, best actor, best singer, etc., suggesting an increased attention to the quality of the craft associated with theatre performance and production.

In Dutch-speaking countries, these competitions were called *landjuweelen* [LAWHNT- yu-vay-lehn] ("jewels of the land"); the earliest of these was recorded in 1413, among six societies performing plays about the Holy Sacrament. They were typically held in large halls or public squares, to enthusiastic crowds; today, the village of Ruigoord in the Netherlands has revived the practice in an annual five-day *landjuweel* festival. Over time, the organization and artistry of these societies became ever more professionalized, with administrative and theatrical duties being differentiated among directors, writers, promoters, costumers – and fools, who could be counted on to entertain the crowds in processions and to perform in a chamber's farces. Few full-length scripts remain, but one features a husband whose wife is seduced by the local priest; other more serious dramas took on higher themes of the day, including the newer forms of Protestant theology sweeping through Europe. Such elements caused the plays to come under the scrutiny of Church authorities, especially during the **Counter-Reformation** (the period in which Catholic authorities sought to suppress the Protestant reforms, between 1545 and 1648). Some chambers were more radical than others in this regard, but historian Gary Waite (2000) suggests a connection between the chambers of rhetoric, theatre, and the growth of Protestant activism in the Low Countries.

Farces were another common form of secular performance, particularly in France. One of the most popular was *La Farce de maître Pierre Pathelin* (*The Farce of Master Peter Pathelin*), from the mid-fifteenth century (Figure 4.3). Like most medieval farces, it features a small cast of characters, in this case focusing on a lawyer and a merchant. Often the farces centered on professions, relationships (among family members, neighbors, servants, and illicit lovers), and various stereotypical figures who are driven by some basic need or desire, such as money, sex, or a cure for a disease. (Of course, these weren't unique to medieval French theatre; recall our Chapter 2 discussions of ancient Roman comedy and Japanese *kyōgen*.)

Also important for the development of theatre in France were the traveling troupes, who often performed indoors at the Hôtel de Bourgogne (described in more detail below), and maintained a repertory dominated by farces combined with a smattering of serious plays. Some of the farce actors became famous in their own day but usually performed under stage names such as Gros-Guillaume (Fat William) (Robert Guérin 1554–1634), Jodelet (Julien Bedeau c.1590–1660), and Valleran le Conte (?–1613). These men, under Valleran's leadership, became the first known *comédiens du roi* (King's Players) in 1598.

Figure 4.3

Scene from the 1457 French farce, *La Farce de maître Pierre Pathelin* (*The Farce of Master Peter Pathelin*), in which the self-proclaimed lawyer Pathelin cajoles a clothier into selling him six yards of cloth on credit, with no means of paying him back. Pathelin will eventually face the clothier in court, defending a shepherd who has been stealing the clothier's sheep, but his clever defense backfires on him.

Source: Wiki, https://commons.wikimedia.org/wiki/File:Pathe-lin_1.png

The *commedia dell'arte* in Italy and its influence in Europe

The scripted farces had much in common with another form of traveling professional theatre that emerged in this period from Italy, the **commedia dell'arte** [kohm-MAY-dee-ah dehl-AHR-tey]. In the *commedia*, however, the action was largely improvised, by troupes of professional actors highly trained in movement. They based their performances on a repertoire of scenarios revolving around stories of love and money. Their influence was felt throughout Europe and elsewhere, eventually making its way into scripted drama as well;

even today, there are *commedia* troupes whose rigorous training regimes are based in techniques developed some four centuries ago.

There is no exact English translation of the term *commedia dell'arte*, a form which most
scholars trace back to the middle of the sixteenth century. (The term first appears in print
some two centuries later, in Carlo Goldoni's 1750 play *Il Comico*.) The term *arte*, in Italian as
well as in older English, can refer to a professional level of craft or technique, so it is usually
left untranslated. *Commedia dell'arte* is distinguished by a number of features:

- Improvised playing based on a repertory of standardized plots, mostly having to do with
  matters of love and intrigue.
- A combination of stock characters, masked and unmasked according to type.
- The use of *lazzi* [LAH-dzee], or highly physical stage routines and comic bits that were
  often associated with the particular prowess of individual performers.
- Mixed-gender casts and companies.
- Professional companies with increasingly formal operations, providing the principal
  livelihood for their members, who performed year-round throughout Italy and Europe.

Origin theories

Although hugely influential on nearly every other European theatre tradition, no one can
say with complete certainty where *commedia dell'arte* itself came from – or if indeed it had
a single, linear genealogy. More likely a number of factors contributed to its development:
the masked, improvised comedy of the Roman Atellan farces (discussed in Chapter 2)
kept alive by traveling mimes; the jugglers, acrobats, singers, dancers, and mountebanks of
public life in medieval Europe; the circulation of plots and characters of ancient Roman
comedies that were often also the subject of the learned Italian drama (**commedia erudita** [kohm-MAY-dee-ah eh-roo-DEE-tah]); and the farces of the earlier sixteenth century
(which flourished in Italy as elsewhere throughout Europe from 1500 to 1550).

If its deeper origins are disputed, many scholars pinpoint the date of 25 February 1545
as the official "birthday" of the *commedia*. That was the date, in Padua, Italy, when director/
manager Ser Maphio signed a letter of incorporation establishing his troupe of performers
as the first known commercial theatre company, organized under a sharing system. Until
then, there was, literally, "no business like show business" as we know it today. The date of 25
February is still celebrated internationally as "*Commedia dell'arte* Day."

Conventionalized plots, individualized lazzi

Because the *commedia* was an improvised form, it relied on standard scenarios that were
adapted in countless ways to accommodate topical themes and local realities, as well as to
capitalize on the talents of individual performers. Before long, professional actresses took the
stage. Vincenza Armani, who appeared in 1566, is the earliest documented, but it is likely
she had predecessors. With actresses performing, scenarios turned from conflicts between
masters and servants to those of romantic intrigue.

A typical *commedia* scenario, like the Roman comedies that may have inspired it, featured
two lovers who were prevented from being together, usually by a parental figure, sometimes
inadvertently by the **innamorato** [in-nah-moh-RAH-toh (m), -tah (f), -tee (pl)], or young
male lead. To overcome this obstacle, comical servants (called **zanni** [ZAHN-nee]) would

be enlisted, or sometimes the *innamorata* in disguise enacted a plot of her own. This general plot outline was often complicated by subplots that could themselves be "dizzyingly complex, involving disguises, misunderstandings, plots within plots, impersonations, and magical deceptions" (Henke 2003: 14).

In addition to the masked servant characters and the young lovers (who played their parts unmasked), the other masked characters of the *commedia* included their parents and a variety of conspirators or unsuitable lovers who provided the central obstacles to their happiness. Isabella Andreini (1562–1604), of the Gelosi troupe, was the most famous of the *innamorati;* over time, young female leads came to be called, simply, "Isabellas." Of the *zanni*, the most famous was Arlecchino, introduced by Tristano Martinelli (c.1555–1630), whose characteristic motley costume would later be codified as "Harlequin" in seventeenth-century France. The elder characters were called **vecchi** [VEHK-kee] – usually men but sometimes their ambitious wives as well (see Figure 4.4). They included:

Figure 4.4

Late sixteenth-century engraving showing three stock characters from the *commedia dell'arte* – from left, Arlecchino, Zanni the cuckold, and Pantalone – serenading an unseen lady in her house on the right.

Source: National Museum Stockholm, G2189-2272-1904.

- Pantalone, a wealthy merchant with a healthy appetite for food and conversation, quick with advice, jealous of his fortune, and often after an inappropriately younger woman;
- Dottore, a learned, lustful philosopher in love with the sound of his own voice, given to feats of virtuosic, if fatuous or even nonsensical punning, alliteration, and other forms of wordplay;
- Capitano, the soldier whose arrogance outstripped his achievements (but who could, at times, be seriously in love);
- Pulcinella, the crafty beak-nosed and hump-backed clown who became "Punch" in the British "Punch and Judy" shows; and
- courtesans and procuresses who served as temptations and distractions for the *innamorati*.

A variety of bit characters drawn from other genres like the pastoral, tragicomedy, and even tragedy rounded out the cast, which could represent a dozen characters or more.

The various plots and subplots of the *commedia* can be considered scaffolds upon which to display the physical and verbal virtuosity of the most popular players, which they cultivated as their particular repertoire of *lazzi*. These bits often bore little relationship to the main action (indeed, they frequently interrupted it, but audiences loved them). One actor, for example, was known for his ability to do a somersault while carrying a full glass of wine, without a spill. Another could do whole scenes while standing on his hands. Acrobatics of all sorts, pantomimes, juggling feats, and elaborate word play were the order of the day.

Verbal improvisation in relation to literacy
Within the basic situations provided by the plot scenarios, all the actors knew very well the relationships between their characters and the others in the troupe, and could draw upon repertoires of praise and compliments for some of them, and insults, threats, and curses for others, depending upon the nature of those relations. It is important to remember that, although improvised, these speeches were themselves very formulaic and rhetorically coded, based on materials carefully recorded in the actors' "commonplace books." These books were compendiums of important passages from longer works that literate people compiled and consulted for personal edification and as inspiration for writing essays and speeches. Thus, although the *commedia* was and is known as an art of improvisation rather than textual interpretation, it was not because the actors couldn't themselves read. They were, in fact, highly literate, often more so than their audiences, and they drew on a variety of written and printed sources, everything from the *commedia erudita* to the latest jokes circulating in the city-state. One **actor-manager** of a *commedia* troupe, Flaminio Scala (1552–1624), published his troupe's scenarios – a risky venture for the time, since that meant any other troupe could appropriate them. His collection of 50 scenarios, published in 1611, tells us much about the state of the *commedia* in his time.

As a type of performance based in physicality and orality, the *commedia* nevertheless maintained a strong relationship to literacy and textuality; it was a form that combined low comedy with literary aspirations. But over the course of the seventeenth century, "a shortage of sufficiently educated *innamorati* and a large number of very talented servants and their prominence in performances tipped the scales in favor of the servants," and by the eighteenth-century *commedia* had grown somewhat stale (Erenstein 1989: 133). As a result, the Italian playwright Carlo Goldoni (1707–1793) tried to "elevate" the *commedia* by bringing the lovers back to center stage, reducing the number of comic masked players to four – and scripting the action in full. (We discuss Goldoni further in Chapter 7.)

Making a living through commedia

Commedia historian Robert Henke (2003) identifies a continuum of business models through which *commedia* performers made their livelihoods. Most enjoyed some form of patronage by a ducal sponsor. Some individual performers may originally have performed regularly in the same designated time and spot, but without a formal contract with their patron; many others were part of *commedia* troupes established as fraternal societies under the seal of a duke. (Such seals functioned as passports and protected performers from imprisonment as vagabonds when they toured in Europe.) Troupes performed at courts and, often, in customs houses, where their audiences came from the growing merchant classes. Eventually, the most successful companies began to operate more independently and entrepreneurially; they were often headed by a *capocomico* responsible for both the business and artistic aspects of the companies, who came to epitomize the troupe itself. The famous Gelosi and Fideli troupes are examples; the former was headed by Giovan Battista Andreini (1576–1654, father-in-law to Isabella); after Isabella's death, her son and his wife left the Gelosi company to form Fideli. So popular was the *commedia* throughout Europe that playwrights of scripted drama – notably Shakespeare and Molière – incorporated many *commedia* elements into their dramas, including character types, masked performances, and plot devices.

Urban growth and the new business of theatre in Europe

As social and political life came increasingly to be organized in the capitals of London, Paris, and Madrid, and in city-states of Italy (the largest being Florence, Milan, and Venice), so too did theatrical activity come to be centered there. The growing popularity of theatre led to the professionalization of the various specializations associated with the theatre (actor, wardrobe manager, prompter, etc.); the increasing commercialization of theatre companies; and the development of permanent structures to house their work. These developments inevitably affected the social status and occasion of theatre, particularly regarding the participation of women on and off stage.

Legal records of English theatre companies show that as early as 1574, playing was referred to as an "arte and facultye," with "arte" signifying a level of technique necessary for belonging to a craft or profession. In 1581, this activity was called a "trade," and in the following year a "profession." It became increasingly possible to make something of a living in the theatre, albeit a difficult one. Audiences could demand a certain standard of craft and technique from performers, but this did not always translate into social respect, a carryover from the days when actors' legal status was "vagabond."

Although the professions of playwright, actor, and actor-manager emerged during this period in Europe, theatres were not a strictly entrepreneurial affair. In England, they depended reputationally, if not financially, upon sponsorship by the crown or the nobility or both, as actors without patrons were subject to severe penalties. In Italy, ducal patronage was important to the *commedia* troupes; in France and Spain, religious charities first ran the theatres as a way to raise money for their good works, and later the various cities took over the public theatre spaces. Almost everywhere, theatre companies needed official licenses to perform. In England, only two companies were granted direct royal **patents**; all others had to be licensed by the "Master of the Revels," an officer of the crown charged with authorizing the production of all plays. In Spain, his counterpart was called, simply, the "Protector." Three charitable organizations dominated public theatre in Spain until 1615, when entrepreneurs began to be granted leases for four years at a time; this practice lasted until 1638, when cities began to take over licensing theatres to companies. Typically, only the largest cities had more than one officially licensed troupe. Meanwhile, France did not permit permanent theatre companies until well into the seventeenth century; after that, the companies at the Hôtel de Bourgogne and the Théâtre du Marais competed against each other.

Not only were authorities rather stingy in granting licenses, they also exerted some control over what could and couldn't be staged, and where. In England, for example, theatrical performances were banned inside the city limits in 1576, effectively removing public theatre to entertainment districts in the various "liberties," areas outside London proper which belonged to the city, but over which it exercised no real control. In Spain and England, there are numerous records of plays being banned or suspended on the very day of performance. In England, the reasons had often to do with suspected political sedition, while in Spain, officers of the **Inquisition** peered over the Protector's shoulder to suppress religious heresy and subversion, sniffing for secular matters of scandal, indecency, and profanity as well. In France, a number of semi-professional troupes comprising student members performed primarily for the elite, but seized every opportunity to play for the common people as well. They generally had relatively easy access to performance spaces in town, but city authorities were often suspicious of the French and Italian professional troupes and sometimes forbade performance, or allowed it only under tight restrictions (not always obeyed).

England and Spain provide the best-documented examples illustrating how the business of theatre was conducted in this period in Europe. Two companies dominated London theatre at the end of the sixteenth and the beginning of the seventeenth century: the Admiral's Men and the Lord Chamberlain's men. (Theatre companies were named after the noblemen who sponsored them.) Theatrical entrepreneur Philip Henslowe (c.1555–1616) backed the Admiral's Men, initially headed by the actor Edward Alleyn (1566–1626) and based at the Rose Theatre; the Burbage family, which owned The Theatre and later the Globe, ran the Lord Chamberlain's Men.

Both companies were founded in 1594, but along very different business models. While the Admiral's Men relied from the outset on Henslowe and Alleyn to underwrite the company's activities, the Lord Chamberlain's Men was run according to the **sharing system**, by which actor-managers, leading actors, and financiers shared in the profits of a given run or theatrical season. Sharing systems were a common way of organizing theatre companies throughout Europe. Playwrights typically did not share in the profits but were paid on a per-play basis. In recognition of the importance of the English companies, King James I (b. 1566, ruled 1603–1625) put the Admiral's Men under the patronage of his son (renaming them Prince Henry's Men) and elevated the Chamberlain's Men to royal patronage (which changed them to the King's Men). Both companies, together with several minor ones, competed for plays and mounted them in outdoor and indoor playhouses as well as in "great rooms" at schools and courts. Rivaling the two companies in popularity during the first decade of the sixteenth century was the Children of the Queen's Revels (earlier known as the Blackfriars Boys), which produced a full range of dramatic genres performed entirely by boys whose voices had yet to change.

While the Admiral's Men produced Christopher Marlowe's popular tragedies, the Chamberlain's Men counted playwright William Shakespeare among its shareholders and controlled the rights to most of the successful plays co-authored by Francis Beaumont (1584–1616) and John Fletcher (1579–1625). Co-authorship was a common practice from 1590 to 1625; Fletcher probably collaborated with Shakespeare on the last three plays attributed to the "Bard of Avon": *Henry VIII* (1613), *The Two Noble Kinsmen* (1613 or 1614), and the now lost *Cardenio* (1613). Playwrights often wrote for several companies, crafting plays with specific actors in mind. Ben Jonson, for example, provided plays to all three of the major performing groups.

Most companies paid top dramatists up front for their work and divided the profits from any subsequent publication among their shareholders. The average payment per play until about 1603 was roughly 6 pounds sterling, a figure that had increased to 10–12 pounds by 1613 – or, by 2024, approximately £2,300 to £2,800 (roughly US$3,000–$3,600).

The public appetite for dramatic variety was healthy, despite the competing attractions of other entertainment options such as bear-baiting and cockfighting in England and bull-fighting in Spain. The English companies maintained a repertory of up to 70 plays to satisfy this demand, with a different play being performed every day of their six-day week, repeated only once every month or so. Because plays weren't published until after they'd been performance-tested, and in many cases only when no longer being performed, actors were given only their own parts to memorize (on long strips of paper called "scrolls"), and must have worked hard between shows to refresh their memories for the next day's performance. In Spain, plays rarely ran for more than a half-dozen performances, and yet the theatres were never closed, except during Lent. As a result, Spanish playwrights like Félix Lope de Vega (1562–1635) had to be prolific in order to keep up with the demand, since he (like most playwrights in Europe) did not share in the profits unless he also acted. Lope de Vega, however, earned about 20 times what a lead actor would have earned for one day's work, and was the only Spanish writer to make his living exclusively in theatre; even so, Lope de Vega depended on private patronage to supplement his income and wrote until his death. In contrast, French playwrights received meager pay until the 1630s. Whenever plays were eventually published, it was often without the playwrights' consent or compensation, and there were no **copyright** laws in Europe to protect their interests.

As companies grew more experienced in their day-to-day operations, professionalization may have led to certain modest economies such as the reuse of props, costumes, and scripts, which made it financially feasible to produce a season of plays, or to tour. While playwrights and actors of principal roles could make a decent living in the theatre, that living depended on many factors outside anyone's control. For example, theatres were often closed due to weather, plague, and periods of royal mourning. In addition, in both Spain and England, anti-theatre sentiment occasionally forced the theatres to shut down.

The establishment of permanent theatre spaces

Noble, royal, and religious patronage may have given acting companies protection from being labeled "vagabonds," but these sponsors only gave money to the troupes when they played before the monarch or at a private event such as a wedding. The rest of the time the companies depended on the box office. Thus, some companies sought the benefits of having a permanent space in which to produce a full season.

Even though the ancient world had permanent theatres, in early Renaissance Europe, theatrical performance often took place in spaces originally created for other purposes (such as public squares, courtyards, and tennis courts). When permanent structures devoted specifically to theatre were built, they were either converted from existing structures, or purpose-built to house professional touring companies, in both cases often maintaining attributes of the original performance spaces.

While permanent theatre spaces were built in Italy as early as 1531, it is likely they were associated with private court rather than public performances. An exception was the Teatro Olimpico (built 1580–1585 in Vicenza). The architect Palladio (1508–1580) modeled its interior on ancient Roman theatre with the intent of housing classical Greek and Roman revivals. The Teatro Olimpico opened in 1585 with a production of *Oedipus Rex* to an audience of academics and nobility. Such productions, however, were mostly occasional, amateur undertakings intended for pedagogical, honorific, celebratory, and scholarly purposes. Renaissance academic theatre might employ professional actors, especially in Italy, but it never challenged the professionals' popularity with the public. Nonetheless, the literary resources of the academic theatre offered substantial opportunities to the early professional troupes. As we have already seen, two major theatrical traditions – *commedia dell'arte* and dramatic, text-based theatre – flowed from the intersection of amateur and professional theatre in the mid-sixteenth century. Teatro Olimpico remains a material manifestation of the age's fascination with the classical past; although it was abandoned soon after it was built, it is still standing after almost half a millennium, and since the mid-1990s has been active again in housing theatre productions.

The earliest of the permanent, public theatres in Europe was built in Paris in 1548, inside the Hôtel de Bourgogne. Its design followed the form of the tennis courts in which visiting troupes to the French capital were accustomed to perform, with seating arranged in galleries and boxes along three interior walls, for more than 1,000 spectators. As in Spain and England, multiple stage settings were conveyed more through language than set or scenery design.

Permanent theatre structures soon appeared in all the major European capitals. In England and Spain, early theatres – like the Red Lion (built 1567 in London) and the first Spanish *corral* [kohr-RAHL] (Seville 1574) – were built to imitate the spaces that had earlier been used for theatrical performances. In France, the models were indoor tennis courts; in contrast in England and Spain, they were outdoor innyards or courtyards enclosed by the exterior walls of adjacent buildings (see Figure 4.5). Risers along three sides of the Red Lion allowed audience members to follow the stage action at one end of the space. In Spain, wealthy patrons used to rent the upper floors and balconies of the buildings surrounding the courtyards, making for a mixture of public and private seating; when designated theatres were built in the latter quarter of the sixteenth century, the custom of dividing the seating by class or occupation and gender carried over into the purpose-built structures, still called *corrales*. Between 1574 and 1628, 18 such theatres were built in Spain and four in its American colonies; in England, between 1575 and 1623, 13 new outdoor theatres were built.

One of the most important London theatres was called simply The Theatre, built in 1576. Unlike the Red Lion and its French and Spanish counterparts, which featured a stage at one end of a rectangular audience space, The Theatre's house was polygonal in shape. It included three galleries where some members of the audience stood or sat, an unroofed yard where

Figure 4.5
"Artist's impression of the interior of the Corral del Principe, by Carlos Dorremochea, c. 1967," in John Allen, *The Reconstruction of a Spanish Golden Age Playhouse: El Corral del Principe (1583–1744)*.
Source: Gainesville: University Press of Florida, 1983, p. 68.

others called the "groundlings" stood, a stage extending into the yard, and a "tiring house" (backstage area, so-called, some believe, because it is where the actors were "attired" before making their entrances). The Theatre was the first example of the distinctive architecture of the Elizabethan public theatre. The design harked back to the Roman amphitheatre, which gave it some degree of classical cachet. But it also maintained some characteristics of the medieval *locus* and *platea* arrangement: audience surrounding a generalized acting area, location suggested through words ("this is the forest of Arden") or context (a conference with the king implying a castle's great hall), and an occasional set piece (like a throne). The Theatre eventually became home to several important theatre companies. In 1598, it was dismantled, rebuilt near the River Thames, and renamed the Globe. The Globe was home to the Chamberlain's Men (later called the King's Men), the company most associated with Shakespeare's plays. (See Figures 4.6 and 14.1 for a recent reconstruction.)

In England, The Theatre and the Globe were open-air structures known as "public" theatres. There were other theatres housed indoors which, although also open to the public, became known as "private" theatres, perhaps in order to skirt requirements that plays be

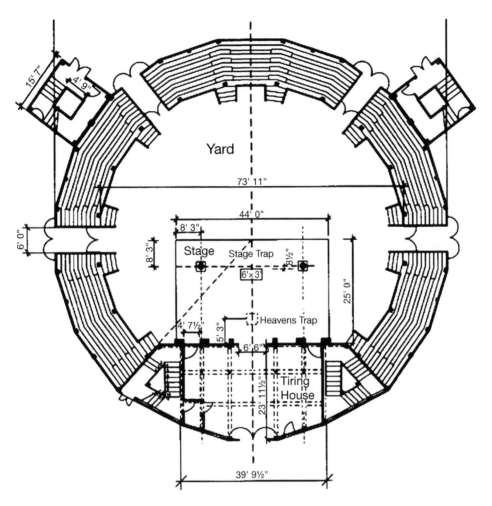

Figure 4.6
A plan for the new Shakespeare's Globe Theatre, completed in 1997, which sought to replicate the Globe of Shakespeare's day (with additional exits for safety reasons). See Chapter 14 for more information on the new Globe.

Source: © Pentagram Design Ltd.

licensed and their companies officially sponsored by the Crown. These theatres were most active in London during the 1570s and 1580s. After 1608, Richard Burbage, lead actor and manager of the King's Men company, took over Blackfriars Theatre, which soon became the company's winter home and the most important English theatre of its day. Although no il-lustrations or plans survive, contemporary accounts suggest that the space was a large indoor hall, with a stage and tiring house at one end, benches for those seated in the **pit**, **galleries** on three sides above the pit, and **boxes** near the stage. Blackfriars, unlike the Globe, was an elite venue, intended for the most refined work of the best playwrights – but other more popular plays were staged there, and it wasn't unusual for spectators to sit or stand on the

Figure 4.7

A 1596 drawing of the interior of the Swan Theatre, London, probably generally similar to the nearby Globe Theatre. Note the figures in the gallery above the two stage doors; this area may have been used as a lord's room and as an acting space. The only picture of the interior of an Elizabethan public theatre, it is a copy by Arend von Buchell of a lost original drawing by his Dutch friend, Johannes DeWitt, who had visited London.

Source: Utrecht University Library, Ms. 842, fol. 132r.

stage, perhaps showing themselves off. Also unlike the Globe, it was used in the evening, probably with the entire room illuminated by candles.

The growing popularity of theatre made it start to seem like a good business proposition, and this, in turn, made indoor theatres increasingly valuable: they allowed companies to perform, and therefore support themselves, year-round. In an age increasingly dependent on selling theatre tickets, a dedicated theatre space allowed the companies to control the audience's entrance, thus assuring they paid the price of admission.

The social occasion of theatre

Early modern audiences in London could attend an outdoor, public playhouse most days of the year, except during the Lenten season and periods of intense heat (and possible plague) in the summer months. For Londoners, a trip to the Globe took them across the River Thames beyond the reach of a city government dominated by Puritans and into an area filled with taverns, brothels, bear-baiting arenas, and other playhouses. The theatres south of the Thames, like others north of the city, drew audiences of all classes. Apprentices, journeymen, soldiers, and others paid a penny (roughly the cost of a loaf of bread) for admittance into the yard of the playhouse, where they could stand to watch the show on the thrust stage, roughly four to six feet high (Figure 4.7). For an additional penny, merchants and their families, courtiers, foreign travelers, and others might purchase a bench seat in one of the galleries. If the Lord Chamberlain himself came to enjoy the troupe he sponsored, he and his retinue might sit in a lord's room behind and above the stage platform, an excellent location to see and be seen. Although the Globe could hold perhaps 2,500 spectators, the average crowd for most performances was probably around 600.

Daytime performances and the configuration of the theatre houses – rectangular as in Spain and France, or the polygonal "wooden O" of the English Globe – meant that audience members had as good a view of each other as they did of the stage. In France, this view was probably better than that of the drama on stage; perhaps that is one reason people tended to refer to "hearing" rather than "seeing" a play. Audiences and seating in Paris during the early 1600s were roughly similar to London's. Theatregoers came from all social classes, but since ticket prices were linked to viewing privileges, seating became segregated by class and other social factors. Most spectators were male, but upper-class women began attending plays in the 1630s, when decorum in drama was becoming more important; however, women from the lower classes probably attended in small numbers long before then. The *parterre* [PAH(r)-tehr] (pit) was crowded mostly with spectators from the lower classes, who were often scorned by the elite for being noisy and quarrelsome. Nevertheless, people from the upper classes could be found in the *parterre* as well, especially writers wishing to be closer to the stage. The boxes were more expensive and reserved for the elite. When *Le Cid* was performed in 1637, it was so popular that well-to-do audience members were allowed to sit on the stage itself, beginning a tradition that the theatres were unable to shed for over a century. However, most playwrights of the early 1600s felt it was important to appeal to all tastes. That too began to change during the 1630s.

In Spain, the *corrales* similarly divided the audience by social class and therefore viewing privilege. Male and female audience members were strictly segregated, and women were not allowed to stand with men in the *patio*, or ground-floor area. Instead, they occupied an upper gallery called the *cazuela*, or "stewpot," where men were not allowed; women were, however, allowed to sit with male relatives in the *aposentos*, or boxes. Other galleries called *tertulias* were reserved for members of the clergy and intelligentsia.

Audiences in the public theatres were vocal and rowdy; theatre as a place of genteel sociability took time to develop, as will be discussed further in Chapter 7. People ate fruit, nuts, pastries, and possibly fish and meat pies, and drank beer or ale. There were no restrooms. In England, "orange wenches" – young women who eked out a living selling oranges (and, often, themselves) – roamed among the spectators. Inter-act and post-show performances often featured highly physical song-and-dance routines.

Because both men and women attended, the theatre of this time afforded an opportunity for the public mingling of sexes outside the sanctioned religious holiday seasons, a matter of no small anxiety to the moral authorities. Throughout Europe, both official and self-appointed watchdogs railed against what they saw as the licentiousness and immorality of the stage. Actors themselves – whether male as in England or male and female everywhere else in Europe – were not held in general respect. Further, limited licensing opportunities made for a kind of hierarchical social ladder for actors everywhere: those associated with permanently licensed companies were at the top of this social schema; actors with touring companies lower down; and individual street performers the lowest of all. But even actors associated with licensed companies were not granted full social esteem. They were banned from London's city limits in 1575; in Spain they were deemed "public sinners" and denied Christian sacraments.

Increasing importance of women in theatre

When a French theatre troupe featuring both male and female players toured to Blackfriars in 1629, they caused such a stir – being "hissed, hooted and pippin-pelted from the stage" – that the Master of the Revels reimbursed some of their license fees (Prynne, qtd. in Adams 1904: 13). Although women frequently appeared in lavish royal court masques throughout Europe, their appearance on public stages was more scandalous. The reasons are complicated, and had much to do with a widely held belief that a woman's place was in the home, away from the gaze of men who had no legal claims on her – unless she was a prostitute. Nevertheless, despite widespread misperceptions of their virtue, women began to appear on stage throughout the continent. The first documented professional actress appeared in Italy, with the *commedia* troupes in the 1560s; in Spain in 1587 (although by 1599 actresses had to be the wives, widows, or daughters of company members); and in France in 1592. In England, boys and young men continued to play all female roles until 1662, when Charles II issued a royal warrant that only women should play women's roles (although there is some evidence that women started appearing on stage in 1660, and men still played older women for a time).

According to theatre historian Eric A. Nicholson,

> Regardless of the country, period, and prevailing religious outlook, female roles distinguish both the drama and society of these centuries. Insofar as the postmedieval and preindustrial world categorized women almost exclusively in terms of their relationship to men, both normative roles – the virginal maid, chaste wife, and celibate widow – and transgressive ones – adulteress, prostitute, courtesan, and procuress or "bawd" – gave prominence to sexuality and the female body, precisely those entities that most demanded – and most threatened – patriarchal domination.
>
> (Nicholson 1993: 296)

The limited roles laid out by Nicholson nevertheless provided an opportunity for playwrights (predominantly men) to expose, explore, exploit, and critique unequal social relations between the genders. Nicholson goes on to trace a number of European plays that treat the contradictory position of women in society in complex ways – at times rehearsing their limited social roles, at others reversing and transforming them (see "Women's Roles in European drama" on the website accompanying this textbook).

FREE

INSTRUCTOR
& STUDENT
RESOURCES

In addition to having men playing the parts of women, Elizabethan playwrights seemed particularly fascinated by the prospects of further crossdressing within the dramatic action. In more than 80 plays, young male actors, playing the parts of women, crossdress *back* into male clothing in order to pursue their female characters' various goals. Examples include Shakespeare's *The Merchant of Venice*, *As You Like It*, and *Twelfth Night*, where crossdressing proves central to the dramatic action. These performances offered audiences the chance to witness the complicated representation of ambiguous sexual tension – between a male character and a female character dressed as and played by a male.

Off-stage, however, **sumptuary laws** restricted clothing choices to their "proper" gender or social class, although some women chose to crossdress in order to travel alone or pursue a trade. In Spain, prohibitions against crossdressing extended to the stage as well. For parts requiring a young woman to dress as a man, actresses were required to wear male clothing above the waist, and a skirt below.

In comparison, as we saw, in both the *zaju* and *kunqu* traditions in China crossdressing was rather free, and women and men shared the spotlight on stage, at least through the late eighteenth century. Then, as regional drama and traveling troupes became popular, single-sex troupes became more of a norm; and while male actors were the majority in later periods, women never disappeared from stage completely. In Japan, as we will see below, female performers were at first central to *kabuki*, but they were eventually outlawed from performing in public. Similarly, crossdressing (both across genders and across social classes) was banned.

Even today, female roles in *kabuki* are played predominantly by males. The *onnagata*, a special-ist in female roles and one of the best-known features of *kabuki*, is discussed in more detail in our case study.

Popular Japanese theatre in a time of cultural seclusion

Civil wars wracked Japanese society from 1467 until 1590. During this chaotic period, only *nō* could be considered professional, although not all *nō* troupes were connected to the court and many toured the country. Various other types of theatrical performance occurred as part of Shinto or Buddhist rituals, or at local festivals, but these were generally per-formed by the villagers themselves, as part of civic life. There were also troupes of itinerant entertainers – actors, dancers, storytellers, musicians, magicians, acrobats, and puppeteers – who roamed the land, but they were considered outcasts (officially classified as "non-humans") and were forbidden to reside in settled villages or towns.

Around 1590, one clan of samurai (professional warriors) gained military power and the long period of civil wars began to subside. In 1603, the Japanese emperor conferred the title of shogun (supreme military ruler) on Tokugawa Ieyasu, the leader of this victorious clan. This act established the Tokugawa shogunate, which moved the capital from Kyoto to Edo (now Tokyo) and enforced the peace until 1868. The period from 1603 to 1868 is therefore called the Tokugawa or Edo era.

The Tokugawa rulers, guided by neo-Confucianism, insisted on having an unchanging so-ciety divided according to hereditary class. As we saw with the sumptuary laws of Europe, each of the four social classes was permitted garments and adornments appropriate to them and for-bidden to others. For example, only the topmost samurai could wear the double swords. Next in the hierarchy were the farmers, followed by artisans and craftspeople. At the bottom were the merchants, thought to contribute nothing to society, because they merely traded items grown or made by others. The three lower classes wore only cotton garments of blue and brown, with little or no pattern. In addition to these four classes, there were those who were outside and above all classes: the imperial family, the nobility, and Buddhist and Shinto priests. They could wear colored silks, embroidered and elaborately patterned. Similarly, there were others who were outside and below the class system, including hereditary outcasts, sorcerers, prostitutes, beggars, and actors. They were all forbidden to wear the trappings of those "inside society."

However, this supposedly inflexible hierarchy was turned upside-down during the long period of peace of the Tokugawa era. Suddenly, money could be spent on leisure instead of war. The *daimyō* (feudal lords of the samurai class) actually became poor because they were required to maintain residences both in their home province and in Edo, and to travel back and forth several times a year.

Unemployed samurai (*rōnin*) sometimes became bandits who ambushed the traveling *daimyō* or lived secretly among the merchants. In contrast, the despised merchants became rich. They secretly defied the law by wearing extravagant silks and bold colors beneath their simple cotton kimono. As many **kabuki** [kah-boo-kee] and **bunraku** [boon-rah-koo] plots demonstrate, the merchants embraced the virtues and values once appropriate to the samurai and feudal lords who no longer possessed them.

The shogunate also feared foreign influences that might undermine their authority. Eu-ropean traders and Christian missionaries threatened to introduce new types of weapons,

Figure 4.8

Detail from a painting showing Okuni, the Japanese female temple dancer/prostitute who originated the performance style eventually called *kabuki*, probably in the late sixteenth century. Note the Christian cross and double samurai swords. Other images show her in male Portuguese garb.

Source: The History Collection/Alamy Stock Photo.

popular foreign goods (such as eyeglasses and clocks), and new ideas. To stem the flow of foreign influence, beginning in the early 1600s, the government enacted a series of laws forbidding contact with foreigners. By 1651, Japan had almost totally isolated itself from the outside world. This isolation continued for over 200 years, ending officially in 1868. It was during this period that *kabuki* developed and flourished.

The birth of kabuki

Around 1600, a dancer named Okuni (c.1578–c.1613) and her mixed-gender troupe appeared in Kyoto, performing Buddhist dances in a dry riverbed to raise funds for a temple. In addition to religious dances, they performed short skits – early plays that were vulgar, irreverent, and often lewd. Their performances became hugely popular, partly because the performers (both male and female) were also prostitutes. Okuni and her troupe ignored the laws against crossdressing, with men playing women and women playing men. They defied rules against proper clothing, wearing forbidden foreign costumes and even Christian crosses. Woodblock prints from around 1600 depict Okuni dressed outrageously in male Portuguese garb, with a Christian cross around her neck and a samurai's double swords at her waist (Figure 4.8).

Like these outcast actors, some young people also flouted the laws. They joined unruly gangs and sported outrageous costumes, shocking hairdos, large and extravagantly decorated swords, and four-foot long tobacco pipes. Like Okuni, they resisted legal dress codes and behaved in anti-social ways. All these counter-cultural people were termed *kabuki-mono*. The word *kabuki* derives from an old verb *kabuku*: "to tilt or slant dangerously to one side." In its origins, *kabuki* was shocking, off-balance, and inappropriate. As long as people performed and dressed outrageously, whether on stage or off, order could not be maintained. Today, however, *kabuki* is considered a "classical" art form, and the word itself is now written differently, using Chinese characters meaning "song-dance-skill."

Soon after Okuni's appearance, copycat *kabuki* troupes appeared, many composed of all women. At least as early as 1612, male prostitutes also formed *kabuki* troupes and competed with the women. By the 1620s, *kabuki* managers had established theatres linked to brothels in all of the major cities of Japan, an entrepreneurial strategy for boosting revenues from both endeavors. The government began to fear that the strict division of classes was breaking down as more and more people attended these outdoor performances and sought out the sexual services of the actors. However, it was not prostitution itself that concerned the neo-Confucians who ran the government. Nor did they suggest that stage acting, crossdressing, or imitation were inherently evil, as many Europeans opposed to theatre did. Rather, they feared class mingling and social rebellion.

The popular success of *kabuki* annoyed the samurai rulers, but at the same time confirmed their self-perceived innate superiority to the rowdy culture of the cities. Thus, although the regime could have stamped out *kabuki* when it first emerged, the shogun and his warriors chose to allow it to continue within limits, fearing that a total ban would lead to worse troubles. In a revealing document, one samurai official stated: "Courtesans, dancers, catamites, streetwalkers, and the like always come to the cities and prospering places of the country. Although the conduct of many is corrupted by them, if they are rigorously suppressed, serious crimes will occur daily" (Shively 2002: 41). This point of view, which underlay the Tokugawa shogunate's policy toward *kabuki* theatre for 250 years, rested on class disdain for merchants and city culture. The combination of traders and workers in wealthy towns, the samurai believed, would always breed criminality. Better for such potential criminals to be distracted by theatrical entertainment, they reasoned, than for these people to turn to "serious crimes."

At the same time, the samurai rulers worried that *kabuki*, if completely unregulated, would corrupt the soldiers and young men of their own class. Although samurai and aristocrats, including high-born women, were forbidden to attend, many flagrantly broke the law. Sometimes they came in disguise; in some periods, they were forced to sit behind screens where they were "invisible." Complaints against the *kabuki* performers in the 1600–1670 period centered on drunken fights and tales of young samurai losing their fortunes and ruining their reputations by chasing after a *kabuki* prostitute. In 1629, the government banned females from performing in *kabuki*. Despite the ban, similar laws were reissued in the 1630s and 1640s, indicating that it took several years for the shogunate to eliminate this popular form of *kabuki*. After 1652, young males were also prohibited from performing *kabuki*, again in an effort to prevent class mingling due to love affairs and prostitution between men. Henceforth, only older males who shaved the forelocks of their hair were allowed to perform in the plays. It was assumed that the male actors would be less sexually appealing (to both males and females in the audience) without their forelocks. Eventually, the actors were required to use scalp coverings and wigs in an ongoing contest of regulation and innovation between the Tokugawa shogunate and the *kabuki* managers. The issue of hair is just one example of the kinds of restrictions and rules that the government tried to enforce.

Although this conflict between the samurai and the theatre managers continued until the end of the Tokugawa regime in 1868, *kabuki* troupes gradually won enough grudging legitimacy from the regime to allow them to elaborate an art form out of this sexually enticing entertainment. After 1652, audiences in Kyoto, Osaka, and Edo began to find more enjoyment in the extended performances by the mature male actors, who now played all the roles on the *kabuki* stage. **Onnagata** [ohn-nah-gah-tah], men who specialized in female roles, gained particular popularity among the merchant spectators (see our case study).

As star actors in the major cities sought better material, *kabuki* playwrights emerged to provide it. Many of the most famous *kabuki* plays began as puppet plays and were later adapted for actors. Many playwrights worked in teams, but a few, such as Chikamatsu Monzaemon (1653–1724), gained recognition for their singular excellence. Chikamatsu preferred writing for puppets rather than for actors who might mangle his words.

Blurring performance genres: Puppets and actors

Japanese puppet theatre (*bunraku*, also called *ningyō joruri* [neen-gyoh joh-roo-ree], which means doll theatre) has a long history, including connections to religious ritual. However, the most representative style, generally known as *bunraku*, is purely secular. Unlike much puppet theatre in the West, *bunraku* is not meant as children's entertainment. The histories of *kabuki* and *bunraku* are closely allied, and the two genres have many performance and script elements in common. Both reached their high points and solidified their most typical characteristics during the mid-seventeenth century, as entertainment for the newly wealthy merchant class. Since both were highly popular, each tried to out-do the other. For example, the puppets became more and more like humans, while the actors tended to mimic puppet movements.

Lifelike puppets can do things that living actors on stage cannot do as believably, such as cutting off heads, gouging out eyes, being eaten by a tiger, or walking to the stars on a rainbow. These effects charmed and thrilled audiences. Consequently, *kabuki* actors sometimes sought to rival the puppets by creating performance skills that were amazing because they seemed almost magical in showing off the actor's versatility. For example, to imitate puppet movement, the actor would perform *ningyō-buri* [neen-gyoh boo-ree], a kind of dance in which black-robed stagehands (**kōken** [koh-kehn] or *kurogo*) acted as puppeteers, literally manipulating the actor as though he were a puppet.

Kabuki soon developed quick on-stage costume changes (such as costumes that seem to turn inside out or that fly off to reveal another costume beneath) that instantly transformed the character right in front of the audience's eyes. Doubles cleverly substituted for star actors so that the star could appear to play multiple roles in a single performance, even apparently acting with himself in the same scene. Special effects developed, such as an actor flying over the audience or appearing magically from a lantern, or a stage set depicting a rooftop that opened to reveal an interior. In response, *bunraku* puppets became more and more lifelike and believable, seeming to breathe, to cry, and to perform delicate, complex dances or activities such as sewing.

Today, *bunraku* puppets are three to four feet tall and highly realistic, with many movable parts – not only arms, legs, and bodies but individual fingers, eyes, and mouths. The puppet for a major character is manipulated by three operators who must work in perfect harmony. The main puppeteer manipulates the head and right arm; the secondary puppeteer manipulates the left arm; and the third puppeteer works the feet and legs. A puppeteer usually spends ten years working the feet and legs, then ten more years working the left arm. Only after 20 years is a puppeteer ready to manipulate the head and right arm (Figure 4.9). Minor puppets may only have a single puppeteer.

The puppeteers do not speak. Instead, there may be a single narrator (called a *gidayū*), an accomplished musician as well, who voices the dialogue for all the characters and all spoken and sung narration, while playing the three-stringed *shamisen*; or a group of chanters (*tayu*) accompanied by *shamisen* music who together provide the narrative function known as

Figure 4.9

Japanese *bunraku* puppets. The head manipulator controls the doll's head and right arm. The secondary manipulator controls the left arm. If needed, a third controls the feet. Photo during a rehearsal of the play *Sonezaki Shinju*, by Japanese photographer Hiroshi Sugimoto, on 9 October 2013 at the Theatre de la Ville in Paris.

Source: Fred Dufour/AFP via Getty Images.

joruri – one conveying the story and the other its emotional essence. Both types of narrators are in full view of the audience. In *kabuki* plays derived from *bunraku* scripts, a *joruri* narrator sometimes chants during certain parts of the play.

The *bunraku* stage is designed so that only the upper portions of the puppeteers' bodies are visible. The front screen covering their lower bodies sometimes serves as a floor for the puppets. The puppeteers often wear black hoods. Even when the audience sees the puppeteer's face, he is considered to be "invisible" – the audience's attention is focused on the puppets and/or the *joruri* narrator. Traditionally, all manipulators are male.

Kabuki and *bunraku* in performance

Early *kabuki* was performed outdoors in dry riverbeds. Later, it began to use a variation of the *nō* stage. After 1724, when indoor theatres became popular, the roof and pillars typical of the *nō* stage were eliminated, and the *hashigakari* [hah-shee-gah-kah-ree] (bridgeway) was moved to extend through the audience. The *kabuki* bridgeway, called the **hanamichi** [hah-nah-mee-chee], is used for major entrances and exits. Unlike its counterpart in *nō*, the *hanamichi* brings the actor into (and above) the audience, creating a highly theatrical

Figure 4.10

A performance of the popular *kabuki* play *Shibaraku* (*Wait a Moment!*), in Tokyo's Nakamura Theatre in the mid-nineteenth century. On the rampway (*hanamichi*) leading to the stage at left, an actor in the robes of the Danjūrō line of actors portrays a commoner who enters to challenge the imminent execution on stage of innocent people by a powerful lord, uttering his famous fierce cry, "*Shibaraku.*" The woodcut triptych by Utagawa Kunisada shows the traditional auditorium (note the seating arrangements) and stage, but with an additional *hanamichi* at right.

Source: Courtesy of Gary Jay and Josephine S. Williams.

and immediate effect. Some plays used two *hanamichi*, one on either side of the auditorium. Originally, the audience sat on the floor on *tatami* mats (woven from rice straw), either in two levels of galleries or in ground-floor boxes (Figure 4.10). Soon, a front curtain of green, orange, and black stripes was added to hide scene shifts (although there had never been a front curtain in *nō*); today, at the play's opening, this curtain is pulled back to the sound of wooden clappers beating faster and faster. Still later, complex mechanical devices for spectacular effects appeared, including revolving sets, devices to fly actors, and traps in the stage floor and the *hanamichi*. Such machines were common in *kabuki* nearly a century before European theatre attempted to use them. Today, *kabuki* theatres can generally seat several thousand spectators.

There are several types of *kabuki* and *bunraku* plays: historical, domestic (about contemporary urban life), and dance plays lacking dialogue. The stories are usually derived from existing sources (legends, epics, novels, or *nō* and *kyōgen* plays), real or imagined history, or current events. Some of the most beautiful and poetic *bunraku* and *kabuki* dramas are Chikamatsu's double-suicide plays. These and other serious plays often focus on an impossible, ultimately tragic conflict between the demands of duty or loyalty to family or lord (*giri*) and personal, human feelings (*ninjō*). All plays are highly choreographed, often including dance or battle sequences and even acrobatics. The two main performance styles in *kabuki* are **aragoto** [ah-rah-goh-toh], or rough-house (popular in Edo), and **wagoto** [wah-goh-toh], or soft-style (popular in Osaka and Kyoto). The *aragoto* style features striking, non-realistic makeup, hugely exaggerated costumes, extreme vocal patterns, and powerful gestures that are based on images of the god Fudō, the patron deity of a Buddhist-Shinto sect of mountain ascetics, whose rituals include terrifying demon-quelling dances. At climactic moments, an *aragoto* actor may toss his head, raise his leg and stamp his foot, pose with open, outreached hand, grunt, and freeze his face in a cross-eyed grimace. Such "punctuation" in acting is called **mie** [mee-eh] (see Figures 4.11 and 7.15). In these moments, the expressive body of the outcast actor incorporates both the Buddhist-Shinto deity and the samurai warrior, suggesting to the merchant audience that they, themselves, partake of both identities.

Music and sound effects are important elements. The vocalization of *kabuki* is unique. The language is unfamiliar to modern audiences; sometimes poetic, its style of enunciation is highly elaborated and often artificial. *Onnagata*, the female-role specialists, speak in a rolling falsetto voice; villains often use a guttural, rough voice.

Makeup and costumes are stylized, colorful, and sometimes fantastic, especially in the *aragoto* style. For example,

Figure 4.11

Danjūrō XII as Sukeroku, the commoner who is an aristocrat of the past in disguise, in the *kabuki* play *Sukeroku: Flower of Edo*. Here, Danjūrō is seen striking a typical *mie* pose.

Source: *Kabukiza* program, Tokyo, January 1995, p. 20. Grand Kabuki Theatre. © Shochiku Co., Ltd.

the hero of the play *Shibaraku* (*Wait a Moment!*) wears a kimono with gigantic, stiff square sleeves. A high-ranking courtesan may wear many layers of colorful kimono, a wide, heavily brocaded and complex *obi* (broad sash) tied around her waist, an elaborate wig decorated with hairpins, jewels, and flowers, and tall, platform-style, lacquered sandals. In *aragoto* plays, everything is bigger than life. In *wagoto* plays, both costumes and makeup are closer to reality. (Chikamatsu's double-suicide plays are examples of the *wagoto* style.)

With rare exception, actors in professional *kabuki* today are male. Most come from *kabuki* families and begin training and performing as children. Those who are not born into an acting family usually begin training at a special school at the National Theatre. If they exhibit sufficient promise, they will apprentice with an established actor and eventually will be adopted into the family. Actors are awarded new personal names as they progress in skill. Actors in *kabuki* and *bunraku* are known by these professional, personal names rather than their family name, unlike other Japanese.

Many now-typical elements of *kabuki* came about as the result of attempts to stifle the art. For example, the *onnagata* developed because both women and boys were banned from the stage. Visual elements became more stunning to attract audiences, scripts became more complex and acting became more polished as the form matured. Keeping actors segregated from the rest of society meant that the children of actors would be forced to learn their craft at an early age. Ironically, official disapproval of *kabuki* actually contributed to its becoming more professional.

CASE STUDY: Realer than real? Imaging "woman" in *kabuki*

Carol Fisher Sorgenfrei

One of the most immediately recognizable features of *kabuki* is the *onnagata* (male actor specializing in female roles). In contemporary Japan, female actors perform in many types of theatre (even occasionally in *nō*), but with few exceptions, *kabuki* remains an all-male genre. This case study will consider some of the historical and aesthetic arguments for and against female actors in *kabuki*. Although the *onnagata* was forged in a patriarchal society in which gender roles off stage were understood to be both biological and fixed, some *onnagata* pushed at those limitations in ways that today's readers may find both strange and familiar.

In 1868, a political revolution known as the Meiji Restoration returned imperial rule to Japan under the Emperor Meiji, inaugurating a series of governmental, military, and industrial reforms, and opening the door to trade with the West. This increased openness brought exposure to many Western technologies and ideas, some more controversial than others. Emerging ideas in the West about feminism and the changing role of women in society caused some social and theatre reformers to call for the *onnagata* to be replaced with actresses, while traditionalists were opposed. Among the latter was a male Japanese theatre scholar who wrote in 1914:

> In Japan, males are superior to females in every way – from the shape of the face, eyes, nose, and mouth to body type and size. Females can be beautiful too, but they usually have some flaw: for example, a lovely face but a short body. Since these flaws do not allow an actress to complement a male lead, it is only obvious that males should continue to perform women onstage.
>
> (Qtd. in Robertson 1998: 57)

On the opposite side, early Japanese feminists and their supporters felt that, as one put it,

> Although the *onnagata* has the weight of history and tradition on his side, all I see is a middle-aged male wearing face powder trying to play the part of a young woman. It is in bad taste and wholly unconvincing. He doesn't even try to hide his Adam's apple!
>
> (Qtd. in Robertson 1998: 58)

Both views tend to miss a key aspect of the power and pleasure of the *onnagata* in performance, which can be more accurately characterized as a performance of the idea of the feminine gender itself, rather than a representation of some actual referent.

Gender, visuality, and the onnagata

A great *onnagata* does not need to appear "beautiful" or even typically "feminine." Rather, he must be a skillful performer, creating a pleasing staged image of "woman." Some *kabuki* connoisseurs actually prefer *onnagata* who are physically unattractive, such as the extraordinarily talented Nakamura Shikan VII (1928–2011), because they feel that an actor's beauty distracts from his skill. One of the twentieth century's most beloved *onnagata*, Onoe Baikō VII (1915–1995) (Figure 4.12) was rather stout, not especially good looking, and behaved in a typically masculine way off stage. Others, such as the internationally renowned Bandō Tamasaburō V (1950–), are quite attractive on stage

Figure 4.12

The well-known Japanese male actor Onoe Baikō in the *onnagata* (female) role as the heroine of *The Lion Dance*, circa 1940 in Japan. He was considered one of the finest *onnagata* of the twentieth century.

Source: Photo by Keystone-France/Gamma-Keystone via Getty Images.

and off. Tamasaburō not only excels in *kabuki*, but portrays realistic, believable women in stage and film roles, such as Blanche DuBois in Tennessee Williams' *A Streetcar Named Desire* or Lady Macbeth (see Figure 4.13).

Although all professional *onnagata* today are male, until the early twentieth century, some actresses – including female *onnagata* – did perform on stage, both in private mansions and in public theatres. Previously, scholars often dismissed them as amateurs, but feminist scholars have shown that this designation is inaccurate (Edelson 2009). One of the most famous female *onnagata* was Ichikawa Kumehachi I (c.1846–1913), who played both male and female roles in *kabuki*. In 1898, critics wrote that "on stage, nobody can tell that she is not a man. When she plays [female] roles . . . , she immediately transforms herself into a blooming beauty or a graceful, virtuous princess" (qtd. in Isaka 2006: 111). Being indistinguishable from a man meant that her body performed in the "authentic" *kabuki* tradition, using the aesthetic ideals developed by male *onnagata*. Over time, distilling down certain indicators of performative gender has become key, regardless of who performs them:

> The roles have been polished to the point where the mere pointing of a finger, swaying of a kimono sleeve, or exclamation of surprise has eliminated everything inessential to the communication of what is conventionally recognized as a womanly presence.
>
> (Leiter 2012: 118)

Historicizing onnagata aesthetics

However, some contemporary theatre scholars (both Japanese and non-Japanese) maintain that only a male *onnagata* can portray the "essence of femininity" and can seem more feminine than a "real" woman. Their comments often echo the 1939 Japanese scholar who maintained, "*onnagata* imparted a flavor that actresses could not hope to pro-

Figure 4.13

The *onnagata* actor Tamasaburō V during his solo performance in *Kanegamisaki* (*The Cape of the Temple Bell*) at the Japan Society, New York, 3 May 1984.

Source: by Jack Vartoogian/Getty Images.

duce" (Robertson 1998: 58). In analyzing such comments, theatre historian James R. Brandon reminds us that:

> We should not forget the historical reason the *onnagata* became part of kabuki theatre … . The *onnagata* was a political expedient and did not need justification on artistic grounds until the ban on actresses was repealed in the late nineteenth century. Then theatre scholars, performers, and culture managers were required to come up with reasons why the *onnagata* should continue. The result was the creation of unsubstantiated myths: only a male actor can suggest the essence of a woman, only a man possesses the physical strength to wear a heavy wig and multiple kimono, and so on. These are not really artistic explanations; they are rationalizations

for why the social institution of male-playing-female should continue undisturbed in the modern era when it was no longer needed or required.

(Brandon 2012: 122)

Although the *onnagata*'s origin was political and not aesthetic, its rationale for bending gender perhaps also masking an unacknowledged homoeroticism, actors and other *kabuki* theatre artists did develop concepts of artistic beauty to justify their art. The great *onnagata* Yoshizawa Ayame I (1673–1729) maintained that the successful *onnagata* must behave like a woman both on stage and in real life, even in private and even if he is married with children. In daily life, he must practice a female's outward behavior and inner thoughts by eating, walking, and gesturing just like a perfect woman – but never copying any specific person. If someone mentions his wife and children, he should really blush in modesty. Even at the public bath, it is said that Ayame would use the women's section. No one objected, and no one was fooled.

According to Ayame, the *onnagata* is not "a male acting in a role in which he becomes a 'woman,'" but rather "a male who is 'a woman' acting a role" (qtd. in Robertson 1998: 54). In other words, before playing a particular female role on stage, the male actor must transform his gender to "woman" (that is, to what society imagines "woman" to be, regardless of biological sex and regardless of specific circumstances). The idea was that an actual woman would not be able to escape her own biological body, so only a male, who was thought to not be hindered by biology, could hope to represent the ideal.

Ayame's ideas are related to certain Buddhist concepts of transformation (*henshin*), which held that females are inherently impure and can only reach enlightenment if their physical bodies are eliminated and they are reborn (after several reincarnations) as male bodies (Robertson 1998: 54). Women were in this view incapable of representing or becoming themselves; they were imperfect copies of an imagined ideal.

Official doctrine of the time concurred. For example, male educators and philosophers encouraged women to follow the Confucian precepts expressed in books such as *Greater Learning for Females* (*Onna daigaku*, 1672) which stated that possessing female sex organs and genitalia actually impeded the ability to be rational and to behave in an appropriately "chaste" fashion. As Jennifer Robertson points out:

> Given the Kabuki theater's mixed reception by the Tokugawa Shogunate, and the low, outsider status of actors during the Edo period, basing the construction and performance of femininity on *Greater Learning for Females* quite likely added a modicum of legitimacy to the urban theatre. . . . An *onnagata*, then, according to Ayame, was . . . the embodiment of patriarchally inscribed, state-regulated "female" gender. The actor was unequivocally Woman, a model for females offstage to emulate and a sex object for males offstage to proposition.
>
> (Robertson 1998: 54–5)

Even today, contemporary Japanese women (who seldom wear kimono except for formal occasions) sometimes view the *onnagata* as "a model to emulate" – but only in terms of how to properly wear (and move gracefully in) kimono. However, even this emulation is not precisely photographic. In Ayame's time, real women performed a half-kneel with the right knee raised while men raised the left knee. Ayame noted that on stage, "it depended upon the look of the thing, and one should not raise the knee that is on the side of the audience. If one only went by consistency, it would not be *kabuki*" (Dunn and Torigoe 1969: 52).

Chikamatsu agreed. He maintained that "art is something that lies in the slender margin between the real and the unreal." When confronted with the argument that absolute realism was desirable, he asked, "would it prove entertaining if an actor, on the grounds that real [samurai] retainers do not make up their faces, were to appear on the stage and perform with his beard growing wild and his head shaven?" (Keene 1960: 389). He felt that too much realism was repulsive; audiences would prefer the tension created by the actor's doubleness, an awareness of opposites in the same body (actor/character, male/female). In other words, aesthetic pleasure is more important than realism.

Some latter-day scholars have suggested that the appeal of the *onnagata* results not from transformation into an ideal, but from the apparent incorporation of both genders within a single body by manipulating (usually visual) cultural gender codes, such as costuming, wigs, makeup, and movement patterns. The audience then "reads" the outer, clothed body as "woman" while simultaneously experiencing an acute awareness of the male/boy "body beneath" (Stallybrass 1992: 70; Mezur 2001: 193, 211).

Although this perspective is both valid and helpful, one cannot help but ask why it doesn't work in reverse. In other words, why aren't male *kabuki* characters performed by biological females? To begin to address this question, we need to remember that we are speaking of a genre that originated in a time when the power to dictate artistic values – like other aspects of power – was controlled by males. Although *kabuki* has changed much over time, most fans think of it as a relatively unchanging historical treasure. Such fans agree that shifting the gender balance would destroy artistic pleasure. (Those who desire to view female bodies performing male roles have a brilliant outlet in the all-female Takarazuka Revue, established in 1914; see Chapter 10.) Then as now, the appeal of the *onnagata* is not fully explicable by simple distinctions between performance on the one hand and biology on the other. Today, that appeal may rely less on long-standing tradition, and more on the complex interplay between the performer's sense of self-identity, the expectations of culture, and the power of performance itself.

Conclusion

Like all vital arts, *kabuki* continues to grow and transform in response to changing times. Over the centuries, it has shifted from a disreputable come-on for prostitution to a classical, national form. Similarly, gender roles and identification differ widely depending on the specific time period and locale. Debates about *kabuki*'s *onnagata* can open diverse avenues to discuss gender and the position of women in various cultures throughout history.

Key references

Audio-visual resources

Tamasaburō talks about being an *onnagata*, in the interview and excerpts of several performances, in this 10-minute clip from the 1995 documentary *The Written Face*, <https://www. youtube.com/watch?v=D_ByGXCey68>.

A 10-minute excerpt of Tamasaburō's performance of the *kabuki* dance *Sagi-Musume* (*The Heron Maiden*), with excellent commentary and example of *hikinuki*, quick on-stage costume change for character transformation, < https://www.youtube.com/watch?v=3wXgh0uUv3k >.

A 10-minute excerpt from a classic *kabuki* dance by Tamasaburō, *Fuji Musume* (*The Wisteria Maiden*), <https://www.youtube.com/watch?v=sPgtX-ljHi4>.

Books and articles

Brandon, J.R. (2008) *Kabuki's Forgotten War 1931–1945*, Honolulu: University of Hawaii Press.

Brandon, J.R. (2012) "Reflections on the *Onnagata*," *Asian Theatre Journal* 29(1): 122–5.

Dunn, C., and B. Torigoe (ed. and trans.) (1969) *The Actors' Analects*, New York: Columbia University Press.

Edelson, L. (2009) *Danjūrō's Girls: Women on the Kabuki Stage*, New York: Palgrave Macmillan.

Episale, P. (2012) "Gender, Tradition, and Culture in Translation: Reading the *Onnagata* in English," *Asian Theatre Journal* 29(1): 89–111.

Isaka, M. (2006) "Women *Onnagata* in the Porous Labyrinth of Femininity: On Ichikawa Kumehachi I," *U.S.-Japan Women's Journal* 30–31: 105–31.

———. (2016) *Onnagata: A Labyrinth of Gendering in Kabuki Theatre*. Seattle: University of Washington Press.

Keene, D. (1960) *Anthology of Japanese Literature: From the Earliest Era to the Mid-Nineteenth Century*, New York: Grove Press.

Leiter, S.L. (2002) "From Gay to *Gei*: The *Onnagata* and the Creation of *Kabuki*'s Female Characters," in Samuel L. Leiter (ed.) *A Kabuki Reader: History and Performance*, Armonk, NY: M. E. Sharpe, 211–29.

Leiter, S.L. (2012) "Is the *Onnagata* Necessary?" *Asian Theatre Journal* 29(1): 112–21.

Mezur, K. (2001) "Undressing the *Onnagata*: Kabuki's Female Role Specialists and the Art of Costuming," in S. Scholz-Ciona and S.L. Leiter (eds.) *Japanese Theatre and the International Stage*, Leiden: Brill, 193–212.

Robertson, J. (1998) *Takarazuka: Sexual Politics and Popular Culture in Modern Japan*, Berkeley and Los Angeles: University of California Press.

Sorgenfrei, C.F. (2007) "Countering 'Theoretical Imperialism': Some Possibilities from Japan," *Theatre Research International* 32(3): 312–24.

Stallybrass, P. (1992) "Transvestism and the 'Body Beneath,'" in S. Zimmerman (ed.) *Erotic Politics: Desire on the Renaissance Stage*, London: Routledge, 64–83.

Summary

The four centuries between 1250 and 1650 saw a tremendous expansion in the kinds and quality of theatre in Asia and Europe, as theatre grew ever more professionalized, secular, and independent of religious and civic cycles of performance. The "business" of theatre was born in this period and was made possible partly by the increasing urbanization of both Europe and Asia. Theatre first occupied outdoor public spaces that had often been designed for other purposes. Eventually, purpose-built structures came to replace them, and then moved indoors to accompany a year-round calendar of performances.

An increasing demand for theatre resulted in a proliferation of theatre forms and thematic explorations. Increasing literacy meant actors were up to the demands of longer scripted drama, and some playwrights wrote their plays with specific actors in mind. Even in the *commedia*, an improvised form, the scenarios were often based on literary sources.

While in all periods in Europe, theatre had included female characters, it was not until this period that actual women began to take the stage and, in some cases, serve as managers of theatre companies. Educated women may have written plays for their own amusement and reading, but as we saw in the case of Hildegard of Bingen in Chapter 3, very little of their work was seen in public. Meanwhile, in Japan, actual women were forced off the stage and replaced by *onnagata*.

With the exception of China, where enjoying drama was principally an activity for the elite, theatre everywhere else was held to be a powerful force in shaping public mores and values, and therefore was subject to careful scrutiny. The presence of actual women on stage, coupled with a growing sense of theatre as a rather rowdy social occasion, made theatre a matter of some concern to the authorities in both Europe and Japan. As a result, there were numerous attempts by authorities to control the theatre through regulations, censorship, and licensing restrictions. As in England, the Japanese shogunate segregated the theatre from other urban activities, and kept the official status of actors near that of thieves and prostitutes. The fact that women were either a principal attraction (as they were in the French, Spanish, and Italian stages) or forbidden from treading the boards at all (as they were in England and Japan) shows how these anxieties frequently were focused on the bodies of women.

And yet, these restrictions did not have a chilling effect on theatrical innovation, as professional troupes and actors found ever more inventive ways to circumvent or work within them. As we move to the next two chapters, we will deepen our exploration of the effects of a burgeoning print culture on both theatre and society. We will also consider the attempts of monarchs to influence or control drama and theatrical production. Whether theatre was constrained for its purported corruptive influence, or harnessed to legitimize the national interest and values (as was the case in neoclassical France), it could be argued that, without the restrictions of monarchy and shogunate, neither Renaissance/neoclassical theatre nor *kabuki* would have developed as they did.

★

CHAPTER 5

Theatre and the print revolution in Europe, 1550–1650

Tobin Nellhaus

Contributors: Bruce McConachie and Tamara Underiner

The political, religious, economic, and cultural upheavals of Europe's **Renaissance** (roughly the fourteenth through sixteenth centuries) often placed theatre in contradictory circumstances. On the one hand, it often honored and drew financial support from monarchs and even religious authorities, and sometimes it partook in religious conflicts. On the other hand, particularly where professionalization allowed theatre greater financial and intellectual independence, at times theatre clashed with the political structures or with religious doctrines, and it faced renewed opposition and even outright suppression.

In this chapter we will focus on the impact of a fundamental change in communication in Europe, the invention of the printing press. That development was closely entwined with the other changes transforming Europe, including the Protestant Reformation and a new approach to science. We begin by sketching those developments and the ways they were connected to the burgeoning print culture. One of the most important was a renewed interest in the literary and scholarly writings of classical Greece and Rome, some of which were newly recovered. Since these works were now readily available thanks to printing, schools began to use them as the mainstays of secular education; boys and occasionally girls studied Latin, and sometimes also ancient Greek. Renaissance writers viewed classical authors such as Terence, Horace and Cicero as the pinnacles of literary style; playwrights sometimes imitated or even lifted plots from Plautus's plays for their comedies. Aristotle was unsurpassable in philosophy, and as we will see, his *Poetics* was assigned a startlingly dictatorial role. Writers found much to seize as their models, summon as their inspiration, or station as their dogmas. European drama during this era fed off the print-enabled influxes of classical texts in ways that shaped it for two centuries.

Partly because of these transformations in culture, and partly because of the development of professional theatre as discussed in the previous chapter, the millennium-long trickle of theatre in Europe burst into a flood, not only in the number of theatres and performances, but also of innovations in dramatic structure and literary style, and in stagecraft too.

DOI: 10.4324/9781003185185-8

This chapter will focus primarily on the rapid and busy developments in England, Spain, and France, and to a lesser extent Italy. In England and Spain, whose fountains of theatre sprang concurrently, the stage aimed to draw a varied audience. Compared to what would happen in France, their playwrights had relatively free rein to write as they wished. Spanish playwrights usually prioritized popular appeal, with plays often centered on the defense of personal honor. In England, dramatists tended to fuse popular styles with literary references attracting the educated elite, and many of their plots drew from Roman comedies and tragedies. In both countries, comedy and tragedy were often mixed in a single play. Professional theatre in France, slowed by domestic turmoil, at first followed a path similar to the other two countries' in its popular appeal. But during the 1500s, Italian scholars developed **neoclassicism**, a misinterpretation of Aristotle which established a set of dramaturgical rules that playwrights were advised to follow, and in 1637 France's monarchical government officially imposed those rules upon the country's dramatists. The neoclassical approach to drama shaped European playwriting for well over a century, in large part because France had evolved into a system of highly centralized rulership, which contributed to establishing itself as the height of style and culture. In all of these places, there began an important shift from the "type" characters of medieval drama and the *commedia dell'arte* to more detailed characters who seemed to have a sense of self, more like individual people. While these developments occurred, new scenic practices also arose, primarily in Italy and then exported to other European countries. Many of these practices involved perspective scenery, an approach to stagecraft that shared many of the ideas behind neoclassicism and flattered the ruler.

Social and cultural upheavals in early modern Europe

The rise of a commercial economy, which included international trade, was one contributor to the transformations that shook Europe. Global colonization was initially undertaken by monarchies, but it soon became the pursuit of private, profit-seeking companies. For example, the massive Dutch East India Company (established in 1602) obtained military, judicial, and diplomatic powers to support its mercantile ventures in Asia, including the establishment of colonies. It was also the first business in the world to issue stock, initiating the modern stock market. The profits from these colonial ventures fed the home economies. Domestically, a growing class of people drew their income from their business activities such as manufacturing, international trade, and banking, slowly forming the modern bourgeoisie – a "middle class" composed of businesspeople, property owners, professionals, and their families. And most importantly for theatre, because cities became business centers and the source of work for former peasants, these economic changes brought rapid urbanization: for example, between 1550 and 1650, Paris's population grew from roughly 300,000 to 450,000, and London's leaped from about 120,000 to 350,000, despite the decimation of each by disastrous plagues. Thus establishing permanent theatres became much more financially viable, leading to the developments discussed in Chapter 4.

Another important shift occurred in several countries' power structures, particularly after 1600: the monarch strove to wrest power from the nobility and place it directly in his or her own hands, and in the administrative, legislative, judicial, and sometimes even religious institutions that he or she controlled. Under this system, known today as **absolutism**, monarchs frequently claimed that their unilateral power was legitimate because they possessed a divine right to rule. Absolutism had important consequences for theatre, which we will touch on in this chapter and explore more fully in Chapter 6.

A third major force behind the social upheavals of this period was the rise of print culture. In Europe, the printing press with movable type (meaning each letter, number, space, and punctuation mark was a separate piece that could be inserted into place and removed for reuse) was invented in Germany around 1440. (As explained in the Introduction to Part II, it had been invented in Asia centuries before, but was far less used.) However, printing didn't have a substantial impact on social life for over 50 years. Printing was also a major commercial activity, which historian Benedict Anderson (1991) has called "print capitalism," and the organization of work in a print shop may have been the first production line. Although initially a printed book was quite expensive, it was less expensive and faster to produce than one copied by hand, so printing houses were able to serve the demands of a readership that was already beginning to grow during the late Middle Ages. Many of printing's effects would take centuries to develop, and they varied depending on social contexts and the ways in which people used print. But the printing press soon made Greek and Roman classical texts and the Bible easily obtainable, especially in vernacular translations, and their availability had major consequences for theatre and drama.

Printing, renaissance humanism, and drama

During the fourteenth century, Italian authors began to view classical Roman texts as the epitome of literary style and elegance intended for the pursuit of moral good. Poet Dante Alighieri (c.1265–1321) exemplified this attitude toward Roman authors when he chose Virgil (70 BCE–19 BCE) as his guide in his trilogy *The Divine Comedy*. These admirers of classical culture were called "**humanists**."

But when the Turks conquered the Byzantine Empire in 1453, scores of scholars fled from the empire to Italy, bringing with them numerous classical Greek manuscripts. Among these writings were several works by Plato and Aristotle that were previously unknown in Western Europe – possibly including a Greek text of Aristotle's *Poetics*, which until then was available only as a Latin translation of an Arabic translation and was virtually ignored.

Printing soon brought these and other classical works beyond in Italy to the continent. Classical Greece and Rome became everywhere esteemed as the Golden Age of culture and political glory. The wealthy and powerful often adopted imagery from those societies, and references to classical literature and art became a staple of European writing. During the century after the printing press was invented, the renaissance of classicism that began during the 1300s in a few Italian cities bloomed into a European Renaissance.

By the early 1500s, one could easily purchase editions of Aristotle's *Poetics*, the major plays of Sophocles, Plautus, Terence, and Seneca, and the illustrated discussions of theatre buildings and scenery by the Roman architect Vitruvius (first century BCE). Fired by an interest in these ancient texts, Renaissance scholars and their aristocratic patrons began writing plays that stylistically imitated the classics, and soon they sought to produce them on stage. In Italy, Gian Giorgio Trissino (1478–1550) wrote and published the first classical-style tragedy, *Sofonisba* (1515). Italian political theorist Niccolò Machiavelli (1469–1527) borrowed the form of classical comedy to write *The Mandrake* (*La Mandragola*, c.1518). Like Machiavelli, university-trained Nicholas Udall (c.1504–1556) in England leaned heavily on

Plautus to shape his *Ralph Roister Doister* sometime in the 1530s. Earlier in the century, classically based entertainments for Iberian royal courts were written by Juan del Encina (1468–c.1529) and Gil Vicente (c.1465–c.1536). Because religious strife wracked France during these years, classically inspired plays and performances developed somewhat later in Paris, with the first of them coming to the French court in the 1550s.

However, playwrights were caught between the cultural value of printing and the drawbacks of the economic environment. On the one hand, along with classical drama, printers published local and foreign tales, myths, legends, chronicles, and histories which inspired many playwrights. Also, by increasing the number of texts available to read and learn from, printing helped to make education more affordable. As a result, more actors were available who could read and memorize lines for large numbers of plays.

On the other hand, playwrights had little incentive to see their own works in print. For most, theatre was something to be heard and seen, and not necessarily read on the page. By the late sixteenth century, there was a growing public eager to read plays they had seen or heard about, which Europe's printers were keen to satisfy; but the playwrights and theatres often resisted publication. There was no copyright protection or royalty system, so playwrights were paid only once: when they sold a play to a theatre. Theatres had a profit motive to guard their plays from piracy by other theatre companies and by publishers, and they seldom allowed a play to be published until it ceased to attract audiences. At that point they might sell the play to a printer in order to squeeze the final drop of money from it, none of which went to the playwright. But once printers had their hands on a script, they reaped all the profit – which could be substantial. So unscrupulous printers stole or enticed the copying of promptbooks (the only "official" record of an entire play in performance, including stage directions), or published the remembered lines of actors that were not necessarily faithful to the playwright's intent. Thus printing under early capitalism threatened playwrights' demonstrations of their literary skill. Modern controversies over the "true" versions of Shakespeare's plays arise from the piracy that this business and legal environment encouraged. Only during the seventeenth century did playwrights start to gain anything – whether money or status – by publishing their works.

Printing and the Protestant reformation

In the Middle Ages, few people read the Bible, not least because it was normally in Latin, and Latin was the language of advanced education; in addition, Bibles were highly expensive. Ordinary priests in local parishes were themselves often ill-educated and lacked Latin. Most people received their religious knowledge primarily through sermons. But even among the elite, the most common religious books were breviaries, psalters, and similar materials for everyday devotional purposes.

Printing changed all that. Not only could a copy of the Bible be easily obtained, it was increasingly translated into the vernacular. Translations were highly desirable to a deeply religious laity: this book was the heart of Christianity. With a translation in hand, lay people's beliefs were released from the authority of the Church, and due to the connection with the vernacular, religious practices increasingly took shape nationally – a tendency that strengthened with geographical distance from Rome. Some laypeople began feeling that individual and small-group Bible-reading could replace the ritual of the Mass.

Starting in 1517, Martin Luther (1483–1546) began to challenge the authority of the Pope. He protested against various Church practices, and taught that the Bible alone was the source of divine knowledge. Luther was not the first to have such ideas or instigate a popular movement to reform the Church: what most distinguished Luther's attack was that his words were rapidly printed throughout Europe, reaching a large discontented laity keen to read them. Within a few years a massive schism within Christianity erupted, known as the Protestant Reformation. The Roman Catholic Church responded with a Counter-Reformation (1545–1648) that sought institutional reforms but also aimed to revive Catholic faith. The two soon became stubbornly adversarial.

Religious conflict grew pervasive. In England, it was central to the tumultuous succession of monarchs from Henry VIII to Elizabeth I; fundamental to England's frequent battles with Spain (including its defeat of the Spanish Armada in 1588); and a factor in the English Civil War that broke out in 1642. In Central Europe, the Thirty Years' War erupted in 1618 primarily on religious grounds, continuing non-stop until 1648. Conflict was not limited to Protestant versus Catholic: Reformation Christianity promptly spawned numerous (and often antagonistic) denominations such as Lutherans, Calvinists, Puritans, and Anabaptists. This sectarianism was itself a product of print culture, as people developed their own interpretations of religious texts. The discord slowed the development of theatre in France, and as we will see, it had an almost cataclysmic effect on English theatre.

Major characteristics of early European book culture

The print culture of early modern Europe had certain traits. One of them appears in its religious practices. In the Middle Ages, people's relationship to the Bible was mediated by the Church through priests, pictures, and other avenues, which treated the Bible in piecemeal fashion as a compendium of stories. The mystery cycles and Passion plays, although generally organized independently from the Church, followed the same pattern. But under Protestantism, religiosity was exercised first and foremost by reading the scriptures oneself. Believers developed a personal relationship to the Bible, and read it whole. For Protestants, reading the Bible provided direct access to God's revealed truth, and their creed was that faith alone was sufficient for salvation. In a related development, legality and validity were increasingly based not in a person's spoken word, but in writing.

These practices slowly inverted the concept of self. People who intensively read books (whether scriptures, scholarship, or literature) tend to develop their interior life, and to define themselves in terms of their ideas, feelings, and beliefs. The classical era and the Middle Ages had been the reverse: people were defined primarily by their outward relationships, such as social role or type (such as soldier, peasant, or merchant). The shift from outward to inward ideas of personhood took two centuries to complete, but one can see it emerging as allegorical and stock characters such as Everyman, Avarice, and wily servant were replaced by more individualized figures such as Shakespeare's characters Hamlet and Viola.

In Protestantism these two tendencies – a strengthening view of writing as the embodiment of truth and individuals' greater inward development – tended to run hand in hand because personal faith was tied to reading the Bible and regarding it as the ultimate truth. In Catholic countries, however, the combination's impact was highly complex, and contradictory trends eventually came to a head in the 1630s when playwriting held Aristotle aloft, science rejected Aristotle in favor of direct perception, and philosophy turned toward pure reason.

During the period covered by this chapter, then, theatre throughout Europe developed in the midst of enormous cultural, religious, scientific, and philosophical ferment and conflict, profoundly shaping society to the present day.

Elizabethan and Jacobean theatre in England, 1558–1642

When Queen Elizabeth I ascended to the English throne in 1558, the trends that would lead to a remarkable era of literature and performance were already beginning to coalesce – in particular, humanism fused with popular performance.

To help students learn their Latin, for several decades the universities and grammar schools had a tradition of performing the works of Roman playwrights and eventually writing new plays in Latin. These plays, along with singing and other types of performance, were often presented for elite audiences, normally indoors.

Writing new plays in Latin led to new plays in English. Comedies in English began to appear with *Ralph Roister Doister* in the 1530s. In 1561, school performances yielded the first blank verse (unrhymed lines of usually ten syllables) tragedy in English: *Gorboduc*, by Thomas Sackville and Thomas Norton. Modeled on Senecan tragedy, it foreshadowed the revenge tragedies that would frequent the English stage a few decades later.

Increasingly, university-educated playwrights turned to the professional theatres to have their plays performed. During the 1580s, most of the prominent Elizabethan playwrights came from the universities. One "university wit" was Thomas Kyd (1558–1594), whose *The Spanish Tragedy* (c.1587) opened the floodgates to murder-heavy "revenge tragedies" on the English stage. In this highly influential play, a man uses a play-within-a-play as cover to avenge the murder of his son. Another university wit was Christopher Marlowe (1564–1593), who mastered episodic plotting in such popular tragedies as *Tamburlaine*, Parts I and II (1587–1588), and *Doctor Faustus* (c.1592) (Figure 5.1), in which a scholar takes up magic and makes a deal with the devil. The 1590s brought the first plays by the two greatest playwrights of the era: William Shakespeare (1564–1616) and Ben Jonson (1572–1637). Unlike their best-known predecessors, neither of them was university-educated: they began their theatre careers as actors. Nevertheless, their grammar school education included Latin and possibly Greek. Thus the humanist tradition and the popular professional tradition merged in Elizabethan theatre.

During the English Renaissance most spectators, like television audiences today, cared little about who wrote a play. According to historian Jeremy Lopez (2003), they enjoyed wordplay (often sexual puns) and characters in disguise. The plays they applauded sometimes included such lurid (and Senecan) plot developments as incest and physical mutilations. Often spectators encountered abrupt shifts in tone, such as between lyricism, suspense, heroics, and grotesquery, and clashes between events and genres were commonplace. For example, low comedy could appear within tragedies (like the porter scene in Shakespeare's *Macbeth*, 1605–1606) or mortally serious moments in comedies (such as the "Kill Claudio" scene in his *Much Ado About Nothing*, 1598). Multileveled experiences were prized, and audiences were alive to possible ironies. They welcomed self-reflexive moments, in which the actors acknowledged the make-believe of their actions or the audience's lively presence. Lopez argues that audiences expected comedies to end in marriage and/or reunion, and the fun often lay in the play's convoluted and implausible pathway. Plays often concluded with superabundance. For example, in Shakespeare's comedy *As You Like It* (1599–1600), marriage piles upon marriage as four couples take vows in the final scene. Likewise, tragedies concluded with a stage full of dead bodies and order restored, yet the very ludicrousness of the heaping corpses contributed to the sense of loss: for example, when *Hamlet* (1599–1601) ends, four characters are dead on stage and Hamlet speaks of silence.

The growing prestige of well-written drama altered acting. In the past, talented performers had been known to go "off-script" because they had been accustomed to a more improvisatory form of theatrical performance. Hamlet makes a frustrated reference to this continuing practice in his famous speech giving advice to the players. (The conflict was scarcely limited to England: for example, as we noted in Chapter 4, the popular Japanese playwright Chikamatsu Monzaemon is said to have become so angry at *kabuki* actors mutilating his scripts that he stopped writing for living actors and shifted to writing plays exclusively for *bunraku* puppets. Similar complaints go back to the Hellenistic age.) By the 1580s, however, performers who might have improvised their way through an evening's

Figure 5.1

Faustus (played by Edward Alleyn) conjures a devil on this title page for a seventeenth-century edition of *The Tragical History of Doctor Faustus*, by Christopher Marlowe. Rumors that "one devil too many" had responded to Alleyn's black magic probably drew audiences to this popular play at the Fortune Theatre.

Source: STC 17436, Folger Shakespeare Library.

entertainment a generation before were increasingly expected to play "by the book." In *A Midsummer Night's Dream* (1595–1596), Shakespeare has even the "rude mechanicals" of his subplot memorize their lines before they mount their performance of "Pyramus and Thisbe."

During the Elizabethan era, English theatre was strongly influenced by Italian performance. Italian styles of every sort were all the rage – Queen Elizabeth herself favored Italian fashion. *Commedia dell'arte* troupes visited England several times during the 1570s, and in the subsequent decades English men of theatre frequently visited the continent and saw *commedia* companies in Italy and at their Parisian residencies. They watched dramatic situations and scenarios familiar throughout Europe (such as young lovers kept apart by their parents) staged by Italian performers, and absorbed these ideas into their own plays, while also transforming *commedia*'s "flat" stock characters into the more "rounded," inwardly de-fined type increasingly evident in English drama (as in *Romeo and Juliet*). And the English saw women such as Isabella Andreini offering powerful performances on stage. Although women could not be actors in London's theatres, the ones in the *commedia* inspired English playwrights to develop fuller female roles for the boy actors to play.

Although few contemporary plays were in print by 1600, humanists were convincing the literate public that dramatic theatre connected their own tastes with the superior culture of the ancients. After 1600, as more contemporary plays reached publication, acting companies and eventually playwrights reaped more direct benefits from the emerging print culture. By 1618, the shareholders of the boys' company Children of the Queen's Revels had published all of the extant plays they had performed. In 1616, Jonson was the first English playwright to edit and publish a collection of his own plays, calling them his *Works* – a term reserved for high literature. It was a major step toward recognizing newly written plays as having literary merit, like the Roman classics, and supplied the crucial precedent for the publi-cation of the "First Folio" in 1623, in which many of Shakespeare's plays, in authorized versions, were presented as literature (Figure 5.2). By the 1640s, it was increasingly common for companies and professional playwrights to arrange for the publication of their dramas.

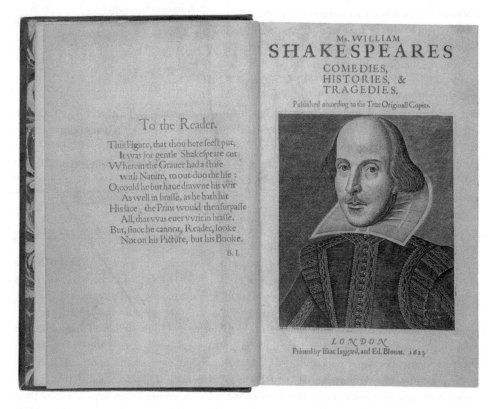

Figure 5.2

Dedication and title page of the First Folio of Shakespeare, 1623.

Source: Library of Congress, https://www.loc.gov/item/2021666879.

In addition, more dramatists were striking deals with their companies to maintain control of their publication rights.

When King James I (1566–1625) began his reign in 1603 – known as the **Jacobean era** – the countries of England and Scotland both came under his rule. In addition, Wales and Ireland had been governed by England for 50 years or more. Thus, for the first time, the British Isles had a single monarch. Shakespeare's *King Lear* (1606), in which the king divides up his kingdom with disastrous results, alludes to King James's unification of the island. James, a firm believer in **absolutism** (discussed in Chapter 6), had frequent conflicts with Parliament over financial matters, and he dissolved Parliament several times.

During James's and his son Charles I's rule, drama continued to flourish. But tragedy became more sensationalist, dark, cynical, sometimes obsessed with (and terrified by) women's sexuality, but sometimes sentimental too. Revenge tragedies became more popular than ever. Strongly influenced by Seneca's morbid plays, they were often filled with gore and broken taboos, and almost specialized in body counts. One of the best known is *The Duchess of Malfi* (1612–1613) by John Webster (c.1580–c.1634), in which one of the Duchess's brothers has her murdered, along with her children, for marrying beneath her and sharing the siblings' inheritance; but then his spy turns the tables and avenges her death. Ten die in all. (*Hamlet* is considered a revenge tragedy.) Comedy now tended toward satirizing the follies of the time, often turning toward London for its subjects. For example, in Jonson's *The Alchemist* (1610) a trio performs preposterous con games that play on their marks' gullibility (see Figure 5.3).

Figure 5.3

Simon Callow (Face), Josie Lawrence (Doll Common), Tim Pigott-Smith (Subtle) in *The Alchemist* by Ben Jonson at the Birmingham Repertory Theatre, 1996, directed by Bill Alexander.

Source: Donald Cooper/Alamy Stock Photo.

More than other playwrights, Jonson also brought a strong dose of classical precepts and wit into his plays, incorporating the neoclassical "rules" discussed later in this chapter. Trag-icomedies abounded too. John Fletcher (1579–1625) wrote many, including *A King and No King* (1611). In it, a young king and his sister, long separated, each feel intense incestuous desires which they struggle against, but all is resolved when they learn that actually they are unrelated.

Elizabethan and Jacobean drama – especially the plays by Shakespeare and Jonson – left long but shifting legacies. During the 1600s and early 1700s, although Shakespeare was much admired and performed, Jonson had greater influence on new plays. But during the eighteenth century, Shakespeare's reputation as the world's greatest playwright began solidi-fying and Jonson passed out of favor. Nevertheless, Shakespeare's preeminence did not create many imitators.

Throughout the sixteenth and seventeenth centuries, many Protestant sects arose in England. One of them, the Puritans, slowly developed considerable clout within the Church of England, educational institutions, and city governments – and they abhorred theatre. Their religious objections to it were partly linked to Protestant print culture, in which morality was tied to reading the Bible. The Puritans feared that imitation and spectacle would turn people away from the biblical path to salvation, and thus corrupt their morals and reason, and teach them to delight in illusion and debauchery. Ordinary people (already inherently depraved, according to the Puritans) would be tempted to commit sinful behaviors such as robbery, sodomy, and even murder if they watched such activities or simply heard them discussed on the stage. Further, the Bible forbade transvestism, which was a regular part of English Renaissance theatre because (as we saw in Chapter 4) all female roles were played by boy actors, and many plot and character devices involved gender bending. In fact, panicked by the very notion of sexuality outside procreation, the Puritans damned every element of theatre as infested with deviance and effeminacy.

Playwrights returned the Puritans' animosity by poking fun at them. For example, the character Malvolio in Shakespeare's *Twelfth Night* is depicted as "a kind of Puritan," and other characters play a few mean practical jokes on him. The Puritans' objections to cross-dressing became the target of Jonson's satire *Bartholomew Fair*, in which a Puritan vehemently censures a hand puppet for wearing women's clothes, and loses the argument when the puppet lifts its skirt to reveal it has no sex at all. (The case study on *Twelfth Night*, located in the *Theatre Histories* website, discusses Elizabethan theatre and sexuality further.)

However, deep trouble was brewing. When Charles I (1600–1649) succeeded James I in 1625, he married the youngest princess of France – a Catholic – raising fears that the Church of England might reunite with the Roman Catholic Church. Despite Charles's sup-port for the Protestants during the Thirty Years' War, some of his actions seemed to justify those fears. Thus the Puritans began to conflict directly with the monarchy. Meanwhile, Par-liament repeatedly clashed with the king, principally over financial matters, leading Charles I to dissolve it. In the late 1630s his religious measures provoked a rebellion in Scotland. To finance his battles with the Scots, Charles recalled Parliament, which refused to provide money except under its own terms. Conflict arose in Ireland as well and ultimately spread to England. The English Civil War broke out in 1642. Led by Oliver Cromwell (1599–1658), opponents of the monarchy beheaded King Charles I in 1649 and declared a Common-wealth that lasted until 1660.

At the start of the Civil War, Parliament, controlled by Puritans, came fully into power in London and the surrounding areas. One of its first acts was to suppress all stage plays. The Puritans initially imposed the ban as a temporary safeguard against civil strife, but they later broadened and extended it. Some theatres managed to continue anyway, even as the Puritans tore down the Globe and all other playhouses. But by the end of the 1640s, theatre in England had become sporadic and usually surreptitious.

Golden age theatre in Spain, 1590–1650

The volume and variety of dramatic output during Spain's Golden Age was enormous, numbering in the tens of thousands of plays. In turn, Spanish drama of this period influenced numerous European playwrights of the time, many of whom borrowed its plots and themes.

While the presentation of religious drama (*autos sacramentales*, see Chapter 3) remained strong throughout the period, and despite Spain's reputation for being an overly zealous Catholic country, the drama of its Golden Age treated many themes central to a humanist understanding of the world. In such drama, the decisions made by everyday men and women – not God, not saints, not allegorical figures – drive the action of the play, as they face conflicts in love, honor, duty, valor, social standing, political power, and so forth. One influence on the drama of this time was the social thought of Spanish philosopher, theologian and jurist Francisco de Vitoria (c.1483–1546), who argued in favor of a "natural law" that was universal and inherent, exercised by human reason rather than delivered of God (Cowling et al. 2021). In some, albeit rare cases, this idea of natural human dignity would extend even to the native peoples of the New World, for example in the drama of its first female playwright, Sor Juana Inés de la Cruz, the subject of our first case study.

In Spain as elsewhere in Europe, it took some time for theatre to separate itself from religious themes and contemporary issues to create a fictional world, or what Spanish Golden Age scholar Melveena McKendrick calls "a self-contained world of its own, a world of the imagination" (1989: 11). Most scholars credit playwright Juan del Encina (c.1468–c.1529) with the beginnings of this movement, especially in his later plays introducing secular themes. Encina was a shoemaker's son who studied law, and his experiences at court in Spain and Rome likely influenced his later work.

Perhaps the principal inaugurator of a truly humanist impulse in Spanish theatre was Bartolomé de Torres Naharro (c.1485–c.1525). He consciously looked back to ancient models from Italy and Greece to derive principles for writing effective drama, both technically and thematically – principles meant to serve as guidelines, in contrast to the ways they became hardened into strict rules and regulations in places like France (discussed below). According to McKendrick, Naharro's plays may never have been staged in Spain, but they were widely read in printed editions and re-editions up until 1557, when they were banned in their entirety by the Spanish Inquisition (which enforced Catholic orthodoxy) for their irreverent themes. His popularity inspired many imitators in print, but it is not clear whether these dramas were ever performed.

As we saw in Chapter 4, once permanent theatres began to be established in the urban centers of Spain, especially in Madrid, the demand for new plays on all kinds of subjects was insatiable.

Just as the public theatres accommodated popular and aristocratic spectators, so too did many of the new plays merge the tastes and values of both groups. The Spanish term for these plays, *comedias* [sing. *comedia*: koh-MEY-dee-ah], refers to a wide variety of plays, both serious and comic, and should not be confused with *commedia dell'arte*. The history plays and romantic dramas successfully fused these traditions and are characterized by their blending of serious and comic elements, usually in a three-act structure. Frequently they featured plots in which a man's or woman's honor was at stake, and which often turned on such devices and developments as mistaken identity, the use of disguises, and swordfights. In fact, swordfights, or the threat of them among men of a certain social rank, were so common as to constitute a subgenre of *comedia* called the *capa y espada* [KAH-pa ee es-PAH-thah] (cape and sword) plays; other recognizable types included pastorals, comedies of manners, "noisy" plays featuring lots of spectacle and stage effects, and dramas based on myth and history.

The illusive nature of reality itself was a frequent preoccupation of Spanish Golden Age playwrights. Theatre and theatricality offered tempting ways for them to explore this theme, in works that staged plays-within-plays, or were themselves *about* plays, or in some other ways showed life itself to be highly theatricalized. So frequently were these metatheatrical device employed in Spanish Golden Age drama that some scholars claim it as a characteristic convention of such drama. In fact, metatheatricality was commonplace throughout European drama during this era; we discuss it further in the second case study in this chapter.

Writing about Spanish Golden Age drama, Alexander A. Parker suggests that the plays operated on five basic principles:

> (1) the primacy of action over character drawing; (2) the primacy of theme over action, with the consequent irrelevance of realistic verisimilitude [lifelike appearance]; (3) dramatic unity in the theme and not in the action; (4) the subordination of the theme to a moral purpose through the principle of poetic justice [where good is rewarded and evil punished], which is not exemplified only by the death of the wrongdoer; and (5) the elucidation of the moral purpose by means of dramatic causality [i.e., all the principal events in the play follow a chain of cause and effect that culminates in the distribution of poetic justice].
>
> (Parker 1971: 29)

Of the voluminous number of plays written and produced, the canon of Golden Age plays in English translation is small, but indicative and provocative. Perhaps the most famous are the historical play *Fuenteovejuna* by Lope de Vega (Figure 5.4); *The Trickster of Seville* by Tirso de Molina (which first introduced to the stage the legendary lothario, Don Juan) (Figure 5.5); and the philosophical drama *Life Is a Dream* by Pedro Calderón de la Barca (who you will recall from Chapter 3 was also the most famous author of *autos sacramentales* in Spain).

The most prolific and renowned playwright of the Golden Age, Lope Félix de Vega Carpio (1562–1635), wrote many *capa y espada* dramas among his more than 800 plays. Although a favorite of the aristocracy, Lope de Vega came from an artisan family, worked to gain more education throughout his life, and eventually became a priest. Two of Lope de Vega's history plays, *The Life and Death of King Bamba* (1597–1598) and *Fuenteovejuna*

Figure 5.4

The Young National Company of Classic Theatre perform *Fuenteovejuna* by Lope de Vega at La Comedia Theatre, in Madrid, Spain, 2017.

Source: Quim Llenas/Getty Images.

Figure 5.5

Spanish actors Mamen Camacho and Raul Prieto in Tirso de Molina's *El burlador de Sevilla* (*The Trickster of Seville*) at the Comedia Theatre, Madrid, Spain, in 2018.

Source: Quim Llenas/Getty Images.

(1612–1614), provide illustrative examples of how the *comedias* blended secular and religious elements. Both alter the historic record for dramatic effect, contrasting peasant wisdom, valor, and humility (backed by Catholic faith) against the foolish and villainous objections of a fractious nobility; both call on the Spanish nobility to draw on history and popular tradition to change their morality. *Fuenteovejuna* (whose title refers to the name of a town named after the local watering hole for sheep) has been frequently re-staged and adapted, for its view of community solidarity against a tyrannical overlord. When this overlord is assassinated, and the royal investigators come to ask "who did it," each community member proclaims, "Fuenteovejuna!" (In Spanish, the answer can become a play on words that further frustrates authority, for if the first syllable is drawn out, as in "*Fue* ..." it also means "It was. ...")

At the invitation of a learned contemporary, Lope de Vega also concerned himself with theorizing drama as well as writing it. The result was his *New Art of Writing Plays for Our Time* (1609), originally delivered in verse as an address to a literary assembly. An informal (and often funny) defense of popular taste as a valid measure of a drama, Lope de Vega's ideas, like Torres Naharro's before him, stand in contrast to the stricter neoclassicism of Italy and France (discussed below), and many scholars view his dramaturgical approach as more aligned with Shakespeare's than with his other European contemporaries.

The role of printing in this period was especially important to female writers, who only rarely, if ever, saw their plays staged, but who nevertheless wrote numerous and worthy dramas that circulated in print and have recently become fertile grounds for scholarship. These playwrights include Ana Caro de Mallén (1590–c.1646), Leonor de la Cueva y Silva (1611–1705), Feliciana Enríquez de Guzmán (c.1569–1644), and María de Zayas y Sotomayor (1590–c.1661). What their plays share most strongly, writes Teresa Scott Soufas, "is an emphasis on male irresponsibility with regard to social mores and gender ideological demands" (1997: ix). These plays seem to ask of their readers: if Spanish society depends upon strict adherence to gendered categories of proper behavior and codes of honor, what happens to its women when the men don't hold up their end of the bargain? According to Soufas, most of these playwrights followed the principles of Lope de Vega's *comedia nueva* (new comedy), but Enríquez's work was consciously concerned with following the form of classical drama, and was meant to appeal to a more learned audience. The verse prologue to her *Tragicomedia de los jardines y campos sabeos* (*Tragicomedy of the Sabean Gardens and Fields*, 1623) called for a return to the formal unities of time and place in drama (as defined by neoclassicism).

During the reign of Philip IV (born 1605; ruled 1621–1665), the Spanish monarchy asserted more control of its kingdom and colonies and also called more frequently on the theatre to bolster its absolutist claims to power. Calderón succeeded Lope de Vega as Spain's most successful playwright, but his energies were split between the public theatres and the court. Writing primarily between 1622 and 1640, Calderón continued and improved upon the previous genres, often blending religious and secular themes. His best-known secular play, *Life Is a Dream* (c.1636), presents the absolute power and agency of kingship as the necessary answer for a royal prince who was imprisoned his whole life and does not know if his return to court has been a dream. After 1640, Calderón mostly abandoned writing for the public theatres so that he could create *autos* and devise entertainments with lavish spectacles to glorify Philip IV and his court.

When Spain began to colonize the Americas, learned men and women there also wrote plays in the tradition of the Golden Age. Perhaps the most important of these American playwrights were Juan Ruiz de Alarcón (whose work was less prolific but more consistently fine than those of his Peninsular counterparts) and Sor Juana Inés de la Cruz. You may recall the brief discussion in Chapter 3 of her *loa* to the *Divine Narcissus*, an allegorical *auto sacramental* that seems to have drawn on the idea of "natural law" mentioned above in affording Native Americans and their gods equal status with Spaniards and theirs. This view was hardly canonical, and Sor Juana paid dearly for her emerging reputation as a free-thinking woman of letters in the early years of print culture in the Americas, as the following case study shows.

CASE STUDY: Sor Juana Inés de la Cruz and the perils of print culture in New Spain

Tamara Underiner

Hardly anything about Sor Juana Inés de la Cruz's life was conventional, and much of it was controversial. Born to an unwed mother in the mid-seventeenth century as Juana Inés de Asbaje y Ramírez de Santillana, she taught herself in the classics she found in her grandfather's library, at a time when only boys received formal education. By the time she was 16, she was as famous at court in New Spain (today's Latin America) for her learning as for her beauty. Four years later, she took the vows of a Catholic nun in order to pursue a life of the mind – a profession impossible for married women in her day. (It is by her religious name, Sor Juana Inés de la Cruz – "Sister Juana Inés of the Cross" – that she is known.) While at the convent of San Jerónimo, she produced hundreds of written works in all literary genres, and wrote numerous philosophical, theological, and scientific essays. She earned a reputation for independent thought,

Figure 5.6
Sor Juana Inés de la Cruz as a nun in the Order of San Jerónimo. *Portrait of Sor Juana Inés de la Cruz* by Miguel Cabrera, c.1750 (Museo Nacional de Historia, Castillo de Chapultepec, Mexico).
Source: DeAgostini/Getty Images.

rooted solidly in her understanding of canonical texts. Her cleverness with language and her fearlessness in the face of textual and religious authority both impressed and threatened her Church superiors, who eventually worked to silence her (Figure 5.6).

Sor Juana's work is important for students of theatre history in two ways. First, her plays are late examples of Spanish Golden Age and Baroque drama that featured at least two innovations: the inversion of gender conventions and the incorporation of non-Spanish culture and thought. Second, she worked under what many scholars refer to as "the shadow of the Inquisition," which led to the central paradox of her life: her apparent capitulation to that authority when she was at the height of her fame and powers. In the end, Sor Juana was caught up in a complex web of oral, written, and print culture.

Sor Juana's dramaturgy

For theatre history, Sor Juana's output is relatively small – three *autos sacramentales*, three *comedias* (two co-authored), and numerous short plays, some devotional, some farcical. Most of these were staged, if they were staged at all, behind convent walls or for the viceregal court in Mexico City. Nevertheless, her work for the stage, even if never realized on one, is noteworthy for its theatrical potential as well as its philosophical qualities and attention to social justice within the concept of natural law, as discussed above. According to Francisco López-Martín:

> In the three autos written by Sor Juana, together with their corresponding loas, the Mexican nun expresses a scathing critique of the conquest of America, with the intention that her voice be heard in Madrid. ... These writings, particularly in their stylistic and aesthetic content, condemn inequality, in particular the unequal treatment of the indigenous people of the New World by the Spanish Crown and its American representatives.
>
> (López-Martín 2021: 54)

As an example, recall our brief discussion in Chapter 3 of Sor Juana's Corpus Christi auto, *The Divine Narcissus*, and its *loa* (one-act prologue, c.1688). Meant for performance in the court at Madrid, both play and *loa* combine the depth of medieval allegory with the height of the Baroque court masques described in Chapter 6. The *loa*, for example, opens with indigenous song and dance in honor of the God of the Seeds. It features four elaborately costumed characters who debate finer points of Christian and native theology; the characterization of Zeal as a blustering Spanish soldier suggests the playwright's opinion on the merits of force in the matter of religious conversion. The play proper reconfigures the Narcissus myth, with Christ as Narcissus falling in love with his own image in Human Nature, dying for that love and being resurrected in the sacraments; Echo is a fallen angel, jealous of that love. In *loa* and play together, Sor Juana figuratively aligns Christ with both the pagan Greek figure of Narcissus and the heathen American God of the Seeds – no small feat artistically, philosophically, and theologically. At the same time, she raises a subtle question about the actual merits and success of the Spanish religious conquest of indigenous Americans.

If the subject of religious conversion sounds appropriately pious for a nun to have undertaken in an auto sacramental, her secular *comedias* were another matter entirely. Sor Juana was familiar with the conventions of the "cape and sword" plays of the Spanish Golden Age, which both circulated in print in Mexico and were staged at court. But in her hands, the convention was transformed from *capa y espada* into what Mexican dramatist and scholar Guillermo Schmidhuber calls "*falda y empeño*" ("petticoats and perseverance"), wherein the perspectives of female protagonists are privileged, as are their "efforts to bettering the condition of women as thinking and social beings" (2000: ix).

Two of her *comedias* were co-authored with male playwrights from Spain and New Spain, both adaptations of older works that feature clever and complex female characters. But it is Sor Juana's solo-authored *comedia* that is best known among theatre scholars and producers, for it is still being written about and staged: *Los empeños de una casa*, translated literally as *Pawns of a House*, and more figuratively as *House of Trials or House of Desires*. It appears to be a take-off of or response to Calderón's *Los empeños de un acaso* (*Determinations of a Chance Happening*, c.1631).

Like the best of the Golden Age dramas, Sor Juana's features the familiar devices of mistaken identity, love triangles, and plenty of swordfighting, by candlelight. The low light of the candles serves at first to mask, and then reveal, a clever plot twist: the person the rivals are fighting over is not the beautiful Doña Leonor, but the clownish manservant Castaño, dressed in her clothes. The men are the "pawns" of the title, masterfully manipulated by the mistress of the house, Doña Ana, for the benefit of Leonor. The language of the scene is full of *double entendres* meant for the pleasure of the knowing audience. It is not clear who actually acted these parts in the original production, but had it been staged in Spain, it would have presented a spectacle of mistaken same-sex desire that reversed the usual set-up for cross-dressing on the Spanish stage, where normally it was actresses who dressed as young men in order to move freely through the world of the play. Scholar Julie Greer Johnson suggests that in *Los empeños de una casa*, Sor Juana argues theatrically that "a woman is suited to other social and cultural roles than the ones she currently occupied, and she demonstrates this by testing, transgressing, and transforming the skewed, conventional spatial boundaries on stage" (Johnson 2001, n.p.).

Sor Juana herself was a transgressor of social norms – cloistered as a good nun should be, but working as a public intellectual by virtue of her writings. Her relations with her superiors were often fraught, but for a time she enjoyed the protection of the vice-regals for whom she wrote this play: the Marquis of la Laguna and his wife María Luisa, countess of Paredes, to whom Sor Juana also addressed many poems of gratitude, admiration, and love. Sor Juana produced the majority of her work during their term in New Spain (between 1680 and 1688), and they were responsible for its eventual publication in Spain. (The strict censorship of books in New Spain would have made their publication there impossible, but copies found their way to the Americas with Spanish travelers.) Under the protection of the vice-regals, she was relatively safe from the Inquisition in New Spain. When they left for Spain in 1688, she came under the increasing scrutiny of Church authorities at home. Dorothy Schons (1949) has suggested that one of her "crimes" was that she was a dramatist at all – let alone a published one who happened to be not just a woman, but a nun – in a period when Mexico City was ruled by an archbishop who did his best to prevent the publishing and staging of theatrical works in Mexico.

A Sermon, two letters, and a famous reply

The story of the end of Sor Juana's life and career revolves around tensions between oral, written, and print cultures. In 1690, at the request of her friend, the Bishop of Puebla, Sor Juana hand-wrote a private letter formalizing comments she had made in conversation with him, about an oral sermon delivered at the Portuguese court and published some 40 years earlier by a Portuguese Jesuit priest. Without her knowledge or permission, she later claimed, the bishop transcribed and printed her letter as a pamphlet entitled *Carta Atenagorica* (*Letter Worthy of Athena*), introducing it with a letter of his own under the feminine pseudonym "Sor Filotea de la Cruz." The bishop's intentions in printing the letter were, ostensibly, to acknowledge Sor Juana's intellectual gifts in a public way. But hiding behind his pseudonym, he actually spent much of his own letter warning her of the dangers to her soul, as a woman, for pursuing humanist learning, and urged her to focus more on the study of religious works in a manner more befitting her vows of obedience as a devout nun.

Within three months, Sor Juana had composed a response, the famous "Respuesta a Sor Filotea" ("Reply to Sor Filotea"), in which she defended the rights of women to knowledge and learning, in the process writing her own spiritual and intellectual biography. Hailed by some as the first feminist manifesto in the New World, it was not published until after she died (and then only in Spain). But her prior work had already brought her under the scrutiny of Church authorities in New Spain, and the Archbishop of Mexico began to issue public calls in support of "Sor Filotea's" position that Sor Juana abandon her worldly studies.

In 1693, she came under investigation by the Church authorities. In 1694, celebrating the 25th anniversary of her vows, she signed certain documents that may have been conventional acts of repentance, or may have been deliberate renunciations of her past life, made under pressure. While her motives may be opaque to us now, it is certainly true that, with the departure of her patrons, her public voice was effectively silenced, since it would have depended upon access to print. We know that she stopped writing in 1694, sold a great number of her books and scientific instruments to help the poor who had suffered through three years of floods, famine, and disease in Mexico City, and devoted her last year of life to nursing ailing nuns in the convent. In 1695, she herself succumbed to the plague that had swept the city.

Feminist scholars have long appreciated the sophistication of Sor Juana's rhetorical strategies in negotiating the various levels of Church and civic power with which she regularly had to contend. As a result, it is difficult to interpret the events of her final year: was she forced by these authorities to abandon all she had once valued, or did she do so of her own choice? Perhaps a clue is in her "Reply":

> But in truth, my Lady, what can we women know, save philosophies of the kitchen? It was well put by Lupercio Leonardo [sic] that one can philosophize quite well while preparing supper. I often say, when I make these little observations, "Had Aristotle cooked he would have written a great deal more." And so to go on with the mode of my cogitations: I declare that all this is so continual in me that I have no need of books.

(De la Cruz 1999: 75)

Not content merely to argue for women's place at the table of learning, Sor Juana suggests that Aristotle himself could have learned and written more had he ventured into the kitchen, that primal domain of women. In this context of her life and work, her claim now to "have no need of books" is a complex statement indeed. For it can be argued that her life and career were both made possible and undone by print culture itself.

Key references

Bemberg, M.L. (2003 DVD, dir.) *I, the Worst of All/Yo, la peor de todas*, First Run Features.

De la Cruz, J. (1997a) *Poems, Protest, and a Dream*, trans. M.S. Peden, New York: Penguin Books.

De la Cruz, J. (1997b) *House of Trials/Los empeños de una casa*, trans. D. Pasto, New York and Oxford: Peter Lang Press.

De la Cruz, J. (1998) *The Divine Narcissus/El divino Narcisso*, trans. P.A. Peters, Albuquerque: University of New Mexico Press.

De la Cruz, J. (1999) *The Answer/La Respuesta*, 2nd edn, trans. E. Arenal and A. Powell, New York: Feminist Press.

De la Cruz, J. (2005a) *House of Desires/Los empeños de una casa*, trans. C. Boyle, London: Oberon Books.

De la Cruz, J. (2005b) *Los empeños de una casa/Pawns of a House*, trans. M. McGaha, Tempe, AZ: Bilingual Review Press.

Johnson, J.G. (2001) "Engendered Theatrical Space and the Colonial Woman in Sor Juana's *Los empeños de una casa*," *Ciberletras,* 5 August. Online, <http://www.lehman.cuny.edu/ciberletras/v05/johnson.html> (accessed 14 July 2023).

López-Martín, F (2021). "The Voice of the Voiceless: Towards Equality and Social Justice in Sor Juana's *El divino Narciso*," in Cowley et al., 53–67.

Merrim, S. (1999) *Feminist Perspectives on Sor Juana Inés de la Cruz*, Detroit: Wayne State University Press.

Paz, O. (1990) *Sor Juana: or, The Traps of Faith*, trans. M.S. Peden, Cambridge, MA: Belknap Press.

Schmidhuber de la Mora, G. (2000) *The Three Secular Plays of Sor Juana Inés de la Cruz*, trans. S. Thacker, Lexington: University Press of Kentucky.

Schons, D. (1949) *Book Censorship in New Spain*, Austin: University of Texas.

French theatre before the triumph of neoclassicism, 1550–1637

Theatre in France began in much the same way as it had in England and Spain: traveling troupes, attracted by the rising population of Paris, eventually established permanent homes in existing buildings or even in purpose-built theatres. Similarly, French playwriting saw popular and humanist plays develop in parallel, a significant number of them written by university students. But from there, French theatre diverged. Its development was slowed by the political and religious turmoil that roiled the country during the last third of the sixteenth century and sporadically well into the seventeenth century. In addition, popular performance in France (unlike England and Spain) was dominated for decades by touring Italian *commedia dell'arte* companies, which were often invited into France by the royalty. Faced with this competition, French popular theatre was strongly shaped by *commedia dell'arte*, which influenced French comedy far into the 1600s.

Drama for the elite was mainly affected by humanism and its more exacting successor, neoclassicism (which we will discuss shortly), which increasingly pushed out popular approaches. By the mid-sixteenth century, the schools and colleges began to generate plays imitating Roman drama but in French vernacular. The first humanist play in France was *Cléopâtre captive*, a tragedy by Étienne Jodelle (1532–1573), which appeared in 1553. It was a resounding success when performed before King Henry II. Comedies and tragicomedies followed, as did plays written in the classical mode but on biblical subjects. Sometimes students toured these plays to towns across France, where they were also warmly received. French humanist drama was spread throughout France through printed editions, which were usually read aloud. However, playwriting barely existed in France until the 1630s, when it rapidly grew in both importance and quality.

The professional players customarily performed a serious play followed by a comedy or a farce, but the farces – often laden with coarse humor or outright obscenity – were by far the most popular and at times dominated the repertory until the 1630s. In Paris, professional companies were occasionally summoned to perform in the palaces and estate houses, bringing exactly the same plays they staged at the Hôtel de Bourgogne (see Chapter 4). But in the early 1600s, the aristocracy began to turn away from farces and instead preferred serious drama and more genteel comedy.

During the first quarter of the seventeenth century, the playwright who dominated the stage was Alexandre Hardy (c.1572–c.1632). Hardy was extraordinarily prolific, claiming authorship of at least 600 plays, although only 34 have survived (having been permitted publication by the acting companies). He wrote mainly for a popular audience, but increased the characters' psychological depth. Although he adopted some of the Senecan style, he combined it with the multiple settings of medieval theatre. His plays frequently mixed genres and have often been disparaged. Nevertheless, as the first professional playwright, he paved the way for the neoclassical playwrights who emerged in the coming decade.

During the 1630s, French theatre developed rapidly. Professional acting companies became increasingly well established in Paris – and like the *commedia* troupes, they included women among the actors. The Comédiens du Roi (mentioned in Chapter 4), led by the actor Bellerose (1592–1670) after Valleran's death in 1613, secured permanent residence at the Hôtel de Bourgogne in 1629. In 1634, Montdory (Guillaume de Gilleberts, 1594–1653), who had been one of the leading actors of the Comédiens du Roi but left that company to start his own, settled his troupe in a new permanent space, the Théâtre du Marais – the first significant challenger to the Hôtel de Bourgogne. Tastes became more sophisticated; audiences probably became less mixed as class divisions took root in French theatre. And humanist approaches to drama, which had continued since the mid-1500s, adopted a new, more rigid form now known as neoclassicism.

Neoclassicism, print, and the controversy over *Le Cid*

Italy – birthplace of the Renaissance humanism that printing helped sweep across Europe – also spawned neoclassicism, an effort to follow the drama theories of classical Greece and Rome as strictly as possible. Its main theorists were Julius Caesar Scaliger (1484–1558) and especially Lodovico Castelvetro (c.1505–1571), who set out to update and improve upon the discussions of drama found in Aristotle's *Poetics*, with some additions from Horace's *Ars Poetica* (see Chapters 1 and 2). But Aristotle's authority was appropriated to justify a dogma that actually drew rather little from the text of the *Poetics*.

Aristotle derived his observations from actual examples of what he considered excellent and lesser plays. Scaliger and Castelvetro reversed Aristotle's method to create prescriptive requirements, or "**rules**," for future plays. The most fundamental requirement was Aristotle's concept of imitation (mimesis), which the neoclassicists developed into the concept of **veri-similitude**: the quality of appearing true to life, realistic, or dramatically probable.

From the concept of verisimilitude flowed further rules. Relying in part on several misunderstandings (and even willful distortions) of Aristotle's notoriously difficult text, Scaliger and Castelvetro required playwrights to maintain three **unities** – of action, time, and place – in constructing their dramas: a play should encompass only one major plot, its fictional time should last no more than a single day, and its scenes should occur in a single location.

The *unity of action* – the only one that actually came from Aristotle's text – prohibited multiple plots, such as those common in English Renaissance and Spanish Golden Age drama. Scaliger and Castelvetro devised the *unity of time* out of Aristotle's comment that the action in most tragedies occurs within a single day, although sometimes longer. Castelvetro not only made this observation an absolute rule, but also urged that 12 hours would better serve verisimilitude. The "ignorant multitude" attending a play, said Castelvetro, would not believe "that several days and nights had passed when their senses tell them that only a few hours have passed" (Carlson 1993: 48–9). Similarly, the *unity of place* was necessary because purportedly, spectators would be bewildered if the stage in front of them portrayed several locations (even though medieval performance had always done exactly that).

One further precept formed the main rules: **decorum** (or propriety), a rule which the neoclassicists took from Horace. It required that playwrights follow the tastes and morals of the day, and it slowly restrained all material that might shock audiences. Decorum preserved class lines by specifying behavior appropriate for each class: for example, in serious drama only lower-class characters could act foolishly. As we will see, one more requirement of neoclassicism would eventually descend from decorum: the principle of poetic justice.

Neoclassicism radically underestimated spectators' imaginative capabilities and flew in the face of most people's actual experience in the popular theatres. But the prejudices of early print culture, plus the current beliefs about social hierarchy, supported Scaliger and Castelvetro. Supposedly, only educated scholars and aristocrats whose imaginations had been stretched and tested by books might be able to understand plays that violated verisimilitude, whereas the "ignorant multitude," with merely their "senses" to guide them, would be lost. Ironically, it was the popular drama that freely presented multiple places, events covering sometimes years, and subplots along with main plots; the upper classes instead demanded plays that carefully narrowed imaginations.

In practice, the unities often conflicted with the goal of verisimilitude. The volume of action in most plays of the era could seldom actually happen in a single day, and was even more unlikely to all occur in a single room or even one building. Consequently, plays frequently stretched the rules and glossed over any contradictions.

However, as historian John Lough points out, despite their apparent rigidity the rules had a crucial result: neoclassical tragedy subordinated physical action to "psychological conflict portrayed at a moment of crisis" (1979: 106). Thus they were part of a larger movement in Western drama – and print culture as a whole – toward a focus on personal internal struggles. Because it was tied to print culture, this orientation became a permanent part of mainstream theatre (and some outside the mainstream), leading, for example, to the **psychological realism** of the 1950s to be discussed in Chapter 12. Even today, numerous plays obey the rules, intentionally or not.

During the early 1600s, the impact of neoclassicism varied across Europe. Most French and Spanish scholars agreed with the Italian theorists, at least in principle, but several popular playwrights voiced objections from the start. As we have seen, Lope de Vega acknowledged the validity of the rules advocated by the Italians and admitted that his plays violated them, but he forthrightly stated his intention to continue pleasing his audiences rather than bow to the theorists. Alexandre Hardy also sought the vindication of public applause over scholarly praise. In England, playwrights other than Jonson almost completely ignored neoclassicism until after the ban on theatre was lifted in 1660. Overall, however, neoclassicism solidified a class division between types of performance: the rule-bound drama of the highly literate elite, and the popular drama which ignored most or all of the rules.

Eventually print culture developed to the point where some of the educated began believing that reading printed plays was superior to watching a live performance. Although that view had been directly contradicted by early neoclassicists like Castelvetro just a few decades previously, some elites developed an antitheatrical prejudice, claiming that the stage was, in effect, the place of bodies and mortality, while the page could attain immortality in the realm of the spirit. Even some dramatists writing for the popular stage supported this view.

The dispute between the popular stage and the academic theorists came to a head in France with the production of *Le Cid*, by Pierre Corneille (1606–1684), in 1637. The play concerned a soldier who, in order to defend his father's honor, is forced to kill the father of the woman he loves. But following his victories in battle and a duel, the king commands their marriage, despite her protests. The play formally accorded with the unities, but the content was more like a popular play: numerous actions were packed into a single day, and the "single place" was the expanse of a city. Moreover, the forced marriage of the woman to her father's killer crashed through the boundaries of decorum. But theatrically it was a success. Thus controversy quickly broke out, and when the resulting "war of pamphlets" became excessively ugly, Cardinal Richelieu (1585–1642) called on the French Academy – established in 1635 to standardize and "purify" the French language, still its role today – to settle the dispute.

Richelieu, who effectively ruled France in the 1620s and 1630s behind the throne of Louis XIII, used the controversy over *Le Cid* to position the monarchy as the final judge of French culture. Although the French Academy had originated as a private organization of scholars, Richelieu pressured its members to adopt state support and to take as its primary goal the codification and regulation of French language and culture. Like the publication of dictionaries and grammars that attempted to standardize Western European languages in the 1600s, the French Academy was itself a product of print culture. By referring the debate over *Le Cid* to the arbitration of the Academy, Richelieu ensured that the French state had control over the future of French theatre and culture, which became a pillar of French absolutism.

Six months later, Richelieu's appointee Jean Chapelain (1595–1674) delivered the Academy's verdict. Chapelain took issue with some of the criticism leveled against Corneille, but condemned the play for breaching verisimilitude and for its lack of ethics. Even though *Le Cid* observes the unity of time, Chapelain complained that Corneille had crowded too many incidents into 24 hours to sustain the play's probability. The Academy argued that the play was particularly offensive because the young woman consents to wedding her father's killer (a trumped-up charge: in actuality, she protests the marriage, which the king has decreed), and so the play transgressed the neoclassical precept of decorum. In his decision, Chapelain had vindicated the unities, upheld decorum, and went beyond the Italian critics in firmly tying the purpose of dramatic theatre to the ideal of **poetic justice** – evil characters should be punished and good ones rewarded – which became part of the neoclassical rules. The rules drove the older approaches to dramaturgy off the elite Parisian stage. In subsequent years, Richelieu and later Louis XIV built France into the main political and cultural force in the continent, and with it, the neoclassical rules soon regulated drama across Europe, not to be toppled for nearly two centuries.

Scenic perspective in print and on stage

Neoclassicism altered theatre architecture and scenic conventions as well as playwriting. In the early seventeenth century, scenic practices on the stages of public playhouses remained indebted to the *platea* and *mansion* arrangements of the medieval theatre (described in Chapter 3). Parisian theatre troupes continued to use small *mansions* or "simultaneous scenery" visible throughout the performance on an unframed stage into the 1630s, when, for example, it was used for *Le Cid*. The French scene designer Laurent Mahelot included many drawings of such settings in his memoirs (Figure 5.7). And in the open-air theatres of England and Spain, the *platea*-like platforms, backed with doors and perhaps an upper level, provided a fluid, unlocalized playing area that could be whatever the characters said

Figure 5.7
Sketch of a set by Laurent Mahelot for Pierre Du Ryer's *Poliarque et Argénis.* This example of simultaneous scenery shows a cave (left), an altar (center), and a ship (right).
Source: Bibliothèque nationale de France.

it was. These scenic practices gradually gave way to a series of single settings that localized the dramatic action – settings that were organized according to the laws of perspective. This convention for staging appeared first in Italian courts and gradually altered public performances throughout Europe.

There are many reasons for the rise and eventual triumph of **perspective scenery**. One was the emergence of perspective in painting. European interest in perspective began in the fourteenth century as part of the Italian humanism discussed earlier in this chapter, stirred by an Arabic treatise on optics. Perspective became highly popular among Italian artists by the middle of the fifteenth century, when printing would carry their ideas across Europe. By 1500, Italian painters had perfected the geometry and graphics of single-point perspective. Soon this mode of illustrating depth on a canvas or on walls began to influence Italian scenographers. By the mid-seventeenth century, perspective scenery had become magic on stage.

But the move toward perspective was also part of a change *in* perspective. Medieval art often portrayed people and objects in terms of their religious significance (e.g., by making them larger), or gathered them together primarily for allegorical or spiritual purposes, rather than for a naturalistic representation. An example of the medieval approach in theatre is *locus* and *mansion* staging, which presents many locations simultaneously. In a sense, this artistic strategy answers the question, "How do things appear in God's eyes?" But perspective painting is more concerned with how things look in a human's eyes – specifically, one's own. It is much more individualistically oriented. That orientation fits well with the interiorized individualism that print culture fostered. Print culture gave perspective painting a new meaning and importance.

Finally, perspective scenery began to appeal to dukes and monarchs for reasons other than their illusionistic and individualistic representations of reality: they noticed that perspective scenery also had a political meaning, since only one person in the theatre could sit where perspective scenery lined up perfectly. This and the techniques of perspective scenery will be taken up in Chapter 6.

European print culture reaches a watershed

Historian Elizabeth Eisenstein observes that printing's impact on religion pointed in two different directions: toward a scholarly humanism on the one hand and orthodoxies on the other (1979: 366–7). One can say that similarly, print's effects on art and scholarship pointed in two opposite directions: toward conformities that leveraged their power by claiming the authority of ancient texts; and toward critical thought willing to start afresh, without the chains of classical views. Orthodoxies made a few books the foundation for all else. The trend toward critical thought was no less dependent on texts, but its dependence was in the form of collecting and comparing them, allowing thinkers both to discover errors and conflicts, and to gather resources and build on the work of others.

In the 1630s these trends reached a tipping point. Neoclassicism began its march toward dominance in the 1560s with Scaliger, and it became orthodoxy in 1637 through the debate over *Le Cid*. Concurrently, paths within critical inquiry were being cut elsewhere in higher learning. In 1632, the Italian scientist Galileo (1564–1642) – arguably the greatest figure of the scientific revolution, and a frequent critic of Aristotle – published his major book on the planets' circling around the sun, and in 1638, a pioneering treatise on physics and mechanics. His method of basing knowledge on the observation of nature is called **empiricism**. Along with the triumph of neoclassicism, 1637 saw a decisive text by French philosopher René Descartes (1596–1650), who held that reason is the sole means of producing truth, and that only absolute, mathematical certainty was acceptable. Part of his effort to establish knowledge independent of ancient opinion was his dictum, "I think, therefore I am" (*cogito ergo sum*): the proof of my existence is that I think. Descartes' **rationalism** was central to much philosophy in subsequent centuries.

Despite their disagreements on the value of ancient texts and the roles of observation versus reasoning, these developments had commonalities. One is the mathematical element in each. This is obvious in Galileo; Descartes was himself an important mathematician, and his desire for absolute certainty had mathematical laws as its model. Neoclassicism's rules are law-like in their apparent clarity (despite any breaches in practice), and the very term "unity" conveys a desire for invariance and the elimination of multiplicity and ambiguity. Although perspective painting arose earlier, its mathematical methodology accorded with these other cultural developments. Perspective organized art around individual perception – and here we find another commonality among these cultural developments. We observed in the Introduction to Part II that the neoclassical unities constrained drama to represent what an individual can perceive, and in this chapter we mentioned how they made psychological conflict the fulcrum of drama. Rationalism and the scientific revolution likewise depended on individual thought and experience as the means for producing knowledge. Print culture was at the heart of new reliance on individual consciousness and the orderliness of knowledge – two of the hallmarks of the next era of Western culture, the Enlightenment. Empiricism, rationalism, and neoclassicism would all become cornerstones of that epoch.

CASE STUDY: Early modern metatheatricality and the print revolution

Tobin Nellhaus

William Shakespeare's *Hamlet*, written around 1600, is famous for its play-within-a-play, "The Murder of Gonzago" (which Hamlet jokingly calls "The Mousetrap") (Figure 5.8). His *Midsummer Night's Dream*, written sometime during 1590–1596, includes the playlet "Pyramus and Thisbe," performed (poorly) by a group of lowly artisans. Ben Jonson's *Bartholomew Fair* (1614) includes a puppet show.

Plays-within-plays are just one type of metatheatricality: theatrical performance that refers to or represents theatrical performance. It is a broad category that includes characters (or even actors) who talk to the audience, characters who observe that they're in a theatre, plays about actors, characters who play roles within the play, conversations about plays, and much more. During the Renaissance, metatheatricality was extraordinarily common – some scholars estimate that around 10 percent of the plays written in England during that period involved at least an instance of metatheatricality.

The interest in metatheatricality wasn't restricted to England, either. Numerous Spanish Golden Age plays had metatheatrical elements. Lope de Vega's *The Great Pretenders* (c.1608) has a play-within-a-play during which a Roman actor ridicules Christians on stage only to be converted while acting the role of a Christian. In Calderón's

Figure 5.8
Alison Halstead (Player Queen) and Nick Howard-Brown (Player King) in the "Murder of Gonzago" (Act III, Scene 2) from the 2021 production of *Hamlet* at the Theatre Royal in Windsor.

Source: Matt Crossick/Alamy Stock Photo.

religious drama *The Great Theatre of the World* (1635), God is an author for whom the world is the stage for human actions. That play is also a prime example of the metaphor "All the world is a stage," which was a commonplace for centuries, yet never so prominent as during this period.

In France too, there were plays-within-plays, such as in Pierre Corneille's *The Theatrical Illusion* (1636) and Jean Rotrou's *The Genuine St. Genest* (1646), the latter on the same subject as *The Great Pretenders*. More frequent in French drama were "performances within plays," in which characters create scenes to dupe another character, often to reveal truths about the dupe. A famous example is in Molière's *Tartuffe* (1664), in which a woman pretends to be attracted to the ultra-religious Tartuffe in order to show her husband that Tartuffe is a lecherous conman. (We will discuss Molière more fully in Chapter 6.)

Why were so many plays across Europe metatheatrical during this time? Metatheatrical techniques are available to all playwrights in every era, and one can find examples throughout theatre history. Yet only in a few eras has it been so frequent. The richest periods in European drama are those spanning roughly 1575–1675, and the period from around 1920 to now (although different metatheatrical techniques were often used). Perhaps these periods indicate no more than a passing fad – or perhaps there are deeper explanations about what makes metatheatricality exceptionally valuable during an era. Given that people in the sixteenth and seventeenth centuries were wrestling with or even fighting over urgent questions about God, nature, thought, and knowledge, one suspects that large social and cultural forces had to be in play.

The years 1550–1650 saw numerous radical social changes – in political structures, economic systems, religious beliefs, and more. But as we have observed throughout this book, none of society's basic structures strikes so close to the inner workings of theatre as changes in communication practices. Theatre is, after all, a form of communication, so it makes sense that when printing became the dominant mode of communication, theatre would be strongly affected.

As we have seen, not long after the printing press became commonplace, it made the Protestant Reformation possible. Just a few decades later, a print-based scientific revolution unleashed new ideas about the world, particularly in such fields as astronomy, mechanics, mathematics, human physiology, and scientific methodology. Between the Middle Ages and the early modern era, there was a radical shift in ideas about God and nature. And yet in actuality, often both the old and the new ideas were active at the same time. Not only did different groups of people perceive things in different ways, but even single individuals could think about religion one way but understand nature in another, or see both perspectives on these subjects.

THINKING THROUGH THEATRE HISTORIES: CRITICAL REALISM

Some of the most basic historical questions are about why cultures and societies change. What were the causes and mechanisms of change? Why did a change occur during one time span rather than another? And why was the change from A to B rather than A to D?

Critical realist historians approach these issues in a particular way. Realism in philosophy is the view that reality (or most of it) exists independent of the mind, in contrast to the notions that the ultimate reality is abstract ideas or just what we perceive. Critical realism is one version of this view, which began in the work of Roy Bhaskar (1944–2014) during the late 1970s. Since then, it has attracted scholars in such diverse fields as philosophy of science, ethics, and especially the social sciences. (The phrase "critical realism" has also been used with a different meaning by other fields, such as theology and aesthetics.) Two of critical realism's positions are particularly important here. First, what is real isn't limited to what we can perceive or detect through instruments: instead, something is real if it has the power to cause changes. So social relationships and thoughts are real, even though they aren't physical. Second, reality is stratified. Most people are acquainted with this notion in the natural sciences: atoms can combine to form molecules, certain molecules create life, living beings evolved to a point where some animals walk on land, and so forth. According to critical realism, society is stratified too. It identifies three main "planes." One plane consists of social structures, such as the economic system. The second consists of agents, that is, people acting within society. Finally, there are cultural discourses, a term encompassing things like words, images, music, ideas, and values. Society can't be boiled down to just one of these layers: all three are necessary, because history consists of their development and interplay. Distinguishing and untangling these planes helps to provide extensive explanations for historical events. In practice, many historians follow this approach, even if they are unaware of critical realism, but the philosophy illuminates the theory behind the practice.

This case study uses critical realism to explore three questions about metatheatricality. One is how to explain why, even though metatheatrical techniques are always available, they're heavily used during some times, much less so in others. Second, since metatheatricality is particularly common during only certain eras, what cultural work does it accomplish that isn't as urgent in other periods? Last, there must be a reason why metatheatrical techniques are particularly effective for this work, otherwise they wouldn't be employed. Such questions concern complex, multileveled interactions and changes in society. The basic theory in this case study is that changes in communication practices (a fundamental social structure) altered the ways people thought about themselves as social agents, and this was expressed discursively through metatheatricality.

In the context of so many cultural changes due to the emergence of print culture, knowledge itself became a crucial issue, full of questions: questions about whether there can be any certainty or truth, and if so, what form it would take; questions about who has (or should have) knowledge; questions about whether the medieval or the early modern approach to knowledge is correct, or if neither one of them is; and many more. An example of the struggle can be seen in Descartes's effort to achieve absolute certainty, leading to his aphorism, "I think, therefore I am": to Descartes, an individual's own self-awareness is all that someone can be categorically sure about. In theatre, doubts about knowledge appeared in the neoclassicists' belief that the lower classes could understand neither multiple plots and locations, nor plots that cover more than a day – a belief that shaped playwrights' ideas of what upper-class audiences could understand.

But to think about problems in thought and knowledge, people must use their thought and knowledge. In other words, during a crisis in knowledge, thought has to be self-consciously reflexive, so that people are aware that they are thinking through problems of thought through the medium of thought itself. "Thought," in this case, means any kind of intellectual activity, including philosophy, religion, fiction, painting, dance, or theatre. The need for self-reflexivity is one reason behind the explosion of metatheatricality at the moment when print culture was becoming dominant. (Self-reflexivity isn't the same as the idea of the self as one's interiority or psychology: one can think about thought, knowledge and truth, and also conceptualize the self as, say, fated by the gods, as in ancient Greece. The concept of self changes historically; it became personal interiority during the transition to print culture.)

There is another reason for the intensive use of metatheatricality, but in order to understand it we need to understand some things about society. Consider being an actor auditioning for roles. When the economy is good, there may be lots of roles to audition for; when the economy is poor, there may be fewer. Also, you may find yourself often being considered for certain kinds of roles, but not others. You might be a "character actor," a "romantic lead," a "heavy," or some other standard type, sometimes whether you like it or not. So you develop your acting career dealing with the economics of theatre on the one hand, and on the other, people's ideas about you and about what theatre should be.

The situation for actors is true for every other person, no matter their age, gender, ethnicity, social class, job, or any other category. There is an important philosophical point here: people necessarily live within certain social preconditions for their actions. Some of these preconditions consist of the economy, political systems, gender-based social relationships, race relations, and so forth: social structures. Other preconditions consist of ideas, beliefs, values, images, and the like that circulate in society through its various communications media: discourses. And then there are people themselves, managing their lives amidst these circumstances. These are the three planes of society noted in the "Thinking Through Theatre Histories" box. According to this view of society, people are social agents, who attempt to achieve their goals under the preconditions of whatever social structures and cultural discourses surround them – and sometimes, in the process of achieving their goals, social agents change the surrounding social structures and discourses.

Theatre, from this perspective, is very similar to society. On the one hand, there is the actor/audience relationship, which is shaped by the physical space of the performance, the conventions for interactions with the audience (such as direct address and an imaginary "**fourth wall**" separating the actors from the audience), and various other factors. This is theatre's structural level. On the other hand, there is either a script, a scenario, or at least a set of improvised character types or situation ideas that actors come up with while performing. These make up theatre's discursive level. The actor (the agent producing performance) is situated between these two elements. Theatre also exists within the society-wide structures and discourses – one might call it a microcosm of society. Strictly speaking, however, all organizations are microcosms of society in the same way. What distinguishes theatre is that it echoes the structure of society one more time: characters act within their *own* (fictive) structural and discursive preconditions. That additional level, consisting of *fictional* structures, agents, and discourses, is unique to theatre. Theatre can even create an additional, interior set of social layers – a play-within-a-play.

Because the constituents of theatrical performance are so similar to what constitutes society, theatre can be described as a model of social agency – it's not only a window onto society, it's also structured like society. The doubled set of layers (actual structures, agents, and discourses doubled by fictional structures, agents, and discourses) arises when at least two people become reflexive about people, using not just talk but their entire bodies. They show how people behave by enacting the behavior, fictionally.

Modes of communication such as printing are among society's structures. When communication structures change, however, it becomes deeply unclear what it means to take action in the world and to be situated in society – not only is knowledge thrown into crisis, but agency is too. New ways of thinking arise, including ideas about selfhood. In medieval society, Christians were taught that they occupied positions along a vertical Great Chain of Being, which placed their existence and action in relationship with God at the top, then angels, descending to the monarch, the clergy, and lords of the manor, peasants, and serfs, then further down to through animals, plants, and finally minerals. But print culture brought a reorientation: relationships strictly among humans started to be primary. Religious plays such as the mystery cycles and moralities were replaced by intrigues of murder, power, and romance. Hamlet struggles over the questions of whether, how, and when to act, and when he ponders whether to take his own life, what stops him is the fear of death: hell is only in the background.

Theatre, as a model of social agency, is a vital arena in which to wrestle with the nature of social agency. That is what plays-within-plays achieve: a group of real people (the audience) watch a group of fictional people in a play, who watch yet *another* group of fictional people in a play. Often the inner play is a poorer form of theatre, for example, dumb shows (silent plays) like the ones in *The Spanish Tragedy* and *Hamlet*, the puppets in *Bartholomew Fair*, and clumsy performances like the one by the "rude mechanicals" in *A Midsummer Night's Dream*. The outer play usually presents a superior kind of social agency. Some of the other metatheatrical techniques mentioned earlier can also accomplish reflexivity about agency, but plays-within-plays present the clearest, most forthright approach.

According to this argument, then, behind the extraordinary increase in metatheatricality in Western drama around the year 1600 were the radical shifts brought about by print culture. Those shifts created a crisis in how to define knowledge and agency. Theatre's connections to communication practices and its multilayered structure made it an especially dynamic medium for embodying and working through this crisis through reflection, which took the form of metatheatricality.

Key references

Archer, M.S. (1995) *Realist Social Theory: The Morphogenetic Approach*, Cambridge: Cambridge University Press.

Bhaskar, R. (1998) *The Possibility of Naturalism: A Philosophical Critique of the Contemporary Human Sciences*, 3rd edn, London: Routledge.

Nellhaus, T. (2010) *Theatre, Communication, Critical Realism*, New York: Palgrave Macmillan.

Summary

Western Europe in the late 1500s and early 1600s experienced enormous social transformations and upheavals. One of the most important changes was in communication. The printing press made books far more available and far less expensive than before. As a result, people of moderate means could afford to purchase Bibles in the vernacular for their religious practices. Reading itself altered and fostered a new sense of interior selfhood, seen most clearly in the new Protestantism, but also evident in secular areas, such as the natural sciences and philosophy.

Printing also disseminated classical works, which became the foundation for most education. As a result, new plays were often written on classical models. In England, Spain, and France, university-educated playwrights began writing for professionals in the popular theatre. Simultaneously, acting troupes produced major writers, and because even grammar schools had a humanist curriculum, they too were influenced by the classics. Print culture affected playwriting in much the way it altered other areas of secular culture: dramatic characters became less like "types" and more like individuals, and plots focused on human activities, not on salvation. Although playwrights sought to please a broad public, they kept an eye on the tastes of their substantial aristocratic audience. In England and Spain, playwrights often alluded to classical literature, and Roman drama frequently inspired their own plots. In France, humanism played an even deeper role, eventually pushing the popular tradition almost to the sidelines. The views of Aristotle and Horace were transformed (with considerable distortion) into strict neoclassical rules. Backed by the increasingly powerful French state, neoclassicism came to dominate playwriting throughout the continent for nearly two centuries.

Meanwhile, during the centuries covered by Chapters 4 and 5, major political and economic changes were afoot. Several European countries began to centralize monarchical power, and some sought to exploit other parts of the world by setting up trade, establishing colonies, and embarking on conquests in East and South Asia, and North and South America. European countries exploited Africa to the utmost by starting an enormous slave trade between there and the Americas. These activities form part of the economic and political background to the next several chapters – developments in which print culture also played indirect and sometimes direct roles.

★

CHAPTER 6

European absolutisms and performance, 1600–1770

Patricia Ybarra and Tobin Nellhaus

Contributors: Bruce McConachie
and Tamara Underiner

As we will see in this chapter, neoclassicism was linked to **absolutism**, as well as to print culture, as noted in Chapter 5. Those who believed in absolutism advanced the new idea that the rightful monarch must monopolize the rule of law and the use of force within the lands that they controlled. This chapter will examine the rise of absolutism in Europe starting in the 1500s and the kinds of theatrical entertainments that supporters of absolutism enjoyed. Emulating the European monarchs and their courts, the aristocracy and most of the rich merchants and professionals applauded festive entertainments, **masques**, **operas**, and finally neoclassical plays in court theatres and public playhouses. With few exceptions, these performances legitimated the values and beliefs of absolutism.

The rise of absolutism coincided with development of **colonialism** in England and France, following the designs of their Spanish and Portuguese counterparts. Colonialism – the policy or practice of acquiring full or partial political control over non-European regions, occupying it with settlers, and exploiting it economically – developed alongside ventures into the violent business of chattel slavery, which allowed people, largely of European descent, to buy and sell other people, largely of African descent, as property. Together participants in these institutions exploited people of non-European descent to garner riches for monarchies in Europe in need of funds to support their regimes. While the entertainments listed above usually stopped short of radically critiquing these institutions, the presence of non-Europeans characters and occasionally non-European performers in masques, neoclassical plays, and ballets of this period suggest that the creators of these entertainments were more ambivalent about colonialism and slavery than they were about the power of the monarch. Some plays from the period attempted to critique or think through new forms of rule, whether they advocated for absolutism or for an enlightened monarch. Sometimes these plays are set outside of Europe, or at least outside of their author's home country. These performances will be explored throughout this chapter. In addition, theatre was performed in sites of colonization in the Americas, including the first French play performed in the

Americas, which mixed Greek mythology and indigenous Mi'kmaq culture in ways echoes *The Masque of Blacknesse*, written just a few years earlier and considered later in this chapter, and Sor Juana Inez de la Cruz's *Divine Narcissus*, discussed in Chapter 5.

On stage, there were significant tensions between neoclassical entertainments and two other kinds of performances. The splendors and enchantments of Baroque opera regularly overwhelmed the rigid strictures of neoclassicism in performances at court until the early 1700s. And **carnivalesque** entertainment, its low delights more popular in fairground theatres than in aristocratic playhouses, also subverted the didactic claims of neoclassicism. In the next chapter, we will discuss a third challenge to neoclassical forms and ideas – the sentimental theatre of the eighteenth century. Partly in response to these alternatives, neoclassicism became so intertwined with the ideology and institutions of absolutism that on the whole, its theatrical genres would not survive absolutism itself.

The rise of absolutism

Absolutism arose in Europe at various points, mainly in large countries but occasionally in small principalities, with diverse structures, intensities, and durations (in Russia, lasting until 1917), but with general features in common. From medieval times through the mid-1600s, within most European countries several overlapping and competing centers of power co-existed. Kings and queens might assert their right to rule their kingdoms, but their actual powers were typically limited by local customs, traditional medieval privileges, strong regional noblemen, and by powerful churchmen. Most kingdoms (and dukedoms and church states) in Europe were little more than bundles of territories held together by allegiance to a ruler. This arrangement had worked well enough before 1500, but it came under intense stress from primarily two directions. On the one hand, the serfs, who benefited from the slow change from paying the lord of the manor in kind to paying money, repeatedly rebelled against the feudal structure, and the economy was gradually shifting from serfdom and medieval guilds to early **capitalism**. On the other hand, several forms of political conflict were erupting, among them the efforts of the nobility to maintain power, and the animosities unleashed by the **Protestant Reformation**, which sparked extreme conflicts and wars. In England, uprisings of varying types marked the reigns of every monarch from Henry VIII to Charles I, which finally ended in civil war in 1642. When the French king tried to exert more direct control in the provinces, French noblemen rebelled twice against the crown in the 1640s and 1650s, even calling in Spanish troops to support them. A still larger conflict erupted in the present areas of Germany, Poland, and Scandinavia, which eventually involved nearly every major country on the continent: the Thirty Years' War (1618–1648), fought mostly among Protestant and Catholic rulers but fundamentally as a contest for land and imperial power. The war devastated populations, towns, and regional economies, and it took decades for these regions to recover.

These upheavals caused many sovereigns and their ministers to recognize that monarchy needed a firmer base of power and authority to survive and flourish. Absolutism was essentially the result of a "bargain": the crown would protect the feudal aristocracy against the restive serfs, but at the cost of stripping the aristocrats' local power (usually unwillingly) and concentrating it within the monarchy, which expanded its own army, often sending it to conquer more land for the aristocrats and increase the monarch's power.

In the Catholic countries, the Church, which had mounted a Counter-Reformation (1545–1648) to fight the rise of Protestantism in northern Europe, provided a source of legitimation by reviving the ideology of the divine right of kings. According to the Vatican, Catholic kings aligned with the teachings of Rome provided their subjects with a beneficent and infallible source of justice. Catholicism strengthened absolutist rule in Spain and Portugal and also aided the Austrian Empire. Cardinal Richelieu, who spoke for the French monarchy in the 1620s and 1630s, linked the crown to the power of the Catholic Church and paved the way for the absolutism of Louis XIV later in the century. Although Protestantism had made inroads in France, the Vatican could rejoice that Richelieu's policies had won another Counter-Reformation victory for Rome.

Among Protestants, the English political philosopher Thomas Hobbes (1588–1679) advanced one of the most vigorous justifications for centralizing all power in the hands of the crown in his 1651 book, *Leviathan*. Hobbes pointed to recent history and the danger of continuous anarchy unless state power were vested in a centralized government that could override all customs, traditional immunities, and even the authority of what some churchmen might claim as the will of God. His treatise provided part of the justification for the **Restoration**, so called because it restored the institution of monarchy to England (in 1660) after the Commonwealth period of the Civil War. The ideas of Hobbes were influential, as well, in Protestant Scandinavia and northern Germany.

Although not the first of its kind – for example, the Tudor and Stuart rulers of England built what might be described as an unfinished absolutism – absolutism reached its zenith in France during the reign of Louis XIV (1643–1715) and became the model (and envy) of other monarchs in Europe. King Louis set about elevating himself as the symbol and embodiment of France. Using the power of print, the king's ministers extended centralized rule into the French provinces through standardized weights and measures, new tax codes, and a disciplined royal army (and the French language itself). Until the late seventeenth century, raising an army had been left to local noblemen, but Louis XIV excluded the fractious aristocracy from that traditional right, made officers dependent on his government, and effectively mobilized the army as an extension of the state. To house his much-enlarged civilian government that managed the realm, and to hobble the provincial noble families by removing them from their own lands and making them more dependent on himself, Louis built a new city in the village of Versailles, about ten miles from Paris. The centerpiece of Versailles was the king's new palace, intended to embody the grandeur of his reign through neoclassical façades, extensive gardens, Baroque paintings and statuary, and the sheer size and extravagance of its public spaces and ballrooms. While holding court at Versailles, Louis XIV divided his daily routines into a series of ritualized acts to elevate his royal body and keep his noblemen envious of each other's privileges; one gentleman, for example, was accorded the honor of holding the right sleeve of the king's nightshirt as he took it off in the morning. The king's propagandists for absolutism advanced the Catholic belief that kings were God's representatives on earth. But they also wrote and preached that royal power, though necessarily absolute, was inevitably reasonable and just, because the king embodied God's will as well as his symbolic power. Because the French monarchy was the most powerful and influential in Europe from the mid-1600s through the 1770s, much of this chapter will center on French political and theatrical practices.

Recognizing that the theatre could influence rebellious aristocrats and wealthy merchants in their kingdoms, absolute monarchs usually sought to control theatrical expression.

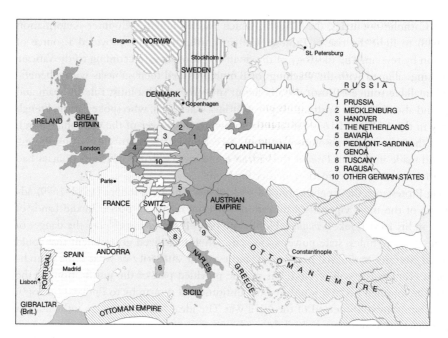

Figure 6.1
Political map of Europe, circa 1730.

They used patronage, monopolistic regulations, state censorship, and sometimes personal interference to support and shape the kinds of theatre that would legitimate their regimes. In addition to paying directly for performances at court, some absolute monarchs provided subsidies to their favorite theatrical companies to finance their public performances. Absolutist governments also granted monopolies to some companies, giving them exclusive rights for the production of certain kinds of theatre; Louis XIVs bureaucrats, for example, restricted operatic, dramatic, and *commedia dell'arte* performances to three different companies and attempted to prohibit other troupes from producing these genres. Finally, believing these restrictions were insufficient, European absolutists also censored their regulated theatres. Companies performing dramatic theatre had to submit their scripts for approval and even operatic and *commedia* troupes performed their shows under the pricked-up ears and watchful eyes of censors, who attended to make sure that their pieces offered no offense to the crown. Nonetheless, as we will see, some approved authors managed to suggest subversive ideas and occasionally entire companies found ways to effectively challenge the monopolistic practices of absolutist regimes.

Entertainments at court

Despite the print-based victory of neoclassicism, most cultured opinion by the 1650s exempted monarchs and their court entertainments from neoclassical standards. This was a major tension in the theatre of absolutism. As we have seen, Louis XIV and other absolute monarchs endorsed neoclassicism – even to the point of censoring artists and theatres that did not meet its rigorous standards. Nevertheless, their major forms of entertainment at court mostly avoided its strictures. For their sumptuous performances, many royals, especially those in the Catholic courts of southern Europe, preferred the **Baroque aesthetic** of playfulness, allegory, metamorphosis, power, and sensuality to the rules of neoclassicism. Despite the extravagant and even voluptuous nature of much Baroque visual art, architecture, and performance, the Catholic Church was one of the most enthusiastic supporters of the Baroque, seeing in its emotional and public appeal a possible counter to the ascetic and private claims of Protestantism. After 1600, the Vatican paid many painters, sculptors, and architects to immerse Rome in the new Baroque style and it sponsored the operas of Claudio Monteverdi (1567–1643), whose lush music initiated Baroque opera with *Orfeo* in 1607.

Baroque aesthetics returned court life to the centrality of visual and oral culture that had predominated in Europe before the rise of print and the new standard of verisimilitude. Although our previous chapter focused on the effects of print culture on European theatre from 1550 to 1650, earlier forms of communication continued to instruct and delight court spectators. Baroque performances borrowed from several of these traditions to flourish in absolutist courts during the 1600s and continued to undercut state-sanctioned neoclassicism into the 1700s. Our discussion of Baroque theatre for the first half of this chapter complements Chapter 5's study of the public career of Sor Juana Inés de la Cruz, who was writing dramas inflected by Baroque playfulness in colonial Mexico in the 1680s.

Typically, when a new medium of communication is introduced and gains cultural power, the old media, although generally less influential, continue to shape the culture, often gaining new niches of authority. This was the case with Baroque spectacles at court, especially performances of seventeenth-century opera. Certainly, the technologies of perspective scenery and the libretti and music for the new operas benefited from print culture; both circulated much more widely in print than would have been possible in a culture that rested on copying manuscripts. But the visual tropes and transformations that linked the power of a king or queen to the magnificence of a Christian God depended on a mode of visual allegory that derived from the manuscript cultures of ancient empires and can be easily traced from Roman times to the courts of medieval Christianity. Music, important to all cultures but diminished in the theatre with the rise of print, reasserted its centrality in the festivals and masques presented at court. As we will see, the values of playfulness and sensuality that the rules of neoclassical thinking had shunted to the wings moved center stage in the spectacular performances of Baroque opera after 1650.

In fact, similar kinds of delights had been a part of court-sponsored festive entertainments in Europe since the late medieval period and into the Renaissance. In addition to weddings and other dynastic events, late medieval rulers celebrated visits of foreign dignitaries, the signing of peace treaties, and the feast days of particular saints with dances, games, and performances throughout their capital cities. Medieval towns returned the favor, staging huge welcoming ceremonies when the monarch paid them a visit. Scenic designers' innovations in Italy began to transform European court entertainments from late medieval practices toward the more complex styles of the Baroque era. Florentine artist and engineer Leonardo da Vinci (1452–1519), for instance, designed a glittering revolving stage that featured moving planets, fabulous beasts, and Roman gods and goddesses to welcome a new duchess to the court of Milan as part of a wedding ceremony in 1490. Called the *Festa del Paradiso*, the spectacle used visual symbols, poetry, and song to suggest that the rulers of Milan descended from a classical version of paradise. Da Vinci's *Festa* mixed pagan with Christian symbols and emphasized lavish display.

As in Milan, most pre-Baroque festivals opened the court to the populace of the city. The counts, dukes, and others who sponsored these events usually took an active part in several of the performances, demonstrating the stability and justice of their rule through the symbolic roles they played, as well as their clothing, horsemanship, and retinue. In the largest of these festivals, the celebrations spread throughout the town, temporarily transforming its squares, churches, and palaces into festive spaces. Although usually centered on the ruler-sponsor, Renaissance festivals were public in the sense that they were accessible to most of the populace and their performances embodied mythic symbols and social relations that all understood to be necessary for the welfare of the whole. In Latin America, festivals of this type were popular throughout the colonial period in the form of the viceregal entry. As representatives of the monarchy, viceroys exerted their control over the territory in similar ways to monarchs on the European continent. While the aesthetics shifted over time to include more baroque elements (as opposed to featuring the mock battles discussed in earlier chapters), these performances persisted as public spectacles in plazas and other urban spaces throughout the late sixteenth and early seventeenth centuries.

In marked contrast, after 1500, in France and England, these festivals began to move indoors, into ducal and royal palaces that usually were off limits to the populace. Because the French and English monarchs had to impress a fractious aristocracy with their power, the audience for their court festivities gradually changed from the populace as a whole to the nobility living at court. By the 1610s, court entertainers and musicians in Paris were mounting lavish **ballet** spectacles – amateur performances featuring the king and court as powerful mythological and allegorical figures. From 1605 until 1640, Inigo Jones (1573–1652) designed court **masques** for English kings, first James I, then Charles I – entertainments similar to the expensive ballet spectacles in France. Jones convinced Charles I to convert two rooms at his court palace for masques. As a demonstration of their political centrality, royal family members often performed in masques and ballet spectacles in London and Paris into the early seventeenth century. Inigo Jones's masques, for instance, typically positioned the king as the pivot around which the costumed courtiers danced. But after the festivities moved indoors, the royalty gradually withdrew from active participation and into positions where they could appear as beneficent overlords to watch the performances of others. To ensure that the glorification of kingship continued to maintain its central focus, many Baroque court spectacles placed a symbolic representative of the monarch on stage.

One of the most controversial of these types of masques was the *Masque of Blacknesse* (1605), designed by Inigo Jones and written by Ben Jonson (1572–1637). Presented on Twelfth Night, the last day of the Christmas holidays, this entertainment (which was Jones and Jonson's first collaboration) was created at the request of James I's wife Queen Anne, who requested an event with masquers, including herself, who would represent Africans. Queen Anne donned black makeup as part of the performance. The character list for the extravagant masque included Oceanus, his 12 other blue-painted attendants, Oceanus's son the river Niger, and his 12 black-painted daughters (Figure 6.2). The masque's plot involves Niger's daughters, distraught at no longer being considered beautiful because of their dark complexion, seeking out a way to become beautiful once more by whitening their skin. These daughters, played by Queen Anne and her female retinue, go to Britannia to seek the sun-like King James I, who can bleach them back to whiteness. This so-called whitening does not happen until the *Masque of Beauty*, which was not performed until 1608, when the performers appeared with light skin. Some scholars speculate that the whitening did not occur during *Masque of Blacknesse* because the makeup simply could not be removed on stage during the Masque. In its own time, the *Masque of Blacknesse* was controversial because of its expense and the appearance of the queen as a blackamoor (a name for white actors painted in blackface to represent "Africans" or "Moors"). In historical context, the novelty of this performance was not that white actors were in blackface – audiences were used to seeing male actors participate in blackface in festivals and weddings, and onstage in roles such as the lead role in *Othello,* which was produced just a year before the masque – but in seeing the queen and her entourage of ladies engage in the practice.

Today the masque is controversial (and much studied) because of its overt ideology of white supremacy, emergent ethnic nationalism, and the creators' employment of the racist practice of blackface (discussed in its eighteenth- and nineteenth-century versions in Chapter 8). For theatre historians, this event suggests that the legacy of blackface performance began in the early modern period (roughly 1450–1800) and that the blackening of the skin in European festive performances had a relationship to conceptions of race from its inception. The interpretation of the masque, beyond its valuation of whiteness as representing beauty and goodness, is complicated by the masques' variety of source materials. A close look at the allegorical text reveals the interweaving of missionary Leo Africanus's (1494–c.1554) map of Africa (1550) with Greek classical allegory; the surviving

Figure 6.2

Daughter of Niger costume for *Masque of Blacknesse*, by Inigo Jones (1605).

Source: The Picture Art Collection/Alamy Stock Photo.

costume sketches reveal the conflation of visual representations of Muslim "others" such as Turks, which were a staple of early modern drama; and creative interpretations of Greek mythological allegorical figures. More specifically, the costume pictured in Figure 6.2 bears a striking resemblance to the 1598 well-to-do Moor drawn by Venice-based artist Cesare Vecellio (1521–1601), whose costume books of world cultures provided wondrous images to curious onlookers, linking these exoticized and often reductive images to early modern print culture. In theatrical terms, these images refer to generic representations of non-Western Muslims, a figure well-known to early modern British audiences. The association between blackness and femininity in the masque displays anxiety about women's unruly bodies (Anne was six months pregnant when she performed), even though Anne's role in creating the masque might be seen as a display of her power within the court. And in political context, rallying to Britannia to be whitened and join under King James's power could be read as an attempt to culturally incorporate Scotland – often represented as ethnically distinct and "darker" – within a consolidated British empire. These multiple interpretations, however, do not erase the fact that the masque's advocacy for a racial hierarchy places whiteness at the pinnacle of power. The fact that many British royals employed Black servants and had contact with Black performers (some of whom were very poorly treated) gives the masque a more pointed valence; for some of its elite audience, the representation of blackness was not an exotification of a distant other, but a fantastical representation of a culturally distinct population (however small) closer to home.

In addition, as scholars such as Kim Hall, Ayanna Thompson, and Mattheiu Chapman argue, the masque's existence also raises questions about how and when African performers were incorporated into early modern theatre culture; how and when the development of anti-Black racism developed in Europe in relationship to their presence rather than their supposed absence; and, lastly, how projection of racial fear interacted with anti-Muslim sentiment. While we cannot answer these questions with certainty, the *Masque of Blacknesse* underscores the relationship between colonialism, absolutism, and Eurocentric modes of thought before the existence of eighteenth century-era conceptions of race.

As in England, in Spain royal entertainments were penned by famous playwrights with equally expensive allegorical representations. When Philip IV of Spain enjoyed *The Greatest Enchantment is Love* in 1635, he watched a symbol of himself as the protagonist of the entertainment. The musical extravaganza, written by Golden Age playwright Calderón and produced by an Italian engineer, featured the temptation of Ulysses by the enchantress Circe, with characters and dramatic situations based on Homer's *Odyssey*. The lavish spectacle, intended to celebrate a saint and honor the opening of the king's new pleasure palace, placed shipwrecks, triumphal chariots, and volcanic destruction on an artificial island in the middle of a small lake within a garden of the new palace. From their seats on gondolas, the court could watch the king enjoy the show or attend to the songs and actions of his representative (Ulysses, in this case) in the entertainment. A paying public was able to see the production in the last days of its performance, and some evidence suggests that because Calderón's *comedia* could stand on its own without the spectacle, it was later performed at the *corrales*. This became standard practice in Spain: the public could see plays at the palace, and the play would then be released to the public theatres. However, at another of the king's palaces, court performances were more restricted, like those in France and England.

The persistence of court entertainments during the middle decades of the seventeenth century was partly related to the successes of absolutism. In Paris, Madrid, and Vienna (then part of the Habsburg Spain) they continued to flourish. In England, however, the extravagance of the masques angered the Puritans and helped motivate the overthrow of the king and the English Civil War in 1642.

Realizing absolutism in stage design

The staging of court ballets and masques was influenced by both aesthetics and politics. One major aesthetic factor was the growing use of perspective in art during the fifteenth century (discussed in Chapter 5). By the middle of the sixteenth century, perspective scenery had been in use for performances at Italian courts for some years. For example, scenographer Sebastiano Serlio (1475–1554) designed several Italian court entertainments in large palace ballrooms and banquet halls. In *Architettura* (1545), he depicted a series of tragic, comic, and pastoral stage settings using perspective. Realizing Serlio's conventional designs in production required a painter and carpenter to construct and hang a painted backdrop at the rear of the playing space and flank the drop with three sets of angled wings, each with two painted sides that receded symmetrically from the front of the stage (Figure 6.3). To contribute to the perspective effect, the upstage floor was sharply raked, sloping upward toward the backdrop. The actors had to perform far downstage on the level flooring, because if they performed within the upstage scenery, their bodies would appear out of proportion to the converging lines of perspective. The scene didn't depict any actually existing location, but rather a fictive "Venice" identified by a few of the buildings, which the audience would also perceive as a theatrical setting for performing a fiction.

When the Teatro Olimpico (mentioned in Chapter 4) was opened in 1585, it integrated perspective scenery into its architecture. Its primary architect, Andrea Palladio (1518–1580),

Figure 6.3

The setting for a comic scene by Sebastiano Serlio, from his *De Architettura*, 1569 edition.

Source: Heritage Image Partnership Ltd/Alamy Stock Photo.

based much of his design on the architectural drawings of the Roman writer Vitruvius (first century BCE), from whom Palladio borrowed the look of the *scenae frons* from the Roman theatre (see Chapter 2) for the Olimpico's scenic façade. After Palladio's death, architect Vincenzo Scamozzi (1552–1616) completed the building's design. Behind each of the five entrances on the façade and two more on either end of the stage, Scamozzi placed perspective scenery. In effect, Palladio and Scamozzi had merged an ancient, Vitruvian design with the Renaissance innovation of perspective painting. However, this manner of putting perspective on stage was not pursued further; Serlio's approach remained predominant.

Baroque aesthetics also influenced art and architecture in the Americas. As on the European continent, where the expansive visual culture of the Baroque allowed for the mixing of Spanish and Moorish elements, so in the Americas did artists mingle Spanish and Native American elements – not only in art and architecture, but also in music, theatre, court entertainments, and the vice-regal entries mentioned earlier.

To emphasize the picturesque qualities of the scenery, theatre architects introduced the **proscenium arch**, still a conventional feature of many theatres today, to create a formal barrier between the area for the spectators and the stage and backstage areas for the actors and technicians by providing two side walls and a horizontal wall that joins them above, creating an opening through which spectators may enjoy the stage action. Because court spectacles before 1640 generally involved scenery in a room used for other purposes, prosceniums were a late addition to the perspective stage. Serlio's angled wings, for example, usually stood alone on temporary platforms without a downstage proscenium to frame them. The move from temporary to architectural prosceniums began in 1587, when the ruler of Florence approved a permanent proscenium for his spectacle room at the Uffizi Palace. After that, as Baroque opera designers and librettists invented more opportunities for elaborate scenic display – such as lavish throne rooms that could be quickly transformed into a scene of pastoral bliss and Olympian gods perched in a cloud machine that gradually descended to the stage – they increasingly relied on permanent proscenium arches to house and hide the machinery that could produce these magical effects.

Theatre historians have examined several reasons for the gradual incorporation of proscenium arches into stage productions at court, among them the suggestiveness of printed illustrations. More quickly than on the stage, the organization of space on an illustrated page in a book shifted historically from the simultaneous representation of several images on a manuscript page to a unified image on a printed one that could take advantage of the discoveries of single-point perspective. Like printers, scenographers thought about space in graphic terms; they shaped the vision of the viewer through unity, symmetry, and the illusion of depth. By the 1540s, printers were using tall arches, modeled after the triumphal arches of Roman times, as a common motif to organize the title page in a book. And even when no printed symmetrical frame dominated the page, the sides of its paper created a visual frame that established every page as a quasi mini-proscenium. By the 1640s, literate Europeans had been looking for 100 years at the pages of books and pamphlets that organized their vision according to a framed perspective. How "natural," then, to expect that a proscenium arch framing perspective stage scenery should mirror this reality.

The politics of absolutism was the other major influence shaping court spectacles. The shift to indoor spectacles had increasingly led court designers to turn to the wonders of Italianate perspective scenery in order to glorify the duke or monarch; the proscenium arch formalized the link between aesthetics of perspective and absolutism. When Serlio and other designers drew and painted three-dimensional scenery onto two-dimensional flats, they needed to fix a vantage point in the auditorium to figure out the mathematics from which it would appear that the perspective on stage was correct. This meant that only one person seated in the auditorium had an optimal view of the scenery; from every other point, the painted perspective looked skewed or even completely awry. Initially designers were inconsistent in their placement of the vantage point – in Serlio's influential plan for a theatre, the best view was from a section seating "women of quality" (Berzal de Dios 2019: 106) – but eventually it belonged to the ruler, seated in the center of the auditorium (later, at the rear center) to organize the visual scene (Figure 6.4). The designer figured out where in the auditorium the ruler sat to gaze on the scene and drew his perspective lines for painting the scenery from that single point toward the vanishing point. The implicit visual demand on the other spectators in the auditorium, of course, was to imagine how the scene looked from the ruler's point of view. But the ruler's centrality also emphasized his role in creating a sumptuous event for everyone's enjoyment and its overall participatory character. This visual power play suited the political dynamics of ruling Italian families in northern Italy, where it was first introduced. As the proscenium arch and single-point perspective scenery spread from Italy to the rest of Europe, this practice also served absolutism at the royal courts of Spain, Austria, and France.

Figure 6.4

Louis XIII, Cardinal Richelieu, and Anne of Austria at a performance of *Mirame* (1641), by Richelieu and Jean Desmaret. Note the proscenium arch and perspective scenery.

Source: © Archives Charmet/Bridgeman Images.

The adoption of proscenium and perspective staging was hastened by the **chariot-and-pole system** of scene changing, invented by Giacomo Torelli (1608–1678), dubbed the Great Sorcerer for his scenic wizardry. Working in Venice, the center of operatic innovation in Europe, Torelli was hired in 1641 to design the stage machinery for the Teatro Novissimo, the only Venetian theatre at the time built solely for operatic production. Torelli got the idea for his new technology from the complex rigging in use by Venetian sailors on their ships. The chariot-and-pole system involves flat wings mounted on the downstage side of long poles, which pass through slots in the stage flooring to small two-wheeled wagons, or "chariots," that run on tracks under the stage. Through a series of ropes, pulleys, winches, and counterweights, all of the chariots under the stage – perhaps as many as ten on both sides for each pair of five wings – could be made to move simultaneously. As one flat moved into view, the flat behind or in front of it receded off stage. The counterweighted flats and drops were linked, as well, to painted borders hanging from the flies. Chariot-and-pole rigging could also include special upstage effects in perspectival miniature and the descents of deities on cloud machines from the heavens. Much as sailors could reorient the sails of a large vessel by turning a few master winches on board, so stagehands could effect a complete scenic transformation from one setting to another in less than a minute through hidden ropes, pulleys, and winches. Sweden's Drottningholm Court Theatre, built in 1766 and still in use today, provides a good illustration of the workings of the chariot-and-pole system (Figure 6.5). There is also a video available to view this more fully.

In 1645, Cardinal Mazarin (1602–1661; succeeded Richelieu in 1642) brought Torelli from Venice to Paris to transform the scenic and playing spaces of French court theatres into fully rigged machines for the production of Baroque opera. Knowing the spectacular marvels that Torelli's accomplishments had facilitated for opera in Venice, Mazarin expected

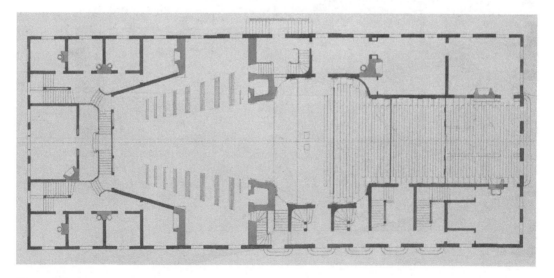

Figure 6.5

Drottningholm Castle Theater floor plan, 1760s.

Source: Wikimedia Commons/Adelcrantz, Carl Fredrik. https://commons.wikimedia.org/wiki/File:Drottningholms_slottsteater_planritning_1760-tal.jpg

the Great Sorcerer's scenic wonders to glorify the new French king, Louis XIV, and to make French theatre the envy of absolutist Europe. Torelli remodeled two royal theatres in 1645 and 1646 and gradually won over the French court to the new mode of scene shifting and design (see Figure 6.6). By the early 1700s, court and public theatres throughout Europe were struggling to catch up with the French mode.

Among the successes of chariot-and-pole staging was the Baroque opera *Hercules in Love*, performed in 1662 for Louis XIV at the new Salle des Machines theatre, built especially to house single-point perspective scenery changed through Torelli's ropes, winches, chariots, and counterweights. Cardinal Mazarin had helped to orchestrate the defeat of those aristocrats who mounted uprisings against royal absolutism between 1648 and 1653. To celebrate this triumph of the king, his recent victories over the Spaniards in war, and his impending marriage to Maria Theresa of Austria, Mazarin spent several years organizing the production of *Hercules in Love* (Figure 6.7). The opera celebrated the suffering of a lustful hero (a stand-in for Louis), who must sacrifice the love of his mistress for the good of the state. According to historian Kristiann Aercke, the court had no difficulty reading Mazarin's allegory as a congratulatory commentary on the well-known political and amatory machinations of the cardinal and the king (Aercke 1994: 165–220). By featuring the changeable qualities of nature through the spectacle of moving scenery – raging storms at sea, the fires of passion, and

Figure 6.6

Giacomo Torelli's setting for Act II of Pierre Corneille's *Andromède* at the Petit-Bourbon Theatre, 1650, in which Torelli's chariot-and-pole scene-shifting machinery was used. Engraving by François Chauveau.

Source: gallica.bnf.fr / Bibliothèque nationale de France.

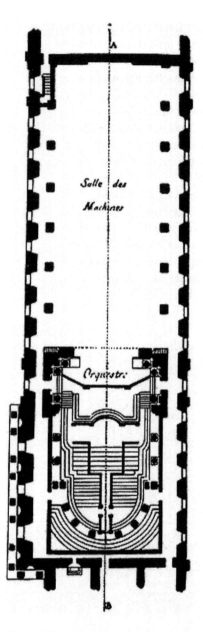

Salle des Machines

Orquestre

frequent interventions from classical gods – the production highlighted the changeable characteristics of the sovereign. Although several viewed the production of this six-hour opus as an artistic failure, Aercke argues that *Hercules in Love* helped to vivify Louis XIV's growing reputation as the Sun King, the embodiment of heavenly power and natural majesty.

The Baroque aesthetics of *Hercules in Love* massively contradicted the neoclassicism that French absolutists had embraced in the controversy over *Le Cid* just 25 years earlier. As noted in the last chapter, Cardinal Richelieu's French Academy severely criticized Corneille's play on the basis of the neoclassical principles of the three unities, verisimilitude, decorum, and poetic justice. In keeping with decorum, *Hercules* glorified the monarch and insisted that the king's rule was absolute in the bedroom as well as in matters of state, but the rest of neoclassicism was nowhere to be found: *Hercules* ignored the unities of time, place, and action – most of its allegorical scenes were set in no particular time or place and the opera featured the character of Hercules in a variety of suffering situations and noble deeds that defied any cohesive plot or logic. While neoclassicism had endorsed verisimilitude, the notion that dramatic scenes should generally mirror situations that could occur in real life, music pervaded the action of *Hercules*, cuing the songs of characters and choruses and the descent of gods from stage machines. *Hercules* broke the neoclassical rules, but no one from the French Academy stepped in to "correct" the cardinal or the king, for the contradiction wasn't arbitrary: it met decorum precisely. The monarch, after all, was deified himself, so he should be greeted in kind. Drama, however, was considered the purview of mortals: gods would never deign to manifest themselves before mere humans, and their interventions occurred only off stage. (In contrast the ancient Greeks, despite being the "source" of neoclassicism, freely let the gods walk among them.) Absolutism allowed the monarchs to adopt Baroque aesthetics for themselves while

Figure 6.7
Plan of the *Salle des Machines*, designed by Gaspar Vigarani (1586–1663) for the 1662 Baroque opera, *Hercules in Love*, an allegorical tribute to Louis XIV. The stage, 140-feet deep, accommodated six sets of side flats and flying machines. At one point in the opera, the entire royal family and attendants were flown in on one machine, 60 by 45 feet wide. The settings, organized around a single, central vanishing point, offered monumental images of a rationally ordered world, seen to fullest advantage by the King seated in his throne front and center.
Source: From L.P. de la Guepière, *Théâtre et Machine* (1888).

insisting on neoclassical restraint for everybody else, a seeming inconsistency that was consistent with their propagandistic logic.

Operatic scenery on the continent gained more Baroque grandeur and monumentality starting in the eighteenth century. This was due in part to the pan-European success of an extended family of architects and designers, the Bibienas. Patriarch Ferdinando Bibiena (1657–1743) gained initial success in Italy and rose to fame in Barcelona and Vienna, where he designed theatres and the scenery for several operas after 1711. His brother Francesco (1659–1739) also enhanced the family's reputation through his international architectural and design work. Three second- and third-generation Bibienas continued the family business: Giuseppe (1696–1757), Antonio (1700–1774), and Carlo (1728–1787). By Carlo's death, the Bibienas had planned theatres in Italy, Austria, and France and had worked as designers with major opera companies in Vienna, London, Paris, Lisbon, St. Petersburg, Berlin, Dresden, and Stockholm. The Bibienas are credited as introducing angle perspective (*scena per angolo* [SHAY-nah pehr AHN-goh-loh]), which used two (or more) vanishing points to visually open up the operatic stage by creating diagonal vistas off to the sides of the stage rather than restricting the vista to a central alley, a requirement of single-point perspective. The concept itself was not new: painters had used angle perspective in the 1400s, and it had already appeared in theatre in 1687 and probably even by 1638, though it was infrequently attempted. What the Bibienas achieved was a new way to implement angle perspective view on stage, essentially reinventing it, to monumental effect. Bibiena designs were especially suitable for flaunting grand architecture such as the palace interiors and courtyards of European rulers – architectural portraits whose truncation by the proscenium paradoxically made the building seem still more imposing. The vertical thrust of the architecture painted on their free-standing flats and drops, which might shoot beyond the proscenium arch, also increased the magnificence of their designs. In theatres that were still lit by candles and mirrors, diagonal vistas and vertical columns or arches could appear to recede and tower into infinity (Figure 6.8). The technique, somewhat in the spirit of the Teatro Olimpico, enabled a larger portion of the audience to enjoy perspective scenery, not just the ruler; the Bibienas even added flats at an angle to mitigate the discrepancies caused by seating. But the massive interior spaces depicted through *scena per angolo* were meant for earth-bound operas; for court entertainments, the Bibienas continued using symmetrical single-point perspective scenery, exuberantly exploiting miraculous machinery that fetched the gods and heroes of classical mythology to flatter the absolutist ruler.

The chariot-and-pole system remained the European standard among premier theatres on the continent until the late nineteenth century. The technologies allowing for easy and flexible scene changes were a triumph for Baroque opera over neoclassical drama. According to neoclassical rules, plays were supposed to occur in one place – all that was needed was one set of stage flats that could suggest a single room or outdoor space. There was little point in putting neoclassical dramas on stages that were built for elaborate and magical transformations. For much of the eighteenth century, however, many European spectators watched neoclassical plays on the same stages that also housed lavish operatic productions. Although most spectators probably were accustomed to the contrast in production styles and values, the possibilities for more elaborate scenic display put pressure on neoclassical staging that could not be accommodated within the rigid rules of the aesthetic. It was not until the early

Figure 6.8

Scena per angolo stage setting designed for a chariot-and-pole theatre by Giuseppe Galli Bibiena. The flats and drop were initially used for an opera produced to celebrate a betrothal between members of the ruling families of Saxony and Poland in 1719.

Source: Peter Jessen, *Meister des Ornamentstichs: eine Auswahl aus vier Jahrhunderten*, Verlag für Kunstwissenschaft, Berlin, [1923], vol. 2, p. 53. https://www.flickr.com/photos/internetarchivebookimages/14761521636/

nineteenth century, with the rise of melodrama and romantic theatre, that non-operatic drama would enjoy the full scenic possibilities of chariot-and-pole staging.

Louis XIV and Molière

Despite its paucity of stage scenery, neoclassicism for spoken drama thrived in France in the 1660s and 1670s. One of Louis XIV's most reliable court entertainers was Jean-Baptiste Poquelin, better known by his stage name, Molière (1622–1673). Molière and his company had been performing in the French provinces when a message from the king's younger brother brought them to Paris in 1658 for their debut at court. Their success with a farcical afterpiece won them permission from Louis XIV to share a Parisian theatre with an Italian *commedia* troupe. Other farces and comedies followed, both at court and in their public theatre, and soon Molière had established himself and his troupe as a royal favorite. But the king kept his popular actor-playwright close. From 1661 until his death 12 years later, Molière devised, directed, and performed several court entertainments, mostly comedy ballets (which alternated scenes of dialogue and dance), to please his royal patron and ensure the continuing employment and success of his company. Molière's relations with the Sun King cooled over the years, however, especially during the long controversy that surrounded one of his most famous plays, *Tartuffe* (1664–1669).

CASE STUDY: Molière and carnival laughter

Gary Jay Williams, with Bruce McConachie

Carnival laughter ... builds its own world versus the official world, its own church versus the official church, its own state versus the official state.

Mikhail Bakhtin (1984)

This case study uses the concept of carnival folk humor proposed by Mikhail M. Bakhtin (1895–1975) to suggest a deep connection between the comic and the controversial sides of Molière's theatre. (For previous commentary on Bakhtin's concept of the carnivalesque, see Chapter 3.) In addition to reading *Tartuffe*, students using this case study may also wish to read one of Molière's short plays, such as *The Precious Damsels* (1659) or *Love's the Best Doctor* (1665), and one of his other five-act verse comedies, such as *The School for Wives* (1662), *The Miser* (1668), or *The Imaginary Invalid* (1673).

Molière's full-length verse plays are regarded as the cornerstone of French comedy. They have been staples in the repertoire of the Comédie Française, France's national theatre, for over three centuries and are revived often in the Western world. Molière served Louis XIV as playwright, actor, and courtier for 15 years, but his middle-class background and profession as an actor set him apart from the court in important ways. He excelled in the leading roles of his own comedies, but also suffered the social stigma attached to the profession. Although the Parisian literati characterized his plays as trifles, some of his satires on the fashionable and foolish made him powerful enemies.

Molière's later five-act plays can stand as comic examples of neoclassicism; many critics have noted his adherence to decorum and the neoclassical unities. Yet Molière never abandoned the kind of disruptive comic elements that are in the spirit of the carnivalesque. Especially important for this study, his plays and performances were strongly influenced by the popular comic theatre traditions of (1) French farce, which had roots in medieval comedy; (2) *commedia dell'arte*, which had plots and character types similar to French farce; and (3) the kind of street medicine show that Molière knew well, in which hawkers sold potions they bragged could cure anything. (Notably, these shows also inspired comic parades in the eighteenth century.)

In previous chapters, we noted that the traditions of medieval farce, *commedia*, and medicine shows have strong links to what Bakhtin calls the spirit of the "carnivalesque" (Figure 6.9). This case study argues that, despite Molière's ties to an absolutist

Figure 6.9

In this farce at a country carnival, a husband is being cuckolded by a monk. Detail from the painting, "Village Festival in Honor of St. Hubert and St. Anthony," by Pieter Breughel the Younger (1564–1637).

Source: IanDagnall Computing/Alamy Stock Photo.

monarchy, the subversive qualities of the carnivalesque spirit are at work in many of his plays. Folk festival entertainments often "marked the suspension or inversion of hierarchical rank, privileges, norms, and prohibitions," according to Bakhtin. In the case of *Tartuffe*, there are key instances of such challenges and inversions. From this point of view, it is not surprising that the French Catholic Church, allied with the absolutism of the monarchy, believed it had to suppress a play that was so close to the seat of power in France.

Elements of carnival humor deriving from oral culture are present throughout Molière's work – early, middle, and late. Molière's early one-act farce *The Precious Damsels* (*Les Précieuses ridicules*, 1659), for example, has many attributes of the carnivalesque. It is a broad parody of the affectations of the salons of fashionable court women (*précieuses*) who were setting the protocols for aristocratic manners, courtship, language, and literature. Two affected young women turn away two potential suitors for lacking faddish manners and language. The young men then contrive a hoax. They send their valets, Mascarille and Jodelet, to visit the young women in the guise of fashionable courtiers, and the foolish women take them to be genuine. According to a surviving account of the performance, when Molière entered as Mascarille in marquis disguise, he wore a hyperbolic parody of a courtier's apparel. His powdered wig (topped by a tiny, fashionable hat) was so large that it swept the area around him every time he made a bow. His lace collar was huge and so were his breeches, the pockets of which sprouted colored tassels. He wore six-inch heels on his beribboned shoes and was carried on stage in a sedan chair by porters, whom he tried to avoid paying (Molière 1971: I:1008; Dock 1992: 53). Molière's scale of exaggeration here is beyond satire; it has the overflow of the carnivalesque about it. It is a festive undoing, a parodic uncrowning of established order writ large on the body. Molière's performance as Mascarille made him a larger-than-life comic icon who burst the seams of both salon decorum and the neoclassical rules for plays that required the restraint of verisimilitude. While his marquis represents an original departure from the stock characters of the *commedia dell'arte*, he functions in the same iconic way: the bold extravagance of the figure testifies to a force of elemental comic energy that explodes the world of over-rationalized drama. Without this kind of elemental comic force, without the precedents of the *commedia dell'arte* and old French farces, it is hard to imagine this performance.

In the original production of *The Precious Damsels*, a comic icon descended from the carnivalesque world was also on stage with Molière. Julian Bedeau, known as Jodelet (1591–1660), Paris's most famous actor of old French farce and Italian comedy, played the other valet, a character who impersonated an old viscount. Known as a good-natured clown, Jodelet always wore clown-white face makeup (probably a vestige of the flour-faced millers of old farce). Mascarille tells the young women, "Don't be surprised at the Viscount's looks. He just got out of bed from an illness that left him so pale" (Molière 1957: 23). Jodelet had recently left a rival theatre company, and Molière jumped at the chance to hire him. Jodelet would have brought with him plays written for him by Paul Scarron (1610–1660), whose parodies Bakhtin cites often, and who influenced Molière. The two comedians go through some ribald jokes involving sexual anatomy under the guise of talking about old war wounds and then they call in musicians for a dance – both typical bits of *commedia* business. Their masters enter to put an end to the deception and the play, beating and stripping their valets of their aristocratic clothes. Bakhtin speaks of thrashings and clothes-changing as a part of the cycle of crownings and uncrownings in carnivalesque fun (Bakhtin 1984: 197). No one gets to lord it for long in festive humor.

Such analysis could be extended through most of Molière's comedies. Two obvious instances of the parodying of "official" language occur in *The Bourgeois Gentleman* and *The Imaginary Invalid*. In the first, a servant dupes Monsieur Jourdain into believing that a long, burlesque ceremony, conducted in an amalgam of pseudo-Turkish, butchered French and Italian, is conferring on him the noble title of "mamamouchi." This ceremony takes place as part of a comic marriage plot in which Jourdain's daughter Lucile's lover, Cleonte, poses as the son of a Grand Turk to persuade Jourdain to let him marry his daughter. Molière's lampooning of Jourdain engages the stereotypical and ridiculous exotification embodied in the stage Turk popular on Western European stages to comic effect – both visually and aurally. (The term "mamamouchi," a Molièreian invention, found its way into the English language as a generic term for someone who thinks themselves more important as they are – a legacy of carni-valesque language, stripped of its Orientalizing roots, in more recent history.)

The second example occurs in *The Imaginary Invalid*, in which Molière satirizes the medical profession (as he does in at least five other plays): an elaborate ceremony ends the play that parodies the granting of degrees to medical doctors. In this case, the profession's Latinate language grants a dunce of a new doctor the right to slash, purge, bleed, and kill his patients at will. The mocking of the "official" language suggests that it has no more truth-value than any other language. The fake Latin, of course, also gestures to *commedia* practice.

Carnival humor's uncrownings of authority also take the form of cuckoldry. A wife's sexual deception of her husband uncrowns his domestic authority, while at the same time parodically crowning his head with horns (Bakhtin 1984: 241). (Horns were a symbol of cuckoldry – originating our word "horny.") A commonplace in medieval farces and *commedia*, cuckoldry or near-cuckoldry is a feature of several of Molière's plays, notably *The School for Wives*, *Don Juan* (1665), and *Amphitryon* (1668). In *The School for Wives*, the foolish Arnolphe has had his prospective young wife raised in the country in convent captivity on the theory that she will be too ignorant to know how to be unfaithful to him, a proposition the play unravels. Carnivalesque sexuality often erupts in this play. Arnolphe, justifying to a doubtful friend his expectation of success in his training of Agnes, says he was delighted when Agnes once came to him much troubled to ask, "In absolute and perfect innocence,/If children are begotten through the ear!" (Molière 1957: 37). Earlier in the same scene, when the zealous Arnolphe is fantasizing about his control of his prospective young wife, a *crème tarte* figures as a salacious sexual reference (Molière 2001: 5, 1971: I, 548). These and several other such moments have the comically subversive merit of suggesting that very powerful sexual forces are surging just below the surface of Arnolphe's controlling behavior. Predict-ably, such bawdiness disturbed decorous court audiences. Rather than being cowed, Molière went on to mock these audiences further in his *Critique of the School for Wives* (1663), one of several episodes in a year-long controversy over the play.

In another variation on carnival humor's upside-down world, the servants in Molière are often wiser than their masters and mistresses (much like those in Plautus's comedies, from which Molière borrowed directly for his *Amphitryon* and *The Miser*). Dorine in *Tartuffe* and Toinette in *The Imaginary Invalid* challenge their masters' de-lusions to a degree that borders on comic domestic anarchy. Similarly, in *Don Juan*, Sganarelle directly challenges the right of his master to seduce women. Street-smart underclass characters in Molière are frequent foils to the self-deluding bourgeoisie. In many of the plays, folk wisdom comes from the servants in the form of proverbs as Molière mines another vein of popular culture.

Finally, let us look through the carnivalesque lens at Molière's *Tartuffe*, in which a clergyman preaches holiness but practices seduction, almost with impunity. It was his most controversial play and, ultimately, the most profitable in his lifetime. Molière first staged it as part of Louis XIV's lavish entertainments at Versailles in 1664, in a version now lost. The king enjoyed it but suppressed it in deference to the outrage of a sect of zealously devout Catholics. The play has many strains of popular folk humor inherited from farce and *commedia*, including a scene of forceful congress in which a woman must fight off a sexual advance, but despite her vulnerability to attack, is nonetheless positioned as literally "on top" of the foolish male head of household. But let us focus here on one profound example of carnival humor in the play.

In the comic spectacles of popular festivals, travesty – the mocking appropriation of the costumes and insignia of authority and identity – was typical. Travesty suggests a slippage between the ideal and the real, between symbol and truth, between the sign and what it signifies – an effect which, for Bakhtin, nourishes positive social change. Molière's plays are full of imposters and poseurs, such as his affected courtiers, his bourgeois would-be gentleman, and all of his mock doctors. Disguised in the vestments and language of authority, such imposters create comic havoc. Tartuffe, as a sexual predator in the guise of a devout, creates more. Molière's play, like theatrical art itself, raises the question of whether we can ever know where the performance of the self ends and a true self begins. Taken seriously, a question about the stability of our knowledge of truth is not one an absolutist church or state can long entertain. Molière's play could be seen not only as irreverent but as a strike at the heart of the Church's authenticity. It is this, perhaps more than the sexual content of the plays, that would account for the deep wrath of the powerful conservative cabal that insisted that the king, who had been Molière's protector in controversies up to this time, suppress the play. One Catholic curate raged in print against *Tartuffe* (Figure 6.10), saying the author was "a demon … dressed like a man," that Molière had held Christ's Church in contempt, and that he should be burned at the stake as a foretaste of what he would surely suffer in hell

LE TARTVFFE

Figure 6.10

Orgon catches Tartuffe (standing at left) in the act of trying to seduce his wife in Act IV of Molière's *Tartuffe*. Engraving by François Chaveau from the 1669 edition of the play.

Source: © Bibliothèque nationale de France.

(Molière 1971: I, 1143–4). When Molière tried to produce a revised version in 1667, the Bishop of Paris closed it down, threatening the excommunication of anyone who performed or read it.

A very persistent Molière finally got his play to the public stage in 1669 in the version that survives today. The ending probably represents his revising process and has been the subject of much debate; it features the last-minute intervention of an emissary from Louis XIV to save Orgon and his home from Tartuffe's grasp. This scene may be understood as a conventional, obsequious compliment from Molière to the king, represented in the emissary's speech as Orgon's omniscient, all-wise sovereign. But some in the original audience may have read this last-act dénouement as an ironic *deus ex machina* [deh-oos ex MAH-khee-nah], which is to say as a carnivalesque parody of power. At the very least, two language zones, as Bakhtin would call them, were in play in the ending – the official and the unofficial – each offering different reception possibilities. The result would have been the kind of dialectic celebrated by Bakhtin that promotes ambivalence and subverts orthodoxy.

In their ribald humor and theatrical artifices drawn from street theatre traditions, Molière's plays, at least momentarily, critiqued decorum and absolutist control, and gestured to the reversals offered by farce before its festive culture was curtailed during the first half of the seventeenth century. Molière persisted in deploying carnivalesque humor throughout his career. Molière, the carnivalesque comic actor and writer, was never elected to the classically rigorous, decorum-conscious French Academy, guardian of French language and literature, a fact that the Academy never has lived down.

Key references

Bakhtin, M. (1984) *Rabelais and His World*, trans. H. Iswolsky, Bloomington: Indiana University Press.

Beam, S. (2007) *Farce and the Making of Absolutism in France*. Ithaca, NY: Cornell University Press.

Dock, S.V. (1992) *Costume and Fashion in the Plays of Jean-Baptiste Poquelin, Molière*, Geneva: Editions Slatkine.

Gaines, J.F. (ed.) (2002) *The Molière Encyclopedia*, Westport, CT: Greenwood Press.

Guynn, N. (2020). *Pure Filth: Ethics, Politics and Religion in Early French Farce*. Philadelphia: University of Pennsylvania.

McCarthy, G. (2002) *The Theatres of Molière*, New York and London: Routledge.

Molière (1953) *Molière, Five Plays*, trans. J. Wood, Baltimore, MD: Penguin Books.

Molière (1957) *Eight Plays by Molière*, trans. M. Bishop, New York: Modern Library.

Molière [Poquelin, J.B.] (1971) *Oeuvres Completes*, ed. G. Couton, Paris: Gallimard. (Scholarly French edition of all the plays and related documents referred to in this study.)

Molière (1993) *Tartuffe*, trans. R. Wilber (1961) in W.B. Worthen (ed.) *The HBJ Anthology of Drama*, Fort Worth, TX: Harcourt Brace Jovanovich. (Includes English translations of Molière's important preface and other documents.)

Molière. (2001) *The Misanthrope, Tartuffe, and Other Plays*, trans. M. Slater, Oxford: Oxford University Press.

Scott, V. (2000) *Molière, A Theatrical Life*, Cambridge: Cambridge University Press.

Absolutism and neoclassicism in France, 1660–1700

By 1660, the French crown was providing financial assistance to four theatre companies that primarily performed neoclassical plays. This practice had begun in the 1630s when Cardinal Richelieu initially arranged subsidies for the acting troupe at the Théâtre du Marais and then extended similar treatment to the other major troupe in Paris performing at the Hôtel de Bourgogne. As other troupes in Paris vied for royal support upon Louis XIV's ascension to the throne in 1643, the new king and his ministers took advantage of the monarchy's position in French culture to continue to tie theatre to the power of the crown. A *commedia dell'arte* company from Italy under the management of Tiberio Fiorillo (also spelled as Fiorilli, 1608–1694), which enjoyed the support of several influential courtiers, gained a subsidy in the mid-1640s that was renewed from 1653 onward. As we have seen, the king also lavished financial assistance on Molière and his company in the 1660s.

Royal support of French neoclassical theatre was capricious and haphazard, however, leading both theatre artists and state bureaucrats to attempt to regularize the arrangements. When Molière died in 1673, rivalry among the Paris acting troupes created a period of flux, with several actors leaving one company to join another. In 1679, the crown forced an end to the conflicts by ordering the two remaining major acting troupes in Paris to combine into one – the Comédie Française. Further, the king's edict also granted a monopoly over spoken drama in French to the new company. (An exception was soon made, however, when Fiorillo's *commedia* troupe won the right to continue to use French in their performances.) Louis XIV's 1679 decree continued the traditional organization of French acting companies, by which the actors shared in the profits of the troupe, but he fixed the number of shares so that no new members could be admitted to the Comédie Française until an old one retired or died. The edict also regulated how actors might be elected as sharing members and the authority the members possessed in selecting plays for production. Finally, the king took control of the internal affairs of the troupe; his decree established his First Gentleman of the Chamber as the arbiter of disputes within the company. Later, in 1701 and 1706, the king imposed censorship on the troupe; the new rules mandated that all scripts be read and approved by a censor in the police department before a public performance in Paris would be allowed.

The success of French neoclassicist playwriting preceded the absolutist consolidation of French dramatic theatre in the Comédie Française. During the 1660s and 1670s, the counterpart in tragic playwriting to Molière's success in comedy and farce was Jean Racine (1639–1699); both were popular in public theatres and at the court of Louis XIV. Following several successes beginning with *Andromaque* in 1667, Racine penned what most critics agree was his masterpiece, *Phèdre*, in 1677. Like several of Racine's tragedies, *Phèdre* plays out the consequences of a maxim by the philosopher René Descartes: "Our passions cannot be directly aroused or removed by the action of our will" (qtd. in Sayer 2006: 258). Proposing a strict separation between human emotions and rational thought – between the needs of the body and the logic of the mind – Descartes and the other rationalists of his day believed they could offer little help to men and women in the grip of "passion." In *Phèdre*, based on an ancient Greek myth, Queen Phèdre is passionately in love with her stepson Hippolyte. Nonetheless, in accordance with neoclassical decorum, Racine spares Phèdre the loss of dignity evident in his play's sources. But the moral code of neoclassical decorum prevents her from acting on her desire. Following the constraints of the three unities, Racine constructs a tightly woven plot in which Phèdre struggles to express and finally to extricate herself from her passion, only to bring on the wrath of her husband, the death of Hippolyte, and her own shame and suicide. As in *Phèdre*, the precepts of neoclassical rules and Cartesian rationalism provided sharp conflicts between duty and desire in many tragedies of the seventeenth century. Long a favorite of French audiences and female tragedy actors, *Phèdre* continues to thrill spectators today, perhaps because of how Racine's character development dovetails with contemporary psychological understandings of human behavior.

While Racine is best known for his adaptations of Greek myths and dramas performed in the professional theatre (he was trained in classical Greek), in his later years he retreated from his life as a professional playwright to become a royal historiographer for Louis XIV, and later held a number of positions in the King's administration. Racine's return to the stage toward the end of his life was at the request of Louis XIV's second wife Madame de Maintenon, for whom he wrote two biblical plays for female students, *Esther* (1689) and *Athalie* (1691). Unlike Molière, Racine was inducted into the French Academy. His closeness to power throughout his life protected him and his family after his death. As Racine's biography demonstrates, neoclassical drama had a close relationship to the absolutism of Louis XIV and the preceding consolidation under Louis XIII.

Fissures in these strictures are also found in representations of gender, race and class as French absolutist solidified. As might be expected, the desire for divine monarchical control necessitated dedication to a strict gender binary within the theatre. Deviations from the norm were often found elsewhere, such as the *Ballet de la Douairière de Billebahaut* (1626), which stages Peruvian indigenous leader Atahualpa's anti-Spanish rebellion. This ballet not only critiqued colonialism, but reimagined indigenous histories complete with "androgenes," third gender figures, not found in official performance scripts. Although the drawings from this ballet may not have correlated with the actual performance, it is clear that these images chipped away at ballet's gendered codes. Anxieties about class, and in particular the possibility of class-mobility, were also often registered in relationship to racial or ethnic Others, as Molière's "mamamouchi" makes clear. Nonetheless, despite the cultural misappropriation in these representations, it is clear that some of these French artists did use non-European cultural sources as a basis for their fictions, and in particular to question forms of absolutism with which they were not fully enthralled or to imagine new ones.

THEATRE IN NEW FRANCE IN THE COLONIAL PERIOD

Dramatic performance was part of the rituals, ceremonies and celebrations of First Nations peoples for centuries before the arrival of French colonizers to what is now Canada. European-style theatre seems to have arrived in 1583, with Sir Humphrey Gilbert's English expeditions performing musical and mumming entertainments for natives and crews alike. In 1606, Marc Lescarbot (1570–1641), interim leader of French colonists in Port Royal in latter-day Nova Scotia, hastily penned what is widely regarded as the first French play to be performed in Canada: *Le Théâtre de Neptune en la Nouvelle-France* (*The Theatre of Neptune in New France*). It was written for and performed by French seamen anxiously awaiting the return of their mothership, which was making an exploratory expedition down the coast and had been gone too long. The performance was meant to boost their morale and prevent rebellion as they faced another hard winter ahead should the ship fail to return with their leader. It did return, and on 14 November 1606, the nautical drama *The Theatre of Neptune* entered theatre history. As the ship approached, it was met with a fantasia blending characters from Greek mythology and the indigenous Mi'kmaq culture, who welcomed the arriving ship bearing armloads of gifts from the local bounty, all proclaimed in rhyming couplets that were the dramatic fashion of the time back in Old France.

Though it only had one performance (for the returning crew and a small gathering of Mi'kmaq locals), *The Theatre of Neptune* has long been of scholarly interest to theatre historians. What we know of it comes from a single source – Lescarbot himself. Although Lescarbot humanizes the Mi'kmaq characters more than many of his European counter-parts did in similar works, to contemporary readers it describes what Alan Filewod terms an "operation of colonialism through spectacle" (2007: 190). In effect, it re-enacted a largely fictional scenario, in redface, of what Julie Burrelle calls "desired conquest," in which native peoples offer gifts, territory, and willing submission to European colonizers (2014: 48). Thus, argues Burrelle, this first instance of French theatre in Canada was also "a foundational spectacle of First Nations' erasure in Canada" (2014: 13).

Theatre participated in that erasure long into the period of colonization in New France as it did in New Spain, where it was used by religious orders to help convert indigenous peoples to Christianity.

> A Jesuit later wrote of a 1640 production [*Le Sage Visionnaire* (*The Wise Visionary*) in honor of the birth of Louis XIV]: "We had a soul of an unbeliever pursued by two demons, who finally hurled it into a hell that vomited forth flames." For the indigenous spectators, "the struggles, cries and shrieks of this soul and of these demons, who spoke in the Algonquin tongue," achieved such a fearful effect that at least one native was having nightmares two days later.
>
> Londré and Watermeier 1998: 77

Theatre was also used for educational purposes in Jesuit schools, and the upper ranks of society enjoyed neoclassical tragedies and comedies, especially during periods of *Carnaval*. *Le Cid* was one of them, as were several others by Corneille and Racine.

Perhaps most famous was an aborted production of Molière's *Tartuffe* in 1694, which became the site of a struggle between religious and civil authorities. Not only did Bishop Saint-Vallier, who ruled Quebec's moral life with an iron hand, find the play to be of an "impious" and "injurious" nature, but he also deemed its producer and principal actor, Lieutenant Jacques-Théodore Cosineau de Mareuil, morally unfit to participate because of his licentious behavior off-stage. In the end, Mareuil was excommunicated and imprisoned (though he was eventually freed and returned to France); and in return for a payment, Governor Frontenac canceled the performance slated to be held at his palace. While most scholars take this as evidence that the same tensions attended the play in New France as in France, Micah True maintains that theatre in New France was selectively produced and sometimes adapted to serve local ends, as suggested by the 1640 religious tragicomedy described above.

Absolutism and neoclassicism in England, 1660–1700

English entertainments also used non-European imagery, even before the official return of theatre. William Davenant's (1606–1668) *The Siege of Rhodes* (1656), which escaped bans on theatre by labeling itself as a "musical entertainment," commented on British politics through the exploration of Ottoman history. In contrast with the negative representation of stage Turks, which extended through 1642, this entertainment exemplified the new fascination and high regard for the Ottoman Empire as a model for Britain's own expansionist designs. After this precursor, regular performances by professional companies would return to England in 1660 (including a revision of *The Siege of Rhodes* in 1661) after the Civil War, with the Restoration of Charles II to the throne. While living in exile at the court of the French monarch, Charles appreciated the control that Louis XIV and his ministers were exercising over French performance. Although Charles did not want to pay the direct theatre subsidies, such as those that allowed the French throne to enjoy entertainments that reflected its absolutist goals, he did believe that he needed to control the stage to legitimate his fragile hold on power. When he returned to England, Charles awarded royal **patents** to two playwright-impresarios, making them the only men allowed to produce plays in London, an unprecedented theatrical monopoly in England. Thomas Killigrew (1612–1683) became the manager of the King's Company, which soon floundered. Davenant, a better theatre manager, supervised the Duke's Company more closely until his death in 1668, when the actors Thomas Betterton (1635–1710) and Henry Harris (1634–1704) assumed artistic control. With the imminent failure of Killigrew's company, the king allowed the two troupes to merge in 1682.

During the reign of Charles II, which lasted until 1685, the London companies generally performed at two indoor theatres, Drury Lane and Lincoln's Inn Fields. Both playhouses accommodated small audiences of mostly aristocratic spectators, who enjoyed bawdy comedies and heroic plays featuring royalist propaganda. Built for wing-and-drop scenery with side flats that slid in grooves on the floor and painted drops lowered from the flies above (the **wing-and-groove system**), these proscenium theatres did not deploy the more expensive chariot-and-pole rigging of many continental playhouses. When the king decided he needed a theatre in which he could entertain foreign dignitaries, he advanced funds from the royal treasury for the completion of a new playhouse in Dorset Garden, which was equipped with a modified version of the chariot- and-pole system for the staging of European opera (Figure 6.11). For ten years after its opening in 1671, the king used Dorset Garden as an extension of his royal power, even though it remained primarily a commercial operation.

Until 1685, the desires and values of King Charles and his aristocratic favorites dominated the English stage. Soon after his return to power, the king had decreed that English companies should now employ women as professional actors, a casting convention he had enjoyed while watching French theatre. Called the "merry monarch" for his sexual affairs, Charles extended his royal prerogatives to taking actresses of his choice as his bedmates. The new female actors were an instant hit on stage (and the convention of men playing young women soon died out). Several women achieved artistic stature, including comedy actor Nell Gwyn (1650–1687), who became Charles's mistress, and tragedian Elizabeth Barry (1658–1713). Many of these women were also immortalized in painted images, often sponsored by their lovers. And, perhaps unsurprisingly given the recent reemergence of women on stage, spectators often commented on actresses' looks as much as their talent. Reviews of actresses' performances also conflated

Figure 6.11
The stage of Dorset Garden Theatre, London, with the setting for Act I, Scene 1 of *The Empress of Morocco*, by E. Settle, produced in 1673. King Charles II's coat of arms is at the center of the proscenium arch. Designed by Christopher Wren, the theatre featured London's best-equipped stage at the time. Engraving by William Dole in the 1673 edition of the play.
Source: © Gary Jay and Josephine S. Williams.

Figure 6.12
Elkanah Settle's *Empress of Morocco*, 1673.
Source: S2678. Folger Shakespeare Library.

their onstage and offstage lives, referring to incidents in their real lives so as to interpret their work on stage. Although a new law (passed to appease the Puritans) made it illegal to produce plays that offended "piety and good manners," many Restoration productions paraded lusty actions and sexual innuendos.

Playwriting between 1660 and 1680 generally reflected royalist values while also grappling with the realities brought on by British colonial expansion and the beginnings of the British slave trade. The slave trade began in 1663 by royal charter, when it created the Royal Adventurers of England, who were later reconstituted as the Royal African Company in 1672 led by the Duke of York, Charles II's brother, who later ascended to the throne as James II (1633–1701) in 1685. Although their early work was not a well-organized business, the Royal African Company's implementation of sugar plantations that used captive labor made slavery an important part of British culture in Stuart England, linking British absolutism with imperial and colonial expansion and the dehumanizing, brutal enslavement of African peoples.

The Indian Queen by John Dryden (1631–1700) and Robert Howard (1626–1698), and Dryden's own two-part *The Conquest of Granada* (1670) followed neoclassical patterns and focused on competitive royal heroes and heroines caught in conflicts between romantic love and duty to the state. Like Racine, his contemporary in France, Dryden attempted to reconcile the philosophy of Descartes with the morality of his heroes and their tragic decisions. Influenced by his correspondence with political philosopher Thomas Hobbes, Dryden celebrated the power of absolute rulers in his early plays. These plays also registered Britain's imperial ambitions. *The Indian Queen* was first presented for Charles II's 1662 wedding to Catherine of Braganza. Catherine was Portuguese, and thus brought with her a number of trading rights, possession of Tangier and Bombay, and the legacy of Portuguese slavery a mere year before England engaged in the trade. The play's plot ends in a marriage between two empires, represented by the Incan Orazia and the Mexican Moctezuma. Despite its butchering of indigenous history and geography, the mixed marriage represented Charles II's own union with the Portuguese queen. For example, the parade of African slaves who carry Zempoalla in the play's final scene gestures both to the legacy of African chattel slavery in the British colonies and to the parade staged as part of Catherine's wedding to Charles, which included ten nude Ethiopians. Yet, as Laura Rosenthal (2020) points out, Dryden called the play a tragedy, suggesting that the failed female lovers, such as Zempoalla, cast aside in the play, might be protagonists rather than supporting players. Dryden's exploration of the uneasy alliance, and the monarchy's imperial project continued with the *Indian Queen*'s sequel, *The Indian Emperor* (1665). The emphasis on mixed marriage is also found in Elkanah Settle's (1648–1724) *The Empress of Morocco* (see Figure 6.12 to see African performers in the foreground), but Settle's play more openly advocates for the benefits of colonizing North Africa, in contrast to Dryden's (perhaps unconscious) ambivalence about Britain's imperial aims. And, in a near parallel with the 1605 *Masque of Blacknesse*, the appearance of a dark queen gestures back to the Queen herself. Portuguese people in this era were not necessarily coded as white, and Catherine's association with the slave trade and Africa more broadly, along with her Southern European roots, made her a dark lady whose prominence cast anxiety over the populace.

By the 1670s, however, Dryden had shifted his focus and began to search for a dramatic vehicle that would allow his spectators to understand greatness through the standard of "generosity," as Descartes had defined it in his writings. According to Descartes, a king could attain "generosity" when he resolved "to undertake and carry out what he judges best" (qtd. in Fletcher 2011: 105). The playwright believed, like Descartes, that such self-esteem allowed the virtuous ruler to rise above his contempt for lesser mortals and judge them with compassion. To this end, Dryden reworked Shakespeare's *Antony and Cleopatra* to express these Cartesian values, changing the title (and emphasis) of the tragedy to *All for Love* (1677). In Dryden's neoclassical version of the final days of these two heroes from Roman times, Antony gradually forsakes the competitive masculinity of Shakespeare's character and eventually finds "generosity" in his continuing concern for Cleopatra, even when both are near their deaths. Dryden also uses the play to advocate for the neoclassical rules of space and time, trimming away the sprawling number of sites in Shakespeare's original, while also meeting the rules of decorum. In doing so, he foreshadowed an important future trend: many "cleaned up" versions of Shakespeare would follow in the eighteenth century, with changed titles and simplified plot structures, to meet new audience expectations.

Today's readers, however, are more familiar with Restoration comedies such as William Wycherley's (1640–1715) *The Country Wife* (1675), George Etherege's (c.1634–1692) *The Man of Mode* (1676), and Aphra Behn's (1640–1689) (Figure 6.13) *The Rover* (1677), which featured witty language and titillating sexual intrigue among the beautiful and privileged. At the center of *The Rover*, for example, are four "Banish'd Cavaliers" (the subtitle of the play), who have traveled to Naples for pleasure and adventure. The subtitle sets the play in the 1650s, when many royalists moved to the continent to escape Puritan rule during the English Civil War. Chief among them is Willmore, who pursues many women, two of whom – Hellena and Angelica – fight for his affections. (Behn's female characters are nearly as sexually voracious as her male Cavaliers.) Behn weaves two more love plots into the action, which involves an English colonel and Florinda, Hellena's sister, and a foolish Cavalier who falls for an Italian prostitute. In addition, a disguised Florinda is nearly raped and Angelica almost shoots Willmore in a jealous rage. In the end, the prostitute robs the Cavalier, Florinda marries the colonel, and Willmore reluctantly agrees to end his roving and marry Hellena.

Other comic writers followed the example of Molière, whose neoclassical comedies provided models on both sides of the English Channel. These and other dramatists wrote for a coterie audience that usually mirrored the king's taste for heroic grandeur and overt sexuality. While a few playwrights, including Anglo-Irish Nahum Tate (1652–1715), who in his adaptations of Shakespeare's *King Lear* and *Richard II*, attempted to articulate anti-absolutist positions through allusive language, most bolstered royalist prejudices.

Charles II's death in 1685 and the political events that followed sometimes affected the era's playwriting in ways not reduced to shifts in genre. For example, it was in this period that Behn, largely known as a writer of witty comedies of intrigue, began to publish plays in timeworn theatrical and print genres that wrestled with British colonialism more openly (although some scholars believe that she critiqued slavery in more covert ways earlier in her career.) Recalling her experience in Suriname in 1662–1663, during the emergence of the slave trade, about which she had remained silent during Charles II's reign, she penned the novel *Oroonoko, the Royal Slave* (1688). During this time, she also wrote the play *Widdow Ranter* (c. 1688), an account of a recent historical event: Bacon's rebellion in Virginia (1666–1667). This rebellion, led by Nathaniel Bacon (1647–1676) and 600 soldiers against loyalist Virginia Governor William Berkeley (1605–1677), was fueled by Bacon's disapproval of Berkeley's attempts to broker peaceful relations with local Indian tribes to retain power and gain land. Bacon, in contrast, advocated driving indigenous people out of Virginia completely. Bacon failed, but within U.S. history, this event was seen as a precursor to the American Revolution and a blow to the use of European indentured labor, perhaps leading to the path toward chattel slavery; for Behn it was a defense of the Loyalist cause, and a critique of the non-Loyalist colonists. While set in different countries, both works looked at conditions in the Americas to critique the rapacity and cruelty of slavery and colonialism. These critiques, as suggested by the plot of the *Widdow Ranter*, did not deter her from her royalist sympathies Instead, she employed noble indigenous and African descended characters as ideal royalists, and used Surinamese and indigenous relationships to land as a model for the British to follow.

Figure 6.13

Aphra Behn, the first woman in England to earn her living as a writer, wrote several plays during the Restoration period, featuring women as central characters. She also wrote novels, poetry, and translations, and served as a spy for Charles II. Sketch by George Scharf from a portrait believed to be lost.

Source: Wiki, https://commons.wikimedia.org/wiki/File:Aphra_Behn.jpg

The political crisis of the 1680s disempowered English absolutism in ways that affected royal control of plays within British theatres. Anti-royalist factions in London took to the streets to perform massive Pope Burning pageants and other demonstrations that linked royal absolutism to the power of Rome. These and other political actions led in 1688 to increased power for Parliament. One patent company continued to dominate theatrical production in London for another ten years, even though they lacked the legal authority of the sort possessed by the Comédie Française to enforce their apparent monopolies. When in 1695 the legal validity of the patents expired, the English throne, which no longer claimed absolute authority, did not revive them. After 1700, although the crown continued to license theatres, it did so unevenly; consequently, many kinds of theatre flourished in England in the early eighteenth century. Soon, neoclassical comedies and tragedies were living, cheek by jowl, with satires and ballad operas as the popular theatres at the Hounslow, Southwark, and Bartholomew fairs competed with the regular London playhouses catering to aristocrats and wealthy merchants.

Reforming Italian and French Baroque opera

As we saw, Italian librettists and composers in the 1600s favored the extravagance of the Baroque over the restraints of neoclassicism for their operas. This began to change in the 1690s, however, as many Italians turned away from the Counter-Reformation ideology of the Vatican, which had pushed the emotional and flamboyant style of the Baroque for over a century, to embrace the Cartesian rationality that Racine, Dryden, and other Europeans had explored and advanced in neoclassical literature and drama. Led by the Arcadian Academy (f. 1690), a group of intellectuals and wealthy patrons in Rome set on modernizing Italian culture, the reformers drew on Aristotle and Renaissance ideals to restore older modes of artistic expression and to urge that artists take up more rational and simplified forms as models for their work. One later Italian critic, looking back on Baroque opera from the perspective of the 1780s after the Arcadian reforms were complete, painted a sharp contrast between the enlightened qualities of present opera and the musical contraptions of the previous century. Baroque opera, he said, presented "an enormous chaos, a concoction of sacred and profane, of historical and fabulous, of mythology, ancient and modern, of true and allegorical, of natural and fantastic, all gathered together to the perpetual shame of Art" (qtd. in Kimbell 1991: 182). As we shall see, however, this critic exaggerated the differences between seventeenth- and eighteenth-century opera.

The reformers of Italian opera began by separating serious from comic opera, establishing two major genres that would endure for the next 80 years – *opera seria* [OH-peh-rah SEH-ree-ah] and *opera buffa* [OH-peh-rah BOOF-fah]. *Opera buffa* drew much of its energy, many of its plots, and most of its stock characters from *commedia dell'arte*, which remained popular among all classes of Italians during the eighteenth century. Our next chapter traces major changes in *commedia dell'arte* during the 1700s, changes that were also reflected in the libretti and music of *opera buffa*. Although reformers also altered *opera seria* (serious opera), the changes were less substantial, primarily because this genre was dominated by one man, Pietro Metastasio (1698–1782), for much of his career as a librettist. Metastasio gained initial fame as a poet in Rome, where he soon turned to writing libretti for operas under the initial sponsorship of the Arcadian Academy. In response to the increasing popularity of *opera seria*

among royals and aristocrats in the Austrian empire, Metastasio moved to Vienna in 1730 and produced several of his most famous libretti, including the words for *Olympiade* and *Clemenza di Tito.*

Bowing to some of the constraints of neoclassicism, Metastasio's libretti reduced the spectacular and allegorical elements of Baroque opera and emphasized intrigues and mistaken identities among historical rulers that turned on conflicts between duty and expediency or virtue and passion, much as the plots of Racine and Dryden had earlier. Unlike their tragedies, however, Metastasio resolved most of his dramatic conflicts happily, often through a change of heart by the hero and the general reconciliation of the principal characters. His libretti suggested that the world of his virtuous aristocrats and royals was more benign than cruel or tragic, if looked at through an enlightened perspective. From the 1730s into the 1770s, many composers found Metastasio's poetic libretti so elegant and captivating that they returned to several of them again and again to re-set them to different music. *Opera seria* in the form and style of Metastasio took much of the pomposity and religiosity out of Baroque opera, but his lyrical libretti departed significantly from the verisimilitude and formal rigor of the neoclassical plays of Racine and Dryden. Regarding the difficulties of European absolutism for its rulers and subjects, the pleasant endings of *opera seria* made these problems seem resolvable. Metastasio's neoclassical libretti may have simplified the plot contortions of Baroque opera, but most of the operas based on his words were performed against the soaring magnificence of Bibiena-designed or –inspired scenery.

Metastasio also regularized the scene structure of *opera seria* by moving most of the action between characters to recitative (dialogue sung in the simple rhythms of natural speech with only slight melodic variation) and leaving the arias of his major characters to mark the ends of scenes. Given this placement of their arias, it was probably inevitable that operatic stars would push composers to lengthen and elaborate their difficulty.

The primary stars of *opera seria*, inspiring devotion in many as well as contempt in a few, were **castrati** [kahs-TRAH-tee], male singers who had been castrated in their youth to preserve their boyish voices so they could deliver *opera seria* arias with supreme virtuosity in a high range. Once castrated, a boy's voice does not deepen by an octave, as normally occurs in males in early adulthood, but usually stays in the soprano range, with a tonal quality half-way between a child's and a woman's. The Catholic Church had been practicing the castration of vocally promising boys (following the dubious consent of their parents) to produce singers for the Papal Choir since the 1500s and castrati sang in Baroque opera in the 1600s.

During the eighteenth century, as *opera seria* spread through Italy and north into the rest of Europe, the practice of castration increased and several more castrati moved from church choirs to operatic stages. Although less than one in a hundred castrati gained a career as a singer, operatic fame meant substantial wealth and aristocratic connections. Among them, Carlo Broschi (1705–1782), who took the stage name Farinelli, was the most popular (Figure 6.14). Following his debut in Naples, Farinelli performed throughout Italy, then toured Europe in the 1720s and 1730s, with stops in Munich, London, and Paris and extensive stays in Vienna, where he befriended Metastasio. Like other castrati, Farinelli primarily performed the masculine heroes of *opera seria*, endowing their arias with intensity, tenderness, force, and passion. While most audiences fawned over castrati opera stars, critics outside of Italy pointed to the hypocrisy underlining the fact that an elite that called itself "enlightened" believed in the need to castrate boys to enable their operatic enjoyment. These critics also noted that castrati performing the roles of powerful rulers were an affront to neoclassical verisimilitude – which is perhaps why castrati were not regularly employed in opera houses in France.

Defining themselves against Italian opera, French opera artists cast the roles played by castrati in Italy with male high tenors. The operas of Jean-Baptiste Lully (1633–1682) sustained normative gender in casting and vocal sound. When male singers were cast in female roles in plays, they were usually roles that were already embodied by male actors, such as the nurse figure played for comic relief in genres such as *commedia* and other genres. The French attitude extended to a lack of eunuch characters in drama, which contrasted with their popularity in English Restoration plays, where they often depicted as chaste guards of female virtue, especially in Orientalist tragedies that depicted Turkish, Persian, or Indian royal courts and other non-European sites (many of the plays discussed in this chapter, including *The Empress of Morocco* (1673), *All for Love*, and *The Mourning Bride* (1697), had eunuch characters). British spectators, although sometimes fascinated with the singers, sometimes spoke negatively about these figures, calling them "Italian castrati," although they also performed in England. The appearance of the castrati – as opposed to eunuch characters – may have caused a different sort of crisis of gender and sexuality. Many female (and male) fans throughout

Figure 6.14

Portrait of Carlo Broschi (Farinelli), soon after the King of Spain made him a Knight of the Order of Calatrava in 1750. Farinelli proudly displays the insignia of the Order on his coat. Painting by Jacopo Amigoni, c.1750–1752.

Source: Classic Image/Alamy Stock Photo.

Europe found castrati quite desirable, suggesting that heterosexuality and gender identity might have been less stable than many thinkers of the time wanted them to be.

For the aristocrats, royal ministers, wealthy merchants, and famous professionals who purchased a box at the theatre for the season, however, opera-going was primarily a social rather than a musical or dramatic occasion. The regularities of *opera seria* and the fact that so many of its stories were familiar enabled spectators to ignore much of what was happening on stage (usually until a castrato began an aria) and to focus instead on social interests and desires. Eighteenth-century architects built opera houses to emphasize the dominance of the boxes, which generally ringed a "U"-shaped auditorium and might be stacked four high, allowing the elite of a city to view the social hierarchy at a glance, parade their wealth and family, and use their opera glasses to get a good look at each other's affairs (Figure 6.15). Most opera houses featured a royal or ducal box, much larger than the others, at the "bottom" of the "U," from which the king (or the local duke, count, or margrave) might watch his subjects and set the social tone for the evening (and enjoy the finest view of

Figure 6.15

The Margrave's theatre in Bayreuth, Germany. Designed by Guiseppe and Carlo Galli
Bibiena and built in 1748, this small Baroque opera house features the typical "U" shape
for its auditorium with a large opera box for the local ruler at its apex. Chairs in the pit
below the boxes were added in the nineteenth century. In the eighteenth century, the pit
probably accommodated temporary benches for servants and others.

Source: Image Professionals GmbH/Alamy Stock Photo.

the perspective scenery). The best boxes, usually placed on the lower levels of the "U" near
the royal box, were actually small parlors, built to accommodate socializing, card playing, and
even dining during the performance. (When not serving their masters, servants might stand
in the pit area below the boxes, which sometimes doubled as a ballroom, or perch on a bench
in a cramped balcony above the royal box, if such a gallery had been built for them.) In Italy
and in many of the small states of Germany, wealthy merchants shared the social ostentation
of the opera with local rulers. In eighteenth-century Lisbon, Vienna, Madrid, and Paris – the
capitals of empires – absolute rulers made sure that operatic spectacle and sociality reflected
and enhanced their power.

   The Paris Opéra in the 1750s provides a good example of the link between absolutism
and opera-going. As music historian James H. Johnson notes:

> At mid-century, the Opéra ... was a royal spectacle, tailored to fit the tastes of the king's
> most distinguished subjects: his closest relatives held their boxes in the most visible rows,
> royal administrators and palace functionaries seldom missed performances, and Louis
> XV himself came with some regularity.
>
> (Johnson 1995: 10)

Instead of the noise of conversations during performances, critics complained that the court etiquette of Versailles prevailed, with many spectators watching the king to see how they should respond. Indeed, in his examination of the records of annual subscribers for first-level boxes over an eight-year period, Johnson found that over 90 percent of them were aristocrats and most of those held high positions in the regime. During the 1750s, Louis XV took a personal interest in the affairs of the Opéra, which, like the Comédie Française, had lost most of its artistic freedom to gain monopolistic privileges. The king established budgets, interfered in personnel decisions, selected operas for performance, and occasionally gave advice during rehearsals. In addition to *opera seria*, the king enjoyed opera ballets (which featured more dancing than singing), pastoral operas (which idealized rural peasant life), and revivals of the lyrical operas by Lully, who had turned Baroque opera away from Italian modes toward French tastes soon after the establishment of the Paris Opéra. Because these operatic genres were royal favorites, they dominated the repertoire in the 1750s.

Absolutism and neoclassicism in the German states and Russia, 1700–1770

While some of the larger courts among the German states and cities in the early 1700s could afford to subsidize regular operatic productions, most of the dukes, counts, princes, and others who ruled in Germany got by with occasional visits from traveling operatic troupes. Public performances consisted mainly of small *commedia dell'arte* companies that toured the area and home-grown fairground troupes that set up temporary stages for seasonal performances. Still recovering from the devastations of the religious wars, most of German society could afford little more than such offerings, which were nonetheless enjoyed by peasants, workers, burgers (middle class citizens), and a few aristocrats (Figure 6.16). Although these troupes performed a variety of genres, the star of most of them was a carnivalesque clown, who

Figure 6.16
At left, touring players on their temporary stage before an audience in a market square in Munich in 1780. From a painting by Joseph Stephan.

Source: © Bayerisches Nationalmuseum, Munich. Photo courtesy: The Deutsches Theatermuseum.

generally enacted a character called Hanswurst. This fun-loving, hard-drinking, and often devilish figure combined attributes from several previous clown-figures seen in Germany, including medieval fools, Falstaffian characters (introduced by English actors who played in Germany during the English Civil War), and Harlequins (known to German audiences from *commedia* tours).

Despite these difficult circumstances for neoclassical theatre, two reformers, the theatre troupe manager Caroline Neuber (1697–1760) and the philosopher and critic Johann Christoph Gottsched (1700–1766) conjoined their shared interest in 1727 to introduce several neoclassical innovations into the German theatre. Gottsched translated and adapted French plays into German, and Neuber staged them and polished their troupe's performance style. Although the Gottsched–Neuber company made some allies among the German aristocracy, the troupe never found a large audience for their neoclassical plays in Leipzig and Hamburg, their primary sites for performance. Both had hoped to rid the stage of Hanswurst and the kind of theatre he represented and "banished" him in a performance in 1737, but Hanswurst plays at fairground theatres remained popular when their troupe broke in two in 1739. Even more than in the theatre of Molière, the carnivalesque undermined neoclassical restraint and Baroque grandeur – at least with popular audiences, if not with many German aristocrats, educated to believe in the superiority of French culture.

Folk and fairground theatrical traditions existed in Russia as well and continued throughout the eighteenth century. But neoclassical ideals, if not direct subsidies for theatrical production, had received a boost during the reign of Tsar Peter the Great (1682–1725), who campaigned to Westernize Russia. By the 1740s, the Russian court was enjoying Italian *opera seria* and French neoclassical plays, produced by troupes of Italian singers and French actors on a chariot-and-pole court stage in St. Petersburg. During the next decade, Alexander Sumarokov (1717–1777) wrote the first successful Russian tragedies and comedies on the French neoclassical model and the empress established and subsidized a state theatre for Russian plays and actors. Russian neoclassical theatre expanded substantially during the reign of Tsarina Catherine II (1762–1796), a playwright herself, bringing more Russian dramas, better subsidies, and the establishment of an acting school. French theatre remained the ideal, however, with translations of neoclassical French plays dominating the repertoire and the French crown's rules for the regulation of the Comédie Française serving as the model for the tsarina's control of the state-supported theatre and opera companies. By 1770, public as well as court theatres had gained a foothold in Russia, but the policies of Catherine II, as well as the domination of theatrical life by the aristocracy and court, ensured that upstart theatre companies would not use their performances to challenge her absolute rule.

The limits of neoclassicism and absolutism in France, 1720–1770

Theatrical neoclassicism spread from Paris throughout France in the 1700s, as large and medium-sized French cities competed with each other to build playhouses that could support touring and eventually permanent companies. About 20 cities enjoyed public performances at their theatres by 1750 and that number jumped to 71 by 1790. By 1789, the date of the French Revolution, France could boast more public theatres outside its capital than any other country in Europe. Funded mostly by local aristocrats and entrepreneurs, these theatres usually housed operatic as well as spoken performances and might also include *commedia dell'arte* troupes and fairground entertainers. Their managers primarily served local nobles, merchants, regional representatives of the crown, and other provincial elites, who socialized and conducted business at the playhouse. Not surprisingly, they looked to Paris for their models of acting, staging, and dramatic or operatic repertoire, which meant in practice that the traditional neoclassicism of Corneille and Racine in playwriting and Lully in opera pervaded the French provinces. Although some Parisian artists challenged neoclassical restraints, the power of the French Catholic Church, the French Academy, and the direct control of Parisian theatre and opera exercised by the French monarchy silenced or sidelined much of the opposition. Officially, all of France was becoming more neoclassical during the 1700–1789 period, even though, in retrospect, neoclassical forms could no longer contain the energies and concerns of the time.

In the 50 years between 1720 and 1770, the most renowned and one of the most popular playwrights of the period was Voltaire, the penname of François-Marie Arouet (1694–1778). Dramatist, pamphleteer, novelist, and historian Voltaire corresponded with many of the rich and powerful throughout Europe to urge reforms in a range of areas, from established religion to absolutist government. Although his plays occasionally took liberties with the three neoclassical unities and with class-bound notions of decorum, Voltaire defended the rules of neoclassicism in several essays. Historian Bettina Knapp calls Voltaire "an innovative theater traditionalist" (2000: 80); she recognizes the tension between Voltaire's push for reforms in staging and costuming (plus his campaigns against arbitrary rules in many areas of French life) and his continued support of neoclassicism.

In part, this tension resulted from the peculiar public position of Voltaire and the other French *philosophes* [fee-loh-zohf] – journalists, encyclopedia writers, and cultural critics of the period who were advocating for reform, but who also believed that they must work within the present absolutist system of government and culture to achieve it. As a leading *philosophe*, Voltaire hoped to influence the powerful to change French life from the top down, and part of this campaign involved a commitment to preserving what he took to be the high moral ground of elite French culture. In addition to attacking the Church, the academy, and other bastions of reactionary power, Voltaire and the other *philosophes* criticized those whom they accused of trivializing the culture of France – including the popular playwright Pierre Marivaux (1688–1763), whose love comedies, the *philosophes* believed, appealed to the vain and frivolous. Hoping to educate the public through elite networks of patronage and sociability and also recognizing that French neoclassical taste was becoming European taste, Voltaire clung to the ideas and forms of neoclassicism and shunned what he saw as the decadence of newer, more popular artistic movements. While a few of the *philosophes*, such as Denis Diderot, believed that some new dramatic genres could be encouraged without compromising traditional standards, all of the reformers saw themselves as the guardians of superior culture. (Diderot will be discussed further in Chapter 7.) By writing plays for the elite, the *philosophes* ensured that theatrical neoclassicism would stay wedded to the politics of absolutism.

Voltaire's point of view about the need for elite power to effect top-down reform is evident in many of his dramas. Although his essays and histories were often didactic and ironic, most of his 52 plays were packed with emotion, often concerning conflicts involving absolutist power and religion. Voltaire understood that emotional appeal was probably the best way to convince the audience at the Comédie Française and local elites in the provinces of the reasonableness of his ideas. In *Zaïre* (1732), one of his most successful tragedies, for example, Christian intolerance leads a "Moslem" Sultan to kill the Christian heroine, Zaïre, whom he loves, and then to take his own life. Voltaire's critics correctly saw his *Mohammed, or Fanaticism* (1741) as a veiled attack on all religions, including Christianity, that spread their gospel through the sword. He had to withdraw this play from production at the Comédie Française after three performances in order to avoid censorship. Both *Zaïre* and *Mohammed* demonstrate the need for rulers to separate religion from the power of the state; the plays suggest that only a virtuous monarch might be able to free humanity from the thrall of religious intolerance, a value he projected onto Islamic characters.

Like other *philosophes*, Voltaire believed that the rational and progressive values of the French **Enlightenment** could lead all of humankind out of superstition and misery. Indeed, many educated people in Europe spoke of the eighteenth century as an "Age of Enlightenment" and foresaw inevitable progress – in the economy, science, religion, the law, and even in governance – for the future. They based their hopes on the scientific and philosophical advances from the previous century, the appearance of reasoned discourse in public affairs, and on the growing prosperity for some Europeans in the 1700s.

While Voltaire's confidence in Enlightenment values helped him to succeed as a dramatist and polemicist, several of his plays exhibited ethnocentrism, even when he created characters from non-European culture as exemplars of Enlightenment reason and tolerance. With little interest in Chinese theatre, Voltaire adapted a Yuan *zaju* (see Chapter 4), translated initially by a Jesuit missionary, as *The Orphan of China* for the French stage in 1755. Although hailed as the first Chinese play to appear in any European language, *The Orphan of China* deleted the songs, changed the verse structure, and telescoped the plot sequence to comply with neoclassical rules. In Voltaire's play, Genghis Khan has recently conquered China, but has also fallen in love with a beautiful Chinese woman. Through her influence, the conqueror decides to spare the life of a royal Chinese orphan, despite the political risks, because nature has taught him tolerance and love. Voltaire believed that established religion undercut morality; in the absence of Christianity and other religions, he held that natural morality would triumph. In *The Orphan of China*, Voltaire altered a traditional Chinese play to preach what he believed was a universal human value. In doing so, however, he selectively chose aspects of "Chinese" culture that supported his own values, such as his rather reductive understanding of Confucianism as a natural religion in line with his own Enlightenment principles. The 1759 British adaptation, by Irish playwright Arthur Murray and starring David Garrick (1717–1779) in the leading role of Zamti, was different from Voltaire's focus on tolerance and love. Murray retained the revenge plot and a diabolical Genghis Khan, while introducing a more powerful "Chinese" female heroine, Mandane, played by Mrs. Yates, who espoused anti-absolutist sentiments as a form of British national pride (Figure 6.17). Both plays, however, tapped into the vogue for China and especially Chinese merchandise in France and England, including Mrs. Yates' costume, which was a premiere example of commodities created in China for European consumption, even though the prologue to Murray's play critiqued the audiences' desire for foreign goods.

The conversion to Enlightenment values on the page did not erase the continual intimate relationship between colonialism, chattel slavery, and absolutism in everyday life. In seventeenth-century France, slavery was encouraged as a way to increase sugar production in the Caribbean. This relationship was formalized in Louis XIVs 1685 Code ("Le Code Noir"), which regulated slavery as a means to keep centralized control over the colonies. This code designated African slaves as property while also insisting on their conversion to Catholicism. It also outlined punishments for non-compliance with these rules. The completion of the code, and its expansion to include new colonies and express restrictions on interracial marriage, occurred in 1724 under Louis XV. Parallel to the uneasiness felt by English authors, the existence of slavery posed a problem for *philosophes* like Voltaire and "popular" playwrights like Marivaux (1688–1763).

In his novel *Candide* (1759), Voltaire seems to decry the violence of slavery in relation to the plight of a Suriname enslaved person; yet this view seems to have more to do with feeling empathy for the oppressed rather than a true antislavery stance. Voltaire, in fact, viewed African descended people as inferior to Europeans in other writings, and profited from slavery in his business ventures. And his critiques of global trade did not openly reckon with France's own practice of slave holding, even when he openly judged the effects of

Figure 6.17

Mrs. Yates as Mandane in the Orphan of China. Painting by Tilly Kettle (1765).

Source: Steve Vidler/Alamy Stock Photo.

colonialism. Voltaire's critical theatrical representations of this violent practice were often set outside of France. *Alzire* (1736), was set in colonial Perú, and its advocacy for humanitarian civilization over brute force was played out in relation to Spanish cruelty in the sixteenth century (echoing Montesquieu's claims in his 1721 *The Persian Letters*). Voltaire displaced his ethical concerns to foreign lands.

Marivaux, meanwhile, created placeless utopias to work out his ideas about proper behavior and social hierarchy. Unlike Voltaire, he made no statements about even an abstracted notion of human bondage as an Enlightenment thinker, yet his plays aren't entirely immune to the practice of slavery. As Scott Sanders (2020) suggests, despite their non-specific settings and non-ethnically marked characters, Marivaux's 1720s island plays evoke the French

Atlantic colonies and their inhabitants through their scenic elements and in their plots about enslaved characters who have escaped captivity, gesturing to the contemporary fear of manumission by French authorities. Marivaux's later play *The Dispute* (1744) is more overt, and includes Black characters, Carise and Mesrou, who are hired as masters of light-skinned children. In their roles, Carise and Mesrou are entrusted with teaching the children romantic fidelity. While we do not know who played these characters, we do know that the play was written at a time when conceptions of race were being debated because of the exhibition of an albino of African descent whose very presence upset notions of race as related to skin color. As in the *Masque of Blacknesse*, the Black characters' skin tones are used as a foil to the light-skinned characters. In *The Dispute*, however, the light-skinned children decry the ugliness of their Black masters, while exhibiting moral ugliness themselves, exemplifying Marivaux's social critique. However metaphorical race might have been in the play, the Black characters indicated that while France tried to maintain that slavery only existed in the colonies outside the continent, there were in fact a small number of African slaves living in France. While not an anti-slavery play, the presence of these characters questioned emerging notions of liberty in France.

These contradictions aside, Voltaire and the *philosophes* (of which Marivaux was not a member) tried to use the power of print and performance to turn the absolutist rulers of their day into enlightened monarchs. Voltaire admired the limited monarchy that was beginning to emerge in Great Britain. He tried to advance these and other reforms at the court of Louis XV in the 1740s, but the king and his ministers ignored him. Voltaire accepted an invitation from King Frederick II of Prussia (1712–1786) to join him in Berlin, but he was again disappointed; King Frederick sponsored the arts and sciences and supported religious toleration, but refused to give up any of his power. Undaunted, Voltaire corresponded with Catherine II of Russia in the 1760s, even after it was obvious that she was using him (and Diderot) as convenient press agents for her consolidation of power and for Russian expansion in Europe. In short, the Enlightenment principles of Voltaire and the other *philosophes* did little directly to change the political realities of European absolutism before the French Revolution in 1789.

Between 1789 and 1792, French revolutionaries turned many Enlightenment principles into national laws, including the disestablishment of the Catholic Church in France, which Voltaire had fought for nearly all of his adult life. Although theatrical neoclassicism, including the plays of Molière, enjoyed a brief resurgence in the 1790s, the Revolution and the Napoleonic wars that followed rechanneled the broader cultural energies that had sustained neoclassicism from the 1500s to the 1720s.

Summary

The absolute monarchs of Europe encouraged two very different styles of dramatic theatre and opera between 1600 and 1770 – Baroque aesthetics and neoclassical restraint. Initially a product of the Renaissance and print culture, neoclassicism had helped many artists to move past the legacies of medieval entertainments and to reimagine how theatre might better serve the needs of elite cultures eager to embrace a new orderliness in their lives. Nonetheless, European rulers favored the power and playfulness of Baroque masques and operas for most of the 1600s. Despite challenges from Baroque allegories and carnivalesque entertainments, theatrical neoclassicism reached the pinnacle of its cultural success in the plays of Molière, Racine, and Dryden between 1660 and 1680. Later, in the hands of the Roman Academy and Metastasio, neoclassicism mustered enough cultural prestige to reform some the excesses of Baroque opera. After 1720, despite the continuing power of neoclassicism in the reformist plays of Voltaire and others, theatrical neoclassicism was doomed to go the way of absolute monarchy in Europe. In addition, despite their adherence to absolutist philosophies, some plays displayed unease with the institution of slavery, and a partial awareness of the consequences of colonialism conveying the power of theatre to subvert even the most orthodox political and formal structures.

★

PART III

Theatre and performance in periodical print cultures

DOI: 10.4324/9781003185185-10

PART III TIMELINE

DATE	THEATRE AND PERFORMANCE	CULTURE AND COMMUNICATION	POLITICS AND ECONOMICS
1644–1912			Qing dynasty, China
c.1650	Introduction of chariot-and-pole scenery system		
c.1650–c.1800		Enlightenment era in Europe	
1653–1724	Chikamatsu Monzaemon, playwright		
1656–1743	Ferdinando Galli Bibiena, scenic designer		
1660			English Restoration; reign of Charles II (to 1685)
1662	Re-opening of theatres in England; women begin to play female roles		
1662–c.1800	Neoclassicism in England, Germany, Russia		
1670–1729	William Congreve, playwright		
1670s	Beginnings of the *aragoto* style of *kabuki* acting, Japan		
c.1675–c.1800			Height of Atlantic slave trade
1680	Comédie Française founded, France		
1685–1750		Johann Sebastian Bach, composer	
1694–1778	Voltaire, playwright and writer		
1697–1764		William Hogarth, artist	
c.1700–c.1750	Sentimental drama in England and France		
1702		First daily newspaper, *Daily Courant*, England	
1705–1782	Farinelli, singer		
1707–1793	Carlo Goldoni, playwright		
1709–1712		*The Tatler* and *The Spectator*, English periodicals	
1712–1778		Jean-Jacques Rousseau, writer	
1717–1779	David Garrick, actor		

PART III TIMELINE

DATE	THEATRE AND PERFORMANCE	CULTURE AND COMMUNICATION	POLITICS AND ECONOMICS
1729–1781	Gotthold Ephraim Lessing, playwright and dramaturg		
1732–1799	Pierre-Augustin Caron Beaumarchais, playwright		
1737	Licensing Act imposes censorship on drama in England; censorship continues until 1968		
1741–1806	Ichikawa Danjiio V, actor		
1749–1832	Johann Wolfgang von Goethe, playwright		
1756–1791	Wolfgang Amadeus Mozart, composer (many operas)		
1759–1805	Friedrich Schiller, playwright		
c.1760–c.1830			Industrial Revolution
c.1760–c.1880			Rise of nationalism in Europe, North America, and South America
1767–1769	Hamburg National Theatre		
1770–1827		Ludwig van Beethoven, composer	
1775–1783			American Revolutionary War
c.1780–c.1870		Romantic era	
1781		Immanuel Kant, *Critique of Pure Reason*	
1789			French Revolution
c.1790	Beginnings of *jingju* (Beijing Opera)		
c.1800	*Ta'ziyeh*, Muslim performance		
c.1800–c.1900	Melodrama in Europe and the U.S.		
c.1800–c.1900		Development of steam-powered railways and ships in Europe and North America enables faster trans- and intercontinental communication	
1807		Georg W.F. Hegel, *Phenomenology of Spirit*	
1813–1883	Richard Wagner, composer (many operas)		

PART III TIMELINE

DATE	THEATRE AND PERFORMANCE	CULTURE AND COMMUNICATION	POLITICS AND ECONOMICS
1826–1914	Georg II, the Duke of Saxe-Meiningen, producer-director		
1828–1906	Henrik Ibsen, playwright		
1830			U.S. begins removing Native Americans to western parts of North America
1830–1962			French colonial rule in North and West Africa, Southeast Asia, and elsewhere
c.1830		Beginnings of modern photography	
1833			U.K. abolishes slavery
1833–1893	Edwin Booth, actor		
c.1835–c.1940	Minstrel shows		
1837		Commercial telegraph	
1840			Modern women's suffrage movement begins
1844–1900		Friedrich Nietzsche, philosopher	
1844–1923	Sarah Bernhardt, actor		
1845–1853			Major U.S. expansion westward
1848–1849			Revolutions throughout Europe
1848–1947			British rule in India
1849–1912	August Strindberg, playwright		
c.1850	Rise of realist stage settings, directors, and playwrights		
c.1850		Copyright laws begin to be passed; enforcement difficult	
c.1850–c.1900	Rise of realism in drama, stage design, and directing		
c.1850–c.1960	Variety shows (e.g., music hall, vaudeville, revues)		
1851		First World's Fair	
1854			External and internal pressures force Japan to open to foreign trade

PART III TIMELINE

DATE	THEATRE AND PERFORMANCE	CULTURE AND COMMUNICATION	POLITICS AND ECONOMICS
1856–1950	George Bernard Shaw, playwright		
1858–1943	André Antoine, director		
1859		Charles Darwin, *On the Origin of Species*	
1860–1904	Anton Chekhov, playwright		
c.1860–c.1925		Impressionism in painting	
1861–1865			U.S. Civil War
1862–1928	Adolphe Appia, stage designer		
1863–1938	Konstantin Stanislavsky, director		
1864–1911	Kawakami Otojiro actor-playwright		
1867		Karl Marx, *Capital* vol. I	
1867–1936	Luigi Pirandello, playwright		
1868			Meiji Restoration in Japan
c.1870–c.1900	Rise of the director		
1871		Charles Darwin, *The Descent of Man*	
1872–1946	Kawakami Sadayakko, actor		
1872–1966	Edward Gordon Craig, theatre theorist		
1876		Electric telephone Phonograph	
1877–1927		Isadora Duncan, dancer	
1879		Electric light bulb	
c.1880–c.1900	Avant-garde theatre, first generation		
1880–1914			"Scramble for Africa": European powers divide Africa among themselves
1881–c.1914	Naturalist movement		
1881–1973		Pablo Picasso, artist	
1882–1971		Igor Stravinsky, composer	

PART III TIMELINE

DATE	THEATRE AND PERFORMANCE	CULTURE AND COMMUNICATION	POLITICS AND ECONOMICS
1884–1885			First Sino-Japanese War
1885		Automobile	
1886–1919	Matsui Sumako, actor		
1887–1896	Théâtre Libre		
1889–c.1930	Symbolist theatre		
1894–1961	Mei Lanfang, actor		
1895		First public motion picture screening, France	
1895		Radio	
c.1895–c.1930	*Shimpa*		
1898			Spanish-American War
1898–	Moscow Art Theatre (various name changes after 1932)		
1900		Sigmund Freud, *The Interpretation of Dreams*	
1903		First successful airplane	
1904		Vacuum tube: beginning of electronics	
1904		Sigmund Freud, *The Psychopathology of Everyday Life*	
1909	*Shingeki*		
c.1910–c.1925		Cubism in art	
c.1910–c.1930	Avant-garde theatre, second generation		
1914–1918			The Great War (aka the First World War)
1914–	Takarazuka Revue		
c.1915–		Jazz	

Introduction: Theatre for bourgeois civil society

Tobin Nellhaus

The SPECTATOR.

Non fumum ex fulgore, sed ex fumo dare lucem
Cogitat, ut speciosa dehinc miracula promat. Hor.

To be Continued every Day.

Thursday, March 1. 1711.

I Have observed, that a Reader seldom peruses a Book with Pleasure 'till he knows whether the Writer of it be a black or a fair Man, of a mild or cholerick Disposition, Married or a Batchelor, with other Particulars of the like nature, that conduce very much to the right Understanding of an Author. To gratify this Curiosity, which is so natural to a Reader, I design this Paper, and my next, as Prefatory Discourses to my following Writings, and shall give some Account in them of the several Persons that are engaged in this Work. As the chief Trouble of Compiling, Digesting and Correcting will fall to my Share, I must do my self the Justice to open the Work with my own History.

I was born to a small Hereditary Estate, which I find, by the Writings of the Family, was bounded by the same Hedges and Ditches in *William* the Conqueror's Time that it is at present, and has been delivered down from Father to Son whole and entire, without the Loss or Acquisition of a single Field or Meadow, during the Space of six hundred Years. There goes a Story in the Family, that when my Mother was gone with Child of me about three Months, she dreamt that she was brought to Bed of a Judge: Whether this might proceed from a Law-Suit which was then depending in the Family, or my Father's being a Justice of the Peace, I cannot determine; for I am not so vain as to think it presaged any Dignity that I should arrive at in my future Life, though that was the Interpretation which the Neighbourhood put upon it. The Gravity of my Behaviour at my very first Appearance in the World, and all the Time that I sucked, seemed to favour my Mother's Dream: For, as she has often told me, I threw away my Rattle before I was two Months old, and would not make use of my Coral 'till they had taken away the Bells from it.

As for the rest of my Infancy, there being nothing in it remarkable, I shall pass it over in Silence. I find, that, during my Nonage, I had the Reputation of a very sullen Youth, but was always a Favourite of my School-Master, who used to say, *that my Parts were solid and would wear well.* I had not been long at the University, before I distinguished my self by a most profound Silence: For during the Space of eight Years, excepting in the publick Exercises of the College, I scarce uttered the Quantity of an hundred Words; and indeed do not remember that I ever spoke three Sentences together in my whole Life. Whilst I was in this Learned Body I applied my self with so much Diligence to my Studies, that there are very few celebrated Books, either in the Learned or the Modern Tongues, which I am not acquainted with.

Upon the Death of my Father I was resolved to travel into Foreign Countries, and therefore left the University, with the Character of an odd unaccountable Fellow, that had a great deal of Learning, if I would but show it. An insatiable Thirst after Knowledge carried me into all the Countries of *Europe*, where there was any thing new or strange to be seen; nay, to such a Degree was my Curiosity raised, that having read the Controversies of some great Men concerning the Antiquities of *Egypt*, I made a Voyage to *Grand Cairo*, on purpose to take the Measure of a Pyramid; and as soon as I had set my self right in that Particular, returned to my Native Country with great Satisfaction.

I have passed my latter Years in this City, where I am frequently seen in most publick Places, tho' there are not above half a dozen of my select Friends that know me; of whom my next Paper shall give a more particular Account. There is no Place of Publick Resort, wherein I do not often make my Appearance; sometimes I am seen thrusting my Head into a Round of Politicians at *Will's*, and listning with great Attention to the Narratives that are made in those little Circular Audiences. Sometimes I smoak a Pipe at *Child's*; and whilst I seem attentive to nothing but the *Post-Man*, over-hear the Conversation of every Table in the Room. I appear on *Sunday* Nights at St. *James's* Coffee-House, and sometimes join the little Committee of Politicks in the Inner-Room, as one who comes there to hear and improve. My Face is likewise very well known at the *Grecian*, the *Cocoa-Tree*, and in the Theaters both of *Drury-Lane*, and the *Hay-Market*. I have been taken for a Merchant upon

Photo PI3

The first page of the first issue of *The Spectator*, 1711.

Source: Lebrecht Music & Arts/Alamy Stock Photo.

During the period spanning roughly 1700–1930, the Western world underwent profound transformations. For the previous two millennia, merchants, tradesmen, manufacturers, and various types of professionals had only modest social and economic power and virtually no cultural influence. Often they were the butt of humor, such as the unintelligible lawyers and quack physicians of *commedia dell'arte* (see Chapter 4) and the ridiculous would-be aristocrat of Molière's *The Bourgeois Gentleman* (1670). Because they lived mainly in the urban centers, this social class was called the **bourgeoisie**, derived from a French word for "city." (The term "capitalists" refers to part of the bourgeoisie: merchants, industrialists, financiers, and other owners of assets used to create private profits – that is, capital – but generally not professionals such as doctors and lawyers.) But starting in the seventeenth century, the bourgeoisie became increasingly affluent and started exercising political power. In England, their rise to power was achieved by Parliament progressively whittling away at the monarch's rule via legislation, starting in 1689; elsewhere it occurred violently, most conspicuously in the American Revolution of 1775–1783, and the French Revolution of 1789–1799. By the nineteenth century, the bourgeoisie was politically ascendant throughout Europe and North America. Absolutism reached its end, and the nation-state came into being.

A development within print culture played a pivotal role in this upheaval. During the seventeenth century, there were various efforts to establish regular newspapers (published weekly or every few days), but these attempts were short-lived. Around 1700, the growth of business and transportation networks made daily newspapers sustainable. As Chapter 7 explains, the development of reliable periodical publication had deep cultural, social, and political effects. The most salient was the formation of what philosopher and social theorist Jürgen Habermas (1989) described as the social and political "public sphere" and historian Benedict Anderson (1991) conceptualized as the "imagined community": the unification of a people, or more precisely a country's bourgeoisie, into a political identity – a nation. Anderson described nations as "communities" because within their borders, their members were portrayed as equals; but they were "imagined" communities because individuals could never know or even hear about everyone in the nation. Newspapers built nationhood because they put a country in conversation with itself and provided an image of the country as a whole.

The shift from purely oral to literate culture and the later rise of print culture involved new technologies; this time, however, dramatic changes in politics and culture arose through a change in how the existing technology was used. Print culture now possessed two main forms: the book and the periodical. Chapter 7 describes how theatre in the Western world participated in these eighteenth-century developments. Sometimes the theatre satirized people and activities which threatened to undermine the premise of equality within the public sphere. But more often, it sought to foster a sense of fellow-feeling (termed "sentiment") among people – the spirit of the public sphere's opposite, the private sphere. Together, the public and private spheres define bourgeois society. Theatre was increasingly recognized as a profession, and actors could be lionized as public figures and their techniques studied. Yet "low" forms of entertainment also thrived, much to the consternation and scorn of the bourgeoisie.

Nationhood was quickly and often simultaneously accompanied by nationalism. Nationalism asserts that countries have strong geographic borders, only those people considered citizens have the right to govern it, and they must be independent of "foreign" powers. Nationalism is complex, and Chapter 8 distinguishes between three kinds, with complex connections among them that varied from nation to nation. The earliest, which expanded the ideas guiding the early eighteenth-century public sphere, emphasized Enlightenment ideals of equal rights and rational discourse. Ironically, these genial ideals became fodder for two revolutions. The American Revolutionary War joined separate British colonies to produce the United States under a constitutional democracy. (Interestingly, one of the revolution's leaders was a newspaper publisher and editorialist: Benjamin Franklin.) However, in the French Revolution, years of political turmoil culminated in a coup led by Napoleon Bonaparte, who soon proclaimed himself emperor and launched a series of wars in a quest to rule Europe. The second form of nationalism focused on the supposed native characteristics of the land and its people's spirit, which were shaped by their history – both its glories and its tragedies. This cultural nationalism rebuffed the universality claimed by the Enlightenment in favor of each country's uniqueness. But in some cases it congealed into racial nationalism, the third type, which fused unity through shared territorial history with unity through a single shared genealogy: "blood and soil." Implicitly undermining the nation-state itself, racism denied the rights of some of the country's residents and sought to unite members of a "ruling race" within an imagined community of common "racial" descent. As a result, the pursuit of equal rights that had fueled eighteenth-century revolutions was sometimes ousted by an ideology of superiority which, well into the twenty-first century, could erupt into state-sanctioned genocides and racial or ethnic civil wars. Chapter 8 traces the rise of these three nationalisms and theatre's place within them, such as national theatres, Romanticism, melodrama, and minstrel shows.

Napoleon's campaign to conquer Europe was a form of imperialism. Imperialism – the formation of empires controlled by a central power – has been part of history for millennia. In modern Europe, it began in earnest with the absolutist monarchies discussed in Chapter 6. An example is the Spanish conquest of the Americas during the sixteenth century, motivated by the desire for both universal Christianity and precious metals. Starting in the eighteenth century, imperialist expansion was increasingly tied to capitalism; in the nineteenth century, driven forward by industries' demands for raw materials and foreign trade, European imperialism massively intensified. Ideologies of bestowing civilization upon "backward" people played a role as well. By the early twentieth century, the British Empire ruled about a fifth of the world's population and a quarter of its land. With these expansions of power came complex attitudes toward foreign cultures, including paternalism, fear, and exoticism. Chapter 9 describes the West's imperialist fascination with (and terror of) foreign cultures, manifested in events such as World Fairs which exhibited "specimens" of non-Westerners, and theatrical performances which showcased the sometimes frightening, sometimes appealing character of foreign peoples.

During the same period, in China – another huge but much older empire, with a quite different social structure – this process was inverted. Far from being intrigued by the provincial cultures, the upper classes in the urban centers at first disdained them. The lower classes, however, were captivated by the unfamiliar performances brought by touring companies.

Eventually, several genres of provincial performance fused and established an enduring form – *jingju*, often called Beijing Opera – that slowly gained upper-class acceptance.

While the modern nation was being born in the late eighteenth century, an **Industrial Revolution** also began. Steam-powered machines increasingly replaced the hands that produced commodities. Over the course of the nineteenth century, industrial capitalism expanded throughout the Western world and became the dominant economic system. Railways connected cities within and between countries; steamers shipped goods, raw materials, and people all over the world; electric power started to light the cities. Industrialists profited handsomely while also bringing significant improvements to urban life – but the working class found themselves stripped of control over their existence and lived hand to mouth, working 12 or more hours a day, six or seven days a week. Whole families, including children, had to work for their meager living, amid highly dangerous conditions where even death was not uncommon. Not surprisingly, the bourgeoisie's industrial revolution was soon met with workers' labor unions and efforts at political revolution. Many workers sought a socialist economy, in which manufacturing would be taken over by the laborers and would produce goods to serve needs rather than profit. German philosopher and economist Karl Marx, a major advocate of socialism, developed highly influential (and to the bourgeoisie, highly subversive) analyses of how capitalism operated and how economic classes struggled for power across history. In the early twentieth century, the pressures of nationalism, capitalism, and imperialism exploded into a world war, followed by a revolution in Russia (eventually creating the Soviet Union) and a failed one in Germany.

These economic and political developments form the background to late nineteenth-century European theatre and its two major legacies, addressed in Chapter 10. One was the producer-director, who wrested financial and artistic control from the actors. This was the first version of the modern director, who determined how (and by whom) a play would be performed, and insisted that actors and designers adhere to those ideas. Although the theatre was certainly no factory, such rigidity and centralization of decision-making was similar to the control that factory bosses had over their workers.

From the beginning, producer-directors pursued aesthetic realism – the second major legacy of the nineteenth century (a style which had begun developing at the middle of the century). Realism fit well with the concept of a public sphere that was rooted in periodical print culture. It also dovetailed with the scientific objectivity needed in designing machinery and pursuing profits. Before long, realism was adopted in North America and Japan. Chapter 9 discusses the major varieties of nineteenth-century realism; more would develop in the twentieth century.

At the end of the century, alternatives to realism began to arise. They substituted the objectivity assumed by realism with subjective or spiritual perspectives (a good fit with the private sphere), and they rejected realistic aesthetics. Realism and the early "avant-gardes" overlapped chronologically so closely that some realist playwrights also wrote in the alternative genres. Chapter 10 surveys the highly diverse first-generation avant-garde movements that developed in the early twentieth century. A cultural separation between mainstream and avant-garde theatre began to take shape, an early twentieth-century legacy continuing today.

The proliferation of stylistic genres had its roots in both book and periodical print culture, and also (as Chapter 10 observes) in the impact of photography, telephones, and phonographs – heralds of new forms of communication. Yet the diversity didn't reflect unfettered imagination: the fact that playwrights could readily switch from an objective to a subjective style hints that there were hidden connections between realism and its opposition. As discussed in Chapter 5, early print culture positioned the individual as the source of perception and knowledge. The seventeenth-century scientific revolution was founded on individuals taking the evidence of their own senses or their own reason as the source of verifiable truth. By the late seventeenth century, science's use of sense experience had ripened into a philosophy called empiricism; French philosopher René Descartes's (1596–1650) focus on reason developed into rationalism. However, both philosophies had an objective cast: objects are perceived and logic is conducted by individuals, but they are independent of individuals as such – anyone else can check their accuracy.

But as we saw, periodical print culture – an organ of bourgeois society – created a division between a public sphere and a private sphere. The latter was the realm of the individual's home and heart, faith and feeling, and only the individual could attest to their own emotions and beliefs. With this division, a true contrast between the objective and the subjective arose – a polarity founded on the bedrock of individualism. The notion that individual experience was the foundation for all knowledge (whether that experience consisted of objective observations or subjective perceptions) provided the fundamental contrast between the realisms and the avant-gardes. This polarity suggests one reason why a dramatist might readily switch from writing highly realist plays to symbolically oriented drama: in many ways, they are the sides of a single coin.

Both the realistic and the avant-garde styles arose out of efforts to define and represent truth, whether that truth was objective or subjective. For example, in 1881, French playwright Émile Zola wrote that "environments, the study of which has transformed the sciences and humanities, must inevitably assume an important place in theatre," because "environment should determine character" (Zola 1881: 365). Likewise, the Belgian Maurice Maeterlinck, considered a Symbolist, wrote in 1896 that "in the ordinary drama, the indispensable dialogue by no means corresponds to reality; and it is just those words that are spoken by the side of the rigid, apparent truth . . . that conform to a deeper truth" (Maeterlinck 1897: 112).

There is yet a third characteristic shared by the realists and the avant-gardes, closely tied to their concern with the presentation of truth on stage: a strong ambivalence toward theatricality, and sometimes even outright antitheatricality. One advocate of realism held that the goal of presenting environments in minute detail is to replace theatrical artifice with "a near-perfect reality, in other words, to drive the 'Theatre' gradually from the theatre" (quoted in K. Williams 2001: 285). Within the early avant-gardes, hostility to theatricality was sometimes equally strong. In 1907, avant-gardist Edward Gordon Craig complained that the actor's inescapable, unreliable body and emotions eliminated the possibility of exact reproduction and perfection, and so he proclaimed, "The actor must go, and in his place comes the inanimate figure – the *Übermarionette*," which he described as a "symbolic creature" (1911: 81, 84). Citing Plato, he criticized the actor as merely "an imitator" who "cannot convey the spirit and essence of an idea," but only "a facsimile of the thing itself" (63). The premises born within Western literate culture 2,000 years earlier about the nature of truth and representation still generated misgivings about theatre.

The director, realism, avant-gardes, and antitheatricality within theatre are still with us. As we will see in Part IV, during the twentieth century, all of them would undergo alterations, sometimes putting into question the idea of individualism and the supposed opposition between theatre and truth. Nevertheless they persist, shaping the majority of theatre today. The path from sentimentalism to realism and avant-gardes presented in Part III is the story of contemporary theatre's beginnings.

★

CHAPTER 7

Sentiment, satire, and acting in bourgeois Europe, 1700–1785

Tobin Nellhaus

Contributor: Bruce McConachie

As the Introduction to Part III observed, European print culture began to change around 1700 with the publication and wide dissemination of newspapers, magazines, and other periodicals. Unlike books, which were printed "for the ages," periodicals were "of the day," like newsfeeds today, intended to bring current news to a broad readership with common interests. Early book culture generally helped to legitimize absolutism; in contrast, **periodical print culture** enabled the new **bourgeoisie** to solidify its values and enlarge the arena of public discourse. Periodical print culture also promoted a sense of private life that helped to underwrite a "sentimental" theatre embracing the morality and feelings of the emerging middle class.

Other types of theatre also thrived in Europe during the eighteenth century. New forms of performance attracted all classes, especially the lower ones. Many of these popular genres involved music and song, which heightened their appeal and, perhaps more importantly, sometimes allowed the theatres to escape the stranglehold that the officially authorized theatres had through their monopolies over tragedy and comedy. Satire played an important role both in the theatres and in political commentary, particularly in England, where popular performance often included political satire so biting that a system of censorship was imposed which lasted until 1968.

In Japan, too, theatre was continually scrutinized. In our first case study, we will discuss how the shoguns regulated *kabuki* to control its potential for social disruption. There were strict limits on intermingling between actors and the public, as well as censorship of *kabuki* performances' moral content.

By the last third of the eighteenth century, sentimentalist thought developed an extreme form more deeply opposed to rationalism, especially the **Enlightenment** rationalism that dominated continental thought and drama. These ideas particularly influenced German drama.

DOI: 10.4324/9781003185185-11

Few plays of eighteenth-century Europe survived the test of time, even if they were enormously popular in their own day, because what actually captured audiences was powerful acting. Although to us, eighteenth-century acting seems stylized and presentational, to the audiences of the time it broke new ground in realism. Many actors became renowned not only in their own countries, but throughout Europe.

The most famous of all was David Garrick, the premier English actor of the mid-eighteenth century. In the second case study, we explore how Garrick encouraged the use of prints and even commissioned paintings in order to strengthen his standing as a lead actor of the age and make him a popular star.

Sentiment and periodical print culture

Although today the word "sentiment" is mildly pejorative, many eighteenth-century European playwrights, actors, and spectators valued sentiments for the refinement, knowledge, and moral uplift they might provide. Sentiments were not the cloying emotions we associate with "sentimentality" today: the term invoked a view of human nature and cultured behavior. A **sentimental** play (or poem or novel) could evoke feelings of sympathy, joy, and sorrow for worthy characters that allowed genteel spectators (and readers) to test the depths of their own emotional responses and to broaden the reach of their moral concerns. People who embraced sentimental culture believed that humans were innately good, and that personal and social bonds would thrive if individuals were true to their "natural" virtues. As we will see, a significant school of eighteenth-century philosophy endorsed this moral and aesthetic point of view. Bourgeois sentimentalism, which emphasized family and marital virtuousness and reconciliations – the constituents of the private sphere – helped to drive Baroque culture out of favor and challenged aristocratic neoclassicism in theatre throughout Europe.

The culture of sentiment did not appear out of thin air: it was created and fostered by a new type of print culture based in the periodical press. Efforts to publish periodicals began as far back as 1600, but most of the earliest newspapers struggled to survive and didn't last long. Generally they were published once a week or every few days, and offered only business information or official government records. It wasn't until the early 1700s that urbanization, business demands, political activity, cultural desires, city and inter-city postal systems, and maritime trade made it financially and logistically feasible to sustain daily publication, and to expand coverage to include topics with broad appeal.

One thing periodicals did *not* require was any change in technology: periodical print culture arose because people utilized the existing technology in a new way. The development of periodical print culture shows that important changes in communication practices are not always tied to changes in communication technology. Economic, political, and other factors play a role in changing communication practices and ways of thinking. For their financial survival, periodicals needed a method for sustaining interest. Books are generally read by solitary individuals at whatever day and time is convenient. A single printing of a book may satisfy reader demand for decades. But newspapers, magazines, and other periodicals are meant to be read by many people throughout a significant geographical area, at roughly the same time, and with each new issue. The challenge in publishing a periodical is ensuring that readers return for subsequent issues. One way a periodical can achieve that goal is by concentrating on a particular subject, such as ever-changing business news, fashion, or ce-lebrity activities; or by giving a picture of the entire society by covering all subjects. Another way is to create a sense of narrative, so that the reader wonders what will happen next.

England was at the forefront in developing daily periodicals. Among the reasons were politics and economics. In 1688 and again in 1714, problems of religion and royal succession led Parliament to install kings of its own choosing from the royal lineage, making absolutism on the French model impossible. Merchants, traders, and investors gained more power in England. The top tier of the English bourgeoisie, who were growing rich on colonial dom-ination, expanding domestic markets and the international slave trade, sought a government that would protect and expand its interests. They required daily newspapers with important business and political news, and as their public roles advanced, they demanded intense parti-sanship as well. They and other middle-class men and women sought periodicals that would keep them up to date on social affairs and culture in London, and justify their emerging cultural values.

Social life, family, fellowship, and culture were the subjects of two early periodicals: *The Tatler*, published three times a week during 1709–1711 and edited by Richard Steele (1672–1729); and *The Spectator*, a daily edited by Steele and Joseph Addison (1672–1719) from 1711 to 1712. Despite the brief spans of their existence, they were enormously important: often distributed in coffeehouses, issues of *The Tatler* and *The Spectator* were read by perhaps 80,000 Londoners and many beyond London, and frequently they were read aloud for oth-ers' enjoyment (Figure 7.1). The two papers present superb examples of how a periodical can unite readers across space and time, creating a social ambience by focusing the papers on the readers themselves, encouraging them to share the paper and eagerly anticipate what might come next. The editors strived to create the sense of a benevolent community among their readers. Addison and Steele published essays advocating mutual trust and self-disclosure within circles of families and friends, and they invited letters to the editor to foster such a circle of affection within their readership. In contrast to aristocratic culture, which empha-sized a hierarchical order and the public projection of social status, Addison and Steele un-derlined the importance of social bonds and fellow-feeling. Unlike today's *Us Weekly*, which celebrates celebrities, *The Tatler* and *The Spectator* were truly about "us." As the models for hundreds of subsequent periodicals seeking bourgeois audiences, *The Tatler* and *The Spectator* broadcast the principles of sentiment in the early eighteenth century. The form as well as the content of the new periodicals thus legitimized bourgeois sentimentalism and broadened its reach.

English sentimental culture drew on the principles of "moral sense" philosophy, which was closely tied to Enlightenment values. Liberal thinkers of the age distinguished their ideas from those of previous philosophers, who had advocated absolutism. For example, in 1651, Thomas Hobbes had written that a strong monarchical government was necessary to control the problems created by rapacious individual interests. In contrast, in 1690 John Locke (1632–1704) – one of the luminaries of the Enlightenment – urged that free individuals in a state of nature might form civil governments that could channel competing interests toward socially beneficial results. Locke, immersed in print culture, also believed that people were like blank pieces of paper when they were born, awaiting the "imprint" of their parents and society.

Locke's ideas about the association of free individuals became a concrete reality through papers such as *The Tatler* and *The Spectator*. These periodicals relegated politics to the margins,

Figure 7.1
Socializing in a London coffee house, c.1700.
Source: Historia/Shutterstock.

contained little or no news (they even ridiculed "newsmongering"), and focused instead on human foibles and promoted a culture of politeness. Their efforts to form a polite society founded on personal character and sensibility helped to create a bourgeois distinction between the **public sphere** where issues of politics, economics, and culture are debated, and the **private sphere**, the realm of the home, family, and friends. The distinction was brought into sentimental drama, and as we will see, it was not the only theatrical genre that contributed to separating the public and private spheres.

Later moral sense philosophers built upon Locke's premises to argue that humanity had an inherent sense of right and wrong and would generally choose the right for its natural beauty and worth. A bad environment, however, could "impress" other values on children, they believed. According to moral sense philosopher Adam Smith (1723–1790), all people had within them an "ideal spectator of our sentiments and conduct" (Kramnick 1995: 287), who, awakened by social pressure, would ensure that each person does his or her moral duty. Like friendly conversation and the sight of strangers in distress, watching the right play could awaken that "ideal spectator" in the mind and steer the playgoer toward affection and beneficence. For the moral sense philosophers, morality was inherent and natural; doing the right thing flowed from emotional sensitivity, not abstract reason.

Sentimental drama in England

Just as periodical publication flourished earliest in England, so too did sentimental theatre. It was in part a response to criticism of the often racy Restoration plays. Early advocates of sentiment found temporary allies among the Puritans. Puritan attacks on the wickedness of the London stage increased in the 1690s, culminating in Jeremy Collier's (1650–1726)

A Short View of the Immorality and Profaneness of the English Stage in 1698. Beginning with the neoclassical precept that "the business of plays is to recommend virtue and discountenance vice," Collier castigated several comedies from the Restoration era for "their smuttiness of expression; their swearing, profaneness, and lewd application of Scripture; their abuse of the clergy; and their making their top characters libertines and giving them success in their debauchery" (qtd. in Dukore 1974: 351–2). Collier's attack aroused indignation in some, struck home for others (a few playwrights even apologized), and garnered public support that altered playwriting. One of Collier's targets was William Congreve (1670–1729), who published an impassioned retort; but stifled by the changed atmosphere, after writing *The Way of the World* (1700) – considered a jewel of Restoration comedy – Congreve quit the stage. Both Collier's reproach and the playwrights' reactions were motivated by the rise of bourgeois culture throughout Europe.

But even before Collier's *Short View*, some playwrights were already softening Restoration cynicism and arranging sentimental endings for their plays. In *Love's Last Shift* (1696), for instance, actor-playwright Colley Cibber (1671–1757) celebrated several characters for their inherent goodness and featured a rakish hero, Loveless, who gladly repents of his compulsive woman-chasing in the last act. While Cibber was writing popular variations on this formula in the first decade of the eighteenth century, playwright George Farquhar (c.1677–1707) took several of his dramatic characters and conflicts out of London into the more sentimental air of the English countryside.

Steele often campaigned in *The Tatler* and *The Spectator* to replace the wittiness and eroticism of Restoration comedy with sentiment. His play *The Conscious Lovers* (1722) demonstrated what he had in mind. The plot centers on Bevil Jr., a chivalrous young man who is in love with a mysterious woman named Indiana, but he also wants to obey his father's instructions to marry a rich friend's daughter. Ultimately a chance discovery reveals that Indiana is the friend's long-lost daughter, permitting Bevil Jr. to both marry his beloved and satisfy his father. Steele created Bevil Jr. partly to prove his claim, declared years earlier in *The Spectator*, that "A man that is temperate, generous, valiant, chaste, faithful, and honest, may, at the same time, have wit, humor, mirth, good breeding, and gallantry" (*The Spectator*, 28 April 1711, in Dukore 1974: 392). *The Conscious Lovers* was wildly successful and drew sympathetic tears as well as laughter from English audiences for the rest of the century.

Notions of sentiment affected tragedy as well as comedy during the 1700s. Beginning early in the century, popular "she-tragedies" featured vulnerable heroines. Other plays partly broke from the neoclassical tragic form, such as *The London Merchant* (1731) by George Lillo (1693–1739), a tragedy that dispensed completely with aristocratic heroes and the constraints of neoclassicism (Figure 7.2). Its protagonist, the naïve apprentice George Barnwell, is enthralled by the prostitute Sarah Millwood, who entices him into stealing money from his bourgeois master, Thorowgood, and later into murdering his rich uncle as well. Throughout the play, Lillo contrasts the optimistic and benevolent sentiments of the merchant with Millwood's deep-rooted resentments (based, interestingly, on her misuse by men, providing the audience with a moment of psychological understanding). Despite Thorowgood's attempts to save him, a repentant Barnwell dies on the gallows – but not before Lillo props him up as an example of the destructiveness of unbridled sexual passion that threatens the social stability that the merchant economy has built. *The London Merchant* achieved immense popularity and inspired several imitations. Real-life London merchants, who expected the

Figure 7.2
George Barnwell murders Thorowgood in Lillo's *The London Merchant,* in a print c.1820.
Source: Chronicle/Alamy Stock Photo.

morality of the play to produce wholesome and profitable results, sent their own apprentices to see the show during the Christmas season for a century, partly as a warning against spending money on prostitutes.

Watching *The Conscious Lovers, The London Merchant,* and other sentimental plays, spectators generally expected to immerse themselves in the feelings of sentimental heroes and other characters. The objects of sympathetic concern in sentimental plays ranged from distraught maidens, to the poor, to general pity for suffering humanity. Among the sentimental protagonists were the enslaved. By the early 1700s, the slave trade, primarily into the Caribbean islands, shifted from a monarchical business to a capitalist industry, and highly popular sentimental dramas assuaged bourgeoise audiences by fantasizing friendship between master and slave, or featuring noble Blacks mistakenly enslaved. Of the latter, the most notable was Thomas Southerne's 1695 stage adaptation of Aphra Behn's novella *Oroonoko,* which was frequently revised and restaged throughout the eighteenth century as part of the abolitionist movement. Bridget Orr (2014) finds that such plays criticized slavery, but usually by arousing a sympathy for their protagonists that flattered the audience's compassion, rather than by directly attacking slavery itself – yet *Oroonoko* also hinted at support for slave rebellion, which by the 1790s made it too subversive to perform. Over the decades England's abolitionist movement grew, but the country's use of slavery continued well into the nineteenth century.

The helpless heroines of sentimental drama were a far cry from the smart, urbane women sparking the stage just a few years before. They reflected the etiquette of the bourgeois private sphere, which restricted women to the domain of gentle domesticity. Similarly, women effectively vanished again from the ranks of new playwrights. In the first decades of the 1700s, Susanna Centlivre (c.1669–1723) was one of the few women who stood as successors to Aphra Behn (discussed in Chapters 4 and 6), but after 1725, new plays by women were rare, and none would achieve popular success for another 50 years.

According to sentimental aesthetics, sympathetic characters and pitiable events on stage would inspire a sentimental response in the genteel viewers, who might then use this response to improve their own sensitivity and morality. Book-oriented neoclassicism instead generally kept spectators at a greater emotional distance and involved them more typically in feelings of awe, disdain, and suspense rather than sympathy, sorrow, and generous good humor. Sentimental drama placed middle-class figures rather than aristocrats as its heroes, endorsed benevolent paternalism instead of royal absolutism for its ethics, and emphasized empathetic responses over judgments. Like *The Tatler* and *The Spectator*, sentimental plays sought to evoke a benevolent community in the audience, and thus contributed to the establishment of the bourgeois private sphere, which (along with the public sphere) was a major byproduct of periodical print culture. By the mid-eighteenth century, the ethos of the private sphere had reconfigured the traditional forms of tragedy and comedy on the London stage. The neoclassical tragedies that had dominated the repertory were fading in popularity for new tragic performances that featured more pathos and tears, and comedies featured sententious moralizing and few laughs. Bourgeois sentimentalism had become firmly entrenched in the dominant culture of England.

Pantomime, satire, and censorship in England

English sentimental drama, including both comedy and tragedy, supported the values of the rising merchant class and the minor aristocracy, the prime constituents of the public sphere. Other types of performance sought to entertain a broader audience, including those at the margins of the bourgeois public sphere, such as tradesmen, workers, soldiers, small-scale shopkeepers, and others from outside the elite. Dances and pantomimes were the most important genres during the early eighteenth century, but there were also songs, performances of instrumental music, acrobatics, and other entertainments. Most of these diversions were performed between acts of a play; the pantomimes usually appeared as afterpieces.

Pantomime originated during Roman imperial rule (see Chapter 2). It re-emerged in fifteenth-century Italy as part of the *commedia dell'arte* tradition. When illegal fairground performances of *commedia* were suppressed in Paris in 1702, a number of performers from the *commedia* tradition sought work in London. Some of *commedia*'s non-verbal comic scenes were set to music and dance, and performed with a few of the key *commedia* characters as "Italian night scenes."

At the beginning of the eighteenth century, pantomimes often had a serious intent or segment. In 1717, the dance master at London's Drury Lane Theatre, John Weaver, created *The Loves of Mars and Venus* featuring dancers impersonating Roman gods. It was advertised

Figure 7.3

John Rich as Arlequin, portrayed in a print from 1753.

Source: agefotostock/Alamy.

as a "new Entertainment in Dancing after the manner of the Antient [*sic*] Pantomimes" (of Rome). Rivaling it, John Rich (1692–1761), dancer, actor, and manager at the Lincoln's Inn Fields theatre, created his own pantomime with characters from Roman mythology, who were magically transformed in the second part of the performance into characters in a knock-about comedy. Rich further developed and popularized this earliest form of British pantomime as "harlequinades" – spectacular performances in which the *commedia* character, Harlequin, magically transformed himself or the scenery with a touch of his magic sword or wand (Figure 7.3). In the 1720s, spectacle and farce became increasingly prominent. But to attract every type of audience, serious scenes based on mythology came to alternate with episodes of farce, fantasy, or intrigue abounding with spectacle, turning British pantomime into a distinctive genre.

The pantomimes became enormously popular, often more popular than the plays. They elicited complaints from the upper-class audience, who felt they degraded the dignity of the stage – and critics scorned them as "irrational entertainments." But they appealed to most people. Some pantomimes enjoyed long runs, and they became a staple of London's theatrical offerings, stirring intense competition between the foremost theatres, Drury Lane and Lincoln's Inn Fields. The pantomimes were a major source of revenue for the theatres; John O'Brien suggests they were a nascent form of the culture industry (O'Brien 2007: 107). In the middle of the eighteenth century, the eminent actor David Garrick (1717–1779), who distanced himself from pantomime and even sought to undercut Harlequin's appeal, nevertheless produced his own pantomimes at Drury Lane, primarily at Christmastime. It was in Garrick's productions that Harlequin first began to speak. His costume of various colored patches also became a literal map for portraying his emotions. Touching red meant love, blue was truth, yellow indicated jealousy, and, to become invisible, Harlequin pointed to a black patch and "disappeared" in order to work his magic. Over the centuries, the genre evolved further, losing the serious portions and eventually becoming a Christmas entertainment primarily for children. But the popularity of pantomimes never abated, and they continue in England to this day, and have even spread to other countries. (To read about the later history of pantomime, see the case study "British

Pantomime" on the *Theatre Histories* website, and the website from the Victoria and Albert Museum in London.)

Pantomime arose in part because theatrical licensing was allowed to slide, allowing four unlicensed theatres to operate in London in 1730, openly competing with the two major theatres, which were Drury Lane and (after 1732) Covent Garden. Aside from pantomimes, the patent theatres had little interest in innovation, and the most exciting developments were at these unlicensed theatres. The English merchant class, which was replacing the aristocracy as the dominant group both in the government and at London playhouses, approved of the fairground theatres no more than the monarchy had and tried to shut them down, without success. By the middle of the decade, there was regular traffic between the fairs and the London theatres. London actors performed frequently at the fairs, and theatre managers borrowed rope dancers and jugglers for *entr'acte* entertainments and incorporated into their plays the political jibes that were common at the fairs.

In fact political **satire** appeared frequently at the unlicensed theatres. The taste for it became especially strong with the production of *The Beggar's Opera* (1728) by John Gay (1685–1732). In an era when opera meant imports from Italy, *The Beggar's Opera* achieved popular appeal by setting new words to popular songs, creating a genre called "ballad opera." Gay's play also parodied sentimental comedy, in part by up-ending the sort of characters it presented: rather than wealthy merchants, honorable shopkeepers, and urbane aristocrats, *The Beggar's Opera* was peopled by thieves, beggars, and prostitutes. Gay's travesty had a political point: by inverting the social pyramid, he implied that the upper classes were no better than robbers, mobsters, and other social leeches. Chief among his targets was the Prime Minister, Robert Walpole (1676–1745).

Walpole was at the opening night performance and seemed to take the digs with good humor. But he had the play's sequel *Polly* (published 1729) banned from the stage, and later, after almost a decade of increasingly savage theatrical attacks on his political manipulations, he lowered the boom and rushed the Licensing Act of 1737 through Parliament. The Act strengthened the censorship exercised by the Lord Chamberlain (to whom the Master of the Revels reported) by requiring companies to submit all scripts for approval before performing them. It also authorized only Drury Lane and Covent Garden in London to perform plays (which paid sizable fees for the privilege). Requiring prior approval for all plays put an end to the attacks on Walpole, and it also ingratiated him with the royal family, whose troubles had led to some theatrical jabs as well. Limiting the number of theatres had an even more drastic effect on performance in London, since it removed all incentive for the licensed theatres to present almost anything but tried and true older plays and farcical afterpieces.

The 1737 Act drove overt satire off the stage and forced some playwrights to couch their criticisms in subtler and more psychological forms. For the most part, though, the Licensing Act transformed London playhouses from arenas of debate and political dissension into models of decorum and false consensus. Walpole had succeeded in pushing the bill through primarily because others in the governing classes also preferred censorship to derisive laughter. English theatre's participation in the public sphere through satire effectively ceased until the Licensing Act was repealed in 1968.

Derisive laughter was nevertheless part of the new distinction between the public and private spheres. As one of the main sites where people gathered, theatre was embedded in the public sphere, and before the Licensing Act it played an active role in the political discourse

Figure 7.4
A Scene from The Beggar's Opera (1729) by William Hogarth. The painting depicts a moment in Act III, Scene 11.
Source: Yale Center for British Art, Paul Mellon Collection.

of the time, no less important than the partisan editorializing that crowded the era's newspapers. William Hogarth (1697–1764), one of the leading artists of the eighteenth century, was especially well known for his satirical engravings caricaturing the politics and morals of the time. Hogarth, who was friends with Gay, even depicted a scene from *The Beggar's Opera* in one of his paintings (Figure 7.4). Walpole showed that although politics in the theatre can have a particularly powerful impact, it is much easier to censor than the press. But sometimes suppression creates interest, as Gay found when the banned *Polly* became a top seller when published. Satire off stage contributed to the vitality of the British public sphere.

Despite its short-term success, the 1737 Act proved unwieldy over time. Designed to protect Walpole and the monarchy, the Act made no provisions for theatre outside of London. Troupes and towns in the rest of the country simply ignored its strictures. Its numerous loopholes also allowed fairground managers and other theatre entrepreneurs to produce plays for lower-class patrons that encouraged a range of antisocial behavior. This led the governing classes to pass the Disorderly Houses Act of 1751, a new strategy in social control that placed responsibility for restraining the masses on those who owned and operated theatres. After 1751, all places for entertainment of any kind within a 20-mile radius of London had to display a license that certified that the managers were liable for the good conduct of their patrons. The local constabulary might revoke the license if order were not maintained. Intended to cut down on the rioting that sometimes accompanied lower-class theatre, the 1751 Act implicitly acknowledged that the Licensing Act of 1737 had not restricted all forms of theatre in the London area. The 1751 law admitted that it would be more effective to make managers responsible for the behavior of popular audiences than to try to dictate the form and content of their entertainments.

CASE STUDY: Censorship in eighteenth-century Japan

Carol Fisher Sorgenfrei

Contributor: Tobin Nellhaus

This chapter mainly concerns a relationship between social class and theatre. In eighteenth-century Europe, the bourgeoisie arose and developed an ideology distinguishing between the private sphere of family, friends and feeling, versus the public sphere of business, politics, class, law and government – a distinction reflected in sentimental plays on the one hand and satire on the other. As we saw, in reaction to the tumbling satires of the British public sphere, Prime Minister Walpole passed a law requiring plays to be vetted by a censor before performance. But theatre has faced censorship in many places, during numerous periods, for differing reasons, and through various methods. Prior censorship such as the Licensing Act has been common. For several centuries, the Church completely banned theatre throughout Europe, nipping its threat in the bud; Russia censored theatre almost as soon theatre existed there. In 1876 India instituted a drama censorship law modeled on the Licensing Act, still on the books. In other cases plays were shut down after their first performances, such as *God of Vengeance* after it opened on Broadway in 1932, largely due to its "immorality" (it portrayed a lesbian relationship). Individual playwrights could be banned, such as Plínio Marcos in Brazil during the 1960s and 70s; some have been imprisoned, including Ngũgĩ Wa Thiong'o in Kenya from 1977 to 1978. But censorship could also be spotty or arbitrary. The Puritan government in seventeenth-century England closed the theatres in London, but unsuccessfully outside the city limits. The Licensing Act barred plays from being staged, but their scripts could be published, and sometimes theatres skirted the law. Throughout Chinese history, plays and performances were frequently censored in varying locations and for varying reasons; for example, in 1781 alone, more than a thousand plays from previous dynasties were "edited" to eliminate anti-Qing materials. But in a country so vast and varied, censorship couldn't be comprehensively enforced and theatre continued to thrive. Political content, religious violations, and sexuality have been the main rationales for imposing censorship, but there have been other reasons too. In this case study, we examine censorship in Japan, partly because in many ways *kabuki* theatrical performance was similar to England's during that era (it was professionalized, it utilized sophisticated scenic technology, audiences were seated by class, and all genders could attend), but mainly because the primary reason for censorship was relatively unusual: to prevent socializing between different social classes.

Kabuki had always been a counter-cultural enterprise. From its start, the government made many attempts to suppress or destroy it, primarily to discourage upper-class samurai and aristocrats from mingling with lower-class merchants and virtually outcast actors. Those who violated the laws were punished severely. An extreme example occurred in 1714, when a raucous theatre party revealed the nine-year love affair between the popular, handsome actor Ikushima Shingorō (1671–1743) and Ejima, a high-ranking lady in the women's quarters of the shogun's castle. Ikushima was banished to a remote island for 18 years; Ejima was banished to another locale and her brother (who it was felt should have controlled her) was executed. The theatre where the party took place – the most popular of the four licensed theatres in Edo – was demolished and its assets and those of its owner were auctioned off. All of the partygoers were punished. The other theatres were closed for three months, and major actors and managers were required to state in writing that they would abide by all laws. For the remainder of the Tokugawa period, there were only three licensed *kabuki* theatres in Edo.

Despite such measures, many samurai and aristocrats secretly attended *kabuki*, sometimes in disguise, and as a practical matter, the authorities understood that limited access to theatre was preferable to a total ban. The government felt that "*kabuki* was, like prostitution, a necessary evil. These were the two wheels of the vehicle of pleasure, useful to assuage the people and divert them from more serious mischief" (Shively 1955: 41). Ironically, many attempts at suppression forced actors and managers to find creative ways to circumvent the laws, ultimately enhancing the art. Examples are the 1629 ban on female actors and the subsequent 1652 ban on handsome young males portraying females, both of which encouraged the creative development of the *onnagata*. Similarly, sumptuary laws, including restrictions and requirements for hair, wigs, and clothing/costumes (both in and out of the theatre), were partly responsible for the *kabuki* actor's distinctive visual style. Playwrights, too, found imaginative ways to avoid censorship.

In eighteenth-century Japan, scripts were censored only after the play opened. (Japan created an office similar to England's Lord Chamberlain, including the power of prior restraint, in 1875.) Japanese theatre of the time, unlike British theatre, did not attempt to satirize or critique the government. When Japanese authorities sought to censor scripts, it was because they deemed the content socially unacceptable or politically dangerous. For example, in 1723, love-suicide plays (often based on actual events) were banned because they seemed to glorify and encourage such behavior. Despite the ban (which lasted only a few years) and harsh punishments for survivors of attempted love-suicides, such works continued to be written, and actual love-suicides continued to occur. Other forbidden subjects were overt sexuality (in spite of the many references to both same-sex and heterosexual love), using the real names of living samurai or aristocrats, and dramatizing actual events after 1600 that involved samurai.

One method for circumventing the law was to substitute the facts and character names in a contemporary event with those from well-known history or legends, a strategy called *mitate*. An example of how playwrights used *mitate* is the play *Sukeroku: Flower of Edo* (1713). Sukeroku is a rowdy commoner in love with a gorgeous courtesan who refuses the advances of an evil samurai named Ikyū. The action takes place in Yoshiwara, Edo's "pleasure district," where theatre, teahouses, and brothels were located. In Sukeroku's danced entrance on the *hanamichi*, he wears a purple headband (a color permitted only to the upper classes), suggesting disdain for society's rules. (For a photo of Sukeroku's entrance, see Chapter 4, Figure 4.11.)

Like the merchants' ideal self, Sukeroku is brave, clever, funny, and a great lover. However, the contemporary surface is revealed as false. He is in disguise, and the time is not the present. He is actually one of the Soga brothers, historical samurai who avenged their murdered father in 1193. He typifies both the pluck of the Edo townsman and the samurai class's abandoned ideals. Sukeroku comically insults and picks fights with various samurai; when the evil Ikyū finally draws his sword, Sukeroku recognizes it as his father's, proving that Ikyū is the murderer. His character hints that common people, not actual samurai, possess the values and behaviors of *bushido* (the traditional "way of the samurai") which, due to a century of peace, seem to have been discarded by the upper classes.

Mitate is crucial in the period's most significant example of script censorship. The actual events took place between 1701 and 1703 and show how deeply the public revered the concept of *bushido*. A young, untutored samurai failed to bribe an elegant superior samurai, who mercilessly taunted him until the younger man drew his sword while in Edo castle, wounding the bully. In punishment, he was ordered to commit *seppuku* (suicide by disembowelment), his lands were confiscated, his retainers became *rōnin* (masterless samurai), and his family line was to be stamped out. On 30 January 1703, his former retainers, who had secretly plotted to avenge his death, attacked and murdered their lord's tormentor, aware that for this act of loyalty, they would be executed.

Their deeds polarized society. Numerous poems and essays extolled their act as an example of loyalty to their master and a heroic demonstration of apparently lost ideals. Others expressed more complex feelings. The Confucian philosopher Ogyū Sorai wrote that because they pursued the vendetta to avenge their lord's shame, and because

> they have followed the path of keeping themselves free from taint, their deed is righteous. However, this deed is appropriate only to their particular group; it amounts therefore to a special exception of the rules. … [T]hey deliberately planned an act of violence without official permission. This cannot be tolerated under the law. … If [they] are pronounced guilty and condemned to commit *seppuku*, in keeping with the traditions of the samurai, the claim of the [wronged] family will be satisfied, and the loyalty of the men will not have been disparaged.
> (Keene 1971: 2–3)

Seppuku, unlike simple execution, was an honorable death. The 46 who were ordered to commit *seppuku* (plus the 47th, admitted to the group posthumously after proving his loyalty) were buried in the same graveyard as their master; their burial place remains to this day a venerated pilgrimage site.

The rapid publication of materials dealing with the incident and subsequent trial ensured a well-informed population. Twelve days after the mass suicide, the first play based on the vendetta was staged, set (like *Sukeroku*) in the medieval world of the Soga brothers. Despite the substitutions, the government closed it after only three performances. Three years later, in a new third act tacked on to an existing play, Chikamatsu set the events in yet another historical era. Probably because it was staged in Osaka, this production was not closed down. It provided the standard "world" for later versions of the tale, including the definitive puppet play *Chūshingura: The Treasury of Loyal Retainers* (1748), subsequently adapted and performed as *kabuki*. Between 1706 and 1748, new versions were staged almost yearly, some with differing interpretations of the characters' motivations, others using new, spectacular staging. As long as the outer form did not violate the law, clever playwriting and staging could appease the censors while pleasing the audience. Even today, new versions continually appear, not only on stage, but as films and even year-long television series.

Key references

Brandon, J.R. (ed. and trans.) (1975) *Sukeroku: The Flower of Edo*, in *Kabuki: Five Classic Plays*, Honolulu: University of Hawaii Press, 49–92.

Keene, D. (trans.) (1971) *Chūshingura: The Treasury of Loyal Retainers*, New York and London: Columbia University Press.

Leiter, S.L. (2002) "From the London Patents to the Edo *Sanza*: A Partial Comparison of the British Stage and *Kabuki*, ca. 1650–1800," in *Frozen Moments: Writings on Kabuki, 1966–2001*, Ithaca, NY: Cornell University East Asia Program, 297–320.

Shively, D.H. (1955) "*Bakufu* versus *Kabuki*," *Harvard Journal of Asiatic Studies* 18 (December), reprinted in S.L. Leiter (ed.), (2001) *A Kabuki Reader: History and Performance*, Armonk, NY: M.E. Sharpe, 33–59.

Shively, D.H. (1978) "The Social Environment of Tokugawa Kabuki," in *Studies in Kabuki: Its Acting, Music and Historical Content*, Honolulu: University of Hawaii Press, 1–61.

Sentiment and satire on the European continent

Sentimentalism emerged on the European continent as well as in England, especially in France, where a culture of tearfulness had already begun forming in Racine's time: throughout the 1700s, French audiences loved to cry at both comedies and tragedies, and plays that failed to elicit tears seldom received favor. Anne Vincent-Buffault observes that the audience's weeping served not only emotional purposes, but also a socio-political one:

> Tears shed in company sealed a kind of social pact of sensibility which turned the theatre into a sort of political assembly. ... In this unanimous assembly of tears, the man whose eye remained dry ... [was thought to] hold himself outside not only the rules of society but those of humanity.

(Vincent-Buffault 1991: 68)

Pierre Marivaux (mentioned in Chapter 6) injected subtle expressions of feeling into his love comedies, most of which he wrote in the 1720s and 1730s, although his heightened prose style kept his plays much less sentimental than Steele's. Beginning in the 1730s French sentimental comedies, called **comédie larmoyante** [koh-meh-dee lahr-mwah-yawnt] (tearful comedy) became popular, such as *The False Antipathy* (1733) and other plays by Pierre-Claude Nivelle de la Chaussée (1692–1754). Some of these plays were often performed for the rest of the century. Like its analogue in England, the *comédie larmoyante* contributed to the increasing distinction between the public and private spheres by making personal relationships and the warmth of home its primary subject – a politics of pushing politics from view.

In the 1750s, the philosopher and writer Denis Diderot (1713–1784) urged the adoption of "middle" genres between comedy and tragedy that would encompass sentimental notions of morality and domesticity. As editor and chief writer of the *Encyclopédie*, the first modern compendium of knowledge and a triumph of Enlightenment culture (which valued individual liberty and rationality), Diderot won many readers throughout literate Europe. In separately published "dialogues," he argued for a type of comedy emphasizing tears and virtues, domestic tragedy called **drame** [drahm] centered on bourgeois family problems, and more realistic dialogue in all plays, and he advocated acting based on the actor's skill rather than their emotions. Diderot's interest in realism extended to staging as well: he was the first to propose that there should be an imaginary **fourth wall** separating the actors from the audience, requiring the actors to perform as though there were no spectators peering in; but this idea was not put into practice for over a century. Although Garrick took steps toward realistic acting, Diderot was the first to conceptualize theatre realism in anything like the modern sense. However, while a few *drames* based on Diderot's ideas saw production in some French theatres, the actors at the Comédie Française saw little in the new genre that would advance their careers, and interest in it faded in France. Even though by the middle of the eighteenth century the country had a significant bourgeoisie, French society was still largely dominated by the nobility and gentry, and the state monopolistic theatres hindered the growth of a sentimental, bourgeois theatre in France until after the Revolution. Consequently, despite the emergence of sentimentalism and *drame*, neoclassicism and its absolutist values remained firmly entrenched in France's official theatres until the 1789 Revolution.

But, as in England, the royally approved theatres did not go unchallenged. A variety of alternative genres and performance venues began developing late in the seventeenth century at the fairgrounds in Paris. Originally the fairs were known for coarse farces, jugglers, pantomimes, dancers, puppeteers, and similar entertainments (the sort of carnivalesque entertainments discussed in Chapter 6), but theatre became increasingly popular. When the Comédie Italienne was expelled from Paris in 1697, some of its actors probably began performing at the fairgrounds; it's clear that *commedia dell'arte* was adapted for performance there. Soon plays were being performed in theatre buildings fully equipped with stage machinery for scenery and special effects.

The fairground theatres posed strong competition to the monopoly theatres. The Comédie Française and the Opéra succeeded in closing them down from time to time, usually by imposing restrictions against spoken drama or the use of music. (However, when the Opéra needed money, it lifted restrictions in exchange for payments.) The fairground theatres soon found ways around the proscriptions, such as using mime, monologues, marionettes, invented languages, and even by having characters pretend to whisper into the ear of an actor, who would then say aloud what the character had said. Perhaps the most striking method of evading the monopoly theatres' prohibitions aimed to circumvent the ban on actors singing:

when a song was supposed to occur, placards were lowered from the flies with lyrics set to a popular tune, and the audience sang the songs. The stratagem soon developed into a new genre, **opéra-comique** (comic opera), which became the most popular type of fairground theatre offering (see Figure 7.5). The adversarial relationship with the official theatres also formed part of the repertory: the fairground theatres produced numerous plays about their difficulties with their rivals, and they parodied nearly every production at the Comédie Française and the Opéra, sometimes just days after their openings – which could only work if much of the audience had seen the original shows. Voltaire's plays were skewered repeatedly, and he disdained the theatres of the fairs. However, despite the popularity of the plays engaged in the battle with the monopoly theatres, most of the plays at the fairground theatres were fantasies, often with characters from *commedia dell'arte*.

The conflict between the conventional and the alternative theatres did not lead to completely polarized encampments: like the audiences, actors, and genres crossed over between them, and several playwrights, including Marivaux, wrote for both. Even so, the fairground theatres held a special attraction for their audience. Their incessant attacks on the Comédie Française and the Opéra established the fairground theatres as contributors to a burgeoning public sphere. There were few explicit criticisms of the monarchy and its government, but as Derek Connon points out:

Figure 7.5

Scene from a Parisian fair theatre play, *The Quarrel of the Theatres*, which satirized two state-supported theatres for stealing from the fair theatres: the Comédie Française, represented by the player on the right, and the Comédie Italienne, represented by the player on the left, which performed the *commedia dell'arte* repertoire and a mix of other works. From Alain René Le Sage and Jacques Autreau d'Orneval, *Le Théâtre de la Foire l'Opéra Comique* (1723).

Source: © Bibliothèque nationale de France.

One of the pleasures for audiences in supporting the underdogs lies in the frisson of danger in doing something that is almost illegal (and may slip over into illegality), in getting one over on the authorities and, ultimately, the monarch who is the source of the laws which are being bent to breaking point. Hence, even if the original reasons for the ban on these theatres is not fundamentally political, the reaction of audiences to it certainly is.
(Connon 2012: 191)

In the mid-1700s, Paris's fairgrounds started to decline, and the theatres began seeking alternative locations. In the early 1750s a new area for popular entertainment developed in the north of Paris on the Boulevard du Temple, closer to the fairground theatres' audience. The locale arose with cabarets, cafés, and marionette booths; soon trained animals, acrobats, and other types of street performance arrived as well. Eventually full-length plays were performed there. In 1759, a permanent theatre was built on the Boulevard; many more soon followed. Over the course of the eighteenth century, these boulevard theatres became home to middle-class dramas of various types.

Italian theatre in the early eighteenth century was in a contradictory state. On the one hand, Venice (the center of theatre in Italy) was able to sustain more theatres than either London or Paris. On the other hand, theatrical performance was still dominated by *commedia dell'arte*, which had long fed theatre everywhere else in Europe, but had deteriorated at home, unable to create new situations or *lazzi*, settling in theatres which they could only half fill. Sentimental drama did not arise in Venice, although French sentimental plays eventually reached there in translation during the 1770s. But two major playwrights – who were mutual antagonists – brought new life to the Venetian stage. Carlo Goldoni (1707–1793) accommodated *commedia* in some respects (he was employed by various *commedia* companies), but at a fundamental level he transformed it. His early play *The Servant of Two Masters* (1745) (Figure 7.6), perhaps his best-known work outside Italy, is in the *commedia*

Figure 7.6
The Servant of Two Masters by Carlo Goldoni, performed at Yale Repertory Theatre in 2010.
Source: © Richard Termine Photography.

style and was initially written as a scenario. (He also gave *commedia dell'arte* its name.) But breaking from *commedia* traditions, Goldoni later eliminated improvisation and insisted that the actors work from the script. These changes switched priority from the actor to the playwright. In pursuit of a more intimate acting style, in 1754 he eliminated masks from his plays altogether. Like reformers elsewhere in Europe, he also banished spectators from the stage. Most of Goldoni's work centered on middle-class characters and values; he favored many proposals championed by Diderot and maintained a correspondence with Voltaire. His greatest innovation was his attention to everyday life, introducing a sense of realism and observation. Many of his plays focused on a new, bourgeois sense of morality which sometimes challenged his audience and criticized aristocratic values. An unusual number of his lead characters were female.

Carlo Gozzi (1720–1806) vehemently resisted Goldoni's innovations – and the whole of Enlightenment culture – passionately defending the older approach to performance (and highly conservative values in general). His earliest play, *The Love for Three Oranges* (1761) used a fantastical fable in order to satirize Goldoni. Although it returned the old *commedia* characters to the Venetian stage and (for the most part) improvisation to the actors, it departed from traditional *commedia* by centering its narrative on a fantasy, which brought the play resounding success. Placing fantasy on stage also contrasted with Goldoni's turn toward everyday life, and Gozzi's plays continued in that vein, to repeated acclaim. However, fantasy required spectacular staging, which conflicted with *commedia*'s barebones tradition. Gozzi's plays outstripped the popularity of Goldoni's for a time, which probably contributed to Goldoni's decision to leave Italy for Paris in 1762, but they soon faded from fashion. Several, however, were later adapted into new plays and operas, most famously Giacomo Puccini's *Turandot* in 1926. In the early twentieth century, Gozzi's plays inspired many anti-realist playwrights and directors.

Despite Gozzi's reactionary approach to theatre and his animosity toward Goldoni, occasionally Gozzi adopted some of Goldoni's reforms, such as increasingly scripting actors' lines and (at his actors' insistence) removing some of the masks. He disdained realism, yet some of his plays gained fuller characters while reducing fantastical elements. And Gozzi occasionally sought tears as well as laughter. More fundamentally, like Goldoni he sought to rescue *commedia* from decay, but his efforts fundamentally changed it and thus contributed to its demise. As Tatiana Korneeva (2019: 4–10) has argued, by striving to turn the audience from passive recipients to an emotionally engaged and critically (including politically) discerning public, both Goldoni and Gozzi helped build the distinction between the public and private spheres.

Italian theatre was greatly affected by French reformers like Diderot and Voltaire, but the streams of influence also flowed the other direction. Although playwright and director Domenico Luigi Barone (1685–1757) was soon forgotten, his activity was not: he pioneered the very modern ideas of perfectionist acting that required even a year of day-long rehearsals, with special attention to gesture, and introduced the technique of staging two or more scenes or dialogues simultaneously. The latter influenced Goldoni, and in *The Paradox of Acting* (discussed later in this chapter) Diderot praised Barone's directorial work without naming him.

The turn to sentimentalism in Germany came with the popularity and influence of Gotthold Ephraim Lessing (1729–1781). Lessing was one of the first writers in Germany to make his living from his pen and he gained success as much from his criticism as his plays. Influenced by Diderot, he advocated domestic tragedy in his writings in the 1750s and used these ideas for his middle-class play, *Miss Sara Sampson* (1755). By 1759, Lessing was attacking Gottsched (see Chapter 6) and French neoclassicism, and advocating Shakespeare as a better model for German theatre. The literary advisor for the Hamburg National Theatre (discussed in Chapter 8, where we address nationalism), Lessing used his *Hamburg Dramaturgy* (1767–1769) to offer a non-neoclassical interpretation of Aristotle's *Poetics* and to urge the writing and production of more sentimental plays. He put this criticism into practice with *Minna von Barnhelm* (1767), a romantic comedy that unites lovers from two sides of a recent war that divided Germany. Like his model, Diderot, Lessing was critical of aristocratic privilege and morality and attacked both in his next influential drama, *Emilia Galotti* (1772). Although Lessing did not intend *Nathan the Wise* (1779) for the stage, his dramatic demonstration of the wisdom of tolerance and understanding among representatives of Judaism, Islam, and Christianity became one of his most widely produced plays in the German theatre. Together with other playwrights and companies after 1750, Lessing had helped to ensure that German drama would gravitate more toward sentimentalism than neoclassicism for the rest of the century.

A German composer, Christoph Willibald Gluck (1714–1787), was primarily responsible for turning *opera seria* away from the neoclassicism of Metastasio and toward European sentimentalism. Like many composers of his time, Gluck traveled to Italy to learn the rudiments of operatic dramatic form and used the libretti of Metastasio for several of his early operas. Influenced by French *opéra-comique* and by a desire to free serious opera from the weight of recitative, Gluck broke with Metastasian tradition in 1762 with the production of *Orfeo ed Euridice*. When composing for the Paris Opéra in the 1770s, Gluck also challenged the domination of operatic castrati, writing lead roles for tenors instead of castrati in a few of his works. According to several Parisian operagoers, Gluck's gloomy and intense operas caused a flood of welcome and sentimental tears, affecting everyone from the king to the intellectuals.

Although generally more classical than sentimental in his style, Wolfgang Amadeus Mozart (1756–1791) benefited from the freedom in operatic composition that Gluck's reforms had accomplished. Born in Salzburg, Austria, Mozart worked there as a court musician for most of the 1770s, finally fleeing to Vienna in 1781, where his operatic career took off. His first production at the court of Emperor Joseph II, *The Abduction from the Seraglio* (1782), an *opera buffa* with a German libretto, was an enormous success. Mozart began collaborating with court librettist Lorenzo da Ponte in 1786; two of their works together, *The Marriage of Figaro* (1786) and *Don Giovanni* (1787), continue to be enjoyed by operagoers today for their compelling drama and emotional range. Through his travels as a child prodigy, his amazing musical memory, and his fluidity and daring in composition, Mozart was able to weave into his mature operas a range of styles from the eighteenth century – the Baroque power and contrapuntal techniques of Bach and Handel, the optimism and charm of Metastasio and his composers, Haydn's astringent clarity and sinuous surprises, and the emotional fervor of Gluck and his imitators – that was unsurpassed in its time. Mozart's final opera, *The Magic Flute* (1791), demonstrated that he could also use German folk tunes and fairy tales to brilliant effect.

Changes and challenges in sentimentalism

In the last third of the eighteenth century, some English playwrights grew impatient with sentimentalism's tepid humor and began to write "laughing comedies," the first significant departure from sentimentalism's velvet grip. Nonetheless, even comic playwrights who disliked sentimentalism still bowed to most of its precepts. Oliver Goldsmith (c.1730–1774), for example, provided much robust humor in *She Stoops to Conquer* (1773), but arranged a sentimental ending for his lovers. Richard Brinsley Sheridan (1751–1816), parliamentarian, theatre manager, and playwright, tweaked the excesses of sentiment and derided those who pose behind a sentimental mask in *The School for Scandal* (1777). But he came down firmly on the side of paternalistic benevolence and morality in wedlock. A few women were finally able to provide plays that proved highly popular, such as Hannah Cowley's (1743–1809) *The Belle's Stratagem* (1780), which joined the drive for "laughing" romantic comedies. Audiences enjoyed both types of comedy.

Although the French Revolution would shatter sentimentalism irreversibly in Europe, there were several deep cracks in the sentimental vase before 1789. At one extreme of eighteenth-century sentimentalism was the cult of sincerity that drew its ideas from Jean-Jacques Rousseau (1712–1778). In his writings, Rousseau criticized Enlightenment rationalism and celebrated an image of natural, sincere, authentic humanity, unencumbered by social masks. These ideas eventually led Rousseau to damn the theatre because he took acting to be duplicitous. Despite Rousseau's antitheatrical prejudices, his ideas carried wide influence in the theatre and culture of his time, both before and after the Revolution, and shaped the work of several playwrights.

Rousseau's extreme version of sentimentalism, which presaged Romanticism (discussed in Chapter 8), fired the imagination of a new generation of German playwrights, young men defecting from the middle-class and loosely grouped together as the Storm and Stress (*Sturm und Drang*) movement. Friedrich Maximilian von Klinger's (1752–1831) play *Sturm und Drang* (1776), set in the American Revolutionary War, posed Rousseau's natural, sentimental humanity against the restrictions of rationality, and gave the movement its name. Not all in this rebellious generation of playwrights embraced Rousseau, but most rejected Lessing's synthesis of sentimental and Enlightenment values and challenged conventional social norms. Recognizing the natural sexual desires of young soldiers, for example, Jakob M.R. Lenz's (1751–1792) *The Soldiers* (1776) advocated state-sponsored prostitution. Although many Storm and Stress plays, including *The Soldiers*, never made it past German censorship into performance, several circulated in print. Three plays from this movement, however, gained some productions and are still in the standard German repertory: *Goetz von Berlichingen* (1773) by Johann Wolfgang von Goethe (1749–1832); and Friedrich Schiller's (1759–1805) *The Robbers* (1782) (Figure 7.7) and *Fiesko* (1783). We will discuss Goethe and Schiller further in Chapter 8.

Rousseau's ideas were important to several of the Storm and Stress playwrights, but their plays also reflected the political situation in Germany – which was that there was no "Germany" at this time. There were over 300 German-speaking principalities, autonomous cities, and bishoprics, but they lacked the political unity that defines a nation. "National" theatres such as Hamburg's strove to create a nation or the idea of a nation, not to represent it. Under King Frederick II (called Frederick the Great, 1712–1786), Prussia began seizing large swaths of German-speaking lands, many of them scattered about toward the west.

Frederick both militarized and bu-reaucratized his lands, beginning the formation of a modern state. His rule did not extend to most of what is now Germany: Hamburg, for example, was not in Prussian control. Prussia was not the nation "Germany," it was one of many German lands. Despite his support for Enlightenment values and his personal military valor, Frederick didn't embody an ideal to the Storm and Stress playwrights: most of them despised his despotism, regimented governance, and power politics. Storm and Stress plays often sought to develop German nationhood as a feeling, with a culture that didn't im-itate French neoclassicism but instead formed on its own terms. Rousseau's ideas of untrammeled genius dove-tailed with these goals; in drama, the protagonist's strength of character and underlying freedom were essential.

Another German playwright, August von Kotzebue (1761–1819), avoided the dramatic and social ex-cesses of the Storm and Stress move-ment, but popularized its rejection of rationalism and its general embrace of Rousseau. Kotzebue's first hit, *Misan-thropy and Repentance* (1787) – a pot-boiler stuffed with Rousseauian senti-ments, pathetic situations, comic relief, romantic love, and moral didacticism – set the formula for his later successes.

Figure 7.7
Illustration for Schiller's *Die Räuber* (*The Robbers*), act 5, scene 2. Copper engraving by Joh. Friedr. Bolt after a draw-ing by Joh. Heinrich Ramberg, 1816.
Source: Interfoto/Alamy Stock Photo.

Several of Kotzebue's more than 200 plays retained popularity for the next 70 years in translations and adaptations in Western Europe, Russia, and the United States. Among his most successful plays were *The Stranger, Pizarro in Peru*, and *Lovers' Vows*. Kotzebue explored the democratic potential of Rousseau's philosophy in theatrical terms. Where most previous sentimental plays had invited middle-class audiences to test their sentimental feelings and ethics within a genteel and rational framework, Kotzebue's dramas appealed to a wider audience by encouraging spec-tators to believe that all people, with or without enlightened reason, were already natural, ethical, and authentic human beings. By downplaying rationality and democratizing senti-ment, Kotzebue's plays anticipated a significant aspect of nineteenth-century melodrama.

Acting in the eighteenth century

In performance, sentimental characters' inward feelings and experiences needed to take outward form. Thus European audiences found acting one of theatre's greatest attractions. With it, actors increasingly played a role in public life as representatives of a nation's culture – a function which rapidly developed into star power. Although actors performed both sentimental and neoclassical plays during the century, and necessarily adapted their playing styles to suit each type of production (not to mention the theatres' increasing size), progressive changes from grand rhetoric toward everyday speech and from heroic to more homely emotions occurred between 1700 and 1790. Acting remained idealized and presentational from today's perspective, with performers striking poses, playing directly to the spectators, and inviting applause in the middle of scenes. Nonetheless, the new emphasis on affecting audience emotions gradually pushed the playing style toward more intimacy and vulnerability.

Print played an important role in turning acting styles toward sentimental culture. Actors continued to rely on their voices to express the dialogue, of course, but after about 1660 they paid as much or more attention to the poses and gestures that made them visually expressive and interesting to spectators. Since the arrival of printing, speech had gradually declined as the culturally dominant mode of communication in Western Europe; sight became more significant than sound. Where previously music and voice had been the path to spiritual transcendence, critics now feared that mere sounds could too easily seduce the other senses. Further, many commentators were laying more emphasis on the importance of gestures in human communication. One treatise written in 1644, for example, suggested that human gestures were a kind of universal alphabet of nature; preachers, actors, and orators must know this alphabet to communicate effectively. Increasingly in society, people were "reading" the appearances of others in addition to listening to their voices to understand human behavior and emotion. To be legible, a character on the stage (like a print "character" on the page) had to look right.

By the eighteenth century, actors were striving to please a print-soaked public eager to read the gestures and poses of their performances. Many treatises and manuals instructed actors in the proper embodiment of their characters' "passions" (emotions). Perhaps the most systematic of these in England was *The Art of Speaking* (1761) by James Burgh. For Burgh, speaking was a whole-body activity that included gestures. The manual offered a series of illustrated "lessons," some of them drawn from plays, demonstrating which pose should accompany each passion so that the audience could understand the desired "affect." By reading books like *The Art of Speaking*, actors learned how to register the progression of poses involved in "Awe – Horror – Fear," for example, with their spectators (Figure 7.8). In addition,

Figure 7.8
The Passions classified: "Terror." From J.J. Engel, *Ideen zu Euer Mimik* (1812).

Source: © P.M. Arnold Semiology Collection, Washington University Libraries.

the theatre-going public praised actors who could hold these poses believably for an extended moment. Not only did actors need to model the right attitude, they also had to manage the transition from one to the next. As Lessing explained in his *Hamburg Dramaturgy*, the actor must prepare for each of his poses "gradually by previous movements, and then must resolve them again into the general tone of the conventional" (Roach 1985: 73). The result in performance was a kind of garlanded effect that alternated between static poses and graceful movement as the actor used a character's lines and emotions to transition from one tableau to the next. It was crucial that each pose make an "impression" on the minds of the spectators before the actor moved on – a printing metaphor widely used in the eighteenth century to describe theatrical communication.

Several significant performers after 1740 embodied the audience's increasing interest in sentiment. On the London stage, for example, Charles Macklin (1699–1797) altered the traditional clownish interpretation of Shylock in *The Merchant of Venice* to

Figure 7.9
Portrait of Mademoiselle Clairon. Lithograph between 1800 and 1820.
Source: Library of Congress, https://loc.gov/pictures/resource/pga.13573/

emphasize the character's domestic affections and fierce ambition. In the 1770s, Friedrich Ludwig Schröder (1744–1816) performed the major plays of Lessing and Shakespeare with his company in Hamburg, Germany, with greater attention to his characters' emotions than had been common in the past. At the Comédie Française in the 1750s, Mademoiselle Clairon (Claire Josèphe Hippolyte Léris Clairon de Latude, 1723–1803) (Figure 7.9) challenged the traditional rhetorical force of French heroic acting by adopting more conversational tones for her tragic roles. Lekain (Henri-Louis Caïn, 1729–1778) followed in her footsteps in the 1760s and garnered applause for his more restrained style in neoclassical tragedy. Because leading actors usually chose their own costumes during this time, Macklin, Schröder, Mlle Clairon, and Lekain also won acclaim for their costuming innovations, which generally shifted stage dress from lavish toward domestic. Together with Macklin, David Garrick revolutionized acting on the English stage by discarding the oratorical style of the past and introducing a more natural style (although still with stylized elements). "His career marks a transition from an insistently aural theatre … to a primarily visual one," Peter Thomson observes (2007: 3). Garrick rapidly became the most renowned actor of his era, and we discuss him in depth in the case study that follows.

CASE STUDY: Theatre iconology and the actor as an icon: David Garrick

Gary Jay Williams

Theatre is a transitory art that thrives in the immediacy of the cultural moment that performer and audience share, most especially, it seems, at times of dynamic cultural change. Past performances cannot be hung in a museum or replayed from a score. To appreciate performances of the past, theatre historians turn to several kinds of primary sources – among them, pictorial representations. These pose both intriguing opportunities and problems. This case study offers examples of iconological analyses of such images. We will discuss four pictorial representations of the famous English actor David Garrick, emphasizing the relation between these images and two culturally important issues for eighteenth-century England: sentimentalism, and England's reinvention of its national identity. Garrick was a significant – and richly signifying – figure in England's construction of itself.

THINKING THROUGH THEATRE HISTORIES: CULTURAL STUDIES AND THEATRE ICONOLOGY

Theatre *iconology* is the interpretive analysis of theatre and performance-related pictorial representations, such as prints, paintings, and photographs, to better understand the cultural work the images were doing and so to better understand the theatre of the past. We use "iconology" here, following Erwin Panofsky (1955), rather than "iconography," a term that is often associated with the work of documentation, such as the thematic cataloging of paintings. Recently scholars have used pictorial sources aware that any representation of performance will itself be the product of many forces at play in the culture of the time. Such images tell us much about the social formations in which actor and audience, painter, and viewer participated, often more than they provide literal depictions of performance.

Analyzing images in this way will involve, as Christopher B. Balme notes, the interpretive task of "uncovering the semantics of a painting's 'sign language' and its relation to the larger social formation" (Balme 1997: 193). Doing so means approaching the image as a system for making meaning within a particular culture that operates with both explicit and tacit conventions and codes. Pictorial representations are always embedded with value choices (Barthes 1973: 117–74). The cultural historian's task may involve some demystification in order to understand the cultural forces at work in an image.

Among the sign-systems in a painting to be considered are the usual compositional ones: choice, size, and placement of the main figure and its spatial relation to other figures, the relation between the figure(s) and their environment, or their clothing, gestures, or postures – but as matters not just of form but as revealing social relations. (The discussion that follows of Hogarth's *Mr. Garrick in "Richard III"* offers examples of this kind of analysis.) Such analysis draws on the field of semiotics, the study of signs, which began with linguistics but expanded to consider how meanings inhere in all kinds of human endeavor, from the use of colors in military uniforms to the rules for social rituals or athletic games. Not only the painting or print itself, but also the circumstances of its production and distribution can tell us what cultural work it was doing. For example, the analyses here point to the fact that the Garrick images were produced in response to a new market for accessibly priced prints of popular actors. This is a symptom of middle-class economic development to which enterprising artists responded, a variation on print capitalism.

The analysis of a painting and print representing a performance may also involve examining it in relation to all the other theatrical primary sources on the performance, such as eyewitness accounts and promptbooks (play texts annotated by those involved in the production), or other related paintings and prints. The analysis of such visual resources requires some understanding of the conventions of the art. For example, portraits of actors in Garrick's day reveal more about individual personalities than did those in the preceding period, which were in the French neoclassical mode that monumentalized actors. To take an eighteenth-century example from Japan, the study of *kabuki* theatre using the contemporary color prints of *kabuki* actors would need to consider the conventions of this special genre of *ukiyo-e* woodcuts. Also, artists derive some of their compositional vocabulary from the works of other artists, as will be seen below in the discussion of Hogarth's composition.

Artists of Garrick's time drew on a widely known illustrated book that offered a science of archetypal facial expressions of emotions (horror, anger, surprise, grief), *Methode pour apprendre à dessiner les Passions* (*A Method for Learning to Delineate the Passions*) by Charles Le Brun (1619–1690), President of the French Academy. Both Hogarth and Garrick knew the work. In Hogarth's painting, *Mr. Garrick in "Richard III"* (Figure 7.10), Garrick's expression of horror and amazement is closer to Le Brun's sketch of an archetypal expression of horror than to a likeness of Garrick. Denis Diderot described Garrick doing a demonstration of Le Brun-like expressions when Garrick visited Paris in 1764 (Diderot 1957: 32–3) (compare Figure 7.8).

Iconological studies may also look at scenery, costumes, and staging arrangements. Pierre-Louis Ducharte's *The Italian Comedy* (1929) draws on 259 prints, paintings, and drawings as sources for the costumes, properties, and poses typical of each of the stock characters of the *commedia dell'arte*. Martin Meisel's *Realizations* (1983) explores relations between nineteenth-century Europe's fiction, painting, and drama.

Figure 7.10

Mr. Garrick in the Charakter of Richard the 3D (1746), engraving by Charles Grignion, after a painting by William Hogarth. This popular image of Shakespeare's version of the English king served several narratives of English national identity in the mid-eighteenth century.

Source: Yale Center for British Art, Gift of Mrs. Lyall Dean, Mrs. Borden Helmer, and the Estate of Bliss Reed Crocker in memory of Mr and Mrs. Edward Bliss Reed, transfer from the Yale University Art Gallery.

As a gifted actor, manager, and playwright, Garrick dominated the British stage and became a focal point in British culture across the mid-century. In his debut, he astonished London as Shakespeare's Richard III in a small, unlicensed theatre in 1741. His first biographer, Thomas Davies, wrote: "Mr. Garrick shone forth like a theatrical Newton; he threw new light on elocution and acting; he banished ranting, bombast, and grimace, and restored nature, ease, simplicity and genuine humor" (Davies 1780: I, 43). All of fashionable London turned out to see him; poet Alexander Pope went three times. Garrick became the leading actor at Drury Lane Theatre, where, within a few years, he won extraordinary acclaim for his performances in his signature roles, tragic and comic, including Hamlet, King Lear, Macbeth, Archer in George Farquhar's *The Beaux' Stratagem* (1707), and Abel Drugger in Garrick's own adaptation of Ben Jonson's *The Alchemist* (1610) in 1743. As the artistic manager of Drury Lane from 1747 to 1776, Garrick was especially dedicated to Shakespeare, staging 26 of the plays and playing leading roles in 14. With his 1769 Shakespeare "Jubilee," he made

Stratford-upon-Avon a site for literary pilgrimages, capping his long promotion of Shakespeare as the national poet. In effect, this dedication to Shakespeare and to Enlightenment England was framed as one and the same.

His successes derived from his genius in the performance on stage and off as the new "natural man" of reason and moral sensibility. Easy and graceful in motion, with a quick intelligence, Garrick offered a nimble, fluent model of the century's ideal of the rational mind and natural sensibility in the confident governance of the self. He planned his performances meticulously, blending physical and vocal grace with the virtuous responses of the Lockean "natural man," which is to say, the self-possessed man of vital moral sympathy, in whose bosom was the potential for the virtue and the benevolence toward others that the new social order required. Garrick, who had been born of a relatively poor family, thus offered the persona of a gentleman by nature more than by class, a persona seen in some of the key plays of the period, such as *The Beaux' Stratagem*, and promoted by the periodicals *The Tatler* and *The Spectator*. This made the actor an appealing figure for an England still negotiating its transition from an old social order, which had its roots in the concept of a divinely ordained, absolutist monarchy, toward a relatively democratized monarchy and a new social order based on civic and personal virtue across the middle class. The middle, merchant class saw itself as the keeper of the moral and economic foundation of a stable society.

Garrick is an ideal figure for iconological studies; portraits of him have been the subject of many articles and exhibitions. The number of engraved portraits of Garrick in the British Museum is exceeded only by those of Queen Victoria. The painting of him as Richard III by William Hogarth is probably the most famous portrait of a Western actor ever done (Figure 7.10 shows the engraving). But many other major English artists painted portraits of him, in his roles or in private life, including Joshua Reynolds, Thomas Gainsborough, Johann Zoffany, Benjamin Wilson, Nathaniel Dance, and Angelica Kauffmann. Louis François Roubiliac created busts of Garrick in marble and bronze, and images of him appeared on porcelain dishes, silver tea caddies, enameled boxes, and medallions. Garrick was arguably the West's first modern, commodified celebrity.

He himself did much to bring that about. He commissioned many paintings and prints of himself in his most successful roles, the prints being intended for wide circulation. Visiting Paris in 1764 as England's most famous actor, he wrote back urgently requesting prints for distribution to friends and fans. He also commissioned portraits of himself in his off-stage role of the natural gentleman, a role that straddled old and new ideas of class.

Moreover, he conceived his performances with a visual acuity that intersected perfectly with trends in English art. Garrick was among the first of a younger generation of actors with a freer physical style and more appeal for the eye than had been the case in the older, declamatory school, which emphasized classical, rhetorical music for the ear. He was, as Michael Wilson has suggested, well aware of the visual lexicon of painters of the time for portraying the passions. Applying this knowledge to his acting, Garrick aligned his performances with the legitimacy of art. Hogarth expert Ronald Paulson makes an acute point about Hogarth's painting of Garrick as Richard III: "If

Hogarth tended to make his painting look like a play, Garrick made his play look like a painting" (Paulson 1992: III, 250). Garrick might be described as an iconic actor in his use of visually arresting poses, which he planned carefully – his acting choices being influenced by his media consciousness, as we shall see. He then had these images popularized through paintings and prints – the visual media of his time. In so doing, he advanced his career and inscribed his performances on the national social consciousness.

Four Richards III

In Hogarth's *Mr. Garrick as "Richard III,"* there is Garrick and more. Garrick debuted in 1741 in the Shakespearean role, as compelling a protean character as any in Western drama. Plotting his ascent from Duke of Gloucester to King of England, Richard vows (in an earlier Shakespeare play that includes him) to deceive everyone like a good actor and to kill anyone between himself and the throne:

> Why I can smile, and murder while I smile,
> And cry "Content" to that which grieves my heart,
> And wet my cheeks with artificial tears,
> And frame my face to all occasions.
> [...]
> I can add colours to the chameleon,
> Change shapes with Proteus for advantages,
> And set the murderous Machiavel to school.
> Can I do this, and cannot get a crown?
> Tut, were it farther off, I'll pluck it down.
> (*Henry VI*, Part 3, Act III, sc. 2: 182–95, in Greenblatt 1997)

His deception and murders bring him to the throne, but they finally result in his overthrow and death in battle at the hands of the decent Earl of Richmond, Henry Tudor.

Hogarth's painting represents the moment when, on the night before the battle, Richard wakes in his tent from a dream in which he has been visited by the ten souls of those he killed, including his king, his brother, his two young nephews, and his wife. Awaking terrified, he cries out, "Give me another horse! Bind up my wounds!/Have mercy, Jesu! – Soft, I did but dream./O coward conscience, how doest thou afflict me?" (*Richard III*, Act V, sc. 5: 131–3). The adaptation of the play by Colley Cibber that Garrick used stressed Richard's villainy heavily, and, in this scene, Cibber added the ghosts' demand that Richard "wake in all the hells of guilt," which he does, though he goes on to fight to his death.

For a mid-eighteenth-century English audience, this anguished recognition of his sins by this, the most evil of men, would have been a critical moral turn, and Garrick turned it into a moral awakening of great visual power, meticulously arranged. Arthur Murphy, a contemporary playwright and Garrick biographer, wrote, "His soliloquy in the tent scene discovered *the inward man* [italics added]," a code phrase in England's age of moral sensibility signifying the natural, inner potential for good in humankind.

Hogarth renders Richard's expression of horror in the wide eyes that stare out over the shoulder of the viewer of the portrait and in the outstretched arm and extended fingers. However, Hogarth does not render Garrick's face with individualized particularity, nor are the figure and costume in the more natural mode of that in his earlier theatrical paintings of *The Beggar's Opera* (Figure 7.4). Rather, the painting of Garrick as Richard III is rendering the theatrical moment in the grand manner of history painting, a genre in which Hogarth had worked in the previous decade. Hogarth took his general composition from Le Brun's *Tent of Darius*; the voluminous flowing robes and other fabrics were painterly strokes to convey nobility. The painting's huge size – over eight feet long and six feet high – is in the mode of history painting, and here it magnifies and ennobles the figure of King Richard. This Richard is, then, a combination of four Richards III: the Richard of Garrick – meticulous master of the morally iconic moment for the age of sensibility; the Richard of English history; the Richard of Shakespeare, the great national poet (whom Garrick was promoting in his playhouse); and the Richard of Hogarth, by then the great English artist. Each presence complements the other. Together they constitute a national narrative aspiring to the status of myth. The buyer, Thomas (William?) Duncombe, paid 200 pounds sterling for the painting, more than had ever been paid to an English painter for a portrait (Paulson 1992: 3, 256–7). The engraving that followed shortly after served the interests of both Garrick and Hogarth. Analyzing the work and its cultural valences today, we can see not only a vestige of Garrick's iconic performance but the ways in which the image was speaking from, and to the English people's construction of their national identity in the eighteenth century.

Figure 7.11
Mr. Garrick in Hamlet, mezzotint print by James McArdell, 1754, after a painting by Benjamin Wilson, depicting Garrick at the moment of Hamlet's encounter with his father's ghost.

Source: © Harvard Theatre Collection. Catalogue of dramatic portraits, vol. 2, p. 98, no. 202. ART File G241 no.94. Folger Shakespeare Library.

Two rivals, two prints

Many of Garrick's other performances resulted in images suitable for framing, including those of his Hamlet and Lear, considered briefly here (Figures 7.7 and 7.8).

Figure 7.12
Mr. Garrick in the Character of King Lear,
hand-colored mezzotint by James McArdell,
after a painting by Benjamin Wilson. With
the mad Lear are Kent behind him (Astley
Bransby) and Edgar (William Havard). The
Fool is missing because the role was eliminated in Nahum Tate's sentimental adaptation. Neoclassicism dictated that comedy and
tragedy should not be mixed.
Source: © Gary Jay and Josephine S. Williams.

James McArdell did mezzotints of him in these roles. Published in 1754 and 1761, respectively, they were based on paintings (both lost) by Benjamin Wilson (1722–1788). (Zoffany also painted the same scene from *Hamlet.*) Both images seem to aspire to the effects of Hogarth's hugely successful portrait of Garrick as Richard III. Both advance Garrick's moral agenda. Collaboration among actor, painter, and printmaker on both is very probable.

The very method of these prints – the mezzotint – represented a new media technology. A special engraving tool was used to create surface texturing on the paper that allowed inking in gradations of shading and subtle chiaroscuro effects. This allowed the capturing of subtler, more emotional facial expression or more emotionally charged landscapes. Both prints also served Garrick's media campaign. Spranger Barry, the "silver-tongued" actor who was a close competitor of Garrick, was playing these same roles at the rival theatre, Covent Garden, at about the time that these Garrick images were published – likely in order to imprint Garrick's triumph in these roles in the public mind.

Garrick had taken special visual care with both scenes. He was proud of the scene from *Hamlet,* performing it in private for friends. He reportedly used a mechanical wig that he could manipulate to make his hair rise in fright, the better to capture Hamlet's horror, as eighteenth-century physiology said it should. The effect seems to be apparent in McArdell's print (Figure 7.11). The print is corroborated by a detailed description of the scene by Georg Christoph Lichtenberg, who saw a performance. Garrick's sentimentalized Lear, seen in Figure 7.12, is frail and vulnerable in the storm scene. Consistent with the Nahum Tate adaptation that Garrick used, his Lear is the sentimentalized father of the family whose demise is tragic in the domestic sphere, that sphere where eighteenth-century Britain had now relocated its national moral center. Tate has Cordelia live to marry Edgar, assuring succession to the throne and a stable future for kingdom and family more than Shakespeare's play does. Both of McArdell's prints were among those Garrick sought supplies of for distribution to friends in Paris.

Thirty Garricks

A century after his Hamlet, Garrick still figured prominently in the British imagination. One comic color print made in the mid-nineteenth century serves both as an amusing index to the Garrick image industry and as an insight into the long English fascination with him. *Garrick and Hogarth or The Artist Puzzled* (1845) by R. Evan Sly was based on an amusing anecdote about a Hogarth–Garrick skirmish that had appeared in a London newspaper several years after Garrick's death (Figure 7.13). Reportedly, every time Hogarth thought he had captured Garrick's likeness in a painting session, the actor mischievously changed his expression; by all accounts, Garrick's expressive face was famously mobile, never at rest, even off stage. Discovering the trick, Hogarth drove Garrick from his studio in a hail of brushes (Paulson 1971: 285–6). Sly used a clever mechanical device to capture the mercurial Garrick face. He placed a rotating wheel on the back of the print so the viewer could change the face of Garrick on Hogarth's canvas and also the face on the seated actor, bringing into view 30 different likenesses of Garrick. These likenesses are, in fact, caricatures of other artists' portraits of him. The faces in the sketches on the floor – caricatures of other Hogarth works – also change

Figure 7.13

Garrick and Hogarth, or The Artist Puzzled. Color print by R. Evan Sly, 1845. The face on Hogarth's canvas and the face of the seated David Garrick can be changed by rotating a wheel on the back of Sly's print, bringing into view 30 different likenesses of Garrick (Figure 7.14). The print is based on an eighteenth-century anecdote about Hogarth painting the actor which is evidence of the public fascination with the protean Garrick.

Source: © The Trustees of the British Museum.

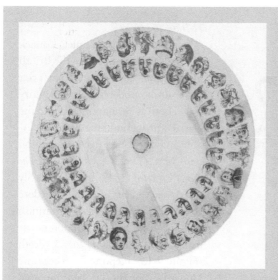

Figure 7.14

"Garrick's faces: thirty different likenesses," on the rotating disk in *Garrick and Hogarth, or The Artist Puzzled* (Figure 7.13).

Source: Billy Rose Theatre Division, The New York Public Library. The New York Public Library Digital Collections. 1730–1900. https://digitalcollections.nypl.org/items/a210f411-fc8b-dfb3-e040-e00a18064589

with a turn of the wheel. The dog on the left, whose knowing look at the viewer heightens the joke on Hogarth, is borrowed by Sly from a Hogarth self-portrait with his own dog, Pug (1745). You can see all the 30 likenesses in Figure 7.14.

The tale on which this print was based was probably an embellished one; its construction and repetition (there was a Gainsborough version) suggest some complexity in the fascination with Garrick. Behind the tale and the print was a paradox that began in his own time: the figure who had become an exemplar of a natural gentleman was an actor, a very adroit member of a profession that was historically suspect, morally and socially. Eighteenth-century English audiences with a hunger for outward signs of interior moral sincerity were enthralled with a talented professional who was skilled in creating meticulous semblances of sincerity. Could an actor adroit with images be a national model of the sincere, natural, virtuous man? Horace Walpole seems to have been aware of the problem when he warned his friend Sir Horace Mann, the British Envoy in Florence, "Be a little on your guard, remember he is an actor" (Shawe-Taylor 2003: 11).

In summary, this case study provides examples of theatre iconology that reads pictorial representations not only for what they might tell us as depictions of performance but for what they tell us about the social formations in which the actor and audience, and painter and viewer all participated. Garrick's performances and the making of the theatrical images of him are parts of a large historical picture, albeit one in which his uses of the media of his time are very recognizable today.

The unabridged version of this case study is available on the Theatre Histories *website.*

Key references

Audio-visual resources

For numerous images of David Garrick, go to the Folger Shakespeare Library's Digital Image Collection at <https://digitalcollections.folger.edu> and search for "Garrick."

Shakespeare & the Players. Website on nineteenth-century paintings, criticism, productions, sound recordings, and video clips of plays by Shakespeare, <http://shakespeare.emory.edu>.

Books and articles

Aliverti, M.I. (1997) "Major Portraits and Minor Series in Eighteenth Century Theatrical Portraiture," *Theatre Research International* 22: 234–54.

Balme, C.B. (1997) "Interpreting the Pictorial Record: Theatre Iconography and the Referential Dilemma," *Theatre Research International* 22: 190–201. (This issue is devoted to articles exploring different possibilities and problems in pictorial analysis.)

Barthes, R. (1973; 1st edn 1957) *Mythologies*, London: Paladin.

Davies, T. (1780) *Memoirs of the Life of David Garrick, Esq.* (2 vols), London: Thomas Davies.

Diderot, D. (1957) *The Paradox of Acting* [c.1778], trans. W.H. Pollock, New York: Hill and Wang.

Ducharte, P.-L. (1929) *The Italian Comedy*, London: Harrap.

Greenblatt, S. (1997) *The Norton Shakespeare*, New York and London: W.W. Norton and Company.

Highfill, P., Jr. and K.A. Burnim. (eds.) (1978) *A Biographical Dictionary of Actors, Actresses, Musicians, Dancers, Managers, and Other Stage Personnel in London, 1660–1800*, Vol. 6, Carbondale: Southern Illinois University Press. (The Garrick entry includes an annotated iconography of Garrick portraits.)

Lennox-Boyd, C., and G. Shaw. (1994) *Theatre: The Age of Garrick*, London: Christopher Lennox-Boyd. (English mezzotints from the collection of the Hon. Christopher Lennox-Boyd, published in conjunction with an exhibition at the Courtauld Institute Galleries.)

Mander, R., and Mitchenson, J. (1980) *Guide to the Maugham Collection of Theatrical Paintings*, London: Heinemann and the National Theatre. (Somerset Maugham's collection, which he gave to London's National Theatre, includes several important Garrick paintings.)

Meisel, M. (1983) *Realizations: Narrative, Pictorial, and Theatrical Arts in Nineteenth-Century England*, Princeton, NJ: Princeton University Press.

Panofsky, E. (1955) "Iconography and Iconology: An Introduction to the Study of Renaissance Art," in E. Panofsky (ed.) *Meaning in the Visual Arts*, New York: Garden City.

Paulson, R. (1971) *Hogarth: His Life, Art, and Times,* 2 vols, New Haven, CT and London: Yale University Press.

Paulson, R. (1992) *Hogarth,* 3 vols, New Brunswick, NJ: Rutgers University Press.

Shawe-Taylor, D. (2003) *Every Look Speaks, Portraits of David Garrick*, Bath: Holbourne Museum. (Catalog for the Exhibit at the Holbourne Museum of Art, Bath, England.)

Wilson, M.S. (1990) "Garrick, Iconic Acting, and the Ideologies of Theatrical Portraiture," *Word and Image* 6: 368–94.

Performers and the public

Few Europeans thought of acting as a profession until print helped to elevate it in public esteem. When the public could read about individual actors' performances in weekly newspapers and monthly journals, the past mystery and opprobrium surrounding their work began to dissipate. The press began its long love affair with actors. In addition to theatre reviews and manuals, actors' pictures appeared in printed plays, in theatre almanacs and books of anecdotes, and in collections of engravings and illustrations, where performers often posed in costumes in evocative moments of their most characteristic roles. Soon after the press began to use actors, actors found ways of using the press – to puff their latest role, to create printed programs that boosted their reputations, and to write articles and memoirs that shaped their recollections of "great" performances. Without the actor–press mutual admiration society, theatrical "stars" could not have been "born." (This was not solely a Western phenomenon: in the nineteenth century, prints of *kabuki* actors – such as Figure 7.15 – were similarly popular in Japan.)

One of the first things that actors did with their newfound authority was to remove spectators from the stage. At various times throughout Europe, the audience sat on public stages and occasionally interrupted the performers – a legacy of the easy flow between spectators and actors in medieval festivals. From the 1600s into the late 1700s, this was an elite practice. Male aristocrats eager to display their wits or wigs often chose to sit among the performers and draw occasional focus from their efforts. With help from the actors, Voltaire pushed for architectural reforms at the Comédie Française that removed Parisian spectators from that stage in 1759. Garrick effected this reform at the Drury Lane Theatre in London in 1762.

The relative ease with which performers were able to claim the stage as their own space reflected their increasing social status in Europe. In subsequent centuries, aided by improved transportation, imagery in printed publicity helped actors become local, national, and ultimately international stars.

Figure 7.15

Three *kabuki* actors in the scene of Kumagai's camp from the *kabuki* play *The Chronicle of the Battle of Ichinotani*, which was first performed in 1811. The actors are striking exaggerated poses (*mie*) in front of a large, blossoming plum tree. This triptych woodblock print is by Utagawa Kunisada (1786–1865), famous for his prints of actors and courtesans (see also Figure 4.3).

Source: Metropolitan Museum of Art. Purchase, Arnold Weinstein Gift, 2001.

Theorizing acting

The eighteenth-century European bourgeoisie, many of them new to the pressures of social performance, welcomed actors as models for enacting their own emotions in public life. Their social anxiety prompted a wide range of investigations into all manner of public performances, the first general outpouring of interest in the topic since classical times. Given the broad interest in acting, it is not surprising that some writers pushed beyond generalities to analyze how actors accomplished their artistic work. Among the most significant writings were reflections by Aaron Hill (1685–1750), an English playwright and critic who published them primarily in his theatrical journal *The Prompter* (1734–1736), and *The Paradox of the Actor*, written by Diderot in 1773 (revised in 1778, and published posthumously in 1830). Both dealt creatively with problems that still concern actors today.

Hill examined the process used by actors for producing emotion and based his conclusions on the mechanistic assumptions about the body that Cartesian philosophy had made popular among many literate Europeans. For Descartes, the body was a machine, following the laws of mechanics. Denouncing those who advocated mere rhetorical technique, Hill depicted a three-step process that involved the will operating the body almost as though it were a robot. First, the actor's imagination was to generate an image of the body expressing a specific emotion. Or, as Hill put it in a poem in *The Prompter* (where he deployed a print metaphor to capture his Cartesian idea): "Previous to art's first act – (till then, *all vain*)/Print the *ideal pathos*, on the *brain* … (Roach 1985: 81; Hill's italics). Next, the actor was to allow the "impressions" of the emotion in his mind to play out in his face. Third, facial expression would impel what Hill took to be the "animal spirits" of the mind and nerves to affect and shape the muscles, so that the actor would fully embody the emotion he had first imagined and thus could speak and act accordingly. In the end, wrote Hill, "the *mov'd* actor *Moves* – and passion shakes" (Roach 1985: 81; Hill's italics). Hill's ideas are similar to modern theories that assume that the actor's mind can trick the body into automatically producing the necessary emotions for a role.

Diderot also built his ideas upon mechanistic Cartesian assumptions, but broke with Hill (and most other acting theorists of his time) to argue that emotion actually got in the way of good acting technique. Like Hill, Diderot believed that the actor must use observation, imagination, and rehearsal to create an inner model of the character, but this preparation provided the basis for enacting an illusion of that character, not embodying the figure's actual emotions in performance. From Diderot's point of view, actors who relied on spontaneity and emotion rather than study and technique reduced the character to themselves, undercut the illusion of the character's emotional life for the audience, and compromised the range of characters they could create. In *The Paradox of the Actor*, Diderot praised performers who could marry a flexible vocal and physical technique to a perfect conception of the role and its emotional dynamics, thus enabling them to present their character in exactly the same way at every performance. Aware that enacting even the illusions of various emotions would tend to involve the actors in experiencing them directly, Diderot drew on Enlightenment science to argue that actors could effectively separate their minds from their bodies and control themselves on stage, much as a puppeteer controls a puppet. As we will see in Chapter 11, Diderot's cool-headed, self-manipulating actor might be compared to the ideal actor of Meyerhold and Brecht in the twentieth century.

Diderot held up Mlle Clairon and David Garrick as exemplars of his theory. He had watched Garrick perform a parlor entertainment in which the great actor shifted his facial expressions instantly to embody a wide range of characters, much to the amazement and delight of his Parisian hosts. Diderot published his *Observations on Garrick* in 1770, and it is clear that the English star significantly influenced his thoughts on acting.

Public interest in performance continued well into the nineteenth century. For example, the elocutionary movement of the mid-1800s in Britain excited numerous lectures and publications that engaged a range of professions from lawyers and merchants to preachers and politicians. In general, the advice given to these budding public speakers was the same as that given to actors before the mid-1700s: coordinate your words with your gestures, express emotions through the attitude of your body as well as your voice, and pause to "impress" your listeners. Attentive readers and listeners also learned to avoid accents and affects that would mark them as Scottish or Irish and how the voice and body could be pressed into the service of marking oneself as a member of a higher social class. But their activities still largely drew on classical ideas of formulated gestures and social comportment, which retained vitality for over a century; although Hill and Diderot differed, what they both articulated was the question of the actor's own mental preparation and emotional engagement – a question that was becoming increasingly central.

Summary

In early eighteenth-century Europe, the development of the periodical press led to profound changes in print culture. Periodicals played a key role in creating the bourgeois division between the public sphere that concerned politics, economics, and cultural interests such as fashion and entertainment, versus the private sphere where family, friends, and feelings abided. Popular magazines established the concept of sentiment, through which refined members of society experienced fellow-feeling, sympathy, and moral improvement. Drama was largely sentimental throughout the century. In England, where the public sphere was able to develop with little interference from the monarchy, satire became prominent as well, until it was suppressed by the government. Censorship was also imposed in Japan, but there the motives concerned class intermingling and morality rather than political control; nevertheless, actors and playwrights skirted the official prohibitions by creative means that sometimes became permanently embedded in *kabuki*. Both there and in Europe, audiences' imaginations were captured by actors and acting. In Europe, this interest was configured according to the public/private distinction as the visual, public enactment of private sentiments. Theatre stars fascinated the nation – or more precisely, the emerging nation-state.

★

CHAPTER 8

Nationalism in the theatre in Europe and the Americas, 1760–1880

Patricia Ybarra
Contributor: Bruce McConachie

Nationalism is relatively new in world history. The idea that a group of people, loosely united by a common language or culture, has an inherent right to its own geographical and political state would have seemed absurd to most Europeans before 1700. (This conception of nation is different from concepts employed by indigenous groups in the Americas.) Before the emergence of nationalism, identities were formed by familial ties, territorial ties, and attachment to cultural practices. When national feeling was present, it was often not attached to the idea of a state. As historian Benedict Anderson notes, the imagined fellowship that undergirds nationalism has to be invented and continuously reaffirmed. Nations, as gatherings of strangers, must both build upon and surpass the affiliations that draw people together as families, townspeople, and social classes. According to Anderson, a nation is "an imagined political community – and imagined as both limited and sovereign" (Anderson 1991: 6). That is, the nation, with its accompanying political state, is imagined as limited with regard to its territorial expanse and sovereign in terms of its ability to take independent political action within its boundaries and against other countries.

Within Europe, citizens in France, England, and the Netherlands were the first to successfully transform their states into national "imagined communities." This development gave their bourgeoisie a decided advantage in international politics and economics over other countries during the continued development of global capitalism in the late eighteenth century. As we have seen, King Louis XIV facilitated this process in France, and the middle classes consolidated nationalism in England after 1688. In the towns and villages of the Netherlands, the Dutch began to embrace nationalism in 1609, after winning independence from Spain. In 1760, however, these nation-states remained the exception in Europe and throughout the world. Despite some commonalities of language and culture, Italy and Germany were divided into small states, and the Austrian Empire encompassed a patchwork of national cultures, including Polish, Hungarian, and Czech. Absolutist emperors or

DOI: 10.4324/978-1003185185-12

monarchs, together with landed aristocrats, ran things in Russia, Spain, and Portugal, where the bourgeoisie were second-class citizens and enjoyed little economic power.

Much of this would change in Europe by 1880. During the nineteenth century, Italian politicians and patriots brought most of Italy under one rule (in 1861) and the Chancellor of Prussia, together with the Prussian army, united most German-speaking lands within the German Empire (in 1871). Meanwhile, in the Americas, the United States established nationhood in the late eighteenth century and most of what is now Latin America had gained independence from Spain and Portugal by 1825. While the push for freedom from colonial rule in the Americas was not based initially in nationalism, but rather the anti-colonial sentiments of native-born elites, it led to the creation of nation-states that became nationalistic in the nineteenth century. The primary matches that lit the flames of nationalism in Europe were the French Revolution of 1789 and the Napoleonic wars that followed until 1815. Unlike earlier European wars, much of the combat after 1795 involved citizen-soldiers who believed they fought to defend people like themselves, not to advance the interests of a king or emperor. As in subsequent wars involving nation-states, the bloodshed of the revolutionary era required justification, and the ideology of nationalism provided ready answers.

In the Americas, these structures were complicated by the racial heterogeneity of their populations and the complex relations between these groups; in some nations, indigenous, mixed-race (*mestizo*), and African-descendent peoples were the majority, despite leadership being largely Latin American-born people of European descent (*Criollo*). Thinking about a common nationality was not just a matter of reaching across social class lines or regional identities, as the subsequent pages will show. Approaching theatre in the national period from this perspective asks us to retain a global frame of cultural development even as we look at particular national performance cultures throughout Europe and the Americas.

This chapter primarily examines the kinds of theatre that helped to legitimate or challenge European and American nationalisms between 1760 and 1880. Theatre participated directly in debates about nationhood and occasionally influenced the rise and fall of governments. Specifically, we will examine three varieties of European and American nationalism and the types of theatre intertwined with each type of nationalism that flourished during these 120 years. The first is *liberal nationalism*, which began in eighteenth-century Europe and involved a commitment to the Enlightenment ideals of individual liberty, private property, and constitutionalism. Although its legitimacy suffered from the wars of the revolutionary era, liberal nationalism continued to inform bourgeois notions of the nation-state during the nineteenth century, including some in the Americas. The basic idea of *cultural nationalism* may also be found in the Enlightenment, but it emerged politically after 1800 as a defensive response to Napoleon's universalizing claims of a benevolent French empire. During the war years of the revolutionary era, roughly 1775–1825, many European and American peoples adopted a version of cultural nationalism, a belief in the uniqueness and greatness of one's language-based culture. It flourished, for disparate reasons, in Europe and the Americas for the rest of the century. As we will see, *racial nationalism* mixed traditional notions of racial superiority with cultural nationalism in various sites in Europe and the Americas. Although our chapter ends at 1880, it will be evident that these three varieties of nationalism, which are intertwined rather than mutually exclusive, also played significant roles in the twentieth century and continue to shape theatre and politics today.

Print, theatre, and liberal nationalism, 1760–1800

Before the French Revolution, periodical print culture helped some bourgeois Europeans to envision themselves as a potential governing class. As literate Europeans read more about current affairs and shared ideas for improving their societies, they developed a sense of themselves as a public, with interests separate from the dukes, kings, and emperors who ruled most of them. As explained in Chapter 7, the news press was especially important in forming this notion of a "public sphere," but so was the theatre. By 1760, many of the same people in Paris, Vienna, London, Hamburg, and other large cities went to the theatre, read plays, and gathered in coffeehouses and salons to discuss developments in science, the arts, and current events. As the press and the theatre influenced each other, both helped to shape an emerging public sphere in their countries.

After 1760, these European publics increasingly thought of themselves as national audiences, with rights that all theatrical spectators could expect to exercise. Royal and aristocratic patronage had waned, especially in England and Germany, and the bourgeoisie had partly taken its place. As theatrical benefactors, they strove to cultivate a theatrical public to sustain a theatre that could explore many of their new ideas. Most of the literate bourgeoisie looked to the power of rational public opinion expressed in print to regulate behavior in the theatre. Stung by the response of a small group of critics to his *The Barber of Seville* in 1775, lawyer-playwright Pierre-Augustin Caron Beaumarchais (1732–1799), for example, addressed a "Temperate Letter" to the reading public of France. "I recognize no other judge than you," wrote Beaumarchais, "not excepting Messieurs the spectators, who – judges only of first resort – often see their sentence overturned by your tribunal" (Peters 2000: 249). Although Beaumarchais might distrust, he knew he could not dismiss, theatrical spectators. Nonetheless, he believed that the reading public, with more time for rational reflection, could gradually educate the theatrical public. Although the state might be mired in royal monopolies, such as the Comédie Française, the public sphere of the nation could support a kind of theatre that could move France toward the political ideals of the Enlightenment. Beaumarchais's views were shaped by the rise and influence of periodical print culture. Newspapers and other periodicals were leading to the standardization of national languages, which facilitated communication among groups within that nation. In effect, print allowed the literate classes with enough leisure time in Europe to imagine the existence of other nationals like them as they read their books, newspapers, and journals. Liberal nationalism, with its commitment to freedom of the press and other Enlightenment values at this time, rested on the imagined coherence of a reading nation.

Influenced by this belief, German critic Johann Friedrich Löwen (1729–1771) published his hope that his new theatre in Hamburg could help to unify the German-speaking-and-reading nation. In the eighteenth century, most Germans lived outside of Prussia and the Austrian Empire, in small states, duchies, and principalities. Löwen's manifesto called for a theatre that would "raise the dignity of German drama" and "inspire the nation's authors to [write] national dramas" (Sosulski 2007: 16). The Hamburg National Theatre opened in 1767. Löwen induced critic-playwright Gotthold Ephraim Lessing to join his troupe as a literary advisor. Lessing thereby became the first dramaturg in Europe, an in-house critic in charge of recommending plays and advising the company on artistic matters (see Chapter 7 on Lessing and sentimentalism). In effect, the German tradition of dramaturgy grew out of the eighteenth-century bourgeois goal of educating a rational theatre public for national responsibilities; dramaturgy was initially a part of liberal nationalism.

Löwen and Lessing's repertoire did not change the Hamburg audience's preferences for farces and ballets, however. Attendance declined and the idealistic enterprise closed after two seasons. Although Lessing had rejected French neoclassical plays as models for German drama, major problems of audience education and taste remained. Lessing's final essay in his *Hamburg Dramaturgy* expressed his deep disappointment that the public had not supported the theatre. More importantly to Lessing, the public apparently had no desire to create something distinctly German (Lessing 1962: 262). Lessing's concern about acting styles was also a part of his political project: he was especially concerned with controlling the emotionality with female actors as part of his reforms. Nonetheless, Lessing's dramaturgical memoir provided an inspirational model for the more than a dozen "national" theatres that flowered in other German-speaking cities before 1800.

Friedrich Schiller, a celebrated historian as well as a playwright and director, shared many of Löwen's and Lessing's hopes for a national theatre. Following his early plays and his tenure as a professor of history at the University of Jena, Schiller returned to the theatre in 1799 in the German principality of Weimar. Like the poet and playwright Johann Wolfgang von Goethe, the director of the Weimar Court Theatre, Schiller had reassessed his earlier embrace of Storm and Stress's more unruly dramaturgical structures; his late plays reflect an interest in classical restraint and Enlightenment morality. Indeed, many Germans would later celebrate the "Weimar classicism" that Schiller and Goethe achieved in their productions at the Court Theatre as models of nationalism that opposed the explicit xenophobia that more fervent German nationalists expressed during the nineteenth century. Our case study for this chapter tests the Weimar experiment against Schiller's concept of a transformative aesthetic experience that could help to shape his ideal of a German nation.

CASE STUDY: Friedrich Schiller's vision of aesthetic education and the German dream of a national theatre

Gary Jay Williams

> ... *If we had a national stage, we would also become a nation.*

> Friedrich Schiller 1784

In recent years, theatre historians have been exploring the relations between theatre/performance and national/cultural identity. This has been fruitful because of theatre's conspicuous place as a mirror of culture in the public sphere. German-speaking peoples, more than most, have aggressively pursued the idea that theatre and the other arts are necessary to the health of a society. In fact, the effort may be rightly characterized as having become an attribute of German culture.

The ideas of playwright, historian, and theorist Friedrich Schiller are significant in that pursuit. This case study explains Schiller's vision, advanced in his *Letters on the Aesthetic Education of Man* (1795), in which he proposes that aesthetic experience can contribute to the social good in its power to better integrate human sensibility.

Basing his ideas on Immanuel Kant's (1724–1804) Enlightenment philosophy of art, Schiller argued that dramatic art could heal the eighteenth-century division between reason and feeling. This case study speculates on whether Schiller's tragedy for the Weimar stage, *Mary Stuart*, probably his finest play, contributed to the kind of aesthetic education he hoped would make humankind whole. In doing so, it raises one of the questions that studies in theatre and national identity often do: Did *Mary Stuart* fulfill the mission of a theatre that aspires to form the life of a nation?

Schiller's vision and its context

Dreaming of a theatre that would be a voice of German culture and a force in shaping it, Schiller wrote in his 1784 essay, "The Stage as a Moral Institution":

> If all our plays were governed by one principle, if our poets were agreed and allied to this end, if a rigorous selection guided their work and their brushes were dedicated only to national matters – in a word, if we had a national theatre, we would also become a nation.
>
> (Schiller 1985: 217–8)

Dismayed by the French Revolution, especially its Reign of Terror that guillotined thousands of French citizens in 1793–1794, Schiller believed that the savagery of the masses after the Revolution showed that the Enlightenment had failed to touch the heart and make humankind whole. In his letters *On the Aesthetic Education of Man* (1795), Schiller looked to the potential of art to heal what he believed to be the fragmented psyche of modern humankind, to restore the balance between reason and feeling, between intuitive and rational processes. This harmony, he asserted, would never be restored by political means or by revolution. Only through aesthetic experience can modern man become whole: "it is only through Beauty that man makes his way to Freedom" (Wilkinson and Willoughby 1967: 9, Letter 2; Sharpe 1991: 146–8). Kant's philosophy provided the credible base for this theory, and Schiller, working especially from Kant's *Critique of Judgment*, hoped to make a case that art could renew the social order.

In Kant's quest to articulate the first principles of human understanding (*Critique of Pure Reason*, 1781), the philosopher argued that through the use of reason any individual will be able to understand and can live up to the basic principles of knowledge and moral action, without recourse to any metaphysics or the divine. Rather, it is through the data of our experience that our reason derives the laws of nature and human conduct. In his *Critique of Judgment* (1791), Kant argues that our aesthetic judgments, though free expressions of individual autonomy, must also be based in cognitive capacities we share with others if such judgments are to have any claim on their assent (Kant 1971: Sections VII and VIII). Yet, this pleasurable exercise is not constrained by rules. It involves "free play" between the imagination and understanding. The aesthetic work of artistic genius cannot properly be judged by how well it conforms to external standards (such as neoclassical rules). Nor can art be judged by whether it fulfills some external, pragmatic purpose (moral instruction). The aesthetic object has an internal purposiveness, stated Kant, a "purposiveness without purpose" (Kant 1971: xv, 386–7).

Schiller wanted to take this idea further and attempted to show that art had the potential to do work in the world, that the aesthetic experience could reintegrate reason and feelings. Schiller certainly agreed with Kant that art should not attempt direct moral instruction. He and Goethe disapproved of the domesticated moralizing of eighteenth-century sentimental drama, and his plays of the 1780s, such as *Passion and Politics* and *Don Carlos,* have a complexity that does not allow them to be reduced to simplistic lessons. Schiller believed the theatre should have the poetic dimension of transcendent, classical art; this would give theatrical productions social efficacy, but of a higher order. Influenced by Kant's notion of the "play-drive" in humankind, Schiller contends that the ultimate form of play is the contemplation of beauty. "Man only plays when he is in the fullest sense of the word a human being, and he is only fully a human being when he plays" (Wilkinson and Willoughby 1967: 107, Letter 15). It is this "play," this contemplation of the beautiful that will restore in humankind that lost unity of sensibility. Schiller's reference point here was an idealized vision of ancient Greece that had allowed for the development of the balanced individual.

Schiller joined Goethe at the Weimar Court Theatre in 1799 for their legendary artistic partnership (Figure 8.1). They made "an open declaration of war on naturalism in art" and sought to create a poetic theatre where they could give their audience experiences that would refine and educate them (Sharpe 1991: 253). Their plays and their carefully disciplined production style became known as "Weimar classicism." Schiller wrote five historical verse dramas for Weimar: *Wallenstein's Camp* (1799), *Mary Stuart* (1800), *The Maid of Orleans* (1801, his St. Joan play), *The Bride of Messina* (1803), and *William Tell* (1804). "For only great affairs will have the power/To stimulate mankind's first principles," wrote Schiller in his prologue for the reopening of the remodeled Weimar with his *Wallenstein's Camp* (Schiller 1991: 9). Goethe staged all of these history plays with historically accurate settings and costumes, the better for audiences to contemplate the magnitude of the issues.

Schiller's vision for German nationhood was probably best expressed in *Mary Stuart,* one of his most enduring works. The playwright creates his tragedy out of the conflict between the famed queens of English Renaissance history, depicting Mary's final days leading up to her execution by her half-sister, Queen Elizabeth. He invents a one-on-one meeting between them for his capstone scene. He characterizes Elizabeth as the woman who has a clear understanding that the throne will often require her to sacrifice herself in order to rule with an iron will. Schiller's Catholic Mary is a charismatic and sometimes impetuous woman who, following her strong passions, has inspired devotion in her followers but also made profound moral errors. The women might be said to exemplify Schiller's view of the modern splintered psyche. Neither character is whole – Elizabeth the rational, political pragmatist or Mary, the emotionally alive, charismatic spirit. Mary, confronting the inevitability of her execution at Elizabeth's hand, achieves grace and serenity at the end. Schiller attempts to embody this spiritual transcendence by having Mary receive the sacraments from a priest before going to her death. At the end of the play, Elizabeth, victim of the necessity of being the guardian of order and power, is left on stage alone.

Figure 8.1

The Weimar Court Theatre interior in 1798. Prosperous bourgeoisie sat on red-covered benches in the orchestra, poorer spectators upstairs in the side galleries, and the duke in the rear center of the gallery. On this stage (approximately 38-feet wide), Schiller and Goethe staged their plays with historical period settings and costumes, an innovation that had wide influence.

Source: Drawing by Alfred Pretzsch in Philipp Stein, *Deutsche Schauspieler, Eine Bildnissammlung*, Berlin 1907, reproduced in Michael Patterson, *The First German Theatre*, Routledge, 1990.

The tragedy was reported to have been successful at Weimar, as were all of Schiller's plays. But if we are to hold Schiller to his vision, we must ask if his theatre produced the kind of transformative aesthetic experience for spectators that Schiller envisioned would result in the healing of the divided modern sensibility. German theatre historian Erika Fischer-Lichte thinks this unlikely, arguing that few audience members at Weimar would have been able to resist emotional identification with the major characters. This would have prevented them from achieving the kind of distance that is implied in Schiller's characterization of the contemplative aesthetic experience from which a balanced self would emerge (Fischer-Lichte 2004: 197–9). To this, we may add that Goethe's occasional autocratic scolding of Weimar audience members from his box and his heavy fining of actors for "extemporizing" and for unrefined comic business in violation of his stringent *Rules for Actors* suggest that audiences were not always experiencing aesthetic contemplation (Schwind 1997: 100, 98). In addition, during Goethe's administration of the theatre until 1826, pieces by August von Kotzebue and A.W. Iffland (1759–1814), plus melodramas, comedies, and other lightweight works, were staged twice as often as plays by Lessing, Goethe, Shakespeare and Schiller

(Sosulski 2007: 27–8). The idealistic Weimar theatre had to offer popular fare to make its budget, only a third of which was covered by its patron, the Duke.

Schiller's dream of an aesthetic experience that could heal the modern psyche probably was never realizable. Nonetheless, many Germans today see a vital connection between the productions of their government-funded theatres, whose work is often challenging and controversial, and their lives as engaged citizens.

THINKING THROUGH THEATRE HISTORIES: STUDIES IN THEATRE AND NATIONAL IDENTITY

The relationship between theatre and nationalism has grown over the last 40 years. The scholarly work in this field is related to the larger issue of how nations define themselves, an interest spurred by many contemporary developments. Among them have been the struggles of once-colonized nations to reshape their identities, "ethnic cleansing" in Europe and Africa, anxiety about newly ethnically and religiously heterogenous populations in Europe, and, of course, globalization, which implicitly challenges notions of national identity. Studies in theatre and national/cultural identity draw on a range of late twentieth-century scholars of cultural history and philosophy. For example, Raymond Williams and Fredric Jameson articulated the implications for literature and the arts of the classical Marxist critique of capitalism and the oppressive social structures it creates, in which nation-states have been complicit. Eric Hobsbawm and others have shown how nations reinvent their "traditions" to try to produce a coherent national narrative. And Benedict Anderson's *Imagined Communities* (1991), much used by theatre historians, offered the concept of nations as imagined political communities. Performance can play a part in creating imagined communities. Patricia Ybarra, for example, has shown how the excavated ruins of Mesoamerican civilizations in Mexico have been used in performances for Mexican audiences of tourists to suggest an imaginary national heritage (Ybarra 2005). Loren Kruger's *The National Stage: Theatre and Cultural Legitimization in England, France, and America* (1992) shows the contradictions between the pretexts and the actual practices of three distinct twentieth-century national theatres. In the process, Kruger raises important questions about the funding of theatres in democracies. (For a detailed reading of the relationship between Nationalism and the development of the Irish theatre, see the case study on the Playboy riots in the *Theatre Histories* website.)

Key references

Anderson, B. (1991) *Imagined Communities*, 2nd edn, London: Verso.

Fischer-Lichte, E. (2004) *History of European Drama and Theatre*, trans. J. Riley, London and New York: Routledge.

Hobsbawm, E., and T. Ranger. (eds.) (1983) *The Invention of Tradition*, Cambridge and New York: Cambridge University Press.

Kant, I. (1971) *Critique of Judgment*, trans. J.H. Bernard (1931), in H. Adams (ed.) *Critical Theory since Plato*, New York: Harcourt Brace Janovich.

Kindermann, H. (1961) *Theatergeschichte Europas*, Vol. IV, Salzburg: Otto Müller Verlag.

Kruger, L. (1992) *The National Stage: Theatre and Cultural Legitimization in England, France and America*, Chicago, IL and London: University of Chicago Press.

Lessing, G.E. (1962) *Hamburg Dramaturgy*, trans. H. Zimmerman with a new introduction by Victor Lange, New York: Dover Publications.

Patterson, M. (1990) *The First German Theatre, Schiller, Goethe, Kleist and Büchner in Performance*, London and New York: Routledge, 1990.

Sharpe, L. (1991) *Friedrich Schiller, Drama, Thought, and Politics*, Cambridge: Cambridge University Press.

Schiller, F. (1962) *Love and Intrigue,* English version by F. Rolf with an introduction by E.P. Kurz, Great Neck, NY: Barron's Education Series.

—————— (1971) *Letters on the Aesthetic Education of Man, in* H. Adams (ed.) *Critical Theory since Plato,* New York: Harcourt Brace Janovich.

—————— (1985) "Theatre Considered as a Moral Institution," trans. By J. Sigerson and J. Chambless, in *Friedrich Schiller, Poet of Freedom,* Schiller Institute. New York: New Benjamin Franklin House, 209–220.

—————— (1991) *Wallenstein* and *Mary Stuart* (ed.) W. Hinderer, *trans.* C.E. Passage. New York: Continuum Publishing.

—————— (1998) *Schiller, Five Plays,* trans. R.D. MacDonald, London: Oberon Books.

Schwind, K. (1997) "'No Laughing!' Autonomous Art and the Body of the Actor in Goethe's Weimar," *Theatre Survey* 38 (November 1997): 89–108.

Sosulski, M.J. (2007) *Theater and Nation in Eighteenth Century Germany*, Williston, Vermont: Ashgate Publishing.

Wilkinson, E.M., and L.A. Willoughby. (1967) (eds.) *Friedrich Schiller: On the Aesthetic Education of Man in a Series of Letters,* Oxford: Oxford University Press.

Ybarra, P. (2005) "Staging the Nation on the Ruins of the Past: An Investigation of Mexican Archeological Performance," in K. Gounaridou (ed.) *Staging Nationalism: Essays on Theatre and National Identity,* Jefferson, NC and London: McFarland, 186–210.

The French Revolution, melodrama, and nationalism

Before the Revolution of 1789, many Europeans looked to France as the most prosperous and civilized country in the world. The French Revolution and the chaos that followed during the 1790s, however, shocked the European bourgeoisie. The civil strife and international wars of the late 1790s brought more bloodshed and confusion, and many Europeans were relieved when Napoleon Bonaparte emerged as a strong leader in 1799. Although Napoleon's rule ensured stability in France, his imperial ambitions soon brought parts of the Revolution to the rest of Europe and the Americas. The former saw intermittent warfare until 1815, while in Latin America the turmoil continued through 1825. We will examine the ramifications of the revolutionary era for the Americas later in this chapter.

Political transformations reconfigured the predominant genres of European theatre. Pre-revolutionary aristocrats and bourgeoisie in France, Great Britain, and Germany had been applauding neoclassical and sentimental comedies and tragedies, together with several minor genres. Twenty years later, by 1810, most European theatregoers in these countries saw nationalistic spectacles, gothic thrillers, and melodramas. In theatres where heroic virtues or genteel pathos had inspired neoclassical or sentimental responses, the emotions of rage, fear, and panic now stirred audiences. For spectators who had weathered the Revolution, either directly or vicariously, the temperate values of pre-revolutionary times seemed quaint and uninteresting. Some pre-1789 plays continued to be performed, but few dramatists after 1800 wrote popular plays within the old conventions. In short, the revolutionary era had transformed the dramatic genres of European theatre. How had this happened?

The shattered expectations of theatregoers in Paris during the Revolution help us understand the transformation. According to historian Matthew S. Buckley, several events occurred between 1791 and 1794 that alienated Parisian playgoers from the kinds of enjoyments that they had come to expect from the old genres. Consequently, the Revolution "became a nightmarish, originary drama of modernism, a material, historical experience of [traditional] drama's failure that could be neither reversed nor banished from cultural awareness" (Buckley 2006: 6). By the start of 1791, many in Paris (including several revolutionaries) expected that the antipathy between the people and the French crown would soon play out like a sentimental comedy, with the king and the revolutionaries agreeing to a constitutional monarchy. After all, the first stages of the Revolution had witnessed the Declaration of the Rights of Man, the abolition of state monopolies, and attempts to separate the French Catholic Church from the power of Rome. In line with these movements, many Parisians assumed that King Louis XVI might decide to accept a limited role in ruling, much like the king of Great Britain.

Instead of a reconciliation, however, King Louis attempted to flee the country with his family in June of 1791. This revealed to many Parisians that the hope of a sentimental ending had been a seductive fiction all along, setting the stage for the king's execution in 1793. During the so-called Reign of Terror in 1793–1794, when the revolutionary leader Maximilian Robespierre and his Committee of Public Safety were attempting to purge the Revolution of its enemies, many Parisians looked upon this lawyer-turned-politician as an incorruptible hero in a neoclassic tragedy and they cheered his attempt to form a republic of virtue. But, instead of sacrificing himself to establish an era of peace and goodness in the neoclassical mode, Robespierre's Terror petered out alongside his botched suicide attempt. Further, the Terror, in which Enlightenment ideas were deployed to justify the legal execution of over 40,000 citizens in France, led many Parisians to conclude that the Enlightenment principles behind many sentimental and neoclassical plays could only end in chaos and horror. When the events of the Revolution rendered old dramatic genres unreliable and irrelevant, Parisians sought new ones.

Many traumatized by revolution, terror, and war found a hopeful replacement for the old plays in the genre of **melodrama**, a form of drama with a simple plot, accompanying music, rigid moral dichotomies, and attendant spectacle. Melodrama, as a distinct genre, emerged in 1800 with the production of *Coelina, Or the Child of Mystery*, by René Charles Guilbert de Pixérécourt (1773–1844). Soon, several other playwrights were writing melodramas and the new genre was all the rage in the boulevard theatres of Paris for the rest of the decade. Melodrama may have reassured a traumatized people, but it could never fully allay the gut-wrenching fears, moral panic, and violence experienced by many Parisians.

Had it not been for the network of periodical print culture in Europe, the traumas of the revolutionary decade in Paris might have remained relatively isolated. Journalists, poets, travelers, and others spread the word about the events of the Revolution, first to the French provinces and then to all European capitals. Reading about these events in Paris produced the feeling that the bottom had dropped out of their world. This sentiment contrasts with the spirit of possibility the Revolution inspired in Haiti, where disparate groups of white planters, artisans, free Blacks and slaves used this example to imagine autonomy from France and freedom from chattel slavery. In Europe, however, such vicarious experiences of violence led playgoers, like their counterparts in Paris, to sense that the older forms of comedy and tragedy could no longer accommodate what they were reading about in their newspapers. In the wake of the Revolution and especially during the European and American wars that followed, melodrama claimed increasingly larger audiences.

Although few of the early melodramas were overtly nationalistic, most undercut the so-called rational and ethical basis of liberal nationalism. The Revolution, coupled with the Rousseauian thinking of the previous decade (see Chapter 7), induced a desire for utopia in which naturally good people might create a society in which evil could be banished from the world. *Coelina* and other plays in the new genre often depicted such a utopia, typically finding it in idealized visions of traditional peasant life. The early melodramas enjoined Europeans to make firm distinctions between hero and villain, French and Prussian, "us" and "them" (Figure 8.2).

These same principles undergirded the ra-

Figure 8.2
This print depicts a scene from Pixerecourt's *The Forest of Bondy*, still popular in 1843 when this illustration (known as a "penny character print") was published. For this exciting melodrama, a dog was trained to jump at the throat of the actor playing the villain, the killer of the dog's master. Penny character print, Mr. Cony-Landri-Webb.
Source: HTC 28, 321. Harvard Theatre Collection.

cial melodramas of the United States (which we will consider later in the chapter) and Orientalist melodramas that created dichotomies between "enlightened" and despotic rulers. Such clear-cut morality might be the ethics of fairy-tale allegories and simplistic (and xenophobic) nationalisms, but it avoided the kinds of hard choices, and emphasis on rationality that Schiller dramatized between his two queens in *Mary Stuart*. Like the plays of Kotzebue, described in the online case study, melodrama elevated nature and intuition over reason as better guides to morality and possible utopia.

Melodrama flourished on European and American stages for the rest of the nineteenth century, reshaping much of their theatre. Because audiences enjoyed melodramatic spectacles, the genre helped to transform the two-dimensionality of chariot-and-pole staging into more realistic scenic illusions. As the size of stages expanded to accommodate the increased demand for spectacle, playwrights called for more three-dimensional scenic units, such as fortresses that could collapse in an explosion and a mountain that a horse and rider could ascend to near the top of the proscenium, for example. By the 1880s, melodramatic ice floes, steaming trains, and galloping horses – the latter done with treadmills and revolving

SCENE FROM "LOST IN LONDON," AT THE ADELPHI THEATRE.

Figure 8.3

Final scene from *Lost in London* at the Adelphi Theatre. This image shows the high contrast of light and dark in melodrama scenography.

Source: *The Illustrated London News*, 6 Apr 1867, p. 341. Courtesy of Adelphi Theatre Collection or Gale.

scenery – were stretching the ingenuity and endurance of technicians and stagehands. As Devin Griffiths claims, in addition to human labor and ingenuity, melodramatic plays also needed the products of extraction – such as oil and gas – to power their stage technologies, especially theatrical lighting. Creating high contrast shadow and light necessary for tableaus and the Manichean morality was part and parcel of the era. (See Figure 8.3.) Today, we might consider melodrama's relation to modernity not only in relation to ideological content, but its participation in an energy regime whose consequences are being debated daily today. The appearance of battles or conflicts between man and machine makes this aspect of melodrama visible.

The wide appeal of melodrama, in part dependent on this technical virtuosity, broadened theatrical audiences. In addition to the middle class, which continued to provide the core audience for melodrama, working-class spectators began attending the theatre in increasing numbers after the 1820s, enjoying plays like *The Carpenter of Rouen* (1837) that pitted plebeian avengers against decadent aristocrats. Moral reform melodramas such as *The Bottle* (1847) and *Uncle Tom's Cabin* (1852) even converted some sober, antitheatrical

Figure 8.4
Henry Irving in his production of *The Bells* at the Lyceum Theatre, London, 1871.
Source: 12/Alamy Stock Photo.

Protestants into playgoers. After 1840, many star-struck spectators enjoyed their favorite actors in melodramatic spectacles, such as English star Henry Irving (1838–1905) (Figure 8.4). Melodrama organized the dramatic plots of many nationalistic war plays, mixing easily with Romantic drama.

European cultural nationalisms, 1815–1848

After 1815, versions of cultural nationalism flourished in most European countries (Figure 8.5). When Enlightenment thinkers looked at history in the eighteenth century, they tried to deduce universal principles about human behavior from the past that they could apply to all nations in the present and future. Historian Johann Gottfried von Herder (1744–1803), however, denied that this was possible. In his *Ideas on the Philosophy of the History of Mankind* (1784), Herder argued that everyone's understanding of the past was necessarily subservient to a ***Volksgeist*** [FOYKLS-gahyst], a German word that means the spirit of a national people. Not even well-trained historians could transcend their particular *Volksgeist* to write universal history because the history of each national people was unique, said Herder, and historical interpretation was necessarily tied to the ideas and values of the *volk*, the nation. Modifications of Herder's ideas shaped most discussions about cultural nationalism

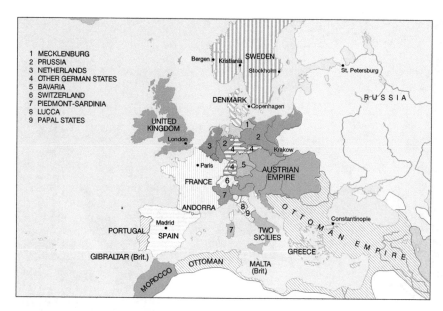

Figure 8.5
Political map of Europe in 1820.

throughout the nineteenth century. Europeans oppressed by the French looked to Herder and his followers to justify their nation's opposition to French imperialism. Although Herder himself never argued that one nation or racial group might be superior to others, several of his later disciples claimed that his historicism justified their sense of national and/or racial superiority. Herder's legacy animated many historians and others to search for the origins of their nation's *Volksgeist*, and to celebrate their own national heroes. Many of Herder's ideas continue to be influential today.

Cultural nationalism based in a version of Herder's ideas played out differently in various European countries. In Great Britain, victorious in the fight against Napoleon, conservative cultural nationalists mostly relived past glories. On the London stage in the 1820s and 1830s, for example, star actor T.P. Cooke (1786–1864) presented the manly and sentimental virtues of an idealized English seaman. Cooke had actually served in the English navy against the French and used this experience to promote his image as the archetypal British sailor. As the beleaguered seaman hero in Douglas Jerrold's *Black-Ey'd Susan* (1829), Cooke found his most popular vehicle, performing it 785 times in his long career. Jerrold's melodrama led to several other plays featuring heroic sailors – and eventually to W.S. Gilbert's brilliant parody of the character type in the operetta, *H.M.S. Pinafore* (1878). Of course, many of these plays also simply gave spectators a chance to enjoy themselves as authors delivered their nationalistic messages.

Also in the 1820s, British theatre artists began working with historians to mount more accurate productions of national historical plays, principally the dramas of Shakespeare. These productions were a part of a movement, **Antiquarianism**, which emerged in the late eighteenth century and aimed to immerse spectators in the details of historical cultures by rendering historically accurate settings and detail. Under Antiquarianism, Shakespearean

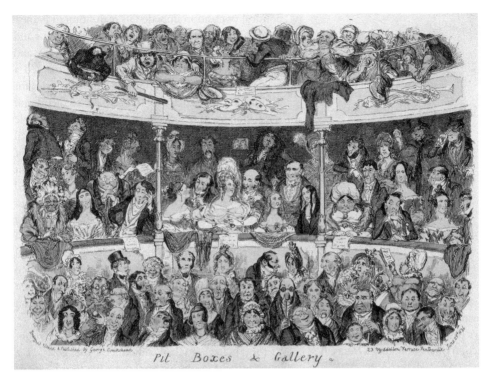

Figure 8.6
George Cruikshank, "Pit, boxes, and Galleries" (1834).
Source: © British Library Board. All Rights Reserved/Bridgeman Images.

productions in England became a means of honoring the genius of the national poet and offering a conservative understanding of the national past. English Antiquarianism began with Charles Kemble's (1775–1854) production of *King John* in 1824. James Robinson Planché (1796–1880) based his costuming of Kemble's actors on scrupulous research into medieval dress, an innovation welcomed by Kemble's bourgeois audience. Planché, a leader in antiquarianism, costumed subsequent Shakespearean productions with attention to historical detail and provided managers with extensive information on the banners and insignia of medieval heraldry (Figure 8.7). William Charles Macready (1793–1873), who dominated the English stage from the 1830s into the early 1840s, popularized the goals of antiquarianism by aiming consistently for historical accuracy in costuming, props, and painted scenery for his major productions. This form of cultural nationalism in England pushed conservative values and emotional attachments to historical artifacts and ancient customs.

In contrast, most French cultural nationalists split into radical, conservative, and reactionary factions, with each group claiming to represent the true identity of France. In addition, liberal nationalists hoped to revive the French constitutionalism of the first three years of the Revolution. After 1815, these factions clashed in several areas of French culture, including the advent of Romanticism on the French stage. **Romanticism** had become popular in England and Germany, and had emerged in Austria and the Italian states, but

Figure 8.7

James Robinson Planché's antiquarian design for the king's costume in Charles Kemble's 1824 production of Shakespeare's *Henry IV, Part 1.*

Source: From Planché's *Costume of Shakespeare's King Henry IV, Parts I and II* (1824). © Lilly Library, Indiana University, Bloomington.

political opposition impeded its realization in France. In brief, Romanticism celebrated artistic genius and ambitious action. In the music of Beethoven and the poetry of Wordsworth, Romanticism marked a new point on the continuum of cultural modes for gaining knowledge about the self. In medieval and early modern times, Western culture taught people to look primarily to external entities – the feudal order, the Church, and absolutist structures – for self-understanding. Beginning with the Protestant Reformation, Western culture increasingly invited humans to discover purpose and understanding from within. Most French radicals and liberals supported Romanticism, although the liberals were skeptical that heroic action could provide a basis for political legitimacy. French reactionaries, however, yearned for a return to a Catholic and absolutist Europe and modeled their hopes for French theatrical culture on the neoclassical era of Molière and Racine.

Leading the liberals was novelist and playwright Victor Hugo, who had announced the goals of a Romantic theatre in his preface to the play *Cromwell* in 1827. The French traditionalists took their stand in 1830 at the Comédie Française's production of Hugo's *Hernani.* Hugo had added some political conservatives to the liberals among his supporters for *Hernani*, a play that intentionally violated many of the rules of neoclassicism and incorporated several scenes of melodramatic action. After an initial three nights of calm, a shouting and shoving match raged for the remaining 36 performances between the Romantics and the traditionalists in the audience, drowning out the actors (Figure 8.8). In the end, most of the Parisian press hailed the Romantics as the victors, chiefly for outlasting their opponents. Following the riots, French Romanticism, with frequent injections of melodrama, achieved widespread success in the 1830s and 1840s. These included the generally liberal plays of Hugo and the conservative costume dramas of Alexandre Dumas (1802–1870), such as *Henri III and His Court* (1829) and his adaptation of *The Three Musketeers* (1844).

Actors were also important to the Revolutionary cause, exemplified in the theatre by the career of actor-playwright Frederick Lemaître (1800–1876). Through the roles he played, Lemaître came to embody the revolutionary values of heroic freedom and working-class grit denied to most French citizens by a conservative French state between 1815 and 1848. While most liberal and conservative artists and critics understood the state and the nation as one, Lemaître's vehicles implicitly divided the French state from the nation of French people in order to criticize the repressive regime installed in Paris after Napoleon's defeat. Lemaître played a wide variety of melodramatic roles between 1825 and 1850 in an emotionally volatile style. Novelist Victor Hugo praised Lemaître as "capable of movements, utterances, cries that could cause an audience to shudder violently, and of astounding flashes which transfigured him and made him appear in the dazzling halo of absolute greatness" (Hemmings 1993: 221).

Lemaître gained fame in 1823 when he played the dashing thief Robert Macaire. Although he used the character to parody the style of early melodrama, he also aimed some pointed barbs at the current French state for its graft and greed, including in the 1834 play *Robert Macaire*. In this vehicle, Lemaître's anti-hero attacked the villainy and hypocrisy of the wealthy, especially those who had profited from the Revolution of 1830 in Paris. Not surprisingly, the authorities eventually banned all melodramas about Macaire, including several other plays that hinted at the character type. This censorship, of course, helped the star to seal his image as the defender of France's revolutionary heritage. In the 1840s, Lemaître chose several vehicles that also positioned him as a champion of the poor. He appeared, for instance, in a feature role in a stage adaptation of *The Mysteries of Paris* in 1844, an exposé of Parisian poverty. Lemaître inspired cultural nationalism in many of his spectators by contrasting present corruption with the remembered glories of 1789.

Figure 8.8

Contemporary illustration of the *Hernani* riots, showing the audience and the final scene of Hugo's play on stage at the Comédie Française in 1830.

Source: Bibliothèque nationale de France.

In Germany and Eastern Europe, nationalism tended to unite radical cultural nationalists and liberal constitutionalists in plans for transforming groups of language-based peoples into nation-states. Earlier German attempts to establish national theatres and write national history plays set the precedent for later cultural nationalists among the small German states and within the Austrian and Russian empires, including Poland, which was partitioned by Russia, Prussia and the Hapsburg Empire, and Hungary (under Hapsburg rule during most of the nineteenth century).

Polish cultural identity in the Polish-Lithuanian Commonwealth was complicated by the association of Polishness with a class of nobility, the *szlachta*, who imagined themselves as descendants of an ancient tribe of Sarmatians, rather than as sharing a common ethnic heritage with those of other classes. Julian Ursyn Niemcewicz's 1791 *Return of the Deputy* satirized the greed of Sarmatian nobles, while arguing for Polish identity to accrue to active citizenship rather than noble status. Not long after, Poland would disappear from European maps for 100 years, but Niemcewicz and other playwrights' ideas would be elaborated upon by Polish Romanticists throughout the nineteenth century. In addition, several Hungarian-language plays in the 1840s dramatized the plight of Hungarian peasants under the rule of Austrian aristocrats. In Prague, cultural nationalists published articles, books, and plays arguing for the independence of Czech lands from the Austrian empire.

These and other national aspirations exploded in the revolutions of 1848. In that year, temporarily bonded coalitions of people demanding constitutional rights, the independence of national groups, and an end to remaining feudal privileges staged revolts in Paris, Copenhagen, Budapest, and Palermo (Sicily). Revolution spread to other cities, and gained support among many liberal groups in central and eastern Europe. In France, Parisians rallied to the barricades to oust an unpopular king, but ended up with the nephew of Napoleon for an emperor. Although Polish, Czech, and Hungarian nationalists threatened for a short time to pull apart the Austrian Empire, the emperor's army routed the rebels and suppressed calls for separate constitutions and independence. An assembly of liberal German delegates met for nearly a year in Frankfurt to form a unified, constitutional German state and offered to make King Frederick of Prussia its constitutional monarch, but he refused, dashing hopes for a liberal German nation. By 1850, serfdom had been abolished throughout Europe (except in Russia) and a few small states had gained more liberal constitutions. None of the stateless European national groups had gained independence, however, and many of their leaders were dead or in prison. Only after the Great War, later known as World War I (1914–1918), and the dissolution of several European empires would cultural nationalists climb to political power within the new nation-states of Ireland, Czechoslovakia, Poland, Finland, and several others. Although the radicals and liberals of 1848–1849 mostly failed to achieve their goals, they did validate the political power of cultural nationalism.

Nationalism in Russia and Italy developed differently than in other parts of Europe. Although Russia, the most agrarian, economically underdeveloped, and politically repressive of European empires had been nurturing pockets of cultural nationalism, both among the majority of Russian-speaking peoples and within its many ethnic minorities, its cultural shifts did not correspond with the revolutions of 1848. Russia was mired in war with many other European countries for much of the first half of the nineteenth century, ending only with the Crimean War (1853–1856). And in the aftermath of the failure of the Decembrist Revolt of 1825, in which a group of nobles refused the leadership of Tsar Nicholas, a series of laws outlining political crimes were placed on the books, leaving autocratic rule in place for most of the rest of the century. Combined with extensive censorship of printed material throughout the nineteenth century, political dissent was greatly discouraged. Nonetheless, there was active construction of Russian identity throughout the century, including within the theatre.

Russian theatre shed the marginal status it had at the beginning of the nineteenth century, resulting in a rich theatre culture. Most performances were in imperial, court and private theatres in Saint Petersburg and Moscow. Serf theatre companies, where serfs (agricultural laborers bound under the feudal system to work for their noble lords) played most or all of the roles, were also immensely popular. Some of these serfs were privately owned by individuals, while others were sold in groups as companies to private theatres. These performers were not free subjects choosing their labors, although some star performers were occasionally freed or permitted social mobility. (Non-serf actors were usually orphans or commoners.) While social hierarchies remained, the theatre was one of the few places where nobles and non-nobles collaborated, although audiences continued to be watched from the parterre. These audiences did not constitute an imagined community as they might have in France, England and Germany. Nonetheless, these audiences saw plays that debated Russian national character; audiences would broaden during the popular theatre movements of the 1860s and 1870s.

Conditions leading up to the War of 1812 marked a turning point in the construction of Russian identity. Until that point, much of the Russian nobility valorized French culture and some did not even speak Russian. Formerly, French-language theatres in Russia received twice the amount of subsidy that Russian theatres did. From 1815 to the 1830s, after the tsar's victory over Napoleon's invading army in 1812, the court and the aristocracy cheered a spate of conservative and reactionary plays and historical dramas. Still influenced by French theatrical forms, however, much of the repertoire Russian theatregoers applauded in the middle decades of the century were melodramas and historical pageants. Notably, the ongoing battle between Francophilic and native Slavophilic cultural identities among the educated nobility continued throughout much of the century as did debates about liberal and orthodox views of the monarchy, and the use of the church versus a social system for the well-being of citizens. Writers, actors, and critics of various aesthetic and political persuasions all made a claim to nationalism.

Censorship, however, inhibited Russian theatre production for native playwrights. The regime did not allow playgoers to see the work of many Russian Romantic playwrights. Like the French Romantics, Russian poet Alexander Pushkin (1799–1837) turned to history for inspiration, but the radical politics of his play *Boris Godunov* (1825), a sprawling masterpiece, kept it out of publication until 1831 and off the stage entirely until 1870. Censorship eased somewhat in the 1850s, allowing the staging of Mikhail Lermontov's (1814–1841) *Masquerade* (1835), inspired by Shakespeare's *Othello*. However, his play *The Spaniards* (1830) – exposing the similarities between Tsar Nicholas I's reign (from 1825 to 1855) and the Spanish Inquisition – was published but not performed during the nineteenth century. (Remarkably, this play was one that contained sympathetic Jewish characters.) Russian comic satirists A.S. Griboyedov (1794–1829) in *Woe from Wit* (1825; performed 1833) and Nikolai Gogol (1809–1852) in *The Inspector General* (1836) had more success with their attacks on individual bumblers, embezzlers, sycophants, and hypocrites, in part because their generally conservative politics offered little offense to the ideology of the autocratic regime. Actors in these plays were often able to explore identity in ways that complicated the content of the plays, however. Mikhail Shchepkin (1888–1863), a former serf, who starred in both *The Inspector General* and *Woe from Wit*, "embodied authentic *narodnost* [national identity] as both Westernizers and Slavophiles had begun to conceptualize it during the interwar years" (Schuler 2009: 175). His style of acting presaged the move to Russian realism, and was highly regarded by playwrights of all political orientations.

Later in the century, the loosening of censorship, the freeing of the serfs in 1861, shifts in the judicial system (1864), and the playwriting of Alexander Ostrovsky (1823–1886) changed the Russian theatre. Ostrovsky wrote in a variety of genres, but found his greatest success in dramas of domestic realism for and about the Russian middle class. *The Thunderstorm* (1859), for example, explores the tragic results of a parent's oppression, while *Enough Stupidity for Every Wise Man* (1868) follows the comic success of a man who manipulates the foibles and stupidities of others. Ostrovsky, whose often ironic tone and focus on domestic situations influenced the plays of his countryman Anton Chekhov (discussed in Chapter 10), encouraged other realist writers to turn to the stage. Given the constraints of tsarist absolutism, Ostrovsky steered clear of overt politics or narrow definitions of Russian nationalism. But by welcoming the emerging Russian bourgeoisie into the theatre with his plays, Ostrovsky ensured a wider, more public audience for future dramatic discussions about Russia. He also brought the tension between adherence to traditional communitarian ideals and liberal individualist action to the stage in his dramas about everyday life. This conversation continued with productions of the historical dramas of Aleksei K. Tolstoy (1817–1875), second cousin to Leo, the great novelist. In his trilogy of plays about three Russian feudal monarchs, *The Death of Ivan the Terrible* (1866), *Tsar Fyodor Ivanovich* (1868), and *Tsar Boris* (1870), Tolstoy focused on the psychological and ethical ramifications of political rule. Most historical plays, however, like many operas and ballets popular with the regime, continued to conflate tsarist rule, Christianity, patriotism, and imperialism until the Russian Revolution of 1917.

Meanwhile, some in Italy began looking for ways to unify their disparate populace. Few people in Southern Italy and Sicily had any interest in nationalism. But patriots in the north were agitating for Italian unification and insurrections broke out in 1848 in several northern cities and in Rome, where a constitutional republic lasted for three months. After the failures of 1848 in Italy, patriots looked to the king of Piedmont as a potential standard-bearer for the military unification of the country. Led by the Piedmontese prime minister and aided by Giuseppe Garibaldi's army in the south, the state of Piedmont unified most of Italy in 1861, later adding Venice and Rome to its territory. But, Italy in 1870 was a nation only in name. Culturally, socially, and economically, the north and south had few interests in common, especially given the subordination of the south to northern capitalistic interests. Lacking a common language, written or spoken, most Italian subjects could not easily communicate across regions; what is now standard, modern Italian only emerged and spread in the twentieth century.

Despite their divisions, Italians in all regions did share a love for opera. Many nationalists celebrated the works of Giuseppe Verdi (1813–1901) for their apparent endorsement of national unity. Ironically, though, Verdi's operas actually had very little to say about Italian nationalism. Verdi was a patriot, but he stayed in Paris during the uprisings of 1848 and for most of the 1850s; and he never considered himself "the maestro of the revolution." Most of his operas center on love triangles among historical characters. His only vaguely nationalistic opera was *The Battle of Legnano* (1849), set in the twelfth century, which praised Italy as "a single people of heroes" in its opening chorus and featured a second act that heaped scorn on Austria (Gilmour 2011: 170). Perhaps because the opera was staged in Rome during its short-lived days as a republic, Italian nationalists seized on *Legnano* as a symbol of Italian independence and unity. It would not be the first (or last) time that nationalists imagined more patriotism and glory for their communities than their national symbols could sustain.

Star tragedian Tommaso Salvini (1829–1915) provided a more genuine nationalistic symbol of Italy than Verdi. In 1849, he fought the Austrians in defense of the Roman Republic and later welcomed Garibaldi and his army into Naples. Salvini's political and cultural nationalism remained a part of his public image. After performing in Italy for most of the 1860s, Salvini embarked on a series of tours in the 1870s and 1880s to South America, the United States, England, France, and even Russia (where a young Konstantin Stanislavsky, to be discussed in Chapter 9, marveled at his power). In addition to roles in Italian plays, Salvini played Othello, Macbeth, King Lear, and other Shakespearean tragic heroes in Italian. Salvini's Othello (Figure 8.9) overwhelmed American novelist Henry James:

His powerful, active, manly frame, his noble, serious, vividly expressive face, his splendid smile, his Italian eye, his superb, voluminous voice, his carriage, his tone, his ease, the assurance he instantly gives that he holds the whole part in his hands and can make of it exactly what he chooses, – all this descends upon the spectator's mind with a richness which immediately converts attention into faith and expectation into sympathy. He is a magnificent creature, and you are already on his side.

(Qtd. in Carlson 1985: 61)

For James and for many other spectators, Salvini's Othello, his most popular role, was related to his Italian identity. Nevertheless Salvini's enactment of Othello participated in blackface practices found from the early modern period forward (see below and Chapter 6). Salvini darkened his skin in "tawny makeup" and chose apparel that alluded to the character's Moorish identity based on fifteenth-century Venetian images of Moorish traders. He based his character on a man he observed in Gibraltar and "Moorish history." Salvini's actions did not make his portrayal authentic; Othello is from Mauritania.

His actions are, however, an example of racial impersonation common throughout the nineteenth century in the United States and Europe. Salvini played many Moorish characters, including Orosmane in Voltaire's *Zaire*,

Figure 8.9
Tommaso Salvini as Othello. Despite his darkened skin and Moorish headdress and costume indicative of the long history of blackface minstrelsy, and the exotification of Muslim Others, Salvini retained his own Italian-style moustache for the role, perhaps to emphasize his Italian heritage.

Source: ART File S185 no.9 photo. Folger Shakespeare Library.

discussed in Chapter 6. While audiences did not mistake him for an African, many viewed his brutality in the role, including the use of a scimitar for his own suicide, as related to his embodiment of savagery and tropical passion – both codes for non-European origin. Although he was northern Italian, his most famous non-Shakespearean role was Sicilian. That audiences read Salvini as both non-white and Italian is not surprising given the racialization of North Africans and Italians (particularly Southern Italians) as "Mediterranean." Compounded with some U.S. citizens' anxiety about both recently emancipated African slaves and an influx of immigrants from Southern Italy fleeing economic hardship, Salvini's popularity likely did stem from his representation of an ethnic Other in ways that mirror and refract the practices of blackface minstrelsy and other forms of racialized performances in the Americas. Salvini was an important symbol of a newly unified Italian nation, but his performance of Othello engaged with U.S. racial nationalism in important ways.

Wagner and racial nationalism in Germany (1848–1880)

Nineteenth-century nationalism in many German-speaking areas turned toward racism. To some extent, racial nationalism exaggerates a major tenet of cultural nationalism; it proposes that the dominant cultural group in a nation is not only different from, but also superior to minority groups. Racial nationalism breaks with cultural nationalism, however, to claim that the essence of a *volk* is in the blood. By conflating culture with a racist notion of biology, the full assimilation of minority Others as equal citizens into the nation becomes impossible. Racism, according to the comparative historian George M. Fredrickson,

> has two components: *difference* and *power*. It originates in a mindset that regards "them" as different from "us" in ways that are permanent and unbridgeable. This sense of difference provides a motive or rationale for using our power advantage to treat the ethno-racial Other in ways that we would regard as cruel or unjust if applied to members of our own group.
>
> (Fredrickson 2002: 9)

This form of racism extends the logic of domination over difference developed under colonialism into a biological logic of exclusion.

Although Herder's cultural nationalism did not assign superiority of one culture over another, nor fail to grant all peoples human status, Herder hoped that Jews and other minorities would assimilate to German culture with the birth of the state. This prejudice against non-German cultures in Europe grew in the nineteenth century; many Germans attacked the rationalism of the "French people" as inferior or sought to elevate the essence of "Germanness" over "Jewishness." Opera composer Richard Wagner (1813–1883) shared these prejudices and advanced them in his political and artistic attempts to facilitate German unification. Like many other German Romantics, Wagner imagined a unified, utopian Germany based in traditions of language, mythology, and ethnic origin, and these ideas shaped his operas.

Several of Wagner's operas before 1848 celebrated German tradition. Wagner set *The Flying Dutchman* (1843) in Nordic legend, for example, and *Tannhäuser* (1845) featured Wartburg castle, a celebrated site for German nationalistic pride. Involved in the idealistic attempt to forge a German nation during the uprisings of 1848–1849, Wagner wrote patriotic poetry, edited a radical newspaper, and aided others in the fight against Prussian domination. Barely escaping arrest, Wagner fled Germany and spent the next 11 years in exile. In 1864, Ludwig II, the new king of Bavaria invited Wagner to join his court and the composer accepted. Both men understood the German *Volksgeist* as an unchanging essence and a possible force in history, if political opportunity was combined with musical genius.

Despite later political friction between them, King Ludwig's support of Wagner allowed him to envision and complete several operas, facilitated the realization of a national theatre for the production of his works, and encouraged Wagner's nationalism to become a racialist one. During his exile, Wagner had begun *The Ring of the Nibelungs*, his tetralogy of operas, completed in 1874. Despite being influenced by the pessimistic philosophy of Schopenhauer, the vast work nonetheless attempts to distill the positive destiny of the German people in what Wagner believed was a truthful fusion of myth and history. The final opera, *Götterdämmerung*, stages the destruction of a decadent order of states, forces, and laws so that a new, utopian Germany might emerge. Throughout, Wagner distinguishes between superior German characters and others who represent corrupt, non-Germanic influences. In one scene in *Siegfried* (1871), the third opera in the cycle, for instance, Wagner signals his rejection of what he had termed "Jewishness in Music" by having his hero, Siegfried, turn away in contempt from a dwarf characterized as a Jew. At other points, blood purity plays an important role in the plots of the four operas.

Wagner finished *The Mastersingers of Nuremberg* (1868) at a crucial time in the push for German unification. Under the leadership of Chancellor Otto von Bismarck, Prussia had won a short war against the Austrian empire in 1866 and was poised to unite Germany under Prussian leadership. Wagner allied with Prussian might. After the success of *The Mastersingers* in Munich, Wagner toured the opera to Berlin in 1870 and scored a triumph in the Prussian capital. In effect, Wagner's nationalistic opera helped to fan the flames for the Franco-Prussian War (1870–1871).

The Prussian victory in that war established a German Empire that facilitated the incorporation of Bavaria and the smaller German states under Prussian rule (Figure 8.10). In response, Wagner composed the "Kaiser March" and conducted it in Berlin, hoping for an appointment in the new regime. But Bismarck had no interest in identifying the German Empire with Wagner's visions, and the composer turned his attention to fundraising for his Festival Theatre at Bayreuth in Bavaria.

Although announced to open in 1867, the first festival did not occur until 1876. Wagner designed the Festival Theatre to achieve his aesthetic and nationalistic goals. Believing that his epic music-dramas could transport his listeners to a spiritual realm of imagined aspiration and unity, Wagner aimed for the total immersion of his audience in his fictions. Accordingly, he attempted to weave together music, drama, singing, scenery, lighting, and all of the other theatrical arts into what he called a ***Gesamtkunstwerk*** [ghe-ZAHMT-koonst-vehrk],

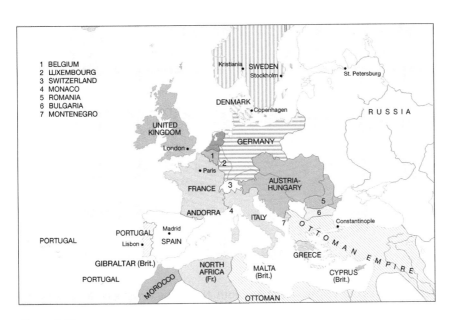

Figure 8.10
Political Map of Europe in 1880.

a totally integrated and unified production. Interested in solidifying the unity of the *volk*, Wagner designed a proscenium theatre that did away with architectural social distinctions in the auditorium, such as private boxes and an upper gallery, and arranged all seats facing the stage (Figure 8.11). In his attempt to ensure that all spectators would sit in rapt attention to the stage illusion, Wagner even eliminated the sight of the pit orchestra, placing it well below the lip of the Bayreuth forestage. In other ways, though, Wagner continued mid-nineteenth-century staging conventions. His theatre relied on painted flats and backdrops, trap doors, gas lighting, and spotlights. Wagner's auditorium design would continue to influence the Western theatre well into the twentieth century.

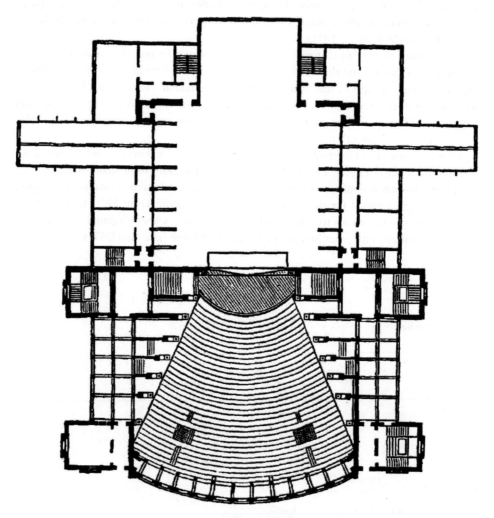

Figure 8.11
Floor plan for Wagner's Festival Theatre at Bayreuth. Notice the fan-shaped seating, with side entrances, the forestage, and the ample depth of the stage area for scenic illusion.

Source: Wiki, https://commons.wikimedia.org/wiki/File:L-Bayrethertheater.png

Wagner staged *Parsifal*, his final opera, at Bayreuth in 1882. In *Parsifal*, religion merges with racism through a plot in which the racial degeneration of the German people must be countered by racial purity so that Germany may be saved from interbreeding and decline. Wagner mixes images of the blood of Christian sacrifice with the blood of racial exclusivity. Even as he was composing his opera, Wagner was writing articles in antisemitic periodicals that sounded the alarm about "racial miscegenation." The Nazis adopted Wagner and his operas as cultural avatars of the Third Reich; Hitler himself was particularly fond of *Parsifal*. While this does not mean that Wagner would have approved Nazi Germany's policy of racial extermination, it should alert us to the long-term political effects that popular theatrical works can unknowingly help to legitimate.

Liberalisms, nationalisms, and theatre in Latin America

The new nation-states of North and South America emerged during the revolutionary era when notions of liberal nationalism, based on principles from the Enlightenment, such as the right of individuals to pursue their interests, predominated. These ideals were continually shaped in the United States and the countries of Latin America through the 1870s. Alongside the European revolutions and U.S. independence, Haiti's independence from France (1804) was also an inspirational model of independence for Latin Americans.

The revolutionary era in Latin America was equally fueled by internal and external conditions. Internally, the colonies' governance was strained by the recent expulsion of the Jesuits, the disenfranchisement of local clergy and other problems stemming from the extraction of resources from the colonies to pay for European Wars. Externally, wars in Europe destabilized colonial governments. When the King of Spain abdicated in 1808, Latin American *Criollos* were ready and rebelled against the Spanish-born viceroys and bureaucrats sent by the King to rule the Spanish colonies. *Criollo* leaders were receptive to independence, even when not allied with secular liberal ideologies of many nationalist movements. Allegiances made between *Criollos*, some *mestizos* (those of mixed Spanish and indigenous heritage) and indigenous people led most of these former colonies to gain freedom from Spain by 1825, although *Peninsulares* (Spanish-born persons), *Criollos*, *mestizos*, indigenous people, and African-descended people fought on various sides of these conflicts at different times and for different reasons (Figure 8.12). In contrast, the white population of Portuguese Brazil, united but vastly outnumbered by African

Figure 8.12

Political map of South America in 1825.

slaves and indigenous people, welcomed the king of Portugal and his court when they had fled from Napoleon's armies. In 1822, the prince regent of Portugal, in alliance with the white Brazilian elite, declared Brazil an independent monarchy, without bloodshed and without disturbing white rule. Cuba and Puerto Rico, meanwhile, remained colonies until 1898, in part because of the Spanish government's tight control of the region in reaction to Haitian Independence; the Dominican Republic emerged as a nation in the mid-nineteenth century after a war of independence against Haiti.

After gaining independence from Spain, the white elites in most of the newly formed nations established liberal constitutions influenced by the early French Revolution and the 1812 Spanish Constitution. Many nations also abolished slavery soon after independence. The new constitutions typically granted universal suffrage to all males in the country, but in practice few people of indigenous, African, and mixed descent participated as citizens. Latin American leaders' interpretation of liberalism led to a series of governing experiments with differing results. Unfortunately, vast inequality and racism were not undone with the emergence of these "liberal" nation-states. In addition, the combination of the lack of ideological homogeneity within ruling groups and the continued coloniality of economic production made many of these early administrations unstable through the first half of the nineteenth century. For example, disputes between Federalists and Centralists abounded in Mexico. Argentina moved into dictatorship soon after Independence; others were still allied with Monarchism, which was not in conflict with commitment to liberalism. The emergence of *caudillos,* strongmen who won the adherence of large parts of the nation due their populist performances, sometimes stymied the rise of effective, elected democratic leadership. The region was also affected by many wars within the hemisphere, including the Argentine-Brazilian War (1825–1828), the U.S.-Mexican War (1846–1848), and the 1879–1883 Chilean War against the Peruvian Bolivian Confederation (also known as The War of the Pacific).

Although *Criollos* were usually the recognized national leaders, there were also important insurgencies against Spanish rule led by indigenous and Black leaders. Haitian independence is the prime example. Another is the Túpac Amaru Rebellion (1780–1783), led by the eponymous indigenous leader in Peru. This uprising presaged how indigenous rebellions, even when they fail, provide inspiration and symbolism for later national movements. This era also showed how theatre inspired revolution. While it cannot be verified that Amaru II read the colonial Quechua-language play *Ollantay*, which staged an indigenous rebellion against empire, the play was banned in 1781 suggesting a connection between onstage and off-stage revolution. The theatre scene in Haiti on the eve of independence featured plays with indigenous and African leaders. The surfeit of plays with indigenous and African-descended heroes in the United States and Latin America in the first half of the nineteenth century suggests how theatrical representation of these rebellions played an important role in the cultural projects of independence and nationalism within the entire hemisphere. This did not mean that Black and indigenous people were treated with respect in everyday life, however. Plays about indigenous and Black heroes were staged in the face of extreme racism against African-descended and indigenous people fueled by the Eurocentric colonial project and Christian ideology.

For example, many Spaniards and Portuguese believed that Jews and Moors who had converted to Christianity were actually incapable of becoming true Catholics; only those who could claim *limpieza de sangre* (purity of blood) through Christian family descent might gain salvation. When they took this belief to their new colonies, the Spaniards and Portuguese usually distinguished between the native indigenous populations, who were deemed capable of salvation, and the slaves imported from Africa, who were not. In addition to blood purity, the pigmentation of the Africans signified to many Catholics that they were descended from the biblical sons of Ham and therefore, as in the Bible, destined by God for slavery. The contrast between the treatments of these two groups by *Criollo* leaders is found in nationalistic dramas throughout the nineteenth century as well as their colonial antecedents.

European desires for dominance were fueled by fear stemming from the reality of their minority rule. At the end of the eighteenth century in Spanish America, only 3.2 of an estimated 17 million people were white, and of these 3.2 million, only 150,000 were born in Spain. This reality manifested in a number of ways, including *casta* (lineages/breeds) designations in paintings that named labeled different combinations of European, *Criollo*, indigenous and Black people. While these often denigrating designations did not find their way into official documents because racial designations were banned in the new nations, the racism behind them persisted. These racial distinctions were complicated by the enslaved, indentured, or free status of said subjects. Fear of non-white people also led authorities to control or eliminate the syncretic religious cultures of Spanish and Portuguese America that combined indigenous, Afro-diasporic, and European Christian practices throughout the late colonial period in ways that were mirrored by theatre censorship throughout the nineteenth century. As might be imagined, political censorship often had a racial valence, and vice-versa.

Despite these instabilities, theatre production in major Latin American cities blossomed. These productions included touring European and domestically written dramas. Spanish and French companies toured opera and theatre productions to major Latin American cities with some regularity to entertain *Criollo* audiences by the mid-1830s. Records of theatre in Buenos Aires and Mexico City for the first half of the nineteenth century show productions of Rossini, Alfieri, Pixérécourt, Kotzebue, Voltaire and Molière, in addition to Spanish classics and native dramas. In Mexico City, the most populous of the post-colonial capitals, President Bustamante started a theatre school in 1831 and the country's entrepreneurs built several theatres in the 1840s and 1850s. Buenos Aires, Montevideo, and Santiago also had active theatre scenes. Play reviews, which include aesthetic, political, and social commentaries, were extensive in the rich periodical culture of Latin American metropoles. The content of the reviews suggests that intellectual statesmen saw theatre as a didactic tool to teach political behavior, emotional comportment, and moral conduct, all of which could support nascent national projects. Theatre spaces became sites to perform nationhood, even when no plays were involved: the Chilean and Peruvian national anthems were debuted in theatres. Theatre performances were also often a part of civic festivals, including Republican (in this instance, meaning commitment to the idea of a Republic, not a political party) festivals extolling independence heroes in the middle of the century.

Buenos Aires offers one example of a burgeoning theatrical public sphere. In the 1810s and 1820s, the state established the Society for Good Taste, which, as Frank Dauster states, used "the theatre as a political instrument" (Dauster 2008: 537). The production of Luis Ambrosio Morante's 1821 *Tupac Amarú* based on the 1780 indigenous rebellion and Camilo Henriquez's *Camila or La Patriota del Sudamérica* (1817) engaged recent Latin American history to advocate and celebrate independence. These plays were sometimes presented within a larger program that might include music, a patriotic poem read by a company actor, and a *sainete* (one act farce or skit with music) or other short piece in addition to a full-length play. Censorship did not stop these or other writers, although the Juan Manuel de Rosas regime (1835–1852), which followed this initial independence era, curbed the productivity of the Argentine theatre.

Despite the continued racism within Latin American nations, some non-European actors were important members of the theatre community. Mixed-race playwright Luis Ambrosio Morante (1784–1837) was also an actor and a company manager of substantial reputation. Alongside Uruguayan-born Trinidad Guevara (1798–1873), he was the most well-known actor of the period in the River Plate region. Yet, his mixed-race background (*pardo*) – which included indigenous, Black and European heritages – was only intermittently mentioned in his time and ours. (It should be noted that colorism might have allowed him more opportunities than dark-skinned African performers.) While his success was exceptional, his situation was not unusual; there were many African-descended performers throughout the River Plate region, especially in musical performance. And, although not common, some slaves were able to navigate to freedom as artists in ways that parallel the experience of serf actors in Russia. Although this fact did not undo racial and class-based hierarchies, theatre production was one of the few occupations in which *Criollo, mestizo, pardo* (a term sometimes used to refer to mixed-race people in Brazil and other parts of South America) and Black persons would work together.

Regulation, however, limited autonomous productions led by non-white artists. A group of *pardo* actors in Montevideo tried to perform a patriotic play in 1837 and were denied the privilege at the exact time that Spanish actor in blackface was playing Othello nearby. In response, this group of actors asked to play *Othello* a short time later. We do not know if they were successful, but the request is illustrative of the complicated relation between race and liberty (hailed in theatrical speeches but often denied in real life) as extended (or not) to non-white theatre actors' experience within the early Latin American national period.

Nationalist ideas, however selectively granted to actual citizens, were worked out by playwrights in various genres, including some European forms. Widely produced Mexican playwright Manuel Eduardo de Gorostiza (1789–1851) wrote neoclassical plays that satirized Romanticism and did not contain any Mexican cultural features. Other Latin American playwrights, however, significantly revised European models or created new genres. For examples, Spanish short forms such as *sainetes, revistas* (revues), *zarzeulas* (dramatic pieces with spoken text and songs), and *teatro bufo* (satirical comic theatre) were hybridized in their new environments through music and content additions and adaptations. New genres were also created, such as full *costumbrista* dramas, gaucho plays, and indigenist tragedies.

Costumbrista theatre, the best known genre of the century, were dramas of everyday life that featured regional customs and idioms. Popular in Argentina, Chile, Colombia, Nicaragua, and Mexico, these plays often represented social stereotypes related to class and region in their depictions of everyday life. The plays' and their playwrights' politics were not uniform. Peruvian playwright Manuel Ascensio Segura (1805–1871), who gained a reputation for his comedies of manners, was a *mestizo* liberal; his fellow Peruvian *costumbrista* playwright, Felipe Pardo y Aliaga (1806–1868) was a conservative who idolized Spanish culture. The satirical plays of both men were popular with audiences, despite their different political orientations.

In Argentina and Uruguay, the *gaucho* drama emerged. Gauchos are landless and vagrant men who performed military support of the nation, even though they suffered from social approbation because of their roughness. Gauchos, on stage and off, often had an independent streak, which was valorized. Precursors to the larger movement are found in the early nineteenth century, but the most famous plays of this type are the theatrical adaptations of the 1884 novel *Juan Moreira*. Gaucho plays' language stems from the oral tradition of epic poetry, contrasting with Neoclassical language used in other plays. The resonances of this genre can still be found in cultural production today in the region.

The most widespread genre in theatre through the Americas, however, is likely *indigenista* drama. These plays engage a representational *indigenismo* that valorized indigenous heritage as national heritage and identity. While political *indigenismo*, which stood to incorporate indigenous subjects into the nation, did not occur until the end of the nineteenth century in Peru and Mexico, the use of indigenous leaders as exemplars of (national) independence within literature was popular beginning in the early nineteenth century. These plays include Morante's *Tupac Amarú* (1821), produced on the Argentine anniversary of independence, Colombian José Fernandez Madrid's (1789–1830) *Atala* (1822) and *Guatimoc* (1825), Cuban José Maria Heredia's (1803–1839) epic *Moctezuma* or *Los Mexicanos* (1819), Ignacio Torres Arroyo's *Teutila* (1828), José María Mangino's *Xicotencatl* (1829) and José María Moreno Buenvecino's *Xicohtencatl* (1828). The indigenous figures in these plays often represented Republican values in addition to proffering non-European exemplars of national heroism. Read as often as they were produced, these plays were primarily pedagogical tools for the educated elites. The resurgence of these *indigenista* images in a later iteration of liberal Mexico included Alfredo Chavero's (1841–1906) *Quetzalcoátl* (1878) and *Xochitl* (1879) both of which incorporated the archeological explorations that established the exhibition of indigenous culture as national culture later in the century. These plays should be remembered alongside the phenomena of "playing Indian" in the United States, which will be discussed below. Indigenous heroes were sometimes used by culture makers as a shield against questioning the morality of chattel slavery. Patrons who supported indigenous drama were often slaveholders. That said, artists, such as Mexican writer José Joaquín Fernandéz de Lizardi (1776–1827), in his melodrama, *El Negro Sensible* (1825), treated its Black protagonist with sensitivity and compassion. A few years later, in 1829, Vicente Guerrero, a Mexican president with Black heritage, banned slavery in his brief term (in 1818, only the trade was banned). Later in the century, frequent staging of *Uncle Tom's Cabin* in Mexico, Cuba, and Brazil (which did not ban slavery until 1888, and remained an empire until 1889) reveals that artists meditated on the (im)morality of slavery within the theatrical public sphere throughout the Americas as liberalism continued to develop.

In the mid- to late nineteenth century, Latin American liberals curtailed the power of the Church, argued for constitutionalism and a civilian army, and for the creation of middle class through property ownership for the working classes (including the breakup of communally worked lands) alongside their new commitment to a "free" (and globalizing) market, which proponents claimed was to benefit all citizens. When these ideals were put in practice, however, the rich enjoyed privileged lives at the expense of the majority of Indians and peasants, most of whom had lost control of their lands to the huge farms and extractive industries that dominated these nation-states.

On a global level, Great Britain, and later the United States, brought the economies of these countries into the emerging global order of nineteenth-century imperialism and new forms of debt-centered capitalism. In exchange for bank loans, transportation, communication, and manufactured goods from the industrialized countries, whites and *mestizos* in Latin America supplied raw materials, mining and farm products, cheap peasant labor, and willing consumers to foreign capitalists. Latin American citizens were not without agency. Many Latin American landowners and merchants worked to integrate their operations with the Europeans and Yankees. After 1850, some of this new wealth was flowing to *mestizos* and others of mixed descent. These groups joined with some of the rich *Criollos* to push for more stable societies based on liberal constitutions, which eventually stressing "order and progress" to serve capitalist development. In Mexico, for example, the liberalism of Zapotec President Benito Juárez (1861–1872) transformed into the liberal dictatorship of Porfirio Díaz (1876, 1877–1880, 1884–1911) fairly rapidly. The new elites were familiar with positivism, an approach to the study of society that relied specifically on empirical scientific evidence. Dedicated to a positivist ideology that saw urban development as a form of modernization, purchased extravagant houses in their capital cities, adorned themselves with the latest European fashions, and built "lavish theatres and opera houses" for their enjoyment (Fowler 2008: 74). This shift in the economic and political basis of Latin American life, and relative stability meant that theatres became again invested in European theatrical imports, especially operas, while retaining the plays. variety entertainments, and *costumbrista* productions of the past. These plays often explicitly supported the values of their patrons: liberal nationalism, positivism and capitalism. In the Southern Cone, by the end of the century, artists chose realistic forms and methods to better reflect these values. Nonetheless, popular performance forms were an important part of the entertainment industry: Circo Criollo (Uruguay and Argentina) and puppet theatre gained popularity at this time.

Although foreign capital reshaped the economy of Brazil as it did the rest of Latin America, Brazil remained an empire for most of the nineteenth century. The country was effectively led by Pedro I (1822–1831), and after he abdicated, Pedro II (1840–1889), with a period of regency in between. Brazil's relative stability (even given a number of political challenges) sparked a surge in conservative nationalism among the court and the group of white creoles who ruled the country in the 1830s. Proponents of nationalism, however, had to justify or ignore Brazil's huge investment in slavery, which at the time constituted roughly half of the population. Portuguese colonial policy had turned Brazil into a sugar plantation dependent upon enslaved labor and the growing and labor-intensive industries of coffee and rubber that increased the demand for more enslaved people.

Slavery's longer life in Brazil (and its large African-descended population) led to both pro- and anti-slavery theatres. Tolerance of, if not open justification for, slavery could be found among the elites and the cultural production they sponsored, including in the Romantic works of conservative Domingos José Gonçalves de Magalhães (1811–1882) and his circle. Magalhães wrote plays and poetry in a neoclassical style and argued for the creation of a Brazilian national theatre. His most famous play, *Antonio José, or the Poet and the Inquisition* (1838), is still celebrated as the first Brazilian tragedy, although set in Portugal. Magalhães' historically based tragic hero is a converted Jew who, though tried and condemned by the Inquisition, nonetheless affirms his Catholic faith in the end and dies a martyr for an open kind of Catholicism. Along with other Brazilian Romantics, Magalhães affirmed that the Catholic faith in Brazil could embrace Jews and Indians – especially those idealized tribes in the interior that might inspire Brazilian nationalists to similar virtues. The Brazilian

Romantics, then, promoted a mix of Catholicism and a Rousseau-inspired belief in the primitive simplicity and natural virtue of Brazil's many indigenous tribes. By idealizing the Amazonian Indians, while abjecting and/or invisibilizing African enslaved people, Magalhães and the Romantics embraced an indigenist nationalism. Pedro II officially endorsed this form of indigenist Romanticism and awarded Magalhães with a series of prestigious diplomatic appointments, which extended his primary residency in Europe.

Pedro II's leadership came after a lost war with Argentina, economic disarray, and fragmentation within the ruling elite which opened up some political opportunities for Brazilian liberals. After a decade of instability, the elite finally closed ranks and backed Pedro II, in part to prevent the enslaved population from capitalizing on this disarray. British warships were dramatically curtailing the slave trade by this point, forcing Brazil to end the trade (but not slavery itself) in 1853.

Although most elite Brazilians favored the continuation of slavery, by the 1850s there was an increasing body of anti-slavery and abolitionist drama, including the works of José de Alencar (1829–1877) and Castro Alves (1847–1871). Alves's work was clearly abolitionist, while Alencar's was merely anti-slavery. Alencar's O Demonio Familiar (1858), advocates replacing enslaved labor in households with the labor of free women. His inscription of traditional gender roles continued with Mãe (1860), which featured the tragic death of a female slave who pretends to be her mulatto son's enslaved person, rather than his mother, so he can succeed as a medical doctor. Her tragic death parallels those found in U.S. melodramas that valorize maternal or female sacrifice. Nonetheless, Alencar did create an Africa-descended female protagonist. By the mid-1870s, the new generation of liberals viewed slavery unfavorably; consequently, theatre of that period and into the 1880s became more openly abolitionist. It was not until 1888, though, that slavery was finally abolished; the establishment of a republic that ended the Brazilian monarchy occurred the following year.

Although its participation in slavery lasted longer than some other nations, Brazil's complex political history and theatre history has many similarities with the rest of Latin America. Conservative liberalism was dominant; an oligarchical group of white elites owned the means of most production; and culture was often utilized for the aims of the state or statesmen. Many performances were part of or adjacent to festivals that celebrated or commemorated important persons or events in Brazilian history; and, in the early decades of the nineteenth century, theatre was considered an important didactic school for the population that could teach ideology and replace (or displace) popular entertainments associated with African-descended people.

In Rio de Janeiro, an active theatre scene emerged despite the poor state of physical performance venues. Many of the primary genres produced were familiar: opera, romantic drama, melodrama, and a national version of comedies of manners that satirized the upper and middle classes. Brazil had a handful of important theatre impresarios. One of these was João Caetano Dos Santos (1808–1863), who directed the first Brazilian acting company. His Teatro de Sao Pedro was the center of theatrical activity in Rio for the first half of the century. There he produced and acted in many plays, including Magalhães' Antonio José. He also developed two important French-inspired theoretical handbooks of acting, Reflexeos Dramaticas (1837) and Liçoes dramaticas (1862). In them, Dos Santos advocated for a state-sponsored Brazilian theatre and for a non-declamatory style of acting. Brazilian theatre

Figure 8.13

Score cover for Carlos Gomes's *Il Guarany*.

Source: Art Collection 3/Alamy Stock Photo.

artists' interest in the French theatre was more pronounced than in the rest of Latin America because they were exposed to touring artists and Rio's French-language print culture. Nationalistic opera creators, however, often adapted French and Italian forms to engage with Latin American culture. The best example of this is Carlos Gomes's *Il Guarany* (1870), a nationalist opera with a deep transnational history. Written and premiered in Milan where Gomes was on fellowship, this opera was based on an Italian translation of Alencar's indigenist novel. (See Figure 8.13.) *Il Guarany* premiered in Italy, tapping into the European desire for exotic locales and subject matter. The opera returned to Brazil, debuting in Rio later that year to mixed reception. While the music, largely European in form, was popular and sometimes applauded, the representation of noble indigenous characters was less well-received. Audiences showed discomfort with both the exoticizing lens of the opera and the invasion of the high opera house by indigenous presence. This reception exposed the contradictions and hypocrisy of *indigenista* cultural production. Nonetheless, because *Il Guarany*'s domestic performance coincided with Brazil's victory over Paraguay and the emergence of its Republican party, the opera linked *indigenismo* and Republicanism, as in other parts of Latin America. Other musical performances, meanwhile, were more pointed in incorporating Afro-Brazilian rhythms into their orchestrations.

Despite this, there were still anxieties about the representations of African-descended peoples on stage. Censorship bodies, which included the participation of many popular Brazilian playwrights, often banned representations of miscegenation. And the presence of Black actors was not openly welcomed after independence. Given the rich legacies of African performance and the popularity of Black performers in the late colonial period, this exclusion is all the more striking. After independence, however, actors were often working-class and non-Black. The most famous version of *Othello* in this period was played by non-Black actors, including Dos Santos, who was inspired by U.S. Black actor Ira Aldridge, discussed below. In addition, the casts of many of the abolitionist plays mentioned above were all-white and sometimes employed blackface. This was the case even for *Uncle Tom's Cabin*, which came to Brazil through its French translation.

As in Brazil, Cuba's independence, and its abolition of slavery, came at the end of the nineteenth century. The Cuban nationalism that preceded independence was an anti-colonial nationalism that entailed new racial formations. Engaging a discourse of *mestizaje*, Cubans claimed that "No Son Negritos, Ni Blanquitos, solo Cubanos" ("They are not little Black ones, or little white ones, only Cubans") as a national creed. Yet for anti-colonial *Criollos*, it was the figure of the *negrito* who came to embody and voice anti-colonial critique in the face of slavery. This theatrical embrace occurred alongside violence and discrimination against Black people, inside and outside of the confines of slavery. Parallel with blackface in the United States, studied below, this figure, and the genre of *teatro bufo* more generally, relied upon racist caricature and marked speech. The most famous company was Bufos Habaneros, which emerged in 1868. This company transculturated Spanish forms, mixing comical short plays and sketches with oft-censored political content and music and dances, including the conga. Cuba, like other Latin American nations, built a few large theatres and opera houses to hold European touring operas, plays and domestic Romantic tragedies by authors such as Gertrudis Gómez de Avellanda (1814–1873) and José Maria Heredia, but it was *bufo* that was most important national form. The Cuban performances reveal a distinct contradiction at the heart of performance in the Americas: the use of virulently racist performance forms to argue for liberal values such as national autonomy or even abolitionism.

Theatre, race, and nationalism in the United States, 1820–1870

In the United States, European settlers wanted land. But the lands were already occupied and stewarded by indigenous people. These settlers also needed to create a new non-British national identity for themselves. To obtain the land, they seized it from indigenous peoples. The approach changed over time. For the first portion of the colonial period, settlers alternated war and diplomacy with indigenous nations throughout the United States and parts of Canada; by the 1820s, President Andrew Jackson implemented genocide and forced removal to the same end, most explicitly in the Indian Removal Act, which passed Congress in 1830. The concretization of these policies coincided with their performative identity projects, which included the proliferation of "playing Indian" (i.e., white people, often men, pretending to be Native American) on stage and in everyday performance, which will be discussed below.

Although they seized indigenous people's communally stewarded land, British imperialists did not force native people on to encomienda-like plantations, as colonists did in Latin America. The nomadic practices of some indigenous nations and the importance of trade with other nations made this impossible. Thus, when the British encouraged their U.S. subjects to begin agricultural and commercial ventures that profited the mother country through trade, they needed a different strategy to obtain the required extensive labor. To meet these needs, the British settler cultures encouraged African slavery, a second form of racial violence crucial to nation building. The stability and success of this system, combined with systemic racist structures and ideologies, made slavery difficult to eradicate in the nineteenth century.

The particularities of British colonialism also supported these structures. The settlers inherited bourgeois mercantile capitalism, Protestantism, and Western expansionism. The legacy of Puritanism, however, preached that the United States might separate itself from the decadence of Europe and lead the world to salvation, which reinforced the country's self-righteousness and the claim of moral exceptionalism. Given this perspective, for most of the nineteenth century, few U.S. citizens understood their conquest of other peoples as imperialism. Although the United States was continuing to practice settler colonialism in its western territories, most citizens believed that the incorporation of new lands into their nation-state expanded freedom and democracy, even when these acquisitions and wars increased the reach of chattel slavery and deprived Native Americans of their homelands and livelihood. Although the Revolution and the Constitution had been fought and ratified primarily on the basis of Enlightenment values, the U.S. form of liberal nationalism excluded Native American lifeways, policed Afro-diasporic practices and denied enslaved people recognition of their humanity for most of the nineteenth century. Although by 1800 most northern states in the United States were gradually abolishing slavery, individual manumissions were increasing in the South. The rising profitability of cotton encouraged many southern planters to double down on their commitment to slavery. A series of presidents who held enslaved people and professed racist views, including Thomas Jefferson and Andrew Jackson, also increased the legitimacy of the trade.

British pressure to end the slave trade, attacks by northern abolitionists, however, and Nat Turner's slave revolt in Virginia (1831) led many southerners in the 1830s to reframe their defense of slavery by extending the breadth of their racism in this period; what had been understood by many as a necessary evil they now proclaimed as a positive good. Many Southern ideologues proclaimed that Blacks were biologically incapable of rational action and ought to be thankful that they had been brought to the United States, where they could learn civilization from a superior race. In the North, some urban workers in northern cities resented competition from free Blacks for scarce jobs and a series of riots occurred in the 1830s that pitted working-class racists against Black citizens and abolitionists. The popular genre of Yankee theatre during the 1830s, which often featured a droll New England character in comic opposition to a free Black figure (usually played in blackface by a white actor) fortified this racism. It was here and elsewhere that U.S. citizens saw both sympathetic and buffoonish characterizations of Black enslaved people and free people of color, by art makers of divergent political persuasions.

The so-called Compromise of 1850, which guaranteed slavery in several western territories, also included a Fugitive Slave Act. This allowed southern masters to pursue their run-away enslaved people in the free states of the North, partly nationalizing the rights of slave owners. Outraged by this attack on Black enslaved families, Harriet Beecher Stowe penned *Uncle Tom's Cabin*, which was quickly adapted for the stage after its appearance as a complete novel in 1852. Although an early adaptation preserved Stowe's abolitionist views, most stage versions of *Uncle Tom's Cabin* compromised her religious and sentimental depiction of enslaved families; some adaptations even endorsed slave holding as a paternalistic institution. Abolitionist objections to slavery were winning more converts in the 1850s, but few commercial theatres in the North were willing to risk their profits to stage abolitionist dramas. In the infamous *Dred Scott* decision of 1857, the Supreme Court gave southern slaveholders the right to take their "private property" with them anywhere in the United

States; the decision implicitly countermanded the ability of Congress to restrict the spread of slavery at all. The rise of the new Republican Party, which opposed extending slavery in the West as a threat to white male farmers who could not afford enslaved people, divided the country and alarmed the South. In reaction, the new Confederate States of America, which began the Civil War in 1861, formed primarily to preserve slavery.

Abolitionism remained a small political movement with little clout at the start of the war; very few Northerners joined the Union army to free Black enslaved people in the South. Knowing that many conservatives in his party feared abolition, President Lincoln initially fought the war on narrow constitutional principles. As the casualties mounted, however, it became apparent to many that abolishing slavery in the ten rebel states would shorten the war and Lincoln issued the Emancipation Proclamation (1863). In 1865, with the end of the war in sight, the Thirteenth Amendment was pushed through Congress, abolishing slavery in the United States. The amendment did not kill racism, of course. The failure of Reconstruction to rectify race-based inequities and their economic and social consequences while reintegrating the Confederate states into the union in the 1870s led to new forms of racial nationalism, whose proponents continued to insist that the United States should guarantee whites preferential treatment over non-white citizens because of their race. Aspects of this form of racial nationalism continue to the present day.

In the United States, American identity was often rehearsed through racial imaginings, including racial (and racist) impersonations such as blackface minstrelsy. They were, however, part of a rich and complex theatre culture that was transnational in its scope. As in Latin America, the ascension of liberal Republicanism and populism pushed many performers of color off the stage in the second half of the century. Until that time, however, the U.S.'s performance culture was quite racially heterogenous, even in the face of violence and racism. This was in part because of the global interconnectedness of performance culture. Immigration of Anglo-Caribbean Black (including mixed-race) workers, the movement of Black performers, many of whom were also maritime workers, and the touring of Anglo theatre companies such as Hallam's that had lengthy stays in Jamaica, created this culture. This reality was part of everyday life in lower Manhattan, which included outdoor pleasure gardens attended by free Blacks and shows of dandy dress by free Blacks on the streets. By the 1820s, the first Black professional theatre in the United States, the African Grove Theatre, had opened in this area, with performers acting in full-length plays, including Shakespeare's works, for racially heterogenous audiences. The shock and controversy of the African Grove was not that Black actors were performing, but that they were performing in "legitimate" full-length plays which were regulated separately. In the U.S. theatre, Black actors regularly performed in genres that were considered minor – such as pantomimes and short musical pieces. This distinction, combined with anti-Black racism, exacerbated by debates about Black male suffrage, may explain the controversy and violence that came when members of the African Grove Theatre were arrested after performing Shakespeare in 1822. The artists' release was predicated on the agreement to only present minor works in the future. The African Grove Theatre, perhaps because of many of the regulatory violence it faced, moved venues often. Eventually, however, founder William Alexander Brown rented a venue located at the center of the theatre district in lower Manhattan, right across from the Park Theatre (incidentally, where *Metamora*, discussed below, debuted several years later). Although it existed for only a short time (1821–1823), there were over 30 actors who performed in

Figure 8.14

African American actor James Hewlett as Richard III (c. 1825) by I. Scoles.

Source: Wiki / TCS 44, Harvard Theatre Collection, Houghton Library, Harvard University. https://commons. wikimedia.org/wiki/File:Houghton_TCS_44_-_James_ Hewlett_as_Richard_the_Third_-_cropped.jpg

the company in those years, including James Hewlett (1778–1849) who played the title role in *Richard III* (Figure 8.14).

The theatre's repertoire included *Julius Caesar, Macbeth, Othello* and a number of non-Shakespearean dramas, including *Obi or Three Fingered Jack, She Would be a Soldier, Tom and Jerry* and the pathbreaking *Drama of King Shotaway*, the first play by a Black author produced in the United States.

The *Drama of King Shotaway* (1823), written by producer William A. Brown, was about an indigenous uprising of Caribs on the island that Haiti and the Dominican Republic now share. Sadly, this script has been lost. Nonetheless, the play's existence demonstrates the dual and interdependent imagining of indigenous and Black desires for freedom and independence. (Brown had staged Kotzebue's *Pizarro*, about a Peruvian native hero, the year before.) Brown may have imagined a more inclusive American identity that combined African, indigenous, and European cultures that Elizabeth Maddox Dillon theorizes as the "performative commons," but his dreams did not become a reality off the stage.

Despite Brown's intentions, the theatre industry did not become more inclusive because of his leadership. One of these Grove's spectators was Charles Mathews, who later performed derisive and demeaning blackface performances about Black Shakespeare performances in the United States in his one man show, *Journey to America* (1824). And the escalation of racist rhetoric and violence against free Blacks in the 1830s and 1840s pushed Black performers off stage, to be replaced by blackface performers. As in most of the Americas, blackface performers in the United States were mostly working-class Euro-descended people who used the form to claim white dominance.

Minstrel shows were in some sense the most successful form of popular entertainment in the northern cities of the United States in the decades before and after the Civil War. These shows featured white performers donning burnt cork and pretending to enact Black caricatures.

In the United States, by the 1850s, minstrel shows usually featured jokes and musical numbers, specialty acts, and a concluding one-act comedy, parody, or farce. Some songs called for the abolition of slavery – but most minstrel troupes of the early 1850s pandered to groups of poor white urban workers who needed to be assured of their racial superiority.

To please these spectators, minstrels generally portrayed Black characters as inept fools, grotesque animals, or sentimental victims. Minstrel plantation skits and musical numbers avoided the realities of slavery – exhausting work, the forced separation of families, and the ever-present threat of violence and death. (This is similar to the phenomenon of "playing Indian," in which the violence of the genocide of indigenous people is erased and/or justified by the racist myth of Euro-Americans superiority.)

The origins of the practice are anything but clear, but many historians of United States minstrelsy begin with Thomas Dartmouth Rice (1806–1860), who was performing minor roles in British-born Samuel Drake's company. When Rice was with this company, he specialized in blackface roles such as Mungo from the eighteenth-century comedy *The Padlock*, which formed the basis for his Jim Crow character. Whether he added additional features from enslaved or free Black performers in unclear. What is clear is that the penchant for apocryphal narratives of stealing from or studying non-white people as the basis for racial impersonation would remain consistent for Rice, including the song and dance that would make him famous – "Jump Jim Crow" – as well as many performers who followed.

Dressed in rags with burnt cork covering his face, neck, and hands, Rice performed several verses of the song. When he danced as a part of a comic afterpiece at the New York Bowery Theatre in 1832, the young, mostly male working-class audience gave him a tumultuous reception. Rice wrote several one-act plays that featured his Jim Crow character and his famous dance and performed them successfully at the end of a regular evening's entertainment for the next 20 years.

The verses of his song, which were taken up by mobs destroying symbols of elite privilege during urban rioting in the 1830s and 1840s, celebrated white working-class victories over their social and economic oppressors. Rice's rough-music and violent gyrations likely reminded his spectators of their own raucous parades through town during holidays, when they blackened their faces to entertain and alarm friends and enemies with scurrilous antics and the noise of tin kettles and cow bells.

This tradition of blackface dated from medieval mummers plays at Christmastime and continued through the nineteenth century and into the twentieth century, as Philadelphia's Mummer's Parades reveal. There was also, of course, a long legacy of blackface characters in European drama from the early modern period (see *Masque of Blacknesse* in Chapter 6). In the United States, however, blackface performance had largely grown from afterpieces by Rice and others into full evenings of entertainment presented by an all-male minstrel troupe of four to ten performers that attracted cross-class audiences by the 1850s. Dozens of minstrel companies played throughout the urban northeast, paying top salaries to their headliners and composers, among them the popular songwriter Stephen Foster (1826–1864). Minstrelsy also existed in other parts of the United States, even pre-Gold Rush California. These racist shows provided apparent "evidence" that Blacks, freed or enslaved, could not participate as the equals of white citizens in a liberal and democratic United States.

These plays and performances were fraught with contradictions endemic to widespread racism. Mid-century minstrelsy parodied abolitionism and anti-slavery productions of *Uncle Tom's Cabin* while abolitionist or anti-slavery versions of the play incorporated minstrelsy performance tropes. And during the Civil War, white performers in blackface praised the bravery of Union soldiers, anguished over the suffering of the wounded and women on the home front, and pushed for a compromise that might end the fighting.

FREE
INSTRUCTOR
& STUDENT
RESOURCES

After the war ended in 1865, minstrel skits demanded that the newly freed enslaved people stay in the South, as wards of their former masters, once again relegating Blacks to second-class citizenship and maintaining the racial basis of nationalism. (For more information on Blackface minstrelsy, see the case study on "Blacking Up" on the website.)

Minstrel shows were gradually incorporated into American vaudeville, but individual minstrel acts continued to amuse white audiences into the 1950s, when Black activism exposed the racism of these forms. Until then, though, some of the premier performers of popular and mass entertainment on stage and screen paraded their talents in blackface – including Al Jolson (1886–1950), Eddie Cantor (1892–1964), Mickey Rooney (1920–2014), and Judy Garland (1922–1969). Notably, there were also African American minstrels, such as George Walker (1873–1911) and Bert Williams (1874–1922), who used the form of blackface minstrelsy to entertain, instruct and simply make a living. These performances sometimes critiqued racism in ways that pleased reformers, while others formed a vernacular form of entertainment for African Americans that Douglas Jones labels the "Black below" (Jones 2020). More on Williams and Walker can be found in Chapter 10.

Blackface minstrelsy was not the only form of theatrical racial impersonation used to construct U.S. national identity. The phenomenon Philip Deloria calls "playing Indian," in which settlers, donning outlandish costumes and makeup, pretended to be "Indians" was also paramount. Deloria traces the practice to the Boston Tea Party, when colonists, angry with British taxes, put on "Indian Dress" (and blackface) and attacked a ship. The conflation of these two modes of racial impersonation was clearly a failure as a disguise, but the performance extended European practices of reversal and misrule so as to create "racial disorder" as a part of a performative rebellion in the United States. U.S. dramatists and theatre makers regularly engaged modes of "playing Indian" from the colonial period throughout much of the nineteenth century. Between 1808 and the 1840s, there were at least 75 plays about "Indians," beginning with James Nelson Baker's *The Indian Princess, or La Belle Sauvage* (1808). By and large, these "Indians" were stereotypical and inauthentic characters played by white settlers that alluded to both Rousseau's noble savage and Republican masculine ideals. The most famous of these plays was John Augustus Stone's *Metamora* (1828/1829), whose eponymous character was played by Edwin Forrest (1806–1872). Based on Chief Metacom/King Philip (1683–1676), a historical Wampanoag leader, Metamora's name alludes to the metamorphosis through which the lead character's death allows Walter, the U.S.-born white male protagonist, to surrogate the Indian chief into his new, American identity. Forrest, who commissioned the play, through his performance made Metamora a masculine figure with an "unschooled" and "natural" delivery style, counter to the prevailing oratorical pedagogy of his day. This style, together with his athletic and muscular body, combined to create Forrest's embodiment of Republican masculinity. It not clear whether Forrest used makeup to darken himself to play Metamora, but it is clear that he did not study with indigenous Choctaw leader Pusha-Ma-Ta or engage any true Choctaw practices to create the role, although this myth has been perpetuated for centuries. Authentic or not, Forrest's portrayal and the play itself was popular in the northeast from its inception in 1829 to the mid-1860s, as were his renditions of Shakespeare (Figure 8.15).

Metamora's dramatic structure and genre combined features from Romantic tragedy and melodrama, the latter being the most popular form of entertainment in the United States. Melodrama was a key mode of entertainment for working through racial anxieties under emergent nationalism. *Metamora*'s staging in the northeast worked in tandem with the project of genocide ("The 1830 Indian Removal Act") under President Andrew Jackson, who was in office from 1829 to 1837. The naturalized "demise" of *Metamora* obfuscated and justified the violent removal of indigenous people from the very areas where Forrest was performing. The play's first productions in the 1830s coincided with exhibitions of conquered indigenous leaders throughout the northeast. Scholars debate the extent to which *Metamora* was a doctrinaire defense of the Indian Removal Act, and audiences clearly read it many ways. There is consensus, however, on the interdependency of policy and "playing Indian" performance on a basic level. The most famous play of the period with a female protagonist, George Washington Custis's *Pocahontas* (1830), also made pro-colonization claims. However, Charlotte Barnes (1818–1863), the daughter of Mary Greenhill Barnes (c.1780–1864), the actress who played Pocahontas in Custis's play, rewrote *Pocahantas* in 1850 as *The Forest Princess* with an explicitly anti-Indian removal message, although it was too late to affect policy.

In the face of this violence, Native American orators and dancers spoke back to white nationalism, instantiating resurgence through oratory and ceremony. Pequot Minister William Apess (1798–1839) for example, performed his *Eulogy for King Philip* in 1835 and 1836 throughout New England,

Figure 8.15
Edwin Forrest as Othello. Published by Johnson, Frye and Co., c.1856. Forrest's stance is consistent in many lithographs, regardless of character.

Source: Billy Rose Theatre Division, The New York Public Library. Mr. Edwin Forrest as Othello https://digitalcollections.nypl.org/items/45cf8f30-5a55-0133-ecd0-00505686d14e

including at the Odeon Theatre in Boston. Apess's *Eulogy* uses communal memory to imagine New England as Native space. Apess's presence contradicted the rhetoric of demise, and expectations by his largely white audience, who, like himself, was likely familiar with the still popular *Metamora*. Unlike Forrest, Apess engaged the rules of elocution – rather than rebelling against them – to make a persuasive case for a model of dual citizenship in the United States and within indigenous nations for indigenous people. Apess then modeled a different form of performing nationalism. Like many other indigenous performers, he made compromises to ensure he was heard and that his family was fed, including touring as an indigenous

Figure 8.16
Ira Francis Aldridge as Othello by Henry Peronet Briggs.
Source: Hi-Story/Alamy Stock Photo.

prophet in 1837 to make ends meet; other performers performed dances for European audiences for the same purpose. Later in the century, however, dance emerged as a revitalized form of resisting nationalistic imperialism. These resurgence rituals, often called the Ghost Dance, occurred from 1889 in relation to the Paiute prophet Wokova. Performers saw their work as ceremony and/or prophesy that would end the domination of settlers and return their rights to them, speaking back to the forms of nationalism considered in this chapter.

Black performers, during the existence of and after the closing of the African Grove Theatre, also made important contributions to theatre culture throughout the century. Ira Aldridge (1807–1867), a free Black citizen of New York City, had a long and important career. Given the anti-Black racism in the United States, and the closure of the African Grove specifically, Aldridge made his living by touring the British Isles and continental Europe from the late 1820s until his death. He played Shakespearean roles such as Othello, Aaron the Moor, King Lear, Macbeth and Shylock in addition to Mungo in the *Padlock*, Zamba in *The Revenge*, Obi in *Three-Fingered Jack*, Gambia in *The Slave*, and Rolla in *Pizarro* (see Figure 8.16). He also performed a number of minstrel songs in the 1830s, including "Jump Jim Crow." This repertoire, then, combined Shakespearean heroes, Black, indigenous or "outsider" characters demanding liberty, and a series of comic roles written for white actors in blackface, the latter of which included demeaning stereotypes. At times, he even played them in the same night.

Aldridge experienced racism in Britain, particularly in London, when he debuted there as Othello in 1833, to many racist reviews, the most egregious of which minstrelized his performances while objecting to his playing Othello with a white actress as Desdemona. (A perhaps apocryphal story suggests Aldridge as Othello dragged the actress playing Desdemona by her hair in the fatal scene, perhaps adding to the myth of his embodiment of brutality; true or not, Tommaso Salvini, mentioned above, seems to have stolen this piece of stage business for his own performances of the role a bit later in the century, making him one of many non-Black actors inspired by Aldridge.) Aldridge's poor reception in the role in London in 1833 was as likely related to concomitant abolition of slavery in the West Indies and Aldridge's marriages to white European women as it was to any "objective" assessment of talent or his performance choices. It was around this time that Aldridge claimed to be an elite Senegalese, instead of Black American. Despite these concessions in his identity construction, Aldridge often adapted plays to make the Black characters less violent or more heroic. Two examples are his alterations of *Titus Andronicus* and the French melodrama *The Black Doctor* (1847). Aldridge never returned to the United States, even after Emancipation, and died in Lodz, Poland, in 1867, where he is buried. As Nicholas M. Evans claims, "Ira Aldridge was neither ... [an] antiracist hero nor a hapless victim of dominant racial discourses, but a deliberate worker of the tensions between the two" (Evans, qtd. in Lindfors 2007: 176). He was also not the only Black Shakespearean of this period to become an "involuntary exile." Samuel Morgan Smith (1833–1882) and Paul Molyneaux Hewlett (1856–1891) had similar career trajectories.

Back in the United States, African American playwrights took up more open critique. William Wells Brown (1814–1884) wrote *The Escape: or, A Leap for Freedom* (1858), which chronicled the actions of an escaped enslaved person. Although *The Escape* used some minstrel stereotypes and staged Judeo-Christian outrage in the face of slavery, Brown's enslaved characters often violently escaped without the aid of white settler allies found in earlier melodramas written by white authors. Brown's play was the first published by an African American in the United States. Meanwhile, mixed-race actress Mary Webb (1828–1859), the child of a mother who escaped slavery and a Spanish father, toured a solo performance/reading of *Uncle Tom's Cabin*. Webb, like Aldridge, became well-known abroad as well as in the eastern United States. In addition to these two figures, Henry Box Brown (1815–1897) performed his personal escape from slavery for audiences. Set up much like a magic trick, these performances nonetheless showed the cruel confinements of slavery within the form of entertainment. Later in the century, Pauline Hopkins (1859–1930), a Black singer, actor, playwright, and novelist from an elite Boston family, wrote the 1879 play *Peculiar Sam*. Hopkins's critique of masculine violence and her concentration on Black characters is unique (there are no white characters in the play). Nonetheless, she employs a "mammy" character who apologizes for slavery, and employed white minstrelsy performer Sam Lucas. The actions of these actor-playwrights reveal that ideological purity may not always be possible in capitalist conditions. Nonetheless, the plays vigorously critique the exclusionary and violent practices of U.S. nationalism. This repertoire of theatrical performance underscores how theatre and performance were crucial to building national identity.

Summary

In Europe and the Americas, numerous theatrical performances reflected and legitimated varieties of nationalism from 1760 to 1880. Liberal nationalism began with the Enlightenment in the eighteenth century and continued to animate people who regarded (or hoped to regard) their country as the home of individual rights and constitutional government. Schiller's plays can stand as a good example of liberal nationalism on stage. Cultural nationalists celebrated their traditions through such varied fare as nautical melodramas, comic operas, and antiquarian revivals. Racial nationalists in Germany furthered their cause within the theatre. In the Americas, the knotted web of liberal nationalism, cultural nationalism, and anti-Black and indigenous racism were foundational to the emergence of political culture and the emergence of the commercial theatre. All of these fusions of nationalism and performance helped to shape the theatre and general culture of several nation-states during the nineteenth century. After 1880, these forms of nationalism influenced historical developments in parts of the world beyond Europe and the Americas, such as Japan and other sovereign countries. In the twentieth century, varieties of nationalism and nationalistic theatre swept the globe, as many nations gained independence from the empires that had dominated them.

★

CHAPTER 9

Theatricalizing modern imperialism and Orientalism, 1790–1914

Daphne P. Lei

Contributors: Carol Fisher Sorgenfrei,
Bruce McConachie and Gary Jay Williams

When the "imagined communities" called nation-states (as discussed in Chapter 8) forcibly transform or absorb other peoples or geographical areas into colonies or controlled regions through military and/or economic force, the result is **imperialism**.

Empires see themselves as the locus of truth, rationality, science, civilization, maturity, and the life of the mind; the rest of the world as the realm of ignorance, child-like naiveté, mystical forces, irrationality, and sensuality (all of which could also be desired, especially within the lingering Romantic imagination earlier expressed by Rousseau, discussed mostly in Chapter 7). Such paternalism can also be a pretense of imperialistic greed. In this chapter, we first examine the rapid, profound shifts in theatrical expression that resulted from modern imperialism in the West, guided by this perception of a "superior self" vs. "inferior Other." The "self/other" dichotomy extends to race/ethnicity, class, philosophy, science, and artistic expression. In Asia, Japan began its imperial expansion, whereas China (already an empire) saw clashes in internal and external imperialisms. In Chapter 8, we saw how theatre bolstered the development of a sense of self for the nation-state; in this chapter, we will discover how artistic practices from areas of the "inferior Others" impacted performance in the imperial heartland.

After a discussion of imperialism, we will explain and expand the concept of **Orientalism**. We consider how international expositions and world fairs showcased overseas colonies and imperial wealth while introducing new visual and aural experiences. In the West and Japan, artists began to incorporate foreign imagery in their work, creating new genres. At the same time, consumers saw and desired exotic items that were formerly available only to the wealthy. In contrast, Chinese internal imperialism resulted in a new genre incorporating styles from regional performance of the mass that were initially outlawed but eventually reached national popularity, almost replacing the older, aristocratic styles. The impact of Western imperialism and modernization led both Japan and China to reexamine their traditional theatrical genres and create new theatre to reflect modernity. In many imperialist

DOI: 10.4324/9781003185185-13

nation-states, the middle and upper classes at first disdained lower-class entertainment, but eventually embraced the popular genres and theatrical forms of the "Other."

A scientific development related to theatrical perception is the rise of anthropology, the study of the human developed in theatre by mid-nineteenth century. Scholar James S. Moy writes, "The anthropological gaze emerged as the mechanism by which the common man came to participate in national dreams of empire" (Moy 1993: 7). Theatrical representation (and reception of such representation) became a way to study, comment, theorize, and often satirize the Other.

Modern imperialisms

Imperialism has existed in many periods of history, including the ancient Roman, Persian, Chinese, Ottoman, Aztec, and Ethiopian Empires, and many others. In contrast to these earlier empires, modern types of imperialism flourish partly due to modern technological advances in travel and communication, the development of international capitalism, and much more powerful military resources.

By the late nineteenth century, British and other European imperial expansion, which had begun in the 1600s with state-supported private investment by entities such as the British and Dutch East India Companies, had reached its peak. In addition to parts of Africa and Asia, Britain had occupied Afghanistan and other areas to prevent Russian expansion. In 1894–1895, European imperial nations (Britain, Germany, France, the Netherlands, Portugal, and others) organized the Berlin Conference to divide the colonized world (especially Africa) into zones to lessen economic competition. They imposed artificial linguistic and cultural boundaries without consulting the colonized peoples whose livelihood would be seriously impacted.

The reasons for imperialism are complex, but overall there are three basic overlapping rationales.

1. *Economic or commercial gain*: the previously foreign areas have something valuable that the imperialists desire. Examples include spices, gold, minerals, oil, water, land, slaves, cheap laborers, agricultural resources, or a convenient route to other parts of the world. Usually, large businesses or corporations work hand-in-hand with the imperial government to maintain economic control and to obtain wealth, preventing colonized areas from achieving further economic development.
2. *Military advantage*: the imperialists want to gain military advantage over the foreign country, or fear it as a potential enemy. They feel a need to protect themselves or to prevent future attacks. In such cases, military forces remain in the colonized areas, often controlling or "advising" the local government, or acting as emissaries of the imperium.
3. *Ideological arrogance*: the imperialists believe their culture, religion, language, and/or way of life is superior to that of the colonized people. A "destiny" to rule others often becomes the rationale for such imperial dominance. They may try to convince their own population and the colonized foreigners that incorporation into the imperial whole (and elimination of cultural differences) will offer the colonized peoples opportunities for "civilization," "modernization" or other advantages, such as material gain, spiritual or religious enlightenment, advanced scientific education, or access to artistic or cultural treasures. The imperialists often impose their language and culture on the colonized.

However, belief in the imperialists' superiority sometimes translates into hatred of the colonized, resulting in racism, oppression, massacres, or even attempted genocide.

One example of these overlapping rationales occurred in the mid-1800s, when European nations and the United States used their military power, desire for economic advantage, and belief in their cultural superiority to force Japan to end its long isolation since the 1600s, allowing Western access and trade. Rather than being colonized, Japan rapidly learned from the West how to be an imperialist nation against other Asian countries. In the three decades between 1868 and 1900, Japan had incorporated most of the scientific, technological, social, economic, artistic, and other innovations that had occurred in the West during their isolation. Japanese imperialism began in earnest when Japan decisively defeated Russia in the Russo-Japanese War of 1904–1905, and gained control of Taiwan from China in 1895. In 1904, Japan made Korea a protectorate and formally annexed it in 1910. That same year, a Japanese play *Korean King* suggested that all Asians would welcome Japanese imperial conquest as progress. By the 1930s, the Japanese Empire included a large number of Asian and Pacific colonies, under the euphemistic heading of "The Great East Asia Co-Prosperity Sphere." Western imperial powers reached China in the mid-1800s as well, through opium, wars, and unequal treaties. The devastating loss inspired multiple revolutions which eventually ended the imperial regime. By 1914, more than 80 percent of the world had been colonized by the West. While except for Hong Kong and Macaw, most of East Asia (such as China) was not under direct Western colonial control, Western and Japanese intra-Asian imperialism significantly affected their nationhood and pursuit of modernity. Almost no one escaped the impact of imperialism and colonialism.

A different example is the U.S. concept of "manifest destiny." Many white settlers in the United States argued that they were fulfilling "manifest destiny" by expanding the nation westward, even though expansion entailed exterminating Native Americans and extending areas of African American slavery. When they reached the west coast, Mexicans (California was part of Mexico until 1848), Native Americans, and after the Gold Rush, Chinese immigrants, became the new obstacles. Violence and political policy were both used to fulfill such destiny. Partly believing that the United States had an inevitable right to expand, and partly to end economic depression, the United States militarily took control of Cuba, Puerto Rico, the Philippines, and Guam in the Spanish-American War of 1898.

Orientalism

In 1978, Edward Said (1935–2003), a professor of comparative literature, published a landmark study of primarily British and French imperial practices, focusing on how intellectual traditions about the "Other" are invented and transmitted. The book, titled *Orientalism*, reconsiders the underlying meaning of visual, aural, literary, and theatrical imagery.

Said defines Orientalism as:

> the corporate institution for dealing with the Orient – dealing with it by making statements about it, authorizing views of it, describing it, by teaching it, settling it, ruling

over it: in short, Orientalism as a Western style for dominating, restructuring, and having authority over the Orient.

(Said 1978: 3)

Orientalist representations take two basic forms. The first is to represent the Other as weak, child-like, uneducated, naïve, submissive, and sexually available. In this view, the Other needs to be saved, educated, and uplifted, or is willing to submit to a morally, spiritually, and physically superior power. Often, the Other is depicted as female, childish, or feminized, while the Self is envisioned as male, mature, or masculinized.

The second type of representation portrays the Other as uncivilized, barbaric, powerful, sexually terrifying, scheming, and intellectually incomprehensible. The Other threatens to devour, attack, murder, rape, or destroy the Self. The Other does not value human life, is a crazed killing machine, and, in contrast to the first version, is usually seen as male. This version of the Other needs to be dominated, controlled, and prevented from undermining the civilization of the Self. Fear and hatred of this version of the Other can lead to war, mass murder, or attempted extermination of the Other.

Often, both versions of Orientalism are simultaneously applied to a specific culture.

Under Orientalism, the "Orient" is a constructed and imagined Other. Although most people today think of "the Orient" as meaning Asia, in earlier eras the term referred primarily to India and the Islamic Middle East under British and French imperialism. The broader definition of Orientalism can include other types of ideological dominance over the Other. To "Orientalize" (to apply Orientalism to) the Other is also a way to define the superior Self. Said writes, "the Orient has helped to define Europe (or the West) as its contrasting image, idea, personality, experience" (1978: 1–2).

Non-Western cultures can also harbor views similar to Orientalism about the West, neighboring countries, or minority populations within their own lands. Orientalism is not only a modern phenomenon, as Euripides's *The Bacchae* demonstrates. In that play, the Greek leader Pentheus fears and hates the "Eastern" or "Asiatic" god Dionysus, whom he views as both feminized and dangerously powerful. He is simultaneously repelled and fascinated by this exotic Other.

Orientalism should not be confused with racism, although often these two ideologies go hand-in-hand; both believe in a fundamental difference between races or between the Orient and the Occident. Racism is defined as prejudices against, and practices aimed at, a specific racial group of people, defined as "inferior" due to their genetic characteristics. The targets of Orientalism, however, may include people of one or more "races" who share some other characteristic in common, such as nationality, gender, or religion.

Orientalist representations can be found in educational, historical, political, or artistic works. According to Said:

> The things to look at are style, figures of speech, setting, narrative devices, historical and social circumstances, *not* the correctness of the representation nor its fidelity to some great original. The exteriority of the representation is always governed by

> some version of the truism that if the Orient could represent itself, it would; since it cannot, the representation does the job, for the West, and *faute de mieux*, for the poor Orient.
>
> (Said 1978: 21)

> Orientalist attitudes are not confined to works produced in the past, or to images of another country. An understanding of Orientalism can be a valuable tool for unearthing subtle prejudices or underlying attitudes about ethnicity, gender, disability, class, and so on in a play's script, costumes, settings, style of acting, musical score, or other aspects of performance, or in the way these things have been analyzed by critics or scholars. To take a step further, minority artists, who are often the Orientalized Other, can use "self-Orientalization" – to "yellow up" – as an artistic strategy to gain acceptance by the global audience; artists can also use self-Orientalization to highlight, satirize, or challenge the Orientalist attitude in mainstream discourse in order to empower themselves.

Performing imperialism and orientalism at the great expositions

The London Exhibition of 1851 was the first of many **world fairs** and expositions presenting the non-Western world as a marketplace for Western tourists and capitalists. Between 1851 and 1920, world fairs and expositions attracted more spectators than any single genre of popular diversion, including the circus. At such events, imperial nations celebrated their conquests by showing off the riches of colonial goods and people, and demonstrated their architectural and technological prowess by erecting mammoth buildings and fabulous arcades. The Eiffel Tower, for example, was built for the 1889 Paris World Fair.

At the Great Crystal Palace Exhibition in London, 1851, millions of visitors gasped at wonders such as huge steam engines, Indian miniatures, giant lumps of coal, classical sculptures, and the interior of a palace identified as a "Nubian Court." Housing many of these spectacles was the Crystal Palace itself, covering almost 19 acres in Hyde Park. The Great Exhibition's success led other imperial nations to present their own events. The Paris *Exposition Universelle* took place in 1855. The Philadelphia Centenary of 1876 celebrated 100 years of U.S. independence. Although originally organized to glorify the progress and superiority of their nation-states, world fairs and expositions soon settled into promoting national empires. For example, in reaction to the loss of two French provinces after the Franco-Prussian War (1870–1871), the French increasingly turned to imperial glory abroad and expositions at home to emphasize their greatness (Figure 9.1).

In fairs from 1889 to 1914, entire "villages" were erected, in which colonized peoples from Africa, Asia, the Middle East, the Pacific Islands, and the Americas were displayed like animals in a zoo. They wore native costume and demonstrated local crafts, traditional dances, food preparation, and so on in carefully recreated surroundings, supposedly presenting a "realistic" image of daily life. Of course, it was all a performance. The imported natives were seldom offered decent pay or housing, they did not speak the language, and many suffered severe culture shock and terrible homesickness.

At the 1893 Chicago Columbian Exposition, colonial subjects from the British and French empires were housed in 17 native settings near the Midway Plaisance, an area that also featured "freak" shows and other carnival acts. At the Pan-American Exposition in

Figure 9.1
A view of the buildings and grounds for the Paris Exposition of 1867. Note the nearby barges in the River Seine for popular amusements. From the *Art Journal Illustrated Catalogue of the Universal Exhibition*. Paul Greenhalgh, *Ephemeral Vistas*, Manchester University Press, 1988.

Source: De Luan/Alamy Stock Photo.

Buffalo, NY, in 1901, Native and African Americans were exhibited along with other "primitive" peoples of the world. Native Americans performed war dances in traditional attire, and African Americans were hired to portray happy antebellum slaves in a popular exhibit called "The Old Plantation."

The organizers claimed that these events offered learning opportunities and promoted international understanding. Under the anthropological gaze, all the peoples on display provided "education" and voyeuristic pleasure for the curious visitors as well as capital gain for the organizers. Imperialism and capitalism worked hand-in-hand.

Although these expositions and fairs were sponsored by and took place in Western empires, other nations often participated, showcasing their own imperial conquests. Mexico, for instance, had a display of Aztec and Mayan "antiquities" in the Madrid Exposition in 1892, as a way to demonstrate their cultures and the modernity of the new government (discussed in Chapter 10). After its successful military expansion in Asia, Japan mounted an impressive display of its imperial possessions at the Japan–British Exhibition of 1910; such exhibit boasted their superiority over other Asian peoples and their role as the savior of all Asian civilization as a successful modernizing nation.

In addition to touting the superiority of their nation, race, and empire, the British deployed strategies solidifying their imperial power around the globe – all through performance. Between 1851 and 1914, Britain organized 33 major expositions in India, Australia, and Great Britain. India, symbolizing British subject colonies, usually provided traditional performers, craftspeople, and models of ancient monuments. Australia, symbolizing all white settler societies, celebrated its progress under the empire through its rising cities and manufacturing. As the "mother country," Great Britain displayed its noble traditions, royal munificence, ships, armaments, and its imperial leadership.

All these identifiably British events cemented the interconnections made possible through empire. As one historian notes:

> Participation at the exhibitions as visiting tourists and actors in pageants was part of the process of building [national and imperial] communities. This was not fantasy as escapism, but the fantasy which integrated experience and imagination, thereby linking citizens and subjects together in a seemingly viable, tangible way.
>
> (Hoffenberg 2001: 243)

Such events were the forerunners of the mass spectacles and rallies that would sweep millions into the political enthusiasms of the twentieth century.

Sometimes science was distorted to justify imperial entertainments. Charles Darwin and others who had examined scientific evidence concluded that humans are related to and evolved from animals, and that evolution results from successful adaptation to the environment. Darwin found that the forces driving evolution were complex and mostly due to variations that arise from generation to generation and their suitability to the natural environment. Although today his theories are widely accepted, they were, and continue to be, controversial for some people because the theories conflict with biblical accounts. They were also adopted and twisted to support ideologies such as Social Darwinism, with which Darwin sharply disagreed.

Social Darwinism argues that all human life is a ruthless competition for material goods, leading to "the survival of the fittest." From a Social Darwinist point of view, white Westerners had proven themselves to be the "fittest," but their morality also instructed them to save more "primitive" peoples from extinction. British poet Rudyard Kipling's 1899 poem "The White Man's Burden" had insisted that Euro-American imperialism would help "civilize" colonial subjects. The poem obliges the world's "white men" to assist "Your new-caught, sullen peoples, /Half-devil and half-child." Social Darwinism is related to Orientalism because both see the "superior Self" as a positive, forward development from an "inferior Other." Both assume the idea of inevitable progress. As we will see in Chapter 10, these ideas are crucial to the philosophy of **positivism** and the development of Naturalism.

Imperialism and orientalism on American stage

Although Asians arrived in Americas as early as in the late sixteenth century, in the United States, "Orientals" did not become a noticeable racial category until the nineteenth century. Unfortunately, the perception of this exotic new race was distorted from the very beginning.

The "Oriental" performers in the early nineteenth century such as "the Siamese Twins" Chang and Eng (1811–1874), who arrived in Boston in 1829, and "the Chinese Lady" Afong Moy, who performed in 1830s, made their fame by displaying their bodily "abnormality" – conjoined bodies and bound feet. Their "freakish" bodies were the interest of medical doctors, voyeuristic audience, and capitalists. The Gold Rush brought "adventurers" from all over the world and laborers from China to California. Chinese theatre (in the form of *yueju,* Cantonese opera) arrived in San Francisco as early as 1852; some troupes (including the first known one) brought their own prefabricated theatres. In the following decades, permanent Chinese theatres were established and performances were popular among Chinese and non-Chinese population, even though the performance was in Chinese. However, while the Western audience enjoyed the acrobatics and costume, they often satirized the Chinese operatic singing and music, comparing the unfamiliar sounds to animals' barking and wailing. Eventually the racial animosity against Chinese led to the Chinese Exclusion Act (1882–1943).

The St. Louis World Fair of 1904 featured several tribes of Philippine villagers "scientifically" classified as representing different stages of civilization. Fresh from their victory in the Spanish-American War, U.S. imperialists could now boast that they had joined Great Britain and France to shoulder "the white man's burden." (No mention was made of the ongoing military campaign to suppress factions of rebellious Filipinos.) While some prominent Americans had actively opposed the trend, by 1900 the United States, a former settler colony which built a nation through slavery and the acquisition of aboriginal lands, had joined the ranks of imperialist nations.

Other popular events such as the "Ethnological Congress" at P.T. Barnum's circus encouraged a "scientific," Social Darwinist view of non-Western peoples as savages in need of imperial civilizing. (For more information on Barnum and the circus, see the Additional Materials on the website.)

Imperialism and orientalism in British theatre

During the 1810s and 1820s, the English actor Edmund Kean performed many "exotic" characters: Turkish kings, Saracen warriors, Arab princes, some half-Greek, half-Turk heroes, a Moorish Othello, and an "Oriental" Shylock, the Jewish moneylender in Shakespeare's *The Merchant of Venice.* Several of Kean's star vehicles, including *The Bride of Abydos* (1827) which was adapted from a poem by Romantic poet George Gordon Byron (generally known as Lord Byron, 1788–1824), featured scenes in a harem. The Western male viewers enjoyed the erotic pleasure and the fantasy of participating; in the Western imperialist dream of rescuing exotic maidens from the control of evil Muslim rulers. Just as romantic, pictorial, scenic antiquarianism was reshaping London's Shakespearean productions, Orientalist scenery helped unify English audiences in regard to British imperial conquests in the Middle East.

Melodramas such as these also celebrated the technology that made imperialism possible. For example, *Freedom* (1882) depicts the British invasion of Egypt as a quest to end the slave trade and save a British financier's daughter from sexual slavery in a harem. Such plays suggest that introducing steamships, railroads, and international trade to Egypt more than made up for the unfortunate deaths of a few Egyptians. In *Khartoum* (1885), a newspaper reporter uses the telegraph and other new modes of communication to tell English imperialists about the dire circumstances in that Sudanese city. The melodrama actually reversed the loss of Khartoum to rebelling Islamic tribesmen the year before. Like later adaptations of *Around the World in Eighty Days* and other plays, these melodramas presented British domination as the forward march of white progress and civilization. Such works were patronized by the middle and upper classes.

CASE STUDY: Imperialism, orientalism, and nineteenth-century Indian theatre

Aparna Dharwadker

Imperialism and Orientalism are key terms in postcolonial studies that usually empha-size the West's construction and appropriation of racial and cultural Others through the processes of colonization, but not the ways in which the colonized Others re-sponded to the Western presence. For example, the chapter which includes this case study focuses on "how artistic practices from areas of the 'inferior Others' impacted performance in the imperial heartland." In such a perspective imperialism is, first and foremost, the territorial control of other countries or regions for the sake of material gain; it is also the ideology that rationalizes the violence of conquest by invoking Western racial, political, scientific, intellectual, and cultural superiority over the col-onized territories. Similarly, the approach to Orientalism in the chapter is based on Edward Said's seminal discussion of it as "a Western style for dominating, restructuring, and having authority over the Orient" – "the Orient" being defined as a region that stretches from Egypt to Japan, serves as the opposite of the Western "Occident," and is paradoxically both contemptible and threatening (Said 1978: 3).

This case study presents five main arguments to demonstrate that nineteenth-century Indian theatre had a distinctly different relationship with both imperialism and Orientalism, even though it emerged during the period of British colonialism. First, for complex historical and cultural reasons this theatre was practiced in major modern Indian languages rather than in the imperial language, English, and relied mainly on Indian narratives and presentational styles in terms of form and content. Second, it benefited greatly from Europe's fascination with India's classical Sanskrit past, which shaped Orientalism as a scholarly field rather than as a form of political and cultural denigration in nineteenth-century India. Third, translations of Sanskrit plays into many modern European and Indian languages, and translations of Euro-pean plays into Indian languages again created relationships of mutual admiration and reciprocity between India and Europe. Fourth, colonial Indian theatre was political from the beginning, and found many different ways to express anticolonial sentiments, often inviting censorship by the colonial state. Finally, the introduction of print during the colonial period transformed the nature of dramatic authorship, and this has given modern Indian theatre as a whole a new kind of visibility in world theatre. The para-graphs that follow explain each of these features in order.

The British conquest of India had begun with the Battle of Plassey in 1757, so when a secular and commercial theatre began to take shape during the 1850s in the colonial metropolises of Calcutta and Bombay, its basic models were Anglo-European (these cities have now been renamed Kolkata and Mumbai, but the old names are retained here for historical accuracy). The new theatre buildings in the two cities followed the architecture of British provincial theatres, the technologies of production emulated the Victorian theatre of spectacle, and the system of ticket sales established the "entertainment for profit" model that British theatre had followed since the late sixteenth century.

However, there were several reasons why theatre was successful in retaining a large degree of cultural autonomy despite India's political subjection to an imperialist regime. Historically, classical Sanskrit emerged from the same Indo-European roots as Greek and Latin, and gave rise to a large number of modern Indian languages by the same processes that connected Greek and Latin to the modern European languages. As a literary culture, India thus had a powerful and continuous tradition of multilingual literacy over a millennium that remained dominant even after English arrived as the colonizer's language around 1800. When new Indian plays began to appear from the 1840s onward, they were written in major modern languages such as Bengali, Marathi, Hindi, Urdu, Kannada, Telugu, and Tamil, and not in English. As an orally performed genre, theatre always has to be fully intelligible to its immediate audience, and the performance culture of the modern Indian languages was already so strong that it could not be displaced by English. The narratives of colonial plays were also based on Indian mythology, history, legend, and folklore as often as on contemporary sociopolitical experience, so that "traditional" Indian subject matter was prominently staged in important new works, and viewers consumed cultural material that was familiar to them, not alien. In addition, the presentation of these narratives invariably involved indigenous styles of music and dance that were adapted to suit the tastes of an educated, middle-class urban audience, and became immensely popular. With some regional variations, these trends anchored the three main varieties of colonial theatre – the Bengali public stage based in Calcutta, the Marathi *sangeet natak* (musical drama) based in Bombay, and the nationally circulating, spectacle-oriented Parsi theatre in Urdu and Hindi. In short, nineteenth-century Indian theatre existed in a colonial environment, but in terms of language, content, and presentational style, it lay beyond the direct control of the British imperial state. European realism in the style of Ibsen and Chekhov did not gain a foothold in Indian theatre until the mid-twentieth century, and as the medium of original composition English lags well behind languages such as Marathi, Bengali, Hindi, and Kannada even in the early twenty-first century.

My second argument – nineteenth-century theatre's unusual connection to Orientalism – has its basis in the deep investment Anglo-European scholars made in retrieving, translating, and disseminating the poetic drama and performance aesthetics of classical Sanskrit playwrights such as Kalidasa, Shudraka, Vishakhadutt, and Bhavabhuti. Groundbreaking translations, especially of Kalidasa's plays, by British Orientalists such as William Jones, H. H. Wilson, and Monier-Williams over the 1789–1853 period positioned drama as the premier Sanskrit genre, ready to be added to the canons of world literature. European valorizations of the classical Sanskrit period as India's "golden age," in turn, encouraged Indian artists and intellectuals to re-claim their past under the transformative conditions of colonialism, and to place its legacies at the center of a national cultural renaissance. In the particular case of theatre, practitioners adopted Sanskrit dramatic theory and the form of the *natak* (serious full-length play based on a mythical or historical narrative) as their conceptual models in a cultural project which sought to restore drama to the pre-eminent literary position it held in the ancient past (see Dharwadker 2019: xlvi–li). This entire field of activity falls under the "earlier" meaning of the term that Said also discusses in his book – "Orientalism" as the academic discipline of "anyone who teaches, writes about, or researches the Orient" (Said 1978: 2). In relation to nineteenth-century Indian theatre, Orientalism therefore functioned as a form of scholarship focused on the philological (and appreciative) study of Sanskrit rather than as a "discourse of domination" (a concept Said borrowed from the Italian political theorist Antonio Gramsci).

The careers of three major nineteenth-century playwrights who wrote in three different languages illustrate the arguments I have offered so far about theatre's relation to imperialism and Orientalism. Michael Madhusudan Dutt (1824–1873), the first important playwright in Bengali, published three significant full-length plays and two farces, all of them written between 1858 and 1860. Among the plays, *Sharmishtha* was based on a well-known episode in the Sanskrit epic, the *Mahabharata*, *Padmavati* on a Greek myth, and *Krishnakumari* on a legend from the Rajasthan region. The two farces, titled *Ekei ki bale sabhyata?* (*Do You Call this Civilization?*) and *Buro saliker ghare ron* (*The Old Fool's Fads*), satirized anglicized young Bengali men and the hypocrisy of the older generation, respectively. The plays of Bhartendu Harishchandra (1850–1885), a foundational figure in modern Hindi poetry and criticism, were not performed in his lifetime, but were written with two explicitly stated purposes: to establish the classical origins and high cultural value of drama as a form, and to give the evolving Hindi language a more prominent place in the theatre. Reflecting Dutt's proclivities in a different language, Bhartendu's plays dealt with mythic and historical subjects (*Satya harishchandran* [*Truthful Harishchandra*, 1876], *Neeldevi* [1881]), or resorted to the forms of allegory and farce for topical political comment (*Bharat durdasha* [*India's Plight*, 1875], *Andher nagari* [*The Upside-Down City*, 1881]).

The third playwright, Krishnaji Prabhakar Khadilkar (1872–1948) belonged fully to the world of colonial commercial theatre, and was the leading figure in the genre of the Marathi *sangeet natak*, which constructed a narrative around virtuosic singing in the Indian classical style. Several of his plays portrayed well-known mythical women (*Menaka*, *Savitri*, *Draupadi*), others dealt with historical figures (*Sawai madhavarao yancha mrityu* [*The Death of Sawai Madhavrao*, 1896]), and still others addressed the complexity of gender relations in a patriarchal society (*Manapman* [*Honor and Dishonor*, 1911]). Khadilkar's outstanding contribution to colonial theatre history, however, was as the author of *Kichaka-vadh* (*The Slaying of Kichaka*, 1907), which became a sensational example of colonial censorship because he was accused of using another very well-known episode in the *Mahabharata* as a screen to incite the murder of British colonial officials (see Solomon 2015 for a comprehensive discussion of this late colonial event). As these examples confirm, Britain as the colonizing culture was either entirely absent from the content of nineteenth-century Indian theatre, or appeared as an object of mockery and critique. Furthermore, the high value these playwrights placed on the drama form was directly related to the Orientalist canonization of Sanskrit.

The careers of Dutt and Harishchandra also illustrate my third main point: from the beginning, translation, adaptation, and transculturation were an intrinsic part of theatre activity, and had the effect of both complicating and reinforcing this theatre's indigenizing energies. During the later nineteenth century, the focus was on translations of Sanskrit drama and Shakespeare, but after 1910 the entire canon of Western and world theatre was gradually and systematically "carried across" into theatrically active Indian languages. Dutt translated Shri Harsha's Sanskrit play *Ratnavali* into English in 1858 so that his patrons, the Rajas of Paikpara, could invite colonial officials, including the Governor of Bengal, to the performance at North Calcutta's Belgatchia Villa Theatre. Harishchandra's major translations from Sanskrit were of *Ratnavali* and Vishakhadutt's political play *Mudrarakshasa* (*The Signet Ring of Rakshasa*), and at his death in 1885 he also left an incomplete Hindi translation of Shakespeare's *The Merchant of Venice* titled *Durlabh bandhu* (*Invaluable Friend*). Translations of Shakespeare became major attractions on the colonial musical stage, and translators were impelled to "Indianize" the original play by recreating it fully in the cultural codes of its receiving audience. The Marathi playwright G. B. Deval's (1855–1916) musical version of *Othello*, titled *Jhunjharrao,* was a sensational success in 1890, and the Gujarati stage mounted an equally successful happy-ending version of the same play, titled *Saubhagya sundari* (*The Fortunate Beauty*) in 1901. Across the literary-popular spectrum, the work of translation simultaneously fulfilled multiple functions: it renewed the classic in the present, demonstrated the strength of the target language and the resilience of its cultural codes, and expanded the theatrical repertory. Once enough original plays had been produced in various theatrically active languages, translation also became a vital conduit for the transregional circulation of successful new works in those languages.

The various forms of opposition to the alien colonial presence in works by all three playwrights discussed above underscore my fourth argument – the anticolonial political orientation of nineteenth-century Indian theatre from the outset. The first major confrontation took place in 1861, when the English translation of Dinabandhu Mitra's play *Nil-darpan* (*The Indigo Mirror*, Bengali 1860) led to the arrest and prosecution, not of the original author or the anonymous translator (who was in fact Michael Madhusudan Dutt), but of the publisher, a liberal-minded Anglican priest named James E. Long. The play criticizes the colonial government's agrarian policies in Bengal, which forced farmers to give up cash crops and cultivate indigo, a very difficult plant to grow, because it was needed in the cotton mills of Manchester. Mitra focused his attack on the "West Indian devils" – demonic overseers brought in from the West Indian plantation colonies to subdue Bengali farmers – and set them on a collision course with members of a landed family modeled on heroic figures from the second famous Sanskrit epic, the *Ramayana*. In 1875–1876, an extended visit by the Prince of Wales Albert Edward, Queen Victoria's eldest son, prompted such a spate of topical political satires that in March 1876, the colonial government passed the Dramatic Performances Control Act, similar to the Licensing Act that had been on the books in England since 1737 (discussed in Chapter 7). The Act allowed the government to prohibit a performance in advance on the basis of the script submitted for police approval, or disrupt it at any stage when it was already in progress. Over the next 50 years, the law was used extensively for censorship and suppression of political theatre, including Khadilkar's *Kichaka-vadha*, and, astonishingly, has remained on the books in post-independence India, despite repeated calls for its repeal since the 1950s. In the late nineteenth century, the Act conveyed a hostility to "native" performance on the part of the colonial government that added other layers of meaning to the preponderance of mythic and historical narratives in theatre – they provided a heroic antidote to the indignities of subjection in the present, and served as indirect (and hence "safer") means for the expression of anticolonial sentiment.

The last feature of colonial Indian theatre that connects productively with Britain's imperial presence is the interrelated dynamic of authorship, print, and performance. Orality and writing were both powerful and unbroken traditions in precolonial India, but the arrival of print around 1800 transformed the workings of multilingual literacy on a historically unprecedented scale. It is important to note in this context that the distinction in India is not between orality and writing, but between orality/writing and print, because as Sheldon Pollock points out, "the dichotomy oral-literate neither encapsulates that of folk-elite nor fits with received European notions of cultural-historical stages. For one thing, written literature continued to be orally performed among most social orders well into the modern period" (Pollock 2003: 22). Print was a technology of mechanical reproduction and mass dissemination that turned Indian viewers and listeners into readers, and permanently altered the conditions for the production and consumption of literary/theatrical forms, pedagogy, disciplinary knowledges, and public discourse of all kinds. In the field of theatre, print enabled the emergence of seminal authors such as Dutt, Harishchandra, and Rabindranath Tagore, for whom playwriting was one important strain in a complex and varied literary career, focusing especially on poetry. If these authors represented the "literary" end of the theatrical spectrum, there were many more playwrights who represented the "popular," commercially successful, and performance-oriented end. But playwrights in the second category, especially major figures like Girish Chandra Ghosh (1844–1912), D. L. Roy (1863–1913), Kshirode Prasad Vidyavinode (1863–1927), G. B. Deval, S. K. Kolhatkar (1871–1934), Khadilkar, and Narayan Prasad Betab (1872–1945), also published their work with the same regularity as their highbrow contemporaries, establishing a lasting connection between drama/theatre and the print medium. As an institution of modern print culture, authorship was therefore a nineteenth-century phenomenon which made many Indian writers comparable to their modern Western counterparts for the first time. In the particular case of theatre, the colonial-era playwright-as-author became foundational to the development of modern Indian theatre in general as a notable formation within contemporary world theatre. When considered collectively, the features I have outlined in this case study bear out my opening claim – that in comparison with British imperial colonies in other parts of the world, colonial Indian theatre has a very unconventional relationship to imperialism and Orientalism.

> Aparna Dharwadker is Professor of English and Interdisciplinary Theatre Studies at the University of Wisconsin-Madison, and a widely published scholar whose most recent monograph is *Cosmo-Modernism and Theatre in India* (Columbia University Press, 2024).

Key references

Dharwadker, A.B. (ed.) (2019) *A Poetics of Modernity: Indian Theatre Theory, 1850 to the Present*, Oxford: Oxford University Press.

Pollock, S. (2003) Introduction. *Literary Cultures in History: Reconstructions from South Asia*, ed. S. Pollock, Berkeley and Los Angeles: University of California Press, 1–36.

Said, E.W. (1978) *Orientalism*, New York: Vintage.

Solomon, R.H. (2015) *Globalization, Nationalism, and the Text of* Kichaka-vadha, London: Anthem.

Variety theatre and music hall

Other new types of popular entertainment also developed, catering to a predominantly working- and lower-class audience. To these audience members, imperial expansion was less important than making it through everyday life. In some ways, they were "internal Others," perceived by the upper classes in the similar negative terms as colonized peoples. Sometimes members of the upper classes would "go slumming" and patronize lower-class entertainments; consequently, aspects of popular entertainment seeped into more aristocratic styles, just as foreign elements had done. At the same time, lower-class audiences both imitated and made fun of aristocratic passions.

 One major form that proliferated after 1850 was **variety theatre**. Variety is simply a series of light entertainments unconnected by any overriding theme, story, or major star. Since the Renaissance, theatre in Western cultures had often incorporated singers, acrobats, performing animals, and other diversions between the acts of a regular drama. In the mid-nineteenth century, however, showmen strung together a series of such "numbers" without providing a regular play as the main attraction. Variety took numerous forms after 1850. One was the blackface minstrel show, which began in the United States (as discussed in Chapter 8) but quickly spread to Europe and to European colonies.

Another form of variety was the **burlesque** show, which began with female performers doing a parody, or "burlesque," of a popular play or work of literature. Eventually, the parodic elements dropped out, and by 1900 the typical burlesque show in England and the United States featured a male comic, several comic sketches, dance acts, and musical pieces, plus highly sexualized females in all of the numbers. The striptease, now identified as the central act of a burlesque show, did not make its appearance in the United States until the 1920s.

Concert saloons, which peddled beer and food along with entertainment, appeared in industrializing cities in Britain during the 1850s. They led to the most resilient and significant form of popular variety theatre, the **music hall**. Although "music hall" is an English Victorian term, it may designate any series of unconnected entertainments on an indoor stage. Music hall entertainment in the United States was called **vaudeville**.

Music hall songs sentimentalized romantic love, delighted in sexual pleasure (a taboo subject for proper Victorians), or derided the entanglements of marriage. Policemen, government clerks, and other figures of authority provided frequent butts for music hall humor. The music hall generally remained culturally and politically conservative. Entertainers might poke fun at factory discipline and lambaste politicians caught up in scandals, but they usually applauded English victories in war and the racism that accompanied English imperialism. Nevertheless, early music hall variety preserved aspects of traditional English customs that provided workers and others with strategies for enduring and occasionally countering the strictures of Victorian life that oppressed them.

By the 1890s, many halls no longer allowed patrons to eat and drink while watching the show. They also featured more homogenized acts that would not offend Victorian tastes. Although gentrification and standard-ization drained the class-based vitality from music hall entertainment after 1890, its anti-Victorian legacy had wide ramifications in the twentieth century – from satiric popular songs and a scandal-mongering penny press to the electoral success of socialism in English politics (Figure 9.2).

In England, music hall lasted longer than variety in other countries and probably had a more enduring effect on the national culture. In 1866, London had over 30 large music halls and more than 200 smaller ones; a few of the larger halls seated over 3,000 spectators. Most English music halls in the 1870s provided entertainment, food, and drink to a predominantly working- and lower-class audience. During the 1880s, some music hall entrepreneurs, seeking higher profits through in-creased respectability, opened new halls in middle- and upper-class neighbor-hoods. The halls reached their high point of popularity around 1910, when competition from silent films began to erode their numbers, which fur-ther declined in the 1930s and 1940s as the radio brought entertainment into homes. In the 1950s, television

Figure 9.2

George Leybourne, a *lion comique* of the music hall stage, who wrote and sang "Champagne Charlie" (c.1867).

Source: Sheridan Libraries/Levy/Gado/Getty Images.

delivered the deathblow to the English music hall. However, aspects of music hall performance found their way into the plays of authors such as Samuel Beckett (1906–1989) and Harold Pinter (1930–2008), both discussed in Chapter 12.

The British musical hall styled entertainment took roots in Sidney, Australia, in the late nineteenth century, generally under the name "Tivoli." Tivoli circuit, which included a wide variety of shows from revue, opera, ballet, singing, musical comedy to minstrelsy, was very popular from 1890s to 1950s.

For a discussion of another form of British popular entertainment, pantomime, see the case study on the website.

Internal and external imperialism in China and the creation of *jingju* (Beijing Opera)

From the First Emperor (259–210 BCE), who united various states to establish an ethnic Han-based Chinese empire (see Chapter 2), China maintained its imperial status despite dynastic changes, until Sun Yat-sen's revolution to establish the modern China in 1912 (Chapter 11). Except for two dynasties – the Yuan (1279–1368) ruled by the Mongols and the Qing (1644–1911) by the Manchus – imperial China was Han-based, with its political power largely centered around the mid-lower Yellow River region, although ethnic Han in different parts of China had different languages, cultures, and theatres. As territorial expansion was essential for empire building, throughout premodern China, the non-Han neighbors such as the Mongols and the Uyghurs – seen as ethnic minorities today but as "barbarians" outside of the "middle kingdom" in premodern times – were always the object of desire of the Chinese empire. Emperor Qianlong (reigned 1735–1795), who consolidated power and wealth by conquering the Mongols, Uyghurs and other ethnic groups, brought China to another historical peak of imperial power in the eighteenth century. The relatively long period of internal peace and territorial expansion made the Qing a very prosperous and populous empire by the mid-nineteenth century; China's population reached around 430 million, more than one third of the world population.

The Mongol rulers abolished the Imperial Examinations, a nation-wide examination system to select scholars to serve at local or central governments (see Chapter 2) and antagonized Chinese elites (Chapter 4); however, the Manchu rulers generally embraced the Chinese artistic and literary tradition and valued the Exam system. Despite the overall change of hair styles and dress codes in daily life as well as the political system, the Manchu imperial court also adopted Chinese customs and many emperors were excellent poets, calligraphers, and lovers of Chinese art and theatre.

Kunqu (discussed in Chapter 4) was the dominant dramatic form from the late fourteenth to mid-eighteenth century. During the mid-to-late eighteenth century, *kunqu* began to wane and regional dramas, which were favored by commoners, proliferated. *Kunqu* was usually authored by famous literati and the scripts were read by the elite as high literature. Regional troupes, however, often created their plays based on stories from popular novels or earlier performances and their authors remained anonymous; the performance, rather than the text, was the focus in regional drama. Among the hundreds of regional forms, the general tradition of Han costume and acting style (dance, gestures, movements, fighting) was similar; however, the local languages, music and singing style, along with unique local cultural characteristics marked the differences among genres. While actresses never completely stopped performing throughout Chinese history, roving troupes of lower-status all-male performers dominated the regional drama scene; some believe that single-sex troupes made traveling more convenient. These troupes catered to the tastes of ordinary people, rather than the elite scholars and aristocrats of big cities. Among the most important regional styles at this time were "clapper operas" (*bangzi qiang* [bahng-dzi chi-ahng]).

Clapper operas feature musical instruments such as stringed fiddles, side-blown flutes, drums and cymbals, and clappers. Clappers include blocks of wood (*bangzi*) that the players strike with a stick, and strips of wood strung together (*ban*) flicked by the players. Overall, the clappers produced a distinctive sound and rhythm; moreover, compared to the earlier *kunqu*, whose music was melodious and elegant, the percussion section of the clapper operas created a mood that was more boisterous and lively.

In 1779, Wei Changsheng (1744–1802), a famous clapper actor from Sichuan Province, brought his troupe to Beijing, hoping to participate in upcoming celebrations for Emperor Qianlong's seventieth birthday. Wei was a male *dan* (a male actor specializing in female roles) who was also an accomplished acrobat skilled in male martial roles. He was sometimes credited for inventing some "feminizing" stage devices (such as hairstyle) and techniques for male *dan* actors. The art of "stilting" (*caiqiao*) created the illusion of bound feet: by fitting the front of the feet into small pointy shoes (*qiao*, stilts), actors performed on tiptoes with the elevated soles covered by pants that were slightly longer than normal. The difficult and painful technique was only necessary when male actors needed to "fake" femininity; however, it was later adopted by actresses in the modern era as a special skill since foot-binding was no longer in practice. The new and exotic performance style of Wei Changsheng's troupe captured people's imagination. They remained in Beijing for six years despite official attempts to censor them. In 1785, they were banned from the stage due to Wei's excessively bawdy acting style. Nevertheless, scholars have called the troupe's arrival and lingering effect "the prelude to the birth of Beijing opera" (Mackerras 1983: 103).

In 1790, troupes from many parts of the empire came to Beijing for the emperor's eightieth birthday. Like the celebrations a decade previously, events were held in public locales – they were intended not for the emperor to see or hear, but to keep the general populace entertained. The court and other aristocrats disdained these popular genres and patronized the more elegant *kunqu*. Troupes from Anhui Province brought distinctive styles, which were combined with local elements and developed into a new genre. This popular new form is known as *jingju* [jing jyu] or *jingxi*. Both terms mean "capital drama," as Beijing was the capital (*jing*) for the last three dynasties of imperial China. In English, the genre is generally termed "Beijing Opera" or "Peking opera." However, this popular opera did not make its debut at the imperial court until 1860. In 1884, the Empress Dowager Cixi (1835–1908) requested *jingju* performances for her own birthday. *Jingju* – once a lower-class regional genre – finally enjoyed imperial patronage.

Western imperialism and Chinese internal imperialism co-existed and did not come into direct conflict until the eighteenth century. In the West, when *Chinoiserie* – items and styles that looked Chinese or were supposedly of Chinese origin – became fashionable, the demand of "Oriental" goods from expensive porcelain tea sets to cheap decorative fans were very desirable. By the end of the century, tea became a necessary commodity for the entire British population. To eliminate the trade deficit caused by importation of tea from China, the British started smuggling opium to China. When the Chinese government tried to ban

Figure 9.3
Jingju actress Wei Hai Min from Taiwan as Yu Ji, performing the farewell sword dance for the Hegemon King of the Chu before the final battle in *Hegemon King Says Farewell to His Queen* (*Bawang bieji*). Mei Lanfang was famous for playing this role. Wei Hai Min was trained in the Mei Lanfang style.
Source: © Nicolas Fan.

the opium import, the British waged wars with advanced weaponry and East Asia became a new ground for British imperial expansion. Other Western imperial powers soon joined the British, trying to take advantage of the weakened Qing Empire; by the end of the nineteenth century, Japan also had a successful imperial expansion in China. The rebalancing of the world powers in the late nineteenth century partially contributed to the international perception of the despicable and feminized "Orientals," such as seen in the previous section on American imperialism. In the twentieth century, *jingju* took on the national mission to restore the Chinese reputation and masculinity on the world stage. The famous male *dan* actor Mei Lanfang (1894–1961) toured Japan, the United States, and the Soviet Union during the 1920s and 1930s. The U.S. tour was designed to demonstrate both Mei's onstage artistic femininity and offstage real masculinity, breaking the stereotype of emasculated "Oriental" men (discussed later in this chapter). The 1935 Moscow visit made a great impression on Stanislavski and Brecht (see the discussion of Brecht in Chapter 11). *Jingju* became a "national opera" of China, both for the Chinese and for the non-Chinese in the first half of the twentieth century; after the end of the Chinese Civil war (1949), it would become part of the nationalist propaganda, both in mainland China and in Taiwan. The birth and growth of *jingju* paralleled the rise and fall of the Qing Empire, the impact of Western and Japanese imperialism, and the long road to modernity, from the late eighteenth to the twentieth century. A local art for the populace that ascended to the power center, *jingju* represented both internal imperialism and nationalism, and a tool to fight external imperialism; nevertheless, its political significance never completely destroyed its appeal to the populace. In today's international arena, *jingju* is a tokenized "Chinese opera" that plays a significant role in theatrical interculturalism and globalization (Figure 9.3).

THINKING THROUGH THEATRE HISTORIES: WESTERN ARTISTS APPROPRIATE NON-WESTERN IMAGERY AND TECHNIQUES

In the West, the popularity of world fairs, exhibitions, and Orientalist plays increased demand for exotic items, from ceramic tea sets, decorative fans, to "native" costumes. In an earlier craze that began in the seventeenth century, Voltaire's *The Orphan of China*, discussed in Chapter 6, is an example of *Chinoiserie* in theatre. After Japan was opened to the West in the late nineteenth century, *Japonisme*, Japanese-like aesthetics became popular in the West. Many famous painters during this period were influenced by or experimented with *Japonisme,* such as Vincent Van Gogh, Pierre-Auguste Renoir, Claude Monet, and Édouard Manet. W. B. Yeats (1865–1929), Irish poet and dramatist, famously used *nō* style and theme in his "plays for dancers," with the participation of the Japanese dancer Itō Michio. His *At the Hawk's Well* (1916) represented another aspect of *Japonisme.*

Both *Chinoiserie* and *Japonisme* can be seen as a personal taste, a fashion statement, or an artistic inspiration for artists who always look for new muses to invigorate their imagination. However, it is sometimes very difficult to distinguish inspiration from borrowing, or borrowing from appropriation. Is *La Courtisane* by Van Gogh a work that imitated or was

Figure 9.4
Vincent Van Gogh's *La Courtisane,*
after Kesai Eisen (1887).
Source: © Heritage Image Partnership Ltd/
Alamy Stock Photo.

Figure 9.5
Claude Monet's *La Japonaise* (1885).
Source: CBW/Alamy Stock Photo.

inspired by the original Japanese woodblock print by Kesai Eisen? (Figure 9.4) Is Monet's *La Japonaise* (Figure 9.5) a fashion statement or an act of appropriation? Appropriation, which means insensitively and inappropriately taking something for one's own use, can be very problematic when the action misrepresents the Other in a power-imbalanced relationship between the borrower and the borrowed. For instance, Peter Brook's *The Mahabharata* (1985), a grand production based on an Indian epic, was often seen as insensitive and even offensive, partially because of the misrepresentation of the Indian classic and partially because of the colonial relationship between British and Indians (see Chapter 14). Western artists who were engaged in *Chinoiserie* or *Japonisme* might not believe Western imperialism or Orientalism played a part in their artistic imagination; on the contrary, some held a Romantic belief that only Asian or ancient art could regenerate the Western culture which was destroyed by industrial revolution – a similar view to

Figure 9.6

Ruth St. Denis performing *Egypta*, one of her "Oriental dances."

Source: Jerome Robbins Dance Division, The New York Public Library. "Ruth St. Denis in Egypta." The New York Public Library Digital Collections. 1910. https://digitalcollections. nypl.org/items/510d47df-854d-a3d9-e040-e00a 18064a99

be repeated in Western avant-garde movements and intercultural theatre in the twentieth century. Nevertheless, the belief that the "Orient" was permanently ancient, classical, naïve, pure, and primitive still played an important part in Western hegemony in the international arena.

In the performing arts, the borrowing from the "Orient" goes beyond décor or text; it is also about kinesthetics and embodiment, such as in choreography and acting. For example, Ruth St. Denis (1879–1968) credited an advertisement for cigarettes depicting Egyptian deities as the sole inspiration for her signature "Oriental" dances; however, she was indeed working closely with the "Nauch" dancers (Indian dancers), whose contribution to her kinesthetic development is often neglected (Figure 9.6). Was inspiration or appropriation of African and Asian art a key factor in her dance creation? As Ruth St. Denis is regarded as a pioneer of American modern dance, we might want to consider the possible Asian influence or multicultural origin of "American" dance.

CASE STUDY: Yellowface

Daphne P. Lei

The theatrical embodiment of the Oriental Other is called **yellowface**. Esther Kim Lee defines yellowface as a "theatrical convention of using makeup, costumes, and visual technology to transform someone to look East Asian" (2022: 1). Although there were earlier performances involving yellowface techniques, such as *The Orphan of China,* the yellowface convention did not become a fashion till the late nineteenth century. Chapter 8 discusses blackface minstrelsy and playing Indian – two types of theatrical representations of the racial Other in the United States; the popularity of such performances in the first half of the nineteenth century, unfortunately, had set a tone for the new national Other, the "Orientals," in theatrical representations. Some yellowface actors also performed in blackface minstrel shows. Under the Orientalist view, the Orient is incapable of representing itself; therefore, yellowface was sometimes considered a better or more "authentic" representation than what Asian actors could offer. For instance, in her visit to San Francisco Chinatown in 1891, the famous French actress Sarah Bernhardt performed "Chinese" songs (with a wailing sound), dance, and imitations of Chinese orchestra and Confucius. Her naturalistic acting style with a sword apparently frightened her Chinese co-actor and brought down the house. "The Western way of playing Chinese appeared more effective and successful than the Chinese way" (Lei 2006: 66).

Yellowface theatrical representations generally fall into two categories, each with some variations. *Comical yellowface* is similar to blackface minstrel shows: the characters of "Chinaman" were played by white actors, with a specific yellowface technique. Unlike in Europe, where the Orient still seemed distant, the United States, especially the West, encountered the first wave of Asian immigrants. Many Chinese men were brought to the United States for working in the gold mines in the 1850s and later in the railroad construction; however, after the completion of the Transcontinental Railroad in 1869, this new ethnic group was seen as an economic threat as they competed in the labor market. Politicians took advantage of such animosity and passed various laws to suppress the Chinese in California and to further curtail immigration. By branding the Chinese as the yellow peril, politicians gained tremendous political power. The culmination was the Chinese Exclusion Act (1882–1943), the first U.S. immigration law to target a specific nationality. "Chinaman," "John Chinaman," "Chinee," and "heathen Chinee" were the derogatory terms for Asians during the nineteenth century in the United States.

Satirizing the racial Other helps fulfill "manifest destiny"; many famous writers and actors were engaged in creating yellowface characters. The comic "Chinese" character "Ah Sin" created by Mark Twain and Bret Harte (1876) was "a particular construction divorced from the experience of Chinese people" (Metzger 2004: 643). He is child-like and ignorant, as well as cunning and despicable. As a Chinese domestic servant working for a white household in California, he is pitied by the matron of the family as a "poor dumb animal, with his tail on top of head instead of where

Figure 9.7

English actor/singer George Grossmith in "yellowface" makeup, as Ko-Ko in the original 1885 production of *The Mikado*.

Source: © Theatre and Performance Collection, V&A Images, Victoria and Albert Museum.

it ought to be" (the male hairstyle in contemporary China was the "queue," a long braid with shaved forehead). For the master of the house, he is a "slant-eyed son of the yellow jaunders" (Williams 1997: 45), "moral cancer," and "unsolvable political problem" (Williams 1997: 46) who always deserves a beating or a kick in the butt. His language and behavior represent the imagined frontier life, such as associating Chinese with laundry business: "You wantee washee-washee? One dollar hap dozen – me plenty washee you" (Williams 1997: 45). Ah Sin also speaks false Spanish: "me no sabee" (I don't know), as the frontier society was racially mixed. According to Mark Twain, Charles T. Parsloe (1836–1898), a former minstrel actor, had "true Mongrel look" because of the gap between his two front teeth. Parsloe presented "East Coast audience how a Chinaman looked and behaved" (Lee 2022: 54–55).

Sometimes yellowface is presented in music and dance in a light-hearted and playful manner, such as *The Mikado* and *The Nutcracker. The Mikado*, a comic operetta by librettist William S. Gilbert (1836–1911) and composer Arthur Sullivan (1842–1900) was an exaggerated version of *Japonisme*. Premiered in Savoy Theatre in London (1885), *The Mikado* was set in a far-away and imaginary place called "Japan," where people had funny names (Nanki-poo, Yum-Yum, Pooh-Bah, Pish-Tush) and sang clever fast-tempo songs. White actresses wore loose-fitting kimonos (without corsets) and wigs, carrying fans and parasols and acting in a childish way; white actors wore Japanese outfits and carried swords, frequently mentioning committing suicide. "Japanese" scenery and music were also incorporated. The humorous yellowface was proven a successful theatrical novelty for the British audience, as *The Mikado* was extremely popular, having one of the longest runs of theatre in London up to that time. It gained international popularity outside of London and is still one of the most produced works of musical theatres today – often with yellowface (Figure 9.7). In 2014, the Gilbert and Sullivan

Society in Seattle produced *The Mikado*, with all but 2 of the 40 Japanese characters played by yellowfaced white actors.

Another famous example is the Tea Dance (or the Chinese dance) of the beloved fairytale ballet *Nutcracker*, with music by the Russian composer Pytor Tchaikovsky and original choreography by Lev Ivanov and Marius Petipa. There are some other famous short "ethnic" dance pieces such as the Chocolate dance (Spanish) and Coffee dance (Arabian). At the premiere performance at the Marinsky Theatre in St. Petersburg in 1892, apparently the audience loved the Tea Dance so much that they requested an encore. The "Chinese style" we are familiar with today is from George Balanchine's 1954 choreography, supposedly based on the original, although it was difficult to verify due to the scanty information available about the original notation. Nevertheless, the child-like innocent smiles, exaggerated makeup, constant bowing, acrobatic-styled high jumping, and pointy index fingers in both hands (some believe they resemble chopsticks) created one of the long-lasting images of the "delightful" Orientals. Many theatres today still rely on *Nutcracker* performances during the Christmas season to generate a large portion of revenues for the entire year.

(Sym)pathetic yellowface is the other theatrical category which seemed to avoid overt racial satire and animosity and even generate sympathy for Asian characters, such as *The First Born* by Francis Powers. Powers spent a few weeks living in San Francisco's Chinatown, so his "Chinatown play" – a tragic story of death and vengeance, supposedly based on real events happened in Chinatown – was believed to have "the most sympathetic portrayal of the Chinese" on the nineteenth-century American stage (Williams 1997: 149). It premiered in San Francisco in 1897 and the revised version continued to be successful in New York and London. The "authentic" play had a "Chinese" set (joss house, temple, wash house, as well as dried fowl and salted fish in store), "Chinese" speech (often inaccurate romanization of Cantonese and "a chatter of Chinese words") sprinkled throughout the play (Williams 1997: 152) and various stage actions in "Chinese style." Such stylized authenticity of Chinese was taken to a much higher level in *The Yellow Jacket* by George C. Hazelton and Harry J. Benrimo (1912). *The Yellow Jacket* is about a rightful heir to the throne overcoming obstacles to reach the happy ending. Instead of the Chinese daily life, it highlights Chinese theatrical conventions as a novelty for the white audience. Traditional Chinese theatre convention requires stagehands (uncostumed) to rearrange the simple set or bring in props, both during the performance and between scenes. There was no drawing curtains or other attempts to hide the actions of the stagehands. Chinese audiences are accustomed to seeing them *not* as part of the theatrical action and understand the co-existence of theatrical action of actors and quotidian behavior of non-actors on stage. In *The Yellow Jacket*, Property Man is a major character, whose non-theatrical action is written into meticulous stage directions, such as entering indifferently, smoking a pipe, moving chairs, and hurts his finger. The common theatrical convention to contemporary Chinese audience would become "quaint" and "amusing" to the American audience with untrained eyes. The play

opened in New York in 1912 and was revived in 1916 and toured around Europe, enjoying an overall overwhelming reception.

Presenting pathetic and tragic yellowfaced Asian characters was another way to generate more pathos. The "romantic" opera *Madama Butterfly* by the Italian composer Giacomo Puccini (1858–1924) created a long-lasting archetype of the beautiful and pathetic Asian woman. *Madama Butterfly* (two-act version, 1904; revised three-act version, 1907) was based on a play by David Belasco (1853–1931), which was inspired by earlier stories. This story involves a 15-year-old Japanese woman named Cio-Cio-san ("Cio-Cio" is butterfly in Japanese, "san" here can be translated as Miss or Madam), who is deeply in love with American Navy Lieutenant Pinkerton. Pinkerton promises to marry her when he leaves. She waits for him faithfully, giving birth to a son in his absence; however, after three years, Pinkerton returns with his American wife, with the intension of bringing his son back to the United States without Cio-Cio-san. Understanding her son would have a better education in the United States, she agrees; however, heartbroken and desperate, she kills herself. Such pathetic suicide by a beautiful Asian woman for her white man for the greater good (to get out of the way for his marriage, to give her son a better chance in life) fulfills the white male fantasy of dominance over beautiful Asian women and the East. (For a more detailed study of *The Mikado* and *Madama Butterfly*, see the case study on website.)

Such archetypes were even more popular when real Asian actresses began to appear in film and theatre. Anna May Wong (1905–1961), the first known Asian American actress on the American silver screen, played Lotus Flower, who committed suicide in the silent film *Toll of the Sea* (1922), a variation of the *Butterfly* story. The anti-miscegenation law in the United States (which was not completely abolished until 1967) made interracial romance a titillating subject but interracial marriage an absolute taboo; the death of the Asian woman to end the interracial relationship intensified theatricality and avoided breaking the law. The 1991 Broadway musical *Miss Saigon* is our modern version of the *Butterfly* syndrome. Set in Saigon during the Vietnam War, a Vietnamese girl falls in love with an American GI, suffering the same fate as Cio-Cio-san – being abandoned, giving up her son, and killing herself.

The rise of anthropology and realism in the nineteenth century provided the background of a "scientific" or "technical" approach to yellowface makeup. Following race scientists' categorization of human races as "Caucasian, Mongolian, and Negro," with whites being the norm, theatrical makeup guides treated the Asian look as deviation from the "neutral" white look; therefore, yellowface, as Esther Kim Lee writes, "relied on the process of stipulating how Asian characters *should* look on white actors" (2022: 116). *How to "Make-Up": A Practical Guide to the Art of Making Up* (under the pseudonym "Haresfoot and Rouge," 1877) was the first English-language book of systematic instructions on theatrical makeup. It described the techniques of making up Chinese characters, including creating a bald forehead and attaching a pigtail, using "Mongolian paste," painting false eyebrows and larger nostrils, and using specific techniques to "give the eyes an almond or elongated appearance" (97).

In film, it was common to have white actors in yellowface to play Asian characters in the first half of the twentieth century. Special yellowface stock characters were created, such as Fu Manchu, a mysterious evil character who first appeared in a silent film *The Mystery of Dr. Fu Manchu* (1923). Many films of Fu Manchu were made, up until the late 1960s, recycling the same stereotypical Asian character in yellowface makeup. Photorealism pushed for more advanced technology to fake the "Oriental" eyes: from using long strips of fish skin and adhesive to pull the eyes upward in early films to gluing latex mode onto the eyelid well into the late twentieth century. The modern *Butterfly* story *Miss Saigon* featured a famous white actor to play a Eurasian character by putting on latex prosthetics over his eyelids to fake the Asian look. This action outraged the communities of Asian actors, who staged protests against the yellowface, finally bringing such unjust practice to the attention of the general public.

Key references

Lee, E.K. (2022) *Made-up Asians: Yellowface During the Exclusion Era*, Ann Arbor: University of Michigan Press.

Lei, D.P. (2006) *Operatic China: Staging Chinese Identity across the Pacific*, London: Palgrave Macmillan.

Metzger, S. (2004) "Charles Parsloe's Chinese Fetish: An Example of Yellowface Performance in Nineteenth-Century American Melodrama," *Theatre Journal* 56(4): 624–51.

Williams, D. (ed.) (1997) *The Chinese Other: 1850–1925: An Anthology of Plays*, Lantham, MD: University Press of America.

Summary

In the West and Japan, imperial expansion joined forces with new ideologies to create the notion of inevitable progress. The "empires" view themselves as the superior Self who ought to control and care for the inferior Other. Orientalism clarifies the ways in which the racial Other is constructed in works of art, theatre, and historical writing. International fairs and expositions demonstrated imperial power and progress, while exposing artists and audiences to the unfamiliar and exotic, creating desire for new material goods and new theatrical imagery.

In the West, imperialism and Orientalism were aided by the development of new technologies such as photography, new philosophies such as positivism, new research disciplines such as anthropology, and new scientific discoveries such as Darwin's theory of evolution. While humans became a research subject under the lens of anthropology, Social Darwinism developed as a distortion and misinterpretation of Darwin's ideas. Such misinterpretation gave rise to racial (and racist) impersonation in the nineteenth century, often with "scientific" reasoning or innovative techniques. As discussed in Chapter 8, blackface minstrelsy in the United States was a way to imagine the American (white) national identity; similarly, yellowface performance, along with fake Spanish or other constructed racial representations were other methods to demonstrate the white racial hegemony. Although blackface and yellowface performances often appeared as comical and frivolous, they deprived Black and Asian actors of their rights to express themselves theatrically and further promoted racial stereotypes in society. Such artistic practice also revealed the anxiety and insecurity of the dominant race in the West at the dawn of modernity, a changing world with increasing internationalization and multiculturalism.

★

CHAPTER 10

Realism, early avant-gardes, commodity capitalism, and circuits of performance

Patricia Ybarra

Contributors: Carol Fisher Sorgenfrei, Bruce McConachie and Gary Jay Williams

In this chapter, we will explore how changes in print and photographic media and commodity capitalism transformed the theatre. This combination of large-scale social changes gave rise to realistic and naturalistic theatre and a series of early avant-garde movements that questioned social reality and the perception of reality onstage. These changes in media and economic structures also affected commercial theatres whose artists and producers were less invested in experimentation. This chapter will also discuss the transformations in the commercial popular and the early avant-garde and modernist theatres together, rather than as antagonistic entities, to understand how new forms of media and commodity capitalism affected theatre culture as a whole.

Some theatre artists used the new modes of photography to argue for a realistic and or naturalistic theatre that reflected social reality by carefully constructing "objective" reality on stage. In contrast, other early **avant-garde** movements opposed realism and Naturalism by countering their positivist assumptions. Artists in Imperial Japan, meanwhile, employed realism to save themselves from domination by European powers, showing the allegiance of political and aesthetic philosophy. Instead of upholding an "objective," materialistic understanding of reality, the European avant-garde artists of the new movements –Symbolism and Aestheticism – told audiences that reality was actually "subjective," spiritual, and more immaterial than photography seemed to show. This embrace of subjective views of reality had emerged earlier in Romanticism, but the influences of positivism and industrialism heightened their importance as a feature of artistic representation that countered these movements. European theatre makers committed to using theatre to assess perceptions of reality often engaged both objective and subjective forms. This tension was already apparent in the final plays of Ibsen, who had embraced the apparent objectivity of realism in the middle of his career with *A Doll House* and *Ghosts*, but moved to the subjective spirituality of Symbolism of *When We Dead Awaken* at the end of it. The tension between these paradigms was heightened by the influence of photography, the newer effects of telephones and

DOI: 10.4324/9781003185185-14

phonographs on perception, spiritualism, and occultism as a religious and social practice. As we will see, **sound-based media**, increasingly influential after 1900, validated realities that could not be photographed – sounds, voices, and music. Inventive dramatists and directors might offer productions that explored both "objective" and "subjective" realities, undermining the idea that a hardline decision had to be made between choosing either an "objective" or "subjective" representation of reality within a theatre constrained by materialist realities of representation. More extensive consideration of later avant-garde movements and those outside of the United States and Europe will occur in subsequent chapters.

This chapter will also consider how commercial theatre forms, such as musical revues, incorporated new social realities and developing forms of media. The emergence and widespread consumption of photography led commercial theatres to frame its most popular actors as commodities whose images could be traded, viewed, and handled in print culture. The theatre also became a place to advertise commodities for new markets of consumers. These innovations led to the further objectification of women's bodies; yet this new population of women working in entertainment transformed the theatre in unanticipated ways. The same could be said for how new modes of making and selling commercial performance led to the development of touring theatres led by immigrant and artists from particular ethnic and racial groups. All of these forms of theatre and performance, and the tensions between them, were part of global theatre culture in the late nineteenth and early twentieth centuries.

New media and new ideologies: Photography, science, and positivism

Forms of modern imperialism discussed in the last chapter developed side-by-side with new concepts and technologies, including the invention of photography and the philosophy of positivism, which we will discuss in this chapter. These new ideas and technologies inspired theatre artists in Europe, the United States, and Japan, but many religious and government leaders feared change and attempted to censor the resulting plays or performances. Aesthetic realism and the Naturalist movement, which grew from these concepts, often featured unorthodox or shocking material. For example, daring European theatre managers such as André Antoine (1858–1943), stage designers such as Alfred Roller (1864–1935), and playwrights such as Henrik Ibsen (1828–1906) and Anton Chekhov (1860–1904) embraced these new modes of perception, foreshadowing the kinds of dramatic structures and theatrical practices that would dominate much of the twentieth century. In Japan, an equally important movement toward realism occurred alongside shifts in their political structures, trade policies, and culture in ways that mirrored, but also sometimes anticipated, these changes in the West.

Henry Fox Talbot invented photography in Britain in 1839, and by the 1860s photographic studios were flourishing throughout Western Europe and North America. By 1900, photography was ubiquitous in Japan as well. While people immersed in a world of orality, writing, or print could easily imagine spiritual and mental realities without material form, viewers of un-retouched photographs were encouraged to believe that the real world "out there" was limited to what they could see with their eyes or capture on film. In other words, photography helped shift many people's perspective of the world, from an emphasis on the immaterial (or "irrational") to a new focus on the material (or "rational").

Both Western and Japanese imperialists, driven by the need for raw materials and new markets, were conquering native peoples around the world, and their photographers were publishing images of peoples from distant lands, framing them as "primitive" to justify their imperialism. Photography was as much a tool of imperialism as print media, steamships, high explosives, and machine guns. For example, numerous photographs inaccurately depicting Korean people as corrupt and backward, in need of the help of Japanese civilization, preceded the Japanese annexation of Korea in 1910. This was occurring not long after European photographers such as Felice Beato were photographing Japan as a pre-industrial paradise.

The widespread experience of taking and viewing photographs suggested an "objective" and materialistic understanding of reality that helped move mainstream playwriting, acting, and design toward aesthetic **realism**. In contrast, non-visual new media (telegraph, telephone, and phonograph) gradually excited an interest in the "subjective" and spiritual side of reality that sharply conflicted with the photographically inspired realism, a trend in twentieth-century avant-garde performance that will be considered later in this chapter.

THINKING THROUGH THEATRE HISTORIES: POSITIVISM

Positivism is a philosophy introduced by Auguste Comte (1798–1857) that insists that only those things that are experienced by the senses and can be measured are real; intuition and subjective feelings are not external behaviors and cannot be measured, and thus they cannot provide truth. This concept was expanded to include the idea that societies are also subject to natural laws that work in a way similar to scientific laws, such as the law of gravity. Positivism maintains that human intellectual development progresses to a high point that is defined by scientific knowledge. It implies that humans can (and will) ultimately understand everything. Clearly, imperial nations with superior weapons and advanced technologies imagined themselves to be closer to knowing the "truth" than those they conquered. Critics of positivism point out that universal understanding is impossible to achieve, since each new scientific breakthrough leads to others, without end.

For the theatre historian, the most important aspect of positivist philosophy is the way that it ties ideas of "truth" and "reality" to a narrow view of science. The aesthetics of Naturalism and realism could only develop in an intellectual climate that supported such ideas. Positivism and theatrical realism continue to be influential – even dominant – in much of the world today.

The rise of realist staging

After 1850, Western theatre artists gradually adapted their techniques to incorporate the new interest in photographic realism. For example, in Irish-American Dion Boucicault's (1820?– 1890) *The Octoroon* (1859), a photograph taken by accident reveals the murderer of a slave boy. In England, the plays of Thomas W. Robertson (1829–1871) revealed character through the actors' handling of realist stage properties. Robertson's "cup and saucer plays" (as they were called), such as *Society* (1865) and *Caste* (1867), also suggested a less Romantic style of acting (Figure 10.1). In Vienna, Ludwig Anzengruber (1839–1889) turned the peasant play, formally a romantic piece meant to evoke nationalistic pieties, toward realist purposes

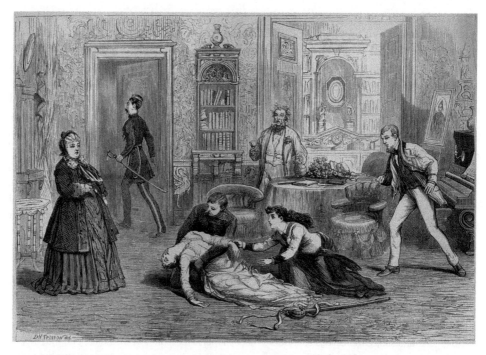

Figure 10.1

An 1879 print illustrating a scene from Thomas W. Robertson's *Caste*, at the Prince of Wales Theatre, 1879. Notice the stage properties on the central table.

Source: © Enthoven Collection, V&A Images, Victoria and Albert Museum.

in the 1870s. As noted in Chapter 8, in Russia, Ostrovsky's *The Thunderstorm* (1859) and *Enough Stupidity for Every Wise Man* (1868) demonstrate a realist handling of melodrama and comedy, and keen attention to the details of middle-class life. Because early nineteenth-century actors usually chose and purchased their own costumes (a costly expense for female actors especially), productions usually lacked a unified appearance. By the 1880s, however, most producers provided costumes for their entire cast to ensure a measure of uniformity and/or authenticity.

After encountering the "box set" in continental Europe, producer/manager, actress, and opera singer Madame Vestris (Lucia Elizabeth Vestris 1797–1856) introduced it to London in 1832. The box set permitted greater photographic realism by creating the illusion of three walls (with the audience peering in through an imaginary **fourth wall**), real doors and windows, and actual furniture.

When electrical stage lighting began to be used in the late 1870s, many designers abandoned two-dimensional scenery. Consequently, improved methods of shifting three-dimensional units and real props and furniture were developed. In 1879, for example, Madison Square Theater in New York rigged elevators for two complete stages, one above the other, to allow one stage to be changed while the other stage served as the playing area. At Henry Irving's Lyceum Theatre in London, workers ripped out the grooves for sliding flats to allow for the "free plantation" (*ad hoc* placement) of scenic units. Less commonly, theatre architects and managers began to abandon the older systems of scene changing, dominant in the West since the seventeenth century, to offer increased off-stage storage space for furniture and three-dimensional units, and clear access from the wings.

Other innovations followed. For example, by 1914, technicians lighted concave, plaster cycloramas in the upstage area to create a variety of outdoor realist illusions. Several German theatres had installed elaborate revolves to wheel on the cumbersome materiality of stage realism. Despite all the interest in Asia, European technicians were unaware that in Japan, revolving stages and other mechanical devices for creating sophisticated stage illusions had been common in *kabuki* since the 1750s.

The American actor William Gillette (1857–1937) performed his star vehicle *Sherlock Holmes* (1899) using realistic properties, costumes, and scenery that looked as though they had been whisked from Victorian London into the United States. British star actor Herbert Beerbohm Tree's (1853–1917) London production of *A Midsummer Night's Dream* in 1900 featured real flowers, mechanical birds, and fairies with battery-operated glow lamps. For its revival in 1911, Tree added live rabbits. In Boucicault's *The Vampire* (1852), thrilling melodramatic staging included a supernatural, instantaneous rescue of the heroine by using a "vampire trap" from which actual red flames and smoke spewed, along with the evil vampire himself.

In Japan, realism had neither been of interest to artists nor was it part of theatre practice. However, after Japan opened up to the West in 1868, there was the perception that adopting and adapting Western technology and ideology might stop Japan from potential colonization by the West (as had happened elsewhere). The commitment to using these technologies to defend themselves from domination forced attitudes to change. Accepting the ideology inherent in positivism, Japan embarked on massive and rapid modernization, including attempts to make Japanese theatre more like Western theatre. Although Japan had been forced to trade with the West, the West had not imposed its own aesthetics on Japan, as it typically did in colonized areas. Rather, the Japanese themselves chose to adopt (and sometimes adapt) realism and other Western artistic modes in order to "join" the modern world on their own terms. Experts in science, technology, education, government, and the arts were sent all over the world to learn the latest Western ideas.

Simultaneously, some theatre artists and managers tried to make *kabuki* more realistic. In 1872, *kabuki* actor Ichikawa Danjūrō IX (1838–1903) appeared in formal Western attire (white tie and tails) instead of the traditional Japanese kimono to inaugurate a new theatre that he promised would cleanse *kabuki* of bawdiness and – in a move that paralleled Western antiquarian Shakespearean performance – would present *kabuki* history plays with authentic-looking costumes, properties, and scenery.

Nō, in contrast, did not attempt to modernize or to add realistic elements, and was almost extinguished due to its connections with pre-Meiji feudalism. In the 1870s, however, the form was revived when Ikawura Tonomi (1825–1883) realized, after a visit to a European opera house, that Japan needed an art form with similar cultural capital that would fend off artistic cultural imperialism. *Nō* became that form. When former United States president Ulysses S. Grant visited in 1879, he also underscored the value of this ancient genre and successfully urged his Japanese hosts to preserve it without change. Although *nō* was in fact "preserved" formally by Japanese artists, by the beginning of the twentieth century, the Japanese government came to use it as an ideological tool to support the state. *Nō*'s history as an elite and religious form (as opposed to *kabuki*, which was largely geared to a merchant class), underscored *nō*'s link to traditional culture.

Other forms of theatre also became culturally potent for a variety of political positions in the Meiji period (1868–1912) despite the presence of censorship in traditional theatre spaces. For example, Japanese artists, like those from many other countries, worked in non-traditional spaces and genres to make their claims. They also adapted and translated Shakespeare with a political purpose. For example, Tsubouchi Shōyō's (1859–1935) 1884 translation of *Julius Caesar* argued for a free government through a prologue and its treatment of Brutus as a tragic hero: Kawashima Keizo's (1856–1933?), in contrast, paints the Meiji Restoration in a positive light. The difference between these translations was often quite subtle. Overall, these translations largely fell into two categories: foreignizing translations that retained the difference of European plays, and naturalizing translations that adapted Shakespearean scenarios to local cultural contexts. This split in translation style was also found in realistic dramas in the first two decades of the twentieth century.

The Japanese government soon embraced the practices of capitalist imperialism perfected by the West. Like the West, Japan rationalized its imperialistic ventures by telling its own people and those it colonized that Japanese expansionism was a positive force that would improve lives by offering the benefits of modern science, technology, and so on.

Among Japan's first imperialistic ventures was the invasion and defeat of northern China in 1894–1895. This invasion offered a pretext for a group of brash young theatre reformers, led by Kawakami Otojirō (1864–1911), to sidestep attempts to alter *kabuki* and instead to create something entirely new, more closely allied to Western models of playwriting and production. They produced *shimpa* [sheem-pah] – literally "new style" – dramas that adapted aspects of nineteenth-century Western dramatic forms to Japanese tastes, but continued the use of an all-male cast. The acting was a cross between highly stylized *kabuki* gesture and vocal patterns, and the comparatively realistic Western acting of the period. One of the earliest *shimpa* plays was *The Sublime, the Delightful Sino-Japanese War* (1894), which was presented like a series of journalistic reports from the front. Like popular historical melodramas in Europe, Kawakami used photographically authentic military uniforms and makeup to depict realistic battle scenes, including heroic re-creations of actual battles. In addition to their political content, *shimpa* were utilized as part of Japan's interventions into Korea as a form of cultural imperialism; they were also the basis for civilization dramas, which were new Chinese forms of spoken drama called *wenmingxi,* discussed in Chapter 11.

The introduction of female performers in Japan

After *shimpa*'s successes, the Japanese government sent Kawakami's troupe on a fact-finding and performance tour of the West. While touring the United States, the lead *onnagata* in *The Geisha and the Knight* (1900) became ill. Although women were still not permitted to perform professionally in Japan, the desire of U.S. audiences to see females playing women's roles prompted Kawakami to allow his wife, Kawakami Sadayakko (1872–1946), a former geisha [gheh-shah] and thus a trained dancer, to perform instead. Audiences adored her, and she continued to play the female lead in subsequent tours of Europe, to great critical acclaim.

The content of plays and dance-dramas such as *The Geisha and the Knight* – and especially the critical and popular praise heaped on Sadayakko – helped create simultaneous and apparently contradictory images of Japan, as suggested in the online case study of *The Mikado* and *Madama Butterfly*. These plays presented Japan as part of the exotic Orient filled with sexually alluring women and fierce male warriors; at the same time, however, they offered the vision of a successful, modern nation that should be considered the military, economic, and cultural equal of the West. In this way, Kawakami and his troupe helped transform Western Orientalist perceptions to Japan's advantage, presenting a revised image of a new, modern Japan to the West. In 1908, Sadayakko founded the Imperial Actress Training Institute, Japan's first acting school for women. *Shimpa* eventually incorporated female actors performing on the same stage as *onnagata*, a practice that continues when *shimpa* is performed today.

Sadayakko's success challenged the exclusion of women from female roles and professional actor training. Some traditionalists feared that replacing *onnagata* would destroy aesthetic pleasure and encourage female sexual promiscuity. Even Osanai Kaoru (1881–1928), whose production of Ibsen's *John Gabriel Borkman* (1909) is considered the first *shingeki* [sheen-gheh-kee] ("new theatre," i.e., modern, Western-style theatre), urged *onnagata* to learn to play modern women.

In contrast, literary critic Tsubouchi Shōyō argued that realist representation demanded women on stage. In 1906, he founded a Theatre Institute to train actors and mount private *shingeki* productions. His 1911 *Hamlet* featured his student Matsui Sumako (1886–1919), Japan's first professionally trained female actor. Later that year, Matsui performed her most famous role, Nora in Ibsen's *A Doll House*, with another *shingeki* troupe. The content of the play, Matsui's performance, and her personal life shocked the country, seeming to crystalize the fears of the traditionalists. However, women acting in realistic plays could not be stopped. Although *shimpa* continued to use both female actors and *onnagata*, by 1930 women routinely performed female roles in *shingeki*. Today, *shingeki* is virtually indistinguishable from contemporary Western theatre.

Takarazuka review

One indicator of the growing acceptance of female actors – as well as an example of how aspects of Western realism supported Japanese imperialism and were transformed to conform to Japanese tastes – was the creation of the all-female Takarazuka Revue. In 1914, Kobayashi Ichizo (1873–1957), a Japanese entrepreneur hoping to lure tourists to his spa in Takarazuka City (near Osaka), offered the first performance of a family friendly "all-girl opera troupe" attached to a music school. Eventually, the music school became a kind of finishing school for girls who were taught not only singing, dance, and music, but how to become "good wives, wise mothers." The phrase indicated women's preferred role in Japan's growing imperialist ventures. They would give birth to and raise strong, patriotic Japanese citizen-soldiers.

At first, the school presented operettas deemed suitable for family entertainment. Later, musical plays, often based on Parisian revues (and, after the Second World War, on Broadway musicals) and exotic, Orientalist tales were joined by elaborately costumed and be-feathered chorus lines, something like a cross between a non-sexualized Las Vegas Revue and the Radio City Music Hall's Rockettes. The word "Takarazuka" now indicates both the city and this unique, all-female performance genre that originated there. Takarazuka is but one form of popular performance that emerged in this period.

Figure 10.2
Kei Aran performs as Oscar François de Jarjayes, a female captain of the royal guards of French Queen Marie-Antoinette during the Takarazuka theatre's *The Rose of Versailles* final rehearsal in Tokyo, 2006. The rigorously trained company, which has performed for nearly a century starring young single women, has drawn generations of devoted, yet decidedly mild-mannered, fans.

Source: Toshifumi Kitamura/AFP/Getty Images.

Today, the Takarazuka Revue's school is one of Japan's most competitive and professional performance training institutions. The students, carefully selected young women, are trained in almost militaristic fashion as professional singer–dancer–actors (Figure 10.2). In addition, as originally envisioned, the school teaches skills such as house cleaning, patriotism, and proper etiquette. The Takarazuka Revue is wildly popular with female spectators of varying ages, including lesbians. Actors specialize in either male or female roles, but male impersonators are the biggest stars. Spectators enjoy the gender ambiguity and idealization of masculinity embodied in the performance of male characters – an idealization that is as much a female fantasy of ideal masculinity as *kabuki*'s *onnagata* is a male fantasy of ideal femininity. In the Takarazuka Revue, the world is transformed into culturally hybrid "fantasy adventure" or "land of dreams" which allows its audiences travel around the world (Yamanashi

2012: 89–90). One might think of Takarazuka's images of Paris in its reviews alongside the *Japonisme* discussed in the previous chapter.

With few exceptions, Takarazuka Revue actors do not perform for more than a few years after graduation. Consequently, almost all are young, usually under 30, enhancing the fantasy element of the performances. Former Revue stars have gone on to successful careers in film and music; most, however, do not.

Scripts, which often foreground gender disguise, range from historical romances set at the time of the French King Louis XIV to spectacular productions of Broadway musicals, original works, and adaptations of Western and Japanese novels, including a musical based on *Gone With the Wind*. Shows are seldom overtly political, but often convey subtle suggestions of Japanese cultural superiority, including the ability to perform "the West." The Takarazuka Revue maintains two major theatres (in Takarazuka City and Tokyo), six permanent touring companies, and its own TV station.

Naturalism on stage

The gradual shift toward theatrical realism after 1850 reached its apex in Europe in the movement known as **Naturalism**. While absolute distinctions between realism and Naturalist aesthetics are probably impossible, realism may be understood as a general style that remains pervasive today, while Naturalism can be seen as a movement that influenced theatre between 1880 and 1914, but then disbanded. Committed Naturalists joined Émile Zola (1840–1902), their leader, in asserting that heredity and the socioeconomic environment are the primary causes of human behavior. Zola argued in *Naturalism in the Theatre* (1881) that play productions must demonstrate the effects of these visible causes (Figure 10.3). In the theatre, stated Zola, "[W]e would need to intensify the illusion [of reality] in reconstructing the environments, less for their picturesque qualities than for dramatic utility. The environment must determine the character" (Zola 1881: 369). Further, photography provided reliable, objective evidence about a character's socioeconomic environment: "You cannot claim to have really seen something until you have photographed it," wrote Zola in 1901 (Sontag 1977: 87). Zola and the Naturalists were well-educated writers, privileged members of the middle and upper classes. Zola's manifestos insist on the use of "rational" or "scientific" methods (including photography) to depict characters who were decidedly Other and "irrational": women forced into prostitution, beggars afflicted with incurable diseases, the uneducated and unemployed, or homeless, downtrodden characters addicted to drink or drugs. Although such plays may seem to suggest social protest and calls for reform, viewing the plays, their authors, and their audiences in socio-historical context suggests that, instead, they may have been exploitative fantasies about characters who did not conform to social, ethical, and economic norms of mainstream society by being productive citizens.

As we have noted, photography helped push realism toward positivism, the claim that scientists could discover an objective reality by dispassionately observing nature. Naturalism joined positivism and photographic realism to Social Darwinism. The Naturalists believed that an accurate rendition of objective, external realities was required to explore positivist and Social Darwinist causation, which, as we saw, has ties to notions of the rational Self and irrational Other.

Although Zola strove to meet his goals by dramatizing his novels, the plays of Henri Becque (1837–1899) were more successful on stage. Becque's *The Crows* (1882) and *La*

Figure 10.3
Emile Zola's naturalistic *The Earth*, directed by André Antoine at the Théâtre Antoine in Paris, 1902.

Source: © Bibliothèque nationale de France.

Parisienne (1885) nearly abandon conventional plotting to present everyday situations in which greedy characters prey on the weak, and a "respectable" wife sleeps with other men to advance her husband's career. The German playwright Gerhart Hauptmann's (1862–1946) influential *The Weavers* (1892) focuses on the exploitation and uprising of German workers in 1844.

Like Hauptmann, an increasing number of theatre artists urged moderate or even radical reform, often focusing on liberalism or socialism. Many of them saw Naturalism as the most powerful genre for impressing their views on their audiences. However, neither liberalism nor socialism meant what most Westerners understood by these terms after 1917. **Liberalism** – defined as the right of individuals to pursue their interests unrestrained by aristocratic privileges or state regulations – had been the banner of reformers since the French Revolution. The bourgeoisie throughout Europe had largely secured these rights by 1850. From the liberals' point of view, the laws of the marketplace and individual effort, if unimpeded, should guarantee economic progress and social justice. However, it had become evident (partly through photographs of slums) that social reforms were needed. Some liberal, Naturalist plays after 1880 railed against social injustice. *A Man's World* (1910) by U.S. playwright Rachel Crothers (1878–1958) critiques the double standard that condemns women for sexual behavior that is accepted in men. In Britain, John Galsworthy's (1867–1933) *Justice* (1910) pleaded for more humane prisons. In *Damaged Goods* (1902), French playwright Eugene Brieux (1858–1932) campaigned against the ignorance and fear that led to the spread of syphilis.

In contrast, **socialism** argued that social needs and equity, rather than private interests, should drive economics. By the late 1800s, many socialists throughout the world had turned to the economic ideas of Karl Marx (1818–1883), who maintained that although capitalism might produce some forms of progress, exploitation of the working class was intrinsic to capitalism. However, large numbers disagreed with his call to revolution; the revolutionaries became known as **communists**. The dramas by Russian socialist Maxim Gorky (1868–1936) include *The Lower Depths* (1902), which centered on impoverished workers and others living in a Moscow flophouse. Like most Naturalist plays, *The Lower Depths* dramatized a photographic "slice of life," with all of its banality, cynicism, sentimentality, and violence (see Figure 10.4).

Women, whether socialists or not, were demanding more equality, including the right to vote, the right to wear less restrictive clothing, safer working conditions, and even the right to birth control. One of the earliest and most radical socialist feminists was Finnish playwright Minna Canth (1844–1897). Her *Children of Misfortune* (1888) depicted the diseases, drunkenness, crimes, and death that degraded the lives of the unemployed, especially women and children.

State censorship throughout much of Europe before 1914 prevented the production of many Naturalist plays. The authorities objected to the plays'

Figure 10.4
The Moscow Art Theatre production of Maxim Gorky's *The Lower Depths*, 1902, with Stanislavsky as Satin (center).

Source: © SCRSS Photo Library – www.scrss.org. uk.

offensive language and feared their political implications. To avoid censorship and produce Naturalist plays, independent (or private) theatres appeared in several countries, offering subscriptions to members. In Paris, André Antoine began the Théâtre Libre (Free Theatre; see Figure 10.5) in 1887 when the censors denied permission for a short season of new plays, including an adaptation of a Zola novel. One of Antoine's early productions was Ibsen's *Ghosts* (1881), forbidden by the censors because it depicts previously taboo subjects, including sexually transmitted disease. The Théâtre Libre also produced several of Becque's plays, *The Power of Darkness* (1886) by Russian novelist Leo Tolstoy (1828–1910), and *Miss Julie* (1893) by Swedish dramatist August Strindberg (1849–1912).

Antoine's theatre provided a model for other free theatres in Europe and Japan. For example, the Freie Bühne (Free Stage) in Berlin produced predominantly Naturalist plays by Ibsen, Becque, Tolstoy, and others and created the first audience for Hauptmann's dramas. London's Independent Theatre, modeled on the other "free" theatres on the continent, opened in 1891 with a production of *Ghosts*. It continued until 1897, mostly showcasing Naturalist plays. Because the Freie Bühne and the Independent Theatre used professional actors who were simultaneously involved with other productions, they could not mount the kind of fully integrated productions that marked the success of the Théâtre Libre, where

Figure 10.5

André Antoine as old Hilse next to his loom in the *Théâtre Libre*'s 1892 production of Hauptmann's *The Weavers*. Color lithograph by Henri-Gabriel Ibels, 1893, on the cover of a portfolio for Antoine's *Théâtre Libre* programs, all of which featured prints by Parisian avant-garde artists.

Source: © Gary Jay and Josephine S. Williams.

Antoine relied on trained amateurs. Nonetheless, all three theatres played a significant role in introducing Europe to the possibilities of stage Naturalism.

Realism and the rise of producer-directors

In Central and Eastern Europe, where subsidized theatrical institutions predominated, a few strong producers championed realism in state- and city-supported theatres. In Western Europe and the United States, by contrast, some producers gradually wrested economic control of commercial theatrical production from the stars, which allowed them to shape both the economic and the artistic fortunes of their theatres. By 1900, both routes had led to the emergence of a new figure who specialized in staging realism: the producer-director. In Japan, the producer-director appeared a few years later. These conflicts highlighted the struggle between those who advocated a contemporary, literary, playwright's theatre and those who wished to modernize *kabuki*'s actor-driven theatre.

The first producer-director to exercise near total control over his productions was Georg II (1826–1914), the Duke of Saxe-Meiningen (an independent duchy in Germany before 1871), although Dominico Luigi Barone, discussed in Chapter 7, had already begun using intensive rehearsals in the eighteenth century. Saxe-Meiningen designed all of the costumes, scenery, and props, even insisting on genuine materials and period furniture for historical authenticity. When the company toured throughout Europe between 1874 and 1890, it set new standards for the aesthetic integration of realist productions, especially in ensemble acting. Most members of Saxe-Meiningen's company played both leading roles and extras; there were no stars. For the first time on a European stage, mob scenes featured individuals with their own character traits speaking intelligible lines, and the mob itself was choreographed to move with a level of reality and power that audiences had never witnessed before (Figure 10.6). The duke achieved these effects by rehearsing for several months, frequently with full sets and costumes, until he believed his productions were ready for the public. By 1890, the troupe had given over 2,500 performances of 41 plays and the duke had demonstrated how an authoritarian producer-director could integrate realist productions.

Konstantin Stanislavsky (1863–1938) saw the Meiningen troupe perform in Moscow in 1890. The ensemble acting and realistic, off-stage sound effects especially impressed him. As he developed his own mode of directing, he would recall the highly disciplined control of this company, and would merge that discipline with an emphasis on non-egotistical, creative, emotionally honest acting that contrasted with the more typical histrionic style of the day. The desired result would be a fully organic production (Benedetti 1999: 40–2). Along with Vladimir Nemirovich-Danchenko (1858–1943), Stanislavsky brought high standards of realist production to Russia after founding the Moscow Art Theatre (MAT) in 1898. He insisted on long rehearsal periods with all of the actors present. Although somewhat less powerful than similar producer-directors, he carried substantial authority due to his membership in the Moscow business elite, connections to wealthy patrons, and growing eminence as an actor and director. The MAT produced the four major plays of Russian playwright Anton Chekhov (1860–1904): *The Seagull* (1896), *Uncle Vanya* (1899), *Three Sisters* (1901), and *The Cherry Orchard* (1904). Stanislavsky paid scrupulous attention to the realities of Russian provincial life on which these plays are based, encouraged ensemble acting, and used a "fourth wall" performance style (Figure 10.7).

Figure 10.6
A crowd scene in the Duke of Saxe-Meiningen's staging of Shakespeare's *Julius Caesar* at Drury Lane Theatre, 1881.
Source: Topfoto.

After 1906, Stanislavsky began working on a "system" to help actors develop commitment to their characters' realities – work he would continue for the rest of his life. Today, most scholars agree that his system combines devotion to finding the character's (not the actor's) personal, emotional truth with intense, physical control of the voice and body. In Chapter 12, we discuss how American interpretations sometimes shifted emphasis away from Stanislavsky's insistence on physical control and toward the actor's (rather than the character's) emotional truth.

In France, for productions at the Théâtre Libre, André Antoine's actors observed the realist convention of the imaginary "fourth wall," occasionally delivering lines with their backs to the audience. Antoine also used the conventions of realism for a different effect in later productions of French classical plays at the state-subsidized Théâtre Odéon. For example, to re-create historically accurate productions of Molière's comedies, he placed costumed actors playing spectators on the stage and hung chandeliers over them. Antoine's productions toured widely in Western Europe and, like Saxe-Meiningen's, shaped a generation of theatre artists.

One of the many artists that Antoine inspired was Japanese director and theatre theorist Kaoru Osanai, whose Free Theatre (Jiyū Gekijō) was named after Antoine's Théâtre Libre. Osanai sought to emulate Antoine's ideals and his theatre was dedicated to experimentation rather than commercial success. This emphasis on art, however, was made possible by the fact that his actors were often also employed by mainstream *kabuki* theatres, effectively subsidizing his theatre. Osanai's form of realism came with a commitment to the importance of the text as the primary element of the theatre and he directed his actors accordingly. His concern echoes the sentiments of many European avant-gardists who, primarily interested

Figure 10.7
V. S. Simov's 1898 naturalistic design for Act I of the Moscow Art Theatre's production of Anton Chekhov's *The Seagull*. Note the painted backdrop.
Source: © SCRSS Photo Library – www.scrss.org.uk

in words and poetry, grew disillusioned with actor-centered commercial theatre. Osanai's shift in emphasis was not only a change in acting style from the highly formal and non-naturalistic vocal styles of *nō* and *kabuki* to realistic "fourth wall" acting but also displaced esoteric embodied acting technique as the heart of Japanese theatre practice. Early in his career, Osanai's interpretation of realism was drawn from his readings of plays, and only later was influenced by his familiarity with productions that used Stanislavsky's acting techniques and Edward Gordon Craig's stagecraft. Osanai's copious writings on the theatre, while sometimes contradictory, nonetheless attempt to combine important insights from these very different European artists. Overall, the development of realism in Japan's rich theatre culture by Osanai and others was multifaceted; artists did not have a common definition of realism, a standardized set of production practices, or a consistent political philosophy.

In China, the humiliations of European imperialism and military defeat to Japan encouraged a shift toward a more cosmopolitan culture, including Western ideas and literature in the May Fourth Movement of 1919. This protest movement was initiated as a student strike, protesting the government and its Confucian values, which they blamed for China's current political condition. Wishing to modernize and embrace some Liberal ideas, progressive Chinese students studying in Japan discovered Harriet Beecher Stowe's novel *Uncle Tom's Cabin*. The theme of freedom and the style of modern Western drama (as they imagined it) resulted in the creation of *The Black Slave's Cry to Heaven* (*Heinu yutian lu*, 1907). They also translated Dumas Fils's *La Dame aux Camelias* (1848) as *The Camilia Lady* in 1906. Many important Chinese authors wrote for *huaju* (Chinese spoken drama), including Cao Yu (1910–1996), whose influential *Thunderstorm* (*Leiyu*, 1934) is a psychologically based family drama. These forms, of course, although imitative of European realism, were quite diverse in form. And, as we will see in the next section, the relationship of realism onstage to the real offstage is an active subject of debate in theatre history.

THINKING THROUGH THEATRE HISTORIES: IDEOLOGY, REALISM, AND THE WELL-MADE PLAY

How "real" is realism? With its selective focus, its relatively unobtrusive exposition, its appearance of real time, its linear sequences of cause-and-effect actions that lead to a third-act crisis, and its careful construction of credible character psychology, aesthetic realism tries to hide the fact that it is a carefully crafted fiction designed to keep the viewer inside the ideology of the middle-class world it represents. Because it emphasizes individual character psychology, it is not well suited to showing how social formations are constructed or how they might be dismantled. In other words, realism encourages an acceptance of things as they currently are.

Raymond Williams has shown that modern realist tragedy, from Ibsen's *A Doll House* through Arthur Miller's *Death of a Salesman* (1949), tracks the struggle and ultimate defeat of the individual who attempts to fulfill her or his desire, but who is ultimately the victim of social formations that are never addressed (Williams 1966: 87–105, 1969: 331–47). Williams shows the inherent contradictions between all the talk of social reform in such plays and the invisible limitations of realism. Williams' one-time student, Terry Eagleton, summarizes the argument:

> The discourse of the play [the liberal tragedy] may be urging change, criticism, rebellion; but the dramatic forms – [that] itemize the furniture and aim for an exact "verisimilitude" – inevitably enforce upon us a sense of the unalterable solidity of this social world, all the way down to the color of the maid's stockings.
>
> (Eagleton 1983: 187)

Consequently, realist plays – even those that appear to be highly critical of society – ultimately support the status quo. The form itself implies that revolutionary change is not possible.

In many ways, realist play structure derives from the very "unreal" structure of "the *well-made play*," a suspenseful genre that had proven its believability for bourgeois audiences since the 1820s, when French playwrights Eugène Scribe (1791–1861) and, later, Victorien Sardou (1831–1908) perfected it. Although the term is usually used in a derogatory sense, the well-made play's structure is central in every significant playwriting and screenwriting textbook in English today.

The well-made play derives from French neoclassicism. The plot results from events happening prior to the play's beginning, demanding much exposition. The plot must follow a strict cause- and-effect pattern, including a series of escalating complications with a final reversal (and/or revelation) that returns the world to a state of order. Well-made plays typically use devices such as letters or other props that are at first misunderstood, but are later revealed as proof of a character's true identity or as a way to unravel plot complications. This structure is also typical of farce. As we will see later in this chapter, Ibsen's plays use techniques derived from farce and the well-made play, but they refuse endings that return the world to a socially acceptable order.

Ibsen and romantic idealism

Norwegian playwright Henrik Ibsen published his first play in 1850 and remained active in the theatre until his death. His career can be seen as a microcosm of the shifting genres of theatre during the late nineteenth and early twentieth centuries. Most of his early dramas were written in verse and set in the Scandinavian past. With *The Pillars of Society* in 1877, Ibsen altered the form and style of his plays from Romanticism to realism, while retaining strong philosophical ties to Romantic idealism. During the 1870s and 1880s, Ibsen was often considered either a realist critic of contemporary society or a Naturalist, intent on revealing the ways in which heredity and environment determined human fate. As noted earlier, many independent theatres, including Antoine's Théâtre Libre, produced his *Ghosts* (1881) as a demonstration of Naturalism. But Ibsen's theatre consistently moved beyond the limitations of realism and the ideology of Naturalism. Rather, Ibsen was drawn to Romantic idealism, a worldview directly influenced by the philosophy of Georg Wilhelm Friedrich Hegel (1770–1831), especially *The Phenomenology of Spirit* (1807). For Hegel, natural and human existence consisted of the process of self-governing and self-developing reason; in humans (both individually and socially), reason seeks self-fulfillment and free spirit. Hegel's view is called idealist in a philosophical sense because it places ideas as the fundamental element or driving force of reality. (Many other thinkers, such as Plato and Kant, are also idealists philosophically.)

Two Romantic plays of Ibsen's mid-career, *Brand* (1865) and *Peer Gynt* (1867), endorse Hegel's commitment to the individual's search for transformational self-fulfillment. Brand is a symbolic Everyman who struggles to transcend earthly fragmentation and live up to the idealist claims of his imagination. Peer Gynt is the comic opposite of Brand, a figure who prefers indirection and compromise to Brand's direct pursuit of perfection. In effect, Peer's foolish,

Figure 10.8

A scene from an Indian adaptation of Ibsen's *Peer Gynt* called *Gundegowdana chaitre*, directed at the Rangayana Theatre in Mysore in 1995 by Rustom Bharucha. Hulugappa Kattimani as Peer, in the white suit, and Manjuatha Belakere, as an Indian folk version of the Button Moulder. The Button Moulder, a messenger of Yama, god of death, in the adaptation, warns Peer of his approaching mortality. Partly because of its universal implications, *Peer Gynt* continues to be performed around the world.

Source: Dennis Kennedy (ed.) *The Oxford Encyclopedia of Theatre and Performance*, Vol. 1, Oxford University Press, 2003, p. 615.

futile life confirms the superiority of Brand's flaming idealism (Figure 10.8). In both plays, Ibsen recognized that self-fulfillment was necessary to strive for but impossible to achieve. In *A Doll House* (1879), he merged Hegel's idealism with a notion of liberal tragedy. (For an interpretation of *A Doll House*, see the case study on the *Theatre Histories* website.)

FREE
INSTRUCTOR
& STUDENT
RESOURCES

Despite the surface realism of Ibsen's later plays, they continued to affirm Hegelian idealism and attacked the limitations of photographic realism. In doing so, they also questioned the representational basis of the theatre. The plot of *Hedda Gabler* (1890), for example, rests on several clichés that had come to be associated with melodramatic versions of the well-made play: a *femme fatale* (Hedda herself, who threatens to lure two good men to their doom), a pair of sensational pistols (which spectators know will be fired), a Mephistophelean figure (who attempts sexual blackmail on Hedda), and the evils of drink, leading to a misplaced manuscript (which nearly drives one man to suicide). Ibsen invites his spectators both to enjoy the operation of these mechanical contrivances of character and plot and to look through them to his language for the more essential action of the play. Mostly through its imagery, *Hedda Gabler* suggests an idealist battle between the forces of light and the forces of darkness.

Ibsen was interested in dramatizing the conflict between imaginative vision and practical reality, the spiritual needs that drive individuals and the limitations of material possibility that constrain and can finally kill them. The problem with staging this conflict in the 1890s (and a problem that remains today), however, is the impossibility of realizing purely spiritual realities on a materialist stage, a conflict that would also haunt the Symbolist movement (discussed later in this chapter). During the era of classical Greece or Baroque opera, writers could lower gods on to the stage to represent spiritual needs and possibilities. But Ibsen, writing for a more realist theatre, can only arrange for his characters to talk about their spiritual yearnings.

In contrast to most realist playwrights' emphasis on photographic reality, Ibsen relied on language rather than spectacle to express his ideas. In *The Master Builder* (1892), he traces the spiritual regeneration of Halvard Solness, a disillusioned middle-aged architect-builder. Solness is urged on a quest for spiritual awakening by Hilde Wangel, a woman in her twenties who shares in his drive for self-perfection. At the end, Solness climbs to the top of an off-stage tower that he built, symbolizing his quest for transcendence, but once there, he falls to his death. Because of the subject matter and because so much action occurs off-stage, *The Master Builder* is dense with dialogue. In summary, Ibsen wrote in many styles, including features later associated with Symbolism and Expressionism.

Chekhov undermines nineteenth-century theatre conventions

Anton Chekhov, while studying to become a medical doctor, wrote sketches, short stories, and one-act plays, several of which were performed in the popular variety theatres of Russian cities. Despite a growing reputation as a dramatist, Chekhov almost abandoned the theatre after the failure of *The Seagull* in 1896. However, Stanislavsky convinced him to allow the Moscow Art Theatre to mount a revival of the play and, following its success, Chekhov composed three more full-length pieces for the MAT. Despite his small output, Chekhov's plays are second only to Shakespeare's as the most produced in the world.

Chekhov, who was interested in the materiality of psychology and history, generally looked with amusement or compassion on people who professed to believe in spiritual

Figure 10.9
Uncle Vanya at The Print Room, London (2012), with Charlotte Emmerson as Sonya, Iain Glen as Vanya, Lucinda Millward as Yelena, and David Yelland as Serebryakov.
Source: Alastair Muir/Shutterstock.

realities. Unlike Ibsen, Chekhov relied on dramatic action and gesture, rather than on speech, to reveal characterization and to undermine the usual genres of nineteenth-century theatre. In the third act of *Uncle Vanya* (1899), for example, Chekhov has his middle-aged protagonist enter a room intending to present a bouquet of flowers to a married woman he is desperately in love with, only to find her in the arms of his best friend. Later in the same act, Vanya chases the woman's husband (an ailing, selfish professor) around the house with a pistol, finally corners him, then shoots at him and misses, twice. Earlier in the play, though, Chekhov paints a sympathetic portrait of Vanya as a man who has wasted his youth and happiness to help others by managing a country estate.

Uncle Vanya combines the genres of French farce and realistic psychological melodrama, making the character of Vanya both ridiculous and pathetic for much of the play (Figure 10.9). Where Ibsen's dramas might use nineteenth-century dramatic genres to indirectly criticize the representational possibilities, Chekhov's plays radically rework and sometimes parody them. For Chekhov, the usual dramatic frames for representing reality could not probe the major psychological and historical conflicts of the modern age. (The online case study on Meyerhold and Chekhov explores two different ways of rejecting the limits of realism in Russian theatre.)

In *The Cherry Orchard* (1904), Chekhov subverts both tragic and comic expectations. The play asks its spectators to respond to a family of aristocrats who return to their debt-ridden estate, waste their time when they should be saving the family legacy, then lose and finally abandon the estate. Should they be understood as tragic or comic figures, or both? Chekhov provides ample possibilities for either interpretation and directors have chosen both extremes, as well as mixing them together in various combinations, as will become clear in the case study below on Stanislavsky and Chekhov.

Whatever the tone of a production, Chekhov's works undermined conventional dramatic forms of representation to theatricalize the downfall of the Russian aristocracy and the rise of the bourgeoisie.

CASE STUDY: Stanislavsky and Chekhov: A collaboration of differences

Paul Fryer

The professional creative relationship between Konstantin Stanislavsky and Anton Chekhov provides us with one of the most important and influential theatrical collaborations of the period. Lasting only six years, this collaboration contributed to the successful establishment of the Moscow Art Theatre (MAT), the resurrection of Chekhov's theatrical career, and the premieres of three of the playwright's most important and enduring plays. Additionally, Chekhov's writing provided ideal material for Stanislavsky to develop his approach to psychological realism, ensemble acting, and detailed, realistic staging and design, revealing a new understanding of the intimacy of Chekhov's writing for the stage. The results of their collaboration helped to shape our contemporary view of theatre.

As well as mutual respect and recognition there was also a significant duality to this relationship, which emerges clearly through an exploration of the four productions that they collaborated upon. Chekhov wrote to Stanislavsky in 1903, as the rehearsals for *The Cherry Orchard* began: "I normally sit in your theatre open mouthed. Without doubt, whatever you do will be beautiful and a hundred times better than I could have imagined" (Benedetti 1991: 180). Stanislavsky spoke of Chekhov's "genius," but their exchanges also revealed tensions. During rehearsals for *Three Sisters,* Stanislavsky wrote, "Your play, which I love more and more as I rehearse it, is such a complete whole ..." (Benedetti 1991: 87). Yet in his memoirs, with hindsight he described the play as having "no resonance, no life, it was long and boring." (Stanislavsky 2008, 205).

Their first working collaboration was on Chekhov's *The Seagull,* which was first staged at the Imperial Alexandrinsky Theatre in St. Petersburg in October 1896. The premiere was a failure with both the audience and the critics. Chekhov was so badly affected that he wrote to his publisher, "stop the printing of the plays .... I shall *never* either write plays or have them acted" (*Letters*: n.p.).

Not everyone who saw the play responded in the same way. Vladimir Nemirovich-Danchenko (1858–1943), the co-founder and co-director of the newly established MAT, who had met Chekhov some years earlier, recognized the qualities of *The Seagull,* and recommended the play to Stanislavsky, realizing that Chekhov's work represented a new, subtle approach to writing for the theatre, offering audiences a genuine insight into the lives of real people caught in real situations. Nemirovich-Danchenko clearly stated his commitment, writing to Chekhov, "I will consider the 'rehabilitation' of this play one of my greatest achievements" (Benedetti 1991: 31). Stanislavsky was not quite so easily convinced, admitting that he had some initial difficulties understanding both the play and the characters. In a letter to Nemirovich-Danchenko, Stanislavsky wrote: "I do not understand myself whether the blocking for *The Seagull* is good or worthless. I only recognize that the play is talented, interesting, but I do not know which way to tackle it" (Senelick 2014: 110).

The play was not traditionally dramatic, and Stanislavsky found it difficult to relate sympathetically to Chekhov's presentation of a quiet, provincial country way of life, where nothing appeared to happen. The play however did offer complex characters, and crucially, "a 'sub-text,' an inner action concealed beneath its largely uneventful surface" (Braun 1982: 62). This was perfect material for Stanislavsky to exercise his new directorial approach, rejecting the artificiality of the old theatre and replacing it with a truthful portrayal of a character's psychological state.

Stanislavsky directed the Moscow production with Nemirovich-Danchenko. He also played Trigorin; Olga Knipper (1868–1959), a founding member of the company who became Chekhov's wife, played Arkadina.

The first performance, in 1898, was received enthusiastically by both the public and the critics. Chekhov did not attend the opening night, but the company sent him a telegram, "… colossal success … Endless curtain calls … We are crazy with delight …" (Senelick 2014: 116). Chekhov finally saw the production more than four months later. He was not entirely happy, writing to Maxim Gorky:

> I can't judge the play with equanimity, because the Seagull herself [Maria Roksanova as Nina] gave such an abominable performance – she blubbered loudly throughout – and the Trigorin (the writer) [Stanislavsky] walked around the stage and spoke like a paralytic. He is not supposed to have a "will of his own" but the way the actor conveyed it was nauseating to behold.
>
> (Karlinsky 1997: 357)

There were obvious synergies between Chekhov's writing and Stanislavsky's approach to direction; however, the tensions between writer and actor/director were to remain a constant feature of their relationship. Although Chekhov had significant reservations about Stanislavski's acting, he was far more impressed by his skills as a director and quickly recognized that the philosophy of the MAT was entirely in tune with his own objectives. The new relationship had begun.

Chekhov intended that *Uncle Vanya*, a re-working of his earlier play *The Wood Demon* (1889) should be produced at Moscow's Maly Theatre, but its theatrical and literary committee found some elements of the play offensive and asked Chekhov to revise it, which he firmly refused to do. Nemirovich-Danchenko took immediate advantage of this opportunity, and the MAT production opened in October 1899. Stanislavsky co-directed with Nemirovich-Danchenko, and played the disillusioned country doctor, Astrov. Olga Knipper played Yelena.

Rehearsals were difficult, exposing a major difference of opinion between the co-directors in their views of the play. Stanislavsky had originally wanted to play the title role, but Nemirovich-Danchenko considered him unsuitable. Seemingly uncomfortable in the role of Astrov, Stanislavsky disrupted rehearsals by failing to learn his lines, and then began to add distractingly fussy and unnecessary business. Nemirovich-Danchenko became increasingly frustrated, complaining, "we have so little time for discussion that one cannot negotiate fully and logically. And we both are aware that it is awkward to disagree during rehearsals. It is embarrassing in front of the actors, don't you think?" (Benedetti 1991: 59). Chekhov was acutely aware of Stanislavsky's tendency to add extraneous detail in his search for creating a complete and natural world for the play. Chekhov was later reported as saying, "Above all … avoid theatricality. Try to be as simple as possible. Remember that they are all ordinary people" (Magarshack 1980: 184).

As Stanislavsky's insecurities receded and his confidence in the role of Astrov grew, the production took shape, and finally settled into a widely acclaimed portrayal. This outcome masked the difficulties encountered in its realization. Meyerhold wrote to Chekhov: "The play is extremely well put together. What I note most of all in the production as a whole is the sense of restraint from beginning to end. For the first time the two directors complement each other perfectly" (Benedetti 1991: 58).

Uncle Vanya was to become a central feature of the company's repertoire, but it was not immediately successful. The initial reviews were mixed: "Though nearly all of them praised the performance highly, few failed to point out defects both in the play and the acting." But opinions changed to general praise "as the staging and acting improved over successive performances and the public understood better its inner meaning and nuances of feeling" (Simmons 1962: 486). Chekhov did not see the play until it came to Yalta the following spring. He expressed himself generally happy with the production, but noted some reservations, particularly the staging of the ending of the third act, where the actress playing Sonya went down on her knees when asking her father to be merciful: he was reported to have said, "You mustn't do that, that isn't what drama is … . The whole meaning or drama of a person lies internally, not in outer manifestations" (Worrall 1986: 48).

Three Sisters premiered at MAT in January 1901, co-directed by Stanislavsky and Nemirovich-Danchenko, Stanislavsky played Vershinin with Olga Knipper as Masha. The MAT had become a central feature of Moscow's theatrical life. The ensemble had also developed sufficiently well for Chekhov not only to write the play especially for the company, but also to create characters specifically for Stanislavsky and Olga Knipper. However, he still harbored reservations about Stanislavsky's approach. He wrote to Olga Knipper, "I can't just hand over four crucial feminine roles, four young intelligent women to Stanislavsky, for all my respect for his talent and understanding. I have to keep half an eye on rehearsals" (Benedetti 1991: 85).

The completion of the play was delayed, and the company did not receive the final act until just over a month before the premiere. Chekhov, however, was still unhappy with the script, he wrote, "The play turned out boring, awkward … and the mood, to coin a phrase, is all gloom and doom…" (Benedetti 1991: 85). From the first read-through of an incomplete draft, one of the earlier problems immediately re-emerged: Chekhov saw his play as a comedy, but the cast had great difficulty in treating it as such. Stanislavsky described a nervous, uncomfortable read-through:

> Once the reading was over, we exchanged impressions, some said it was a drama, others a tragedy, without noticing that these titles bewildered Chekhov…. He was convinced that he had written an amusing comedy, but when it was read everyone took it as a drama, and wept. That made Chekhov think that his play had been misunderstood and was a failure.
>
> (Stanislavsky 2008: 204–05)

Stanislavsky approached the play with confidence, but initially he had great difficulty in bringing the characters and situations to life. The rehearsals were "agonizing and de-energized" (Senelick 2014: 135). But as he began to get a better grasp of the play, Stanislavsky started to explore the subtext and experimented with variations on Chekhov's stage directions, creating a more independent interpretation. Although Stanislavsky was not satisfied with his own performance, he was very pleased with the final production: "In terms of acting and directing this production was one of the best things we had done… [The cast] can be considered exemplary in their creation of classic Chekhovian characters" (Stanislavsky 2008: 207).

Chekhov had remained in Moscow during the early rehearsals, but in December he travelled to Nice, France, and Pisa, Italy, partly because of his ill health. Stanislavsky later stated that he thought Chekhov had left because of his worries about the play. By the time of the first performance, after many revisions the play had changed significantly.

Although Nemirovich-Danchenko was impressed by Stanislavsky's staging, he also considered it "overloaded with details and business" (Senelick 2014: 138), by now a common criticism of his directorial approach. The play opened on 31 January 1901, to a mixed critical reception. However, audiences reacted positively, many considering that it was the company's most successful production to date. Shortly afterwards, the MAT toured to St. Petersburg, where Gorky saw the play, declaring it "wonderful! Better than Uncle Vanya. Music, not acting…" (Benedetti 1991: 103). The company, however, was given a hostile reception by the conservative press, prompting Chekhov to repeat his threat that he would never write for the theatre again. Fortunately, he did not carry out this threat.

The Cherry Orchard was first staged at MAT in January 1904, directed by Stanislavsky. While writing the play Chekhov's health deteriorated dramatically and the consequent delays caused him added frustration and doubtless contributed to his hypersensitivity over the initial reception of the script.

Following the previous disagreements between author and director, a major and all too familiar divergence occurred over this, their final collaboration: Chekhov firmly intended his play to be a comedy, and he stated this very clearly to Nemirovich-Danchenko, but Stanislavsky decided to emphasize what he saw as the tragic aspects of the story. After reading the play he sent a telegram to Chekhov: "Deeply moved…. In unaccustomed raptures. Consider play best of all your beautiful writings. Cordial congratulations to brilliant author…" (Senelick 2014: 166). But Chekhov was not reassured and registered his doubts and insecurities: "he calls my play a work of genius; which means he's overpraising it and removing from it a good half of the success it might have under optimal conditions" (Senelick 2014: 166). Stanislavsky maintained his position that this was "not a comedy nor a farce … it's a tragedy, whatever outlet to a better life you may reveal in the last act" (Senelick 2014: 167), viewing the play as a "potentially tragic drama of the vanishing life of the gentry, crushed by economic demands of vulgar commercialism" (Simmons 1962: 612).

Chekhov arrived in Moscow at the beginning of December and devoted most of his time to attending rehearsals. Of the rehearsal process, Stanislavsky wrote, "The beginning was difficult… The play is difficult. Its attraction lies in its deeply hidden, elusive fragrance" (Stanislavsky 2008: 235). He realized that he had not yet refined the precise skills of his actors sufficiently, particularly in relation to their use of affective (emotion) memory, in order to tackle such an "elusive" play. He later admitted that he tried to fill this gap by using excessive scenic elements, lighting and sound effects.

One of the major concerns of the MAT, and of particular interest to Stanislavsky, was the creation of authentic and naturalistic scenic designs. The "realistic" potential of Chekhov's plays positively supported and encouraged this approach. These plays provided an ideal opportunity for Stanislavsky and his designer, Viktor Simov (1858–1935), "a naturalistic designer of outstanding talent" (Braun 1982: 61), to experiment with the *mise en scène* in an entirely new way. Simov admitted that they departed from Chekhov's stage directions. He felt that visually Chekhov's plays were closest in spirit to the work of the artist Isaac Levitan, describing Chekhov's work as having "simplicity, softness of tone, subdued colour and mood, with no extraneous detail" (Simov 2020: 205).

Stanislavsky later recalled Chekhov's disapproval of his approach to scenographic detail:

> Chekhov said to someone, so that I could hear, 'I am going to write a new play and it opens with: How wonderful, how quiet! No birds, no dogs, no cuckoos, no owls, no nightingales, no jingling bells, no clocks, not a single cricket.' One in the eye for me.
>
> (Stanislavsky 2008: 236)

Chekhov felt unable to effectively convey his ideas to the actors in rehearsal, and began to feel that the approach being taken by Stanislavsky was so wrong that it was actually impossible to stage the play.

The premiere was scheduled for 17 January 1904, to coincide with Chekhov's 44th birthday and his 25th anniversary as a writer. Either in order to avoid the planned celebrations, or in anticipation of what he felt convinced would be a failure, Chekhov decided not to attend. However, Nemirovich-Danchenko sent him a note saying that the audience and the company demanded to see him in the theatre, and he arrived before the final curtain, greeted with great rejoicing, speeches, flowers, messages of congratulations and general celebrations. The play, however, was not well-received. The press criticized the acting and, although not condemning the play as whole, obviously agreed with Stanislavsky that it was closer to tragedy than comedy.

Chekhov continued to maintain that the production was a misinterpretation of his work. Three months before his death, he wrote, "Why do they persist in calling my play a drama… Nemirovich and Stanislavsky absolutely do not see in my play what I actually wrote…" (Benedetti 1991: 190).

Ironically, *The Cherry Orchard* became the MAT's most successful Chekhov play, being performed over 1,200 times.

Chekhov died in the German spa resort of Badenweiler on 2 July 1904. A week later, Stanislavsky wrote: "Poor Anton Pavlovich never leaves my mind. I am rereading his stories and love and treasure him all the more… He didn't have long to live. I cannot imagine life without him…" (Senelick 2014: 185). Stanislavsky suffered a major heart attack during a performance as Vershinin in Act I of Chekhov's *Three Sisters* in a gala marking the 30th anniversary of the MAT, in 1928. It was his last appearance as an actor.

Paul Fryer is a Visiting Professor and Co-Director of the Stanislavsky Research Centre, University of Leeds (UK), and series editor of *Stanislavsky And…*

(Routledge)

Key references

Benedetti, J. (1991) *The Moscow Art Theatre Letters*, New York: Routledge/Theatre Arts.

Braun, E. (1982) *The Director and The Stage*, London: Methuen Drama.

Karlinsky, S. (1997) *Anton Chekhov's Life and Thought: Selected Letters and Commentary*, Evanston, IL: Northwestern University Press.

Letters of Anton Chekhov. Project Gutenberg, https://www.gutenberg.org/files/6408/6408-h/6408-h.htm#link2H_4_0008

Magarshack, D. (1980) *Chekhov the Dramatist*, London: Eyre Methuen.

Senelick, L. (2014) *Stanislavsky, A Life in Letters*, London: Routledge.

Simmons, E.J. (1962) *Chekhov, A Biography*, Boston, MA: Little, Brown and Co.

Simov, V. (2020) "Fragments from Memories," in P. Fryer and A. Toros (ed.) *Viktor Simov, Stanislavsky's Designer*, London: Routledge, 180–233.

Stanislavsky, K. (2008) *My Life in Art*, trans. Benedetti, J. London: Routledge.

Worrall, N. (1986) *File on Chekhov*, London: Methuen.

Ibsen, Chekhov, and the critique of photography

Although theatre historians hail the influence of photography on the development of realism in the theatre, both Ibsen and Chekhov – two of the most significant playwrights identified with early realism – believed that photography had little to reveal about human experience.

Chekhov sets up photography for ridicule in the first act of *Three Sisters*, when a minor character, Fedotik, has everyone pose for a photograph. Of course, photos freeze the flow of life in a static pose, and Chekhov uses this fact to explore the changes that actually occur. The happy faces frozen in the Act I photograph are no longer possible by the play's end. In Act III, a fire burns up all of Fedotik's photos, and by Act IV, taking photos has become a sour joke.

Similarly, Ibsen sets much of *The Wild Duck* (1884) in a photographer's studio, but his photographer, Hjalmar Ekdal, is a fool who cannot see beyond the surfaces of his photos. Like many photographers in the 1880s, Ekdal's clients want him to retouch his photos to conform to their sentimental self-images. His clients actually reject the documentary evidence of photography, wanting the images to be more like idealized paintings. Ekdal gives much of this retouching work to his adolescent daughter, even though the strain on her eyes is gradually blinding her. The implications are clear: those who believe that photographs are truthful may lead themselves and others into sentimentality and moral blindness. Thus, while working within the conventions of realism, both playwrights questioned the psychological effects and social uses of photography. This critique contrasts with the use of the camera in Boucicault's *Octoroon* 25 years earlier, and the subsequent embrace of positivism and realism photography inspired in the theatre.

Sound-based media after 1870

Despite this domination of print's influence in the theatre, other media were beginning to alter, narrow, and divide older modes of dramatic communication. Two sound-based media, the telephone and phonograph (invented in 1876 and 1877 respectively), initially appeared to complement and extend the power of print-based theatre. Before 1900, from the point of view of most theatre makers, telephone conversations and the ability to record the human voice simply made it easier to produce, manage, and publicize all theatrical productions. And it made it possible to add a character to a play without adding an actor – many plays in the first half of the twentieth century have characters only present on the telephone.

But telephones and phonographs did more than serve practical purposes. The new sound-based media excited an interest in the "subjective," spiritual, and non-visual sides of reality and began to challenge the implicit positivism of photography. The telephone and phonograph separated the human voice from the materiality of the body. Apart from their wires and machinery, these media carried the intimacy and immediacy of music and the human voice on sound waves that lacked the visibility and concreteness of previous media. In the past, "hearing voices" had been a sign of religious possession, Spiritualist congress with the dead, or mental instability, and these traditional attributes clung to the affects (and the sociocultural effects) of these new media. Conversing on the phone and listening to music and voices from strange new machines revived an interest in religion, altered musical composition, and played on age-old fears of alien "others." It also tended to validate belief in the new psychoanalytic techniques of Sigmund Freud (1856–1939) and his followers.

Freud, in fact, understood phonographic recording as a metaphor for part of the work of the analyst. Convinced that sound revealed the realities of the unconscious mind, Freud urged the accurate recording of patient vocalizations as the first step in a psychoanalytic session. He advised psychoanalysts to transcribe all of the vocal mistakes of the patient in order to understand patients and their psychological problems. Freud's view of vocalization was part of a wider notion that, as we will see, would have a formative influence on the early avant-garde movement known as Symbolism.

The emergence of avant-garde theatre

Photography inspired the development of Naturalism and realism in the theatre. Both movements began as avant-gardes, although realism was incorporated into mainstream commercial production by 1900. Simultaneously, in 1890s Europe, a minority of artists began demanding that the theatre must not ignore the spiritual and subjective qualities of reality most evident to them in poetic and aural symbols. This urgency was exacerbated by awareness of the *fin de siècle,* the end of the nineteenth century, which was thought to be ushering in a new era. These artists called themselves Symbolists and many theatre historians point to Symbolism as the first movement of the avant-garde.

"Avant-garde" was originally a French military term referring to the forward line of soldiers – those leading the charge into battle. Likewise, avant-garde artists thought of themselves as marching in the front ranks of artistic progress, fighting bourgeois propriety to expand the boundaries of the possible. Avant-garde movements proliferated in the theatre between 1880 and 1930. Both first- and second-generation avant-garde movements began in small groups of artists and spectators who reinforced each other in their rebellion against established cultural institutions and their desire for change. They published manifestos to proclaim their ideology and elevate their work over that of conventional artists and rival avant-garde groups. While some of these movements flamed out within a few years, others burned for two decades or longer and exerted a significant impact on twentieth-century theatre.

Avant-garde theatre did not exist before the end of the nineteenth century. Innovative theatre artists in earlier times might have rejected the prevailing norms of artistry, but they did not form movements, write manifestos, and attempt to set the terms by which their art should be understood. Avant-garde movements began to flourish in all of the arts after 1870, partly as a result of industrial capitalism, but also due to the traditions of revolutionary Romanticism, still a usable past for artists in the West. In earlier decades and centuries, most artists had worked directly for rich patrons, whose interests partly sheltered them from direct competition for survival. Nineteenth-century capitalism forced many artists, commercial and avant-garde, to compete in the marketplace as entrepreneurs. This situation and their new-found freedom, by turns both liberating and terrifying, led many artists to mine the legacy of Romanticism for sensibilities, values, and roles, including the role of the Romantic rebel.

Avant-garde innovators in the theatre after 1880 exploited a brand-new technology to alter stage production – electricity. Electrical illumination allowed for the full dimming of house lights during performances, which left audiences, for the first time in theatre history, in the dark. When spectators could no longer observe each other during performances, theatre-going shifted from a generally social to a much more individualistic experience.

Increasingly, modern audiences after 1880 no longer started a riot if the show displeased them; nor did they often interrupt the show to applaud star actors after an impressive speech. Musical performers still gained applause at the end of a song or dance number, but musicals, too, kept the house lights turned off except during intermissions. This more private mode of spectating generally suited the goals of the Naturalists, as we have seen, and also heightened the kinds of effects sought by the Symbolists and by other movements in the first generation of the avant-garde. This darkening of the house also de-emphasized the importance of playing to and audience observation of prominent spectators. These artists' ambivalence toward bourgeois spectators forms part of the lore of avant-garde reception, as evidenced by the reception of *Ubu Roi* – an event steeped in theatrical myth-making. (We will examine second-generation avant-garde movements, which roughly spanned the years from 1910 to 1930, in Chapter 11.)

Despite significant differences between the two generations of the avant-garde, they shared a common cultural situation. With the questioning of traditional religious faith and the rise of positivism, some Westerners were beginning to suspect that all values might be relative. The influential philosopher Friedrich Nietzsche (1844–1900) held that conventional western morality was based on flawed and destructive assumptions, including claims of universal validity, and that modern people had not progressed over time in moral understanding. Perhaps, as some linguists, anthropologists, and philosophers were beginning to affirm after 1900, this cultural relativism extended to all claims of truth; maybe there was no position beyond human language and culture that allowed for objectivity. Complementing this cultural relativism was the recognition that human subjectivity was much more complex and irrational than people had realized. Could it be that humans were chiefly animated by a "will to power," as Nietzsche thought? Or, perhaps an unconscious sexual drive motivated humanity, which meant that bourgeois society was little more than a machine of sexual repression? This, in more scientific language, was the pessimistic conclusion of Freud's *Civilization and Its Discontents* (1930). Avant-garde innovators would explore these and other possible paths for the next 40 years.

Most of the avant-garde movements could claim some legitimacy for their work within their national cultures. Since the eighteenth century, French culture had provided public forums for debates among the intelligentsia (a recognized elite of artists, academics, critics, philosophers and others) on topics ranging from the nature of art to the nature of being. This tradition spread to other national cultures strongly influenced by France or containing a significant level of public debate about the arts – notably Italy, Germany, Poland, and Russia. In contrast, artists in the United States and England did not have much in the way of an established public forum in which to discuss new work. Although avant-garde artists were active in all of the major cities of the West between 1880 and 1930, avant-garde movements tended to flourish best in cities that supported an influential intelligentsia.

On the European continent, they often gathered in cabarets. "Bohemians," typically university-educated members of the urban youth culture, plus artists and other intelligentsia constituted the primary participants and spectators for cabaret entertainment, which emerged in Paris in the 1880s. After 1900, cabarets in several major European cities – the Mirliton in Paris, Motley Stage in Berlin, Green Balloon in Krakow, Stray Dog in St. Petersburg, and Cabaret Voltaire in Zurich – hosted artists in many of the avant-garde movements of the twentieth century. Performances at these venues might include puppet shows, poetry readings, political skits, art songs, satirical and literary tableaux, and occasionally one-act plays. In general, cabarets provided a hot-house environment where avant-gardists could explore new performance ideas with little risk before sympathetic audiences. These cabarets were different in kind than the commercial ventures found in the United States, excepting the Harlem cabaret scene in the 1920s and 1930s, whose legacy is more politically complex.

Symbolism and aestheticism

Exulting in what they took to be subjective experience, the Symbolists urged viewers to look through the photo-like surface of appearances to discover true realities within – spiritual realities that they believed the realists and Naturalists had ignored. This frustration was parallel to Ibsen's frustration with the materialist nature of the theatre discussed above. Seeking to advance a theatre of immanent spirituality, Gustave Kahn (1859–1936) wrote the first manifesto of theatrical **Symbolism** in 1889. Other manifestos followed. According to Symbolist Pierre Quillard (1864–1912) in 1891, "The human voice is a precious instrument; it vibrates in the soul of each spectator" (Schumacher 1996: 87). Quillard advised artists to avoid the trap of material décor on the stage, so that the chanting of verse could be "freed to fulfil its essential and exclusive function: the lyrical expression of the characters' souls" (90). The early Symbolists, primarily located in Paris, included the French poet Stephane Mallarmé (1842–1898), Rachilde (1860–1953), Jean Marie Mathias Phillipe August, Comte de Villiers de l'Isle-adam (1838–1839), and Belgian playwright Maurice Maeterlinck (1862–1949). They drew inspiration from the gothic mysteries of Edgar Allan Poe (1809–1849), German idealist philosophy, the imagistic poetry of Charles-Pierre Baudelaire (1821–1867), the decadent movement, and the myth-laden music-dramas of Richard Wagner. Many Symbolists praised Wagner's aesthetic goals (discussed in Chapter 8) and attempted to mount similarly integrated works of art in their own productions.

The Symbolists' engagement with Wagner's work was focused on the musical aspects of his operas rather than their theatricality, which the Symbolists often rejected. Their interest, as Quillard's manifesto claimed, was in language and musicality, not spectacle. It was no accident that many of the Symbolists were poets rather than playwrights. Their manifestos could be read as anti-theatrical, but in practice these artists were most concerned with the theatre's inability to transcend the material world, including a frustration with the limitations of the physical body. This concern led many Symbolists to de-emphasize the role of the actor who represented flesh and blood characters within their productions. Maeterlinck even went so far as to suggest the use of marionettes to solve this problem. Ironically, Symbolist principles were most successfully rendered in theatre productions or staged readings, rather than on the page; many of the movement's non-verse dramas read more realistically than the authors intended when confined to print.

The first theatre dedicated to the new Symbolist art was Paul Fort's Théâtre d'Art. Fort (1872–1960) was just 18 when he started producing theatre. In the short years of Théâtre d'Art's existence (1890–1892), the theatre presented Shelley's *The Cenci* (originally written in 1819), Quillard's *The Girl with the Cutoff Hands* (1891), Rachilde's *La Voix du Sang* (*The Voice of Blood*) (1890) and *Madame La Mort* (*Madame Death*) (1891), and Maeterlinck's *Intruder* (1891). These plays, often one-acts, were usually staged or read in evening programs that might include music, poetry and art exhibition. In production, many Symbolist artists attempted to counter the representationalism of real-istic theatre. In *Madame La Mort*'s second act for example, a hooded and faceless Georgette Camée (d. 1957) portrayed a female personification of death through slow and deliberate movement. Her hieratic recitation of the lines further dis-tanced her from human existence. Drawings by Odilon Re-don (1840–1916) accompanied the production, but did not represent scenes in the play. This play shared its fascination with death with Rachilde's *Crystal Spider* (1892), a one act in which a young male character kills himself by shattering a mirror. Rachilde (Figure 10.10) was not only an important writer but also a patron of the Symbolist theatre of Alfred Jarry (1873–1907). Like many of the avant-gardists of this period, Rachilde created a persona whose public appear-ance at salons rivaled the attention given to their writing. And, like Sarah Bernhardt (1844–1923), discussed later in the chapter, Rachilde as a self-promoter who used this fame quite successfully.

Figure 10.10
Image of Rachilde, c 1899.
Source: Historic Images/Alamy Stock Photo.

Although Fort had the support of the *Mercure de France* (in part through Rachilde's influence), he closed the The-atre d'Art in 1892 because it was struggling financially. The last play he had planned to produce became the first produced by the subsequent Thea-tre de l'Oeuvre: Maeterlinck's *Pelias and Melisande* (1893), directed by Aurélien Lugné-Poe (1869–1940). (Lugné-Poe, who was a popular Symbolist actor, added the "Poe" to his name in honor of the American author Edgar Allen Poe.) Like other of Maeterlinck's early plays, *Pelléas and Mélisande* evokes a mood of mystery through multiple symbols, eerie sound effects, and ominous silences. With little overt action, *Pelléas and Mélisande* relies as much on sound as sight. Following Quillard's advice to avoid realist décor, Lugné-Poe produced Maeterlinck's play on a semi-dark stage with grey backdrops and gauze curtains separating performers and spectators. In accord with the Symbolists' desire to foreground the aurality of language, the actors chanted or whispered many of their lines, and they moved with ritual-like solemnity. Maeterlinck's Symbolist plays mystified and irritated some spectators, but they also fascinated others. In his theatre, Lugné-Poe also experimented with synesthesia (the combination of distinct senses, as in "hearing green") in an attempt to engage all of the senses in the theatrical experience. Théâtre de l'Oeuvre became the center of Symbolist performance in Western Europe. The theatre produced plays in many styles and from many periods (including a translation of the Indian Sanskrit drama *The Little Clay Cart*) until 1929, but continues to be known for its Symbolist experiments in its early years. This included Symbolist productions of Ibsen plays such as *Rosmersholm* (1886) and *An Enemy of the People* (1892), the latter of which, in Lunge-Poe's hands and with poet and anarchist Laurent Tailhade's (1854–1919) preface, was considered sympathetic to anarchism and to anarchist violence.

Although Ibsen never endorsed the principles of Symbolism, his final four plays investigated many of the interior and spiritual themes of the Symbolists. The first of these, *The Master Builder* (1892), uses a variety of symbols to contrast vaulting spirit-uality with earthly cowardice, old age, and death. Despite its realistic settings, the overt symbolism of the play moves it sharply toward a dream-like allegory. *When We Dead Awaken* (1899), the last drama of the playwright's career, depicts the evolution of human spirituality through the works of a sculptor, Rubek, who began by crafting half-human, half-animal shapes and finally created an idealized nude of a young woman. The play, which ends ambiguously, opposes spirituality to physicality, art to life, without embracing either side.

The Parisian Symbolists influenced two centers of Symbolist production in Russia. In Moscow, Valery Bryusov (1873–1924) argued that the naïve lyricism of Russian folk drama made it appropriate for the Symbolist stage. Viacheslav Ivanov (1866–1949) led the St. Petersburg Symbolists with manifestos calling for a theatre in which actor-priests would facilitate the creation of mythic dramas with audience-congregants, primarily through the chanting of archaic language. Although Stanislavsky produced several Symbolist pieces at the Moscow Art Theatre, Vsevolod Meyerhold (1874–1940) had more success with Symbolism in St. Petersburg. Meyerhold's production of *Hedda Gabler*, for example, ignored Ibsen's realist stage directions and deployed bold colors and sculpted, repetitious movements to evoke the claustrophobia of Hedda's world.

Two theatrical visionaries, Adolphe Appia (1862–1928) and Edward Gordon Craig (1872–1966), borrowed many of their ideas from the Symbolists. Both urged a radical break with the pictorial illusionism of the past through the innovations made possible by electricity. They understood that the new lighting could add dynamism to the image of the actor moving within sculpted scenery rather than pasted against stage flats. Eager to perfect a scenic equivalent to the soaring music of Wagner's operas, Appia published *The Staging of Wagner's Musical Dramas* in 1895 and *Music and Stage Setting* in 1899. In these and later works, Appia agreed with Wagner that the aesthetic unity of opera depended on synthesizing all of the stage elements – crucially the music, scenery, lighting, and the performers. This led him to recommend steps, platforms, vertical columns, and other non-realist, three-dimensional units in scenic design (Figure 10.11). Appia emphasized musical rhythm as the key to aesthetic coherence, following the ideas of the "Eurhythmics" movement. Eurhythmics, begun by Émile Jaques-Dalcroze (1865–1950), trained musicians and dancers to learn music through movement. For Appia, sound-based communication was the proper basis for artistic unity and the key to true reality. Most theatre practitioners ignored Appia's ideas before 1910, but his precepts exerted significant influence after the Great War (the name given to World War I by the war's contemporaries) when German Expressionist experiments with sound, scenery, and light gave his ideas new cogency.

Craig's visionary statements about the need to revolutionize the stage were more broadly published. In a series of books beginning in 1905 and in a periodical, *The Mask*, which he edited sporadically between 1908 and 1929, Craig argued for aesthetic and atmospheric coherence through designs that integrated the actor with three-dimensional, abstract set pieces through the bold use of light and sound. Unlike Appia, Craig favored a single setting for an entire performance to evoke the spirit of the play, with minor changes effected through the movement and lighting of towering, vertical screens. Craig also urged that the theatre – which he believed was an individual, not a collective art – must bow to the control of a master-artist. Influenced by Wagner's call for stage production as a *Gesamtkunstwerk* and by Nietzsche's desire for a *ubermensch* (superior person) who could bear the burden of life's contradictions, Craig sought a total artist of the theatre who could combine playwriting,

Figure 10.11
Adolphe Appia's design for Christoph Willibald Gluck's opera, *Orpheus and Eurydice*, 1913, at Hellerau, as realized through computer-assisted design.
Source: © 3D Visualization Group, School of Theatre Studies, University of Warwick.

designing, and directing. At one point, Craig proposed that this directorial master artist might even control the acting during performances. Despairing of the intransigence of stars and the materiality of actors' bodies, he, influenced by Maeterlinck, suggested that live performers should be replaced by large puppets – *Übermarionettes* [EW-behr-marionettes] he called them – that could evoke spiritual realities and would be easier to control. Both Craig and Appia advocated abstract scenery and flexibility in lighting, and pushed the stage director toward the role of an *auteur* [oh-tur], a figure (like some film directors) who takes author-like control of all the elements of a production. We will discuss a series of *auteur* directors who followed Appia and Craig in Chapter 13.

Appia and Craig shared some commonalities with the Aestheticist movement, which also praised Wagner's concept of artistic unity. In general, though, **Aestheticism** turned its back on the spiritual yearnings of the Symbolists; the Aestheticists attempted stage productions that encouraged spectators to escape the workaday world and revel in heightened aesthetic sensations. Believing in "art for art's sake," they often chose contents and styles from the theatrical past to inspire new emotional responses. In *Salomé* (1893), for example, Oscar Wilde hoped that his imagistically charged dialogue and tension-filled stage pictures would move his audience to experience the anger, lust, cruelty, and revenge of his major characters from the biblical story. He offered the play to Sarah Bernhardt, who planned to produce it, but this plan failed

Figure 10.12

Aida Overton Walker as Salomé (1912).

Source: Library of Congress, https://www.loc.gov/
item/97502075/.

because *Salomé* was censored in the U.K. Although the play was produced by the Théâtre de l'Oeuvre in Paris in 1896, with Lugné-Poe as Herod, Wilde never got to see it because he was jailed for sodomy at the time of its production.

Wilde was not the only artist obsessed with Salome. Her image had been important to the Decadent movement within visual arts, and afterward a phenomenon called "Salomania" followed the 1907 production of Strauss's opera version of the play. In Europe and the United States, dancers and actresses often uprooted the "dance of the seven veils" mentioned in Wilde's play and created sensual choreographies for commercial consumption. Some alluded to the character Salome's Jewishness through Orientalist tropes; but some performers, including African American Aida Overton Walker (1880–1914), made the dance their own. (See Figure 10.12.) While most versions of the dance were designed to titillate spectators and make money, Overton Walker's version was designed as high art, and part of her project of racial uplift, on its own and within the 1908 Broadway musical *Bandanna Land* (although this performance also contained a parodic performance of the dance). The movements of Salomania underscore the fact that a hard line between commercial and art theatre perhaps never existed, despite the theoretical antipathy between the two.

Aestheticism also shaped the neo-romanticism of Hugo von Hofmannsthal (1874–1929) in Germany. The playwright and poet invited a meditative response from audiences with a group of short plays in the 1890s, including *Death and the Fool* (1893) in which allegorical characters speak a poetic language. The French dramatist Edmond Rostand (1868–1918), best known for his *Cyrano de Bergerac* (1898), also embraced the goals of the Aestheticists early in his career. Sarah Bernhardt lent her soaring, lilting voice to the lead character in Rostand's *La Samaritaine* (1897), a biblical drama inspired by the story of a woman from Samaria.

Aestheticism traveled under the name of **Retrospectivism** in Russia. Aleksandr Blok (1880–1921), earlier hailed as a major Symbolist poet and dramatist, came to reject Symbolism for what he took to be its empty mysticism. Meyerhold, too, moved beyond Symbolism after 1905. His 1906 production of Blok's tragi-farce, *The Puppet Show*, combined *commedia dell'arte* comic techniques with grotesque effects to underline Blok's poetic and absurdist vision. In addition to its satirical intent, the aim of this production, and of cultural Retrospectivism in general, was to recover older forms of theatre as a means of transporting audiences into heightened aesthetic experiences. Like the Aestheticists, the Retrospectivists believed in immersing themselves in artistry for relief and enjoyment. Nikolai Evreinov (1879–1953) became the major proponent of Retrospectivism in Russia. He drew on Nietzsche's praise of the aesthetic life to propose that the artist-hero transform his own life into a work of art.

In a series of manifestos, essays, and plays, Evreinov urged the production of monodramas – monologues about the self – to externalize the consciousness of the artist-protagonist. He co-founded a theatre in St. Petersburg to explore his ideas and later served as artistic director at the Maly Theatre in Moscow, where he directed harlequinades, pantomimes, and monodramas.

William Butler Yeats and poetic modernism

The early avant-garde movements and some second-generation avant-garde movements lived alongside what might be called poetic modernism. Most critics and historians begin their definitions of theatrical **modernism** by noting that this twentieth-century orientation to the arts emphasized the vision of the dramatist as the primary carrier of meaning in the theatre. In a broader sense, modernism encompassed many of the avant-garde movements of the first half of the twentieth century, which were reacting to the modernization of contemporary life and its effects on social, spiritual and political life, which will be discussed in more detail in the next chapter. In this section, however, we will concentrate on what we call poetic modernists, who focused on the possibilities of poetry as text as the basis for their dramatic works. (See the online case study on modernism for an exploration of the term and movement.)

FREE

INSTRUCTOR & STUDENT RESOURCES

To emphasize his imagistic poetry, Irish writer and theatre manager William Butler Yeats (1865–1939) tried to alter the actor's embodiment of a character, the basis of theatrical representation. As a young man, Yeats saw several Symbolist productions at the Théâtre de l'Oeuvre and returned to Dublin convinced that Ireland needed a poetic stage and a national theatre. Intrigued by Craig's interest in substituting marionettes for actors, Yeats experimented with some of the actors at the Abbey Theatre to see if he could minimize their physical expressiveness and turn them into mouthpieces for his words. Although his experiments to turn spectators into readers were initially unsuccessful, Yeats bragged that he had "been the advocate of poetry against the actor" and vowed to keep trying (2002: 129).

Yeats had more success with a Westernized version of *nō*. In 1915, the poet Ezra Pound introduced Yeats to Itō Michio (1892–1961), a dancer from Japan who had studied eurhythmics and performed dances in a style that combined European and Japanese traditions. Yeats had been reading translations of some Asian plays, including Tagore's *The Post Office* (1912) and several *nō* dramas, and was eager to adopt *nō* as a partial model for his poetic theatre. With two other Japanese performers, Itō introduced a Europeanized, invented version of *nō* dancing to Yeats. Yeats revised the script of *At the Hawk's Well* (1914–1916) for Itō, who choreographed and performed a major role in the production in 1916. As described in Chapter 2, *nō* uses musical accompaniment behind a chorus of voices, sometimes speaking the words of the main character, to tell a story, while other performers dance the action. Likewise, *At the Hawk's Well* separates much of the spoken narrative from the embodied action. A chorus of three "musicians," as Yeats calls them, frames the entire performance by introducing the characters, narrating the action, and occasionally adding their own commentary. In addition, they set the scene by appealing to the imagination of each spectator. Instead of looking at actual scenery on the stage, the audience is encouraged by the narrator-musicians to envision "A well long choked up and dry/And boughs long stripped by the wind" in their imaginations (Yeats 1952: 399). Even after the actors enter playing specific characters, Yeats's musicians comment on their actions, reducing the actors to doing what the musicians report, so that the narrators created a tension between what they say and the mimetic actions of the actors. Yeats's actors also wore masks, further marking their distance from realistic acting. Yeats wrote several more plays based, like *Hawk's Well*, on a mythic Irish past and evocative language. He recognized that his poetic theatre would never be popular, but hoped to inspire a coterie audience with his poetic visions.

Yeats also continued to adapt forms he saw as *nō*-like, although he did not adhere to the formal features of *nō* acting or dramaturgical practices. Yeats exemplified a modernist fascination with the "East" later followed by Antonin Artaud (1896–1948), Bertolt Brecht (1898–1956), and contemporary European adaptations of *butoh*, while also engaging a form of *Japonisme* discussed in the previous chapter. He was interested in both creating drama that would speak to Irish anti-colonial national spirit, and solving a formal problem: the difficulty of creating a truly poetic theatre of the soul, which was impossible with either realistic or melodramatic acting styles and textual conventions. Yeats's initial appropriation in his Celtic-*nō* adaptations, became a truly transnational and transcultural phenomenon in conception and reality. Ironically, Yeats saw his drama as linked to anti-colonial movements in India and other global sites, even as he only selectively understood each country's contemporary politics and he participated in cultural imperialism himself.

Yeats's collaborations with Itō led to a circuit of dance-theatre performances for the Japanese dancer, including tours of *Hawk's Well* which he directed and performed in through the 1930s. Adaptations of *Hawk's Well* are still part of contemporary *nō* repertoires. Itō's own repertoire as performer, teacher, and choreographer was diverse, including adaptations of *nō* plays with U.S. and European actors, dance spectacles and roles in U.S.-authored plays in the early twentieth century. Itō's work was not free from the Orientalist and exoticist practices embodied by other Asian and Asian American performers trying to make a living in theatre and film. He created the role of the Congo Witch Doctor in O'Neill's *Emperor Jones* in 1920 and Orientalized himself in commercial Hollywood films. Despite this, his long career reveals the breadth of transnational circuits of modernist intercultural performance.

Media, consumerism, and the theatre

In this section, we will consider how developments in print and photographic media also impacted the commercial theatre, which often thrived within the ongoing dominance of industrial capitalism and emerging forms of consumerism, commodification of the body, and entrepreneurial self-promotion in this period. Our objects of study include musical comedies, theatrical revues, and the influence of performances featuring international stars. We will also begin to explore circuits of touring, itinerant, and non-urban performances by African American, Asian American, Jewish, and Mexican artists, whose popular performances created new audiences and performance cultures within capitalism. These developments existed alongside the avant-garde experiments described above, and as our section on gender, sexuality and capitalism will show, the desire of avant-garde artists to sequester themselves away from capitalist conditions did not always work. Recognizing commercial theatre and avant-garde theatre as coexisting in a larger theatre culture presents a more dynamic and robust understanding of theatre in this period.

Print culture for stars and playwrights

Within the theatre, international stars and popular playwrights benefited from print-based modes of marketing performances. Photography widened the appeal of theatrical stars and the prestige of print helped to win playwrights international copyright protection.

After 1870, it was common for stars to arrange for the sale of small pictures of themselves in their performances, typically costumed in the roles of their favorite characters. By 1900, photographic images splashed on posters and throughout newspapers told the public that a star had hit the town. Photos helped make possible the great era of international stars that toured from Tokyo to New York to St. Petersburg from the 1870s into the 1920s. National-turned-international stars Tommaso Salvini and Eleanora Duse (1858–1924) from Italy, Henry Irving (1838–1905) and Ellen Terry (1847–1928) from England, Kawakami Otojirō and his wife Kawakami Sadayakko from Japan, and Edwin Booth (1833–1893) and Richard Mansfield (1857–1907) from the United States performed (in their native languages) before millions of fans. International starring on this scale had not been possible before telegraphs, railroads, and steamships allowed agents to schedule theatres, plan mass publicity campaigns, and transport their precious cargoes to the desired site on the right night with efficiency and economy.

Figure 10.13
Sarah Bernhardt as Camille in *The Lady of the Camellias*, one of her greatest romantic roles. From the International Library of Famous Literature Published in London.

Source: © V&A Images, Victoria and Albert Museum.

From among these luminaries, most critics around 1900 would likely have ranked Sarah Bernhardt (1844–1923) at the top of the firmament (Figure 10.13). Following her success at the Comédie Française and elsewhere, Bernhardt quit the Comédie at the height of her popularity in 1880 to form her own company for a series of international tours, primarily to England and the United States. During a career of more than 60 years, Bernhardt performed over 130 characters, nearly half of them written specifically for her. Twenty-five of her 130+ roles were male, Hamlet among them, her cross-gender role-playing facilitated by her thin, athletic, sometimes androgynous body and flexible, yet powerful voice.

Novelist Anatole France suggested some of the chief reasons for her magnetic attractiveness in male roles in a comment about her performance as a young poet in Alfred de Musset's (1810–1857) *Lorenzaccio* (Figure 10.14):

> We know what a work of art this great actress can make of herself. All the same, in her latest transformation, she is astounding. She has formed her very substance into a melancholy youth, truthful and poetic. She has created a living masterpiece by her sureness

of gesture, the tragic beauty of her pose and glance, the increased power in the timbre of her voice, and the suppleness and breadth of her diction – through her gifts, in the end, for mystery and horror.

(qtd. in Gold and Fizdale 1991: 261)

Bernhardt, who played more male roles later in her career, once said that a woman was better suited to play roles like Hamlet than a young man who could not understand the philosophy or an older man who does not have the look of the boy. "The woman more readily looks the part, yet has the maturity of mind to grasp it" (Ockman 2005: 41–2). As Pamela Corbin suggests, Bernhardt acted across gender and age, defying female norms of aging, including the retirement of post-menopausal women from public life. Her athleticism, showcased in form-fitting male costumes at that age was a contrast to younger actresses who played "girl-boy" roles such as Eva Tanguay (1878–1947) (Figure 10.15), Maude Adams (1872–1953), and Nina Boucicault (1867–1950), who were her contemporaries, or those of an earlier generations such Adah Issacs Menken (1835–1868), whose pants roles were designed to show off her youthful body.

Bernhardt, despite her exceptional career, was part of a sizable group of Jewish performers in the nineteenth and early twentieth centuries, including Fanny Brice (1891–1951), Alla Nazimova (1879–1945), and Sophie Tucker (1886–1966). Unlike most of these performers, however, Bernhardt acted almost exclusively in legitimate dramas. A Catholic convert, her embodiment of her Jewish identity was often subtle or displaced onstage; she sometimes mentioned it and sometimes denied it. Less subtle was her form of self-promotion and entrepreneurialism that presaged contemporary celebrity culture. Bernhardt advertised herself as a distinctive individual and social critic as well as an actress. Ironically, her histrionic attitude was posthumously attributed to her Jewish identity.

Her millions of devoted fans returned often to enjoy *la divine Sarah*, not only for her latest physical and vocal transformations, but also for her conscious sculpting of self and role into a "living masterpiece" of art. Further, Bernhardt found numerous ways of sharing her emotions with the audience, inducing them to feel the same "mystery and horror" experienced by herself as the character. Due to a backstage accident, Bernhardt had to have her right leg amputated in 1915, at the age of 70. Nonetheless, she continued to perform, often

Figure 10.14
Poster of Sarah Bernhardt in the title role of the young male poet in Alfred de Musset's *Lorenzacchio*. Bernhardt played 25 male roles during her career, including Hamlet and the Hamlet-like Lorenzacchio. The poster is by Alphonse Mucha, the Czech artist whose distinctive style became known as *Art Nouveau*. Bernhardt signed a six-year contract with Mucha for a now-famous series of posters.
Source: Artefact/Alamy Stock Photo.

seated or completely static, still thrilling spectators with her vocal power, range, diction, and emotional expressiveness. Despite her many photogenic qualities, Bernhardt may be best remembered for her voice. In many ways, she was the perfect star for a culture that was becoming more aware of the potential mystery and luminescence of the human voice.

While Bernhardt and other international stars had the power to hire and fire directors, designers, and promoters at will, by 1900 they had to pay for the right to perform the plays of living dramatists upon which their stardom depended. Earlier, around 1870, most dramatic authors, like other self-employed writers, had gained legal **copyright** protections for the publication of their plays. Control over performance rights, however, remained elusive. Since the sixteenth century, stars and acting companies could purchase plays outright from their authors, perhaps paying them an additional sum after the third night of its opening performance if the play were a success. After that, the performance rights normally belonged to the company or star and the playwright received no royalties.

Figure 10.15

U.S. vaudeville star Eva Tanguay, in a publicity photo for a 1908 performance in Kentucky.

Source: © Keith/Albee Vaudeville Theatre Collection, University of Iowa Libraries, Iowa City, Iowa.

This began to change in the 1850s, when powerful playwright-producers such as Dion Boucicault (father of Nina Boucicault) secured some legal protection for future performances of their plays. Nonetheless, it remained a common practice for managers to pirate published and unpublished plays from other theatres, make a few minor alterations, and pay nothing to the original playwrights when they produced the piece under a different title. The international traffic in pirated plays was even higher because, prior to 1886, no treaties protected the rights of non-national authors. By 1900, although European and U.S. dramatists continued to have difficulties collecting payments due from theatre managers, they had won the cultural and legal battle for full copyright protection. The emphasis on print-based rights for dramatic material created a separation between a dramatic text and its interpretation in production, a new distinction which shifted commercial theatre practices in ways that exceeded the rights of dramatists to claim a share of the profits from performances as well as from the publication of their plays. Thus, for the first time in the United States, the text of the play stood apart as a piece of intellectual property autonomous from the creative practice of actors and directors. Scholar Julia Walker (2009) sees this ability to separate Expressionist production techniques from Expressionist playwriting as an important part of the American Expressionist movement, discussed in the next chapter.

Authorship governed by the logic of print culture continues to be a significant keystone of theatrical power to the present day. Despite the rise of star actors, producers, and directors after 1870, the playwright, designer, and choreographer could claim legal protection for his or her work, but actors and (until very recently) directors could not copyright their work. When a U.S. director around 1900 tried to claim copyright protection for a bit of stage business he had invented, for example, the courts did not allow it. Musical rights were also sometimes unprotected as we discuss below. As we will see in Part IV, the power of authorship continued as an important economic foundation of the theatre, even as new media began challenging the centrality of print culture.

Commodity capitalism and new forms of popular theatre

The previous section of this chapter explored how the dissemination of print images of performers buoyed the careers of theatrical stars. These proliferating photographs of their bodies, however, also made them commodities, expanding spectatorship and the escalating interest in their consumption inside and outside of entertainment venues. Yet the marriage of commodity capitalism and new media went further than expanding audiences – it actually helped create the conditions for new forms of entertainment.

For instance, photography advanced musical theatre, which featured spectacular stars, in addition to hummable music. Although musical theatre traditionally meant opera in Europe, light operatic entertainment (**operetta**) emerged in the mid-nineteenth century in Vienna, Paris, and London to amuse mostly bourgeois spectators. In London in the 1890s, musical comedies challenged and soon replaced operetta in popularity – including the concoctions of William S. Gilbert and Arthur Sullivan, discussed in the last chapter. While there is no firm distinction between operetta and the musical, pre-1910 musicals typically featured a script with a girl-gets-boy love story, songs that could be marketed by the new popular music industry that expanded from the sale of sheet music to phonograph recordings, and an attractive female chorus line. Indeed, the first important impresario of musicals was George Edwardes (1852–1915), who made his initial reputation through shows highlighting the Gaiety Girls chorus at his theatre in London. Audience interest in the chorus girl rose with the influence of photography, and by 1900, the commodification of the chorus girl's sexual allure was a chief feature of the musical stage. Not surprisingly, photographs of chorus girls and other spectacular females of the theatre (including legit actresses such as Adah Issacs Menken), in various states of undress, were popular after 1870. These images could be considered early forms of musical theatre "merch" that lived alongside the images discussed above that made actresses. These items often assumed male heterosexual spectators, although regimes of spectatorship are complicated, as the contemporary version of Takarazuka theatre reminds us.

A variety of musical theatre forms flourished on U.S. and European stages from 1895 to the Great War (1914–1918). Several U.S. musicals, such as Victor Herbert's (1859–1924) *Babes in Toyland* and the first of several versions of *The Wizard of Oz* (both 1903), mixed whimsy and fantasy with light satire. Austro-Hungarian composer Franz Lehár's (1870–1948) *The Merry Widow* (1905 in Vienna and 1907 in London) reminded audiences of the soaring musical tones of operetta. Others, like George M. Cohan's (1878–1942) *Little*

Johnny Jones (1904), made a splash with catchy tunes ("I'm a Yankee-Doodle Dandy," for example), wise-cracking humor, and polished dancing. London saw a run of musicals with "girl" in the title – *The Earl and the Girl* (1904), *The Girl in the Taxi* (1912), *The Shop Girl* (1894), and *The Quaker Girl* (1910), for instance. Cohan's musicals were patriotic and he and his peers often created shows that supported turn of the century U.S. imperial efforts, such as a series of gunboat musicals with xenophobic depictions of non-European people. Others demonstrated fascination with and optimism about emergent technologies such as the automobile, such as *The Auto Race* (1907) and *The International Cup* (1910), that each ran over 300 performances at The Hippodrome, which seated over 5,000 people. Smaller scale musicals were developed a few years later at the Princess Theatre, which seated just under 300 people. These modest-budget musicals, composed between 1915 and 1918 by Jerome Kern (1885–1945) and written by Guy Bolton (1884–1979) depended as much on plot as music for character development. Although a point of debate, scholars sometimes see them as harbingers of the musicals of the 1940s discussed in Chapter 12. Surprisingly, few musicals engaged with the Great War itself. Anti-European, and in particular anti-German sentiment, however, diminished the number of imported operettas produced on U.S. stages, in this period opening the doors to a rise in domestic U.S. musical theatre production.

This era also saw theatre artists newly as laborers by emerging labor movements in this era. Between 1910 and 1920, many unions were founded to protect theatre workers including The Dramatists Guild (1912) (known as The Authors Guild until 1921), the American Society of Composers Authors and Publishers (1914), and Actors' Equity (1913). (The International Alliance of Theatrical Stage Employees had already been founded in 1893.) Until the foundation of Actor's Equity, actors were not paid for rehearsals, and producers set pay scales and working conditions. Before a group of artists including Victor Herbert and Irving Berlin (1888–1989) formed ASCAP (American Society of Composers, Authors and Publishers), composers, songwriters, lyricists and publishers could not protect the copyright and public performance of their works, meaning songs were often performed live without credit or payment to the artists who created them. The Actors' Equity strike in 1919 created solidarity amongst existing unions, but did not protect everyone – chorus dancers, for example, were left out in the cold. Together, the actions taken by the unions diminished the absolute power of producers. This decade also saw the demise of the Erland Syndicate (a loose consortium of producers that emerged in the 1890s) and the rise of the Shuberts, who came to dominate theatre production in the following era.

These economic changes did not hamper the development of Broadway as the center of the musical theatre industry. The 1920s gave rise to a boom in New York's population and the building of Broadway theatres. In 1918, there were 48 Broadway theatres, by 1928, there were 76, a number which has never been surpassed. Between January 1920 and December 1929, 549 musical shows opened. This boom was possible in part because of reasonable production costs, which meant that shows could turn a profit after a few months. In addition, ticket prices rose so slowly over the 1920s, that working-class and middle-class spectators could see the shows from the mezzanine fairly regularly, growing audiences (Jones 2003: 61).

The repertoire of these theatres was varied, including musical comedies, operettas, revues (discussed below) and, at times, all-Black cast shows.

All Black-cast musicals had been produced before the 1920s on Broadway. In New York, African American artists, wrote and performed and produced several successful musicals with Vaudevillian elements, including *A Trip to Coontown* (1898), and Bert Williams and George Walker's *In Dahomey* (1903), *Abyssania* (1906), and *Bandanna Land* (1908), which went on to tour Europe. The difference in the 1920s was who was producing the shows. In 1921, *Shuffle Along* became a surprise hit on Broadway, inspiring other white producers to produce all-Black cast shows. In retrospect, the movement of all-Black shows from Black to white producers traces an end to Black artists' control of their representation on stage.

The era between the wars also saw the rise of Jewish-American lyricists and composers in the musical theatre; some, like Irving Berlin (1888–1989) and Ira Gershwin (1896–1983), had earned their fame as Tin Pan Alley popular songwriters, others like Jerome Kern and Oscar Hammerstein II (1895–1960) were formally educated musicians. These men contributed greatly to musical theatre history through their popular songs and contributions to musicals such as Hammerstein II and Kern's *Showboat* (1927), which followed the lives of performers on a showboat over a 40-year period, including a series of personal romances. This mixed-cast musical is criticized today for its depiction of Black characters, which fell into stereotypes, although some argue that the musical also critiqued the racial bigotry of the era. What is not disputed is that *Showboat* demonstrated the possibilities of the musical with a unified plot and set of characters, although that form would not become the norm until after World War II.

The Great Depression, and the rise of the more affordable tickets to the "talkies" (films with sound) affected theatre production in the 1930s – some two-thirds of Manhattan's theatres were shut during 1931 – although Broadway was far from unoccupied in this period. The show went on, if in fewer theatres and with significantly reduced budgets. Although U.S. producers struggled, and often served up escapist fluff, there were also significant satires such as *Of Thee I Sing* (1931), and serious works such as Gershwin's 1935 Opera *Porgy and Bess*, and Marc Blitzstein's controversial "play in music" *The Cradle Will Rock* (1937) produced by the Federal Theatre Project.

Theatrical revues and vaudeville, mentioned in the last chapter, also flourished on European and U.S. stages between 1900 and 1930. This genre mixed chorus girls with the musical, comic, and sketch traditions of the variety stage. Paris led the way with spectacular revues at the Folies-Bergère and elsewhere in the 1880s that involved dancing girls and glamorous tableaux. By 1900, high-priced variety shows in Germany and Austria typically ended the evening as spectacular revues. Florenz Ziegfeld (1867–1932) popularized revues in the United States with his lavish *Follies*, staged yearly between 1907 and 1931. The "follies," "shows," "scandals," "vanities," and "revues" of these years in U.S. entertainment typically featured top talent, from Eddie Cantor (1892–1964) to Bert Williams and exciting music by the likes of George Gershwin and Irving Berlin. The legacy of these spectacular revues may be seen today in the night club acts at Las Vegas and on the Takarazuka stages of Japan, whose repertoire, discussed above, often adapted Parisian forms of U.S. revues to Japanese forms.

Gender, performance, and capitalism

The intersection of the rise of the musical revue and the chorus girl intersected with changes in gendered labor practices and industrial and consumer capitalism more broadly. In the United States, between 1890 and 1930, the number of women working in professional careers grew 226 percent; the number of women in college classes grew to 40 percent. Women without college educations took up professions in service work, including waitressing, office work and retail sales; women who could move out of domestic work did. As might be expected, women were paid less than men; salaries were often modest. For working-class single women, being a chorus girl, a staple of vaudeville entertainment from the 1890s forward, was both a fantasy for escaping poor work conditions and a real opportunity for women to work outside of traditional "female" professions for pay that was equivalent or higher than those other professions. (Because chorus girls often worked in the same area in New York as sex workers, chorus girls and other female entertainers were often categorized as or assumed to also be sex workers.) Commercial chorus girls emerged alongside the New Woman, a term used to describe independent and economically and sexually autonomous women. Although chorus girls were often from less elite socioeconomic classes and dependent upon male patronage to gain upper class status, they were part of a panoply of changing roles for women at the turn of the century.

Black women in the United States were not part of the new class of shopgirls and waitresses, and were usually excluded from the category of New Woman due to segregation, racism, and classism. Some Black women, did, however, become chorus girls on segregated stages; they also worked as trainers for white performers. Despite these conditions, and the stigma of association with sex work, some Black female dancers saw this profession as a form of freedom to live differently – enacting what Saidya Hartman uses as the title of her 2019 book on independent Black women laborers in New York: *Wayward Lives, Beautiful Experiments*. Aida Overton Walker, who transformed the role of a dancer into one that upheld Black respectability, was a model for many young Black women who came to work in the city a generation after the great migration of African American workers from the South to the North beginning in the 1910s, even if they did not have the cultural capital she enjoyed as a light-skinned woman who has already a part of an established theatre company.

Working women were not just laborers but also consumers within the burgeoning entertainment and retail industries. *The Ziegfeld Follies* produced almost every year between 1907 and 1931, forged a link between female beauty and consumer culture. Miss America pageants, Macy's Thanksgiving Day Parades, fashion shows in department stores, and many other institutions and events in American life between the 1920s and the 1960s owe much of their popularity to Ziegfeld's success in promoting high fashion. In fact, much of the initial influence of the *Ziegfeld Follies* rested on the ties between periodical print culture, touring Broadway shows, and department store marketing that had emerged in U.S. cities by 1900. Publishers of high-gloss photo magazines had discovered that pictures of star actors and expensive shows could attract readers to their journals. The new department store capitalists needed to reach high-end consumers with their magazine advertisements. And Broadway producers knew their productions could make more money on the road (i.e., outside of New York) if they arranged for tie-ins with local businessmen. The merchandisers who organized some of the world's first department stores, together with their allies in journalism and "showbiz," began the transition toward consumer capitalism that would utterly transform the economy of the United States by 1990.

Most of the women in Ziegfeld's audiences were not average consumers of inexpensive entertainments, of course; tickets for the *Ziegfeld Follies* cost more than the average household often spent on entertainment. And Ziegfeld positioned spectators in his audience as consumers of beauty; like shoppers watching a department store fashion show, his spectators saw woman and costume as one in the *Follies*, a single object of envy and desire. As feminist scholar Linda Mizejewski points out, this conflation of women and clothes confuses "the abstract consumable and the abstract consumer" (Mizejewski 1999: 97).

Ziegfeld's emphasis on high fashion earned him the reputation in New York of refining the stereotype of the low-class chorus girl and racializing her as middle-class, graceful and white. All of Ziegfeld's showgirls were white, of Nordic-looking ethnicity (no Jews, Eastern Europeans or non-Europeans allowed) and fit a particular body type. Ziegfeld even paid his dancers not to tan in the summer, even though he asked them to wear tawny makeup for certain numbers. Nonetheless, Ziegfeld's dancers were trained by Ethel Williams, a Black *Darktown Follies* (1914) performer, who, in her own performances, refused the standardization of chorus line dancing. She never received credit for this work; and because she was Black,

Figure 10.16

Dolores (Kathleen Mary Rose Wilkinson), originally a Duff Gordon mannequin model, who became a Ziegfeld star.

Source: Billy Rose Theatre Division, The New York Public Library. Dolores in Ziegfeld's *Midnight Frolic* (Town and Country, 20 Dec. 1919). https://digitalcollections.nypl.org/items/b850e 8be-5f1f-ff08-e040-e00a180669022

Ziegfeld would not hire her as a dancer, despite her well-recognized talent. Nonetheless, Ziegfeld's dancers incorporated Black vernacular dance into the whitened Follies, Ziegfeld's intervention was especially striking given the working-class backgrounds and non-Anglo ethnicity of many popular female entertainers in the decades before, during and after the emergence of the Follies.

The training of the chorus girl as was also a mode of bodily discipline related to developments in capitalism. In 1890s Britain, John Tiller (1854–1925) started a school for chorus girls designed to train young working-class women whose only other choice was factory work; this training, however, was not unlike the mechanization of the factory. The dancers were often taken from families as children and often trained for 14 hours a day. The emphasis on synchrony and identical precision was an embodied reflection of industrial capitalism. Meanwhile, some 20 years later, Ziegfeld hired trend-setter Lady Duff ("Lucile") Gordon (1863–1935) to design his fashionable costumes and choreographer Ned Wayburn (1874–1942) to teach his performers how to walk in them.

Wayburn taught the showgirl models a mode of erect posture and slow gait that came to be called "the Ziegfeld Walk" (Figure 10.16). From the 1915 revue onwards, the fashion mannequins/dancers generally paraded down a steep, curved staircase, moved to the down-center area of the stage where they turned on their charms for the spectators, and then moved to the side to make way for the next model. As Wayburn explained it, the women needed to practice a difficult thrust of the hip and shoulder in order to avoid falling over; "the Ziegfeld walk" could cause broken bones.

The deep relationship between consumer capitalism and performance was not limited to European capitals. The Takarazuka Revue's founder Kobayashi Ichizo was also the creator of train station malls which included rooftop restaurants and the revue theatre, linking theatre, shopping and dining. The rigid training of Ziegfeld's dancers was met with a parallel in the Japanese form of revue. This training was commented upon when the performers toured abroad.

In addition, new modes of labor and emerging forms of consumer capitalism deeply affected the embodiment, performance and representation of gender from 1890 to 1930. As suggested throughout this chapter and the next, performance was a site of challenge to gender roles and gender expression throughout the era. Commercial actresses and performers modeled new modes of female behavior as laborers and social beings. Not surprisingly, their actions were celebrated or criticized in equal measure, anticipating modes of disciplining gender through celebrity culture we see today. Ideas of masculinity, femininity, and gender expression were challenged in other ways. Many of the avant-garde artists erased the line between art and life in public space. These performances included dandyism, crossdressing, and other forms of performance of the self that called into question ideas of Victorian manhood and womanhood. Prohibitions on homosexuality were also challenged. Rachilde, for example, although assigned female at birth, used masculine pronouns for part of her life, and applied for permission from the Parisian prefecture of police to wear men's clothes. Interestingly, her justification for cross dressing was economic: women's clothes were too flimsy and expensive for her to maintain and men's were more sustainable, inherently linking consumer capitalism and gender performance. Additionally, educated women were sometimes gendered male in the early twentieth century, suggesting that advanced education also gendered people, despite the clothing they wore.

Oscar Wilde, although married, wore dandyish clothes and did not completely obfuscate his homosexual relationships. Although neither of these figures was fully accepted, they modeled new possibilities, especially within entertainment venues in which spectators of all genders consumed entertainment. Anxiety about these spaces of performance and their homoeroticism fueled many a warning, if not always outright censorship. When one looks at these figures today, one might see the roots of queer culture, or frame artists such as Rachilde as transgender artists. Being sensitive to historical specificity and the complicated lives these artists led may temper this impulse. For example, Rachilde, although gender nonconforming, publicly rejected feminism, and created misogynistic depictions of women like other Symbolist playwrights. Nonetheless, it is important to recognize the convergence of public queerness, gender expression and consumer culture that remains to the present day.

The creation of new entertainment markets also created opportunities for immigrants, and non-Anglo racial and ethnic groups. Artists from these groups, despite prejudice and oppression, created vibrant theatre and performance communities and spaces. These included playwrights and performers centered in New York City, such as Harlem Renaissance writers such as Langston Hughes (1901–1967) and Zora Neale Hurston (1891–1960), who wrote plays alongside other forms. While the center of this movement was in New York, the creation of complex depictions of Black life by Black writers in this movement affected theatre far outside of the isle of Manhattan, as Lisa Anderson's case study demonstrates.

CASE STUDY: Karamu Theatre and the Harlem Renaissance

Lisa M. Anderson

The Harlem Renaissance is typically thought of as the decade of the 1920s, although it extends from the 1910s to the mid-1930s, when it faded as a result of the Great Depression. The period refers to Harlem specifically, because of the outpouring of arts that emerged there. In the midst of the financial boom of the period, post-World War I, patrons, both Black and white, funded artists across the United States. However, this flurry of artistic production wasn't confined to New York, and was also reflected in many of the cities which had significant Black populations.

The origin of this period of artistic flourishing began with the Great Migration. Beginning about 1915, millions of Black people left the explicit racism and violence that was the Jim Crow South for better jobs – and better lives – in the industrial cities of the North, including New York City, Philadelphia, Baltimore, Pittsburgh, Cleveland, Detroit, and Chicago, among many others. This influx of people, who were largely from rural areas, in addition to new European immigrants, generated a need for spaces through which these people new to cities could go for assistance in adjusting to their new cities. For Black migrants, this cause was largely taken up by Black women's clubs, who led the effort to better integrate their Southern peers into city life. For the European immigrant, settlement houses grew up from the late nineteenth through the early twentieth centuries. The most famous of these was Hull House in Chicago, which catered to new European immigrants; less well known was the unique Neighborhood Association Settlement House in Cleveland, which would change its name in the 1940s to Karamu House (which is generally now used to refer to its entire history). Naming the settlement house Karamu would follow the naming of its best-known project, Karamu Theatre.

A settlement house in Cleveland, and a theatre

The Cleveland settlement house was founded by Russell (1891–1980) and Rowena (1892–1992) Jelliffe in 1915 as the Neighborhood Association Settlement House, a space for the community – which then comprised Black migrants and European immigrants – to engage in activities that would both acclimate and educate them. While most settlement houses were focused on European immigrants, Karamu was unique because both its neighborhood (at first) and its settlement house were integrated. This reflected the Jelliffes' commitment to racial integration and the improvement of all communities. These efforts began with a children's theatre, and the arts would become central to Karamu's mission in what would become a predominantly Black neighborhood in Cleveland. (Technically, it was part of the Little Theatre movement that emerged in the 1910s and reached its heyday in the mid-1920s; aside from Karamu, they were relatively short-lived.)

The early years were stressful in many ways. The Jelliffes' philosophy was in stark contrast to the common de facto segregation of the time, even in a Northern city like Cleveland. Their progressive vision made some residents of the "Roaring Third" neighborhood nervous and reluctant to participate (Selby 1966: 11). Like other settlement houses, the Cleveland settlement house had a wide-ranging set of programs designed to help the community, especially arts programs for women and their children, and engaged in activism around civic reforms that supported unions, better wages and better working conditions. Raising money was also a challenge, since not all of those with money – mostly white – were willing to give. The Jelliffes continued undaunted, and in 1917, they put on their first play: *Cinderella*, a children's play, with an interracial cast. While the interracial cast did make some nervous, by all accounts the children's theatre became a success. In 1920, the success of its Children's Theatre inspired the Settlement House to create "the Dumas Dramatic Club for Adults" (Alkebulan 2005: 2).

Their first adult production was *The Little Stone House* by George Middleton (Selby 1966: 44). The group's leader Rose Griffiths hoped that they could subtly avoid the issue of race, since the play was set in Russia. As was typical for the plays produced by the Cleveland settlement house at this time, the casting was "color-blind," since the specifics of the play were, at least in theory, distant from the contemporary issues of Cleveland in 1920. It was a fine production, but the Jelliffes were interested in representing Black people as themselves on stage. Their challenge would be two-fold. First, the dramatic literature that represented Black Americans was minimal, and most of what was available relied on stereotyped and racist characterizations of Blackness. Second, the white public of Cleveland was not necessarily interested in seeing Black people on stage, let alone in roles that reflected the lived experiences of Black people in the late 1910s and early 1920s. At the very least, the Jelliffes needed the artistic output of the Harlem Renaissance in order to provide them with material for productions.

In 1922, the club changed its name to the Gilpin Players, named for Charles Gilpin (1878–1930), who had become famous for creating the lead role in Eugene O'Neill's *The Emperor Jones* at the Provincetown Playhouse (which was also a part of the Little Theatre movement). Gilpin made a controversial visit to the Neighborhood Association in 1922, not long after he won recognition from the New York Drama League for his role in *The Emperor Jones*. The visit was controversial because while Gilpin was hailed by many white theatre critics of the time, neither the Black press nor many Black people were excited about Gilpin or the role he played. Some considered *The Emperor Jones* to be as bad in its representation of Black people as the film *Birth of a Nation*. In spite of this, the Jelliffes recognized Gilpin's considerable talent, and thought that he would have advice for the club members who were interested in pursuing theatre.

The members of the dramatic club were surprised by his speech. In it, Gilpin did not apologize for playing the Emperor, which perhaps the club members expected. He "told the Dumas troupe to look within themselves, to see their own lives and to ape no one" (Hill and Hatch 2003: 228). The speech was encouraging, envisioning a future with a real body of Black literature that they could perform. His support for them was backed up with a donation of 50 dollars, a significant sum in the 1920s. He encouraged them and considered the future of Black theatre. Perhaps his explanation of why he took the role of Emperor, and the complexity with which he tried to portray his character, changed minds about Gilpin and his politics. With their perspective about him transformed, they renamed their club for him.

The Gilpin Players set about to produce a play about Black people. This would not be easy, since the dearth of dramatic literature that took seriously the lives of Black people made it very difficult to find appropriate material. The theatre groups were Rowena's focus, and she would take this goal as central during this period. They would finally produce their first play focused on Black people in 1925. Rowena's choice was Ridgely Torrence's *Granny Maumee* (1917), which had already been produced by a Black Little Theatre group in New York. Torrence had written a collection of plays called *Three Plays for a Negro Theater* (1917). Unfortunately, Torrence was Irish, not Black, and the play showed only some familiarity with Black Americans. The Players' Black members were not thrilled; they thought the play derogatory to Black people. The white audience was also not terribly excited by the play (or the players); some felt that the pursuit of the arts took away from encouraging the newly relocated population of the Roaring Third to work rather than to engage in artistic pursuits. Clearly, the Gilpin Players needed a new source of dramatic literature, and fortunately, the creativity that would emerge from this period – in Harlem, certainly, but also in other cities – would provide material for the players that reflected the diversity of Black life.

The creative burst of the Harlem renaissance

Karamu was able to take advantage of the flurry of plays that were written during the Harlem Renaissance. This outpouring of literature resulted in all kinds of drama being written and produced. Two things drove this expansion of writing. The financial boom of the 1920s made it possible for wealthy people – mostly white, with a few Black exceptions – to provide patronage to Black artists of all kinds, including writers. Second, W. E. B. Du Bois (1868–1963), Montgomery Gregory (1887–1971), and Alain Locke (1885–1954) encouraged the writing of plays about Black experiences. These plays were called "native dramas" (Perkins 1990), and were foundational to the Little Negro Theatre Movement, of which the Gilpin Players/Karamu was a part. As Kathy Perkins notes, these were both dramas and comedies, and "could be divided into two distinct categories: 'race or propaganda plays' and 'folk plays'" (Perkins 1990: 3).

Many of the plays that were written by Black writers during this period were "folk" plays, set in Southern rural settings, and dealt with the challenges that Black people faced in the rural South. Georgia Douglas Johnson's *A Sunday Morning in the South* (1925) took up lynching as its topic; Jean Toomer's (1894–1967) *Balo* (1922) is a drama in which a young man has a mystical revelation of God. Willis Richardson (1889–1977) wrote plays of Black rural life, and in 1930 he published a collection entitled *Plays and Pageants from the Life of the Negro*. These folk plays were strongly supported by philosopher and Howard University professor Alain Locke, who strongly believed in the importance not only of art, but of drama that captured the quotidian and varied life of Black people.

While plays about rural life were certainly popular, there were other aspects of Black life that those plays did not capture. Race and propaganda plays were sometimes plays about the lives of urban Blacks, who dealt with different kinds of challenges than their rural counterparts did. These were sometimes more strongly activist, pushing for equality in significant ways. Angelina Weld Grimke's (1881–1958) *Rachel* (1917), published in W. E. B. Du Bois's journal *Crisis*, would be one example of this type of play. Some of the activist plays were written by Black women, like Mary Burrill (1881–1946), whose plays addressed racial violence (*Aftermath*, 1919) and women's reproductive freedom (*They That Sit in Darkness*, 1919). Many of the plays written by Black women during the Harlem Renaissance period did take up contemporary issues; they also included anti-lynching dramas, as the post–World War I period had seen a rise in racial violence (through a resurgence of the Ku Klux Klan, who were intolerant of Black soldiers returned from World War I who challenged the Jim Crow racial order).

Willis Richardson's *Compromise* (1925), also in the arena of the folk drama, became the first play by a Black playwright to be produced at Karamu. *Compromise* was produced in February of 1926. Richardson's work was frequently taken up by amateur groups for production (Hatch and Shine 1996: 217), and Karamu was no exception. They also produced Paul Green's (1894–1981) *The No 'Count Boy* (1925) in the spring of 1926. Some of the plays produced were adaptations of short stories written by Rowena Jelliffe.

A theatre at last

The Jelliffes were able to acquire a theatre space of their own in 1927; the theatre was called Karamu from that point. The settlement house would take on the name Karamu House in 1941. According to Selby, their first production in the 120-seat theatre included three one-act plays: *Off Nag's Head* by Douglas MacMillan; *The Medicine Show*, by Stuart Walker; and *Simon the Cyrenian*, by Ridgley Torrence (Selby 1966: 60). This amateur playhouse would go on to attract professionals, and also to train amateurs who would go on to be professionals. According to Selby, it was the first integrated theatre in the United States. It was decorated with African designs, researched at the local public library by theatre members.

The key tension that existed for Karamu would continue into the early 1930s: while the players were Black, and the neighborhood increasingly so, the audience was largely white. Middle-class white patrons had the disposable income during this period to enjoy the arts, and Karamu put on quality work. While the players were excited to put on plays that featured Black life, the audiences were not as interested. As the actors – and Rowena as director – became more adept, they took on bigger challenges. They expanded beyond theatre to include other performing arts, and their audience would become more Black as Karamu embraced its place as an incubator of the Black performing arts.

Inevitably, the neighborhood changed, as many neighborhoods did in the period following the Great Migration. European immigrants, having acculturated to the United States, moved to whiter neighborhoods, and the area that was the "Roaring Third" became a Black neighborhood. The Jelliffes would continue their investment in Karamu House as the neighborhood changed, seeking to fulfill their vision of racial equality.

With the Jelliffes, Karamu was able to attract important playwrights of the period to workshop and premier their plays there. At least five of Langston Hughes's plays were first done by Karamu; of course, having grown up in Cleveland, Hughes also studied there in his youth. Notably, Karamu was the place where *Mule Bone*, co-authored by Hughes and Zora Neale Hurston, was first workshopped there. "The Gilpin Players wanted very much to do the play. Mrs. Jelliffe was enthusiastic" (Robert Hemenway, qtd. in Houston and Gates 1996: 167). Unfortunately, a deep conflict between Hurston and Hughes meant that the play was never fully produced there. But that was one glitch in a long history of Black theatre production, which continues to today (karamuhouse.org).

Lisa M. Anderson is a professor in the School of Social Transformation at Arizona State University, and the author of *Black Women and the Changing Television Landscape* (Bloomsbury 2023)

Key references

Books and articles

Alkebulan, A. (2005) "The Karamu House," in M. Kete Asante and A. Mazama (ed.) *Encyclopedia of Black Studies*, Thousand Oaks, CA: SAGE Publications, 289–90.

Blood, M.N.(1996) "Theatre in Settlement Houses: Hull-House Players, Neighborhood Playhouse, and Karamu Theatre," *Theatre History Studies* 16: 45.

Hatch, J.V., and T. Shine. (1996) *Black Theatre USA: Plays by African Americans, 1847 to Today*, rev. and exp. edn, New York: The Free Press.

Hemenway, R. (1991) Excerpt from *Zora Neale Hurston: A Literary Biography*. In G.H. Bass and H.L. Gates, Jr. (eds.) *Mule Bone: A Comedy of Negro Life*. New York: Harper Perennial, 161–188.

Hill, E., and J. Hatch. (2003) *A History of African American Theatre*, New York: Cambridge University Press.

Hughes, L. and Z. N. Hurston. (1991) *Mule Bone: A Comedy of Negro Life*, ed. G.H. Bass and H.L. Gates, Jr., New York: Harper Perennial.

Perkins, K. (1990) *Black Female Playwrights: An Anthology of Plays before 1950*, Bloomington: Indiana University Press.

Richardson, W. ed., with an introduction by C.R. Gray. (1993) *Plays and Pageants from the Life of the Negro*, Jackson: University of Mississippi Press.

Selby, J. (1966) *Beyond Civil Rights*, Cleveland and New York: The World Publishing Company.

Websites

Karamu House. *History*. https://karamuhouse.org/history/

Circuits of U.S. popular performance

As Lisa Anderson's case study shows, many popular entertainments were produced and/or developed outside of New York City. A sizable portion of these productions were created by immigrant artists and artists of color, many of whom faced discrimination by the white majority. Some forms of entertainment were designed primarily for audiences from their own communities, while others were designed for Anglo spectators. Some of these forms became incorporated into mainstream commercial theatres, while others did not. Nonetheless, these circuits of performance were an important part of U.S. theatre culture.

On the West coast, the development of San Francisco's Chinatown during the Gold Rush led to extensive productions of Chinese performance. This repertoire featured Cantonese opera, a southern form distinguished from the better-known *jingju* (Beijing Opera). Cantonese Opera's era of popularity began with Hong Fook Tong Company's debut in 1852 and until 1871. The Chinese Exclusion Act of 1882, which curtailed Chinese immigration to the United States, including performers, affected the industry greatly. The 1870s heyday supported several theatres including the Royal Chinese Theatre (founded c. 1874), the Gem of Mount Quan (founded 1878), the Peacock Theatre (founded 1877), and Grand Theatre (founded 1879). Other cities with large Chinese populations, such as Portland, Oregon, also had theatres. The fact that these performances were designed for Chinese spectators did not stop interested white spectators from fascination with these forms. Sarah Bernhardt was one of those spectators. Unfortunately, she decided to perform a Chinese dance herself in San Francisco, making her one of many performers who used racial impersonation in ways discussed in Chapters 8 and 9.

A second era of vibrancy emerged in the 1920s, when Cantonese opera groups moved their operations to the United States, and also toured Mexico and Cuba, supported in part by prosperous merchant immigrants. In this era, changes in immigration rules also allowed Chinese performers entrance into the United States, when political conditions in China made touring attractive again. San Francisco was once again a major hub although New York also had a substantial presence of Chinese theatre forms. With the opening of the Great China Theatre in San Francisco came complex scenography and a more modern building influenced by opera practices in southern mainland China. In contrast to the 1870s, the 1920s era brought troupes of female performers, and, as changes were made on the mainland, a rise in scripted operas, elaborate playbills, and an elaborate star system featuring actresses known to Chinese and non-Chinese spectators alike.

Anglo spectators' desire to see "China" eventually led to the Chop Suey Circuit in the 1930s. Named after an Americanized Chinese noodle dish, these touring performances featuring Chinese performers were created for Anglo audiences. While we can criticize the framing of these performances as performing the "Orient" for white audiences, this set of touring shows nonetheless employed many Asian American actors in the first half of the twentieth century. And, together, these performers had an impact on the development of U.S. performance culture which has rarely been recognized.

The Borscht Belt, a term coined by *Variety* magazine in the 1930s, referred to the Jewish summer resort area in the Catskills that housed Jewish entertainers well into the second half of the twentieth century. These resorts existed to provide vacation options for Jews who were regularly denied lodging and services in many U.S. resorts and hotels. Beginning in the 1920s entertainers in these resorts included comedians and out-of-work vaudevillian performers, some of whom had worked in New York City. While the performances were primarily in English, they included some in Yiddish. The social directors of these hotels created shows, including musical revues, for the Jewish patrons in indoor and outdoor theatres. In addition to providing entertainment for Jewish citizens, the Borscht Belt entertainment circuit nurtured the talents of many Jewish entertainers and led to the creation of a certain style of Jewish humor, important to the development of American comedy. This type of humor is exemplified by the stars who performed in these resorts, including Jerry Lewis (1926–2017), Danny Kaye (1911–1987) (who worked as an entertainment director in a resort in addition to being a singer and performer), Jackie Mason (1928–2021), Red Buttons (1919–2006), Rodney Dangerfield (1921–2004), and Henny Youngman (1906–1998). Moss Hart (1904–1961), who went on to stage write *My Fair Lady* and many other canonical American musicals, was also a Catskills alumnus, linking the history of Broadway to the Belt. The Belt became a testing ground for future entertainers, who travelled to the area to be seen and vetted before performing in New York City. Although the popularity of the Borscht Belt declined by the 1960s, the legacy of these performance sites remains present in performance history.

The so-called Chitlin Circuit brought Black performance revues to largely Black audiences in the 1930s, alongside performance circuits in the Borscht Belt. Begun by Black Indianapolis entrepreneurs Sea (1899–1974) and Denver (1895–1957) Ferguson in 1930, this circuit of Black performers toured Black-owned clubs in the southern and midwestern cities along the East Coast. Although the term Chitlin Circuit was informally and belatedly coined, these tours existed from the 1930s to end of formal racial segregation in the 1960s. The circuit launched the careers of many popular performers who later became mainstream, such as B.B. King (1925–2015). The conditions under which these performers worked were less than ideal; they often worked for less money and had poorer touring and hotel accommodation than white performers. They also worked most days out of the year. These conditions were common for jazz musicians and some cabaret performers discussed earlier in the chapter. The commercial goals of the circuit contrasted with the goals of the Harlem Renaissance, dedicated to social and racial uplift, although they shared audiences.

The itinerant nature of performance was also important for the development of the Mexican *carpa*. These forms of tent theatre were especially popular in the U.S.-Mexico borderlands between northern Mexico and what is now the U.S. southwest. Performed in Spanish, these entertainments often incorporated political humor, wordplay, and physical comedy. The actors in the *carpas* were greatly talented physical comedians, not unlike Italian *commedia* actors of the earlier centuries. While we do not know the names of many of these performers, famous Mexican film actor Cantinflas (1911–1993) started as a *carpa* actor (Figure 10.17), as did Felipe Cantú (1919–1988), one of the most famous actors in the Chicano labor theatre Teatro Campesino (discussed in Chapter 13). *Carpa* audiences included many working-class spectators, who saw the shows after hard days of labor. Perhaps this is why Luis Valdez, the founder of El Teatro Campesino, consciously used *carpa* acting techniques combined with Brechtian forms to reach farmworker audiences in the 1960s.

Popular theatre forms in the United States, then, were not solely based in Euroamerican forms, or only aimed at Euroamerican audiences, even if they were later incorporated into mainstream urban commercial theatre. As this section on popular theatre reminds us, commodity capitalism had the effect of rapidly creating heterogenous audiences for newly introduced theatrical forms. Immigrant artists were part of, rather than separate from, these circuits of performance. In addition, popular theatre was just as important as a cultural form as its innovative avant-garde counterparts in Paris, Berlin and Zurich.

Summary

As economic and social disparities grew wider and the plight of the poor and marginalized became more visible, in part due to the power of photography, theatre artists began to create works reflecting the changes in reality. Inspired by changes in print and photographic media, and the developing philosophy of positivism, theatre directors and designers developed methods to enhance the photographic reality of plays, and powerful stage directors emerged who championed these new ideas. For example, Stanislavsky worked to make acting more believable by de-emphasizing the actors' performance of themselves, emphasizing instead their performance of the character's inner life through vocal and physical means. Naturalism, created by middle- and upper-class authors, emphasized poverty, and other dark aspects associated with "irrational" or unfortunate persons. Naturalists embraced Social Darwinism, believing that the ills of the world are the result of one's inborn nature and environment. In contrast, realism offered a more balanced perspective and remains the dominant genre today. Realist authors (including early feminists) who depicted life's ills suggested that these might be mended if the causal economic or social factors improved. In Japan, debates about Westernization resulted not only in the creation of the new genres of *shimpa* and realistic *shingeki*, but in the gradual acceptance of women on stage. The great masters of realism, Ibsen and Chekhov, wrote plays demonstrating the complexities and confusions not only of society, but of theatre in a process of transformation.

Figure 10.17
Cantinflas (born Mario Moreno), photographed 1960.

Source: Columbia/Kobal/Shutterstock.

Instead of depending on the external, material realities of biological evolution and industrial capitalism to undergird their theatre, the Symbolists looked to the evanescence of sound and the inner promptings of religion and psychology to shape dramas that called forth universal yearnings wrapped in gauze and half-light and performed through poetic evocation and ritual chanting. The Aestheticists pushed this subjective faith in new directions, idealizing artistic experience as a realm apart from the workaday world. Despite their rejection of conventional society, first-generation avant-gardists helped to shift conventional Western theatre away from the constraints of stage realism and toward new possibilities of theatrical expression. While these movements are clearly differentiated in theatre history narratives, they nevertheless shared many formal traits, such as emphasis on vocal expression, non-realistic movement and innovative stagecraft.

At the same time, commercial theatre utilized print and photographic media in different ways in line with the emergence of consumer capitalism. This included the emergence of star performers as commodities, the use of the theatre to advertise products, and the commodification of sexuality and femininity in new ways. While these forms of capitalism could be harmful, the resulting dissemination of performances to ethnically and class diverse audiences supported new forms of popular performance, and new circuits of presentation that innovated and transformed the popular theatre, particularly, musical theatre. As this chapter has shown, the roots of popular musical theatre in the early twentieth-century United States were diverse, and the form is particularly indebted to African American musical forms, Jewish American performers, composers and writers and the ingenuity of producers from various backgrounds (although power still lay with white producers).

This chapter concludes Parts II and III of our textbook, both of which focused on the causal relations among print culture, historical contexts, and the theatre. Looking back, it is clear that the divide between differing views of reality that structured many of the conflicts in Western theatre in this period was partly due to a division that emerged with periodical print culture between the public and private spheres. Newspapers, treatises, and many other public print media propagated "hard" facts and often partisan contention, while the private sphere of confessionals, novels, and most popular magazines thrived on "soft" psychological insights and domestic affairs. Specific historical pressures from photographic and sound-based media shifted the terms of the debate about the real and that these changes were felt in the theatre.

In retrospect, the nineteenth century's photographic and sound-based media probably did as much to extend the life of theatre based on print culture as to undermine it by demonstrating its internal conflicts. Combined with the emergence of consumer capitalism and the increased mechanization of industrial capitalism, these new forms of media greatly undermined long-standing belief systems. Different artist reactions to these changes created a rich and diverse theatre culture.

As we will see in the next chapter, the Great War and motion pictures would further question many of the assumptions, beliefs, and procedures upon which European and U.S. cultures had been based. We are still picking up the pieces from the after-effects of the Great War, and film was only the first of many media shocks to the system – shocks that would proliferate with increasing speed into the twenty-first century. Part IV of our book brings the story of media, history, and the theatre up to the present.

★

Theatre and performance in electric and electronic communication culture

DOI: 10.4324/9781003185185-15

PART IV TIMELINE

DATE	THEATRE AND PERFORMANCE	CULTURE AND COMMUNICATION	POLITICS AND ECONOMICS
1856–1950	George Bernard Shaw, playwright		
1858–1943	André Antoine, director		
1859		Charles Darwin, *On the Origin of Species*	
1860–1904	Anton Chekhov, playwright		
1861–1941	Rabindranath Tagore, playwright		
1863–1938	Konstantin Stanislavsky, director		
1867		Karl Marx, *Capital* vol. 1	
1867–1936	Luigi Pirandello, playwright		
1872–1946	Kawakami Sadayakko, actor		
1868			Meiji Restoration
1872–1966	Edward Gordon Craig, theatre theorist		
1876		Electric telephone	
1876–1948	Susan Glaspell, playwright		
1877		Phonograph	
1877–1927		Isadora Duncan, dancer	
1879		Electric light bulb	
c.1880–c.1900	Avant-garde theatre, first generation		
1880–1914			"Scramble for Africa": European powers divide Africa among themselves
1881-c.1914	Naturalist movement		
1881–1973		Pablo Picasso, artist	
1882–1971		Igor Stravinsky, composer	
1894–1855			First Sino-Japanese War
1885		Automobiles	
1887–1896	Théâtre Libre		
1888–1953	Eugene O'Neill, playwright		

PART IV TIMELINE

DATE	THEATRE AND PERFORMANCE	CULTURE AND COMMUNICATION	POLITICS AND ECONOMICS
1894–1855			First Sino-Japanese War
1894–1961	Mei Lanfang, actor		
1894–1991		Martha Graham, dancer-choreographer	
1895		First public motion picture screening, France Radio	
c.1895–c.1930	*Shimpa*		
1896–1948	Antonin Artaud, actor and theorist		
1898			Spanish-American War
1898–1948		Sergei Eisenstein, film director	
1898–1956	Bertolt Brecht, playwright		
1898–	Moscow Art Theatre (various name changes after 1932)		
1900		Sigmund Freud, *The Interpretation of Dreams*	
c.1900–c.1970	Modernist stage design	Modernism in art and literature	
1903		First successful airplane	
1904		Vacuum tube: beginning of electronics Sigmund Freud, *The Psychopathology of Everyday Life*	
1906–1989	Samuel Beckett, playwright		
1907–	*Huaju*		
1909–	*Shingeki*		
c.1910–c.1925		Cubism in art	
c.1910–c.1930	Avant-garde theatre, second generation		
1911–1983	Tennessee Williams, playwright		
1914–1918			Great War (aka First World War)
1914–	Takarazuka Revue		
c.1915–c.1930	Expressionist theatre in the U.S.		

PART IV TIMELINE

DATE	THEATRE AND PERFORMANCE	CULTURE AND COMMUNICATION	POLITICS AND ECONOMICS
c.1915–		Jazz	
1915–2005	Arthur Miller, playwright		
1917			Russian Revolution
c.1918–c. 1935		Harlem Renaissance	
1918–2007		Ingmar Bergman, film and theatre director	
c.1920–	Musical theatre		
1922–1991			Soviet Union
1923		First public screening of sound film	
1925–1970	Mishima Yukio, playwright		
1925–2022	Peter Brook, director		
1926–	Dario Fo, performer-playwright		
1930–c.1940			Great Depression worldwide
1930–1965	Lorraine Hansberry, playwright		
1930–2008	Harold Pinter, playwright		
1930–2021	Stephen Sondheim, musical theatre composer-lyricist		
1931–2009	Augusto Boal, theatre creator and theorist		
1932–	Athol Fugard, playwright		
1933–1945			Nazi concentration and labor camps in Germany and Eastern Europe
1933–1999	Jerzy Grotowski, director		
1934–2014	Amiri Baraka (aka LeRoi Jones), playwright		
1934–	Wole Soyinka, playwright		
1935–1939	Federal Theatre Project, U.S.		
1935–1983	Terayama Shuji, playwright and director		
1936		Television broadcasting	

PART IV TIMELINE

DATE	THEATRE AND PERFORMANCE	CULTURE AND COMMUNICATION	POLITICS AND ECONOMICS
1937–	Tom Stoppard, playwright		
1938–	Caryl Churchill, playwright		
1939–1945			Second World War
1939–	Suzuki Tadashi, director		
c.1940–c.1970	"Golden Age" of Broadway musical theatre		
1940–	Gao Xingjian, playwright Luis Valdez, playwright-director		
1941–	Robert Wilson, director-designer		
1942–2023	Ama Ata Aidoo, playwright		
1942		All-electronic computer	
1943	*Oklahoma!*		
1945			Nuclear bomb used on Hiroshima and Nagasaki, Japan
1945–2005	August Wilson, playwright		
1947		Transistor: basis of all modern electronic equipment	
1947–1991			Cold War: the U.S. and its allies vs. Soviet Union and its allies
1947–	Living Theatre, U.S.		
1949	Berliner Ensemble founded		People's Republic of China (Communist China) established
1950–1953			Korean War
1951–1980			African independence movements
c.1955		Television becomes an important medium	
1955–1975			Vietnam War
1956–	Tony Kushner, playwright		
1957			Sputnik 1 (Soviet satellite)
1957–	David Henry Hwang, playwright		
1959		Beginning of *butoh* dance	

PART IV TIMELINE

DATE	THEATRE AND PERFORMANCE	CULTURE AND COMMUNICATION	POLITICS AND ECONOMICS
1959–c.1990	Happenings		
c.1960	Beginnings of Civil Rights era theatre movements		
c.1965–c.1975	Main period of political theatre		
c.1960–	Performance art		
c.1962–	*Angura*		
c.1962–		Rock music	
1963–	Suzan-Lori Parks, playwright		
1964		Communications satellites	
1964–1971			Worldwide protests against the Vietnam War
c.1965	Beginnings of feminist, Latinx, gay, and lesbian theatre		
1966–1976			Chinese Cultural Revolution
c.1966–	*Yangbanxi* (Chinese revolutionary opera)		
1967		Jacques Derrida, *Of Grammatology*	
1967–			European Community (starting point of the European Union)
1968	U.K. ends theatre censorship		May 1968 events in France Martin Luther King assassinated, U.S.
1969		Moon landing First network of computer networks (beginning of the Internet)	
c.1970–c.1985	Nuevo Teatro Popular		
1973		Birth of Hip Hop and rap	
1974			U.S. President Richard Nixon resigns
1976		Satellite television Michel Foucault, *The History of Sexuality*	
1977		Mass-market personal computers	
1978		Text-based online virtual worlds	
c.1980			AIDS crisis begins

PART IV TIMELINE

DATE	THEATRE AND PERFORMANCE	CULTURE AND COMMUNICATION	POLITICS AND ECONOMICS
1980–	Lin-Manuel Miranda, musical theatre composer, dramatist and lyricist		
1983		Commercially available mobile phones	
1989			Berlin Wall falls, Germany Tiananmen Square protests, China
c.1990		Commercially available digital cameras	
1991		World Wide Web	Break-up of the Soviet Union
1993–			European Union
1994		Web-based social networking	
2000		Smartphones	
2001			September 11th attacks on the World Trade Center and Pentagon, U.S.
2001–2014			Wars in Afghanistan and Iraq
2003–2011			Iraq War
2007–2009			Great Recession worldwide
2010–2012			Arab Spring
2016			U.K. votes to leaves the European Union
2019–2023			COVID-19 pandemic worldwide
2020	"We See You, White American Theater" statement		
2021			Far right rioters attempt to overturn the U.S. Presidential election
2021–2023		Publicly available image- and text-generating artificial intelligence systems introduced	
2022–?			Russian invasion and partial occupation of Ukraine

Introduction: Theatre and the unceasing communications revolutions

Tobin Nellhaus

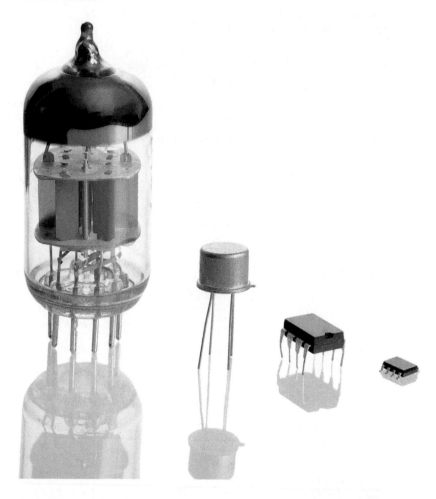

Photo PI4
A vacuum tube, a transistor, and microchips.
Source: vlabo/Shutterstock.

Beginning in the twentieth century, invention and upheaval wracked the globe. There were two world wars, several genocides, a massive economic depression, plus smaller versions of each. Some major countries had political revolutions; many more achieved independence from imperialist control, but sometimes only to plummet into dictatorships or civil wars. Liberalizations of cultural values and the creation of social support programs were followed by conservative reactions in a repeated cycle. Much like the 1600s, religious faith could congeal into a fanaticism that led people to repress and even kill others; so too could political party affiliation. Cars and planes transformed transportation, and rockets landed men on the moon. **Globalization** knotted national economies together and enabled people around the world to talk with each other. Simultaneously, it highlighted the uniqueness of the local, although occasionally fragmenting societies. Human-caused global heating began to unleash drastic environmental conditions and events.

While the use of fossil fuels continued unabated, a new form of energy became a key force behind many of those constant sea changes: electricity, which starting in the late nineteenth century could be produced at an industrial scale. One technology after another manipulated electricity with ever-greater sophistication; each day brought it further into people's lives, to the point that without a source of electrical power, nearly all devices and machines today would be no better than rocks. Communication media in particular were radically and repeatedly altered or invented. During the early phase of this period, they included telegraphs, photography, typewriters, telephones, phonographs, radios, and silent films. Most of them utilized electricity as a source of power to move mechanical parts, but also – in the form of electromagnetic radiation, namely light – as a catalyst for chemical reactions (which is how photography worked). In these ways, electricity became an element in the very production and transmission of words, sounds, and images – culture itself. Not only did political, economic, and social events strongly affect theatrical developments, especially topically, but also the unending innovations in communication played a fundamental role in changing the styles and methods of performance. These developments are the focus of Part IV.

We described in Chapter 10 how some of these early electricity-based communication media influenced theatre in multiple and sometimes opposite ways, especially the contrast that emerged between Naturalism and Symbolism. By the close of the nineteenth century, theatre had divided into two major artistic branches: mainstream realism and the avant-garde. The contrast and even antagonism between them rapidly intensified. The avant-garde, already split from the mainstream aesthetically, began to produce plays that aimed to subvert bourgeois culture. At the same time, some Naturalist playwrights incorporated political critique within their plays. These varying approaches soon also appeared in theatre's rapidly growing relative, the movies.

The era covered by Part IV started with two developments that in different ways shook the world, as Chapter 11 explains. One was the Great War (1914–1918, later known as the First World War) and its aftermath, which accelerated theatrical movements against bourgeois society. Anti-capitalist playwrights increasingly joined the avant-garde in rejecting Naturalist styles, and a number of second-generation avant-gardists rejected capitalism. A third branch of theatrical performance also emerged: political theatre with a non-realistic style. Nevertheless, realism (whether or not political) and the apolitical avant-garde remained stronger than the political theatre. The impulses behind these two branches were conjoined in modernism, a form of theatre that utilized some avant-garde techniques; however, its aim was not to challenge bourgeois society but to renovate it, mainly though formal innovations.

The other development was technological. In 1904, the vacuum tube was invented, which made it possible to control electricity in highly refined ways. It was the first electronic technology: it used electricity not just for energy, but also to store, control, send, and receive information. By 1930, vacuum tubes had dramatically improved, commercializing radios and phonographs, and allowed images and sound to be synchronized on film. As Chapter 11 shows, radio and especially sound film (the "talkies") had major effects on the theatre of the time, sometimes to be used, sometimes to be resisted. However, the applications of vacuum tubes did not end there: they could manipulate light waves, and they could be combined into complex switches. The former led to television, and broadcasting to the public began in 1936. The latter resulted in the first wholly electronic computer, which was built in 1942. One generation later, these devices would upend the world.

The Second World War (1939–1945) involved nearly every country around the globe and was even more devastating than its predecessor. Afterward, the victorious countries split into two camps: the capitalist countries and the Communist ones, leading to a "Cold War" fought largely through propaganda and proxy wars in small countries such as Vietnam. The governments on both sides of the Cold War sought to quell any opposition, even imagined opposition, resulting in varying degrees of conformism that in the capitalist countries only lessened during the 1960s.

As Chapter 12 observes, few of the second-generation avant-gardes survived the war; some had faded away even before then. Nevertheless, to varying extents in each country, theatre in the postwar era continued the three rough types from before: psychological or social realism, which sometimes adopted elements of avant-garde styles, and sometimes had a politically critical edge; avant-garde genres with varying relationships with bourgeois culture; and political non-realism. Theatre in the United States predominantly focused on psychological realism, generally within a naturalistic setting, but at times in a more abstract style similar to modernism or Expressionism. Even plays critical of mainstream politics tended to employ psychological realism. Musical theatre in the United States reached a new level of sophistication – its "Golden Age" – which had aspects in common with psychological realism as well. Soviet state policy locked theatre into "socialist realism," which stylistically differed little from bourgeois realism. But political theatre became an important trend in South Asia, Africa, and Latin America. Europe and Japan contended with both the destruction left by the warfare, and the political and moral legacies of fascism, genocide, and the atomic bomb. Thus the war raised profoundly disturbing questions and disillusionment with Enlightenment ideas of truth, reason, and progress, which was often reflected in non-realist drama. However, in the midst of the recovering economy of the late 1950s, alternative forms of performance arose in the United States, Europe, Japan, and elsewhere, some tied to protests against postwar conformism and political inequities, and some wholly unlike theatre itself.

One element in both the recovery and the emergence of non-conformism in the 1950s was yet another transformative technology: the invention of the transistor in 1947. Transistors did the same things vacuum tubes did, but they were more reliable, smaller – and soon, cheaper. They revolutionized all of the previous devices, found new applications, and enabled whole new technologies. The vacuum tube had introduced a few electronic devices to people's homes; the transistor made electronics utterly ubiquitous. In the mid-1950s, the portable transistor radio became the first mass-produced mobile device. We fully entered the era of **electric and electronic communication culture**.

Now largely transistorized, televisions started residing in most living rooms, reshaping culture and influencing politics. By the mid-1960s, about 94 percent of homes in the U.S. and Japan, 86 percent in the U.K., and the majority of households in other industrialized countries owned television sets – and millions of viewers saw the war in Vietnam. The protests against the war were part of a turning point in world history: throughout the late 1960s and early 1970s, a wide range of political and cultural clashes erupted worldwide, some of them in opposition to global politics, some of them in opposition to domestic authoritarianism and lack of political equality. Chapter 13 shows how theatre worldwide often participated in the activism of the last third of the twentieth century, whether directly in political theatre, or through challenges to theatre's traditional hierarchies, such as the authority of the dramatic text.

The 1960s launched the current era of accelerating globalization, in which national economies – driven by multinational corporations, international trade agreements, supranational organizations such as the World Trade Organization, worldwide transportation systems, and global telecommunications – have become deeply interdependent, to some extent making nationalism moot. But this has had complex effects. Globally, treaties unify world economies and legal frameworks, businesses in one continent decide what farmers should grow in another, and McDonald's and Hollywood cover the planet. Locally, many people experience declining self-governance, the disappearance of regional culture, environmental damage caused by import and export, and other effects. Sometimes the local and global have blended, for instance, in regional versions of rap music. In Chapter 14, we discuss how these forces and concerns have been manifested in theatre, in everything from musicals to the preservation of indigenous performance genres, to borrowing from foreign traditions. Theatre for social change has also been affected by the combined pressures of the global and the local.

The past 50 years have been marked by the rampant growth of consumer electronics. A staggering list of devices permeated life in the industrialized countries, and increasingly in the developing world as well, including music players, cameras, video recorders, mobile telephones, and most importantly, computers. Devices that fit on a desktop became portable, portable became hand-held, hand-held became pocket-sized, pocket-sized became watch-sized – and these small devices packed together an increasing array of unrelated functions.

The most fundamental advance occurred during that same turning point. In 1969, two computers were linked by telephone. A few more were soon added, forming a network. In 1971, the first email was sent, heralding the coming expansion of computers from advanced calculators to a new communication medium. Meanwhile, other computer networks were created. The networks swelled and interconnected, and in the early 1980s, the **internet** was born. Then in 1990, a standardized way to link electronic documents via the internet was developed and established the World Wide Web. Internet usage grew spectacularly. As early as 1995, 0.5 percent or so of the world's population used the internet, facilitated by the Web. In 2000, it connected about 7 percent of the world, around 400 million people. By 2010, that figure had leapt to 2 billion, around 30 percent. Just five years later, the number surpassed 44 percent – over 3.2 billion people. In 2023, about 5.2 billion people, nearly 65 percent of world's population, could access the internet. Increasingly, they connected through sophisticated smartphones, integrating a large number of electronic devices (including a telephone, camera, web browser, multimedia players, and geographical positioning system) into one hand-held unit, along with numerous software applications ("apps") putting the hardware to use. Never before were so many communication media available to so many people.

The internet established a mode of communication with several crucial differences from print and most previous electric/electronic communication technologies. Those largely conducted one-way communication to large numbers of people, whether through the dissemination of physical books, recordings and photographs, or through on-air broadcasts. For most people, only the telephone allowed person-to-person communication. The internet, however, combines two-way communication with broadcast communication. In principle, any individual can get in touch with any other individual. But also in principle, anyone can present whatever thoughts, pictures, or videos they choose before the entire world – and in principle, anyone can respond back. And all of that happens instantly. Thus the internet not only networks computers, it networks people. In addition, digital media provide new textual, mechanical, and visual tools. Chapter 15 explores a number of these issues as they emerge in performance. It focuses first on changes in the performer, such as her representation through projections, augmentation by electronic equipment, replacement by robots, and re-embodiment by avatars. Next, it looks at new types of performance spaces – not just virtual realities, but also textual realms such as X (formerly Twitter), and uses of public spaces. The chapter concludes by considering how concepts and practices derived from the virtual world are manifested in real-world performance genres and methodologies.

Networked culture is generating social changes in unpredictable ways. In Part III, we saw the pivotal role periodical print culture played in establishing the distinction between the public sphere and the private sphere within bourgeois society; in the overthrow of absolutism and the creation of nation-states, usually with some type of democracy; and in transforming the audience's emotional response to dramatic characters. It is becoming increasingly clear that as networked culture begins, it is likewise presenting threats and changes to the established political, economic, and cultural order, particularly due to its push-pull of expanded democratic practices, rabbit holes of conspiracy theories, voluminous personal data collection, and "deep fakes." The governments of China, Iran, and elsewhere attempt to prevent or impede dangers to their power by censoring, restricting, or even shutting down their country's internet, and sometimes even its phone network; the U.S., the U.K., and other governments have or had programs to collect data on the personal communications of everyone in the country. In fact, when it comes to information – both its content and its ownership – the very concepts of public and private are now the subject of fierce arguments and legal battles. Businesses, seeking sales, extensively mine personal data; they also aggressively protect their copyrights, sometimes even subverting the right to fair use. At the same time, private property is challenged by the view that books, music, and films are or should be publicly available for free and without permission – a view some people hold unconsciously, others take as permission for theft, and still others propose as a fundamental principle based on a recognition of the importance of information and culture in society. Left unconsidered by this view is how the artists are supposed to survive, a problem massively intensified when it was industrialized by artificial intelligence (AI), in which computer systems devour vast quantities of writers' and visual artists' work unpaid, and entertainment industry giants seek to store performers' image and voice to be used and reused indefinitely. AI was science fiction in 2020, and suddenly became public reality; we cannot even guess what the situation will be a mere five years from now – accommodation, deterioration, improvement, maybe all three?

We also cannot predict how networked culture may alter two fundamental concepts: the nature of knowledge and personhood. Both concepts directly affect theatre and performance. As we observed at several points in this book, arguments about truth have been wielded as a weapon against theatre, whether to condemn it as a hotbed of falsity and sham or to dismiss it as an empty distraction from wiser pursuits. Such antitheatricality, we have noted, has even appeared within theatre. Late twentieth-century "experimental" theatre might be either the last gasp of the insistence that theatre justify its existence by becoming a kind of laboratory, or the opening round in a new struggle to make performance a fully legitimate part of global culture. It could be the forge of performance methods that will become the theatrical norm expressing a new consensus about knowledge and theatre's relation to it. Certainly, networked culture has led to new platforms for theatre, such as online video (accelerated by the COVID pandemic of 2019–2023), and even non-human actors such as robots.

Developments of that sort contribute to potential alterations in the concept of personhood, which directly shapes the portrayal of dramatic character, which in turn influences the stories theatres are likely to tell. As we saw in Part II, psychological interiority was born with print, and in Part III, we described how periodical print culture ripened that interiority as part of the public/private distinction. If that distinction is now an area of conflict and change, the idea that a character should reveal a private self must surely become dubious as well. Some forms of theatre described in Part IV – such as those which discard the traditional division between actor and audience in favor of the participant, or abandon linear plot development for episodes, pastiche, simultaneity, and/or associative connections – make one wonder if such explorations in personhood have already begun.

In an era of unceasing communications revolutions when our everyday choices about how to communicate can have unexpected long-term consequences, we can be sure that such explorations will be ongoing. As we have seen throughout this book, changes in communication practices affect theatre on fundamental levels. But those changes are seldom immediate, and often lead in directions no one could foretell.

★

CHAPTER 11

Revolutionary times, 1910–1950

Patricia Ybarra
Contributor: Bruce McConachie

This chapter begins with a focus on two major causes of change in the theatre of the early twentieth century: the Great War and the movies. Both affected Western bourgeois culture, animating some theatre artists to demand radical change and leaving others to search for forms of aesthetic transformation. The war led to the emergence of political theatre, which contributed to the atmosphere which allowed the Russian Revolution of 1917 to succeed. Following the Revolution, new models of political theatre from the Soviet Union (which included most of the former Russian Empire) proliferated in Europe, the United States, India, and China. Film destabilized conventional notions of the self and society and directly challenged mainstream theatrical practice in the West. Theatre artists reacted to these changes with new formal innovations, which we will explore below.

War and the movies

The Great War (1914–1918) was a catastrophe for mainstream Western culture. Most immediately, it wreaked unprecedented devastation on lives, wealth, and established political power. The war broke apart four major European empires – the German, Austro-Hungarian, Russian, and Ottoman empires – and left many new nations, including Finland and Poland in northern Europe and Hungary and Bulgaria further south, to struggle for independence and national coherence in the 1920s and 1930s (see Figure 11.1). The Great War was a direct cause of the Russian Revolution and civil war (1917–1921), which led to the first anti-capitalist regime in modern times. The upheavals of the Russian Revolution, especially when joined with earlier revolutions in China (1911–1912) and Mexico (1910–1921), animated widespread global desire for radical change. Indirectly, the 1914–1918 war precipitated the decline of Western imperialism around the world, contributed to the rise of European fascism in the 1920s, and helped to cause the worldwide economic Depression of the 1930s.

DOI: 10.4324/9781003185185-16

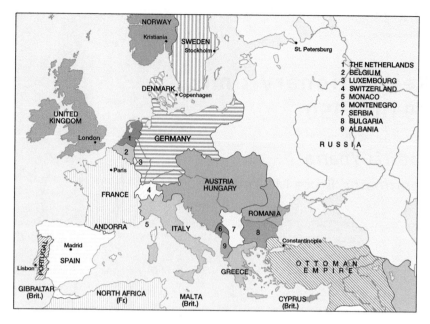

Figure 11.1
Political maps of Europe before (1914) and after (1920) the Great War.

In these and other ways, the Great War fractured Western bourgeois culture and introduced new realities and possibilities undreamed of before 1914.

The war and its aftermath altered all of the major areas of theatrical activity in the West. In political theatre, the Russian Revolution undermined the deterministic side of

Naturalism and sparked widespread theatrical activism. The initial success of the Revolution converted many avant-gardists in Russia, Germany, and elsewhere to **communism** and they began to experiment with a variety of forms and styles to move people to political action. Before 1914, all of the significant avant-garde movements had been international, with artists freely trading ideas and performances across borders, which was not always possible during the conflict. After the war, political differences affected avant-garde networks. By the mid-1930s, with Europe preparing for another war, these avant-garde movements ceased to exist as important forces, although politically left internationalism continued to exist.

The international popularity of silent films after the Great War radically altered popular entertainments at circuses, world fairs, and on variety stages – never more popular than in the decade before 1914 – and drove some out of business. All forms of live entertainment declined after 1918, a trend accelerated by the arrival of the "talkies" in 1927. The telephone and phonograph, much more widespread in the 1920s than before, increased their challenges to print culture and photography, which dominated theatrical representation before the war. In addition to these older sound-based media, radio listening rapidly gained in popularity from the late 1920s through the 1930s, despite the Depression. Among all media, however, it was the movies that offered the most provocations to pre-1914 culture in the West. The cultural fragmentations caused by the war and the popularity of film animated radical theatre artists in the West to question the older premises of theatrical representation and gave rise to a movement known as modernism, which serves as an umbrella for many of the "isms" (Futurism, Expressionism, Dadaism) discussed in subsequent sections of this chapter.

Modernism, more broadly, usually refers to a series of artistic movements in the West reacting against Victorian and other socially and religion-based forms of morality and the dehumanization of industrialization. Many of the artworks deemed as modernist were formally innovative and dedicated to "making it new." There were great variations, however, in how this dictum was expressed: some artist's works were explicitly political, while other works were created to be autonomous from politics; some were non-representational while others were realistic; some were explicitly non-commercial, while others reimagined commercial art blurring the line between popular and high art. Modernist movements in the theatre usually saw themselves as part of a revolutionary cultural transformation.

Powering some of the optimism about possibilities for revolutionary change was electricity. Following inventions such as Thomas Edison's (1847–1931) telephone, Nikola Tesla's (1856–1943) alternating current, and others in the late nineteenth century, economic and political elites used electrical power to illuminate their businesses and public buildings and to run their factories and theatres by 1910. In Chapter 10, we noted that electric lights made possible more realistic effects and a more private viewing experience for theatrical audiences. But coal and gas continued to heat the homes and shops and to illuminate the dwellings and streets of most Westerners. After the war, the rapid electrification of cities in the West transformed the everyday lives of many citizens. In addition to illumination, electricity powered heating, hot water, and an increasing range of appliances, from vacuum cleaners and irons to refrigerators and toasters, in the homes of many urbanites by 1930. The power generated to run the new phonographs and movies (initially shot and projected by hand-cranking) was a part of the general electrification of Western culture.

Following France in 1895, the first public exhibition of a film in the United States occurred at a New York vaudeville house in 1896. Soon "nickelodeons" (a name that combined a reference to the five-cent entry fee and the term for a site for musical performance) sprang up in major urban centers in the United States. By 1914, most variety theatres had integrated silent films into their entertainments, a trend that undermined the presentation of live acts and made the vaudeville stage much less popular. Early French and U.S. filmmakers borrowed extensively from the theatre, taking variety acts, scenic conventions, modes of storytelling, acting styles, and musical underscoring (played by musicians during the screening) from the popular stage. French film director Georges Méliès (1861–1938), for example, built a proscenium stage at his film studio, equipped with the machinery and two-dimensional scenery of a typical Parisian theatre, so that he could provide the kinds of pleasures in his films, such as *A Trip to the Moon* (1902) that delighted popular theatrical audiences. Australia also had a huge film industry, and screened the first multi-reel film about bushranger Ned Kelly, *The Story of the Kelly Gang* in 1906. The ban on bushranger films hurt the industry, allowing the United States to become dominant.

The U.S. director D.W. Griffith (1875–1948), who had largely failed as an actor and playwright, brought with him a strong taste for melodramatic stage scripts, associated acting styles, and paternalistic control as a director when he switched from live theatre to the moving picture business in 1907. He based one of his most successful and notorious films, *The Birth of a Nation* (1915), on earlier stage performances of *The Clansmen* that celebrated the rise of the white-supremacist Ku Klux Klan in the American South after the Civil War, and the film's popularity throughout the country was symptomatic of the nation's endemic racism. Until 1915, theatre artists dismissed film as entertainment of little artistic worth. However, by the end of the Great War, when better technology had led to a much wider range of shots, locations, and editing possibilities and when mass distribution was attracting the middle classes for feature-length films starring Charlie Chaplin (1889–1977) and other international stars, theatre artists became more interested in it. From the 1920s onward, film had more of an influence on the stage than the other way around.

As an extension of photography, film seemed to uphold an "objective," positivistic view of the world, even though the subject matter of most films was clearly imagined and "subjective." But shooting and editing for film also cut up the perceived world into various points of view; the pieced-together nature of films, despite Hollywood editing techniques that suggested a seamless flow of images, underlined the fragmented nature of human perception. Sometimes, it seemed, people saw reality in close up, while at other times, they perceived the world in long perspective or even as a whirling nightmare; the movies heightened the suspicion that reality might be inherently unstable.

Nonetheless, by the mid-1920s, the largely unconscious effects of the movies were less important for many audiences than the expectation that film offered a revolutionary potential for altering modern life. It was clear to all that the movies could effectively persuade others of important values and ideas. During the 1920s, revolutionary movements around the globe were using the new medium, along with the theatre, to challenge the political and ideological status quo.

One result of the ubiquity of film after the war was to popularize some of the innovations that avant-gardists had been pushing since the 1890s. Many of the Symbolists and

Expressionists had explored a wide variety of locales in their productions, a fluid use of space impossible to achieve in realist and Naturalist productions, and, more broadly, in the material apparatus of the theatre itself. Film could easily take spectators into numerous places, and audiences began to expect the same kinds of flexibility while watching a play on stage. Appia, Craig, and others had anticipated filmic effects in their suggestions that lighting instruments could be used to heighten an actor's presence, gain design flexibility, and speed playing time. Many directors and designers in the 1920s, taking advantage of darkened house lights, effectively turned follow-spots into cameras. Before film scripts demonstrated the power of short scenes with little dialogue and heightened action, playwrights Strindberg, Kaiser, and Blok had already explored these possibilities. In East Asia, other techniques anticipated these filmic changes, for example the use of the Japanese *mie* and Chinese *liangxiang*, in which performers struck poses to focus spectator attention on them to the exclusion of other stage actions.

By the 1920s, German Expressionism, discussed later in the chapter, had largely focused on the shattered bodies and psyches left by the war, although it also offered some utopian visions to heal them. Even as the theatrical side of the movement was waning, however, the Expressionist films of Fritz Lang (1890–1976), especially *Dr. Mabuse* (1922) and *Metropolis* (1927), and of other film directors, kept Expressionist acting and design before the public. This was done in part by employing many of Expressionist theatre's most famous actors, such as Fritz Kortner (1892–1970). As we will see, some of the politically oriented theatre artists under discussion in this chapter struggled both to acknowledge the changing nature of society, including its instability, and to suggest a vision that might unite or improve human conditions, while others chose to simply expose the nonsensical aspects of the era. Still others, less interested in political or social change, invoked idealized truths or reimagined ancient myths and traditional religion. In the process, they championed the importance of the playwright and the printed word against the fractured world suggested by film and war-based trauma.

Revolutionary predecessors

As noted, three major revolutions rocked the bourgeois world of the 1910–1920 decade. In 1910, revolutionaries in Mexico ousted Porfirio Díaz (1830–1915), a dictator who used his ties to U.S. imperialists to concentrate wealth is the hands of the wealthy. The revolutionaries established a constitution in 1917 in the midst of a civil war, and continued to fight for radical change, including land redistribution to those who worked it, into the 1920s. Secretly transported back to Russia by the Germans during the Great War, Vladimir Lenin (1870–1924) helped to transform an uprising against tsarist rule in Russia into the Communist Revolution in 1917. By the early 1920s, Communists under Lenin and others had consolidated their power in most of the former Russian Empire and embarked on a campaign of political agitation and upheaval in much of Europe and Asia that would last for the next 30 years.

Great political transformation was also happening in China. Led initially by Sun Yat-sen (1866–1925), the Chinese Nationalist Party fought primarily against Western-backed warlords during the first decade of the revolution in an attempt to unify China under one government. Sun Yat-sen started promoting his revolution ideas and established the Nationalist party in 1894; after many failed uprisings, finally the 1911 Revolution led to the establishment of the Republic of China in 1912. His political vision was mixed with liberalism, socialism, and nationalism (which was initially anti-Manchu, but later included all ethnicities in its imagining).

For a few years during the 1920s, the Nationalists collaborated with Russian-based Communists to purge China of foreign imperialists, an alliance that was revived in 1937 when the Sino-Japanese War started. Japan had invaded and occupied Manchuria in China since 1931 and gradually moved its force down to coastal Chinese cities, and later to southeast Asia, the Indian Ocean, and the Pacific Ocean; the later part of the battles which involved the Allies to fight the Japanese imperialism is called the Pacific War (1941–1945). The defeat of Japan in the Second World War finally ended a century of foreign domination in China. The Chinese Communists, who won the civil war against the Nationalists in 1949, benefited throughout this period from the perceived alliance between communism and anti-imperialism. All of these movements would radically transform the theatre, as we discuss below.

Before 1910, however, there were already political and theatrical signs of the radical challenges that might lie ahead. Since the 1890s, many Europeans believing in socialism had warned that the increasing disparities in power and wealth between capitalists and workers could lead to revolution. Socialists pointed out that market forces caused frequent depressions and argued that unimpeded capitalism would lead to long-term misery for most of the population. By 1890, socialist political parties with a base in the working class, sometimes called labor parties, were electing representatives in democratic industrial countries, including the United States, where such parties were actively squashed by the government. Socialists throughout the world drew on Marx's arguments about the inherent class conflict between workers and capitalists, but often differed on the question of revolution. Most argued that political and economic reform might alter the capitalist system to produce more economic justice, while a minority believed that only violent revolution could truly transform the system.

Before the Russian Revolution most socialist playwrights and audiences gravitated to Naturalism. (Lenin's wife later proclaimed Hauptmann's *The Weavers*, about a worker rebellion, one of her favorite plays.) For some socialists concerned about effecting change, however, a major problem with Naturalism was its deterministic point of view, as discussed in Chapter 10. Naturalism could examine the brutalities of capitalism with photo-like acumen, but its basis in Social Darwinism and positivism suggested that the masses, once degraded by heredity and their socioeconomic environment, rarely roused themselves from their situation to take control of their lives. Or, if they started a revolt, the authorities would quickly intervene to restore order, as related by Hauptmann in his historically based play. Most socialists continued to write Naturalist dramas that exposed the problems of capitalism, but there was a tension between their pessimistic plays and their hopeful politics. Later socialists and communists, such as Vsevolod Meyerhold, Erwin Piscator (1893–1966), and Bertolt Brecht, would reject Naturalism for this reason.

George Bernard Shaw's (1856–1950) response to the deterministic tendencies of Naturalism made him the most outspoken socialist playwright of the 1890–1914 period. Shaw became a socialist in 1882 and soon after joined the Fabian Society, a group of British journalists, professionals, and others who campaigned to end capitalist oppression by gradualist, political means. Shaw's first plays in the 1890s carried Fabianism into the London theatre by attacking slum-landlordism, capitalist profits from prostitution, and the foolishness of armies and war.

In *Man and Superman* and *Major Barbara* (both performed in 1905), Shaw dramatized a political philosophy that joined socialism to vitalism, the belief in a "life force" that could make it possible for people to control evolution. With these plays, Shaw discarded the Social Darwinist side of Naturalism to emphasize that human agency could work through evolution to effect progressive change. In *Major Barbara*, Shaw's audience learned that social conscience without economic power is useless and unethical (Figure 11.2). Further, *Man and Superman* demonstrated that all the political power in the world cannot alter material reality unless it works in conjunction with evolution. The hundred-page preface to his epic five-act play *Back to Methuselah* (1922) outlines the intellectual genealogy of his form of creative evolution. Shaw's Fabian vitalism argued against the pessimistic conclusions that many Social Darwinists predicted for humankind. Shaw's interest in vitalism and evolution also led him to embrace eugenics, the attempt to shape the future of humankind by manipulating the gene pool, causing him to be widely critiqued and dismissed in subsequent years. While Shaw's philosophy and the plays that embodied it may no longer seem politically relevant, or may even be considered misguided or offensive, Fabian vitalism did change political discourse in England before 1914. Shaw's efforts helped to lay the groundwork for the eventual political triumph of the Labour Party after the Second World War and its commitment to democratic socialism in Great Britain. His comedies from this period continue to startle playgoers with their combative debates and acute social analyses. Stylistically, however, his plays, even when fantastical, were often orthodox in structure and characterization.

In addition to the socialists, several second-generation avant-garde movements also attacked bourgeois society, warned of possible chaos to come, and proposed utopian alternatives to conventional, middle-class life. As literary theorist Peter Bürger

Figure 11.2

Photograph from the 1905 production of Shaw's *Major Barbara* at the Royal Court Theatre, London. Louis Calvert played Undershaft and Granville Barker (with drum), who also directed, performed Cusins. The photo appeared with others from this production in the *Illustrated Sporting and Dramatic News* (20 January 1906), one of several news magazines in Europe and the United States after 1900 that regularly ran photographs of current events.

Source: Hulton Archive/Getty Images.

insists, avant-garde artists could not break their ties to the dominant culture until they attacked "the status of art in bourgeois society" (Bürger 1984: 49). Accordingly, second-generation avant-garde movements stopped treating "the arts" as a separate arena of practice within bourgeois society and began to reconfigure their artistic work as the genuine basis for a utopian society. Instead of producing individual works that might (or might not) have some limited effects on the dominant culture, as the Naturalists and Symbolists had done, avant-gardists started to use their own theatres to explore the possibilities of new modes of experience and social organization. The Futurists and Dadaists took the first tentative steps toward realizing this challenge; Expressionists and Surrealists were less programmatic, but also reconsidered perception and spirituality through theatrical means.

Most of the movements also undercut the representational basis of the theatre. As noted in Chapter 10, early avant-gardists did not completely overturn the assumption that the theatre should somehow imitate and represent "reality" (whatever that might be) espoused by professional artists in mainstream theatre. Thus, some artists chose to incorporate avant-garde experiments into their commercial productions, as we will see at the end of this chapter. In 1896, however, one avant-garde production openly attacked the mimetic basis of the stage – *Ubu Roi* (*King Ubu*), by Alfred Jarry. The play satirized a bourgeois anti-hero as a gross, ambitious, and murderous idiot; Ubu simply slaughters others for pleasure and power. Jarry combined characters and situations from *Macbeth* with conventions from rural French puppet theatre (where he had worked), put them on the stage of the Théâtre de l'Oeuvre with deliberately crude and highly stylized scenery, and instructed his actors to perform mechanically, like marionettes (Figure 11.3). As this description suggests, *Ubu* did not fit completely within any of the representational commercial or avant-garde movements of the day; it mocked realism and Naturalism and avoided the principles and beliefs of Symbolism and Aestheticism, although he was supported by Symbolist playwright Rachilde. Instead of representing reality, the production of *Ubu* was forthrightly presentational; spectators were made aware that they were in a theatre watching actors present a strange and disturbing piece of fiction.

Despite only having two performances, *Ubu* gained a kind of mythic notoriety for shocking the bourgeoisie and causing a riot that fed the imaginations of second-generation avant-gardists through the 1920s. The facts of its production, however, contradict the myth propagated by Rachilde. According to the evidence, there were some calculated confrontations of support and opposition among the invited intelligentsia at the preview performance. Many of these spectators had read previously published excerpts of the play and planned to demonstrate, as had vocal claques at other Parisian performances throughout the century. But there was no riot among a scandalized bourgeoisie. Such theatregoers did attend the official opening on the second night and some may have been shocked, but the performance passed without incident. Why the myth of scandal and riot? Part of it was apparently the result of Jarry's self-promotion, but its perpetuation also stems from the need for later avant-garde artists and their allies to create an us/them situation of persecuted Romantic artists vs. a foolish and angry bourgeoisie. (Unfortunately, some accounts of *Ubu* continue to recount this myth.) More important than the play's manufactured scandal was its radical break with the accepted theatre practices of the 1890s.

Figure 11.3
Alfred Jarry's lithographed program for the 1896 Paris premiere of his play, *Ubu Roi* (*King Ubu*), at the Theatre de L'Oeuvre, staged by Aurélien Lugné-Poë. It was published by the journal, *La Critique,* with other programs for the theatre's season. The corrupt Ubu carries the "pshitt sword" he refers to in the play and a bag of money. The burning house probably depicts the home of one of Ubu's subjects who did not pay his taxes.

Source: Minneapolis Institute of Art, The Mary and Robyn Campbell Fund for Art Books.

Futurism and dada

Perhaps hoping for similar alleged shock effects, Filippo Marinetti (1876–1944) began **Futurism** in Italy with the publication of "The Founding and Manifesto of Futurism" in 1909. The manifesto damned the art of the past, including museums, concert halls, and conventional theatre, and, in a slap at Symbolism, called for artistic forms that would exalt the speed and dynamism of the machine age. More manifestos followed, and soon Marinetti was producing "Futurist evenings" in large auditoriums that included lectures, poetry readings, art displays, and theatrical skits. Some skits resembled conventional variety sketches, but others explored themes and conflicts that were anti-positivist, a-logical, and abstract. They were occasionally thrilling and visionary. The short plays the Futurists staged were called *sintesi*. Like Jarry, Marinetti also experimented with performer–spectator dynamics, usually in an attempt to outrage bourgeois audiences. He never let his audience forget that they were watching a performance that rarely attempted to represent "reality." Marinetti was interested in theatre because of its social reach, but was also interested in dance. In 1917, he wrote a manifesto on Futurist dance, which featured "The Dance of the Machine Gun," "The Dance of the Aeroplane," and the "Dance of the Shrapnel." Unlike many other theatre artists, by the end of First World War, Marinetti embraced the revolutionary potential of film to transform the theatre.

Marinetti has a complex legacy in theatre history. He glorified warfare as a necessary source of modern dynamism, and allied himself with the Fascist Party for a short period. Nonetheless, he was inconsistently attached to a political program. Until 1915, Marinetti's work was primarily aesthetic. Once Italy entered the war, and Marinetti became a soldier, he joined his political and artistic aims. Marinetti even performed Futurist plays at Red Cross benefits for soldiers. After 1920, he once again became mostly interested in aesthetics. Futurist art continued throughout the 1920s and 1930s, and became more integrated into mainstream theatre production. Marinetti's connection with Fascism, however, has led art from the later period to be dismissed, ignored, or vilified until recently.

Even though many of the Italian Futurist manifestos exhibited misogyny and embraced war rhetoric obsessed with masculinist virility, some of the Futurists' anti-bourgeois stances challenged traditional gender roles, attracting intellectual female artists to the movement. For example, French artist Valentine de Saint-Point (1875–1953), who wrote "Manifesto of the Futurist Woman" (1912) and "Futurist Manifesto of Lust" (1913) directly engaged with and countered Marinetti's assumptions about gender, sex and female virility, eventually collaborating with him. Saint-Point also had a close connection to theatre – she performed a dance theatre piece called *Metachorie* in 1913 as a total fusion of the arts, including set design, lighting, music, and movement. In 1931, during the second wave of the Futurist movement, Giannina Censi (1913–1995) staged aero-dances imagined by Marinetti in his "Manifesto on Futurist Dance" that incorporated Futurist idealizations of machine and motion into performance. Censi often improvised these dances as Marinetti read poetry in the wings of the theatre. These performances resonated with avant-garde experiments that rejected sentimental and emotional acting styles found in the commercial theatre. As Anja Klöck has suggested, these dances also engaged, willingly or not, with Fascist and Futurist discourses of the period. Meaning Censi's dances not only referenced Marinetti's manifesto, but also made use of the airplane imagery important to Fascist imaginings. Photos of this dance even made their way into a physical education book designed to prime women to develop the muscular strength to procreate – an ironic use given many Futurist feminist critiques of the previous era (Klöck 1999).

Interest in the potential of Futurism to inspire a machine-age heaven-on-earth blossomed in Russia. The Russian Futurists, like their Italian counterparts, scoffed at the idealizing mysticism of the Symbolists and looked to the machine and to film as engines for utopian change. Soon after the 1917 Revolution, Vladimir Mayakovsky (1893–1930), leader of Futurism in Russia, aligned the movement with communism and worked to create effective propaganda for the struggling regime. With Meyerhold, Mayakovsky co-directed his play *Mystery-Bouffe* (1918), which depicts the establishment of a Futurist paradise. As we will see, this production helped to move Meyerhold away from Futurism toward his eventual embrace of Constructivism, the major avant-garde movement to emerge from the Russian Revolution.

While the Futurist movements were strongest in Italy and the Soviet Union, they also blossomed around the globe in divergent forms. Marinetti's 1909 Manifesto was published in the Parisian newspaper *Le Figaro*, and was quickly translated by artists in many countries. Later movements were often responses to the manifestos rather than Futurist artwork. Nonetheless, Futurism was a global phenomenon throughout the early to mid-twentieth century, as the subsequent section on Latin America shows.

The Dadaists (who apparently chose their name randomly by opening a dictionary), in contrast, rejected the rationality that they believed had led to war. The artist-refugees, who founded the movement, which included Hugo Ball (1886–1927) and Emmy Hemmings (1885–1948), initiated **Dada** at the Cabaret Voltaire, a cabaret theatre in neutral Zurich in Switzerland during the Great War. Partly inspired by the myth of *Ubu Roi*, as well as by Marinetti's Futurist experiments (despite their ideological divergence from the glorification of war), the Dadaists played with satire and anarchy in their cabaret performances. Unlike the Futurists, however, the Dadaists leavened their oppositional anger against bourgeois art with greater experimentation and a wider range of playful visions, including conscious incitement of audience reaction. Several Dadaist musicians included a variety of everyday sounds in their compositions, for example. The Dadaists also questioned the causal connections between sensations and behaviors that provided the basis for representational theatre. During and after the war, some of the Zurich Dadaists attempted to live according to the notions of chance, fragmentation, and simultaneity that they were exploring in their art. The Dadaists' productions at the Cabaret Voltaire included Jarry's plays and *The Gas Heart* (1921) by Tristan Tzara (1896–1963) that featured absurd dialogue between body parts, interrupted by ballet numbers.

Like the Futurists, the Dadaists eventually became international through the publication and dissemination of manifestos. But the theatre was also important to the movement. In fact, one of the movement's founders, Hugo Ball, originated his artistic career as an actor, having moved to Berlin in 1910 to collaborate with Max Reinhardt (1873–1943), while Emmy Hemmings lived as an itinerant performer before the movement and was a key performer throughout its heyday.

German Expressionism

While German Expressionistic theatre had its roots in the first generation of the avant-garde, it also extended into second-generation concerns centered on utopian hopes and social transformation, in relationship to the Great War and its devastation.

The term "**Expressionism**" was initially used by François Delsarte (1811–1871), who attempted to systematize the actor's physical and vocal expression of ideas and emotions related to what he conceived to be the physical, mental, and spiritual parts of the performer's body. By the end of the nineteenth century, Delsarte's system had become the basis for many programs of actor training. The theatre artists in Germany who began calling themselves Expressionists around 1910 were especially interested in the spiritual dynamics of Delsarte's system. After 1900, art critics also used the term to denote a non-realist painting suffused with the subjective emotions of the artist; this general connotation also applied to the new theatrical movement.

The late plays of August Strindberg (1849–1912) provided significant models for Expressionism as well. Following such Naturalistic dramas as *Miss Julie* and a difficult period of mental instability the dramatist called his "inferno," the Swedish playwright strove for a theatre that he hoped might synthesize the objectivity of Naturalism with the spirituality of the Symbolists. His post-inferno plays, notably *To Damascus*, a trilogy (1898–1901), *A Dream Play* (1902), and *The Ghost Sonata* (1907), attempted to embody the experiences of mythical journeys and spiritual dreams. One of his initial titles for the play was "Kama-Loka: A Buddhist Drama." On a draft page for *Ghost Sonata*, Strindberg wrote, "Maya = the World-weaveress, the Spider, the Illusion, the Folly, Matter" (Malekin 2010: 134). These notes reveal that Strindberg had been reading some of the works of H.P. Blavatsky (1831–1891), whose "theosophical" ideas in the 1880s mixed together Buddhist and Platonic beliefs in ways that many turn-of-the-century thinkers found convincing. Strindberg's interests in spirituality, strong emotions, the tricks of perception, and grotesque sounds and images were given fuller rein in theatrical Expressionism.

Early German Expressionist plays called for such anti-realist techniques as grotesquely painted scenery, exaggerated movement, and "telegraphic" dialogue, so named because it copied the abbreviated, mechanistic quality of a telegraph message. These features were evident in several Expressionist plays, including Walter Hasenclever's (1890–1940) *The Son* (1914) and George Kaiser (1878–1945)s *From Morn to Midnight* (1912). While both plays invite spectators to view the distorted dramatic action through the fevered eyes of the protagonist (who also represents much of the author's point of view), neither drama ignores the very real material factors that constrain the protagonist's spiritual longings. The younger generation's revolt against the restraints of bourgeois society in *The Son* acknowledges that the title character cannot realize his ecstatic hopes without killing his father, a symbol of conventional order and repression. Many of the conflicts in German Expressionist plays were staged as between men, leaving female characters marginalized or absent. Other portrayals reveal a profound anxiety and fear of the feminine by their creators, which read as misogynistic today. For example, Oskar Kokoschka (1886–1980)s *Murder, Hope of Women* (1909), often cited as the first Expressionist play, limns female sexuality and animality, replicating turn of the century pseudo-scientific theories. The play is a battle between the sexes that ultimately ends in a woman's murder.

Although censorship before and during the Great War prevented most Expressionist plays from reaching the stage, Expressionism flourished in German theatre immediately after the war. Optimism about the imminent overthrow of conventional German society after Germany's defeat and the 1917 revolution in Russia turned some Expressionists toward utopian socialism. When *The Son* finally reached the stage in 1918, the director's statements about the production summed up the goals of the movement for the public. Expressionism, he said, was "the exteriorization of innermost feelings," a "volcanic eruption of the motions of the soul"; it involved "the boundless ecstasy of heightened expression" (Berghaus 2005: 85). Georg Kaiser's vision now embraced pacifism in his anti-war play *Gas* (1918), which took the poison gas used by troops in the Great War as a metaphor for the spread of social corruption. In the same year, with some Germans still inspired by the news of the Russian Revolution, Ernst Toller (1893–1939) advocated a revolution in Germany in *Transfiguration* (1918) (Figure 11.4). Other Expressionists combined the generational rage that had fueled several pre-war plays with a more general call for the spiritual and material regeneration of German society. To model their hoped-for utopia, several productions sought to forge

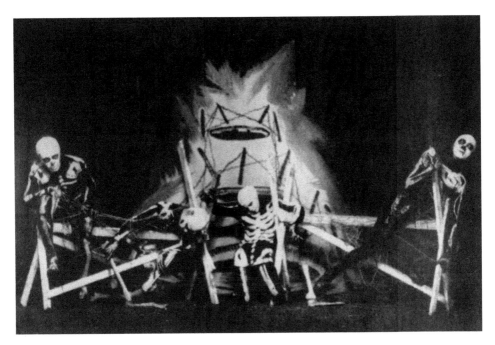

Figure 11.4
Contemporary print of a scene from the 1919 Expressionist production of *Transfiguration*
(*Die Wandlung*, 1918), by Ernst Toller.
Source: C. Oskar Fischel, *Bildernerische der Scene* (1931), Abb. 125.

a spiritual union between actors and spectators by abolishing the proscenium arch, eliminating illusionistic scenery, and mounting direct calls for a new world. Ecstatic acting often
powered Expressionist performance with revolutionary urgency. According to one review
praising actor Fritz Kortner, for example, "Words coagulate and dissolve in a rhythmic
fashion. Screams erupt and vanish again. Movements surge back and forth. . . . Kortner's
playing pushed himself beyond the limits of the stage and made him burst into the auditorium" (Berghaus 2005: 87). Kortner, like his fellow Expressionist actor Leopold Jessner
(1878–1945) was Jewish and fled Germany in 1933 when Hitler came to power. This was
also true of many female actors and performers, such as pathbreaking cabaret star, actress,
and dancer Valeska Gert (1892–1978), who performed in Toller's *Transfiguration* and Oskar
Kokoschka's *Hiob* (1917).

Revolutionary fervor was short-lived in German Expressionism, however. Kaiser ended
Gas II (1920), his sequel to the 1918 play, with the apocalyptic destruction of the world
to indicate his growing despair with politics. Toller, initially a more politically radical
writer than Kaiser, used irony to express his disillusionment with socialism in *Hurrah, We
Live!* (1927). The uneasy fusion of subjective vision and revolutionary politics in post-war
German Expressionism quickly faded in the theatre after 1924. More so than Symbolism or
Aestheticism, German Expressionism had explored the relativity of extreme perceptions and
emotions on the stage. At the same time, however, most Expressionists tried to claim that

the objective, material world was just as real as inner, subjective feelings. Although today we might say that these two realities actually met in the bodies of Expressionist actors, such a synthesis was not recognizable to most Germans in the 1920s.

Expressionism in the United States

U.S. Expressionism in the early 1920s was a separate artistic movement. Before American artists and audiences had seen much German Expressionism, playwrights Eugene O'Neill (1888–1953) and Elmer Rice (1892–1967) used the term "expressionism" to point to similarities between their dramas and the expressive culture movement, a broad-based program in the United States that sought to counter anxieties about the modern world by drawing on the performing arts. S.S. Curry (1847–1921) combined Delsarte's methods with an emphasis on oral expression of the self, forming the basis of a performance method shared by actors and orators that centered the use of human voice; although related to German Expressionist acting practices, American Expressionist acting was more secular than spiritual, focusing on pushing against capitalist alienation.

U.S. Expressionist playwriting also confronted the violence of capitalism and mechanization. Elmer Rice's best-known play, *The Adding Machine* (1923), depicts the recycling of an alienated office worker, Mr. Zero. In this Nietzschean grotesque comedy, Zero refuses possible freedom and floats from a pointless job adding up figures, through death and finally to eventual reincarnation as another cowardly office worker. The short scenes of the play tend to build cinematically, partly a result of Rice's earlier work as a screenwriter in Hollywood. Sophie Treadwell (1885–1970), another U.S. Expressionist, demonstrated the need for a middle-class woman to rebel against her robotic life in *Machinal* (1928). Treadwell's protagonist murders her husband, an act which eventually sends her to the electric chair. Like Susan Glaspell's plays discussed below, Treadwell's dramas mixed formal innovation with feminist critique in her depictions of violence against women and violence enacted by women who were suffering under patriarchy and advanced capitalism. She also gestured to the fragmentation of the body and gendered labor by placing emphasis on how the typewriter replaced hand-written script. Given the increase in female stenographers and typists in this period, the contrast between the mechanization of the typewriter and the emphasis on the protagonist's pretty hands, *Machinal's* repetitive phrasing is an important aspect of the play. Julia Walker emphasizes S.S. Curry's influence on college-educated Treadwell's dramaturgy (Walker 2009: 227).

One might also see the work produced by the Provincetown Players a few years earlier, as partly expressionist, particularly the plays of O'Neill and Susan Glaspell (1876–1948). The Provincetowners started an artists' colony in New England in 1916, during the Great War, and drew their energy from a mix of American pragmatism, the politics of anarchism, and the philosophy of Nietzsche. By 1922, when the group disbanded, they had produced nearly a hundred plays, a few of them by Glaspell and O'Neill. Glaspell wrote *The Verge* (1921) in an Expressionist style that merges feminism with a Nietzschean will to power in order to explore a female artist's attempts to push beyond convention to true innovation. Like the work of other U.S. Expressionists, *The Verge* places the protagonist in a recognizably objective social world, but also finds ways of exploring her subjective, psychological sides. By the 1920s, O'Neill had moved from the realism of his early one-acts to write two Expressionist plays,

The Emperor Jones (1920) and *The Hairy Ape* (1921). The first is a peeling-away of the layers of civilization in the mind of a Black man and the second focuses on a working-class loner struggling to find a group where he feels he "belongs." O'Neill's staging of African American identity exhibited a form of primitivism, which projected the idea of "pre-civilization" onto non-Western persons. O'Neill's staging was representative of modernism and part of a long tradition of thinking about class in the United States through representations of race. Both O'Neill and Treadwell gained artistic and box office success in New York, where the Provincetowners had opened a commercial theatre.

Although O'Neill left Expressionism behind in the early 1920s, he continued to explore the staging of "subjective" experience in his plays' themes and forms. In *Desire Under the Elms* for example, he explores Freudian unconscious desire as the primary motivation for an adulterous affair between the young wife (Abbie) of an old man (Old Cabot) and her mature stepson (Eben) (Figure 11.5). The 1924 production shocked many theatregoers in the United States because the play effectively excuses the young couple's immoral behavior as inevitable. If "desire" is unconscious and powerful, as Freudian psychoanalysis seemed to suggest, how could society blame Abbie and Eben for their crime, which also included the murder of their newborn child? O'Neill's plot sends the couple to jail in the end, but the play's sympathies lie with them as victims of a force beyond their control. (See the online case study on O'Neill for more about this play.) Psychoanalysis and its spinoffs in popular psychology would continue to shape the American theatre for the next 40 years. It infused multiple genres, including the psychological realism that became the dominant mode of representation in the 40s and 50s, exemplified by Arthur Miller, Tennessee Williams, and their contemporaries, that we will explore in Chapter 12.

FREE
INSTRUCTOR & STUDENT RESOURCES

Figure 11.5
Old Cabot (Walter Huston) looks down on Abbie, his young wife (Marry Morris), who is comforting Eben Cabot (Charles Ellis) in O'Neill's *Desire Under the Elms*. The Experimental Theatre, an outgrowth of the Provincetown Players, produced the drama in 1924.

Source: © Museum of the City of New York.

Theatricalizing the Russian Revolution

The victory of communism in Russia in 1921 sharply altered the dynamics of political theatre in the West. Only later would democratic socialists discover that the Soviet Union under the Russian Communist Party would not function as a democracy. After the Revolution, however, the short-term sacrifice of some democratic rights seemed to many European socialists a small price to pay for the opportunity to transform an entire economy and society. Despite the setbacks caused by the Great War, eager socialists renewed revolutionary action in Eastern and Central Europe and nearly toppled some post-war liberal regimes, including the fragile German state opposed by some of the politically radical Expressionists. Although liberal governments were soon established in the nations of the former German and Austro-Hungarian empires, a new, revolutionary form of Russian theatre soon spread from the Soviet Union to socialists around the world.

To teach peasants and workers the basics of communism, the Communists organized Blue Blouse troupes, named for the color of workers' shirts, and fostered their establishment around the country. A collection of short skits legitimating the radical changes brought by the Revolution, many of these Blue Blouse revues were called "living newspapers" – a term adopted later by U.S. political theatre makers. Through speech, music, gestures, and spectacle, Blue Blouse troupes instructed the many Russians who could not read. In style and ideology, their revues were anti-capitalist and anti-representational. Through presentational skits that directly acknowledged the presence of the audience, they asserted that workers and peasants could take control of their lives and effect radical change. Many Russian vaudeville performers, mostly unemployed since the war and Revolution, joined the Communist Party to write sketches and participate in the Blue Blouse movement. By 1927, more than 5,000 Blue Blouse troupes were active in the Soviet Union.

Inspiring some of the Blue Blouse innovations was the work of avant-garde artist Vsevolod Meyerhold. Meyerhold had journeyed from Naturalism to Symbolism and into Retrospectivism by 1907. From 1907 to 1917, Meyerhold had directed operas, plays, and entertainments at the Imperial Theatres in St. Petersburg, while also working under a pseudonym to stage more than 20 experimental pieces in little theatres, private apartments, and cabarets around the city. By 1917, he had also been teaching regularly and directing short films. Meyerhold welcomed the Revolution and led members from several factions of the Russian avant-garde into active collaboration with the Communists. While holding several leadership positions in the new government, Meyerhold also continued his theatrical experiments, which included a system of actor training known as biomechanics and the elaboration of Constructivism, the final avant-garde movement of his career.

Partly a synthesis of Retrospectivism and Futurism, **Constructivism** sought to energize audiences with actors and designs that demonstrated how human beings could use their bodies and machines to produce engaging art and a more productive life. Meyerhold collaborated with Lyubov Popova (1889–1924) on a Constructivist set for *The Magnificent Cuckold* (1922), for instance, that used platforms, ramps, slides, ladders, and three moving wheels to suggest a mill that had been transformed into a huge mechanical toy (Figure 11.6). Lyubov Popova's set designs were an important part of the Constructivist theatre. She was, however, just one of many women set designers who were part of the development of Russian scenography. Other important figures include Alexandra Ekster (1882–1949), who designed

Figure 11.6
Lyubov Popova's constructivist set for Meyerhold's 1922 production of *The Magnanimous Cuckold*, by Fernand Crommelynck. The ramps and machinery provided a practical playground for biomechanical acting.
Source: © SCRSS Photo Library – www.scrss.org.uk.

Alexander Tairov's (1885–1950) 1917 production of *Salome*, and Natalia Goncharova (1881–1962), who designed sets for the Ballet Russes.

In *Cuckold*, as the actors performed, the wheels of the mill turned to complement their timing. In effect, the production fused the clowning of Retrospectivism with the mechanical rhythms of Futurism. During the 1920s, Meyerhold applied his presentational Constructivist style to several plays that advocated Communist propaganda, to Mayakovsky's grotesque Futurist dramas, and to a range of Russian classics. In one scene of his Constructivist production of Gogol's *The Inspector General* in 1926, 15 officials popped out of 15 doors around the stage to offer a bribe to the man they took for an inspector.

As these examples suggest, Meyerhold drew direct inspiration from filmic techniques. "Let us carry through the 'cinefication' of the theatre, let us equip the theatre with all the technical refinements of the cinema," he wrote in 1930 (Meyerhold 1969: 254). His work also influenced the great Russian film director Sergei Eisenstein (1898–1948), best known for his *Battleship Potemkin* (1925) and *Ivan the Terrible* (1944). Eisenstein, a student of Meyerhold's, claimed that he learned the filmic technique of montage from Meyerhold's inventive sequencing of stage actions for his productions. These techniques greatly contrasted with the U.S. commercial film techniques discussed earlier in the chapter.

Increasingly out of favor with Joseph Stalin (who ruled the Soviet Union from 1924 until his death in 1953) and tethered by the dictates of **socialist realism**, an official policy that required artists to celebrate the victories of the Communist state in a mode of heroic realism, Meyerhold lost his theatre in 1938. In retrospect, it is clear that Lenin, Stalin, and other Communist leaders had needed Meyerhold and the Russian avant-garde in the early 1920s to stabilize their regime internally and to give it credibility and influence outside Russia, especially since the Soviets desired to foment international revolution. After the mid-1920s, however, when hopes for worldwide revolution had dimmed, Stalin and his functionaries began tightening the funding and freedoms of the avant-garde. They pushed out and eventually executed Meyerhold and others who would not conform to the narrow political and aesthetic constraints of socialist realism. After Stalin's death in 1953 and the 1956 "thaw" in the Cold War, however, the ideas and images of Meyerhold's Constructivist theatre and his biomechanical training for actors began to emerge. They influenced theatrical practice throughout the world, especially in England, Germany, Japan, and Eastern Europe.

CASE STUDY: Lenin's Taylorism and Meyerhold's biomechanics

Bruce McConachie

Ironically, the Russian Communists, soon after attaining power in the early 1920s, borrowed extensively from the ideas of Frederick W. Taylor (1856–1915). Taylor, the American originator of "scientific management," had helped to make U.S. capitalism more efficient and profitable. Taylor had observed and tested the physical motions of workers in factories to discover how they might streamline their tasks even if it meant that each worker was performing repetitive actions. Taylor believed that this was the best way to perform all factory jobs and all workers should conform to that ideal, and to a top-down approach – where directives came down from knowledgeable managers to compliant workers. A few Communist engineers had also witnessed the wonders of Henry Ford's assembly line manufacturing and believed, as did many Americans and Russians, that Ford and similar modern industrialists had simply translated Taylor's "time-and-motion" principles into industrial practice. Although the Communists despised capitalism, they also realized that they had to adopt systematic management techniques as well as new technologies if they were to modernize production in the Soviet Union. Lenin had read essays about Taylorism, as Taylor's principles had come to be called, and he was impressed by Russian engineers who had studied some of Taylor's publications, including *The Principles of Scientific Management* (1911).

Soon after the Revolution, Lenin spoke publicly about the transformational possibilities of Taylorism. His 1918 address, Lenin claimed that the "The Taylor system"

is a combination of the subtle brutality of bourgeois exploitation and a number of its greatest scientific achievements in the field of analyzing mechanical motions during work. The elimination of superfluous and awkward motions, the working out of correct methods of work, the introduction of the best system of accounting and control, etc. The Soviet Republic must at all costs adopt all that is valuable in the achievements of science and technology in this field. . . . We must organize in Russia the study and teaching of the Taylor system and systematically try it out and adapt it to our purposes.

(Hughes 1989: 256)

Lenin surely knew that Taylorism had also encountered stiff resistance from U.S. workers, but he apparently believed that the benefits to be gained for all Soviet citizens outweighed the problem of the loss of worker control on the factory floor.

Soon after Lenin's death in 1924, Joseph Stalin celebrated the synthesis of American Taylorism and Russian energy as the primary legacy of their fallen leader: "American efficiency is that indomitable force which neither knows nor recognizes obstacles . . . and without which serious constructive work is inconceivable. . . . The combination of the Russian Revolutionary sweep with American efficiency is the essence of Lenin-ism" (Hughes 1989: 251). Although other efficiency experts in the United States were already improving on Taylor's principles by 1924, Taylorism would help to transform industrial production in the Soviet Union during the 1920s and 1930s.

Under Meyerhold's leadership, Taylorism would also help to transform a significant segment of post-revolutionary theatre in the new Communist nation. Soon after the October Revolution of 1917, Meyerhold had been the first major theatre artist to meet with the Communists to discuss the future of theatre and culture in the new na-tion; in contrast, most of his colleagues at the Imperial Theatres were horrified by the Revolution. Meyerhold severed his links with those artists, managed to mount signif-icant productions during the difficult days of 1918, and staged theatricals for the Red Army in the midst of civil war. By 1920, when the regime summoned him from St. Petersburg to Moscow, Meyerhold was one of the most accomplished and politically radical theatre artists in the new Soviet Union. He was also ready to reimagine and rebuild Russian theatre practice in accordance with the revolutionary ideas of Lenin.

Whether Meyerhold fully shared Lenin's faith in the revolutionary possibilities of Taylorism for training actors cannot be known. But it is clear that he took Lenin's advice to "adapt" much of Taylor's system when he began workshops for his company in 1921. In addition to the kinds of exercises Meyerhold had used before to train young actors, he required all of his performers to participate in a one-hour activity called **biomechanics**. Although the term was new, the notion that actors should seek to fuse the biology of their bodies with the motions of machinery was straight out of Taylorism. The term "biomechanics" also included a nod to the psychology of Ivan Pavlov, who had discovered that animals could be trained to behave in certain ways through positive conditioning. Introducing his ideas to the public in 1922, Meyerhold directly compared biomechanics to the "scientific" principles of Taylor. He also stated:

In the past the actor has always conformed to the society for which his art was intended. In future, the actor must go even further in relating his technique to the industrial situation. For he will be working in a society where labor is no longer regarded as a curse, but as a joyful vital necessity. In these conditions of ideal labor, art clearly requires a new foundation. . . . Art should be based on scientific principles; the entire creative act should be a conscious process. The art of the actor consists in organizing his material; that is, in his capacity to utilize correctly his body's means of expression.

(Braun 1995: 172–3)

By invoking conformity, industry, the joy of labor, a new foundation, scientific principles, and a correct way of movement, Meyerhold knew he was speaking a Taylorist discourse that would please the new Soviet intelligentsia.

Several of Meyerhold's workshop exercises practiced the Taylorism that he preached. Underlying Meyerhold's concept of an "acting cycle," for example, was Taylor's notion of a "working cycle." Following Taylor's language, Meyerhold instructed his actors to think in terms of three "invariable stages" (Braun 1995: 174) when they performed a task on stage – intention, realization, and reaction. Meyerhold developed what he called "études" to give his actors practice in working through a complete acting cycle. In his "Shooting a Bow" étude, for example, the actor pantomimes a series of rhythmic movements that suggest running toward a quarry, shooting an imaginary arrow, and celebrating the kill. The exercise involves a thorough workout of the pursuit of an "intention," the various muscular tensions involved in its "realization," and the release (or "reaction") the actor feels when the task is complete. Central to this kind of work is training actors to manipulate their body as a physical object, the same kind of control that Taylor required of workers under his supervision (see Figure 11.7). The études, like several other of Meyerhold's physical exercises, trained actors in the efficient use of their bodies.

However, Meyerhold gave his actors much more freedom than Taylor allowed his factory workers. As a teacher and director, Meyerhold sometimes gave direct orders to students and actors, but he preferred to encourage their own decision-making. Knowing they had to make hundreds of choices to put together a performance, he praised the brains of his students and actors as well as their bodies. Meyerhold also understood that an actor's movements invariably triggered emotional states within the performer.

As Meyerhold developed biomechanics during the 1920s, he devoted more attention to the complex dynamics linking physical activity to emotional stimulus and response. In 1934, Russian actor Igor Ilinsky (1901–1987) emphasized the comprehensive nature of biomechanics:

People think that essentially biomechanical acting is rather like acrobatics. . . . But not many realize that the biomechanical system of acting, starting from a series of devices designed to develop the ability to control one's body within the stage space in the most advantageous way, leads on to the most complex questions of acting technique. . . . The emotional state of the actor, his temperament, his excitability, the emotional sympathy between the actor as artist and the imaginative processes of the character he is performing – all these are fundamental elements in the complex system of biomechanics.

(Braun 1995: 176–7)

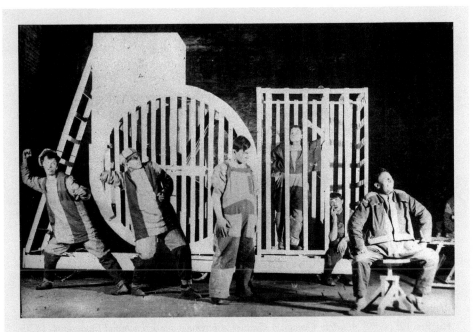

Figure 11.7
The "meat mincer" setting, designed by Varvara Stepanova, for Meyerhold's 1922 production of *The Death of Tarelkin*, by Alexander Kobylin. Stepanova referred to her set pieces as "acting instruments," designed to enable vigorous biomechanical performance.
Source: Album/Alamy Stock Photo.

By 1930, Meyerhold had expanded biomechanics to include more freedom for his actors and a firmer link to their emotional lives on stage.

Biomechanics had also proven its practical applicability. One of Meyerhold's first successes with his biomechanically trained actors was *The Magnanimous Cuckold*. Igor Ilinsky, quoted above, also deployed several types to depict his character Bruno. He even undercut his most prominent characterization of the miller with clowning. As a fellow actor stated:

> Bruno . . . stood before the audience, his face pale and motionless, and with unvarying intonation, a monotonous declamatory style, and identical sweeping gestures he uttered his grandiloquent monologues. But at the same time this Bruno was being ridiculed by the actor performing acrobatic stunts at the most impassioned moments of his speeches, belching, and comically rolling his eyes whilst enduring the most dramatic anguish.
>
> (Braun 1995: 183–4)

By all reports, the workers who enjoyed *The Magnanimous Cuckold* often burst into raucous laughter. Avoiding psychological characterization, Meyerhold's use of biomechanics with his actors helped them to induce a more direct response from his audience. By training his actors to physicalize social types for the stage through biomechanics, Meyerhold wanted to call attention to the kinds of physical and social transformations necessary to build the new Soviet Union.

From his other writings, it is clear that Meyerhold conceived of spectators as similar to a group of filmgoers whose physical responses to his productions would help to transform the new nation. For Meyerhold, spectators could become self-conscious viewers aware, like him, of the construction of a film and its potential meanings. Rather than creating an illusion on the stage, Meyerhold sought to invent a kind of carnival in the entire auditorium, and he often had his actors breaking the illusion of the fourth wall or even running through the playhouse to engage spectators directly, to activate them to helping create toward a communist utopia, first imagined in the theatre. Ironically, he drew on the work of an American capitalist to do it.

Key references

Banta, M. (1993) *Narrative Productions in the Age of Taylor, Veblen, and Ford*, Chicago, IL: University of Chicago Press.

Braun, E. (1995) *Meyerhold: A Revolution in Theatre*, Iowa City, IA: University of Iowa Press.

Hughes, T.P. (1989) *American Genesis: A Century of Invention and Technological Enthusiasm, 1870– 1970*, New York: Viking.

Leach, R. (1989) *Vsevolod Meyerhold*, Cambridge: Cambridge University Press.

Meyerhold, V. (1969) *Meyerhold on Theatre*, trans. and ed. E. Braun, New York: Hill and Wang.

Radical theatre in Europe after the Russian Revolution

The failure of post-war revolutionaries in Germany to establish a communist state led to the cessation of theatrical Expressionism and to a counter-reaction. In the mid-1920s, German socialists began experimenting with more dispassionate means of inducing audiences to alter their society. By the time a Russian Blue Blouse company visited Germany in 1927, German troupes had been performing Russian-inspired revues for several years. At Berlin's Volksbühne (People's Theatre), director Erwin Piscator expanded on the techniques of the Blue Blouse troupes to teach straightforward lessons about socialism that emphasized that the working class could exercise power. Piscator used situations of class conflict, film clips of historical scenes, and a panoply of on-stage technological devices to create presentational history lessons in socialism. Piscator termed his plays documentary "montages," in recognition of his debt to the artistry of film to Eisenstein.

Dramatist and director Bertolt Brecht (1898–1956) also worked in film as well as the theatre. Influenced by his experience as a medical orderly in the Great War and by the failure of Expressionist utopianism in Germany, including his own early play *Baal* (1923), Brecht gained commercial success with his cynical *The Threepenny Opera* in 1927 and then turned his back on bourgeois theatre to embrace communist politics in 1928. Convinced that German communists needed to discipline themselves for the long fight against capitalism, Brecht wrote a series of presentational *lehrstücke* (learning plays) in the early 1930s before fleeing the rise of Nazi power in 1933. In exile in Scandinavia and the United States until 1947, Brecht expanded his vision of what he called his "epic theatre" to tell historical and allegorical tales that encouraged spectators to look at the present world of capitalism and **fascism** critically. Aware of the persuasive charisma of politicians, the dangerous emotions of populist nationalism, and the callous manipulations of the economically powerful, Brecht sought to educate, entertain, and empower his audiences. Several of the plays he wrote while in exile – which often mixed representational scenes with presentational performance modes – have been celebrated as masterpieces of the twentieth-century stage, including *The Life of Galileo, Mother Courage and Her Children, The Good Person of Szechwan*, and *The Caucasian Chalk Circle* (all four written 1937–1945; first produced 1941–1948). (Please see the case study on the website on Brecht's direction of *Mother Courage* to read more about his directing work.)

In addition to playwriting, Brecht's epic theatre forged several innovations in production and performance. To prepare his spectators to accept his Marxist understanding of the economic circumstances of the twentieth century, Brecht generally wanted them to view the

actions of his main characters with a critical distance rather than with psychological absorption. Brecht interrupted the story of *The Good Person of Szechwan*, for example, with songs and poetry to encourage his audience to step back perceive the social and economic circumstances of Shen Te, the good prostitute of the title, who is forced to invent an evil male cousin (Shui Ta) to save her from the consequences of her desire to love others and share her wealth. As the play points out in several ways, acts of goodness under capitalism can only lead good people into economic ruin. Brecht called his technique *Verfremdungseffekt* [fehr-FREHM-dungs-eh-fehkt], a term he coined to indicate his interest in arousing audience curiosity about his characters and their situations for the purpose of revolutionary change. Sometimes mistranslated as "alienation effect," *Verfremdungseffekt* is better understood as the effect of making something on stage "strange" or "distant," so that it arouses audience interest and curiosity. Brecht meant the term to stand as the German translation of a Russian word used by the aesthetician Victor Shklovsky (1893–1984) to describe an interest in making events "strange" to spark audience interest and to underscore the social and political structure of which they were a part, so as to spark social and economic change.

In addition to using music and poetry to comment on character actions in his plots, Brecht often found ways to keep his spectators aware of the inherent doubleness of all actor/characters on his stage. In *Good*

Figure 11.8
Helene Weigel as Mother Courage from Brecht's staging of *Mother Courage and Her Children* in Berlin, 1949. Mother Courage bites the coin to test its authenticity.

Source: Universal History Archive/UIG/Shutterstock.

Person, for instance, the audience always knows that Shen Te and Shui Ta are the same person, even though that insight is not available to the other characters in the drama. Brecht also instructed his actors to emphasize the social position rather than the inner psychology of their characters, so that spectators could better understand how economic circumstances shaped their actions. In keeping with this idea, he asked his actors to underline the social and economic choices their characters must make, which he understood as a part of the actors' *gestus* [GHE-stoos], a term which refers both to the individual gestures made by an actor and to the general movement of all of the actors on stage that embody social attitudes and relationships.

At one point in *Good Person,* Shen Te must decide whether to marry for love or to transform herself into her businessman cousin so that he can call off the wedding. Brecht has the actor playing Shen Te use gestures to weigh both possibilities; she finally adopts the mask of Shui Ta, the businessman, who abruptly cancels the wedding to avoid economic calamity. Brecht urged directors to pay close attention to the groupings of his actor/characters so that the audience could read the economic relations among them from the stage picture. Overall, Brecht sought to induce his audiences to respond rationally rather than emotionally to productions of his plays. Following our overview of radical and anti-colonial theatre outside of Europe, our second case study examines Brecht's influence in a global perspective.

Other radical theatres flourished in France in the wake of the Russian Revolution. Russian Blue Blouse troupes traveled to France in the 1920s and helped to turn **Surrealism,**

Figure 11.9
Katrin, Mother Courage's daughter, beats her drum to warn the townspeople in the 1949 production of Bertolt Brecht's *Mother Courage.*

Source: Lebrecht Music & Arts/Alamy Stock Photo.

the last major European avant-garde movement of the interwar years, toward communism. André Breton (1896–1966) and other Parisians had been experimenting with "automatic writing," in the belief that chance, spontaneity, and the unconscious might lead a writer into a dreamlike state in which he or she could discover the source of aesthetic truth. In 1924, Breton issued a manifesto proclaiming his allegiance to "Surrealism," which isolated the Dada anarchists from the psychoanalytic aims of Breton's followers. Breton took the new name from Guillaume Apollinaire (1880–1918), who had subtitled his fanciful 1903 play, *The Breasts of Tiresias*, a "*drame surrealiste.*" Although the 1924 manifesto was heavily indebted to Freud and mostly apolitical, Breton's next manifesto in 1929 embraced communism. Suspicious of theatre and eager to make Surrealism more militant, Breton denounced many former colleagues after this manifesto, including all of those who wished to use Surrealism on stage. Breton appointed Antonin Artaud (1896–1948) his first director of research for Surrealism in 1924, but then kicked him out of his coterie two years later. In response, Artaud and others staged Surrealistic productions in a space they named the Théâtre Alfred Jarry. Artaud wrote manifestos and struggled to start new theatres until psychiatrists institutionalized him for insanity in 1937.

Despite his mental illness, Artaud's manifestos, published in 1938 as *The Theatre and Its Double*, gained substantial influence among other theatre avant-gardists after his death in 1949. Writing in the tradition of Rousseau, who believed that civilization had corrupted humankind, Artaud argued for a theatre that would return modern humans to what he called "primitive" mysteries through their bodies. He urged theatre artists to reject the dramatic masterpieces of the Western tradition – in fact, to throw out all text-based theatre – and embrace performances involving music, dance, and spectacle. Artaud conjured what he called a **Theatre of Cruelty**, a kind of production that could unite actors and audiences in a collective purgation of their rational restraints and individual freedoms.

Artaud's conception of The Theatre of Cruelty was a reaction to his experimentations with peyote in the indigenous Tarahamura land of Chihuahua, Mexico. Artaud's fascination with Mexico, which existed before his trip, certainly employs an exotification similar to the Orientalist constructs discussed in Chapter 9 and to the racialized idea of the "primitive" mentioned above. Nonetheless, he was not completely ignorant of Mexican political life; in fact, it was his deep disappointment with the orthodox Marxist revolutionary paradigms he experienced in Mexico City that led him to go on the trip to Chihuahua in the first place.

Although critics such as theatre historian Kimberley Jannarone have recently noted similarities between Artaud's Theatre of Cruelty and the fascist rallies that were occurring in France and the rest of Europe in the 1930s, *The Theatre and Its Double* had little influence on theatrical practice during Artaud's life. Avant-garde theatre artists unfamiliar with Artaud's attraction to fascism, however, would be inspired by his visions in the 1960s and 1970s, as we will see in Chapter 13. (See also the case study on the website on "Artaud and the Crisis of Representation.")

Breton broke with Artaud over the theatre, but he embraced the revolutionary potential of film for Surrealism. Indeed, Surrealists Salvador Dali (1904–1989) and Luis Buñuel (1900–1983) had already made *Un chien Andalou* (*An Andalusian Dog*) in 1928, on the eve of Breton's second manifesto. By the mid-1930s, several French Surrealists, including Jean Cocteau (1892–1963), were working again in the theatre as well as film. He directed seven feature films in addition to his copious work as a playwright and director for the stage. While

Surrealism is largely associated with Paris, many of the surrealists (including Artaud) lived in Mexico for portions of the 1930s, given its lenient immigration laws, revealing the global character of avant-garde movements.

Socialism and communism gained many theatrical adherents among English-speaking artists and spectators as well. In Great Britain, Canada, Australia, and the United States, amateur workers' theatre groups performed Blue Blouse-like revues in union halls and at factory strikes. Called **agitprop** plays – short for agitation and propaganda – these short pieces generally involved stereotypical characters and a chorus of workers in class-conflict situations. Relying on bold gestures, mass chants, evocative tableaux, and emblematic props and costuming, agitprop performances helped workers to organize politically and motivated their economic demands. Amateur agit-prop theatre proliferated during the early years of the Great Depression.

In addition to amateur theatre, international communism influenced many left-wing theatre artists and groups after 1920. In Ireland, Sean O'Casey (1880–1964) wrote socialist plays for production at the Abbey Theatre. His Dublin trilogy, *The Shadow of a Gunman, Juno and the Paycock*, and *The Plough and the Stars* (1923–1926), presents incidents in the Irish fight for independence from the anti-heroic view of people living in the Dublin slums. Even in the United States, there were a few socialist plays, such as John Howard Lawson's (1894–1977) *Processional* (1925) and *The Internationale* (1928), which departed from the generally conservative politics of the country in the 1920s. Socialist hopes also shaped some of the many productions of the Federal Theatre Project (FTP) in the United States. Under President Franklin Delano Roosevelt's New Deal, the government organized and funded the FTP in 1935 to create jobs for out-of-work theatre professionals during the Depression. FTP "living newspapers," which derived from the Blue Blouse form and dramatized such social and economic problems as housing, agriculture, and electrical power through large-cast shows, were among the organization's most distinctive productions. In 1936, the FTP produced a celebrated production of *It Can't Happen Here*, an adaptation of Sinclair Lewis's novel about the election of a fascist as U.S. President and the imposition of dictatorship (Figure 11.10). This play opened simultaneously around the country, and has received attention again in recent years. However, the U.S. Congress, fearing the influence of communism in the nation, shut down the FTP in 1939.

The avant-garde outside of Europe and the United States: Global revolutionary theatres

Many of the avant-garde artistic movements in Latin America and Asia developed alongside the revolutionary, anti-imperialist and post-colonial movements throughout the twentieth century, leading to many different timelines and culturally specific forms. Of course, many forms of theatre outside of Europe and the United States engendered some of the formal innovations of the European avant-garde, such as non-linear storytelling, multiple media and abstract characterization. For example, it has been argued that *Ta'ziyeh* is Iranian avant-garde theatre and that African pre- and post-colonial theatres exhibit these avant-garde techniques, decentering Europe as the birthplace of the avant-garde (Harding and Rouse 2006). Many of the non-European avant-garde and revolutionary movements were in dialogue with, but were not merely imitative of, the European avant-garde.

Figure 11.10
Production Photo of the Work Progress Administration's *It Can't Happen Here* (1935).
Source: Wiki/U.S. National Archives and Records Administration NARA – 195740, https://commons.wikimedia.org/wiki/File:WPA_Federal_Theater_Project_in_New_York-%22It_Can%27t_Happen_Here%22_-_NARA_-_195740.tif

For example, Murayama Tomoyoshi (1901–1977), after visiting Germany and seeing Expressionist art in 1922, came back to Japan and founded the Mavo group, which advocated revolutionary and radical art that was to be experienced, not observed. Murayama's aesthetic philosophy echoed German Expressionism and anticipated Artaud (Eckersall in Harding and Rouse 2006). Murayama was openly socialist and theorized Marxist methods in his essays. He was also a visual artist who designed a production of Kaiser's *From Morn to Midnight* for the Tsujki Little Theatre in 1924. His later experiments included hybrid forms that combined *bunraku* with theatrical aspects of Jarry's *Ubu Roi*. Osanai Kaoru, a proponent of realism in his early career, also experimented with Expressionist forms. Enthralled with the writings of Edward Gordon Craig, and having seen Craig's production of *Hamlet* at the Moscow Art Theatre, Osanai collaborated with designer Kisaku Itō (1899–1967) on a production that combined Expressionist acting with Craig-inspired stylized scenery, a combination that some audiences found confusing. Japan's Expressionist movement occurred in the midst of a cosmopolitan period that included new form of mass consumer culture, not unlike those in Europe and the United States. The Little Theatre's repertoire was eclectic, and like many early avant-garde theatres in Europe, it produced an almost dizzying number of plays, some of which would run in repertoire. These plays included Aestheticist productions such as Osanai's and political productions by communist artists such as designer Kenkichi Yoshida

(1897–1982) and actor Koreya Senda (1904–1994), who attempted, mostly unsuccessfully, to convert *The Merchant of Venice* into a play about class conflict.

These political Japanese artists became more marginalized by the end of the decade, when Emperor Hirohito came into power. For example, in Japan, Marxist *shingeki* (Western-style plays) mentioned in Chapter 10, were adapted to introduce the possibilities of socialism. One of the best was *The Land of Volcanic Ash* (1938), by Kubo Sakae (1900–1958), who was also an important translator of German drama. In Kubo's celebrated play, an agricultural scientist tries to reclaim land polluted by volcanic ash on the island of Hokkaido. The six-hour, two-part play portrays the difficult lives of many social groups in this rural environment and also features the hero's inner conflict over his growing commitment to communism. Due to the play's Marxism and Kubo's communist beliefs, the Japanese government prohibited production of the play and sentenced Kubo to house arrest or jail for much of the war. Until its defeat in the Second World War (1945), imperial Japan closed Marxist *shingeki* theatres, censored all theatrical productions, and even turned performances of traditional *nō* plays to patriotic purposes. Proletarian amateur theatres lived alongside professional companies in this period, supporting socialist values.

In contrast, some Japanese professional theatre artists who embraced Western drama avoided express political content. One of the most significant was Kishida Kunio (1890–1954), also a member of the Tsukiji Little Theatre who studied in France with Jacques Copeau in 1921 and 1922. Like many European poetic modernists, Kishida attempted to evoke humanistic idealism through his plays. His play's apparent lack of political content protected Kishida during the Second World War, when more outspoken (often Marxist) playwrights, actors, and directors who criticized the militarist government were jailed. Kishida advocated for the playwright as the primary theatre artist, whereas traditional Japanese performances were actor centered. In contrast to the stylized, non-realistic (and sometimes incomprehensible) vocal delivery of *nō* or *kabuki*, Kishida insisted,

> The theatre must depend on the words of the play. Surely the theatre will come to demonstrate the essential importance, not of "plays for the eye," but of "plays for the ear." A playwright, more than anything else, must now be a "poet."
>
> (Rimer 1974: 137–8)

As discussed in the last chapter, the emphasis on playwright was common to many early twentieth-century Japanese artists, whose emphasis on poetry overshadowed a commitment to an ideologically consistent political theatre.

In Latin America, avant-garde movements were especially active in Mexico, Argentina, Brazil, Chile, Cuba, and Peru. These movements flourished during the early twentieth century when many European countries imported raw materials from Latin America, including rubber and coffee, and sold these materials back in the form of manufactured goods. This system of exportation incorporated many Latin American countries into the periphery of capitalism. Latin American avant-garde artists first responded by creating a form of modernism that espoused art for art's sake, whose proponents attempted to sever the relationship between art and commerce. The avant-garde movements that followed rejected this aestheticism, while overtly critiquing the violence of capitalism.

As was the case in Europe, these emergent avant-garde movements were transnational, continental, nationalist, and at times, local. Latin American intellectuals were aware of some of the avant-garde movements in Europe, primarily through the published manifestos. For example, the 1909 Futurist Manifesto was translated and published in different forms in Montevideo and Buenos Aires less than a month after it appeared in *Le Figaro*. Nicaraguan poet Ruben Dario (1867–1916) translated it again a month along with a critical commentary on the Futurist movement. Others simply read the French original. Additionally, Latin American artists and intellectuals of means traveled to New York and European capitals. And some European artists (such as Artaud) traveled to major cities in Latin America, particularly Buenos Aires and Mexico City.

Many of the Latin American avant-gardists were political, although their politics did not always programmatically correspond to their artistic programs. In the midst of emerging cultural nationalisms, and state sponsored modernization efforts, Latin American avant-garde movements took on nationalist characteristics in ways that some European artists abjured, but that Italian and Russian Futurists embraced. Russian Communist theorist and revolutionary Leon Trotsky (1879–1940) saw uneven development as crucial to Futurism's success in Russia and Italy. Theatre historian Sarah Townsend reminds us that this uneven development was also a factor in Latin America avant-gardism, perhaps explaining why the Futurist movement was so often embraced in the Americas, even when critiqued or modified. Almost all revolutionary theatres in Latin America were committed to linking art to political practice, effectively embracing the erasure of the boundary between art and life. Latin American artists were not, however, as deeply invested in destroying commercial theatre apparatuses as their European counterparts, given that storied institutions of bourgeois art production did not exist there.

In Mexico, several leftist theatres and avant-garde groups began performing in the capital after the Revolution and the passage of the Constitution of 1917. Enthusiastic Mexican artists and anthropologists collaborated on huge outdoor performances that used music and dance to celebrate the nation's Aztec (Mexica) roots and its new independence from U.S. and European imperialism. Other festivals, such events sponsored by Theatre Murciélago, consciously fused Mexican festive traditions, framed and staged by anthropologists with short pieces inspired by Russian cabaret, which one of the artists had seen in New York.

Some of these artists' "synthetic theatre" gestured to Marinetti's *sintesi*; however, the Mexican short plays were quite different from Marinetti's. The Mexican "synthetic theatre" was often composed of short skits or presentations of indigenous life from all regions of the country. The idea of synthesis in these works included the idea of racial synthesis of indigenous and European roots that was key to the Mexican national project, adding another layer to idea of synthesis. These enactments of racial synthesis were not besotted with technology or speed like their Italian counterparts. In fact, one of the more interesting performance manifestos of the period, *Magnavox 26* (1926) by Xavier Icaza (1892–1969), questions whether the role of radio, which had become a major mass medium, was positive or negative. Written as a play, but likely unperformable, the text features volcanoes with internal speakers that emit speeches representing a variety of different political positions. Yet, it is only the unamplified and live voice of Mexican muralist and nationalist figure Diego Rivera (1886–1957) that stirred the scripted audience of the piece. This is an important critique given the rise of radio dramas during this period.

Figure 11.11

Photo of Salvador Novo (1904–1974).

Source: Album/Alamy Stock Photo.

More influential was the Teatro Ulises, which included some of the most important Mexican playwrights of the era, including Salvador Novo (1904–1974) (Figure 11.11) and Xavier Villaurrutia (1903–1950). Teatro Ulises opened in 1928. There, Villaurrutia and Novo staged European avant-garde plays, including the works of Cocteau and Roger Vildrac, for the first time for Mexican audiences.

In 1933, Juan Bustillo Oro (1904–1989) and Mauricio Magdeleno (1906–1986) founded the Teatro de Ahora to stage political plays with more direct relationships to the audience. Bustillo Oro's stagecraft and dramaturgy were influenced by Piscator's work in Germany. His play *Masses*, for example, put the audience in the midst of political rallies and strikes with film clips and loudspeakers to tell the story of a corrupt revolutionary leader's fall from power. Mexico's avant-garde, like Europe's, was aesthetically diverse and deeply invested in the power of the manifesto; almost all of the groups listed above announced themselves with polemical statements on the purpose of theatre in society. Many artists also made claims in little magazines, linking poetry, performance, political activism, and print culture.

In Argentina, different groups of theatre artists debated the merits of European-inspired political theatre in journal articles and stage productions during the 1930s. One theatre collective in Buenos Aires, the People's Theatre, produced and toured a range of productions to diverse audiences and engaged them in often heated post-performance discussions. This theatre began the rich independent theatre scene still active in Buenos Aires today. The People's Theatre's most renowned dramatist was Roberto Arlt (1900–1942), whose 1930s plays critiqued contemporary fascism, brought to Argentina by Italian expatriates loyal to Benito Mussolini, the dictator of Italy during that decade. In *Saverio el Cruel* (1936), Arlt used the Argentine tradition of *criollo grotesco*, a form of drama that combined content about immigrant life with the formal metatheatricality found in Pirandello's plays. His *Trescientos Millones* (1932) also demonstrates this form of metatheatricality. Arlt and his colleagues formed the political avant-garde; in contrast, the La Florida group, whose members included Argentina's most famous modern writer José Luis Borges (1899–1986), who was primarily aestheticist, demonstrate the divide in avant-garde practices.

Chile's avant-garde theatre scene was less extensive; however, Vicente Huidobro (1893–1948) plays and manifestos made important contributions. He played with Futurist and Dadaist forms in his poetry before writing a play, *En la Luna* (1934), that dealt with the period's politics through metatheatrical means. His travels (made possible by his extensive wealth) made him a true internationalist despite his concern with domestic politics. He wrote many of his works in French.

Meanwhile, Brazil's avant-garde revolution had a more auspicious start. The Brazilian avant-garde began during Week of Modern Art in February 1922 at the Theatro Municipal in Sao Paolo, Brazil's rapidly developing second city. The Week of Modern Art was planned to coincide with and to critique the country's centenary. The artists who participated distinguished themselves from both the "arts for art's sake" poets and Brazil's nationalist and commercial opera industry. Gomes's indigenist *Il Guarany* (1870), discussed in Chapter 8, was a frequent target of derision for these new artists, especially given its starring role in Brazilian cultural life. Although the Week of Modern Art was originally to be titled a Week of Futurist Art, Brazilian Futurism was often invoked in name only. And, despite the drama of the event which drew an unruly crowd, there was little theatre in this event or in the movement.

Two important exceptions are works by the two modernist Andrades: Oswald de Andrade (1890–1954) and Mário de Andrade (1893–1945) that greatly affected the development of the avant-garde in Brazil. Mário de Andrade's main contributions were his manifestos and subsequent attempts to create a mixed-race identity for Brazilians through his novels and opera adaptations. He used his role as a producer at the Theatro Municipal to do this work. Oswald de Andrade, who joined the Communist Party after the revolution of 1930, had a more lasting impact on the theatre through his plays and his 1928 "Cannibalist Manifesto." This manifesto was an anti-capitalist polemic that argued for the cannibalism of the West by native people. The valorization of the indigenous cannibal – an admittedly colonialist and racist figure – was an ironic comment on figures like the title character of *Il Guarany*. Andrade's manifesto also made the links between colonialism and capitalism explicit, providing an important frame for understanding the aesthetics of Brazilian literature and theatre for the rest of the century.

Oswald de Andrade's influence is all the more remarkable considering that his plays were never staged in his lifetime. *Man and a Horse* (1934) was censored because of its political ideology. *The Candle King* (1934), which tears economic imperialism apart limb by limb in what Sarah Townsend calls "a Brazilian spin on *Ubu Roi*" (Townsend and Taylor 2008: 146) was not produced in Brazil until the late 1960s. Like many Latin American avant-gardists, Oswald de Andrade's influences included commercial and avant-garde forms (Russian Constructivist theatre and film), which he eclectically combined to criticize the racial and class-based aspects of capitalism. Overall, then, Latin American avant-garde theatre exemplifies the transnational mobilization of politics and print culture, combining domestic and European forms. Rather than being simply derivative, these movements were transcultural and revolutionary.

Revolutionary theatre's global character is also exemplified by Japanese director Seki Sano (1905–1966), who had studied with Meyerhold and went on to become an innovator of Latin American theatre. Sano became interested in theatre after the Japanese imposition of martial law and the violent murder of many Koreans, leftists and members of non-Japanese ethnic groups. He and his fellow students began to study theatre, including European plays, in part by attending the Tsukiji Little Theatre. Sano became a Marxist soon after, eventually staging a successful production of Soviet playwright Anatoly Lunacharsky (1875–1933)s *Don Quixote Liberated* in 1926.

Sano was forced into exile because of his Marxist views. He left Japan in 1930, eventually settling in Mexico in 1939 after being expelled from the Soviet Union and rejected from U.S. residency. In Mexico, Sano had a profound influence on generations of theatre artists (including Alicia Martinez Medrano, discussed in Chapter 14). In his first seven years there, he used theatre to propagate antifascist rhetoric and to support labor causes. He staged a variety of contemporary political plays, including a 1941 production of Clifford Odets's *Waiting for Lefty*. Sano trained his actors with methods that combined Stanislavsky's and Meyerhold's teachings. His overt political theatre activity continued until 1947, after which he began to participate in more mainstream and commercial theatre. This work included directing the Mexican debut of *A Streetcar Named Desire* (1948) and several films. Despite his commercial turn, he inspired many popular theatres in Latin America, including Colombia's Teatro la Candelaria. He opened an acting school in Bogotá and stayed until he was again exiled because of suspected Communist affiliation. His contribution to acting training continues to be recognized to the present day.

Theatres of anti-imperialism, 1910–1950

In addition to its influence in the West, the Russian Revolution also speeded revolts against imperial domination. By 1914, the imperial powers – chiefly England, France, the Netherlands, Germany, the United States, and Japan – had occupied crucial islands in the Caribbean and Pacific, solidified their control in most of South Asia, and extracted sizeable regions of the Ottoman and Chinese empires and Africa. Although rebellions against foreign capitalists had occurred before 1914, nationalistic movements in India, China, and elsewhere gained more leverage against the imperial powers during and shortly after the Great War, when the combatants in Europe needed their help. The war in Europe, however, emboldened Japanese imperialists, who saw the decline of European power in China and the Pacific as a chance to expand their hegemony. The triumph of the Communists in Russia inspired nationalists in the colonized countries, in part because they too identified imperialism with capitalism. If workers in one country had destroyed capitalism, nationalists might destroy imperialism in their own.

Many educated members of colonized countries also worked against imperialism after 1914 because they saw widening differences in standards of living, democratic rights, and literacy between the populations of their own countries and those in Japan and the West. In per capita income alone, the imperial powers surpassed the rest by 2:1 in 1880. By 1914, the ratio was 3:1 and it rose to 5:1 by 1950. While many European and Euro-Americans enjoyed some individual and political rights, slavery and various forms of serfdom persisted in many parts of the colonized world. Literacy increased rapidly and widely after 1850 in Europe, Japan, and North America, but remained a privilege of the social and economic elite in most areas of Africa, Asia, and Latin America. Although the imperial powers generally believed they were civilizing and improving their subjects, the realities of empire bred orientalism, racism, exploitation, and degradation.

The link between theatre and revolution in China began much earlier, in the late Qing period (1644–1911). The Qing dynasty was ruled by the Manchus, a non-Han ethnic group from northeast China; therefore, many late-Qing revolutions bore a racial significance. Theatre and performative activities helped push China toward modernity. Despite the overall change of dress code under the Manchu rule, in theatre, the Han costume tradition was kept and attending theatrical performance was to reinforce the belief of a Han China. Outside of theatre, both the Taiping Rebellion in the south (1851–1864) and the Boxer Rebellion in the north (1900) – the largest late-Qing revolutions which affected lives of millions, their leaders theatricalized their revolutions. The Boxer Rebellion's focus was anti-Western. Their use of stagecraft, spiritual performance, and magical acts – a form of revolutionary theatricality – was seen as the best way to fight Western imperialism. The Taiping Rebellion promoted anti-Qing rhetoric and reinterpretation of certain Western ideology (including Christianity). Li Wenmao, a Cantonese opera actor specializing in martial roles, led a troupe of actors and theatre craftsmen to join in the rebellion; he later established his own kingdom, organizing his imperial court based on theatre conventions, transforming theatrical acts into daily court rituals. Ironically, he banned theatrical performance in his kingdom because his court solely controlled the theatricality. His uprising, widely popular though short-lived, led to censorship of Cantonese Opera from 1855 through 1871. The ban of Cantonese opera sent actors across the ocean to perform in San Francisco's Chinatown (discussed in Chapters 9 and 10).

The development of Chinese theatre in the first half of the twentieth century followed the political fortunes of the country. As in Japan, Western realist theatre had been introduced before the Great War and began to flourish in the 1920s with the founding of modern theatres, an increase in translations and performances of Western plays, the establishment of new training centers for actors, and greatly increasing the casting of women. Many of these innovations were based in Shanghai, where Chinese adaptations of Japanese *shimpa* were also staged. This form of early twentieth-century theatre, called *wenmingxi* (civilization dramas), was culturally hybrid, commercial, nationalist and often political. These dramas were credited with supporting the 1911 revolution. *Wenmingxi* sometimes refers to Western-styled theatre in general, such as spoken drama. After the revolution, these plays often reflected Chinese fears of national demise in the face of renewed Japanese imperial machinations to warn against complicity or apathy. Other plays called out the need to topple or kill corrupt leaders. Ultimately, however, many of the companies that produced these dramas folded by 1920 as its actors left theatre to join the film industry.

As noted in Chapter 9, *jingju* (Beijing opera) remained the dominant genre throughout China, and became the nexus (although not the sole artistic form) for the development of national drama and drama research as part of the Republic's Chinese nationalism project; *jingju* also became the ambassador of China in Western countries. Simultaneously, several Communist troupes emerged in the 1930s to protest Japanese imperialism; their "living newspapers," modeled on the Soviet example, appealed to thousands in the countryside and in cities unoccupied by the Japanese. Both Chinese Nationalists and Communists used theatre to rally patriotic support against the Japanese.

Within Communist-controlled areas of the country, Chinese artists developed a new form of theatre called *yanggeju* [yahng guh jyu], based on *yangge*, a traditional folk dance during Spring Festival, and fused with folk songs and dramatization. Featuring 20 to 30 dancers accompanied by drums, flute, and other instruments, *yanggeju* formed part of the basis for the emergence of a new national drama called *geju* [guh jyu], or song drama. *Geju* was designed as the Chinese equivalent of Western opera, based on Chinese music, folk songs and musical elements from traditional theatre. Originally developed in the 1920s, it flourished after the Communist victory in 1949. While *yangge* had its rustic origin, *geju* was generally created by the elites as part of the nationalist project. *Geju* typically involved disputes among villagers over abusive social practices and village ethics, performed in a question-and-response pattern. Hugely popular, *The White-Haired Girl* (1945) is considered a milestone, inspiring later *geju* glorifying communist heroism. *The White-Hair Girl* was later made into film, *jingju*, and ballet (one of the original eight model dramas). By the 1960s, other types of state-sponsored performances featured thousands of professional and amateur performers and integrated the music and dance traditions of several minority groups within China. The performances both embodied and propagated the ideology of strength through collective effort put forward by Mao Zedong (1893–1976), the revolutionary leader and political dictator of China until 1976. More than a thousand performers staged *The East Is Red* in 1964, for example, a nationally famous spectacle.

In India, by the nineteenth century, there was a rich theatre and performance culture, with plays staged in a variety of regional forms and in many languages, in addition to Western-style spoken drama. The introduction of European forms in India inspired two closely related theatrical movements that continued into the twentieth century. The first was social drama, which criticized the inequalities of India's traditional socio-economic system and argued for liberal reform. By the late 1800s, some British and Indian writers were attacking traditions that relegated most Indians to low caste status, kept many peasants working in compulsory positions on huge landed estates, and trapped numerous young women in arranged marriages. Reformers in southern India began mounting protest plays in 1929 with the production of *From the Kitchen to the Stage*, by V.T. Bhattathiripad (1896–1982), which opposed polygamy and the marriage of high-caste old men to young girls. A later play, *Rental Arrears*, focused on the eviction of a tenant farmer from the land and its effects on his family. Some social dramas drew thousands of spectators in open-air, rural theatres during the 1930s and 1940s. Though aimed primarily at social and economic arrangements, these plays occasionally attacked the Raj (as British imperial rule in India was termed) for supporting traditional customs.

The second type, anti-colonial drama, directly resisted English culture and British authority. An 1872 production of *Indigo Mirror* (*Nil Darpan*), by Kolkata playwright Dinabandhu Mitra (1830–1873) began this movement; *Indigo Mirror* focused on the plight of peasant workers oppressed by British indigo planters. The play stirred a controversy and created open hostility between planters and the missionaries, the latter of whom helped publish the play. Although initially an obscure play by an unknown playwright, *Indigo Mirror* quickly entered the global stage. It also spawned a surge in nationalist drama, including *The Tea Planter's Mirror* (*Chakar Darpan*) (1875), which exposed the exploitation in the tea industry, and *The Mirror of Baroda* (*Gaekwar Darpan*), which criticized the British annexation of Baroda in 1875. The establishment of the Great National Theatre in Calcutta happened in the same year. (Calcutta is the former colonial name of Kolkata.) Eventually, this theatre toured productions in other parts of the subcontinent, meeting its founders' goals of drumming up nationalist sentiment. Given its political potential, theatre was subject to censorship and control by the Dramatic Performances Control Act of 1876, enacted by the Supreme Legislative Council in Calcutta; later, controls on print inhibited anti-colonial and nationalist Indian playwrights from many regions. Many playwrights came to lean on allegory to make their critiques, such as Krishnaji Prabhakar Khadilkar (1872–1948), who wrote the famous Marathi anti-colonial classic *Kichaka Vadha* (1909), which advocated for radical methods of the

Indian National Congress, while masquerading as an adaptation of the *Mahabharata*. These plays were popular in Kolkata starting in the late nineteenth century and became very popular in North India by the 1920s, where they also performed allegorical nationalism often accompanied by elaborate stagecraft. These plays drew in middle-class audiences, reforming the reputation of theatre that had been dismissed as deviant by British officials.

The British banned more openly anti-imperialist plays, such as *Sirajuddaula* by Bengali playwright Girish Chandra Ghosh (1844–1912) in 1905, for inciting Indian nationalism. Anti-colonialism intensified in India after the Great War and the Russian Revolution, and reached a peak during the Second World War. In 1943, the Communist Party of India founded the Indian People's Theatre Association (IPTA), which established regional centers throughout the country to produce anti-colonial plays. IPTA was inspired both by indigenous traditions, such as the *jatra* of Bengal, *tamasha* of Maharastra, and the *burrakatha* of Andhra Pradesh and by many of the global theatres of revolution discussed in this chapter, Soviet theatre, and the United States's WPA troupe. The IPTA often toured. To reach diverse audiences, they performed in many regional languages, incorporating details about the villages they performed in for diverse audiences; they also often performed outdoors, which necessitated flexible stagecraft. IPTA adapted the 1926 Soviet play *Roar China!* in 1942, but its best-known production was Bijon Bhattacharya's (1917–1978) *New Harvest* (*Nabanna*) in 1944, which incited anger against British failures to help the starving during a Bengali famine that killed more than 3 million people. The IPTA fragmented in 1947 following India and Pakistan's independence from Britain. Given their "affiliation with popular drama" the IPTA "has remained largely unacknowledged in the dominant discourse of Indian cultural history" (Bhatia 2004: 78).

There were also anticolonial productions of Shakespeare, whose political commentary belied the idea of the Bard's humanist universality. An 1880 adaptation of *The Merchant of Venice* titled *Dependable Friend* (*Durlabh Bandhu*) by Bharatendhu Harishchandra critiqued the practices of the colonial court and its attempts to expand British power. This form of anti-colonial adaptation transmuted into postcolonial critique during the 1960s and 1970s. In addition, Marathi theatre artists began to stage realist European classics in the 1930s, perhaps as a reaction to the hegemony of film. Although Marathi playwrights chose to blunt the critiques of gender roles in their adaptations of Ibsen and Bjornson, their producers made the radical choice to cast female actors, including the famous Jyotsna Keshav Bhole (1914–2001), in lead roles, such as in the 1933 debut of *A Gauntlet* in Mumbai.

Internationally, the most famous playwright and theatre artist to emerge in India in the 1910–1950 period was Rabindranath Tagore (1861–1941). Tagore was acclaimed for his lyrical plays, mystical poetry, paintings, and songs and for his insightful short stories and essays on subjects ranging from educational reform to nationalism, which he denounced in favor of universal humanism. Tagore's poetry and prose won him the Nobel Prize in Literature in 1913; he was the first non-European so awarded. Although Tagore denounced the British Raj, he was best known as a social and educational reformer in Bengal, in northeastern India. Several of his many plays, including *Sacrifice* (1890) and *The Post Office* (1912), achieved Indian and international successes. In *Sacrifice*, Tagore used historical events to pit a devout Maharaja against a fanatical head priest in order to denounce cruel and superstitious rites. The more mystical *Post Office* focuses on a sick boy who falls asleep (and probably dies), according to Tagore, to gain spiritual release from "the world of hoarded wealth and certi-fied creeds" (Tagore 1961:123–4). Contemporary Indian theatre artists continue to venerate Tagore for his imaginative fusion of traditional forms and modern ideas.

Despite the rich innovations of the Indian playwrights, certain constants remained; one of these was the circumscribed role for women within many plays, especially anticolonial dramas appealing to social justice. Often, the cruelty of the British oppressors included the rape of Indian female characters, who committed suicide due to these violent attacks. These tropes were politically effective in showing the cruelty of colonial rule and were persuasive to the growing colonial Indian audiences, including educated Indian nationalists who bris-tled under colonial rule. While the virtue of these Indian female characters countered British propaganda that staged Indian people as uncivilized, the politics of respectability for female subjects limited women's roles within a patriarchal frame. It also allowed censors to ban plays in which women were brutalized as obscene. Given that women had begun acting on stage in Bengal in the 1870s (female performers had largely been pushed from the stage under British colonialism), this policy was all the more pointed.

Indian actresses, like actresses in other global sites and in other historical periods, were considered morally dubious and faced social censure. Some of the first Bengali actresses were prostitutes; and when they were not, actresses were conflated with prostitutes in the public imagination. In this early period, however, Indian actresses mostly played divine characters, which was seen as more acceptable. As suggested above, however, by the 1930s, some actresses had begun to star in realis-tic dramas playing middle class characters in other areas of the country. While the history of actresses in India is fraught, it is worth noting that famous actresses par-ticipated in celebrity culture in ways that paralleled their U.S. and European coun-terparts. The premiere example is Noti Binodini (1863–1941), a woman who be-gan her life as a prostitute but went on to star in over 80 roles in the Bengali theatre, became an entrepreneur, and wrote an au-tobiography in 1913 (Figure 11.12). She is still an important figure about whom many contemporary plays and movies have been made.

In summary, China and India had rich traditions of revolutionary, anticolonial drama that combined indigenous and non-indigenous forms of drama. Participants in theatrical production were sometimes activists and fighters and at other times intellectuals shielded from combat. None-theless, each and every participant had a role to play in these struggles.

Figure 11.12
Image of Binodini Dasi.
Source: Historic Collection/Alamy Stock Photo.

CASE STUDY: Global Brecht

Tobin Nellhaus

Many figures in twentieth-century theatre have been internationally influential: Stanislavsky, Artaud, and playwright Samuel Beckett (discussed in Chapter 12) spring to mind. But few can be considered truly *global*: both absorbing the world into themselves and transforming theatre across the globe, from Finland to South Africa, Japan to Argentina, New Delhi to New York. Such was Bertolt Brecht, and his global impact began shortly before his death.

To understand "global Brecht," one must start with Brecht himself. As a young man Brecht found an affinity to Taoism, and somewhat later he became interested in *nō*. Most of his plays are set outside Germany, including England, India, China, the Caucasus, Finland, Italy, and three in the United States – but often they are exuberantly fantastical locations, in no sense realistic, or else generalizable in a way that allowed later adaptations to easily localize. For instance, his free adaptations of Chinese themes in plays such as *Caucasian Chalk Circle* and *The Good Person of Szechwan* had thin connections to their sources. Even so, the plays have frequently been localized into productions such as *The Central Avenue Chalk Circle* in Los Angeles and *Bhalomanusher Pala* in Bengal.

In his late twenties Brecht began reading Marx and committed himself to communism. In Marx's view, capitalism is an international system based on exploitation, and its overthrow requires the workers of the world to unite. Marx also argued that slavery in the United States was integral to Western capitalism's development, and he vigorously supported the rebellions by the enslaved. In the early twentieth century, Marxists began theorizing imperialism as a stage of capitalism.

Inspired by Marxism, Brecht began developing approaches to performance aiming to politicize the audience. An important step came through Brecht's encounter in Moscow with the classical Chinese actor Mei Lanfang in 1935. Although Brecht misunderstood the nature of Mei's performance, it was crucial to Brecht's theorization, and his essay on it introduced his concept of the *Verfremdungseffekt*. Brecht's intercultural contact with Mei produced one of the most vital ideas of twentieth-century artistic practice, resonating not just in theatre but also in movies, novels, even painting.

When the Nazis gained power in Germany in 1933, Brecht was forced into exile, becoming a nomadic refugee fleeing from country to country for 15 years – years that carved globalism into his very life. After the war he landed in 1949 in what had become East Berlin, where he founded the Berliner Ensemble and spent his last years.

The Berliner Ensemble finally enabled Brecht to direct his plays largely on his own terms (for example, in his production of *Mother Courage*; see Figures 11.8 and 11.9), and his work became not just internationally famous, but globally transformative. Before and after Brecht's death the Berliner Ensemble attracted visitors from abroad and toured to other European countries. Theatre practitioners from as far away as India, China, Egypt and Latin America saw his productions and brought his approach home with them. Where Brecht's work couldn't be attended in person, his impact came via his plays and even more through the English translations of his theoretical writings published in 1964, sometimes retranslated into the local language.

However, when one considers Brecht's work as a whole, one finds that there are many Brechts, each with his own potential impact upon other theatre practitioners. There's Brecht the playwright, whose epic theatre employs tactics such as an episodic structure, songs, and a focus on characters' decisions in order to encourage the audience to respond more critically than emotionally. There's Brecht the director, who introduced the stylistic techniques of the *Verfremdungseffekt*, the social *gestus*, and a version of Piscator's non-naturalistic staging that incorporated a strong dose of popular performance. There's Brecht the leftist, aiming to use theatre to critique class relations and seek political change. And there's Brecht the philosopher, who adopted a particular theory of society and history that created an understanding of realism in theatre very different from the Naturalist approach. For some people, Brechtian theatre means all of these together; for others, it means only two or three of them, or even just one. And none of these Brechts was static, for over the years his methods, arguments and perspectives adjusted.

Brecht's impact differed between the Western versus the non-Western worlds. The Berliner Ensemble's tours in the 1950s energized directors and playwrights throughout Europe. Major directors such as Ariane Mnouchkine in France and Giorgio Strehler in Italy became advocates of Brecht's work. The company's performances in England transfigured British playwriting and directing virtually overnight, and numerous British theatre practitioners are indebted to Brecht, such as Edward Bond, Joan Littlewood, John McGrath, and Peter Brook. His impact remains visible in the work of British playwrights such as Caryl Churchill and Mark Ravenhill; in the United States, companies like the Wooster Group owe much to Brecht, Tony Kushner names Brecht as one of his influences, and some of Suzan-Lori Parks's plays are considered Brechtian. However, after his death Brecht the playwright largely became a "classic" — standard fare in literature and drama courses, and mostly produced by colleges and occasionally mainstream theatres. At the latter, his plays are often politically defanged; audiences are encouraged to empathize with Mother Courage and Galileo, and *The Threepenny Opera* became an opportunity for fun rather than critique. Brechtian staging has been absorbed throughout Western theatre as an aesthetic without political teeth.

Outside the West, Brecht's impact tended to be more gradual, not least because of the need for translations, but it was more profound. Although in many countries Brecht's work eventually wound up in the same position as in the West, for decades he offered approaches that opened new and sometimes vital paths for non-Western theatre: Brecht became truly global. For instance, in 1968, more than half of the countries producing Brecht's plays were outside the West (Youssef 1979: 657). Nor did the interest turn merely academic: in 1986, when the International Brecht Society met in Hong Kong under the theme, "Brecht in Asia and Africa," attendees included 125 scholars from around the world – and 176 actors, directors, and stage designers (Weber 1989: 30).

What appealed to non-Western theatre practitioners naturally varied from country to country, and even person to person, but there were several basic trends. First and foremost was Brecht's extraordinary indigenization: often his performance methods – the use of song, stylized makeup and *gestus*, lack of a fourth wall, episodes rather than closely knit plots, and so forth – felt remarkably like the local forms of folk performance. People could quip, only half-jokingly, "Wasn't Brecht an African writer?" (Richards 1989). Behind this tendency, however, lay the specific political and cultural context of reception.

One of the countries most deeply impacted by his work is India. An Indian theatre scholar visited the Berliner Ensemble before Brecht's death, and more went afterward. His greatest impact was in Bengal, which (as we saw) already had a tradition of political theatre. Brecht's theories drew more focus than his plays or even his politics, partly due to his interest in Eastern performance. Theatre practitioners observed that many of Brecht's techniques were commonplace in India's traditional folk performances, making it easy to adapt Brecht's plays into those forms to make them accessible to local audiences. The point was to concentrate on the plays' political relevance, even if at the expense of Brecht's methods; but by some lights the absorption into traditional forms could turn his plays into ordinary entertainment. Others preferred to translate his plays as written and stage them according to his own techniques, sometimes imitating the Berliner Ensemble's productions based on their documentation. However, according to some, the emphasis on Brecht's formal innovations tended to depoliticize the plays, ignoring the goal of the techniques and turning his work into another version of what he might call "culinary theater." Occasionally his plays were so depoliticized that they were performed like mainstream productions. Thus there were two basic and antipathetic interpretations of Brechtian theatre in India: one that emphasized his politics at the expense of his form and methods, assimilating them into the local traditional theatre; the other adopting a formalist approach at the expense of his politics. Despite this conflict, Brecht's work was taught at the premier theatre schools throughout the country, and productions of his plays were second only to Shakespeare. Slowly, new plays were written that incorporated Brecht's ideas.

A similar pattern of Brecht's theories having more impact than his plays or practices and the development of disputes over what truly constitutes Brechtian theatre – especially between politics and formalism – was to a greater or lesser extent replicated elsewhere. The problems and opportunities were particularly complicated in Asian countries because Brecht had been inspired by various traditional East Asian performance forms and modeled some of his work on them, which encouraged the indigenization of his plays. But these issues were always affected by the local context, not least the political situation, as well as familiarity with European theatre.

We can see this especially clearly in Brecht's reception in China. Brecht was fascinated by classical Chinese acting (as noted above), but misunderstood it; before his death China began to return the favor, but misunderstood him. The Chinese reception of Brecht was primarily influenced by the assimilation of Brecht's interest in classical

Chinese performance into modern Chinese performance, and by the seesawing policies of the authoritarian Chinese government. The Communist Party of China swung
between allowing study and performance of Brecht, then condemning Brecht as a
bourgeois Westerner during the Cultural Revolution and making even study of him
dangerous, and later reviving him as his Marxism redeemed him. Most scholars and
directors emphasized his absorption of classical Chinese performance, literature, and
philosophy, without concern over his misinterpretations; moreover, the aspects of classical Chinese acting that Brecht found estranging were completely ordinary to Chinese audiences. Thus although some of these thinkers recognized differences between
classical Chinese theatre and Brecht's work, others depicted his theatre as "already
Chinese," and even that classical Chinese theatre was already Brechtian. At first Chinese directors focused on the *Verfremdungseffekt*, understanding it only formalistically,
so that introducing its staging techniques to Chinese audiences had little political
sting; later productions cloaked their political character to dodge the authorities' ire.
Nonetheless, occasionally a Brecht production could be highly provocative. Brecht
attained premier authority, becoming a required part of theatre education; but his political and social goals were seldom pursued and muffled when they were, so that from
later perspectives, "the reception of Brecht in China was marked by depoliticization"
(Feng 2020: 203).

Brecht's impact in Japan took a different course. The rebellions against the
Stanislavskian realism dominating *shingeki* (the "modern theater") followed three main
streams: existentialist, Absurdist, and Brechtian. As political protests intensified during
the 1960s, so too did interest in Brecht, especially his theories; it didn't hurt that
because he didn't conform to socialist realism, the staid Japanese Communist Party
considered him a heretic. Brecht's plays affected the newer Japanese playwrights. But
despite Brecht's use of *nō* as a model in some of his plays, there was little interest in
assimilating him, and when the *angura* ("underground" avant-garde) theatres arose as
another form of opposition to mainstream theatre, most preferred to turn away from
European forms altogether. The major exception was Black Tent 68/71, later renamed
Black Tent Theater, which has continued to use Brechtian approaches to stage production to this day.

Latin American theatre practitioners were among the Berliner Ensemble's audiences when Brecht was still alive. For varying reasons theatre-makers increasingly
desired some form of political theatre, and the Cuban Revolution's overthrow of
its dictator in 1959 became an inspiration for many leftists. Cuba embraced Brecht;
his plays began to be performed across South America continent in the mid-1960s,
and his theories grabbed practitioners' interest. Initially playwrights and performers
modeled their work on Brecht's theories and practices, and he played an important
role in the development of the Nuevo Teatro Popular (see Chapter 13). But it eventually became apparent that the problems roiling Latin American were different from
Brecht's Europe and theatre practitioners needed to follow not the letter of his work,
but its goal of permeating performance with politics. Many experimented with new

approaches to producing political theatre, especially collective creation leading to a script, and audience involvement that sometimes operated without a script at all – a performance culture that led to Boal's "theater of the oppressed" and long-lived theatre companies such as Yuyachkani – in keeping with Brecht's desire for an actively thinking audience, albeit not the way he likely imagined it. As Santiago Garcia, the director of the esteemed director of the Colombian Teatro La Candelaria put it, "our practice with Brecht reveals that we can be most Brechtian by not reproducing his plays in Latin America, but by using Brecht's principles to create our own Latin American dramaturgy" (qtd. in Baycroft 1986: 43). Thus even though Brecht's plays were seldom performed and his ideas fell into the background, his spirit imbued much Latin American theatre.

Africa was almost completely colonized between 1884 and 1914, mainly by Great Britain and France – a grotesque era of imperialist expansion. During the Second World War, decolonization began, and continued in fits and starts over the decades until by 1977 it was virtually complete. Colonization had wrought often severe economic, political, social and cultural wreckage and drastic differences in development, from which many countries are still recovering. Hence for most African writers and artists, the culture of the colonial powers left a bitter taste, including its theatre, with a prominent exception: as one person put it, "If European theater at all, then Brecht" (qtd. in Gugelberger 1987: 372). Part of Brecht's appeal lay in the political and didactic character of his work, which spoke to the issues wracking the continent; in addition, directorially Brecht aimed for theatrical performance bearing affinities with indigenous performance, fostering some of the assimilation we saw elsewhere, though not to India's extent. But, as in Latin America, for some African theatre practitioners the class consciousness of Brecht's work did not align with their political realities, such as the infliction of violent and kleptocratic state power upon all classes. Moreover, while audiences in South Africa (the most "Western" country on the continent) generally interpret Brecht productions more or less the way audiences in Western countries do, Brian Crow (2009) finds that elsewhere in sub-Saharan Africa, despite the outward similarities between Brechtian theatre and indigenous performance there is a major cultural difference: the audiences' responses are complicated by a tendency to assess characters and actions according to a fixed moral system rather than viewing them as the product of social relationships. As a result, they can arrive at highly un-Brechtian interpretations of his plays.

Brecht's global impact is complex but with several distinct tendencies, themselves having historical and regional dimensions. In Europe, Brecht has been influential primarily as a director, initially through practitioners' attendance at the Berliner Ensemble's performances, later through their encounters with his theories. These formal elements (the *Verfremdungseffekt*, anti-naturalistic staging and so forth) have not always stayed connected to Brecht the leftist: they were generally stripped of their politics and absorbed into mainstream theatre, which, in turn, fostered depoliticizing his plays or skipping actual production. However, we can add here that his politicized directorial approach has also been applied to other arts (especially filmmaking) and theatre with other philosophical orientations (including feminism, queer theory, and as we will see shortly, postcolonialism).

In the non-Western world, in contrast, his theatre often had powerful similarities to indigenous performance, which could lead Brecht's plays to be largely indigenized stylistically, sometimes in the process again being depoliticized. But where Brecht was understood as a leftist in theatre, non-Western theatre practitioners often found that his philosophical focus on economic class didn't fit local politics, leading to fewer productions of his plays as written, but inspiring adaptations and the invention of new approaches to political theatre. Thus Brecht has met his greatest success outside the West: as performance scholar Diana Taylor puts it, "Brecht was a common source of inspiration to dramatists from many colonized and marginalized societies, responsible, indirectly, for introducing them to each other" (2000: 183).

Although today Brecht's plays may not be staged as often as they once were, they synthesize his many sides, which each achieved a life of its own. His approaches to theatre have had lasting impact on productions, performance companies, and aesthetic theory. No other twentieth-century theatre practitioner has affected theatre in so many different ways, so deeply, upon so many other arts, and so globally.

Key references

Baycroft, B. (1986) "Brecht in Latin America: The Ideology and Aesthetics of the New Theater," *Communications from the International Brecht Society* 15(2): 43–7.

Crow, B. (2009) "African Brecht," *Research in African Literatures* 40(2): 190–207.

Dharwadker, A. (1995) "John Gay, Bertolt Brecht, and Postcolonial Antinationalisms," *Modern Drama* 38(1): 4–21. https://doi.org/10.1353/mdr.1995.0044.

Feng, W. (2020) *Intercultural Aesthetics in Traditional Chinese Theatre from 1978 to the Present*, Cham: Palgrave Macmillan.

Gugelberger, G.M. (1987) "'When Evil-Doing Comes Like Falling Rain': Brecht, Alioum Fantouré, Ngugi Wa Thiong'o," *Comparative Literature Studies* 24(4): 370–86.

Richards, S. (1989) "Wasn't Brecht an African Writer? Parallels with Contemporary Nigerian Drama," in J. Fuegi (ed.) *Brecht in Asia and Africa, The Brecht Yearbook/Das Brecht-Jahrbuch* 14, Hong Kong: University of Hong Kong, 168–83. https://search.library.wisc.edu/digital/AVQ2V5BUHHEAXF8H.

Taylor, D. (2000) "Brecht and Latin America's 'Theatre of Revolution,'" in C. Martin and H. Bial (eds.) *Brecht Sourcebook*, London: Routledge, 173–84.

Weber, C. (1989) "Brecht Is at Home in Asia: A Report on the IBS Symposium in Hong Kong, December 1986," in J. Fuegi (ed.) *Brecht in Asia and Africa, The Brecht Yearbook/Das Brecht-Jahrbuch* 14, Hong Kong: University of Hong Kong, 30–43.

Youssef, M. (1979) "The Reception of Bertholt [sic] Brecht in Egypt," in E. Kushner, R. Struc, and M.V. Dimic (eds.) *Actes du VIIe Congrès de l'Association Internationale de Littérature Comparée/Proceedings of the 7th Congress of the International Comparative Literature Association*, Stuttgart: Bieber, 2: 657–61.

Theatre experimentation between the wars

There were theatre artists who, rather than consciously organizing themselves into exclusive groups, publishing manifestos, and adhering to a specific style, decided to work within the conventional arrangements of the commercial theatre and print culture to meet their artistic goals. These artists aimed to separate the imaginations of their spectators from the mundane realities of the stage by focusing audience attention on voice and language, and transport them to a unified aesthetic world. They also employed metatheatricality, which (as discussed in Chapter 5) often frames the fiction of the theatrical illusion within another fiction to create a play-within-a-play. By calling attention to the artificiality of the stage, metatheatricality interrupts the flow of a performance and temporarily undercuts its representational effects. Spectators frequently reminded of the fictive nature of a play cannot immerse themselves in a Wagnerian *Gesamtkunstwerk* or any other representational performance.

Luigi Pirandello (1867–1936) did not directly attack the representational link between actors and characters, but rather subverted the believability of the conventional theatre through metatheatricality. Although he had written a few plays during 20 years of publishing poetry, novels, and short stories, Pirandello turned more frequently to drama during the Great War, when Italy began to slide toward social and political disorder. The post-war period added wrenching economic problems and, like many Italians, Pirandello sought order in the midst of this apparent chaos. Attempting to dramatize this conflict between the reality of art and the illusory qualities of lived experience, Pirandello soon crystallized this insight in the play that would make him famous, *Six Characters in Search of an Author* (1921). *Six Characters* succeeded in Milan in 1922, then Paris, and eventually throughout the world.

Six Characters contrasts the lives of actors – Pirandello's symbols of people with no firm identity – with those of fictitious characters whose identity has been written for them. Abandoned by their author, however, the six characters cannot escape from their melodramatic conflicts, and they seek a resolution to their ongoing drama from the actors. The result is a play within a play, in which the actors put aside the production they have been rehearsing and attempt to enact the roles and relationships of the six characters before them. By showing how the actors utterly fail, Pirandello critiques the general failure of the stage to represent ideal reality. A larger point, though, is that authors writing literature can approach the enduring truths of idealized character types, but the attempt at truth on the stage will always be compromised by the imperfect and mortal bodies of the performers. Only an author can help the six characters, implies Pirandello; the stage will always fail them. To emphasize the unchanging truths of art, Pirandello instructed the actors playing the six characters to wear masks. Although the play seems to throw up its hands about the nature of truth and illusion, Pirandello does not endorse relativism; art is true and life is illusory.

Pirandello's search for order through art led him to explore the themes and techniques of *Six Characters* in several subsequent plays. These included *Naked* (1922), *Each in His Own Way* (1924), *Tonight We Improvise* (1930), and *Henry IV* (1922), in which Pirandello worked through the problem of time and art touched on in *Six Characters*, through the situation of a man pretending to be insane. These plays, too, relied on metatheatricality to interrupt and undermine theatrical representation, challenging spectators to question their own illusions. Unfortunately, Pirandello joined the Fascist Party in 1924 and remained a Fascist until his death in 1936.

Other modernists turned to Christianity, to gain relief from the fragmentations of everyday life. Like Pirandello and Yeats (discussed in Chapter 10), the Christian modernists looked back to the spirituality of the Symbolists and, before them, to nineteenth-century Romanticism. French diplomat, poet, and playwright Paul Claudel celebrated the mysteries and saving grace of Catholicism and the Catholic Church in several plays over a long career. His most famous work, *The Satin Slipper*, a seven-hour epic written between 1919 and 1924, is set in the Spanish Golden Age. In formal, elevated language, Claudel's stately pageant explores the religious fervor that drove the Spanish conquest of the New World and the need to sacrifice earthly passions for the sake of divine salvation. *The Satin Slipper* received an influential production at the Comédie Française in 1943, which led to a Claudel revival in the post-war period.

Although U.S. novelist and dramatist Thornton Wilder (1897–1975) was less insistently religious than Claudel, his faith in a benign American Protestant God is evident in many of his plays. In *Our Town* (1938), a folksy, God-like Stage Manager calls forth actors who demonstrate that people are destined to repeat universal patterns designed by "the mind of God" without knowing that they are doing so. *Our Town* illustrated Wilder's belief that the theatre was uniquely suited, as he said, "to raise the exhibited individual action into the realm of idea and type and universal" (Bigsby 1982: 262). Wilder's *Skin of Our Teeth* (1942) was more formally innovative, utilizing direct address, dispensing with linear narrative, and combining contemporary situations with biblical events, and human and non-human characters, combining philosophy with formal innovation. The relevance of the play is underscored by the well-received 2022 revival, directed by Lileana Blain-Cruz, on the 125th anniversary of Wilder's birth.

Theatricalizing modernism

After the Great War, pictorial Shakespeare, such as the kind advocated by Herbert Beerbohm Tree as discussed in Chapter 10, seemed cumbersome and unbelievable, mostly because of the movies. A succession of directors at London's Old Vic Theatre incorporated several modernist innovations that moved Shakespearean performance away from the clutter of realism. Chief among them was Tyrone Guthrie (1900–1971), artistic director of the Old Vic from 1937 to 1945. Guthrie deployed Appia-like settings of ramps and platforms, mostly realist props and costumes, rapid movement and speech by the actors, and quick lighting changes to lend Shakespearean production the speedier rhythms and heightened contrasts of the cinema (Figure 11.13).

Meanwhile, actors John Gielgud (1904–2000), Sybil Thorndike (1882–1976), Laurence Olivier (1907–1989), and others developed playing styles that emphasized the psychology of their characters rather than their realist situations. Olivier's success in filming several Shakespearean plays – notably his *Henry V* (1944) and *Richard III* (1955) – confirmed the popularity of a more cinematic acting style for Shakespeare on the stage. For spectators attuned to the perceived effects of the movies, Guthrie's and Olivier's modernist staging and acting rejuvenated Shakespearean production in the 1930s and 1940s. For these artists, Shakespeare, rightly staged, could elevate spectators to appreciate and enjoy universal meanings.

The fragmentations of the modern world also troubled many theatrical modernists in France. In the 1930s and 1940s, several directors and playwrights drew on their heritage

Figure 11.13

The Old Vic production of Shakespeare's *The Tempest*, 1934, with Charles Laughton as Prospero and Elsa Lanchester as Ariel.

Source: © V&A Images, Victoria and Albert Museum.

of Racinean tragedy and the comedy of Molière to fashion a distinctive theatre of lyric abstraction, which emphasized the lyricism of the French language in often minimalist and allegorical settings. Even before then, the work of Jacques Copeau (1879–1949) turned the French stage toward modernism. Like the Shakespearean modernists, Copeau, a critic turned producer-director, eliminated realist details to emphasize the work of his actors in the French classics. At his small theatre, the Vieux-Colombier, Copeau produced several plays before 1914 with minimal realism for audiences of only 400 people (Figure 11.14). He resumed productions at the Vieux-Colombier for a short time after the war and later directed at the Comédie Française from 1936 until 1940. Copeau and his successors enlivened the character types and generalized themes of the French classics with a fresh, lyrical energy. He applied this style to Shakespearean productions and modern plays. Directors who modeled their artistry on Copeau's – a group that included Louis Jouvet (1887–1951) and Charles Dullin (1885–1949) – emphasized adherence to the language and rhythms of the script and strove to invest their stylized costumes and minimalist scenery with symbolic significance. After the Second World War, two of Dullin's students, directors Jean-Louis Barrault (1910– 1994) and Jean Vilar (1912–1971), continued to refine and extend this tradition.

French playwrights influenced by lyric abstraction tended to write allegories in which the general problems of humanity predominated over historical or psychological concerns.

Figure 11.14

Stage of the *Vieux Colombier*, designed by Jacques Copeau, as adapted for Shakespeare's *Twelfth Night*.

Source: Redrawn from *Theatre Arts Magazine*, 1924.

The first major playwright to work in this style was Jean Giraudoux (1882–1944), who collaborated closely with Jouvet to stage his plays. These included *The Trojan War Shall Not Take Place* (1935) and *The Madwoman of Chaillot* (1945), an amusing attack on the excesses of French capitalism. Similarly, Jean Anouilh (1910–1987) wrote light comedies with fairy-tale-like resolutions, such as *Thieves' Carnival* (1938), and dark allegories, such as *Antigone*, composed in 1943 during the German occupation of France.

Institutionalizing the avant-garde

A few directors involved in first-generation avant-garde groups, such as Antoine and Meyerhold, worked in both avant-garde and mainstream theatres. Others, like Stanislavsky, who produced several Symbolist as well as Naturalist works at the Moscow Art Theatre, temporarily embraced one or another of the avant-garde movements. Although most avant-garde artists had declared their independence from conventional theatre, this did not stop those directors committed to mainstream theatres from borrowing from the avant-garde to shape their own productions. These successful directors and their institutions helped to popularize first-generation avant-garde styles with a wider audience.

German director Max Reinhardt was one of the most influential mediators between the early avant-garde movements and the bourgeoisie during the first third of the twentieth century. Believing that no single style suited all plays and theatrical occasions, Reinhardt directed Naturalist, Symbolist, and Expressionist plays in Germany and Austria often to wide public acclaim. Reinhardt honed his Expressionist style during and immediately after the Great War by directing several of Strindberg's post-inferno plays. He incorporated the innovations of Appia, Craig, and others in lighting and design and sought out new training techniques for his actors. Reinhardt was able to embrace such eclecticism because he worked closely with his collaborators while insisting on final artistic control. He also maintained a significant degree of stage realism in his productions; his actors generally used realistic props and costumes and typically did not acknowledge the presence of the audience. Reinhardt's production of Frank Wedekind's *Spring's Awakening* in 1906, for example, featured frilly transparent curtains (of the kind that proper bourgeoisie used to dress their windows) over much of the stage opening and created innovative lighting effects, but kept his actors behind the proscenium frame (Figure 11.15). After the Great War, Reinhardt staged many of his productions in churches and other non-theatre settings, such as public squares. Reinhardt's success exerted an immense influence in German-speaking theatre between 1910 and 1925.

Several other pre-1930 directors followed Reinhardt's lead, adapting relevant avant-garde techniques to their mainstream productions. As director of the Odéon in Paris, Firmin

Figure 11.15
Karl Walzer's rendering of his design for a scene from Reinhardt's production of Wedekind's *Spring's Awakening*, 1906. Wedekind's play about adolescent sexuality and the repressiveness of German culture created a scandal when it was published.

Source: Max Reinhardt Archive, Binghamton University Libraries' Special Collections and University Archives Binghamton University.

Gémier (1869–1933), an early proponent of bringing theatre to all of the French people through tent productions, produced and directed an eclectic mix of conventional and avant-garde styles in the 1920s. In Germany, Leopold Jessner (1878–1945), director of the Berlin State Theatre from 1919 until 1933, incorporated several Expressionist design principles into many of his productions. These often featured Appia-inspired flights of stairs, non-realist lighting, and symbolic costuming. In the United States, the Theatre Guild, which enjoyed a broad subscription base of spectators, brought a few avant-garde productions to audiences from 1919 into the 1930s. Through the influence of these directors and their institutions, plus the adoption of similar innovative practices elsewhere, the early avant-garde gradually altered the expectations of mainstream audiences in the United States and Europe.

Summary
The revolutionary decades between 1910 and 1950 spawned immense political and theatrical changes. The Great War and the Russian, Chinese, and Mexican revolutions shattered the old order and generated demands for radical political changes that played out in the theatres of Meyerhold, Brecht, and other revolutionary theatre artists. These movements reshaped the theatres of many European and Latin American countries, and generated anti-imperialist theatres in India and China. Filmic fragmentation – the recognition that the movies could take apart and reassemble reality in innumerable ways – ensured that most practitioners of the new political theatre would not return to the kinds of representational theatre offered by realism. Nonetheless, as we will see in the next chapter, the comforts of bourgeois realism on the stage enjoyed a resurgence after the Second World War.

★

CHAPTER 12

The aftermath of the Second World War and theatres of the Cold War, 1940–1970

Daphne P. Lei

Contributors: Carol Fisher Sorgenfrei and Bruce McConachie

As we saw in Chapters 10 and 11, the shock of the Great War and the widespread use of radio and film deeply affected society and theatre. In this and the following chapter, we will consider similarly profound responses to the Second World War and the subsequent Cold War.

The origins of the Second World War lay in the end of the Great War. Germany had been forced to accept concessions and blame. In response, the fascist Nazi Party formed, attaining power in 1933; it then strived to dominate Europe. Germany's 1939 invasion of Poland instigated the Second World War in Europe. Meanwhile, Japan sought control over Asia, and its invasion of Manchuria (China) in 1931 foreshadowed the war in China (1937–1945). The League of Nations (a predecessor of the United Nations) lacked the force to counter these aggressions. Japan's further attacks and occupation of Hong Kong, Burma, Malaysia, and regions of the Pacific Basin launched "the Pacific War." The Japanese attack on Pearl Harbor in Hawaii in December 1941 forced the United States to join the conflict; the U.S. government also responded with deporting and relocating many Japanese Americans into internment camps (1942–1945).

Only about two decades separated the 1918 Armistice ending the Great War and the outbreak of the Second World War. Between them lay the worldwide Great Depression. Often soldiers who had fought and survived the Great War as 20-year-olds were called back into service in their 40s – sometimes along with their own sons. By 1945, when the Second World War was ended by atomic bombs that devastated the Japanese cities of Hiroshima and Nagasaki, soldiers had spent many years in battle; civilians had suffered decades of destruction and deprivation; and around 11 million people had been murdered by the Nazis. Refugees from the war-ravaged lands sought new lives, adopting new languages and cultures. In much of Europe, Asia, the Pacific, and Africa – where the brutal battles of the Second World War had been fought – cities were wrecked and food remained scarce. Rebuilding ruined

DOI: 10.4324/9781003185185-17

lives and ruined cities was costly, time-consuming, and emotionally difficult. All these survivors (soldiers and civilians, the victors and the defeated) desired a world of peace.

Because the United States had escaped such physical devastation, it emerged from the war far richer than the rest of the world. This fact, combined with the desire to solidify its military and political position as the main opponent of communism, meant that the United States became the central purveyor of money and goods for rebuilding the postwar world.

With the end of the Second World War, hostility between two superpowers – the United States and the Soviet Union, former allies who had been victorious over the Nazis – hardened into an ideological divide between "free market" capitalism and authoritarian communism. This conflict, which lasted over 40 years, was named the Cold War because it never broke out into direct combat; nevertheless, nuclear warfare that would lead to mutually assured destruction remained a constant threat. Other nations were pressured to align themselves with the Soviet Union or the United States. Although a few like India remained neutral, most succumbed through military might, economic power, coups, and/or diplomatic leverage. The potential of China's rise as a major world power widened the scope of the Cold War. All three superpowers engaged in various "proxy wars," injecting their influence and sometimes their troops into regional and civil conflicts in countries such as Korea and Vietnam. In other words, the war was not exactly "cold" in those countries who were at the frontlines of the conflicts of the superpowers. By the 1960s, the Cold War lens of "us versus them" became a common way to view domestic and international conflicts.

Nevertheless, anti-imperialist sentiment and nationalist political action (often including violent revolutions) grew in the colonized areas. As colonies became independent countries, the old empires began to crumble. Although decolonization had been encouraged by the League of Nations following the Great War, little actually took place until after the Second World War. When the Great War began in 1914, there were more than 120 colonized territories in the world. Africa changed the most rapidly. As noted in Chapter 9, the Berlin Conference of 1894–1895 had divided Africa into numerous European colonies. By 1905, the only non-colonized areas in Africa were Liberia (founded by African Americans and Afro-Caribbeans) and Ethiopia (which had successfully resisted Italian colonization). By the start of the Second World War, a total of only five African nations were independent. However, between 1951 and 1960, 25 African nations gained independence. From 1961 to 1980, they were joined by 26 more, with another three following by 1993. By 2023, the United Nations listed only 17 non-self-governing territories and only one is in Africa.

Conflict seemed both ubiquitous and unending in the process of decolonization. Not only were many decolonizing nations embroiled in rebellion and war as they fought for independence, but after winning independence, internal fighting for political power often ensued. As each proxy war was fought, another seemed always around the corner. Thus, the initial feeling of relief and peace at the end of the Second World War soon shifted to concerns over ongoing warfare and nuclear threat throughout the world.

Conflict also grew within the wealthy Western countries. With their common enemy, the Nazis, defeated, the victorious countries began to question their own value systems. Economic growth nourished desires for greater democracy, which were blocked by the conservative values of anti-communism; nevertheless, many countries began striving for political, legal, social, cultural, and even economic equality.

Television became affordable in wealthy Western countries in the 1950s but did not become available worldwide till the 1960s. However, it brought not only entertainment into people's living rooms, but also vivid images of distressing world events, many of them the direct result of Cold War politics. In the mid-1960s, students and some disadvantaged populations in many parts of the world rebelled against the status quo, demanding an end to war, poverty, racism, sexism, colonialism, and unreasonable university policies. The dramatic changes and upheavals across the world led to a global crisis often marked by the year 1968.

In this chapter, we first consider the devastating impact of the Second World War on Europe and Japan, noting how a new postwar understanding of reality altered theatrical styles. We then turn to theatre during the Cold War. The United States was relatively unscathed and became obsessed with communism and the Cold War. Most other countries, in contrast, were still recovering from the impact of the war: they were deeply disturbed by the meaning of the war, attempting to extract themselves from imperialist power, or occupied themselves in building a national narrative on either side of the Cold War divide; both the postwar trauma and Cold War tension were daily reality. As a result, theatre in the United States sharply differed from elsewhere. While film and radio continued to influence approaches to theatre and drama, the biggest advancement of media was probably the popularization of television, which created the sense of interconnectivity and closeness around the world. Finally, we take a first look at the alternative theatres that developed in the United States just before the turning point of 1968 (discussed in the next chapter).

The impact of the Second World War on the victors and the defeated

In Europe and Asia, where the war had devastated many cities and created massive civilian death and suffering, theatre artists turned increasingly to new philosophical or political perspectives in order to make sense of the world. For many, prewar modernism, revolutionary theatre, or the first-generation avant-gardes could not adequately express contemporary reality. New approaches appeared, including variations of Brecht's political theatre, revisions of the surrealist ideas of Artaud, a revised modernism, various alternative forms of theatre, and a "Theatre of the Absurd."

Beckett and the end of high modernism

One of the key theatrical and literary voices in the early postwar period was Samuel Beckett (1906–1989). Although born in Ireland, Beckett lived in Paris for most of his life and wrote many of his plays in French. He felt that using his second language forced him to constantly be aware of the precise meaning of every word. Beckett's stage plays kept film's insistent realism at bay by a poetic minimalism that tightly controlled what his actors could do and what his audience experienced as reality. At the same time, he experimented with film, radio, and tape recording.

Beckett's plays may be seen as transitional because they contain aspects of both prewar modernism and the sense of futility and lack of meaning that characterized many postwar plays. They also have elements that were later adapted by postmodernism. However, Beckett's modernism differs from that of his predecessors. Modernists from Ibsen to Eliot had built their theatrical world on the premise that there was another reality, idealist or religious, that transcended

Figure 12.1

Patrick Stewart (Vladimir, left) and Ian McKellen (Estragon, right) in Samuel Beckett's *Waiting for Godot*, directed by Sean Mathias, at the Theatre Royal Haymarket, London, 2009.

Source: Donald Cooper/Alamy Stock Photo.

Figure 12.2

Teresita Garcia Suro as Nell (left) and Alan Mandell as Nagg (right) in *Endgame*, written and directed by Samuel Beckett, produced by San Quentin Drama Workshop at the Young Vic Theatre, London, 1980.

Source: Donald Cooper/Alamy Stock Photo.

the modern, material world. Beckett's characters can find no relief in a spiritual realm from the mundane tedium of their very material lives; how to pass the time in everyday existence becomes an obsession for many of them. Time is a fundamental concern in the action of two of Beckett's early plays, *Waiting for Godot* (1952) and *Endgame* (1957) (Figures 12.1 and 12.2). The main "story" of *Waiting for Godot* is about two tramps waiting for a mysterious man, Godot, who never shows up. It is the act of waiting, instead of something or someone that one is waiting for that constitutes the significance of the play. These lines summarize the "action" (or non-action) of the play well: "Nothing happens, nobody comes, nobody goes, it's awful" (Beckett 1954: 41). Act 1 and Act 2 both end with the very similar dialogue: "Well, shall we go?/Yes, let's go. (*They do not move*)" (Beckett 1954: 35); and "Well? Shall we go? / Yes, let's go. (*They do not move*)" (Beckett 1954: 60).

Concerning the theme of time and *Waiting for Godot*, Martin Esslin, the author of *Theatre of the Absurd*, writes, "it is in the act of waiting that we experience the flow of *time* in its purest, most evident form" (Esslin 1980: 50). *Waiting for Godot* becomes a symbol for enduring the course of time in difficult circumstances. In 1957, Herbert Blau directed the San Francisco Actors' Workshop to perform the play at the San Quentin State Prison, to an audience of 1,400 male convicts. The audience members, who were literally "doing time," felt the immense impact of the play. During the COVID-19 global pandemic shutdown in 2020, this play was also used as a symbol for the inability of escaping the cruelty of time.

Beckett's theatrical ideas and practices extend and complicate techniques typical of **high modernism**, such as his use of metatheatricality. In *Endgame*, for example, when one character asks another what keeps him "here," a reference to the room that the two characters occupy, the other answers, "The dialogue" (Beckett 1958: 58); "here" has changed from a represented place in the drama to suggest the real place, the stage. Beckett's theatrical minimalism and precisely crafted action rarely allow spectators to forget that they are in a theatre. In *Ohio Impromptu* (1981), Beckett places two men, dressed identically, sitting across from one another at a table with their heads bowed, in a precise mirror image of each other. There is nothing else on stage to suggest a theatrical illusion; the two are surrounded by darkness. They sit nearly motionless for the 15 minutes of the play, while one reads the "sad tale" of the other's life from a book. At the end, Beckett's stage directions specify that the two "[s]imultaneously … lower their right hands to table, raise their heads and look at each other. Unblinking. Expressionless. Ten seconds. Fade out" (Beckett 1984: 288). Beckett gives us no illusion to get lost in. This performance style – like that of *Breath* (1969), a stage play with no actors, no dialogue, and no visual action – is nearly as far from an enveloping Wagnerian *Gesamtkunstwerk* as the theatre can take its spectators. In terms of philosophy, Beckett's theatre is a clear statement of the disillusionment and sense of helplessness felt by many people in the postwar era. Beckett emphasizes the concrete "here" and offers no religious or spiritual alternatives to the apparent meaninglessness of existence.

Like earlier high modernists, Beckett attacked the mimetic basis of acting. He severely restricted the freedom that actors usually have to interpret and embody their characters. As Beckett director Alan Schneider once noted, "Actors feel like impersonal or even disembodied puppets of his [Beckett's] will" (Puchner 2002: 159), a remark that recalls Craig's and Yeats's interest in substituting large puppets for live actors. Beckett placed actors in trash barrels (*Endgame*), encased them up to their necks in dirt (*Happy Days*, 1961), and entombed them in urns (*Play*, 1963). This practice not only restricts the actors' movements, but visually expresses the idea of the futility of action. Sometimes he reduced the actors to mouthpieces for his words, as in *Not I* (1972), where all of the words spoken during the minimal action of the play emanate from a female character named Mouth. The actor playing Mouth must stand on a platform behind a painted black wall or curtain with a small hole in it and place her head against a padded frame behind the hole so that only her lips can be seen by spectators as she speaks. In rehearsing *Not I*, the actor Billie Whitelaw (1932–2014) reported extreme "sensory deprivation": "I felt I had no body; I could not relate to where I was; … I was becoming very dizzy and felt like an astronaut tumbling into space" (Worthen 1992: 138). Critic W. B. Worthen compares the rigors of Beckettian acting to physical torture. Beckett insisted that other directors follow his printed scripts precisely – including all stage directions – and he actually sued the American Repertory Theatre over their 1984 production of *Endgame* because he objected to casting women in male roles and to setting the action in a realistic underground train station that was being used as a shelter following a nuclear war, rather than the abstract time and place that the printed script specified. Beckett's position was that as long as he was alive, actors and directors should respect his scripts' words and stage directions. This point is crystalized in *Act Without Words I* (1956) and *Act Without Words II* (1956), stage plays totally lacking dialogue. The scripts consist entirely of stage directions that the actors and technicians must follow as precisely as choreography for a ballet.

Such power over actors and directors corresponds to Beckett's worldview, in which unknowable forces and seemingly arbitrary events control our lives. In *Waiting for Godot*, for example, strangers come in the black of night, kicking and beating the two tramps for no reason; a character who once had sight is inexplicably struck blind; and day after day, Godot keeps sending word that he is delayed.

Beckett was also intrigued by new modes of communication. He realized that electronic media could control what the audience – and the characters – experience. In *Krapp's Last Tape* (1958), Krapp listens to his recorded voice from the past, almost as though it is a stranger's voice lacking meaning, and repeatedly fast-forwards just before a major revelation that the audience never hears. Beckett wrote several plays for radio, including *All That Fall* (for the BBC, 1956) and *Nacht und Träume* (for German radio, 1982). He also wrote *Film* (1965), a silent movie starring Buster Keaton. While silent films or radio plays – media that deprive the audience/listeners of sound or vision – were popular earlier, Beckett's use of these forms instead of theatre of all senses confront the audience/listeners the meaning of theatre. He wrote several works for television, including *Eh, Joe* (1965) and *Quad I+II* (1981).

THINKING THROUGH THEATRE HISTORIES: EXISTENTIALISM AND THE "THEATRE OF THE ABSURD"

Historians in every field frequently debate the validity and application of commonly used terminology and periodization. For example, the usefulness and specific meanings of terms such as "the Renaissance," "the modern period," "the Elizabethan age" or even "the Sixties" are contested. Many historians use terms such as "the long eighteenth century" (1688–1815 or 1660–1830, in reference to Britain), or the "long nineteenth century" (1789–1914); the twentieth century is both called "the short twentieth century" (1914–1991) and "the long twentieth century" (1870–2010) in terms of capitalism and state formation. Because change is usually gradual and proceeds at uneven paces, some artists and thinkers are said to be "ahead of their time" or "behind the times." Different countries reach "modernity" at different times and different speeds. The old definitions of style and genre can become overly generalized and need to be challenged in a new era. One of the historian's problems is how to use commonly accepted but often misunderstood or deceptive terms. "Absurdism" offers an example.

"Absurdism" is a term that is used to depict some of the sentiment and aesthetics of the tumultuous twentieth century. It is frequently associated with existentialist philosophy. Søren Kierkegaard (1813–1855) is usually said to be the first existentialist philosopher, but Jean-Paul Sartre (1905–1980) and Albert Camus (1913–1960) are often viewed as its main exponents, although Camus denied being an existentialist.

Existentialism came into its own during and after the devastation and horrors of the Second World War, and was in many ways a response to that war. According to this philosophy, "existence precedes essence." Each individual is responsible for their own actions. One's own consciousness dictates who an individual is – one's choices define one's concrete "existence." There is no eternal "essence" outside the individual – no identity based on concepts such as the soul, truth, beauty, God, politics, race, gender, and so on. To become oneself, one must act "authentically," that is, according to a deep understanding of one's personal needs and desires, not according to some outwardly imposed code (such as religious or civil law). However, authentic action is not simply self-interest. Rather, it demands that each person respects the existential needs and realities of others, implying a kind of innate or natural morality.

Sartre also wrote plays to make his philosophy accessible to more people. In *No Exit* (1944), he uses a realistic dramatic style and structure to demonstrate the terrifying results of living an inauthentic life. In this play, the dead confront neither God nor the devil, but instead must live eternally with others in whose eyes they are defined. In the play's most famous line, they realize that "Hell is other people" and there is indeed "no exit" from their tormented existence.

Such ideas conflict with many traditional worldviews. For example, Plato and his followers insisted that only abstract ideas exist, and that what we see and experience are merely imperfect reflections of the true reality. Most religions and many political ideologies share such ideas, offering hope of a better future in which justice prevails, with the good being rewarded and the evil punished.

In contrast, existentialism suggests that the universe is random and lacks purpose, as demonstrated by the horrors of both the Great War and Second World War. Only human actions and how we interpret those actions define and create meaning. Consequently, the cruelties and injustices of life appear incomprehensible, arbitrary, and meaningless, in other words, absurd.

Albert Camus, who was born to a poor family in French Algeria, passionately advocated Algerian independence and an end to poverty. Like Sartre and Beckett, he was active in the French Resistance (an underground movement in the Second World War that fought against the Nazi Occupation of France). His philosophical essay "The Myth of Sisyphus" (1942) is often cited as the first clear depiction of "Absurdism." He explains:

> A world that can be explained by reasoning, however faulty, is a familiar world. But in a universe that is suddenly deprived of illusions and of light, man feels a stranger. His is an irremediable exile, because he is deprived of memories of a lost homeland as much as he lacks the hope of a promised land to come. This divorce between man and his life, the actor and his setting, truly constitutes the feeling of Absurdity.
>
> (Qtd. in Esslin, 1980: 23)

In this essay, Camus compares modern life to the Greek myth of Sisyphus, who was condemned to push the same rock eternally up a hill, despite the fact that each time he almost reaches his goal, the rock rolls back to the bottom of the hill. The randomness, meaninglessness, and futility of modern life describes our absurd existence.

The term "**Theatre of the Absurd**" was introduced in 1961 by the Hungarian-British critic Martin Esslin (1918–2002), whose book of that title noted certain philosophical and stylistic similarities in diverse postwar plays. Esslin points out the original meaning of absurd is "out of harmony" in a musical context; he cites Eugène Ionesco, one of the best known "Absurdist playwrights" to further define the term for "Theatre of the Absurd": "Absurd is that which is devoid of purpose … . Cut off from his religious, metaphysical, and transcendental roots, man is lost; all his actions become senseless, absurd, useless" (qtd. in Esslin 1980: 23). "Theatre of the Absurd" was not intentionally created as a new genre or a conscious and coherent movement by an artist with a manifesto. Rather, each artist, working independently (and often unaware of the others), happened to develop plays with shared characteristics. They were responding in the only way they could to an incomprehensible reality, the sense of absurdity.

Unlike existentialism, "Theatre of the Absurd" is generally unconcerned with individual choice and authenticity; however, it shares with existentialism a focus on the meaninglessness of action, the cruelty or arbitrariness of life, and an emphasis on the here-and-now. Playwrights usually considered "Absurdist" include Samuel Beckett (generally considered to be the most significant writer), Eugène Ionesco (1909–1994), Harold Pinter (1930–2008; early works only), Sławomir Mrożek (1930–2013), Abe Kōbō (1924–1993; also known as Kōbō Abe – Abe is his family name), Edward Albee (1928–2016; early works only), and many others. In addition to meaninglessness, arbitrariness, and inaction, their plays are often characterized by apparently nonsensical dialogue coupled with black comedy or an uncanny feeling of menace.

Despite the fact that these playwrights never defined themselves as "Absurdists," and that some, such as Albee, actually refused the label, various critics and historians have found the concept useful. For example, in his influential *Shakespeare Our Contemporary* (1964), Jan Kott (1914–2001) read Shakespeare from the perspectives of existentialism, Absurdism, and his own experiences as a Pole in war-ravaged Europe. Others have suggested that, because the dialogue and action are so often illogical or dreamlike, "Absurdist" plays are descended from Surrealism. Later playwrights living under authoritarianism sometimes used Absurdist style to express the senselessness of life under such regime without being overtly political. The Nobel Laureate Gao Xingjian's *Bus Stop* (discussed in the next chapter) is a good example.

Transforming modernism in Europe

Ever since the first generation of modernism, modernists in the theatre had struggled against the constraints of photographic realism. As a moving "picture," film continued photography's ties to the literal, material world. Because the high modernists had privileged the representational validity of print, they had also regarded film with suspicion. Nevertheless, film had been transforming the expectations of theatre audiences and artists since the 1920s; many postwar directors who grew up watching the movies would employ filmic techniques to create new models of modernist theatre in the West during the 1940–1970 era.

One such director in England is Peter Hall (1930–2017). Although well known for directing Shakespeare, in 1955 Hall mounted the first English-language production of Beckett's *Waiting for Godot* at his Arts Theatre in London. Even after becoming artistic director of the new Royal Shakespeare Company (previously called the Shakespeare Memorial Theatre) in 1961, he continued to alternate contemporary and classical productions. By the mid-1960s, Hall had developed a distinctive style for all of his projects, a heightened realism that mixed close attention to the language of the play, a generally spare but distinctive use of design elements, and carefully crafted, often forceful movement. It was a modernist style that worked as well for the plays of Harold Pinter as for those of William Shakespeare.

At first, Pinter's darkly comic plays mystified but intrigued the British public with their strange oppressors, panic-stricken artists (*The Birthday Party*, 1958), and garrulous drifters (*The Caretaker*, 1960). When Hall directed a Royal Shakespeare cast in Pinter's *The Homecoming* in 1965, some British theatregoers and critics were outraged by the dramatist's send-up of conventional family values, but the play ran for 18 months. Initial appearances of the characters to the contrary, *The Homecoming* gradually reveals a working-class family as a group of animalistic thugs and pimps and shows the home-comers of the title – a seemingly abstracted academic and his attractive middle-class wife from America – to be as heartless and bestial as the rest of the family (Figure 12.3). The success of the U.S. production in 1967 (with most of the same cast) confirmed the play as a modernist classic.

The rhythms of Pinter's dialogue, including its many pauses, reveal an ear attuned to the bleak comedy of Beckett's early plays and also show the influence of radio, for which Pinter had written several one-acts. Like many of his plays, *The Homecoming* explores the dynamics of dominance, exploitation, and victimization, themes that Pinter first dramatized in personal and psychological terms and which he would later treat in more directly political ways.

The Polish playwright Sławomir Mrożek began as a newspaper humor writer and cartoonist. His early one-acts set up ironic mod-

Figure 12.3

Playwright Harold Pinter acting on stage with actress Jane Lowe in his own play *The Homecoming* at Palace Theatre, Watford, UK, 1969.

Source: Tony Prime/ANL/Shutterstock.

els of political power and undercut them through their own logic. *The Police* (1958), for example, depicts a perfect but radically dysfunctional police state. In *Out at Sea* (1961), three starving characters on a raft establish a socialist republic, then proceed to define justice and freedom in such a way that two of them are able to eat the third, who agrees with the logic of his sacrifice. Mrożek fled Poland in 1963, but continued to write plays that barely skirted censorship and delighted Polish audiences. Critics Martin Esslin and Jan Kott placed Mrożek in the tradition of Polish political Surrealist dramatists Stanislaw Ignacy Witkiewicz (1885–1939) and Witold Gombrowicz (1904–1969). Like Pinter and Beckett, Mrożek was introduced to London audiences by Peter Hall. Mrożek's most important play, *Tango* (1965), was produced by Hall's Royal Shakespeare Company in 1966 at the Aldwych Theatre in London. *Tango* is a black comedy that satirically deploys the tired form of domestic family comedy to examine the failure to stop Europe's slide into totalitarianism. In Mrożek's parable family, each of the three generations represents a different political view, from the 1920s to the 1960s. Perhaps the most foolish are the grandparents, who prattle on in the language of the Dadaists and Surrealists while raw power takes over the household. The irony is that the victory of the idealistic but conservative Hamlet-like son over his bohemian family results in stifling totalitarianism. *Tango* was one of the first works directed by Trevor Nunn (1940–), who later served as artistic director of both the Royal Shakespeare Company (1968–1986) and the National Theatre (1996–2003) in the United Kingdom, and as stage director of numerous plays, including international mega-musical hits such as *Cats* (1981) and *Les Misérables* (1985). The translation of *Tango* by Nicholas Bethell was further polished by the then-unknown playwright Tom Stoppard (1937–), who gained fame the following year with the National Theatre production of his *Rosencrantz and Guildenstern are Dead* (which, like *Tango*, eerily reflects and reconsiders *Hamlet*).

Other playwrights from this era – especially those from Eastern Europe – also wrote politically inflected works. For example, Eugène Ionesco's *Rhinoceros* (1959) depicts a society where all the citizens, except one man, blindly rush to transform into wild beasts. The memory of wartime horror was not far from the surface in many major European plays of this period.

Postwar theatre in a defeated Germany

The advent of Nazism in 1933 closed left-wing and avant-garde theatres in Germany, silencing or exiling many of Germany's best theatre artists. After the war, the defeated nation was divided into two. The DDR (Deutsche Demokratische Republik, also called the German Democratic Republic or East Germany) became a Communist nation aligned with the Soviet Bloc, while the BRD (Bundesrepublik Deutschland, also called the Federal Republic of Germany or West Germany) was a capitalist nation aligned with Western Europe and the United States. The former capital city, Berlin, which was fully within the borders of East Germany, was itself divided into East Berlin (a part of East Germany) and West Berlin (which, despite its location, was legally a part of West Germany). Germany would not be reunited until 1990. In East and West Germany after 1945, local governments quickly rebuilt their playhouses as a matter of civic pride, but a national German theatre emerged more slowly.

Until the mid-1950s, the Berliner Ensemble (in East Berlin) was the only German theatre with an international reputation. Bertolt Brecht and his wife, actress Helene Weigel (1900–1971), established the Ensemble in 1949. Even though the Berliner Ensemble was located in East Berlin, many socialist artists in both East and West Germany looked to the Ensemble's productions as models for their work. In addition to Brecht's plays, the Berliner Ensemble regularly produced the dramas of Shakespeare and the German classics. Brecht's death in 1956 and the assumption of the Ensemble's leadership by Helene Weigel did not diminish the influence of Brechtian theatre (and may even have enhanced it). It became the most influential socialist theatre of the postwar era. (See Chapter 11 and its case study for further discussion of Brecht's theories, practice, and global impact.)

In the 1960s, a new generation of German theatre artists also looked to the documentary tradition of the German stage to examine the Holocaust and the Nazi past. Several socialist playwrights, including Rolf Hochhuth (1931–2020) and Peter Weiss (1916–1982), used documentary devices to expose the extent to which thousands of ordinary Germans, not just the Nazis in command, had been responsible for the extermination of millions of Jews, Slavs, Romani, homosexuals, and other minorities. A firestorm of controversy swirled around Hochhuth's play, *The Deputy*, when it opened in 1963. The play drew on written evidence to suggest that many German Catholics and even the Pope himself had condoned the slaughter of European Jews. In *The Investigation* (1965), Peter Weiss used dialogue taken directly from official transcripts of the investigations into the Auschwitz extermination camp. In their lack of spectacle, both *The Deputy* and *The Investigation* suggest that emotion-laden images of the Holocaust, whether photographs or films, would detract from the necessity of probing Germany's guilty past. The assumption was that understanding an event of such magnitude and preventing a recurrence of the attitudes that fostered it requires close attention to the logic and morality of its perpetrators. Other German documentary plays of the 1960s used similar minimalist methods to focus audience attention on British war crimes, European imperialism, the development of the hydrogen bomb in the United States, and the U.S. war in Vietnam. This socialist "theatre of fact," as it was called, generally shunned complex technology and spectacle to rely on the theatre's oldest tools, the actor's craft, and the moral imagination of the audience.

German-language playwrights outside of Germany also adopted some of Brecht's politics and methods. For example, the Swiss playwright Friedrich Dürrenmatt (1921–1990) combined Brechtian techniques with other styles to critique both totalitarianism and capitalism in his best-known work, the macabre black comedy *The Visit* (1956).

Although some of the techniques of the "theatre of fact" departed from the general aesthetic approach of the Berliner Ensemble, Brechtian and documentary German theatre shared the same general moral and political point of view in the 1960s. In East Germany, the work of playwright Heiner Müller (1929–1995) and director Peter Palitzsch (1918–2004) (who began with the Ensemble and later moved to West Germany) derived from, but went beyond, Brecht. Müller's later works, such as *Hamletmachine* (1977), have been crucial in defining postmodernism (considered in Chapter 13).

Japanese theatrical responses to defeat in the Second World War

Like much of Europe, some areas and infrastructure in Japan were in ruins by the end of the war. Japan surrendered only after Hiroshima and Nagasaki were destroyed by atomic bombs. The Japanese and the world gradually learned that these new, incomprehensibly powerful weapons could not only kill and even obliterate all living beings near the blast's epicenter, but that nuclear fallout could contaminate the environment, cause cancer in survivors, and create genetic mutations in the unborn for generations to come. The Japanese people would also learn about the brutal war crimes inflicted by their own soldiers and military leaders on enemy combatants and civilians.

One way to respond to such unspeakable horrors of the war is to abandon words completely. Turning to the body, some postwar Japanese choreographers created **butoh** [boo-toh] (also romanized as *butō*), a non-verbal performance genre that rejects both traditional Japanese and Western aesthetic concepts. Originally called *ankoku butoh* "dance of darkness"), the first public performance took place in 1959. The creators of this movement offered divergent approaches. Hijikata Tatsumi (1928–1986) choreographed and performed intentionally crude, contorted movements that derived from his childhood memories of poverty in rural, northeastern Japan. In contrast, Ōno Kazuo (1906–2010) created gentle, nostalgic, often mystical works that emphasized the feminine. Many variations followed. Among the later *butoh* performers are the duo Eiko & Koma (Eiko Otake, 1952–, and Takashi Koma Otake, 1948–). *Butoh*'s extreme physical and mental rigor achieved international notoriety in 1985 when Takada Yoshiyuku, a dancer from the troupe Sankai Juku, performing hanging upside down outside a building in Seattle, fell to his death. Regardless of the specific style, *butoh* is generally characterized by dead-white, full-body makeup, grotesque or contorted physical gestures, extreme slowness, and a suggestion of the forbidden and taboo. Using various styles that sometimes fuse *butoh* with local popular culture, *butoh* troupes now exist throughout the world. The genre has powerfully impacted modern dance worldwide.

After the war, the Japanese government was forcibly transformed by the imposition of Western-style institutions. From 1945 to 1952, the U.S. military essentially ruled Japan in what is called the Occupation. The goal of the Occupation was to turn a former enemy into a permanent ally by substituting American-style democracy for traditional Japanese values. However, long-held cultural practices and traditional beliefs were not eliminated.

To curb the possibility of rebellion and to encourage the growth of constitutional democracy in Japan, the Occupation practiced censorship. Because many *kabuki* plays celebrated the values of revenge, feudalism, emperor worship, and the subjugation of women, *kabuki* theatre in general was suppressed, while Western-derived, realist *shingeki* plays flourished. Thus, Japan's first postwar production – just four months after the surrender – was a revival of Chekhov's *The Cherry Orchard*. Many characters in *The Cherry Orchard* are nostalgic for a vanished past. They also fear a rapidly transforming present and a future they cannot comprehend. Such emotions resonated deeply with the audience in a devastated, postwar Japan.

Despite the Occupation's efforts to prevent the return of militarist ideology, one of the most popular *shingeki* playwrights of the postwar era was the poet, novelist and playwright Mishima Yukio (1925–1970), also well known outside Japan as Yukio Mishima. He was best known for his novels *The Temple of the Golden Pavilion* and *Forbidden Colors*. Mishima was an ultranationalist who despised Westernization and longed for a return to samurai values; he committed suicide in the traditional *seppuku* style as a way to protest Japan's postwar constitution. Nevertheless, he wrote Western-style *shingeki* plays, adapted the stories of *nō* plays into *shingeki*, using modern settings and psychology, and was an important author of new *kabuki* plays, including one inspired by Racine's *Phèdre*. Japanese critics and audiences consistently name his all-female *Madame de Sade* (1965) the best Japanese postwar play. *Madame de Sade* has had several important English-language productions, including one at London's Donmar Warehouse in 2009, starring Judi Dench (1934–).

Another key *shingeki* playwright, Kinoshita Junji (1914–2006), moved beyond the constraints of realism. His *Twilight Crane* (1949), based on folklore, remains the most produced play in Japan. In this play, Kinoshita turned to his nation's mythic past to create a new artistic genre, reliant on a fresh vernacular dialect and a notion of "pure Japanese essence" uncontaminated by the West. In contrast, his realist *Between God and Man* (1970) is one of the few dramatic attempts to come to terms with Japanese war crimes.

Anti-*shingeki* artists began to appear around the time that Japanese radicals and workers staged mass protests in 1960 against the ratification of the United States–Japan Mutual Security Treaty. The treaty, still in effect in 2024, essentially places Japan under the military protection of the United States. The protestors were demanding a return to Japanese autonomy and an end to the use of Japan as a base for American soldiers and nuclear submarines. A new generation of artists – the playwright Betsuyaku Minoru (1937–2020), playwright/director Terayama Shūji (1935–1983), and directors Suzuki Tadashi (1939–) and Ninagawa Yukio (1935–2016) emerged in the 1960s (Ninagawa's work is discussed in the case study on "Global Shakespeare" on the website). Betsuyaku's *The Elephant* (*Zō*, 1962), which deals with the horrors of nuclear contamination in a style inspired by *kyōgen* and *Waiting for Godot*, is generally considered the first *angura* [ahn-goo-rah; underground] play. Waseda Little Theatre, created by Suzuki, Betsuyaku and others in 1966, is credited to have started Japan's Little Theatre Movement. Akimoto Matsuyo (1911–2001), one of Japan's first modern female playwrights, wrote *Kaison, the Priest of Hitachi* (1965), which features a young man who escapes from his historical burden of war guilt into mythic time to become Kaison, a twelfth-century warrior.

Postwar theatre and the Cold War

As we described in the introduction to this chapter, the Second World War had left massive destruction and dislocation in its wake, especially in Europe and Japan, profoundly affecting their view of the world. Communism and anti-communist ideologies also shaped national policies and the development of arts in many countries. Although the U.S. mainland had escaped the bombardment from the war, there were still significant sociopolitical consequences on American people.

Psychological realism in the United States

Many American women who had developed a professional career during the war found themselves replaced by returning male soldiers. They were forced into less satisfactory or lower-paying jobs or retreated to their prewar domestic roles. Similarly, many minority soldiers still found themselves subject to legal segregation or discrimination. Japanese Americans, who had voluntarily joined the military to demonstrate patriotism and allegiance, returned to find that their service abroad had not changed their second-class status at home. Americans had little direct contact with communism, compared to South Korea, Taiwan, or countries in Eastern Europe; however, the phobia against communism, known as the Red Scare, still dominated the political narrative and stifled arts and literature.

The indirect war impact did not push the postwar U.S. theatre to engage in a soul-searching type of reflection, such as intense philosophical inquiries or aesthetic revolution, as seen in existentialism and Theatre of the Absurd in Europe. Political and economic pressures, a legacy of realist theatre, a self-flattering notion of popular psychology, plus the emphatically realistic quality of film and TV, had encouraged the adoption of psychological realism in the United States. Although the roots of this style date from the late nineteenth century and include many of the plays of Eugene O'Neill, we see an intensified development of psychological realism in terms of stage practices: acting, directing, and design.

During the 1930s, Lee Strasberg (1901–1982) and other members of the Group Theatre in New York had applied what they took to be Stanislavsky's precepts about acting to their work on realist plays. They gradually forged their own acting "systems" that helped actors to empathize deeply with their stage characters. After the war, Strasberg's version – usually called the "**Method**" – trained a generation of actors. Unlike Stanislavsky's System, Strasberg's Method emphasized the actor's memory of their personal experiences and emotions, in order to connect to the character. Stella Adler (1903–1992), also an original member of the Group, briefly studied with Stanislavsky and believed that Strasberg's Method was flawed. Instead of the actor's personal emotions, she focused on "the given circumstances" of the drama as written – including historical period, location, culture, and so on. Thus Adler stressed what the character in the play (not the actor) experienced. She trained actors such as Marlon Brando (1924–2004). Other notable actors trained in some version of the Method or of Stanislavsky's System include Marilyn Monroe (1926–1962), Robert De Niro (1943–), and Johnny Depp (1963–). By the 1950s, Method Acting and its variations dominated theatrical performance in the United States. This acting style, psychologically attuned directing, and fluid scenography had produced a theatre of **psychological realism** that became a distinctive national style.

While the influence of Appia and Craig (discussed in Chapter 10) during the decade of the Great War had moved some U.S. stage design away from literal realism, most scenic and lighting designs for dramatic productions in the 1920s and 1930s continued to emphasize the massiveness of realist rooms and exteriors. However, Jo Mielziner (1901–1976) and a few other designers of Broadway productions drew on European ideas to discover more abstract solutions for staging realist plays. At the same time, the pressure from film to create quick shifts of scenic locales inspired theatre artists to move away from realism and to use more lightweight, lyrical designs. This led Mielziner, especially, toward a visual poetic realism with the use of color and soaring vertical lines in scene designs that left rooms without ceilings and substituted transparent walls made of painted scrim for the material solidity of regular stage flats.

Consequently, when Mielziner designed Tennessee Williams's *The Glass Menagerie* in 1945, he knew he could regulate the flow between the scenes of narration in the present and the scenes of memory in the past through the manipulation of scrim and lighting. When lit from the front, scrim can give the illusion of a solid wall. Illuminated from behind as well, the wall of scrim becomes transparent, allowing spectators to see objects and actors through a gauzy grain. Mielziner's painterly, soft-edged designs nicely complemented the psychological realism of Williams's plays. He designed seven modernist productions for Williams between 1945 and 1963, including *A Streetcar Named Desire* (1947) and *Cat on a Hot Tin Roof* (1955).

Mielziner's use of lighting and scrim to shift between locales or atmospheric effects permitted a "filmic" kind of scenic transformation; the technique also borrowed from the sound transition that radio drama producers called a "segue." By the 1940s, many popular radio serials used a musical or vocal bridge that faded in and out to move from one scene to another. At times, the segue moved the listener inside the narrator's head, sharing intimate thoughts, daydreams, or flashbacks.

The principle of the radio segue shaped playwriting as well as design on the postwar American stage. The lingering trauma from the returned soldiers, the Red phobia promoted by the government, and social discontent found no outlets and had to be internalized. "Inside the head" became a unique feature of U.S. theatre during the Cold War. "Inside of His Head" was actually Arthur Miller's initial title for *Death of a Salesman* (1949), which deploys several radio-drama techniques to tell the story of the dreams of material and capitalistic success that push salesman Willy Loman to suicide. Mielziner's design for *Salesman* used lighting-and-scrim shifts to move spectators inside Willy's head, where they could see the world from the perspective of Miller's Everyman character (Figure 12.4). Audiences familiar with the "voice-over" convention of radio drama – a narrator taking the listener directly to a new episode in the plot – had no difficulty following Willy's vocal transitions from present time and place into his daydreams located in the past. Many radio plays divided the internal psychology of the protagonist into different voices and sounds so that the split desires of the main character could be dramatized. Miller, who had written radio plays in the early 1940s, achieves a similar effect in *Salesman* by dividing the voices "inside of his [Willy's] head" among several characters. Directly shaped by the techniques and effects of radio drama, *Death of a Salesman* was a milestone in American psychological realism.

Salesman was directed by Elia Kazan (1909–2003), the premier director of psychological realism in the United States from the late 1940s through the 1950s. During those years, Kazan also enjoyed a successful career in Hollywood and brought several of the techniques of film directing to his work in New York. Kazan had been a member of the Group Theatre in the 1930s and, like several of his cohort, continued to use Method Acting and its variations with actors in stage productions such as Miller's *All My Sons* (1947) and Williams's *Sweet Bird of Youth* (1959), and in such films as *On the Waterfront* (1954) and *East of Eden* (1955). Kazan directed both

Figure 12.4
A rendering of Jo Mielziner's setting for Arthur Miller's *Death of the Salesman*, 1949.
Source: © Peter A. Juley & Son Collection, Smithsonian American Art Museum.

the stage and film versions of Williams's *A Streetcar Named Desire* (1947, 1951). He carefully coached his actors and used their edgy, high-strung psychological rhythms to shape their stage movements and his camera shots. Kazan's success helped to ensure that psychological realism would unite the film screens and the theatrical stages of modern America. Such filmic images of psychological realism achieved international renown as uniquely American aesthetics.

In the United States, mainstream theatre artists generally thought of themselves as apolitical. Most productions supported capitalist notions of individual success, consumer choice, and corporate power, while accepting limits on democracy and on the government's responsibility to improve economic and racial equity. These basic values were apparent in most musicals with comic elements, especially those by Rodgers and Hammerstein. In the intense psychological dramas that relied on Method Acting, the focus tended to be on personal struggle. While the audience might have felt empathetic with the characters, these plays were less likely to incite actions toward social change.

A few mainstream playwrights dissented from the consensus. Lorraine Hansberry's (1930–1965) *A Raisin in the Sun* (1959) managed to offer a mostly white audience a realistic view of the daily lives of African Americans and the problems they faced due to racial inequality, which the burgeoning civil rights movement had begun to contest. Hansberry was the first African American woman playwright to have a Broadway production, and the play's director, Lloyd Richards (1919–2006), was Broadway's first African American director. Tennessee Williams attacked homophobia and consumerist values in *Cat on a Hot Tin Roof* (1955) (Figure 12.5), while Arthur Miller's *The Crucible* (1953) equated U.S. anti-communist hysteria and blacklisting with the Salem witch trials of 1692–1693. The blacklisting referred to the activities of the Congressional hearings led by Senator Joseph McCarthy and the House

Figure 12.5
James Earl Jones (left) and Phylicia Rashad performing as Big Daddy and Big Mama in Tennessee Williams's *Cat on a Hot Tin Roof*, directed by Debbie Allen at The Novello Theatre in London, 2009.
Source: Nobby Clark/Popperfoto via Getty Images.

Committee on Un-American Activities (HUAC). HUAC forced many theatre and film artists to testify, asking them "Are you now or have you ever been a member of the Communist Party?" Those who refused to answer or who were merely named by others were subsequently "blacklisted," which meant that they were forbidden to work in the industry. Kazan was among those who "named names," informing HUAC of those who had been associated with Communist Party. Some blacklisted artists survived as ghostwriters, but many never recovered their careers. Fear of communism fueled many Hollywood films, especially science fiction films which often presented the threat of alien invasion and mind control.

The Cold War and theatre outside the United States
The Red Scare permeated the literary and artistic circles during the McCarthy era and foreign playwrights such as Bertolt Brecht, who had settled in California, went back to Europe; however, the U.S. government did not overtly promote anti-communist drama. In some countries devastated by wars against communism, a new genre to express anti-communist sentiment flourished in the 1950s and early 1960s. This transitional genre – diverse in forms and content in different countries was instituted by governments as propaganda, written as self-expression of patriotism, or co-sponsored by American organizations to comply with the U.S. Cold War international policy. While scholars today might question the literary

value because of its propagandic nature and right-wing leaning ideology, some might argue that anti-communist drama was a pragmatic way to sustain theatre and artists' livelihood in the challenging postwar time. Not only did it allow artists to continue their training, in some cases, it also established the foundation of modern theatre movements for these countries.

The defeat of Japan in 1945 concluded Japanese colonialism in Korea, but the U.S. military occupation (1945–48) immediately controlled the southern Korean peninsula. Social realism was a popular form for modern Korean playwrights' response to the turmoil they were in; however, many socialist intellectuals and artists fled to the North at the outbreak of the Korean War (1950–1953). In the South, the National Theatre closed down only 57 days after its opening in 1950, and anti-communism became the national policy. Yoo Chi-jin (or Yu Chi-jin, or Yu Chijing, 1905–1974), already a well-known playwright, was instrumental in bringing modern Korean theatre to a new level and international dimension by aligning Korean theatre with American anti-communist ideology during the Cold War. Yoo was an active theatre artist and expert on Anglo-American theatre; his right-wing anti-communist agenda and reputation made him a perfect candidate to collaborate with the Rockefeller Foundation and other philanthropies to promote the anti-communist Western liberal ideology. Some university students also benefited from such sponsorship through intra-university drama competitions, although many opposed the right-wing leaning intervention. Yoo's decade-long advocacy resulted in the Drama Center, which opened in Seoul in 1962. This 500-seat theatre – along with a drama school and library – is one of the oldest modern theatres in Korea today. Although Yoo's right-wing ideology might seem controversial today, it helped sustain theatre in South Korea during a very challenging time. Other famous playwrights during this period include Lee Haerang (1916–1989), Lee Keunsam (1929–2003), and Cha Beomseok (1924–2006). Cha's *Burning Mountain* (1962) realistically depicts the violence of the war and the plight of local people caused by the division of the country. Lee Haerang, expert in Western drama, later became the head of the Drama Center.

Communism also forever changed the lives of the modern Chinese. In 1949, the retreat of the Republic government led by Chiang Kai-shek's Nationalist Party (KMT) to Taiwan established two things: the separation of the Communist China on the mainland and the Republic government in Taiwan, and the positioning of Taiwan as a strategic frontline in the Pacific for Western democracy during the Cold War. In 1950, leaders of the literary circle in Taiwan set up a committee to award the best literary works in this new era. This committee, heavily subsidized by the government, played a crucial role in promoting newly written anti-communist works, from lyrics, poetry, to novels and drama. The postwar economic devastation made these large awards extremely attractive, and thousands of plays were written during a few years in the 1950s. Lee Man-Kuei (Li Mangui, 1907–1975), a feminist playwright and educator, was instrumental both in promoting the government-sponsored anti-communist drama and in cultivating modern theatre artists in Taiwan. In 1960, after her visit to the United States and Europe, she started the "Little Theatre Movement," which would become the leading force behind modern theatre in Taiwan for the next decades (see Chapter 13).

Jingju (Beijing opera), a popular pastime for the soldiers, also migrated to Taiwan along with the Nationalist troops. The Chinese morality promoted in *jingju* plays solidified the government's ideological wars against communism, which aimed to destroy old values. Starting in 1950, military-sponsored *jingju* troupes were established to train youngsters to carry on the tradition. American aid for Taiwan in the 1950s and 1960s, which was to stabilize the postwar economy and to curtail the further expansion of Chinese communism, helped sustain traditional theatre as well as establish a foundation for modern theatre. Taiwan was also cultivated as the new cultural center for diasporic Chinese in Asia, as many students from South and Southeast Asia would study Chinese language and literature in colleges in Taiwan.

As seen in Chapter 11, Brecht continued to impact the theatre world during the Cold War and beyond. For example, following the influential European tour of the Berliner Ensemble in 1956, English playwrights John Arden (1930–2012) and Edward Bond (1934–2024), director Joan Littlewood (1914–2002), and others were inspired to use Brechtian style to stage socially critical plays that had begun to flourish in the United Kingdom after the war. Italian Giorgio Strehler (1921–1997) also directed productions of Brecht's plays. Brechtian theatre was an alternative response to conforming to the ideology of superpowers.

In Latin America, long dominated by U.S. interests, Brechtian theatre was especially influential during the 1960s. Argentinean playwright and director Osvaldo Dragún (1929–1999) modeled many of his short plays in the 1950s and 1960s on Brecht's dramas to point up the sacrifice in human dignity demanded by capitalist economics. Brechtian theatre influenced several Mexican playwrights and directors, such as Luisa Josefina Hernández (1928–2023), who translated Brecht into Spanish and used his techniques to express social concerns in her own work, notably *La fiesta del mulato* (1966). Her *La fiesta del mulato* (1966), for example, used epic theatre devices to examine social injustice from the intersecting dimensions of race, culture, and socioeconomics. In Colombia, Enrique Buenaventura (1925–2003) led the charge, staging Brechtian productions, writing plays with revolutionary messages, and helping to reorganize the university theatre movement in the country for radical purposes. Although the authorities suppressed the collective theatre movement Buenaventura had helped to begin, its legacy continued in Bogotá and other major cities, with radical street theatre and plays that dramatized Colombia's oppressive history. In São Paulo, Brazil, the Arena Theatre modified Brechtian techniques to search for a specifically Brazilian stage language for social criticism. International activist Augusto Boal (1931–2009) joined Arena in 1956, wrote and directed several politically radical plays, and began experimenting with participatory forms of theatre, which later found expression in his 1974 book *Theater of the Oppressed*, discussed in more detail in Chapter 14. Along with Buenaventura, Boal would have enormous influence in the New Popular Theatre (Nuevo Teatro Popular) movement in Latin America during the 1970s and 1980s (see Chapter 13).

More significant than Brecht for Mexican oppositional theatre was the legacy of Surrealism, which Mexican playwrights began to transform for their own uses soon after the Second World War. The leading dramatist of the postwar generation, Emilio Carballido (1925–2008), freely mixed reality and fantasy in a wide range of genres, from film scripts and children's theatre pieces to over 100 works written for the professional stage. A critic of traditional Mexican culture in his opposition to patriarchy, the divisions been rich and poor, and his focus on serious socio-political concerns (often under the mask of farce), Carballido also engaged the positive possibilities of Catholicism and celebrated some of Mexico's founding national myths.

His most famous play, *Yo también hablo de la rosa* (*I, Too, Speak of the Rose*, 1966), has been identified as a surreal allegory, a Brechtian parody, and a postmodern paradox, to note only a few of the critical tags it has evoked. Through popular storytelling and songs, send-ups of Freudian and Marxist rhetoric, news accounts and poetic metaphors, and even occasional snippets of dramatic realism, the play depicts multiple representations of the same train derailment, as well as several versions of the events that led up to it and the responses that followed. Even as this multi-layered pastiche invites several interpretations, it also makes fun of the act of interpretation itself. At the same time, a rough populist energy animates the play; marginal members of Mexican society pushed the powerful train off its tracks and proceeded to loot it when it was down. This oppositional and possibly revolutionary action remains a potent fact during the performance, despite the ridiculous attempts of others in Mexican society to explain what happened. *I, Too, Speak of the Rose* presents a warning to those who controlled the public discourses of Mexican society that the poor will not be ignored.

In contrast, the Soviet Union's ideology of socialist realism, plus censorship and control, kept most Soviet theatre within the boundaries of Cold War communism, even after the death of Stalin in 1953. A few directors, however, including Nikolai Okhlopkov (1900–1967), were permitted to experiment with new ideas and forms (Figure 12.6). While approving of Brecht's Marxism, the Soviets kept Brechtian theatre at arm's length; they recognized that its antimilitarism and democratic socialism subverted their authoritarian power.

Theatre and politics intersected in India's social drama, as seen in the case study below.

Figure 12.6
Okhlopkov's production of *Hamlet* relied on a triptych-like design to suggest the prince's imprisonment in traditional culture. Produced at the Mayakovsky Theatre in Moscow in 1954, soon after the death of Stalin.

Source: © SCRSS Photo Library – www.scrss.org.uk

CASE STUDY: Social drama in Kerala, India: Staging the "revolution"

Phillip B. Zarrilli, with Carol Fisher Sorgenfrei

> There once was a time like this. A time when human lives burned in the "test fires" of social change.
>
> Tooppil Bhaasi, playwright and director, Kerala

Indian theatres of decolonization

Anti-colonial nationalism intensified in British-ruled India after the Great War and the Russian Revolution, reaching a peak during the Second World War. After Indian independence in 1947, many leftists joined with some of the liberal reformers to begin new theatre troupes in Indian cities. Among the most influential was the Group Theatre in Calcutta (now renamed Kolkata), which challenged the dominant, Western-style commercial theatre of the city. Where the old imperial theatres had featured British plays, occasional hybrid shows written by Indians, and the latest hits from London, the Group produced modernist European classics (Chekhov, Pirandello, and Ibsen, for example) and several politically radical plays by Brecht and others. By performing canonical Western plays in an Indian context, the Group hoped to cultivate an audience of serious theatregoers who would reject the frivolous entertainments of imperial times for politically engaged drama. Director Sombhu Mitra (1914–1997) worked briefly with the Group and then founded his own company, Bohurupee. Mitra directed a localized version of Ibsen's *A Doll House* for Bohurupee in 1958 and successfully adapted several plays by Rabindranath Tagore (1860–1941), one of the leading writers of the early twentieth century, whose plays had resisted modern modes of staging until that time. Mitra's modernist vision for his theatre led him to stage productions of *Oedipus the King* and Tagore's *Rājā* on consecutive nights in 1964.

Far to the south, in the state of Kerala, a very different form of grassroots, anti-colonialist theatre developed.

Tooppil Bhaasi and the Kerala people's arts club

Tooppil Bhaasi (1924–1992) was born in Vallikkunu, a typical agricultural village in south central Kerala, India. He was educated in a Sanskrit school and went on to pass his examination in traditional Indian medicine (*Ayurveda*). However, Bhaasi never pursued a career in medicine. Rather, like many other young men receiving an education during this turbulent period, he became a student activist and leader, working in the student congress movement as part of the national drive toward independence from British colonial rule. He later joined the Communist movement. He had been arrested for his activities of organizing low-caste agricultural workers, protesting against the hoarding of food grains and black-marketeering by wealthy landholders, for the cultivation of waste land, and for attempting to overturn the hierarchical caste system. The ultimate goal of this movement was to replace the old social and economic order with progressive social-democratic models that would gradually and peacefully move from capitalism toward socialism by creating extensive governmental support systems.

THINKING THROUGH THEATRE HISTORIES: POLITICS, IDEOLOGY, HISTORY, AND PERFORMANCE

Janelle Reinelt raises several important questions about writing histories of theatre when she asks, "what is the relationship of politics [and ideology] to culture? How does social change result in cultural change – or can various cultural practices initiate or precipitate change?" (Reinelt 1996: 1).

Throughout this book, we have attempted to locate various types of theatre within their specific historical, political, cultural, and ideological frameworks. We have emphasized how ideologies change over time, and how specific social or political realities are reflected in – or even brought about by – local theatre. In the current chapter, for example, we suggest that various responses to the traumatic events of the Second World War and the subsequent Cold War – whether in the form of resistance or compliance – can solidify the survival and emergence of certain styles and genres of performance. Theatre is live art; as long as it is kept alive, there is hope for it to grow and blossom, despite its sometimes challenging social and political milieu. As seen in the examples above, some anti-communist theatres in East Asia kept theatre alive during the Cold War and helped establish solid foundation for experimental theatres in the next decades.

Cultural theorist Terry Eagleton maintains that "there is one place above all where … consciousness may be transformed almost literally overnight, and that is in active political struggle" (Eagleton 1991: 223–4).

This case study examines the interconnections between theatre and political struggle in the state of Kerala in a newly postcolonial India.

Between 1946 and 1952, the Communist Party of India was advocating active and sometimes violent revolutionary struggle against the new Indian government. As a Communist, Bhaasi and other activists were forced to live in hiding because some of their activities were declared illegal. While in hiding, in 1952 he wrote his first play, *You Made Me a Communist*, and the Kerala People's Arts Club (KPAC) almost immediately produced it. Founded in 1950 by a group of student activists at the Law College in Ernakulam Town, KPAC began to produce dramas as one means of raising socio-political issues. The group first used shadow puppets and then staged the political drama *My Son is Right*. But it was their production of Bhaasi's *You Made Me a Communist* that launched KPAC on to the path toward becoming Kerala's most visible contemporary theatre company.

You Made Me a Communist enacts the struggles of agricultural laborers and poor peasants for a better life by focusing on how Paramu Pillai, a conservative farmer, makes the decision to become a Communist. The play focuses on his change in socio-political consciousness and calls for the revolutionary overthrow of landlordism. With its very loose structure, and with characters who burst into song at unexpected moments during the course of the story, *You Made Me a Communist* swept across the length and breadth of Kerala and became a powerful inspiration for people to fight against social injustice and for their rights.

There can be no doubt that attending a performance of *You Made Me a Communist* in 1952–1953 was a special event. It was not simply a dramatic representation of a fictionalized story and its characters, but part of an unfolding and evolving socio-political revolution as it was happening. Journalist, essayist, playwright, and activist Kaniyapuram Ramachandran explained both the timeliness and excitement generated by this interrelationship between stage and life in Bhaasi's early social dramas, and in *You Made Me a Communist* in particular:

> [The] dividing line between stage and audience was simply erased! What they saw there was their real lives! The workers, agricultural laborers, people coming on stage and speaking their own dialects and ordinary language – not literary language. The ultimate aim is to make the audience part of the experience. There is no detachment, but attachment. So with the social issues in the play – it was all so relevant. At the end of a performance the entire audience would come to its feet. So, *You Made Me a Communist* wasn't a drama at all! The social relevance of the play made people forget everything when they saw it. It was a drama for the people, by the people. It gave people what they wanted to see at the right time. It was a magic wand. The audience was like a mental vacuum that sucked up what was given … . In 1951 it was so apt! It was the medicine that the patient was waiting for. People were ready for that message of social change.
>
> Bhaasi always wanted the audience to first understand his plays. They should be clear and straight. He was speaking to the heart, and not the intellect. He used to talk to the emotions, and through the emotions, people would change their thinking.
>
> (Ramachandran 1993)

The impact of the production of this play on people in Kerala was remarkable. So important was it for the spread of the Communist point of view from 1952 to 1954 that some commentators have suggested that without it the emergence of the first democratically elected Communist government to the newly established state of Kerala in 1957 would never have happened.

Since 1952, *You Made Me a Communist* has been performed well over 2,000 times and continues to be part of KPAC's active repertory of social dramas. Bhaasi went on to become one of Kerala's most important playwrights, providing KPAC with a series of highly popular social dramas, including *The Prodigal Son* (1956), in which a wayward, selfish rowdy is transformed into a champion of the low castes. His *Aswameetam* (1962) explores the social stigma of leprosy. His political satire, *Power House* (1990), focuses on the irresponsible behavior of a government institution – the Kerala State Electricity Board. *Memories in Hiding*, which won the Kerala Best Play Award in 1992, was his final play. In *Memories in Hiding*, a tenant-farmer, whose family has for generations devotedly served a landlord as virtual slaves, realizes that the landlord will not step forward to aid the tenant-farmer's falsely arrested son. The tenant-farmer then courageously declares his independence and walks out (Figures 12.7 and 12.8).

From its nineteenth-century realities as a hierarchically ordered, feudal social system ridden with caste and class conflicts, with high birth and infant mortality rates, Kerala was gradually transformed into a turn-of-the-twentieth-century social-democratic state with radical reductions in population growth and infant mortality rates. Illiteracy was virtually eradicated, many previously dispossessed peasants and communities were enfranchised, and there was extensive land reform, with the redistribution of considerable amounts of land to the landless. This transformation of Kerala in just over 100 years into a new model of social development has taken place peacefully within a democratic framework and without the outside assistance of global institutions such as the International Monetary Fund or the World Bank (Parayil 2000: 1–15).

Spoken drama and theatre, together with numerous modes of public performance, have clearly played an essential role in redefining individual, social, and political awareness

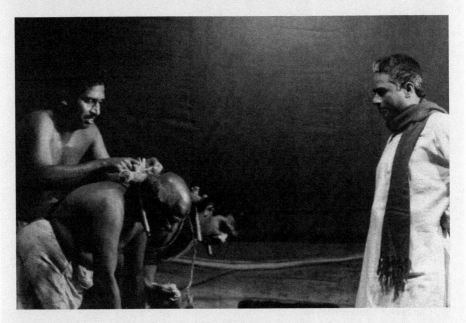

Figure 12.7

In a 1993 production of *Memories in Hiding* by Tooppil Bhaasi, in Thiruvananthapuram, Kerala, the Landlord (right, with scarf) forces Teevan to yoke together his father, Ceenan, and Paramu Naayar to plough a paddy field.

Source: © Phillip B. Zarrilli.

Figure 12.8

In *Memories in Hiding,* the jailed Paramu Naayar shouts defiantly near the end: "Our voices will be heard even after we die. They are the voices of revolution."
Source: © Phillip B. Zarrilli.

in contemporary Kerala. A more detailed version of this case study, including additional historical, political, and cultural background, can be found on our website.

Even traditional theatre such as *kutiyattam*, the Kerala-based Sanskrit drama (discussed in Chapter 2) went through a reform to become more "democratized," largely thanks to the maestro and performer Painkulam Rama Chakyar (1905–1980). His vision to welcome anyone to learn the form, which had been restricted to certain caste members and specific religious space, is the major reason why such *kutiyattam* is still alive today can still survive the thrive today.

Key references

Bhaasi, T. (1996) *Memories in Hiding*, trans. J. George and P.B. Zarrilli, Calcutta: Seagull.

Eagleton, T. (1991) *Ideology: An Introduction*, London: Verso.

Handelman, D. (1990) *Models and Mirrors: Towards an Anthropology of Public Events*, Cambridge: Cambridge University Press.

Namboodiripad, E.M.S. (1976) *How I Became a Communist*, Trivandrum: Chinta Publications.

Parayil, G. (ed.) (2000) *Kerala: The Development Experience*, London: Zed Books.

Ramachandran, K. (1993) Interview with the author.

Reinelt, J. (ed.) (1996) *Crucible of Crisis: Performing Social Change*, Ann Arbor: University of Michigan Press.

The rise of the American musical

As previous chapters showed, prior to the emergence of the distinctive form of American musicals, there were many popular forms of performance that heavily relied on music, such as vaudeville, minstrelsy, and cabaret.

American musicals came of age in the 1940s and 1950s, which is considered by many scholars to be Broadway musical theatre's "golden age" (Wollman 2017: 78). But the Great Depression had caused lasting damage to Broadway: over the following decades, the number of venues sharply declined and the number of new shows each year tumbled from over 100 before the Depression to a mere handful. Meanwhile ticket prices rapidly spiraled upward. At the same time, with new technology and cheaper ticket prices, movies became the glamorous lure that stole Broadway audience, soon compounded by TV. Many theatre artists also left Broadway for Hollywood.

Broadway musicals were predominantly diversionary and had a rather loose structure, but beginning in the 1940s formal innovations became the backbone of modern musicals. The breakthrough occurred even before the Second World War was over. In 1943, *Oklahoma!*, with music by Richard Rodgers (1902–1979), script ("book") and lyrics by Oscar Hammerstein II (1895–1960), choreography by Agnes De Mille (1905–1993), and based on the 1930 play *Green Grow the Lilacs* by gay Cherokee playwright Lynn Riggs, perfected what had been attempted a few times before: the formally **integrated musical**, in which the characters, storylines, dialogue, lyrics, music and dance all contribute to a whole, driven by characters' motivations and following logical (and usually romantic) plots – the model for musicals ever since. (The word "integrated" didn't yet refer to racial integration; today we might prefer "formally coherent." However, the term persists.) *Oklahoma!* smashed performance records. Rodgers and Hammerstein wrote numerous other hit musicals, including *South Pacific* (1949), *The King and I* (1951), *Flower Drum Song* (1958) and *The Sound of Music* (1959). Hammerstein's scripts often sought to critique prejudices and urge tolerance (although today we can see his limitations).

By the 1950s, U.S. culture had become rigid and conservative. The Red Scare intensified. Nevertheless there were crosscurrents of criticism and dissent, especially by the mid-1950s: for example, *The Organization Man* by William H. Whyte (1956) attacked the "bureaucratic ethic" that had settled into the middle class; Betty Friedan's *The Feminine Mystique* (1963) almost single-handedly launched a new wave of feminism; and the Civil Rights movement fought against anti-Black discrimination and for legal equality, eventually winning major court cases and legislation.

As always, Broadway during the 1950s had plenty of light fare, such as *Guys and Dolls* (1950, music and lyrics by Frank Loesser, book by Jo Swerling and Abe Burrows). But beyond Rodgers and Hammerstein's work, probably the most innovative musical of the 1950s was also highly topical (and controversial): *West Side Story* (1957), an adaptation of *Romeo and Juliet* set as a conflict between two street gangs of different ethnicities and cultures, with music by Leonard Bernstein (1918–1990), book by Arthur Laurents (1917–2011), lyrics by Stephen Sondheim (1930–2021), and choreography by Jerome Robbins (1918–1998).

Since the 1920s, an overwhelming proportion of composers and writers of American musicals, including everyone mentioned above, was Jewish or half-Jewish – John Bush Jones suggests at least 90 percent (Jones 2003: 205). Although Jewish themes didn't appear in musicals until 1961 with *Milk and Honey*, Andrea Most believes that "the Broadway stage was a space where Jews subtly wrote themselves into that scenario as accepted members of the mainstream American community" (Most 2004: 1–2). For example, written at the height of antisemitism of the 1940s, *Oklahoma!* may have expressed the anxiety of recently immigrated Jews and advocated for assimilation and acceptance of immigrants by having everyone – including an immigrant among other native-born characters – singing "We know we belong to the land" together at the end of the show. The year 1964 saw two major hits of Jewish-themed musicals. The first, *Funny Girl*, about the performer Fanny Brice (1891–1951), was primarily notable for starring Barbara Streisand (1942–). And then *Fiddler on the Roof* (music by Jerry Bock, book by Joseph Stein, lyrics by Sheldon Harnick) took the city by storm, attracting a broad audience with its themes of generational change, prejudice, and community survival, sweetened with a dollop of sentimentality; it blew through *Oklahoma!*'s performance record by almost 50 percent.

The triumph of the formally coherent (or integrated) musical, with its orientation around characters' motivations driving a (more or less) logical plot, was in keeping with the rise of psychological realism in American drama, such as Williams's and Miller's plays. Musicals of course can never be fully realistic – people don't ordinarily break out in song to express their feelings and intentions, and support such expressions with dance. Nevertheless the genre developed in the same general direction as Tennessee Williams's and Arthur Miller's plays.

CASE STUDY: "Asian" Broadway musicals: Rodgers & Hammerstein's *South Pacific* and *The King and I*

Stacy Wolf

In 1950, an advertisement in *Life* magazine for Breck shampoo featured a photo of Mary Martin, then starring on Broadway in Rodgers and Hammerstein's *South Pacific*. That Martin's endorsement would sell the brand underlines the importance of Broadway musical theatre in the mid twentieth-century U.S. Songs from musicals played on the radio, original cast albums landed on the Billboard Top 40 chart, and Broadway performers appeared on television variety shows like the *Ed Sullivan Show*, one of the most popular on the new, growing entertainment platform.

Broadway musical theatre's ubiquity in U.S. middle-class culture meant that this commercial, profit-seeking entertainment served up cultural messages about gender and race alongside tuneful melodies and virtuosic dances. Richard Rodgers and Oscar Hammerstein II, the most influential and prolific musical theatre team of the 1940s and 1950s, had highbrow intentions for their shows in both content and form. They wanted to elevate musical comedies – frothy escapist fare – by writing musical plays: dramatic stories that tackled social issues, such as male violence (*Carousel*, 1945), miscegenation (*South Pacific*, 1949), and Nazism (*The Sound of Music*, 1959). Rodgers and Hammerstein also wanted to weave together the disparate parts of a musical – music, lyrics, dance, speech, and design – into a unified "integrated" whole, which signified a more sophisticated version of a thoroughly entertaining and popular genre. Rodgers and Hammerstein's shows won accolades from critics and audiences alike.

Many of the conventions developed by Rodgers and Hammerstein and their peers, such as Lerner and Loewe (*My Fair Lady*, 1957; *Camelot*, 1960) and Frank Loesser (*Guys & Dolls*, 1950; *Fiorello*, 1959), set audiences' and critics' expectations for musical theatre: that a dramatic story provides the spine of the show; that the music of the show is unified – a score rather than a collection of musically unrelated songs; that characters' songs reflect who they are, in both lyrics and music; that musical numbers are functional and either move the plot along, develop character, or reflect the setting; that characters move "naturally" into song or dance at moments of extreme emotion.

Alongside these formal conventions, Rodgers and Hammerstein and their peers built heterosexual romance narratives into each show's structure – the classic "boy-meets-girl, boy-loses-girl, boy-gets-girl." Most musicals of the era feature a male and female principal who dislike each other at the start but who sing together, foreshadowing that they will indeed become a couple by the show's end. Many musicals also feature a secondary couple with a parallel, often comic romance plot. In a musical's "marriage plot," each leading character represents different, opposing U.S. values that are reconciled by the end of the show, performing America's unity.

Musical theatre does its cultural and political work through pleasure and emotional engagement. Rodgers and Hammerstein's songs are catchy; audiences leave the theatre humming the melodies. Exciting choreography encourages spectators to tap their toes. Beautiful sets, costumes, and lighting seduce audiences through visual spectacle. And because the music of Broadway was the popular music of the day, Americans heard the songs from *South Pacific* and *The King and I* on the radio in their homes and public places. Knowingly or not, everyday people found themselves singing songs that justified U.S. involvement in East Asia.

In the late 1940s and early 1950s, eager to gain geopolitical power in the East and the Pacific, the U.S. military established bases in Japan, Korea, Taiwan, Philippines, Guam, Hawaii and other Pacific regions. Thailand – the setting of *The King and I* – was a U.S. ally; after China became a Communist country in 1949, the United States invested money for development in Thailand. By the time *The King and I* opened in 1951, the United States was involved in the Korean War to combat communism in the East. While the United States expanded its geographical influence abroad, Cold War politics at home encouraged containment and fueled paranoia about communism. Like all popular performance, *South Pacific* and *The King and I* conversed with issues of the day, revealing U.S. perspectives on Asia and effectively functioning as propaganda to support U.S. intervention in Asia.

Rodgers and Hammerstein were the most successful musical theatre team in Broadway history. As liberal, upper-middle class Jews during the McCarthy era, they were attuned to the politically risky association between Jews, the liberal causes that they supported, and communism. Rodgers was active in various Jewish organizations, and Hammerstein was a committed internationalist who advocated for strong bonds between the United States and other countries. Hammerstein also donated time and money to organizations that supported orphans from Asia. *South Pacific* and *The King and I* reveal – through the multivalent modes of music, lyrics, dance, speech, and design – the men's Jewish liberalism.

U.S. culture was fascinated with Asia from the nineteenth century on, so Rodgers and Hammerstein's interest in representing Asia and Asian characters was unsurprising, but their desire to humanize Asian characters was unusual at the time. In addition to *South Pacific* and *The King & I*, Rodgers and Hammerstein adapted a novel by C. Y. Lee to create *Flower Drum Song* (1958; movie 1961; revisal [revival with a new, revised libretto by David Henry Hwang] 2002), which is set in then-contemporary San Francisco and features Chinese and Chinese American characters. Rodgers and Hammerstein's Asian characters have objectives to follow, character arcs, and they sing, which demonstrates their importance.

South Pacific and *The King and I* perform "Asia" as imagined by U.S. ideology and politics. Although Rodgers and Hammerstein intended to represent Asian characters in a positive light, which most middle-class white spectators at the time absorbed, from an Asian point of view and from a contemporary perspective their shows look and sound conservative and even racist. They present Asian cultures as childish and immature, in need of Westernizing, and they reproduce negative stereotypes of Asians. The protagonist of each musical is a white woman who elects to stay in Asia to raise Asian (or biracial) children, joining imperialism with the high value placed on women and the home during the Cold War. (Nellie in *South Pacific* and Anna in *The King and I* are excellent roles for white women, but they come at the expense of the Asian characters' humanity.) As charismatic and sympathetic characters (leading ladies who sing the most songs in their shows), the women rationalize U.S. expansion in Asia.

South Pacific (1949)

Based on *Tales of the South Pacific* (1947) by James Michener, *South Pacific* takes place during the Second World War on two remote, fictitious islands, though it bathes the actual brutality of war in a nostalgic glow. Nellie Forbush, a nurse in the navy stationed on one island, meets and falls in love with Emile de Beque, a European plantation owner and widower with two mixed-race children. The secondary love story centers around Princeton-educated Lt Joe Cable, who falls in love with a young Asian woman, Liat. Both Nellie and Joe struggle with their racism, which, Joe insists, is neither natural nor necessary but, as he famously sings, "carefully taught." By the end of the show, Nellie has come to accept and love Emile's children, and Joe, having decided that he will marry Liat and remain on the island, is killed in battle. The musical, which pushes the actual war into the background, ends with a tableau of Nellie, Emile, and the children seated at a table – a new, mixed race heterosexual family. The show received critical acclaim, including the Pulitzer Prize, and was wildly popular with audiences.

Through much of *South Pacific*'s history, white middle-class audiences and critics interpreted it as an argument against prejudice and in favor of mixed-race relationships.

The song, "You've Got to Be Carefully Taught" expresses this perspective directly when Cable sings. "You've got to be taught to be afraid/Of people whose eyes are oddly made,/And people whose skin is a different shade." When the show went on national tour in 1950, in fact, two legislators in Georgia who objected to the musical's interracial relationships introduced a bill to outlaw its performance.

South Pacific is centered on the two white American characters who change and presumably become less racist. Cable believes that he can reject his white wealthy conservative family to stay on Bali Hai, but he dies in battle. Thus Rodgers and Hammerstein kill off the character so that he dies nobly, but his relationship with Liat never moves beyond a one-night stand. Nellie finally accepts Emile's mixed-race children, but her future husband is a white European man (that is, similar to her racially) and a plantation owner (that is, an oppressor). As the heroine of the musical, Nellie is idealized as the best American – tolerant of difference and able to change.

Nellie is exuberant and energetic, the embodiment of white American postwar optimism. She changes from a "knucklehead" to efficient and responsible, from independent ("Washin' that Man") to a wife and mother. Nellie leaves her hometown of Little Rock, but not domesticity. The end of the show isn't romantic but familial, which aligns with the Cold War values at the time. The show endorses a feminine maternal love in which the mother is present but doesn't sing; as the final stage directions read, "her voice [is] gone."

Over time, *South Pacific*'s contradictions have become more evident to spectators and scholars, and its demeaning representations of Asians obvious. Bloody Mary, who has no real name, only the nickname given to her by the Seabees, embodies the stereotype of the Asian dragon lady. She is a ruthless and "primitive" businesswoman who takes advantage of and is entirely dependent on the young American men. She is described in the script as "small, yellow, with Oriental eyes" that are "crafty" and she has "betel-stained teeth." Before she speaks, "she gives out a shrill cackle of laughter." She speaks in broken English, but nonetheless sings "Bali Hai," the most beautiful song in the score, as a siren song to seduce the men, and she offers up her daughter, Liat, to Cable, almost like a pimp. Liat, although she is the leading lady of the secondary romance plot, neither speaks nor sings and merely has sex with Cable and plays finger games to Bloody Mary's "Happy Talk." Liat is an exoticized, silenced, childlike Other. Two important Asian characters in the musical are one-dimensional and without agency.

The King and I (1951)

Adapted from Margaret Landon's novel, which was based on Anna Leonowen's heavily fictionalized memoirs of her time living in Siam in the 1860s, the musical follows Anna, a widow with a son, who travels to Siam to teach the king's numerous children and wives at his request. Anna and the King are a combative pair as they get to know each other, and she tries to influence his behavior and Westernize the palace. He grows to trust her and relies on her for diplomatic maneuvers to maintain Siam's independence. The secondary plot involves Tuptim, a Burmese slave to the King and protégée of Anna's, who attempts to escape the palace to elope with her lover, but they are caught, and he is killed. The final scene finds the King on his deathbed. Anna has grown to love him, and his son, the Crown Prince, is prepared to lead in a Western style. *The King and I* was an immediate hit with U.S. critics and audiences, though the 1956 movie version was banned in Thailand.

Rodgers and Hammerstein were unapologetic about their imagined representation of Siam. As Rodgers explained, Western audiences "would not find this kind of [authentically Siamese] music attractive" (Rodgers's memoir, qtd. in Most 2004: 187). He used some instruments from Eastern music to evoke exotic otherness in melodies that followed conventions of Broadway popular songs. Similarly, Jerome Robbins's famous choreography for the "minstrel show" version of *Uncle Tom's Cabin*, "The Small House of Uncle Thomas," borrowed stereotypical gestures and movements from various Asian cultures to create an imitation of Siamese dance.

Like *South Pacific*, the main character in *The King and I* (which the title confirms) is a white woman who leaves her home country in the West and confronts cultural differences in the East. Though Anna is British, she, like Nellie, symbolizes America and justifies U.S. involvement in Asia. But while Nellie plays the role of the student, learning from Cable that she must reject the racism of her southern U.S. home, Anna plays the teacher who criticizes the habits and politics of Siam and the King's household. She refuses to bow down to him, chides him for breaking his promise of providing a separate house for her, then later, advises him on diplomatic relations with English visitors. In her first scene with the children and the wives, she displays a Mercator map of the world, revealing that in truth, Siam is a tiny country, the same size as England. Then she leads them in a charming number, "Getting to Know You," which persuades them (and the audience) that her way, a Western perspective and Western habits, is best.

Anna is both masculinized and feminized in the musical. She wears a traditionally feminine late-nineteenth-century corset and hoop skirt but carries masculine power because she is from the West, is educated ("scientific"), and she brings the power and authority of a teacher (they call her "sir"). Anna wants a house, which signifies both domesticity (feminine) and property (masculine). Anna overshadows the King and serves as an intellectual mother for the young Prince.

The leading man in *The King and I* is Asian. The King is a forceful, dynamic character who sings "A Puzzlement," in which he muses over Siam's position in the world and calculates political risks. Still, he is often ridiculed or infantilized in the musical. Barefoot and shirtless, feminized by his Asianness, the King speaks halting, broken English (similar to Bloody Mary in *South Pacific*) and acts like a petulant child. He has numerous wives, his polygamy a sure sign of his barbarism, and is tied to traditionalism. Despite the King's performance of bravado, the audience knows that Anna, the Westerner – and by extension, Westernization – will win. Indeed, as much as Anna infuriates the King, he comes to rely on her, which reinforces the idea that she knows him, his country, and Siamese culture better than he does (a typical Orientalist gesture).

The relationship between Anna and the King follows the conventional trajectory of heterosexual romance of many mid-twentieth-century musicals, even though their romance is neither overt nor consummated. They begin with antipathy laced with fascinated attraction, then develop sympathy, which culminates in the effervescent polka, "Shall We Dance." This number expresses their connection in a Western dance form and Western courtship ritual; Anna teaches the King the dance and its meaning. The two finally admit their mutual respect and even love, and the King dies. Just as Rodgers and Hammerstein could not represent Cable and Liat in marriage, neither could they bring Anna and the King together as an interracial couple. The musicals argue for tolerance within a Western imperialist framework.

Both *South Pacific* and *The King and I* were cast according to practices of mid-twentieth-century Broadway theatre that would warrant scrutiny today. None of the leading Asian characters were played by Asian actors in the original Broadway productions or the first film versions. Yul Brynner, of Russian and Swiss-German descent, was cast as the King in a prime example of yellowface casting. Juanita Hall, who was Black, achieved stardom when she played Bloody Mary on Broadway and film, and Rita Moreno, who would go on to play Anita in *West Side Story*, played Tuptim in the movie. The children in *The King and I*, according to Rodgers, were "Oriental, Negro, and Puerto Rican"; that is, undifferentiated children of color (James Poling, qtd. in McConachie 2003: 158). Today, productions typically cast Asian American actors as Asian characters, though seldom specifically Polynesian or Thai actors.

These shows are part of the musical theatre canon, so they continue to be frequently performed at regional theatres, community theatres, and schools across the United States. Contemporary production teams strive to challenge the shows' negative stereotypes of Asians and signal their own interpretation to their audience. Still, *South Pacific* and *The King and I* tell stories of Western domination that reveal the expansionist ideology of the Cold War United States.

> Stacy Wolf is Professor of Theater and American Studies at Princeton University. Her latest book is *Beyond Broadway: The Pleasure and Promise of Musical Theatre Across America*.

Key references

Klein, C. (2003) *Cold War Orientalism: Asia in the Middlebrow Imagination, 1945–1961*, Berkeley: University of California Press.

Ma, S. (2003) "Rodgers and Hammerstein's 'Chopsticks' Musicals," *Film and Literature Quarterly* 31(1): 17–26.

McConachie, B. (2003) *American Theater in the Culture of the Cold War: Producing and Contesting Containment, 1947–1962*, Iowa City: University of Iowa Press.

Most, A. (2004) *Making Americans: Jews and the Broadway Musical*, Cambridge, MA: Harvard University Press.

Videos

The King and I (1956) "Shall We Dance," https://www.youtube.com/watch?v=QgVPnWmUqd4

South Pacific (1958) "You've Got to Be Carefully Taught," https://www.youtube.com/watch?v=VPf6ITsjsgk

Happenings, protest, and the growth of alternative theatre in the United States

Some of the most radical political performance during the 1960s flourished on the margins of mainstream theatre in the United States. The agitprop tradition, a significant part of working-class theatre in the United States during the 1930s, blossomed again in the mid-1960s, as small groups on college campuses and elsewhere sought to protest the war in Vietnam. Vietnam had become a pawn in the Cold War, and the United States gradually ramped up its military commitment to prevent what it feared would be a Communist takeover of the country.

Theatre and other artists also practiced new tactics to destroy audience complacency. Allan Kaprow (1927–2006) was a painter and aesthetic theorist who popularized concepts such as performance art, environmental art (including theatre), and **Happenings**. A typical Happening might involve spectators at an art gallery who would encounter not only paintings and sculptures, but performers engaged in unrelated, random activities. Happenings could occur anywhere, sometimes without the audience realizing they would be involved. Participatory and interactive, Happenings aimed to destroy the fourth wall between performer and audience. Kaprow first used the term "Happening" in a 1958 essay; by the early 1960s, they had become significant in the art world.

Related to Happenings was an avant-garde movement called Fluxus, a loose international alliance of musicians and performers dedicated to continuing the experiments of composer John Cage (1912–1992) with chance events, mundane sounds, and the embodiment of everyday rituals in performance. Fluxus began in 1948 when Cage and dancer Merce Cunningham (1919–2009) worked together at Black Mountain College in North Carolina. Like the Futurists and Dadaists, Cage had been experimenting with everyday sounds and chance occurrences to expand the range of "music." His most remembered piece *4'33"* (1952) is a three-movement composition of "silence" for piano for three minutes and 33 seconds. Cunningham explored modes of movement that might correspond with Cage's mix of unconventional sounds. Both objected to the modernist removal of aesthetics from everyday life and the utilitarian narrowness of Cold War American society. An untitled performance of theirs in 1952 included reading a Dadaist poem, showing a film on the ceiling, and pouring water from one bucket into another.

Cage's class in experimental music at the New School for Social Research in 1958 generated several Fluxus events, as did his international travels and collaborations in Europe and Japan during the 1960s. One event, *Snowstorm No. 1* (1965), put together by Czech Fluxus artist Milan Knížák (1940–), simply instructs the facilitators to distribute paper airplanes to the expectant audience and invite them to fly the planes around the auditorium. For Knížák, the point was to enjoy the beauty of the gliding paper and the fun of exchanging the planes with others. At a time when many real airplanes carried atomic bombs, however, some saw the Fluxus event as a demonstration for peace.

Cage also influenced the Living Theatre, a group begun by Julian Beck (1925–1985) and Judith Malina (1926–2015) in 1951. In 1960, they produced a theatre piece that played with Cage's combinations of sounds, props, and actions. The year before, Beck and Malina had produced *The Connection*, a play by Jack Gelber (1932–2003) that purposefully invited audience confusion about whether the drug addicts and jazz players on stage were real people or fictional characters. Their Pirandellian experiments with reality and illusion soon combined with an interest in the ideas of Artaud after the initial publication in English of his *The The-atre and Its Double* in 1958.

Less strident in its demands but no less utopian in its politics was the Bread and Puppet Theater, founded by Peter Schumann (1934–) in 1961. Schumann began aligning his puppet pageants and street shows with anti-war demonstrations in 1964. For the rest of the 1960s, the oversized puppet heads of his peasants, washerwomen, and workers, plus his bad guys like King Herod and Uncle Fatso (a capitalist-exploiter dressed like Uncle Sam), were marching against the war, homelessness, and nuclear arms. Schumann and his loose collective of pup-pet animators also mounted parable-like productions, such as *The Great Warrior* (1963) and *The Cry of the People for Meat* (1969), that explored mostly timeless problems of peace and justice through slow-moving puppets that were sometimes 30 feet tall (Figure 12.9).

The San Francisco Mime Troupe also used a traditional form, *commedia dell'arte*, to satirize the U.S. war in Vietnam and push for social justice. Begun in 1959 by actors interested in exploring the traditions of *commedia*, the group moved toward Marxist politics in the 1960s

Figure 12.9
A scene by Bread and Puppet Theatre depicting the life and work of Archbishop Óscar Romero of El Salvador, assassinated in March of 1980 for his frequent public denunciations of the Salvadoran government's repressions and abuses of basic human rights. The troupe has been performing puppetry-based, politically engaged theatre since 1963. This photo was taken on 11 November 2022 in Tempe, AZ, during a stop on its national tour.
Source: Tamara Underiner.

and formed itself into a collectively run theatre in 1970. The Mime Troupe denounced the war in their adaptation of a traditional *commedia* script by Carlo Goldoni, *L'Amant militaire* (1967). In later productions, the company used comic-book stereotypes and fast-action farce to demand women's rights and expose the lies of local politicians.

Enraged by the slow pace of civil rights progress and continuing racism in the United States, the Black Arts Movement (BAM) called for revolutionary action in the 1960s. Scorning moderate Black artists and religious leaders in the United States, the BAM artists allied themselves with the Black Power movement of the late 1960s and called for the cultivation of Black consciousness and the political overthrow of white regimes. In manifestos, plays, and performances, leaders Amiri Baraka (formerly LeRoi Jones, 1934–2014) and Ed Bullins (1935–2021) demanded the abolition of mainstream white culture and the immersion of Black audiences in ritual-like experiences to enable them to gain a physical understanding of their past. In an article originally commissioned in December 1964 by *The New York Times*, but which that paper subsequently refused to publish, Baraka (still called LeRoi Jones then) called for a "Revolutionary Theatre" that would

> force change ….The Revolutionary Theatre must EXPOSE! Show up the insides of these humans, look into black skulls. White men will cower before this theatre because it hates them. Because they themselves have been trained to hate. The Revolutionary Theatre must hate them for hating. For presuming with their technology to deny the supremacy of the Spirit…. It should stagger through our universe correcting, insulting, preaching, spitting craziness – but a craziness taught to us in our most rational moments….The Revolutionary Theatre is shaped by the world, and moves to reshape the world….
>
> (Jones 1965: 1–3)

One of Baraka's most compelling works is *Dutchman* (1964), a dramatized encounter between a mild-mannered Black man and a flirtatious white woman on a New York subway. The racial tension, gender dynamics, political and social conflicts, and a "passage" which ends with the violent death of the Black man confront a painful part of American history. Baraka started the Black Arts Repertory Theatre in Harlem in 1965 and premiered his ritualized historical pageant *Slave Ship* in 1967 at Spirit House in Newark, New Jersey (Figure 12.10). After 1970, Baraka devoted most of his energy to social action rather than theatre, and Bullins, who produced his plays with the New Lafayette Theatre Company in Harlem, came to prominence. Bullins used ritualistic, often jazz-inspired structures for his plays, such as *In the Wine Time* (1968), which explored the limitations and possibilities for Black revolutionary action. Bullins's plays were sometimes criticized as languishing in despair. Other playwrights chose to focus on the quiet heroism of ordinary Black people, rather than Baraka's active revolution or Bullins's victimhood and despair. For example, Alice Childress (1916–1994) wrote *Wedding Band: A Love/Hate Story in Black and White* (written 1962, premiere 1966), about a forbidden, interracial love affair. Although the U.S. Supreme Court ruled anti-miscegenation laws – some of which dated back as early as the late seventeenth century – unconstitutional in 1967, it took decades for all states to repeal their state anti-miscegenation laws. *Wedding Band* was considered so shocking that it was not produced in New York until 1972. When it was filmed for TV, some stations refused to air it.

Figure 12.10
Scene from the Chelsea Theater Center production of Amiri Baraka's "Slave Ship" during Brooklyn Academy of Music's Fall Series, 1969.
Source: BAM Archives/Deidi von Schaewen.

Summary
In this chapter, we explored how the direct and indirect impact of the World Wars generated new philosophical thinking and political ideologies; it also affected both the form and content of theatre in the Cold War era. In Europe, new developments reflected the devastation of the war. Such developments included the philosophy of existentialism and "Theatre of the Absurd." In the defeated nations of Germany and Japan, playwrights found various ways to come to terms with their nations' past and present, most noticeably through non-verbal expression in *butoh*. For regions directly impacted by communism during the Cold War, ideological and propagandic theatre was common as a transitional genre to stabilize the national narrative in a tumultuous time. Although later generations might doubt their literary or artistic value, serving as the government's mouthpiece gave theatre a chance to sustain itself during the harshest times.

Because the United States had experienced far less damage than the rest of the world during the Second World War, it had emerged as a wealthy superpower. As an art form, theatre in the United States had less urgency to find new aesthetics to respond to the atrocity of the war and continued to grow in the convention of psychological realism. In terms of content, the Red Scare further depoliticized mainstream theatre, and the discontent against government or society was internalized and expressed as something personal or psychological. This was also the time when American musicals flourished and some reflected American expansionism over the contemporary Asia along with the fantasy of the old exotic Orient. Although rebellious and innovative ideas began to appear in the U.S. theatre during this time, not until the late 1960s did we see the blossoming of dissent reflected both in political movements and in theatre.

Media played an important role in both disseminating information and influencing theatre. During the 1950s, television became more common in the West. Events in distant areas seemed more significant, and protests against unpopular wars or social injustices became more relevant and more people could get involved. Television sometimes altered the way theatre was made. Especially in the United Kingdom and the United States, television permitted more people to see great actors performing in important plays, broadcast live (not pre-recorded) from the studio. Although highly popular in its heyday, live theatre on commercial TV fell out of favor after the 1970s. Nevertheless, media (television, radio, newspaper, and movies) exponentially increased the speed of circulation of the most crucial political, societal, and technological information and directly help propel the social movements of the late 1960s.

★

CHAPTER 13

Art, politics, identity, 1968–2023

Daphne P. Lei

Contributors: Carol Fisher Sorgenfrei, Gary Jay Williams, Tamara Underiner, Patricia Ybarra, Bruce McConachie and Tobin Nellhaus

For many people, "the Sixties" (1960s) was a pivotal point in history, with numerous efforts toward diversity, justice, and progress. We can find traces of the upheavals launched in that period in almost every area of life today, particularly in politics, economics, sexuality, culture, arts, and the media. In the West, the liberating spirit of the Sixties was a great catalyst for experimental performances and the emergence of underrepresented artists during the 1970s and 1980s. Outside of the developed Western countries, however, "the Sixties" often meant cruel wars, authoritarianism, and economic devastation, all of which created a hostile environment for art; a post-traumatic recovery needed to happen before artistic innovations could take place at the end of the twentieth century. Very often, a transnational perspective or alliance, either among developing countries or between diasporic and at-home artists, became necessary for artistic expression when local political resistance was not possible.

Here we focus on the 1960s through the early 2020s, an era that saw the rise of transnationalism and forerunners of **globalization** in the theatre world. As a transnational view enables us to learn more from the populations of the so-called ethnic minorities or marginalized cultures from many parts of the world, we realize that such multiple "minority" groups actually constitute the "global majority." Understanding that power plays an essential part in determining "majority" and "minority" is the first step toward world justice.

Because many well-established Western theatre artists today began their work in the Sixties, there is often a romantic and nostalgic view of the period. We hope to view the Sixties from a less nostalgic and Euro-American perspective. We will address five major topics. Escalating political tensions in the early 1960s led to an explosion of sometimes controversial theatre advocating or participating in political and cultural change. Many theatre artists radically challenged the meaning of author, text, and even theatre itself. We discuss "theatre business," including the changing circumstances of subsidized national theatres and

DOI: 10.4324/9781003185185-18

the development of not-for-profit theatres. Women and underrepresented authors and artists significantly shaped the theatre scene locally and globally. Finally, we pay attention to theatre development from a transnational and global point of view.

The Sixties: A historical crossroads

Historians sometimes define "The Sixties" as lasting from c.1958 to c.1974, when major cultural shifts occurred throughout the world. Focusing on Europe and the United States, Arthur Marwick notes specific characteristics of this crucial period, including criticism of established society; individualism; youth power; technological advances; public spectacles; international cultural exchange; improvements in material life; upheavals in race, class and family relationships; sexual permissiveness; new modes of self-presentation; rock music as a universal language; original developments in elite thought and culture; growth of progressive ideology in institutions of authority; reactionary and violent responses by police and some religious bodies; increased concern for civil and personal rights; and awareness of multiculturalism. The concepts "counterculture" and "underground" defined developments in theatre and the arts (Marwick 1998: 16–20). Additionally, there was a strong desire to search for alternative and non-orthodox means to expand the mind, in order to enhance and heal oneself mentally and physically, including herbal medicine, shamanistic healing, mysticism, lesser-known religious practices and philosophical beliefs, and psychedelic drugs.

Outside Western Europe and North America, there were also significant cultural, political, and artistic transformations. In the People's Republic of China (PRC), the Cultural Revolution (1966–1976) attempted to eliminate vestiges of traditional Chinese culture and capitalist and imperial influence. Many artists, academics, landowners, and other "elitists" were sent into the countryside and forbidden to practice their professions; religious activities and worshipping places were generally shut down; and Chinese Communist orthodoxy was rigorously enforced, both in politics and in arts and literature. The Cultural Revolution generally resulted in economic and political stagnation as well as an irreversible impact on arts, especially in the destruction of books and artifacts and the interruption of oral and intangible traditions, although such destruction subsequently inspired overseas Chinese to both protect traditional Chinese arts and redefine and recreate Chineseness in the diaspora. Within China, Scar Literature, a literary genre documenting or depicting the suffering of the Cultural Revolution, emerged in the late 1970s; it affected the development of Chinese arts and literature for decades.

Many nations broke free of colonial subjugation or partition, resulting in political and economic instabilities that were often accompanied by wars, bloody coups, terrorism, mass killings, poverty, and starvation, all of which caused transnational migrations. The Cuban Revolution contributed to a wave of national experiments with socialism throughout Latin America, and then reactions to these experiments, not all of them peaceful. While the lingering colonial control in many parts of the society still deeply affected people's daily lives, the continuing Cold War between the United States and the Soviet Union exacerbated existing political problems and often created neocolonial domination in these regions in the postcolonial era.

The year 1968 is often chosen as the dividing line between the more complacent "Fifties" and the radically transforming "Sixties" in the West. A few key events of 1967–1969 will demonstrate the cataclysmic nature of the cultural shift and the complex, ever-changing emotions of people throughout the world.

On 14 January 1967, the first "Human Be-In" took place in San Francisco's Golden Gate Park. This self-described "gathering of the tribes" was populated by "hippies," anti-establishment youth rejecting conformity, war, and materialism and advocating communal sharing. The Human Be-In inspired *Hair: The American Tribal Love-Rock Musical* (1967; book and lyrics by James Rado and Gerome Ragni, music by Galt MacDermot). It was at the Human Be-In that Timothy Leary (1920–1996), a former Harvard professor who advocated the use of psychedelic drugs such as LSD, first urged the world's youth to "turn on, tune in, drop out," to heighten their consciousness, be sensitive to the surroundings, and resist involuntary or unconscious commitment (Leary 1983: 253). The Human Be-In gave rise to the 1967 "Summer of Love," when about 100,000 "flower children" gathered peacefully in San Francisco's Haight-Ashbury district, openly taking psychedelic drugs, enjoying music, and engaging in uninhibited sex.

The imagined idyll of the Summer of Love was followed by the harsh brutalities of 1968. In France, Japan, Italy, the U.S., the U.K., Germany, Mexico, and elsewhere, protests by students and workers against the Vietnam War, authoritarian governments, social/racial inequality, and conservative educational systems resulted in violent police and military responses. Historians often cite the upheavals in France during May 1968 as the defining moment. Following extensive student protests, the closure of universities, and violent military responses, over 11 million workers – more than one-fifth of the population of France – went on strike (including spontaneous "wildcat" strikes) for two weeks, virtually shutting down the French economy and threatening to topple the government.

In Poland, strikes by university students and intellectuals were harshly suppressed by Russian-backed security forces. Soon after, an antisemitic campaign forced the mass emigration of Polish Jews. In what was then Czechoslovakia, a movement for political change (the "Prague Spring") was crushed by the invasion of Soviet and Eastern Bloc troops. Police brutality in Northern Ireland signaled the beginning of a long-lasting insurrection against British rule ("The Troubles"). In Japan, students' and intellectuals' protests against the government's policies and the Vietnam War were suppressed by the riot police, which led to many university shutdowns by early 1968.

The year 1968 was traumatic in the United States as well. Both Black civil rights leader Dr. Martin Luther King, Jr. and probable Democratic Presidential nominee Robert F. Kennedy were assassinated; riots, looting, and arson erupted in over 100 poor, Black, urban neighborhoods, eliciting police and National Guard brutality. Between 1968 and 1971, on university campuses, massive student protests were held against the government's drafting college-age males to fight in the Vietnam War. The authorities responded violently to student demonstrations and strikes at the University of California at Berkeley, Columbia, and other universities, and to anti-Vietnam War demonstrations at the Democratic National Convention in Chicago. Agitprop groups, calling themselves guerrilla theatre companies (after the jungle-fighter revolutionaries in Latin America), performed at rallies and elsewhere to protest the war. By 1970, there were probably 400 student guerilla theatre troupes in the United States. Students in Western European cities formed similar troupes to protest American militarism in Vietnam.

There were also important advances in awareness of social welfare and civil rights and in science and technology. An estimated 650 million television viewers (53 million in the United States) watched the U.S. astronauts land on the moon in July 1969, planting the nation's flag on its surface. As a technological triumph and landmark media event, it symbolized a new era, a new global consciousness and spectatorship, and a U.S. public relations victory in the Cold War. In 1972, the U.S.'s National Aeronautics and Space Administration (NASA) released its famous "blue marble" color satellite photos, showing the planet earth floating in space. Circulating on global television, the beautiful marble represented the hope and connectivity of mankind and the fragility of the earth. Between the 1950s and the 1990s, radio, film, television, satellite television, video cassettes and compact discs, and finally the internet significantly changed the ways in which information and performance are recorded and disseminated, and the 1960s marked the beginning of such rapid development of media and increasing global interconnectivities. Anything under the sun – violent and traumatic wars and protests, exciting Olympic Games, or glamorous Oscar award ceremonies – became part of the consumable spectacle. In 1989, the Chinese government's military crackdown on students' pro-democracy protest at the Tiananmen Square on 4 June and the fall of the Berlin Wall that separated East and West Germany since 1945 on 9 November were both watched as TV "drama." The global viewership also had the function of "bearing witness." The camera footage of the beating of Rodney King by police in Los Angeles in 1991 significantly changed the racial dialogue in the United States. In the 1990s, the World Wide Web and cell phones (or mobile phones) joined in the media force. By the end of the millennium, the concept of total global connection, rapid information dissemination, and world viewership became the norm.

Theatre and electronic media

Media technologies have had an obvious impact on the forms, styles, and techniques of the theatre. As we saw in Chapter 12, Arthur Miller's *Death of a Salesman* had roots in radio, and Jo Mielziner's setting offered a film-like effect. By the 1980s, digitization made the interplay between human bodies and media much more fluid. "Multimedia" was a new term to describe a live performance incorporating sound, light, projections, and video as part of the theatrical narrative; sometimes, verbal expressions were secondary. Scenic spectacularism became a star performer in big-budget American and British musicals, such as *The Phantom of the Opera* (1984). Musicals and some non-musical plays began to equip actors with wireless microphones and to manually balance and distribute blends of singers and orchestras, creating soundscapes that differ greatly from traditional (non-amplified) live performance. Stage musicals were recycled into films, soundtrack albums, and videos and toured for international audiences. Technological "advancement" also had an irreversible impact on traditional performing arts, both in performance style and in training. For instance, wireless microphones began to appear in Chinese opera in the 1990s and significantly affected the voice training process and singing style of the classical art. New recording technology was essential in documenting and transmitting traditional arts; for instance, karaoke (which literally means "empty orchestra") was originally invented for popular entertainment and was adopted by Chinese opera practitioners in the diaspora as the "orchestra" during the training sessions because live musicians were not available.

Radical theatre for social change in Europe

Many theatre groups advocated political change long before 1968, such as the U.S.'s Living Theatre, San Francisco Mime Troupe, and Bread and Puppet Theatre (Chapter 12). The uprisings of 1968 had further awakened a generation of theatre artists eager to push for political change through their art. They recognized the power disparities caused by class, racial, gender, and/or regional differences and hoped to forge an alternative culture to help workers, peasants, and others to oppose capitalist power and political injustice. They typically performed in parks, community centers, popular demonstrations, village squares, churches, and similar gathering places.

In Provence, France, the Lo Teatre de la Carrièra emphasized southern France's unique culture by using the Occitan dialect and by decrying the region's industrialization by Parisian "imperialists." In Berlin, the West German GRIPS Theater produced radical plays for children and youth. In Spain, despite rigorous censorship, theatres opposed dictator Francisco Franco during the early 1970s. These included Barcelona's Els Joglars, agitating for Basque independence in northern Spain, and Madrid's Tabaño, which mocked Spanish consumerism, authoritarianism, and the Catholic Church.

In 1971, British playwright/theorist John McGrath (1935–2002) founded 7:84, a theatre company named for a statistic published in 1966 in *The Economist* stating that 7 percent of the population of Great Britain owned 84 percent of the capital wealth. His productions, using broad humor, catchy tunes, and identifiable locations, were performed in working-class halls and pubs throughout the 1970s. His highly Brechtian *The Cheviot, the Stag and the Black, Black Oil* (1973) demonstrated that capitalists' desire to profit from North Sea oil was simply one more episode in the long exploitation of the Scottish poor by the English rich.

In 1968, Italian playwright-performer Dario Fo (1926–2016) and his wife, playwright-actor Franca Rame (1929–2013) (Figure 13.1), established a noncommercial theatrical cooperative, which soon produced *Mistero Buffo* (1969), a one-person show (with Fo as court jester) that satirized Catholicism. *Accidental Death of an Anarchist* (1970) was a farcical attack on police corruption. During the 1970s and 1980s, Fo explored Italian folk drama, including commedia dell'arte, wrote several more plays, and expanded his repertoire of theatrical clowning. Rame wrote and performed feminist pieces, such as *All Bed, Board and Church* (1977), which excoriated Italian patriarchy. Fo and Rame often donated their performance proceeds

Figure 13.1

Italian actor and director Dario Fo and his wife Italian actress Franca Rame performing in *Settimo: ruba un po' meno* (*Seventh Commandment: Steal a Little Less*), Milan, 1964.

Source: Angelo Cozzi/Mondadori via Getty Images.

to radical political movements. These proceeds might be quite substantial; in the mid-1980s, Fo often attracted over 10,000 spectators per performance. In 1997, he was awarded the Nobel Prize for Literature. His Nobel Prize speech can be found on the website, under Links.

Social activism and theatre in postcolonial Africa

The end of colonialism in Africa often resulted in poverty, political instability, and ethnic wars. After independence, some indigenous theatre artists began to reclaim tribal myths and performance practices and, at the same time, develop new, often politically themed works that assessed the damage of colonialism or critiqued the neocolonial regimes; these artists were often imprisoned or forced into exile.

Nigeria, which became independent of the Britain in 1960, includes several distinct ethnicities and languages. This diverse culture offers a wide spectrum of theatrical styles and perspectives. Hubert Ogunde (1916–1990) founded the Ogunde Concert Party, Nigeria's first professional theatre company, in 1945. Both his anticolonial plays before independence (many of which were banned) and his post-independence *Yoruba Awake!* (1964) drew on Yoruba myths. During Nigeria's civil war, Wole Soyinka (1934–), Nigeria's best-known playwright and winner of the 1986 Nobel Prize for Literature, was detained without trial and subsequently went into exile. His *Madmen and Specialists* (1971) was a bitter, enigmatic

play inspired by those events. Soyinka's *Death and the King's Horseman* (1975) used a Yoruba religious ritual called *Egúngún* masquerade to critique colonialism (see the Yoruba *Egúngún* case study on the website). After returning from exile, Soyinka staged *Opera Wonyosi* (1977), a Nigerian amalgam of *The Beggar's Opera* (1728) by John Gay (1685–1732) and Brecht's *Threepenny Opera* (1928). It satirized a self-proclaimed African emperor and the Nigerian middle class. Fellow Nigerian Femi Osofisan (1946–), influenced by Marx and Brecht, looked unfavorably on Soyinka's sometimes abstruse metaphysics. Osofisan's plays reflected both his own aesthetic interests and his passionate advocacy of social justice. His *Once Upon Four Robbers* (1980) satirized the Nigerian military government, and his adaptation of Nikolai Gogol's *The Inspector General* (1836) mocked the ruling elite. Osofisan used traditional dance, music, myth, and folklore to explore modern class polarities in *The Chattering and the Song* (1976). His *Tegonni: An African Antigone* (1999) critiqued both colonial and patriarchal authority by juxtaposing the classical Greek character with a nineteenth-century Yoruba princess.

Soyinka and Osofisan primarily write in English, although their incorporation of indigenous elements is a powerful anticolonial statement. For some other writers, the choice of an indigenous language is essential for decolonization. In Sierra Leone, independent of the Britain since 1961, Thomas Decker (1916–1978) promoted theatre in Krio, an urban, English-based Creole language that developed in the interchange among freed slaves in Freetown, the Europeans, and the indigenous people of the region. Krio theatre served a wide cross-section of society and inspired a number of playwrights, including the radical Yulisa Amadu Maddy (1936–2014). His play *Big Berrin* (*Big Death* 1976) was critical of the plight of the urban poor and resulted in his imprisonment. The most influential writer advocating native languages in postcolonial Africa was probably Ngũgĩ wa Thiong'o (1938–), the prolific novelist, playwright, essayist, and theorist who has been considered in multiple years a front-runner for the Nobel Prize in Literature. While British colonial rule ended in 1962 and the first president of the Republic of Kenya was elected in 1964, the colonial legacy and oppression remained. Ngũgĩ advocated linguistic decolonization as the first step for "decolonizing the mind" (Ngũgĩ 1986), denouncing English and writing in his native language Gikuyu. In the Gikuyu play *I Will Marry When I Want* (*Ngaahika Ndeenda*, co-written with Ngũgĩ wa Mirii, 1977), marriage was used as a theme to critique class, gender, and religious inequity and to illustrate the conflicts between tradition and modernity in postcolonial Kenya. This play was considered politically provocative and may have prompted his imprisonment. He later left the country and has been dedicating himself for decades to education, translation, and writing, mostly in the United States. His other better-known plays include *The Trial of Dedan Kimathi* (co-written with Micere Githae Mugo 1976) and *Mother, Sing for Me* (1982), a multilingual musical play.

South Africa became an independent state in 1934, but a legacy of Dutch and then British colonial practices remained. Despite being the minority, white descendants of the colonizers controlled the government. In 1948, they formally instituted a legal system called apartheid (a Dutch and Afrikaans word meaning "apartness"), a segregation policy that relegated Blacks to separate inferior living and working conditions until 1990. Apartheid classified people into four racial groups: Black, white, colored (mixed race), and Indian. It implemented strict racial segregation in public spaces, anti-miscegenation laws, and resettlement. To create white-only space, over three and half million people were forcefully relocated into "townships." Other non-white residents such as Chinese and Indians were also discriminated against. In 1990, the ruling National Party renounced apartheid, and in 1994, Nelson Mandela (1918–2013), who had been a political prisoner from 1963 to 1990 because of his anti-apartheid resistance, was elected the nation's first Black president.

Both Black and white artists used theatre to protest apartheid policy since the 1960s; cross-racial collaboration played an important part in bearing witness and performing resistance as racial trespassing was forbidden in real life. For instance, the internationally well-known anti-apartheid play *The Island* (1973) was created through improvisation by John Kani (1943–) and Winston Ntshona (1941–2018), along with the white actor-playwright Athol Fugard (1932–). *The Island* is about two Black political prisoners rehearsing Sophocles' *Antigone*, drawing a connection between the Greek classic and contemporary South Africa regarding senseless authoritarian laws. Fugard later became probably the best-known South African playwright of the twentieth century to the world. One of his most studied plays in the West is *Master Harold and the Boys* (1982), which examines the destructive force of white supremacy over basic humanity in an originally loving relationship between a white boy and his Black servants and caretakers. A case study of Athol Fugard can be found on the website.

Another well-known cross-racial collaboration is *Woza Albert!* (1980), which was created by Mbongeni Ngema (1955–2023), Percy Mtwa (1954–), and the white writer Barney Simon (1932–1995). This political satire depicts Jesus's return to Earth in South Africa (Figure 13.2). Mbongeni Ngema's best-known work was *Sarafina!* (premiered on Broadway in 1988); it was adapted into a musical drama (1992), which became an international success, and was nominated for the Tony and Grammy Awards. In 1976, Barney Simon and Mannie Manim transformed Johannesburg's Indian Fruit Market (built in 1913) into the "Market

Figure 13.2

Percy Mtwa and Mbongeni Ngema in the "pink-nose" mimicry scene in *Woza Albert!*, by Percy Mtwa, Mbongeni Ngema, and Barney Simon, directed by Barney Simon, at the Market Theatre, Johannesburg, South Africa, 1982.

Source: © Ruphin Coudyzer, The Market Theatre.

Theatre," an anti-apartheid theatre internationally known as "South Africa's Theatre of the Struggle." The Market Theatre, renamed John Kani Theatre in 2014, continues to be a cultural icon in South Africa today.

In 1995, the South African government established the "Truth and Reconciliation Commission" (TRC) to solicit testimonies from victims and perpetrators of human rights violations; the commission focused on reconciliation and reparation instead of retaliation as a way for the country to move forward. For many, this nation-building strategy did not effectively address the fundamental issues of violence and injustice of apartheid, and it was not adequately executed. Many theatrical works were inspired by TRC, such as *Ubu and the Truth Commission* (1997) by Jane Taylor and William Kentridge with the Handspring Puppet Company. With the characters Pa Ubu and Ma Ubu (referring to *Ubu Roi*, Alfred Jarry's 1896 play, discussed in Chapter 11), this multimedia performance with puppetry presented people's ambivalence and critique about TRC in the post-apartheid era.

Even though traditional patriarchy continued to affect women's literacy and economic independence in postcolonial Africa, many women wrote and spoke up. Ama Ata Aidoo (1942–2023), probably the most famous and influential African female playwright, was a Ghanaian feminist, writer, scholar, and educator who also served as the country's Minister of Education (1982–1983). Her plays *The Dilemma of a Ghost* (1964) and *Anowa* (1971) are modern classics of postcolonial theatre that are taught and produced today and discussed in the case study. Violet Barungi (1943–, from Uganda), Tsitsi Dangarembga (1959–, from Zimbabwe), and Goretti Kyomuhendo (1965–, from Uganda) are some other significant African female playwrights. One of the most important organizations that promoted African women's writing is FEMRITE, which was founded in 1995 in Uganda. With its focus on Uganda and East Africa, FEMRITE publishes women's writing and offers programs regarding women's issues, such as education, health, and women's rights.

CASE STUDY: Ama Ata Aidoo's dramas: Gender, diaspora, and slavery in *The Dilemma of a Ghost* and *Anowa*

Ketu H. Katrak

Ama Ata Aidoo (1940–2023), born in Central Ghana, was a Fante woman (part of the Akan group of people). Her family ancestry is "royal"; her father, as an enlightened Chief, started a girls' school that Aidoo attended. In this matrilineal society, her mother and other women served as strong role models. Aidoo's vision – historical, feminist, and diasporic – was committed to the welfare of Black people in Africa and the diaspora. She was a renowned dramatist, as well as a poet, novelist, short story writer, essayist, professor, and public intellectual.

Orality in Aidoo's written drama

The dynamism of orality [is what] Africa can give to the world.

Ama Ata Aidoo (James 1990: 23)

Ghana was a British colony (1874–1957, previously the Gold Coast). Aidoo writes in English inflected with local Ghanaian idioms, traditional African dramatic forms, and Akan folk forms of orality, including proverbs, communal choral characters, preludes, and "dilemma tales" that pose choices to listeners, often raising "ethical, moral or legal issues" (Brown 1981: 85). Aidoo remarks that of the various literary forms, "I am happiest with drama. Given some other circumstance, I would have liked to write more plays" (James 1990: 22). She traces her playwriting to "a people who told stories ... My mother 'talks' stories and sings songs ... [She] is definitely a direct antecedent" (James 1990: 23). Her play *Anowa* is dedicated to her mother, who told Aidoo the story (as a song) of a disobedient daughter, like the precocious Anowa, who faced a bitter fate. Aidoo believes that "the art of the speaking voice" enables her to "write for listeners" rather than for readers only (Duerden and Pieterse 1972: 24).

Diaspora and Pan-Africanism

Aidoo is unique among African writers for her singular diasporic-feminist vision, displayed in *The Dilemma of a Ghost* (hereafter *Dilemma*) and *Anowa*. Most other writers on the Black diaspora are located outside the African continent (the Black and Creole communities of the Americas and Caribbean), and most are male, seldom adopting a feminist stance.

Aidoo's awareness of prominent Black people outside Africa and her remarkable Pan-Africanism were rooted in her 1960s upbringing, an exhilarating time of Pan-African connections spearheaded by Kwame Nkrumah, the inaugural President of Ghana, which was also the first African nation to gain independence (1957) from the British. Intellectuals such as W. E. B. Du Bois and George Padmore came to Ghana seeking diasporic connections. Aidoo's Pan-Africanist vision in her dramas makes a significant contribution to excavating historical links among people of African origin.

However, Ghana's involvement in the European slave trade as represented in Aidoo's plays was uncomfortable for local Ghanaians, who were "nervous about people from the diaspora," remarks Aidoo:

> Because we don't want to deal with the slave trade, or with colonization. The relationship between us and the African diaspora is charged . . . [and] very complicated. It is one of the issues that the entire continent needs to go through; [to undertake] some debriefing. Our inability almost to go forward is part of this, part of the mess we are in.
>
> (Badoe 2014)

For Aidoo, this is a fundamental, albeit painful reality that must be faced honestly by Black people on both sides of the Atlantic.

Aidoo embraces "the continent through tough love," remarks Ngũgĩ wa Thiong'o, "being able to see its beauty because she is also able to see clearly her warts." Such "warts" include the taboo subject of Ghanaians participating in the slave trade, as in *Anowa*, or a family's rejecting African American Eulalie Rush in *Dilemma* only because of her enslaved ancestors. Aidoo wrote *Dilemma*, her first play, at 24 years. Ivor Agyeman-Duah describes *Dilemma* as "Aidoo's literary trade-mark . . . For years a standard textbook of the West African Examination Council [and] for its . . . historical confrontation of the colony and the Civil Rights Movement as a dimension of the slave trade" (Agyeman-Duah 2012: 409).

Eulalie, a young Black woman, meets Ghanaian Ato Yawson in a U.S. college. They get married without Ato telling his family since he dreams, with his shallow Westernization, that as two individuals, he and Eulalie would "create a paradise" with or without children. Naïve Ato has "forgotten" his people's expectation of marriage with children.

Eulalie's mythical views of Africa – "palm trees, the azure sea, the sun and golden beaches" – result partly from her limited, even misleading education in the United States. Nor does Ato explain his family's customs to Eulalie, for instance, the incident when Ato's mother Esi Kom brings live snails, considered a delicacy and Ato's favorite, to the young couple's house. Eulalie is shocked at the sight of the crawling creatures and throws them away. The colliding worlds in Eulalie as a "wayfarer," a foreigner descended from enslaved Africans, place her in a state of "internal exile" where she feels like an outsider to her own body within patriarchal domination.

Slavery, gender, and compulsory motherhood

Aidoo skillfully links slavery with gender – in *Dilemma*, a weak male protagonist cannot defend Eulalie from being rejected by Nana, his grandmother, as coming from "a doubtful stock," "an offspring of slaves" (19–20). Eulalie can hardly defend herself; she does not know the local language and has to rely on Ato, an ineffectual go-between.

Aidoo represents women characters carrying patriarchal burdens of compulsory fertility and motherhood. In *Dilemma*, 1st and 2nd Woman as the chorus (an aspect of orality) represent two contrasting states of motherhood – one burdened with children and the other stigmatized for having none. Fertility equals womanhood; hence, a childless woman is unjustly denied even her personhood (Figure 13.3).

Eulalie and Ato decide to practice birth control, a modern family planning method unknown and alien to Ato's community. In fact, the family gathers their traditional medicines "to wash Eulalie's stomach" to help her conceive. Ato is inept in explaining this reproductive option to his family. The choral women wonder if the "stranger woman" is infertile, or with her foreign needs for "machines" such as a stove and a refrigerator that she is pregnant with "a machine child."

As cultural collisions and miscommunications mount, Ato slaps Eulalie; she leaves the scene. He is distraught and finally explains birth control to his mother, who is

Figure 13.3
Fiifi Coleman (left), actor and director of Ama Ata Aidoo's *The Dilemma of a Ghost*, in a production in honor of Aidoo, National Theatre, Accra, Ghana, 2023.

Source: Photo by Prempeh Yeboah-Afari. © Fiifi Coleman, FC Productions.

shocked; she thinks only a barren woman would present such an idea. Ato tries weakly to protest, "But Maami, in these days of civilization." His mother is enraged:

> Why did you not tell us that you and your wife are gods and you can create your own children when you want them? You do not even tell us about anything and we assemble our medicines together. While all the time your wife laughs at us because we do not understand such things . . . and we are angry because we think you are both not doing what is good for you.
>
> (51)

Esi Kom blames her son since Eulalie is a "stranger" who cannot break any law, explained by a proverb: "Before the stranger should dip his finger/Into the thick palm nut soup,/It is a townsman/Must have told him to."

When Eulalie stumbles back, Esi Kom takes her hand, welcoming her daughter-in-law for the first time into the family home. Both connect as women while Ato is left like the ghost "bewildered and lost" at the crossroads. His dilemma is unresolved – will he win Eulalie back? Will he find a compromise between his Westernized ways and his traditions?

Ato is disturbed by a children's song that evokes the stark reality of Cape Coast and Elmina, slave "castles," a euphemism for dungeons: "I went to Elmina Junction/And there and there/I saw a wretched ghost/Singing to himself/'Shall I go to Cape Coast/Or to Elmina/I don't know/I can't tell'" (28). The song reflects Ato's indecisiveness. Aidoo does not romanticize tradition showing its fault lines. Simultaneously, she is critical of Ghana's Western-educated people who place themselves above the locals as if their degrees have given them wisdom! Ato is called the "One Scholar" who had drained family resources for his U.S. education.

Aidoo shared in an interview that "as a sickly child," when her mother took her to the big hospitals in Cape Coast, they had to drive by the castles but no one talked about what they represented. When Aidoo finally found out that they held slaves, she "was traumatized and [she] couldn't get the story out of [her] mind" (Mugo 2012: 34) – a visceral, personal response that encapsulates the horrors of the political past.

Anowa: a defier of tradition

Set in 1870, *Anowa* portrays an exceptional, self-possessed, bold woman who stands up for her convictions. Anowa is way ahead of her time and echoes modern untraditional women (the play was published in 1970). Anowa, exceptionally beautiful, has refused, although past puberty, to marry until she falls in love with Kofi Ako and decides to marry him. As a rebellious daughter, she fights her mother Badua's objections to this match and leaves Yebi, her hometown, to "make something" of Kofi, who Badua rightly judges as lazy.

This unusual, multi-layered heroine is judged as "wild," with "feet nimble enough to dance for the gods." The community believes that she should be apprenticed as a priestess, living celibate. Ironically, Badua opposes this, wanting her only daughter to get married and have children. The community's judgment to confine Anowa to a priestess is a way to contain her headstrong, even modern ideas.

Old Man and Old Woman, described symbolically as "the mouth-that-eats-salt-and pepper," serve as the chorus in *Anowa*; salt as necessary for the taste, whereas pepper as an additional spice to add flavor. Old Man, sympathetic to Anowa, represents salt. Old Woman (ironically upholding internalized patriarchy), harsh about Anowa's untraditional ideas, adds pepper to any situation: "Who is she to bring us new rules to live by?" Anowa's opposition to her husband acquiring slaves elicits this response: "The dumbest man is/always better than a woman./Or *he* thinks he is!/And so Kofi shall teach Anowa/He is a man!" (102, original emphasis).

When Anowa does not conceive, the fault is assumed to be hers, biologically, whereas the truth that drives her husband to shame and a tragic death is that he is sterile. When Anowa is worried about not conceiving a child, she encourages Kofi to take another wife; he refuses, perhaps to bury his doubts about fathering a child.

Kofi, unable to become a father, decides to get "one or two men" to help him. Anowa, appalled, insists that slavery is wrong and evil. She begins to consider herself a "wayfarer," someone with no roots and no home, since she had vowed not to return to her hometown. Anowa's opposition is physicalized in her sadness and isolation; she dresses like a beggar while her husband "is resplendent in brilliant kente or velvet cloth and he is over-flowing with gold jewelry from the crown on his head to the rings on his toes" (104). Anowa, barefoot, wears old clothes, recalling a time when as a child she heard her grandmother recounting her travels. Anowa learns about "the pale men" who built big houses to keep slaves. "What is a slave, Nana?" asks the child, who is told that the slaves were sold by the people of the land. When more questions follow, she is told to "shut up" and reprimanded harshly with the words: "It is too long ago! ... All good men and women try to forget:/They have forgotten" (106).

These images stay in the child's consciousness since "that night, [she] woke up screaming hot; my body burning and sweating from a horrible dream" (106). The nightmare shows Anowa as a large woman, Mother Africa, from whom men, women, and children are born in a "hot sea" with "giant, boiled lobsters" who destroy people. This psychic turbulence led to Anowa becoming very ill; that is, when talk began of apprenticing her to a priestess, "I don't know what came of it," notes Anowa, "But since then, any time there is mention of a slave, I see a woman who is me and a bursting of a ripe tomato or a swollen pod" (106–107). Anowa's empathy, indeed identification with slaves, is rooted in this childhood trauma.

In *Anowa*, the marriage that started out with dreams of being "the new man and the new woman" is over when Kofi wants to send Anowa away but, not knowing why, she refuses. The hurtful truth finally rears its ugly head, and Anowa is shocked but blurts this humiliation out in public: "My husband is a woman now. [*She giggles.*] He is a corpse. He is dead wood" (122). Kofi leaves the scene and we hear a gunshot off-stage. Anowa's mental state is profoundly strained as she sits in the gilded chair, giggling, her feet dangling.

Aidoo provides two endings for *Anowa* – in one, we leave Anowa alive at the end; in the other, the chorus returns to comment that Anowa drowned herself. Old Woman echoes a traditional belief that Kofi consumed his manhood acquiring wealth, but she is ruthlessly vicious against Anowa: "What man prospers, married to a woman like Anowa? . . . Was it not that Anowa who made [Kofi] shoot himself?" (123–124). However, Old Man remarks wisely: "It is men who make men mad. Who knows if Anowa would have been a better woman, a better person if we had not been what we are?" He accepts society's responsibility for both tragic outcomes. Old Man also notes that "Anowa behaved as though she were a heroine in a story" – the disobedient daughter who came to a bad end. Yet, she remained "true to herself. She refused to come back here to Yebi, to our gossiping and our judgements." But since the parents are bringing the two dead bodies to Yebi, Old Man remarks that "Anowa's spirit will certainly have something to say about that" (124).

Anowa represents Aidoo's feminist stance remarkably. As she notes forthrightly in an essay:

> When people ask me rather bluntly every now and then whether I am a feminist, I not only answer yes, but I go on to insist that every woman and every man should be a feminist – especially if they believe that Africans should take charge of our land, its wealth, our lives, and the burden of our own development. Because it is not possible to advocate independence for our continent without also believing that African women must have the best that the environment can offer. For some of us, this is the crucial element of our feminism.
>
> (Aidoo 1992: 323)

Theatricality

Both plays' theatricality emerges through the written text woven with orality – the dramatic story is told through communal judgments via the Choral figures, proverbs, and idioms such as "the mouth must not tell everything," "one must take time to dissect an ant in order to discover its entrails," and Eulalie's African American English with the double negative: "I don't care neither." Aidoo's plays structurally build suspense. *Dilemma* opens with a prelude and has five acts. The action in *Dilemma* unfolds in the Odumna Clan's house courtyard; the foreground leads beyond the domestic sphere to the river, farm, and market. *Anowa* is structured in three phases. A prologue situates the drama within the historic Atlantic slave trade: "Those forts standing at the door / Of the great ocean" (66), and "the Bond of 1844 . . . Binding us to the white men/Who came from beyond the horizon" (68), signed 30 years before 1874 when the play is set. Aidoo links Europe's greedy human trade to Kofi's "Big House at Oguaa" with opulent furniture, carpet, fireplace, and "a picture of Queen Victoria unamused" (103). *Anowa* includes extensive production notes about the setting, costume, lighting, music, and two endings.

In conclusion, both protagonists are "free" yet bound under patriarchy and lack family or community support during their ordeals that place them in "slavery kinlessness occasioned by . . . ostracism, estrangement, banishment . . . [that are] extraordinary form(s) of living death" (Houchins 2012: 259). As "wayfarers" without belonging, they echo Saidiya Hartman's delineation of a slave as "a stranger torn from kin and community . . . the outsider . . . the perpetual outcast, the coerced migrant, the foreigner, the shamefaced child in the lineage" (qtd. in Houchins 2012: 259). Both plays demonstrate Aidoo's use of orality and her excavation of gender, slavery, and diaspora through a feminist lens. In *Dilemma*, the resolution is characteristically open-ended as in a "dilemma tale." *Anowa* ends tragically with a glimmer of Anowa's strong spirit returning to play a role in her community:

Ketu H. Katrak is Professor Emerita of Research, University of California, Irvine. Her latest book is on the South African choreographer, theatre director and curator, *Jay Pather, Performance, and Spatial Politics in South Africa* (Indiana University Press, 2021).

Key references

Agyeman-Duah, I. (2012) "Ama Ata Aidoo: Whose Dilemma Could It Be?" in A. V. Adams (ed.) *Essays in Honour of Ama Ata Aidoo at 70*, Oxfordshire: Ayebia Clarke Publishing, 407–14.

Aidoo, A.A. (1985) *Two Plays: The Dilemma of a Ghost and Anowa*, Harlow and New York: Longman.

Aidoo, A.A. (1992) "The African Woman Today," *Dissent* 39: 319–25.

Badoe, Y. (2014) *The Art of Ama Ata Aidoo*, DVD, Fadoa Films. www.amaatafilm.com. (Documentary film.)

Brown, L.W. (1981). *Women Writers in Black Africa*, Westport, CT: Greenwood Press.

Duerden, D., and C. Pieterse. (eds.) (1972) *African Writers Talking: A Collection of Interviews*, London: Heinemann, 19–27 (1967 interview).

Houchins, S. (ed.) (2012) "Paradoxical Queenmother of the Diaspora," in A. V. Adams (ed.) *Essays in Honour of Ama Ata Aidoo at 70*, Oxfordshire: Ayebia Clarke Publishing, 257–76.

James, A. (ed.) (1990) *In Their Own Voices: African Women Writers Talk*, London: Heinemann.

Katrak, K.H. (2006) *Politics of the Female Body: Postcolonial Women Writers*, New Brunswick, NJ: Rutgers University Press.

Mugo, M. (2012). "A Conversation Ama Ata Aidoo with Micere Githae Mugo," in A. V. Adams (ed.) *Essays in Honour of Ama Ata Aidoo at 70*, Oxfordshire: Ayebia Clarke Publishing, 29–45.

Ngũgĩ wa Thiong'o. (2012) "Ama Ata Aidoo: A Personal Celebration," In A. V. Adams (ed.) *Essays in Honour of Ama Ata Aidoo at 70*, Oxfordshire: Ayebia Clarke Publishing, 426–38.

Theatre and resistance in the Philippines

Perhaps the most successful political theatre in the developing world has been the Philippine Educational Theater Association (PETA), founded in 1967. The Philippines was colonized and occupied by various imperial powers – Spain, Great Britain, the United States, and

Japan – from 1565 to 1946. The modern independent Philippines was not free from political turmoil, such as the dictatorship and corruption of Ferdinand Marcos (president from 1965 to 1986), who instituted martial law (1972–1986). With the vision of a Philippine Theatre engaged in anti-imperialism and socialism and the development of people and society, PETA started staging plays in Filipino (Tagalog) and trained members in theatrical and improvisational skills and community organizing. They also went into the countryside to help locals to create theatre analyzing the social, economic, and political conditions of the disadvantaged communities and suggesting solutions. By the 1990s, PETA had produced some 300 plays, with its network composed of numerous local theatres run by fishermen, peasants, students, industrial workers, and others. Later PETA focused on examining and protesting the effects of local, national, and global policies on everyday lives. PETA had many touring shows and mounted large productions in Manila. In 1995, PETA collaborated with the San Francisco Mime Troupe on a musical satire about elections in the Philippines. In 1996, the play *1896* was staged to mark the centennial of the Filipino revolution against Spain (Figure 13.4). In 2005, PETA moved into its permanent home, the PETA Theater Center, which has become a landmark in Philippine Arts and Culture that offers professional theatre repertory performances, workshops, and community and outreach programs.

Figure 13.4
The Philippine Educational Theatre Association's *1896*, performed in 1995 and 1996. Libretto by Charley de la Paz; music by Lucian Leteba; directed by Soxie Topacio.
Source: © PETA.

Theatre and resistance in South Korea

The Korean War ended in 1953. With the "Red Scare" as a strategy, the Korean government ruled the country with a military dictatorship till the 1980s. As seen in Chapter 12, the government-supported mainstream theatre was right-wing leaning. Under severe censorship, some theatre artists experimented with non-realistic forms to stage their resistance; some produced translated Western "absurdist" plays by Beckett, Ionesco, and others; and some incorporated traditional Korean performance in Western experimental theatre. One significant development was a theatrical form called **madangguk** [mah-DAHNG-g(u)k] or **madanggeuk** (*madang* means yard or open square, *guk* or *geuk* means theatre), a combination of elements from traditional mask dance-drama (*talchum*, discussed in Chapter 2), agitprop, and Forum Theatre (discussed in Chapter 14). As a form of guerrilla theatre for resistance and social change, *madang* theatre critiqued the government and satirized the corrupt ruling class; the performers used improvisations and engaged the audience in a direct address-response format. The time and location of the performances were secretly communicated, and the audience dispersed immediately after the performance to avoid trouble. *Madangguk* was most popular during the 1970s–1980s, especially with university students, significantly contributing to the social movement of that time. **Madangnori** [mah-DAHNG-no-ri], a form developed from *madangguk* in the 1980s, played emphasis on the comical play or satire (*nori* means play) as entertainment. Today, *madangguk* and *madangnori* are sometimes used interchangeably; they can be performed indoors or outdoors, free or ticketed. Their original form – traditional folk elements and direct audience interaction – remains similar, but the performances are much more refined, entertainment-based, and have lost the radical political edge of the guerrilla theatre of resistance.

Theatre experimentation in the Middle East

The diversity of cultures and languages in the region means we cannot speak of Middle Eastern theatre in the singular. However, the road to modern theatre was similar across the region. Western-styled theatre, as a major component of the general modernization movement (or sometimes referred to as a "renaissance" or "awakening"), started in the mid-nineteenth century, although traditional forms like singing and storytelling continued to be popular (see Chapter 9). European plays were translated and adapted in the beginning, but different cultures, languages, politics, and artistic traditions marked distinctive types of Middle Eastern theatre. In general, modern theatre has been shaped by wars, revolutions, and sociopolitical changes in the region.

The best-known dramatist of the Arab world in the twentieth century was probably Tawfiq al-Hakim (1898–1987, Egypt), who lived in France for a few years and experimented with various Western theatrical traditions in his writing. He wrote more than 80 plays in diverse styles from 1920s to 1970s, establishing a solid foundation for modern Egyptian theatre. His most famous play *The Tree Climber* (*Ya Tali' al-Shajarah*) was written in the style of Theatre of the Absurd and premiered at the Pocket Theatre, Egypt's first experimental theatre, in 1964. Alfred Farag (1929–2005), who wrote more than 50 plays, was regarded as the most important Egyptian playwright after al-Hakim. His *Fire and Olives* (1970), which centered on Palestinian issues, was done in a Brechtian documentary style.

A highly convoluted history of conflicts involving political rule, inhabitation, the Second World War, antisemitism, and the Holocaust led to the establishment of modern Israel in

1948. In the June 1967 ("Six-Day") War between Israel and a coalition of its Arab neighbors, Egypt, Jordan, and Syria lost territory to Israel, including the Gaza Strip, West Bank, Golan Heights, and Sinai Peninsula. Around 1 million Palestinians came under Israel's administrative rule; others fled or were deported. In subsequent years, Israel returned some regions and annexed others, but the West Bank and Gaza remained as occupied or blockaded territories. The volatile and ever-unfolding situation has yet to be resolved.

Under Israeli rule in 1967, Palestinian nationalism resurged and, with it, cultural resistance that included new theatre troupes and projects that emerged in the 1970s. El Hakawati (founded in 1983) established the Palestinian National Theatre (PNT) in 1984, which was the only arts and culture center for the Palestinian community in Jerusalem for many years.

ASHTAR, a Palestinian theatre established in 1991 in Jerusalem, uses the format of Forum Theatre to create an active dialogue with audience. ASHTAR is still an important theatre today that promotes change in society. Another prominent Palestinian theatre, The Freedom Theatre, was established in the Jenin refugee camp in the northern part of the West Bank in 2006. Theatre is seen as an empowering tool for the young generation to deal with daily hardship under occupation.

Hebrew and Yiddish theatres existed centuries around the world before the founding of Israel in 1948. The Habima Theatre, a Hebrew theatre originally founded in Russia in 1912, became the National Theatre of Israel in 1958. Hanoch Levine (1943–1999), who wrote more than 60 plays and directed many himself, was probably the most famous Israeli playwright of the twentieth century. Other significant Israeli plays include *A Night in May* (1969) by A.B. Yehoshua (1936–2022), *Around and Around* (1970) by Jesef Mundi (1935–1994), and *Soul of a Jew* (1983) by Yehoshua Sobol (1939–). As a pluralist and multicultural country, Israeli playwrights often deal with complicated Israeli-Jewish-Hebrew identity, Zionism versus Jewishness, and other political (often controversial) issues in their work. The Acre Festival for Alternative Theatre was established in 1980, allowing more diverse voices to be presented.

Modern theatre became very important for Iranian intellectuals after the Constitutional Revolution (1905–1907), and the first theatre journal *Tiart* (*Theatre*) was launched in 1908. Both adaptations of Western plays and newly written Iranian-themed plays were performed. Bahram Beyzai (1938–), a prolific writer, theatre and film director, and scholar, was probably the most revered theatre figure of the twentieth century and is still highly respected today. His play *Death of Yazdgerd* (1979) was about the inequitable society on the eve of Islamic conquest in the mid-seventh century. This play has been translated into numerous languages and performed in many countries. His scholarship on *Ta'ziyeh* and pre-Islamic Persian culture, as well as his groundbreaking book *A Study on Iranian Theatre* (1965), made significant contributions to the writing of Iranian theatre history. Another distinguished and prolific playwright of the twentieth century was Akbar Radi (1939–2007), known for offering social commentary in realistic playwriting. *Melody of Rainy City* was one of his most famous plays. Naghmeh Samini (1973–) was probably the first internationally known Iranian female playwright. Her plays, often written with magical realism and a non-linear structure, are among the most significant works in Iranian theatre in the twenty-first century. *The King and the Mathematician: A Legend* (2012) was selected by UNESCO as one of the cultural achievements of the year.

Theatre and resistance in Latin America

In the Americas, the Cold War between the Soviet Union and the United States played itself out in revolutions and rebellions (as in Cuba and Colombia), and in dictatorships and dirty wars seeking to quell all opposition (as in Brazil, Guatemala, Chile, Argentina, and Peru), often with the support of the superpowers interested in protecting both ideological and business interests.

In the transitional period of the 1960s, there were many influential playwrights whose work powerfully presented the shifting sociopolitical and historical power relationships in the general region as well as issues related to violence, economics, colonialism, and identity in their own countries. The examples are *Night of the Assassins* (*La noche de los asesinos* (1965) by Jose Triana (1931–2018, Cuba); *Siamese Twins* (*Los siameses*, 1965) and *The Camp* (*El campo*, 1967) by Griselda Gambaro (1928–, Argentina); *The Day They Let the Lions Loose* (*El día que se soltaron los leones*, 1960) and *I Too Speak of the Rose* (*Yo también hablo de la rosa*, 1965, discussed in Chapter 12) by Emilio Carballido (1925–2008, Mexico); *Documents from Hell* (*Los papeles del infierno*, 1968) by Enrique Buenaventura (1925–2003, Colombia); and *Paper Flowers* (*Flores de papel*, 1970) by Egon Wolff (1926–2016, Chile) (Taylor 1991: 9).

Soon after the Cuban Revolution in 1959, leader Fidel Castro (1926–2016) and his deputies began to use a type of **theatre for development** (further discussed in Chapter 14) to transform Cuba. In 1969, they sent a professional theatre company into the Escambray region, where counter-revolutionary groups had been active in the early 1960s, to prepare the traditional small farmers and peasants for collectivization. Mixing revolutionary propaganda with participatory techniques and developmental strategies, Teatro Escambray became a model for Cuban revolutionary theatre by the mid-1970s.

The combination of radical political theatre and theatre for development exemplified by Teatro Escambray exerted wide influence in Latin America during the 1970s and 1980s. Some companies pushed for a Cuban-style revolution, but many more worked toward versions of democratic socialism. In Mexico, where over 200 theatres joined socialist politics for community development, this movement was called Nuevo Teatro Popular (New Popular Theatre), a term that can be applied to the movement as a whole.

Throughout Latin America, Nuevo Teatro Popular was nearly as various as it was huge, embracing amateurs and professionals, performing in agitprop and realistic styles, drawing urban intellectual and village peasant audiences, and ranging widely among aesthetic and political priorities. Many artists drew from theatre traditions of Brecht and Grotowski; many used "collective creation" as a central method, such as Teatro La Candelaria in Columbia and Teatro El Galpon in Uruguay. Nuevo Teatro Popular helped to empower peasants and workers in Colombia, Peru, and Mexico; worked against repressive dictatorships in Brazil, Argentina, and Uruguay; and supported democratic socialist regimes in Chile and Nicaragua. Nuevo Teatro Popular was both local and transnational: exiled artists worked with artists from other countries and troupes met regularly in international festivals or conferences. Cuba led hemispheric meetings of theatre artists and troupes in 1964 and 1967.

After 1990, with the end of the Cold War, the decline of Cuba, and the fall of most dictatorial governments in Latin America, the Nuevo Teatro movement lost momentum. Nevertheless, many troupes made a successful transition to the globalization era. For instance, Grupo Cultural Yuyachkani in Peru, established in 1971, is one of the most renowned and longest-running theatre ensembles in Latin America. "Yuyachkani" means "I am thinking,

I am remembering" in Quechua, a major indigenous language in Latin America and an official language of Peru. Often incorporating folkloric performance traditions, Yuyachkani documents and responds to the most pressing, immediate realities of the country, such as the violence against indigenous and rural mestizo populations by the "The Shining Path." Plays such as *Against the Wind* (*Contraelviento*, 1989), based on a survivor's testimony about a 1986 massacre, and *Good-bye Ayacucho* (*Adios Ayacucho*, 1990), about a ghost of a murdered peasant searching for a proper burial, make Yuyachkani a "testimonial theatre company" (Weiss et al. 1993: 197). Yuyachkani won Peru's National Human Rights Award in 2000.

In Chile, universities played a crucial role in developing, supporting, and financing theatre productions, starting in the 1940s. Two major university theatre programs, TEUCH and TEUC trained important artists and cultivated a vibrant theatre culture before the dictatorship of Augusto Pinochet (1973–1990); universities also helped sustain the art through the harshest period of authoritarianism. Under the dictatorship, theatre artists were intimidated, some forced into exile and some disappeared; theatre groups were also heavily taxed and strictly controlled. One intimidation tactic, for instance, was a 1973 "accident" that burned down a circus tent used to stage Jaime Vadell's popular show containing anti-government messages. Nevertheless, many forms of theatre survived: non-political commercial theatre, amateur theatre, popular theatre (Teatro Popular, such as El Telon), independent theatre (such as productions *Pedro, Juan, and Diego* by David Benavente and ICTUS in 1976 and *The Clowns of Hope* by the Taller de Investigación Teatral in 1977), workers theatre (such as El Riel), as well as theatre activities and festivals by students. Jorge Díaz (1930–2007), Ramón Griffero (1954–), and Omar Saavedra Santis (1944–2021) were playwrights who were instrumental in creating and sustaining Chilean theatre during the Pinochet era. One of the most successful and prolific Chilean directors of the late twentieth century was Andrés Pérez (1951–2002), who founded Gran Circo Teatro in 1988, with the intention of reaching mass audience. He incorporated multicultural elements into his productions, such as Chilean popular culture, techniques from Théâtre du Soleil (where he was a resident artist), and *nō*. His popular musical *Black Ester* (*La Negra Ester*, 1988) is said to have the most viewership in the history of Chilean theatre. Another influential and prolific playwright was Isidora Aguirre (1919–2011), whose works dealt with social injustice and sometimes served as historical witnesses. *The Altar of Yumbel* (*Retablo de Yumbel*) was based on testimonials of relatives of disappeared peasants. CADA (Colectivo Acciones de Arte) was an activist artist group that used "art action" to stage an intervention in public space during the 1970s and 1980s. The disruption of normalized routines of daily life was a way to challenge Pinochet's dictatorship.

Brazilian director Augusto Boal (1931–2009) was a key influence on the Nuevo Teatro movement. Boal recognized that theatre could oppose, from the ground up, the imposition of capitalist ideologies and the social inequities they produced. Boal wanted theatre to be a space where audiences could "rehearse the revolution," both on-stage and off-stage. His methods continue to be utilized by grassroots movements throughout the world. After adapting international classics for the Arena Theatre in São Paulo, he began working with Brazilian playwrights. However, beginning in 1964, his cultural activism made him a target of Brazil's military dictatorship. He was kidnapped and tortured, and in 1971, he was exiled to Argentina. While in exile, he developed his influential "Theatre of the Oppressed," described in Chapter 14.

Politics and theatre in China

Politics and theatre were closely intertwined in mainland China in this period. Artists and writers had to negotiate with strict censorship and control but could also benefit from government sponsorship. Political theatre was an important part of the entertainment industry, not outside of it.

During the Cultural Revolution (1966–1976), most forms of traditional theatre and spoken drama were forbidden by Maoist extremists who considered them decadent and counter-revolutionary. Instead, a new form of musical theatre – "model drama" (*yangbanxi* [yahng bahn shee]) – was created. Model drama combined traditional *jingju* and Western performance traditions. Some were based on traditional plays, rewritten to eliminate "feudal" elements and to emphasize Communist ideology. The first model drama was *Taking Tiger Mountain by Strategy* (*Zhiqu Weihushan* 1969), based on a novel inspired by an actual 1946 incident from the Chinese Civil War. It was filled with patriotic fervor and revolutionary thought. Other famous "model" works include ballet dramas such as *The White-Haired Girl* (see Chapter 11) and *The Red Detachment of Women* (*Hongse niangzijun* 1964), which was based on the 1962 film of the same title; it was later adapted into *jingju* in 1972.

China began to open up in the 1980s, gradually accepting capitalism and globalization. Many theatre artists experimented with non-illusionistic and Brechtian styles, sometimes combining Chinese "tradition" and Western "modernity." The theorist/director Huang Zuolin (1906–1994) was a prominent figure who had been advocating such an approach: he introduced a version of Stanislavsky's acting method to China in 1938–1940, and in the 1960s, he advocated acting styles combining methods of Brecht, Piscator, Meyerhold, and traditional Chinese aesthetics. In comparison with Western realism, he proposed the theory of "essentialism" (*xieyi*), based on traditional Chinese theatrical aesthetics and conventions which focused on the essence of the play through extracted, elevated, and refined language, movement, and décor. While many playwrights and directors were engaged in stylistic experiments, criticism of the Communist Party was still censored. Sha Yexin's (1939–2018) *What If I Were Real* (*Jiaru wo shi zhende* 1979) and Gao Xingjian's (1940–) *Bus Stop* (*Chezhan* 1983) were the most famous examples of banned plays during the post-Mao period.

At the end of the twentieth century, artists continued to experiment with forms and styles, although political critique was still suppressed and often took form in social satire or personal stories. Experimental theatre director Meng Jinghui (1964–) explored intersections among theatre, architecture, music, installations, and multi-media. He started experimental work with translated absurdist works such as Harold Pinter's *The Dumb Waiter* (1990) and Eugène Ionesco's *The Bald Soprano* (1991). In 1999, he directed Shen Lin's (1958–) *Bootleg Faust* (*Daoban Fushide*), satirizing Chinese popular consumer culture by intermingling elements from Goethe's *Faust* with Chinese slang, classical Chinese poetry, Greek mythology, and Chinese television.

Student movements had been instrumental in modern reforms in China, such as the May Fourth Movement in 1919 (discussed in Chapter 9). In the late 1980s, students began to express their pro-democracy ideas in various demonstrations across the country, and the death of a pro-reform official in April 1989 drew many students to demonstrate at Tiananmen Square in Beijing. For about two months, pro-democracy student demonstrators tried to initiate a dialogue with the government through letters, speeches, performances, and hunger strikes. The government imposed martial law but the student movement gained more momentum. On 4 June, the government took military action against student demonstrators. There was a large presence of Western media in Beijing because of the Sino-Russia Summit in May; as a result, the world was able to witness the historic event. This massacre led to more severe censorship of media and arts, subsequent arrests and prosecution of the suspects, and a significant "brain drain" as many Chinese intellectuals fled to foreign countries and overseas students refused to return home; a number of well-known performers also sought political asylum in foreign countries. The June Fourth/Tiananmen Incident became a taboo subject within China until today, but it serves as a symbol for pro-democracy movements outside China. Moreover, the June Fourth/Tiananmen Incident contributed to the growth of a transnational Sinophone theatre collaboration (see the case study below).

CASE STUDY: Contemporary Sinophone theatre

Daphne P. Lei

The second half of the twentieth century was a tumultuous time, both for Chinese citizens and for ethnic Chinese outside of the People's Republic of China (PRC). People in Taiwan (Republic of China), Hong Kong and Macau (Special Administrative Regions), Singapore (with an ethnically Chinese majority), and the Chinese diaspora in South and Southeast Asia and around the world felt a need to reposition themselves politically, culturally, and artistically. In the 1980s, the aftermath of the Cultural Revolution, the anxiety about Hong Kong's postcolonial future after the signing of Sino-British Joint Declaration (1984), and the political transformation of Taiwan – the formation of a major oppositional party (1986) and the end of martial law (1987) – gave birth to a new academic discipline, Sinophone studies: the study of the complexity and alterity of Chinese cultures and identity beyond PRC and Chinese nationalism. "Sinophone" became a preferred term to cover a broad spectrum of Chinese ethnicity, language, and culture, because the English word "Chinese," with its inevitable association with China, seemed limited in describing the rich multiplicity of cultures in these regions. Sinophone, which means Sinic (Chinese) languages or Chinese-speaking, is an inclusive term to discuss identities beyond Chinese nationality. While the Han is the largest Chinese ethnic group (nearly one-fifth of the world's population) and Mandarin is the most spoken Chinese language today, each Sinophone region has nevertheless developed its unique local arts and culture. The aftermath of the Tiananmen Incident, a new attitude toward "flexible citizenship" (Ong 1999), and the rise of transnationalism and globalization in the late twentieth century further confirmed that "Sinophone" instead of "Chinese" would be a new approach to better understand the multiplicity, complexity, and ambiguity of "Chineseness." Sinophone theatre is thus an inclusive way to study theatrical performances related to Sinophone languages, cultures, and people beyond national boundaries.

The following section discusses contemporary Western-style theatres created in regions of large ethnic Chinese populations outside of mainland China, from a transnational angle. The abundance of artistic styles, languages, philosophy, and political agendas of Sinophone theatres, which are both distinctively local and transnationally similar, presents great challenges for studying the topic. The brief introduction of four major Sinophone artists, each represented by one signature production in their early careers, provides a sketch of this complicated topic. Gao Xingjian (1940–), Kuo Pao Kun (Guo Baokun 1939–2002), Danny Yung (Yung Ning Tsun/Rong Nianzeng 1946–), and Stan Lai (Lai Shengch'uan 1954–) represent important voices from the Chinese diaspora, Singapore, Hong Kong, and Taiwan.

Before Gao Xingjian (1940–), émigré dramatist and novelist from China who became the first Chinese Nobel laureate in 2000, there was very little recognition of modern Chinese theatre and drama on the world stage. Orientalist views often suggest a "temporal disjunction between the Orient and Occident" and the non-Western countries are seen as lagging behind in time, thus incapable of producing modern theatre (Lei 2006: 73). Gao Xingjian proved the contrary. He left China for France in 1987 and became a French citizen in 1998. His dramatic works, with their abstract setting and absurdist style, were often compared with Samuel Beckett and Eugène Ionesco and considered avant-garde theatre in China. *Bus Stop* (*Chezhan* 1983) is one of his best-known plays. A few people are waiting for a bus to go to the city; they chat about their lives, argue, and philosophize. Buses come but never stop. The waiting turns from hours to days to a year, and they finally realize that the bus stop no longer functions and they have been waiting in vain. *Bus Stop* was attacked by the Chinese Communist Party officials as "spiritual pollution" when it had its premiere in Beijing.

Many of Gao's plays were banned in China because of their possible critiques of the regime; therefore, it was the translations of his works (plays, essays, and fiction) into Western languages that gave him a wider readership and spectatorship. His work was recognized by the Nobel Prize committee as an "oeuvre of universal validity, bitter insights and linguistic ingenuity." The reception of Gao's prize in China was mixed. Many believed that his "universal" writing style, his diasporic status, and his translated work made him accessible to the Western evaluation system which gave him the award. To this day, he is possibly the most recognized Sinophone playwright outside of Asia.

The effort of pushing for a transnational alternative narrative to Chinese theatre had begun in Asia in the 1980s. Singapore, an independent nation with three-quarters of its residents of Chinese ethnicities and easy access from South/Southeast Asian countries with large diasporic Chinese, was in a good position to advocate trans-Asian Sinophone theatre. Playwright-director Kuo Pao Kun (1939–2002), often called the "father of modern Singapore theatre," was such a pioneer and influential figure in the history of Sinophone theatre. Singapore is an island city nation proud of its clean, safe, orderly, and beautiful environment and multicultural and multiracial society. With its official "Multiracial Model" policy, the Singapore government stipulates English as the language of administration, whereas Mandarin, Tamil, and Malay were "mother tongues." Other Chinese languages (such as Cantonese, Hokkien, and Teochew) and non-Chinese languages are also widely spoken, though not considered official.

One of Kuo's most famous plays, *The Coffin Is Too Big for the Hole* (*Guancai taida dongtaixiao*, first written in English in 1984, then translated into Chinese), satirizes and challenges the uncompromising bureaucracy, law and order, nationalism, and tradition in Singapore. This one-person play is about a man recounting his grandfather's funeral: the respected old man has had custom-made a luxurious grand coffin for himself before his death. A large crowd gathers at the spectacular ceremony but realizes that the coffin is too big for the hole assigned for him by the government at the graveyard. The state only permits standardized burial plots so the whole graveyard will appear orderly and beautiful, and "there is no room for exceptions!" Personal liberty and in-dividualism come into direct conflict with the Confucian tradition of filial piety and the state's order of standardization and homogenization. The long negotiation process between the family members and state officials reveals the absurdity of state policy and bureaucracy against humanity. The satirical and daring short play was a new milestone both in Singaporean and in Sinophone theatre.

Throughout the twentieth century, Hong Kong, the "Pearl of the Orient," was an important center for world finance, entertainment industry, and tourism; however, its subjectivity was greatly controlled by British imperialism and Chinese neocolonial-ism. After the loss of Opium Wars in the mid-nineteenth century, China was forced to be open to Western imperialism. As a result, Hong Kong was under British control till 1997. The Beijing and British governments, after meeting behind closed doors for years, announced the Sino–British Joint Declaration in 1984 to stipulate that Hong Kong would be handed over to the PRC but would obtain a temporary status as a Special Administrative Region (SAR) and maintain its status quo for 50 years. The anxiety over Hong Kong's future and sovereignty loomed large in the 1980s, and the "97 Doomsday" became a popular topic for artistic expression. Danny Yung, the "Cultural Godfather of Hong Kong," started exploring the dilemma and anxiety related to Hong Kong/Chinese identity, and in 1982, he founded Zuni Icosahedron (*Jinnian ershimianti*, or Zuni for short). Yung usually stays away from conventional characters, dialogues, and realistic plots and instead relies on images, sounds, and im-provisation. Zuni embodies the cutting-edge experimental spirit in a highly capitalist society in Hong Kong. *Opium War – Four Letters Addressed to Deng Xiaoping* (*Yapian zhanzheng, gei Deng Xiaoping de sifengxin*, 1984) was an early and important produc-tion that addressed the anxiety, confusion, frustration, and identity crisis of Hong Kongers. The years 1842 (the end of the first Opium War), 1997 (the Hong Kong handover), and 1492 (the beginning of the Western colonization of Americas) are linked together as historical events that ultimately decided the fate of Hong Kong. *Opium War* was a four-night sequence, each representing a letter to God, Father, Lover, and Self, respectively. Calling them letters to Deng Xiaoping (the leader of the PRC at that time) was to symbolize the aloof and distant position of the Beijing government which would never care to receive such letters from Hong Kongers. Various actors representing different strata of society entered and exited, crossed the stage, brought in, took out, sat on a chair, or spoke random lines. The audience had to decide the meaning of the play themselves. The audience was encouraged to take part in the last night's performance, and this enraged the theatre authorities. The power was cut off and the curtain lowered but the actors finished the performance with calm and determination. Zuni remains the most important avant-garde theatre in Hong Kong today. Yung's boundary-breaking spirit and his critical reflection on Hong Kong identity versus conventional Chineseness are still the central themes of his work today.

A large migration followed Chiang Kai-shek's republic government (ROC) to Taiwan on the eve of the establishment of the Chinese Communist Party in 1949. For decades, Taiwan was seen by the world as another China, the old China, or the democratic China, and the anti-communist theatre sponsored by the government during the height of the Cold War was to promote Taiwan as the *real* China (discussed in Chapter 12). However, the United Nations officially recognized the PRC in 1971, and the United States terminated its official relation with Taiwan in 1979. Taiwan was left in limbo, a complete political entity without internationally recognized sovereignty or nationhood. Locally, different ethnic groups – the new migrants from different regions of China, the earlier settlers from southern China, and the island's indigenous population – had to cohabit and negotiate a new identity. Stan Lai founded the Performance Workshop (*Biaoyan gongzuofang*) in 1984 and their first play, *That Night We Became Crosstalk Comedians* (*Nayiye, women shuo xiangsheng* 1985), addressed the identity crisis in Taiwan. *That Night* was a simple two-person play mixing tongue-in-cheek humor, slapstick, philosophical satire, and political commentary. Two minor entertainers were forced to perform crosstalk in place of two famous master performers. Crosstalk (*xiangsheng*), a two-person improvisational-style standup comedy from the Beijing area, a traditional performing art for the populace transplanted from China along with the Nationalist Party's retreat to Taiwan, was quickly disappearing in the multicultural and Westernized society in Taiwan. Decades after the retreat from mainland China, the parents' nostalgia for the cultural and artistic memories of the old China was fading, but the new Taiwan identity was also not yet formed. The hilarious comedy with daring social commentary ingeniously reflected the anxiety and critique of the politics of 1980s Taiwan and became an overnight success. The audiotapes of the performance sold millions of copies – a record-breaking number in the history of Sinophone theatre. The Performance Workshop still has great popularity today in the entire Chinese-speaking world; their *Secret Love in Peach Blossom Land* (*Anlian Taohuayuan*, premiered in 1986, film version in 1992) (Figure 13.5) is probably the most commercially successful Sinophone theatre. Stan Lai's *Dream Like a Dream* (world premiere in Hong Kong 2002) is an epic production with performances lasting up to eight hours about life, death, illness, storytelling, and dream. Audiences sit in chairs on wheels in a center surrounded by unfolding dramatic actions from all four sides. Many consider this the most significant Sinophone theatre in the twenty-first century.

Despite the multitude and diversity of Sinophone theatres in different regions, they share some characteristics. While the playwrights or directors are of Chinese ethnicity and some emigrated from China, most Sinophone theatre excludes China proper (the PRC). The works can be performed in different Sinophone languages (such as Cantonese, Mandarin, Hokkien) or non-Sinophone languages. Bi/multilingual performances

Figure 13.5
Secret Love in Peach Blossom Land (Anlian Taohuayuan), directed by Stan Lai (Lai Shengch'uan), at the Performance Workshop, Taiwan, 1999.
Photo by Chung-Wei Pan.
Source: © The Performance Workshop.

and multicultural references are common. There are resemblances among the works across the region in their intercultural and global awareness, and their constant critical reflection on the topic of Chineseness in relation to both local subjectivities and Chinese political and economic hegemony. Transnational collaborations and dialogues are common; this is usually done in the form of theatre festivals, play competitions, or academic conferences. There is a strong Western and intercultural influence, as many artists and playwrights have lived, studied, and/or trained in multiple countries: Kuo Pao Kun (Singapore, Australia), Stan Lai (Taiwan, United States), Gao Xingjian (China, France), and Danny Yung (Hong Kong, United States). Grotowski-inspired physical training, absurdist-influenced playwriting, abstract and minimalist settings, Brecht and Boal-inspired dramaturgy, and other traces of Western experimental theatre are often present in these works.

Key references

Lei, D.P. (2006) *Operatic China: Staging Chinese Identity Across the Pacific*, New York: Palgrave Macmillan.

Ong, A. (1999) *Flexible Citizenship: the Cultural Logics of Transnationality*, Durham, NC and London: Duke University Press.

Questioning the author(ity)

"Question authority" was a characteristic slogan of the Sixties. Some important intellectuals challenged the concept of authority of texts and authorship in literary criticism. In 1967, Roland Barthes (1915–1980) wrote an essay titled "The Death of the Author." Barthes argued that meaning arises only through the interaction between the reader and text, not through an author's intentions or personal/historical circumstances. Michel Foucault's (1926–1984) article "What Is an Author?" (1969) proposed that instead of a person, we should think about authorship as "author function," a discursive function surrounding a body of work in various constructions. And in *Of Grammatology* (1967), Jacques Derrida (1930–2004) "deconstructed" texts to show the instability of their meaning and their self-contradictions.

In theatre circles, the author was being similarly questioned. Scripts were not always unassailable; other aspects of theatrical performance sometimes took center stage. To some, the key element was the performer, especially the performer's body and embodied encounter with the audience. To others, the director's vision was uppermost. The play text – or any text – could be used as mere raw material, to be manipulated or uprooted for performance. Possibly texts were unnecessary: observation, personal interactions, and staged imagery could constitute performance. In short, many theatre artists decided that the play/text was *not* the thing: performance was the act of challenging the author(ity), creating new forms of theatre, and even new author(ities) for the next generation.

Performing in the flesh

Antonin Artaud, whose influence was moderate during his own time, was "resurrected" and embraced during the Sixties. Many of his theories, such as denouncing masterpieces from the past, searching for a direct, primal access to the forces at the heart of human existence, forsaking psychological realism and melodrama, emphasizing the *mise-en-scène*, non-verbal expression, and corporeality. Moreover, his theorization of the "Oriental theatre" (such as Balinese dance) as a necessary inspiration for "Occidental theatre" was put into practice by many experimental theatre artists, especially those anti-author(ity) artists who were looking for a sensuous performance style instead of illusionistic representation.

The Living Theatre's collectively created *Paradise Now* (1968) was probably the most Artaudian of their productions. It was structured around rituals, outcries against oppression, and calls for audience participation, including joining a nude quasi-orgy on stage, with a concluding procession out to the streets. The goal was to break down the boundary between performers and audience as a step toward political freedom.

Similarly, *Dionysus in '69* (1968), a rendering of Euripides's *The Bacchae* by Richard Schechner (1934–) with his Performance Group (1967–1980), combined narrative and extra-textual, faux-ritual scenes. It not only pitted Dionysian sexual freedom against repression but also hinted at the dangers of unrestrained freedom. Like *Paradise Now*, it was notorious for orgiastic nude scenes that included audience members and hoped to have a political effect. *Dionysus in '69* also demonstrated Schechner's ideas of "environmental theatre": no demarcation between actor and spectator space; multiple competing events to diffuse any single focus; and actors interacting with audience members in character and personally (Aronson 2000: 97–102). The roots of environmental theatre are in the ideas of Allan Kaprow (see Chapter 12).

The Polish director Jerzy Grotowski's (1934–1999) body-oriented approach to performance was very influential. His "**poor theatre**" advocated stripping away elaborate production elements typical of the commercial stage but relying on performers. Scripts would emphasize archetypal human dimensions and productions would be forged in collective collaborations. The "holy actor" would be an ascetic athlete of the soul, physicalizing the sufferings and ecstasies of the human spirit, uniting psychic and bodily powers to achieve "translumination" (Grotowski 1968: 15–59). The actor would become theatre's chief poet, creating "his own psychoanalytic language of sounds and gestures in the same way that a great poet creates his own language of words." The actor would sacrifice personal psychology and eliminate bodily resistance to full expression through *via negativa*: "a process of elimination" (Grotowski 1968: 133). Actors should remove their physical and psychological blocks in order to be truly present on stage.

Grotowski limited his audiences to 100 to assure immediacy and intimacy. His theoretical language was sometimes obscure and mystical, redolent of both his Polish Catholic background and his existentialist despair. But clearly, performance itself was the authentic center, the object and subject of performance, rather than a realistic representation of another thing. Grotowski's sources included Stanislavsky's method of physical actions, Meyerhold's biomechanics, traditional Asian techniques such as Indian *kathakali*, and Carl Jung's theory of archetypes that activate the collective unconscious.

Figure 13.6
Ryszard Cieslak as Esau, one of the Jewish prisoners in Auschwitz, dreaming of the freedom of the life of a hunter, in Jerzy Grotowski's production of *Akropolis* at the Polish Laboratory Theatre, Wroclaw, 1962.

Source: Laboratory Theatre/The Grotowski Institute Archive.

Grotowski's productions in his Laboratory Theatre in Wroclaw included *Akropolis* (1962), a free adaptation of a work by Polish playwright Stanislav Wyspiański (1869–1907). The original play was set in the Royal Palace at Krakow (a Polish version of the Athenian Acropolis – "the height of civilization"), where figures from its tapestries come alive and are led by the resurrected Christ to redeem Europe. In Grotowski's dark, ironic conception, the acropolis was the Nazi extermination camp at Auschwitz (not far from Krakow). In this symbolic cemetery of Western civilization, Jewish prisoners labored to build cremation ovens and fantasized about love and happiness (Figure 13.6). In this production and *Apocalypse cum figuris* (1969), Grotowski's key actor, Ryszard Cieslak (1937–1990), reportedly achieved a trance-like state. His interpenetration of the actor and role realized Grotowski's vision of externalizing inner suffering – the actor becoming both subject and object.

Grotowski focused his work on "Objective Drama" in the 1980s. A portion of the experiment was carried out at the University of California, Irvine, where a yurt and a barn – his performance laboratory – still function as performance and rehearsal space and a symbol of his legacy today. Objective Drama focused on the elements distilled from traditional performing arts and their "precise therefore objective impact on participants" (Robert Cohen, qtd. in Wolford 1991: 165). Along with his assistants, including "technical specialists" from different traditional cultures, Grotowski conducted workshops that had tremendous and even long-lasting effects. Many of his students (including international ones) started their own experimental groups with such psychophysiological emphasis after studying with him. For instance, Liu Ruoyu (Liu Ching-min 1956–), who received a year of training with Grotowski at the University of California, Irvine, founded U Theatre (1988–) in the mountains in Taiwan. With unique actor training that combines rituals, martial arts, folk theatre, drumming, Grotowski methods and site-specific outdoor performances, U Theatre represents one of the many Grotowski-inspired theatre groups around the world. Grotowski died in 1999, but his global impact can still be felt today.

Japanese director Suzuki Tadashi (1939–, sometimes known in the West as Tadashi Suzuki) developed a physical training method for actors (the Suzuki Method) now used internationally. The Suzuki Method posits a constant tension between the upper body (seen as the origin of the conceptual and the conscious) and the lower body (seen as the origin of the physical and the unconscious). His acting exercises, which incorporate elements of *nō, kabuki, kathakali* and Japanese martial arts, include slow movements, rhythmic foot stamping and sliding, crouching, and tension-informed stances, combined with vocalizations (Carruthers and Takahashi 2004: 70–97). The aim of the Suzuki training is to strengthen the body, voice, and concentration of the actors and help create a powerful stage presence with energized but restrained physical motions. He established Suzuki Company of Toga (SCOT) in the remote mountain village Toga in Japan in 1976. In 1992, Suzuki and American director Anne Bogart (1951–) founded Saratoga International Theatre Institute (SITI) in New York State to train performers using both Suzuki Method and Bogart's own method, called Viewpoints. Many international artists take pilgrimage-like trips to Toga or Saratoga to experience the unique trainings. SITI had its last production season in 2022 but their training center continues.

Performance art

Artists' questioning of authority – the authority of art itself – gave birth to **performance art** in the 1960s. Performance art – like Dada and other avant-garde movements of the early twentieth century – questioned the definition, aesthetics, and judgment of art, as well as the modes and venue of production. Performance artists often rejected the boundaries between artistic genres, and even between life and art, such as performing artists' blending of theatre with painting, sculpture, and dance. Early performance art (called "**live art**" in the U.K., or "performance" elsewhere) was clearly influenced by Kaprow's Happenings (Chapter 12). It often stays away from a conventional dramatic narrative line or imposes an aesthetic standard, but aims to demystify high art and call attention to the social processes that "confirm" art as art.

Performance artists often use their own bodies as performance instruments and their own lives as subjects. They may use video, dance, sculpture, painting, and music, or strange media such as food, and often perform at non-conventional sites: on roofs, in shop windows, in airports, in lobbies, or on street corners. Performance artists often associated themselves with the visual arts instead of theatre. Some have performed works only once, creating a never-to-be-repeated experience that could not be purchased or commodified. In contrast, other performance artists repeated the event and charged admission, and even performed in conventional venues. Well-known performance artists of this period include Carolee Schneemann (1939–2019), Chris Burden (1946–2015), Marina Abramović (1946–), Laurie Anderson (1947–), Guillermo Gómez-Peña (1955–), Karen Finley (1956–), Coco Fusco (1960–), and Denise Uyehara (1966–). Each is unique in style, vision, and goal.

While early performance art was sometimes criticized as too personal or self-indulgent, we should also consider that "personal is political" was an important concept behind performance art. Some later artists are engaged with specific social issues such as race, gender, and social inequity. For instance, Guillermo Gómez-Peña is a prolific artist whose work often centers on race and border-crossing. Born in Mexico and coming to the United States in 1978, he calls himself:

> a nomadic Mexican artist/writer in the process of Chicanization, which means I am slowly heading North. . . . I make art about the misunderstandings that take place at the border zone. But for me, the border is no longer located at any fixed geopolitical site. I carry the border with me, and I find new borders wherever I go.
>
> (Gómez-Peña 1996: 1, 5)

Working solo or in collaboration with such artists as Coco Fusco and Roberto Sifuentes (1967–), Guillermo Gómez-Peña challenges the constructed national and cultural identities, in the context of Latinx (or Latine) experience in the United States. In 1994–1996, Gómez-Peña and Sifuentes collaborated on the *Temple of Confessions*, in which they became exhibits in Plexiglas booths, like archeological relics or scientific specimens. They were advertised as the last living *santos* (saints) from an "unknown border region." Spectators were invited to experience this "pagan temple" and to confess their "intercultural fears and desires" to the artists, who embodied a hybrid identity of Mexican beasts and living santos." The "confessions" ranged from guilt to anger to sexual desire (Gómez-Peña 2000: 35).

The director as auteur

By the late 1960s, the idea of the director as the primary artist, or at least a coequal with the playwright, was emerging. It was becoming commonplace to speak not of Shakespeare's but Peter Brook's *A Midsummer Night's Dream* (1970), not of Molière's but Roger Planchon's *Tartuffe* (1962, 1973), not of Euripides's but Suzuki Tadashi's *The Trojan Women* (1974). We call these directors *auteurs*, a French word meaning "authors." An **auteur director** (a term borrowed from film criticism) – not the playwright or the actor – is the primary "author" of the performance. Although many *auteur* directors, especially ones working in mainstream theatre, direct written plays, they deemphasize the text and shift authority to their own vision. In this way, *auteur* directors produce their own interpretations by exerting total control

of the **mise en scène**. Although many performance artists write, direct, and perform their own work with the total control of the aesthetics, the term *auteur* is usually reserved for *maestro/a* directors with high recognition; it is also often coded with white-maleness, especially in the earlier period. We will look at some of the *auteur* directors' work here.

British director Peter Brook (1925–2022) was a very important *auteur* director in the English-speaking world. His wide array of theatrical experiments over half a century established him as one of the most innovative, sometimes controversial, directors in twentieth-century theatre. He brought Artaud, Brecht, and Beckett to bear on his 1962 *King Lear* with the then-new Royal Shakespeare Company (RSC). His production sought to emphasize an existential vision of a cruel, godless universe. For instance, when the elderly Gloucester's eyes are gouged out, Brook located the scene downstage close to the audience with house lights up, confronting the audience with the theatrical horror in a very direct way.

Brook conducted Theatre of Cruelty experiments in 1964, culminating with RSC's production of *The Persecution and Assassination of Jean-Paul Marat as Performed by the Inmates of the Asylum of Charenton under the Direction of the Marquis de Sade* (usually called *Marat/Sade*) by German-born playwright Peter Weiss (1916–1982) (Figure 13.7). Weiss's verse text, about the assassination of a leader of the French Revolution, rendered a morally chaotic world in grim corporeal imagery, graphically physicalizing the inmates' madness in a claustrophobic acting space where they perform their play within the play. Charlotte Corday's murder of Marat in his bath was performed in a ritualistic manner, visually echoing Jacques-Louis David's 1793 painting *The Death of Marat*. The inmates' frenzied attempt to take over the asylum created an unforgettable scene of chaos and horror. The play closes with an indictment of complacency toward poverty and political repression – an echo of Marat's own deepest concerns.

In his manifesto *The Empty Space* (1968), Brook called for a "holy theatre" marked by sincerity and authenticity to replace the pre-packaged "deadly theatre" of a consumer society. His *A Midsummer Night's Dream* (RSC 1970) (Figure 13.8) moved away from realism-based staging: the set was a simple non-illusionistic white box setting, the characters were dressed in contemporary flower-children styles, and the fairies were clad in bright colors, swinging on trapezes. The playful eroticism and romantic love in a fresh "Sixties" style offered a promise of both challenging the old social order and artistic imagination of Shakespeare. Brook's *Dream* toured internationally for three years.

French director Roger Planchon (1931–2009) viewed the director as equal to the author. Influenced by Artaud, Brecht, and Marx, Planchon's politically committed productions utilized what he called "scenic writing," that is, vivid stage images that conveyed his vision of a play (Bradby and Williams 1988: 51–6). For many years, he headed the Théâtre National Populaire (TNP) in Villeurbanne (a suburb of Lyon), desiring to bring theatre to the working classes outside of Paris.

For his 1962 staging of Molière's *Tartuffe*, Orgon's home was a kind of mini-Versailles palace. Orgon's devotion to the bogus cleric Tartuffe suggested unconscious homosexual yearning, adding sexual confusion to blind religious devotion. When Orgon is saved at the last instant, the staging evoked a chilling

Figure 13.7

Patrick Magee (as Marquis de Sade) and Glenda Jackson (as Charlotte Corday) in *Marat/Sade* by Peter Weiss, directed by Peter Brook, Royal Shakespeare Company, 1964.

Source: Morris Newcome/ArenaPAL.

Figure 13.8

Oberon (Alan Howard) casts a spell on Titania (Sara Kestelman) in her "bower," assisted by Puck (John Kane), in Shakespeare's *A Midsummer Night's Dream,* directed by Peter Brook with the Royal Shakespeare Company, 1970. Setting by Sally Jacobs.

Source: Thomas Holte © Shakespeare Birthplace Trust.

demonstration of Louis XIV's absolute power. Directing the same play in 1973, Planchon had Orgon's house dismantled room by room. Orgon and his family were herded into a dungeon beneath the stage floor before being released (see the case study in Chapter 6 for other interpretations of *Tartuffe*).

In Suzuki Tadashi's radical adaptation of *The Trojan Women* in 1974, new poetry and styles such as *nō, shingeki,* and Suzuki method were incorporated. Ultimately condemning all wars and military atrocities, Suzuki presented the traumas of Hiroshima and Nagasaki with memorable images and scenes. For instance, the chorus women were homeless sur-vivors of both Troy and Hiroshima/Nagasaki; the Greek soldiers were samurai who vi-

olently raped Andromache and dismembered her son (a doll) on stage. Major characters were presented in a *kabuki*-style dumb show (*danmari* [dahn-mah-ree]). Japan was always presented as both a defeated victim and a militaristic victimizer. Suzuki is very clear about his role as an *auteur* director. Speaking of his freedom with Shakespeare's text in his *Tale of Lear* (1988), he said: "[T]he first responsibility of a director is to define what interests him the most, what resonates with his current concerns" (Mulryne 1998: 84). Suzuki's *Lear* is set in a nursing home/mental hospital. Shakespeare's King Lear is gradually going mad throughout the course of the play; Suzuki's *Lear* has already gone mad before the play begins.

The Bacchae (1974, at the Schaubühne in Berlin) by the German *auteur* director Klaus-Michael Grüber (1941–2008) offered a very different look from Schechner's *Dionysus in '69*. The performance began with the weakened Dionysus, god of the theatre, being rolled out on a hospital gurney, barely able to speak his name in the opening line, "I am Dionysius, the son of Zeus" (Euripides 1959: 155). Grüber's staging was a never-ending process of stitching and restitching fragments from the classic together, with the result open to varying readings (Fischer-Lichte 1999: 16–7). Critics describe his approach as "postmodern." **Postmodernism** is a concept that emerged in the 1970s that can be used in many contexts, such as philosophy, literary criticism, and arts. Postmodernism is not about "after modernism" but about the rejection of meaning, narrative, high art, self-enclosed truth, and value that modernism embraces. Philosopher Jean-François Lyotard wrote: "Lamenting the 'loss of meaning' in postmodernity boils down to mourning the fact that knowledge is no longer principally narrative" (Lyotard 1984 [1979]: 26). Instead, postmodernism implies "a deep incredulity toward metanarratives" (Lyotard 1984: xxiv). In theatre, postmodern productions tend to have non-linear narratives, pastiches, or samplings of pre-existing but unrelated texts and images; they are open to multiple and endless interpretations but refuse to prescribe meanings. In contrast to traditional and modernist approaches to drama, which seemed to hold out a promise of eternal, redeeming truths lying behind the plays, postmodern performance offers only the "empty presence" of the here and now (Connor 1989: 140–1). Another famous *auteur* director, Robert Wilson (1944–), whose work is often described as postmodern, will be discussed in the section below.

Ariane Mnouchkine (1939–) founded Théâtre du Soleil in 1964 in Paris. Her signature style usually blends a wide range of performance traditions, such as commedia dell'arte, puppetry, physical theatre, and ensemble acting. Her concept of egalitarian theatre community eliminates hierarchy among leadership roles and actors, and audiences are often invited to watch actors getting ready for the performance. Her incorporation of Asian traditional arts in her adaptations of Western classics sometimes draws criticism, although she is the only world-recognized female director of intercultural theatre in the twentieth century and the only female artist who has received the International Ibsen Award (more below and in Chapter 14).

Joanne Akalaitis (1937–) and Martha Clarke (1944–) are both important award-winning American *auteur* theatre directors with unique artistic approach. Akalaitis co-founded the avant-garde theatre Mabou Mines in New York (1970). With an emphasis on physicality, she choreographs actors' movements and considers architecture, light, and sound as compositional elements in order to form images as a sculptor creating a piece of artwork. Her theatrical space is also psychological and emotional space. To her, the most essential part of theatre is "the inside and outside coming together" (Saivetz 1988: 132). Working with cutting-edge artists like composer Philip Glass (1937–), her work is sometimes considered iconoclastic and controversial (see more about the controversy of her production of *Endgame* in Chapter 12). Martha Clarke is known for her innovative and multidisciplinary approach to theatre, dance, and opera, strongly inspired by visual art. Her *Garden of Earthly Delights* (1984), a sensational reimagination of the famous painting by Hieronymus Bosch (1450–1516), is a dance drama combing evocative music and images and stage aerial art (flying), creating an unforgettable theatrical experience for audience.

THINKING THROUGH THEATRE HISTORIES: FUNCTIONS OF THE CLASSICS

The term "classics" usually refers to well-recognized and well-aged texts of high quality; "classics" also suggests a sense of familiarity and deference from the readership. In theatre history, the term "classics" often refers to Shakespeare or ancient Greek plays in the West. These canonical texts, which have been translated into many languages and performed frequently, become "universal" classics through colonization and globalization. There are also classics outside of the Western canon, such as *Mahabharata* in India and *The Peony Pavilion* in China. Classics denote authority and power, and they constitute the canon to be studied throughout history. These famous texts' purported "universal" value and their authority make them highly adaptable in different contexts for specific purposes. For instance, as explained in the previous section, many *auteur* directors transform Western classics into their signature works with distinctive interpretations of the texts and unique directing theories and styles. The familiarity of the original texts makes it easier for the audience to understand the deviation from the original and to appreciate the innovation of the director. The audience of Peter Brook's *Midsummer Night's Dream* did not need to make sense of his daring artistic choices staging because they already knew Shakespeare by heart; Brook's ingenious staging or new interpretation of the old story would be the new focus.

Similarly, classics can be adapted effectively in intercultural and postcolonial performances, and in any performances of resistance. For instance, Prospero's dominance over Caliban and Ariel in *The Tempest* creates a perfect scenario for a "canonical counter-discourse" from a postcolonial perspective. *A Tempest* (*Une tempête*, 1969) is an early and influential postcolonial adaptation by Aimé Césaire (1913–2008), the famous Afro-Caribbean writer from Martinique (a Caribbean island and overseas region of France). The Black native hero Caliban and the mulatto Ariel elucidate the relationship of master/slave and colonial/indigenous. *A Branch of the Blue Nile* by Derek Walcott (1930–2017), the Nobel laureate of 1992 from St. Lucia (a Caribbean island nation), is another famous example of rewriting Shakespeare (*Anthony and Cleopatra*). Transposed into the Trinidad context, *Blue Nile* examines the predicament of local Black actors in the global theatre market as their skin color destroys their chances to be in any classics on the global stage (Gilbert and Tompkins 1996: 15–52).

In the context of intercultural theatre, Western classics (as text) are often paired with non-Western artistic traditions (as raw material and labor). Some works of the French director Ariane Mnouchkine and the American director Richard Schechner belong to this category. For more on this intercultural model – Hegemonic Intercultural Theatre (HIT), see Chapter 14. Very often, the Western notion of universality is forced upon non-Western artists and audience, and the relationship among intercultural collaborators might not be equal because of their power differences. When non-Western classics are used in such intercultural productions, more controversies might surface, such as Peter Brook's *The Mahabharata* (1984; see Chapter 14).

Ironically, the supposed universality of Western classics creates an opportunity for artists from non-Western countries to be accepted in a global setting. For instance, a Chinese opera or Indian dance version of a Shakespearean play will have a higher chance of being invited to an international Shakespeare festival than a traditional Chinese opera production. The familiarity of the Western classics helps the global audience appreciate the intercultural experiment without worrying about linguistic barrier. In many instances, non-Western artists might intentionally adopt a Western gaze for their traditional art in intercultural performances. We discuss intercultural theatre further in Chapter 14.

Creating "performance texts"

Instead of treating theatrical production as a process "from page to stage," or as the materialization of the script, constructing a **performance text** is a new way of imagining and interrogating the meaning and creative process of theatre. Artaud's notion of *mise en scène* and eliminating the author is the essence of performance text. The "text" is only completed when the theatrical creation is done: the performance text can be a collage of images with music, a compilation of vignettes of verbal or physical expressions, or multimedia presentations. Many of the *auteur* directors discussed above can be better described as creators of performance texts instead of directors of plays.

For example, in Paris in 1968, Jean-Louis Barrault (1910–1994) staged a three-hour adaptation of writings by sixteenth-century French author François Rabelais, and Ariane Mnouchkine's Théâtre du Soleil assembled a collage of sketches on the French Revolution titled *1789* (1970). Both emphasized the relation of French history and culture to the then-current spectacle of student uprisings and the desire to free body and spirit from traditional restraints. *The Serpent* (1969), created by American director Joseph Chaikin (1935–2003) with his Open Theatre company, was a collage of material from the Bible and scenes from the assassinations of U.S. President John F. Kennedy and Black civil rights leader Martin Luther King, Jr. Suzuki Tadashi created several collages which he titled *On the Dramatic Passions* (1969), including scenes from classical and contemporary Japanese plays as well as Western drama. Polish director Tadeusz Kantor's (1915–1990) *The Dead Class* (1975) staged "Old Men" with aphasia and amnesia, recounting fragmented and distorted memories; each old man is accompanied by a mannequin representing their childhood. Kantor was on stage, both performing and continuing to create the performance text.

The "text" of Peter Brook's *Orghast* (1971) was an arrangement of musical phonemes and fragments of ancient languages compiled by poet Ted Hughes, intoned by the actors along with ancient music. Performed in the ruins of Persepolis at the Shiraz Festival in Iran, it opened with the Prometheus myth. Romanian director Andrei Serban (1943–) brought new rigor to the American experimental scene at Ellen Stewart's (1919–2011) La Mama Experimental Theatre Club (founded 1961) in the early 1970s. The performance text of Serban's *Fragments of a Trilogy* (1974) was a non-verbal, aural score to communicate the power and passion in portions of Euripides's *Medea*, *Electra*, and *The Trojan Women*. Fragments of Senecan Latin, Greek, and English were woven together with primitive-sounding vocalizations and Elizabeth Swados's (1951–2016) original score. *Trilogy* was staged throughout an empty, rectangular, galleried hall, and the audience moved to follow the action.

The Wooster Group developed from Schechner's Performance Group beginning in 1975, taking its formal name in 1980. It continues to emphasize radical reworkings of canonical plays, developing its pieces in collective improvisations, from which director Elizabeth Le-Compte (1944–) shapes the final collage product. *Route 1 & 9* (1981) juxtaposed portions of the modern classic *Our Town* (1938) by Thornton Wilder (1897–1975) with a recreation of a routine called "The Party," recorded in 1965 by Black artist Pigmeat Martin, and a sexually graphic film. The intent was to explode Wilder's picture of an all-white, small-town America as an embodiment of universal human experience. *L.S.D. (. . . Just the High Points . . .)* (Figure 13.9) (1984) critiqued Arthur Miller's *The Crucible* (1953), which, as noted in Chapter 12, draws parallels between the Salem witch trials and anti-communist hysteria. In "Part Two – Salem," portions of the dialogue were read at a table with microphones, seeming to evoke and query both the infamous televised McCarthy hearings and Miller's play itself as processes leading to truth. The production incorporated controversial minstrel-style black-face in order to probe the authority of Miller's representation of race in America.

Sometimes, the performance conventions rather than canonical texts become the subject of deconstruction and experimentation. For instance, in Japan, the works of Terayama Shūji suggest a desire to shake audiences out of complacency by disrupting theatrical conventions.

Figure 13.9
The Crucible sequence from the Wooster Group's *L.S.D. (. . . Just the High Points . . .)*, directed by Elizabeth LeCompte, 1984.
Source: © Elizabeth LeCompte.

Plays such as *Opium War* (*Ahen sensō*, 1972), *Blindman's Letter* (*Mōjin shokan*, 1973), and *A Journal of the Plague Year* (*Ekibyō ryūkōki*, 1975) were described by Terayama as "invisible theatre" that plunged audiences into terrifying total darkness or into private, curtained rooms. The assault on the audience's senses sometimes led to claustrophobia, hysteria, violence, and even police intervention.

The furthest possible questioning of authorship is its complete elimination. Terayama's outdoor "city drama" (*shigaigeki*, city-street drama) which resembled Happenings, completely eliminated authorship and text and both actors and spectators relied on a series of chance events "in the moments." For example, *Knock* (*Nokku*, 1975) consisted of sites and events spread across 27 locations throughout a district of Tokyo, to which participants (sometimes blindfolded) could journey over a 30-hour period.

Theatre of images

In the 1970s, some theatre artists, dancers, and choreographers began to create performances using visual and aural landscapes that defied conventional concepts of artistic order, continuity, and time. These came to be known as "Theatre of Images." The term was first applied to the theatre productions of the American *auteur* Robert Wilson (1944–). His works present abstract landscapes of discontinuous, dream-like images, encompassed by music, sound, and light. Meticulously choreographed performers slowly move in and out of tableaux, following the carefully executed lighting movements, in front of giant projection screens or among surrealist objects, with or without spoken words. He calls himself a "formal" director, with directorial emphasis on forms instead of content, meaning, or psychology of actors. The refined visual aesthetic does not prescribe meaning in Wilson's "performance text." He even says: "I often use nonsense, but the audience tries to make sense of nonsense" (Lei 2011: 150). Arnold Aronson notes, Wilson's spectacles demand "a new kind of watching" (Aronson 2000: 125).

Wilson's *Life and Times of Joseph Stalin* at the Brooklyn Academy of Music in 1973 was a 12-hour "opera" in seven acts, requiring 140 actors. *Einstein on the Beach* (1976), written with composer Philip Glass, and choreographed by Lucinda Childs (1940–), presented Einstein as a dreamer and scientist, with an overall orchestration of images, trance-like music, and hypnotic movement (Figure 13.10). Its repeated images of a train, a spaceship, and a trial seemed to raise issues about scientific progress. Wilson's monumental *the CIVIL warS: a tree is best measured when it is down* (1984) dealt generally with human conflict at many levels through evocative images and icons, among them battlefield gunfire and a pageant of historical and fictional figures that included King Lear, Marx, Abraham Lincoln, and a Native American tribe.

Théâtre de Complicité is a London-based company that began in 1983 as a collective of actors trained in the methods of Jacques Lecoq. It specializes in a Theatre of Images based on "extreme movement," mime, and clowning techniques. They achieved international acclaim with the 1992 *The Street of Crocodiles*, based on the life of Polish writer Bruno Schulz, in which the poetic and surreal aspects of Schulz's memoirs were theatricalized by the collective in music, image, rhythm, movement, and action.

Some works of Chinese American director Ping Chong (1946–) might also be described stylistically as Theatre of Images. Chong's productions of the 1970s and 1980s were

Figure 13.10
Performers in the "Spaceship" section of *Einstein on the Beach* (by Robert Wilson and Philip Glass) at the Brooklyn Academy of Music's Howard Gilman Opera House, Brooklyn, New York, 8 December 1984.
Source: Jack Vartoogian/Getty Images.

collaboratively developed, plotless, carefully choreographed, sometimes meditative but always very experimental works. He had studied and collaborated with Meredith Monk (1942–), the important composer, vocalist, and interdisciplinary performance artist. Born in Toronto and raised in New York's Chinatown, Ping Chong often expresses a sense of spiritual and cultural dislocation and alienation in his works, based on his own experience as an outsider in the white America. *A.M./A.M – the Articulated Man* (1982) took up the Frankenstein legend and featured a robot who, unable to become socialized, kills and flees into the city. This almost wordless, music-driven performance took place in a white set with all white furniture, a reference to the sense of spiritual dislocation of many Asian Americans. Chong said of this production, "When human beings in a society fail to have a rich psychic life, then it's ripe for fascism" (Leiter 1994: 62). *Kind Ness* (1986) is about the friendship of six elementary school classmates, one of whom is a gorilla. *Deshima* (1990) and *Chinoiserie* (1994) were about East/West encounters, which fused historical events and traditional visual elements in an experimental style. His most ambitious project is *Undesirable Elements*, which expanded from 1992 till today, with over 60 productions in different communities both in the United States and abroad. The interview-based project involves oral history told/performed by community members, mixed with other theatrical elements.

Authors and innovation in playwriting

Despite the radical questioning of the author, playwrights and play texts never disappeared. Some of the most important theatre after 1968 involved text-based new plays. For example, *Angels in America* (1992) (Figure 13.11), the two-play, Pulitzer Prize–winning epic by American playwright Tony Kushner (1956–), combined rich language with scenic collages to juxtapose scenes such as an angel bursting through the bedroom ceiling of a gay man suffering from AIDS, a political conservative's discovery of his homosexuality, a Cold Warrior's visitations by a ghost from his past, and an agoraphobic Mormon woman's hallucinatory friends.

Many mainstream playwrights and directors found ways to depart from psychological realism, such as Harold Pinter, Sam Shepard (1943–2017), and David Mamet (1947–), who probed the emotionally volatile and destructive forces beneath the surfaces of language. With the focus on exploring deep and even dark male psychology, their work is sometimes criticized as misogynistic.

Documentary plays influenced by film and television also proliferated. African American writer/actor Anna Deavere Smith's (1950–) one-person shows on urban unrest in the United States, *Fires in the Mirror* (1992) and *Twilight: Los Angeles, 1992* (1994; later adapted for ensemble performance), focused on language but drew from film and video documentary techniques. Smith interviewed many people from the communities involved in the events (riots in Crown Heights and Los Angeles, respectively). She performed their actual words (verbatim) and gestures, selecting the "shots" and editing the results (Jensen 2007). Another important "verbatim" play was *The Laramie Project* (2000) by Moisés Kaufman and the Tectonic Theatre Project, based on the 1998 murder of a young gay man Matthew Shepard in Laramie, Wyoming. The play was based on hundreds of interviews conducted by the company, exposing the homophobic hate crime. The "playwright" obviously edits the "verbatim" text and incorporates other text; nevertheless, many believe that the "real" words spoken by a "real person" about a "real" event – a new type of mimesis – create greater impact than the conventional theatre of psychological realism.

Some playwrights defended the primacy of the text on legal grounds. Arthur Miller threatened legal action, insisting his copyright of *The Crucible* had been violated in the Wooster Group's *L.S.D. (. . . Just the High Points . . .)*. In 1984, Samuel Beckett and Grove Press filed a lawsuit against the American Repertory Theatre over director Joanne Akalaitis's production of *Endgame* (see Chapter 12). Especially after the early 2000s, the Dramatists' Guild of America (a professional association for U.S. playwrights, composers, lyricists, and librettists) energetically advocated legal action against directors and/or theatres that cut or changed scripts (including stage directions and casting requirements) without the playwright's approval. Although upheavals in communications were altering attitudes, print culture's concept of copyright was still very much alive, until the 2020s, when Artificial Intelligence (AI) became part of "creative" authorship (discussed in Chapter 15).

A new era of playwriting by women

Women write – they wrote throughout history and continue writing; however, only a very small number of female playwrights were recognized as part of the dramatic canon, such as Hrostvitha, Aphra Behn, and Susan Glaspell. It is true that many cultures deliberately kept girls and women from receiving proper education, and it is also true that theatre traditionally

Figure 13.11

The appearance of the angel in the final scene of Tony Kushner's *Angels in America: Millennium Approaches* (1990). From the 1992 production of the Royal National Theatre, London, directed by Declan Donnellan, with Stephen Spinella as Prior Walter and Nancy Crane as the Angel.

Source: © John Haynes/Bridgeman Images.

was a public art dominated by men and that theatre history is a discipline controlled by men. The cultivation of women's playwriting, therefore, goes beyond personal education; it relies on the change in the sociopolitical and economic environment of theatre. In the late twentieth century, many women playwrights flourished; their works have continued to shape the theatre scene and reconstruct the dramatic canon for the next century. They have explored suppressed and controversial topics, interrogated and rebelled against patriarchy, experimented with dramaturgy and narrative style, and envisioned a new playwriting method that could be more nuanced, compassionate, and attentive to gender and other issues that might have been neglected in canonical playwriting; they have demonstrated to the world that women can and should write; many were also devoted to peer-mentoring and educating the next generation.

One of the most prolific and influential figures of the twentieth and twenty-first century is the British playwright Caryl Churchill (1938–), whose dramatic works interrogate power and sexual politics, with a feminist approach and often non-realistic setting. Her plays have been well recognized, widely staged, translated, and anthologized around the world. Her award-winning plays include *Cloud Nine* (1979, 1982 Obie Playwriting award), *Top Girls* (1983, 1983 Obie Playwriting Award), *Serious Money* (1987, 1987 Obie Best New American Play, and 1987 Laurence Olivier Award for Best New Play), and *A Number* (2002, 2005 Obie Playwriting Award). She also received Obie Award for Lifetime Achievement in 2002. *Top Girls*, possibly Churchill's most famous work, opens with a dinner party, hosted by a successful career woman, with a group of iconic historical or fictional women, such as a character from Boccaccio's *Decameron* and a Victorian female explorer. The characters reveal their struggles and secrets and discuss what a woman needs to do in order to succeed in a men's world, including mimicking the ridiculous male behavior. Many critics see her works as rebellions against the conservative ideology of Margaret Thatcher, the British prime minister from 1975 to 1990. Churchill famously said, "there is no such thing as right-wing feminism" (Fitzsimmons 1989: 61).

An important figure of American theatre was Cuban-born American Maria Irene Fornes (1930–2018). (We write her name the way she did, without vowel accents.) Her emotionally compressed works, including *Fefu and Her Friends* (1977), *Mud* (1983), and *Conduct of Life* (1985), highlight the subjugation of women, appealing to both feminist and Latin American audiences. Fornes often directed her own plays and her direction challenged conventional spectatorship. The second part of *Fefu and Her Friends* contained four scenes, which were performed simultaneously in different locations four times, and the audience moved around and watched the scenes in different sequences. Fornes disrupted the temporal and spatial order and challenged the convention of narrative and perspective in theatre. Her *And What of the Night?* was a 1990 Pulitzer Prize finalist.

Fornes was instrumental in shaping the American theatre scene through her long-term commitment in cultivating the next generation of playwrights: many Latinx playwrights such as Cherríe Moraga (1952–), Eduardo Machado (1953–), Migdalia Cruz (1958–), Nilo Cruz (1960–), and Caridad Svich (1963–) received her close mentorship when she directed the INTAR (International Arts Relations) Hispanic Playwrights-in-Residence Lab in the 1980s and 1990s in New York City. Pulitzer Prize-winning writers such as Tony Kushner, Paula Vogel, Sam Shepard, and Edward Albee all credit Fornes as an inspiration and influence.

The American playwright Paula Vogel (1951–) has been tremendously influential since the late twentieth century, in her playwriting, social activism, and mentoring. Vogel's most famous work, *How I Learned to Drive* (1997), uses driving as a metaphor to explore issues related to pedophilia, incest, manipulation, misogyny, and alcoholism. Although the topics are extremely disturbing, Vogel treats her characters with humanity, respect, and even with humor. The play received many awards, including the Obie (1996) and the Pulitzer Prize (1998).

Like Fornes, Vogel's dedication in teaching has helped shape the American theatre canon of the twenty-first century; her former students include Pulitzer-winning playwrights Nilo Cruz, Lynn Nottage (1964–; Pulitzer twice; Obie), Quiara Alegría Hudes (1977–; Pulitzer), and Sarah Ruhl (1974–, MacArthur Fellow).

Other important female playwrights during this period include African writers such as Ama Ata Aidoo (discussed in the case study above) and Violet Barungi. African American writer Anna Deavere Smith, Elena Garro (1916–1998), Griselda Gambaro (1928–), Adrienne Kennedy (1931–), Hélène Cixous (1937–), Marsha Norman (1947–), Ntozake Shange (1948–2018), Wendy Wasserstein (1950–2006), Cherrie Moraga, Valina Hasu Houston (1957–), Suzan-Lori Parks (1963–), Naomi Iizuka (1965–), and Sarah Kane (1971–1999) are some of the most representative female playwrights who have contributed to deconstructing the male canon in playwriting around the world.

The growth of non-commercial theatres

Starting in the 1960s, many countries developed extensive networks of theatre outside the commercial arena. Several new national (i.e., government-subsidized) theatres were created, while older ones occasionally found themselves in complex circumstances. Numerous small theatre companies arose, sometimes to serve a particular audience community. Many companies decided to maintain a "non-profit" status, relying on donations and low ticket prices without paying taxes. Here "profit" means earnings beyond those needed to pay reasonable salaries and expenses. (Not-for-profit is a U.S. federal tax category of organizations exempt from taxes; the U.K. equivalent is a registered charity.)

In the United Kingdom, the Royal National Theatre (known as "the National" or NT) and the Royal Shakespeare Company (RSC) vied for government funding. The National was opened in 1963 under the artistic direction of Sir Laurence Olivier, with a production of *Hamlet* starring Peter O'Toole. In 1976, it moved to its current home, a three-theatre complex on the south bank of the Thames in London that cost over $32 million (U.S.) to construct. In 1982, the RSC, which makes Shakespearean production central to its mission and had been producing Shakespeare in Stratford-upon-Avon since 1961, added two performance spaces at London's Barbican, making it the world's largest theatrical institution. By the mid-1980s, both companies needed big budgets. Both theatres have produced some of the best-known classical and contemporary theatre and boasted world-class companies and artistic directors. Trevor Nunn (1940–) managed the RSC from 1968 until 1986, and Peter Hall, who had resigned from the RSC, replaced Laurence Olivier as director of the National in 1973 (Figure 13.12). Despite their international theatrical prestige and financial gain from tourism, both theatres were sometimes caught between national budgetary constraints and international expectations of grand productions (such as RSC's *Les Misérables* 1985). The

Figure 13.12
Peter Hall's 1984 production of Shakespeare's *Coriolanus* at the National Theatre, starring
Ian McKellen and Irene Worth. Hall resigned from the National in 1988 to found his own
company.
Source: © John Haynes/Bridgeman Images.

RSC gave up its London theatres in 2002. Shakespeare's Globe, which was opened in 1997,
is a top site for Shakespeare tourism in London (see Chapter 14).

A somewhat similar conflict faced the major theatres of Berlin. During the Cold
War – before German reunification in 1990 – East and West Germany lavished subsidies on
several theatres in East and West Berlin. They became international showplaces for the two
superpowers' rival cultures. In West Berlin, the Schiller Theater offered bourgeois classics and
contemporary plays from Western Europe and the United States. The city hosted yearly festivals to display the best West German productions to the world. In East Berlin, the Berliner
Ensemble, the Volksbühne, and the Deutsches Theater (once the center of Max Reinhardt's
theatrical enterprises) flourished during the 1970s and 1980s.

But after reunification in 1990, Germany could no longer afford to support all these
world-class theatres in Berlin, partly because state subsidies in Germany typically covered
about 80 percent of all operating costs. The competition for spectators and subsidies, plus
major reorganization in several companies, forced some, including the Schiller Theater, to
close. The Berliner Ensemble lessened its ties to the traditions of Brechtian production –
offering a variety of plays, including those of Brecht, directed in a variety of styles. To
enhance the reputation of Berlin as a center for global performances, *Theatertreffen*, the festival that showcases the year's best German-language productions, added a few international

productions and now offers English supertitles for selected shows. Like London, Berlin remains a center of globalized theatre.

National theatres were created in many parts of the world. For example, the National Theatre of Japan was opened in 1966, followed by the National Nō Theatre in 1983, and the National Bunraku Theatre in 1984. South Korea's National Theatre was established in 1950, although it had to close shortly afterward because of the Korean War. Mexico's National Theatre Company was founded in 1977. Taiwan's (ROC) National Theatre opened in 1987. There is no national theatre in the United States.

In the not-for-profit world, markets are often defined in terms of values and purposes, but the practice of seeking a specific audience is essentially the same. In the United States, for example, regional not-for-profit theatres aim to attract season subscriptions from up-scale, educated, and "cultured" audiences in urban areas. Many were created starting in the early 1960s, first with support from private grant foundations and later with the help of government grants. Large and mid-size regional theatres often use a combination of local actors supplemented by the occasional well-known star. Some smaller companies retain semi-permanent ensembles. These theatres see themselves as non-commercial alternatives to Broadway.

Another development in the 1970s and 1980s was the construction of performing arts centers (containing both theatres and concert halls) in regional urban areas, modeled on venues such as New York City's Lincoln Center or London's South Bank.

In the United States, Broadway remains so prominent in American theatre that the loss of a major figure can cause national and international sorrow. At 6:30 p.m. on Wednesday, 8 December 2021, every Broadway marquee dimmed its lights for a full minute, in honor of the passing of Stephen Sondheim (1930–2021). Sondheim's songs could be heard on the radio from the 1960s forward, and five of his musicals were adapted into films (one of them twice). He was mentored by Oscar Hammerstein II and, in turn, mentored artists Jonathan Larson (1960–1996) (*Tick, Tick . . . Boom!, Rent*) and Lin-Manuel Miranda (1980–) (*In the Heights, Hamilton*). Many scholars, critics, and aficionados credit Sondheim with elevating the American musical to a serious art form, pointing to the sophistication of his music and his lyrics. His works treat themes that challenge anyone to equate musical theatre with froth (though *A Funny Thing Happened on the Way to the Forum* [1962] and *Follies* [1971] were plenty frothy). Sondheim began his Broadway career writing the lyrics for *West Side Story* (1957), a collaboration with Leonard Bernstein and Arthur Laurents, but five years later, with *Forum* he was writing the music as well. If Golden Age musicals relied on the melodramatic certainties of good triumphing over evil and love winning the day, Sondheim's work instead made existential doubt and moral ambivalence the central drivers of his works, whether they were ostensibly light-hearted like *Company* (1970), *A Little Night Music* (1973), *Into the Woods* (1987), or *Merrily We Roll Along* (1981); already grim like *Sweeney Todd, the Demon Barber of Fleet Street* (1979) or *Assassins* (1990); or something altogether different like *Pacific Overtures* (1976), which treats the forced opening of Japan to the West in the late nineteenth century. He won one Academy Award, eight Tonies, eight Grammies, an Olivier, and a Pulitzer, among others. His work continues to be produced, including a highly acclaimed Broadway revival of *Sweeney Todd* in 2023.

However, smaller-sized theatres also thrived "Off Broadway." "Off-Broadway" theatres, which may or may not be in or near the Broadway area, generally means theatres that have under 500 seats and employ Equity actors (Equity is the trade union to which professional actors belong). The still smaller "Off-Off-Broadway" theatres have 99 or fewer seats or employ non-Equity actors. Thus, the designations refer more to the business of theatre (How large is the audience? How much money are the actors paid?) than to the location, or the content or style of production. "Fringe Theatre" is the term experimental groups prefer now at the international level. The Little Theatre movement in Japan was similar to Off-Off-Broadway. The co-existence of "Broadway" and "Off/Off-Off-Broadway," mainstream and fringe theatres, both in the United States and as equivalent forms in other countries, has formed a theatre ecosystem of our time.

Theatre of underrepresented voices: Local minorities or global majorities?

One of the most revolutionary developments in the theatre world of the 1960s was the rise of underrepresented, often called "minority" voices. It is important to note that the term "minority" is problematic and needs to be contextualized first in any historical moment. Today, both "minority" and "majority" are best understood as political terms, not numeric ones: a "minority" person, such as a non-white person in the United States, is actually part of the global majority; a "minority" voice might belong to a country's majority population, such as the case in South Africa. "Minority," therefore, often refers to the lack of representation and political and economic power, which may or may not correspond to the percent of population. In the 1960s, theatres in many countries began to reexamine the power relations between the dominant and dominated cultures and dedicate to audiences defined by their interests in issues of race, ethnicity, culture, gender, or political views. In the United States, the Civil Rights Movement inspired many underrepresented artists to form theatre companies to challenge the white heteronormative mainstream theatre. Some of these theatres provided the first homes for "minority" artists who later met with success on Broadway or the West End. By the end of the twentieth century, theatres of "minority" voices flourished and significantly changed the theatre scene of the world; even mainstream and commercial theatres started including plays by "minority" playwrights in their seasons. "To tell/hear our own stories" might have been the original desire for artists and audience from underrepresented communities; however, as the world becomes increasingly global and intercultural, diversity becomes a new justification for the production and consumption of theatre.

As noted in Chapter 12, African American theatres developed in the United States following the Civil Rights movement. Among the most notable were the Free Southern Theater (1963–1980), the Harlem-based New Lafayette Theatre (1967–1973), and the Negro Ensemble Company, founded in 1968. The spirit of the Black Arts Movement also paved the way for Black playwrights whose works critically examine American histories and racial dynamics. Significant twentieth-century African American playwrights include Adrienne Kennedy, George C. Wolfe, Anna Deavere Smith, and Ntozake Shange. Two playwrights are especially notable, although they belong to different generations and write in very different styles: August Wilson (1945–2005), whose plays are mostly in the style of realism, and Suzan-Lori Parks (1963–), who sometimes writes in an experimental style. Both playwrights have been produced on Broadway and by major regional theatres. Wilson's ten-play cycle, each play set during a different decade of the twentieth century and all but one in Pittsburgh, represents a century of African American history and experience. Set in the 1950s, his Pulitzer and Tony winning *Fences* (1985) depicts a middle-aged Black man who had to give up his dream to join the Major League Baseball because of the color barrier; now stuck in a menial job; his anger and frustration affect his family. *The Piano Lesson* (1987) is set in the 1930s. The piano, a family inheritance, is the object of struggle between siblings; the man wants to sell it to buy some land, but his sister refuses because carved into the piano are figures of their entire family history. This play too won the Pulitzer Prize. Other plays in the cycle include *Ma Rainey's Black Bottom* (1984) and *Joe Turner's Come and Gone* (1986). Some of his plays incorporate supernatural moments.

Parks's *Topdog/Underdog* (2002), which won the Pulitzer Prize, dramatizes sibling love and rivalry of two brothers, Lincoln and Booth, names given to them as a joke. Lincoln actually makes a living impersonating President Lincoln in an arcade. The brothers' struggle with poverty, racism, and their haunted past makes this play a dark fable of African American historical inevitability of past, present, and future. Parks's other important plays include *The Red Letter Plays: In the Blood* (1999) and *Fucking A* (2000). Both plays feature Hester, a single mother who struggles under extreme hardship, sexism, injustice, poverty, and violence.

In the new millennium, more Black American playwrights attained prominence. Lynn Nottage is the only woman who won the Pulitzer Prize twice. *Ruined* dramatizes women's struggle in the war-torn Congo, contending with rape, female genital mutilation, and other horrors; the play won the Pulitzer Prize in 2009. Based on extensive research, Nottage's *Sweat* (2015) dramatizes the financial devastation of steel workers in one of the poorest towns in the United States. *Sweat* was Nottage's Broadway debut (2017) and won the Pulitzer Prize and Obie Award in 2017. One of her most popular plays is *Intimate Apparel* (2003), which tells the story of a Black seamstress who sews undergarments (intimate apparel) for women ranging from rich white women to prostitutes. Branden Jacobs-Jenkins, one of the newest American Black playwrights, won the 2014 Obie Award for his two plays *Appropriate* and *An Octoroon*. *An Octoroon* is an adaptation of Dion Boucicault's melodrama *The Octoroon, or Life in Louisiana* (1859) (Chapter 10). Generally following the original plot, characters, and even dialogue, Jacobs-Jenkins invites the audience to critique the far-reaching legacy of slavery in contemporary U.S. society in a Brechtian rewriting of the original play. Another major new voice in African American drama is Jackie Sibblies Drury (1981–), whose *Fairview* (2018) won the Pulitzer in 2019. The play starts as a television sitcom episode about a Black family, repeated in mimed in act 2 while we hear whites discussing which race each would choose to be; in the final act, the white speakers assume some characters' roles, playing grotesque stereotypes, until the Black teenaged daughter stops the action to talk with the theatre audience about Blacks trying to tell their own stories. The 2020 Pulitzer for Drama and Tony for Musicals went to Michael R. Jackson (1981–) for his musical *A Strange Loop* (2019), described in Chapter 14. Jackson's previous work was mostly in writing for television soap operas, a genre he lovingly lampooned in *White Girl in Danger* (2023), about a young Black woman trying to break out of the blackground into the racy drama of three white high school girls and their rock band. In 2024 the Pulitzer was awarded to *Primary Trust* by Eboni Booth.

Following the lead of African American theatre, other theatres for specific U.S. audiences developed. El Teatro Campesino (The Farmworkers' Theater) was founded in 1965 by Luis Valdez (1947–), who had worked with the San Francisco Mime Troupe and was inspired by its use of agitprop and guerrilla theatre. The initial intention was to educate Mexican American farm workers in California about unionizations and exploitation. The real campesinos (farmworkers) collectively created and performed *actos*, a kind of "short, usually comical sketch, often created through improvisation, designed to be performed anywhere" (Huerta 2016: 30). *Los Vendidos* (*The Sellouts*, 1967) is one such *acto* with simple characters (often character types and stereotypes) and staging, and a clear message. From a small amateur campesino theatre involved in César Chávez's unionization effort in the early Chicano Movement, El Teatro Campesino became the first Chicano theatre to have a breakthrough into the mainstream entertainment industry. Valdez's *Zoot Suit* and *La Bamba* were examples of Chicano art going beyond its community to have a popular appeal, partially because of their music: *Zoot Suit* was performed on Broadway (1979) after regional success and later produced as a film (1981), and *La Bamba* (1987) was extremely popular with general audiences. Both Valdez and El Teatro Campesino (based in San Juan Bautista since 1971) are still very active today, committed to arts education, community building, and social justice.

In addition to Chicano theatre, diverse theatre groups representing Cuban and Puerto Rican cultures proliferated in the 1980s. INTAR Theatre in New York, now under the direction of Eduardo Machado (1950–), is devoted to producing new plays by Latinx writers – many of whom were taught by Fornes, as discussed earlier. Jose Rivera (1955–), one of the best-known Nuyorican (New York Puerto Rican) playwrights, received an Obie award in 1992 (*Marisol*) and in 2001 (*References to Salvador Dali Make Me Hot*).

Latinx theatre has grown since then, honoring its transnational roots in collective practice while nurturing many important individual artists. One such ensemble, California-based Culture Clash – formed in 1984 by Marga Gomez, Monica Palacios, Herbert Siguenza, Ric Salinas, Richard Montoya, and Jose Antonio Burcíaga, and now composed of Siguenza, Montoya and Salinas – has created a series of comical and sometimes satirical plays, including *Chavez Ravine* (2003), which tells the story of the Latinx enclave that existed on the site where Dodger Stadium now sits. Gomez and Palacios have gone on to successful solo careers, like New York City-based queer artist Carmelita Tropicana's.

This era has also seen the success of innovative Latinx playwrights in regional, independent, and off-Broadway venues, such as Kristoffer Diaz, Virginia Grise, Jesús I. Valles, and Victor I. Cazares. Taken together, their plays consider the popular themes from the canon of Latinx theatre such as immigration and the complexities of contemporary urban life, including gentrification, labor oppression, identity, and queer survival through new lenses. Diaz's *The Elaborate Entrance of Chad Deity* (2011), a Pulitzer Prize finalist, portrays encounters between Asian, Black, and Latinx characters in the professional wrestling world, while Cazares, Grise, and Valles place queer lives at the center of their stories. While their plays are stylistically different, these playwrights share a commitment to formal experimentalism. Their work is produced alongside works by Octavio Solís and Migdalia Cruz, who have been active since the 1990s.

Latinx artists have also had recent success on Broadway. Lin-Manuel Miranda and Quiara Alegría Hudes's *In the Heights* (2008), about a young college student returning to her home in the predominantly Latinx Washington Heights neighborhood of New York City after a tough year at college, was a smash success, won the Tony Award for best musical, and was a Pulitzer Prize finalist. This musical, largely centered on Dominican residents of Washington

Heights, also introduced Latinx characters from throughout the hemisphere. Hudes's *Water by the Spoonful* (2012), a Pulitzer Prize winner, is the second play in the "Elliot trilogy" about the Ortiz family of North Philadelphia, in which Elliot returns home after the Iraq War to face a battle against addiction in his own family. Miranda's *Hamilton* (2015), discussed in Chapter 15, focused on the eponymous character as an immigrant (and became controversial for its casting call asking for mostly non-white actors). It also popularized Hip Hop in a mainstream Broadway musical. *Hamilton* was awarded the Pulitzer.

The expansion in the number of professional Latinx theatre artists led to the creation of two organizations to support Latinx theatre: the Latino (now Latinx) Theatre Commons, founded in 2013 by artists including Karen Zacarias and Tlaloc Rivas to support U.S.-based Latinx artists through festivals, conferences, publications and mutual aid, and the New York City-based Sol Project, dedicated to producing Latinx playwrights. Attention to Latinx artists also led to a call to support Afro-Latinx artists. Although some writer-performers such as Josefina Baez, who wrote the influential *Domincanish* (2000), were recognized at the time, she was an exception. Today, a new generation of artists such as Guadalís del Carmen are leading the new generation.

In 1965, Japanese American actor Mako (Makoto Iwamatsu 1933–2006) and others, frustrated by the lack of opportunities and representation for Asian Americans on stage, founded East West Players in Los Angeles, the first theatre devoted to the Asian American experience. In 1998, it moved from a 99-seat theatre to a 240-seat Equity house in the Little Tokyo area of downtown Los Angeles. The "new" permanent home had historical significance for Japanese Americans – the former Union Church built in 1923 was used as a congregation site for Japanese Americans on their way to the War Relocation Center (internment camp) at Manzanar, California. In Seattle, the Northwest Asian American Theatre grew out of the earlier Theatrical Ensemble of Asians, founded in 1974 at the University of Washington. New York's Pan Asian Repertory Theatre emerged in 1978 and Ma-Yi Theater Company in 1989. Theatre Mu in Minneapolis-St. Paul was founded in 1992.

Among Asian American playwrights, the best known is David Henry Hwang (1957–), whose *M. Butterfly* (1988) won the Tony Award – the first for an Asian American playwright – in 1988. It investigates Orientalist perceptions by combining Puccini's opera *Madama Butterfly* (discussed in Chapter 9) with a fictionalized account of a real love affair between a French diplomat and a *jingju* actor. The interracial sexual relationship also illustrates the East/West power dynamics. All of Hwang's plays deal with some aspect of Asian American identity, and their mainstream success is a matter of Asian American pride. Other significant Asian American playwrights of the twentieth century include Wakako Yamauchi (1924–2018), Frank Chin (1940–), Ping Chong, Philip Kan Gotanda (1951–), Velina Hasu Houston (1957–), Chay Yew (1965–), and Denise Uyehara (1965–). Many early Japanese American plays deal with issues related to historical trauma, immigration, assimilation, intergenerational conflicts between the Japanese immigrant parents (*issei*, first generation) and the American-born children (*nisei*, second generation). For instance, Yamauchi's *And the Soul Shall Dance* (1977) describes the displacement, isolation, and hardship of Japanese immigrants, as observed by a young American-born Japanese girl. Houston's *Tea* (1981) uses different types of tea to explore the lives of Japanese war brides (the Japanese women who married American service men during the American occupation in Japan in the Second World War).

The struggles over identities – Asian, American, Asian American – in American society is another major topic in early plays. Chin's *Chickencoop Chinaman* (1972) attacks the stereotype "John Chinaman" and its long-emasculating impact on Asian Americans. Gotanda's *Yankee Dawg You Die* (1988) dramatizes the struggles of Asians in the American entertainment industry. Later writers explored more diverse topics and forms, such as Chay Yew's *A Language of Their Own* (1995) centering on gay love and sexuality in the age of AIDS. In *Hello (Sex) Kitty: Mad Asian Bitch on Wheels* (1994), Denise Uyehara uses the one-woman show format to discuss sex, love, respect, violence, and relationship in various personae such as Mad Kabuki Woman, Chick, and Asian Guy. Ping Chong boldly experimented with various styles in his work, as seen in earlier discussion.

The new millennium saw a new generation of playwrights, such as Young Jean Lee (1974–), Qui Nguyen (1976–), Kristina Wong (1978–), and Lauren Yee (1985–). Lee's daring and absurdist funny works include *Straight White Men* (2014), the first Broadway production by an Asian American woman (2018). Nguyen employs racy, foul, and hilarious language: *She Kills Monsters* (2011) engages the fantasy adventures in a very popular tabletop role-playing game; *Viet Gone* (2015) and *Poor Yella Rednecks* (2019) tell stories of Vietnamese refugees with Hip Hop and a highly sexualized acting style. Yee rediscovers the horror of the Khmer Rouge regime with psychedelic rock by Dengue Fever (a Los Angeles-based band) in the *Cambodian Rock Band* (2018). Wong, a solo-performance artist, often uses foul language and vulgar humor (very often referring to female genitalia) to make social commentaries. She dramatizes her experience of volunteering in sewing masks during the crisis of facial mask shortage in the COVID-19 pandemic in *Sweatshop Overlord* (2020 online; 2021 on stage, for which she was a Pulitzer Prize finalist in 2022). Drastically different from earlier writers, these younger playwrights are defiant, funny, angry, unapologetic, and engage in non-realistic experimental styles. Established playwright David Henry Hwang explores bilingualism and transnationalism in *Chinglish* (2011) and *Soft Power* (2018). *Soft Power* is done in the form of American musical, to tell a reversed story of *The King and I*.

Theatre artists of Asian descent are also active in other non-Asian countries. Because of its colonial history, British Asian theatres in the U.K. started with immigrants (or their children) from South Asia such as India, Pakistan, and Bangladesh, unlike Asian American theatres, which were first started by artists of East Asian descent. Key British South Asian theatre companies include Tara Arts (founded in 1977) and Tamasha (founded in 1989). Yellow Earth Theatre (founded in 1995, renamed as New Earth Theatre) is a theatre with an East Asian emphasis. In Canada, the important fu-Gen Theatre (founded in 2002 in Toronto) is the longest-running Asian Canadian theatre.

Political injustice is often an urgent cause for theatre creation to reflect minority voices. Pakistani American playwright Ayad Akhtar's (1970–) *Disgraced*, which examines Islamphobia in the post-9/11 America, won the 2013 Pulitzer Prize. Iranian American playwright Sanaz Toossi's *English*, a reaction to the travel ban against Muslim countries in 2017, won the Pulitzer Prize in 2023.

Gender and sexualities are almost inescapable topics in the plays after the 1960s, especially after women began to take major roles in creating new plays, and LGBTQ artists also began to be recognized by mainstream theatres. The Lilith Theatre in San Francisco and the Women's Project of the American Place Theatre in New York (later becoming independent and re-named WP Theater) promote the work of women writers and directors. Founded in 1976 as a feminist collective, the performance group Spiderwoman evolved into a company that primarily showcases the experiences of Native American women. Some companies specialize in producing shows with an all-female cast, such as the Los Angeles Women's Shakespeare Company (LAWSC), founded in 1993.

Some artists and companies use gender and sexual orientation as the major or even sole focus of their works. The Ridiculous Theatrical Company, founded in New York in 1967 by actor/playwright Charles Ludlam (1943–87), created comic, campy, pastiche-gothic plays that had special appeal for the gay community. Split Britches, co-founded in 1980 in New York by performer/writers Peggy Shaw (1946–), Lois Weaver (1951–), and Deb Margolin (1953–), uses a broadly satirical, gender-bending style to highlight lesbian and feminist issues. Founded in 1982, the Celebration Theatre in West Hollywood, California, offers a wide range of plays exploring gay, lesbian, bisexual, transgender, and queer issues. In the U.K., the feminist troupe Siren, founded in 1979 by members of the band The Devil's Dykes' Jane Boston, Tash Fairbanks, and Debs Trethewey, pursues similar themes. It has been more challenging for plays treating lesbian themes to find their way to Broadway. One success was Paula Vogel's *Indecent* (2015), which explored the controversy surrounding the 1923 play *God of Vengeance* by Sholem Asch, which was a love story between a prostitute and the daughter of the brothel's owner; Asch's play was shut down, and the producer and cast were arrested. Another was the 2015 musical *Fun Home*, adapted by Lisa Kron and Jeanine Tesori from Alison Bechdel's 2006 memoir (which is also about her father's coming out); it won the Tony award for best musical and was a Pulitzer finalist.

The AIDS crisis of the 1980s did much to bring awareness of the realities of gay men's lives to the mainstream, with plays like Larry Kramer's *The Normal Heart* (1985) and Tony Kushner's epic *Angels in America* (1993). Harvey Fierstein's *Torch Song Trilogy* (1979) both celebrated and domesticated the drama of the drag queen, as had *La Cage aux Folles* by Jean Poiret (1973). More recently, Tarell Alvin McCraney used drag to interrogate masculinity and gender in his 2008 play *Wig Out*, which explores what it means to be Black and gay (also a key theme in *A Strange Loop*). As trans rights increasingly draw social commentary and controversy, so have trans artists taken to the stage to tell their particular tales. Notable is the prolific British playwright Jo Clifford, who has been writing plays with trans themes since the late 1980s; her adaptation of *Great Expectations* marked the first time an openly trans playwright has had their work staged in the West End. Some shows have been memorable for staging these realities without overtly calling attention to them; notable among them are Jonathan Larson's Tony- and Pulitzer Prize-winning *Rent* (1996), which included without fanfare two queer couples: bisexual Maureen, partnered with Joanne; and the transgender or drag queen (depending on the production) Angel, in a relationship with Collins, each with very different love stories. Finally, there is playwright and performance artist Taylor Mac (1973–), whose category-defying artistry combines camp, drag, music, and nonconformity of virtually every kind. Mac's *24-Decade History of Popular Music* was a 24-hour show merging nightclub act, drag show, and participatory performance art, and was performed in its entirety only once, in 2016 (portions were performed previously and subsequently). In it, Mac covered all of U.S. history, decade by decade, through 246 songs – some popular, some not especially, mostly American but a few by modern British musicians – placing them in historical context, with a queer and critical perspective that creatively opened space in U.S. history for those who have been excluded and oppressed. The work was a Pulitzer Prize finalist.

As many former colonized countries became independent in the twentieth century, theatre artists were looking for new ways to convey new sentiments related to their new postcolonial identities. For many postcolonial countries, the process of decolonization was also an opportunity to revive indigenous performance traditions and to inspire new indigenous artists. In Australia, the first work by an indigenous playwright to break into mainstream theatre was *The Cherry Pickers* (1968) by Kevin Gilbert (1933–1993), a member of the Wiradjuri and Kamilaroi nations. The Noongar playwright Jack Davis (1917–2000) combined traditional Aboriginal visual and performance culture with historical and contemporary stories in plays such as *The Dreamers* (1982). Nindethana, Australia's first indigenous theatre, was founded in 1972. Bangarra Dance Theatre, founded in 1989, is an Aboriginal and Torres Strait Islanders company, fusing traditional culture, contemporary dance, and theatre. Bangarra is an internationally known company that tours around the world. Canada's best-known Aboriginal playwright is probably Tomson Highway (1951–), a Cree. Among his works are the multiple award-winners *The Rez Sisters* (1986) and *Dry Lips Oughta Move to Kapuskasing* (1989). Margo Kane (1951–) is a Cree-Saulteaux writer and performing artist who founded Full Circle: First Nations Performance in Vancouver in 1992. Full Circle is intended to provide opportunities for First Nations artists and writers to tell their stories. In the United States, an important Native American playwright and artist is Hanay Geiogamah (1945–, Kiowa and Delaware), who started his career in the early 1970s. In 1973, he renamed his theatre ensemble to Native American Theatre Ensemble (NATE) and toured around the United States; he formed the American Indian Dance Theatre in 1987. The first major anthology of Native American plays was published in 1998 (*Seventh Generation: An Anthology of Native American Plays*, edited by Mini D'Aponte). In 2023, Larissa FastHorse (Scangu Lakota; MacArthur Fellow 2020) became the first Native American female playwright to have a play (*The Thanksgiving Play* 2020) produced on Broadway. Los Angeles-based TeAda Productions (established in 1994) is a theatre devoted to immigrants and refugees, with an emphasis on Pacific Islanders. *Masters of Currents* (2017) addresses issues of Pacific Islanders as climate refugees as the result of global warming.

Singapore, a former British colony that is now a multicultural, multilingual nation, is home to both small and large theatre companies. Among them is TheatreWorks, founded in 1985 by the innovative director Ong Keng Sen (1963–). Singapore also hosts an international festival of the arts (SIFA), which includes theatre offerings from many countries. Another former British colony, Hong Kong, has developed a vibrant theatre culture, both locally and as part of the Sinophone region (see the case study above); its movie and popular music industry has had great impact in Asia and around the world. Local and international festivals are considered in greater detail in Chapter 14.

India became independent from the British in 1947. The postcolonial Indian theatres were diverse in styles and purposes in the multicultural and multilingual society. As seen in Chapter 12, Calcutta's (now Kolkata) "group theatre" operated against the commercial star system and produced both contemporary Indian plays and Western plays in the Indian context. Badal Sircar (1925–2011) was an influential and prolific dramatist writing in Bengali.

Summary

The Sixties brought momentous political, social, cultural, and technological changes. People all over the world were suddenly able to witness historical events as they happened, transforming how they thought of themselves and the universe. The tensions that had started to emerge in the early 1960s erupted into demonstrations, riots, sometimes even revolutions, wars, and de-colonization movements. Although the post-traumatic recovery was lengthy for some countries, theatre artists worldwide explored ways in which performance could contribute to social, political, and cultural change. Influences from Brecht, Grotowski, Boal, and absurdism appeared in many theatrical experimentations around the world; the rise of guerrilla-style, site-specific, less formal but nevertheless very powerful small theatres was also directly linked to the cries for social change. At the same time, there was a significant shift from the primacy of the written script to that of the *auteur* director, from the power of words to the power of images and flesh, and from play text to performance text. Collective or ensemble script creation and active audience participation were not uncommon. As technology advanced, live and mediatized genres were intermingled and multimedia performances were common. The institutional landscape was transfigured too, as non-commercial venues became commonplace, some producing mainstream drama, others producing theatre for particular communities. By the end of the twentieth century, a "new normal" had become established, in which the non-commercial and the commercial, the experimental and the mainstream, and the political and the staid all found opportunities to flow into each other. What was originally considered "minority" theatre targeting specific audiences on the margin sometimes became part of the mainstream, as the theatre audience population became more diverse. For instance, in the United States, works by August Wilson, David Henry Hwang, and Luis Valdez are anthologized, studied widely, and often performed today. The regional transnational collaborations, such as in Sinophone theatres and Latin American theatres, and international theatre festivals/tourism such as in TOGA and Shakespeare's Globe, became a norm by the end of the twentieth century. Our next chapter explores the more fully developed theatre of globalization in the twenty-first century.

★

CHAPTER 14

Theatres of local roots and global reach, 1970–2023

Tamara Underiner

Contributors: Bruce McConachie, Gary Jay Williams, Daphne P. Lei and Patricia Ybarra

In 1962, Canadian media theorist Marshall McLuhan suggested that "the new electronic interdependence recreates the world in the image of a global village" (McLuhan 1962: 31). His prediction of a shrinking world has in many ways been realized. Migration has made the world's cities much more culturally and ethnically complex than they were when McLuhan was writing. International travel by the middle class of wealthier nations has become a major industry. International concert tours have become commonplace, as have educational exchanges. Since 2013, more than 150 countries have signed on to China's Belt and Road Initiative, arguably the world's largest transportation and communications infrastructure development program, sometimes called the new "Silk Road" of global trade. Above all, as McLuhan predicted, electronic media – television, radio, video and audio recordings, and the internet – have become key factors in negotiations of cultural change, even though the effects, positive and negative, remain unevenly distributed.

As a result, it is common to speak of ours as the era of **globalization**. The first transcontinental trade route or trans-oceanic crossing centuries ago may have initiated the process, but today the speed of information and its ability to connect peoples who otherwise might know nothing of each other distinguishes the current era of globalization from previous periods of global exploration and exploitation. Neither governments nor the corporate electronic media are wholly in control of the processes or technologies whereby the world's peoples now connect and interact, nor of the social, economic, and political relations that result.

The focus of this chapter is the effect of globalization on culture – particularly theatre culture – and, in turn, the way theatre culture might affect these processes. Responses to globalization move in different and often opposed directions, as the title of this chapter suggests. They range from an embrace of the global reach of "world culture" in music, fashion, cuisine, and consumer products to the promotion and assertion of resolutely local roots in resistance to the pressures of global conformity on local ways of living. Falling somewhere between these two extremes – of **cultural homogenization** on the one hand and **cultural**

DOI: 10.4324/9781003185185-19

differentiation on the other – is the phenomenon of **cultural hybridity** or the fusion of material from two or more cultures. Some type of hybridity results any time cultures come into contact with each other and intermingle for any length of time. (That's how McDonald's, perhaps *the* symbol of globalization, has come to offer shrimp burgers in Japan and Singapore, "Big Brekkie Burgers" in Australia, and "McAloo Tikki" vegetable burgers in India.) Some call this process "**glocalization**," a term made popular by sociologist Roland Robertson.

We pursue four general themes and movements important for understanding "theatres of local roots and global reach" in the decades since 1968. The first is global theatre culture, as exemplified by the increasing importance of international theatre festivals and the emergence of the mega-musical in the United Kingdom and North America. The next is theatre of cultural differentiation, which celebrates local heritage and national patrimony, often in touristic settings, and offers a site for the critique of globalization's more all-encompassing tendencies. Third, we explore theatre as a zone of contact within and between cultures, often resulting in new fusions and hybrid forms. Finally, we consider theatre for social change, a term given to theatre that has some kind of social aim at its heart and is manifested in both local and global (and sometimes local-to-global) forms. Our case study considers the global reach and inter- and multicultural dynamics at play in the theatrical form known as "Chinese Opera."

To illustrate the distinctions and overlaps among these four themes, we open with an examination of Shakespeare's iconic status as an international presence.

Local roots, global reach, hybrid play, and social change in "Shakespeare"

FREE

INSTRUCTOR & STUDENT RESOURCES

William Shakespeare remains the most-performed playwright on the planet. His plays have been translated into every major language (and many less widely spoken ones as well), produced all over the world, and adapted into popular films for markets far away from his native England. As Gary Jay Williams points out in his online case study "Global Shakespeare," "[a]ll of this could be claimed as evidence of Shakespeare's universality, of the ease with which his plays (ostensibly) leap all historical, linguistic, and cultural boundaries." However, as Williams also observes, Shakespeare's stature has also grown from the economic and cultural power it might confer on those who produce the work. Seen this way, writes Williams, "globalized Shakespeare has become a marketable prestige commodity, a *Shakespeare*™ ready to be packaged and distributed by global capitalism through all its technological platforms. Global Shakespeare is exemplary of a Western modernity to which developing nations aspire, a problematic byproduct of colonialism." When we put quotation marks around "Shakespeare," as we have in the heading of this section, it is to highlight his status as a global icon or industry.

At the same time, "even in the West, each age and nation has, to a considerable degree, reinvented the Shakespeare it needed," argues Williams. Thus, productions of Shakespeare's plays also function within the other paradigms we discuss in this chapter: as examples of cultural or nationalist differentiation (through heritage promotion); as examples of cultural hybridity, in which artists adapt Shakespeare's plays to local and contemporary norms and customs; and even as theatre for social change, as initiatives like "Shakespeare Behind Bars"

Figure 14.1
Interior of the reconstructed Globe Theatre, London, which opened in 1997. Shown is
a scene from an all-male production of *Twelfth Night*, with Mark Rylance as Olivia and
Michael Brown as Viola/Cesario.

Source: John Tramper, © Shakespeare's Globe Picture Archive.

and recent examinations of "anti-racist Shakespeare" also illustrate. England's National Theatre and Royal Shakespeare Company (discussed in Chapter 13) are examples of theatre
for nationalist differentiation. While both the National and (to a lesser degree) the RSC
produce works outside the Shakespearean canon, the newer Shakespeare's Globe (which
opened in 1997, see Figure 14.1) trades more overtly on a notion of authenticity related to
Shakespeare's relationship as house playwright for the Globe Theatre.

The brainchild of American actor/director Sam Wanamaker (1919–1993), under the patronage of the late Prince Phillip, the new Globe was built on the south bank of the River
Thames, close to the site of the original "wooden O," as a scrupulous replica of its namesake.
Shakespeare's Globe considers itself to be a laboratory for the ongoing exploration of Shakespeare's plays in performance, pursued through the close approximation of architecture and
stage conventions based on the company's meticulous research (with requisite concession to
contemporary safety considerations). Over the years, it has broadened its agenda to include
re-conceptions of Shakespeare's plays and the commission of new work.

The new Globe's claim to historical authenticity has troubled some critics. Some doubt
the possibility of such a recreation at all, given the scarcity of evidence available about the
old Globe, gleaned from one sketchy drawing of another theatre of the time, some incomplete archaeological evidence, visitors' accounts, and whatever evidence the available

texts of the plays themselves might yield. As a result, scholars are still debating some of the decisions made. For example, some question the choice to feature permanent, highly decorated painted décor inside the new Globe, maintaining that the wood of the original interior had been left plain and temporary decorations hung for each play. Since the facts of the Globe's history will always be elusive, other critics are suspicious of the motives behind and effects of the desire for production authenticity. One concern is that, even if one could find all the necessary facts, museum-quality attention to detail may not speak across the ages and might stifle the drama. Another is that this desire serves to uncritically reinforce the idea of Shakespeare as the "world's most important playwright." Still, other critics have fretted that the attention to architectural and stage detail has come at the expense of the contributions of the actor's voice and body and of the Shakespearean text itself.

Despite these concerns, Shakespeare's Globe has thrived. In recent years, it has expanded its focus on original practices to include new adaptations – such as *Henry VIII* as seen from the Spanish point of view – and premieres of new work and other types of events. In 2013, an indoor playhouse opened, allowing for year-round programming. Then, in 2021, Shakespeare's Globe partnered with Cambridge University Press to offer a series of webinars devoted to "Anti-Racist Shakespeare," inviting scholars and artists to examine the body of Shakespeare's work from the lens of social and racial justice. Curated by education director Farah Karim-Cooper, the webinars draw on a growing body of scholarship on such themes in Shakespeare's works. The webinars explore the language, character dynamics, and plotting of Shakespeare's plays to reveal their gendered and racialized aesthetic and moral logics that have, precisely because of the power of "Shakespeare," subtly structured audience understandings of gender and race over the generations.

Thus, although the National, RSC, and Shakespeare's Globe all began as national(ist) ventures to celebrate English theatre for English-speaking audiences, a combination of international tourism, global criticism, high aesthetic expectations, and responsiveness to contemporary social concerns has put all in the world's limelight.

Across the pond in Canada, the annual Stratford Festival has come to represent a flashpoint in ongoing conflicts between national and international priorities over "Shakespeare" as a figure for cultural heritage. Begun in 1953 in a town named after Shakespeare's birthplace in the province of Ontario, the Stratford Festival is now the largest repertory company in North America and is heavily subsidized by the Canadian government.

In his *Shakespeare and Canada*, Canadian theatre historian Ric Knowles points out several ironies that have dogged the Stratford Festival since its beginnings. Many Canadians understood the initial success of the Festival as a marker of Canada's maturity as a nation-state – whose authority rested on the reputation of a famous English playwright and which borrowed most of its actors and its first artistic director (Tyrone Guthrie, 1900–1971) from the country that had once ruled it as a colony. Thus, from the late 1960s through the 1970s, Stratford's board struggled to find a more "Canadian" identity: appointing a Canadian artistic director and hiring more Canadian actors, eventually even dropping "Shakespeare" from the official title of the festival. During the 1980s and into the 1990s, many Canadian playwrights and directors targeted "Shakespeare" at Stratford for satiric attack and re-appropriated the Bard's plays for their own uses, which might be described as culturally hybrid approaches. Black Theatre Canada produced a "Caribbean" *A Midsummer Night's Dream* in 1983, for instance, while Skylight Theatre set *The Tempest* (1987) in aboriginal Canada, and Theatre

Under the Bridge staged an urban *Romeo and Juliet* (1993), literally under a bridge in downtown Toronto.

By the 1990s, the Stratford Festival had begun to look to multinational corporate sponsors, international consumers, and global critics for its legitimacy and prestige. Knowles examined Stratford during the 1993 season and concluded that globalization had triumphed over national priorities. The subsequent history of the Festival reveals ongoing ambivalences in the strategic use of "Shakespeare" (in the title and in the season) for the Festival's purposes. By 2022, within the Festival's 15-play season, four were Shakespeare's; the rest were new works registering a commitment to explorations of diversity, equity, and inclusion, along with tried-and-true revenue-generators such as *Rent* and Monty Python's *Spamalot*. Such combinations marked the negotiations many major theatre-producing institutions were facing in the second decade of the twentieth century, as they simultaneously stepped up to their ethical responsibilities as brokers of cultural representation, and expanded their budgetary horizons accordingly.

Despite its undeniable influence on contemporary theatre production, it would be a mistake to think of "Shakespeare" as a theatrical juggernaut, absorbing all interpretive possibilities unto itself in its global reach. As we'll see next, the history of "Shakespeare" in Asia and two multicultural productions of *Romeo and Juliet* in New York City (one by Black Americans and one by indigenous Mexicans) stand against such a claim, illustrating how strategically hybrid adaptations of Shakespeare's plays can serve quite powerful local purposes.

"Shakespeare" arrived in Asia through different routes and for different purposes. As early as 1619, performances of Shakespearean drama were brought to Indonesia by Dutch merchants. Under colonialism, his plays were performed in India to entertain British officers, and the texts were incorporated into colonial education there and in the Philippines. In Japan, the plays were employed as a tool for Westernization and modernization after the Meiji Restoration (1868).

Early Asian translations of Shakespeare's works often leaned toward free adaptation rather than full literal translation. Charles and Mary Lamb's *Tales from Shakespeare* (1801) served as the base for many Asian translations, such as Lin Shu's (1852–1924) in China. The Chinese scholar and translator Liang Shiqiu (1903–1987) embarked on a mission to translate all of Shakespeare's works; he eventually published the 40-volume *Shakespeare in Chinese* in Taiwan in 1967.

In the twentieth century, Shakespeare's plays were performed all over Asia, either in English (often abridged) as part of English-language education or in free adaptation in local languages and Western style. Since the late twentieth century, Shakespearean drama in Asia has taken on a form of intercultural or experimental theatre: it is often rewritten to fit local cultures and staged in local languages and performance traditions. The style varies widely and often bears little resemblance to more conventional European stagings. Examples include Contemporary Legend Theater's *Kingdom of Desire* (*Macbeth; jingju*, 1986, Taiwan); Suzuki Tadashi's *Tale of Lear* (Suzuki style 1988, Japan); Ong Keng Sen's *Desdemona* (multiple Asian styles, Singapore 2000); and Norzizi Zulkifli's Makyung *Drops of Magic* (*A Midnight Summer Night's Dream; makyung* dance-drama, Malaysia, 2009). Although Asian intercultural Shakespeare still travels to global festivals, it is completely decentered from London and has become what Bi-qi Beatrice Lei calls a new "living organism" in different cultures and geographical locations (B. Lei 2020: 74).

Two relatively recent illustrations of "Shakespeare's" malleability across time and geographical location occurred in multicultural adaptations of *Romeo and Juliet* in New York City parks. One, from the summer of 2014, is the Classical Theatre of Harlem's *Romeo N Juliet*, staged in Marcus Garvey Park. Adapted and directed by Justin Emeka (1972–), the original served as the backdrop to foreground the visual, aural, and musical cultures of the African diaspora, extending from the African continent to the islands of the Caribbean and the urban centers of the United States. African ancestors provided a kind of chorus of observers to the dramatic action, which paid homage to the icons both of Black American culture (such as the Black Panthers) and of the play itself (see Figure 14.2).

Another richly layered example occurred during Joseph Papp's Festival Latino for the Public Theater in 1990, when a company of indigenous Mexican performers was invited to restage their tri-lingual adaptation of *Romeo y Julieta* in Central Park. Under the direction of Maria Alicia Martínez Medrano (1937–2018), El Laboratorio de Teatro Campesino e Indígena (Indigenous and Farmworker Theater Lab) sets the story of two doomed lovers on a debt-slavery plantation on the Yucatán peninsula in the early twentieth century.

Of course, *Romeo and Juliet* seems meant for adaptations that explore interracial or intercultural conflict, and many theatre companies have done just that over the years. The LTCI production was unique, however, in its exploration of a little-known aspect of pre-Revolutionary Mexican history. The Maya of southeastern Mexico and the Mayo of the northwest are two of more than 50 indigenous groups in Mexico. They do not share a bloodline, language, or customs and would likely never have encountered much of each other had the Mayo not actively opposed the Mexican government under Porfirio Díaz (1830–1915; in office 1876–1880 and 1884–1911). Many Mayo were rounded up from the northwest and sent to work on the Yucatán plantations in southeastern Mexico for rebelling against Díaz. The local Maya, themselves working in serf-like conditions, did not welcome them. Martínez Medrano used this history to set the stage for a Mayo Romeo to fall in love with a Maya Julieta. By situating the conflict between two indigenous groups – and by casting indigenous actors, speaking "Shakespeare in tongues he surely never heard," as one *New York Times* critic put it – LTCI expanded the horizon for understanding Mexican theatre in general and its indigenous cultural history in particular. By incorporating indigenous languages, it suggested that history is not over. By having those languages translate Shakespearean English, it subtly reminded audiences that indigenous cultures are not somehow removed from Western history either, but participant within it. Finally, the Mexican setting allowed audiences to reflect on the role the indigenous peoples have played within Mexican history and politics – and not always as a unified front.

"Shakespeare in tongues he surely never heard" appears all over the world. Interestingly, in those places where English is not the principal language, there is far more latitude of adaptation than we see where the English of Shakespeare is no longer spoken, but is nevertheless revered. Our discussion of "Shakespeare" the icon has allowed us to introduce the four main themes we focus on in this chapter: global theatre culture, theatre of cultural differentiation, theatre as a zone of (inter)cultural contact, and theatre for social change. In the remaining sections of this chapter, we look, in turn, at other examples of these overlapping categories.

Figure 14.2
The Classical Theater of Harlem presented their version of Shakespeare's classic under the title *Romeo N Juliet,* adapted and directed by Justin Emeka, at the Richard Rodgers Amphitheater in Marcus Garvey Park, New York City, on 5 July 2014. From left: Natalie Paul and Sheldon Best.

Source: Hiroyuki Ito/Getty Images.

Global theatre culture

While electronic media have contributed to the spread of knowledge about theatre in the world, two developments in global theatre culture still depend on live, real-time interaction between players and audiences: the growth of international festivals and the increasing popularity of the mega-musical, both of which allow some forms of theatre to achieve a kind of global reach.

International festivals

Since the middle of the last century, the growth of transnational festivals – invited gatherings of several theatre companies in a limited area for a limited time – has become a key factor in theatrical globalization. Such festivals tend to internationalize aesthetic trends and provide an important showcase for directors with global reputations (or, as was the case with Bertolt Brecht, can create such reputations). For producers, festivals are a chance to re-mount their best shows, usually with low production costs and excellent publicity. Because many festivals invite small companies as well as large ones, some marginalized and experimental troupes can gain more international exposure. For theatregoers, festivals typically offer the opportunity to see a number of critically acclaimed productions in a few days.

Two notable festivals, both founded in 1947, are the Avignon Festival, founded by director Jean Vilar (1912–1971), and the Edinburgh Festival, directed by civic and cultural leaders. Both were established to bring high culture to common people, featuring theatre as an instrument for international understanding, and both were eventually challenged by alternative ("**fringe**") festivals that have come to rival the originals in attendance. These fringe festivals also provide a chance for some troupes to emerge as globally known companies.

By 1963, Avignon was attracting over 50,000 spectators for French theatre. Vilar added new spaces and brought in younger directors. Although several of Vilar's productions and those he championed at Avignon had challenged the French status quo, the radical Living Theatre from the United States (see Chapters 12 and 13) led demonstrations in 1968 against his "reactionary" leadership and demanded that the Festival open its doors to all comers at no admission charge. The next year, several French-language troupes began offering fringe performances at Avignon. These unofficial groups proliferated in the 1970s and 1980s – amateur and professional troupes performing everything from edgy minimalism to fully staged classics – and eventually became a second Festival, called "Avignoff," or simply "Off."

In 1994, the official Festival began to internationalize its own offerings, although French-language productions still predominated. Avignon/Off now boasts over 1,400 productions throughout the month of July, with most of the theatrical events occurring at the Off by a ratio of about 10:1. French subsidies and corporate sponsorship, however, have elevated the official Festival to the status of global culture. There, locals can mingle with international playgoers and critics, enjoying a mix of tier-priced theatrical fare and free workshops, panels, film screenings, and exhibitions.

Avignon's two-track festival model may have emulated the Edinburgh Festival in the United Kingdom, whose Fringe is now the largest annual arts festival in the world. Its origins were humble: eight theatre companies organized their own separate event in the first year of the larger International Festival. Edinburgh officially recognized its Fringe as a separate operation much sooner than did the organizers of the Avignon, and its openness to alternative selection criteria has resulted in an explosion of more than 25 parallel festivals, organized by different sponsors but understood as part of one big summer-long arts festival in the city, visited by hundreds of thousands of international visitors each year.

A hemisphere away to the south, the center/fringe model has been adopted by the National Arts Festival of Makhanda (formerly Grahamstown), South Africa. Held annually since 1974, it rivals the Edinburgh Fringe in size and scope, with thousands of performances in all genres spread across scores of venues and many parallel festivals. In 2021, it combined online and live performances due to the COVID-19 pandemic – another feature common to many international festivals in the 2021 season.

Using theatre for greater international understanding has been a key strategy of UNESCO – the United Nations Education, Scientific, and Cultural Organization. Formed in 1945 to promote world peace through a variety of initiatives, among them the preservation and promotion of cultural expressions, in 1948 UNESCO launched the International Theatre Institute (ITI). In 1957, ITI sponsored the first of many annual "Theatre of the Nations" festivals in Paris. The festival showcased the theatre of ten different countries, including *jingju* (Beijing opera), *kabuki*, and dramatic work from the Moscow Arts Theatre and the Berliner Ensemble. Starting in 1972, the festival began to be hosted by other participating cities, which helped to confer on them a certain status as international theatre capitals. Thus, according to Latin American theatre scholar Juan Villegas, the year the Theatre of the Nations festival came to Santiago, 1993, marked an important moment in the internationalization of Chilean theatre. Not only did this bring a large roster of international theatre companies to Chilean audiences but it also registered the power of theatre to function as an instrument of cultural and political legitimation in the country's return to democracy after the military dictatorship (1973–1990) ended. Chile has since then maintained an active international theatre presence, between 2005 and 2013 exporting more than 500 works to festivals around the world. Since 1994, it has hosted its own annual Santiago a Mil International Theatre Festival, regularly attracting artists from more than two dozen countries around the world.

The notion of "exporting" productions suggests that the internationalization of theatre, whatever laudable nationalist purposes it may also serve on the stage of international visibility, runs the risk of turning theatre into a "product" in an international marketplace. Villegas and other theatre scholars have examined the costs to cultural specificity such commodification might exact, as the plays are selected (and perhaps developed) with audiences in mind who may otherwise know very little of local realities. Perhaps the biggest drawback of international festivals is this decontextualization. Most productions at festivals have originated in a different city and with a local audience, one that might not share the interests and concerns of the national and international spectators attending the festival. Many directors and companies get around this problem by mounting well-known plays for festival spectators – the plays of Shakespeare, Beckett, and Chekhov, for example. Perhaps that is why, when the du Maurier World Stage festival in Toronto invited Brazil's Grupo Galpão, a street theatre troupe, to perform in 1998, the results were disorienting for most of the audience. Few Toronto spectators could understand the conventions of the neo-medieval biblical pageant that the Grupo Galpão had reshaped for their radical political purposes. The production, thrust from its normal context in the streets of Brazil, became mostly an exercise in exotic tourism (see below on theatre and tourism). Not all festival productions suffer this level of decontextualization, of course, but those that veer very far from the expectations of international audiences risk the most (Figure 14.3).

Figure 14.3

A touring production of *Romeu & Julieta* by Grupo Galpão in 2000, which met with more success among global spectators than some of their earlier work.

Source: Sheila Burnett.

Despite such tensions between the local and the global, international festivals have increased. The Vienna Festival in Austria, begun soon after the Second World War like the Avignon and the Edinburgh, has long featured companies from Russia and Eastern Europe. Its popularity, coupled with the ongoing success of the pre-war Bayreuth and Salzburg music festivals, has helped to foment the international festival spirit in other German-speaking areas. The Bonn Biennale and Ruhr Triennale, for example, began in 1992 and 2002, respectively. Many other cities around the globe now sponsor one or more international festivals. As nation-states have lost power in the globalization process, large cities have gained it, and hosting an important festival boosts a city's international reputation (sometimes through the strategic showcasing of Western-style theatrical fare). These cities include Singapore, Montreal, Toronto, Los Angeles, Miami, Cádiz, Mexico City, Buenos Aires, Wellington (New Zealand), Sydney, Melbourne, Hong Kong, Tokyo, Athens, Rome, Paris, London, and Dublin, to name some of the most prominent. In addition, large cities have been hosting the International Theatre Olympics, a festival lasting over two months, which has staged more than 880 productions between 1995 and 2019. More than half of these were in 2018 alone, when New Delhi and Mumbai hosted the opening and closing of the festival, held throughout 17 different cities in India; 2019 marked the first time it was hosted by cities in two different countries, Russia and Japan.

Mega-musicals on Broadway and beyond

Another form global theatre culture takes, the mega-musical, seems to begin and end on Broadway, at least symbolically. In his study of the Broadway musical over the past 80 years, David Savran suggests that "the thoroughfare embedded in its name is less a real street than a phantasmatic origin and terminus in the global culture industry" (Savran 2023: 11). Even if some of these musicals began in London's West End, as with *Cats* (1981) and *Phantom of the Opera* (1986), or in Paris as with *Les Misérables* (1980), their success on Broadway and subsequent tours to Europe and Asia (in English and translation) have resulted in a kind of Broadway "branding." More recently, the brand is being experimented with abroad, with new musicals being created and exported back to Broadway in forms simultaneously familiar and fresh.

Cats and its offspring have been called mega-musicals for their spectacular visual and aural effects, enormous investments, high ticket prices, and potential for huge profits. They are sometimes disparagingly referred to as "McTheatre" because, as Dan Rebellato writes in *Theatre and Globalization*:

> There is something very distinctive and unusual about the way these shows have prolif-erated around the world. When you buy the rights to put on *Phantom of the Opera*, you're not given a score and a script and told to get on with it; you buy the original produc-tions: sets, costumes, direction, lighting, the poster, and all the merchandise. This means that all productions of *The Phantom of the Opera* are, to a very significant extent, identical.
>
> (Rebellato 2009: 41)

This homogenization not only works on the level of individual play productions but over time has come to represent a certain aesthetic dominated by lavish production values and songs that cross over into popular music. After some time in New York and with the "Broad-way" label affixed to its price tag, a mega-musical can be exported to the international mar-ket, *The Lion King* has not stopped touring since 1998. With few exceptions, its audiences go to see not the latest new conception of *The Lion King*, but the original production they've already heard so much about, without any risk that this particular production might be a flop. They attend in large numbers, paying relatively high ticket prices, a quarter or more of which goes directly back to the financial investors (more on that in a bit).

But while the franchising of many mega-musicals does demand much standardization of production elements, there are two other interesting phenomena at play, increasingly so since the beginning of this century. First, as Savran also argues, local circumstances can make the results quite distinct (such as the casting and interpretations of specific actors, local contexts of perfor-mance, and audience response) (Savran 2014: *passim*). Second, if Broadway-style mega-musicals dominated global theatre culture in the late twentieth century, a new "global musical theatre ecology" has emerged, in which international currents of musical theatre flow *back into* the hubs of Broadway and the West End (Blair 2023: 153). Thus, we see successful Broadway-style exports such as *The Last Empress* (1995) and *Hero: The Musical* (2009) from South Korea, both directed by Yun Ho-jin, with premieres in Seoul before productions at Lincoln Center and subsequent world tours. Both generously adapted aesthetic conventions of the mega-musical to celebrate Korea's nationalist struggles against Japanese imperialism (Savran 2023:17), making them touring examples of what we later describe as theatres of cultural differentiation. (For more history on how Broadway became the launching pad for global mega-musicals and sim-ilar entertainments, see our online case study "The Vortex of Times Square.")

FREE

INSTRUCTOR & STUDENT RESOURCES

THE BUSINESS OF SHOW BUSINESS

In the past, theatre producers (sometimes in partnership with theatre owners) might form short-term corporations to finance productions. Today, producers of mega-musicals are more likely to be global corporations, long-standing firms with investments in a range of products. The transition to risk sharing and corporate production for mega-musicals began in the 1980s. When Cameron Mackintosh (1946–) teamed up with Andrew Lloyd Webber

(1948–) to produce *Cats* in 1981, the lush pop music and grand spectacle of this dance-based production outclassed most of the other musical offerings in London and New York. The show began an international run that lasted more than 20 years. Mackintosh followed with other musical hits in the 1980s – *Les Misérables* (1985), *Phantom of the Opera* (1986), and *Miss Saigon* (1989). Following his work with Mackintosh, Lloyd Webber formed a corporation, Really Useful Group, to produce his subsequent musicals, which have included *Sunset Boulevard* (1993), *Bombay Dreams* (2002), and the sequel to *Phantom of the Opera*, *Love Never Dies* (2010).

More corporations entered the mega-musical business in the 1990s. In Toronto and New York, Livent produced two musical splashes, including *Ragtime* (1996, Toronto), before ending in bankruptcy. The Walt Disney Corporation began producing on Broadway in 1994 with *Beauty and the Beast*; it renovated a theatre on 42nd Street to house *The Lion King* and future productions (see Figure 14.4). In London's West End, Disney co-produced *Mary Poppins* with Mackintosh in 2004. Clear Channel Communications (now iHeartMedia), a corporation with major investments in radio and television, also began developing mega-musicals (usually with other producers), but its major interest, in corporate lingo, was "feeding the road": creating musical products that supplied its road companies with profitable fare. To ensure these profits, both conglomerates primarily featured "family entertainment," such as *Rugrats – A Live Adventure* (1998) and *Aladdin* (2016).

Figure 14.4
The cast of the musical *The Lion King* performs at the 62nd Annual Tony Awards in New York, Sunday, 15 June 2008.
Source: Theo Wargo/WireImage.

Breaking down the costs of a mega-musical

By the second decade of the twenty-first century, a mega-musical in New York cost about $10 million to produce and roughly half a million per week to run. With a possible weekly gross of around $800,000, most musicals must play for a year and a half before they break even. (*Wicked* cost approximately $14 million to mount in 2003, recuperating its initial investment some 14 months later.) Ticket prices are therefore high; in 2021–2022, the average was $132 a seat (some of which may reflect pandemic impacts, whose long-term effects are difficult to predict). Of that average Broadway ticket price, here's how the costs would be allocated to the various people and functions involved to bring a show to the stage:

- Artistic salaries (actors, musicians, including union dues): $27
- Royalties (to playwright, composer, and designers or to cover prior advances): $20
- Reserves against loss after the show opens (10–15 percent of total production budget): $14
- Administrative expenses (producer and general manager fees, insurance, payroll and accounting services, box office): $13
- Creative fees for artistic directors, designers, music, vocal, and dialect coaches, etc.: $9
- Bonds and deposits for actors, stagehands, wardrobe, manager, and press agent unions: $9
- Scenery (materials and associated expenses): $8
- Music (instruments, rentals, copying): $5
- Management salaries (general, company, "child wrangler"): $5
- Costumes (materials, rentals, wigs, accessories): $4
- Rehearsal expenses (space, script copies) $4
- Publicity (press agent, photographer, opening night party): $4
- Sound (prep, permissions, music): $3
- Production salaries (crews, assistants, benefits, payroll taxes): $3
- Lighting (electrical prep, gels, practicals): $2
- Advertising (print, electronic, outdoor, front-of-house, design services): $2

Adapted from information in Schwartz (2023: 553–4), from 2016 averages.

Wicked's total expenses run to $872,000 per week and more. Although that is above average for Broadway, *Wicked*'s box office returns are also higher than average, between $1 and $2 million per week. Part of the reason for its enduring popularity may be its innovation in content, which we turn to next.

If the last two decades of the twentieth century inaugurated the corporate mega-musical that could travel the world with tamely entertaining content, the first two decades of the twenty-first brought two bolder experiments with the form that proved just as profitable: At the time of this writing, *Wicked* (2003) and *Hamilton* (2015) are the #2 and #4 highest-grossing Broadway shows ever (not adjusted for inflation), behind *The Lion King*. (To clarify, *Hamilton* is not a mega-musical per se because it was not designed to be a global franchise, though it has achieved international acclaim.)

Based on the 1995 best-selling novel by Gregory Maguire, *Wicked* tells the story of how the Wicked Witch of the West came to be both wicked – or so she seems – and green. While in some ways it can be considered a mega-musical – especially given its global marketing and distribution – musical theatre scholar Stacy Wolf argues that in other respects, it follows the more traditional conventions of the "integrated musicals" of the mid-twentieth century. However, whereas these other musicals tend to uphold white, heterosexual norms, *Wicked* upends them. It emphasizes instead the bonds of female friendship between a green witch who is "wicked" and a white one who is "good" (or at least, "popular"), upholds the inter-species solidarity between humans and animals, and tells a love story that breaks with the usual happily-ever-after protocols of musical romances. For Wolf, *Wicked*'s distinction lies in "how it uses a very traditional musical theatre formula, but infuses the formula with newly gendered and queered content and relationships that are in large part responsible for its enormous theatrical and financial success" (Wolf 2008: 6). For its part, *Hamilton*, the brain-child of songwriter and theatre artist Lin-Manuel Miranda, upends similar expectations of U.S. history itself. Via Hip Hop music and deliberate cross-racial casting, its retelling of the biography of founding father Alexander Hamilton invites a critical reflection on what it means to be heirs to the legacy of American independence.

As the investment of time and money continues to rise for all types of theatre production, many theatre companies have taken the safe route of staging revivals to bring audiences in. Others have adapted some of the strategies of the global producing corporations to ensure success. Some non-commercial theatre producers, for example, have partnered with global producing corporations to share their risks. When the U.S. non-profit regional theatre movement began in the late 1950s, companies in Chicago, Minneapolis, San Francisco, and elsewhere looked primarily to European theatres and classical plays for their models, not to commercial Broadway. Few even produced musicals on a regular basis until the 1980s. However, the success of *A Chorus Line* (1975) at the Public Theater in New York and its transfer to Broadway for a 15-year run, with the resulting infusion of millions of dollars back to the Public, permanently altered the non-profit landscape. The La Jolla Playhouse in San Diego has transferred several musicals to New York, including *The Who's Tommy* (1993) and many revivals. Since 2008, under the direction of Diane Paulus (1966–), Boston's American Repertory Theatre has premiered numerous shows that later found success on Broadway, including *Finding Neverland* and *Pippin*. The corporations have also partnered with larger non-profits for out-of-town tryouts for new works: Disney opened an initial version of its *Aida* (1998) at the non-profit Alliance Theatre in Atlanta; and in 1999, Mackintosh took his production of *Martin Guerre* to the Guthrie Theater in Minneapolis to prepare it for a Broadway opening. To bring the discussion full circle, the Public Theater launched *Hamilton* in 2015 (filmed for Disney+ in 2020). Once indifferent to each other's fortunes, many non-profits and commercial theatres are now cooperating in the hope of leveraging increasing interest in musical theatre spectaculars, if not mega-musicals per se.

Another strategy in recent years has been to deepen the interdependence Broadway has long had with other media, extending back to the 1960s with the influence of rock musicals and concept albums like *Jesus Christ Superstar, Tommy*, and *Evita*. If in the earlier part of this period Broadway's "mediascape" counted on vinyl and radio for both source inspiration and reach, now it does so with film, TV, and social media (Blair 2023: 151). Of course, *The Lion King, Beauty and the Beast,* and *Frozen* (2018) were animated films before they were

Broadway mega-musicals. *Spiderman: Turn Off the Dark* (2011) was based on the Marvel comic book series and film franchise. Producers and investors are more likely to take risks on new shows if they've been tested out of town – or if film stars have top billing in them. (This is an especially apt strategy for revivals: Hugh Jackman starring in the 2022 revival of *The Music Man* could command ticket prices of close to $700.) More and more film studios are becoming theatre producers on Times Square; in addition to Disney, the list includes 20th Century Fox, Sony Pictures, MGM, Warner Bros, and Global Creatures, producer of *Moulin Rouge* (a musical without original music). Popular songs remain popular sources of inspiration for the so-called jukebox musicals; examples are *Mamma Mia!* (1999), based on songs by ABBA; *Jersey Boys* (2005), based on those of Frankie Valli and the Four Seasons; and *Girl from the North Country* (2017), based on the Bob Dylan songbook.

This section's focus on the mega-musical should not obscure the fact that smaller-scale musicals remain popular, continuing to develop as a serious art form, and garnering international attention. Over this period, musicals have grappled with themes unheard of in their Golden Age, or in ways that declined to sanitize them. If Rodgers and Hammerstein's *Sound of Music* (1959) turned on a triumphal escape from Nazism, Kander and Ebb's *Cabaret* (1966) sounded a darker note about being blind to and trapped within its rise. Qui Nguyen's (1976 –) Hip Hop-inflected *Vietgone* (2016), a comedy about his parents' love story, was also a politically charged look at the ramifications of immigration from the immigrant point of view. Shows like Jonathan Larson's *Rent* (1996) and Anais Mitchell's (1981–) *Hadestown* (2019), both adaptations of other tales (respectively Puccini's opera *La Bohème* and the Greek myth of Orpheus and Eurydice), tackled serious topics like poverty and HIV/AIDS in the first case and climate change in the second. Another adaptation, the 1990 *Miss Saigon* mentioned above, came to New York from London amid great controversy, illustrating a shift in how seriously musicals were beginning to be taken as representational practices. Based on the opera *Madame Butterfly*, it featured a Eurasian central character named "Engineer," played in the successful West End run by white British actor Jonathan Pryce. When it transferred to Broadway, despite initial protests by Actors Equity and others, no attempts were made to find an Asian or Asian-American for the role, and Pryce reprised it, in a performance viewed by many as a contemporary instance of "yellowface." Nevertheless, the buzz created by this controversy showed the seriousness with which critics and audiences were coming to take their Broadway fare as the last century drew to a close.

Two final examples are noteworthy for the way they reflect, embody, and critique several of the trends described above. *The Band's Visit* (2018), a touring musical based on the internationally acclaimed 2007 Israeli film of the same name, began with an off-Broadway trial run, and includes characters, actors, and musical motifs (in this case Middle Eastern) not traditionally seen or heard on Broadway in much depth. This last point – Broadway's slowness to become truly inclusive – is also a theme in Michael R. Jackson's Pulitzer Prize-winning, metatheatrical sendup/takedown of Broadway musicals, *A Strange Loop* (2019), which brings us back full circle to the mega-musical. Here the principal character, an "Usher" for *The Lion King*, thinks and sings out loud with his embodied "Thoughts" about what it is to be big, Black, and queer on the Broadway stage, while trying to write a Broadway show himself.

Of course, Broadway wouldn't be Broadway today without the significant presence of international tourists, who descend upon Times Square not only to attend the theatre but also to shop at the various emporia devoted to American mass culture that surround the Square, fueling homogenization of both theatrical and consumer varieties. In the next section, we explore the phenomenon of tourists pursuing quite opposite desires and loci of performance – experiences of cultural difference, often via quite culturally specific local venues. This tourist desire often intersects with a desire on the part of local performers and authorities to assert local cultural expression in the face of globalization's homogenizing pressures. The next section looks at these strategies of cultural differentiation both as celebrations of local roots and as negotiations with international spectatorship.

Theatres of cultural differentiation

In this section, we pursue the second strain of theatrical activity within globalization, exploring several examples in which theatre and performance are used to assert cultural differentiation. The examples cover three principal trends: (1) theatre for the preservation and articulation of local culture meant principally for local audiences; (2) the emergence of theatre meant to restore and promote cultural heritage, for both local and wider audiences; and (3) the increasing variety of performances aimed at satisfying tourist curiosity about local culture. In all three, the local and the global intersect; what distinguishes them from performances described later on in this chapter is the degree to which cultural differentiation is held up as a key virtue. In its own way, each also illustrates that even the most local of celebrations and theatrical explorations of culture can enter into complicated and often contentious relationships with national and international interests.

Theatre for cultural preservation and assertion

Two examples from southern Mexico reveal how theatre has been used to assert local knowledge, even (and especially) under pressure of national and global processes of homogenization. In the middle of the last century, many cultural observers, both local and foreign, became concerned about the erosion of indigenous languages in Mexico in the wake of national programs of modernization and Spanish-language literacy. In response, a group of Mayans collaborated with anthropologists to form a multilingual writers' collective in 1983, publishing works in local Mayan and Spanish languages; by 1985, they added a puppet theatre company called Lo'il Maxil (Tzotzil Maya for "Monkey Business"). Eventually, the troupe grew to incorporate live performances to supplement their Mayan-language literacy workshops and publishing endeavors. Two members of the troupe, Isabel Juárez Espinosa (1958–2023) and Petrona de la Cruz (1965–), went on in 1994 to form La Fomma (an acronym for the Spanish "Strength of the Mayan Woman"). This collective, devoted to improving the lives of local Mayan women, also used theatre as part of their multilingual programming.

Both troupes began as attempts to preserve local culture and languages through the recuperation of local legends and the staging of local realities; both received significant Mexican and international support for cultural heritage preservation. In contrast to the *Rabinal Achi* in neighboring Guatemala, which is more a "performance of patrimony" of the sort described below, the new Mayan theatre in Mexico is also concerned with problems of pressing contemporary concern, exploring them through theatre techniques they have appropriated from other performance traditions, which they study through collaborations with visiting artists and participation in international theatre festivals.

For example, in 1994 Lo'il Maxil explored the roots of indigenous unrest that had led to the Zapatista uprising earlier the same year. This indigenous-led action took the name of a national hero of the earlier Mexican Revolution, Emiliano Zapata, invoking his legacy to take the Mexican government to task for its failure to consider indigenous perspectives in its rapidly globalizing economic policies. The play *De todos para todos* (*From All, For All*, 1994) examined the situation of a rural Mayan community robbed of its lands and banished to the jungle. Although the people take up arms to reclaim their heritage, the ending of the play recommends negotiation with the Mexican government, not the continuation of armed rebellion. La Fomma has also looked closely at national issues, with particular attention to their effects on women and children. In addition to producing plays aimed at assisting women with a variety of new social problems, their dramas target the economic policies that have forced the separation of Mayan family members. Other plays, such as *Échame la mano* (*Lend Me a Hand*) (2001), explore the dangers for women of participating in the international tourist trade.

Performances of national patrimony

> With the dawn of the new millennium, we are witnessing the rise of a new paradigm: a veritable wave of "**patrimonialization**" is sweeping the entire world. The list of acts and displays declared to be cultural heritage over the past 10 years – the Argentine tango and the Mediterranean diet, Mongolian chants and human pyramids in Spain, the *nō* theater of Japan and the carnivals of Colombia, just to name a few – reads more like a poem by Borges than the official program of a supranational organization. It is, in sum, a politically correct and updated expansion of the Seven Wonders of the World.
>
> (Vignolo 2012: 4)

There's a lot at work in Colombian performance studies scholar Paolo Vignolo's observation here. First, he suggests that the ephemera of culture – notably, performance culture – have now become monumentalized as cultural patrimony, testaments to the unique contributions of a given nation, ethnic group, or region to the larger world. While at one time, natural and human-made structures were what made a place a destination, a "wonder of the world," now it is more likely some tradition of song, dance, or theatre that merits special consideration. (UNESCO's 2005 proclamation of the Guatemalan *Rabinal Achi* as a "Masterpiece of the Oral and Intangible Heritage of Humanity" is an example of this trend.) Second, he points to the contingent nature of this wave – that is, that there are no generally enforceable standards about what constitutes patrimony that some "supranational organization" (not even UNESCO, which is Vignolo's referent) can impose, because culture is so heterogenous. Finally, his reference to political correctness suggests a discomfort with the phenomenon in general. On the one hand, it may be laudable to move away from a classical, old-world sense of what is wondrous in the world to incorporate heretofore under-recognized "wonders." On the other hand, somebody (or some political body) will still be making decisions about what is included and what is excluded from a given people's "patrimony" – and such a process is never agenda-free. (Add to that UNESCO's policy to make its designations within nation-state boundaries – whereas cultural identifications often exceed such borders – and one can see how fraught such complications can become.)

Vignolo is concerned specifically with the particular Colombian carnival tradition of Barranquilla – claimed by Colombia's tourism bureau as "The Most Colorful Carnival in the World," second in scale only to that of Rio de Janeiro. For more than a century, the Carnival was sponsored by political patrons seeking to gain the favor of the electorate; in 1991, it was privatized and is now owned by a company of local elites, who installed seats and stages, sold advertising space, and began to charge admissions and fees. Writes Vignolo, "In short, a collective festival was transformed into an economic engine for profit" (Vignolo 2012: 2). Ironically, in 2003 UNESCO designated the Carnival as a masterpiece of world heritage, precisely to reduce "cultural alienation produced by commercialization" (qtd. in Vignolo 2012: 2). While the aim of most patrimonial policies is to preserve heritage and to strengthen cultural identities, the support of the state often makes them more attractive to economic interests as well. This can give living traditions the unwelcome flavor of museum pieces. In the case of Barranquilla, what started out as a local celebration soon became an important international tourist attraction that, in order to perpetuate itself, must work harder at "preservation" than at presenting changing notions of identity – ethnic, gender, sexual, etc. – within Colombia (see Figure 14.5). As a result, some groups have begun to stage their own dissident parades a few streets over from the main parade route.

"Performing patrimony" can take place anywhere. For an extended discussion of a small Wisconsin town's annual staging of its own Swiss roots, see our online case study,

Figure 14.5
A scene from the Colombian Carnival of Barranquilla. Here, a local tradition begun in 1888 has come to draw thousands of international tourists, especially since its designation in 2003 by UNESCO as a Masterpiece of Oral and Intangible World Heritage.
Source: Federico Rios.

"Backstage/frontstage: Ethnic tourist performances and identity in 'America's Little Switzerland,'" by Phillip B. Zarrilli.

Performances of (and against) "authenticity" in the context of tourism

The desire to explore other lands and know other cultures is evident in the travel literature and travel pictures of many cultures over many centuries, which record pilgrimages to capital cities, religious shrines, and scenic natural wonders. By the end of the seventeenth century in Europe, the "grand tour" to sites of classical monuments and to museums and galleries became a regular rite of passage for the sons of aristocracy and gentry. Over the next two centuries, the development of a middle class with increasing leisure time led to an increase in tourism. Tourist destinations responded with improved and added attractions, many of which traded on an appetite for exotic and ethnic differences. It was not uncommon in nineteenth-century Chinatown, for example, for a tourist's day to include visits to the narrow alleys of an urban bazaar, an opium den, and a leper shelter, followed by a local meal, then an evening at the theatre – where he and his traveling companions could poke fun at the "bizarre" stage practices they did not understand. Today, national and international tourism is a major industry, serving a large middle class in all developed nations. Sites once remote have become more accessible through air travel and package tours.

Whether travelers seek historic sites or different cultures, they pursue their own sensuous confirmation of the existence of a world they have imagined and anticipated. Further, as contemporary life becomes ever more socially mediated, many tourists also travel in search of an experience of authenticity. Often, local performances of various kinds are an important part of their experience. As noted, theatre festivals and Shakespeare's Globe serve as pilgrimage destinations for some. Tourism companies and state agencies have also helped develop performances or exhibitions for travelers that draw on the music and dance traditions of local and indigenous cultures. In Seville, Spain, for example, tourists may cap a visit to the Museum of Flamenco with a Museum-sponsored flamenco dance exhibition, or choose another tourist package that features an evening of dinner and flamenco without the educational contextualization. *Kathakali* continues to draw international tourists to Kerala, India, as does *jingju* in Beijing, and *kabuki* and *nō* in Japan. These examples illustrate that language difference is not always an obstacle.

In some parts of the world, everyday life itself has been theatricalized and consciously staged for tourist consumption, sometimes under the rubric of education and cultural exchange, sometimes as frankly commercial ventures. Such ventures allow local communities to participate in global trade, offering aspects of their cultural distinction as commodities for exchange in the international marketplace. These kinds of performances have given rise to questions about the desire for and pursuit of authenticity as a function of privilege, unevenly distributed across the world, questions taken up by artists in performances that challenge this desire.

In 2002, for example, performance theorist Richard Schechner described how in India Jaipur's Rex Tours arranged for urbanized Rajasthanis and foreign visitors to observe "authentic" rural Indian life in a specially built village, where they could watch craftsmen work and enjoy traditional food, dance, and music. The tour company brochure invited the traveler to "take a peek into the lives of rural folk, their abodes, social setup [sic], religious beliefs, and innovative cuisine" (qtd. in Schechner 2002: 236). In Rio de Janeiro, a company called

"Be a Local Tours" offers insider tours of the city, including not only Rio's famous Carnival but also its infamous *favelas*, where its poorest residents live. In Ireland, the Bunratty Folk Park functions as a "living reconstruction" of a nineteenth-century village – complete with school, shops, post office, and pub, worked by costumed personnel who demonstrate their various occupations – located conveniently near Shannon Airport.

Another set of examples comes from the relatively recent phenomenon of "dark tourism," where tourists visit sites of death, disaster, conflict, or tragedy, often themselves taking on the roles of the historical participants. Sometimes referred to as "immersive tourism," examples include simulated experiences of the Underground Railroad in the United States; illegal border crossing in Mexico; and "Escape from the U.S.S.R.," a simulated prison break in Latvia.

Whenever ethnic or economic "Others" are the principal attraction for tourists, such performances raise ethical questions. When are these performances meaningful examples of cultural exchange and sustainability, and when do they become demeaning exhibitions for the consuming gaze of tourists? While historical villages and heritage tours may be creating jobs and keeping a local economy going, are they also fabricating an appealing "eternal past" that spectators can view with comfortable detachment, even nostalgia – a past unconnected to any problems in the present? Are tourists seeking escape, or will they have opportunities to be active rather than passive and to ask questions about such issues?

Some performance artists have devised presentations for tourist settings that confront tourists with the very issue of the touristic gaze. Mexican American performance artist Guillermo Gómez-Peña (see Chapter 13) and Cuban American performance artist Coco Fusco (1960–), famously arranged such an event in 1992 in Madrid's Columbus Square on the 500th anniversary of Christopher Columbus's "discovery" of America. It was designed to help spectators recognize the ways in which "exotic peoples" have been exploited and colonized, literally and conceptually, since they were first toured to Europe as part of Columbus's return entourage. The artists set up a 12-foot square golden cage in which they portrayed two recently discovered "primitive" native residents of the entirely fictive "Guatinaui" people, supposedly from an island in the Gulf of Mexico. The couple was dressed exotically, spoke gibberish, watched TV, and posed for photos (Figure 14.6). Ethnographic handouts described the "specimens" and their typical behavior. Over the next two years, the exhibit toured art galleries and museums in the United States, and spectators' responses varied widely. Some believed they were seeing rare natives; some complained that the display was inhumane; some, especially patrons of elite art galleries, saw the performance as a performance (Schechner 2002: 261). Whatever the interpretation and ethical ramifications (for example, some questioned the wisdom of allowing school-age children to interact with the "natives"), the notion of humans on display was not itself completely foreign to visitors to the installation. The 1993 documentary *Couple in the Cage*, produced by Fusco and Paula Heredia, captures these varying interpretations, as well as much of the history of human display, a common practice in the nineteenth century meant both to entertain and "educate" about the supposed natural inferiority of non-white races (see Chapter 9).

For the Vienna Festival in the summer of 2000, German director Christoph Schlingensief (1960–2010) created a performance work that scandalized Austria, the more so for being set up next to the Vienna State Opera, a prime site for the tourists it was designed to reach. Entitled *Please Love Austria*, it employed a "residential container" in which 12 actual (though

Figure 14.6
A tourist photographs the performance work *Two Amerindians Visit the West*. Guillermo Gómez-Peña and Coco Fusco played fictive "Amerindians" as caged, exotic specimens in this performance piece, created in 1992 in Madrid's Columbus Square on the 500th anniversary of Christopher Columbus's "discovery" of America.
Source: © Coco Fusco.

unnamed) refugees from different countries who were seeking asylum in Austria stayed awaiting their fate. They were guarded and their daily routines were filmed and shown on television screens in the plaza. Over the container was a slogan representative of the extreme right-wing politics of Austria's Freedom Party and its leader, Jörg Haider (1950–2008), "*Ausländer raus*" ("Foreigners out"). Schlingensief shouted extreme right-wing slogans from a nearby rooftop and shocked tourists in the plaza below by welcoming them to Austria, "the Nazi factory." As Gitta Honegger explains, "The container installation was the simulation of a culture that had absorbed Haider's extremist rhetoric" (Honegger 2001: 5).

THINKING THROUGH THEATRE HISTORIES: DOING THEATRE HISTORY IN A LOCAL/GLOBAL WORLD

Cross-cultural conversations are not new in theatre history. Japan was importing masked dance forms from Korea, China, and India between the sixth and eighth centuries CE. Roman drama and theatre architecture were the godchildren of Greek forms. When the Italian humanist academies of the sixteenth century attempted to resurrect Greek tragedy, it resulted in the fusion we know as opera. Some later Renaissance playwrights borrowed from the plays of ancient Rome. The *kathakali* dance-drama was woven from strands of several indigenous performance traditions, including the Sanskrit temple dance-drama, *kutiyattam*. Japan's *shingeki* (new theatre) movement introduced Western dramatic and acting styles to Japan in the late nineteenth century. Irish playwright William Butler Yeats was influenced by Japanese *nō* drama. Bertolt Brecht's theories of acting were based in part on his observation of the Chinese actor Mei Lanfang. These could be considered early examples of intercultural theatre, latter-day examples of which we'll discuss more below. Such historical perspective reminds us that cultures are never completely uniform nor unchanging, and it would be a mistake to suppose that traditional theatre genres (*kabuki*, for example) exist today in pure and unchanging form. Nor does culture tend to fit neatly within national borders. Some nations have, at least in theory, built their identities on the mixture of cultures and linguistic traditions they comprise. (Consider India, a nation in which there are 18 official languages and more than 1,500 different spoken ones.) Others are continuing to work out the relationships between aboriginals and European settler/colonizers. Uneven development even within nation-states has also contributed to internal migration from the countryside to the cities, changing the nature of urban culture as well as the lived experience of rural emigrants. The theatre that emerges from these realities is often called **multicultural** theatre (as we do in this text).

But when they appear before the word "cultural," prefixes like "inter" and "multi" almost force us to view cultures as rather stable, even when we know they are not. This can be a hindrance to tracking the movements of people and objects (including theatrical practices) in zones of contact, but it can also serve as an important caution. There are legitimate reasons both to celebrate the new forms that emerge when different cultures meet each other and to be wary of cultural "borrowings" that are really (sometimes violent) appropriations; note that Yeats and Brecht never became experts in the Asian artistry that influenced them, whereas mastery of the Western style of realism was profound in Japan. Therefore, it is important to approach a given instance of inter- or multicultural theatre with careful attention to its historical and contemporary contextual pressures.

In this section, we have examined touristic performance as a zone of contact between cultures. The theatre itself has always been such a zone, offering artists and audiences the opportunity to "visit" other times, places, and peoples. The next section explores some of the issues involved in these cross–cultural encounters.

Theatre as a zone of contact within and between cultures

Although they may to some degree engage both local and global influences and effects, the examples we have been discussing so far have tended to move in one or the other of our first two directions: either toward global theatre culture or toward a more local theatre of cultural differentiation. Next, we explore a third direction of theatre in globalization: theatre as a zone of cultural contact, where the local and the global influence each at a fundamental level. We focus here on three broad types of theatrical activity:

multicultural, intercultural, and hybrid theatres, in several different contexts. Our online case study, "Imagining Contemporary China," discusses a multicultural Chinese play that also features intercultural and hybrid elements.

Multicultural theatre

Multicultural theatre combines performance modes from different cultural traditions or communities within nation-state boundaries, rather than across them (which we describe as intercultural theatre). *Jingju*, as discussed in Chapter 9, is an example because it draws on various performance traditions from within China. At its most ideal, such theatre has inclusion at the heart of its mission, staging both form and content understood to represent the variety of cultural contributions to the society in which the theatre finds itself. An early example of such a theatre is the San Francisco Mime Troupe, which we discussed in Chapter 12. Formed in 1959 as an avant-garde company devoted to exploring politically charged themes through alternative theatrical forms, the troupe eventually became a multiracial collective. It became a touring company in 1965 with *A Minstrel Show, or Civil Rights in a Cracker Barrel*, which used the exploitative form of nineteenth-century minstrelsy to stage a critique of twentieth-century racism.

While for the San Francisco Mime troupe multiculturalism is a practice, for Mixed Blood Theatre in Minneapolis, Minnesota, it is the point. Founded in 1976 by artistic director Jack Reuler (1954–), Mixed Blood's original mission was to promote "cultural pluralism and individual equality through artistic excellence, using theater to address artificial barriers that keep people from succeeding in American society" (Mixed Blood Theatre 2015). Mixed Blood's seasons thus typically explored a range of American lived experiences and social issues, both historical and contemporary, native and immigrant; nearly half of its more than 175 productions have been American or world premieres. Some of its plays are presented in both English and the relevant immigrant language (see Figure 14.7). While most of its productions feature characters and themes reflecting the changing face of America, the company has also staged plays written by non-American playwrights about their local perspectives on global issues. In recent years, the company's mission has expanded to include theatre-making in the community for various community-building ends in the city that was the hometown of George Floyd, a Black man whose murder at the hands of the police sparked local, national, and global protests against racial injustice. Similarly, not far away in St. Paul, Penumbra Theatre (founded in 1976 by Lou Bellamy [1944–] and known for launching the careers of African American playwrights such as August Wilson) announced in 2020, it was transforming its operations into a Center for Racial Healing.

In the small city of Victoria in British Columbia, Canada, Chilean émigré Lina de Guevara (1933–) has developed another model of multicultural theatre. In 1988, she founded PUENTE Theatre; its name means "bridge" in Spanish, and its mission is to "build bridges between cultures." In the 1970s, many emigrants from Central and South America fled the violence and political strife of their countries, seeking new beginnings in Canada, with its open territory and similarly open immigration policies. In Canada, however, they met with a rhetoric of multicultural inclusion that didn't seem to match daily life. PUENTE was formed as a way for new Latina/o Canadians to come together to devise theatrical works based on their lived experiences in Canada. Their works, developed collectively, explored issues of racism, workplace discrimination, human rights abuses, sexual

Figure 14.7
Rehearsal of *The Primary English Class* at Mixed Blood Theater in October 2001. Teacher Amy Colon attempts to teach an English as a Second Language class where no one speaks the same first language. Here she starts with the phrase "God bless you" which she enunciates with expansive hand gestures. The actors are, left to right: Ann Kim and Maria Cheng in the front row, and Raul Ramos, Michael Tezla and Warren Bowles in the back.
Source: Duane Braley/*Star Tribune* via Getty Images.

harassment, and other forms of oppression. Today, second and third generations of participants are exploring their mixed legacy, under the artistic direction of Guevara's successor, Mercedes Bátiz-Benét (1977–).

In other contexts, multicultural theatre has not been so successful and has been critiqued as a form of tokenism that keeps intact the privilege and priorities of the dominant culture. This can be seen, for example, in attempts by some large non-profit theatres to "diversify the season" through the inclusion of one or two [name the minority] plays or in the choice to colorblind cast canonical works rather than to stage lesser-known but deeper explorations of local experience, for fear of losing the subscriber base. Such matters were the motivation behind the "The Ground We Stand On" collective of theatre makers self-identifying as Black, Indigenous, and People of Color who, in response both to civil unrest in society following George Floyd's murder by police in May 2020 and pervasive racism in its cultural institutions, in the summer of 2020 wrote an open letter to mainstream theatre outlining a series of tenets, principles, and demands for a more just American theatre. "We See You, White American Theater" became a rallying cry for a thorough overhaul of practices, processes, systems, and outcomes in American theatre production.

Intercultural theatre: Four examples in three waves

We define **intercultural** theatre as the practice in which theatre artists use the texts, acting styles, music, costumes, masks, dance, and/or scenic vocabularies of one culture and adapt and modify them for audiences of another culture, across national boundaries rather than within them. Since the 1970s, productions of this kind have developed in the context of globalization, with its imbalances of power and wealth, and against the backdrop of historical colonialism. Intercultural theatre is both filled with the promise of cultural exchange and fraught with the possibility of cultural appropriation, depending on the relationship between the source material and the production results and contexts. In this section, we consider four different combinations to illustrate the key issues involved in international theatre production, in three successive and overlapping historical waves of interculturalism and performance, as identified by Daphne Lei and Charlotte McIvor (2020).

The first wave is characterized by the work of Western artists (often charismatic white men) who have mixed elements of West and East (and sometimes the global south) together in their work. Initially produced to wide acclaim (largely due to an unequal distribution of critical voices who might speak out against them), such productions have in recent years come under new scrutiny. The second wave occurs when work is packaged for global consumption, as exemplified by international theatre festivals. Second-wave productions tour internationally, their spectacle and music playing a large role in the endeavor to make them accessible to audiences of different cultures and languages. Many have been especially designed for festival venues. A third, more recent wave, represents the exchange of culture from the ground up, work which arises "from migrant and/or minoritarian practices and practitioners, often in collaborative and community-based interculturalism-from-below" (Lei and McIvor 2020: 241).

Our first two examples come from the first and second waves of intercultural theatre: productions in which Western artists have borrowed (some have said "kidnapped") East and South Asian performance modes, and then gone on to tour the productions widely. Their varied critical reception illustrates the contours of concern over such productions. The first involves the staging of a non-Western text, the Indian epic the *Mahabharata*, within a Western mode of theatrical production. The second considers the staging of four Greek tragedies using non-Western theatrical conventions. Do these examples represent latter-day "Orientalist" approaches that demonstrate the West's belief in its own superiority, or is something more complex at work?

In 1985, British director Peter Brook (1925–2022) collaborated with French writer Jean-Claude Carrière to create a French-language adaptation of the *Mahabharata*, which premiered at the Avignon Festival. It was then adapted into English and toured to six countries in 1987–1988 (Figure 14.8). The production was monumental in scope and generated much critical conversation.

Vijay Mishra's favorable review, for example, found the production added a new dimension to the *Mahabharata* texts that would "radically challenge (if not alter) the Indian regimes of reading" (qtd. in Williams 1991: 204). Indian critic and director Rustom Bharucha (1988) thought otherwise, arguing that the reworking of an Indian religious text for insertion into a secular Western theatre mode represented an insensitive use of the source material – an insensitivity that extended to the communities for whom the *Mahabharata* is still very much alive and sacred. Here, intercultural theatre may mirror some of the problems and

Figure 14.8
Actors perform British director Peter Brook's adaptation of *The Mahabharata* on stage at Théâtre des Bouffes du Nord in Paris in 1987. Brook collaborated with French scriptwriter Jean-Claude Carrière.

Source: Julio Donoso/Sygma via Getty Images.

opportunities inherent in globalization: on the one hand, the forced encounter between powerful and less powerful cultures has the potential to overrun the cultural identities of the less-resourced cultures of the world as they are absorbed into more dominant forms; on the other hand, it also presents an opportunity to break down problematic Western attitudes of superiority to these cultures. Unfortunately, so long as Western artists view non-Western forms as "raw materials" to be tapped for their own artistry, and audiences aren't given the tools to critically examine the dynamics at play and demand different results, such intercultural exchanges are likely to remain uneven.

Our second exemplar reverses the relationship between source text and theatrical modality: Ariane Mnouchkine's 1990–1993 staging of four Greek tragedies in Paris, presented in a non-traditional theatre space and relying extensively on Asian performance conventions. Reconstructing the glories of ancient Greece – the usual Western humanistic mode of production – was not the goal here. For Mnouchkine (1939–) and her Théâtre du Soleil company, the staging of the tragedies (under the collective title *Les Atrides – House of Atreus*) was an experiment in recovering them as works to be acted, danced, and sung, in this case using *kathakali* dance and Chinese costume influences. She hoped to liberate the Greek tragedies from text-oriented, literary scholarship and Western staging conventions, and additionally to introduce a feminist point of entry and reflection in the work (see Figure 14.9).

Figure 14.9
Dancing chorus members in Euripides' *Iphigenia in Aulus*, in the *Les Atrides* cycle as staged by the Théâtre du Soleil, directed by Ariane Mnouchkine at the Cartoucherie, Paris, 1990.
Source: © Martine Franck/Magnum Photos

Audiences entered the auditorium of the hangar-like building that houses the Théâtre du Soleil by crossing a bridge over a simulation of the site of the archaeological dig in China which had recently uncovered thousands of life-size terracotta Chinese soldiers. The costumes of the principals in the Greek tragedies were based on those worn by the Chinese figures. Each production began with a long crescendo from a large tier of ancient percussion instruments located on a large platform above stage left. Drums propelled the chorus on stage and drove the plays forward thereafter. The chorus dances were derived mostly from *kathakali*, as were their costumes of black tunics and white skirts over pantaloons and elaborate headdresses. Their faces were whitened and their eyes were dramatically highlighted. Individual chorus members hovered around the action, peering over the walls and around panels in front of the enclosing walls.

Mnouchkine's production was successful with audiences in France and on tour in Vienna, Montreal, and New York. It was less criticized than Brook's *Mahabharata*, perhaps because Mnouchkine had not reworked an Eastern text. For some, her production's exotic, fable-like milieu sometimes seemed a remote cultural fantasy; for others, Mnouchkine's vision was transcultural and epic, offering a god-like view of the human condition. As with other intercultural productions, its global touring life – with its Asian visual vocabulary and its performances always in French – raises the question of what it meant, or could have meant, for its various audiences. To make themselves available to international audiences, intercultural theatre productions must rely on labor-intensive translations or on the non-verbal languages of the theatre – scenic spectacle, music, and dance. Such considerations, increasingly common in the late twentieth and early twenty-first centuries, have given rise to what Daphne Lei has termed "Hegemonic Intercultural Theatre" (Lei 2011: 571); notable artists such as Ong Keng Sen and Suzuki Tadashi have contributed to an Eastern version of this model.

Turning to the emergent third wave of interculturalism in theatre, which looks at life from a more minoritarian perspective, we consider two examples originating outside of Western cultural capitals. In New Delhi in 2004, director Amal Allana (1947–) staged *Eréndira*, an adaptation of a story by Colombian Gabriel García Márquez (1928–2014), who won the Nobel Prize for Literature in 1982. The New Delhi company adapted his early short novel *The Incredible and Sad Tale of Innocent Eréndira and Her Heartless Grandmother* into the Rajasthani dialect of Hindi. It is a tale that blurs the lines between fantasy and reality. A grandmother who was once a prostitute and who has pretensions to grandeur is served, hand and foot, by her granddaughter, Eréndira. Blaming Eréndira for a fire that destroys their home, the evil grandmother prostitutes her. She takes her, chained to her bed, on an epic journey lasting years, with men lining up for miles to enjoy the legendary Eréndira. The New Delhi company of six women and one man staged the journey in a sequence of striking visual images intended both to correlate with Márquez's verbally rich narrative and to bring out resonances with North Indian culture and rituals. They used music, dance, and masks, drawing on Indian and American sources, including Rajasthani folk music and Colombian carnivals. *Eréndira* toured in India and played in Singapore and London, always using supertitles in English.

Figure 14.10

Cover image from playbill for *eXtras*, Mexico City, 2003, starring "two of the three Bichir brothers" – popular Mexican movie stars – on any given night. Part of the fun was waiting to see which two would star in the production as the extras heading to Hollywood – and which would actually *be* an extra in this production.

Source: *Theatre Journal*, Volume 56, Number 3, October 2004, p. 438

While the example of *Eréndira* shows how local traditions can be used in dialogue with a foreign text, our final example shows how a foreign text can be more fully transplanted into local soil, this time to make a critique of globalization. Mexican playwright Sabina Berman (1955–) saw fascinating intercultural possibilities in the Irish playwright Marie Jones's 1999 play, *Stones in His Pockets*, which won the Olivier Award for Best Comedy in London and was subsequently produced throughout Europe and finally on Broadway. Berman is known internationally for her theatrical explorations of the seams and tears of gendered, cultural, and cross-cultural identifications; in 2003, she translated, produced, and directed Jones's play in Mexico City with the new title of *eXtras*, which enjoyed a run of several years there (Figure 14.10).

The original play features two characters – Jake Quinn and Charlie Conlon – who play extras in a Hollywood movie being filmed in their hometown in County Kerry, as well as extra roles in the play proper. The title refers to the fate of a young local whose dreams of stardom are crushed by the filmmakers; he fills his pockets with stones and drowns himself.

In response to this tragedy, the villagers rise up against the foreign producers and the erosive threat they represent to local culture and values. In the end, the two principals, now playing themselves, decide to make their own film, casting the dead boy in the lead role and Hollywood stars as extras.

Jones intends their story to represent "the whole disintegration of rural Ireland" (qtd. in Bixler 2004: 431). Given the similarity in economic conditions between rural Ireland and rural Mexico, Berman saw possibilities in a close adaptation. Jake and Charlie become José and Charlie, County Kerry becomes Chiconcuac, a poor pueblo in the state of Morelos, and the shoes that were used to represent character and identity changes become red bandannas, a familiar symbol of the Mexican revolution (1910–1917) with contemporary resonances to the ongoing Zapatista revolutionary movement. According to scholar Jacqueline Eyring Bixler:

> Berman recognized that the acts of adaptation and translation themselves convey what is perhaps the most important message of *Stones in His Pockets*, which is that U.S. culture – particularly that produced and marketed by Hollywood – has a pervasive and pernicious effect on the rural, impoverished, desperate, and brainwashed masses, not only in Ireland but throughout the world. In other words, the act of translating the play is itself a form of intercultural performance, or what [Marvin] Carlson calls "the weaving of complex patterns of contact with other cultures or other cultural performances."
>
> (Bixler 2004: 432)

CASE STUDY: Chinese opera in the age of interculturalism and globalization

Daphne P. Lei

In previous chapters, we learned about various traditional forms of Chinese theatre such as *zaju*, *kunqu*, and *jingju* throughout history. These traditional forms, synthesizing music, singing, dialogue, recitation, stylized movements, elaborate costumes, and symbolic makeup, are generally categorized by the Chinese as *xiqu* (*xi* for drama, *qu* for music), as opposed to *huaju* (spoken drama). Hundreds of forms of *xiqu*, diverse in performance style, language, and music, exist today.

The term "Chinese opera" is an invented concept, becoming a synonym for various *xiqu* performances since the 1920s. The new term is closely related to American modernity. As "theatre" and "drama" were reserved for the increasingly realism-based form of spoken performance, and "musical" was a unique new American form, "opera" became a term that implied foreign and archaic, non-modern and non-American. Moreover, to refer to Chinese theatre as "opera," or classical Indian theatre as "dance," is to define theatrical performance in a very narrow, Orientalist view; "Chinese opera is a term coined in the West, reflecting the Western cultural hegemony and logocentrism which separate text and music and prioritize drama over opera" (Lei 2020: n.p.). To demystify "Chinese opera," therefore, we need to recognize the form as neither

"Chinese" (as representing the entire nation or culture) nor "opera" (as a non-t-heatrical form). In other words, from the very beginning, the term "Chinese opera" implies a racial and cultural Other in the East/West dichotomy in the context of interculturalism.

Chinese opera is alive today in many ways: it is preserved as a cultural heritage and practiced as a living tradition; it is experimented upon, often manipulated and misrepresented in intercultural theatre; it is tokenized as the Oriental other, both by Chinese and non-Chinese; finally, it is an important tool to connect theatre (or art and cultures) and global capitalism, an essential element of globalization. This case study first briefly explains how the earliest East/West encounter of Chinese opera has set up the expectation of the art for today's globalized audience; it later lays out the three stages of Chinese opera in the international and multicultural context, with the focus on Chinese opera and globalization, from the late twentieth century until now.

The earliest substantial direct encounter between traditional Chinese theatre and the West was in the 1850s in San Francisco's Chinatown. *Yueju* (Cantonese opera) was enjoyed by Chinese residents, international gold seekers, and tourists. The international audiences loved the spectacle (splendid costume and magnificent acrobatics), but could not tolerate the music and singing. The whining string music and loud percussion, nasal singing, and falsetto were satirized to the extreme as animal howling or braying, only "pleasant to the auricular nerves of the natives" (Soulé et al. 1999: 382). This early reception has influenced later adaptations of Chinese opera: the Chinese "opera" becomes a stylized mime or dance without any singing; if music is included, it is modified and exoticized to suit the Western ears, as exemplified by Rodgers's comment on the "Siamese" music for *The King and I* (Chapter 13).

The three stages of the development of Chinese opera since the late twentieth century are explained below. They are all ongoing developments and are often intertwined and overlapping.

UNESCO-ing Chinese Opera: the pros and cons of institutionalized cultural heritage

Chinese opera, like all traditional arts, declined in the second half of the twentieth century, and by the 1980s, it had lost most of its commercial viability. Although the major genres continued to survive and even occasionally thrive, some minor genres became unsustainable. In 2001, UNESCO launched the Proclamation of Masterpieces of the Oral and Intangible Heritage of Humanity as a way to raise awareness of the declining intangible heritage, and "Kun Qu Opera" (*kunqu*, Kun opera), the oldest form of Chinese opera still performed, received that honor. Subsequently, "*yueju* opera" (*yueju*, Cantonese opera) received this recognition in 2009 and "Peking opera" (*jingju*, Beijing opera) in 2010. UNESCO's move, the first external attempt to safeguard traditional Chinese theatre on a global scale, aroused both artistic alarm and nationalist pride. However, as noted above, UNESCO limits such honors within national boundaries, and all these recognitions were marked as "China," so the contribution of other

Sinophone regions that have preserved some of the most precious traditions were not acknowledged. UNESCO's proclamations have generated a great deal of local and national enthusiasm and financial support; it is exactly the boost that the declining "old" art needed in the new millennium. However, one might worry about the further fossilization of traditional arts as well as national intervention from above, which might lead to unfair distribution of resources, all of which will speed up the decline or even extinction of minor artistic genres.

Interculturalizing Chinese opera: inspiration, appropriation, or self-Orientalization

Modernization and Westernization always went hand in hand in non-Western countries; in other words, ever since the late nineteenth century, even simple attempts to modernize Chinese opera such as the use of electric lighting and the proscenium stage or incorporation of modern themes can be seen as a form of interculturalization. Contemporary Legend Theater's *Kingdom of Desire* (1986), as seen above, was one of the groundbreaking indigenous intercultural productions. Wu Hsing-kuo (Wu Xingguo 1953–), a *jingju*-trained actor, set out to revive the dying tradition with new modern and intercultural energy, such as breaking the strict *jingju* rules and incorporating modern dance. He later famously performed *Lear Is Here* (2001), a solo performance in which he played ten characters from *King Lear* in *jingju* style. Wu's performances incorporate a great deal of *jingju* singing, unlike most contemporary intercultural performances with more emphasis on movement or spectacle. The Singaporean director Ong Keng Sen, who usually mixes multiple artistic traditions in his productions, also experiments with Chinese opera movements. With multicultural Singaporean and global audiences in mind, his productions sometimes engage elements of spectacular self-Orientalization (to further exoticize or Orientalize oneself in order to gain acceptance or empowerment, as discussed in Chapter 9). The Hong Kong avant-garde director Danny Yung (discussed in Chapter 13) has experimented with *kunqu* since 2010. *Flee by Night* (*Yeben*, premiered 2010) is one of the most significant recent pieces. It dramatizes a stage crew member witnessing the evolution of the traditional play *Flee by Night* over the span of 450 years. Starting in 2017, he also used the simple concept of "one table and two chairs" (the basic "set" for Chinese opera) to connect with theatre artists both from the Sinophone regions and other countries to create new experimental theatre.

The search for "Oriental" inspirations is still a major motivation for Western artists to experiment with Chinese opera today; this is similar to the attempts by such earlier artists as Yeats, Meyerhold, and Artaud. There are two basic formulas: the first engages a traditional performer in intercultural performance, so the traditional elements are preserved within the performer's body; the result might be considered a hybrid performance. The second engages a Chinese opera master to train Western actors in basic movements for a short period of time and lets the actors freely experiment with their new corporeal knowledge during the rehearsal process; the result is usually a Western-styled performance decorated with quasi-Chinese opera movements.

Peter Sellars's *The Peony Pavilion* (1997) involving *kunqu* master Hua Wenyi (1941–2022) is the first kind: Hua's exquisite traditional performance was almost uncontaminated in a wild multimedia production with avant-garde music. Illustrating the other is the RSC's 2012 production of *Orphan of Zhao*, which had a cast of non-East Asian actors (except for very minor roles) performing in quasi-Chinese opera style in Chinese costume. Similarly, Mary Zimmerman's (1960–) *The White Snake* (2012) engages lavish and fantastical Oriental spectacle, but the actors performed in a realism-based acting style.

Globalizing Chinese opera: national soft power and global capitalism

Here we consider Chinese opera in two types of globalization. The first type is when a Chinese opera product is toured or broadcast around the world and is a source of national and cultural pride as well as a form of soft power. The second type is when artists or organizations converge on a play or a concept related to Chinese opera at a global scale, or engage in a similar idea in different parts of the world, without partnering with one other. In other words, the first type is a product going to the world, whereas the second type involves the world coming to a single idea/product.

The first successful example of globalized Chinese opera of the first type was probably *The Peony Pavilion: The Young Lovers' Edition*, the *kunqu* classic reimagined by the Taiwanese writer Kenneth Hsien-yung Pai (discussed in Chapter 4). It has toured around the world since 2004 and continued having sold-out performances – an unprecedented phenomenon for Chinese performance. In 2008, an epic-scale *jingju* production *Red Cliff* (*Chibi*) premiered in the National Theatre in Beijing. With dazzling high-tech stagecraft (such as a burning ship and flying arrows), large-number dance and acrobatic spectacle, and symphonic music, *Red Cliff* resembled a grand Western opera or an American mega-musical, despite the traditional *jingju* singing. In 2009, *Red Cliff* was broadcast on giant screens in Times Square, where international tourists frequent. Although passersby only glanced for seconds and moved on, it is a symbolic participation of the world mega-musicals on Broadway.

In 2008, an estimated 2 billion people (then almost a third of the world's population) witnessed the grandiose Beijing Olympics opening ceremony. Among all the most iconic Chinese images, from terracotta soldiers to *taikonauts* (Chinese astronauts), were segments of quasi-Chinese opera spectacle. Although these fragments – like the glimpses captured by tourists in Times Square – did not take place in a theatre proper, they were seen and acknowledged by the global audience. While a nation can arm itself with military force or economic sanctions, it is equally important to demonstrate its soft power in international relations. Soft power includes arts, culture, diplomacy, or politics; it can be a strategic move when hard power does not function well, or it can further glorify a nation. Chinese opera, as seen in the multiple examples above, is an excellent soft power generator.

The second type of globalizing Chinese opera is organized around a single play or a similar topic. As explained earlier, Chinese opera is often misunderstood as a dance spectacle instead of a musical performance in the international context. One perfect example is the Monkey character. Sun Wukong, normally known as Monkey King in the West, is a monkey-transformed character from the sixteenth-century novel *Journey to the West* (*Xiyou ji*), whose authorship is usually attributed to Wu Cheng'en (1506–1582). One of the possible origins of this character is Hanuman, the mythical monkey character from the Hindu epic *Ramayana* (see Chapter 3). He accompanies his master, a Buddhist monk, to the "West" (India) to obtain Buddhist sutras. The magical monkey with his transformative superpower becomes a unique role type in Chinese opera training. As a stage character, his fantastical acrobatic and fighting skills, comical facial expressions, rebellious and eccentric personality, and endless adventures – all expressed in the half-human and half-monkey body – have made him a well-loved character by adults and children (often as their introduction piece to Chinese opera).

The movement-based characteristics along with the concept of a journey to the "West" are intercultural in nature and very attractive to Westerners. There were numerous experimental performances produced outside of China, usually with the involvement of Chinese artists. One example is *Monkey: Journey to the West*, originally conceived by the Chinese director Chen Shi-Zheng (1963–) with music by British musician Damon Albarn (1968–) and visual design by the British animator Jamie Hewlett (1968–). (Albarn and Hewlett are best known for their virtual band Gorillaz, which premiered at the Manchester International Festival in 2007 and later performed in various venues such as the Paris théâtre du Châtelet in 2007, London's Royal Opera House in 2008, and Lincoln Center in 2013; see Figure 14.11.) It was a spectacular pastiche of acrobatics, tai chi, aerial art, special effects, and projected animation – everything "Oriental" to draw a "wow" response from the British audience. Theatre scholar Ashley Thorpe believes this Sino-British collaboration is motivated by British awareness of China's growing economic power and its intention to bid for the 2012 Olympics (the United Kingdom successfully won the bid to host the next game) (Thorpe 2016: 208).

A smaller-scale Monkey performance with an educational purpose was *The Forbidden Phoenix* (2009), with a script by the Asian Canadian playwright Marty Chan (1965–) and music by Robert Walsh. Here, Monkey King was localized in the context of Asian Canadian immigration history. With a multiracial cast, the performance emphasized the visual effect – the heavy makeup masked the racial differences, whereas the acrobatic-based performance avoided Chinese-language singing. School children were brought to the performance and a study guide was designed to teach them about Chinese opera and Chinese immigration history. However, Chinese opera was reduced to a form of Orientalized dance spectacle in order to contribute to the process of incorporating Chineseness into Canadian multiculturalism.

Chu Luhao (Chu Lu-hao or Zhu Luhao, 1954–), famously known as *the* Monkey King of Taiwan (in *jingju* style), returned to perform the traditional repertoire of *Monkey King* in Taiwan (2021) and Singapore (2023), after having announced his retirement from the role 17 years earlier. In the age when numerous "monkeys" were generated in intercultural, hybrid, multimedia or mixed media contexts, Chu's return

Figure 14.11

Chinese actors perform in *Monkey, Journey to the West,* in September 2007 at the théâtre du Châtelet in Paris. The opera was a collaboration between Chen Shi-Zheng of China, who conceptualized it, and Britain's Damon Albarn and Jamie Hewlett of Gorillaz music, who designed the music and scenery.

Source: Thomas Coex/AFP via Getty Images.

to perform this extremely physically demanding role in the traditional style (perhaps for the last time) is also a declaration of ownership of the theatre tradition.

Finally, "time" instead of themes or artistic forms became a way to imagine global Chinese opera. The year 2016 was a year of cross-cultural coincidence – the 400-year anniversary of the death of two great playwrights, the Bard and Tang Xianzu, the author of *The Peony Pavilion*. Intercultural comparison in theatre often derives from a Western point of view, as the West tries to understand the enigmatic and exotic Other by comparing the latter with themselves. For instance, both Tang Xianzu (1550–1616) and the Japanese playwright Chikamatsu (1653–1724) are sometimes called the "Chinese/Japanese Shakespeare," despite the invalidity of such comparisons in many aspects. Nevertheless, the 2016 anniversary was a raison d'être for numerous theatre activities at a global level. For example, the "Shakespeare-Tang Project: Celebrating a 400 Year Legacy" made connections between the University of Leeds (UK) and the University of International Business and Economics (UIBE, China), and between *Midsummer Night's Dream* and *The Dream of Nanke* (*Nanke Ji,* c.1600) by Tang Xianzu. Students experimented with retelling the stories and mixed acting styles (realism and quasi-*jingju* style). A much bigger operation was the collaboration between RSC, the British Council, the Chinese Ministry of Culture, JP Morgan (an American financial firm), and others – which sponsored a tour of RSC's production of *Henry IV* (Parts I and II) and *Henry V* to Beijing, Shanghai, and Hong Kong. A connection between Shakespeare and *kungqu* was foregrounded during this multi-city engagement for a few months. In Hong Kong, a former British colony, Shakespeare's First Folio was displayed for free for the public in the Hong Kong Arts Festival; *The Tragedy of Macbeth*, directed by the well-known experimental Hong Kong director Tang Shu-Wing (Deng Shurong 1959–) and premiered in Shakespeare's Globe in 2015, was a highlight of the festival. Experimenting with Western physical theatre, Chinese opera movement and instrumentation, gender-bending, and Cantonese dialogue (the local language of Hong Kong), *The Tragedy of Macbeth* was a total reimagination of Shakespeare into Chinese opera.

Summary

At a time when many indigenous cultures and languages are disappearing at record speed every day, Chinese opera would have died decades ago if not for various interventions, direct and indirect – UNESCO-ing, interculturalizing, and globalizing. One essential aspect of the Chinese opera's survival is its ability to participate in the global economy; like Shakespeare, Chinese opera is the most recognized classic of Chinese culture and can generate tremendous soft power. As a treasure trove or rich source, Chinese opera is malleable and offers great potential for intercultural experimentations. In the process of travel, exchange, reimagination, experimentation, and marketing today, Chinese opera is inevitably tokenized, fragmented, and misrepresented. Nevertheless, the tradition survives and even thrives in alternative ways, in spite (and because) of the unstoppable power of globalization.

Key references

Audio-visual resources

For a taste of a traditional "Monkey" performance by Chu Luhao's troupe, watch this promotional video, https://www.youtube.com/watch?v=MAR8UNwveXM.

For clips from the touring production of *Monkey: Journey to the West* by Chen Shi-Zheng and Damon Albarn, see https://www.youtube.com/watch?v=NR7EEoOwIdg.

Books and articles

Lei, D.P. (2020) "Neither Chinese Nor Opera: Demystifying and Retheatricalizing 'Chinese Opera,'" in D. Caddy (ed.) *Theatricality and the Challenge of Definitions* series, *Naxos Musicology International*, https://naxosmusicology.com, 16 September.

Soulé, F., J. H. Gihon, and J. Nisbet (1999) *Annals of San Francisco*, Berkeley: Berkeley Hills Books.

Thorpe, A. (2016) *Performing China on the London Stage: Chinese Opera and Global Power, 1759–2008*, London: Palgrave Macmillan.

Form in fusion: Where the local and global influence each other

The performances described above are among the many manifestations of the cultural hybridity resulting from the movements of people, ideas, and art forms in the era of globalization, whereby different systems of beliefs, social practices, or aesthetics are merged together. The resulting fusions may represent disproportionate influence by the dominant power, as historically has happened in eras of colonialism, with its military conquests, religious evangelism, settlement, and commerce. But this is not always the case, as an example from music suggests. In 1977, the British rock group Queen (whose lead singer Freddie Mercury/ Farrokh Bulsara was a Parsi Indian of Iranian descent) recorded "We Will Rock You," known to millions as a thundering victory chant performed at athletic events worldwide. What may be less well known is that its beat was derived from the rhythms of a Muslim rite of self-flagellation practiced by Iranian males.

Hybridity of form and practice in theatrical performance is also quite common. The Japanese dance theatre form of *butoh*, introduced in Chapter 12, provides an example. Having declined in Japan, it experienced a resurgence outside that country beginning in the 1980s, when troupes began to tour (Figure 14.12). Since then, *butoh* has gained in global awareness not only as a form in and of itself but also as a training technique for performers preparing for non-*butoh* work, incorporating aspects of it into other types of dance and theatrical performance. In fact, it is now better known abroad than it is in Japan. Many of these international performers are of Japanese descent, but many more are not. In Europe, Canada, and Africa new *butoh* or *butoh*-inspired troupes have emerged, their work ranging from the minimalist to the spectacular. In West Africa, Eseohe Arhebamen (1981–) combined *butoh* with elements of traditional Nigerian dance styles, mixing them with song, speech, gestures, sign language, spoken word poetry, and experimental vocalizations in a very hybrid new form. While in some cases the darkness of *butoh*'s Japanese origins seems to be erased by its abstraction into pure style, others maintain its original intent to have the dancing body bear the enormous burden of history; the 2003 piece *Fagaala*, a collaboration between Yamazaki Kota (1959–) and Germaine Acogny (1944–) of the Senegalese company Jant-Bi, used *butoh* to explore the Rwandan genocide of the mid-1990s.

Another example of local-to-global adaptation and interpenetration comes from Indonesia and illustrates the interplay of influence between patrimonial assertion, globalization, and electronic media culture: the **wayang golek** [wah-YAHNG goh-lek]. This centuries-old tradition of puppetry in West Java has in recent years adapted itself to the medium of television. In *wayang golek*, three-dimensional, carved, and painted wooden rod puppets tell stories in the Sundanese language. In contrast, the Indonesian shadow puppets of the **wayang kulit** [wah-YAHNG koo-lit] are two-dimensional silhouettes and transparencies. Both, however, draw on the Hindu epics of the *Mahabharata* and the *Ramayana* and probably arrived in Indonesia with Hinduism and Buddhism during the first century CE. (See Figure 14.13.) In their original form, *wayang golek* performances are extremely social occasions, drawing large crowds and lasting for hours. The puppets represent a metaphysical view of the human condition and are manipulated by artists adept at improvising based on audience responses, as the old tales may take on some contemporary resonance. As Indonesia modernized and entered the global economy, *wayang golek* artists created hybrid forms that took advantage of the new communication technologies, beginning with audio cassettes in the 1970s and moving to national television in the 1980s. These new technologies resulted in changes to

Figure 14.12
Japanese dancer and choreographer Akaji Maro (right), founder and director of *butoh* troupe Dairakudakan ("Great Camel Battleship"), performs in his work *The Five Rings* at City Center, New York, New York, April 8, 1987.
Source: Jack Vartoogian/Getty Images.

the form, as they had to fit a shorter time frame, and could take advantage of multiple camera perspectives. However, these studio productions lacked live audience responses – a factor that suited the Suharto government then in power (1967–1998).

This began to change in 1996, when one well-known puppeteer, Asep Sunandar Sunarya (1955–2014), developed a new *wayang golek* derivative for television, a hybrid comic form featuring the traditional puppet character Cepot. This simple, country bumpkin figure's earthy lifestyle served as a foil for the excesses and corruptions of the Suharto regime, then in its last years in power, in new versions of the old tales. *The Asep Show* thus harnessed contemporary media to a traditional puppet theatre form, in order to make targeted critiques of the contemporary national situation in Indonesia. (An expanded discussion of this example appears on the website.)

A final example from Ghana, West Africa, illustrates the resiliency that culturally hybrid forms often enjoy because of their adaptability to change over time, and points ahead to our section on theatre for social change. Since the 1930s, the "concert party" has been a staple of popular entertainment for a wide swathe of society in what was then termed the "Gold Coast."

Figure 14.13
Backstage of a *wayang kulit* shadow theatre in the city of Yogyakarta, Indonesia, where a *dalang* (puppeteer) manipulates his puppets behind the screen, accompanied by musicians, in a performance of a play about the Pandava brothers derived from the *Mahabharata*.
Source: © Juliet Highet. All rights reserved 2023/Bridgeman Images.

Its roots extend back to the English-language concert and musical performances imported by the British to the area's urban centers in the late nineteenth and early twentieth centuries. Audiences for these performances came to include both English-speaking elites and educated "intermediate" professional classes who attended to show their sophistication, despite tensions between them. The concert party, and the term itself, emerged in the 1930s to denote a structured program of performances, rather than a European concert or African open-air festival.

These performances were usually an hour or two long, started with opening songs and moved to scenarios enacted by trios who played a series of stock characters, including the Lady, the Gentleman, and the houseboy or the "Bob" who lived by his wits. Performers were usually English-speaking male children of civil servants of the intermediate class, who were not able to access clerical employment.

The performers incorporated African cultural traditions, including the performative tricks of Anansi, a spider trickster, into their shows, often through the figure of the Bob. Although sometimes shunned by their families, these early performers took advantage of the conditions created by industrialization and international trade, including the creation of railways. The concert party groups traveled the rail lines where they met migrant workers hungry for entertainment, often timing their tours with the payday schedules of workers. At other times, they followed the harvest schedule, arriving in rural areas and trading sites at opportune times.

From the 1930s until the Second World War, concert parties became itinerant polyglot performance, which, while largely English, also included Akan, Twi, and Hausa. After the war, these shows, which had not carried political content, began to include commentary on social realities. As Catherine Cole (2001) notes, concert parties performed by much larger groups, with longer program times, became a way for audiences to process their experiences as they moved toward Ghanaian independence in 1957; the move into more intensive use of African languages happened during this nationalist period.

The subsequent Golden Age of the concert party in the 1960s was short-lived; the economic depression of the 1970s caused its performers, now including some women, to fall on hard times. Yet, the form is surprisingly resilient, finding ways to survive and, at times, contest the corporatization that came with Ghana's economic liberalization. David Donkor (2016) attributes this resilience to the use of Anansesem, a form of trickster storytelling whose mode of open-ended multivocality allows concert party performers to speak circuitously and cleverly against power. This legacy began with Ghanaian comedian Bob Johnson (1904–1985) and continues with contemporary performers.

Such strategies illustrate the fluidity and adaptability of traditional theatre practices within globalization, and help to ensure their continuance without becoming exoticized museum pieces.

As the global village becomes ever smaller through the electronic media, the unequal distribution of its resources becomes harder and harder to ignore. Our fourth route through theatre in globalization illustrates how local communities the world over are using theatre to address some of these issues.

The global reach of theatre for social change

"**Theatre for social change**" is an umbrella term that captures several related movements – among them, Theater of the Oppressed, "theatre for development" and community-based theatre – that have as their aim the use of theatre to explore and address pressing social problems. While all theatres have the possibility to affect and effect social change in any number of ways, and certain manifestations of what we describe below can be found in earlier periods, "theatre for social change" began to emerge as a distinct category of theatrical practice during the 1970s. It is a broad and generous category, encompassing a variety of forms, working methods, and performance settings. In general, "theatre for social change" is distinguished from commercial or non-profit theatre that occurs in a formal theatre building; its workers are professionals who perform with participants and audiences who may or may not care about theatre as an art form per se. What matters most, as its name suggests, is that it aims to address, if not solve, social problems of concern to its participants. In this section, we focus particularly on those kinds of theatre for social change in which the local and global intersect in some way.

Theater of the Oppressed

Many of these movements draw on the theories and techniques of Brazilian theatre director Augusto Boal's **Theater of the Oppressed**, mentioned in Chapters 12 and 13. Strongly influenced by the ideas of educational theorist Paulo Freire in his 1968 book, *Pedagogy of the Oppressed*, Boal developed a series of theatrical innovations and interventions designed to raise awareness of the causes of oppression, identify key problems facing a given community, seek collective solutions to them, and implement them not only on stage but also in societal and political venues. In later years, working in exile in countries where the forms of oppression were less overt than those exercised by dictators, Boal developed his ideas into what he called "The Rainbow of Desire," which helped participants to become aware of "the cop" in their own heads – in other words, the subtle ways oppressions can become internalized.

In such theatre, trained practitioners work with groups – usually communities coming together around a specific cause, within an identified system of oppression, or within zones of ethnic or intercultural conflict – to collectively advance their aims. Practitioners affiliate through such organizations as Pedagogy and Theater of the Oppressed, Inc., a global forum for "people whose work challenges oppressive systems by promoting critical thinking and social justice through liberatory theatre and popular education" (ptoweb.org).

Key characteristics of Theater of the Oppressed are the inclusion of a facilitator (or "difficultator") called "The Joker," and an understanding of the audience as "spect-actors," called upon to actively propose and enact the contours of and solutions to the problem being explored, rather than be passive "spectators" who simply sit back and watch. Forms and techniques of Theater of the Oppressed include:

- Image theatre, where participants use their bodies to form wordless images of a situation under discussion;
- Forum theatre, whereby different solutions to a given problem are proposed by the spect-actors, who then test them by acting them out in improvised scenarios;
- Newspaper theatre, drawing on an early form of documentary theatre to offer techniques for groups wishing to explore contemporary issues in their world;
- Invisible theatre, where individuals trained in Theater of the Oppressed techniques publicly enact a scenario that calls attention to a social injustice, in a context where it regularly occurs, without calling attention to itself as theatre; and
- Legislative theatre, a type of forum theatre that takes place in town halls and houses of legislature, where a given law, policy, or statute is being debated.

Boal's ideas have become internationalized in a variety of movements that draw on his Theater of the Oppressed techniques to serve particular purposes. Since Boal's death in 2009, Julian Boal has taken up his father's work, conducting workshops across the world when he is not engaged in his own work with Escola de Teatro Popular (the Popular Theatre School) in Rio de Janeiro, Brazil.

Theatre for development

The term "**theatre for development**" (TFD) originated in Botswana, Africa, in the mid-1970s to describe performances intended to help communities address their difficulties with health, agriculture, literacy, and similar issues. The basic model, as it emerged in a series of conferences and workshops, involved theatre activists researching a community problem, creating a play through debate and improvisation, presenting the piece to the community, and following the performance with discussion and community planning. Well-funded by non-governmental organizations (NGOs), themselves often based in powerful countries far away, this model spread throughout English-speaking Africa in the 1980s. Many theatre and community leaders, however, criticized the early phase of TFD for its crude modernization ideology, its failure to involve community participants, and its blindness to local customs and political power struggles.

Most present versions of TFD have taken these criticisms to heart and have remained an important strategy for activists seeking theatrical means to improve the lives of many Africans. The Nigerian Popular Theatre Alliance (NPTA), for example, through its Theatre for Development [training] Centre, works in the areas of adolescent health and education, democratic citizenship, economic empowerment, and conflict resolution, an important concern for many Nigerians because of the bitter history of civil war in that country. Affiliated with a local university, the Centre also educates future leaders on the problems and possibilities of TFD.

In Zambia, SEKA, the acronym for Sensitisation and Education through Kunda Arts, works through university teachers, community activists, and theatre artists to tackle many of the problems of village life in central southern Africa. Among these are child labor, rampaging elephants, and HIV/AIDS, particularly rife in rural Zambia. To involve the villagers in their programs, SEKA relies primarily on interactive theatre that uses stories and songs from local life to demystify problems and create collective solutions (Figure 14.14). Partly to fund their major programs, SEKA also creates customized productions for conferences and performs traditional Zambian culture for tourists. SEKA's stated goal is an appropriate summary of the aims of many TFDs: "We believe in changing circumstances by changing minds and changing minds through the arts – theatre and stories in particular" (seka-theatre.com).

Community-based theatre and community plays

Though not a coordinated movement, **community-based theatre** is a worldwide phenomenon. It overlaps with theatre for development initiatives in Africa and India, and is sometimes referred to as "theatre for community cultural development" in the United States, "community theatre" and "community plays" in the United Kingdom and Canada, and *teatro comunitario* in Latin America. Not to be confused with "community theatre" in the United States that restages mainstream theatre with non-professional actors, community-based theatre draws on the legacy of Theater of the Oppressed, Nuevo Teatro Popular (see Chapter 13), and other socially engaged work that mixes political agitation and developmental strategies. Community plays also depend upon ongoing dialogue between artists and spectators, and explore ways of maximizing the agency of a local audience.

Unlike the radical theatre movements of the 1960s, however, the political beliefs of artists committed to community-based work are not necessarily oriented to revolutionary action or democratic socialism, but grow out of their commitment to a local community or social group. Although most espouse liberal political values, some are motivated by a more conservative desire to preserve the past or to pursue notions of community development that align with the global development initiatives that have also inspired theatre for development movements. Not surprisingly, these political differences often translate into competing definitions of the term "community," which can serve one or more groups identified by a sense of regional, ethnic, or social class belonging. Community-based theatre's commitment to a "community" has been both a strength and a weakness, energizing some groups for self-improvement and progressive change, and limiting the social, political, and aesthetic reach of

Figure 14.14
A SEKA performer in a large mask clowns for Zambian villagers.
Source: © Miranda Guhrs of Seka (www.seka–theatre.com).

others. For those communities caught up in problems related to globalization, community-based theatre has primarily led to smart tactics and long-term adjustment or resistance, but at times also to a reliance on rather inflexible identity formations.

There are thousands of community-based theatres around the globe. In Western Europe and North America, community-based artists and facilitators have focused much of their attention on empowering marginalized groups, celebrating the useable past of a community, and helping people to energize communities that have been damaged or destroyed. For example, Stut Theater in Utrecht, the Netherlands, devised a production involving Dutch, Turkish, and Moroccan young people and their parents to recognize the needs of the two marginalized groups and encourage intercultural understanding. In England, playwright and facilitator Ann Jellicoe (1927–2017) helped several communities to celebrate their histories. Swamp Gravy, located in a small town in Georgia in the United States, draws on local tradition and African American Christianity to bridge the racial divide in the American South. The LAPD seeks to generate a sense of community among the residents of Skid Row in Los Angeles; an acronym for the Los Angeles Poverty Department, its shared initials with the police department draws ironic attention to the failures of the city's safety nets.

Several companies work toward all of the goals noted above. In the United States, one of the more established such groups is Cornerstone Theater. Now based in Los Angeles, Cornerstone began in 1986 as a traveling ensemble working with rural communities in the United States to bring their stories to the stage, and including members of the communities in the productions. Since 1992 they have focused more on urban issues and collaborations. Their model of theatre utilizes community-based, peer-to-peer education methods, based on gathering stories from community members and creating plays inspired by those stories. These plays are organized around themes and staged in multi-year cycles; since 1992 they have included the Watts Cycle (building bridges between African American and Latino residents of the Watts neighborhood of Los Angeles); the Faith-Based Cycle (exploring the city's communities of faith); the Justice Cycle (exploring the relationship of law to community); and the Hunger Cycle, around issues of food justice. Cornerstone has also partnered with the National Day Laborer Organizing Network to help launch the Teatro Jornalero Sin Fronteras (Day Laborer Theater Without Borders), an ensemble of day laborers who use Cornerstone methodologies to educate immigrant workers about their rights and to humanize the immigration debate for the larger community. The company has recently collaborated with playwright Larissa FastHorse (of the Sicangu Lakota Nation) on a three-part series with U.S. indigenous communities in South Dakota, Los Angeles, and Phoenix, AZ.

Community-based theatres sometimes combine theatre work with social and economic transformation. In Brazil, Nos do Morro (Us from the Hillside) produces theatre for the poor citizens who live in the hills above the wealthy beach areas of Rio de Janeiro. While the theatre space also serves as a local community center that provides participatory entertainment, the company members engage in various interventions to help the workers, street children, and dispossessed of the area. In the Philippines and the Marshall Islands, respectively, the Philippine Educational Theatre Association (discussed in Chapter 13) and Jodrik-drik ñan Jodrikdrik ilo Ejmour (Youth to Youth in Health) train squads of young people to lead outreach programs using theatrical techniques that help other youth adjust to the many problems that accompany globalization to the islands, including AIDS, increasing alcoholism, and the disruption of traditional culture. In Kenya, the Kawuonda Woman's Group shows the continuing influence of theatre on development programs in a small village. When the women dramatize one of their stories for the village, they typically rehearse them while doing the laundry or picking coffee beans, and they perform their short scenes within a circle of dancers and singers to demonstrate their female solidarity.

Many of the artists involved with these community-based theatres have adopted strategies to moderate or resist some of the effects of globalization that are changing the lives of the populations they assist. Global media, especially from the United States, now saturate the lives of young people around the globe and are fast replacing traditional cultures as a common point of reference in most societies. Jodrikdrik recognizes this fact and encourages their participants to mix island traditions with popular songs and media genres from the United States in their annual talent show, called, appropriately, *Showtime!* In Rio, Nos do Morro has found film and television work for several of the young actors who have performed on its stage. Other community-based theatres, including PETA, La Fomma, and Aguamarina, have helped their participants to organize collectives to maintain the economic viability of traditional crafts in competition with international corporations.

The pressures of globalization are also changing the organizational strategies of community-based work. Yuyachkani in Peru not only maintains its company identity but also facilitates the work of individual members to pursue projects related to company goals. Ground Zero in Toronto has abandoned the notion of a theatre company altogether. Its founder, Don Bouzek, now works with temporary alliances of funders, clients, and artists to produce theatre pieces that will advance progressive causes and alliances in Canada. In the United States, Sojourn Theatre, founded by Michael Rohd (1967–), operates on a similar model. Two scholars of contemporary interventionist theatre, Alan Filewod and David Watt, argue that such "strategic ventures" involving like-minded artists and activists collaborating together on specific projects, provide the best strategy for transforming communities in the global future (Filewod and Watt 2001: *passim*). Indeed, in urban centers the world over, which have become both internationalized and interculturalized through centuries of globalization, growing numbers of minoritarian theatre companies now work from different business and production models (and often collaboratively with each other) to challenge both the dominance of traditional cultural institutions and definitions of community itself.

Summary

Theatre has always been a site for cultures to come into contact with each other, materially and imaginatively. While globalization itself is not new, with the advent of the "global village" since the middle of the last century, the possibilities for such contact have been both broadened and deepened.

In this chapter, we have seen how theatre culture in the era of globalization has taken a variety of forms, ranging from the rather homogenized aesthetic of the mega-musical to the radically local and culturally specific performances of everyday life offered for tourists. Many theatre artists, seeking to advance and reanimate their practice, have looked to other traditions for inspiration, or have found new ways to reach international audiences for their work via festivals and other touring circuits. At the local level, many performance traditions like the *wayang golek* puppet theatre have proven themselves adaptable to new media, in the process achieving a new political life. The processes of globalization have prompted theatrical responses that both preserve patrimony and urgently question its contours in contexts of international spectatorship. Finally, we have discussed a variety of instances and types of theatre that have as their heartbeat an impulse to change the world, community by community.

The notion of theatre as a "zone of (inter)cultural contact" carries with it the full gamut of possible outcomes, ranging from embrace of the foreign to active resistance against its incursions. One result is that theatre in the era of globalization functions within changing norms of formal and cultural hybridity. Like any other social institution, theatre operates within power relations that are often highly imbalanced. An important task of the critic and historian, therefore, is to pay careful attention to how that power, a matter of cultural as well as political and economic capital, is flowing.

★

CHAPTER 15

Theatre in networked culture, 1990–2023

Tamara Underiner

Contributors: Bruce McConachie

"Give me four trestles, four boards, two actors and a passion," Lope de Vega reputedly said, "and I will give you a play." A favorite adage among theatre people, it calls attention to theatre's most basic elements and alludes to its infinite possibilities. As we have seen throughout this book, theatre artists have frequently experimented with these elements. We have also seen how developments in theatre history have always been in conversation with changes in the culture that surrounds them; new technologies, communications and otherwise, have both enabled innovation and, on occasion, spurred the desire to get "back to basics." Now is no different.

As brick-and-mortar theatre spaces continue to produce work for live audiences, with live actors performing scripted drama on three-dimensional sets, the pandemic foregrounded theatrical solutions that before may have been deemed more experimental, both accelerating and normalizing those experiments. Today, the "four trestles and four boards" may be a smart stage, in which actors trigger sensors that trigger lights and sounds, or a **virtual** stage altogether. Of the "two actors," one might be a robot or appear on a screen to interact with the other actor. The "passion" or driving force behind a theatrical experience may not be the vision of a single playwright or director, but arise instead from the collective experiments of a theatre ensemble, possibly rehearsing and performing over Zoom from multiple countries and time zones. The "plays" that result from these new combinations produce new audience experiences, including live and virtual interaction, in which audience contributions influence the action. Finally, the "I" who "give[s] you a play" need no longer be human, as advancements in **artificial intelligence** (AI) expand the authorial horizons of the playwright.

In this chapter, we discuss the interaction not only between human and non-human theatre makers but also between "**networked culture**" as a whole and performance practices on and off the formal stage. While in a fundamental sense, human history is itself a history of networked culture, over the past two decades, new media technologies have made it easier than ever for people to connect with each other and to remain aware of personal and world developments in real time. In North America, Europe, and Australasia, **internet** usage has surpassed television viewing, and mobile internet now accounts for more than half of the world's total web traffic. These new technologies, so central to everyday life, are also becoming increasingly integral to performance on stage, going far beyond their potential as special effects. At the same time, off-stage, social media such as TikTok, YouTube, Meta Platforms' Facebook and Instagram, and X (formerly Twitter) create opportunities for people to "stage" themselves, whether they see themselves as performers or not.

But "networked culture" does not refer only to the computational technologies that make real-time connectivity possible. It also refers to the way these technologies have influenced the ways we are or can imagine being social together. In this culture, "the network" is not merely a technologized byproduct *of* social relations, but is quickly becoming the dominant organizational paradigm for society itself, extending deeply *into* social, cultural, and political conditions. The results reach down to the level of the individual, now conceived as a node in a network composed of both humans and objects (the "internet of things"). There have never been more affordable outlets and channels for individual creative expression, even as the increasing consolidation of media companies into huge conglomerates such as Disney, Sony, and Paramount has concentrated commercial and economic power in the hands of a very few. Audiences for art have become more and more participatory in its experience, if not its creation. Increasingly, new works are being developed by appreciators of visual and performing arts (including film, music, and theatre), who adapt and mix together elements from other works and post the results via open platforms like YouTube. This kind of borrowing, mixing, and adaptation in order to make something new has itself borrowed a term from the music industry – the **remix** – and has become the prevalent aesthetic of networked culture.

Therefore, while much theatres being produced today continues earlier practices, in this chapter, we focus particularly on theatre that registers network culture's varied and ever-changing influences and interactions. To organize the fluid array of ideas and examples available, we divide our coverage into three broad sections, roughly reminiscent of Lope's adage – players, platforms, and performances that respond to the logic of the network in different ways. We open with a brief discussion of how the pandemic mobilized the network to keep theatre alive in a most precarious moment in its history. And because this chapter is also the culmination of this particular theatre histories textbook, we take the opportunity to look not only *at* "theatre in networked culture" but also *through* it to examine how theatre (one of the original "social media") has changed over time as a forum for reflection about society.

Along the way, we should keep in mind that while some characteristics of "networked culture" may seem to represent differences in kind from what came before, others are better understood as differences of degree. Consider, for example, what the ancient Greek philosopher Aristotle held to be the key to effective dramatic plotting: the careful selection and arrangement of incidents from stories already in circulation and well known to the culture for whom the classic Greek playwrights wrote. Is there something essentially different between those playwrights and the aggregators and remixers of today, who re-assemble the raw materials of the story as circulated by their own media and social networks?

Other aspects of networked culture may prove more distinctive. Take the matter of time and space in dramatic action and theatrical performance. While the French neoclassicists may have insisted on preserving the unities of time, place, and dramatic action, theatre artists in all other times and places have taken great liberties with all three aspects of drama, and audiences follow along. But until very recently in theatre history, the performance of stage plays – no matter how long their action was presumed to take, in however many locales – has unfolded in real time before their audience and in a shared physical space. Do today's technologies of connectivity, and the subsequent experiments they allow in performance, represent a new phase in an ongoing evolution of temporal and spatial experimentation on stage or a more radical disruption in the nature of theatrical time and space itself? The examples we follow in this chapter are meant to raise and shed light on such questions, rather than to definitively answer them. For example, our case study below on Hip Hop theatre asks us to consider how this art form, called by Daniel Banks the "theatre of now," also serves as a register of a centuries-old heritage of theatrical practices. Our online case study on online roleplaying also raises interesting questions. To what extent are such experiences related to theatre – do they just "resemble" it, or are they a new type of theatre altogether? And if so, how significant are their differences from traditional theatre in terms of social or cultural factors?

FREE
INSTRUCTOR & STUDENT RESOURCES

Global effects of the pandemic on theatre

Between the last edition of this textbook and the one you're now reading, a global pandemic shut down most of the world's theatres. Few sectors were hit harder economically than the performing arts, few professions were impacted more than those of the individual artists that comprise it, and many of them were self-employed. In the United States, the revenues of performing arts presenters (including festivals) fell by nearly 72.8 percent between 2019 and 2020, while those of performing arts organizations contracted by 50.9 percent. The situation was similar in England; there, producer Andrew Lloyd Weber reported that he was losing £1,000,000 per month by February of 2021 keeping his seven London venues closed. Tens, if not hundreds, of thousands of jobs were lost, many of them never to return. And yet, though the theatres were closed, the shows in many cases went on, as theatre companies first struggled against, and then began to embrace, the new restraints (Figure 15.1). In what follows, we discuss in broad outlines some of the principal strategies adopted by enterprising artists and performing arts organizations via a selection of exemplars and consider the longer-term ramifications of the adjustments made and innovations introduced. (Some of these innovations stand as examples *par excellence* of "theatre in networked culture" and are saved for later discussion.)

Early on, larger theatre companies like the National Theatre in London were able to stream their back catalogs of previously recorded productions, and streaming platforms like Broadway HD, which had that capability since 2016 for Broadway shows, enjoyed a surge in popularity via their "pay per view" options. As the pandemic wore on, some companies also were able to develop new productions staged in carefully controlled conditions and livestream them to people viewing at home or in their COVID "cells."

But within a week of the theatre shutdown in London, British actor and author Robert Myles created *The Show Must Go Online*, which eventually would reimagine the complete plays of Shakespeare on Zoom, livestreaming them weekly to an audience of over 200,000, with actors drawn from all over the world. Similarly, actors of note were drawn to "Lockdown

Figure 15.1

French humorists Othman (left) and Kalvin perform onstage at the Apollo Theatre in Paris during their live-streaming show with 20 spectators in a videoconference on 14 May 2020.

Source: Franck Fife/AFP via Getty Images.

Theatre" in England and "First Reads," a branch of the Oregon Shakespeare's Play on Shakespeare initiative; both featured Zoom table reads of new conceptualizations of canonical works.

 Artists whose commissions were canceled or indefinitely postponed found ways to keep their planned projects inventively alive. One example, blending new and old-school technologies, was Virginia Grise's (1976–) 2020 *A Farm for Meme*. A project of the "Innovations in Socially Distant Performance" Initiative of Princeton University's Lewis Center for the Arts, *A Farm for Meme* combined box puppets made out of construction paper, string, and cardboard; shadow play; filmed monologue; and archival footage set to an evocative score. It tells, in English and Spanish spoken versions accompanied by American Sign Language, two parallel and richly layered stories revolving around a 14-acre farm that was planted and briefly thrived on a vacant lot in the middle of South Central Los Angeles. This lot was the former site of a local revolt that garnered national attention sparked by the 1992 police beating of Rodney King before it was bulldozed by private interests. One story is that of three-year-old Emanuel (the "Meme" of the title, Meme [meh-meh] being the short form of Emanuel), who lives with his mother and two brothers in an encampment in South Central LA in 1992. The other is that of the contemporary queer Latinx family of the narrator and her contemporary, multicultural South Central neighborhood, and all the story seeds that continue to be planted and grow there.

As this example suggests, commissions of new work and critical and scholarly coverage of it soon followed. Very early on, the Public Theater in New York commissioned what *New Yorker* theatre critic Alexandra Schwartz called "the first great original play of quarantine" – Richard Nelson's (1950–) *What Do We Need to Talk About?*, which streamed via YouTube on 29 April 2020. It featured a family meeting up on Zoom to discuss, among other things, the death by the coronavirus of the actor Mark Blum, whom the actors playing the family members likely knew personally. The same review suggested that Molière in the Park's migrated-to-Zoom version of *The Misanthrope* a few days later, featuring actors in front of specially designed background/interiors and allowing audience interactions and encouragements during the inevitable technical glitches, may have hit on the right formula for lockdown theatre: "Choose a classic text — preferably not too long, preferably funny—get good actors to perform it into their devices, and voilà" (Schwartz 2020: n.p.)

Many of these productions served as benefits for the performers or companies involved. In her study of 49 such performances between the onset of social distancing and 26 May 2020, when protests began after the murder of George Floyd, theatre scholar Dani Snyder-Young noted:

> Even performances that did not generate direct revenue for artists in this way looked to generate clicks and views attesting to the value of the work within the context of the attention economy . . . ; such attention holds the possibility of generating later opportunities for the artists.
>
> (Snyder-Young 2022a: 5)

Snyder-Young's research team found that, overwhelmingly, the theme of "we are in this together" permeated much of this work; however, she cautions against assuming a collective "we" that experienced the pandemic all in the same way. She illustrates her point via the piece *How Are We?*, commissioned by the Onassis Foundation as part of their "ENTER" project, a series of works created within 120 hours to capture the "here and now" of quarantine. *How Are We* is a 25-minute digital film featuring 90-second, movement-based works by 18 different artists, developed by Emily Mast and Yehuda Duenyas. In contrast to the other pieces the team studied, which portrayed a rather flattened experience from the predominant focus on being "in it together," *How We Are* focused instead on difference:

> A young nonbinary person (Shannon Hafez) playing in their yard with their dog (0:49), is not the same as a woman (Jennie MaryTai Liu) who cannot get out of bed to attend to a house full of small children (5:45), is not the same as a Black man (David Adrian Freeland Jr) bottling rage and fear to put on a composed and pleasant face (15:28). Each separately authored piece reflects a distinct experience and understanding of quarantined isolation.
>
> (Snyder-Young 2022b: E4)

For their part, disabled communities pointed out that accessibility gains made possible by the newly ubiquitous digital delivery modalities were long overdue (especially for people with vision, hearing, and mobility constraints), while continuing to call attention to the limits of other workarounds that paid too little heed to such constraints. For example, some outdoor theatre options that otherwise followed COVID safety protocols may not necessarily have provided support for the audio-visually impaired or wheelchair-bound. "Walking tours, promenade-style projects, and physically distanced outdoor stages have all recently been introduced, but they are highly unregulated in terms of mandatory venue accessibility accommodations" (Marotta 2020: n.p.). Many expressed concern that even if addressed, such accommodations would prove temporary, due to such factors as expense and the sustained activism required to keep attention on them.

On Wednesday evening, 4 August 2021, the first new play to be staged in person on Broadway since the lockdown was Antoinette Chinonye Nwandu's (1980–) *Pass Over*, a comedy-drama about two young Black men afraid to leave the safety of a streetlight's circle at night for fear of encountering police violence. Mixing *Waiting for Godot* with the bible story of Exodus, it was significant for its address of racist realities that were as front and central in public mind as the pandemic and for being the first of seven plays on Broadway that year written by Black playwrights.

At this writing, current producers of live theatre are concerned about three factors affecting its future: attendance has yet to recover to its pre-pandemic levels; ticket revenues are also down; and expenses are up (due to higher safety protocols as well as general inflation and rent increases). Further, during the first year and a half of the pandemic, governments and private relief organizations stepped in to support artists and arts organizations to keep them afloat; that support has largely ended. In response to these concerns, large companies are changing everything from the way they govern and fundraise to their entire business models. Smaller, scrappier companies are finding new ways to partner with other organizations that share their artistic visions (including potential landlords) in order to meet their operational needs. Speaking to a National Public Radio host in early 2023, Randi Berry, executive director of IndieSpace, a nonprofit that provides support to New York's independent theatre community by finding and offering untapped rehearsal space at deep discounts (or even free for some performing arts organizations), summed up the situation this way:

> As we saw during the pandemic, arts organizations that were working on their own were struggling on their own. When we have an amazing resource for the community, the more people that can get their hands in it, the better.
>
> (qtd. in Veltman 2023: n.p.)

This isn't the first pandemic theatre has come through, and it will likely not be the last. For instance, for more than half of the last decade of Shakespeare's life, the theatres were closed due to epidemics (78 months in all). To learn more about the history of theatre's relationship to plague and pestilence, take a look at Maria Ristani's excellent historical overview, "Theatre and Epidemics: An Age-Old Link" available online from criticalstages.org. As we've argued so far, in order to survive the current one as well as it did, theatre artists and producers mobilized various networks to keep themselves and their work relevant. In the sections that follow, we take a closer look at the historical developments that made such adjustments possible at all.

New players

As we've seen in previous chapters, the role of the actor in society – whether elevated as celebrity or denigrated as vagabond – derives from the power actors are believed to have in shaping human values. Their larger-than-life significance is due, in part, to the double reality they inhabit on stage, a reality that borders on the virtual. They transform and extend themselves through both external means (costume, makeup) and internal means (physical, psychological, and emotional training and preparation), all the while remaining present to their audiences both as themselves and as their characters. They are both real and unreal; or, as Richard Schechner has elaborated, they are both "not me" and "not not me" (Schechner 1985: 112).

Until very recently, however, actors have always been co-present with their spectators, sharing physical proximity with them in real time. In fact, for many, it is this property of "presence" that has distinguished theatre from other forms of narrative and representational media. However, we can and often do experience this sense of presence with and through media as well, as when we watch a "livestream" of a performance or communicate with an online chatbot (and we notice it keenly when our devices "die"). Understood this way, the question of "presence" has moved away from its traditional domain in the theatrical form and has taken up residence in the audience's experience of the form, if not in the technology itself. And that form has increasingly come to entangle together live and media "performers."

Experiments with live, virtual, and machine actors

Perhaps the earliest performance pairing a live actor with a virtual performer was in a 1914 vaudeville act by Winsor McCay (c.1866–1934), who interacted with a film animation of Gertie the dinosaur. Since then, experiments have grown in complexity and sophistication. In the early days of the internet, performance artists and theatre companies were quick to explore the question of live/virtual performance. In 1995, Guillermo Gómez-Peña and Roberto Sifuentes (see Chapter 13) collaborated with James Luna (1950–2018) on an in-stallation/performance called *The Shame Man and El Mexican't Meet the CyberVato*. Over the course of five days at an art gallery at Rice University, Luna as The Shame Man and Gómez-Peña as El Mexican't performed various incarnations of how "Native Americans" and "Mexicans" should look, behave, and perform in the 1990s, based on suggestions posted by visitors to the performance's website, which also appeared on monitors in the performance space. Meanwhile, the character CyberVato (Sifuentes), an exaggerated Chicano gang member decked out in techno-gadgetry, captured images of his collaborators' transformations, and transmitted them daily to the Web via video teleconferencing. The intent was "to politicize the debates around digital technologies and to infect virtual space with Chicano humor and *linguas polutas* (such as Spanglish)" (Gómez-Peña 2003: 38).

The following year, the San Francisco-based troupe George Coates Performance Works premiered *Twisted Pairs*, whose characters were based on personality types making early appearances in online chatrooms and bulletin boards; its action was structured according to the associative logic of internet surfing. (The title refers to the way electrical wires are twisted together to cancel out electromagnetic interference from other sources, key to clarity in telecommunications.) The plot, similarly convoluted, revolved around an Amish farmgirl who discovered a laptop by accident and went on to become an internet celebrity calling herself "Annette Diva." Other characters were developed out of recognizable online personas and the live actors interacted with video projections and telecasts. At the time, such technologies were new enough that a glossary of internet terms was necessary for audience members – many of whom were not sufficiently literate in internet lingo to get many of the jokes.

In 2000, Steve Dixon, Paul Murphy, and Wendy Reed of Chameleons Group developed *Chameleons 3: Net Congestion*, which experimented with combinations of live actors with remote audiences and with recorded characters. Actors performing on three separate stages in a black box studio interacted with pre-recorded characters projected on screens behind them, while the audience – none of whom was there in the studios, but watching over the internet – typed in suggestions for the performers to use or play with. Dixon writes, "Whilst a 'high-tech' project, the stage configuration itself harked back to the pageant wagon staging of Medieval Mystery Plays" (Dixon n.d.).

More recently, the age-old theatrical art of puppetry too has achieved new life at a new scale through the boost of more modern technologies like animatronics. Two examples are *The Sultan's Elephant* (2005), created by the French Royal de Luxe theatre company to celebrate the centenary of Jules Verne's death, and *Little Amal* (2021) (see Figure 15.2), created by

Figure 15.2
The giant puppet Little Amal, representing a young Syrian refugee, continues her pilgrimage through the world's cities with a stop in Lviv, Ukraine, in May 2022.
Source: Ruslan Lytvyn, Shutterstock Images.

the South African Handspring Puppet Company for a project called The Walk, to celebrate migration and cultural diversity. Both featured breathtaking parades through city streets that left spectators astonished at the spectacles. *The Sultan's Elephant* featured a giant, 42-ton wood and leather elephant manipulated by 22 puppeteers operating its internal machinery (which included the aforementioned hydraulic lifts); a separate marionette of a giant "little" girl (arriving by a rocket in clouds of smoke) was lifted to its back and paraded around the cities they visited. *Little Amal* was born in 2021 to bring awareness to the plight of Syrian refugees. Three and a half meters (11.5 feet) tall, she is operated by three external puppeteers with the aid of internal animatronics. Her first five-month walk covered 65 different cities from the Syria-Turkey border to London; since then, she has made appearances elsewhere on the continent. While the reception is almost universally positive, she has also been pelted by spectators expressing anti-Muslim sentiment. Word spread quickly about both of the phenomena through social media, bringing an international spectatorship both synchronously and asynchronously through platforms like YouTube.

While technology has allowed actors and puppeteers to connect with audiences across time and space, new advancements in medical and cyber-technology have prompted many theatre and performance artists to explore the limits of "the human" itself in their work.

Exploring and expanding the limits of the human

The theatrical stage has always been a site for magic, where the supernatural and the uperhuman can appear to have tangible reality. Today, a performer can do more than amplify the sound of their voice with a wireless mike; they can also manipulate other elements of the theatrical environment that previously had been run by crews behind the scenes. For example, their costume can be a smart one, outfitted with movement sensors that trigger sound, music, lights, and so forth, at their command. In one sense, this is an extension of centuries of experimentation with theatrical illusion and special effects. In another sense, the new possibilities for extending human powers through technology have raised compelling questions about where the human ends and the machine begins. Human–machine interactions have produced new ideas about being human in this digital, mediatized – some say posthuman – age. Theatre scholar Jennifer Parker-Starbuck refers to a "cyborg theatre" (2011), which explores this merging of human and technology, both literally and figuratively, toward moving past traditional notions of biology-based humanity. The only line that appears to have been drawn in the sand has to do with AI and the creative professions: during the writers' and actors' strikes of 2023, actors called for contract protections against their identities and talents being exploited by AI without their consent or compensation. Beyond that the lines begin to blur.

For example, some artists have undergone extreme modifications of their own bodies in work that calls the "givenness" of that body into serious question as they experiment with body type, gender stereotype, and even human/animal hybridity. (Many of these experiments have come through the work of individual performance artists; for more information on performance art itself, see the section in Chapter 13). For example, the work of the Australian digital/live performance artist Stelarc (1946–) has included both cybernetic performance and body modification. In the 1990s, Stelarc created a series of live/internet performances in which his body was remotely controlled through interfaces with remote viewers and with the internet itself, resulting in his body being, literally, jerked around by

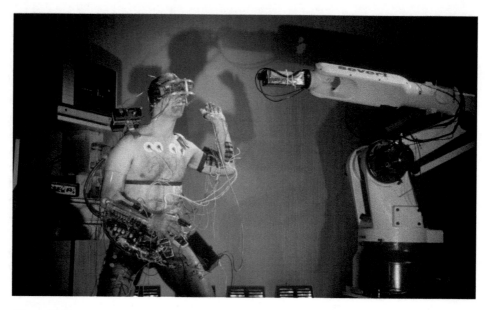

Figure 15.3
Australian performance artist Stelarc in his 1994 work, *Amplified Body*.
Source: Jan Sprij.

remote controllers (Figure 15.3). More recently, Stelarc has been experimenting with more extreme and permanent body modification. In 2006, for example, he began work on an ongoing project in which he is growing an ear on his left forearm; it has been fitted with a microphone and wireless transmitter that allows remote listeners to hear what his arm/ear is "hearing" (through its built-in microphone) in real time over the internet. A 2020 installation called "Reclining Stickman" is a nine-meter (29.5 feet) high human–robot interaction activated by visitors via the control panel, by remote control via the internet, or by an algorithm running in the background when no one else is there. As a result of his experiments and speculations, Stelarc has come to consider the body increasingly obsolete – at least in terms of its former physiological limitations.

Actors and robots, robots as actors – and authors

Still, other artists have experimented with humanoid robots to question our confidence in how special we humans might really be. Japanese playwright Hirata Oriza (1962–) collaborates with robot designer Hiroshi Ishiguro at Osaka University to stage humans and android robots together. Their 2010 play *Sayonara* is about a young woman with a terminal disease whose parents hire an extremely human-looking android to care for her, so that they can then abandon her. The voice and gestures of the android, "Geminoid F" (see Figure 15.4), were created off stage by an actress in a soundproof chamber, fed to the android via camera and replicated on stage. In 2012, *Sayonara II* featured a defective robot reading poems to comfort a girl dying of radiation exposure from the damaged nuclear power plant at

Fukushima after the 2011 earthquake. Another collaboration resulted in the 2011 *I, Worker*, which features two non-humanoid robot maids. All have at their center an exploration of what it is to be human, forced into stark relief by robots (a frequent theme of science fiction, not yet fully realizable on stage).

Not every experiment with robotic performances has profound philosophical questions as its inspiration. In 2006, the Les Frères Corbusier production of Elizabeth Meriwether's *Heddatron* also featured live actors sharing the stage with radio-controlled robots, their operators off stage. Designed by Cindy Jeffers and Meredith Finkelstein of Botmatrix, an art robotics collective, the robots in *Heddatron* entice an unhappy housewife from Ypsilanti, Michigan, to the jungles of Ecuador, where they force her to perform the title role of Ibsen's *Hedda Gabler* (1890). They perform the supporting roles and that of Ibsen himself – who is, like his heroine, portrayed as suffering within a stifling marriage. Originating in New York, *Heddatron* has been produced in several other theatres across the United States, to generally enthusiastic reviews. Interestingly, these reviews tended to focus as much on the show's premise and themes – the identification of a contemporary woman with a character written over a century before her birth, and the redemptive possibilities of theatre itself – as they did on the fact that more than half the cast were robots.

One reviewer called attention to the robots' perfect comic timing, which raises an interesting point for theatre history. Unlike fully human actors, robots are able to achieve exact repetition from performance to performance, a fact that recalls certain other moments in theatre history. On the one hand, live theatre's unrepeatability is, for some, what makes it uniquely attractive. On the other, theatre history has also been marked by frequent demands to deliver fidelity to the playwright's text, and consistent, if not identical, performances along the course of a show's run. In the Hellenistic age, for example, proscriptions against actor improvisations were common. Also recall our discussion in Chapter 7 of Denis Diderot's eighteenth-century *The Paradox of the Actor*, in which the French philosopher praised performers who could separate their emotions from their actions, their minds from their bodies, so that they could present their character in exactly the same way at every performance. Diderot argued that, to effectively move an audience, the actor must remain himself/herself unmoved. This idea was later expanded upon by Gordon Craig (see Chapter 10), who longed to replace actors entirely with large puppets, or *Übermarionettes*, because they would be easier to control than live human beings.

But what price is such control? Today, theatre artists are paying closer attention to the cost to the emotional health and well-being of actors as they prepare, in ways that Diderot and Craig (and for that matter Stanislavsky and Meyerhold) could not have imagined. Over the past 25 years, in theatre training and rehearsal settings, the role of intimacy coaches, directors, choreographers, and dramaturgs has become increasingly important to help actors and actors-in-training identify and manage personal boundaries in order to distinguish self from character, especially when the roles they are asked to play may trigger past traumas or create new ones – whether emotional, sexual, racial or physical in nature. In 2016, Intimacy Directors International became the first organization to begin to collate and codify the skills, techniques, and methodologies associated with this work.

And while the replacement of actors on stage by robots may be unlikely, there is a growing area within the networked culture in which virtual bodies take center stage – and the stage itself is also a virtual one. Our online case study takes a closer look at the phenomenon of online role-playing as a new form of theatre.

Finally, could an artificially intelligent playwright produce a speech as convincingly trippingly for the tongue as its human equivalent? These experiments too are underway. In 2020, for example, to mark the 100th anniversary of Karel Čapek's (1890–1938) play *RUR* (*Rossum's Universal Robots* – which introduced the term "robot" into the global lexicon) – THEaiTRE project produced the first fully computer-generated drama, premiering online because of COVID. It has since been staged by Švand Theatre in Prague, where Čapek lived and worked, under the direction of Daniel Hrbek. Advertised as "Snippets from the life of artificial intelligence in its own words. A futuristic post-pandemic Little Prince," it was also described by one critic as "surprisingly vulgar in places" (Svoboda 2021: n.p.). It should be noted that the creative team, a collaboration among machine language and theatre experts, included a human dramaturg. A second play, *Permeation,* was developed by the company in 2022 to support Ukrainian refugees. The project website listed the director as Erwin Maas, project author as Tomas Studenik, and playwright as "artificial intelligence" (rehearsalfortruth.org).

Changing platforms for theatre and performance

Another change brought about by networked culture is the expansion of possible platforms for performance beyond the material "four trestles" and "four boards" once required of the formal stage. Sometimes, the new platforms are digital, in full or in part: theatre increasingly houses digital sets and scenic elements or is being presented on wholly virtual platforms. But theatre is also taking place off the formal stage and in the "real" world, in ways that are themselves enabled by social media, used to attract both live and remote spectators.

Digital platforms

Live theatre has utilized film and electronic media for decades; as long ago as 1898, playwright Lincoln J. Carter (1865–1926) designed filmed scenery as a backdrop to his stage action. Performances have long used closed-circuit television, motion-controlled projections, or online streaming media to add characters or create a setting on stage. In 1996, for example, the University of Kansas's Institute for Exploration of Virtual Reality staged Arthur Kopit's (1937–2021) *Wings* (1978), using a completely electronic set design, which audience members accessed through virtual reality headsets (Figure 15.5). (The play, which explores the effects of stroke on the language and mental processes of its victim, was originally written as a radio play.)

Figure 15.5
An early experiment combining live and virtual performance elements, by the University of Kansas's Institute for Exploration of Virtual Reality, in 1996. This scene is from Arthur Kopit's *Wings*, about a woman recovering from a stroke. Audience members watched the play through head-mounted displays, which allowed them to see through the computer graphics and live video being projected on their devices to the production's live actors and digital projections. (Director Ronald A. Willis, Designer/Technologist Mark Reaney, and Video Director Lance Gharavi.)
Source: © Mark Reaney.

Today, projections are commonly employed both as virtual scenery and as interactive elements in stage plays. Online, whole plays have been performed within a virtual world (often designed for the event), with the actors' lines expressed through voice, typing, or even icons. For instance, in the online virtual world of *Second Life*, people are able to create custom animations to make their avatars (which they also create) move in a programmed way (walk, dance, hug, etc.; see Figure 15.6). This capability was used in a performance of Sophocles's *Oedipus Rex* staged by the Avatar Repertory Theater in 2010–2011. The audience's avatars sat on cushions while they watched the play. Then, when the performance reached the play's choral odes, the cushions triggered animations that made the spectators move and gesture, in unison, so that they became part of the performance itself – a new way to break down the actor/audience division (Figure 15.7). The Australian performance artist Stelarc, mentioned above, has created performances within *Second Life* as well.

Downloadable podplays, the descendants of the radio plays of the mid-twentieth century, now let listeners access a variety of plays, some meant to be experienced anywhere and some custom written for specific places and experiences. Roy Williams's *846*, for example, is

Figure 15.6
The Realm of Mystara, a role-playing setting in *Second Life.*
Source: © Tobin Nellhaus.

Figure 15.7
Oedipus Rex as performed in *Second Life* by the Avatar Repertory Theater, performed in 2010–11. The spectators' avatars move and gesture through animations programmed into the cushions they sat on and triggered by a member of the theatre company.
Source: Courtesy of Mary Linn Crouse.

a collection of 14 short audio plays by British playwrights of color, released as a podcast in July 2020 in response to the murder of George Floyd; the title refers to the 8 minutes and 46 seconds that the police officer had his knee on Floyd's neck.

Other artists have experimented with simultaneous stage spaces via network technology. For example, media artist Adriene Jenik's (1964–) 2007 *Open_Borders: Improvisation Across Networks, Distance, Time Zones*, used Skype technology to unite 41 artists from 12 countries in 11 time zones, in a single performance. Jenik's work highlighted not only questions of how liveness operates through technology but also questions about how technology serves to collapse and stretch both time and space.

When the mini-blogging platform Twitter (now X) debuted in 2006, theatre companies were quick to see its potential for generating interest in productions that could be instantly reviewed by artistic staff and audiences. Innovations in both staging and dramaturgy soon followed. Audience tweets in response to a production could be projected onto screens on stage, used as prompts for improvisation or to develop the plot of the drama itself in participatory forms of theatre.

There have also been a number of experiments in playwriting, leading to a burgeoning body of "Twitter plays." Theatre scholar John H. Muse has identified two broad categories encompassing four types of Twitter plays: short-form "nanodramas" consisting of a single tweet; and long-form plays tweeted as a series of updates among the characters over the course of several days or weeks. Within the longer form are three subgenres: original works, impersonations of famous people (historical or fictional), and adaptations, all of which are performed in real time but in virtual spaces, and which take advantage of the conventions of Twitter to provide additional insight into characters' motivations and emotions (Muse 2012).

Many nanodramas have been inspired by challenges posed by the New York Neo-Futurists, a collective devoted to staging non-illusionistic theatre that foregrounds an awareness and inclusion of the actual world; their work often appears on material stages but embraces electronic platforms as well. In 2009, they began issuing calls for single-tweet plays that had to contain or be constrained by certain elements – e.g., at least three characters, the use of a certain prop, or a particular action such as "a big kiss." Within two years, some 800 Twitter playwrights responded, with more than 4,000 plays.

The first long-form Twitter play was created by Jeremy Gable (1982–); his *140: A Twitter Performance* followed four fictional characters from Idaho, whose story unfolded over the course of some 300 updates during a two-month period in the summer of 2009. Two years later, the Reorbit Project was launched as an experiment in social media "[c]alling all writers to inhabit a historical or fictional character in real-time over Twitter" (Reorbit 2010). The principal criterion, apart from the 140-character limit, was fidelity to the original character's persona; hence, tweets from a teenaged "Samuel Beckett" such as this: "Writing this way, writing in bits, has an appeal, has a pleasing brevity, the momentary pause discovered between dry heave and stomach cramp" (quoted in Muse 2012: 47). The most popular long-form Twitter plays have been adaptations, a prominent example being *Such Tweet Sorrow*, a 2010 co-production of the Royal Shakespeare Company and the Evanston, Illinois-based Mudlark Theater. Set in modern-day London, this version of Shakespeare's *Romeo and Juliet* had the actors playing the six principal characters post updates about their characters' dilemmas over the course of five weeks.

For Muse, Twitter plays, with their combination of compression and concision, and their appearance (in the longer form) of transpiring over the course of real character time, offer an opportunity to reflect on the nature of theatre itself. Can a play really be expressed in 140 characters? Is Twitter drama a new form of closet drama (meant to be read, rather than staged)? Or does the fact that it is "performed" via text in real-time updates make a significant difference? Is it more similar to serialized radio drama, or does the fact that it is "seen" and not heard significant? And what does the evolving nature of the #hashtag – originally a search mechanism, now increasingly used to make meta-commentary on the tweet itself – suggest about the way the tweeter performs the self? "To examine the ways artists are enlisting Twitter for theatrical ends reveals not only that playwrights are colonizing Twitter," Muse writes, "but also the extent to which social media are making playwrights, performers, and spectators of us all" (2012: 43), a point well illustrated by our next two examples, which highlight the interpenetration of theatre and the video-sharing platform TikTok.

Even more than X/Twitter, TikTok functions as a stage in its own right, allowing anyone with a smartphone camera to be the star of their own short show, the catchier the better. It has reached more than 2 billion users worldwide. During the pandemic, the New York-based arts collective Fake Friends produced a TikTok-dependent production called *Circle Jerk* that was a "homopessimist" satire of the news cycle and internet culture from all sides of it, becoming a finalist for the Pulitzer Prize in Drama in 2020. Audiences at home watched a live theatre version of the cast producing their own TikToks and turning them into theatre, including a frenetically paced "meme ballet" involving multiple costume changes. Critic, scholar, and TikTok expert Trevor Boffone noted:

> TikTok aesthetics informed *Circle Jerk* as it delved into the relentless internet meme culture that has come to define Millennial and Gen Z experiences. As *Circle Jerk* erupted into its infamous meme ballet, the more we associated with the piece, the more we recognized, the more implicated we became. Where does TikTok end and where does digital theatre begin? Or, are they one in the same? Does a distinction even matter?
>
> Boffone 2021: n.p.

Another inventive use of TikTok was to crowd-source the creation of *Ratatouille, the TikTok Musical*. Over the fall of 2020, after an original "Ode to Remy" (the rat protagonist of the Disney animated movie) was uploaded by schoolteacher Emily Jacobsen, then scored in a Disney style by Daniel Mertzlufft, fans and artists began adding their own contributions – music, scene design, choreography, playbill, and so on. Eventually, it gained Disney endorsement, a director (Lucy Moss), librettists (two members of Fake Friends, Michael Breslin and Patrick Foley), and a professional cast (collaborating with some of the original non-professional contributors), accompanied by the Broadway Sinfonietta, a 20-piece all-female orchestra. It premiered on 1 January 2021 as an hour-long benefit concert for the Actors' Fund, raising some $2 million for the cause.

Thinking back to Chapter 13's discussion about how the primacy of the text and author have been questioned since the 1960s – does X/Twitter and TikTok theatre, with their actor/improvisers and audience interaction, represent a new phase of this democratizing creative impulse, or perhaps its ultimate fulfillment, at least among those with access to social media?

Socio-spatial performance experiments in the material world

For many artists and activists, social media and online archiving have literally turned the world into a stage for their artistic and political agendas. Their work ranges from runs of full productions taking place in a designated extra-theatrical space, to "pop-up" performances that come and go very quickly. At both ends of the spectrum, the performance and the space in which it happens are in conversation with each other and are enhanced, if not enabled, by social media.

In the days before the construction of purpose-built theatre spaces, theatre was performed in and arguably conditioned by the particulars of the spaces in which it had to appear, be they tennis courts or city streets. The York Cycle's pageant wagons, for example, provided a near backdrop for the plays, and the city's buildings a further one; the staging of the cycle plays turned the entire city into something of a holy site once a year. Today, theatre artists sometimes specifically choose sites outside of existing theatre structures, for particular purposes and to make particular points. An example from 2007 is *Girls Just Wanna Have Fund$*, commissioned by the arts arm of the World Financial Center in New York City. This series of six 10-minute plays was developed by writers and directors associated with the Women's Project Theater Lab and presented 13 times over the course of four days in various public areas of the World Financial Center. The plays explored different aspects of women's relationship (or lack of relationship) to wealth. No one could buy a ticket for the performances, but audiences grew over the course of the three weekdays and one Saturday as word spread through social media.

Free theatre offered in public spaces is not new; since the middle of the last century, such performances have usually been subsidized by theatre companies in partnership with arts granting organizations and municipalities. (A prominent example is the Public Theater's *Shakespeare in the Park* in New York City.) But networked culture is further democratizing the experience, changing our expectation of who might appear on these new platforms, and who might be invited to the "show." The flashmobs of the past 25 years or so are one illustration. Here, organizers count on social media as well as the power of a seemingly spontaneous performance to gather audiences in the moment – and to ensure the performance has a virtual life afterward on platforms such as YouTube. One of the earliest and most frequently imitated such performances is based on Michael Jackson's 1982 song *Thriller* (Figure 15.8), which has not only motivated dozens of Halloween performances every year but has also been used to make political statements. In 2011 hundreds of Chilean students, angered by the fees charged by their increasingly privatized school system, choreographed a performance of *Thriller* outside the presidential mansion to protest their plight. The videos taken on personal cellphones soon went viral, subverting the "official coverage" and censorship of the Chilean news corporations.

GPS technology has inspired new forms of theatricality in unexpected places. For example, in 2008, Pittsburgh artists Robin Hewlett and Ben Kinsley created "Street with a View," a simulated street scene including both actors and local residents, who staged scenes specifically for the moment when the Google Street View vehicle was passing through their Northside neighborhood in May of that year. Their scenes included a parade, a garage band practice, a cat being rescued by firemen, and even a swordfight in seventeenth-century costume. Thus, for a time, when Google Map users later sought street views of those locations, they were treated to specially staged dramatic tableaux.

Figure 15.8
Fans of singer Michael Jackson flashmob on the steps of the Municipal Theater in São Paulo dancing *Thriller* on the day the singer would have turned 60 (29 August 2018).
Source: Cris Faga/NurPhoto via Getty Images.

New performance structures and processes

As these experiments and innovations suggest, social media and the logic of networked culture within globalization have inspired new forms of staging and more democratized relations of theatrical production. In this section, we will expand the focus to examine how this logic, if not the technology itself, has worked its way into dramatic structure, with new developments in **immersive theatre**. We also consider how these influences have affected how plays come to be, with a brief look at recent developments in **postdramatic** and **devised theatre**.

Since 1994, New York City-based The Builders Association, founded by Marianne Weems (1960–), has been experimenting with all these developments in highly mediatized, collaborative work (Figure 15.9). Its inaugural piece, an adaptation of Henrik Ibsen's *Master Builder*, was developed over the course of seven months in a Chelsea warehouse. The set was a full-scale, dilapidated three-story family home, sections of which were gradually demolished over the course of the performance to reveal other thematic infrastructures at play. It was wired with MIDI triggers the actors activated, bringing the house itself alive with sound effects and music; there was also a complex sound and video score that featured Buster Keaton films, industrial films from the 1950s, clips from the "This Old House" television series, and Led Zeppelin rock and roll music. Most recently in 2022, the group presented the fully online *I Agree to the Terms*, in collaboration with MTurk Workers (short for Amazon's Mechanical Turk), microworkers who "train the algorithms that shape our online experience" (thebuildersassociation. org). Audience members entered the 45-minute experience to train with actual workers, compete for jobs, and get paid in virtual "Builders Coin." Along the way, they learned about the invisible labor force behind not just our online but much of our material reality.

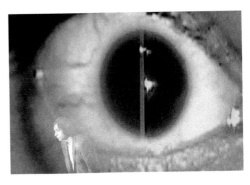

Figure 15.9

Rizwan Mirza as The Ugandan/Indian Traveller rehearses a production of the Builders Association's *Super Vision*, a multimedia theatrical examination of life in the post-privacy era, for the L.A. premiere at Redcat Theatre, Disney Hall, directed by Marianne Weems.

Source: Ricardo DeAratanha/Los Angeles Times via Getty Images.

Cultural critics often point to data mining and aggregation as key characteristics of networked culture, features that distinguish its conventions of information organization from those of prior periods. While in the past, information archiving depended upon some kind of ordering principle – even if only as simple as "keep" vs. "toss" – nowadays everything that can be turned into data is storable as such. The organization of all of this information depends not on *a priori* selections, but on the search preferences of the end user. The vast amounts of information now instantly

available to searchers have contributed to the prevailing aesthetic of the remix we identified in the introduction to this chapter.

In 2011, the New York City-based theatre ensemble Elevator Repair Service incorporated both the technology and the logic of data mining and remixing into their work *Shuffle*, produced in collaboration with installation artist Ben Rubin and UCLA statistician Mark Hansen. The company had been working with adaptations and inventively staged readings of the novels *The Great Gatsby* (F. Scott Fitzgerald 1925), *The Sound and the Fury* (William Faulkner 1929), and *The Sun Also Rises* (Ernest Hemingway 1926). Taking these sources as both inspiration and data, in 2011 they did a mashup of all three in the New York Public Library. Scripts were generated by digital algorithms drawn from the novels' "data"; the performers from the past productions now improvised upon the new remixed scripts in this one. Audience members were free to wander among the performers, as though they themselves were browsers, while they improvised. The point was not to preserve original plot lines and intentions but to call attention to the ways data mining and creative data analysis can produce startling juxtapositions and new, far-from-intended meanings.

Social media has also highlighted the pliable nature of time and space in globalization, with its tendency to increase speed and shrink distance. What is the human experience of time in such circumstances? One notable theatrical response to this question was Robert Lepage (1957–) and Ex Machina's 2001 *Zulu Time*, a "techno-cabaret" collaboration with musician Peter Gabriel (see Figure 15.10). The title refers to what the military and civil aviation call Greenwich Mean Time (GMT), the central – if somewhat arbitrary – point of reference for setting time across the world. The piece was divided into 26 sections, one for each letter of the military phonetic alphabet code (from A for Alpha to Z for Zulu). Each section featured a setting where time seems suspended – in waiting areas, airport restaurants

Figure 15.10
A scene from Robert Lepage's *Zulu Time* (2001).
Source: © Emmanuel Valette.

and bars, hotel rooms, terminal walkways, and so forth, most having to do with travel and the in-between state that travel produces (neither here/home nor there/away). The stage set design was multi-level and dynamic and included film and video projections; the acrobatic actors moved between levels and interacted with flying insect- and animal-like robots. Each vignette was distinct and not overtly connected to the others in terms of character, plot, or even dramatic tone. Performance scholar Steve Dixon describes the production this way:

> Characters talk in different languages; a lounge singer croons and tells jokes in Spanish and German, which no one understands; a woman listens to her erotic messages in a hotel room; we watch a screen display of a pregnant woman's unborn baby as she undergoes a hospital scan. Though characters do meet (and even dance and make love) the vignettes are generally far more about isolation and disconnection. The flight attendants, terrorists, drug-traffickers, and other dazed, time-lagged travelers are misplaced, lonely, and predominantly alone. . . . [I]n the sleepy somnambulance of transatlantic flight, each abandons his or her body to become [what Patrice Pavis called] "a machine that defies time, catches up with it, or at least neutralizes it, a short moment of eternity."
>
> (Dixon 2007: 521)

In *Zulu Time*, air travel becomes a symbol of globalization's ability to collapse time and space together, producing at once the opportunity for high-level connectedness and extreme isolation. One of the scenes was eerily prescient of an event that would itself indelibly mark a certain day as a watershed moment in recent world history: the "K for Kilo" section contained a remarkably detailed scene concerning a plane bombing, which caused the cancellation of the show's North American premiere in New York City, scheduled for ten days after September 11, 2001.

That date indeed became a pivotal point in world history, and we now live in a world marked "post-9/11." For a discussion about how theatre registered its effects, see our online discussion.

Immersive theatre

In the second decade of this century, immersive theatre has been a prevalent trend. In this theatre, audiences play some kind of a role in the action of the play in performance, whether as a witness or as a character. Often, as in the case of *Shuffle*, they are allowed to roam freely around the performance space, choosing the order of their experience much as surfers on the internet move from point to point on the web. At times, they may be invited by the performers to take a more active role in the action.

Immersive theatre seems to be inspired by a number of factors in networked culture: the associative logic of browsing, the increasingly immersive environment of "choose your adventure" online roleplaying and video games, and possibly a sense of wanting to get out and interact with live human beings, albeit in the kind of impersonal way conditioned by social media, which can produce a sense of isolation despite its being all about connectivity. Two of the better-known examples of immersive theatre are Punchdrunk's production of *Sleep No More* (2003), based on Shakespeare's *Macbeth*, and Third Rail Projects' *Then She Fell* (2012), inspired by Lewis Carroll's life and writings, including his *Alice in Wonderland*.

Originally developed in London in 2003, *Sleep No More* has been restaged in Boston, New York, and Shanghai. In Boston, the playing space was an old-school building; in New York, three abandoned warehouses were converted for the purpose into the fictional "McKittrick Hotel," featuring nearly a hundred different playing spaces distributed among five floors. The rooms in this hotel (named after the hotel in Alfred Hitchcock's 1958 film, *Vertigo*) are not typical hotel rooms; rather, they range from indoor spaces such as shops, padded cells, and doctor's offices to outdoor spaces such as a cemetery. After entering the first-floor lounge, audience members are given masks to wear, then move on to other floors and rooms, where they witness the actions that take place within them – all silent, all inspired in some way by the Shakespearean original, but in style not historically accurate, as the unmasked performers wear makeup and costume evocative of the style of *film noir*. Audience members are free to follow the actor/action of their choice, or to move around from place to place, in groups or alone, or to explore the other areas of the "hotel," for up to three hours, and are also free to leave whenever they wish (Figure 15.11).

A number of factors make the experience of *Sleep No More* something like a live version of a video or online role-playing experience. The masks worn by the audience members protect their anonymity. As in immersive online environments like *Second Life*, they are free to explore the space as they wish and to follow their curiosity where it may lead them – or not. Because there is no spoken or written text, nor prescribed order to the scenes an audience member might experience, it is up to individual audience members to create for

Figure 15.11

Masked audience members surround a silent actor performing alone in a room/scene of *Sleep No More*, New York production.

Source: Yaniv Schulman.

themselves any narrative throughline. Far from having any kind of "unified action," *Sleep No More* gathers audience members at the beginning of the night in the lounge and then sends them off to different floors and doesn't bring them back together until the very end of the performance when everyone watches the banquet scene. And yet, the choices are not infinite and completely open-ended, and neither are audience members meant to do more than witness the action; they do not influence it or direct it in any way.

Although there are some similarities to *Sleep No More*, Third Rail's *Then She Fell* is a very different type of immersive theatre. Like *Sleep No More*, it is based on other work – in this case, the life and work of Lewis Carroll, familiarity with which helps to situate the spectator in its otherwise dreamlike landscape. Audience members are encouraged to rummage through the cabinets, trunks, and drawers containing Carroll's writings and other items. It too is staged in a found space, this time the Greenpoint Hospital in Brooklyn, New York, with rooms set up as individual performance spaces that audience members move into and out of. But *Then She Fell* allows only 15 (unmasked) audience members at a time to participate, breaking them up into increasingly smaller groups as they travel through the spaces, their routes controlled by company members. They may end up alone with one actor by the end of the evening. As a result, *Then She Fell* makes for a more intimate experience than *Sleep No More*.

The COVID pandemic spawned its own varieties of immersive and interactive theatre as artists moved outdoors for safety's sake – or, as in the case of Tectonic Theatre's *Seven Deadly Sins* – asked audiences to, watching from the streets as the titular "Sins" performed in storefronts in New York's meatpacking district in April of 2021. Immersive experiences that were already outdoors enjoyed more popularity during the pandemic. *Endure*, for example, a Run Woman Show production, began in 2012 as an audio-theatre experience in which audience members outfitted with headsets followed a solo marathoner/performer as she spoke her thoughts aloud in interaction with the natural park settings in which she trained. It gained new traction in the pandemic when few other live theatre options were available.

Immersive theatre is not limited to non-theatre spaces, however. Over the same period of time we've been discussing, major theatre companies have also experimented with some aspects of immersive theatre in various ways and toward various ends. In 2019, for example, the American Repertory Theatre closed a ten-year run of *The Donkey Show*, a club-theatre mashup inspired by *Midsummer Night's Dream* that experimented with space, storytelling, and the relationship between actors and audiences. And more recently, the Broadway Theatre in Manhattan was gutted and its infrastructure radically transformed to house the musical *Here Lies Love* in 2023. Under the direction of Alex Timbers (1978–), this immersive piece about the life of Imelda Marcos (1928–) wife of Philippine dictator Ferdinand Marcos (1917–1989, ruled 1965–1986) is set in a disco ballroom to the original music of David Byrne and Fatboy Slim. A hit off-Broadway ten years earlier at the Public Theater, with stagings as well in Seattle and London (Figure 15.12), it was transferred to the Broadway

Figure 15.12
A scene from the 2014 London production of *Here Lies Love*, starring Natalie Mendoza as Imelda Marcos.

Source: Donald Cooper/Shutterstock.

and made more fully immersive, with only 42 seats and more room for audience members to dance to the hypnotic beat along with the legendarily disco-loving protagonist – who was also an enthusiastic participant in her government's theft of billions of pesos from the Filipino people. It was designed to give audiences the uncomfortable experience, if they allowed themselves to realize it, of getting swept up in the similarly hypnotic spectacle of oppressive politics itself, and to ask themselves where else they might be tempted to "dance along" in their own lives.

As social networking technology can lead to both expansive socializing and increased isolation, so can immersive live theatre work in both directions. The actors may interact more with the audience members, but only as their characters or personae. *Sleep No More* audience members stay safely behind their masks, while individual *Then She Fell* audience members grow increasingly separated from the other 14 members. Audience/club attendees in *Here Lies Love* may simply have a great time dancing to the beat without ever grasping that they are symbolically implicating themselves in the corrupt regime they are dancing along with. In this sense, is immersive theatre radically different from theatre that has come before? To some degree, theatre has also always produced this tension, functioning both as a social space that can generate dialogue and as an event experienced differently from audience member to audience member, each of whom arrives with individual sets of desires and expectations and leaves with independent personal reflections.

Postdramatic theatre

The works described above, often developed collectively and compelling audiences to be more active than traditional spectators, call attention to another hallmark of networked culture: interaction and collaboration. Such work often relies more on the pleasures of the immersion and discovery within the performance event, than on absorptions into ordered plots and character dramas. Theatre that emphasizes experience over narrative, plot, or character has been labeled "postdramatic theatre" by German performance scholar Hans-Thies Lehmann (1999). Lehmann includes a variety of performance forms in his study, ranging from visual and performance art to stage plays and from single-authored works to collective creations. What characterizes this work is another kind of immersiveness, in which the dramatic text – if there is one – is subsumed to the other meaning-making elements of the production, including the acting, design, direction, and audience (see Figure 15.13).

Experiments with form and against narrative in drama were certainly taking place in the various avant-garde periods of theatre history described earlier in this book. Lehmann argues that recent postdramatic theatre marks a paradigm shift away from the centrality of dramatic action and toward a more interactive experience both among the elements of production and between the production and audience. For Lehmann, the point of such theatre is expressly not to communicate something; rather, it is about the proximity of and to the various elements involved in the theatre experience – in other words, a privileging of presence and aggregation over ultimate communicative effect. While multiple factors in theatre history have contributed to the emergence of postdramatic theatre, some aspects may seem familiar to students of networked culture, with its decentered, non-hierarchical approach to meaning-making, and the freedom it allows users to make their own connections and conclusions.

Figure 15.13
British playwright Sarah Kane's *4:48 Psychosis*, an exploration of depression, features no character attribution or stage directions, and is one example of a postdramatic theatre. Shown here in the U.S. premiere is, from left, Jo McInnes, Marin Ireland, and Jason Hughes.
Source: Anne Cusack/Los Angeles Times via Getty Images.

Collaborative theatre devisement

Throughout much of theatre history, hierarchies have tended to prevail, with companies and productions centering themselves on a playwright, a playtext, a star performer, or, more recently, a director held to be the key person responsible for the overall experience. But since the 1960s, there has been a trend toward collaborative theatrical devising by an ensemble or theatre collective. (Some historians trace the devising impulse back to *commedia dell'arte* – see Chapter 4.) An early commercial example was the dark musical comedy *Oh, What a Lovely War!* (1963), developed by the Theatre Workshop under the direction of Joan Littlewood (1914–2002). Drawing on the tradition of the English music hall, the piece was meant to expose in an ironic mode the horrors and vulgarity of war. It was performed by actors in Pierrot costumes, wearing First World War helmets and singing tunes originally meant to glorify the war. Much of the work in theatre for social change discussed in Chapter 14 has considered the democratic process of devisement to be as important as the end results, when that process adopts a consciously egalitarian approach. Networked culture has accelerated this trend.

Increasingly, work is being brought to the stage that has not been authored by a single playwright but rather devised by a group of actors, sometimes with and sometimes without a director (Figure 15.14). While collective creation does not necessarily result in nonlinear plot structures, much devised theatre of recent years does tend to resemble scenic

Figure 15.14

Actors perform the devised work *The Fall* during the 10th Annual Youth Expression Festival at the State Theatre on 6 June 2018 in Tshwane, South Africa. *The Fall*, based on the recent University of Cape Town's #RhodesMustFall movement, was the devised work of seven UCT Drama graduates who shared their personal experiences.

Source: Gallo Images/Alet Pretorius/Getty Images.

variations on a theme – which are often developed through ensemble improvisation – than a straightforward development of plot, navigated by recognizable characters portrayed by actors trained in psychological realism or Method Acting.

Devised theatre today often starts with an idea or an inspiration, which the group explores together to bring to the stage. For example in 2012, Washington, DC's Impossible Theater Company began a project simply with the idea of "missed connections." The company members' widely varying ideas were discussed, debated, and improvised upon over the course of six months before being condensed into an 80-minute piece called *[missed connections]* which revolved around the question: "If you had one chance to be the person you always wanted to be, what would you do?" (Desaulniers 2012).

The company's six-month rehearsal schedule would be a luxury for most commercially oriented theatres. Devised theatre does not fit easily into existing producing structures, and for Equity houses especially such theatre would be extremely expensive. Still, Vanessa Garcia of the Florida-based ensemble touring troupe The Krane considers how "going mainstream" for devising companies might benefit theatre in general:

> Technology, which so often aids and abets devised theater, is trying to obliterate surface, after all. Our computers are getting thinner and thinner, inching towards a kind

of space where there will be no surface, only a digital projection in air. And so, how do we make art in a world that seems obsessed with surface – a surface that is, technologically, and, ironically, about to disappear? The answer for theater, I believe, lies in devised theater – an art form that plays upon multiple surfaces in flux (the human body for one), and multimedia – all in order to reinstate a kind of underground. In a world in which surface is fetishized, devised theater tells the viewer, now you see surface, now you don't, playing with the appearance and disappearance of said surface and echoing back, always, towards something deeper.

(Garcia 2013)

The U.S.-based InHEIRitance Project illustrates Garcia's point, using devised theatre with and in communities to help them go past the surface of differences that divide them to get at the deeper, more difficult conversations. The project began in 2014 with plays based on biblical texts matched to topical civic concerns arrived at through a joint exploration process with various citizen groups the artists met with in each of the cities they visited throughout the United States; it has since expanded internationally. The process tends to triangulate on the connections between the themes in the chosen sacred text, the history of the city, and the experiences of the people who live in it; working together over the course of several weeks, the play begins to take shape. The work is meant to give participants a focus for dialogue about their shared cultural touchpoints, even as they may have deeply felt differences in experience from each other, and to find new ways to relate to each other through theatrical expression.

The final case study of our book considers a particular form of theatre in which the interplay between surface and depth – not to mention modern and ancient, technological and human, aesthetic and political, and local and global – all feature prominently: Hip Hop theatre.

CASE STUDY: Hip Hop theatre

Tamara Underiner

In 2004, Regina Taylor's (1960–) *Drowning Crow* premiered on Broadway, three years after its world premiere at the Goodman Theatre in Chicago. An adaptation of Chekhov's *The Seagull*, it was set in the present-day Gullah Islands of South Carolina, with an African American cast. Like the original, it featured a main character suffering from unrequited love, and struggling with his desire to forge a new form of theatre, one that would depart from the tired, "sold-out" traditions of the stage to capture the sensibility of a new age. In Chekhov's play, the new form was Russian symbolism. In Taylor's, it was Hip Hop theatre.

To many observers, the success of the musical *Hamilton* in 2015 has come to represent a fulfillment of that dream: a departure from a mainstream theatre culture perceived as elitist and entrenched in outmoded themes and means of production. Hip Hop theatre emerges from within a larger international culture of the same name, one with its own worldview, ethics, and aesthetics and that this culture has ancient roots. Born of political struggle and creative urgency, this culture represents not only a rupture with mainstream culture – which often works to commercialize and absorb it – but also a continuity with African-derived performance traditions that are themselves thousands of years old.

In this case study, we examine **Hip Hop theatre** both as a performance form and as a historiographic practice in itself – that is, as a way of telling history. We cover its history, aesthetics, worldview, and relationship to culture – both ancient and contemporary – paying particular attention to its innovative use of communication technologies. Every form of communication is present in Hip Hop theatre: from oral and written expression through highly mediated production and distribution technologies, with stylized vocabularies of movement and gesture added to the mix.

Hip Hop history, worldview, and aesthetics

Most narratives of Hip Hop culture situate its origins at a back-to-school party in the Bronx, DJ'd by Clive Campbell (DJ Kool Herc [1955–]) in August 1973, but its general roots were in the economic collapse of New York City in the early 1970s, and similar expressions arose in other urban centers around the same time. As white flight to the suburbs left behind unsaleable properties in the urban cores, absentee landlords found it more profitable to burn their holdings to the ground and collect the insurance money than to convert them to affordable housing; meanwhile, municipalities created policies of "planned shrinkage" that resulted in dispossession, unemployment, reduced social services, and increased poverty. Many responses to this situation were violent, as rival gangs fought over shrinking territory. The first artistic responses were made by visual artists, using inexpensive materials like spray paint, applied to available surfaces like building walls and subway train cars – these were the precursors to the aerosol art form known as Hip Hop *writing*. Of course, these artistic expressions were not seen as such by building owners and transit authorities, but that was part of the artists' point: to assert a creative presence in the face of forced displacement, marginalization, and accelerated urban "decay."

With ever-decreasing opportunities to gather together, some young people with good record collections and the right equipment – among them Cindy Campbell and her brother Kool Herc, Grandmaster Flash (1958–), Grand Wizard Theodore (1963–), and Afrika Bambaataa (1957–) – began playing recorded music in public parks and basketball courts (*DJ'ing*). Before long they had developed a particular technique of playing records on more than one turntable, enhancing and combining them with digital synthesizers (*sampling* and *remixing*), and incorporating spoken word, rhythmically delivered (*rapping, MC'ing*). The gathered young people soon developed new dance styles in response to the sampled and repeated *breakbeat* manipulated by the DJs' techniques, including *breakdancing* and *locking* (and eventually on the West Coast, *popping*). Soon, *B-boys* and *B-girls* began to engage in competitions of dance moves or improvisational spoken wordplay – *battling*, where two contestants face each other from within a circle formed by their communities of supporters (the Hip Hop *cipher*). These forms came before the advent of Hip Hop culture and then were integrated and innovated within it (see Figure 15.15).

Figure 15.15

B-boys breakdancing in San Francisco, 2008. As hip-hop has become more popular, the cipher has expanded to include tourists and passers-by.

Source: Wiki/Cam Vilay.

http://en.wikipedia.org/wiki/B-boying#mediaviewer/File:Breakdancer_vilay.jpg

The content of these performances is both explicit and coded. Many spoken word performances and rap songs call specific attention to the histories of oppression, police brutality, and economic exploitation that have produced the pervasive disenfranchise-ment of economically and culturally marginalized young people in some urban areas. They do so through recourse to a new vocabulary that has worked its way into main-stream culture, a vocabulary of word, movement, fashion, and gesture that calls members into a growing, global community. This community is networked through Hip Hop academies, workshops, and theatre festivals now appearing in many world capitals. Cul-tural historian Jeff Chang calls Hip Hop "one of the big ideas of this generation, a grand expression of our collective creative powers" (2006: x). As such, this "big idea" encom-passes a worldview that extends beyond the form's aesthetic elements, even as those elements have come to influence virtually every genre and form of artistic expression.

Certain aspects of the Hip Hop aesthetic have lent themselves to commercializa-tion over the first half-century of its existence and indeed, many moguls and tycoons have emerged from its ranks; historian Jeffrey O.G. Ogbar reported that by 2006, the ten wealthiest people in Hip Hop were worth more $2 billion due to ventures in film, restaurants, real estate, clothing lines, recording equipment, and more (Ogbar 2007: 176–7). But it is also an example of global interculture sharing certain recognizable elements of style and a general stance that speaks truth to power. As such, it can also be characterized as a grassroots movement that connects practitioners globally from the ground up, and understands itself as both a culture and an art form that proclaims unity, peaceful resolution of conflict, democratic participation, and targeted social analysis and critique and can serve as an "effective organizing tool for reaching youth and disenfranchised populations" (Uno 2006: 300). In the United States and internationally, its music has become the soundtrack of the Black Lives Matter movement, increasingly so since the murder of George Floyd.

Internationally, it has taken on widely divergent characteristics suited to the local contexts in which it finds itself. Ogbar's survey of such work finds it has taken hold in places as diverse as Africa, Brazil, Poland, Germany, Spain, Southern Italy, and Cuba. In some places, rap is used to uphold indigenous language expression, in others to express the dilemma of the immigrant; some Europeans use it to express frustration with poverty and political apathy and others to proclaim a multi-millennial allegiance with their African ancestry. In general, he suggests, the emphasis of international Hip Hop is more political than are U.S. varieties, but not all are explicitly so, nor overtly resistant to racism.

In France, as Felicia McCarren has studied, Hip Hop in dance has become increasingly professionalized through studio training and performances in concerts and festivals. The dancers are largely immigrants or immigrant-descended, and the venues they train and perform in are often subsidized through state support, which is ironic (but not unique, even in the United States) for a form born in anti-authoritarianism and a critique of institutions. The results are necessarily inflected by the traditions the dancers bring with them, and tend to reflect a preference in France for a more generic "universalism" in Hip Hop itself that refers back to U.S. culture.

As Hip Hop celebrated its 50th anniversary in 2023, the slogan "Hip Hop is Universal" was tempting to get behind. But the label was troubling for some critics. As we turn next to a closer look at Hip Hop theatre, it is worth considering a caution from U.S.-based artist-scholar Nicole Hodges Persley, who chafes at the ways Hip Hop itself is in danger of cultural appropriation, or for being emptied of its African American specificity in service of other aims. In her work on sampling and remixing in Hip Hop theatre, Hodges Persley targets performances and performers whose appreciation for the form veers into appropriation when they otherwise have little claim to, or accountability for, the lived experiences and cultural history that gave it its original purpose, form, and momentum. Her targets are especially those who can "shed" at will their association with the Black identities that are at the heart of Hip Hop; even *Hamilton* comes under her scrutiny for its treatment of the more complex history of slavery glossed over in its selective samplings from the historical record (more on that below).

Hip Hop theatre: roots, functions, structures, and themes

Hamilton is perhaps the most visible of Hip Hop theatre's recent contributions to theatre history for its Broadway presence and international tours. To understand Hip Hop theatre's emergence and importance, and in the spirit of Hodges Persley's critique, we focus on the deep traditions upon which the more grassroots movement draws. According to Danny Hoch (1970–), founder of the New York Hip-Hop Theater Festival, the aesthetics that inform Hip Hop theatre have as much to do with New York's demographics as they do with the socio-economic circumstances that produced so much urban blight and bleakness:

> Southern blacks living alongside Puerto Ricans, Dominicans, Jamaicans and a handful of working-poor whites, all of whom drew upon both inherited and appropriated cultures in the face of urban decay and accelerated technology – created a legacy of art forms and language that would wind up being inherited by various races, colors and classes around the world.
>
> (Hoch 2004: n.p.)

Like the indigenous and diasporic African and American cultures from which it draws, Hip Hop theatre has shown itself to be a capacious form that can absorb many influences and, in turn, influence many other forms. The "inherited cultures" include those of the African and Caribbean continuum of storytelling and art, manifest in the "polycultural traditions of immigrants and migrants" (Hoch 2004: n.p.). The "appropriated cultures" include European traditions, amplified through Japanese audio-visual technologies.

In its insistence on the power of the live, spoken word, artists and scholars see parallels between the MC and the storytelling traditions of Africa – specifically, the *griot* or *griotte* storyteller of West Africa (described in Chapter 1), and the *djeli* of Mande, the person who carries culture in stories, song, dances, riddles, and proverbs, oral traditions from which Hip Hop derives its status as a "method of sustenance and sustainability" (Banks 2011: 12). While in its rhythmic wordplay there are parallels with a variety of other performance traditions and types, including Djelyi, *kabuki* theatre, R&B, opera recitative, and the patter songs of Gilbert and Sullivan, in most cases, the content of Hip Hop theatre is of urgent social, community, or spiritual concern. Poet/playwright/head Marc Bamuthi Joseph (1975–) has spoken of the DJ's function as a community historiographer, telling the stories from the perspective of the people he/she represents, particularly young people:

> Like Hip Hop, spoken word reflects American diversity and engenders a community of young artists who reach across demographic boundaries toward self-exploration and growth, providing a platform where conflicts are resolved on the page or the stage, rather than on the street.
>
> (Joseph 2006: 17)

Among others, scholar/Hip Hop theatre artist Daniel Banks has argued that Hip Hop theatre exists on a historico-cultural continuum that includes epic poetry and the classic tragedy of ancient Greece: "Within a Hip Hop Theatre audience, there is a spectrum of trauma, oppression, and marginalization, and Hip Hop Theatre, perhaps like Athenian tragedy, is a safe space in which to express concerns, rehearse empowerment, and imagine solutions" (Banks 2010: 242). As Banks points out, there are some distinct theatrical predecessors as well – among them, the non-linear poetic and political drama of the Black Arts Movement of the 1960s and 1970s, and later work that incorporated text, music, and movement, often in a non-linear plotline, specifically to tell the stories of the disenfranchised. Some appeared on Broadway; many more in communities further afield – such as through the work of Junebug Productions in New Orleans and Cultural Odyssey in San Francisco.

From these diverse yet intertwined roots, Hip Hop theatre emerged in the early 1990s. Multidisciplinary performance and visual artist Holly Bass (1975–) was the first to use the term "hip-hop theatre" in print, in 1999, in reference to its status as a special category of performance in the National Black Theatre Festival that year in Winston-Salem, North Carolina. Jeff Chang situates its debut on stage seven years earlier with GhettOriginal Production Dance Company's 1992 production of *So What Happens Now?* at PS 122 in New York City, about the rise and fall of 1980s-style B-boying. This production inspired Hoch, Clyde Valentin, Kamilah Forbes, and others to establish the first Hip-Hop Theater Festival in New York City in 2000.

Playwright/poet Eisa Davis (1971–), who is credited with popularizing the term among practitioners, speaks to this theatre's capacity for both specificity and inclusion:

> I like the name "hip-hop theatre," because when it's ascriptive, voluntary and utilized by a self-described hip-hop generation that speaks through theatre, we are *found* in translation. Finally, a form that describes and comprises our multi-ness. When U.K.-based artist Benji Reid dances his monologues, it's new, and it's the best kind of new – the kind that plays with conventions and serves up their permutations. And we've got all kinds of historical precedents. Art forms progress when they mimic other art forms, whether it's Langston Hughes writing the blues on the page or Aaron Copland building symphonies from folk tunes or Lee Strasberg bringing the therapist's couch into acting. The purists shriek, the open-minded are jazzed, and the culture follows.
>
> (Davis 2004: n.p.)

Further, Hip Hop theatre allies political urgency to ritual function, which as we've seen, has long been associated with theatre in many times and places:

> Like any culture's ritual theater, Hip Hop Theater is where members from within the culture come for reassurance, to find the values of the culture reiterated, to hear the history retold, and to locate ourselves inside of our own cultural frame. It is not just about information. Equally important is the cultural mind-set and logic. In terms of form, a Hip Hop head will, most likely, feel at home in a poetic, nonlinear, fragmented narrative with multiple ethnicities represented on the stage and multiple languages spoken. And the storytelling would almost certainly need to be interdisciplinary.
>
> (Banks 2011: 11)

The theatrical expression of this mindset and logic has manifested itself in a wide variety of original works and classical adaptations. Banks's comments appear in the introduction to his edited anthology of Hip Hop plays, *Say Word! Voices from Hip Hop Theater* (2011). It organizes its nine plays according to the formal categories "Spoken Word Theater," which focuses on heightened, poetic language; "Hip Hop Theater Plays," which both reference and include specific elements of Hip Hop culture; and "Solo Performance," which Banks argues manifest the links to a long tradition of oral culture and storytelling. A haunting example of the first category is Rickerby Hinds's 2013 *Dreamscape*, based on a true story of a 19-year-old African American woman who was shot to death by a policeman while she was sleeping in her car. As the DJ/coroner attempts to categorize each of the 12 bullet wounds that led to her death, the young woman dances scenes of her childhood and more recent past. By the end of the play, her line, "You know me," challenges the audience to move past viewing her as yet another unfortunate statistic. "Hip Hop Theater Plays" feature characters in plot-lines aimed at recovering Hip Hop history, dealing with contemporary issues of self-expression in what is often viewed as an illicit art form, or, as in the case of Zakkiyah Alexander's *Blurring Shine* (2003), provide a blistering critique of the larger cultural industries that exploit young men in Hip Hop culture. The section on solo performances includes the link to a storyboard and script of a beatbox theatre piece, *From Tel Aviv to Ramallah* (2006), by Rachel Havrelock with Yuri Lane and Sharif Ezzat, which tells the story of two young men living on either side of the border between Israel and Palestine. This piece illustrates the scope of Hip Hop's reach and speaks to its "ethic of inclusion" (Banks 2011: 1).

This scope and ethic is also manifest in dramaturg Kim Euell and playwright Robert Alexander's 2009 anthology, *Playz from the Boom Box Galaxy*, whose ten works are organized according to their content rather than their form. The plays collected under the theme "ruminations on identity" focus on the playwrights' search for individual self-formation within and against institutional archetypes and stereotypes of race, class, and gender. While these plays tend to focus on personal and internal struggles, those in the next section, "cautionary tales," target the institutions themselves and the ways that capitalism intersects with racism and sexism to produce many forms of social violence. One of these plays, Aya de León's *Thieves in the Temple* (Figure 15.16), was also featured in a recent study by Patricia Herrera highlighting the connection between Nuyorican feminism and Hip Hop theatre aesthetics. The plays in the final section, "transformationals," deepen the relationships and tensions between self and society, marshaling spirituality and creativity as key conditions for cultural survival.

Many writers refer to Hip Hop theatre as a "genre," which suggests a similarity of form, style, structure, or subject matter across its productions. What makes Hip Hop theatre recognizably "Hip Hop," however, is not so easy to pin down. To be sure, most plays explore some aspect of contemporary Hip Hop culture in their subject matter, even as they may draw on sources deep in African history, and most feature language drawn from well inside Hip Hop culture. Most also include one or more of Hip Hop's

Figure 15.16

Aya de León's *Thieves in the Temple: The Reclaiming of Hip-Hop* (2003) is a one-woman show that critiques sexism in hip-hop. Among other characters, she plays a DJ with a form of Tourette's syndrome that forces him to reveal his sensitive side, and a blonde sex object on the verge of a nervous breakdown.

Source: Aya de Leon.

four principal elements (DJ'ing, MC'ing, breaking, and writing graffiti), but that is not required. For example, Ben Snyder's 2001 *In Case You Forget* is about a young graffiti writer's awakening to both love and political commitment; but, its form is straightforward realism, no music or dancing is called for, and its action unfolds over two tightly structured acts covering the days before the main character will be sentenced to serve time. In general, however, Hip Hop theatre favors other styles over straight realism. Many plays follow a more epic, Brechtian structure, in which the action is episodic and interspersed with song and dance numbers or parodic interludes, and the fourth wall is broken (if it is even there to begin with) by DJs and MCs and choruses, which function much as they did in ancient Greece.

While many Hip Hop plays deal with tragic events and their aftermath, others have employed rollicking comedy. Kristoffer Diaz's 2002 *Welcome to Arroyo's*, for example, uses the DJ/rapper duo of Trip Goldstein and Nelson Cardenal (aka the "Tripnel Cartel") to narrate, interrupt, comment on, and sometimes even rewind and replay the action developing over the play's 39 short scenes. These scenes combine two love stories with a mystery about a Latina DJ and point to Latina contributions to early Hip Hop culture.

While some Hip Hop plays experiment with dramatic structure (e.g., *Dreamscape*), others are distinguished for their experiments with character and language. The late Chadwick Boseman's *Deep Azure* (2005) includes the allegorical character of "Street Knowledge," described as a "Duo angelic chorus" comprising Twin Lovers: Street Knowledge of Good (SK Good) and "Street Knowledge of Evil" (SK Evil). They transform into other characters in a play exploring the aftermath of a wrongful death by police – a common Hip Hop theme (Banks 2011: 93). *Deep Azure* is written almost completely in verse that sounds both like spoken word and like Shakespeare. In the following passage, SK Evil ponders the truth behind the killing; "prince" refers to the victim, Bloods and Crip to rival gangs who wear red and blue, respectively:

> SK Evil: To what set and name falls the blame of this heinous deed?
> Witnesses saw no Bloods, 'cept blood the prince did bleed
> And though that boy was of blue, he showed no signs of Crip
> But hear this lie, more true than truth from my very lips.
> T'was an officer of "peace" that waged war on our warrior of light
> How this brutality came to a fatality one night, that is the question.
> What had he done? Possession?
> No gun. No boat. No bud. No crack. No transgression.

The poetic rhythms here invoke two cultures – Hip Hop and Elizabethan – and, for Banks, serve to decenter Shakespeare's place in the history of dramatic storytelling, placing him on a continuum between oral culture and Hip Hop. Perhaps this shift is also registered in the fact that Hip Hop theatre and spoken-word open mikes have begun to appear in a number of Shakespeare festivals around the world. While clearly there is an audience-development component to this phenomenon, it is also worth pointing out the growing scholarship on the similarities between spoken word and Shakespeare, which notes affinities of lyrical and rhythmic complexity, and in the demands on the listener made by both. A 2014 study by designer/coder/data analyst Matt Daniels determined that some rap music artists' vocabularies and new word coinages are, in fact, larger than Shakespeare's over a similar body of work.

Hip Hop theatre is also known for its "remixes" of the classics, as suggested in the example of *Drowning Crow* above, with Greek tragedy and Shakespeare as frequent sources. While Hip Hop has the potential to create vibrant new interpretations of classic texts, Hoch and others are concerned that such remixings will be taken simply as bids for legitimacy, casting Hip Hop elements as adornment rather than serious artistry, or sacrificing opportunities to stage stories emerging from Hip Hop culture itself. (All of these are possible interpretations of *Drowning Crow*, an adaptation of one of Chekhov's most open-to-interpretation plays.)

Thus, content and intent matter as much as form and structure. For Hoch, what makes a Hip Hop play a Hip Hop play is not that it includes all or even any of Hip Hop's four principal elements of DJ'ing, MC'ing, breaking, or writing graffiti. It is instead that it must be "*by, about* and *for* the Hip Hop generation, participants in

Hip Hop culture or both" (Hoch 2004: n.p., original emphasis). Finally, Hip Hop playwright Will Power (1968–) argues for a "fifth element" of Hip Hop culture as important as the first four: collective knowledge production. Seen this way, Hip Hop theatre serves for today's performers and audiences much the same function discussed in Part I of this book: as a key preserver of social memory for a culture not content to allow larger narratives to constrain or co-opt it.

Theatre historians and critics play a role in documenting and preserving this form of social memory as well, but have some catching up to do. As Roberta Uno, founder of the New World Theater in Amherst, reminds us:

> Hip-hop artists state that critics lack a genre exposure. . . . They may like what they see without knowing breaking from B'boying; popping from locking; or toprocking from uprocking – the point is that even when hip-hop forms are noticed, they are not understood or critiqued from within the discipline vocabulary. This type of technical knowledge is as important as historical, cultural and self-knowledge. At the end of the day, it is this fifth element, glaringly absent from the marketplace, that may provide the space where art can flourish.
>
> (Uno 2006: 305)

Hamilton's popularity illustrates Uno's point. Lin-Manuel Miranda's musical prominently features elements of Hip Hop music and dance in an otherwise period piece, set in the quarter century following the American Revolution of 1776. Widely acclaimed by audiences and critics, it has been praised for its deft homage to, and re-imagining of, America's past, through the lens of a multi-racial present (although the perspectives of Native Americans and enslaved persons were absent in the final production – especially those of the latter who were serving dinner "in the room when it happened" [Monteiro 2016: 94, qtd. in Gentry; see also Hodges Persley]). But in its early years, few reviewers acknowledged Hip Hop's contributions, because they had not been trained to recognize or critique it in the same way they would other elements of theatrical production. In fact, Hip Hop may be its signal contribution, says musicologist Philip Gentry:

> As has been noted by most reviewers, the story is actually quite traditional and sentimental, complete with a finale in which the characters pedantically instruct us in the work's moral in the manner of *Don Giovanni*. The historical subject matter is no great innovation, with such precedents as *1776* (1969) and *Bloody Bloody Andrew Jackson* (2008). The racial dynamics of the casting are not unheard-of, even if Miranda and his team exercised particular care in casting people of color in all major roles save that of King George and his defender, Samuel Seabury. No, the innovation that seems most likely to emerge from *Hamilton* is Miranda's fluid synthesis of hip-hop idioms into the traditional Broadway vernacular.
>
> (Gentry 2017: 273)

In 2011, Daniel Banks called Hip Hop theatre the "theater of now" (2011: 20). Ten years later, as mainstream theatres re-opened after the pandemic, many were taking hard looks at their missions, seasons, practices, and habits of mind, in response to "We See You, White American Theatre" (see Chapter 14) and to the Google spreadsheet circulated on "Theaters Not Speaking Out" about injustices to Black people, that grew to some 400 theatres in the two weeks following George Floyd's murder. It became common to speak of "multiple pandemics" and their effects on the theatre scene, to lament the economic devastation the coronavirus wrought and to call attention to the role, and action, theatre can take in exposing the other pandemics lurking under the social surface in terms of racist (and ableist) discrimination. At this writing, Hip Hop theatre is itself still coming back. A 2021 restaging by the Studio Theatre in Washington, DC of Will Power's 2003 *Flow* (Figure 15.17) nicely illustrates the themes of this case study with its blend of African storytelling and urban community building, perhaps a sign that, like many mainstream theatres, Hip Hop theatre will be rediscovering its own canon in the post-pandemic era. This period may mark an inflection point for the form, which is always in dialogue with the external contexts in which it finds itself. It will be interesting to see if future historians, with their penchant for assigning labels that characterize an era, will look back at this period of theatre history and refer to it as an "age of Hip Hop" that came and went. Or, considering the success of *Hamilton* as evidence of Hip Hop's capacity to absorb and influence other forms, perhaps it will always be known as the "theatre of now."

Key references

Banks, D. (2010) "From Homer to Hip Hop: Orature and Griots, Ancient and Present," *Classical World* 103(2) (Winter): 238–45.

Banks, D. (ed.) (2011) *Say Word! Voices from Hip Hop Theater*, Ann Arbor: University of Michigan Press.

Bass, H. (1999) "Blowin' Up the Set," *American Theater* 16(9) (November): 18–20.

Chang, J. (ed.) (2006) *Total Chaos: The Art and Aesthetics of Hip-Hop*, New York: Basic Civitas Books.

Davis, E. (2004) "Found in Translation: Hip-Hop Theatre Fuses the Thought and the Word, the Rhythm and the Rhyme, the Old and the New," https://www.thefreelibrary.com/Found+in+translation%3A+hip-hop+theatre+fuses+the+thought+and+the+word%2C...-a0119310489 (Accessed 20 August 2023).

Euell, K., and R. Alexander. (2009) *Playz from the Boom Box Galaxy*, New York: Theatre Communications Group Books.

Forman, M. and Neal, M.A. (eds.) (2004) *That's the Joint! The Hip-Hop Studies Reader*, New York and London: Routledge.

Gentry, P. (2017) "Hamilton's Ghosts," *American Music* 35(2): 271–80.

George, N. (1993) "Hip-Hop's Founding Fathers Speak the Truth," *The Source* (November) 50: 44–50.

George, N. (2005) *Hip Hop America*, New York: Penguin Books.

Figure 15.17

Actor, rapper, and playwright Will Power rehearses for his Sydney Festival production of *Flow* at The Studio, Sydney Opera House on 23 January 2007 in Sydney, Australia. *Flow* is an 80-minute one-man hip hop theatre show that takes in rapping, DJing, break-dancing and graffiti, fusing original music and rhymes with choreography to narrate urban tales about destructive social forces. It was reprised in May 2021 at the Studio Theatre in Washington with Justin Weaks, under the direction of Psalmayene 24 and with choreography by Tony Thomas.

Source: Patrick Riviere/Getty Images.

Hoch, D. (2004) "Here We Go, Yo . . . A Manifesto for a New Hip-Hop Arts Movement," https://www.thefreelibrary.com/Here+we+go%2C+Yo+...+a+manifesto+for+a+new+hip-hop+arts+movement%3A+the...-a0126388759 (Accessed 20 August 2023).

Hodges Persley, N. (2021) *Sampling and Remixing Blackness in Hip-Hop Theater and Performance*, Ann Arbor: University of Michigan Press.

Johnson, K. (2018) "A Beginner's Guide to Implementing Hip Hop Theatre," in K. Perkins, S. Richards, R. A. Craft, and T. DeFrantz (eds.) *The Routledge Companion to African American Theatre and Performance*, U.K.: Taylor & Francis, 395–9.

Joseph, M.B. (2006) "(Yet Another) Letter to a Young Poet," in J. Chang (ed.) *Total Chaos: The Art and Aesthetics of Hip-Hop*, New York: Basic Civitas Books, 11–17.

McCarren, F. (2013) *French Moves: The Cultural Politics of Le Hip Hop*, Oxford: Oxford University Press, 2013.

Monteiro, L. (2016) "Race-Conscious Casting and the Erasure of the Black Past in Lin-Manuel Miranda's Hamilton," *Public Historian* 38(1) (February 1): 89–98.

Ogbar, J. O.G. (2007) *Hip-Hop Revolution: The Culture and Politics of Rap*, Lawrence: University Press of Kansas.

Uno, R. (2006) "Theatres Crossing the Divide: A Baby Boomer's Defense of Hip-Hop Aesthetics," in J. Chang (ed.) *Total Chaos: The Art and Aesthetics of Hip-Hop*, New York: Basic Civitas Books, 300–5.

Deep thanks to Daniel Banks for his insights in the development of this case study.

Summary: Thinking through theatre histories

In this chapter, we have considered how theatre has registered the influence of networked culture on the most basic elements of performer, stage, and performance type. More than ever, the experience of a play has come to depend not on the meanings "held" in a prewritten script authored by a single playwright, but on the complex interplay among a variety of factors, including collective devising and audience participation, that are manifest both on stage and online. We have seen how theatre's manipulation of new social media and other technologies has called attention to received notions of time, space, bodies, and theatre itself. The adage that opened this chapter situated theatre as a special event that takes place on "four trestles and four boards" established for the purpose – but networked culture has come increasingly to blur the lines between theatre and everyday life, taking advantage of other platforms originally designed for other purposes.

Some of this is new, to be sure, and some an extension of theatre's historic adaptability and responsiveness. Throughout this chapter and this book, we have considered how communication practices shape social structures and cultural dynamics, and how these cultural dynamics, in turn, shape theatrical activity. Thinking through this centuries-old interaction, we might ask ourselves the following questions:

- Throughout this book, we have seen theatre play a variety of roles in society: as a way to convey religious knowledge and values, especially in Chapter 3; as an instrument of state or political control such as in Chapters 2 and 6; as a form of political activism in

Chapters 11 and 13; and of course in all periods, as a form of entertainment. How and why does theatre change its social role and how does that affect its meaning and impact?

- In Chapter 5, we discussed the way print culture fostered a sense of personal interiority, and ultimately, individualism. How do communication practices alter our understanding of selfhood and the way we engage with the world?
- We saw in Chapter 7 that periodicals were crucial to the development of the public and private spheres and the concept of the nation-state. The larger question we can ask, then, is how do communication practices affect the way we interact with each other and thereby influence the way we imagine and shape society?
- Chapter 10 considered photography's role in the rise of positivist philosophy, which portrays the world as wholly understandable through sense perception and objective facts. In what ways do communication practices shape our understanding of reality and truth?
- And how, finally, are such transformations manifested in performer/audience relationships, acting styles, stage design, character qualities, plot construction, and other aspects of theatrical performance?

The sky has been declared to have fallen on theatre many times over the period covered in Part IV, as communication technologies have proliferated the possibilities for storytelling by other means, and a pandemic nearly delivered a near deathblow to its economic infrastructure. Yet, the sky remains above, where it now might share cloud space with TikTok musicals, and theatre continues to transform in response to these evolving technologies. Some theatre artists have incorporated them into the formal performance space, be it stage, gallery, or street; others have engaged with these technologies at the level of their underlying logic, exploring at a fundamental level what theatre might be, do, and become in an increasingly networked age. As it always has, theatre in this age continues to offer us a distinctive glimpse of who we are, where we've come from, and what we might become.

★

Media resources

Japanese theatre

The best single online source for *nō*, *kyōgen*, *kabuki*, and *bunraku* – video clips (*nō* and *kyōgen*), photos (*kabuki*), historical prints, and other materials – is provided by the National Theatre of Japan at http://www.ntj.jac.go.jp/english

Video introductions to these traditional forms are also available at http://www2.ntj.jac.go.jp/unesco/noh/en/

All U.S. Japanese Consulates (and the Embassy) have cultural attaché offices which lend out for free a wide selection of videos and DVDs about Japan, including excellent videos on *nō*, *kabuki*, *bunraku*, and modern theatre. The selection at each consulate varies. Contact the one closest to your physical location several weeks before planning to show the videos; they will ship them to you or you may pick them up personally. There are consulates in New York, Chicago, Los Angeles, and San Francisco as well as the Embassy in Washington, DC.

Many videos, including the brief sampling below of titles we recommend, are for sale from Insight Media: http://www.insight-media.com

- *Bunraku: The Classical Puppets of Japan* (29 minutes).
- *Kyōgen* classic: *Poison Sugar* (Busu) (28 minutes).
- *The Tradition of Performing Arts in Japan* (42 minutes).
- Overview of *nō*, *kabuki*, and *bunraku*: *Theatre in Japan: Yesterday and Today* (52 minutes). Dated, but includes interviews with performers including Suzuki Tadashi on modern and traditional Japanese theatre.

Japanese Theatre 1: Nō: https://www.youtube.com/watch?v=_T5RqW8TWWY. After a short general introduction to three classical forms, *nō*, *kabuki*, and *bunraku*, the video offers excerpts of a *nō* play with excellent commentary. The video is about 15 minutes.

A complete resource of factual material about *nō* is available at http://www.the-noh.com/

A 3-minute sequence of a fast-paced climactic dance: https://www.youtube.com/watch?v=lu5Vn1vQ5i4

Many videos of complete plays or substantial excerpts, in Japanese, without subtitles, are available online. For example:

- *Hagoromo*: https://www.youtube.com/watch?v=1M-GrlxbhTA.
- *Aoi no ue*: https://www.youtube.com/watch?v=Euq03OKDhF8

Kutiyattam

The following videos are available at www.keralatourism.org/video-clips. See the following videos on the *kutiyattam* temple-theatre tradition; enter the site and look for the complete list of clips.

(1) *Kutiyattam*
(2) *Koothiyattam* (a variant spelling of *kutiyattam*)
(3) *Chakyarkoothu* (solo performance of the *vidusaka* or clown-like comic figure)
(4) *Nangyarkoothu* (solo performance of the Nangyars or women who perform the female roles).

Kailasodharanam (Ravana: The Lifting of Mount Kailasa). On YouTube, search *kutiyattam* and then scroll for this title. This is a famous *kutiyattam* scene in which the actor playing the ten-headed demon-king, Ravana, mimetically enacts his tremendous power by "lifting" Mount Kailasa.

Richmond, F. (1999) *Kutiyattam: Sanskrit Theater of Kerala*, Ann Arbor: University of Michigan Press (CD-ROM). Audio and video clips. (See the University of Michigan Press listing online for computer requirements.)

Carnival

To "visit" carnivals from around the world, tour the New Mexico Museum of International Folk Art's excellent exhibition at http://www.carnavalexhibit.org/

European medieval theatre

The Play of Daniel: YouTube recording of the 1958 Pro Musica production of *The Play of Daniel,* Noah Greenberg directing. https://www.youtube.com/watch?v=rXyK7yVwBVA&t=3s

The Play of Herod, New York Pro Musica, Noah Greenberg, musical director. Scored by Noah Greenberg and staged by Nikos Psacharopoulos. Brayton Lewis as Herod. Decca Records, DL 710,095–6 (1964).

Mystery of Elche (*Misteri d'Elx*), YouTube videos: for an excellent overview, visit UNESCO: https://www.youtube.com/watch?v=bj34GC4giGM; for recordings of the individual parts search: "Misteri d'Elx" (Part I: descent of the angels from heaven to Mary); "Coronation of the Virgin Mary" and/or "Coronación Elche" (the conclusion of Part II); "Misteri o festa" (series of images from Parts I and II).

There is an online simulator showing the path and the sequence of plays in the York Corpus Christi Cycle at http://jerz.setonhill.edu/resources/PSim/applet/

For links to online resources, such as medieval play texts and bibliographies; to databases of research projects such as Records of Early English Drama; and to various groups devoted to research on and production of medieval plays, see https://www.medievalists. net/2021/02/records-early-english-drama-resouces/

Ta'ziyeh

YouTube video: see https://www.youtube.com/watch?v=kD8TG7S2QTs. There are others as well; search for "Ta'ziyeh" and "Persian Passion Play."

Purim shpiln

There are numerous YouTube videos that show homegrown versions of this "Jewish carnival" tradition. Enter the search term "Purim Shpiel."

Ramlila

There are many YouTube videos covering *Ramlila* performances, in Ramnagar and elsewhere, as well as other kinds of art inspired by *Ramlila*. UNESCO provides an overview of the *Ramlila* story in performance: https://youtu.be/89dtCI4oNzU

Karagöz and ortaoyunu

A U.S.-based traditional Turkish theatre company provides background and videoclips on their work in both forms: https://karagoztheatre.com/about-ortaoyunu-traditional-turkish-theatre/

Talchum

"Talchum named UNESCO cultural heritage": a brief video of different genres of *talchum*. https://www.youtube.com/watch?v=uxxYOV0NjYQ
 "Masks & the Mask Dance":
 https://www.korea.net/NewsFocus/Culture/view?articleId=121401
 https://www.korea.net/NewsFocus/Culture/view?articleId=122081

Media resources – Part II

Commedia dell'arte

A video introduction to the world of *Commedia dell'arte*, its stock characters' status, physical shapes and characteristics: https://www.youtube.com/watch?v=h_0TAXWt8hY (a film by Deborah May of a two-day workshop with young actors held at the National Theatre of England with Didi Hopkins from Commediaworks).

Kunqu

"*Kunqu*: The Mother of All Chinese Drama": short introduction and excerpt from *Peony Pavilion* https://www.youtube.com/watch?v=qNGUhRTfBhE
 Injustice Done to Dou E (Snow in Midsummer), originally written as a *zaju*. This is a six-minute video recording of a *kun*-style performance, with annotated clips: https://www.youtube.com/watch?v=5HNK7XI9hqQ

Japanese theatre

See listings in Part I for overall material on classical Japanese theatre (*nō*, *kyōgen*, *kabuki*, and *bunraku*). Many of these include all or several of these genres. Specific material for *kabuki* and *bunraku* follows.

Kabuki

Japanese Theatre 3: Kabuki: 13-minute introduction with excerpts from plays and commentary https://www.youtube.com/watch?v=F3IHdm2Tf8g
 Ennosuke III: Kabuki Actor: a documentary made in 1984, about an important and innovative *kabuki* actor (now retired), including backstage scenes as well as excerpts of plays: https://www.youtube.com/watch?v=kEUQNvn8EJQ

Bunraku

Titled "Japanese Theatre 2: *Bunraku*": an introduction to *bunraku* with excerpts from plays and excellent commentary, total running time 9.5 minutes: https://www.youtube.com/watch?v=4TKt67ouaqM
 The Japan Foundation produced an 11-minute introduction, in Japanese but with English subtitles: https://www.youtube.com/watch?v=8F-xtbiTtjQ

Printing press

The Atlas of Early Printing has animations showing how the printing press worked and the spread of printing during the fifteenth century: http://atlas.lib.uiowa.edu

There is a brief video on the history of the printing press at https://www.history.com/topics/inventions/mankind-the-story-of-all-of-us-videos-the-printing-press, and a demonstration at http://youtu.be/ksLaBnZVRnM

Renaissance and Baroque theatre
Molière's Tartuffe, video recording of the Royal Shakespeare Company production, directed by Bill Alexander, with Antony Sher as Tartuffe (1984)

A 10-minute tour of the reconstructed Globe Theatre, excerpted from the online course "Shakespeare's Hamlet: The Ghost": https://youtu.be/95ec5xtt6Hs

On the Agas interactive map of London, select "playhouses" to see the location of the theatres during the Renaissance: https://mapoflondon.uvic.ca/agas.htm

The Morgan Library & Museum has an extensive collection of Italian Baroque stage designs (including many by the Bibienas) at https://www.themorgan.org/exhibitions/stage-designs

The Drottningholm Theatre has a video showing its backstage, the operation of its machinery, and scene changes at https://vimeo.com/291460936

There is a video of a complete performance of the early *opéra-comique Les Troqueurs* (*The Barterers*) by the French composer Antoine Dauvergne (1713–1797), as reconstructed and staged at the Baroque theatre in Český Krumlov, showing chariot-and-pole scenery changes and the use of other stage machinery: https://www.youtube.com/watch?v=y4Iu9ZTtd6o

Zaju
A modern reconstruction of the original photo of the Guangsheng Temple mural in the Shanxi province, shown in Chapter 4, describing a Yuan *zaju* performance of the fourteenth century, featuring the actress Zhongduxiu: https://commons.wikimedia.org/wiki/File:Yuan_qu.jpg

Media resources – Part III
German expressionism
http://Everything2.com/index.pl?node_id=166783 (2009), website (on German Expressionism, with many links to other sources).

German Expressionism Collection (2008), DVD-video (4-disc set, includes *Cabinet of Dr. Caligari* and other films).

Variety theatre
Vintage Variety Stage and Vaudeville Film Collection (2009), DVD, Bestsellers in Movies and TV.

Pantomime
The Victoria and Albert Museum's "The Story of Pantomime" https://www.vam.ac.uk/articles/the-story-of-pantomime discusses the evolution of British pantomime from its beginnings to 1900, with many illustrations.

Blackface minstrelsy
"Stephen Foster," American Experience Series (Public Broadcasting System 2000): http://www.pbs.org/wgbh/amex/foster/sfeature/sf_minstrelsy.html.

"Blackface Minstrelsy, 1830–1852," http://www.iath.virginia.edu/utc/minstrel/mihp.html

Japonisme
"Curator's Perspective: Vincent Van Gogh and Japan" – an illustrated lecture by art historian (1 hour, 2 minutes) at https://www.youtube.com/watch?v=-mnBo87-T80

The Mikado
A full production by D'Oyly Carte Opera, 1992 (2 hours, 22 minutes): https://www.youtube.com/watch?v=f2TW90OEU-U

Full-length feature film *Topsy-Turvy* by Mike Leigh detailing the partnership of Gilbert and Sullivan, specifically the creation of *The Mikado*. Includes many scenes replicating the original production, costuming, and rehearsals as well as other aspects of Victorian life and theatre: https://www.youtube.com/watch?v=hjoxdw69xCo

Madama Butterfly
Filmed version, filmed realistically in Japan (not on stage) with English subtitles (2 hours, 14 minutes): https://www.youtube.com/watch?v=3stgof-xyN0

Media resources – Part IV

Early cinema
Melies, G.A. *A Trip to the Moon* (1902) can be watched at https://www.youtube.com/watch?v=xLVChRVfZ74

Second-generation avant-gardes
"Futurism" website, including Marinetti's manifesto and other documents: http://www.unknown.nu/futurism/

"MoMA Dada": http://www.moma.org/learn/moma_learning/themes/dada

"Surrealism" websites include http://surrealism-plays.com and the British Research Centre for the Study of Surrealism and its Legacies site: http://www.surrealismcentre.ac.uk

"UbuWeb: Historical," a resource for the historical documents and manifestos on Dadaism, Surrealism, and Futurism, is at http://www.ubu.com/historical/

A reconstruction of Meyerhold's biomechanics training: https://www.youtube.com/watch?v=eoq8_90id2o&t=829s

"Federal Theatre Project Collection," website (Library of Congress), http://memory.loc.gov/ammem/fedtp/

Chinese theatre
The White-Haired Girl (1950), website with film: http://archive.org/details/the_white_haired_girl

Yang Ban Xi: The Eight Model Works (2006) can be watched on Vimeo: https://vimeo.com/114648184

Postwar theatre

The Samuel Beckett Web Links page by Mantex Information Design (http://samuel-beckett.net/) contains a useful (albeit not entirely updated) set of links to various resources on Beckett.

Jerzy Grotowski: A recording of *Akropolis* is available through Arthur Cantor Films in New York. The film *Training at Grotowski's "Laboratorium" in Wrocław in 1972* can be purchased from http://www.artfilm.co.uk. In addition, search YouTube for "Grotowski" for clips of performances and training sessions.

The Living Theatre: Some clips of *Paradise Now* can be viewed on YouTube at: https://www.youtube.com/watch?v=8ef51VmIWf8. There is also a montage of excerpts from major productions: "A Video Retrospective: The Living Theatre": https://www.youtube.com/watch?v=KVeuNhmaTEQ

Dionysus in '69: filmed by Brian De Palma, can be seen at https://hdl.handle.net/2333.1/mcvdncsq

Suzuki Tadashi: A film of his *The Trojan Women* (*Toroia no Onna*) is in vol. 2 of *The Theater Goer's Collection, The Classics of Contemporary Japanese Theater*, DVDs published by Kazumo Co., Ltd., Tokyo, Japan. In addition, search YouTube for "Suzuki training" for clips of training sessions.

Suzuki Tadashi's philosophy, artistic vision, publications, as well as production records can be found in this website: https://www.scot-suzukicompany.com/en/

The SITI Company's home page is https://siti.org/

Robert Wilson: There are numerous excerpts of his work on YouTube, plus a two-part documentary called *Einstein on the Beach: The Changing Face of Opera*

PETA website: https://www.petatheater.com/

Danny Yung's experimental theatre Zuni Icosahedron: https://zuniseason.org.hk/en/home/

Stan Lai's Performance Workshop: https://www.pwshop.com/en/

Secret Love in Peach Blossom Land. Film version of the play: https://www.youtube.com/watch?v=75gRkRffzYg (without subtitles). For a 2-minute video with the 2015 Oregon Shakespeare English production, see https://www.youtube.com/watch?v=cEzk8y-kuBc

Some examples of *madangguk* performance: https://www.youtube.com/watch?v=RjZ0vjplOvs and https://www.youtube.com/watch?v=Parl5Bmr2T4

An example of *madangnori*: https://www.youtube.com/watch?v=99qpZ4mIqc4

ASHTAR Theatre: https://www.ashtar-theatre.org/

The Freedom Theatre: https://thefreedomtheatre.org/

Globalized, localized, and political performance

For a quick online tour of Shakespeare's Globe, visit: https://www.youtube.com/watch?v=ZRKJ4QrrfHI

To learn more about UNESCO's International Theatre Institute, which sponsors the Theatre of Nations festivals and other activities, visit: https://www.youtube.com/watch?v=kpgMW6rqbGY

Augusto Boal and Theatre of the Oppressed: YouTube has several videos demonstrating exercises and applications of Boal's methods, and a short interview from 2007 with Boal himself: https://www.youtube.com/watch?v=HOgv91qQyJc.

Nigerian Popular Theatre Alliance: https://npta.org.ng/

Sensitisation and Education through Kunda Arts: https://seka-theatre.com/seka-zambia/

Bread and Puppet Theater: A three-part documentary called *Ah! The Hopeful Pageantry of Bread and Puppet* can be found at https://archive.org/details/ah_the_hopeful_pageantry_of_bread_and_puppet. Excerpts of shows are available on YouTube.

Mahabharata: Peter Brook's stage production has been made into a film and TV series (3 episodes): see the full version (5.5 hours) here: https://www.youtube.com/watch?v=IEE_yGjsR0w

A 10-minute overview of Guillermo Gómez-Peña and Coco Fusco's performance installation, *Two Undiscovered Amerindians Visit the West,* with clips from Fusco and Paula Heredia's documentary about the project, *Couple in the Cage*, is available on YouTube: https://www.youtube.com/watch?v=saBoY-nQAtY

Guillermo Gómez-Peña's philosophy, artistic vision, publications, as well as production records can be found in this website: https://www.guillermogomezpena.com/

El Teatro Campesino: For the history of the theatre, the archive of previous productions and introduction of Luis Valdez, visit https://elteatrocampesino.com/

The Hemispheric Institute (https://hemisphericinstitute.org/en/hidvl.html) has an extensive collection of online performance videos including:

- Latin American theatre such as Yuyachkani and FOMMA
- Social-group focused theatre such as Split Britches and El Teatro Campesino
- Performance artists like Guillermo Gómez-Peña
- Hip Hop performers such as Danny Hoch

Mega-musicals: There are many YouTube videos offering flavors of (and in some case full) productions of mega-musicals such as *Phantom of the Opera* and *Wicked*.

For the full text of the open letter to the theatre community articulating principles for building more anti-racist theatre systems known as "We See You, White American Theater," see https://www.weseeyouwat.com/

To see videoclips from Ong Keng Sen's 2000 *Desdemona* in Japan, an adaptation of Shakespeare's *Othello,* featuring a fusion of different Asian performance styles, visit https://www.youtube.com/watch?v=spwN6H_NMc8

Bunratty Folk Park: https://www.bunrattycastle.ie/folk-park/the-village-street/

Peony Pavilion: The Young Lovers' Edition. It celebrated its twentieth anniversary in 2024. https://www.youtube.com/watch?v=R4T6Ic84AZI

Theatre in networked culture

Chilean Students "Thriller" Protest: see http://www.huffingtonpost.com/2011/06/25/chilethriller-protest-students-michaeljackson-dance_n_884531.html

Gertie the Dinosaur and Winsor McCay: https://www.youtube.com/watch?v=32pzHWUTcPc

George Coates Performance Works: http://stevemobia.com/WriteSubPages/George_Coates.htm

Stelarc: For an overview of the performance artist's work in body modification, visit https://www.youtube.com/watch?v=6z_CK6Fm4_g

Street with a View: http://benkinsley.com/street-with-a-view/

Play on Shakespeare initiative to "translate" the Bard, broadly construed: https://playonshakespeare.org/

For an overview and links to English and Spanish-language videos and a radio play of *A Farm for Meme*, visit https://www.sociallydistantperformance.com/productions/a-farm-for-meme

To watch the videos in the *How Are We* project, visit https://howarewe.xyz/

A 2018 performance of *Pass Over* filmed by Spike Lee is available through Amazon Prime Video.

Robot theatre: Hirata Oriza's robots in dramatic action are viewable in these videos from Seinendan Theater Company and the Osaka University Robot Theater Project at https://www.youtube.com/watch?v=BVPcjuyLfho. The first one features Geminoid F and the second the maids in *I, Worker*.

YouTube videos for The Sultan's Elephant and Little Amal are plentiful. Some recommendations include:

Sultan's Elephant in London, 2006: https://www.youtube.com/watch?v=Bc0PoWfPzmI
Sultan's Elephant returning after lockdown in France (where it was born): https://www.youtube.com/watch?v=oDh6T7_3-Bg
Little Amal Highlight reel: https://www.youtube.com/watch?v=iqYABB9AIf0
At United Nations: https://www.youtube.com/watch?v=bJIrp3l1K4w
In Manhattan: https://www.youtube.com/watch?v=ZBXUzDBn1HE
In U.K.: https://www.youtube.com/watch?v=lwsPUgKXGJA

Theatre by artificial intelligence is available through the THEaiTRE website: https://www.theaitre.com/, including a demo of the robot tool and available downloads of the robot-generated script.

An excerpt from the Builders Association's *I Agree to the Terms* is available through their website: https://thebuildersassociation.org/shows/i-agree-to-the-terms/

A 10-minute documentary on the InHEIRitance Project is available here: https://youtu.be/6dSnWb70XiA

Pronunciation guide

There are also recorded pronunciations by native speakers on the *Theatre Histories* website.

TERM	TRANSCRIPTION
Angura	ahn-goo-rah
Aragoto	ah-rah-goh-toh
Auteur	oh-TUR
Auto sacramental	OW-toh sahk-rah-men-TAHL
Bhava	BAH-v
Bunraku	boon-rah-koo
Butoh	boo-toh
Capa y espada	KAH-pa ee es-PAH-thah
Castrato, -ti	kahs-TRAH-toh, -tee
Catharsis	keh-THAHR-sis
Comedia	koh-MEY-dee-ah
Comédie larmoyante	koh-meh-DEE lahr-mwah-YAWNT
Commedia dell'arte	kohm-MAY-dee-ah dehl-AHR-tey
Commedia erudita	kohm-MAY-dee-ah eh-roo-DEE-tah
Corral	kohr-RAHL
Costumbrismo	kos-toom-BREES-moh

Danmari	dahn-mah-ree
Dengaku	dehn-gah-koo
Deus ex machina	deh-oos ex MAH-kee-nah
Dithyramb	DIH-thih-ram
Einfühlung	ahyn-FEW-lung
Geisha	gheh-shah
Geju	guh jyu
Gesamtkunstwerk	ghe-ZAHMT-koonst-vehrk
Gestus	GHE-stus
Hanamichi	hah-nah-mee-chee
Hashigakari	hah-shee-gah-kah-ree
Innamorato, -ta, -ti	in-nah-moh-RAH-toh, -tah, -tee
Jingju	jing jyu
Kabuki	kah-boo-kee
Kathakali	k-TAH-kah-lee
Kōken	koh-kehn
Kunqu	kwun chyu
Kutiyattam	koo-DYAH-tum
Kyōgen	kyoh-ghen
Landjuweelen	LAWNT-yu-vay-lehn
Lazzi	LAH-dzee
Locus	LAW-loos
Ludi	LOO-dee
Madangguk	mah-DAHNG-g(u)k
Madangnori	mah-DAHNG-no-ri
Mie	mee-eh
Mise en scène	meez on sehn
Monomane	moh-noh-mah-neh
Natyasastra	NAH-tyah-shas-tr
Naumachia	naw-MAH-kee-ah
Nō	noh
Onnagata	ohn-nah-gah-tah
Opera buffa	OH-peh-rah BOO-fah
Opera seria	OH-peh-rah SEH-ree-ah
Parterre	PAH(r)-tehr

Philosophe	fee-loh-zohf
Platea	plah-TEH-ah
Polis	POH-lis
Rabinal Achi	drah-vee-NAHL ah-CHEE
Ramlila	rahm-LEE-lah
Rasa	RAH-s(eh)
Sarugaku	sah-roo-gah-koo
Scena per angolo	SHAY-nah pair AHN-goh-loh
Shimpa	sheem-pah
Shingeki	sheen-gheh-kee
Shite	sh-teh
Shpil (plural, shpiln)	shpihl
Ta'ziyeh	TAH-zee-yeh
Theatron	THAY-ah-tron
Tsure	tsoo-reh
Übermarionette	EW-behr-marionette
Vecchi	VEH-kee
Verfremdungseffekt	fehr-FREHM-doongs-eh-fehkt
Volksgeist	FOHLKS-gahyst
Wagoto	wah-goh-toh
Waki	wah-kee
Wayang golek	wah-YAHNG goh-lek
Wayang kulit	wah-YAHNG koo-lit
Yangbanxi	yahng bahn shee
Yanggeju	yahng guh jyu
Yūgen	yoo-ghehn
Zaju	zah jyu
Zanni	ZAHN-nee

Case studies library

The following are the case studies in the book and on the website for each chapter.

Chapter 1
Book
Hopi kachinas and clowns
Website
The Yoruba *Egúngún* ritual as "play," and "contingency" in the ritual process
Korean shamanism and the power of speech

Chapter 2
Book
Plautus's plays: What's so funny? (abridged)
The *nō* play *Dōjōji*
Website
Plautus's plays: What's so funny? (unabridged)
Kutiyattam Sanskrit theatre of India: *Rasa-bhava* aesthetic theory and the question of taste
Kathakali dance-drama: Divine "play" and human suffering on stage

Chapter 3
Book
Christians and Moors: Medieval performance in Spain and the New World Ramlila
Playful Gods: The *Ramlila* in North India
Website
[None]

Chapter 4
Book
Realer than real? Imaging "woman" in *kabuki*
Website
[None]

Chapter 5
Book
Early modern metatheatricality and the print revolution
Sor Juana Inés de la Cruz and the perils of print culture in New Spain
Website
Sexuality in Shakespeare's *Twelfth Night*

Chapter 6
Book
Molière and carnival laughter
Website
[None]

Chapter 7
Book
Censorship in eighteenth-century Japan
Theatre iconology and the actor as icon: David Garrick (abridged)
Website
Theatre iconology and the actor as icon: David Garrick (unabridged)

Chapter 8
Book
Friedrich Schiller's vision of aesthetic education and the German dream of a national theatre
Website
"Blacking up" on the U.S. stage
Theatre and cultural hegemony: Comparing popular melodramas
The *Playboy* riots: Nationalism in the Irish theatre

Chapter 9
Book
Imperialism, Orientalism, and nineteenth-century Indian theatre
Yellowface
Website
Inventing Japan: *The Mikado* and *Madama Butterfly*
British pantomime: How "bad" theatre remains popular

Chapter 15
Book
Hip Hop theatre
Website
The vortex of Times Square
Online role-playing as theatre

Works cited

Adams, W.D. (1904) *A Dictionary of the Drama*, Philadelphia, PA: J.B. Lippincott.

Aercke, K.P. (1994) *Gods of Play: Baroque Festive Performances as Rhetorical Discourse*, Albany: State University of New York Press.

Aghaie, K.S. (2005) "The Origins of the Sunnite–Shi'ite Divide and the Emergence of the Ta'ziyeh Tradition," *TDR: The Drama Review* 49(4): 42–7.

Ajayi, O.S. (1998) *Yoruba Dance*, Trenton, NJ: Africa World Press.

Akkeren, R. van (1999) "Sacrifice at the Maize Tree: *Rab'inal Achi* in Its Historical and Symbolic Context," *Ancient Mesoamerica* 10: 281–95.

Anderson, B. (1991) *Imagined Communities*, 2nd ed, London: Verso.

Archer, M.S. (1995) *Realist Social Theory: The Morphogenetic Approach*, Cambridge: Cambridge University Press.

Aronson, A. (2000) *American Avant-garde Theatre: A History*, London and New York: Routledge.

Artaud, A. (1958) *The Theatre and Its Double*, trans. M.C. Richards, New York: Grove Press. (Originally published in French in 1938.)

Auslander, P. (1992) *Presence and Resistance: Postmodernism and Cultural Politics in Contemporary American Performance*, Ann Arbor: University of Michigan Press.

Bakhtin, M.M. (1981) *The Dialogic Imagination: Four Essays*, ed. M. Holquist, trans. C. Emerson and M. Holquist, Austin: University of Texas Press.

Bakhtin, M.M. (1984) *Rabelais and His World*, trans. H. Iswolsky, Bloomington: Indiana University Press.

Barish, J. (1981) *The Antitheatrical Prejudice*, Berkeley: University of California Press.

Beckett, S. (1954) *Waiting for Godot: A Tragicomedy in Two Acts*, New York: Grove Press.

Beckett, S. (1958) *Endgame*, New York: Grove Press.

Beckett, S. (1984) *The Collected Shorter Plays*, New York: Grove Press.

Benedetti, J. (1999) *Stanislavski: His Life and Art*, 3rd edn, London: Methuen.

Bennett, S. (1990) *Theatre Audiences: A Theory of Production and Reception*, London: Routledge.

Berghaus, G. (2005) *Theatre, Performance, and the Historical Avant-Garde*, New York: Palgrave Macmillan.

Berzal de Dios, J. (2019) *Visual Experiences in Cinquecento Theatrical Spaces*, Toronto: University of Toronto Press.

Bharata (1961, 1967) *Natyasastra*, 2nd edn, trans. and ed. M. Ghosh, vol. I, Calcutta: Manisha Granthalaya, 1961; vol. II, Calcutta: Asiatic Society, 1967.

Bharucha, R. (1988) "Peter Brook's *Mahabharata*: A View from India," *Economic and Political Weekly* 23(32): 1642–7.

Bharucha, R. (2000) *The Politics of Cultural Practice: Thinking Through Theatre in an Age of Globalization*, Hanover, NH and London: Wesleyan University Press.

Bhatia, N. (2004) *Acts of Authority/Acts of Resistance: Theater and Politics in Colonial and Postcolonial India*, Ann Arbor, MI: University of Michigan.

Bigsby, C.W.E. (1982) *A Critical Introduction to Twentieth-Century American Drama*, Vol. 1, Cambridge: Cambridge University Press.

Bixler, J.E. (1997) *Convention and Transgression: The Theatre of Emilio Carballido*, Lewisburg, PA: Bucknell University Press.

Bixler, J.E. (2004) "Performing Culture(s): Extras and Extra-Texts in Sabina Berman's *eXtras*," *Theatre Journal* 56(3): 429–544.

Blair, K. (2023) "Since the 1980s: The Global Musical Theatre Ecology," in MacDonald and Donovan, 150–64.

Boffone, T. (2021) "All the TikTok's a Digital Stage," *Theatre Times*, 31 July, https://thetheatretimes.com/all-the-tiktoks-a-digital-stage/.

Borneoco. (n.d.) "Zuhe Niao Performances," http://www.borneoco.nl/zuhe-niao-performances.php.

Bradby, D., and D. Williams. (1988) *Directors' Theatre*, London: Macmillan.

Buckley, M. (2006) *Tragedy Walks the Streets: The French Revolution in the Making of Modern Drama*, Baltimore, MD: Johns Hopkins University Press.

Burelle, J.S.V. (2014). *Encounters on Contested Lands: First Nations Performances of Sovereignty and Nationhood in Quebec*, ProQuest Dissertations & Theses Global (1548325709).

Bürger, P. (1984) *Theory of the Avant Garde*, trans. M. Shaw, Minneapolis: University of Minnesota Press.

Camus, A. (1942). *Le Mythe de Sisyphe*. Paris: Gallimard.

Carlson, M. (1985) *The Italian Shakespearians: Performances by Ristori, Salvini, and Rossi in England and America*, Washington, DC: Folger Books.

Carlson, M. (1993) *Theories of Theatre*, expanded edn, Ithaca, NY and London: Cornell University Press.

Carruthers, I., and Y. Takahashi. (2004) *The Theatre of Suzuki Tadashi*, Cambridge: Cambridge University Press.

Case, S. E. (1985) "Classic Drag: The Greek Creation of Female Parts," *Theatre Journal* 37: 317–427.

Castelvetro, L. (1570 [2000]) *The Poetics of Aristotle*, Selections, in D. Gerould (ed.) *Theatre/Theory/Theatre: The Major Critical Texts from Aristotle and Zeami to Soyinka and Havel*, New York: Applause, 109–16.

Chapman, M. (2017) *Anti-Black Racism in Early Modern Drama*, New York and London: Routledge.

Clifford, J. (2005) "Diasporas," in A. Abbas and J.N. Erni (eds.) *Internationalizing Cultural Studies*, Malden: Blackwell Publishing, 524–58.

Cole, C. (2001) *Ghana's Concert Party Theatre*, Bloomington: Indiana University Press.

Connerton, P. (1989) *How Societies Remember*, Cambridge: Cambridge University Press.

Connon, D. (2012) "The Theatre of the Parisian Fairs and Reality," *Romance Studies* 30(3–4): 186–92.

Connor, S. (1989) *Postmodernist Culture: An Introduction to Theories of the Contemporary*, Oxford and New York: Basil Blackwell.

Connor, W.R. (1989) "City Dionysia and Athenian Democracy," *Classica et Mediaevalia* 40: 7–32.

Cowling, E.A., G.Y. Nieto Cuebas, M. García Jordán, and T. de Miguel Magro. (eds.) (2021) *Social Justice in Spanish Golden Age Theatre*, Toronto: University of Toronto Press.

Craig, E.G. (1911) *On the Art of the Theatre*, London: Heinemann.

D'Aponte, M.G. (ed.) (1999) *Seventh Generation: An Anthology of Native American Plays*, New York: Theatre Communications Group.

Dauster, F. (2008) "Spanish American Theatre of the Nineteenth Century," in *The Cambridge History of Latin American Literature (online)*, Cambridge: Cambridge University Press, 536–555.

Delora, P.J. (1998) *Playing Indian*, New Haven, CT: Yale University Press.

Derr, H. (2023) "Shared Leadership: Theatres Find an Inclusive Model Spurs More Diversity and Innovation," *Southern Theatre* 64(1): 36–51.

Desaulniers, A. (2012) "Devised Theatre: The Art of the Impossible," http://theatrewashington.org/content/devised-theatre-art-impossible.

Dillon, E.M. (2014) *New World Drama: The Performative Drama and the Atlantic World, 1649–1849*, Durham, NC: Duke University Press.

Dirks, N. (2001) *Castes of Mind: Colonialism and the Making of Modern India*, Princeton, NJ: Princeton University Press.

Dixon, S. (2007) *Digital Performance: A History of New Media in Theater, Dance, Performance Art, and Installation*, Cambridge: Massachusetts Institute of Technology Press.

Dixon, S. (n.d.) "Practice: Chameleons 3: Net Congestion," *Absent Fields* https://www.primidi.com/steve_dixon_actor/the_chameleons_group/chameleons_3_-_net_congestion.

Dobson, R.B. (1997) "Craft Guilds and City: The Historical Origins of the York Mystery Plays Reassessed," in A.E. Knight (ed.) *The Stage as Mirror: Civic Theatre in Late Medieval Europe*, Cambridge: D.S. Brewer, 91–105.

Donkor, D. (2016) *Spiders of the Market: Ghanaian Trickster Performance in a Web of Neoliberalism*, Bloomington: Indiana University Press.

Duckworth, G.E. (1942) *The Complete Roman Drama*, vol. I, New York: Random House.

Dukore, B.F. (ed.) (1974) *Dramatic Theory and Criticism*, New York: Holt, Rinehart and Winston.

Eagleton, T. (1983) *Literary Theory: An Introduction*, Minneapolis: University of Minnesota Press.

Eisenstein, E.L. (1979) *The Printing Press as an Agent of Change*, Cambridge: Cambridge University Press.

Else, G. (1965) *The Origin and Early Form of Greek Tragedy*. New York: W.W. Norton.

Erenstein, R. (1989) "The Humour of the Commedia dell'Arte," in C. Cairns (ed.) *The Commedia dell'Arte from the Renaissance to Dario Fo*, Lewiston/Queenston/Lampeter: Edwin Mellen Press, 118–41.

Esslin, M. (1980) *The Theatre of the Absurd,* 3rd edn, London and New York: Penguin Books.

Euripides. (1959) *The Bacchae*, trans. W. Arrowsmith, in D. Grene and R. Lattimore (eds.) *Euripides V, The Complete Greek Tragedies*, Chicago, IL: University of Chicago Press, 154–220.

Filewod, A. (2007) "Colonial Spectacle," review of *Spectacle of Empire: Marc Lescarbot's "Theatre of Neptune in New France,* J. Wasserman (ed.), *Canadian Literature* no. 195: 190–91.

Filewod, A. and D. Watt. (2001) *Workers' Playtime: Theatre and the Labour Movement since 1970*, Sydney: Currency Press.

Fischer-Lichte, E. (1999) "Between Text and Cultural Performance: Staging Greek Tragedies in Germany," *Theatre Survey* 40(1): 1–29.

Fitzsimmons, L. (ed.) *File on Churchill*, London: Methuen.

Fletcher, A. (2011) *Evolving Hamlet: Seventeenth-Century English Tragedy and the Ethics of Natural Selection*, New York: Palgrave.

Fletcher, J. (2002) *The Egyptian Book of Living and Dying*, London: Duncan Baird Publishers.

Foley, H.P. (1981) "The Concept of Women in Athenian Drama," in H.P. Foley (comp.) *Reflections on Women in Antiquity*, London: Gordon and Breach, 127–68.

Fowler, W. (2008) *Latin America Since 1780*, London: Hodder Education Press.

Fredrickson, G. (2002) *Racism: A Short History*, Princeton, NJ: Princeton University Press.

Fujita, M., and M. Shapiro. (2021) *Transvestism and the Onnagata Traditions in Shakespeare and Kabuki*, London: Brill.

Garcia, V. (2013) "The Paradox of Devised Theater on the Twenty–First Century Stage," *Howlround*, 21 July, http://howlround.com/the-paradox-of-devised-theater-on-the-twenty-first-century-stage.

Gaster, T. (1950) *Thespis, Ritual, Myth and Drama in the Ancient Near East*, New York: Henry Schuman.

Gellius, A. (1927) *The Attic Nights of Aulus Gellius*, trans. J.C. Rolfe, Cambridge, MA: Harvard University Press.

Gerow, E. (1981) "*Rasa* as a Category of Literary Criticism," in R. van M. Baumer and J.R. Brandon (eds.) *Sanskrit Drama in Performance*, Honolulu: University of Hawaii, 226–57.

Gilbert, H., and J. Tompkins. (1996) *Post-Colonial Drama*, London and New York: Routledge.

Gilmour, D. (2011) *The Pursuit of Italy: A History of a Land, its Regions and their Peoples*, London: Penguin.

Gold, A., and Fizdale, F. (1991) *Divine Sarah: A Life of Sarah Bernhardt*, New York: Vintage.

Goldhill, S. (1990) "The Great Dionysia and Civic Ideology," in J.J. Winkler and F.I. Zeitlin (eds.) *Nothing to Do with Dionysus? Athenian Drama in Its Social Context*, Princeton, NJ: Princeton University Press, 97–129.

Gómez-Peña, G. (1996) *The New World Border*, San Francisco, CA: City Lights Books.

Gómez-Peña, G. (2003) *Dangerous Border Crossers*, New York: Routledge.

Goodman, D. (trans.) (1986) *After Apocalypse: Four Japanese Plays of Hiroshima and Nagasaki*, New York: Columbia University Press.

Griffiths, D. (2018) "Petrodrama: Melodrama and Energetic Modernity," *Victorian Studies* 60(4): 611–38.

Grotowski, J. (1968) *Towards a Poor Theatre*, ed. E. Barba, New York: Simon and Schuster.

Guan, H. (1972) *Injustice to Tou O (Tou O Yuan)*, trans. Chung-wen Shih, Cambridge: Cambridge University Press.

Habermas, J. (1989) *The Structural Transformation of the Public Sphere: An Inquiry Into a Category of Bourgeois Society*, trans. T. Burger, Cambridge, MA: MIT Press.

Hall, K. (1995) *Things of Darkness: Economies of Race and Gender in Early Modern England*, Ithaca, NY and London: Cornell U Press.

Harding, J., and J. Rouse. (2006) *Not the Other Avant-Garde: The Transnational Foundations of Avant-Garde Performance*, Ann Arbor: University of Michigan Press.

Harris, M. (1994) "The Arrival of the Europeans: Folk Dramatizations of Conquest and Conversion in New Mexico," *Comparative Drama* 28: 141–65.

Harris, M. (2000) *Aztecs, Moors and Christians*, Austin: University of Texas Press.

Harrison, T. (2000) *The Emptiness of Asia*, London: Duckworth.

Hartman, S. (2019) *Wayward Lives, Beautiful Experiments*, New York: W.W. Norton Press.

Havelock, E.A. (1963) *Preface to Plato*, Cambridge, MA: Belknap Press of Harvard University Press.

Hemmings, F.W.J. (1993) *The Theatre Industry in Nineteenth-Century France*, Cambridge: Cambridge University Press.

Henke, R. (2003) *Performance and Literature in the Commedia dell'Arte*, Cambridge: Cambridge University Press.

Henke, R., and M.A. Katritzky. (2016) *European Theatre Performance Practice, 1580–1750*, London: Routledge.

Hoffenberg, P.H. (2001) *An Empire on Display: English, Indian, and Australian Exhibitions from the Crystal Palace to the Great War*, Berkeley and Los Angeles: University of California Press.

Homer. (1967) *The Odyssey of Homer*, trans. R. Lattimore, New York: Harper and Row.

Honegger, G. (2001) "Austria: School for Scandal," *Western European Stages* 13: 5–12.

Huerta, J. (2016) "El Teatro's Living Legacy," *American Theatre* (December): 28–32.

Hughes, B. (2018) "The Indispensable Indian: Edwin Forrest, Pushmataha, and *Metamora*," *Theatre Survey* 59(1): 23–44.

Jannarone, K. (2010) *Artaud and His Doubles*, Ann Arbor, MI: University of Michigan.

Johnson, J.H. (1995) *Listening in Paris: A Cultural History*, Berkeley: University of California Press.

Johnson, O. (2010) "Unspeakable Histories: Terror, Spectacle, and Genocidal Memory," in H. Bial and S. Magelssen (ed.) *Theatre Historiography: Critical Interventions,* Ann Arbor: University of Michigan Press, 11–21.

Jones, D.A., Jr. (2021) "'The Black Below': Minstrelsy, Satire and the Threat of Vernacularity," *Theatre Journal* 73: 129–46.

Jones, J.B. (2003) *Our Musicals, Ourselves: A Social History of the American Musical Theatre* Waltham, MA: Brandeis University Press.

Jones, L. (1965) "The Revolutionary Theatre," *The Liberator,* http://nationalhumanitiescenter.org/pds/maai3/protest/text12/barakatheatre.pdf.

Jonson, B. (1969) "*Masque of Blackness*," in B, Jonson *The Complete Masques*, ed. S. Orgel, New Haven, CT: Yale University Press, 47–60.

Kale, P. (1974) *The Theatric Universe*, Bombay: Popular Prakashan.

Keenan, S. (2014) *Acting Companies and Their Plays in Shakespeare's London*, London and New York: A&C Black.

Kimbell, D. (1991) *Italian Opera*, Cambridge: Cambridge University Press.

King, P.M. (2012) "John Heywood, *The Play of the Weather*," in T. Betteridge and G. Walker (eds.) *Oxford Handbook of Tudor Drama*, Oxford: Oxford University Press, 207–23.

Kirshenblatt-Gimblett, B. (1980) "Contraband: Text and Analysis of a 'Purim Shpil,'" *TDR: The Drama Review* 24(3): 5–16.

Klöck, A. (1999) "Of Cyborg Technologies and Fascistized Mermaids: Giannina Censi's Aerodanze in 1930s Italy," *Theatre Journal* 51(4): 395–415.

Knapp, B.L. (2000) *Voltaire Revisited*, New York: Twayne Publishers.

Knight, A.E. (1983) *Aspects of Genre in Late Medieval French Drama*, Manchester: Manchester University Press.

Knight, A.E. (ed.) (1997) *The Stage as Mirror: Civic Theatre in Late Medieval Europe*, Cambridge: D.S. Grewer.

Korneeva, T. (2019) *The Dramaturgy of the Spectator: Italian Theatre and the Public Sphere, 1600–1800*, Toronto: University of Toronto Press.

Kort, M. (2011) "The Whole Megilla," *Ms. Magazine,* 20 March, https://msmagazine.com/2011/03/20/the-whole-megillah/.

Kramnick, I. (ed.) (1995) *The Portable Enlightenment Reader*, London: Penguin.

Lam, J.S.C. (n.d.) "*Kunqu*: The Classical Opera of Globalized China: A Long Story Briefly Told," http://www.confucius.umich.edu/uploads/HcHLEQLsVE6yBvqVb726.pdf. Last accessed on 10 November 2015.

Langston, S. (2022) "The Pandemic Nearly Killed Theatre – the Creative Way It Fought Back Could Leave It Stronger," *The Conversation,* 21 February, https://theconversation.com/the-pandemic-nearly-killed-theatre-the-creative-way-it-fought-back-could-leave-it-stronger-176185.

Leary, T. (1983). *Flashbacks: A Personal and Cultural History of an Era*, Los Angeles: J. P. Tarcher.

Lee, E.K. (2022) *Made-up Asians: Yellowface During the Exclusion Era*, Ann Arbor: University of Michigan Press.

Lehmann, H.T. (1999/2006) *Postdramatic Theatre*, London and New York: Routledge.

Lei, B. (2020) "Decentering Asian Shakespeare: Approaching Intercultural Theatre as a Living Organism," in D. Lei and McIvor, 63–77.

Lei, D.P. (2006) *Operatic China: Staging Chinese Identity across the Pacific*, London: Palgrave Macmillan.

Lei, D.P. (2011) "Interruption, Intervention, Interculturalism: Robert Wilson's HIT Productions in Taiwan," *Theatre Journal* 63(4): 571–86.

Lei, D.P. (2015) "Dance Your Opera, Mime Your Words: (Mis)Translate the Asian Body on the International Stage," in N. George (ed.) *The Oxford Handbook of Dance and Theatre*, Oxford and New York: Oxford University Press, 669–90.

Lei, D.P. (2019) *Uncrossing the Borders: Performing Chinese in Gendered (Trans)Nationalism*. Ann Arbor: University of Michigan Press.

Lei, D., and C. McIvor. (eds.) (2020) *The Methuen Drama Handbook of Interculturalism and Performance*, London: Bloomsbury.

Leiter, S. (1994) *The Great Stage Directors*, New York: Facts on File.

Leprohon, R.J. (2007) "Ritual Drama in Ancient Egypt," in E. Csapo and M.C. Miller (eds.), *The Origins of Theater in Ancient Greece and Beyond: From Ritual to Drama*, Cambridge: Cambridge University Press, 259–92.

Lessing, G.E. (1962) *Hamburg Dramaturgy*, trans. H. Zimmerman, intro. V. Lange, New York: Dover.

Li, L. (2015) *Popular Religion of Modern China: the New Role of Nuo*, New York: Routledge.

Lindfors, B. (2007) *Ira Aldridge, The African Rocius*, Rochester, NY: University of Rochester.

Londré, F.H., and D.J. Watermeier. (1998) *The History of North American Theater: from Pre-Columbian Times to the Present*, London and New York: Continuum.

Lopez, J. (2003) *Theatrical Convention and Audience Response in Early Modern Drama*, Cambridge: Cambridge University Press.

Lough, J. (1979) *Seventeenth-Century French Drama: The Background*, Oxford: Clarendon Press; New York: Oxford University Press.

Lutgendorf, P. (1991) *The Life of a Text: Performing the Ramcaritmanas of Tulsidas*, Berkeley: University of California Press.

Lyotard, J.-F. (1984) *The Postmodern Condition, A Report on Knowledge*, trans. G. Bennington and B. Massumi, foreword by F. Jameson, Minneapolis: University of Minneapolis Press.

MacDonald, L., and R. Donovan. (eds.) (2023) *The Routledge Companion to Musical Theatre*, London and New York: Routledge.

Mackerras, C. (ed.) (1983) *Chinese Theatre from its Origins to the Present Day*, Honolulu: University of Hawaii Press.

Maeterlinck, M. (1897) "The Tragical in Everyday Life," in *The Works of Maurice Maeterlinck (1913–1914)*, New York: Dodd, Mead, 95–120.

Manning, B.J. (2022) *Played Out: The Race Man in Twenty-First-Century Satire*, New Brunswick, NJ: Rutgers University.

Marotta, A. (2020) "The Ableist Effects of Creating 'Post-Pandemic Theatre' During a Pandemic," *Howlround*, 8 December, https://howlround.com/ableist-effects-creating-post-pandemic-theatre-during-pandemic.

Marwick, A. (1998) *The Sixties*, Oxford: Oxford University Press.

May, E. (1988) *Homeward Bound: American Families in the Cold War Era*, New York: Basic Books.

McKendrick, M. (1989) *Theatre in Spain 1490–1500*, Cambridge: Cambridge University Press.

McKinley, J. (2002) "And the Stub Is All Yours," *New York Times*, 19 May, http://www.nytimes.com/2002/05/19/arts/theater/19TICKET.html.

McLuhan, M. (1962) *The Gutenberg Galaxy: The Making of Typographic Man*, Toronto: University of Toronto Press.

Metzger, S. (2004) "Charles Parsloe's Chinese Fetish: An Example of Yellowface Performance in Nineteenth-Century American Melodrama," *Theatre Journal* 56: 624–51.

Meyerhold, V. (1969) *Meyerhold on Theatre*, trans. and ed. E. Braun, New York: Hill and Wang.

Mixed Blood Theatre. (2015) "Our Mission," http://www.mixedblood.com.

Mizejewski, L. (1999) *Ziegfeld Girl: Image and Icon in Culture and Cinema*, Durham, NC: Duke University Press.

Most, A. (2004) *Making Americans: Jews and the Broadway Musical*, Cambridge, MA: Harvard University Press.

Moy, J.S. (1993) *Marginal Sights: Staging the Chinese in America*. Iowa City: University of Iowa Press.

Mulryne, J.R. (1998) "The Perils and Profits of Interculturalism and the Theatre Art of Tadashi Suzuki," in T. Sasayama, J.R. Mulryne, and M. Shewring (eds.) *Shakespeare and the Japanese Stage*, Cambridge: Cambridge University Press, 71–93.

Murray, P. and T.S. Dorsch. (trans.) (2000) *Classical Literary Criticism*, rev. edn, Harmondsworth: Penguin Books.

Muse, J.H. (2012) "140 Characters in Search of a Theater: Twitter Plays," *Theater* 42(2): 42–63.

Nagler, A.M. (1952) *A Source Book in Theatrical History*, New York: Dover Publications, citing *The Works of Lucian of Samosata*, trans. H.W. Fowler and F.G. Fowler, Oxford: Clarendon Press, III, 249–63.

National Endowment for the Arts. (2022) "New Data Show Economic Impact of COVID-19 on Arts and Culture Sector," online report 15 March, https://www.arts.gov/news/press-releases/2022/new-data-show-economic-impact-covid-19-arts-culture-sector.

Nellhaus, T. (2010) *Theatre, Communication, Critical Realism*, New York: Palgrave Macmillan.

Ngũgĩ wa Thiong'o (1986) *Decolonising the Mind: The Politics of Language in African Literature*, London: Heinemann.

Nicholson, E.A. (1993) "The Theater," in N.Z. Davis and A. Farge (eds.) *History of Women in the West, Vol. III: Renaissance and Enlightenment Paradoxes*, Cambridge, MA: Belknap Press, 295–314.

Noriega, J.A., and J. Schildcrout, J. (eds.) (2022) *Fifty Key Figures in Queer US Theatre*, London and New York: Routledge.

O'Brien, J. (2007) "Pantomime," in J. Moody and D. O'Quinn (eds.) *The Cambridge Companion to British Theatre, 1730–1830*, Cambridge: Cambridge University Press, 103–14.

O'Neill, P.G. (1958) *Early Noh Drama*, London: Lund Humphries.

Ockman, C. (2005) "Was She Magnificent? Sarah Bernhardt's Reach," in C. Ockman and K. Silver (eds.) *Sarah Bernhardt, The Art of High Drama*, produced for the Bernhardt exhibit of the Jewish Museum, New York, 2005–2006, New Haven, CT: Yale University Press.

Ong, A. (1999) *Flexible Citizenship: The Cultural Logics of Transnationality*, Durham and London: Duke University Press.

Orr, B. (2014) "Empire, Sentiment, and Theatre," in J. Swindells and D.F. Taylor (eds.) *The Oxford Handbook of the Georgian Theatre, 1737–1832*, Oxford: Oxford University Press, 621–37.

Parker, A.A. (1971) *The Approach to the Drama of the Spanish Golden Age*, London: Hispanic and Luso-Brazilian Councils.

Parker-Starbuck, J. (2011) *Cyborg Theater: Corporeal/Technological Intersections in Multimedia Performance*, London: Palgrave Macmillan.

Pattie, D. (2000) *The Complete Critical Guide to Samuel Beckett*, London: Routledge.

Paulose, K.G. (ed.) (1993) *Natankusa: A Critique on Dramaturgy*, Tripunithura: Government Sanskrit College Committee [Ravivarma Samskrta Grathavali–26].

Peters, J.S. (2000) *Theatre of the Book, 1480–1880: Print, Text, and Performance in Europe*, Oxford: Oxford University Press.

Pettys, R.A. (2005) "The Ta'ziyeh of the Martyrdom of Hussein," *TDR: The Drama Review* 49(4): 28–41.

Plass, P. (1995) *The Game of Death in Ancient Rome: Arena Sport and Political Suicide*, Madison: University of Wisconsin Press.

Pocha Nostra. (n.d.) "Ethno-Cyborgs," http://www.pochanostra.com/antes/jazz_pocha2/mainpages/ethno.htm.

Puchner, M. (2002) *Stage Fright: Modernism, Anti-Theatricality, and Drama*, Baltimore, MD and London: Johns Hopkins University Press.

Rebellato, D. (2009) *Theatre and Globalization*, Basingstoke: Palgrave Macmillan.

Rehearsal for Truth Theatre Festival Honoring Vaclav Havel, https://www.rehearsalfortruth.org/program/permeation.

Rehm, R. (2002) *The Play of Space: Spatial Transformation in Greek Tragedy*, Princeton, NJ: Princeton University Press.

Reorbit. (2010) https://twitter.com/reorbitproject.

Richlin, A. (2005) *Rome and the Mysterious Orient: Three Plays by Plautus*, Berkeley: University of California Press.

Rimer, J.T. (1974) *Toward a Modern Japanese Theatre: Kishida Kunio*, Princeton, NJ: Princeton University Press.

Ristani, M. (2020) "Theatre and Epidemics: An Age-Old Link," *IATC Journal,* June, https://www.critical-stages.org/21/theatre-and-epidemics-an-age-old-link/.

Roach, J.R. (1985; reprint 1993) *The Player's Passion: Studies in the Science of Acting,* Ann Arbor: University of Michigan Press.

Rolf, R., and J.K. Gillespie. (eds.) (1992) *Alternative Japanese Drama: Ten Plays,* Honolulu: University of Hawaii Press.

Roselli, D.K. (2011) *Theater of the People: Spectators and Society in Ancient Athens,* Austin: University of Texas Press.

Rosenthal, L. (2020) *Ways of the World: Theatre and Cosmopolitanism in the Restoration and Beyond,* Ithaca, NY and London: Cornell University Press.

Rouse, J. (1992) "Textuality and Authority in Theater and Drama: Some Contemporary Possibilities," in J.G. Reinelt and J.R. Roach (eds.) *Critical Theory and Performance,* Ann Arbor: University of Michigan Press, 146–57.

Said, E. (1978) *Orientalism,* New York: Vintage.

Saivetz, D. (1998) "An Event in Space: The Integration of Acting and Design in the Theatre of JoAnne Akalaitis," *The Drama Review* 42(2): 132–56.

Salmi, H. (1999) *Imagined Germany: Richard Wagner's National Utopia,* New York: Peter Lang.

Sanders, S. (2020) "Code Noir in Marivaux's Theatre," *Eighteenth Century Fiction* 32(2): 271–96.

Savran, D. (2014) "Trafficking in Transnational Brands: The New 'Broadway-Style' Musical," *Theatre Survey* 55: 318–42.

Savran, D. (2023) "Musical Theatre Mobilities: Around the World in Eighty Years," in MacDonald and Donovan, 9–24.

Sayer, J. (2006) *Jean Racine: Life and Legend,* Bern: Peter Lang.

Schechner, R. (1985, rpt. 2011) *Between Theater and Anthropology,* Philadelphia: University of Pennsylvania Press.

Schechner, R. (2002) *Performance Studies: An Introduction,* London and New York: Routledge.

Schuler, C. (2009) *Theatre and Identity in Imperial Russia,* Iowa City: University of Iowa Press.

Schumacher, C. (ed.) (1996) *Naturalism and Symbolism in European Theatre,* Cambridge: Cambridge University Press.

Schwartz, A. (2020) "The First Great Original Play of Quarantine," *New Yorker,* 11 May, https://www.newyorker.com/magazine/2020/05/18/the-first-great-original-play-of-quarantine.

Schwartz, M. (2023) "Art Isn't Easy (and Neither Is Commerce): The Musical Stays in the Money," in MacDonald and Donovan, 552–66.

Scullion, S. (2002) "'Nothing to Do with Dionysus': Tragedy Misconceived as Ritual," *Classical Quarterly* 52: 102–37.

Senda, A. (1997) *The Voyage of Contemporary Japanese Theatre,* trans. T. Rimer, Honolulu: University of Hawaii Press.

Shah, I. (2000) *The Oxford History of Ancient Egypt,* Oxford: Oxford University Press.

Shakespeare Behind Bars (SBB) (2014) "Mission & Vision," http://www.shakespearebehindbars.org/about/mission/.

Shih, C.W. (2015) *Golden Age of Chinese Drama: Yuan Tsa-Chu,* Princeton, NJ: Princeton University Press.

Shimazaki, S. (2016) *Edo Kabuki in Transition: From the Worlds of the Samurai to the Vengeful Female Ghost,* New York: Columbia University Press.

Shively, D.H. (2002) "*Bakufu* versus *Kabuki*," in S. Leiter (ed.) *A Kabuki Reader: History and Performance,* Armonk, NY: M.E. Sharpe.

Sieber, P., and R. Llamas. (2022) *How to Read Chinese Drama: A Guided Anthology,* New York: Columbia University Press.

Snyder-Young, D. (2022a) "We're All in This Together: Digital Performances and Socially Distanced Spectatorship," *Theatre Journal* 74(1): 1–15.

Snyder-Young, D. (2022b) "Performing Quarantined Isolation in the Spring of 2020," online support material for 2022a essay, https://jhuptheatre.org/theatre-journal/online-content/issue/volume-74-issue-1-march-2022/performing-quarantined-isolation.

Sontag, S. (1977) *On Photography*, New York: Delta Books.

Sorgenfrei, C.F. (2005a) "Remembering and Forgetting: Greek Tragedy as National History in Postwar Japan," in K. Gounaridou (ed.) *Staging Nationalism*, Jefferson, NY: McFarland and Co., 126–40.

Sorgenfrei, C.F. (2005b) *Unspeakable Acts: The Avant-Garde Theatre of Terayama Shūji and Postwar Japan*, Honolulu: University of Hawaii Press.

Sosulski, M.J. (2007) *Theater and Nation in Eighteenth Century Germany*, Williston, VT: Ashgate Publishing.

Soufas, T.S. (ed.) (1997) *Women's Acts: Plays by Women Dramatists of Spain's Golden Age*, Lexington: University Press of Kentucky.

Sten, M. (1982) *Vida y muerte del teatro náhuatl*, Veracruz, Mexico: Universidad Veracruzana.

Svoboda, J. (2021) "Švanda's Theater Presented a Play Written by Artificial Intelligence," *CzechCrunch*, February, https://cc.cz/2021/02/svandovo-divadlo-uvedlo-hru-napsanou-umelou-inteligenci-misty-je-prekvapive-vulgarni-a-reflektuje-dnesni-dobu/.

Tagore, R. (1961) *A Tagore Reader* (ed.) A. Chakravarty, Boston, MA: Beacon Press.

Taylor. D. (1991) *Theatre of Crisis: Drama and Politics in Latin America*, Lexington: University Press of Kentucky.

Taylor, D. (2004) "Scenes of Cognition: Performance and Conquest," *Theatre Journal* 56: 353–72.

Taylor, D., and S.J. Townsend. (2008) *Stages of Conflict: A Critical Anthology of Latin American Theatre and Performance*, Ann Arbor: University of Michigan Press.

Tedlock, D. (1985; 2nd edn 1996) *Popul Vuh: The Mayan Book of the Dawn of Life*, New York: Simon and Schuster.

Tedlock, D. (2003) *Rabinal Achi: A Mayan Drama of War and Sacrifice*, Oxford: Oxford University Press.

Thompson, A. (2008) *Performing Race and Torture on the Early Modern Stage*, New York and London: Routledge.

Townsend, S.J. (2018) *The Unfinished Art of Theater: Avant-Garde Intellectuals in Mexico and Brazil*, Evanston, IL: Northwestern University Press.

True, M. (2015) "Beyond the 'Affaire "Tartuffe"': Seventeenth-Century French Theatre in Colonial Quebec," *Romance Notes* 55(3): 451–61. https://doi.org/10.1353/rmc.2015.0066.

Vatsyayan, K. (1968) *Classical Indian Dance in Literature and the Arts*, New Delhi: Sangeet Natak Akademi.

Vatsyayan, K. (1996) *Bharata: Natyasastra*, New Delhi: Sahitya Akademi.

Veltman, C. (2023) "Theater Never Recovered from COVID – and Now Change Is No Longer a Choice," transcript of NPR *Morning Edition* radio broadcast, 6 February, https://www.npr.org/2023/02/06/1153453450/oregon-shakespeare-control-group-productions-west-village-co-op-theater.

Versényi, A. (1989) "Getting under the Aztecs' Skin: Evangelical Theatre in the New World," *New Theatre Quarterly* 19: 217–326.

Vignolo, P. (2012) Cultural Heritage as the Ultimate Utopia: Disputes Around the Origins of the Carnival of Barranquilla, speech presented at the David Rockefeller Center for Latin American Studies at Harvard University, Cambridge, MA.

Vince, R. (1989) *A Companion to the Medieval Theatre*, New York: Greenwood Press.

Vincent-Buffault, A. (1991) *The History of Tears: Sensibility and Sentimentality in France*, Houndmills, Basingstoke: Macmillan.

Waite, G. (2000) *Reformers on Stage: Popular Drama and Religious Propaganda in the Low Countries of Charles V, 1515–1556*, Toronto: University of Toronto Press.

Walker, J. (2009) *Expressionism and Modernism in the American Theatre*, Cambridge: Cambridge University Press.

Ward, D. (2006) "All Heaven Breaks Loose," *Guardian*, 5 October, http://www.theguardian.com/music/2006/oct/06/classicalmusicandopera.

Weiss J.A. et al. *Latin American Popular Theatre: The First Five Centuries.* Albuquerque: University of New Mexico Press.

Wheatcroft, A. (2004) *Infidels: A History of the Conflict between Christendom and Islam*, New York: Random House.

Wichmann, S. (1999) *Japonisme: The Japanese Influence on Western Art Since 1858*, London: Thames and Hudson.

Wiles, D. (2000) *Greek Theatre Performance: An Introduction*, Cambridge: Cambridge University Press.

Williams, D. (ed.) (1991) *Peter Brook and The Mahabharata: Critical Perspectives*, London and New York: Routledge.

Williams, D. (ed.) (1997) *The Chinese Other: 1850–1925: An Anthology of Plays*, Lantham, MD: University Press of America.

Williams, G.J. (1997) *Our Moonlight Revels: A Midsummer Night's Dream in the Theatre*, Iowa City: University of Iowa Press.

Williams, K. (2001) "Anti-Theatricality and the Limits of Naturalism," *Modern Drama* 44(3): 284–29.

Williams, R. (1966) *Modern Tragedy*, Stanford, CA: Stanford University Press.

Williams, R. (1969) *Drama from Ibsen to Brecht*, New York: Oxford University Press.

Winkler, J.J. (1990) "The Ephebes' Song: *Tragoidia* and *Polis*," in J.J. Winkler and F.I. Zeitlin (eds.) *Nothing to Do with Dionysus? Athenian Drama in its Social Context*, Princeton, NJ: Princeton University Press, 20–62.

Wise, J. (1998) *Dionysus Writes: The Invention of Theatre in Ancient Greece*, Ithaca, NY: Cornell University Press.

Wolf, S. (2008) "'Defying Gravity': Queer Conventions in the Musical *Wicked*," *Theatre Journal* 60(1): 1–21.

Wolford, L. (1991) "Subjective Reflections on Objective Work: Grotowski in Irvine," *The Drama Review* 35(1): 165–80.

Wollman, E.L. (2017) *A Critical Companion to the American Stage Musical*, London: Methuen Drama.

Woodhouse, J. and G. Hutton. (2021) "Covid-19 and the Arts and Culture Sectors" (House of Commons briefing paper CBP 9018, 25 February, https://researchbriefings.files.parliament.uk/documents/CBP-9018/CBP-9018.pdf.

Worthen, W.B. (1992) *Modern Drama and the Rhetoric of Theater*, Berkeley: University of California Press.

Worthen, W.B. (2003) *Shakespeare and the Force of Modern Performance*, Cambridge: Cambridge University Press.

Yamanashi, M. (2012) *A History of the Takarazuka Review since 1914: Modernity, Girls' Culture, Japanese Pop*, Boston: Global Oriental.

Yeats, W.B. (1952) *The Collected Plays*, New York: Macmillan.

Zola, É. (1881) "Naturalism in the Theatre," in E. Bentley (ed.) *The Theory of the Modern Stage*, London: Penguin, 1968, 351–72.

Index